Dictionary of Literary Biography

Dictionary of Literary Biography Documentary Series

12 *Southern Women Writers: Flannery O'Connor, Katherine Anne Porter, Eudora Welty,* edited by Mary Ann Wimsatt and Karen L. Rood (1994)

13 *The House of Scribner, 1846–1904,* edited by John Delaney (1996)

14 *Four Women Writers for Children, 1868–1918,* edited by Caroline C. Hunt (1996)

15 *American Expatriate Writers: Paris in the Twenties,* edited by Matthew J. Bruccoli and Robert W. Trogdon (1997)

16 *The House of Scribner, 1905–1930,* edited by John Delaney (1997)

17 *The House of Scribner, 1931–1984,* edited by John Delaney (1998)

18 *British Poets of The Great War: Sassoon, Graves, Owen,* edited by Patrick Quinn (1999)

19 *James Dickey,* edited by Judith S. Baughman (1999)

See also DLB 210, 216, 219, 222, 224, 229, 237, 247, 253, 254, 263, 269, 273, 274, 280, 284, 288, 291, 294, 298, 301, 304, 308, 309, 315, 316, 320, 324

Dictionary of Literary Biography Yearbooks

1980 edited by Karen L. Rood, Jean W. Ross, and Richard Ziegfeld (1981)

1981 edited by Karen L. Rood, Jean W. Ross, and Richard Ziegfeld (1982)

1982 edited by Richard Ziegfeld; associate editors: Jean W. Ross and Lynne C. Zeigler (1983)

1983 edited by Mary Bruccoli and Jean W. Ross; associate editor Richard Ziegfeld (1984)

1984 edited by Jean W. Ross (1985)

1985 edited by Jean W. Ross (1986)

1986 edited by J. M. Brook (1987)

1987 edited by J. M. Brook (1988)

1988 edited by J. M. Brook (1989)

1989 edited by J. M. Brook (1990)

1990 edited by James W. Hipp (1991)

1991 edited by James W. Hipp (1992)

1992 edited by James W. Hipp (1993)

1993 edited by James W. Hipp, contributing editor George Garrett (1994)

1994 edited by James W. Hipp, contributing editor George Garrett (1995)

1995 edited by James W. Hipp, contributing editor George Garrett (1996)

1996 edited by Samuel W. Bruce and L. Kay Webster, contributing editor George Garrett (1997)

1997 edited by Matthew J. Bruccoli and George Garrett, with the assistance of L. Kay Webster (1998)

1998 edited by Matthew J. Bruccoli, contributing editor George Garrett, with the assistance of D. W. Thomas (1999)

1999 edited by Matthew J. Bruccoli, contributing editor George Garrett, with the assistance of D. W. Thomas (2000)

2000 edited by Matthew J. Bruccoli, contributing editor George Garrett, with the assistance of George Parker Anderson (2001)

2001 edited by Matthew J. Bruccoli, contributing editor George Garrett, with the assistance of George Parker Anderson (2002)

2002 edited by Matthew J. Bruccoli and George Garrett; George Parker Anderson, Assistant Editor (2003)

Concise Series

Concise Dictionary of American Literary Biography, 7 volumes (1988–1999): *The New Consciousness, 1941–1968; Colonization to the American Renaissance, 1640–1865; Realism, Naturalism, and Local Color, 1865–1917; The Twenties, 1917–1929; The Age of Maturity, 1929–1941; Broadening Views, 1968–1988; Supplement: Modern Writers, 1900–1998.*

Concise Dictionary of British Literary Biography, 8 volumes (1991–1992): *Writers of the Middle Ages and Renaissance Before 1660; Writers of the Restoration and Eighteenth Century, 1660–1789; Writers of the Romantic Period, 1789–1832; Victorian Writers, 1832–1890; Late-Victorian and Edwardian Writers, 1890–1914; Modern Writers, 1914–1945; Writers After World War II, 1945–1960; Contemporary Writers, 1960 to Present.*

Concise Dictionary of World Literary Biography, 4 volumes (1999–2000): *Ancient Greek and Roman Writers; German Writers; African, Caribbean, and Latin American Writers; South Slavic and Eastern European Writers.*

Castilian Writers, 1200–1400

Dictionary of Literary Biography® • Volume Three Hundred Thirty-Seven

Castilian Writers, 1200–1400

George D. Greenia
College of William and Mary
and
Frank A. Domínguez
University of North Carolina at Chapel Hill

A Bruccoli Clark Layman Book

Detroit • New York • San Francisco • New Haven, Conn. • Waterville, Maine • London • Munich

THOMSON
GALE

Dictionary of Literary Biography
Volume 337: Castilian Writers, 1200–1400
George D. Greenia and Frank A. Domínguez

LIBRARY OF CONGRESS CATALOGING-IN-PUBLICATION DATA

Castilian writers, 1200–1400 / edited by Frank A. Dominguez and George D. Greenia.
    p. cm. — (Dictionary of literary biography ; v. 337)
  "A Bruccoli Clark Layman Book."
  Includes bibliographical references and index.
  ISBN-13: 978–0–7876–8155–5 (hardcover)
  ISBN-10: 0–7876–8155–5 (hardcover)
  1. Spanish literature—To 1500—Bio-bibliography—Dictionaries. 2. Authors, Spanish—
To 1500—Biography—Dictionaries. I. Domínguez, Frank, 1945–   . II. Greenia, George D.
III. Gale Group. IV. Series.
    PQ6058.C36 2007
    869.9'001—dc22
    [B]
                    2007025179

Printed in the United States of America
10 9 8 7 6 5 4 3 2 1

*For Thomas B. Wood, loving spouse
and fellow pilgrim*

*A mi madre, Nena, con todo el
cariño posible—Paco*

Contents

Plan of the Series

. . . Almost the most prodigious asset of a country, and perhaps its most precious possession, is its native literary product—when that product is fine and noble and enduring.

Mark Twain*

The advisory board, the editors, and the publisher of the *Dictionary of Literary Biography* are joined in endorsing Mark Twain's declaration. The literature of a nation provides an inexhaustible resource of permanent worth. Our purpose is to make literature and its creators better understood and more accessible to students and the reading public, while satisfying the needs of teachers and researchers.

To meet these requirements, *literary biography* has been construed in terms of the author's achievement. The most important thing about a writer is his writing. Accordingly, the entries in *DLB* are career biographies, tracing the development of the author's canon and the evolution of his reputation.

The purpose of *DLB* is not only to provide reliable information in a usable format but also to place the figures in the larger perspective of literary history and to offer appraisals of their accomplishments by qualified scholars.

The publication plan for *DLB* resulted from two years of preparation. The project was proposed to Bruccoli Clark by Frederick G. Ruffner, president of the Gale Research Company, in November 1975. After specimen entries were prepared and typeset, an advisory board was formed to refine the entry format and develop the series rationale. In meetings held during 1976, the publisher, series editors, and advisory board approved the scheme for a comprehensive biographical dictionary of persons who contributed to literature. Editorial work on the first volume began in January 1977, and it was published in 1978. In order to make *DLB* more than a dictionary and to compile volumes that individually have claim to status as literary history, it was decided to organize volumes by topic, period, or genre. Each of these freestanding volumes provides a

*From an unpublished section of Mark Twain's autobiography, copyright by the Mark Twain Company

biographical-bibliographical guide and overview for a particular area of literature. We are convinced that this organization—as opposed to a single alphabet method—constitutes a valuable innovation in the presentation of reference material. The volume plan necessarily requires many decisions for the placement and treatment of authors. Certain figures will be included in separate volumes, but with different entries emphasizing the aspect of his career appropriate to each volume. Ernest Hemingway, for example, is represented in *American Writers in Paris, 1920–1939* by an entry focusing on his expatriate apprenticeship; he is also in *American Novelists, 1910–1945* with an entry surveying his entire career, as well as in *American Short-Story Writers, 1910–1945, Second Series* with an entry concentrating on his short fiction. Each volume includes a cumulative index of the subject authors and articles.

Between 1981 and 2002 the series was augmented and updated by the *DLB Yearbooks.* There have also been nineteen *DLB Documentary Series* volumes, which provide illustrations, facsimiles, and biographical and critical source materials for figures, works, or groups judged to have particular interest for students. In 1999 the *Documentary Series* was incorporated into the *DLB* volume numbering system beginning with *DLB 210: Ernest Hemingway.*

We define literature as the *intellectual commerce of a nation:* not merely as belles lettres but as that ample and complex process by which ideas are generated, shaped, and transmitted. *DLB* entries are not limited to "creative writers" but extend to other figures who in their time and in their way influenced the mind of a people. Thus the series encompasses historians, journalists, publishers, book collectors, and screenwriters. By this means readers of *DLB* may be aided to perceive literature not as cult scripture in the keeping of intellectual high priests but firmly positioned at the center of a nation's life.

DLB includes the major writers appropriate to each volume and those standing in the ranks behind them. Scholarly and critical counsel has been sought in deciding which minor figures to include and how full their entries should be. Wherever possible, useful references are made to figures who do not warrant separate entries.

Each *DLB* volume has an expert volume editor responsible for planning the volume, selecting the figures for inclusion, and assigning the entries. Volume editors are also responsible for preparing, where appropriate, appendices surveying the major periodicals and literary and intellectual movements for their volumes, as well as lists of further readings. Work on the series as a whole is coordinated at the Bruccoli Clark Layman editorial center in Columbia, South Carolina, where the editorial staff is responsible for accuracy and utility of the published volumes.

One feature that distinguishes *DLB* is the illustration policy—its concern with the iconography of literature. Just as an author is influenced by his surroundings, so is the reader's understanding of the author enhanced by a knowledge of his environment. Therefore *DLB*

volumes include not only drawings, paintings, and photographs of authors, often depicting them at various stages in their careers, but also illustrations of their families and places where they lived. Title pages are regularly reproduced in facsimile along with dust jackets for modern authors. The dust jackets are a special feature of *DLB* because they often document better than anything else the way in which an author's work was perceived in its own time. Specimens of the writers' manuscripts and letters are included when feasible.

Samuel Johnson rightly decreed that "The chief glory of every people arises from its authors." The purpose of the *Dictionary of Literary Biography* is to compile literary history in the surest way available to us—by accurate and comprehensive treatment of the lives and work of those who contributed to it.

The *DLB* Advisory Board

Introduction

Though published second, *Castilian Writers, 1200–1400* is chronologically the first of two *Dictionary of Literary Biography* volumes devoted to medieval Spanish literature: the other is *DLB 286: Castilian Writers: 1400–1500* (2004). This division by centuries has been adopted for practical reasons of volume length; the tumultuous record of Iberian literature cannot be parceled out in such tidy periods. Some entries in each volume explore authors, works, genres, or themes that transcend the period of the book in which they appear and even the time frame of both volumes.

The origins of Spanish literature are deeply bound up with national identity and national pride; but Spain did not truly emerge as a nation until the late fifteenth century, when the marriage of the Catholic Monarchs, Fernando II of Aragon and Isabel of Castile (better known to English speakers as Christopher Columbus's patrons, Ferdinand and Isabella), brought together the two principal kingdoms of the peninsula and the last Arab redoubt in Granada fell to their united forces. When Isabel died in 1504, the kingdoms were briefly divided again; but on Fernando's death in 1516 they were joined definitively under Fernando and Isabel's grandson, Charles I of Spain, who became Holy Roman Emperor Charles V three years later.

But modern Spain is still riddled with distinctive ethnic and regional histories that exert a centrifugal effect on the nation. Many Spaniards recognize that their divided loyalties look back to the Middle Ages, when the Iberian Peninsula was a conglomerate of principalities with divergent cultures, languages, and literatures. Only the traditions of the Christian majority survive in a continuous stream into the modern period; during the thirteenth to the fifteenth centuries many writers and readers moved readily between Hebrew, Arabic, and the welter of Romance dialects that coalesced during this period into Catalan, Portuguese, and, above all, Castilian. Christian Spaniards also corresponded with and were missionized by fellow Catholics from outside the peninsula, trading ideas and impressions in a patois of Mediterranean Romance tongues or in the true lingua franca of their faith, Latin.

These volumes pay special attention to Castilian as the mightiest of the medieval linguistic streams but with full knowledge that each of Iberia's ethnic communities echoed with the cadences of their neighbors'—and their rivals'—tongues, songs, and attitudes. Jews, a minority under both Muslim and Christian overlords, served as conduits of cultural transfer between those military opponents. But the Moorish and Christian populations also had unmediated points of contact; warrior princes on both sides routinely incorporated areas populated by members of the opposing faith and linguistic group; and residents of the fluid frontier regions were adept in the customs and languages of the opposing culture. The contributors of the entries in the two *DLB* volumes on medieval Castilian writers repeatedly recognize the fitful but steady cultural commerce within the literate communities that shared an Iberian homeland, called al-Andalus by the Muslims, Sepharad by the Jews, and las Españas (the Spains) by the Christians.

For five centuries prior to the period covered in *Castilian Writers, 1200–1400* the territory that had been designated more than a millennium and a half earlier by the Romans as the provinces of "Hispania" was divided by religion into two areas. A unified and extensive Muslim kingdom in the central and southern part of the peninsula constituted itself as an emirate after the Arab invasion of 711; within a century it became a caliphate, and its cultural achievements and influence rivaled anything in the rest of the Muslim world. In the north and northeast several peripheral Christian principalities slowly took shape as Christians fled Muslim rule. By the beginning of the tenth century these principalities consisted of the county of Barcelona and the kingdoms of Navarre; León, which included the county of Aragon; Asturias; and Galicia. The four kingdoms were bisected by the road to Santiago de Compostela, which attracted streams of pilgrims from across the breadth of Christendom. In the earliest stages, however, the bulk of the Christian population remained in Arab territory. It is estimated that in the opening decades of Muslim domination as few as eleven thousand Moors controlled a Hispano-Visigothic population of several million, and the latter came under pressure to convert to Islam. But before the formerly Christian masses were completely acculturated, centuries of accommodation and *convivencia* (coexistence) left the earliest remains of literary expression in a nonstandardized proto-Romance language.

These first traces of vernacular Romance appeared in the late tenth and early eleventh centuries. In the south they consist of *kharjas* (in Spanish, *jarchas*): concluding lines, often mere couplets, attached to Arabic or Hebrew poems and written down in those alphabets. The absence of vowels in Arabic and Hebrew makes the reconstruction of the *kharjas* difficult, but great energy has been lavished on their interpretation and evaluation as expressions of a bilingual community in Muslim-dominated territories in medieval Spain. These studies indicate that the popular lyric, the evolution of which is difficult to document in the oral tradition, existed as the language evolved from Latin to a dialect that many scholars call "Ibero-romance." The early dating of the *kharjas,* at first hotly disputed, gave Spain bragging rights over its European neighbors in retaining the oldest remnants of a true vernacular national literature.

The earliest record of Romance words from the northern provinces is found in the *Glosas Emilianenses* (Glosses of Emilianus), late-tenth- or early-eleventh-century marginal glosses to a Latin document that is still held as a national treasure at its place of origin, the Monastery of San Millán de la Cogolla. Oral epic poetry flourished, but its written record is complex. Nationalistic claims of ancient or early medieval Germanic roots for Spanish epic are now largely discredited, because no remnants date from the era recounted by extant epics.

In the tenth century the king of León was also king of Galicia, Asturias, and a border territory that was known as Castile because of its many castles. Count Fernán González exploited Leonese weakness and used a cunning marriage policy to make Castile a hereditary fief for his family. The *Poema de Fernán González* (between 1251 and 1258, Poem of Fernán González) retells this history for a thirteenth-century Castilian audience. The county of Castile had become a kingdom under Fernando I in 1035.

The strategic importance of Castile was obvious from the beginning. Its location on the eastern edge of the Kingdom of León made it the scene of frequent battles with neighboring Navarre. It was also exposed to Moorish raids from the south and was the logical region from which to launch the reconquest of Muslim-held Toledo.

This goal would have been more difficult to achieve if the political and military unity of Muslim Spain had not disintegrated. Between 1009 and 1031 the Caliphate of Cordova fragmented into small, independent *reinos de taifa* (factional or "party" kingdoms) centered around principal Muslim cities. The southern borders of the Christian kingdoms faced the *taifa* of Saragossa to the east, Toledo in the center, and Badajoz to the west. These *taifa* kingdoms were less able to stave off Christian incursions than the caliphate had been. Toledo fell to Alfonso VI, King of Castile and León, in 1085. On Alfonso's eastern flank lay powerful warlords: the masters of Muslim Saragossa and Valencia and the Christian count of Barcelona. They were engaged and neutralized by a former member of Alfonso's court who had been sent into exile: Rodrigo Díaz de Vivar, known to history by the honorific Arabic title bestowed on him by the Moors: the "Cid" (leader). Forced to become a sword for hire, Díaz fought ably for the king of Saragossa; but like most Christian mercenaries of the age, he had conflicting feelings about serving a Muslim employer. After he had gathered sufficient military strength of his own, he took the glittering prize of Valencia and much of its outlying fertile lands and became a liege lord in his own right. His death in that city–in bed and of natural causes–in 1099 was soon followed by its recapture by Moorish forces. But the sporadic and testy alliances of Díaz and his kinsman Alfonso VI had allowed the Castilian king to regain as much land from the Moors as Díaz did and to do so far more permanently.

Despite a century of invasions by fundamentalist Berbers–first Almoravids and then Almohads–most of the Toledan lands were integrated into Castile and resettled by Christians. Portugal on the west and Aragon on the east were also bent on gnawing into the rich Muslim lands on their southern frontiers. All were driven by the Iberian notion of *Reconquista* (the reconquest of their lost lands) and by the international Christian obsession with religious Crusade. Moorish armies dealt a devastating blow to the northern allies in the battle of Alarcos in 1195; had they pressed their advantage, they might have retaken a large part of the peninsula. But the routed Christian king, Alfonso VIII of Castile, escaped to forge a new coalition, whose victory at Las Navas de Tolosa in 1212 generated an unstoppable momentum. Fernando III of Castile launched successful campaigns against Cordova in 1236, Murcia in 1243–1244, Jaén in 1246, and Seville in 1248; his son Alfonso X *el Sabio* (the Learned) consolidated administrative control over those lands and pressed the enemy into a beleaguered containment that lasted until the fall of the rump state of Granada in 1492.

The few surviving texts of epic tales in Castilian all have to do with the Castilian expansion from the eleventh through the thirteenth centuries and are presumed to reflect a vast corpus of oral tales that were sung for hundreds of years in many versions by *juglares* (minstrels) in taverns and palaces. The principal exemplars are, in order of their composition, *Los siete infantes de Lara* (The Seven Young Noblemen of Lara), recounting events from the late tenth century but preserved in a manuscript from the thirteenth century; the *Cantar de mio Cid* (circa 1200; translated as *Poem of the Cid,* 1879), preserved in a manuscript from the late thirteenth or early fourteenth century; the *Poema de Fernán González,* preserved in a manuscript from the mid thirteenth century; and *Las Mocedades de Rodrigo* (circa 1300; translated as *Las Mocedades de Rodrigo: The Youthful Deeds of Rodrigo, the Cid,* 2007), preserved in a manuscript from the third quarter of the fourteenth century. The *Poema de Fernán González,* set during the period of the founding of the county of Castile around 950, is a learned creation of uneven artistry and a weak reflection of the oral tradition it must have used for its raw materials. Of the four poems, only the *Cantar de mio Cid* exists in a version close to its original form.

Spain is, indeed, fortunate that the unique and nearly intact manuscript of the *Cantar de mio Cid,* its sole surviving medieval epic, eluded the perils of fire, war, and neglect; the work is an undisputed masterpiece of world literature. The poem opens with Díaz being sent into exile by Alfonso VI. The recovery of his good name, his wealth, and the favor of his king comprise the basic plot of the work. He is not only a clever military strategist but also a brawling swordsman: in one encounter he slices a foe in two from head to waist with one blow of his sword. The Cid is just as admirable as a family man, and some of the most touching scenes are those shared with his devoted wife, Jimena, and his two compliant and admiring daughters. The longest dramatic episode of the tale involves the daughters' marriage, at the king's insistence, to unworthy—indeed, homicidal—suitors. The *Cantar de mio Cid* shows many of the hallmarks of poems crafted "on the fly" by skilled singers who could draw on a repertoire of rhetorical formulas to deal with almost any stock situation, such as pitched battles, long marches, farewells, and duels.

The preeminent figure of twentieth-century Hispano-medieval studies, Ramón Menéndez Pidal, spent a good part of his long career plumbing the *Cantar de mio Cid* and confirming its status as a national epic. His interpretation of the poem was based on a belief in its essential historicity, a characteristic he accepted as a trait of all medieval and postmedieval Spanish literature. Most critics now agree that while the *Cantar de mio Cid* reflects a great deal of historical fact, in part owing to the documentary sources used by the poet to assemble his tale, the impression of factuality is largely an artistic effect produced by the way the story is told with a confident aura of historical truth.

The date of composition of the *Cantar de mio Cid* is crucial to interpreting the work. Pidal and his school of "neotraditionalists" believed that it was composed shortly after the hero's death in 1099. This line of thinking dominated in the first half of the twentieth century, with Spanish critics, in particular, presuming a vast, unbroken, but undocumentable succession of oral reworkings of a poem that was essentially complete by 1140 and was set down in the surviving manuscript much later. Other scholars, many of them British and American, called "positivists" because of their insistence on hard evidence for supposed early transitional adaptations of texts, hold that the ephemeral oral tradition cannot be used to justify a reading of a version recorded at a much later date. Neither school has triumphed in the debate. The *Cantar de mio Cid* has too much artistic unity and internal cohesion to be ascribed to collective composition over several centuries; yet, it clearly belongs to an age and an audience that enjoyed oral performance and expected all the established conventions of oral epic to be present. Just as clearly, there is a learned background to many of the plot elements, from the structure of formal prayers such as Jimena's farewell blessing on her departing husband, which has unmistakably liturgical precedents, to the legal niceties of arranging a trial by combat so that neither party is forced to fight with the sun in his eyes. There are also abundant features that only make sense in the context of a dramatic presentation of the poem, such as the constant use of deictics (pointing words), which would have served as virtual stage directions to choreograph the gestures of the *juglar* who was declaiming the story to a circle of listeners. Both sides of the debate have offered engaging insights on the oral culture of the Middle Ages and the participation of literate members of medieval societies in their vernacular oral literature.

Latin learning is reflected in several of the authors and works surveyed in this volume. The Latin chronicles of the opening decades of the thirteenth century by Lucas de Túy, Rodrigo Jiménez de Rada, Juan de Soria, and Fray Gil de Zamora are imposing narratives that present the official perspective of the regime in power when the histories were composed and often of the historians' personal patrons. The vernacular recasting of the origins of the Crown of Castile in *cuaderna vía* (fourfold way), a learned genre of metrical composition, in the *Poema de Fernán González* also supports the status quo, although not favoring any one ruler, and draws on both oral and Latin sources.

A more intense training in Latin is evident in other *cuaderna vía* poetry: churchly training in the case of Gonzalo de Berceo's lives of saints and *Los Milagros de Nuestra Señora* (before 1246–after 1252; translated as *Miracles of Our Lady,* 1997); and academic training in the cases of the triumphalist *Libro de Alexandre* (early thirteenth century, Book of Alexander), with its trove of lore about foreign lands and its imperialistic musings, and the moralizing adventure story *Libro de Apolonio* (late thirteenth century, translated as *The Book of Apollonius,* 1936). French models inspired the various lives of

Santa María Egipçiaca (St. Mary of Egypt), some of the moralistic—or religiously antagonistic—debate poems in which Christians defeat Jews in staged intellectual contests, and poems influenced by the goliards or the troubadours, such as the *Razón de amor con los denuestos del agua y el vino* (1230–1250, Treatise on Love with the Debate between Water and Wine). Petrus Alfonsi wrote in Latin, and his works acquired a huge international readership over the following centuries. The Latin historians Jiménez de Rada and Lucas de Túy had much less luck in finding readers; but when their chronicles were translated into Castilian and incorporated into narratives of national, or at least dynastic, history, they inspired a profusion of works that continued into the sixteenth century and beyond.

Much of the production of Castilian literature in Latin, Galician, and Castilian has to do with the phase of the Reconquest that surrounded the reign of Fernando III. Fernando—who was canonized as St. Fernando in 1671 in tribute to his Crusading ways—encouraged the use of Castilian, along with Latin, as the official languages of his royal chancery. His son, Alfonso X, the most erudite monarch of his century in all Christendom, made the use of Castilian mandatory but retained trained Latinists for his voluminous international correspondence and to support educational ventures such as the university in Salamanca and one announced, but perhaps never actually founded, in Seville. He energetically promoted scholarly enterprises in an unheard of range of areas, commissioning translations of Arabic and Latin works and personally supervising vast encyclopedia projects in Castilian. Alfonso's greatest literary achievement, however, was the social and educational engineering that made the Castilian language a fit instrument for every form of public and scholarly discourse throughout his realm.

Alfonso's royal scriptorium was charged with different projects from those of the chancery, although they no doubt traded resources and key personnel from time to time. The scriptorium took on scientific tasks of personal interest to the king, such as manufacturing timepieces and making astronomical calculations, both of which were connected with casting accurate horoscopes. Astrology and astronomy were virtually synonymous during this period, and Alfonso viewed them as a single science with practical applications. For the next two centuries much of Europe relied on the calculations of the movements of planets and stars made by Alfonso's team of scientists from the meridian of Toledo. The handsomely illustrated *Lapidario* (Book of Stones), translated in 1250, with the only surviving copy produced in the king's workshop between 1276 and 1279, is a compendium of translations of treatises on the medicinal and magical properties of minerals

when used during the ascendancy of stars and planets that promoted their maximum efficacy.

The great team of historiographers commissioned by Alfonso produced constantly evolving projects whose various phases are now given the titles *Estoria de España* (circa 1270–circa 1284, History of Spain) or *Primera Crónica General* (First General Chronicle) and *General Estoria* (circa 1272–circa 1280, General History). Earlier scholarly assumptions that these works were intended as distinct intellectual ventures with separate agendas are now widely questioned.

Alfonso's legal scholars undertook an almost impossibly ambitious merger of Spanish customary law, both codified municipal law and the common law of local practices; canonical law; and reconstituted forms of Roman jurisprudence that had recently been imported into Iberia by Italian law professors. The results range from legal codes as specific as the *Leyes para los adelantados* (1255? Laws for Frontier Governors) and the *Ordenamiento de las tafurerías* (1276, Manual for Gambling Houses) to massive corpora as comprehensive as the *Siete partidas* (1256–after 1272, Seven-Part Law), which still forms the basis of Spanish national law, a large part of the Napoleonic Code, and, through the latter, some of the legal framework of the American state of Louisiana. In 1931 the *Siete partidas* received a full translation into English commissioned by the American Bar Association, and a portrait of the Learned King, carved in marble, hangs in the United States House of Representatives in tribute to his international stature as a legislator.

Alfonso's greatest artistic achievement is his *Cantigas de Santa María* (circa 1257–1282; translated as *Songs of Holy Mary of Alfonso X, the Wise,* 2000), an anthology of 420 songs to the Virgin Mary that express the king's personal piety and Mary's medieval configuration as a spiritual resource for Christian believers. The songs are written in the tongue of Alfonso's childhood, the Galician-Portuguese dialect of northwest Iberia that was favored for courtly lyrics by the literary tastemakers of the peninsula and even in some French territories. After the king's death in 1284, the *Cantigas de Santa María* were virtually ignored until the late twentieth century; since then the four royal scriptorium manuscripts have been recognized as the greatest compilation of Marian miracle narratives, popular music, vernacular poetry, and manuscript illuminations to have been preserved from any country of the period.

The literary and cultural milieu of thirteenth- and fourteenth-century Castile and its neighbors is marked by the ascendancy of Christian Spain over its Muslim antagonists to the south. The entry in this volume on Ramón Llull, the visionary, if eccentric, Christian scholar who wrote in Latin and Catalan and interacted with Castilians at home and with Muslims as far away as North Africa, deals with part of the process. Since no one at the time could know that the last decisive battles had been fought, such celebrated Christian victories as that at Las Navas de Tolosa in 1212 brought no sense of calm or complacency to Christian princes and nobles: the experience of previous centuries was that Moorish Africa was an inexhaustible well of invading armies and that Christian territorial gains were always hard-won and precarious. In the last quarter of the thirteenth century armed bands led by kings or by freelancing noble marauders turned from crusading to fighting each other over sparsely settled and unpacified territories within their expanded borders. They continued to feel threatened by the Moors for another two centuries.

The great shared experience of the thirteenth century may have been mobility. For the masses, travel often meant pilgrimage: on a small and local scale in the form of *romerías* (pious excursions) to neighboring shrines but, above all, the journey to Santiago to pray at the tomb of St. James the Apostle. Europeans of all ranks and stations tramped the open roads and wooded byways to the *Sede Compostelana* (See of Compostela), bringing with them safe-conduct documents, letters of introduction and credit, devotional literature, and private missives to be delivered along the way. A large portion of the hagiographic literature of this period—the works of Berceo, the lives of Santa María Egipçiaca and of a dozen other saints, and, perhaps, even some of the tales of epic heroes—is thought to be the residue of edifying lessons recited to these *peregrinos* (pilgrims). Johann Wolfgang von Goethe remarked that the *Camino de Santiago* (Road to Santiago) "made Europe," and its contribution to cultural exchange cannot be underestimated. Pilgrimage to Santiago became so common among Spaniards, either during their lifetimes or as a testamentary requirement for their heirs, that by the end of the Middle Ages a popular quip was "En vida o en muerte, has de ir a Santiago" (In life or in death, you are bound to go to Santiago).

Much travel was redirected to secular sites during the thirteenth century as land was retaken from Muslim hands and placed under Christian administration. The frontiers could not be consolidated by the remnant Christian minorities in the reconquered lands nor by the soldiers who had won them: settlers and colonists—farmers and artisans and a middle class—were needed. When he started compiling the *Cantigas de Santa María,* Alfonso X drew on well-known tales of Mary's intervention from almost anywhere in Europe; but as the collection—and his territorial holdings—grew, more and more miracle stories were recorded from new shrine sites in underpopulated southern provinces. Alfonso probably believed that these miracles actually took place in towns, such as Santa María del Puerto, that he had brought under his rule, and he no doubt thought that it was good public policy to let those open to relocating there know that the Virgin had a history of assisting the local populace in those places.

Mobility also meant royal armies and privateering raiders foraging through lands available to those with the horses, lances, and swords needed to take and hold them. Those who came south created power struggles by their presence and power vacuums by their absence. Noble clans gained greater reach across the peninsula and prominence in court politics but also found themselves stretched thin by the displacement of expeditionary forces. This climate was not a propitious one for underwriting costly entertainments for a courtly circle: most travelers preferred amusements of a portable variety that could be carried in the memories of balladeers and *juglares.* Alfonso X sustained—at no small cost—the best traditions of courtly song and story established by his predecessors, Alfonso VIII and Fernando III; but the Learned King was a monarch in motion, with no fixed court or castle. His constant wanderings required a baggage train of mules pulling carts piled high with charters, privileges, and the inevitable paper trail of a large bureaucracy, as well as books and musicians with their instruments.

The more stable and cultured courts of this period were those of the episcopal palaces. Led by the scions of many of the same noble families who were privateering in the south, these bastions of church authority enjoyed the regular income of their benefices, a steady stream of foreign and domestic dignitaries, institutions of clerical training that expanded their ranks without their having to wage war or negotiate expensive betrothal contracts, and access to international channels of information and influence. Much of the accumulated learning into which Alfonso X tapped for his great literary projects was borrowed from the libraries of these princes of the church, who could also appreciate a good song and a feast with guests from among the laity. The primates of Santiago de Compostela and Toledo vied with each other for cultural, as well as administrative, leadership of the Spanish church. The governing ecclesiastics in dozens of other cities, and scores of convents and monasteries, were the nuclei that preserved and cultivated the graphic arts and the pleasures of the word that have come down as debate literature, translations of Latin and Semitic learning, moral treatises, and anthologies of exemplary tales, many of which were assembled as preachers' aids. Figures whose ecclesiastical courts in Toledo produced or facilitated outstanding works of Castilian literature include Jiménez de Rada in the early thirteenth century, who wrote the *Historia de rebus Hispaniae sive Historia Gothica*

(1243, History of the Affairs of Spain or History of the Goths) and may have written the *Auto de los reyes magos* (Drama of the Magi), and the "Mozarabic Cardinal" Gonzalo Pérez Gudiel at the end of the century, who possibly assisted the scriptorium of Sancho IV with the *Castigos del rey don Sancho IV* (1292–1293, Lessons of King Sancho IV) and the *Libro del caballero Zifar* (circa 1300–1325; translated as *The Book of the Knight Zifar*, 1983).

Two literary giants mark the early part of the following century: Juan Manuel, a grandson of Fernando III, and Juan Ruiz, Archpriest of Hita. About the former a significant amount is known, because he was one of the principal noblemen of the period, as well as an outstanding writer. Juan Manuel reached manhood at the end of the reign of Sancho IV, Alfonso X's son, who rebelled against his father and took the crown when Alfonso died. Juan Manuel opposed attempts by Fernando IV and Alfonso XI to centralize their power and fought for his rights as a noble of Castile–so much so that Joseph F. O'Callaghan calls him "a born conspirator." His concern for rank shows throughout many of his eight extant works, but especially in the *Libro de los estados* (1326–1330, Book of the Estates), a dialogue between an old knight and a young prince that serves as a narrative frame for a series of exempla. In the second part of the work Juan Manuel argues for the certainty of achieving salvation by acting within one's own estate, or social class. This concern is shared by the piece for which he is best known: *El conde Lucanor* (1335; translated as *Count Lucanor; or, The Fifty Pleasant Tales of Patronio,* 1868), in which a nobleman asks his adviser a series of practical questions and receives answers in the form of exempla.

Less worry about rank but greater anxiety about salvation mark Ruiz's *Libro de buen amor* (circa 1330–1343; translated as *Book of Good Love,* 1933). In contrast to the situation with Juan Manuel, virtually nothing is known with certainty about this author's life; what can be extrapolated about him from his single work is highly conjectural. As the entry in this volume maintains, however, that work provides ample fuel for scholarly speculation about Ruiz and about the literature of the period. The *Libro de buen amor* is a richly woven tapestry incorporating a wide gamut of materials ranging from religious doctrine, didactic tales, clerical jests, legal knowledge, and Aesopian fables to an adaptation of medieval drama, sermon materials, treatises on sin and redemption, instruction on poetic techniques, and folklore. It gives insights into what people were reading and thinking and into the heterogeneity of Castile's population; it raises questions about the role that various genres had on its creation; it exemplifies the shift from Galician-Portuguese to Castilian as a poetic medium;

and, above all, it is suffused with an ambiguity that provides a rich vein for scholars to explore.

The fourteenth century closes with the royal chronicler Pero López de Ayala and Leonor López de Córdoba; their lives encompass the highly significant change of dynasty that occurred in 1369 with the accession of Enrique II, an illegitimate son of Alfonso XI, and the murder of his legitimate half brother Pedro I. It will probably never be known how much of the political instability of Castile was caused by the first outbreaks of the plague, but the period is characterized by such turbulence–indeed, by civil war–that many of the works produced at this time are marked by pessimism.

López de Ayala translated moral and historical works such as Giovanni Boccaccio's *De casibus virorum illustrium* (1355–1360, On the Downfall of Famous Men) as *Cayda de príncipes* (The Fall of Princes), Livy's *Decades,* and Pope Gregory the Great's *Moralia in Job,* and produced chronicles of the reigns of Pedro I, Enrique II, Juan I, and Enrique III. As a poet he was the last author of note to use the already antiquated *cuaderna vía* strophe: he chose it for his best-known work, *El Rimado de Palacio* (1367–1407, The Poem about the Palace), which condemns the system of court favorites and criticizes the venality of public officials. In spite of his choice of an obsolete verse style, López de Ayala represents a literary type that became prevalent in the fifteenth century: the noble who takes up letters as an avocation. Among those who followed his example were Íñigo López de Mendoza, Marqué de Santillana, and the most famous poet of the Castilian fifteenth century, Jorge Manrique.

Unlike López de Ayala, who left a significant body of work, López de Córdoba is the author of only one short piece: the *Memorias* (circa 1400; translated as "To Restore Honor and Fortune: The Autobiography of Leonor López de Córdoba," 1984), an account of her early life. Unknown for most of its existence, the *Memorias* was rediscovered in the late eighteenth century but did not attract much interest until 1977. Since then it has been included in many anthologies of medieval texts and become one of the most frequently read works of the Spanish Middle Ages, because it has the distinction of being the first or second autobiographical work of the Castilian Middle Ages and provides an independent account of the death of Pedro I of Castile and the execution of Leonor's father, Martín López de Córdoba, *maestre* (Grand Master) of Alcántara and Calatrava. It also raises complex questions concerning historical evidence in a narrative written for unclear purposes.

The volume concludes with appendices that survey various genres of Castilian letters during the period. "Medieval Spanish Exempla Literature" treats the short stories and fables that entertained the masses and were retold in subtle ways by the learned to prove sometimes contradictory morals. Other essays deal with the Alfonsine legal codes, Latin histories and chronicles, debate literature, epics, spiritual literature, and theater. Finally, as in all *DLB* volumes, an extensive list of readings that go beyond the bibliographies of the individual entries is provided. The essays in this volume and *DLB 286,* while selective, at least suggest the richness of culture and language awaiting those who explore the literary pathways of medieval Castile and the authors who wrote for its polyglot populations.

—George D. Greenia and Frank A. Domínguez

Acknowledgments

This book was produced by Bruccoli Clark Layman, Inc. Philip B. Dematteis was the in-house editor.

Production manager is Philip B. Dematteis.

Administrative support was provided by Carol A. Cheschi.

Accountant is Ann-Marie Holland.

Copyediting supervisor is Sally R. Evans. The copyediting staff includes Phyllis A. Avant, Caryl Brown, and Rebecca Mayo. Freelance copyeditors are Brenda L. Cabra, Jennifer E. Cooper, and David C. King.

Pipeline manager is James F. Tidd Jr.

Editorial associates are Elizabeth Leverton and Dickson Monk.

Permissions editor is Amber L. Coker.

Office manager is Kathy Lawler Merlette.

Photography editor is Kourtnay King.

Digital photographic copy work was performed by Kourtnay King.

Systems manager is James Sellers.

Typesetting supervisor is Kathleen M. Flanagan. The typesetting staff includes Patricia M. Flanagan.

Library research was facilitated by the following librarians at the Thomas Cooper Library of the University of South Carolina: Elizabeth Sudduth and the rare-book department; Jo Cottingham, interlibrary loan department; circulation department head Tucker Taylor; reference department head Virginia W. Weathers; reference department staff Marilee Birchfield, Karen Brown, Mary Bull, Gerri Corson, Joshua Garris, Beki Gettys, Laura Ladwig, Tom Marcil, Anthony Diana McKissick, Bob Skinder, and Sharon Verba; interlibrary loan department head Marna Hostetler; and interlibrary loan staff Robert Amerson and Timothy Simmons.

Castilian Writers, 1200–1400

Dictionary of Literary Biography

Alfonso X

(23 November 1221 – 4 April 1284)

Richard P. Kinkade
University of Arizona

and

Joseph T. Snow
Michigan State University

WORKS: *Cantigas de Santa María* (circa 1257–1282)

Manuscripts: Biblioteca Nacional, Madrid, MS. 10069, known as manuscript *To,* owing to its provenance in the cathedral of Toledo, 160 folios containing 127 *cantigas*; Real Biblioteca del Monasterio de El Escorial, MS. I.b.2, known as manuscript E and dubbed *Códice de los músicos* (Codex of the Musicians) because of its more than forty miniatures depicting musicians and their instruments, 361 folios containing 420 *cantigas* (the actual number is 427, but 7 are repeated); Real Biblioteca del Monasterio de El Escorial, MS. T.I.1, known as Manuscript T, called the *Códice rico* (Rich Codex) because of its lavish full-page color illuminations of each *cantiga* divided into six panels and, for every numbered *cantiga* ending in 5 (5, 15, 25, and so on), twelve panels spread over two facing folio sides, 256 folios containing 196 poems with musical notations in roughly the same sequence as Manuscript E; National Library of Florence, Magliabechiano MS. Banco Rari 20, known as Manuscript F, 131 folios in a bound volume matching the *Códice rico* in format and style and, despite some modifications, undoubtedly created as the companion volume to it but left incomplete (space has been allotted for texts, illuminations, and musical notation, but only 113 *cantigas* have been copied onto the pages; on many pages designed for musical notation only the staves have been finished, but no notation has been copied).

Statue of Alfonso X at the Biblioteca Nacional, Madrid (from <http://www.flickr.com/photos/zaqarbal>)

Facsimile editions: *El "Códice rico" de las Cantigas de Alfonso X el Sabio: ms. T.I.1 de la Biblioteca de El Escorial* (Madrid: Edilán, 1979); *Cantigas de Santa*

María: Edición facsímil del códice B.R.20 de la Biblioteca Nazionale Centrale de Florencia, siglo XIII, 2 volumes, edited by Ana Domínguez Rodríguez, Agustín Santiago Luque, and María Victoria Chico Picaza (Madrid: Edilán, 1989, 1991).

First publication: *Las "Cantigas de Santa Maria,"* edited by Leopoldo A. de Cueto and Marqués de Valmar, 2 volumes (Madrid: Real Academia de la Lengua Española, 1889; republished, 1990, 1991).

Standard editions: *Cantigas de Santa Maria,* 4 volumes, edited by Walter Mettmann (Coimbra: Acta Universitas Conimbrigensis, 1959–1972; republished, 2 volumes, Vigo: Xerais de Galicia, 1981; republished, 3 volumes, Madrid: Castalia, 1986–1989); *Cantigas de Santa Maria,* edited by José Filgueira Valverde (Madrid: Castalia, Odres nuevos, 1985); *Las cantigas de loor de Alfonso X el Sabio,* edited by Luis Beltrán (Madrid: Ediciones Júcar, 1990); *Cuarenta y cinco cantigas del Códice rico de Alfonso el Sabio,* edited by Beltrán (Palma de Mallorca: José J. de Olañeta, 1997); *Cantigas,* edited by Jesús Montoya (Madrid: Cátedra, 1988).

Edition in English: *Songs of Holy Mary of Alfonso X, the Wise,* translated by K. Kulp-Hill (Tempe: Arizona Center for Medieval and Renaissance Studies, 2000).

Estoria de España (circa 1270–circa 1284)

Manuscripts: The *Estoria de España* (History of Spain) was extensively revised both during and after the reign of Alfonso X. It is extant in partial or fragmentary form in more than one hundred codices from the thirteenth to the sixteenth centuries. Further complicating the matter is that the various versions of the *Estoria de España* are found both in separate manuscripts and in *crónicas* (chronicles) composed at later dates and using different sources and methodological criteria from those that guided the original historical projects of the Alfonsine royal scriptorium. Of the extant codices, only Real Biblioteca del Monasterio de El Escorial, MS. Y.I.2 and the first eighteen folios of Real Biblioteca del Monasterio de El Escorial, MS. X.I.4 are from the royal scriptorium.

Editions: *Primera Crónica General de España que mandó componer Alfonso el Sabio y se continuaba bajo Sancho IV en 1289,* edited by Ramón Menéndez Pidal, Nueva Biblioteca de Autores Españoles, volume 5 (Madrid: Bailly-Bailliere, 1906; republished, Madrid: Gredos, 1977); *Estoria de España (EE1): Biblioteca del Escorial, Y.I.2 (1270–1284) and Estoria de España (EE2): Biblioteca del Escorial, X.I.4 (1284?–1345?),* in *The Electronic Texts and Concordances of the Prose Works of Alfonso X, el Sabio,* edited by Lloyd A. Kasten, John J. Nitti, and Wilhelmina Jonxis-Henkemans, CD-ROM Series 1 (Madison, Wis.: Hispanic Seminary of Medieval Studies, 1997); *Versión crítica de la Estoria de España. Estudio y Edición desde Pelayo hasta Ordoño II,* edited by Inés Fernández-Ordóñez (Madrid: Universidad Autónoma y Fundación R. Menéndez Pidal, 1993).

General Estoria (circa 1272–circa 1280)

Manuscripts: The *General Estoria* (General History or History of the World) is extant in six major divisions corresponding to the medieval concept of the *sex aetates mundi* (six ages of the world) symbolically linked to the biblical week of Creation; each age represents approximately a thousand years. It survives in more than ninety-five manuscripts from the thirteenth through the sixteenth centuries, only two of which are from the original Alfonsine scriptorium: Biblioteca Nacional, Madrid, MS. 816 and Vatican Library, Rome, MS. Urbinas Lat. 539.

Editions: *General Estoria: Parte I,* edited by Antonio García Solalinde (Madrid: Junta para Ampliación de Estudios e Investigaciones Científicas, Centro de Estudios Históricos [J. Molina], 1930); *General Estoria: Segunda Parte,* 2 volumes, edited by Solalinde, Lloyd A. Kasten, and Victor Oelschläger (Madrid: Consejo Superior de Investigaciones Científicas and Instituto "Miguel de Cervantes," 1957); *General Estoria: Tercera parte,* volume 4: *Libros de Salomón: Cantar de los cantares, Proverbios, Sabiduría y Eclesiastés,* edited by Pedro Sánchez-Prieto Borja and Bautista Horcajada Diezma (Madrid: Gredos, 1994)–six additional volumes are projected for this series; *General Estoria I; General Estoria II, Biblioteca Nacional, Madrid, MS 10237; General Estoria IV, Biblioteca Vaticana Urb. Lat., Rome, MS 539; General Estoria V, Biblioteca del Escorial, MS R.I.10; General Estoria V, Biblioteca del Escorial, MS I.I.2; and General Estoria VI, Biblioteca de la Catedral, Toledo, MS n.° 20, Cajón 43,* edited by Lloyd A. Kasten, John J. Nitti, and Wilhelmina Jonxis-Henkemans, in *The Electronic Texts and Concordances of the Prose Works of Alfonso X, el Sabio,* CD-ROM Series 1 (Madison, Wis.: Hispanic Seminary of Medieval Studies, 1997); *General estoria,* 2 volumes of 10 projected, edited by Pedro Sánchez Prieto and Inés Fernández Ordóñez (Madrid: Patronato de la Fundación José Antonio Castro, 2001)–comprises *Tomo I. Génesis; Tomo 2: Exodo, Levítico, Números y Deuteronomio.*

Alfonso X *el Sabio* (the Learned), king of Castile and León, is universally praised for his learning, his poetic endeavors, and his sponsorship of translations of classical and medieval texts. He compiled one of the early verse monuments of the Iberian Middle Ages, the *Cantigas de Santa María* (circa 1257–1282, Songs of Holy Mary); many of his translations from Latin, Greek, Arabic and Hebrew were used for his major historiographic projects, the *Estoria de España* (circa 1270–circa 1284, History of Spain); and the *General Estoria* (circa 1274–circa 1280, General History); and he institutionalized earlier attempts by his father, Fernando III, to make Castilian the language of administration and law within his realms, while directing the compilation of the major law codes of Castile. Translations of Arabic works brought astronomy, applied science such as the construction and use of astrolabes, and medical lore into the European Christian tradition. His efforts were so exemplary that Robert I. Burns has dubbed him the "Emperor of Culture."

Alfonso was born in Toledo on 23 November 1221 to Fernando III, the conqueror of Andalucía, and Queen Beatriz. Through his mother, the daughter of Philip of Swabia, Alfonso was related to the Hohenstaufen family, which included the Holy Roman Emperor Frederick II. Alfonso was raised near Burgos but as a youth spent a good deal of time in Galicia, a region to which he often referred fondly in later life; he acquired a love of the Galician-Portuguese language, which he used extensively in his poetry. Alfonso had six younger brothers and a sister. After Beatriz died in 1235, Fernando III married Jeanne de Ponthieu; the union produced four sons and a daughter.

As a young man, Alfonso was active in the Reconquest of Andalusia from the Moors and came into conflict with Jaime I of Aragon when both were intent on subjugating the Islamic population of Murcia. To heal the rift, a marriage was arranged between Alfonso and Jaime's eldest daughter, thirteen-year-old Violante. The wedding took place in Valladolid on 29 January 1249; the couple had eleven children. Alfonso also had four illegitimate children, including his favorite, Beatriz.

On the death of his father in 1252, Alfonso inherited the throne of Castile and León; through the conquests of Cordova in 1236, Jaén in 1244, and Seville in 1248, the kingdom had come to include much of Andalusia. His immediate concern was to repopulate the vast expanse of land to the south that had been largely abandoned by its former Muslim owners. The internal politics of Andalusia, however, were dictated by the Muslim rulers of North Africa, and Alfonso decided that the security of his realm would best be assured through the conquest of that area.

When Emperor Frederick II died in 1250, his Crown of the Two Sicilies, comprising the kingdoms of Naples and Sicily and including most of the Italian peninsula south of Rome, passed to his son Conrad IV. The title of Holy Roman Emperor, however, was retained by the papacy, which had struggled for years to counter the rising influence of the Hohenstaufens. Through his mother, Alfonso envisioned himself as a candidate to inherit the duchy of Swabia and eventually to contend for the emperorship. Pope Innocent IV, however, rejected his arguments and named William of Holland duke. When both the Pope and Conrad died in 1254, Alfonso pressed his claim with Innocent's successor, Alexander IV, who was at first well disposed toward the king's ambitions. Alfonso's pursuit of his imperial ambitions depleted his kingdom's reserves, forcing him to resort to several currency devaluations, increased taxes on the nobility and church, and other fiscal chicanery. His constant economic depredations engendered ill will among even his staunchest supporters.

The nobles were also provoked by Alfonso's massive recodification of the laws of the land, which they believed was calculated to deprive them of their feudal rights. The *Fuero real* (Royal Charter) and the *Espéculo* (Mirror of Laws) were most likely promulgated during the *cortes* (parliament) held in Toledo in 1254. The *Fuero real* was meant to replace the older *fueros,* which were municipal codes of traditional or common law in use throughout the kingdom, while the *Espéculo* was a set of universal laws that could be used to adjudicate appeals from lower courts governed by the *Fuero real.* By his application of the *Fuero real* throughout Castile and Extremadura and the *Espéculo* in the royal court, Alfonso invoked the principle of equality before the law, denying the nobility the right to be tried by their peers, the *alcaldes de Castilla* (noble judges of Castile).

A delegation of electors traveled to Spain from Pisa in 1256 to propose that Alfonso accept nomination as a candidate for emperor of the Holy Roman Empire. He was elected king of the Romans the following year in preparation for his investiture as emperor; but the election was disputed, and he lost the title in a second round of voting.

Between 1256 and 1265, the period when he entertained his greatest hopes for securing the crown of the Holy Roman Empire, Alfonso directed the compilation of his most important contribution to jurisprudence: the *Libro de las leyes* (Book of the Laws), an extensive revision of the *Espéculo* emphasizing his imperial role together with a synthesis of Roman and canon law condensed into seven parts; it has been known since the fourteenth century as the *Siete Partidas* (Seven-Part Law). There can be little doubt that Alfonso's significant legislative activity during this

Illumination of Alfonso X with his musicians and scribes in the prologue to the Códice rico *(Rich Codex) of the* Cantigas de Santa María
(Real Biblioteca del Monasterio de El Escorial, MS. T.I.1)

period was largely motivated by his desire to be recognized as a monarch thoroughly familiar with Roman law and capable of implementing Roman jurisprudence not only in his own kingdom but also throughout the Holy Roman Empire.

In 1266 Alfonso granted the petition of his five-year-old grandson Prince Dinis of Portugal to release that country from certain feudal obligations. Many of his noble advisers considered the move a foolish dilution of the king's authority that indirectly weakened their own prerogatives. They organized a conspiracy against Alfonso that was led by the king's brother Felipe and by the *Adelantado Mayor* (Governor of the Frontier) Núño González de Lara, Felipe's uncle by marriage, who had been a boyhood friend of Alfonso's. The plotters were soon joined by Lope Díaz de Haro, Lord of Vizcaya, and Esteban Fernández de Castro, governor of Galicia. The rebels thus included not only factions within the royal house but also the three most significant families of the realm: the Laras, the Haros, and the Castros.

Alfonso's son Fernando de la Cerda, the heir apparent, and Blanche, the daughter of King Louis IX of France, were married in November 1269. The ceremony and accompanying festivities committed the Crown to enormous expenses, which, combined with the monarch's insatiable need for revenue to finance his imperial aspirations, forced him to increase taxes again. Alfonso took the opportunity provided by the gathering for the wedding of nobles, prelates, and members of the third estate to summon a *cortes* in Burgos in December 1269. For their part, the rebellious nobles used the occasion to further their conspiratorial schemes. They tried to persuade Alfonso's father-in-law, Jaime I of Aragon, to side with them, but Jaime adroitly evaded the issue. Alfonso was sufficiently concerned by the threat of rebellion to spend several days seeking Jaime's counsel, accompanying him on his return journey to Aragon as far as Tarazona. On his way back to Castile, Alfonso fell gravely ill in Fitero de Navarra from injuries he had sustained when he was kicked by a horse while in Burgos. Informed of the accident, Jaime brought the Aragonese royal physician, Mestre Ioan, to treat Alfonso, and they stayed with him for several days until he was well enough to travel. The injury required a convalescence of nearly a month and a half. The gravity of the condition suggests that Alfonso was most likely kicked not in the *"cama"* (leg), as recorded in Jaime's *Crónica* (Chronicle), but in the *"cara"* (face), and that the resulting fracture led to a slow-growing cancer (squamous-cell carcinoma) that spread through the bones of his face. The accumulation of fluid within his sinuses exerted enormous pressure, which was followed by a rapid remission of symptoms when it drained; then the cycle would start again. During the winter of 1276–1277 and the summer of 1280 the pressure forced the king's left eye from its socket. The illness, whose symptoms often mimicked leprosy, rendered him unable to rule and gave rise to many of the myths that later surrounded his reign, including the legend that he lost his crown while gazing too fondly at the stars—a reference to his desertion of royal responsibilities in pursuit of literary, cultural, scientific, and historical interests during the last two decades of his life.

By September 1272, when Alfonso convoked another *cortes* in Burgos, the conspirators had enlisted the support of Henry I of Navarre and the kings of Granada and Morocco. In the middle of November, having received evidence of renewed interest abroad in his quest to be named Holy Roman Emperor, Alfonso summoned all his diplomatic skills and agreed to the nobility's demands that he submit to arbitration and restore the old *fueros*. Finding their support shriveling, the conspirators withdrew from the *cortes*, declared themselves in revolt, and fled to the kingdom of Granada. There they pledged homage and fealty to the emir Ibn al-Ahmar.

The emir died in January 1273. Alfonso, anxious to secure peace in order to pursue his imperial quest, called the rebels to an assembly in Almagro in March to meet with the emir's heir, Muhammad II; Alfonso's brother Fadrique; and Queen Violante. The meeting severely reduced the credibility of the conspirators. In April, Pope Gregory X called for a council of European prelates and sovereigns to commence in Lyon in May 1274 to seek a solution to the question of the imperial crown. Also in April, Alfonso convoked an assembly of the representatives of the towns of León and Extremadura in Ávila. There Prince Felipe's brother-in-law, Ferrán Ruiz de Castro, and his followers defected from the conspiracy. For the moment it seemed that Alfonso had defused the insurrection.

In June, Alfonso left Ávila for Segovia. From there he sent a letter informing his son Fernando of his illness during the assembly in Ávila; it is one of the first documented references to Alfonso's chronic infirmity and its symptoms: "Era en Ávila, que venía allí por fablar con los concejos de tierra de León e de las Estremaduras que fize allí ayuntar, e ove enfermedat de romadizo e de calentura poca. Et pesóme mucho porque en tal tienpo me acaesciera" (I was in Ávila, where I came to speak with the councils of León and Extremadura, which I convoked there, and I was sick with rheum and a little fever, and I was greatly distressed that this should happen to me at such a time). The illness explains why he did not accompany Queen Violante to a meeting in Cordova with his son Fernando and the rebels in March.

At the end of August 1273 Alfonso met with his father-in-law in Requena, a small town thirty-seven miles west of Valencia. They discussed the intractable aristocracies in both their realms, the forthcoming papal council in Lyon, and the possibility of an invasion of their kingdoms by the emir of Morocco, Abu Yusuf. After the meeting, Jaime returned to Valencia, but Alfonso stayed in Requena to recover from a tertian fever. The normal flow of correspondence and other documents from the king's chancellery ceased during August, suggesting a serious disability. According to *Cantiga de Santa María* 235, "en Requena este Rey mal enfermou, / u duicavan que morresse, daquel mal ben o sãou; / fez por el este miragre" (in Requena this king became gravely ill / and just as they thought he would die, he recovered from that malady; / she [the Virgin Mary] worked this miracle for him). In October the king was in Burgos, where he probably received the news of the election of Rudolf of Hapsburg as king of Germany on 29 September.

In May 1274 Jaime I arrived at the papal court in Lyon as his son-in-law's representative at the council of European prelates and princes. Alfonso had chosen not to attend in person; he was aware of the Pope's predilection for Rudolf of Hapsburg, whose candidacy for the imperial throne seemed assured in light of his election as king of Germany the previous year. The financial outlay for the journey was formidable: Alfonso wanted to give the impression that he was capable of meeting the lavish expenses incumbent on a Holy Roman Emperor. Jaime was obliged to pledge his royal diadem as security to meet his own expenditures for the trip. Alfonso would also have to muster a strong show of internal support for his claims to the imperial crown, and neither the nobility nor the church had shown themselves supportive of this nebulous enterprise. He therefore convoked an assembly of nobles, jurists, and prelates in Zamora in June and July. On 22 July a further complication arose when the death of Henry of Navarre set the stage for a power struggle in Pamplona among political factions allied with Castile, France, and Aragon. Alfonso, mindful of the need for peninsular unity, advanced his own rather tenuous claims to the Navarrese throne.

Meanwhile, at the Council of Lyon, Pope Gregory X was determined to settle the imperial question once and for all but was unwilling to yield to Alfonso's demands. Yet, he could not afford to ignore the claims of a powerful political figure around whom many of the Ghibelline factions of northern Italy had rallied. The pontiff was also aware of the need to enlist Alfonso's support in a new Crusade. He therefore issued a papal bull condemning the divisive stratagems of the recalcitrant nobles, who had thwarted Castilian efforts to subdue the Moors while inviting Muslim intervention in the south of Spain. Gregory also offered Alfonso one-tenth of all ecclesiastical revenues for six years if the monarch would desist from his imperial pretensions and devote his efforts to a Crusade on his southern frontier. The extent of Alfonso's obsession with the imperial crown may be measured by his refusal of this magnanimous bid on the part of the Pope, though he did not reject the notion of a Crusade.

Alfonso renounced his claim to the Navarrese throne in favor of his son Fernando, who marched without delay toward Pamplona and laid siege to the town of Viana in September; when his efforts in this area were frustrated, he besieged Mendavia. Displeased by this display of strife among Christian nations, the Pope confirmed the German princes' election of Rudolf of Hapsburg as king of Germany on 26 September 1274. When Alfonso learned of Rudolf's confirmation, he must have reasoned that any further delay in meeting with Gregory would jeopardize his imperial aspirations. He arrived in Alicante on 16 October, in Valencia around the middle of November, and in Barcelona during the Christmas holidays. Jaime I spared no expense in accommodating his royal son-in-law, and Alfonso remained in Barcelona until the end of January. He then made his way with an Aragonese escort as far north as Perpignan on the French border, where he left the queen, their children, and many of his retainers and proceeded to Montpellier. He spent fifteen days in the city, famous for its schools of law and medicine. During his stay he received a message from the Pope proposing an interview in Beaucaire, a small town on the Rhone thirty-one miles away, instead of Lyon, where the council had concluded its yearlong deliberations. The location was, perhaps, chosen out of consideration for the king's health, which was once again in crisis: Lyon would have required a journey more than five times as far. *Cantiga* 235 says that "quando da terra sayu e que foi veer / o Papa que enton era, foi tan mal adoecer / que o teveron por morto" (when he left his land and went to see / the Pope of that time, he fell so gravely ill / that they thought he would surely die). This information is at variance with the lighthearted account of the contemporary Catalan chronicler Ramon Muntaner, who emphasizes the festive air surrounding the entire expedition.

The Pope was in Beaucaire on 14 May 1275, and one may suppose that Alfonso arrived there at about the same time. Their discussions lasted until the end of July but were inconclusive. The Pope was committed to the idea of embarking on an expedition to the Holy Land with Alfonso's assistance but was unyielding in his demand that the king renounce all claims to the throne of the Holy Roman Empire; equally obdurate,

Alfonso never repudiated his imperial aspirations in writing.

Alfonso had received word in late May or early June that the vanguard of a new Muslim invasion had disembarked in Tarifa on 13 May, no doubt encouraged by the divisive activities of the rebellious Spanish nobles. The advance troops were followed on 16 August by Abu Yusuf and the main Moorish assault forces. Alfonso probably returned to Montpellier in late August. *Cantiga* 235 recalls: "E pois a Monpisler vo e tan mal adoeceu / que quantos fisicos eran, cada hûu ben creeu / que sen duvida mort'era; mas ben o per guareceu / a Virgen Santa Maria, como Sennor mui leal" (Then he arrived in Montpellier and became so seriously ill / that of all the physicians there each and every one firmly believed / that he was surely dead; but he was completely cured by / the Holy Virgin, faithful Lady that she is). This information, found nowhere else, is of the utmost consequence for understanding Alfonso's actions in the next few months, a pivotal period in the history of Castile. In Montpellier he learned of the death on 24 or 25 July of his twenty-year-old son and heir, Fernando de la Cerda, who had fallen victim to an unidentified illness in Villareal. Alfonso also had to bear the loss of his daughter Leonor and his nephew Alfonso, the son of his youngest brother, Prince Manuel, who had both also died in July.

The Muslim army routed the Castilians in Ecija on 7 September 1275, killing one of the principal rebels, Nuño González de Lara. On 15 October Pope Gregory announced to the princes of Europe that Alfonso had abandoned his claim to the Holy Roman crown. Jaime I's son Sancho, the archbishop of Toledo, was captured during the Battle of Martos on 20 October and was beheaded the following day. On 23 October the invaders were at the gates of Seville, but they were unable to breach the city walls. Menaced by a naval blockade organized by Alfonso's seventeen-year-old son, Prince Sancho, that would eventually cut off their supplies, the invaders pillaged the western Andalusian countryside; by the middle of November they had returned to Algeciras with their booty. Sometime after the middle of December, Alfonso arrived in Alcalá de Henares, where he spent Christmas. Peace talks with the Muslims, in which Prince Sancho was one of the main negotiators for the Castilians, were concluded by the end of the year.

Gregory X died in December 1275. Innocent V became Pope on 21 January 1276 and died on 22 June; he was succeeded on 11 July by Adrian V, who died on 18 August. On 8 September the College of Cardinals elevated the Portuguese Pedro Juliano Rebello, known as Petrus Hispanus, to the papacy as John XXI.

On 4 January 1276 the king was in Toledo. In the following weeks he met with Sancho and Lope Díaz de Haro, Lord of Vizcaya, to discuss the succession to the throne. On his deathbed Fernando de la Cerda had reportedly sworn his vassal Juan Núñez de Lara, the son of the late Nuño González, to promote the claim of Fernando's firstborn son, Alfonso, to the throne, thereby committing the powerful house of Lara to the de la Cerda cause. At the same time Lope Díaz de Haro had made a pact with Sancho to support him as the rightful heir apparent. The situation was further complicated by the fact that Alfonso de la Cerda's mother, Blanche, was the sister of the king of France, Philip III, who had every reason to believe that his nephew would be proclaimed heir to the throne of Castile and León; any challenge to the de la Cerda claim would be hotly contested by the French monarch.

Alfonso X was in a legal quandary: he had ruled in the *Espéculo,* promulgated in 1255, and again in the *Siete Partidas,* published before 1265, that legal succession to the throne descended in a direct line from father to firstborn son to grandson. Thus, he was bound by his own legal pronouncements to favor his grandson by Fernando; on the other hand, he was faced with his own illness, the probability of renewed Muslim invasions on his southern flank, and the fact that Alfonso de la Cerda, five years old at the time of his father's death, would be unable to rule until he reached his majority, while Sancho was a battle-tested warrior and negotiator who commanded the allegiance of many of the most powerful lords of the realm. Perhaps unable to take a decisive stance because of his illness, Alfonso returned to the north, arriving in Valladolid in February 1276. In April he was back in Burgos, where he summoned a *cortes* that met from May through July. Unable further to postpone a decision on the succession to the throne, he confirmed Sancho as his heir, securing the approval of the *cortes* at the beginning of July.

Philip III reacted to Alfonso's failure to ratify the right of his nephew to the throne of Castile by invading the peninsula. At the same time he dispatched troops under the command of Blanche's brother Robert, Count of Artois, to Pamplona to defend French claims in Navarre. Alfonso reacted to the latter move by sending forces under the command of his brother, Prince Fadrique, and the prince's son-in-law, Simón Ruiz de los Cameros, to Pamplona. The expected battle never materialized: inexplicably, the Castilian army marched to Monreal, a few miles southeast of Pamplona, and remained there without making any effort to relieve the beleaguered Castilian partisans, who were defeated by the French.

By 5 September, Alfonso had taken up residence in Vitoria. Philip moved on him, but an unusually rainy

Panel of illuminations for Cantiga *42 in the* Códice rico *of the* Cantigas de Santa María *(Real Biblioteca del Monasterio de El Escorial, MS. T.I.1)*

fall and a lack of supplies obliged the French forces to abandon their campaign at Sauveterre-de-Béarn, thirty miles east of Bayonne. Near the end of October, Philip sent emissaries to Vitoria to sue for peace. The two sides reached an understanding on 7 November 1276.

During the winter of 1276–1277 Alfonso suffered an excruciating recurrence of his illness that *Cantiga* 209 recounts in detail, claiming that he was once again near death. In the meantime the king of France, frustrated in his bid to dominate Castilian and Navarrese politics by force and in an attempt to coerce a resolution favorable to his nephew, was courting clandestine factions in Castile hostile to Alfonso, while Prince Sancho and his allies were working to consolidate the second-born's claim to the throne.

Apparently without warning, Prince Fadrique and his son-in-law, Simón Ruiz de los Cameros, were executed on Alfonso's order at the end of April or the beginning of May 1277. Ruiz was burned at the stake, and Fadrique was *"afogado"* (strangled), most likely with a golden silk cord symbolic of his royal rank and his right to die a more dignified death than an individual of inferior station. No conclusive information concerning the reason for the executions is available. *Cantiga* 235, which comments in rigorous chronological order on several events in Alfonso's life during the 1270s, makes an oblique reference to the incident: it says that Alfonso, with divine assistance, wreaked royal vengeance on those who had attempted to evict him from his own domain; those of his enemies who did not love women—a veiled allusion to the crime of sodomy—were burned at the stake. The implication would seem to be that Fadrique and Ruiz were discovered in flagrante delicto and dispatched without benefit of trial. The liberal-minded Alfonso would probably have been tolerant of a homosexual relationship between Fadrique and Ruiz; but when faced with their support of the rebellious nobles and the threat that they might use the Castilian army stationed in Navarre to overthrow him, he likely seized on their liaison as a justification for fratricide. Nevertheless, Sancho publicly rebuked his father for murdering Fadrique *"sin causa"* (without cause), and, in an act that would seem to belie either the validity of the charge of homosexuality or the seriousness with which the crime was viewed in Castile, ordered the body of his uncle removed from "un lixoso lugar do el rey don Alfonso lo mandó enterrar" (the filthy place in which Alfonso had him interred) and gave him an honorable burial in the Trinitarian monastery in Burgos.

A *cortes* convened in Burgos in the late spring of 1277 and ended sometime before Pentecost, which fell on 16 May. On 16 May, Lope Díaz de Haro, having abandoned his allegiance to Alfonso, signed a receipt in Pamplona for monies advanced for feudal service to the king of France. Alfonso lost another ally with the death on 20 May of the Portuguese Pope John XXI. In July, Alfonso's cousin, Fernán Pérez Ponce, received his advance for services to Philip III. The Haros, supporters of Sancho, and the Laras, champions of the de la Cerda cause, were thus united on the side of the French against their own monarch. The defection of the nobles to the French can only be explained by the same conspiracy that had cost Fadrique and Ruiz their lives.

In the late spring of 1277 a Moroccan expeditionary force ravaged the countryside along the southern frontier. The raiders were followed by a much larger army under the command of Abu Yusuf, who disembarked in Tarifa on 1 July to pursue a now and more vigorous jihad. *Cantiga* 235 reports that "E pois sayr de Castela, el Rey con mui gran sabor / ouve d'ir aa fronteira; mas a mui bõa Sennor / non quis que enton y fosse, se non sãasse mellor; / porend' en todo o corpo lle deu febre geral" (After leaving Castile, the king was eager / to go to the frontier; but the virtuous Lady / did not wish him to go there just then, until he recovered more fully; / therefore, she gave him a general fever throughout his body). Alfonso remained in Burgos for the rest of the year. On 3 August, Abu Yusuf arrived at Seville, where he defeated Castilian forces under Alfonso Fernández. The Moroccans attacked Jerez on 15 September and Cordova on 30 October.

In January 1278 Queen Violante, her grandchildren Alfonso and Fernando de la Cerda, and their mother, Blanche, abandoned the king in Burgos and fled to the protection of the queen's brother, Pedro III, who had succeeded Jaime I as king of Aragon in 1276. Pedro and his nephew, Sancho, had hatched the scheme to promote their mutual interests: sequestering the children in Aragon removed a major obstacle to Sancho's accession to the throne and secured a bargaining chip for Pedro to use against the children's uncle, Philip III. Isolated by his illness, Alfonso was apparently unaware of the deception and was confused by Violante's actions, which further compromised the monarch's dwindling prestige and authority.

Alfonso left Burgos in March, passed through Peñafiel on 24 March, and arrived in Valladolid on Sunday of Holy Week, 10 April 1278. He spent the week in the agony of death, his physicians having abandoned all hope for his recovery. Then, on Easter Day, 17 April, according to *Cantiga* 235, the Virgin miraculously healed him. Alfonso had sufficiently recovered by the middle of May to attend the *cortes* in Segovia, where he turned over many of his royal responsibilities to Sancho. Reaching Seville during the summer of 1279, Alfonso, who had forged an alliance with Muhammad II of Granada, proposed that they blockade Algeciras to prevent it from falling into the hands of Abu Yusuf and the Moroccan invaders. The cost of maintaining a siege on land and sea soon depleted Alfonso's coffers, and Muhammad II, sensing the collapse of the blockade, repudiated the pact and sided with the invaders. The king attempted to raise funds through yet another tax levy, but Sancho used the money to help his mother, Violante, repay the debts she had accumulated during her stay in Aragon. The gesture allowed her to return to Castile. While the king was willing to pardon Violante's duplicity, the funds diverted to her forced him to abandon the blockade of Algeciras and allowed Abu Yusuf to capture the city. The emir then turned on his erstwhile ally, Muhammad II, who had refused to surrender Málaga to the Moroccans, and proposed a pact with Castile for a joint attack on Granada. Unable to participate in the campaign because of a recrudescence of his malady, which threatened him with the loss of his left eye, Alfonso sent Sancho to besiege Granada. Although the Castilians and Moroccans succeeded in ravaging the countryside around the city, they were unable to breech the walls. The successive failures of the blockade of Algeciras and the siege of Granada left the ailing monarch with enormous debts that he could only settle by yet greater taxation. Convinced that his principal tax collector, Zag de la Maleha, had betrayed him by handing over to Sancho the revenue collected for the siege of Algeciras, Alfonso had Zag executed before the gates of Sancho's residence in Seville. He then arrested all of the Jews in the kingdom, forcing them to pay a huge ransom for their release. Sancho was strongly opposed to these moves and was becoming an ever more attractive alternative to his father's increasingly irrational rule.

Pope Nicholas III regarded the rift between Alfonso and Philip III as an impediment to his plans for a Crusade to liberate the Holy Land and arranged a summit between the two sovereigns, who met before Christmas 1280. Alfonso was aware that Philip's enmity toward him was rooted in his decision to disinherit his grandchildren, the infantes de la Cerda in favor of Sancho. To appease Philip, Alfonso offered to invest Alfonso de la Cerda with the kingdom of Jaén. Although Philip rejected the proposal as inadequate, Sancho was enraged that his father had considered depriving him of a large part of his inheritance and fragmenting the realm. As Alfonso's health and judgment continued to deteriorate, Sancho recognized that his firmest ally might be his uncle, Pedro III of Aragon, who was embroiled in a conflict with Alfonso X over claims to the kingdom of Navarre and Aragonese support of the rebellious nobles lodged in Vizcaya. Sancho met secretly with Pedro and promised to relinquish all rights to Navarre and other disputed territories as soon as he became king. These agreements and Sancho's alli-

ance with Pedro quickly became known, reconfirming Alfonso's waning authority and Sancho's growing influence in peninsular affairs.

Alfonso became obsessed with wreaking vengeance on Muhammad II of Granada for betraying him. He convoked a *cortes* in Seville in the fall of 1281 to garner support and raise revenues for a campaign against Granada. To secure the financing for the impending war, Alfonso proposed further debasement of the coinage; to avoid renewed hostilities with France, he resumed negotiations to offer Philip III's grandson Alfonso de la Cerda the kingdom of Jaén. Alarmed by his father's renewed insistence on a scheme designed to diminish his future domains, Sancho prepared to revolt. At the same time, the representatives of towns and cities throughout the realm, dismayed at the economic disarray that would be caused by the debasement, organized an open rebellion that culminated in the convocation of an unlawful *cortes* in Valladolid in April 1282. Sancho had the support and backing of his mother, Queen Violante; his paternal uncle Manuel; his brothers Pedro, Juan, and Jaime; and a large contingent of prelates and nobles who banded together with townsmen throughout the peninsula in *hermandades* (brotherhoods) whose immediate concern was the protection and strengthening of their local *fueros*. Among the few municipalities that remained loyal to Alfonso were Seville, Murcia, and Toledo. His rejection by so many others and the groundswell of support for Sancho's rebellion led the king to seek an alliance with his former foe, Abu Yusuf of Morocco. Pledging his crown as collateral, Alfonso received from the Marinid emir a loan of 100,000 gold dinars and the promise of troops to besiege Cordova, where Sancho had established a stronghold in September. Abu Yusuf took advantage of the agreement to ravage the land as far north as Toledo before withdrawing to Algeciras. Though offended, as were most Christians, by Alfonso's coalition with the Moroccan, Pope Martin IV condemned Sancho's treasonous revolt by excommunicating him; he also placed an interdict on the people of Spain until they renewed their allegiance to the monarch. Alfonso cursed and disinherited Sancho and declared the infantes de la Cerda his heirs. Several attempts were made to reconcile father and son but to no avail.

In January 1284 the dying monarch revised his last will and testament to recognize and reward those who had supported him but with no mention of the infantes de la Cerda. He stipulated that the *Cantigas de Santa Maria* should be given to the Cathedral of Seville, where he was to be buried, and that they were to be sung there on the Virgin's feast days. He died on 4 April. A repentant Sancho remarked on his own death-

Illumination for Cantiga 71 *of the* Cantigas de Santa María, *showing the Virgin Mary curing Alfonso, who was thought to be dying, in Valladolid (National Library of Florence, Magliabechiano MS. Banco Rari 20)*

bed in 1295 that his end had been hastened by his betrayal and his father's curse.

Among the most significant literary works associated with Alfonso is the *Cantigas de Santa María,* a collection of more than four hundred poems in Galician-Portuguese verse form, many with written musical accompaniment, recounting miracles performed by the Virgin Mary. Many of the poems are illustrated in the manuscripts with full-page illuminations.

Devotion to Mary not only as *Theotokos* (Mother of God; literally, "God Bearer" in Greek), as she was designated by the Council of Ephesus in the fifth century, but also as a personal advocate for sinners on Judgment Day grew with particular force in Europe from the late tenth century onward and rose sharply with the preaching of Dominican and Franciscan friars in the thirteenth century. It manifested itself in hundreds of Latin anthologies of miracle narratives that attested her interventions on behalf of those who called on her for aid and protection in their daily lives. These accounts were often adapted to heighten the fame of local shrines to Mary, whose custodians hoped to increase the flow of pilgrims to their locales.

Adgar, a cleric based in London and writing in Anglo-Norman, seems to have begun the fashion with thirty-eight accounts of Mary's wondrous acts in the 1190s. They were followed by the fifty-nine accounts in the *Miracles de Nostre Dame* (Miracles of Our Lady), written in French by Gautier de Coincy around 1230; Gonzalo de Berceo's twenty-five accounts in Castilian, the *Milagros de Nuestra Señora* (circa 1260, Miracles of Our Lady), twenty-four drawn from a Latin prose original with the addition of a new Iberian-based miracle of unknown provenance; and the fifty miracles in the Latin *Liber Mariae* (Book of Mary), composed by a member of Alfonso's court, the friar Juan Gil de Zamora.

The *Cantigas de Santa María* was once attributed in its entirety to Alfonso, but most of the poems are now believed to have been written by many authors within his court circle; court conventions allowed the poets to adopt the king's voice and persona. Alfonso might have written as few as ten poems and as many as forty. Airas Nunes is believed to have written some of the *cantigas;* his name appears twice in marginal manuscript notations. Another candidate is Gil de Zamora, since a few of the miracle accounts in his *Liber Mariae* are found in versified adaptations in the *Cantigas de Santa María*. Nothing is known with certainty regarding other possible contributors to the *Cantigas de Santa María*.

The Galician-Portuguese language of the poems had long been used in secular lyric compositions of three types: *cantigas d'amigo* (songs of a friend), in which a girl laments the absence of her male lover or "friend"; *cantigas d'amor* (songs of love), in which a male lover sings the praises or defends the virtues of an inaccessible liege lady; and *cantigas d'escarnho e de mal-dizer* (songs of mocking and denigration) directed against rivals or enemies. Alfonso is known to have joined in poetic jousts and to have produced about three dozen *cantigas,* some of which predate his ascension to the throne in 1252. One of these secular compositions is a fragment of a *loor* (praise song) modeled on an *alba* (dawn song) composed by the Provençal troubadour Cadenet but dedicated to the Virgin. This fragment coincides with *Cantiga* 340 and suggests that Alfonso may have begun to experiment with the more-intimate *cantigas d'amor*. Of the three genres of Galician-Portuguese secular song poems, only the *cantiga d'amigo* was not cultivated by the monarch. The first redaction of the *Cantigas de Santa María* is found in the Toledo Manuscript, known as manuscript *To,* and can be dated to the first half of the 1260s by references it makes to events that occurred in those years.

The rosary is so named because of the association of the aesthetic perfection of the rose and the mystical perfection of the Virgin Mary, who was called "Mystical Rose" in her medieval litany, and the *Cantigas de Santa María* forms a sort of poetic rosary. The poems are gathered in groups of ten: nine *miragres* (miracle accounts) representing the nine small beads are capped by a *loor* that exalts Mary's wondrous attributes and powers, representing the larger bead of the early rosary. The fifth poem in each unit of ten is normally a longer miracle account. Each decade of poems is interlocked with the following decade throughout the collection in an endlessly recyclable structure that mirrors a central theme of the *Cantigas de Santa María:* that Mary's *bees e mercees* (good qualities and mercies) are inexhaustible. This sentiment is the theme of *Cantiga* 110, a *loor* in which the impossibility of sufficiently praising the Virgin is evoked in the image of a man who writes for his entire life, with the sky for parchment and the sea for ink, but leaves the vast majority of her qualities and miracles unmentioned.

According to Walter Mettmann, the editor of a modern edition of the *Cantigas* (1959–1972), the poems are grouped by hundreds—a procedure that roughly reflects the manner in which the compilation grew. The first seventy-five are about miracles that take place out-side Iberia; fourteen are Iberian miracles, one of which is of a personal nature. (The *loores,* which are nonnarrative, do not figure in Mettmann's calculation.) In the second hundred the pan-European miracles decrease to forty-six, and the national ones increase to forty-four; three of the latter are personal. In the third hundred the extra-Iberian total drops to thirty-six miracles, and the national tally rises to fifty-four, with eight of the latter being personal. The fourth grouping exceeds one hundred, as Mettmann takes the appendix poems into account: here only nineteen miracles are international, sixty-eight are Iberian, and thirteen of the latter deal with Alfonso directly.

One of the ways in which the *Cantigas de Santa María* diverges from the typical Marian compilation is by transforming otherwise unrelated miracle accounts into a coherent narrative around the king. This transformation casts Mary as a lady who is loved by an *entendedor* (troubadour suitor), a self-confessed sinner without any specific failing other than his fallen human condition and need for spiritual succor. The *Cantigas de Santa María* begins with two Prologue poems, traditionally designated A and B. In Prologue A, Alfonso is called "dos Romãos Rey" (the King of the Romans), a title he could only have used after his election in 1257. After listing all of the lands over which he rules, Prologue A notes that Alfonso "made" the *Cantigas de Santa María* in honor and praise of Mary and that he composed its *cantares e sões* (lyrics and music). In Prologue B an unnamed first-person speaker fears that he may not be up to the task of praising his beloved and places his trust in God to help him find the proper voice for this monumental task. He declares himself desirous of becoming the troubadour of Mary and beseeches her to accept him in her service, for she is known not to fail those who ask for aid. He hopes that she will consider the songs offered to her as a living token of his unswerving service and devotion. He adds that if she does see fit to reward him, all those who come after him will still find ample reason to *trobar* (sing) her praise. He declares that "des oge mais" (from this day forward) he will sing only for and of his beloved Virgin Mary. The same sentiment is heard in *Cantiga* 10, where he continues his request to be accepted as Mary's *entendedor*. After a detailed paean to Mary in which she is declared unique among women and invoked under her honorific titles as Rose of Roses, Flower of Flowers, and Lady of Ladies, he says that should he be given the opportunity to earn her love, he vows to renounce "os outros amores" (all other loves). This renunciation, he says, must be sincere, for Mary would know if it were not so.

Cantiga 100 praises the Virgin for placing sinners on the correct path to God and ends by affirming that since Heaven is a reward for believers, the troubadour would be pleased, should Mary approve, if his soul were accepted into the divine fellowship. In *Cantiga* 180 he declares his love not for a mortal *domna* (lady) but for Mary, Virgin and Mother, Wife and Handmaiden to God. She is the one sinless woman, chosen by God for the redemption and salvation of sinners, who will undo the harm caused by Eve, whose Original Sin all other humans have borne from birth. She will play the role of *mediatrix* (mediator) and *avogada* (advocate) for sinners on Judgment Day. *Cantiga* 200 blurs the line between the voice of the troubadour and that of Alfonso by noting that she allowed him to be the king of his people, attended him in illness, and provided for his safety. He prays that when his life on Earth is over, he may be granted the gift of being able to contemplate her face forever.

Confirmation of the efficacy of Mary's power comes in *Cantiga* 209, which is narrated in the first person. Alfonso falls ill in Vitoria on his return trip from seeing the Pope in Beaucaire in 1275. Physicians cannot cure the king; but when he commands that the book of *cantigas* to Mary be placed on his ailing body, his pain disappears in an instant. In *Cantiga* 295 the troubadour is informed of his hoped-for salvation by some devout nuns to whom Mary appears in dream visions; the experience will make the king serve Mary even more assiduously thereafter. Internal references link several poems together and refer to the king's journeys. In *Cantiga* 366 Mary is "A que en nossos cantares / nos chamamos Fror das flores" (She whom in our songs / we have called Flower of Flowers), which he had done in *Cantiga* 10. *Cantiga* 235 recalls the illness, detailed in *Cantiga* 209, that forced the king to remain in Vitoria.

In *Cantiga* 260 the speaker chides other poets for being slow to take up the praise of Mary: "Dezid', ai trobadores, / a Sennor das sennores, / porqué a non loades?" (Tell me, o troubadours, / why you do not praise / the Woman of Women?). These other troubadours while away their time pursuing "outros amores" (other loves) that the speaker has renounced. In *Cantiga* 300 the speaker urges all humankind to praise Mary, who aids sinners to return to God's true path, and he beseeches Mary to come to his aid and fight his enemies, some of whom begrudge the time he has devoted to composing poetry in praise of her. He repents of having trusted certain men who have only repaid him with treason and falsehood. In *Cantiga* 400 he admits that despite his best efforts he has not adequately praised his beloved Mary; he knows, however, that God will judge not the quantity of the "love tokens" that he has presented to her but the spirit in which they have been offered. He pleads with Mary to accept his *cantigas* in the name of Christ, her son. In *Cantiga* 401 he says that Mary will intercede as his advocate and win him a place in Paradise; but while he lives, he needs wisdom to deal with his enemies and strength to defeat the Saracen infidels. He declares that if he is rewarded for his service in composing these songs, it should be because they are an example and a stimulus to others—a theme first broached in Prologue B. *Cantiga* 402 insists again on the smallness of the poet's service to the Virgin when compared to her munificence, should he be found worthy of her favors.

Cantigas 209, 235, 279, 366, and 367 are of inestimable benefit to historians for the explicit descriptions they provide of the king's ill health, which is not mentioned in other contemporary sources. *Cantiga* 235, described and extensively annotated by Richard P. Kinkade in a 1992 article, is the most valuable of these compositions both for its broad historical perspective and for its rigorous chronological ordering of significant episodes. Most likely composed by the monarch himself and spanning the decade from 1269 to 1278, *Cantiga* 235 recounts a series of personal disasters—the treachery of his relatives, the rebellion and renunciation of feudal obligations to the Crown by many of Castile's most powerful nobles, a cycle of nearly fatal illnesses, the abandonment of his cherished claims to the throne of the Holy Roman Empire, and the deaths in the same year of his son and heir Fernando and his youngest daughter Leonor—events from which Alfonso recovered, according to the *cantiga,* only because of the personal intervention of the Virgin.

Escorial manuscript T.I.1, known as Manuscript T and called the *Códice rico* (Rich Codex) because of its lavish illuminations, profusely illustrates 192 *cantigas*—approximately one half of the total—in more than 1,600 miniature paintings. Every miracle account and song of praise is accompanied by a pictorial representation in six panels on a single page, except those ending in 5 (*Cantigas* 5, 15, 25, and so forth). These longer miracle accounts are represented by facing pages of six panels each, which means that the song would have been sung from memory or performed from another copy while the audience enjoyed the visual display in the open book before them. The *Códice rico* was left incomplete by the royal scriptorium around the time of Alfonso's death; the last *cantiga* that is datable refers to an event that happened in 1281 and must have been composed not long afterward. An identical layout and format characterizes Manuscript F, which must be an unfinished continuation of the *Códice rico* and is believed to have made its way to Florence in the seventeenth century. If all the miniatures in the two manuscripts had been completed, there would have been about 2,640 of them, making them one of the largest programs of illumination conceived in the Middle Ages and rivaled only by the French "moralized Bibles" of the 1220s and 1230s.

The miniatures paint a canvas of life in the thirteenth century, providing diverse views of urban, rural, and marine landscapes; foreign lands; and social classes. The artists, who may have come from both inside and outside the peninsula—the influence of French painting conventions in the "international Gothic" style has been detected—painstakingly reproduced the exteriors and interiors of fortresses, castles, churches, tradesmen's shops, and humble homes. The illustrations depict carpenters, pharmacists, stonemasons, silk farmers, mule drivers, and dozens of other craftsmen and craftswomen with the tools of their trades. There are travelers, pilgrims, runaway nuns, hook-nosed Jews, turbaned Moors, physicians, jugglers, hunters, merchants, peddlers, kings, emperors, queens, harlots, thieves, and seamen; scenes of construction and demolition, war and peace, and health and illness; open wounds, children of all ages, bedroom scenes, ships and shipwrecks, day and night, Earth and heaven, shrines to Mary, and the sun, moon, and stars. The story lines of the individual narratives served as a general guide for the artists, but their imaginations were free to supply details. The illustrations of the *loores* feature Mary and her liturgical symbols more prominently than do those of the miracle accounts. These illustrations routinely portray Alfonso as a beardless youth, wearing a crown and robes embroidered with his regal insignia, in various attitudes of worship before the Queen of Heaven.

The illuminations add layers of complexity to the retelling of common-stock miracle stories. In *Cantiga* 42 a young man in Germany is betrothed to a maiden, who has given him a ring. The village church is undergoing construction, and the image of Mary has been placed outside under the portico while the workmen labor inside. When his companions invite the young man to join them in a ball game in an adjoining field, he looks for a safe place to leave his engagement ring and wanders over to the portico. Overcome with the beauty of the woman depicted in the statue, he impulsively takes off the ring, places it on the finger of her open, upraised hand, and declares:

"Oi mais non m'encha
. . . .
Daquela que eu amava, ca eu ben jur' a Deus
que nunca tan bela cousa viron estes ollos meus;
poren daqui adeante serei eu dos servos teus,
e est' anel tan fermoso ti dou porend' en sinal."

("From this day onward
. . . .

The lady I used to love is of no importance to me, for I swear before God
that these eyes of mine have never seen such loveliness;
so from now on I will be one of your servants,
and I give you this beautiful ring as a sign of my resolve.")

Before his startled eyes the hand of the statue closes on the ring in acceptance. His excited shouts bring his friends running from their game, and they urge him to fulfill his vow by joining the Benedictine monastery. But the allure of his prior arrangement is too strong; he goes through with the wedding ceremony and retires to the bridal suite with his new wife. But the Virgin Mary is not ready to let herself be displaced by a mortal woman. She appears to the groom in a dream, sternly insisting on her claim and his free pledge of commitment. When he tries to ward her off, she lies down between her reluctant suitor and his sleeping bride, piling up recriminations and threats like any jilted mistress. He sees his true duty and abandons the marriage bed to become a holy hermit.

The illuminations that appear with this *cantiga* in the *Códice rico* tell their own story. The text is almost pure narration, with little description of setting. The painters, who were probably working under Alfonso's supervision, could not violate the sense or the spirit of the narrative, but they enjoyed a good deal of freedom to embellish the story. The serenity of the Virgin's sheltered arcade contrasts with the busy building scene in the adjoining space and the hustle of the ball game in the next panel. The poem merely mentions young men playing ball in a meadow; the illustration shows them playing something akin to American baseball. As John E. Keller points out in his *Alfonso X, el Sabio* (1967), the players telescope time and space: the "outfielders" are bunched up behind the pitcher, who has already released the next ball before the last one has been caught. The third panel depicts the private revelation granted to the youth as the statue of the Virgin miraculously closes her hand around his engagement ring. The wedding banquet is not mentioned in the poem, but the miniaturists show the dinner table, flatware (knives were the only eating tools used at that time), guests and servants gathered around, the bride wearing her dowry in the form of showy gold ornaments, and an apparently cross-eyed mother of the bride scowling at the girl's side. The text does not mention sex, although the Virgin is obviously trying to prevent it by lying between the groom and his bride. The artists guarantee the girl's innocence by showing her fast asleep. Abandoned by her husband before the consummation of their union, the girl is free to return to her family with her reputation and dowry intact and to arrange another honorable marriage.

sta e de loor de santa maria

Illuminations from the Códice de los músicos *(Codex of the Musicians) of the* Cantigas de Santa María, *showing musicians playing harps, plucked lutes, and a zither (Real Biblioteca del Monasterio de El Escorial, MS. I.b.2)*

The illumination of *Cantiga* 1 in Escorial MS. I.b.2, known as manuscript E and called *Códice de los músicos* (Codex of the Musicians), depicts the composition of the *Cantigas de Santa Maria.* The king, young and beardless, is seated on a low platform in the center of five arches that span the page. He is holding a folio in his lap and facing four kneeling and seated men in the arch to his right, one of whom holds writing materials and paper and seems to be copying the words spoken by the king. In the corresponding arch to the king's left sit another four figures, who seem to be listening to the king with rapt attention. In the outer arches are musicians, two on the right and two on the left, facing the center. Some have their instruments at the ready, as though listening for a cue from the king to begin a performance.

Miniatures accompanying the *loores* in the *Códice de los músicos* have been a rich source for historical investigation, for it is assumed that the musical instruments, and perhaps even the performances, depicted in them were painted from life. The musicians are routinely depicted in pairs but are not placed in a standard pose; the number and variety of their stances and facial expressions is impressive. Feet and instruments frequently extend beyond the borders of the miniatures. Some of the musicians playing nonwind instruments are depicted as singing. In most instances the musicians are Castilian or Galician-Portuguese, but a Castilian is paired with a Moorish musician in the illumination for *Cantiga* 120, and in the illumination for *Cantiga* 300 a male musician is paired with a *juglaresa* (female minstrel) who is playing a percussion instrument—shoulder drums or wooden blocks—and may be singing, as well. These miniatures are visual reminders that the *cantigas* are more than poetic texts: they were performed by troubadours and minstrels for a sophisticated audience.

The variety of musical instruments depicted in the miniatures is considerable: there are bowed and plucked fidulas and rebecs, plucked citterns or guitars, mandolas, psalteries, zithers, and harps; among wind instruments one can make out the single and double shawm, flutes and recorders, trumpets and horns, bagpipes and portable organs; there are also percussion instruments such as drums and tabors, castanets, cymbals, and ranks of graduated bells—an image clearly copied from contemporary Bible illustrations of King David performing his psalms but having no known iconographical precedent among those produced by Alfonso's graphic artists.

While Prologue A claims that Alfonso composed the lyrics and music for the *cantigas,* modern scholars believe that, as with the texts, one must be cautious in assigning to the king any significant portion of credit for the musical notations displayed in the collection. That all four of the extant manuscripts contain, or were meant to contain, complete musical scores to accompany the texts is significant in the history of music. Little musical notation survives elsewhere in the Galician-Portuguese poetic repertory, especially for nonliturgical compositions: few musical transcriptions accompany the more than 1,600 poems in the three major manuscripts that contain the bulk of all secular poetry in Galician-Portuguese. It is likely that the major musical influence on the *Cantigas de Santa María* was from Latin liturgical sources and from contemporary popular melodies, particularly the French *virelai,* to which many of the complex metrical patterns are easily traced.

The illuminations in the *Cantigas de Santa María* manuscripts consistently indicate that the *cantigas* were performed. The formatting of the manuscripts also shows that the compilers desired that all of the texts be accompanied by their musical notation. And Alfonso's last will and testament commanded that the *cantigas* be sung on appropriate feast days. On the basis of evidence in the miniatures, some scholars believe that a solo voice sang the stanzas, and a chorus sang the refrains. In *Cantiga* 409 the refrain begins, "cantando e con dança seja por nos loada" (singing and dancing let us praise the Virgin), and the illustration of *Cantiga* 5 supports the notion that public dancing accompanied the sung performance of the compositions.

When Alfonso's grandson, King Diniz of Portugal, a prolific poet in the Galician-Portuguese idiom, died in 1325, Galician-Portuguese was already considered moribund as a literary language in Castile, and spoken and written Galician and Portuguese were continuing their increasingly divergent evolutionary paths. Castilian had become the lyric language of choice in Iberian lands, and it took increasing effort to express oneself in the language of the *Cantigas de Santa María;* poets who did so were aware of the archaic flavor it gave their compositions. It was usually reserved for a passing homage to the literary past, and its use for this purpose can be found as late as the early years of the fifteenth century. Alfonso is credited with only one short attempt at a poem in Castilian.

Alfonso also undertook the composition of the *General Estoria,* a history of the world from Genesis to the time of Christ, and the *Estoria de España,* a history of Spain from its founding as a Roman colony in 38 B.C. to the death of his father in 1252. He was motivated by a desire not only to extend human knowledge but also to promote his own political aspirations. In the introduction to the *Setenario,* a *speculum principum* (manual for princes) written sometime after 1275, Alfonso asserts that his father "En rrazón del enperio, quisiera que ffuesse así llamado ssu sseñorío e non rregno, e que ffuese él coronado por enperador segunt lo ffueron otros de su linage" (In the matter of empire, he wished his sovereignty to be referred to thus and not as a kingdom, and that he should be crowned as emperor even as were others of his lineage). The *General Estoria* draws a direct line of descent from Adam to David to Christ to the first king of the world, Nimrod, and ultimately to Alfonso himself: "E del linaje deste rrey vinieron los rreyes de França e los emperadores de Rroma, e de los emperadores de Rroma e de los rreyes de França por linna vino la muy noble señora rreyna Beatriz, muger que fue del muy noble e muy alto señor e sancto don Fernando, rrey de Castilla e de Leon, e padre e madre que fueron del muy noble e alto rrey don Alphonso, que fizo fazer estas historias e muchas otras" (And from the lineage of this king came the kings of France and the emperors of Rome and from the lineage of the emperors of Rome and the kings of France came the very noble lady Queen Doña Beatriz, who was the wife of the very high and noble lord and saint Don Fernando, king of Castile and León, who were the father and mother of the most high and noble king Don Alfonso, who commissioned these histories and many others). The same lineage links Alfonso's cousin, the Holy Roman Emperor Frederick II, with the god Jupiter. The *Estoria de España* establishes a direct line of descent from Hercules to Hispan, the first king of Spain; no such descent is mentioned in Alfonso's main Latin source, the *Historia de rebus Hispanie sive Historia Gothica* (1243, History of the Affairs of Spain; or, History of the Goths), written by his mentor, Rodrigo Jiménez de Rada, archbishop of Toledo.

Further justification for the king's historical project is found in the *Setenario*, where he recalls that his father expressed the desire that a *speculum principum* be written to serve as a model of regal comportment that the people of his kingdom "oyesen a menudo, con que se costunbrasen para sser bien acostunbrados. . . . Et que lo ouyesen por ffuero e por ley conplida e çierta" (might listen to frequently, one with which they might learn how to act. . . . So that it might serve them as a complete and sure source of laws). This quest for a single source of laws, doctrines, and general knowledge is, according to Diego Catalán in *La estoria de España de Alfonso X: Creación y evolución* (1992, Alfonso X's History: Creation and Evolution), a unifying principle of all of Alfonso's intellectual production, initially defined by the monarch in the *Setenario* and later expanded to include his historical, scientific, and legal works. In this regard Alfonso echoed the guiding principles of Jiménez de Rada, who affirmed in *Historia de rebus Hispanie* that "Regis ad exemplum totus componitur orbis" (All men model themselves after their King); the comment is paraphrased in the *Estoria de España* as "todos los omnes del mundo se forman et se assemeian a manera de su rey" (all men are formed and act according to the model provided by their king). Rulers who neglect this

admonition will bring about their own downfall and the ruin of their kingdoms, for "non guardando la uerdad nin el derecho que deuieran y guardar por quexa de ganar el sennorio mal et torticieramientre como non deuien, por ende los otros omnes que fueron otrossi en sus tiempos dellos formaron se con ellos et semeiaron les en los peccados; e por esta razon auiuose la yra de Dios sobrellos" (failing to maintain truth and righteousness as they should by desiring to obtain dominion by wrong and wicked means as they should not, those who lived in their kingdoms were formed and acted in sin even as they did; and for this reason God rose up in anger against them). Alfonso expresses this same doctrine in the *Fuero Real* and the prologue to the first part of the *Siete Partidas*.

To address such an ambitious undertaking, the king assembled in Seville a scriptorium with teams of archivists, translators, and historians. When the source works for the two history projects had been determined and the location of the codices ascertained, Alfonso personally wrote to the monastic archives holding the manuscripts to request their loan. Extant copies of this correspondence have facilitated the identification of the source works for both projects: in addition to the Bible and Jiménez de Rada's *Historia de rebus Hispanie sive Historia Gothica,* they include Eusebius of Caesarea's *Chronicorum canonum* (Ecclesiastical History), translated into Latin by St. Jerome; Eutropius's synopsis of Livy's *Breviarium ab urbe condita* (Comprehensive History of Rome from Its Beginnings); Paulus Diaconus's *Historia romana* (Roman History); Jordanes's *De summa temporum* (Origin and Deeds of the Roman People); Landolfus Sagax's *Historia romana;* Lucan's *Pharsalia,* or *Bellum Civile* (Civil War); Peter Comestor's *Historia scholastica* (Scholastic History); Pompeius Trogus's *Historiae Philippicae* (Philippine History) as preserved in Justin's *Epitome;* Paulus Orosius's *Historia adversus paganos* (Histories against the Pagans); Sigebert of Gembloux's *Chronica;* Lucas de Tuy's *Chronicon mundi* (History of the World); Abu al-Bakri's *Geography of Spain;* and Wasif-Sah al-Misri's *History of Egypt.* Royal receipts acknowledging acceptance of these archival materials establish January 1270 as a terminus a quo for the composition of the *Estoria de España;* the Bible is used extensively in the *General Estoria;* because it was translated much earlier, the project may have commenced well before 1270. The *General Estoria* was still in progress as late as 1280, since one of the three original extant manuscripts from the Alfonsine scriptorium, Manuscript U (Vatican Library, Rome, MS. Urbinas Lat. 539), corresponding to part 5, states that "Este libro fue acabado en Era de mil et trezientos et diziocho annos" (This book was completed in the Era of one thousand three hundred and eighteen years): the *era española* (Spanish Era) takes 38 B.C., when Spain became a Roman province, as its starting date, so

Page from one of the two extant manuscripts of the Estoria de España *that were produced by Alfonso's scriptorium (Real Biblioteca del Monasterio de El Escorial, MS. X.I.4)*

that 1318 is equivalent to A.D. 1280. The *Estoria de España* was apparently neglected from 1275 until the final years of Alfonso's reign, when it was extensively revised in the *versión crítica* (critical version). References in this version to Sancho's rebellion date the text to the period following Alfonso's expedition against Cordova in September 1282.

Until the 1980s most scholars held that the *Estoria de España* was composed before the *General Estoria* because of several passages in the latter referring to information that "fablamos nos enla nuestra Estoria que fiziemos en Espanna" (we have spoken of in our Estoria de Espanna). More-recent studies by Catalán and Inés Fernández Ordóñez dealing with the organization and procedures of the Alfonsine historical workshops have shown that both projects were probably launched at the same time. They were assigned to different teams of historians; both teams appear to have been working with the same materials, which were compiled and translated by yet a third team. Each of the two main groups then freely adapted the source materials according to distinct criteria: an all-inclusive chronological approach for the *General Estoria* and a narrow methodology of *señoríos* (sovereignties) for the *Estoria de España*. Sharing of sources is evident in such episodes as the histories of Hercules and of Dido and the kingdom of Carthage, composed for the *General Estoria* and later used in the second part of the *Estoria de España*, and the chapters concerning the origin of the Goths, the political system of the Romans, the wars of Pompey and Julius Caesar in Spain, and the first years of the reign of Caesar Augustus composed for the *Estoria de España*, which are also found in the third and fifth parts of the *General Estoria*.

To tell the story of the world from the Creation to the time of his own reign, Alfonso initially employed a modified version of the medieval concept of the "world week" or *sex aetates mundi* (six ages of the world), which was linked to the biblical week of Creation. Each age was thought to have lasted approximately a thousand years; the first extended from Adam to Noah, the second from Noah to Abraham, the third from Abraham to David, the fourth from David to the Babylonian Captivity, the fifth from the Captivity to Jesus, and the sixth from the time of Jesus to Judgment Day. Within this scheme Alfonso imposed a more rigorous chronological design, using the sequence of events described in Eusebius's *Chronicorum canonum* as a model. Until the second year of the reign of Darius, when the Jews were sent into Babylonian exile, the history is structured according to the lives of the Hebrew patriarchs, judges, and kings. Subsequent to the Babylonian Captivity, at which time the Jews became slaves and lost their *imperium* (rule), the history is structured according to the political principle of *translatio imperii* (transmission of

authority and power) to princes, whose reigns represent individual *señoríos*. Following Lucan, the sixth age is said to begin with Julius Caesar being made emperor of the world. From this point onward his *señorío* and those of his successors become the calendar to which all other chronologies are referred.

The synchronization of the various chronologies with the sources, which were often at odds with each other concerning the details of events or the time at which they occurred, presented a constant challenge. The creation of the world, the Flood, the construction of the Tower of Babel, the birth of Abraham, the destruction of Troy, and the founding of Rome served as moments to which other chronologies could be related and synchronized. The books of the Old Testament prophets, which the chroniclers considered indivisible units, were inserted as autonomous divisions within the reigns in which the events described took place. The Alfonsine plan was, thus, first to establish the biblical structure of history, then to relate the sources of pagan history to the Bible. Nonbiblical sources such as Eusebius were integrated into and synchronized with the overall biblical structure.

The *General Estoria* is meant to be exhaustive: "Queremos contar la estoria toda como contescio e non dexar della ninguna cosa de lo que de dezir fuesse" (We desire to relate all of history exactly as it happened without excluding anything that was said). To this end all written sources will be used: "Yo don Alfonsso . . . fiz ende fazer este libro, e mande y poner todos los fechos sennalados tan bien delas estorias dela Biblia, como delas otras grandes cosas que acahesçieron por el mundo, desde que fue començado fastal nuestro tiempo" (I, don Alfonso . . . caused this book to be made and I commanded that in it be placed all things of note including the histories of the Bible as well as other great things which happened in the world from its beginnings up until our own time). This all-inclusive approach, going beyond the Hebrew Bible to the written sources of antiquity, including works of pagan mythology such as Ovid's *Metamorphoses*, required the history to be glossed with explanations that would make such works intelligible to contemporary readers. The history says of the *Metamorphoses*, which is referred to as *"Ouidio mayor"* (major Ovid): "e el Ouidio mayor non es al entrellos si non la theologia e la biblia dello entre los gentiles" (the major Ovid is nothing other among them than the theology and the Bible of the Gentiles). Most pagan works are interpreted with reference to their symbolic meaning, so that even in regard to a sexually explicit story such as the union of Pasiphae and the bull that begets the Minotaur the reader is told, "ca el que las sus razones bien catare e las entendiere fallara que non ay fabliella ninguna, nin frey-res predigadores e los menores que se trabaian de tornarlo en la nuestra theologia non lo farien si assi fuesse, mas todo es dicho en figura e en semeiança de al" (if one looks well and understands, he will find that there is no tale here, nor would Dominicans nor Franciscan preachers attempt to render it in terms of our own theology were it so, but everything said here is referred to symbolically, in the likeness of something else).

While the *General Estoria* is to be as comprehensive as possible, the *Estoria de España* is restricted to events that took place on the Iberian Peninsula. The *Estoria de España* most often summarizes its sources or states that the particulars may be found in "other books." In this way the *Estoria de España* is not based solely on the chronological procession of *señoríos* but on the thematic development of history according to the Alfonsine point of view. The first 121 chapters eschew chronological sequence, using instead the organizational principle of the sovereignty of the various peoples who ruled Spain until the beginning of the Roman Empire under Caesar Augustus. From this point forward, every year is accounted for with reference first to the Roman emperor, then to the Roman people, then to the *era española,* and finally to the Christian calendar. This system is used until the Arab invasion in 711; after that point the chronology is ordered with reference to Pelayo and his Asturian, Leonese, and Castilian successors, who are considered to be the true descendants and heirs of the former Gothic monarchy. The history never recognizes Arab sovereignty, though for the purpose of synchronization and accuracy it frequently refers to the reigns of individual Arab rulers; their dates are subordinated to those of the Asturian, Leonese, and Castilian monarchs. The reigns of the Navarrese, Aragonese, and Portuguese kings are likewise excluded, since they are not part of the hereditary line of the Goths; these dynasties are mentioned in chapters dealing with the ways in which they are linked with the Leonese-Castilian dynasties. This treatment was most likely based on the paradigm provided by Jiménez de Rada's *Historia de rebus Hispanie sive Historia Gothica,* though the Alfonsine historians rarely if ever paraphrase the archbishop. Chapters 1 to 3 of the *Estoria de España* deal with biblical and mythological history; chapters 4 to 13 with the rule of the Greeks, descendants of Japhet; chapters 14 and 15 with the rule of the "almujuces"; chapters 16 to 22 with the rule of the Africans and Carthaginians; chapters 23 to 364 with Roman rule; chapters 365 to 385 with the rule of the barbarian tribes of the Vandals, Suevi, Huns, Alani, and Silingi; chapters 386 to 559 with Gothic rule; chapters 560 to 565 with the Arab invasion and the establishment of Pelayo as the first king of Asturias; chapters 566 to 801 with the Asturian-Leonese kingdoms; and chapters 802 to 1035 with the Leonese-Castilian kingdoms.

Known to posterity as "the Learned" or "the Wise," Alfonso X was certainly one of the most cultured monarchs of the thirteenth century. His early efforts to record and extend human knowledge with a series of scholarly and encyclopedic works written in the vernacular rather than in Latin, the customary language of learning, promoted the growth and eventual dominance of Castilian as the principal language for scientific and historical works on the Iberian Peninsula. His efforts to translate all that was known about astronomy gave rise to astronomical works and tables that were standard in Europe for centuries. While his attempts to normalize the legal system throughout the peninsula met with opposition during his lifetime, his reforms were subsequently adopted everywhere in the Spanish-speaking world, including areas in what later became the southwestern United States. He provided financial and legal support for the nascent University of Salamanca and personally assisted in the founding of the University of Seville in 1254; his court there became the principal center of intellectual life in Spain.

Bibliographies:

Joseph T. Snow, *The Poetry of Alfonso el Sabio: A Critical Bibliography* (London: Grant & Cutler, 1977);

Anthony J. Cárdenas, Jerry R. Craddock, and Barbara de Marco, "A Decade of Alfonsine Studies: Working Notes and Bibliography," *Romance Philology,* 49 (November 1995): 192–244;

Arthur L.-F. Askins, Charles B. Faulhaber, and Harvey L. Sharrer, eds., "BETA/Bibliografía Española de Textos Antiguos," in *PhiloBiblon: Electronic Bibliographies of Medieval Catalan, Galician, Portuguese, and Spanish Texts; Bibliografia de Textos Antigos Galegos e Portugueses (BITAGAP)*; *Bibliografia de Textos Catalans Antics (BITECA)*; *Bibliografía Española de Textos Antiguos (BETA)* (Berkeley, Cal.: Bancroft Library, 1999) <http://sunsite.berkeley.edu/PhiloBiblon/phhm.html>.

References:

José Andrés-Gallego, José María Blázquez, and others, eds., *Historia de la historiografía española* (Madrid: Encuentro, 2000);

Antonio Ballesteros Beretta, *Alfonso X el Sabio,* edited by José M. Pérez Prendes (Barcelona & Madrid: Salvat, 1963; republished with indexes by Miquel Rodríguez Llopis, Barcelona: El Albir, 1984);

Benito Brancaforte, *Las Metamorfosis y las Heroidas de Ovidio en la General Estoria de Alfonso el Sabio* (Madison, Wis.: Hispanic Seminary of Medieval Studies, 1990);

Robert I. Burns, ed., *Emperor of Culture: Alfonso X the Learned of Castile and His Thirteenth-Century Renaissance* (Philadelphia: University of Pennsylvania Press, 1990);

Fernando Carmona and Francisco J. Flores, eds. *La lengua y la literatura en tiempos de Alfonso X* (Murcia: Departamento de Letras Románicas, Facultad de Letras, Universidad de Murcia, 1985);

Diego Catalán, *De la silva textual al taller historiográfico alfonsí: Códices, crónicas, versiones y cuadernos de trabajo* (Madrid: Fundación Ramón Menéndez Pidal / UA Ediciones, Universidad Autónoma de Madrid, 1997);

Catalán, *La estoria de España de Alfonso X: Creación y evolución* (Madrid: Seminario Menéndez Pidal, Universidad Complutense de Madrid / Fundación Ramón Menéndez Pidal / Universidad Autónoma de Madrid, 1992);

Center for the Study of the Cantigas de Santa Maria *of Oxford University* <http://csm.mml.ox.ac.uk/>;

Alan Deyermond, "The Death and Rebirth of Visigothic Spain in the *Estoria de Espanna,*" *Revista Canadiense de Estudios Hispánicos,* 9 (1985): 345–367;

Francisco Javier Díez de Revenga, "La condición de autor literario en Alfonso X el Sabio: *Crónica General,*" *Miscelánea Medieval Murciana,* 13 (1986): 117–129,;

Díez de Revenga, "Literatura en las obras históricas de Alfonso X el Sabio," *Mester,* 17 (1988): 39–50;

Ana Domínguez Rodríguez, "Imágenes de presentación de la miniatura alfonsí," *Goya,* 131 (1976): 287–291;

Domínguez Rodríguez, "Imágenes de un rey trovador de Santa María (Alfonso X en las *Cantigas* [Escorial T.I.1])," in *Il medio Oriente e l'Occidente nell'Arte del XII secolo,* edited by Hans Belting (Bologna: Editrice Bologna, 1982), pp. 229–239;

Daniel Eisenberg, "The *General Estoria*: Sources and Source Treatment," *Zeitschrift für Romanische Philologie,* 89 (1973): 206–227;

Carlos Estepa Díez, and others, eds., *Alfonso X: Aportaciones de un rey castellano a la construcción de Europa* (Murcia: Región de Murcia, Consejería de Cultura y Educación, 1997);

Inés Fernández Ordóñez, "La historiografía alfonsí y post-alfonsí en sus textos: Nuevo panorama," *Cahiers de Linguistique Hispanique Médiévale,* 18–19 (1993–1994): 101–132;

Fernández Ordóñez, *Las Estorias de Alfonso el Sabio* (Madrid: Istmo, 1992);

Fernández Ordóñez, ed., *Alfonso X el Sabio y las Crónicas de España* (Valladolid: Fundación Santander Central Hispano-Centro para la Edición de los Clásicos Españoles, 2000);

David A. Flory, *Marian Representations in the Miracle Tales of Thirteenth-Century Spain and France* (Washington, D.C.: Catholic University of America Press, 2000);

Charles F. Fraker, *The Scope of History: Studies in the Historiography of Alfonso el Sabio* (Ann Arbor: University of Michigan Press, 1996);

Leonardo Funes, *El modelo historiográfico alfonsí: Una caracterización* (London: Department of Hispanic Studies, Queen Mary and Westfield College, 1997);

Amparo García Cuadrado, *Las Cantigas: El Códice de Florencia* (Murcia: Universidad de Murcia, 1993;

Alfonso García Gallo, ed., "El 'Libro de las leyes' de Alfonso el Sabio: Del *Espéculo* a las *Partidas,*" *Anuario de Historia del Derecho Español,* 21–22 (1951): 345–528;

Fernando Gómez Redondo, *Historia de la prosa medieval castellana, I: La creación del discurso prosístico. El entramado cortesano* (Madrid: Cátedra, 1998);

Roberto J. González Casanovas, "La historiografía alfonsí: Estado actual de la investigación," in *Actas del 6 Congreso Internacional de la Asociación Hispánica de Literatura Medieval,* 2 volumes (Alcalá de Henares: Universidad de Alcalá, 1997), I: 87–110;

Tomás González Rolán, "San Isidoro de Sevilla como fuente de Alfonso X el Sabio: Un nuevo texto de las *Etimologías* (L. XIV) en la *General Estoria* (40 parte)," *Revista de Filología Española,* 61 (1981): 225–233;

George D. Greenia, "The Court of Alfonso X in Words and Pictures: The '*Cantigas,*" in *Courtly Literature: Culture and Context,* edited by Keith Busby & Erik Kooper (Amsterdam & Philadelphia: Benjamins, 1990), pp. 227–237;

Greenia, "The Politics of Piety: Manuscript Illumination and Narration in the *Cantigas de Santa Maria,*" *Hispanic Review,* 61 (Summer 1993): 325–344;

José Guerrero Lovillo, *Las Cantigas: Estudio arqueológico de sus miniaturas* (Madrid: Consejo Superior de Investigaciones Científicas, 1949);

Gerardo V. Huseby, "Musical Analysis and Poetic Structure in the *Cantigas de Santa Maria,*" in *Florilegium Hispanicum: Medieval and Golden Age Studies Presented to Dorothy Clotelle Clarke* (Madison, Wis.: Hispanic Seminary of Medieval Studies, 1983), pp. 81–101;

Israel J. Katz and John E. Keller, eds., *Studies on the* Cantigas de Santa Maria: *Art, Music, and Poetry* (Madison, Wis.: Hispanic Seminary of Medieval Studies, 1987);

John E. Keller, *Alfonso X, el Sabio* (New York: Twayne, 1967);

Keller and Annette Grant Cash, *Daily Life Depicted in the* Cantigas de Santa Maria (Lexington: University Press of Kentucky, 1998);

Lawrence B. Kiddle, "The Prose *Thèbes* and the *General Estoria:* An Illustration of the Alphonsine Method of Using Source Material," *Hispanic Review,* 6 (1938): 120–132;

Kiddle, "A Source of the *General Estoria:* The French Prose Redaction of the *Roman de Thèbes,*" *Hispanic Review,* 4 (1936): 264–271;

Richard P. Kinkade, "Alfonso X, *Cantiga* 235, and the Events of 1269–1278," *Speculum,* 67 (1992): 284–323;

Kinkade and Keller, "Myth and Reality in the Miracle of Cantiga 29," *La corónica,* 28, no. 1 (1999): 35–69;

María Rosa Lida de Malkiel, "La *General Estoria:* Notas literarias y filológicas," *Romance Philology,* 12 (1958–1959): 111–142; 13 (1959–1960): 1–30;

Peter Linehan, *History and the Historians of Medieval Spain* (Oxford: Clarendon Press, 1993);

Francesco Márquez Villanueva and Carlos Vega, eds., *Alfonso X of Castile, the Learned King, 1221–1284: An International Symposium, Harvard University, 17 November 1984* (Cambridge, Mass.: Department of Romance Languages and Literatures of Harvard University, 1990);

Georges Martin, *Histoires de l'Espagne médiévale: Historiographie, geste, romancero,* Annexes des Cahiers de Linguistique Hispanique Médiévales, volume 11 (Paris: Klincksieck, 1997);

Jesús Montoya Martínez and Ana Domínguez Rodríguez, eds., *El scriptorium alfonsí: De los Libros de Astrología a las "Cantigas de Santa María"* (Madrid: Editorial Complutense, 1999);

Montoya Martínez and José Mondéjar, eds., *Estudios alfonsíes: Lexicografía, lírica, estética y política de Alfonso el Sabio* (Granada: Universidad de Granada, 1985);

Francisco Mundi Pedret and Anabel Sáiz Ripoll, *Las prosificaciones de las Cantigas de Alfonso X el Sabio* (Barcelona: Promociones y Publicaciones Universitarias, 1987);

Ramon Muntaner, *Crònica,* in *Les quatre grans cròniques,* edited by Ferrán Soldevila (Barcelona: Selecta, 1971);

Joseph F. O'Callaghan, *Alfonso X and the* Cantigas de Santa Maria: *A Poetic Biography* (Leiden: Brill, 1998);

O'Callaghan, *Alfonso X, the Cortes, and Government in Medieval Spain* (Aldershot, U.K. & Brookfield, Mass.: Ashgate, 1998);

O'Callaghan, *The Learned King: The Reign of Alfonso X of Castile* (Philadelphia: University of Pennsylvania Press, 1993);

Carmen Orcástegui Gros, *La historia en la Edad Media: Historiografía e historiadores en Europa Occidental, siglos V–XIII* (Madrid: Cátedra, 1991);

Stephen Parkinson, ed., *Cobras e son: Papers of the Text, Music and Manuscripts of the "Cantigas de Santa Maria"* (Oxford: European Humanities Research Centre of the University of Oxford, 2000);

David G. Pattison, *From Legend to Chronicle: The Treatment of Epic Material in Alphonsine Historiography* (Oxford: Society for the Study of Mediaeval Languages and Literature, 1983);

Julián Ribera, *La música de las Cantigas: Estudio sobre su origen y naturaleza, con reproducciones fotográficas del texto y transcripción moderna* (Madrid: Revista de archivos, 1922);

Francisco Rico, *Alfonso el Sabio y la "General estoria": Tres lecciones,* revised and enlarged edition (Barcelona: Ariel, 1984);

Connie L. Scarborough, *Women in Thirteenth-Century Spain as Portrayed in Alfonso X's "Cantigas de Santa Maria"* (Lewiston, N.Y.: Edwin Mellen, 1993);

Antonio Solalinde, "Fuentes de la *General Estoria* de Alfonso el Sabio," *Revista de Filología Española,* 21 (1934): 1–28; 23 (1936): 113–142;

Joseph T. Snow, "The Central Role of the Troubadour *Persona* of Alfonso X in the *Cantigas de Santa Maria,*" *Bulletin of Hispanic Studies,* 56 (1979): 305–316;

Snow, "Self-Conscious References and the Organic Narrative Pattern of the *Cantigas de Santa Maria,*" in *Medieval, Renaissance and Folklore Studies in Honor of John Esten Keller,* edited by Joseph Ramon Jones (Newark, Del.: Juan de la Cuesta, 1980), pp. 53-66;

Symposium: Alfonso X el Sabio y la música (Madrid: Sociedad española de musicología, 1987);

Leopoldo Augusto de Cueto, Marqués de Valmar, *Estudio histórico, crítico y filosófico sobre las Cantigas del rey D. Alfonso el Sabio* (Madrid: Sucesores de Rivadeneyra, 1897);

Mercedes Vaquero, *Tradiciones orales en la historiografía de fines de la Edad Media* (Madison, Wis.: Hispanic Seminary of Medieval Studies, 1990);

Keith Whinnom, *Spanish Literary Historiography: Three Forms of Distortion* (Exeter, U.K.: University of Exeter, 1967).

Cantar de mio Cid

(circa 1200)

Alberto Montaner
Universidad de Zaragoza

Manuscript: The *Cantar de mio Cid* is extant in a unique fourteenth-century manuscript: Biblioteca Nacional, Madrid, MS. Vitr. 7-17. This parchment codex comprises seventy-four folios and is missing at least three more: an initial sheet and internal ones between folios 47 and 48 and folios 69 and 70. This lack implies a loss of some 150 verses, compared to the 3,730 that survive. The manuscript was copied from another, whose concluding colophon was transcribed, as well, thanks to which it is known that the now-lost source manuscript was copied by Per Abbat in May 1207. That date, therefore, constitutes the last possible one by which the *Cantar de mio Cid* could have been composed. The Biblioteca Nacional also holds, as MS. 6328, a handwritten copy of the fourteenth-century codex, transcribed in the sixteenth century by the genealogist Juan Ruiz de Ulibarri and corrected by José Antonio Pellicer in the eighteenth century. This version was the basis for the first printed edition of the *Cantar de mio Cid* in 1779. The missing folios were already lost when the transcription was done, so there is no way to recover the current gaps in the text.

First publication: *Poema del Cid,* in *Colección de poesías castellanas anteriores al siglo XV,* volume 1, edited by Tomás Antonio Sánchez (Madrid: Printed by Antonio de Sancha, 1779), pp. 220–404.

Facsimile editions: *Poema de Mio Cid,* 2 volumes, edited by Ramón Menéndez Pidal (Madrid: Dirección General de Archivos y Bibliotecas, 1961); *Poema de Mio Cid,* 2 volumes, edited by Hipólito Escolar (Burgos: Ayuntamiento, 1982); *Cantar de Mio Cid: Manuscrito de Per Abbat,* edited by Lourdes Sanz, Tesoros de la Biblioteca Nacional, no. 1 (Madrid: Biblioteca Nacional, 1998 [CD-ROM]);
Poema de mio Cid: Edición commemorativa del VIII Centenario (Madrid: Círculo Científico, 2007).

Critical editions: *Cantar de mio Cid: Texto, gramática y vocabulario,* 3 volumes, edited by Ramón Menéndez Pidal (Madrid: Bailly-Baillière, 1908–1911;

Statue of the Cid by Juan Cristóbal at the San Pablo Bridge in Burgos (from Francisco López Estrada, Panorama crítico sobre el Poema del Cid, *1982; Thomas Cooper Library, University of South Carolina)*

revised edition, Madrid: Espasa-Calpe, 1944–1946); *Poema de mio Cid,* edited by Colin Smith (Oxford: Clarendon Press, 1972); *The Poem of the Cid: A New Critical Edition of the Spanish Text,* edited by Ian Michael, translated by Rita Hamilton and Janet Perry (Manchester, U.K.: Manchester University Press, 1975; New York: Viking Penguin, 1984); *Cantar de mio Cid,* 2 volumes, edited by Jules Horrent (Gand: Story-Scientia, 1982); *Cantar de mio Cid,* edited by Alberto Montaner, preliminary study by Francisco Rico (Barcelona: Crítica, 1993; revised edition, Barcelona: Galaxia Gutenberg, 2007).

Translations into modern Spanish: *Poema del Cid,* prose translation by Alfonso Reyes (Madrid: Espasa-Calpe, 1919); *Poema de Mio Cid,* verse translation by Pedro Salinas (Madrid: Revista de Occidente, 1926); *Poema del Cid,* verse translation by Francisco López Estrada (New York: Eliseo Torres, 1955; Valencia: Castalia, 1955); *Poema de mio Cid,* prose translation by Cedomil Goic (Santiago: Universidad de Santiago de Chile, 1955); *Poema de mío Cid,* verse translation by A. Manent (Barcelona: Juventud, 1968).

Editions in English: *Poem of the Cid,* translated by J. Ormsby (London: Langmans, 1879); *Poem of the Cid,* 3 volumes, translated by Archer M. Huntington (New York: Putnam, 1897–1903); *Poem of the Cid,* translated by Lesley B. Simpson (Berkeley: University of California Press, 1957); *The Poem of the Cid,* translated by W. S. Merwin (London: Dent, 1959; New York: New American Library, 1962); *The Epic of the Cid,* translated by J. Gerald Markley (Indianapolis & New York: Bobbs-Merrill, 1961); *The Poem of the Cid: A New Critical Edition of the Spanish Text,* edited by Ian Michael, translated by Rita Hamilton and Janet Perry (Manchester, U.K.: Manchester University Press, 1975; New York: Viking Penguin, 1984); *The Poem of My Cid (Poema de Mio Cid),* translated by Peter Such and John Hodgkinson (Warminster, U.K.: Aris & Phillips, 1987); *Poem of the Cid,* translated by Paul Blackburn (New York: American R.D.M. Corporation, 1966; republished, with a foreword by George Economou and an introduction by Luis Cortest, Norman: University of Oklahoma Press, 1998).

The anonymous twelfth- or thirteenth-century epic poem *Cantar de mio Cid* (Song of My Cid; translated as *Poem of the Cid,* 1879) recounts the deeds of Rodrigo "Ruy" Díaz de Vivar, known as *El Campeador* (The Battler or The Champion Warrior) and as *El Cid* from the Arabic *Sidi* (My Lord). King Alfonso VI has banished the Cid from Castile after being persuaded by envious courtiers, led by Count García Ordóñez, that the Cid had kept for himself a portion of the tribute he was sent to collect from a Moorish vassal, the king of Seville. As the poem opens, the Cid sadly glances around his home in the town of Vivar, which has been quickly stripped for his unplanned departure. With his few followers, he rides to the neighboring town of Burgos. While the adults cower behind closed shutters and doors, a nine-year-old girl tells him that by command of the king no one can offer him shelter or provisions. She asks him to move along in peace and with their blessing.

The Cid sets up camp on the bank of a nearby river. There he is joined by a knight from Burgos, Martín Antolínez, who suggests that he pawn with the Jewish moneylenders Raquel and Vidas a set of chests that purportedly contain purloined Moorish tribute but are actually filled with sand. After doing so, the Cid goes to the monastery of San Pedro de Cardeña, where he has arranged for shelter for his wife, Jimena, and their two daughters. That night he has a dream in which the Archangel Gabriel assures him that all will turn out well. The next day he crosses the frontier between Castile and the Muslim kingdom of Toledo and begins the life of a warrior in exile. He launches his first campaign in the Henares River Valley; while he takes the town of Castejón, his chief lieutenant, Álvar Fáñez, carries out raids downstream. Both operations pay off handsomely, and the Cid advances to a second campaign in the Jalón River basin. He extracts tribute from a succession of villages and takes the strategic town of Alcocer, where the defeated residents praise his temperance and fair play. The Moorish populace seeks the aid of King Tamín of Valencia, who sends his two finest generals, Fáriz and Galve, against the Cid; they are routed. Deputizing Álvar Fáñez to bear a portion of the spoils to Alfonso as a gift and a first gambit toward winning his pardon, the Cid proceeds down the valley of the Jiloca River and then to the east to the region of the Maestrazgo, which is under the protection of the count of Barcelona. The count confronts the Cid with a large but rather effete army; once again, the Cid emerges triumphant, thanks to his hearty men and shrewd battle tactics. His spoils include the sword Colada, worth 1,000 marks of silver. The count is taken captive and goes on a petulant hunger strike but is cajoled by his jovial host into joining in the feast that celebrates his own defeat. The Cid releases him unharmed and generously outfitted for his embarrassing return home.

The Cid then begins his campaign in the eastern marches. He is no longer interested in pillaging and temporary occupation, as at Castejón and Alcocer, but in the total conquest of the region of Valencia, which he wishes to make a homestead and family possession. After he takes Murviedro (modern Sagunto), Valencian Moors try to halt his advance; but the Cid's troops defeat them resoundingly. At the end of three years the Cid and his band have taken the provincial seaboard as far as the coast, leaving the city of Valencia cut off. At last the city is starved into surrendering. When the news reaches him, the king of Seville tries to retake Valencia but fails. Even greater booty is taken, including the sword Tizón, which is also worth 1,000 marks of gold.

The Cid appoints Jerónimo (Jerome), a French bishop who is also handy with a sword, to administer Valencia. He sends Álvar Fáñez once more with gifts of booty for King Alfonso and a request for permission for his family to join him in Valencia. The mission is a success but provokes the envy and greed of certain members of the court, including the young Leonese infantes de Carrión, Diego and Fernando. Through intermediaries they propose marriage to the Cid's daughters, hoping thereby to gain a portion of the Cid's wealth.

Under the protection of Álvar Fáñez, the Cid's wife and daughters and the maidens in their service arrive in Valencia to great rejoicing. The interlude of calm and festivity is shattered by an assault by King Yúcuf of Morocco, which unleashes the greatest battle described in the *Cantar de mio Cid*. Jimena and the girls watch the bloody engagement from the city battlements; the Cid had asked his daughters to witness it so that they could see "cómmo se gana el pan" (how one earns one's bread). After a clever tactic by the Cid wins the battle, he presents himself to his womenfolk with courtly gestures but also shows them his bloodied sword and sweating horse. He modestly gives thanks to God for the victory.

The massive booty taken from the king of Morocco allows the hero to send a third and even greater embassy of gifts to Alfonso, who grants his pardon and takes personal responsibility for arranging the marriage of the infantes de Carrión to the Cid's daughters. The reconciliation of the monarch and the Cid takes place in a solemn assembly of the court on the bank of the Tagus River; feudal ties are restored, and magnificent gifts are given. Afterward, the Cid and his company return to Valencia with the infantes and many lords of Castile. The joint weddings are celebrated over a two-week span of sumptuous feasting and games. The Cid gives the swords Colada and Tizón to his sons-in-law as wedding gifts.

One day the Cid's pet lion slips out of its cage. The infantes' frantic scramble for safety inspires laughter and derision among the Cid's men, who form a human shield between the beast and their sleeping lord. The Cid awakes, calmly leads the lion by the mane back to his cage, and orders those who witnessed the boys' pitiful display to keep silent. Their cowardice is soon confirmed, however, when King Búcar's forces arrive from Morocco in an effort to retake the city. During the battle the Cid's men perform admirably, but Diego and Fernando flee before the foe.

The infantes leave Valencia under the pretext of taking their wives to see their new landholdings in Carrión, but they actually plan to commit outrages against

the girls along the way. After a final night of sex in the Robledo de Corpes (Oak Grove at Corpes), they beat the girls savagely. The girls plead for martyrdom at the edges of the famous swords their father bestowed on his sons-in-law, but the infantes compete in a whipping contest until the girls lose consciousness. They then abandon the girls in the wilderness.

Fortunately, the girls' cousin, Féliz Muñoz, has been trailing the party. He arrives on the scene, assists the girls, and sends word of the outrage to their father. The Cid appoints Muño Gustioz to carry his demand for justice to Alfonso. The king convenes a royal judicial court in Toledo. The Cid demands the return of the swords Colada and Tizón; thinking that they have gotten off lightly, the infantes return the weapons. But the Cid's next demand is for repayment of the dowry he had bestowed on the young men on their departure from Valencia. The money has already been spent, and they are forced to draw on the resources of their extended families and lands. Finally, the Cid demands satisfaction in the form of judicial duels, pitting three of his knights against the infantes and their blustering older brother, Asur González. The brothers balk, because their opponents will be armed with the famous blades that the Cid has just repossessed; but after having conceded their faults so plainly, they are unable to back out. Three weeks later, a public trial by combat is joined in Carrión; the Cid's champions emerge victorious, while the vanquished are allowed to live but are consigned to disgrace. Princes of Navarre and Aragon arrive to seek the hands of the Cid's abandoned daughters. Thus, the Cid has recovered his honor and has grafted his family line onto those of the principal rising dynasties of Spain. Nothing is left to tell, the narrator concludes, except that his death took place peacefully at home on the solemn feast of Pentecost.

The story is based on the real-life adventures of Rodrigo Díaz, who was born around 1045 to 1049 in Vivar and raised in the court of Fernando I of Castile and León. In his youth he was a member of the *schola regis* (royal squad) in the inner circle of Sancho II, who became king in 1065. Sancho died in 1072, and his brother succeeded to the throne as Alfonso VI. Alfonso continued to show favor to Díaz, sending him as royal ambassador to the Moorish king of Seville in 1079. The following year, however, Díaz carried out an unauthorized military operation in the Muslim kingdom of Toledo, and Alfonso banished him in 1081. Díaz placed himself in the service of the Moorish king of Saragossa and achieved renown as a fighter. He finally made peace with Alfonso, and he returned to Castile in 1086. Alfonso sent him on expeditions to the realms of Valencia, but in 1089 a new falling-out resulted in Díaz's second and permanent exile. He then decided to wage battles of acquisition in his own name, gnawing away at the province of Valencia and in 1094 seizing its capital. He married his daughter María to Ramiro, Lord of Monzón, a member of the royal house of Navarre, and his daughter Cristina to Ramón Berenguer III, the Count of Barcelona. After additional conquests, he died of natural causes in 1099. His wife, Jimena, maintained control of Valencia until 1102, when a renewed onslaught by the Almoravids—a Moroccan tribe that had invaded the peninsula in 1093—forced the Christians to abandon the city. Jimena reburied her husband at the Benedictine monastery of San Pedro de Cardeña near Burgos.

The *Cantar de mio Cid* thus takes Díaz's first exile as its starting point and follows his career rather faithfully from 1089 onward except for colorful details of its own invention. The marriage of the Cid's daughters to the infantes de Carrión, for example, is made up out of whole cloth.

The relationship between truth and fiction in the *Cantar de mio Cid* has played a central role in the debate over the authorship and date of composition of the poem. Ramón Menéndez Pidal at first regarded the *Cantar de mio Cid* as the work of a *juglar* (singer of tales) from Medinaceli, a Castilian town on the border of Muslim-held Spain, who composed around 1140—less than half a century after Díaz's death—a folk poem faithful to the historical incidents. Later, to account for shifts of style and content that belonged to a slightly later age, Menéndez Pidal posited the existence of two *juglares*. The first, whom he associated with San Esteban de Gormaz, a town not far from Medinaceli, composed the more historically accurate elements of the text around 1110. The Medinaceli *juglar* then added the fictional features around 1140. Menéndez Pidal's theory as to the type of author, if not necessarily as to the dates, has been embraced by "oralists" such as Joseph J. Duggan who maintain that the poem was improvised by a *juglar* to be copied down from dictation.

At the other pole is the British literary historian Colin Smith, who defends the authority of the colophon of the extant manuscript of the *Cantar de mio Cid*:

Quien escrivió este libro, dél' Dios paraíso, ¡amén!
Per Abbat le escrivió en el mes de mayo
en era de mill e dozcientos e cuaraenta e cinco años.

E el romanz es leído,
datnos el vino;
si non tenedes dineros,
echad allá unos peños,
que bien nos lo darán sobr'ellos.

(May God grant the one who wrote out this book paradise, amen!

Per Abbat wrote it out in the month of May
In the Era of 1245.

The poem is read,
give us the wine;
if you don't have coins
toss down some possessions of your own
for they'll surely give us wine for them.)

The "Spanish Era" is dated from 38 B.C., when Spain became a Roman province; thus, the 1245 in the colophon is equivalent to 1207. Smith identified Per Abbat as a lawyer who practiced in Burgos at the beginning of the thirteenth century. Thus, according to Smith, the author of the *Cantar de mio Cid* was a legal expert who knew of Díaz's life from archived documents and whose modes of expression owed nothing to a traditional popular style; instead, the poem was modeled on French chansons de geste and on classical and medieval Latin precursors. In his final publications on the subject Smith conceded that Per Abbat was probably the copyist and not the author of the poem; the colophon represents the typical way scribes signed their projects. Smith insisted, however, that the true author, whoever he was, must have been a man of expansive culture and familiarity with the law; that he composed the work around 1207; and that if he did not invent the Spanish epic, he at least transformed it profoundly. Although modern critics no longer attempt to name the author, they accept the later dating of the poem and the notion of a poet of considerable learning who worked out his composition in writing rather than orally.

None of the proposals for pinning the author down to a specific locale has been supported by solid arguments. Menéndez Pidal's theories were based on the belief that the geographic detail given for the regions of San Esteban de Gormaz and Medinaceli (now in the province of Soria) is a consequence of the author or authors coming from those towns; but a writer could know those sorts of details from reading or hearing about them, and there is just as much precision as to place-names and other information for other areas, such as the region around Calatayud and the basin of the Jiloca River.

The only element that points in a specific direction is a persistent awareness of the laws governing frontier life, in particular the regulations set out in the *Fuero de Cuenca* (circa 1189–1193, Code of Cuenca). This feature makes one think of an author from the southeast borderlands of Castile; roughly, from Toledo in the south to Cuenca in the east, a span of a hundred miles. Given the preeminent role of Álvar Fáñez in the *Cantar de mio Cid,* one might think of the region around La Alcarria (in the modern province of Guadalajara), where the town of Zorita de los Canes is located: the

Cid's lieutenant was governor of that locale between 1097 and 1117, as one line of the poem notes anachronistically. It also lies in a zone that governed itself by one of the versions of the *Fuero de Cuenca*. The place-names of this area are recorded with unusual exactness. The Cid wages his first campaigns there after going into exile; while these events are apparently fictitious, they might echo memories of the true role played by Álvar Fáñez in this frontier region.

Scholars such as Jules Horrent defend Menéndez Pidal's notion of successive reworkings and elaborations of the narrative. This stance presupposes a gradual evolution of the work from an early oral version that was shorter and closer to the historical events and was retold until the tale reached the written version in the copy that exists today. But the extant poem does not give the impression of a work cobbled together over time out of preexisting texts by singers of varying levels of skill. On the contrary, the *Cantar de mio Cid* displays an essential unity of plot structure, style, and narrative purpose. The overwhelming impression is of the craftsmanship of a single author who was intimately familiar with the traditional Spanish epic, the new French styles, and the law, and who had at least a healthy smattering of Latin letters.

The only substantial argument for the 1140 date is a Latin poem composed around 1147 to 1149, the *Prefatio de Almeria* (Preface of Almería), which hails the hero as "Ipse Rodericus, Meo Cidi sepe vocatus, / de quo cantatur quod ab hostibus haud superatur" (That very Rodrigo, often called the Cid, / of whom is it sung that he was never defeated by his enemies). This mention of a song about the Cid might be taken to indicate that the *Cantar de mio Cid* was being sung by the late 1140s; on the other hand, in the Middle Ages the phrase could simply mean "it is well known that he was never defeated." If internal evidence in the *Cantar de mio Cid* leads to a later dating, the reference in the *Prefatio de Almeria* could be to some earlier verse tribute to the Cid that might have been a source for the *Cantar de mio Cid*. This view seems the most plausible, since there are considerations that push the composition of the *Cantar de mio Cid* toward the end of the twelfth century. Neither the *sobregonel* (open skirt) worn by the knight nor the *cuberturas* (drapery) that covers his horse are documented on the Iberian Peninsula until 1186. Nor were *armas de señal* (heraldic devices) widespread in Spanish lands until around that time. The same holds true for the administrative vocabulary of the *Cantar de mio Cid,* in particular two key terms employed to describe social relations: *hidalgo* (knight of hereditary rank)—a contraction of *hijo de algo* (son of property)—and *ricohombre* (man of wealth), which first appear in documentary sources in 1177 and around 1194, respectively. During this

same period monarchs acquired the title of *señor natural* (lord by birth), meaning that the king is the immediate and common sovereign of all the natives of a kingdom, independent of bonds of vassalage. This notion justifies the Cid's feelings of loyalty to the monarch even during his exile, when he was not a vassal of Alfonso.

A further important aspect of the hero's comportment is his treatment of the Moors he defeats. There is no ethos in the *Cantar de mio Cid* of "crusade," with its absolutes of conversion or death. Muslims are targets of opportunity for practical reasons such as simple survival and, in the long run, as a source of wealth. Religious confrontation is present in the poem only as an incidental factor, and two Muslim populations are clearly differentiated: the resident Andalusian Moors and the North Africans who invaded the peninsula in the eleventh and twelfth centuries. The latter are objects of hatred and war, while the former are allowed to live as neighbors of the Christians and labeled *moros de paz* (Moors of peace)—Muslims who fell under terms of capitulation or peace treaties. This social class emerged in the eleventh century, but invasions by fundamentalist Moroccan tribes—the Almoravids in 1093 and the Almohades in 1146—led Christians to opt for the expulsion of the Muslim population from newly conquered territories. Only at the end of the twelfth century was the attitude of tolerance that is reflected in this poem reinstated and communities of *mudéjares* (resident client Moors under the authority of Christian overlords) folded back into the social landscape.

This change in attitude coincides with an important renewal of Castilian law that culminated in the *fueros de extremadura* (law codes for the frontier), promulgated between 1185 and 1190, and the compilation of formalized privileges for the nobility, the *Fuero Viejo de Castilla* (Old Code of Castile), the first drafts of which date from the beginning of the thirteenth century. The *Cantar de mio Cid* alludes to these administrative procedures in matters as central to its plot as rights and duties before the king, the organization of war bands, the just distribution of booty, and judicial challenges between nobles. These features are not casual additions to the *Cantar de mio Cid* but thematic and structural building blocks that stand apart from any inherited narrative tradition, and they make it possible to fix the creation of the work to the period around the year 1200.

It is more difficult to ascertain where the poet obtained the historical data about his hero's life a century after Díaz's demise. Scholars have pointed to several possible sources, including now-lost poems about the Cid's exploits that were composed during or shortly after his lifetime and benefited from eyewitness testimony; legal documents, such as those now held at the Cathedral of Burgos and the Diocesan Museum of Salamanca, one of which contains his only known autograph signature; and the *Historia Roderici* (History of Rodrigo), a fairly complete Latin biography written around 1185. The counterargument to the hypothesis of preexisting poems is the lack of evidence of such *cantares noticieros* (news-bearing songs). The problem with the suggestion that the poet looked up some of his information in archives is that the legal instruments dealing with Díaz's life, like medieval documents in general, do not offer much grist for a narrative of epic proportions. Still, the inclusion of characters who were companions of the Cid, and of figures who had nothing to do with him but who were his contemporaries, hints that the poet undertook some sort of research to round out his work.

The third theory is the most promising, because of the pronounced similarities between the *Historia Roderici* and the *Cantar de mio Cid,* above all in regard to the conquest of Valencia. The principal objection to a connection between the Latin history and the vernacular poem is the silence of the latter about the Cid's career as a hired sword under the orders of the king of Saragossa, a topic that the *Historia Roderici* covers at length. Yet, the same sort of textual selectivity is seen in two other texts that are certainly derived from the Latin biography: the *Linaje de Rodrigo Díaz* (Lineage of Rodrigo Díaz), a Navarrese genealogy accompanied by a biographical sketch of the hero, and the *Carmen Campidoctoris* (Poem of the Warrior), a Latin panegyric that recounts the Cid's principal battle. Since both of these compositions can be dated to within a few years of 1194, everything points to the final decade of the twelfth century as the moment when the legend of the Cid coalesced into one of a steadfast foe of the Moors—a fact that would encourage the deletion of any reference to his services to a Muslim prince of Saragossa.

Finally, oral references to the famous Rodrigo Díaz de Vivar were still echoing in the time of King Alfonso X *el Sabio* (the Learned) of Castile, whose teams of scholars were collecting materials around 1270 for their *Estoria de España* (History of Spain). The poet of the *Cantar de mio Cid* could have gathered this sort of oral history, full of bits of historical fact and anecdote, even more easily some seventy or eighty years earlier.

In the end, one may conclude that the poet probably took his raw material from the *Historia Roderici* and from casual sources, especially the oral tradition, but that he also took advantage of documents and maybe some earlier epic telling of his hero's exploits. Consideration of his sources does nothing, however, to lessen one's esteem for his masterful disposition of the building blocks of narrative in forging his own artistic whole.

The *Cantar de mio Cid* could have ended perfectly satisfactorily when the Cid receives his royal pardon after the conquest of Valencia. But the poet prolongs the work with a fictitious episode that enhances the hero's stature and ends with his daughters in regal second marriages, a legendary version of their actual fates. This well-crafted fusion of inherited incidents with invented episodes results in a finely plotted narrative turning on two thematic axes: the reconciliation of the Cid with his king and the restoration of his family honor after its defilement at the hands of the infantes de Carrión. The plot trajectory of the *Cantar de mio Cid* can be diagramed as a *W,* with a double downward plunge and recovery. In each case a dramatic conflict—first the exile, then the outrage at Corpes—breaks a state of equilibrium to generate the abasement of the hero, who then not only recovers the lost ground but also achieves an even higher position than he held previously. From his loss of royal favor and forfeiture of lands and property in Castile, the Cid winds his way through a series of adventures to become lord of Valencia, powerful enough to treat his king nearly as an equal. Then, after the abuse and abandonment of his daughters, he attains through a hard-fought legal battle an even more exalted status when his offspring contract marriages with the crown princes of Navarre and Aragon. These two sequences are not merely juxtaposed: the second flows directly from the effects of the first. The triumphs of the Cid allow for a reconciliation with the king and also inspire the infantes to inaugurate their matrimonial pretensions. The king pardons the Cid after learning of the infantes' intentions, perhaps because the proposed liaison reassures him that the court would welcome such a move, and he pursues the arrangement because he thinks that betrothals to high-born grooms show favor to the Cid. For his part, the Cid is keenly aware from the outset of the poem that his banishment will make it difficult to arrange appropriate unions for his daughters. Later, he has misgivings about the wisdom of the proposed family ties, acceding only to comply with the desires of his lord and not in the wholehearted way he does at the end with the royal unions. At the conclusion the two narrative streams are brought together when those who defamed the Cid and caused his exile are conflated with the infantes through Count García Ordóñez's dishonorable bona fides for Diego and Fernando in court and the reversals that they all suffer before the royal magistrate and on the field of judicial battle.

In addition to the interconnections of plot, the two narrative lines display an unusual cohesion in ideology between the lower classes of the nobility and the frontiersmen of the *extremadura*. In Spanish society at this period the higher nobility in the heartlands, where the Cid's enemies held sway, lived off the payments of retainers on their lands and based their privileged position on their families' prestige and hereditary rights. The colonizers of the frontier lands, in contrast, owed their wealth to the looting of the adjacent Muslim territories. In recognition of the danger of their circumstances and the losses they suffered, these lower-ranking squires and country folk could be elevated to the status of knights and thereby secure some of the entitlements of the nobility: exemption from taxes, certain rights of due process, and, above all, the honor inherent in the knightly status. The men of the borderlands wanted their hard-won merit recognized as earned rather than inherited, as was the case with the established aristocracy of the north. The Cid was not a frontiersman, but his life's upheavals and triumphs, turned into literature, were the perfect expression of the virtues needed for war against the Moorish foe and of the chance to shine on one's own and not in the reflected glory of ancient arms and bloodline. It would, of course, be anachronistic to speak of any sort of democratic spirit in the *Cantar de mio Cid*, since there is no rejection of the nobility of blood as a determiner of social class. What is championed is a limited social mobility from peasant to knight and from knight to full noble by virtue of one's personal achievements.

These notions are evident in the exile narrative in the poem. When the Cid marches out of Castile, he is determined to win the king's pardon through booty gained in a series of bellicose adventures. The king will thereby be put on notice that the former vassal has not been neutralized: he is potent and on the move, and it would be a good idea to count him in again. Furthermore, even though the Cid is no longer bound by the rules of vassalage, he sends Alfonso a share of the spoils as if he were. This action carries dual implications: whoever behaves in this way would never have embezzled from the tribute of the king of Seville, as his defamers charged; and despite his unjust treatment at his lord's hands, he remains loyal. The Cid's freewill offerings become increasingly expansive, in proof of his steady climb, and they work their desired effect of swaying the impressionable Alfonso and eventually winning a royal pardon. The Cid's men, too, earn tangible benefits from their shared campaigns: "los que fueron de pie, cavalleros se fazen" (those who were foot soldiers are made knights). The way the hero reestablishes himself in the king's favor is a perfect expression of the *espíritu de frontera* (frontier spirit).

This ethos is, perhaps, less apparent in the second part of the poem, but it still underlies the motivations of the characters. On the one hand, the infantes are cast as scions of the court, puffed up about their lineage and looking to marriage to the Cid's daughters as a way of tapping into his wealth; in turn, the Cid and his family will receive the honor of being related to them. This attitude awakens the shrewd distrust of the hero, who nonetheless deals with his sons-in-law in good faith. The pretentious, foppishly dressed youths soil their expensive clothing when bolting for cover from the escaped lion. Their cowardice is repeated in the battle with the forces of Búcar and confirmed when they seek vengeance on helpless victims—the Cid's daughters—instead of proving themselves before the Cid and his lieutenants. A polarity is struck between these courtly dandies and the knights flanking the Cid, heightening the differences between those lofty noblemen who cling to the past but cannot prove themselves on their own and the warriors of the borderlands whose swordsmanship has won all they possess. This contrast extends to their personal finances: the infantes derive their pride from their lands in Carrión but are cash poor, while the Cid and his followers, who endured the confiscations of their estates, owe their abundant money and jewels to their exploits in war.

The confrontation of the two lifestyles and the ideologies that underlie them reaches a pitch at the end of the *Cantar de mio Cid* when those who had maligned the Cid and the perpetrators of the outrages against his daughters gather in a single faction bent on besting him on their home turf: the royal court. Instead, the Cid defeats all of his foes and the social order they represent. In the first part of the story he proved that he could recover his public honor by force of arms; he now shows that he is equally capable of vindicating his private honor by his command of legal avenues. By making disgrace fall on the heads of his earlier slanderous foes and his upstart adversaries, he establishes that in war or in peace his core values are preferable to those of jealous and sclerotic blue bloods. That stagnant caste, too long sheltered behind the battlements of pride and lordly privilege, is incapable of accomplishing anything on its own and ends up debased before the Cid and his band, who are humbler in family name but as superior to the aristocrats in morality as they are in arms.

The outcome of the story makes clear how the *Cantar de mio Cid* relies on the judicial principles of a specific historical period for both its ideological stance and its aesthetic logic. The initial conflict is unambiguously blocked out in judicial terms, since the Cid is banished under the formal aegis of expulsion as the penalty for incurring the *ira regis* (wrath of the king). This "wrath" is not the personal pique of the monarch; it is a legal status, like being in contempt of court or a persona non grata for diplomatic purposes. It indicates the rupture of the bonds of vassalage between king and subject and the forced departure of the latter from the king's lands. It is a sentence without appeal, since the condemned party has no higher authority to whom he might plead his case. This dead end for due process would make little difference in the case of crimes directly against the regime, such as rebellion or defiance of a royal mandate, but here it stems from false accusations leveled by *mestureros* (slanderers) against someone who can do nothing to reverse the king's summary judgment.

To make matters worse, the *Cantar de mio Cid* describes an unusually harsh order of banishment. First, the Cid's property is confiscated; historically, this action was taken only in cases of treason, which is clearly not the case here. Second, the exiled individual could normally take thirty days to set out with his personal *mesnada* (war band); the Cid is given only nine days. Finally, the inhabitants of Burgos are—amazingly—forbidden to provision the Cid and his companions. Such details betray a vengeful application of the full rigors of the law, enhancing the obstacles the Cid will have to overcome and heightening his stature in the process. The severity and arbitrariness of the sentence serve a dark judgment on the medieval institution of "the wrath of the king," depicting it as an ideologically biased maneuver practiced by unworthy courtiers against enemies they cannot confront by other means. This negative presentation does not amount to an outright condemnation of the practice but does resonate with the background sentiments of the *cortes* (advisory assembly) of nobles of the kingdom of León, before whom Alfonso IX swore in 1198 that anyone accused by *mestureros* would have the right to be heard in his own defense.

In the face of the injustice committed against him, the Cid could have risen in rebellion against the king; one reads of such rebel vassals in French epics of the period. On the contrary, the Castilian hero opts to comply with this exercise of royal prerogatives and sets himself the task of regaining his monarch's favor through legal channels. According to the *Fuero Viejo de Castilla,* if the exiled person and his attending knights were to attack the lands of the king in the course of their service to another lord, they were obligated to convey to him a portion of their booty. Even in the absence of any obligation to do so, since he deliberately never attacks the king's lands nor those of the king's vassals, the Cid lets himself be ruled by these strictures in portioning out his winnings; given his beleaguered circumstances, this practice underscores his loyalty and promotes his eventual reconciliation with his liege. The legal procedures of the period also indicate that among the causes for revocation of the *ira regis* was the performance of signal services to the king by the exiled individual.

Legal practices in force at the time of composition of the poem also surface in the internal management of the Cid's growing army. The plainest case in point is the distribution of booty, the prime motivation of the freelance squadrons of armed men working the frontier.

Precalculated portions were allotted to each rank: after the leader took a fifth of the total, the remainder was divided up so that one part went to each *peón* (foot soldier) and two parts to each *caballero villano* (horseman). Promotion in rank was also formalized: a man who could afford the expenses of a horse and equipment could rise from *peón* to *caballero villano,* gaining thereby some of the entitlements of a hidalgo.

The reconciliation of Alfonso and the Cid and the marriages of the Cid's daughters to the infantes de Carrión play out in accordance with set procedures in which special attention is paid to juridical formalisms—the performance of specific words and gestures without which the act lacks the force of law. The best example is the *besamanos,* the ritualized kissing of the hands of the lord by a vassal accepting an enfeoffment. In the eyes of medieval participants and their witnesses, it was not enough that the two principals should agree on the terms of their arrangement; they had to act out the full stage business called for by the legal process for the feudal pact to take effect. In the *Cantar de mio Cid* the legal formalities become dramatic imperatives in the climactic confrontation in court. The epic genre normally propels the offended parties to a quite different set of actions: after an affront like the one suffered by the Cid's daughters, one would expect the father to channel his energies into private vengeance, marshaling his knights and hurling all the might he could assemble into a frontal assault on the infantes de Carrión and their entire clan, slaying whomever they could and torching their lands and dwellings. The hero of this story, however, chooses to avail himself of procedures governed by codes of laws that dictated how members of the upper class could denounce and challenge their equals. Precisely to deflect cycles of vengeance and reprisal that could end up as endemic clan warfare among the powerful, two institutionalized procedures arose during the second half of the twelfth century: a quasi-contractual "amity" among hidalgos and the ritual of denunciation. The former implied a pact of mutual loyalty and presumed convergence of interests among all those of noble blood, in virtue of which none of them could impute offense on the part of another without a prior declaration of enmity. The latter required that a noble wishing to lodge a complaint against another had to frame it as a formal denunciation followed by a demand for satisfaction, a demand normally handled through single combat between accuser and accused or by their chosen alternates. If the accuser won, the charge was considered justified; the accused sank into permanent infamy and lost some of the privileges associated with his noble rank. The *Cantar de mio Cid* follows all of the formal requirements for challenges of this sort with exacting care. The *cortes* of the realm is convoked; the *Campeador* lays out his charges against the infantes; two of his lieutenants challenge them to give satisfaction; the king validates the challenges, and all proceed to the performance of the judicial duels, in which three champions for the aggrieved are pitted against the infantes and their older brother. The Cid's men secure their victories without slaying their opponents and practically without bloodshed: one brother surrenders after the first blows; another is knocked unconscious and wounded but spared, and the third flees the terrain marked out for the contests—all in accordance with the most exacting legal stipulations of the period.

The integration of legal detail into the story line is just as clear in the first part of the narrative, when the hero, instead of assuming the part of an outlaw, behaves as if he were still a loyal subject. This choice reflects one of the key components of the Cid's moral character in the poem: his measured restraint. Another, obviously, is his military prowess. He fulfills the classical characterization of one who displays *sapientia et fortitudo* (wisdom and strength). This wisdom is not, of course, erudition; it is worldly wisdom, a sense of proportion, foresight, and, above all, prudence. As for strength, it is not mere brute force, necessary though that kind of strength would be in armed conflict between medieval fighters. It suggests, instead, decisive action, an ability to lead, and a commanding persona both for war and for upholding what is right.

The Cid's *sapientia* is, above all, *mesura* (moderation or equilibrium), which expresses itself according to the circumstances as reflectiveness, sagacity, or even resignation. In the opening strophe the Cid thanks God for the tests to which he is being put by being banished. From this moment onward the hero and his company will have to rise or fall on their own. They are sentenced to this fate, but it also opens up a future filled with opportunity; the Cid recognizes it as such when he exclaims to his lieutenant, "¡Albricia, Álvar Fáñez, ca echados somos de tierra!" (Good tidings, Álvar Fáñez, for we are thrown out of this land!). The banishment commences a new chapter in the Cid's life, and he makes the most of it. His success results from the measured self-possession that carries him through a course of actions realized without haste or desperation, his compassionate treatment of the frontier Moors he conquers, and his shrewd organization of the governance of Valencia. In the second phase of the narrative that same inner balance leads the Cid to achieve his vindication through legal channels rather than the wholesale slaughter of his foes, a pursuit of justice that matches his astute campaigns on the battlefield.

The Cid's *fortitudo* shows to full advantage in his mighty arm, his endurance in battle, his capacity for focused engagement, and, above all, the force of his will. It allows him to work through the bitter moments of his departure, when he bids farewell to his family: "así' parten unos d'otros commo la uña de la carne" (and so they took leave of each other as [painfully as] a nail is pulled from the flesh). He sets off on an unstoppable march that lifts him to the ownership of Valencia, reunion with his family, and, finally, a royal pardon. In the second narrative block his *fortitudo* allows him to rise to the outrage perpetrated by the infantes: although he renounces blood-soaked reprisals, the public vindication he accomplishes is just as complete. Like his *sapientia,* his *fortitudo* is as effective in peace as in war. The frontier ethos prized personal effectiveness that brought about the social advancement of the individual without contravening existing class structures.

This model of heroism may trace its roots to classical times, but in the epic genre of the Spanish Middle Ages it takes unique form in the *Cantar de mio Cid.* The majority of works in that tradition are far more disposed to excesses of violence than to the restraint of the Cid, and, paradoxically, they concern themselves far more with internecine struggles within their Christian kingdoms than with military challenges from their Muslim enemies. Formally, the *Cantar de mio Cid* may be an amalgam of traditional and new approaches; but it is hard to specify exactly how, since none of the epic poems that supposedly preceded it have survived except in prose distillations embedded in the chronicles of the thirteenth and fourteenth centuries. It is, however, likely that the poem represents a novel renovation of the epic tradition in Spain, in part owing to elements clearly derived from French epics and probably from contemporary Latin histories, as well.

The aspect of the *Cantar de mio Cid* that seems most in harmony with the generic conventions of medieval Castilian epic is its meter, which is based on an end pause that marks the border between verses and on a caesura that divides each verse into two hemistiches. The hemistiches comprise between three and eleven syllables, with the most common length being six to eight syllables. In theory, then, full lines should be between six and twenty-two syllables long; but the tendency is to compensate for a short hemistich with a longer-than-average complementary one, so that line lengths range from nine to twenty syllables with the majority comprising fourteen to sixteen syllables. This variability indicates that medieval epic prosody is based not on syllable count, as is modern Spanish verse, but on an accentual rhythm consisting of a certain number of stressed syllables per line. In the *Cantar de mio Cid,* with the exception of hemistiches of less than five syllables, there are routinely two stresses per hemistich—three if the hemistich contains nine or more syllables.

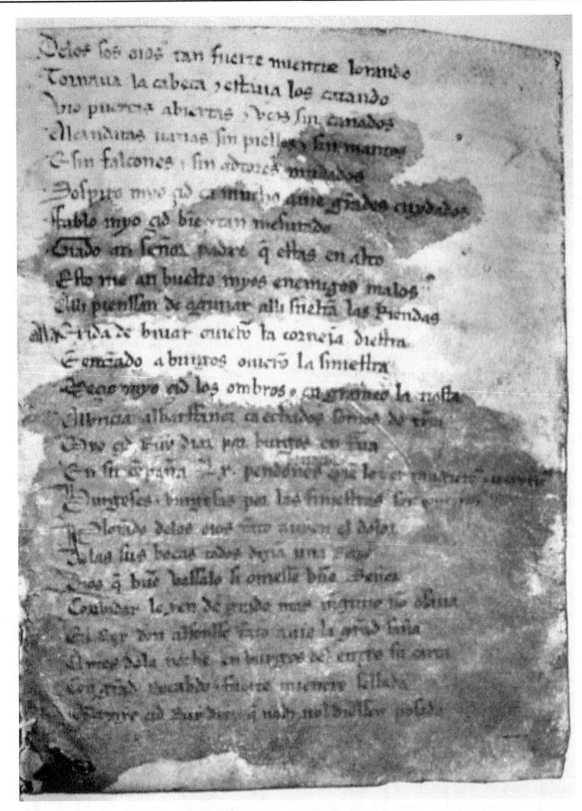

Recto and verso from the only surviving manuscript of the Cantar de mio Cid. *The recto shows damage from reagents used by a former owner of the work (Biblioteca Nacional, Madrid, MS. Vitr. 7-17; photograph courtesy of Albert Montaner).*

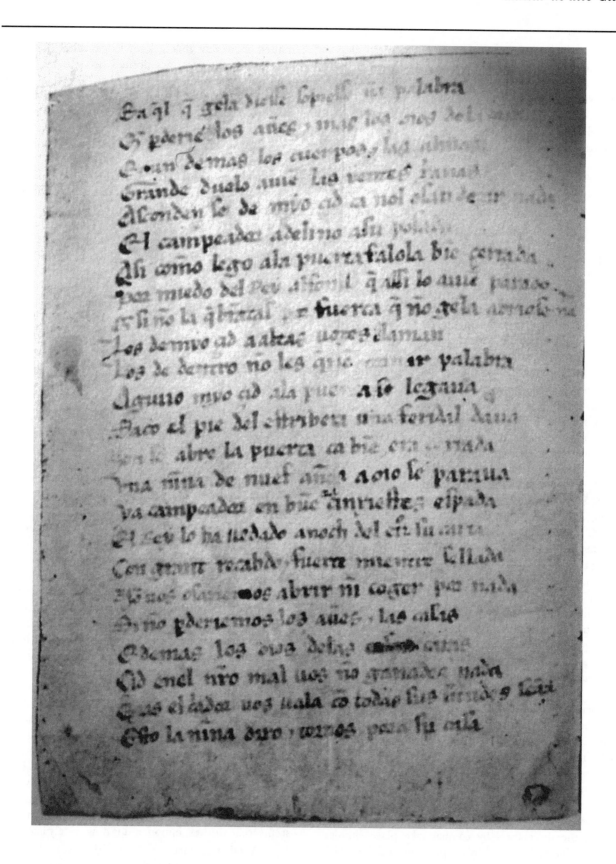

The other required element of the metrical system seen in the *Cantar de mio Cid* is assonantal rhyme: *mál, Bivár, picár, fár,* and *casár* all rhyme with each other. If a stressed vowel is followed by an unstressed one, both vowels count for the rhyme, unless the unstressed vowel is an *e;* thus, *pinár* and *mensáje* function as a rhyming pair. The stressed vowel *ó* can rhyme with either *ú* or *ué* and can be followed by an unstressed *e* or *o,* so that *Campeadór, nómbre, Alfónso, fuért,* and *súyo* would be acceptable rhymes.

A series of verses sharing the same rhyme constitutes a *tirada* (strophe); a *tirada* can have any number of lines. *Tiradas* tend to display a unity of sense and an ability to stand alone, though there are "run-on strophes" where one or two verses take up the theme or story line of the following strophe. There are even cases where the same phrase is split between two consecutive *tiradas,* and once in a while one comes across a strophe with no discernible unifying theme.

Normally, an episode spans several *tiradas.* Therefore, a change in rhyme pattern, which signals the start of a new strophe, is no guarantee that the content of the poem is taking a new tack. The poet's habitual procedure seems to be to start a new strophe when he considers some aspect of his narrative to be concluded. For example, the first strophe in the poem tells of the Cid's departure from Vivar; the second, the trip from Vivar to Burgos. Up to this point each strophe refers to a discrete unit of the action. The stopover in Burgos, however, is one unit with two scenes, each with its own *tirada* and its own internal drama: the third strophe relates the troubled reception of the Cid by the townsfolk; the fourth tells how, despite their sympathy for his plight, the citizens dare not disobey the royal mandate forbidding shelter to the banished hero, forcing him and his band to camp by the river. New strophes are also triggered by shifts such as the prelude to a battle, the engagement proper, and the aftermath. Other strophes are launched to introduce a new character or to set off an extended monologue. At still other times the poet starts a new *tirada* to set off part of the narrative that suspends the linear progress of events, a practice that can be disorienting to the modern reader. Such is the case in the so-called *series gemelas* (twinned series), in which one strophe recapitulates in a more detailed way or from another perspective what was reported in the previous strophe. There are also parallel series, which recount in successive strophes events that are occurring at the same time. For example, near the end of the poem the three trials by combat take place simultaneously but are reported by the poet one at a time, each in its own *tirada.*

Finally, the strophes are clustered into *cantares* (songs), though the surviving manuscript is not for-matted in a way that acknowledges these divisions. Nineteenth-century critics posited two *cantares,* with a transition point after verses 2,776–2,777: "¡Las coplas d'este cantar, aquís' van acabando, / el Criador vos vala con todos los sos santos!" (The verses of this *cantar* come to their end here; / may the Creator bless you with all his saints!). This division establishes a long first *cantar,* made up of verses 1 through 2,777, which recounts all of the events connected with the exile of the Cid from the order of banishment to the marriage of his daughters to the infantes de Carrión. The second *cantar* embraces verses 2,778 through 3,730, concluding with an explicit closure to the entire *Cantar de mio Cid:* "en este logar se acaba esta razón" (at this point the tale is finished). Later, Menéndez Pidal argued for division into three *cantares,* with the second beginning at verse 1,085: "Aquís' compieça la gesta de mio Cid el de Bivar" (Here begin the exploits of my Cid from Vivar), with *gesta* (exploits or deeds or a poem recounting them) understood as a "chapter in an epic poem." He dubbed the three parts "Cantar del Destierro" (The Song of Exile), verses 1 through 1,084; "Cantar de las Bodas" (The Song of the Marriages), verses 1,085 though 1,277; and "Cantar de la Afrenta de Corpes" (The Song of the Outrage at Corpes), verses 1,278 through 1,370. The two-part division better accommodates the thematic structure of the *Cantar de mio Cid.* It also meshes well with the fact that in medieval Castilian the word *gesta* is used only in the sense of *hazaña* (mighty deed) or *proeza* (notable accomplishment); by this reasoning verse 1,085 does not refer to an epic poem, a composition that was generally called in this period a *cantar* or *fabla de gesta* (tale of deeds) and still less to a chapter in such a story. On the other hand, the three-part division breaks up the narrative into units of similar length that roughly match what a singer could deliver in a single performance. Then verse 1,085 suggests a shift from what has just been recounted to the memorable event that is about to be told–a rhetorical marker much in the style of the start of a work and one found in the *Historia Roderici,* which starts in exactly the same way: "Hic incipit gesta de Roderici Campidocti" (Here begins the story of Rodrigo the Battler). Since the deed about to be told is the conquest of Valencia, the greatest military exploit of the Cid's career, it is not difficult to believe that the author wanted to single it out in a section of its own. Thus, even though the dividing line noted by verse 1,085 is much less important than the one at verse 2,777, a segmentation into three parts seems to be the best option and is now widely accepted.

Another distinctive feature of the *Cantar de mio Cid* is its reliance on formulaic diction. This rhetorical mode systematically reworks a battery of familiar epic phrases to allow them to do duty in varying metrical contexts.

The formulas in the *Cantar de mio Cid* are linked to twelfth-century French epic; they could not have come from earlier Spanish epics, because the *Cantar de mio Cid* deals with innovations of content and theme that belong to its own historical period and not to those in which its predecessors were composed. An obvious example is the description of combat, which is highly stylized but reflects ways of handling battle lances that emerged during the late eleventh and early twelfth centuries. These descriptions have already settled into routinized phrases but are incompatible with poems supposedly composed in the tenth or eleventh centuries.

A formula is a reusable statement of a single idea that is expressed two or more times in a poetic text. It is used to fill out a hemistich, and if that halfline is in the second position, it provides the rhyme word for the line. An example is found in verse 2,901, "¿Ó eres, Muño Gustioz, mio vassallo de pro?" (Where are you, Muño Gustioz, my trusty vassal?), and verse 3,193, "A Martín Antolínez, mio vassallo de pro" (Martín Antolínez, my trusty vassal). A "variant formula" or "formulaic segment" occurs when a phrase is repeated not verbatim but with a slight modulation that leaves it metrically intact, as in verse 402, "a la Figueruela mio Cid iva posar" (Off to Figueruela my Cid went to set up camp), and verse 415, "a la Sierra de Miedes ellos ivan posar" (Off to the Miedes Mountains they went to set up camp). In addition to whole phrases and parts of phrases used in the same way each time, a third mode of formulaic composition consists of phrases whose internal elements are rearranged. This option is the most versatile and can be seen in verse 500, "que empleye la lança e al espada meta mano" (Let him use his lance and take up sword in hand); verse 2,387, "el astil á quebrado e metió mano al espada" (the lance shaft snapped, and he set hand to sword); and verse 3,648, "Martín Antolínez mano metió al espada" (Martín Antolínez set his hand to his sword).

Three classes of formulas can be distinguished according to rhetorical function. The first class, delimiting formulas, mark a turning point in the action or a shift in the mode of presentation; sometimes they include a direct address to the audience to draw them into the tale. Delimiting formulas are further divided into elocution formulas, which function as a formal prelude to a speech by one of the characters; transitional formulas, which mark changes in theme or focus of attention; and presentation formulas, which summon the listeners to renewed alertness. Elocution formulas are made up of a verb for a speech act and its subject, usually the name of the speaker, such as "Essora dixo Minaya: 'De buena voluntad'" (Then up spoke Minaya: "Most willingly") and "Essora dixo el rey:

'Plazme de coraçón'" (Then up spoke the king: "This warms my heart"). In these cases the formulaic phrase takes over the first hemistich, leaving the second to communicate the character's words. At other times the second half-line is given over to an elocution formula, such as "Fabló Martín Antolínez, odredes lo que á dicho" (Martín Antolínez spoke, you will hear what he said) and "Diego Gonçález odredes lo que dixo" (Diego Gonçález, you will hear what he spoke). Sometimes an elocution formula marks a spontaneous reaction or retort by one speaker to another: "Respuso el conde: '¡Esto non será verdad!'" (The count replied: "That will not come true!"); "Respuso Minaya: 'Esto non me á por qué pesar'" (Minaya replied: "There is no reason that should grieve me").

Transitional formulas are directed to the listeners in the second person to prepare them when the story shifts attention from one character to another. Two variants of this kind of formula occur in the *Cantar de mio Cid,* each of which has two instances. The first occurs in "Dirévos de los cavalleros que llevaron el mensaje" (I will tell you of the horsemen, how they carried the message) and "Los dos han arrancado, dirévos de Muño Gustioz" (The two have set out, I will tell you about Muño Gustioz). The second variant occurs in "Quiérovos dezir del que en buen ora cinxo espada" (I wish to tell you of he who girds on his sword in a fateful hour) and "Dezirvos quiero nuevas de allent partes del mar" (I wish to tell you of news from the far shores of the sea).

Presentation formulas are of two kinds: those that are built of the deictics (pointing words) *afévos* (here you have) and *felos en* (there they are in) and those that use the verb *ver* (to see), which are used especially in descriptions of combat. Deictics only have a formulaic character when they start a hemistich and are followed by a noun, as in "Afévos doña Ximena, con sus fijas dó va llegando" (Here you have Lady Jimena, as she comes forward there with her daughters) and "Felos en Valencia con mio Cid el Campeador" (There they are in Valencia with my Cid the Campeador). *Veriedes* (you will see) produces a formula in "Veriedes cavalleros venir de todas partes" (You would see knights coming from everywhere) and "Veriedes cavalleros que bien andantes son" (You would see knights, how finely they ride). Two other techniques that sometimes take on a formulaic quality are exclamations and rhetorical questions. The first technique is of the form "¡Dios qué (bien). . . !" (Lord, what a [good]. . . !) or, with a slight modification, "¡Dios, cómmo. . . !" (Lord, how . . . !), as seen in "¡Dios, qué bien tovieron armas el Cid e sus vassallos!" (Lord, how well the Cid and his vassals handled their weapons!) and "¡A Minaya e a las dueñas, Dios, cómmo las ondrava!" (Minaya and his daughters,

Lord, how he honored them!). The second technique is seen in "el oro e la plata, ¿quién vos lo podrié contar?" (the gold and the silver, who could reckon it all for you?) and "e los otros averes, ¿quién lo podrié contar?" (and the other goods, who could reckon it all?).

The second main class of formulas, descriptive formulas, characterize some element introduced into the narrative. They can be made up of the habitual association of an adjective and a noun, as in "buen cavallo" (good horse) and "buenos cavallos" (good horses), with more elaborate variations such as "cavallos gruessos e corredores" (heavy and swift horses). They may also consist of a qualifying phrase that can be applied to various elements and that might pertain to the same class of things, such as "e Peña Cadiella, que es una peña fuert" (and Peña Cadiella, a castle on a crag) and "A siniestro dexan Atienza, una peña muy fuert" (on the left they passed Atienza, a castle on a crag), or to different classes of things, as in "En medio de una montaña maravillosa e grand" (in the midst of the wilderness, wondrous and vast), "de la ganancia que an fecha, maravillosa e grand" (the spoils they have taken, wondrous and vast), and "Venció la batalla maravillosa e grant" (He conquered in the battle, one wondrous and great).

A technique linked to descriptive formulas is the use of epic epithets, which consist of fixed expressions—although not so fixed that they cannot be modified according to the needs of the line and its syntax—to designate or characterize a given figure in the narrative, always in a positive light; the Cid's enemies are never given personal epithets. The usual arrangement is a noun in apposition with a person's name, or the name with a modifying phrase or adjective that singles the person out from everyone else and does not just describe a passing state. In the *Cantar de mio Cid* the hero is the beneficiary of the greatest variety of epithets, such as "el Campeador contado" (the Battler of whom stories are told) and "la barba vellida" (the flowing beard). Some are of a quasi-astrological character, alluding to propitious astral influence at the moment of the Cid's birth and when he was dubbed a knight: "el que en buen ora nasco" (he who was born at a lucky hour) and "el que en buen ora cinxo espada" (he who gird on his sword in a lucky hour). Almost all of the characters within the Cid's inner circle receive an epithet, including Jimena, who is "muger ondrada" (an honorable woman), and Álvar Fáñez, who is "el bueno de Minaya" (the trusty Minaya) and, in the Cid's own words, "mio diestro braço" (my right arm). The king is "el buen rey don Alfonso" (the good king Alfonso) or "rey ondrado" (honorable king).

The third main class of formulas, narrative formulas, allow the poet to report recurrent events. Narra-tive formulas can refer to the passage of time, physical gestures, the expression of emotion, bodily movement, or combat. The first kind mark the chronology of events, such as "otro día mañana" (the next day in the morning) and "cuando saliesse el sol" (at the rising of the sun), or the duration of an event, such as "las noches e los días" (for nights and days). The second kind are applied to a limited set of gestures that possess a special significance; for example, "la cara se santiguó" (he made the sign of the cross on his face), a gesture of surprise; "prisos' a la barba" (he took his beard in his hand), which the hero does in grave or solemn moments; and "las manos le besó" (he kissed his hands), the legal enactment of an oath of fealty. The formulaic expression of emotions includes collective or individualized expressions of joy or grief: "grandes son los gozos y grandes son los pesares" (great are their joys and great are their sorrows), "alegre era" (joyful was he), "plogo a" (it pleased him), and "pesó a" (it grieved him). These formulas can be reinforced to make them more emphatic: "plógol' de coraçón" (it pleased him to his heart) and "pesól' de coraçón" (it grieved him to his heart). Physical movements are indicated in formulas about actions in general, such as "aguijan a espolón" (they picked with their spurs) and "luego cavalgava" (and then he rode), and in reference to specific routes and directions, such as "trocen las Alcarrias e ivan adelant" (they cross the Alcarrias and go on ahead) and "trocieron Arbuxuelo e llegaron a Salón" (They crossed Arbuxuelo and came to Salón). The largest repertoire of formulas is devoted to open-field combat. It is often narrated in a flowing succession of formulas that allows for its description in eight distinct phases, each with a variety of formulas based on meter, rhyme, and style: first, general references, such as "a menos de batalla" (unless [he/they] engage in battle) and "pora huebos de lidiar" (out of need for combat); second, references to arming and outfitting, such as "metedos en las armas" (put on your armor) and "de todas guarnizones" (of all their gear); third, battle cries, such as "¡feridlos, cavalleros!" (Lay on them, knights!) and "¡yo só Ruy Díaz!" (I am Ruy Díaz!); fourth, descriptions of the charge into battle, such as "embraçan los escudos delant los coraçones" (they lifted their shields before their hearts), "abaxan las lanzas a bueltas de los pendones" (they lower their lances together with their pennants), "enclinaron las caras de suso de los arçones" (they inclined their faces above the saddle horns), and "ívan-los ferir" (they went to deal them blows); fifth, descriptions of the clash, such as "fiérense en los escudos" (they laid blows on each other's shields), "da(va)nle grandes colpes" (they laid great blows against him), "falssóle la guarnizón" (he pierced his armor), and "el espada en la mano" (sword in hand); sixth, accounts of pursuit of fleeing enemies, such as "de los que alcan-çava" (those that he overtook) and "duró el segudar" (the pursuit lasted); seventh, relations of the outcome, such as "arrancólos del campo" (he swept the field before them), "oviéronlos de arrancar" (they were swept away), and "(mal) ferido es de muert" (he is wounded [even] to death); and eighth, accounts of the aftermath of the violence, such as "por el cobdo ayuso la sangre destellando" (the blood running down his elbow) and "la cofia fronzida" (his hood pushed back). The use of such reiterative templates at specific junctures generates a style of composition guided by theme and incident. The structure adopted by the poet depends on the type of episode with which he is dealing, and its distinct phases are processed through a formalized sequence of expressions. In other circumstances the use of formulas is more variable. An example of the latter are the embassies the Cid sends to the king, which unfold in seven stages: the entrusting of the mission, the departure of the envoy, the journey to the court, the appearance before the king, the revelation of the mission, the response of the monarch, and the return of the messenger.

In these cases, as in most of the *Cantar de mio Cid,* the narrative follows the chronological order of the events. But there are times, as in the case of the twinned and the parallel *tiradas,* when the poem departs from that mold. The first such instance happens at the outset of the poem, at least as far as can be determined from the reconstruction of the first folio from later sources. The missing opening was about fifty lines in length, too brief to recount all of the events leading up to the hero's exile. Thus, the poem probably did not start from the true beginning of the story, with the Cid being sent to Seville to take delivery of the tribute owed to Alfonso, but in medias res, with the Cid receiving his order of banishment. Those background events are recapitulated in retrospect in verses 109 through 115.

Another situation in which the linear flow of the story is broken occurs when simultaneous events are related; for example, when the story follows some character other than the hero: Minaya pursuing his own sortie down the Henares River Valley while the Cid conquers Castejón; the Cid sending envoys with gifts for Alfonso; or the king and the Cid traveling to the rendezvous site for their reconciliation. In some cases what is happening to the hero while the other events transpire is skipped over, but most of the time both branches of the tale are told in interweaving and alternating scenes with clear markers of transitions from one plotline to the other.

Less familiar to modern readers is another technique characteristic of epic storytelling: double narration, the recitation of the same events in successive passages. This technique takes two forms. In the first, the verses that provide the transition echo the final verses of the strophe that has just concluded, thereby assisting the audience in following the thread of the narrative. The second form is a "prospective" mode that tells a story up to a certain point and then retells the same events in greater detail or from a complementary point of view. *Series gemelas* are employed by the poet in this way, with the change of strophe alerting the listener to the shift in narrative flow. It is somewhat more difficult to identify double narration when it occurs in longer passages and even more so when it spans strophic boundaries. This situation arises when the Cid offers the count of Barcelona his freedom: it happens only once but is related twice, each time with a different coloration.

Another aspect of the epic that tends to confuse the modern reader is a brusque jumping between the *pretérito* (past tense) and the "historical present." One determinant here is the rhyme scheme, since the verb endings provide the vowels that fall into rhyming position, but these temporal leaps do not occur only in rhyming words. The assignment of verb tenses also points to some actions as completed and others as in progress: a given episode may be reported mostly in the *imperfecto* (continuing past tense), with a shift to the *pretérito* signaling the completion of the action. Furthermore, verbs whose inherent meaning is one of uncompleted action or state of being tend to be in the present; those that construe completed events and actions gravitate toward the *pretérito*–unless the action is negative, which tends to generate the historical present tense. Scholars have also detected a correlation between the number of the subject and the verb tense: if the subject is singular, the verb tends to be in the preterit, while if the subject is plural, the verb is in the present. Both occur in the same sentence in "espidiós de todos los que sos amigos son" (he took his leave of all those who are his friends). Finally, certain events are highlighted by being drawn into the immediate temporal plane of the listener through the use of the historical present. When the Cid humbles himself before King Alfonso at their encounter at the Tagus, the hero's specific actions are presented in the simple past tense: "los inojos e las manos en tierra los fincó, / las yerbas del campo a dientes las tomó" (he went down on his hands and knees, he took the grasses of the field in his teeth). But the point of the scene is given in the present tense: "así sabe dar omildança a Alfonso so señor" (Thus he knows how to render homage to Alfonso his lord).

The *Cantar de mio Cid* is told by an omniscient narrator who can offer the reader or listener more information than the characters possess. Depending on the situation, this gap in knowledge can provide humor or dramatic tension. In the *Cantar de mio Cid* it usually tends toward the latter: for example, when the infantes de Carrión depart from Valencia with their wives, the hero is unaware of their intentions; but the audience is fully informed about their plans and has to wait helplessly for them to be carried out. Humor prevails, however, when the Cid barters with the Jewish moneylenders Rachel and Vidas over the chests of sand; when the hero teases the distrustful count of Barcelona; and when the narrator contrasts the responses to the escaped lion of the terrified infantes de Carrión, the alarmed but stalwart palace guard, and the totally unfazed hero.

The narrator of the *Cantar de mio Cid* does not assume a neutral position but is a partisan for his hero; he has no qualms about dismissing the count of Barcelona as a *follón* (blowhard) or about labeling the infantes de Carrión *malos* (evil) after they devise their ignoble plan for avenging themselves on the Cid. He rejoices with the victors when he exclaims, "¡Dios, qué alegre era todo cristianismo, / que en tierras de Valencia señor avié obispo!" (Lord, how joyful all Christendom was, / to have a bishop in Valencian lands!). He also displays his lack of neutrality by dropping out of third-person reportage to address his audience in the second person or to speak in the first person.

Despite his omniscience, the narrator never delves into the minds of his characters to expose their thoughts and motivations. And while he makes no pretense of neutrality, neither does he indulge in moral stereotyping of his subjects—although he does provide some signposts as to their character in the epic epithets he uses. Character is reliably displayed through the subjects' actions and through their words. The latter technique tends to increase the incidence of direct address, with the result that the *Cantar de mio Cid* displays one of the highest ratios of speech to narrative in all of medieval literature.

In rendering the utterances of his characters the narrator may let them speak in their own words; he may paraphrase what they said in full or in summary; or he may use a sort of free indirect discourse, similar to reported speech but without the syntactic subordination that usually indicates dialogue. The first option is the most common one in the *Cantar de mio Cid*: the narrator routinely yields the floor to the character by means of rhetorical formulas and similar gambits or by using a verb that functions in the same way in the context—for example, *sonreír* (to smile), which only occurs as a prelude to direct address. Only when one character replies to another can all transitional markers be omitted:

> mio Cid el Campeador al alcácar entrava,
> recibiólo doña Ximena e sus fijas amas:
> "¡Venides, Campeador, en buena ora cinxiestes espada,
> muchos días vos veamos con los ojos de las caras!"
> "¡Grado al Criador, vengo, mugier ondrada!"

(my Cid the Battler has come into the fortress.
Lady Jimena received him, and both their daughters:
"You have come, Battler, in a happy hour you girt on your sword,
may we see you with our own eyes for many days to come!"
"Thanks be to the Creator, I come, honored wife!")

Indirect discourse is indicated by a verb of speaking or its functional equivalent, which, in addition to introducing the characters' reported discourse, allows for its coloration, as in "Mandó mio Cid a los que ha en su casa / que guardassen el alcácar e las otras torres altas" (The Cid commanded those who were in his household / that they guard the keep and the other high towers) and "Díxoles fuertemientre que andidiessen de día e de noch, / aduxiessen a sus fijas a Valencia la mayor" (He told them sternly to march by day and night, / that they bring his daughters to Valencia the city). When the indirect discourse records a character's thoughts, recourse is had to verbs that mean "to think" or "to ponder," as in "ya veyé mio Cid que Dios le iva valiendo" (the Cid now saw that God was helping him along) or "Todos se cuedan que ferido es de muert" (All were convinced that he was dealt a mortal blow). These occasional references do not negate the narrator's staunch resistance to peeking into his characters' minds: he is passing along impressions, rather than actual thoughts. The same is true when he describes the emotions that result from certain actions: "Mucho pesa a los de Teca e a los de Terrer non plaze" (It grieves those in Teca and pleases not those in Terrer); "Cuando esto oyó el conde ya s'iva alegrando" (When he heard this, the count's spirits perked up).

In free indirect discourse the verbs introducing speech are replaced by transition markers from narration to spoken expression. This technique is used in the *Cantar de mio Cid* primarily in situations that are somewhat impersonal, such as the reception of communiqués or the contents of a document: "a aquel rey de Sevilla el mandado llegava / que presa es Valencia, que no ge la enparan" (word reached the king of Seville that unless someone comes to its aid, Valencia will fall), "llegaron las nuevas al conde de Barcilona / que mio Cid Ruy Díaz quel' corrié la tierra toda" (the news reached the count of Barcelona that my Cid Ruy Díaz was scouring the land before him), "el Poyo de mio Cid asíl' dirán por carta" (the documents will show that this was the Cid's Hilltop). Like direct discourse, it is only rarely used to convey someone's thoughts: "commo ellos tenién, crecerles ía la ganancia" (they thought that their wealth would grow). And like the variation in verb tenses, different forms of presenting speech can be combined. This passage starts with indirect, switches to direct, and concludes with free indirect discourse:

> mandó mio Cid Ruy Díaz, que en buen hora nasco,
> que fita soviesse la tienda e non la tolliese dent cristiano:
> "Tal tienda commo ésta, que de Marruecos á passado,
> enviarla quiero a Alfonso el castellano,"
> que croviesse sos nuevas de mio Cid, que avié algo.

> ([Thus] commanded my Cid Ruy Díaz, who was born in a good hour,
> that the tent should remain standing and no one remove it from there:
> "Such a tent as this, come all the way from Morocco,
> I want to send it to Alfonso of Castile,"
> and so the news would grow of my Cid and the wealth he possessed.)

As for individualized expression, the only significant difference between the characters and the narrator is that they are not allowed the same latitude in tense. This difference can be explained by the narrator's need for a more complex repertoire of expressive options than the actors in his story, who only speak to their immediate circumstances and do not have to worry about variety of style or shifts in perspective. An exception to the similarity of the manner of speech of the various characters is that the oath "Sant Esidro!" (St. Isidore!) is reserved for King Alfonso, a reference to the historical king's devotion to the saint. Also, the formal second-person plural, *vós,* which is equivalent to *usted* (the polite singular "you") in modern Spanish, is not found in the speech of Moorish characters; they use the second-person singular *tú,* the normal form in the Arabized Romance language spoken in the southern and Muslim portions of the peninsula—in Arabic, plural forms are used to show respect only in the most solemn of contexts. The one exception is the Cid's *amigo de paz* (ally by pact of friendship) Avengalbón, who betrays by his use of *vós* his assimilation to his Christian neighbors.

The characters are distinguished by what they say, not how they say it. Their attitudes, intentions, and actions differentiate them. There are good characters and bad ones, and those categories are based on whether they support or oppose the hero. Still, their virtues and vices are not assigned mechanically; everyone gets his own shading. For example, the count of Barcelona, the infantes de Carrión, and García Ordóñez share a courtly hauteur and disdain for the Cid, but each has his quirks. The count is a braggart but can handle himself in battle and ends up not quite as blackened as the infantes; Diego and Fernando are grasping, deceitful, and cowardly and are clearly the most morally debased characters in the *Cantar de mio Cid,* a fact that the narrator underscores; and García Ordóñez tries

to defame the hero and ends up shamed himself. Accordingly, the Cid does not treat all of his foes in the same fashion. With the count he first displays a jocular irony and then a ruefully dismissive tone. The infantes are handled with appropriate courtesy while they reside in Valencia but afterward with a profound disregard that sinks to the point of labeling them "canes traidores" (traitorous curs). The Cid's changing attitude to his sons-in-law, from distrust to attachment to total rejection, shows that the characters in the *Cantar de mio Cid* are allowed scope to evolve. The clearest case is that of King Alfonso: he gradually lets go of his early wrath and comes to feel a profound affection for the Cid, whom he finally admires so much that he declares before his court "¡Maguer que a algunos pesa, mejor sodes que nós!" (Although it might grieve others [to hear/say it], you are a better man than I). The characterizations are fairly nuanced, especially that of the Cid: he is capable of showing grief and joy with his family, vacillation and resolve in his military campaigns, camaraderie with his men, stateliness at court, and even—an unexpected quality in an epic hero—an unabashed sense of humor that is revealed not only with the count of Barcelona but also when he is in pursuit of King Búcar.

The absence of psychological descriptions, which forces the task of characterization onto speeches and actions, is matched by a lack of descriptions of the physical appearance of the characters. The Cid's daughters receive the greatest number of descriptive phrases, and even those are scant. When they stand with their mother on the battlements of Valencia, gazing out on the vast holdings of the Cid, their "ojos vellidos catan a todas partes" (lovely eyes glanced in every direction). The Cid himself says that his daughters are "tan blancas commo el sol" (as white as the sun). The latter comparison is also used for tunics of polished mail, a shirt, and a head scarf or hood, which might lead one to suppose that it is conventional and empty of special meaning. But the use of this formulaic expression is so limited that one is led to assume that each of these items is outstanding in its own way.

One signal physical trait is associated with the Cid from the beginning of the poem: a flowing beard that grows to imposing length as a result of his self-imposed vow not to cut it until he recovers his king's favor. This aspect of his appearance becomes so essential that he regularly acquires epic epithets that allude to it, such as "el de la luenga barba" (he of the long beard), "el de la barba grant" (he of the great beard), "barba tan conplida" (beard so excellent), and "la barba vellida" (the comely beard). In contrast, García Ordóñez sports a disfigured growth, for during an earlier dispute the Cid marked him for life by ripping out a piece of his beard. This act was a grave insult in the Middle Ages, one that the *fueros* reckoned as equivalent to castration, and the fact that García Ordóñez never dared to demand reparation from the Cid for this ritual mutilation symbolized for contemporaries the gap of honor that existed between the two. As for the infantes de Carrión, the general opinion is that they are two of a kind; Pero Vermúez says to one of them, "e eres fermoso, mas mal varragán" (You are good-looking enough, but not much of a man). A final descriptive detail is assigned to don Jerónimo, the French bishop installed by the Cid as Valencia's prelate, who displays his clerical state by being *coronado* (tonsured).

The dearth of descriptions in the *Cantar de mio Cid* suggests that the ones that do exist fulfill a deliberate purpose and are not mere ornamental touches. The same is true for the objects named: whenever something is pointed to, the intention is to make it and the person who owns it stand out. For example, the Cid's spotless tunic, shirt, and hood receive the same attributes as his daughters. Usually the poet limits himself to mentioning the quality of the object, without going into specific details: thus, he often speaks formulaically of "buenos cavallos," as is natural in a poem that exalts the feats of mounted knights. Clothing gets the same sort of treatment when the Cid grants the count of Barcelona his freedom: to send him off outfitted as befits his rank—and to show off the Cid's generosity—"Danle tres palafrés muy bien ensellados / e buenas vestiduras de pelliçones e de mantos" (They give him three riding mounts with fine saddles / and good clothing with gowns and capes). Occasionally, however, more particulars are provided: "Saca las espadas e relumbra toda la cort, / las maçanas e los arriazes todos d'oro son" (He brings out the swords and they dazzle the assembled court, / the pommels and crosspieces all of gold). At the suit against the infantes the Cid appears in raiment of the finest sort, whose rich materials and perfect fit inspires rapturous wonder in those present: "en él abrién que ver cuantos que ý son" (all who were there had to pause to admire him). Other expressions of approval are more veiled and subtle. For example, when the Cid finishes a battle, one glimpses "la cofia fronzida" (his hood [or helmet liner] crumpled and distressed) or "la cara fronzida" (his face furrowed and distressed): the hero's skin and the lining of his battle gear have been battered by the press of the chain mail and metal of his armor and the exertion of his feats of arms, implying an essential unity of character and indicating the punishment he has endured during the clash of warriors.

Another technique used by the *Cantar de mio Cid* to heighten the impact of its descriptions is carefully weighed pairings. Some seem to be merely instances of the formulaic diction that suffuses the work; but when one considers that some of the descriptive comparisons are rather obvious, it becomes clear that their repetition is styled to accomplish a specific artistic effect. When King Alfonso readies himself for the rendezvous on the banks of the Tagus where he will grant the Cid's pardon, the narrator surveys his entourage in a prolonged series of rhetorical questions:

> ¿quién vio por Castiella tanta mula preciada
> e tanto palafré que bien anda,
> cavallos gruessos e corredores sin falla,
> tanto buen pendón meter en buenas astas,
> escudos boclados con oro e con plata,
> mantos e pielles e buenos cendales d'Andria?

> (Who throughout Castile ever saw so many handsome mules
> so many fine stepping riding mounts,
> sturdy horses who can gallop so surely,
> so many stout pennants on so many strong lances
> shields with gold and silver bosses,
> cloaks and lined furs and smooth silks from Andros?)

This passage displays the typical features of many descriptions in the *Cantar de mio Cid;* their impact is enhanced by the accumulation of precious objects, by the insistent use of *tanto* (so many), and by the question format. The Castilian monarch's adorning and outfitting of himself is paralleled in the next *tirada* by the simultaneous actions of the hero:

> Dentro en Valencia mio Cid el Campeador
> non lo detarda, pora las vistas se adobó:
> ¡tanta gruessa mula e tanto palafré de sazón,
> tanta buena arma e tanto buen cavallo corredor,
> tanta buena capa e mantos e pelliçones!
> Chicos e grandes vestidos son de colores.

> (Within Valencia my Cid the Battler
> does not tarry, and dressed himself for the encounter:
> so many sturdy mules and so many riding mounts in their prime,
> so many fine arms and so many clean-hoofed chargers,
> so many good capes and cloaks and lined furs!
> Young and old are decked out in bright colors.)

One can see how closely these lines are kept in step with the ones that precede them, but it would be a mistake to attribute the similarities to habits of formalized speech, since they share only a couple of formulaic phrases. The poet is making a conscious effort to collate the statures of the two figures. The Cid does not ride out to receive his royal pardon because he is destitute without it; he is now the lord of a realm of his own, and his riches are nearly as great as those of the Castilian court. The hero desires reconciliation with his king because Alfonso is his *señor natural,* and to be in harmony with the monarch allows all things to recover their preordained order and balance. When the rendezvous on the banks of the Tagus comes to its conclusion, the Cid bestows on the king and his nobles gifts that take on the rhetoric and resonance of the previous enumerations:

> Aquís' metió en nuevas mio Cid el Campeador:
> tanta gruessa mula e tanto palafré de sazón,
> tantas buenas vestiduras que d'alfaya son,
> compeçó mio Cid a dar a quien quiere prender so don;
> cada uno lo que pide nadi nol' dize de no.

> (Here my Cid the Battler performed another resounding gesture:
> so many sturdy mules and so many riding mounts in their prime,
> so many good garments of richest finery,
> my Cid set himself to give away to whoever would like to take his gifts;
> he gave to each what he asked for, and said no to no one.)

The undeniable use of formulaic composition in this passage does not weaken its force. The parallelism of these verses with those describing the Cid's preparations for the rendezvous suggests that the hero can dole out livestock and clothing of the same quality as his own—a noteworthy point, because largesse was one of the most esteemed qualities in the world of knightly comportment.

The use of parallel features and calculated contrasts is one of the stylistic constants of the *Cantar de mio Cid.* When the Cid faces his estranged king at their rendezvous, he prostrates himself and kisses Alfonso's feet—a conventional gesture of assuming bonds of fealty. The king invites the Cid to rise and kiss his hands instead, an action that is also sufficient to reestablish their bond. The Cid does rise but kisses Alfonso on the mouth: a sign of friendship. Those three moments visually recapitulate the Cid's career as recounted in the epic: abasement, recovery, and finally an elevation that leaves him nearly equal to his lord. There is also an echo of the rapprochement achieved through the three envoys the *Campeador* sent to his *señor natural* with gifts: the first was accepted with a certain coolness; the second was warmly received and resulted in permission for the Cid's family to rejoin him in Valencia; and the third prompted a fulsome spectacle of renewed friendship and the granting of pardon. Similar structural principles inform the beginning of the poem: the Cid leaves the doors of his house in Vivar hanging open, a mute expression of abandoned home and hearth; the image is repeated in even darker colors when he finds the doors in Burgos closed to him; but the symbolism of homelessness is inverted when the doors of the monastery of

Cardeña swing open in welcome, for the shelter and hospitality proffered by the monks provide at least a transitional new home for his family. In a similar way, the emergence of the infantes de Carrión on the scene recycles various details of the prior intervention of the moneylenders Raquel and Vidas. Both pairs of characters are bent on taking advantage of the Cid. The Jews are duped; the aristocrats profit handsomely, but their wealth is not won by their efforts or even derived from their solidarity with the band who earned it, and therefore, within the ethical world of the poem, they clearly lack the right to possess and enjoy it. This play of repetitions and contrasts throughout the poem contributes to a sense of cohesion and craftsmanship that is one of the greatest artistic achievements of the *Cantar de mio Cid.*

Yet another factor is the majesty of style. According to medieval tenets of composition, epic poetry concerns itself with elevated themes in an elevated, dignified, and sober style. In the earliest days of critical attention to the work, Menéndez Pidal argued that the loftiness of tone in the *Cantar de mio Cid* is achieved in part through the archaic cast of its language. Scholars are no longer quite as sure about this supposed old-fashioned solemnity of expression: too few twelfth-century vernacular texts exist to allow one to get a reliable idea of what might have felt archaic to an audience around 1200. Traits that do help to produce a sense of solemnity include the use of learned words and expressions adapted from church Latin and the language of the law, among them *criminal* applied specifically to criminal calumny, *monumento* (tomb), *tus* (incense), *virtos* (host or army), and *vocación* (vocation or calling). There is also an expansive repertoire of Spanish military terms: *loriga* (coat of mail), *almófar* (the hood of mail whose links are continuous with the coat), *belmez* (padded tunic worn under the coat of mail), *arrobda* (patrol), *art* (feint or gambit as a maneuver in battle), *az* (line or formation of soldiers), *compaña* (war band, troops), *fierro* (iron point on a lance), and *huesa* (horseman's sturdy high boot). This sort of diction is natural in a poem about military exploits, but one is caught off guard by the quite different diction of legal process, which is ample in range and deployed with precision. This language does not appear only in the final judicial confrontation in Alfonso's royal court of appeal; it is found throughout the work. Apart from the Latinate terminology, one could point to the Spanish *alcalde* (in the antique sense of "judge" rather than the modern "mayor"), *entención* (an allegation in legal proceedings), *juvizio* (judgment or sentence), *manfestar* (juridical confirmation of an alleged crime), *rencura* (civil or criminal suit), and *riepto* (formal accusation with judicial challenge for satisfaction). There are also pairs of apparent synonyms that one would expect to encounter not in a poetic work but in a legal instrument where exact terminology is required. The pairings of roughly equivalent terms specify subtle differences in sense that are not to be blurred: "a rey e a señor" (to king and liege lord), "pensó e comidió" (he pondered and weighed), and "a ondra e a bendición" (honorable and sanctioned [in reference to a legally contracted matrimonial union]). Other pairs indicate a totality by listing the constituents: "grandes e chicos" (adults and minors [that is, everyone, regardless of age]), "moros e cristianos" (Moors and Christians [that is, all citizens or inhabitants of every class and standing]), "nin mugier nin varón" (neither woman nor man), "el oro e la plata" (the gold and the silver), "en yermo o en poblado" (in desert or town [that is, in open countryside or in incorporated district under a code of law]), and "de noche de día" (by night or by day [that is, at any time]).

Reduplicative phrasing can also be noted in more-complex structures that fill out a verse and use the caesura as their hinge point, such as "grandes averes priso e mucho sobejanos" (bountiful possessions he seized, and ones greatly to be prized) and "a priessa vos guarnid e metedos en las armas" (swiftly outfit yourselves and put on your arms), both of which are examples of twinned complements, and "antes perderé el cuerpo e dexaré el alma" (before [that] I will forfeit my body and forsake my soul) and "comed, conde, d'este pan e beved d'este vino" (eat, Count, of this bread and drink of this wine), examples of inclusive complements. The first class includes curious cases of synonymy by contrast—that is, expressions that are apparently contradictory but in fact mean the same thing, such as "venido es a moros, exido es de cristianos" (he has come to Moors, he has come out from Christians) and "passada es la noche, venida es la mañana" (the night has passed, the morning has come). This rhetorical turn can also be used to indicate true antithesis: "e faziendo yo a él mal e él a mí grand pro" (and I doing to him great harm and he to me great benefit).

Another type of locution that is characteristic of the poem is the "physical phrase," which emphasizes an action by redundantly specifying the part of the body that performs it: "plorando de los ojos, tanto avién el dolor" (crying from his eyes, so great was his sorrow); "de la su boca compeçó de fablar" (he began to speak with his mouth). It is possible that these expressions were a form of stage directions indicating the movements and posture the *juglar* should assume during his recitation of the poem, but it is just as likely that their vividness obviated the need for acting them out. Besides, it is difficult to imagine how the performer would play them out except by exaggerated histrionics

that would violate the solemnity characteristic of the epic.

The intonation to be given to the text is more obvious. Exclamations, questions, and the declarative voice are employed by the narrator and by the characters. One use of exclamation is in the war cries of the two sides: "Los moros llaman '¡Mafómat!' e los cristianos 'Santi Yagüe'!" (The Moors shout "Muhammad!" and the Christians "St. James!"). And one should note the rhetorical questions posed by the Cid in his formal denunciation of the infantes before the judicial *cortes* in Toledo, an address that ends, movingly, "Cuando las non queriedes, ya canes traidores, / ¿por qué las sacávades de Valencia, sus honores? / ¿A qué las firiestes a cinchas e a espolones?" (Since you did not love them, you traitorous dogs, why did you take them from Valencia, them and their riches? Why did you whip them with cinches and spurs?).

Not much is known of how the *juglares* made their texts come alive. The performer's colophon at the end of the manuscript makes it clear that this copy of the *Cantar de mio Cid* would sometimes be read aloud. Nonetheless, the most frequent sort of delivery must have been done from memory and sung to music that some researchers imagine—without much evidence—to have been a variation of Gregorian chant. The delivery was probably fairly stiff and formalized, and the use of any instrument that required two hands to play would have hobbled the performer's dramatic style even further. Recitations were done in the street or the town square at the request of the passersby or by commission of the town council, which contracted with performers to enliven local festivals. It was just as common for a *juglar* to stage his artistry in private at a family occasion such as a wedding or baptism. When the audience had the wherewithal, it was common to hire performers to provide after-dinner entertainment. The length of the *Cantar de mio Cid* militates against its having been performed in its entirety on any given occasion. The most that might have been recited at a single performance would have been one *cantar* of the three identified by Menéndez Pidal; often, probably, only selected episodes would have been presented, according to the taste of those gathered. No documentation exists to indicate which audiences fancied which passages, although the popularity of the old ballad of the king who lost Valencia—"Helo, helo por do viene / el moro por la calzada" (See him, see him, as he comes along / the Moor along the highway)—might allow one to venture a guess that the pursuit of King Búcar was a favorite of audiences. As with all works that were oral in origin, it is hard to know what sort of success the *Cantar de mio Cid* had in its inaugural generation; but proof of the durability of its appeal is as close as the extant manuscript, produced more than a century after its original model in anticipation of live performances for fourteenth-century audiences. The prestige of the work is shown by the persistent echoes of it in a great deal of later Castilian epic poetry—especially in the other extant poem about its central figure, the *Mocedades de Rodrigo* (circa 1300, Youthful Deeds of Rodrigo)—and bits can be found in works and authors of quite different genres, such as Gonzalo de Berceo. A prose version was worked into Alfonso X's *Estoria de España,* and other chronicle accounts are based on it. After the Middle Ages, the memory of the deeds of the Cid were kept alive by these sources until the first publication of the *Cantar de mio Cid* in 1779 brought a new generation's attention to bear on the text.

Esteemed by universal consensus as the foremost work in the Spanish literary canon, the *Cantar de mio Cid* continues to draw the interest of specialists and the cultured public alike. It has been published in many modern editions and been the subject of an imposing body of scholarship, but it has also inspired artists and writers to generate their own diverse reimaginings of the story and its hero in works of literature, paintings and sculptures, motion pictures, and comic books.

References:

Carlos Alvar, Fernando Gómez Redondo, and Georges Martin, eds., *El Cid: De la materia épica a las crónicas caballerescas* (Alcalá de Henares: Universidad de Alcalá, 2002);

César Hernández Alonso, ed., *Actas del Congreso Internacional El Cid, Poema e Historia* (Burgos: Ayuntamiento, 2000);

Matthew Bailey, *The "Poema del Cid" and the "Poema de Fernán González": The Transformation of an Epic Tradition* (Madison, Wis.: Hispanic Seminary of Medieval Studies, 1993);

Simon Barton and Richard Fletcher, *The World of the Cid: Chronicles of the Spanish Conquest* (Manchester, U.K. & New York: Manchester University Press, 2000);

James F. Burke, *Structures from the Trivium in the "Cantar de Mio Cid"* (Toronto & London: University of Toronto Press, 1991);

Edmund de Chasca, *El arte juglaresco en el "Cantar de mio Cid,"* second edition (Madrid: Gredos, 1972);

Alan Deyermond, *El "Cantar de mio Cid" y la épica medieval española* (Barcelona: Sirmio, 1987);

Deyermond, "Structural and Stylistic Patterns in the *Cantar de Mio Cid*," in *Medieval Studies in Honor of Robert White Linker,* edited by Brian Dutton, James Woodrow Hassell, and John E. Keller (Madrid: Castalia, 1973), pp. 55–71;

Deyermond, ed., *Mio Cid Studies* (London: Tamesis, 1977);

Deyermond, David G. Pattison, and Eric Southworth, eds., *Mio Cid Fifty Years On,* Papers of the Medieval Hispanic Research Seminar, no. 20 (London: Queen Mary, University of London, 2000);

Joseph J. Duggan, *The "Cantar de Mio Cid": Poetic Creation in Its Economical and Social Contexts* (Cambridge: Cambridge University Press, 1989);

Duggan, "Formulaic Diction in the *Cantar de Mio Cid* and the Old French Epic," *Forum for Modern Language Studies,* 10 (1974): 206–209;

Nancy J. Dyer, *El "Mio Cid" del taller alfonsí: Versión en prosa en la "Primera Crónica General" y en la "Crónica de veinte reyes"* (Newark, N.J.: Juan de la Cuesta, 1995);

Richard Fletcher, *The Quest for El Cid* (New York: Oxford University Press, 1989; London: Century Hutchinson, 1989);

José Manuel Fradejas Rueda, *Crono-Bibliografía Cidiana* (Burgos: Ayuntamiento, 1999);

Luis Galván, *El "Poema del Cid" en España, 1779–1936: Recepción, mediación, historia de la filología* (Pamplona: EUNSA, 2001);

Michel García and Georges Martin, *Études Cidiennes: Actes du Colloque "Cantar de Mio Cid"* (Limoges: Presses Universitaires de Limoges, 1994);

Miguel Garci-Gómez, *"Mio Cid": Estudios de endocrítica* (Barcelona: Planeta, 1975);

Stephen Gilman, *Tiempos y formas temporales en el "Poema del Cid"* (Madrid: Gredos, 1961);

José Luis Girón Alconchel, *Las formas del discurso referido en el "Cantar de Mio Cid"* (Madrid: Real Academia Española, 1989);

Michael Harney, *Kinship and Polity in the "Poema de mio Cid"* (West Lafayette, Ind.: Purdue University Press, 1993);

David Hook, "Some Problems in Romance Epic Phraseology," in *Cultures in Contact in Medieval Spain,* King's College Medieval Studies, no. 3 (London: King's College Press, 1990), pp. 127–150;

Jules Horrent, *Historia y poesía en torno al "Cantar del Cid"* (Barcelona: Ariel, 1973);

María Eugenia Lacarra, *El "Poema de mio Cid": Realidad histórica e ideología* (Madrid: Porrúa, 1980);

Francisco López Estrada, *Panorama crítico sobre el* Poema del Cid (Madrid: Castalia, 1982);

Albert B. Lord, *The Singer of Tales* (Cambridge, Mass.: Harvard University Press, 1960), pp. 127, 206;

Michael Magnotta, *Historia y bibliografía de la crítica sobre el "Poema del Cid"* (Chapel Hill: University of North Carolina Press, 1976);

Gonzalo Martínez Díez, *El Cid histórico* (Barcelona: Planeta, 1999);

Ramón Menéndez Pidal, *En torno al "Poema del Cid"* (Barcelona: Edhasa, 1963);

Menéndez Pidal, *La España del Cid,* 2 volumes (Madrid: Plutarco, 1929; revised edition, Madrid: Espasa-Calpe, 1969);

Ian Michael, "Tres duelos en el *Poema de Mio Cid,*" in *El comentario de textos,* volume 4: *La poesía medieval* (Madrid: Castalia, 1983), pp. 85–104;

Alberto Montaner, "El Cid: Mito y símbolo," *Boletín del Museo e Instituto "Camón Aznar,"* 27 (1987): 121–340;

Montaner, "Un posible eco del *Cantar de mio Cid* en Gonzalo de Berceo," in *Actas del VI Congreso Internacional de la Asociación Hispánica de Literatura Medieval,* 2 volumes (Alcalá de Henares: Universidad de Alcalá, 1997), II: 1057–1067;

Milija N. Pavlović and Roger Walker, "Roman Forensic Procedure in the *Cort* Scene in the *Poema de Mio Cid,*" *Bulletin of Hispanic Studies* (Liverpool), 60 (1983): 95–107;

Francisco Javier Peña Pérez, *El Cid Campeador: Historia, leyenda y mito* (Burgos: Dossoles, 2000);

Brian Powell and Geoffrey West, eds., *"Al que en buen hora naçio": Essays on the Spanish Epic and Ballad in Honour of Colin Smith* (Liverpool; Liverpool University Press/Modern Humanities Research Association, 1996);

Peter Russell, *Temas de "La Celestina" y otros estudios: Del "Cid" al "Quijote"* (Barcelona: Ariel, 1978);

Colin Smith, *Estudios cidianos* (Madrid: Cupsa, 1977);

Smith, *The Making of the "Poema de mio Cid"* (Cambridge: Cambridge University Press, 1983);

Story Weavers and Textual Critics Interpret the "Poema de Mio Cid," special issue of *La Corónica,* edited by Oscar Martín, 32, no. 2 (2005);

Antonio Ubieto, *El "Cantar de mio Cid" y algunos problemas históricos* (Valencia: Anubar, 1973);

Irene Zaderenko, *Problemas de autoría, de estructura y de fuentes en el "Poema de mio Cid"* (Alcalá de Henares: Universidad de Alcalá, 1998).

Cantigas in the Galician-Portuguese Cancioneiros

Janice Wright
College of Charleston

WORKS: *Pergamiño Vindel* (end of thirteenth or beginning of fourteenth century)

Manuscript: Pierpont Morgan Library, New York, MS. 979, one folio. This single parchment leaf preserves seven *cantigas de amigo* by the Galician composer Martin Codax. The scribe divides the songs in four columns without illuminations and only modest initial letters. Six of the *cantigas* have musical notations. The parchment was discovered in Madrid by Pedro Vindel, a dealer in rare books, who published it in 1915.

Editions: *Martin Codax: Las siete canciones de amor, poema musical del siglo XII,* edited by Pedro Vindel (Madrid: Printed by the successors of M. Minuesa de los Ríos, 1915); *O Cancioneiro de Martin Codax,* edited by Celso Ferreira da Cunha (Rio de Janeiro: Departamento de Imprensa Nacional, 1956); I. Fernández de la Cuesta, "Les cantigas de amigo de Martin Codax," *Cahiers de Civilisation Médiévale,* 25 (1982): 179–185.

Sharrer Manuscript (end of thirteenth or beginning of fourteenth century)

Manuscript: "Pergaminho Sharrer," Torre do Tombo, Fragmentos, caixa 20, n. 2 [Casa Forte], one mutilated parchment folio discovered in 1990 in the Arquivo Nacional of the Torre do Tombo by Harvey L. Sharrer. It contains seven *cantigas de amor* by King Denis with musical notations. The large sheet is written in three columns on both sides. Given its size and arrangement, it may be a fragment of a general or genre songbook.

Edition: Harvey L. Sharrer, "Fragmentos de sete cantigas de D. Denis, musicadas—uma descoberta," *Actas do IV Congresso da Associação Hispânica de Literatura Medieval,* volume 1 (Lisbon: Cosmos, 1991), pp. 13–29.

Cancioneiro de Ajuda (first quarter of the fourteenth century)

Manuscript: Biblioteca de Ajuda, Lisbon, MS. 118, 127 surviving folios. Illuminations accompany the first 224 songs, and all begin with ornate initials. Copying of the collection seems to have been interrupted, since the miniatures are incomplete and there is no accompanying musical notation.

Editions: *Cancioneiro de Ajuda,* 2 volumes, edited by Carolina Michaëlis de Vasconcellos (Halle: Niemeyer, 1904; republished, with glossary and introduction, by Ivo Castro, Lisbon: Imprensa Nacional-Casa da Moeda, 1990); *Cancioneiro da Ajuda: A Diplomatic Edition,* edited by H. R. Carter (New York & London: Modern Language Association of America, 1941); *Cancioneiro da Ajuda: Edição fac-similada do Códice existente na Biblioteca de Ajuda* (Lisbon: Távola Redonda, 1994).

Cancioneiro da Biblioteca Apostólica da Vaticana (copied in Italy, 1490–1530)

Manuscript: Vatican Library, Rome, MS. Vat. lat. 4803 (sixteenth-century copy of lost fourteenth-century original), 235 folios, made under the direction of the Italian humanist Angelo Colocci. The scribe was probably not a professional, judging by his use of cursive script and corrosive ink; there are also frequent lacunas. Colocci's notes are in the margins.

Editions: *Il grande Canzoniere Portoghese della Biblioteca Vaticana,* edited by Ernesto Monaci (Halle: Niemeyer, 1875); *Cancioneiro Português da biblioteca Vaticana (Cód. 4803),* facsimile edition, edited by L. F. Lindley Cintra (Lisbon: Centro de Estudos filológicos-Instituto de Alta Cultura, 1973).

Cancioneiro da Biblioteca Nacional de Lisboa (Colocci-Brancuti; sixteenth-century copy of a lost fourteenth-century original)

Manuscript: Biblioteca Nacional, Lisbon, Códice 10991, 335 folios. Contains *cantigas de amor, de amigo,* and *de escarnho e maldizer.* It was discovered by Costantino Corvisieri and Enrico Molteni in the library of Count Paolo Antonio Brancuti in Cagli; the manuscript was purchased by the Portuguese government in 1924 and renamed *Cancioneiro da Biblioteca Nacional.* The first part of this songbook, the most complete collection of Galician-Portuguese poetry, corresponds to the *Cancioneiro de Ajuda* and also includes all of the songs collected in the *Cancioneiro da Biblioteca Apostólica da Vaticana.*

Editions: *Il canzoniere portoghese Colocci-Brancuti pubblicato nele parte che completano il Codice vaticano 4803,* edited by Enrico Molteni (Halle: Niemeyer, 1880); *Cancioneiro da Biblioteca Nacional,* 8 volumes, edited by Elza Pacheco Machado and José Pedro Machado, (Lisbon: Revista de Portugal, 1949–1964); *Cancioneiro da Biblioteca Nacional (Colocci-Brancuti), Cód. 10991,* facsimile edition, edited by Luís F. Lindley Cintra (Lisbon: Biblioteca Nacional/Imprensa Nacional-Casa da Moeda, 1982).

Arte de Trovar (sixteenth century?)

Manuscript: The *Arte de Trovar* is a fragment of an *ars poetica* included in the *Cancioneiro da Biblioteca Nacional de Lisboa (Colocci-Brancuti),* Cód. 10991, folios iiir–ivv.

Editions: "Arte de Trovar," in *Cancioneiro da biblioteca nacional (antigo Colocci-Brancuti),* edited by Elsa Pacheco and José Pedro Machado (Lisbon: Revista de Portugal 1, 1949), pp. 15–30; Jean Marie D'Heur, "L'art de trouver du chasonnier Colocci-Brancuti," in *Recherches internes sur la lyrique amoureuse des troubadours galiciens-portugais (XII–XIV siècles): Contribution a l'étude du "corpus des troubadours"* (Liége: Faculté de Lettres, 1975), pp. 97–171; Elsa Pacheco, "'Arte de Trovar' Portuguesa," *Revista da Faculdade de Letras,* second series, 13 (1994): 53–60; Giuseppe Tavani, *Arte de trovar do Cancioneiro da Biblioteca Nacional de Lisboa* (Lisbon: Edições Colibri, 1999).

OTHER COLLECTIONS: José Joaquim Nunes, ed., *Cantigas d'amigo dos Trovadores Galego-Portugueses,* 3 volumes (Coimbra: Imprensa da Universidad, 1926–1928; New York: Kraus Reprint, 1971);

Nunes, ed., *Cantigas de amor dos trovadores galego-portugueses: Edição crítica acompanhada de introdução, comentário, variantes e glossário* (Coimbra: Imprensa da Universidade, 1932);

Manuel Rodrigues Lapa, ed., *Cantigas d'escarnho e de mal dizer* (Vigo: Galaxia, 1965; revised edition, 1970);

Carlos Alvar and Vicenç Beltran, eds., *Antología de la poesía gallego-portuguesa* (Madrid: Alhambra, 1985);

Paredes Núñez, *El cancionero profano de Alfonso X el Sabio* (Rome: Japadre, 2001).

In the thirteenth century the courts of the Castilian monarchs Alfonso VIII, Fernando III, and Alfonso X and other noble courts sheltered *trovador* (troubadour) poets from Iberia and southern France. They enjoyed and sponsored songs written in Galician-Portuguese, a literary language rooted in one of the living languages of the western part of the peninsula, while favoring Castilian for epic and narrative poetry. The same division occurred in France, where for a time Old French was used for narrative poetry and Occitan for the lyric. The songs also flourished from the second half of the thirteenth century through the first quarter of the fourteenth century in the Portuguese courts of King Afonso III and his poet son, King Denis. According to António de Resende de Oliveira, the Portuguese court troubadours were mostly from Galicia and Portugal, favored the indigenous *cantiga de amigo,* and were less susceptible to Occitan influence. These songs are preserved in three large *cancioneiros* (songbooks) and two additional small manuscripts. The surviving record of the Galician Portuguese lyric is relatively poor compared with those of the Occitan, Italian, and Catalán-Provençal lyrics of the fourteenth century. Even the extensive *Cantigas de Santa María* (Songs of Holy Mary), the great thirteenth-century sacred anthology by Alfonso XI *el Sabio* (the Learned), king of Castile and León, has survived only in the four songbooks produced during his reign. The other extant manuscripts were compiled in the first quarter of the fourteen century in the Portuguese courts of Afonso III and Denis, rather than in Galicia, the northwestern territories that remained part of the Spanish kingdoms after Afonso Henríquez established the independence of Portugal in 1179 and became King Afonso I. Since the court poets were Leonese, Castilian, Galician, and Portuguese, however, the songs are considered the literary patrimony of both Spain and Portugal.

Although the *cancioneiro* poems are assigned to individual poets, scant biographical information is available for most of them. The Portuguese historian António José Saraiva believes that the earliest of the poets was João Soares de Paiva, born in 1141 during the reign of the Portuguese king Sancho I, and the latest was Count Pedro, son of King Denis, who died in 1354.

Quite a few noble *trovadores* existed, since writing poetry was in style among noblemen in the peninsular courts of the time; little is known about them other than their names. The powerful Coelho family not only produced poets but was also politically active. João Soares Coelho and Estevão Coelho wrote lyric poetry; the latter was either the father or brother of Pero Coelho, who was sentenced to death in 1360 for participating in the murder of Inés de Castro. Mem Rodrigues Tenoiro was also a noble Galician poet; King Pedro I handed him over to the Castilian king of the same name in exchange for the men responsible for the death of Inés. The *segrels* (lower-class nobles) also lived in the courts and made their living writing poetry. The prolific Bernardo de

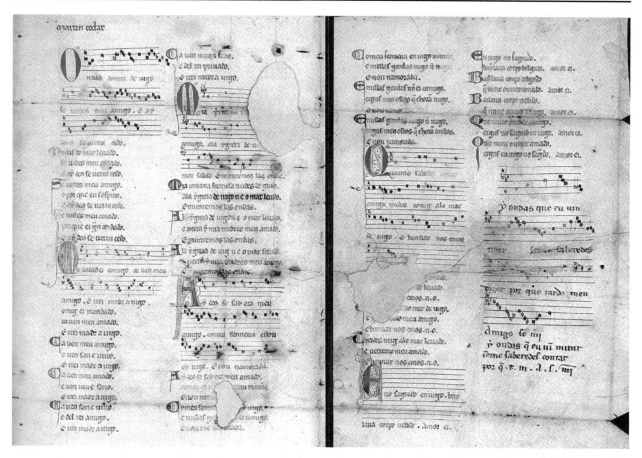

The Pergamiño Vindel, *comprising seven* cantigas de amigo *by the Galician composer Martin Codax (Pierpont Morgan Library, New York, MS. 979)*

Bonaval and Pero da Ponte are members of this group. Pero Amigo de Sevilha, Pero d'Armea, and João Baveca probably lived in the court of Alfonso X. Almost nothing is known about the bourgeois troubadours; Sancho Sanchez and Airas Nunes were clergy in the court of Alfonso X, and João Airas de Santiago traveled in the general area and spent some time in Portugal. The common person who earned his living by reciting his own poetry and that of others was a *jograr*. No biographical information is available about any of these poets. Martin Codax was, perhaps, a contemporary of Afonso III. Lourenço is said to have made an effort to raise himself to a higher level, probably in the court of Alfonso X or Denis, resulting in his exile by the more influential poets. Nuno Peres was one of fourteen poets who, as far as is known, wrote nothing other than *cantigas de amigo*.

The anonymous handbook *Arte de trovar* (Art of Poetry), which was probably composed in the sixteenth century, defines the two types of love songs in the Galician-Portuguese songbooks concisely: if the song "se move a razón dele" (is in male voice), it is a *cantiga de amor;* if it "se move a razón dela" (is in female voice), it is a *cantiga de amigo*. The male sings to or about his *senhor* (lady), and the woman sings to or about a man. The most widely accepted classification of the *cantiga de amor* divides it into two groups: songs in which the *trovador* sings directly to his lady and in which an invocation to his *senhor, senhor fremosa* (lovely lady), or *mia senhor* (my lady) is found in the first two lines, and songs in which the *trovador* sings about his lady in the third person. In the latter the poet may address his friends, God, love, or his lady's eyes, but in most cases the audience is unidentified.

The court of Alfonso X was a refuge for troubadours fleeing southern France during the persecution of the Albigensian heresy, and the influence of the Occitan lyric on Iberian poets composing *cantigas de amor* in Galician-Portuguese added nuances and variations. The peninsular poets were particularly inspired by the idea of *amor cortés* (courtly love), unrequited love as service to an inaccessible lady. Since dynastic marriages occurred at a young age in Provence, the Occitan songs were sung to young married women who were often of higher rank than the poets. Love was also considered incompatible with marriage, because marriages were determined by family obligations, while love was to be given freely. Since property was inherited only by the eldest son, the other sons were left to seek their fortunes as clergymen or knights. The knights, who did not marry to bond clans or merge estates, were raised in the courts of their fathers' lords, where they played at games of courtly love. Parodying the role of vassals in the feudal system, these young men chose their lords' wives as their "ladies" and sang to them in the hope of an amorous reward. The more the lady resisted these advances, the more glory the aspiring lover enjoyed as a stalwart and long-suffering suitor. In this game only male desire could exist; the lady's role was that of passive ennobler of the masculine spirit. The "game master" was probably the lord himself, who used the activity to keep his men under control and to encourage poetic competition among young nobles in order to create a more sophisticated atmosphere in his court.

Courtly love could never totally fit into thirteenth- and fourteenth-century western Iberian society. Connie L. Scarborough and M. Carmen Pallares point out that women were much less powerful in the peninsula than in France. Also, there were far fewer noble courts in Spain than in Provence; thus, the *cantigas* were cultivated only in the courts of the kings and those of a few grandees. Since there were few noble married ladies to pursue, the peninsular *trovadores* replaced the married lady with a single woman. Peninsular poets were, however, well aware of the Occitan influence on their songs. King Denis, for example, makes a direct reference to the songs from Provence:

> Quer'eu en maneira de proençal
> fazer agora un cantar d'amor;
> e querrei muit'I loar mia senhor,
> a que prez nen fremosura non fal,
> nen bondade; e mais vos direi en:
> tanto a fez Deus comprida de ben
> que mais que todas las do mundo val.

> (I want in Provençal style
> to write a song of love;
> and I want to praise my lady in it,
> who is not lacking in value nor beauty,
> nor kindness; and I will tell you more about her:
> God made her so full of grace
> that she is worth more than all other women in the world.)

The influence of the Occitan lyric on peninsular poets is evident beyond questions of genre and vocabulary. In the *cantiga de amor* the Galician-Portuguese *trovador*, like the Provençal troubadour, is obligated to work his way up from a timid *fenhedor* (pretender) who dares not openly express his love for his lady to a supplicant *pregador* (suitor;

literally, "beseecher") who confesses his love and finally to an *entendedor* (confidant; literally, "man in the know") whose lady has accepted his love. This last stage has traditionally been understood as a spiritual relationship; Vicenç Beltran writes that the desensualization of the Occitan lyric is one of the basic characteristics of the *cantiga de amor*. Nevertheless, the possibility exists, especially in the more insistently erotic poems, that the relationship may be physical. The Provençal *drutz* (sexual lover) who has received his lady's physical favors is parodied in an ironic *cantiga de escarnho e maldizer*:

> Dade-m' alvíssara, Pedr' Agudo,
> e ôi-mais sodes guarido:
> vossa molher á bon drudo,
> baroncinho mui velido.
> Dade-m' alvíssara, Pedr' Agudo,
> vossa molher á bon drudo.

> (Give me a reward, Pedro Agudo [Smart],
> and from today on be more fortunate:
> your wife has a good lover,
> A handsome little fellow.
> Give me a reward, Pedro Agudo,
> Your wife has a good lover.)

The peninsular game of courtly love is governed by several aspects of the Occitan lyric's code of behavior. According to Saraiva, the *trovador* must, first of all, keep the lady's name a secret. Since in Provence the woman was married, the suitor had to be extremely discreet; in the Galician-Portuguese lyric, where there is no husband to fear, the rules of the game are imposed by the woman herself. She sees *mesura* (self-control) as one of the lover's highest qualities, since lack of it would cause her to fall into *desmesura* (disgrace). In response, she might *estranhar* (ignore) his attentions, react to him with *desamparo* (studied indifference), *dar penas* (show disrespect) for him, *fazer mal* (wound) him, or display *sanha* (vengeful anger) for him. Second, the *trovador* must be adept at giving and receiving *prendas* (love tokens) and *dõas* (gifts). Third, he must not take his leave without her permission. Fourth, he must live in a state of continual suffering, always ready to *morrer de amor* (die of love) for her. Finally, and most important, his love songs must reflect this tension, in accordance with the Occitan idea that for the true male lover no resolution is possible.

In the Galician-Portuguese love lyric the lady is called *molher* (woman), *moça* (young girl), *donzela* (young lady), or *amiga* (lady friend). Her physical description is reduced to generalities: she has *bon parecer* or *bon semellar* (good looks), *ben talhada* (a good figure), *buen prez* (charm), and *fremosura* or *beleza* (beauty). The lady's moral qualities—her *ben falar* (well-spoken words), *siso* (good sense), and *dozura* (sweetness)—are praised more extensively than her physical ones.

There are few indications of concrete space and time in the *cantiga de amor*. The Occitan lyric's setting in a beautiful garden on a spring day is usually absent, and the only characters mentioned in most cases are the *trovador*, his lady, and *Deus* (God). The *trovadores* realized that there was an aesthetic difference between their songs and those of the Occitan poets, and they wondered about the sincerity of the latter. King Denis writes:

Proençaes soen mui ben trobar
e dizen eles que é con amor;
mais os que troban no tempo da frol
e non en outro, sei eu ben que non
an tan gran coita no seu coraçon
qual m'eu por mia senhor vejo levar.

(Poets from Provence know how to write songs
and they say that it is done with love;
but those who write in the flowering springtime
alone, I know well that they do not
suffer pangs of love in their hearts
like the ones that weigh me down for my lady.)

The *Morrer de amor* topos is shared with the Occitan lyric. Love in the *cantiga de amor* is almost always overwrought, and the majority of the songs revolve around the *trovador's coita* (suffering in love). His feelings are expressed in nouns such as *doo* (pain), *dano* (harm), *pena* (feeling sad), and *pesar* (feeling sorry) and in verbs such as *sofrer* (suffer), *lazerar* (exacerbate), and *tromentar* (torment). He is *desnortado* (confused), *desventurado* (ill-fated), *desesperado* (desperate), *cativo* (imprisoned by love), and *mal día nado* (born under an unlucky star). He may even be driven to insanity as *minguar o sen* (reason falters) or *perder o sén* (reason fails); he may *ensandecer* (become unhinged) or suffer *sandede* or *sandeu* (craziness), *loucura* (madness), and *folía* (folly).

Some critics attribute the reduction of the *cantiga de amor* to the theme of the suffering of the male lover to the idea that the talent of a true artist lay not in his originality but in his ability to manipulate details to introduce a new variation on an overworked theme. As a result, the *cantiga de amor* analyzes to the point of exhaustion the feelings and psychology of the unrequited male lover, and the songbooks include only works that best represent this definition of art. Nevertheless, some texts that deviate from the norm have been preserved: satirical elements intrude into the *amor* genre in Paay Soarez de Taveyros's humorous song about a man in love with a female relative, in Roy Queymado's singing that he has saved himself from dying of love by cutting off his relationship with his *sen-*

hor, and in Pai Gómez Charinho's declaration that he loves his *senhor* but not enough to die of love for her.

Most researchers consider the *cantiga de amigo* a courtly elaboration of an earlier popular folk lyric. Nevertheless, the existence of *zéjel* manuscripts that consist of a *villancico* (initial refrain), three *mudanzas* (monorhyme line strophes), and a *vuelta* (fourth line that rhymes with the refrain) has led some scholars to believe that the genre was cultivated in the peninsula half a century before the first *albas* (dawn songs) were written in southern France. The *zéjel* was a poem written in the spoken language that at times included romance words. In 1919 Ramón Menéndez Pidal presented his traditionalist theory, which postulates the existence of a Castillian lyric parallel to the Galician-Portuguese. He believed that the *zéjel* had been imitated by the Provençal poets, as well as the Galician-Portuguese, Italian, and Spanish. In 1948 Samuel M. Stern discovered the *kharjas* (closing lines written in mozárabe) of twenty *muwashshahas* (formal poems written in Arabic or Hebrew) dated in the second half of the eleventh century; he published his findings that same year in his article "Les vers finaux en espagnol dans les *muwassahas* hispano-hébraïques" (Spanish End Verses in the Hispano-Hebrew *muwashshaha*). This discovery dealt a second blow to the theory of the Occitan origin of the peninsular lyric.

Two lyric subgenres of the Galician-Portuguese *cantiga de amigo* that have traditionally been considered of Occitan origin are the *pastorela*, which corresponds to the Occitan *pastourelle*, and the *alba*. The former is a chance meeting between a gentleman on horseback and a shepherdess; the latter is a dawn song of farewell after the lovers have spent the night together. Careful readings, however, place the Occitan origin of these subgenres in doubt. In the *pastorela* the dialogue between the gentleman and the shepherdess that is found in the Occitan *pastourelle* is often eliminated: the peninsular poem is reduced to the male listening to the young woman sing a *cantiga de amigo* about her happiness and sadness in love, and she may not even be aware of his presence. A typical example is King Denis's "Ua pastor se queixava" (The shepherdess complained), in which the male listens as a country girl lying in a meadow of flowers sings about her suffering because her lover is marrying another. Also, the word *pastora* in Galician-Portuguese may mean simply a young woman rather than a shepherdess. In the Occitan *alba* the threat of violence always comes from outside the lovers' hideaway in the person of the husband or the *lauzengiers* (court gossipers), while the Galician-Portuguese speaker may find herself threatened not only by the outside world but also by the

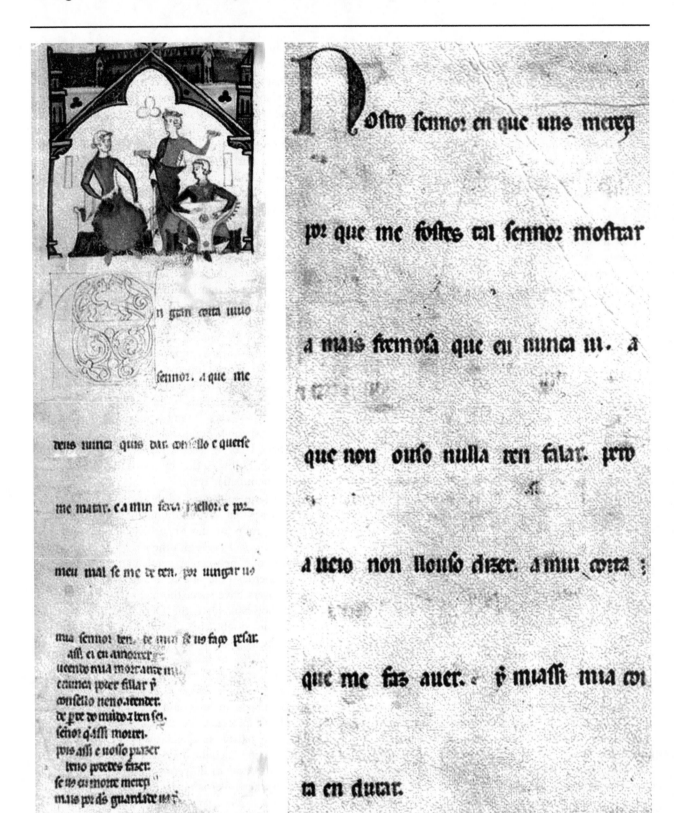

Pages from the manuscript of the Cancioneiro de Ajuda *(Biblioteca de Ajuda, Lisbon, MS. 118)*

predatory lover himself. Other subgenres of the *cantiga de amigo* are *bailadas* (dance songs), *marinhas* (sea songs), and *romarias* (pilgrimage songs). There are also dialogue songs between the girl and her mother or a female friend or between her and her lover. Some of the best poets, such as Pero Meogo, composed works in almost all of the subgenres. Scholars today are no longer concerned with classifying these songs but with studying individual poets.

The *cantiga de amigo* can be divided into two types according to form: simpler poems, properly characterized as parallelistic songs, and *cantigas de meestria* (mastery songs), which use some of the techniques of the Provençal lyric and in which the game of courtly love is often played. The parallelistic *cantiga de amigo* is thought to have originated in the dances and collective songs associated with pagan rites that are seen as typical of the rural communities of northwestern Iberia. In contrast to the lack of physical setting in the *cantiga de amor,* the parallelistic *cantiga de amigo* is rooted in local life: the *romarias,* for example, celebrate pilgrimages to the shrines of Galician and northern Portuguese saints. The regional characteristics of the bucolic landscape include fauna such as deer and various types of birds, flora that consists, as today, of pine and hazelnut trees, the Ria de Vigo and other rivers and fjords of the Iberian northwest, and the sea. The themes reflect the rural life of the people, especially that of the girl who goes to the fountain or river to wash her hair or clothes and meets her lover there. These deceptively simple poems with their stylized patterns are filled with nature and pagan symbolism; for example, the first sexual encounters between the lovers often take place at a fountain or river where mountain stags stir up the still waters.

Saraiva mentions the traces of phonetic archaism found in the parallelistic songs, such as the intervocalic *n* in key words such as *fontana/louçana* (fountain/lovely girl). Early in the study of these songs, Ernesto Monaci was of the opinion that the appearance in the parallelistic songs of words that had disappeared by the thirteenth century proved that the poems existed before the influence of the troubadour school of Provence spread to the peninsula. Carolina Michaëlis de Vasconcellos claims in her edition of the *Cancioneiro de Ajuda* (1904) that the first parallelistic *cantiga de amigo* was written by Sancho I before 1200 and was perhaps inspired by his lover, the "Ribeirinha" (Maria Pais Ribeiro), the daughter of Paay Moniz:

> ¡Ay eu coitada!
> ¡Como vivo en gram cuidado
> por meu amigo
> que ei alongado!
> ¡Muito me tarda
> o meu amigo na Guarda!

> ¡Ay eu coitada!
> ¡Como vivo en gram desejo
> por meu amigo
> que tarda e não vejo!
> ¡Muito me tarda
> o meu amigo na Guarda!

> (Oh poor me!
> How I live in longing
> for my lover
> who is far from me!
> He tarries so long
> my lover in Guarda!

> Oh poor me!
> How I live in great desire
> for my lover
> who tarries and I don't see!
> He tarries so long
> my lover in Guarda!)

Some forty of these simpler *cantigas* are extant. They usually consist of two lines per strophe of assonant rhyme, with a tonic (stressed) vowel *i* or *e* in one of the distichs of each pair and *a* in the other, as in *pio/amigo* (pine/friend) and *ramo/amado* (branch/lover). The rhythmic unity is found not in the strophe but in a pair of strophes or distichs that express the same notions and differ only, or almost only, in the rhyme words. The last verse of each strophe is the first verse of the next strophe, and each strophe is divided by a repeating refrain. Using this system of parallelism, it is possible to construct a composition of six to eight strophes and eighteen to twenty-four lines in which there are only five or six completely different lines, including the refrain. The structure of this type of *cantiga de amigo* can be understood by imagining two speakers, each of whom sings one or more strophes. Each successive strophe repeats the preceding one but with a change of assonance. A *cantiga* by King Denis is a good example of this type of song:

> ¿–Ai flores, ai flores do verde pio,
> se sabedes novas do meu amigo?
> ¿ai, Deus, e u é?
> ¿Ai, flores, ai flores do verde ramo,
> se sabedes novas do meu amado?
> ¿ai, Deus, e u é?
> ¿Se sabedes novas do meu amigo,
> aquel que mentiu do que pôs comigo?
> ¿ai, Deus, e u é?
> ¿Se sabedes novas do meu amado.
> aquel que mentiu do que mi á jurado?
> ¿ai, Deus, e u é?

> ¿–Vos me preguntades polo voss' amigo?
> ¿E eu ben vos digo que é sã' e vivo:
> ¿ai, Deus, e u é?

¿Vós me preguntades polo voss' amado?
E eu ben vos digo que é viv' e são:
¿ai, Deus, e u é?
E eu ben vos digo que é sã; e vivo
e seerá vosc' ant' o prazo saido:
¿ai, Deus, e u é?
E eu ben vos digo que é viv' e são
e s[e]erá vosc' ant' o prazo passado:
¿ai, Deus, e u é?

(–Oh flowers, oh flowers of the green pine tree,
have you news of my friend?
oh, God, and where is he?
Oh flowers, oh flowers of the green branch,
have you news of my lover?
oh, God, and where is he?
have you news of my friend,
the one who lied when he set a date with me?
oh, God, and where is he?
have you news of my lover,
the one who lied about what he swore to me?
oh, God, and where is he?

–Are you asking me about your friend?
I am truly telling you that he is well and alive:
oh, God, and where is he?
Are you asking me about your lover?
I am truly telling you that he is alive and well:
oh, God, and where is he?
I am truly telling you that he is well and alive
and he will be with you before his [military] service
    [against the Moors] is up;
oh, God, and where is he?
I am truly telling you that he is alive and well
and he will be with you before his service is over:
oh, God, and where is he?)

In a parallelistic *cantiga de amigo* by Pero Meogo, the young woman is talking to her mother on her return from a meeting with her lover at the fountain:

–Digades, filha, mia filha velida:
¿porque tardastes na fontana fria?
os amores ei.
Digades, filha, mia filha louçana:
¿porque tardastes na fria fontana?
os amores ei.

–Tardei, mia madre, na fontana fria,
cervos do monte a augua volvian:
os amores ei.
Tardei, mia madre, na fria fontana,
cervos do monte volvian a augua:
os amores ei.

–Mentir, mia filha, mentir por amigo:
nunca vi cervo que volvess'o rio:
os amores ei.
Mentir, mis filha, mentir por amado:
nunca vi cervo que volvess'o alto:
os amores ei.

(–Tell [me], daughter, my beautiful daughter:
why did you tarry at the cold fountain?
I am in love.
Tell, daughter, my lovely daughter:
why did you tarry at the fountain so cold?
I am in love.

–I tarried, my mother, at the cold fountain,
mountain stags stirred up the water:
I am in love.
I tarried, my mother, at the fountain so cold,
mountain stags stirred up the water:
I am in love.

–You are lying, my daughter, lying for a friend:
I never saw a stag stir up the river:
I am in love.
You are lying, my daughter, lying for a lover:
I never saw a stag stir up the deep water:
I am in love.)

In a parallelistic poem the first lines indicate the time and place at which the poem is set; they thus have a narrative character that one would expect to see developed in the rest of the composition. This development does not take place, however; the remaining strophes repeat the initial situation with few variations. All of the information given in the poem is present in the first strophe. The symmetrical repetition of the lines, the final rhymes, and the refrain, along with the repetition of pauses, reduce the already weak logical relationship between the lines. Menéndez Pidal writes in "La primitiva lírica española" (1944, The Primitive Spanish Lyric) that the use of parallelism expands, slows, or stops the flow of the girl's feelings about being in love. This repetitive structure builds and multiplies the emotional force of the song, creating an extremely lyric quality.

Purely parallelistic songs were written by members of the high nobility; many of the poems of King Denis are of this type. This fact has traditionally been explained by attributing popularity to folkloric-type poetry, after a phase in which the Provençal style was imitated at court. The poets of Denis's circle are thought to have collected, imitated, and revised traditional songs learned from the common people. This theory would explain the existence of variations of the same song by different poets, such as the two versions of "Balada Avelaneiras Floridas" (Ballad of the Flowering Almond Trees) by the *poeta culto* (cult poet) Airas Nunes and the *jograr* João Zorro.

In the second type of *cantiga de amigo,* the *meestria* song, the poet often plays the Provençal game of courtly love and uses several of the techniques of Occitan poetry. In these songs there are few narrative or descriptive elements; the setting is vague, and all is subordinated to the poet's expression of the pleasure and pain of the young woman in love. *Cantigas de meestria* have a more complicated structure than parallelistic songs: the refrain is frequently placed within a strophe, increasing the number of lines and breaking up their pairing. The anaphoric parallelism of the other group, which includes identical or similar lines at the beginning of the paired strophes, is reduced in the *cantiga de meestria* to a simple parallelism in rhyme. This development tends to eliminate the archaic vocabulary and the repetitions, including those of the refrain.

In these poems the *trovador* presents the ups and downs of the relationship between the lovers, interpreting the way a woman in love would react to the presence or absence of her lover according to the tenets of courtly love as the *trovador fidalgo* (noble peninsular poet) conceived it: happiness when he arrives, sadness and loneliness when he leaves. The women are aware of their beauty, and the poet indirectly praises himself by presenting a beautiful woman dying of love for him. As in the parallelistic songs, the young woman may speak to her mother, a pretty young friend, Love, God, the saints, or nature. This type of dialogue gives the *cantiga de meestria* a dramatic quality that, along with the narrative and lyric components, adds to its charm. The *coita* of the *trovador* in the *cantigas de amor* is here transferred to the woman.

In this song the man has broken one of the rules of the courtly love game by leaving without the permission of his lady. She is complaining to one of her friends, another beautiful girl:

Ai, Deus a vó-lo digo:
foi-s'or' o meu amigo:
ie se o verei, velida!
Quen m'end'ora soubesse
verdad'e mi dissesse:
ie se o verei, velida!
Foi-se'el mui sen meu grado
e non sei eu mandado:
ie se o verei, velida!
Que fremosa que sejo,
morrendo con desejo:
e se o verei, velida.

(Oh, God I am telling you:
my friend has now left:
and if I will see him [again], pretty one!
Who might know and
tell me the truth:
and if I will see him, pretty one!
He left very much without my approval
and I do not know of the order [a military order or the fact that she did not order him to leave]:
and if I will see him, pretty one!
How beautiful I am,
dying of desire:
and if I will see him, pretty one.)

Doris Earnshaw and Cynthia P. Bagley have discarded the theory of the folkloric origins of the genre and proposed a textually oriented approach that sees both the simple parallelistic and the more complex *meestria* songs as the creation of male troubadours who composed and sang them for the entertainment of an aristocratic audience at court. Earnshaw states that the two types of *cantiga de amigo* were used by the Galician-Portuguese troubadours simply to add variety to their performances. According to Bagley, there is no clear proof of an oral lyric tradition, and the assumption of another persona was a common part of the poet's craft. Her arguments, based on manuscript assignment, the fact that each poem has a specific author, and the introduction of a pretended speaker, minimize the differences between a popular women's song and the male voice in the *cantiga de amor*: the former is seen as a product of the latter, and the only feature that differentiates them from one another is the stipulation in the *Arte de Trovar* that the *cantiga de amor* have a male speaker and the *cantiga de amigo* a female speaker.

The idea that both the parallelistic and *meestria* songs are exclusively the work of male court poets during the thirteenth and fourteenth centuries, and that these poets did not have recourse to an existing body of women's songs on which to base their poems, is extreme. Women's songs existed in almost all medieval cultures, and they were certainly present in Galicia and northern Portugal. The traditional view that credits the origin of the parallelistic *cantigas de amigo* to traditional women's songs of an earlier precourtly society is probably valid: these poems do seem to be elaborations of traditional peninsular lyrics. Earnshaw and Bagley's view that the poems are exclusively the work of individual poets is, however, applicable to *meestria* songs. Earnshaw contends that in this form the male voice speaks of a newer social ethic that contrasts with the "traditional rhythms and rhymes" of the speech of the *amigas*. This feature is certainly evident in the *pastorelas* and in many dialogue songs.

The masculine elaboration of women's song paralleled the growth of the male-dominated aristocratic class and accompanied further linguistic changes. It is possible that the archaic, exclamatory speech of the *cantigas de amigo* was perceived by aristocratic audiences as old-fashioned or even laughable and provided a means of contrasting countrified speech with the more sophisticated language of the court. The "cut-and-paste" style of the *meestria* poems thus fulfills a cultural need of the new ruling class as it tried out its power to change the older rural organization of society.

Trovadores and *jograres* also wrote satirical songs, known as *cantigas de escarnho* and *cantigas de maldizer*, about the battles, individual "crusades," and court events they witnessed. Alfonso X, for example, wrote *cantigas de escarnho* and *cantigas de maldizer* about those in his circle of retainers and unreliable allies who displayed crassness or cowardice. By the mid thirteenth century a corpus of satirical songs had been created.

These songs were censored for their obscene language from the moment of their composition. Manuel Rodrigues Lapa notes in his edition of these *cantigas* (1965; revised, 1970) that Alfonso X's own code of law, *Las siete partidas* (The Seven Parts), forbade the singing of the songs he himself composed: "que ningun ome non fuese osado de cantar cantiga nin decir rimas nin dictados que fuesen fechos por deshonra o por denuesto de otro" (No one should dare to sing a *cantiga* or recite verses or compositions made to dishonor or defame another).

The form of these satirical songs is similar to the other genres in their use of parallelistic and refrain styles. They have been the least studied of the *cantiga* genres because their rich and varied vocabulary, wordplay, and use of colloquialisms make the texts more difficult to decipher. The first scholar to analyze these songs was Michaëlis, who tried to clarify some of the more difficult passages in fifteen studies she published between 1896 and 1905. There has been a resurgence of interest in the genre.

Rodrigues Lapa points out that the Galician-Portuguese satirical songs, also called *serventeses,* were influenced by the Occitan *sirventés.* The latter are divided into three categories: the first comprises moral or religious complaints about the decadent and rude habits of the nobility, satires against women, and attacks on the corruption of the clergy; the second consists of political comments on the events of the times, mostly about the wars between the English and the French and the Albigensian Crusade; and the third embraces personal attacks on individuals' personal and professional lives. Some Galician-Portuguese poets, such as Martim Moxa and Airas Nunes, imitated the Occitan *sirventés* closely, writing moral or social criticism that provides an interesting picture of the time. Saraiva notes that Alfonso X wrote a poem satirizing a group of nobles who deserted the Christian forces in a battle to take Granada, the last Moorish stronghold, and two compositions accusing two nobles of betraying King Sancho II in the civil war of 1245.

Personal satire and attack is the strong point of the peninsular songs. Rodrigues Lapa lists many verbs meaning to "make fun of" someone, often viciously: *fazer jogo, escarnir, escarnecer, chufar, desdizer, profaçar,* and *travar.* The nicknames the poets give to their targets heap ridicule on their bearers: Nuno Porco (Pig), Nuno Peres Sandeu (Crazy), Fernand' Esquio (Sneaky), Airas

Corpancho (Widebody), Coxas-Caentes (Hot Thighs), and so forth.

In addition to *cantigas de escarnho* and *cantigas de maldizer,* Rodrigues Lapa identifies four other types of satirical song: the *joguete d'arteiro* (wisecrack song), which the *Arte de Trovar* classifies as a *cantiga d'escarnho;* the *cantiga de seguir* (imitation or plagiarized song), a parody of an existing song; the satirical *tençao* (debate song), a debate in verse among the poets of the several nationalities that lived in the peninsular courts—Giuseppe Tavani states that this form was mainly limited to the court of Alfonso X; and the *cantiga de risadilha* (joking song), which the *Arte de Trovar* defines as a simple song, probably popular satire and older than the courtly lyric. Saraiva says that in the *Cancioneiro da Biblioteca Nacional* a note is written next to one of these songs indicating that it is an imitation of a *cantiga de vilão* (country bumpkin's song), a subgenre also mentioned in the *Arte de Trovar.*

The *escarnho* poem is ironic and full of double meanings and does not name the person being satirized. Rodrigues Lapa cites as an example of this type of song one by Afonso Mendes de Besteiros that makes fun of João Pires de Vasconcelos, a Portuguese noble living in the Castilian court who was afraid to fight in the wars of the Reconquest. Nicknamed "o Tenreiro" (young and tender one), he is compared to a calf:

> Don Foão, que eu sei que á preço de ligeiro,
> vedes que fez ena guerra—daquesto son verdadeiro:
> sol que viu os genetes, come bezerro tenreiro,
> sacudiu-se [e] revolveu-se,
> alçou rab' e foi sa via a Portugal.

> (Sir So and So, who I know has a reputation as a light-
> weight [coward],
> see what he did in the war—in this true song:
> as soon as he saw the horsemen, like a tender young calf,
> he shook himself off and spun around,
> he turned tail and took off on his way to Portugal.)

The *maldizer* song accuses or makes fun of people openly, using direct, frank language. Many of the Galician-Portuguese *serventeses* are of this type. Some were composed in contests in which groups of bawdy poets took part. One of the most famous contests is known as the *ciclo das amas* (cycle of the wet nurses) and was devoted to ridiculing the *jograr* Lourenço for composing songs in praise of a wet nurse. Another group of *serventeses* was composed about the *soldadeiras* (girls for hire) who accompanied male performers as singers or dancers and were prostitutes, as well. Maria Peres Balteira is the best-known *soldadeira* because of the large number of satirical songs about her amorous adventures. The preference for satirical verse

Illuminations from the Cancioneiro de Ajuda *(Biblioteca de Ajuda, Lisbon, MS. 118)*

was accentuated in the fourteenth century: twenty-eight of the thirty-five poems by Estevan da Guarda are of this type, as are seven of Count Pedro's eleven songs.

The *cantigas de escarnho e maldizer* are the best documentation available for the variable fortunes, decadence, and ruin of the thirteenth- and fourteenth-century peninsular nobility, who were impoverished by war and by their own ostentation. As the Reconquest progressed, prestigious noble houses fell, and opportunities were opened for landless sons and members of the lower nobility to climb the social ladder. Pero da Ponte, a famous *segrel* in the Castilian courts of Fernando III and Alfonso X, was the best of the poets who satirized nobles.

These satirical poems reveal a society in which the royal and noble courts included people from the king and high nobles to bohemian types, court *trovadores, jograres,* and *soldadeiras.* The last two groups were present only to entertain, but everyone socialized together, and this mixing encouraged pleasures forbidden by law and by the Church. Everyone was aware of the amorous escapades, vices, and weaknesses of everyone else. Anyone with the talent to do so, whether king, *trovador,* or *jograr,* amused the court by composing satirical songs that made fun of even the most embarrassing and intimate encounters. The songs include gossip about women of dubious morals, about liaisons between noble gentlemen and lower-class women, and about performers whose talents have been ruined by drink. The songs have no general theme, but grievances are frequently encountered between lowly *jograres* and the upper-class *trovadores.* The former wanted to compose their own songs, while the latter defended the traditional hierarchy that limited the *jograr* to singing and accompanying the songs composed by the *trovador.* Some songs complain about the stinginess of the higher nobility, who did not reward poets for their services to the degree that they wished.

The Galician-Portuguese school of lyric poetry was an important part of Romance letters in the thirteenth century, but by the beginning of the fourteenth century these songs were sung less frequently in Castilian courts. Although Spanish poets began to write some lyrics in Castilian in the thirteenth century, Galician-Portuguese verse is still present in the *Cancionero de Baena,* one of the three important Spanish songbooks of the fifteenth century. *Trovador* activity in Portugal diminished after King Denis's death in 1325. Its last strongholds were the smaller courts of noble Galician and Portuguese poets and the regional court of one of Denis's illegitimate sons, Count Pedro of Barcelos. Even though Pedro continued to compose songs in Galician-Portuguese, his court was unable to sustain its literary production, and the movement was greatly reduced or nonexistent by the middle of the fourteenth century.

At the death of Denis, the group of poets who lived and wrote in his court was dispersed because the new king, Afonso IV, did not have his father's literary bent and, embroiled in a civil war with his half brother, Afonso Sanchez, had little leisure to distract himself with court poets. It seems that Denis had intended to legitimize Afonso Sanchez, who was also a poet, and name him king, but the conflict ended with the pretender's death in 1329. In spite of the political turmoil, poets continued to live and write in other venues. A few were themselves landed aristocrats who could afford to continue their literary pursuits in their own courts and take in other, less fortunate poets, as well. Count Pedro, who wrote, collected, and transcribed texts until the last years of his life, is a distinguished example.

The badly truncated surviving copy of the *Arte de Trovar* is the best extant guide to the general principles shared by the practitioners of the *cantiga* tradition. Although it is clearly influenced by the practices of Occitan lyric, knowledge of which helps to fill in some of the gaps, the fragmentary text of the *Arte de Trovar* is difficult to understand. The complete work had six parts, each of which was divided into chapters. The first two parts, which discussed the *amor* and *amigo* songs, have been lost. The third part deals with the *escarnho* and *maldizer* songs; the first three of its nine chapters are missing. Many of the guidelines of this part may be applied to all three genres.

The first and most important guideline in the surviving passages of the *Arte de Trovar* is the statement that the rhythm of the verse is dependent on that of the song. This rule reinforces rhythmic regularity, especially in the parallelistic *cantigas de amigo.* The frequent presence of hiatus and dieresis, imposed by the tendency to archaize the language, affects syllable count; sinaloepha and syneresis are also prevalent, based on vowel tone and frequency of use of the words involved. The *Arte de Trovar* classifies hiatus as an error but seems to accept it as long as vowels of the same tone are not involved. The length of the strophe, called a *cobra* or *talho,* varies from two to ten *palavras* (lines), and each poem should have three or more strophes. They should have the same rhyme, as in Occitan song; but the peninsular poets were not particularly concerned with obeying this rule and used *rims singulars* (discrete and changeable rhymes).

The date of the *Arte de Trovar* is uncertain, but, like most didactic manuals, it was probably a product of the end of the movement. Rodrigues Lapa dates it after 1356, when the Occitan treatise on metrics known as the *Leys d'amours* (Laws of Love Lyrics) appeared, because the author of the *Arte de Trovar* was familiar with Old French and Provençal verse. But if Count Pedro was the author, as has been conjectured, it must have been written before 1354, the year of his death.

For a century and a half, the Provençal and Iberian poets continued to sing about the same thing. The similarity of the *cantigas de amor* to the Occitan lyric and the monotony of reading hundreds of songs about males suffering unrequited love for their ladies has led the genre to be underappreciated. Saraiva states, for example, that the songs are characterized by a simplification and immaturity in their imitation of Occitan poetry. In his opinion the poets, although aware of the learned formulae, usually simplify them to short expressions that emphasize unity through apparent contradiction: *prazer/pesar* (pleasure/pain), *vivir/morrer* (to live/to die), and *bem/mal* (good/bad). This repetitious uniformity raises another problem for modern readers: that of sincerity. The sentiment of the courtly love lyric is considered part of a "game" that has little to do with real feelings.

It is difficult not to judge these medieval songs from a modern perspective, but today's concepts of originality cannot be applied retroactively to the Middle Ages. For the medieval *trovador* the art of the *cantiga de amor* consisted of cleverly reworking known themes and presenting the most subtle nuances of the mind and heart of the male in love. Critics are now engaging in systematic and chronological readings to look for any possible evolution of the genre. Beltran sees the use of a type of parallelistic structure and a prefiguration of the Spanish Baroque writer Baltasar Gracián's ideas about *conceptismo* (subtleties of words and notions) as giving a special aesthetic value to the *cantiga de amor*. He considers the unity and distribution of internal content of the later parallelistic lyric to be the strength of medieval literature and repetition to be the preferred rhetorical figure of the short poem of the time. In the *cantiga de amor*, he suggests, the orientation of the *preludio* (introduction), the particular wordplay used, and variations in word patterning are evidence that the compositions were evolving. He also argues that, at least for the most talented poets, the logical framework of the introduction, the repetitions, and the surprise of the final strophe change the interpretation or the sense of the song and are exceptional in the rhetorical tradition of medieval poetics. Although many poets failed to maintain the balance, thematic unity, and harmony of the Occitan songs, he says, the *cantigas de amor* make excellent use of their preferred rhetorical figure, and he calls their art one of subtle quality rather than energetic departures. He believes that the poets knew their limitations and transcended them through the effective use of tone,

ambiguity, irony, parody, and even obvious subversions of the admired Occitan system.

Scholars still puzzle over a variety of problems, including the origins of a lyric tradition that began with the *cantiga de amor,* embraced the *cantiga de amigo,* and expanded to include the *cantiga de escarnho e maldizer.* The role of the *Arte de Trovar* in the *cantigas* merits continued study, as does the search for information about the lives of the poets. The amount of satire in the songs, especially in the *cantiga de amigo,* has sparked additional interest, as has the relationship between French troubadour verse and other Iberian *trovador* poetry. Manuscript studies continue to clarify the stages of evolution of the surviving compositions, and research needs to continue on the manuscripts with musical notations.

Bibliographies:

Martín de Riquer, *Los trovadores: Historia literaria y textos,* 3 volumes (Barcelona: Planeta, 1975);

Joseph T. Snow, *The Poetry of Alfonso X: A Critical Bibliography,* Research Bibliographies and Checklists, volume 19 (London: Grant & Cutler, 1977);

Silvio Pellegrini and G. Marroni, *Nuovo repertorio bibliográfico della prima lirica galego-portoghese* (L'Aquila: Japadre, 1981);

Vicenç Beltran, ed., *Boletín Bibliográfico de la Asociación Hispánica de Literatura Medieval* (1987–) <http://griso.cti.unav.es/medieval/ahlm/principal.html>;

Janice Wright, "Reference Bibliography for Critical Cluster on the Galician-Portuguese Lyric: New Critical Approaches," *La corónica,* 26, no. 2 (1998): 91–129.

References:

Sheila R. Ackerlind, *King Dinis of Portugal and the Alfonsine Heritage* (New York: Peter Lang, 1990);

Eugenio Asensio, *Poesía y Realidad en el cancionero peninsular de la Edad Media,* second edition (Madrid: Gredos, 1970);

Cynthia P. Bagley, "*Cantigas de Amigo* and *Cantigas de Amor,*" *Bulletin of Hispanic Studies,* 43 (1966): 241–252;

Vicenç Beltran, *A Cantiga de Amor* (Vigo: Edición Xerais de Galicia, 1995);

Josiah Blackmore, "Locating the Obscene: Approaching a Poetic Canon," *La corónica,* 26, no. 2 (1998): 9–16;

Mercedes Brea, ed., *Lírica Profana Galego-Portuguesa* (Santiago de Compostela: Xunta de Galicia, 1996);

Charles Brewer, "The *Cantigas d'amigo* of Martin Codax in the Context of Medieval Latin Secular Song," *La corónica,* 26, no. 2 (1998): 17–28;

Hernani Cidade, ed., *Poesia Medieval,* volume 1: *Cantigas de amigo,* fourth edition (Lisbon: Textos Literários, Autores de Língua Portuguesa, 1959);

Celso F. da Cunha, *Estudos de Poética Trovadoresca,* Coleção de Filologia, volume 2 (Rio de Janeiro: Instituto Nacional do Livro, 1961);

A. D. Deyermond, "The Earliest Lyric and Its Descendants," in his *A Literary History of Spain: The Middle Ages* (London: Benn, 1971; New York: Barnes & Noble, 1971), pp. 1–23;

Peter Dronke, *The Medieval Lyric,* second edition (Cambridge: Cambridge University Press, 1977);

Doris Earnshaw, *The Female Voice in Medieval Romance Lyric,* American University Studies, Series II: Romance Languages and Literatures, no. 68 (New York: Peter Lang, 1988);

Ana Paula Ferreira, "A 'Outra Arte' das soldadeiras," *Luso-Brazilian Review,* 30 (1993): 155–166;

Manuel Pedro Ferreira, *O som de Martin Codax: Sobre a dimensão musical da lírica galego-portuguesa (séculos XII–XIV)* (Lisbon: Unisys, 1986);

José Filgueira Valverde, "Lírica medieval gallega y portuguesa," in *Historia general de las literaturas hispánicas,* volume 1, edited by Guillermo Díaz-Plaja (Barcelona: Barna, 1949), pp. 545–642;

Denise K. Filios, "Jokes on soldadeiras in the Cantigas de Escarnio e de Mal Dizer," *La corónica,* 26, no. 2 (1998): 29–39;

Margit Frenk Alatorre, *Las jarchas mozárabes* (Mexico City: El Colegio de México, 1975);

Frenk Alatorre, *Lírica hispánica de tipo popular: Edad Media y Renacimiento* (Mexico City: Universidad Nacional Autónoma, 1966);

Emilio García Gómez, *Las jarchas romances de la serie árabe en su marco* (Madrid: Sociedad de Estudios y Publicaciones, 1965);

García Gómez, *Todo ben Quzman* (Madrid: Editorial Grecos, 1973);

Elsa Gonçalves and Ana Maria Ramos, *A lírica galego-portuguesa* (Lisbon: Comunicação, 1983);

F. R. Holiday, "Extraneous Elements in the *cantigas de amigo:* The Frontiers of Love and Satire in the Galician-Portuguese Medieval Lyric," *Bulletin of Hispanic Studies,* 39, no. 1 (1962): 34–42;

John Esten Keller, *Alfonso X, el Sabio* (New York: Twayne, 1967);

Benjamin Liu, "Obscenidad y transgresión en una *cantiga de escarnio,*" in *Erotismo en las letras hispánicas: Aspectos, modos y fronteras,*" edited by Luce López Baralt and Francisco Márquez Villanueva, Publicaciones de la *Nueva Revista de Filología Hispánica,* no. 7 (Mexico City: Centro de Estudios Lingüísticos y Literarios, El Colegio de México, 1995), pp. 203–217;

Liu, "Risabelha: A Poetics of Laughter?" *La corónica,* 26, no. 2 (1998): 42–47;

C. de Lollis, "Cantigas de amor e de maldizer di Alfonso el Sabio re di Castiglia," *Studi di Filologia Romanza,* 2 (1887): 31–66;

Ramón Menéndez Pidal, "La primitiva lírica española," in his *Estudios literarios,* fifth edition (Buenos Aires: Espasa-Calpe, 1944), pp. 197–264;

Menéndez Pidal, "La primitiva lírica hispana y los orígenes de las literaturas románicas," in his *España y su historia,* volume 1 (Madrid: Minotauro, 1957), pp. 499–514;

Carolina Michaëlis de Vasconcellos, "Randglossen zum altportugiesischen Liederbuch. XV. Vasco Martínez und D. Afonso Sánchez," *Zeitschrift für Romanische Philologie,* 29 (1905): 683–711;

Ernesto Monaci, *Cantos de Ledino, tratti del grande Canzoniere Portoghese della biblioteca Vaticana,* second edition (Halle: E. Karras, 1875);

William D. Paden, "Contrafracture between Occitan and Galician-Portuguese (II): The Case of Bonifacio Calvo," *Tenso,* 13 (Spring 1998): 50–71;

Paden, "The Troubadour's Lady: Her Marital Status and Social Rank," *Studies in Philology,* 72, no. 1 (1975): 28–50;

M. Carmen Pallares, "Las mujeres en la sociedad gallega bajomedieval," in *Relaciones de poder, de producción y parentesco en la Edad Media y Moderna,* edited by Reyna Pastor (Madrid: Consejo Superior de Investigaciones Científicas, 1990), n.pag.;

Juan Paredes Núñez, *La guerra de Granada en las Cantigas de Alfonso X el Sabio* (Granada: Universidad de Granada, 1991);

Silvio Pellegrini, *Studi su trove e trovatori della prima lirica ispano-portoghese* (Turin: Gambino, 1937);

António Resende de Oliveira, "A Cultura Trovadoresca no Ocidente Peninsular: Trovadores e Jograis Galegos," *Biblos,* 63 (1987): 1–22;

Resende de Oliveira, *Trobadores e xograres,* translated by Valentin Arias (Vigo: Edicións Xerais de Galicia, 1994);

Martín de Riquer, *Los trovadores: Historia literaria y textos,* 3 volumes (Barcelona: Planeta, 1975);

Manuel Rodrigues Lapa, *Lições de literatura portuguesa, Epoca medieval,* revised edition (Portugal: Coimbra, 1970);

Antonio Sánchez Jiménez, "Catalan and Occitan Troubadours at the Court of Alfonso VIII," *La corónica,* 32, no. 2 (2004): 101–120;

Antonio José Saraiva and Oscar Lopes, *História da Literatura Portuguesa,* fourth edition (Porto: Porto Editora, 1964);

Connie L. Scarborough, "Privileges, Property and Power: Women in Thirteenth-Century Castile-Leon," *Anuario Medieval,* 3 (1991): 217–231;

Kenneth R. Scholberg, *Sátira e invectiva en la España medieval* (Madrid: Gredos, 1971);

Samuel M. Stern, *Les chansons mozarabes* (Palermo: U. Manfredi, 1953);

Stern, "Les vers finaux en espagnol dans les muwassahas hispano-hébraiques," *Al Andaluz,* 13 (1948): 299–346;

Laura Tato Fontaiña, "Cantigas de amor. Cantigas de amigo," in *Historia da Literatura Galega,* A Nosa Terra, volume 2, fascicle 3 (Vigo: Asociación Socio-Pedagóxica Galega, 1996), pp. 66–96;

Giuseppe Tavani, *A poesía lírica galego-portuguesa* (Vigo: Galaxia Ensaio e Investigación, 1984);

Yara Frateschi Vieira, "Carolina Michaëlis e a Lírica Galego-Portuguesa," *Revista da Faculdad de Letras, Linguas e Literaturas, Porto,* 18 (2001): 73–78;

Vieira, "O escândalo das amas e tecedeiras nos cancioneiros galego-portugueses," *Colóquio-Letras,* 3 (1983): 19–25;

Julian Weiss, "On the Conventionality of the Cantigas d'amor," in *Medieval Lyric: Genres in Historical Context,* edited by William D. Paden (Urbana: University of Illinois Press, 2000), pp. 126–145;

Janice Wright, "The Enemy Within: A Galician-Portuguese Dawn Song," *La córonica,* 26, no. 2 (1998): 79–90.

La doncella Theodor

(late-thirteenth or fourteenth century)

Pablo Pastrana-Pérez
Western Michigan University

Manuscripts: Two Arabic manuscripts are extant: Real Academia de la Historia, Madrid, MS. Gayangos 71, twenty-three folios, late thirteenth or early fourteenth century; and *Cuento de la Doncella Theodor,* Escuela de Estudios Árabes, Granada, MS. IIº A-5-20, folios 75v–100r, after the fourteenth century. Five Castilian manuscripts are extant, all from the fifteenth century: an untitled fragment, Biblioteca Nacional, Madrid, MS. 9055, folios 69r–74r; *Capítulo que fabla de los enxemplos et castigos de Theodor la donzella,* Real Biblioteca del Monasterio de El Escorial, MS. h.III.6, folios 119r–124v; *Capítulo que fabla de las preguntas que fizieron a la donzella Theodor,* Biblioteca Nacional, Madrid, MS. 17853, folios 112r–117r; *Capítulo que fabla de los enxemplos de Theodor donsella,* Biblioteca Nacional, Madrid, MS. 17822, folios 117v–123v; and an untitled fragment dated "4 febrero 1433," Biblioteca de la Universidad de Salamanca, MS. 1866, folios 91v–96v.

Early editions: Untitled fragment (Toledo: Pedro Hagembach, circa 1500–1503); *Hystoria de la donzella Theodor* (Seville: Juan Varela de Salamanca, circa 1516–1520); *Historia de la donzella Teodor* (Seville: Jacobo Cromberger, circa 1526–1528); *Hystoria de la donzella Teodor* (Saragossa: Juana Milián, 1540); *La donzella Theodor–Hystoria de la donzella Teodor* (Seville: Domenico de Robertis, 1543); *La donzella Teodor–Historia de la donzella Theodor* (Toledo: Fernando de Santa Catalina, 1543); *Historia de la donzella Teodor* (Seville: Juan Cromberger, 1545); *La historia de la muy sabia y discreta donzella Teodor* (Burgos: Juan de Junta, 1554); *Historia de la Donzella Teodor* (Segovia: Juan de la Cuesta?, circa 1590); *Historia de la Sabia Donzella Teodor* (Alcalá de Henares: Juan Gracián, 1607); *Historia de la donzella Teodor* (Salamanca: Antonia Ramírez, 1625); *Historia de la donzella Teodor* (Cuenca: Salvador de Viader, 1628); *Historia de la donzella Teodor* (Jaén: Pedro de la Cuesta, 1628); *Historia de la donzella Teodor* (Seville: Pedro Gómez

de Pastrana, 1641); *La Historia de la Donzella Theodor* (Valencia: Bernardo Nogués, 1643).

Editions in modern Arabic: *Mittheilungen aus dem Eskurial,* edited by Hermann Knust (Tübingen: Literarischen Verein in Stuttgart, 1879), pp. 507–517; "Una versión en árabe granadino del *Cuento de la Doncella Teodor,*" edited by J. Vázquez Ruiz, *Prohemio,* 2 (1971): 331–365.

Editions in modern Castilian: "*La historia de la donzella Teodor;* Ein spanisches Volksbuch arabischen Ursprungs Untersuchung und kritische Ausgabe der ältesten bekannten Fassungen," edited by Walter Mettmann, *Akademie der Wissenschaften und der Literatur,* 3 (1962): 74–173; *Narrativa popular de la edad media: La doncella Teodor, Flores y Blancaflor, París y Viana,* edited by Nieves Baranda and Víctor Infantes (Madrid: Akal, 1995), pp. 58–83; *The Story of a Story across Cultures: The Case of the* Doncella Teodor, edited by Margaret R. Parker (London: Tamesis, 1996), pp. 33–76; Historia de la donzella Teodor: *Edition and Study,* edited by Isidro Rivera and Donna Rogers (Binghamton, N.Y.: Binghamton University Center for Medieval and Renaissance Studies, 2000).

La doncella Theodor (Lady Theodor)–or the *Historia de la doncella Teodor* (Story of Lady Teodor), as it was commonly known after the sixteenth century–achieved a degree of popularity matched by few other medieval stories. Its legacy is attested by many manuscripts and editions. It was widely known in the Islamic world as the tale of the slave girl Tawaddud; the Arabic name of the heroine became Theodor in medieval Castilian, Teodor throughout the sixteenth century, Theodora in a 1735 Portuguese translation, and Teodora after 1846.

José Simón Díaz's bibliographical study records only one other text, *Crónica troyana* (The Trojan Chronicle), with more printed editions between 1480 and 1560–a total of thirteen–than *La doncella Theodor,* which was printed twelve times along with another popular text of didactic fiction, *Calila e Dimna* (circa 1251, Calila and Dimna). Only one other pre-1400 didactic story, *Historia de los siete sabios* (The Story of the Seven Sages), has had as long a literary life as *La doncella Theodor*. Carlos Ferreira published a Portuguese translation in 1735 as *Historia da donzella Theodora;* but as Marcelino Menéndez y Pelayo points out, it must have been translated into that language at least a century earlier if the *Auto ou Historia de Theodora donzella* (Act or Story of Lady Theodora) listed in the *Index Expurgatorius* of 1624 is the same story. The work survives in more than a dozen Portuguese chapbooks.

The popularity of the story is not limited to the Iberian Peninsula. It is registered in Irving Albert Leonard's *The Books of the Brave: Being an Account of Books and of Men in the Spanish Conquest and Settlement of the Sixteenth-Century New World* (1949) as a common shipboard item in the overseas voyages of the conquistadors. It reached the Philippines, where it appeared in a verse edition in Tagalog that is detailed by Samuel G. Armistead and James T. Monroe. It surfaced in the Mayan culture of Mesoamerica in the Chilam Balam (Jaguar Oracle Priest) books. Theodor's influence has been detected in traditional Argentinean poetry, a whole section of which, following J. A. Carrizo's 1945 study, is classified as "Tema 68: de las preguntas de la *Doncella Teodor*" (Theme 68: Of Lady Teodor's Questions). It has also spread into Brazil, where it has been included in the *livros do povo* (books of the people).

Aside from the abundant copies of the text, the frequent literary allusions to the story also indicate its popularity. In *El razonamiento que hizo Palmyreno a los regidores de su patria* (circa 1550, The Speech That Palmireno Delivered to the Rulers of His Land), the humanist Juan Lorenzo Palmireno cites the work as an example of the art of capturing the audience's attention. The main character is mentioned in Francisco López de Úbeda's *La pícara Justina* (1604). Lope de Vega's comedy *La doncella Teodor* (1604–1617) follows the basic plot of the medieval story. A character in Tirso de Molina's play *El vergonzoso en palacio* (1621, The Bashful Man in the Palace) cites Teodor as the epitome of an educated woman: "Miren aquí qué criatura, o qué doncella Teodor" (Look here what a child, what a lady Teodor). Puntillas, a character in "Fisiología y chistes del cigarro" (Physiology and Jokes of the Cigarette), the last story in Serafín Estébanez Calderón's *Escenas andaluzas* (1847, Andalusian Scenes), says, "tengo más respuestas y acertijos que la doncella Teodora" (I have more answers and riddles than Lady Teodora).

The only version of the story to survive from its Oriental past is included in *The Arabian Nights* under the title "Hikayat tawaddud al-gariya" (Story of the Slave Girl Tawaddud); in most modern editions the tale is told between nights 436 and 462. The collection did not take its present form until the fourteenth or fifteenth century; the Arabic story probably circulated independently in North Africa and Muslim Spain after the tenth century. Abu'l-Husn (Abulhasán in modern Spanish translations), the son of a Baghdad merchant, squanders his inheritance after his father's death. All that is left is the slave girl Tawaddud, the embodiment of beauty and wisdom. At her suggestion Abu'l-Husn tries to sell her to the emir Harun al-Rashid for 10,000 dinars. The emir asks her to justify the high price by listing the sciences she knows; she claims to be versed in grammar, poetry, law, music, geometry, astronomy, medicine, the Koran, mathematics, philosophy, logic, rhetoric, dialectics, and music. The emir demands that her wisdom be tested by seven sages in the areas of Koranic law, theology, astronomy, medicine, philosophy, poetry, and logic. Tawaddud not only confounds the sages with her knowledge but also challenges her examiners with questions and riddles that they are unable to answer, and they all admit defeat. After the examination, Tawaddud proves that she is also expert in chess, backgammon, and cards. Finally, she demonstrates her musical prowess by playing the lute and singing. Marveling at her wisdom and grace, the emir grants her a wish; she asks to be returned to her master. The emir agrees, and Tawaddud is reunited with Abu'l-Husn; thanks to the emir's generosity, their financial struggles come to an end.

The unreliability of existing copies of *The Arabian Nights* as representative of a pre-thirteenth-century text or collection of texts makes it impossible to ascertain whether the story of Tawaddud is similar to any version of the tale that might have circulated in medieval Spain; but as María del Pino Valero Cuadra points out, there was a custom in Al-Andalus of employing learned female slaves, called *jariyas,* who were purchased for large sums and provided amusement for their masters with their talents and knowledge. Ibn Bassam's eleventh-century *Dajira* (Treasury) tells of a famous slave similar to Tawaddud whose knowledge was superior to that of any man. *The Arabian Nights* also includes the stories of *jariyas* such as Sofia, Umar al-Numan's concubine, and her daughter, Nuzhat al-Zaman; it also tells of a nonslave, Ibriza, the daughter of King Hardub. All are models of eloquence and beautiful diction that astonish kings and dignitaries.

The Tawaddud tale might have begun spreading northward from Arabia during the eleventh century, a time of intense intellectual activity in western Europe when Arabic literature, mathematics, philosophy, and the sciences migrated into the Continent with Sicily and Al-Andalus as the major ports of entry. In the twelfth century Archbishop Raimundo helped to disseminate Arabic cultural production throughout Spain by establishing an important center of translation in Toledo. As Isidro Rivera and Donna Rogers point out, translations from Arabic into Latin and the European vernacular languages abound in this period thanks to the work of translators such as Raimundo, Gerard of Cremona, Adelard of Bath, Hermann the German, and Robert of Chester. The tale of Tawaddud as it is known today probably remained in Islamic territory, including Al-Andalus, until the twelfth or thirteenth centuries, when the material was refashioned for Christian audiences. It must have been recast and translated into Castilian during the reign of Alfonso X in the second half of the thirteenth century, following the same path as texts such as *Calila e Dimna; Barlaam e Josafat* (circa 1250, Barlaam and Josafat); the *Poridat de las poridades* (circa 1250, Secret of Secrets), also known as the *Secreto de secretos;* the *Libro de los buenos proverbios* (circa 1250, Book of Good Proverbs)*;* the *Libro de los engaños e de los assayamientos de las mugeres* (circa 1253, Book of the Deceits and Wiles of Women), also known as *Sendebar;* the *Bocados de oro* (circa 1257, Golden Morsels); and *Flores de Filosofía* (circa 1290, Flowers of Philosophy).

The various manifestations of the core narrative of *La doncella Theodor* can be divided into three groups: the first is conveyed in the two extant Arabic manuscripts, the second in the five Castilian manuscripts, and the third in the many printed editions. The Arabic manuscripts follow the narrative line of the so-called long version, nights 436 through 462 of *The Arabian Nights*. Nevertheless, they differ from one another, as well as from *The Arabian Nights* tale and from the Castilian manuscripts. They are both considered a recasting of an earlier version attributed to Abu Bark al-Warrak, a famous fabulist during the second century of the Hegira. Of the two Arabic manuscripts, MS. Gayangos 71 at the Real Academia de la Historia in Madrid, which was probably originally composed in the late thirteenth or early fourteenth century, represents an older and shorter version, and shares more similarities with the Castilian manuscript versions than the other. It remains unedited. The second Arabic manuscript, MS. IIº A-5-20 in the Escuela de Estudios Árabes de Granada, is inserted in a codex containing other works and was discovered and edited by José Vázquez Ruiz. The story of the *jariya* Tudur is part of a collection of stories written in Maghrebi/Granadine script without title, author, or date. The story of Tudur is longer than that of the other Arabic version, with poems interpolated throughout, and is farther removed from the Castilian manuscripts. One must presuppose the existence of other versions in Arabic, now lost, that were more closely related to the medieval Castilian version.

The five extant Castilian manuscripts all seem to derive from an early-fifteenth- or late-fourteenth-century text that is now lost. Menéndez y Pelayo believed that the handwriting in one of the Castilian manuscripts, Escorial MS. h.III.6, was from the fourteenth century and suggested that it was one of two slightly different versions of the story derived from a thirteenth-century original. The first version is contained in a single manuscript, Biblioteca Nacional de Madrid MS. 9055; it is an untitled fragment appended to the *Libro del conoscimiento de todos los rregnos* (circa 1390, Book of Knowledge of All Kingdoms), with pages missing before, within, and following the fragment. In the second version, represented by Escorial MS. h.III.6, Biblioteca Nacional de Madrid MSS. 1722 and 17853, and Biblioteca de la Universidad de Salamanca MS. 1866, the story appears as an addendum to the *Bocados de oro* (Choice Golden Morsels), a Castilian translation of the eleventh-century Arabic *Mukhtar al-hikam wa-mahasin al-kalim* (The Choicest Maxims and Best Sayings) that was produced in the second half of the thirteenth century, probably under the auspices of Alfonso X.

Aside from their relative brevity, the Castilian manuscripts differ from the Arabic versions in reducing the number of examiners from seven to three: a wise *alfaquí* (Muslim judge or doctor of law) with knowledge of the law, a physician, and an expert in grammar, logic, and "la buena fabla" (good speech). Tawaddud becomes the young Christian slave Theodor, and the caliph Harun Arraxid becomes King Abomelique Almanzor. Surprisingly, the locale changes from Baghdad to the more temporally remote Babilonia (Babylon). The Castilian translator has eliminated almost all questions referring to the Koran and Muslim jurisprudence, leaving those related to physics, medicine, natural history, astronomy, and practical morality. Even more tellingly, the section on matrimonial hygiene and sexology appears less obscene in the Castilian versions as the portrait of desirable female beauty loses its vulgar sensuality to become more stylized. The chess game and the musical performance have also been eliminated in the Castilian manuscripts. The brevity fit the parameters set by the incipient publishing industry for popular fiction during the final years of the fifteenth century and the first half of the sixteenth: such works were to take up no more than thirty-two pages in the popular quarto-size *pliego* format, making them easier and faster to copy.

The many early editions of *La doncella Theodor* can be divided into four groups. The first group comprises the two earliest witnesses: an untitled fragment printed by Pedro Hagembach in Toledo, around 1500 to 1503, and Juan Varela de Salamanca's edition printed between 1516 and 1520. Both derive from a common source, probably a printed one, that is unknown today.

The novelties of these versions include further Christianization and a setting recognizable to an Iberian readership. The main locale has moved from Babylon to Tunisia; the merchant, Teodor's master, is from Hungary; and Teodor is "una doncella christiana que era de las partes de España" (a Christian lady from the parts of Spain). The first examiner is a Christian theologian; the second is an expert in natural philosophy, logic, medicine, and astrology; and the third, Abraham, has been transformed into a Jewish troubadour and music master. The anti-Semitism prevalent in the late fifteenth and early sixteenth centuries transforms Abraham into a fitting antagonist whose pride, vanity, and arrogance stand in diametrical contrast to Teodor's discretion, moderation, and humility. If Teodor is the incarnation of medieval Christian perfection, Abraham has been made into a ridiculous and laughable character for the story's new commercial public.

Aside from these elements, the chief difference between the inaugural print editions and the extant manuscript tradition is the inclusion in the former of material from the *Repertorio de los tiempos* (Repertory of the Times), printed in Saragossa by Andrés de Li in 1492, to accommodate the story to the early-sixteenth-century Castilian audience's utilitarian concerns and interest in popular scientific writing. The emphasis shifts to practical knowledge of farming, astrology, and the *ars amatoria* (art of love).

The second group of early printed works is made up of six editions: those produced in Seville by Jacobo Cromberger around 1526 to 1528, Domenico de Robertis in 1543, and Juan Cromberger in 1545; in Toledo by Fernando de Santa Catalina in 1543; in Burgos by Juan de Junta in 1554; and in Segovia, probably by Juan de la Cuesta, around 1590. This second recasting constitutes the basis of a new genre, labeled "editorial fiction" by Víctor Infantes. The characteristics of this version won a popular favor that propelled the text into the early years of the twentieth century. The emphasis on farming and agriculture that mark the first group is eliminated, although praise of a holistic knowledge of all arts and sciences survives. A mostly rural world is replaced by an urban one characterized by a predilection for astrology and medicine, especially the art of bleeding. Teodor's extensive enumeration of her abilities and wisdom is reduced to a reference to the fact that she knows many other arts and sciences, and the *ars amatoria* and all questions related to it are suppressed. Such brevity is typical of editorial fiction, in which the action is condensed to the bare minimum.

The later sixteenth-century editions exhibit a gradation in the attitudes of the three wise men that is absent in the earlier versions. The first sage addresses Teodor with a petition: "Donzella, plégate de no te eno-

IDystoria dela donzella Theodor.

Title page from the 1516–1520 edition, published in Seville by Juan Varela de Salamanca (Biblioteca de don Bartolomé March, Palma de Mallorca)

jar" (Lady, I beg you to not be angry); the second, having seen his partner humiliated, is more irritable; and the third, the Jew, expresses his wrath to the point of betting his clothes against Teodor's ability to come up with an answer. As in the manuscript versions, the last wise man mistrusts the other two, and Teodor bets her own clothes with him; in the manuscripts, however, the wager is the wise man's initiative, while in the printed versions the suggestion comes from Teodor. Her superiority having been proven, she shows mercy and grants Abraham's petition to forfeit his money instead of his clothes. Only after his humiliation is complete and her authority confirmed beyond doubt does Teodor return to her lord and master. The editions of the second group also include many woodcuts illustrating the zodiac and the figure of the *homo astrologicus* (a human body traced over an astrological map).

The third group of early printed versions of the story consists of editions printed in Saragossa by Juana Milián on 15 May 1540, in Alcalá de Henares by Juan Gracián in 1607, in Salamanca by Antonia Ramírez in 1625, in Cuenca by Salvador de Viader in 1628, and in Jaén by Pedro de la Cuesta in 1628. As Infantes and Nieves Baranda and Walter Suchier have noted, the novel feature of this group is the incorporation of several questions taken from *El emperador Adriano y el infante Epitus* (before 1528, Emperor Adrian and Prince Epictetus), a work of a similar exemplary and didactic nature with which it had already shared elements in its fifteenth-century manuscript tradition.

The fourth and final group of early printings established a version of the story that remained largely unchanged until the early twentieth century. The two most important editions of this group were printed in Seville by Pedro Gómez de Pastrana in 1641 and in Valencia by Bernardo Nogués in 1643. In this version, prepared for the press by Francisco Pinardo and "agora nuevamente corregida è historiada" (newly corrected and illustrated), the only substantive alterations are the addition of a few questions on marriage posed by the king after the dispute with the three sages has ended and the inclusion of maxims by Diogenes to fill in the remaining space in the chapbook.

Editions of *La doncella Teodor* continued to appear during the eighteenth century and reached the nineteenth century as *literatura de cordel* (string literature), semi-infantilized popular narratives. The prevailing characteristic of these later editions is an emphasis on edifying and pious doctrine, including a declaration of the mysteries of the Mass. The "scientific" information on astronomy, meteorology, medicine, and so on was replaced by more-contemporary pedantries favored by the new audiences of Romanticism and modernism.

Depending on the version, the emphasis of *La doncella Theodor* is either on Koranic/Islamic law or on Christian values; on ancestral knowledge or on more-scholastic disciplines; on popular folkloric pedagogy or on more-dogmatic, exclusionary academicism; and on ethics or on spirituality. The subjects of Theodor's knowledge may shift from the rural, agricultural practices to the more urban fields of medicine, astrology, and the *ars amatoria*. There can be either an overt stress on sexuality and earthy vulgarities, or on scrupulous morality and righteousness. Wisdom may be proved with well-documented answers, including names and events in history, or with the shorter and more trivial solutions to mere puzzles and riddles. But the defining

essence of *La doncella Theodor* is the dexterity and discretion of a young woman whose vast knowledge, intellectual acumen, and moral fiber can act as the motor force in the restoration of order and fortune.

La doncella Theodor belongs to the venerable medieval genre of didactic literature, but the core of the story adheres both to the traditional medieval pattern of the scholastic *disputatio* (dispute), a "game" of dialectical dexterity in which one proved one's wisdom and persuasiveness, and to the Latin *quaestiones* (questions), written collections of questions and answers that were popular after the ninth century and of great importance in the teaching of disciplines such as philosophy, theology, and medicine. A series of questions asked by an authority elicited answers in a well-orchestrated pattern of climactic progression. The question-and-answer format lent itself to public recitation, allowing the didactic message to be disseminated in an entertaining way. *La doncella Theodor* is thus related to *El emperador Adriano y el infante Epitus, El filósofo Segundo* (second century, Secundus the Philosopher), and the medieval genre of the *Joca Monacharum* (Amusements of Monks), all of which consist of questions and answers. It is also related to texts composed of riddles, hints, and practical counsel, which emphasized the playful dimension of orchestrated demonstrations of wisdom. This aspect helped guarantee its popularity in the sixteenth century, a period during which games of questions and answers became courtly pastimes.

The story of Theodor serves several purposes. As wisdom literature it is a repository of insights from the Indo-Persian, Arabic, and Graeco-Roman traditions: it contains the fundamentals of the natural sciences, medicine, and the liberal arts, as well as endorsing dance and poetry. Such a rich blend of wisdom from several traditions may be taken as evidence of the often-disputed *convivencia* (harmonious coexistence) of cultures during much of the Iberian Middle Ages. On another level, however, it is a vivid example of the appropriation of Arabic discourse to legitimize Christian dominance over Muslim enemies: as Christianity became the dominant faith in the Iberian Peninsula, the Arabic and Semitic elements of the original text were reduced in importance. As a defense of women's intellectual prowess the story of Theodor continues the tradition of the Queen of Sheba, who dared to probe Solomon's wisdom; the difference is that Theodor is the one being put to the test and forced to prove the scope of her knowledge. Margaret R. Parker argues that a closer parallel to Theodor can be found in another learned woman of Byzantine times, St. Catherine of Alexandria in the fourth century. Persecuted by a pagan emperor, she confronted him in a disputation from which she emerged victorious. The humiliated emperor then gathered fifty of his wisest men to probe Catherine's wisdom. After she won every debate and persuaded each of the fifty sages to convert to Catholicism, the emperor had her imprisoned, tortured, and decapitated. Other learned women capable of acquitting themselves against male opponents include Tarsiana, King Apollonius's daughter in the *Libro de Apolonio* (translated as *The Book of Apollonius*, 1936), a thirteenth-century Castilian translation of Simphosius's sixth-century *Historia Apollonii Regis Tyri* (History of Apollonius, King of Tyre); and the intercalated tale "De las preguntas que fizo un padre a su fija, sobre los amores de las mujeres" (About the Questions That a Father Asked His Daughter Pertaining to Women's Love) in the *Libro del caballero Zifar* (circa 1332–1333, Book of the Knight Zifar). Theodor is also an echo of Scheherazade in *The Arabian Nights,* who is threatened by sages and scrutinized by a king but triumphs thanks to her eloquence and astuteness.

Aside from her learned ways, Theodor is *discreta* (discreet) and *mesurada* (restrained). During the Middle Ages the virtues of discretion and restraint were the basic pillars of masculine moral superiority; epic heroes and elevated figures such as Alexander the Great, Charlemagne, and El Cid are vivid personifications of them. By exhibiting these typically masculine traits and behaviors Theodor is not only masculinized but also elevated above men; this element became a literary commonplace in the treatment of other female protagonists in brief narratives, such as Joan of Arc in the anonymous *Poncella de Francia* (1533, The Maid of France). Rivera and Rogers point out that by subjecting herself to the interrogations of masters, Theodor must adopt a masculine disposition and act like a man in her responses; she must not only avoid subjecting herself to the wisdom of a man but also assert herself over him if she is to conquer the art of the *disputatio*. Helen Solterer notes that the Ovidian and the Aristotelian models of mastering a woman were essential components of scholarly training in the medieval university debating tradition. Much like a student in the early universities, Theodor must behave with masculine authority. Solterer adds that while women were believed to be literalminded readers, Theodor is adept at extracting symbolic meanings from the riddles she poses to her examiners.

As a final note about the masculine/feminine tensions in the story, one must add that while Theodor is not the prototypical medieval female, since she is able to confront men intellectually and emerge victorious, there are echoes of medieval misogyny in her dialogue when she speaks of intercourse, details the ages of women, and parrots the accepted portrait of female beauty. A desirable woman must be young and have a long body, neck, and fingers; a small mouth, nose, and

feet; broad hips, back, and forehead; white skin, teeth, and sclera; black hair, eyebrows, and pupils; and red cheeks, lips, and gums. This organization in triads—three parts of the woman's body that must be long, three parts that must be small, three that must be broad, three that must be white, three that must be black, and three that must be red—can be found in the *Llibre de tres* (second half of the fourteenth century, Book of Three), attributed to the Catalan author Anselm Turmeda. This placement of misogynistic discourse in the mouth of a female has prompted Emily Francomano to affirm that Theodor is, in fact, assuming authority, as she is reproducing the received knowledge about women in antiquity and the Middle Ages and thus rendering herself unable to question prior authority. Francomano asserts that Theodor represents not a woman per se but "Sabiduría" (Wisdom), a personification of wisdom. This interpretation accords with María Eugenia Lacarra's argument that the role of the wise woman in medieval literature is not to question masculine wisdom but to reinforce it, even to the point of denigrating women.

Theodor's education showcases the liberal arts, which were divided into the trivium of grammar, rhetoric, and dialectics (logic) and the quadrivium of arithmetic, geometry, astronomy, and music. Her command of the trivium is evident both in her long and elaborate answers to difficult questions and in her short and proverbial ripostes to riddles and puzzles. Astronomy included astrology, which dealt with human anatomy, medicine, diet, and health: the movements and positions of planets and constellations explained behaviors and ailments and provided a rationale for prescriptions and treatments. Much of the medical lore and notions of hygiene in *La doncella Theodor* derive from the *Sirr-al-asrâr* (circa 950–970, Secret of Secrets; in Castilian, *Poridat de las poridades* or *Secreto de los secretos*). Another popular treatise, Ibn Habib's *Mujtasar fi al-tibb* (second half of the ninth century, Compendium of Medicine), included the medicinal value of certain foods, such as the quince and the pomegranate, both of which are mentioned in the Arabic versions of *La doncella Theodor*. Theodor is well versed in phlebotomy, a therapy derived from the theories of authorities such as Hippocrates and Galen, which required knowing which months of the year and astrological signs were propitious for bleeding certain organs.

Two elements are indispensable to *La doncella Theodor* as it circulates in various cultures and languages. First, Theodor, a woman of unparalleled knowledge, upholds her worthiness before a succession of well-schooled men who test her thoroughly but fail to defeat her, thus defying the conventional association of wisdom with men and with old age; her knowledge of all arts and sciences, her wisdom, and her discretion earn her the Moorish king's favor and love and restore order and financial solvency to her master. Second, the story is characterized by its emphasis on scientific and practical disciplines and arts. Focus on any particular science or discipline, such as agriculture, medicine, astrology, or *ars amatoria,* or any sphere of life, such as sex, marriage, or beauty, allowed the story to adapt to new times, places, and audiences and accounts in part for its continuing popularity.

Bibliography:

José Simón Díaz, "La literatura medieval castellana y sus ediciones españolas de 1501 a 1560," in *El libro antiguo español: Actas del primer Coloquio Internacional: Madrid, 18 al 20 de diciembre de 1986,* edited by María Luisa López Vidriero and Pedro M. Cátedra (Salamanca: Ediciones de la Universidad de Salamanca, 1988), pp. 371–396.

References:

María L. Águila, "Las mujeres 'sabias' en Al-Andalus," in *La mujer en Al-Andalus: Reflejos históricos de su actividad y categorías sociales,* edited by María J. Viguera (Madrid: Universidad Autónoma, 1989), pp. 139–184;

Samuel G. Armistead and James T. Monroe, "Celestina's Muslim Sisters," *Celestinesca,* 13 (1989): 3–27;

Nieves Baranda and Víctor Infantes, *Narrativa popular de la edad media: La doncella Teodor, Flores y Blancaflor, París y Viana,* Nuestros Clásicos, no. 14 (Madrid: Akal, 1995);

Baranda and Infantes, "Post Mettmann: Variantes textuales y transmisión editorial de la *Historia de la donzella Teodor,*" *La corónica,* 22, no. 2 (1994): 61–88;

Claude Bremond and Bernard Darbord, "Tawaddud et Teodor: Les enjeux ludiques du savoir," in *L'Enciclopedismo Medievale,* edited by Michelangelo Picone (Ravenna: Longo, 1994), pp. 253–273;

J. A. Carrizo, *Antecedentes hispanos-medievales de la poesía tradicional argentina* (Buenos Aires: Estudios Hispánicos, 1945);

Dwayne E. Carpenter, "Social Perception and Literary Portrayal: Jews and Muslims in Medieval Spanish Literature," in *Convivencia: Jews, Muslims, and Christians in Medieval Spain,* edited by Vivian Mann, Thomas Glick, and Jerrilynn Dodds (New York: Braziller, 1992), pp. 61–81;

Thomas E. Case, "Gender and Dress in Lope's *La doncella Teodor,*" *Bulletin of the Comediantes,* 46 (1994): 187–206;

Thomas Frederick Crane, *Italian Social Customs of the Sixteenth Century and Their Influence on the Literatures of Europe* (New Haven: Yale University Press, 1920);

Bernard Darbord, "La tradición del saber en la *Doncella Teodor,*" in *Medioevo y Literatura: Actas del V Congreso de la Asociación Hispánica de Literatura Medieval: Granada, 27 de septiembre–1 de octubre de 1993,* 4 volumes, edited by Juan de Peredes (Granada: Universidad de Granada, 1995), I: 13–30;

Alan Deyermond, "The Lost Genres of Medieval Spanish Literature," *Hispanic Review,* 43, no. 3 (1975): 231–259;

Deyermond, *The Middle Ages* (London: Benn, 1971; New York: Barnes & Noble, 1971), pp. 100–101, 106;

Emily Francomano, "'¿Qué dices de las mugeres?': *Donzella Teodor* as the Conclusion to *Bocados de oro,*" *La corónica,* 30, no. 1 (2001): 87–110;

Claudine Gerresch, "Un récit des *Mille et une Nuits:* Tawaddud," *Bulletin de l'Institut Fondamental D'Afrique Noir, Série B: Sciences Humaines,* 35 (1973): 57–175;

Harriet Goldberg, "Women Riddlers in Hispanic Folklore and Literature," *Hispanic Review,* 59 (1991): 57–75;

Ángel González Palencia, *Historia de la literatura arábigo-española* (Barcelona: Labor, 1925), pp. 120, 316–321;

Marta Haro Cortés, "Erotismo y arte amatoria en el discurso médico de la *Historia de la doncella Teodor,*" *Revista de Literatura Medieval,* 5 (1993): 113–125;

Víctor Infantes, "La prosa de ficción renacentista: Entre los géneros literarios y el género editorial," *Journal of Hispanic Philology,* 13 (1989): 115–124;

Danielle Jacquart and Claude Thomasset, *Sexuality and Medicine in the Middle Ages* (Princeton: Princeton University Press, 1988), p. 137;

María Eugenia Lacarra, "Parámetros para la representación de la sexualidad femenina en la literatura medieval castellana," in *La mujer en la literatura hispánica de la Edad Media y el Siglo de Oro,* edited by Rina Walthaus (Amsterdam & Atlanta: Rodopi, 1993), pp. 23–43;

Lacarra, "Representaciones de mujeres en la literatura española de la Edad Media (escrita en castellano)," in *La mujer en la literatura española: Modos de representación desde la Edad Media hasta el siglo XVII,* volume 2 of *Breve historia feminista de la literatura española en lengua castellana,* edited by Iris M. Zavala (Barcelona: Antropos, 1993), pp. 21–68;

María Jesús Lacarra, "El arquetipo de la mujer sabia en la literatura medieval," in *La mujer en la literatura hispánica de la Edad Media y el Siglo de Oro,* pp. 11–22;

Irving Albert Leonard, *Books of the Brave: Being an Account of Books and of Men in the Spanish Conquest and Settlement of the Sixteenth-Century New World* (Cambridge, Mass.: Harvard University Press, 1949), pp. 98, 111, 319, 441;

Marcelino Menéndez y Pelayo, "La doncella Teodor (Un cuento de *Las mil y una noches,* un libro de cordel y una comedia de Lope de Vega)," in *Homenaje a D. Francisco Codera en su jubilación del profesorado: Estudios de erudición oriental,* edited by Eduardo Saavedra (Saragossa: M. Escar, 1904), pp. 483–511;

María Rosa Menocal, *The Arabic Role in Medieval Literary History: A Forgotten Heritage* (Philadelphia: University of Pennsylvania Press, 1987), pp. xiv, 35, 60, 141;

Menocal, *The Ornament of the World: How Muslims, Jews, and Christians Created a Culture of Tolerance in Medieval Spain* (Boston: Little, Brown, 2002), pp. 21, 24, 91, 154, 225, 273–274;

Walter Mettmann, "*La historia de la donzella Teodor:* Ein spanisches Volksbuch arabischen Ursprungs Untersuchung und kritische Ausgabe der ältesten bekannten Fassungen," *Akademie der Wissenschaften und der Literatur,* 3 (1962): 74–173;

Mettmann, "Spruchweisheit und Spruchdichtung in der spanishchen und katalanishchen Literatur des Mittelalters," *Zeitschrift für Romanische Philologie,* 76 (1960): 94–117;

Margaret R. Parker, *The Story of a Story across Cultures: The Case of the* Doncella Teodor, Monografías, no. 161 (London: Tamesis, 1996);

Isidro Rivera, "Negotiation of Scientific Discourse in the First Printed Edition of the *Historia de la Donzella Teodor* (Toledo: Pedro Hagenbach, ca. 1500)," *Hispanic Review,* 66, no. 4 (1998): 415–432;

Rivera and Donna Rogers, Historia de la donzella Teodor: *Edition and Study* (Binghamton, N.Y.: Binghamtom University Center for Medieval and Renaissance Studies, 2000);

Helen Solterer, *The Master and Minerva: Disputing Women in French Medieval Culture* (Berkeley: University of California Press, 1995);

Walther Suchier, *L'enfant sage (das gespräch des kaisers Hadrian mit dem klugen kinde Epitus)* (Dresden: Niemeyer, 1910);

Suchier, *Das Mittellateinische Gespräch Adrian und Epictetus nebst verwandten texten (Joca Monacharum)* (Tübingen: Niemeyer, 1955);

Barry Taylor, "Old Spanish Wisdom Texts: Some Relationships," *La corónica,* 14 (1985): 71–85;

María del Pino Valero Cuadra, La doncella Teodor: *Un cuento hispanoárabe* (Alicante: Instituto de Cultura "Juan Gil-Albert," 1996);

Valero Cuadra, "El mito literario medieval de la mujer sabia: La doncella Teodor," in *Las sabias mujeres: Educación, saber y autoría (siglos III–XVIII),* edited by María del Mar Graña Cid (Madrid: Asociación Al-Mudayna, 1994), pp. 147–154;

José Vázquez Ruiz, "Una nueva versión árabe del cuento de la doncella Teodor," *Miscelánea de Estudios Árabes y Hebreos,* 1 (1952): 149–153;

Vázquez Ruiz, "Una versión en árabe granadino del *Cuento de la Doncella Teodor,*" *Prohemio,* 2 (1971): 331–365;

Juan Vernet, *Las mil y una noches y su influencia en la novelística medieval española* (Barcelona: Real Academia de Buenas Letras, 1959), pp. 23, 25;

John K. Walsh, "More on Arabic vs. Western Descriptive Modes in Hispanic Literature: Brantôme's 'Spanish' Formula," *Kentucky Romance Quarterly,* 18 (1971): 3–16.

Juan Fernández de Heredia

(circa 1310 – March 1396)

Conrado Guardiola Alcover
Rutgers, The State University of New Jersey

WORKS: *Cartulario Magno* (1349–1354)

Manuscript: Archivo Histórico Nacional, Madrid, MS. 648–653. The *Cartulario Magno* of the Castellany of Amposta comprises documents concerning the Order of the Hospital of St. John of Jerusalem. It was copied by the public notaries Domingo Carcases and Gonzalo López de San Martín in six volumes. No edition of the work as a whole has been published, although researchers have published some of the documents.

Paulus Orosius, *Orosio, Paulo Orosio,* or *Historia contra paganos,* sponsored by Heredia (after 1372)

Manuscripts: Biblioteca Nacional, Madrid, MS. 10200; Biblioteca Universitaria, Valencia, MS. 189; Biblioteca del Patriarca, Universidad Pontificia, Valencia, MS. V-27. Paulus Orosius wrote the work at the request of St. Augustine to refute the idea that the evils that afflicted the Roman empire were the fault of Christianity.

Paleographic edition: John N. Nitti and Lloyd Kasten, eds., *The Electronic Texts and Concordances of Medieval Navarro-Aragonese Manuscripts* (Madison, Wis.: Hispanic Seminary of Medieval Studies, 1997 [CD-ROM]).

Grant Crónica de Espanya (1385)

Manuscripts: The first part of the three-part *Grant Crónica de Espanya* survives in Biblioteca National, Madrid, MS. 10133. The fourteen books contain the history of ancient worthies until the Visigoths in a manner similar to that of the *Primera crónica General* of Alfonso X. It was copied by Alvar Pérez de Sevilla, canon of the Cathedral of Jaén. The second part is lost. The third part, "Aqui conta la istoria de otras cosas que se avinieron en el Real de los cristianos et de la prision de Algezira," was copied between 1383 and 1393 by Ferdinandus (probably Ferdinandus Metinenssis), copyist of MS. Z.I.2 of the Real Biblioteca del Monasterio de El Escorial, and survives in Biblioteca Nacional, Madrid, MS. 10134.

Paleographic edition: John J. Nitti and Lloyd Kasten, eds., *The Electronic Texts and Concordances of Medieval Navarro-Aragonese Manuscripts* (Madison, Wis.: Hispanic Seminary of Medieval Studies, 1997 [CD-ROM]).

Edition: *La Grant Crónica de Espanya, libros 1–2: Edición según el manuscrito 10133 de la Biblioteca Nacional de Madrid,* edited by Regina af Geijerstam (Uppsala: Almqvist & Wiksell, 1964).

Thucydides, *Plutarco,* sponsored by Heredia (between 1385 and 1388)

Manuscripts: A partial translation of the *Parallel Lives,* it survives in Bibliothèque National, Paris, MSS. 70, 71, and 72, and Biblioteca Nacional, Madrid, MSS. 2211, 10133, 10134, 10190, and 12.367.

Paleographic edition: John J. Nitti and Lloyd Kasten, eds., *The Electronic Texts and Concordances of Medieval Navarro-Aragonese Manuscripts* (Madison, Wis.: Hispanic Seminary of Medieval Studies, 1997 [CD-ROM]).

Editions: A. Álvarez Rodríguez, "Las 'Vidas de hombres ilustres' (Nos. 70–72 de la Biblioteca Nacional de Paris): Estudio y edición," dissertation, Universidad Complutense, 1983; *Las vidas de hombres ilustres, Aragonese Translation of the Lives of Plutarch: A Partial Edition,* edited by Edward Whitman Irvine (Ottawa: National Library of Canada, 1984).

Paulus Diaconus, *Eutropio,* sponsored by Heredia (between 1385 and 1393?)

Manuscript: Bibliothèque de l'Arsenal, Paris, MS. 8324. The manuscript attributes the work to Eutropius, but the text corresponds not to his *Breviarium ab urbe condita* but to Paulus Diaconus's Christianization of the *Breviarium,* the *Historia romana.* The work includes a summary of Paulus Diaconus's *Historia longobardorum.*

Paleographic edition: John J. Nitti and Lloyd Kasten, eds., *The Electronic Texts and Concordances of Medieval Navarro-Aragonese Manuscripts* (Madison, Wis.: Hispanic Seminary of Medieval Studies,

1997 [CD-ROM]).

Edition: Porter Conerly, "An Edition, Study and Glossary of the 'Eutropio' of Juan Fernández de Heredia," dissertation, University of North Carolina at Chapel Hill, 1979.

Hayton, *Flor de las ystorias de Orient* or *Hayton,* sponsored by Heredia (between 1385 and 1393)

Manuscript: Real Biblioteca del Monasterio de El Escorial, MS. Z.I.2, folios 1r–57v. The work takes its second name from the Armenian prince who dictated the work in 1397 to Nicolás Falcón, who translated it into Latin for Pope Clement V. It includes a description of Asiatic princes and places, including an account of the Tartar victories over the Arabs in Palestine.

Paleographic edition: John J. Nitti and Lloyd Kasten, eds., *The Electronic Texts and Concordances of Medieval Navarro-Aragonese Manuscripts* (Madison, Wis.: Hispanic Seminary of Medieval Studies, 1997 [CD-ROM]).

Edition: *Flor de las ystorias de Orient,* edited by Wesley Robertson Long (Chicago: University of Chicago Press, 1934).

Marco Polo, sponsored by Heredia (between 1385 and 1393)

Manuscript: Real Biblioteca del Monasterio de El Escorial, MS. Z.I.2, folios 58r–104v. The work is the Aragonese translation of the Venetian adventurer's journey to Asia.

Paleographic edition: John J. Nitti and Lloyd Kasten, eds., *The Electronic Texts and Concordances of Medieval Navarro-Aragonese Manuscripts* (Madison, Wis.: Hispanic Seminary of Medieval Studies, 1997 [CD-ROM]).

Edition: *El Libro de Marco Polo,* edited by Hermann Knust and Rudolf Stübe (Leipzig: Seele, 1902); John J. Nitti, "An Edition, Study and Vocabulary of the Unique Aragonese 'Book of Marco Polo,' Translated by Juan Fernandez de Heredia," dissertation, University of Wisconsin–Madison, 1972; *Juan Fernández de Heredia's Aragonese Version of the Libro de Marco Polo,* edited by Nitti (Madison, Wis.: Hispanic Seminary of Medieval Studies, 1980).

Rams de flores or *Libro de actoridades* (between 1385 and 1393)

Manuscript: Real Biblioteca del Monasterio de El Escorial, MS. Z.I.2, folios 105r–224v. The manuscript was copied by Ferdinandus Metinenssis. The work is a compilation of the *Communiloquium* or *Summa Collationum* of Juan de Gales and includes a selection of the *Facta et dicta memorabilia* of Valerius Maximus. The *Rams de flores* is based on a Catalan translation of both works.

Editions: M. R. C. Leslie, "An Edition of Juan Fernández de Heredia's 'Rams de Flores' with a Study of the Dialectal Features of Its Language," dissertation, University of Oxford, 1966; "Edición y estudio del 'Libro de Actoridades' de Juan Fernández de Heredia, tesis doctoral dirigida por D. César Hernández Alonso (Valladolid, 1990)," dissertation, Universidad de Valladolid, 1992; *Rams de flores, o, Libros de actoridades: Obra compilada bajola protección de Juan Fernández de Heredia, Maestre de la Orden de San Juan de Jerusalén: Edición del ms. de la Real Biblioteca de El Escorial Z-I-2,* edited by Conrado Guardiola Alcover (Saragossa: Institución Fernando el Católico, 1998).

Paleographic edition: John J. Nitti and Lloyd Kasten, eds., *The Electronic Texts and Concordances of Medieval Navarro-Aragonese Manuscripts* (Madison, Wis.: Hispanic Seminary of Medieval Studies, 1997 [CD-ROM]).

Partial edition: George W. Umphrey, "Aragonese Texts Now Edited for the First Time," *Revue Hispanique,* 16 (1907): 244–287.

Secreto secretorum or *Pseudo-Aristóteles,* sponsored by Heredia (between 1385 and 1393)

Manuscript: Real Biblioteca del Monasterio de El Escorial, MS. Z.I.2, folios 254r–312v. The work is a collection of maxims on government supposedly written by Aristotle for Alexander the Great; it was widely translated in the Middle Ages.

Paleographic edition: John J. Nitti and Lloyd Kasten, eds., *The Electronic Texts and Concordances of Medieval Navarro-Aragonese Manuscripts* (Madison, Wis.: Hispanic Seminary of Medieval Studies, 1997 [CD-ROM]].

Edition: Lloyd Kasten, "'Secreto de los secretos' translated by Juan Fernandez de Heredia," dissertation, University of Wisconsin–Madison, 1931.

Juan Zonaras, *Libro de los enperadores, Crónica de los enperadores,* or *Zonaras,* sponsored by Heredia (1393)

Manuscript: Biblioteca Nacional, Madrid, MS. 10131, folios 1r–182r. The *Libro de los enperadores,* also known as the *Crónica de los enperadores* and *Zonaras,* was copied by Bernardo de Jaca and signed on 5 March 1393. It consists of a translation of the last four books of Juan Zonaras, a twelfth-century Byzantine historian and canonist. It covers Byzantine history until the death of Alexis Comnenus in 1118.

Paleographic edition: John J. Nitti and Lloyd Kasten, eds., *The Electronic Texts and Concordances of Medieval Navarro-Aragonese Manuscripts* (Madison, Wis.: Hispanic Seminary of Medieval Studies, 1997 [CD-ROM]).

Detail of a fresco by Andrea Bonaiuti in the Spanish Chapel of Santa María Novella in Florence. The white-bearded figure at top right, wearing the robe of a knight of St. John, may be Juan Fernández de Heredia (photograph courtesy of Conrado Guardiola Alcover).

Editions: Thomas Dean Spaccarelli, "An Edition, Study and Glossary of the 'Libro de los enperadores' Translated from the Greek for Juan Fernández de Heredia," dissertation, University of Wisconsin–Madison, 1975; Joannes Zonaras, *Libro de los emperadores: Versión aragonesa del Compendio de historia universal patrocinada por Juan Fernández de Heredia,* edited by Adelino Álvarez Rodríguez, with contributions by Francisco Martín García and Ángeles Romero Cambrón (Saragossa: Prensas Universitarias de Zaragoza: Institución Fernando el Católico / Huesca: Instituto de Estudios Altoaragoneses / Saragossa: Departamento de Educación, Cultura y Deporte del Gobierno de Aragón, 2006).

Libro de los fechos et conquistas del principado de la Morea (1393)

Manuscript: Biblioteca Nacional, Madrid, MS. 10131, folios 183r–265r. The manuscript was copied by Bernardo de Jaca and signed on 24 October 1393.

Paleographic edition: John J. Nitti and Lloyd Kasten, eds., *The Electronic Texts and Concordances of Medieval Navarro-Aragonese Manuscripts* (Madison, Wis.: Hispanic Seminary of Medieval Studies, 1997 [CD-ROM]).

Edition: *Libro de los fechos et conquistas del principado de la Morea compilado por mandamiento de Don Fray Johan Fernández de Heredia,* edited by A. Morel-Fatio (Geneva: Jules-Guillaume Fick, 1885).

Guido delle Colonne, *Crónica troyana,* sponsored by Heredia (after 1393)

Manuscript: Biblioteca Nacional, Madrid, MS. 10801, folios 71r–253v. The translation of Colonne's *Historia destructionis Troiae* was thought to be related to the 1367 Catalan translation by Jaume Conesa, but Robert T. Dunstan has shown that Conesa's work was not used by Heredia.

Paleographic edition: John J. Nitti and Lloyd Kasten, eds., *The Electronic Texts and Concordances of Medieval Navarro-Aragonese Manuscripts* (Madison, Wis.: Hispanic Seminary of Medieval Studies, 1997 [CD-ROM]).

Editions: Robert T. Dunstan, "A Critical Edition of Fernández Heredia's Translation into Aragonese of Guido Delle Colonne's 'Cronica troyana,'" dissertation, University of Wisconsin–Madison, 1928; Evangeline V. Parker, "The Aragonese Version of Guido delle Collone's 'Historia destructionis Troiae': Critical Text and Classified Vocabulary," dissertation, Indiana University, 1971.

Corónica de los conquiridores (between 1385 and after 1396)

Manuscripts: The work is divided into two parts: Biblioteca Nacional, Madrid, MSS. 2211, 12367, and 10190; and MS. 10134bis. The *Corónica de los conquiridores* was finished after Heredia's death, but some of its themes are included in the *Grant Crónica de Espanya.* The first part comprises sixteen books on famous warriors of classical antiquity from Nino to Julius Caesar; the second part consists of eighteen books devoted to Roman, Germanic, Arab, Oriental, and European personages, concluding with Fernando III *el Santo* and Jaime I *el Conquistador.*

Paleographic edition: John J. Nitti and Lloyd Kasten, eds., *The Electronic Texts and Concordances of Medieval Navarro-Aragonese Manuscripts* (Madison, Wis.: Hispanic Seminary of Medieval Studies, 1997 [CD-ROM]).

Partial editions: Jesús Domínguez Bordona, "La

primera parte de la 'Crónica de Conquisidores' de Fernández de Heredia," *Revista de Filología Española,* 10 (1923): 380–388; Joseph A. Palumbo Jr., "An Edition, Study and Glossary of the Second Part of the 'Coronica delos conquiridores' by Juan Fernandez de Heredia," dissertation, University of Wisconsin–Madison, 1976.

Thucydides, *Tucídides* or *Guerra del Peloponeso,* sponsored by Heredia (late fourteenth century)

Manuscript: Biblioteca Nacional, Madrid, MS. 10801, folios 1r–69v. Heredia is not named as the translator, but a close study of the manuscript reveals that it shares characteristics with other texts by him.

Paleographic edition: John J. Nitti and Lloyd Kasten, eds., *The Electronic Texts and Concordances of Medieval Navarro-Aragonese Manuscripts* (Madison, Wis.: Hispanic Seminary of Medieval Studies, 1997 [CD-ROM]).

Edition: *Tucídides romanceado en el siglo XIV,* edited by Luis López Molina (Madrid: Real Academia Española, 1960).

Counselor of kings and popes, politician, and bibliophile, Juan Fernández de Heredia was a knight and grand master of the Order of the Hospital of St. John of Jerusalem. Little was known of Heredia's early life until recently, and most of what was "known" was incorrect. Some biographers gave Heredia's father's name as Lorenzo and maintained that he was a member of the lower aristocracy of Aragon; others, such as Giacomo Bosio, said that Heredia was born in Valencia. Today it is known that his father was García Fernández de Heredia, a knight of Jaime II in charge of the defense of the Castle of Ródenas in 1301, and that Juan was probably illegitimate. It was traditionally believed that he was born in Munébrega (Calatayud), but on the basis of unpublished information from Anthony Lutrell, Jean Gilkison Mackenzie suggests that he was born in Albarracín around 1308. He seems to have become a Hospitaller around 1327. In 1333 he was second in command to the knight-commander of Alfambra, and he received the commanderies of Alfambra in 1337, of Villel at an undetermined date, and of Saragossa in 1344. His children—Toda, Donosa, Juan, and Teresa—were all born after he became a Hospitaller and were illegitimate.

The Aragonese kings were fearful of the economic power of the Order of St. John after it received the possessions of the Order of the Temple (Knights Templars), which was dissolved in 1312; they kept a watchful eye over the order's direction and demanded that the chatelain of Amposta do homage to and uphold the rights of the kings of Aragon. Heredia's maneuvers to obtain the chatellaincy made his relations with King Pedro IV *el Ceremonioso* (the Ceremonious) difficult while Sancho, the king's uncle, held the position. After Sancho died in 1346, Heredia became chatelaine, and Pedro IV, who shared Heredia's passion for books and hawking, named him a counselor and used him for diplomatic tasks.

Heredia's frequent visits to Avignon reflect the high esteem in which he was held at the papal court, where he represented his order and defended Pedro IV's interests. Pope Clement VI assigned Heredia to prevent a confrontation between Edward III of England and Philip VI of France in the Hundred Years War; Heredia is said by some historians to have been imprisoned at Crécy by the English in 1346, but it is doubtful that this event actually took place. Heredia helped Pedro in his struggles against the antimonarchist Union of Aragon in 1347–1348, his relations with Mallorca in 1349, and his disputes with Castile, undertaking several missions to Castile and Navarre on behalf of the king.

Heredia's activities in the Order of St. John are marked by his efforts to reorganize the administration and economic structure of the chatelaincy of Amposta, particularly after the outbreak of the Black Death in 1348. In 1350 he commanded that all "privilegios reales, bulas pontificias, donaciones y otras escrituras" (royal privileges, papal bulls, donations, and other writings) related to the patrimony of the order and the chatelaincy of Amposta be copied. The resulting work, the *Cartulario magno* (Great Book of Charts), consists of about three thousand documents in six volumes; the manuscript is held at the Archivo Histórico Nacional in Madrid. The economic help he gave students, bachelors, and masters to attend their local Estudios de Artes (Arts Studies) in Teruel and Daroca and the Estudios Generales (General Studies) at the Universities of Lerida, Perpignan, and Montpellier had the objective of creating a cadre of notaries, lawyers, judges, and scribes able to act in the defense of the order's interests. He visited Rhodes in 1354–1355 to reinforce its discipline. He was named prior of Castile and León in 1355 and of Saint-Gilles in Provence in 1356.

The Pope sent Heredia to prevent the battle of Poitiers in 1356 and placed him in charge of the defense of Avignon from the mercenaries who roamed southern France. In this capacity he was named captain-general of the county of Venaison and of the diocese of Avignon and put in charge of the fortification and defense of the city between 1357 and 1376. He also organized and directed the fleet that took Gregory XI from Marseilles to Rome, and he served as the Pope's standard-bearer. Heredia was also involved with Gregory's attempt to stop the spread of Turkish influence in the Balkans. Heredia's good relations with the Pope kept

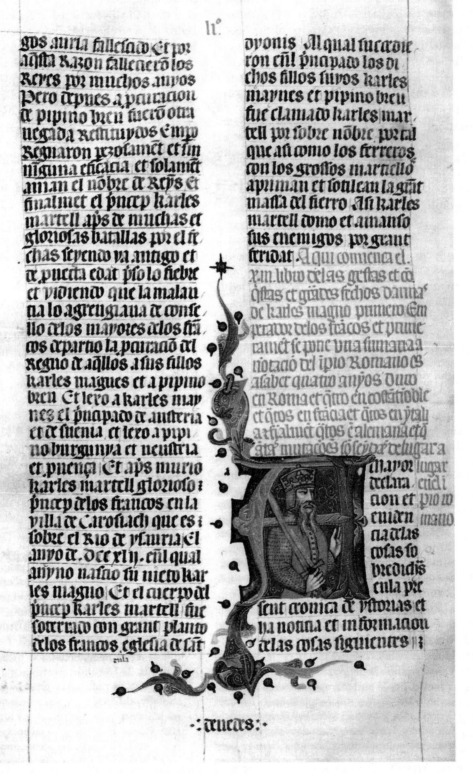

Page from a manuscript of Fernández de Heredia's Corónica de los conquiridores, possibly depicting the author in the illuminated initial (Biblioteca Nacional, Madrid, MS. 10134bis, folio 192v; photograph courtesy of Conrado Guardiola Alcover)

Pedro IV from being excommunicated when he seized several papal properties during his war with Castile.

A 1360 document confers legitimacy on Heredia's eldest son and namesake so that the latter can inherit the lordship of Zurita. Heredia was named prior of Catalonia in 1369. When Robert de Jully, Grand Master of the Order of St. John, died in Rhodes, the Pope invested Heredia with the office on 24 November 1377.

On Gregory XI's death in 1378 the Avignonese elected Clement VII Pope, while the Roman cardinals elected Urban VI. This division, known as the Western Schism, affected the Order of St. John. A few of its knights accepted the Roman Pope; the majority, guided by Heredia, followed Clement VII.

In 1378 Heredia headed a naval fleet that was successful at Vonitza and perhaps at Lepanto and Patrás, but during a sortie in Arta against the Albanian prince Ghin Boua Spata he was taken prisoner and sold to the Ottomans. He was held prisoner until the order paid his ransom in 1379. He spent the following three years in Rhodes, arranging for its defense and the reorganization of the order. From these years stems Heredia's interest in Hellenistic culture, which is reflected in the translation of Thucydides known as the *Plutarco* (between 1385 and 1388, Plutarch) that he sponsored.

In 1382 Heredia returned to Avignon to deal with the election of an anti-grandmaster and the organization of another expedition against the Turks in Greece and Macedonia. He was successful in the first task, and by 1384 he was in total control of the order. The second task, however, ended in failure because of the economic difficulties facing the order.

Heredia remained in Avignon for the rest of his life. Surrounding himself with collaborators, he took advantage of his access to the papal library and his contacts with Italian humanists to compile and translate books that transmitted the culture of the past. Although the dated manuscripts fall between 1377 and 1396, they build on an interest formerly manifested by the *Cartulario magno,* his patronage of students, and his correspondence with Pedro IV from 1362 to 1371. This correspondence, collected in Antonio Rubió y Lluch's *Documents per l'historia de la cultura catalana mig-eval* (1908, 1921, Documents on the History of Medieval Catalan Culture), shows that Heredia's search for books to copy and translate antedates most of his works. Nevertheless, the bulk of the production of Heredia's scriptorium belongs to his last years at Avignon. These works comprise the greatest literary corpus of Aragon and are comparable in Spain only to the production of the scriptorium of Alfonso X *el sabio* (the Learned) of Castile. Heredia's involvement in the production of his corpus is also comparable to that of Alfonso X. Most

often, according to the manuscripts, "mandó escreuir" (he commanded it be written), "fizo translatar" (he had it translated), or "ordenó et fizo" (he ordered and caused). Occasionally, however, there is evidence of more direct participation: "he ordenado aquesti libro . . . al qual he posado nombre *Rams de flores*" (I have ordered this book to be written . . . which I called *Rams de flores*); "si por auentura era trobada diuerssitat en las allegaçiones que yo he posadas en aquesti libro de los actores, no me pienso que por aquesto yo diga mentira" (if by chance there is disagreement among the different sayings of the authors that I have placed in this book, do not think that because of this I lie). In spite of these statements, it is not possible to determine the extent to which Heredia was involved in the composition of the works that bear his name.

Books from Heredia's scriptorium are written in an Aragonese Gothic script that is easy to read. With their rich decoration, most of the manuscripts appear to be finished products destined to be possessed by a great noble. Art critics have determined that the illustrations belong to the Italianizing school of Juan de Tolosa, which was active in Avignon at the end of the fourteenth century. The miniatures have been ascribed to the Spanish painter Sancho Gontier, although scholars have also found traces of French style.

The Heredian scriptorium did its work in six phases. First came the gathering of materials and the production of a draft. The resulting text was revised by a corrector, who normalized it according to a standard, eliminated strange linguistic forms and Catalanisms, and abbreviated or expanded passages. A redactor then ordered the text, adding or suppressing passages. A clean draft was produced by several copyists. This draft received some last-minute additions. Finally, a prologue and indexes were added. Errors in some of the manuscripts indicate that they may be preliminary drafts; others may be copies of a final draft produced by a scribe belonging to a different linguistic camp. Heredia says in the prologue of *Rams de flores* that he had it written by "scriuano qui no era de la mía lengua" (a scribe from a different tongue). In some cases the copyist, for whatever reason, corrects the beginning of a phrase and leaves the rest uncorrected. Still other errors reflect a lack of understanding of the original phrase. In sum, many hands took part in the creation of a Heredian work, and each left his mark on the manuscript. The names of three of Heredia's copyists are known: Alvar Pérez de Sevilla, Ferdinandus Metinenssis, and Bernardo de Jaca; little else is known about them.

Heredia's literary corpus consists of about fifteen compilations and translations, all composed with a cultural, political, or instructive goal. Of particular interest to critics are the works that deal with Greek culture.

Some see in them a reflection of the need to know that culture with a practical end in mind: the establishment of the Knights Hospitallers in Morea. Others see these works as precursors of fifteenth-century humanist interests in the classical past. Heredia's translations of Greek authors are the first to be made in the West and reflect the Aragonese cultural milieu toward the end of the Middle Ages. They are, accordingly, of great interest to students of the development of Western thought in Spain and in Europe.

Heredia died in Avignon in March 1396; according to a bull of Benedict XIII, he was more than a hundred years old. His remains were taken to the Aragonese city of Caspe and interred in the church of the convent of San Juan, which Heredia had founded for this purpose in 1394.

Juan Fernández de Heredia's works have aroused scholarly interest since the late nineteenth century. An edition of the *Libro de los fechos et conquistas del principado de la Morea* (Book about the Deeds and Conquests of the Principality of Morea) was published in 1885 and an edition of the *Libro de Marco Polo* (Book of Marco Polo) in 1902. Editions of various works appeared as dissertations or as published books in 1928, 1931, 1934, 1960, 1964, 1966, 1971, 1972, 1975, 1976, 1980, and 1983. In 1997 all of his texts except the *Cartulario Magno*, the *Ysidoro menor* (Lesser Isidore), and the *Historia Gothorum* (History of the Goths) appeared on CD-ROM in paleographic editions, providing a basis for subsequent critical editions. Mackenzie's lexicon of Heredia's works (1984) has helped to establish a norm for medieval Aragonese.

References:

María Bonet Donato, *La Orden del Hospital en la corona de Aragón: Poder y gobierno en la Castellanía de Amposta (ss. XII–XV)* (Madrid: Consejo Superior de Investigaciones Científicas, 1994);

Giacomo Bosio, *Dell'istoria della sacra religione et illustrissima militia di San Giovanni Gerosolimitano*, 2 volumes (Rome: Stamperia Apost. Vaticana, 1629);

José Manuel Cacho Blecua, *El Gran Maestre Juan Fernández de Heredia* (Saragossa: Caja de Ahorros de la Inmaculada, 1997);

Miguel Cortés Arrese, "Manuscritos miniados para Don Juan Fernández de Heredia conservados en España: II. Textos e imágenes," *Seminario de Arte Aragonés*, 41 (1987): 237–263;

J. Delaville Le Roulx, *Les Hospitaliers à Rhodes jusqu'à la mort de Philibert de Naillac (1310–1421)* (Paris: E. Leroux, 1913); republished with an introduction by Anthony Lutrell (London: Variorum Reprints, 1974);

Jesús Domínguez Bordona, "Los libros miniados en Aviñón para D. Juan Fernández de Heredia," *Museum: Revista mensual de arte español antiguo y moderno*, 6 (1920): 319–327;

Aurora Egido and José María Enguita, eds., *Juan Fernández de Heredia y su época: IV Curso sobre Lengua y Literatura en Aragón* (Saragossa: Institución Fernando el Católico, 1996);

Juan Agustín de Funes, *Corónica de la Ilustrísima Milicia y Sagrada Religión de San Juan Bautista de Jerusalem* (Valencia: Miguel Sorolla, 1626);

Karl Herquet, *Juan Fernández de Heredia, Grossmeister des Johanniter Ordens (1377–1396)* (Mühlhausen: A. Foerster, 1878);

Anthony Lutrell, "Juan Fernández de Heredia and Education in Aragón: 1349–1369," *Anuario de Estudios Medievales*, 17 (1987): 237–244;

Lutrell, "Juan Fernández de Heredia at Avignon: 1351–67," in *El cardenal Albornoz y el Colegio de España*, volume 1, edited by Evelio Verdera y Tuells (Bologna: Publicaciones del Colegio de España, 1972), pp. 287–316;

Jean Gilkison Mackenzie, *A Lexicon of the 14th-Century Aragonese Manuscripts of Juan Fernández de Heredia* (Madison, Wis.: Hispanic Seminary of Medieval Studies, 1984);

Alberto Montaner Frutos, "Una aproximación a Juan Fernández de Heredia," *Turia*, 35–36 (1996): 253–283;

Antonio Rubió y Lluch, ed., *Documents per l'Historia de la Cultura Catalana Mig-eval*, 2 volumes (Barcelona: Institut d'Estudis Catalans, 1908, 1921);

Manuel Serrano y Sanz, *Vida y escritos de D. Juan Fernández de Heredia, Gran Maestre de la Orden de San Juan de Jerusalén* (Saragossa: La Editorial, 1913);

René Aubert Vertot, *Histoire des Chevaliers Hospitaliers de Saint Jean de Jerusalem, appellés depuis Chevaliers de Rhodes, et aujour d'hui Chevaliers de Malte, par l'abbé de Vertot*, volume 2 (Paris: Rollin, 1726), pp. 79–112;

José Vives, *Juan Fernández de Heredia, Gran Maestre de Rodas: Vida, obras, formas dialectales* (Barcelona: Biblioteca Balmes, 1927).

Flores y Blancaflor

(circa 1375 – 1400)

Patricia E. Grieve
Columbia University

Manuscript: The only extant manuscript of the medieval Spanish version of the legend of Floire and Blancheflor, which is distinct from the version found in the sixteenth-century printed editions, is Biblioteca Nacional, Madrid, MS. 7583, 207 folios, copied in the fourteenth or fifteenth century from a late-thirteenth-century original. The *Crónica de Flores y Blancaflor* is interpolated intermittently into Alfonso X's *Estoria de España,* also known as the *Primera crónica general,* between chapters 564 and 783.

First publications: *La historia de los dos enamorados Flores y Blancaflor* (Alcalá de Henares: Arnao Guillén de Brocar, 1512); *La historia de los dos enamorados Flores y Blancaflor* (Seville: Cromberger, 1524?); *La historia de los dos enamorados Flores y Blancaflor* (Seville: Cromberger, 1532).

Standard editions: *La historia de los dos enamorados Flores y Blancaflor,* edited by A. Bonilla y San Martín (Madrid: Ruiz Hermanos, 1916); "Flores y Blancaflor," edited by José Gómez Pérez, *Anuario de Filología* (Maracaibo), 2-3 (1963-1964): 35-94; "Flores y Blancaflor," in *Narrativa popular de la Edad Media,* edited by Nieves Baranda and Victor Infantes, Nuestros clásicos, no. 14 (Madrid: Akal, 1995), pp. 84-127.

The popular medieval legend of Floire and Blancheflor circulated for centuries in multiple versions in many languages. Although not familiar to a modern audience like the stories of Tristan and Iseult or Lancelot and Guinevere, it was one of the most beloved tales of the Middle Ages, and elements of it can be found in modern reworkings in the twenty-first century.

According to the legend, on the death of her husband Countess Berthe of France and her father set out on a pilgrimage to Santiago de Compostela to give thanks for the child with which Berthe is pregnant. While plundering and pillaging northern Spain, the Muslim king Felix encounters the hapless pilgrims; he has his soldiers kill the father and take Berthe prisoner.

At his court in Andalusia in southern Spain his wife, who is also pregnant, befriends the Christian captive. On Palm Sunday (Pentecost in some versions) the queen gives birth to a boy, Floire, and Berthe to a girl, Blancheflor. The children fall in love and use their study time to write love poems in Latin and daydream about each other. The king is dismayed—in some versions because he considers Blancheflor socially inferior to his son, in others because her Christianity poses a threat to his kingdom. To separate the children, the king and queen send Floire away to stay with relatives; they then accuse Blancheflor of trying to poison the king, and they sell her to slave merchants. They take her to Cairo, where she quickly becomes the favorite in the emir's harem. Meanwhile, the king and queen have ordered the erection of an elaborately decorated tomb to make Floire believe that Blancheflor has died. By virtue of a magic ring, Floire realizes that Blancheflor is alive but in danger. When the queen realizes that her son may die of melancholy and despair, she admits that Blancheflor is alive. Vowing not to return to his father's kingdom until he has recovered Blancheflor, Floire travels to Cairo and discovers that Blancheflor is one of many maidens kept in a tower by the emir. Inside the tower is a garden with a magic tree beneath which the maidens walk each day; that night the emir takes to bed the one on whom a flower has fallen. The next day she is beheaded, and the process continues. Floire challenges the tower's porter to a game of chess; if Floire wins, the porter will help him enter the tower. To bolster the porter's confidence, Floire lets him win the first time, then roundly defeats him in subsequent games. The porter carries Floire into the tower in a basket of flowers (in some versions the basket is hoisted up the side of the tower). Floire is discovered in the basket by Blancheflor's friend Claris (or Gloris), which leads to much merriment in the harem and sexual joking about "knowing this flower well." Claris explains Blancheflor's absence by telling the emir that she is sleeping because she was up late reading the night before, but the emir goes to Blancheflor's quarters and discovers the lovers in bed. After a lengthy trial, the lovers are exonerated and return to Spain. In most versions Floire converts to Christianity, which removes the one remaining obstacle to their marriage, and the lovers live happily ever after.

Separation and adversity drive the plots of medieval romances in general, and *Floire and Blancheflor* is no exception. Floire and Blancheflor fall in love as children and remain steadfast in their devotion to each other through a long separation. The tale includes many other staples of romance, including beautiful gardens and lush scenery, bejeweled objects, and a false tomb. In *Floire and Blancheflor* exotic details add to the excitement of the story: love between a French Christian woman and a Spanish Muslim man, women in sexual peril in an Islamic harem, magic rings, and travels to Cairo and other exotic locations.

Most nineteenth-century critics believed that two twelfth-century poems in Old French, preserved in thirteenth- and fourteenth-century French manuscripts, were the oldest surviving texts of the legend. The poems reflect two strains of the legend, which Edélestand du Méril called the aristocratic and the popular versions. Some critics considered the French poems to derive from a lost earlier French work; Italo Pizzi believed that they originated in Persia; René Basset, Gédéon Huet, and Jan ten Brink thought that the poems had Arabic origins; Hugo Brunner argued that similar episodes in *Floire et Blancheflor* and *Aucassin et Nicolete* demonstrated a Hispano-Arabic common ancestor; and du Méril argued for the existence of an original Byzantine tale, since lost. But most critics accepted Hans Herzog's view that the aristocratic version originated in France and that the popular version came from Greece and passed through Spanish and Italian versions before serving as a basis for the French version. Joachim Henry Reinhold denied the existence of Spanish and Italian versions, arguing that the popular version derived from the aristocratic version and another lost French poem. Finally, Gaston Paris postulated the existence of a third version, which he called the "third strain," in French, Spanish, or Italian, that had Italo-Spanish or Hispano-Arabic origins; combined features of the aristocratic and popular versions; and was earlier than either the aristocratic or the popular version. For nationalistic and ideological reasons, Paris's hypothesis of a non-French origin of the beloved legend was rejected by his countrymen.

A Spanish version of the legend existed in the form of a sixteenth-century prose romance, *Historia de los dos enamorados Flores y Blancaflor* (History of the Lovers Flores and Blancaflor). Some critics suspected that there must have been an earlier Spanish version, but no one could prove it until José Gómez Pérez, a bibliographer working with Ramón Menéndez Pidal's team of researchers at the Biblioteca Nacional in Madrid in the late 1950s, discovered an uncatalogued manuscript. The team was gathering chronicles composed during the reign of King Alfonso X *el Sabio* (the Learned) of Castile and León in an attempt to reconstruct the archetype of the encyclopedic *Estoria de España* (History of Spain), also known as *Primera crónica general* (First General Chronicle), written in the second half of the thirteenth century. As a late-fourteenth- or early-fifteenth-century copy of part of the *Primera crónica general,* the uncatalogued manuscript was deemed unnecessary to the project. Only Gómez Pérez appears to have recognized its importance for the history of *Floire and Blancheflor.* Interpolated at various points between chapters 564 and 783 of the *Primera crónica general,* which deal with the Moorish kings of southern Spain, were about fifty folios containing a complete version of the story, the *Crónica de Flores y Blancaflor* (Chronicle of Flores and Blancaflor). It was followed by *Berta,* the tale of Berta of Laon, the wife of Pépin III and mother of Charlemagne; Berta is depicted as Flores and Blancaflor's daughter. Her story takes place during the reign of Flores and Blancaflor as king and queen of Spain, and her adventures are interspersed with episodes about her father's political activities, particularly his dealings with the Christian king Fruela of Asturias in northern Spain. *Berta,* in turn, is followed by *Mainete,* about the young Charlemagne.

Gómez Pérez published his transcription of the *Crónica de Flores y Blancaflor* in the 1964–1965 volume of an obscure Venezuelan journal, *Anuario de Filología* (Philological Annual), under a title, "Leyendas carolingias en España" (Carolingian Legends in Spain), that did not indicate its relationship to Floire and Blancheflor. Hence, even in the *Bibliography of Old Spanish Texts* (1984) the manuscript is listed as a late and insignificant partial copy of the *Primera crónica general,* with no indication that it also includes *Flores y Blancaflor.* Until the publication of Patricia E. Grieve's *"Floire and Blancheflor" and the European Romance* (1997), the chronicle version remained unknown outside of Hispanic studies and to only a limited extent within the field, being mentioned briefly in José Fradejas Lebrero's 1981 article on fourteenth-century Spanish prose fiction. Therefore, a vast amount of criticism has been produced in ignorance of the existence of the Spanish chronicle version.

Aside from its importance as a much earlier Spanish witness of the legend than the sixteenth-century prose romance, the *Crónica de Flores y Blancaflor* is the only extant witness of Paris's hypothesized "third strain": as he predicted, it combines features of the aristocratic and popular French versions. For example, in the aristocratic versions of the story, but not in the popular versions, Berthe is Floire's daughter, while in the popular versions, but not in the aristocratic ones,

Floire's father's court is in Almería. In the *Crónica de Flores y Blancaflor,* however, Floire is Berthe's father, and the court is in Almería. It also predates Giovanni Boccaccio's *Il Filocolo* (circa 1336, Love's Labor) and shows itself to be an important influence on the Italian writer's lengthy romance. Much of what was considered original with Boccaccio, because it was not found in the Old French poems, occurs in the Spanish chronicle.

The manuscript, now catalogued as BN Madrid 7583, lacks the first few folios and begins with events from the first half of the eighth century of the Spanish Era; since the Spanish Era takes 38 B.C., when Spain became a Roman province, as its starting date, that period is approximately equivalent to the years 739 to 768. The manuscript lists the territories and bishoprics that had once been under Christian control but were conquered by the Muslims. This material corresponds to Chapter 576 of the *Primera crónica general.* The interpolation of the story of Flores and Blancaflor begins after what would be chapter 581 of the *Primera crónica general* with the lineages of the hero and heroine. The early chapters that do not deal with the love story of Flores and Blancaflor include an account of the occupation of southern Spain by Moorish kings and their confrontations with the Asturian defenders that is faithful to the *Primera crónica general* except that they incorporate Fines—the father of Flores—and Flores himself into the skirmishes.

The Spanish version differs from the basic legend of Floire and Blancheflor in many details and episodes. For example, whereas in the French versions one adviser from Floire's father's court accompanies Floire on his journey to rescue Blancheflor, in the Spanish chronicle an adviser and a tutor are present and serve different purposes. An episode unique to the Spanish chronicle is Flores's effort to free the king of Babylon from the caliph's prison. Also, in the Spanish tale the trial of the lovers in the emir's court is extremely lengthy and seems to follow recognizable precepts of Islamic law. Finally, Flores and Blancaflor are shipwrecked on a Mediterranean island inhabited by monks; St. Augustine appears and tells the monks that Flores and Blancaflor will desire baptism and that the sailors should convert, as well.

At the end of the *Crónica de Flores y Blancaflor* additional episodes extend Flores's conversion to Christianity to include all of Spain as Flores converts his Muslim subjects; these episodes are also found in Boccaccio's *Il Filocolo* and the *Historia de los dos enamorados Flores y Blancaflor.* The *Crónica de Flores y Blancaflor* is, thus, both a Christian romance and a conversion narrative that fictionally overturns the victory of the Muslims in 711, when Rodrigo's Visigothic kingdom fell to invaders from North Africa. It fits in well with the grand national histories composed in the late thirteenth century that described the Iberian Peninsula as "Espanna" (Spain) as if it were a single country when it was actually a collection of independent states ruled by Christian kings and Muslim caliphs.

An important feature of these grand national histories was the tendency to record the facts as part of a larger providential design. The method involved depicting the land as a paradise on earth, a latter-day Garden of Eden that was assailed by outsiders who wanted to possess such a treasure but were unworthy of it. Military defeats and victories are then recorded as a series of falls and redemptions that are part of God's divine plan for the country. These general tendencies of medieval historiography are present in the *Crónica de Flores y Blancaflor* and help to explain why the story appeared time and again: it could be used as a political allegory in various periods.

BN Madrid 7583 is a fourteenth- or fifteenth-century copy of a lost manuscript that seems to date from the reign of Sancho IV, who ruled Castile from 1284 to 1295. In 1269 Alfonso X had married his son Fernando de la Cerda to Princess Blanche, the daughter of Louis IX, who was a descendant of Charlemagne. The marriage thus forged both a political alliance with France and a link to the emperor's lineage. Fernando died in 1275, leaving two young sons. Conflict developed when the supporters of Alfonso X's surviving son, Sancho, argued that the Castilian throne should pass to him and not to Fernando's son, the half-French Alfonso de la Cerda. The nobles also criticized Alfonso for allowing Roman legists in the law courts, arguing that Castilian nobles should be judged by their peers and not by foreigners. When Alfonso died in 1284, Sancho became king as Sancho IV; but King Philip IV of France—Blanche's brother and, therefore, Alfonso de la Cerda's uncle—supported Alfonso as the rightful heir. The names Fernando and Blanche—or Blanca, as she was called in Spain—recall Flores and Blancaflor. There was no greater role model for a Christian prince—especially an ambitious one such as Alfonso X, who wanted to be Holy Roman Emperor himself—than Charlemagne; Blanche was a descendant of Charlemagne, and Blancaflor is Charlemagne's grandmother: in the *Crónica de Flores y Blancaflor* Blancaflor's captive mother is comforted by a prophecy that she will be the great-grandmother of an emperor. That prophecy becomes a reality in the two stories that follow the *Crónica de Flores y Blancaflor* in BN Madrid 7583, *Berta* and *Mainete.* The *Crónica de Flores y Blancaflor* thus recalls the association of the Spanish kings with Charlemagne. Furthermore, in the *Crónica de Flores y Blancaflor* young King Flores is visited by Roman jurists, who give him advice that is better than that of his own counselors. The reader is not told what the advice is; but even Flores's tutor, who had refused to convert to Christianity, finds it persuasive. By having Flores become the Christian king of Spain and foretelling that Flores and Blancaflor will be Charlemagne's grandparents, the *Crónica de Flores y Blancaflor* argues for the importance of being true to a legitimate lineage linking the thrones of Spain and France.

One might wonder what would lead a scribe to make a copy of the legend in the late fourteenth or early fifteenth century, aside from the fact that it is an entertaining story. The answer could be that political activity in the late fourteenth century once again focused on Franco-Castilian relations. During the Western Schism of 1378–1417, which divided the Papacy between Avignon and Rome, supporters of the rival Popes vied for the allegiance of Castile. The *Crónica de Flores y Blancaflor* clearly supports the view that the Pope and the seat of the Church are in Rome.

Unlike the French versions of the tale, which focus on the love story, the *Crónica de Flores y Blancaflor* places the legend within a coherent narrative of Christian providential design that really alludes to a contemporary reign. Similarly, the sixteenth-century prose romance *Historia de los dos enamorados Flores y Blancaflor* was printed for the first time in 1512. This story in this printing parallels the political ambitions of another Spanish king, Charles I, who campaigned successfully to become Holy Roman Emperor being crowned by the Pope as Emperor Charles V in 1519.

Retellings of the version of the legend in the *Crónica de Flores y Blancaflor* include an Icelandic epic poem and prose saga and a Spanish ballad, "Hermanas reina y cautiva" (Queen and Captive Sisters), that is still sung in communities of Sephardic Jews. The ballad ignores the two lovers and makes the Christian captive and the Saracen queen long-lost sisters. It expresses painful sentiments of expulsion, exile, captivity, and longing for the homeland. Anthropologists have found that villagers in certain regions of Spain, including Cáceres, tell a folktale called "Blancaflor" to convey differing male and female views of courtship and marriage. The oral tale stresses the journey to maturity that the young suitor must undergo, implies that men and women should learn to accept their differences, and places much emphasis on the power of a woman's love to overcome obstacles. Although there are some odd transformations of the Christian elements in the medieval version of the story, many of the details survive in these modern retellings.

Bibliographies:

Marvin J. Ward, *"Floire et Blancheflor:* A Bibliography," *Bulletin of Bibliography,* 40 (1983): 45–64;

Charles B. Faulhaber and others, *Bibliography of Old Spanish Texts* (Madison, Wis.: Hispanic Seminary of Medieval Studies, 1984), entry 1544.

References:

Samuel G. Armistead, *El romancero judeo-español en el Archivo Menéndez Pidal: Catálogo-índice de romances y canciones,* volume 1 (Madrid: CSMP, 1978);

René Basset, "Les sources arabes de *Floire et Blanchefleur,*" *Revue des Traditions Populaires,* 22 (1907): 241–245;

Hugo Brunner, *Über Aucassin et Nicolete* (Halle, 1880), pp. 6–21;

Mario Cacciaglia, "Appunti sul problema delle fonti del romanzo di *Floire et Blancheflor,*" *Zeitschrift für romanische Philologie,* 80 (1964): 241–255;

Juan Manuel Cacho Blecua, "'Nunca quiso mamar lech del mugier rafez': Notas sobre lactancia, del *Libro de Alexandre* a don Juan Manuel," in *Actas del I Congreso de la Asociación Hispánica de Literatura Medieval,* edited by Vicenç Beltrán (Barcelona: PPU, 1988), pp. 209–224;

Jan ten Brink, *Geschiedenis der Nederlandsche Letterkunde* (Amsterdam: Elsevir, 1897), pp. 113–118;

William C. Calin, "Flower Imagery in *Floire et Blancheflor,*" *French Studies,* 18 (1964): 103–111;

Georges Cirot, "El *celoso extremeño* et l'Histoire de Floire et de Blanceflor," *Bulletin Hispanique,* 31 (1929): 138–143;

Edélestand du Méril, *Floire et Blanceflor: Poèmes du XIIIe siècle, publiés d'apres les manuscrits* (Paris: P. Jannet, 1856);

José Fradejas Lebrero, "Algunas notas sobre *Enrique fi de Oliva,* novela del siglo XIV," in *Actas del I Simposio de Literatura Española, Salamanca, del 7 al 11 de mayo de 1979,* edited by Alberto Navarro González, Acta Salmanticensia, Filosofía y Letras, no. 125 (Salamanca: Ediciones Universidad de Salamanca, 1981), pp. 309–360;

Roberto Giacone, *"Floris and Blauncheflur:* Critical Issues," *Rivista di Studi Classici,* 27 (1979): 395–405;

José Gómez Pérez, "Leyendas carolingias en España," *Anuario de Filología* (Maracaibo), 4 (1964–1965): 121–148;

Patricia E. Grieve, *"Floire and Blancheflor" and the European Romance,* Cambridge Studies in Medieval Literature, volume 32 (Cambridge & New York: Cambridge University Press, 1997);

Hans Herzog, *Die beiden Sagenkreise von Flore und Blancheflur: Eine litterarhistorische Studie* (Vienna: Verlag des Verfassers, 1884);

Gédéon Huet, "Encore *Floire et Blanchefleur,*" *Romania,* 35 (1906): 95–100;

Huet, "Sur l'origine de *Floire et Blanchefleur*," *Romania*, 28 (1899): 348–359;

Oliver Martin Johnston, "The Description of the Emir's Orchard in *Floire et Blancheflor*," *Zeitschrift für romanische Philologie*, 32 (1908): 705–710;

Johnston, "Origin of the Legend of *Floire and Blancheflor*," in *Matzke Memorial Volume*, edited by E. Flugel and others (Palo Alto, Cal.: Stanford University Press, 1911), pp. 125–138;

Jean Luc Leclanche, "La Date du conte de *Floire et Blancheflor*," *Romania*, 92 (1971): 556–567;

Myrrha Lot-Borodine, *Le Roman idyllique au môyen-age* (Paris: A. Picard, 1913), pp. 9–74;

Gaston Paris, *Poèmes et légèndes du Môyen Age* (Paris: Société d'Edition Artistique, 1900);

Paris, "Review of *Il Cantare di Fiorio e Biancifiore*," edited by V. Crescini, *Romania*, 28 (1899): 439–447;

Italo Pizzi, *Le somiglianze e le relazione tra la poesia persiana e la nostra del medio evo: Memoria* (Turin: Clausen, 1892);

Jocelyn Price, "*Floire et Blancheflor*: The Magic and Mechanics of Love," *Reading Medieval Studies*, 8 (1982): 12–33;

Joachim Henry Reinhold, "Chronique au sujet de *Floire et Blancheflor*," *Romania*, 35 (1906): 335–336;

Reinhold, *Floire et Blancheflor: Etude de littérature comparée* (Paris: E. Larose, 1906);

Harvey L. Sharrer, "Eighteenth-Century Chapbook Adaptations of the *Historia de Flores y Blancaflor* by Antonio da Silva, Mestre de Gramatica," *Hispanic Review*, 52 (1984): 59–74;

John Webster Spargo, "The Basket Incident in *Floire et Blancflor*," *Neuphilologische Mitteilungen*, 28 (1927): 69–75;

Heinrich Sundmacher, *Die altfranzösische und die mittelhochdeutsche Bearbeitung der Sage von Flore und Blanscheflur* (Göttingen: Druck der Dieterischschen Universität, 1872);

James M. Taggart, *Enchanted Maidens: Gender Relations in Spanish Folktales of Courtship and Marriage* (Princeton: Princeton University Press, 1990), pp. 165–199;

Karl P. Wentersdorf, "Iconographic Elements in *Floris and Blancheflour*," *Annuale Mediaevale*, 20 (1981): 76–96.

Gonzalo de Berceo

(circa 1195 – circa 1264)

James W. Marchand
University of Illinois at Urbana-Champaign

WORKS: *Vida de San Millán de la Cogolla* (circa 1230)

Manuscripts: Biblioteca de la Real Academia Española, Madrid, MS. 4 (fourteenth century); Monastery of Santo Domingo de Silos, MS. 56 (eighteenth century); Monastery of Santo Domingo de Silos, MS. 110 (1775–1779), copy of lost thirteenth-century original; Monastery of Santo Domingo de Silos, tomo 36 of the Papeles de la Congregación de Valladolid, and Biblioteca Nacional, Madrid, MS. 13149, two parts of an eighteenth-century copy of a lost thirteenth-century original.

Facsimile edition: *Poemas: Edición facsímil del manuscrito del siglo XIV de la Real Academia Española* (Madrid: Real Academia Española, 1983).

Modern editions: *La Vida de San Millán de la Cogolla*, volume 1 of *Gonzalo de Berceo, Obras completas*, edited by Brian Dutton (London: Tamesis, 1978); "Vida de San Millán de la Cogolla," in *Gonzalo de Berceo, Obra completa*, edited by Dutton and others, coordinated by Isabel Uría Maqua (Madrid: Espasa-Calpe, 1992), pp. 117–249; "Vida de San Millán de la Cogolla," in *Obras completas de Gonzalo de Berceo*, edited by Jorge García López and Carlos Clavería (Madrid: Fundación José Antonio de Castro, 2003), pp. 299–372.

Translation into modern Spanish: *Milagros de Nuestra Señora, Vida de Santo Domingo de Silos, Vida de San Millán de la Cogolla, Vida de Santa Oria, Martirio de San Lorenzo*, edited by Amancio Bolaño e Isla (Mexico City: Porrúa, 1965), pp. 327–421.

Vida de Santo Domingo de Silos (circa 1236)

Manuscripts: Monastery of Santo Domingo de Silos, MS. 12 (late thirteenth century); Biblioteca de la Real Academia Española, Madrid, MS. 4, folios 146r–194v (fourteenth century); Academia de la Historia, Madrid, MS. 12-4-1 (second half of the fourteenth century), a copy of Silos MS. 12.

Facsimile edition: *Poemas: Edición facsímil del manuscrito del siglo XIV de la Real Academia Española* (Madrid: Real Academia Española, 1983).

Early editions: *Vida y milagros de el thaumaturgo español Moyses segundo redemptor de cautivos, abogado de los felices partos, Sto. Domingo Manso, abad benedictino, reparador de el real monasterio de Silos*, edited by Sebastián de Vergara (Madrid: Francisco Hierro, 1736); *Colección de poesías castellanas anteriores al siglo XV*, volume 2, edited by Tomás Antonio Sánchez (Madrid, 1780); *Poetas castellanos anteriores al siglo XV*, edited by Florencio Janer, Biblioteca de Autores Castellanos, volume 57 (Madrid: Rivadeneyra, 1864).

Modern editions: *Vida de Santo Domingo de Silos*, critical edition and palaeographic text, edited by Fr. Alfonso Andrés (Madrid: Padres Benedictinos, 1958); *Vida de Santo Domingo de Silos*, edited by Germán Orduna (Salamanca: Anaya, 1968); *Vida de Santo Domingo de Silos*, edited by Teresa Labarta de Chávez (Madrid: Castalia, 1972); *La Vida de Santo Domingo de Silos*, volume 4 of *Gonzalo de Berceo, Obras completas*, edited by Brian Dutton (London: Tamesis, 1978); "Vida de Santo Domingo de Silos," in *Gonzalo de Berceo, Obra completa*, edited by Dutton and others, coordinated by Isabel Uría Maqua (Madrid: Espasa-Calpe, 1992); pp. 257–453; "Vida de Santo Domingo de Silos," in *Text and Concordance of Obras de Gonzalo de Berceo: Real Academia Española MS. 4*, edited by Edward Baranowski and Matt Mayers (Madison, Wis.: Hispanic Seminary of Medieval Studies, 1994 [microform]); *Vida de Santo Domingo de Silos. Manuscrito conservado en el Archivo del Monasterio de Santo Domingo de Silos*, edited by José Antonio Fernández Flórez (Burgos: Universidad de Burgos, 2000); "Vida de Santo Domingo de Silos," in *Obras completas de Gonzalo de Berceo*, edited by Jorge García López and Carlos Clavería (Madrid: Fundación José Antonio de Castro, 2003), pp. 373–488.

Translation into modern Spanish: *Milagros de Nuestra Señora, Vida de Santo Domingo de Silos, Vida de San Millán de la Cogolla, Vida de Santa Oria, Mar-*

tirio de San Lorenzo, edited by Amancio Bolaño e Isla (Mexico: Porrúa, 1965), pp. 179–325.

Del Sacrificio de la Misa (date uncertain)

Manuscript: Biblioteca Nacional, Madrid, MS. 1533 (fourteenth century); Monastery of Santo Domingo de Silos, MS. 110 (1775–1779), copy of lost thirteenth-century original.

Modern editions: "El Sacrificio de la Misa," in *Gonzalo de Berceo, Obras completas,* volume 5, edited by Brian Dutton (London: Tamesis, 1981), pp. 3–80; *Gonzalo de Berceo, Obra completa,* edited by Dutton and others, coordinated by Isabel Uría Maqua (Madrid: Espasa-Calpe, Gobierno de la Rioja, 1992), pp. 933–1033; "Del Sacrificio de la Misa," in *Text and Concordance of Obras de Gonzalo de Berceo: Real Academia Española MS. 4,* edited by Edward Baranowski and Matt Mayers (Madison, Wis.: Hispanic Seminary of Medieval Studies, 1994 [microform]); "Del Sacrificio de la Misa," in *Obras completas de Gonzalo de Berceo,* edited by Jorge García López and Carlos Clavería (Madrid: Fundación José Antonio de Castro, 2003), pp. 153–197.

El Duelo de la Virgen (date uncertain)

Manuscripts: Monastery of Santo Domingo de Silos, MS. 110 (1775–1779), copy of lost thirteenth-century original; Monastery of Santo Domingo de Silos, tomo 36 of the Papeles de la Congregación de Valladolid, and Biblioteca Nacional, Madrid, MS. 13149, two parts of eighteenth-century copy of lost thirteenth-century original.

Modern editions: "El Duelo de la Virgen," in *Gonzalo de Berceo, Obras completas,* volume 3, edited by Brian Dutton (London: Tamesis, 1975), pp. 7–58; "El Duelo de la Virgen," in *Gonzalo de Berceo, Obra completa,* by Dutton and others, coordinated by Isabel Uría Maqua (Madrid: Espasa-Calpe, Gobierno de la Rioja, 1992), pp. 797–857; "El Duelo de la Virgen," in *Text and Concordance of Obras de Gonzalo de Berceo: Real Academia Española MS. 4,* edited by Edward Baranowski and Matt Mayers (Madison, Wis.: Hispanic Seminary of Medieval Studies, 1994 [microform]); "El Duelo de la Virgen," in *Obras completas de Gonzalo de Berceo,* edited by Jorge García López and Carlos Clavería (Madrid: Fundación José Antonio de Castro, 2003), pp. 221–252.

Himnos (date uncertain)

Manuscripts: Monastery of Santo Domingo de Silos, MS. 110 (1775–1779), copy of lost thirteenth-century original; Biblioteca Nacional, Madrid, MS. 13149, eighteenth-century copy of lost thirteenth-century original.

Modern editions: "Los Himnos," in *Gonzalo de Berceo, Obras completas,* volume 3, edited by Brian Dutton (London: Tamesis, 1975), pp. 61–66; "Himnos," in *Gonzalo de Berceo, Obra completa,* edited by Dutton and others, coordinated by Isabel Uría Maqua (Madrid: Espasa-Calpe, Gobierno de la Rioja, 1992), pp. 1063–1075; "Himnos," in *Text and Concordance of Obras de Gonzalo de Berceo: Real Academia Española MS. 4,* edited by Edward Baranowski and Matt Mayers (Madison, Wis.: Hispanic Seminary of Medieval Studies, 1994) [microform]; "Himnos," in *Obras completas de Gonzalo de Berceo,* edited by Jorge García López and Carlos Clavería (Madrid: Fundación José Antonio de Castro, 2003), pp. 213–220.

Edition in English: James W. Marchand, "The Hymns of Gonzalo de Berceo and Their Latin Sources," *Allegorica,* 3 (1979): 105–125.

Loores de Nuestra Señora (date uncertain)

Manuscripts: Monastery of Santo Domingo de Silos, MS. 110 (1775–1779), copy of lost thirteenth-century original; Monastery of Santo Domingo de Silos, tomo 36 of the Papeles de la Congregación de Valladolid, and Madrid, Biblioteca Nacional, MS. 13149, two parts of eighteenth-century copy of lost thirteenth-century original.

Modern editions: "Los Loores de Nuestra Señora," in *Gonzalo de Berceo, Obras completas,* volume 3, edited by Brian Dutton (London: Tamesis, 1975), pp. 69–117; "Loores de Nuestra Señora," in *Gonzalo de Berceo, Obra completa,* edited by Dutton and others, coordinated by Isabel Uría Maqua (Madrid: Espasa-Calpe, Gobierno de la Rioja, 1992), pp. 859–931; "Loores de Nuestra Señora," in *Text and Concordance of Obras de Gonzalo de Berceo: Real Academia Española MS. 4,* edited by Edward Baranowski and Matt Mayers. (Madison, Wis.: Hispanic Seminary of Medieval Studies, 1994) [microform]; "Loores de Nuestra Señora," in *Obras completas de Gonzalo de Berceo,* edited by Jorge García López and Carlos Clavería (Madrid: Fundación José Antonio de Castro, 2003), pp. 253–294.

Los Signos de Juicio Final (date uncertain)

Manuscripts: Monastery of Santo Domingo de Silos, MS. 110 (1775–1779), copy of lost thirteenth-century original; Biblioteca Nacional, Madrid, MS. 13149.

Modern editions: "Los Signos de Juicio Final," in *Gonzalo de Berceo, Obras completas,* volume 3, edited by Brian Dutton (London: Tamesis, 1975), pp. 121–144; "Los Signos de Juicio Final," in *Gonzalo de Berceo, Obra completa,* edited by Dutton and others, coordinated by Isabel Uría Maqua (Madrid:

Espasa-Calpe, Gobierno de la Rioja, 1992), pp. 1035–1061; "Los Signos de Juicio Final," in *Text and Concordance of Obras de Gonzalo de Berceo: Real Academia Española MS. 4,* edited by Edward Baranowski and Matt Mayers (Madison, Wis.: Hispanic Seminary of Medieval Studies, 1994) [microform]; "Los Signos de Juicio Final," in *Obras completas de Gonzalo de Berceo,* edited by Jorge García López and Carlos Clavería (Madrid: Fundación José Antonio de Castro, 2003), pp. 199–212.

Los Milagros de Nuestra Señora (before 1246–after 1252)

Manuscripts: Biblioteca de la Real Academia Española, Madrid, MS. 4, folios 50v–101r (fourteenth century); Monastery of Santo Domingo de Silos, MS. 110 (1775–1779), copy of lost thirteenth-century original; Biblioteca Nacional, Madrid, MS. 13149, eighteenth-century copy of lost thirteenth-century original.

Facsimile edition: *Poemas: Edicion facsímil del manuscrito del siglo XIV de la Real Academia Española* (Madrid: Real Academia Española, 1983).

Modern editions: *Gonzalo de Berceo, Milagros de Nuestra Señora,* edited by Antonio García Solalinde, Clásicos Castellanos, no. 44 (Madrid: Espasa-Calpe, 1922); *Milagros de Nuestra Señora,* edited by Daniel Devoto, second edition (Madrid: Castalia, 1965); "Los Milagros de Nuestra Señora," in *Gonzalo de Berceo, Obras completas,* volume 2, edited by Brian Dutton (London: Tamesis, 1971); *Milagros de Nuestra Señora,* edited by Michael Gerli (Madrid: Cátedra, 1985); "Los Milagros de Nuestra Señora," in *Gonzalo de Berceo, Obra completa,* edited by Dutton and others, coordinated by Isabel Uría Maqua (Madrid: Espasa-Calpe, Gobierno de la Rioja, 1992), pp. 553–795; "Los Milagros de Nuestra Señora," in *Text and Concordance of Obras de Gonzalo de Berceo: Real Academia Española MS. 4,* edited by Edward Baranowski and Matt Mayers (Madison, Wis.: Hispanic Seminary of Medieval Studies, 1994 [microform]); "Los Milagros de Nuestra Señora," in *Obras completas de Gonzalo de Berceo,* edited by Jorge García López and Carlos Clavería (Madrid: Fundación José Antonio de Castro, 2003), pp. 1–152.

Translation into modern Spanish: *Milagros de Nuestra Señora, Vida de Santo Domingo de Silos, Vida de San Millán de la Cogolla, Vida de Santa Oria, Martirio de San Lorenzo,* edited by Amancio Bolaño e Isla (Mexico: Porrúa, 1965), pp. 1–177.

Edition in English: *Miracles of Our Lady,* translated by Richard Terry Mount and Annette Grant Cash (Lexington: University Press of Kentucky, 1997).

Poema de Santa Oria (date uncertain)

Manuscripts: Madrid, Biblioteca de la Real Academia Española, MS. 4, folios 101v–114v (fourteenth century, only stanzas 1–205); Monastery of Santo Domingo de Silos, MS. 110 (1775–1779), copy of lost thirteenth-century original.

Facsimile edition: *Poemas: Edición facsímil del manuscrito del siglo XIV de la Real Academia Española* (Madrid: Real Academia Española, 1983).

Modern editions: "La Vida de Santa Oria," in *Gonzalo de Berceo, Obras completas,* volume 5, edited by Brian Dutton (London: Tamesis, 1981), pp. 83–136; "Poema de Santa Oria," in *Gonzalo de Berceo, Obra completa,* edited by Dutton and others, coordinated by Isabel Uría Maqua (Madrid: Espasa-Calpe, 1992), pp. 491–551; "Poema de Santa Oria," in *Text and Concordance of Obras de Gonzalo de Berceo: Real Academia Española MS. 4,* edited by Edward Baranowski and Matt Mayers (Madison, Wis.: Hispanic Seminary of Medieval Studies, 1994) [microform]; "Poema de Santa Oria," in *Obras completas de Gonzalo de Berceo,* edited by Jorge García López and Carlos Clavería (Madrid: Fundación José Antonio de Castro, 2003), pp. 507–543.

Translations into modern Spanish: *Milagros de Nuestra Señora, Vida de Santo Domingo de Silos, Vida de San Millán de la Cogolla, Vida de Santa Oria, Martirio de San Lorenzo,* edited by Amancio Bolaño e Isla (Mexico: Porrúa, 1965), pp. 423–463; *Berceo's "Vida de Santa Oria": Text, Translation and Commentary,* edited by Anthony Lappin (Oxford: European Humanities Research Centre, 2000).

Edition in English: *Berceo's "Vida de Santa Oria": Text, Translation, and Commentary,* edited by Anthony Lappin (Oxford: Legenda [European Humanities Research Centre], 2000).

El Martirio de San Lorenzo (date uncertain; possibly interrupted by Berceo's death)

Manuscripts: Monastery of Santo Domingo de Silos, MS. 110 (1775–1779), copy of lost thirteenth-century original; Monastery of Santo Domingo de Silos, tomo 36 of the Papeles de la Congregación de Valladolid, eighteenth-century copy of lost thirteenth-century original.

Modern editions: "El Martirio de San Lorenzo," in *Gonzalo de Berceo, Obras completas,* volume 5, edited by Brian Dutton (London: Tamesis, 1981), pp. 139–180; "Martirio de San Lorenzo," in *Gonzalo de Berceo, Obra completa,* edited by Dutton and others, coordinated by Isabel Uría Maqua (Madrid: Espasa-Calpe, 1992), pp. 455–489;

Del mortal enemigo tu gracia nos defienda,
danos como vivamos en paz e sin contienda:
tu sey nostra guion, cubra nos la tu tienda
qui escusar podamos toda mala facienda.

Danos vencido que podamos al Padre entender,
à bueltas con el Padre al Fijo conoscer,
de si como tengamos creencia e saber,
como eres con ambos un Dios e un poder.

Looz sea al Padre, è al su engendrado
à ti Creator Spiritu de ambos aspirado
el Fijo que por nos fue en cruz marteriado
embie nos la gracia de el Spiritu sagrado.

Cathalogo de las obras poeticas
de J. Gonzalo de Berceo,
que se conservan en el Archivo de S. Millan
Año 1752 =

Del sacrificio de la Missa
De las señales previas al Juicio
Del Duelo de la Virgen
Laudes de la Virgen, y en este poema que es largo se incluye
Vida y muerte de Cristo
Glosa del Veni creator, y del Christe qui lux
Milagros de la Virgen
Vida de Sta Aurea, ù Oria
Vida de S. Millan
Votos de Castilla à S. Millan
Vida de ~~xxxx~~
Passion de S. Lorenzo = falta el fin =
Vida de S. Domingo de Silos = Xelose à S. Monast.

Vivia año 1222 como consta de diversas escrituras q. estan en un libro q. Ramon Bulario

Page from an eighteenth-century copy of the 1230 manuscript of Gonzalo de Berceo's Vida de San Millán de la Cogolla
(Biblioteca Nacional, Madrid, MS. 13149)

"Martirio de San Lorenzo," in *Text and Concordance of Obras de Gonzalo de Berceo: Real Academia Española MS. 4,* edited by Edward Baranowski and Matt Mayers (Madison, Wis.: Hispanic Seminary of Medieval Studies, 1994) [microform]); "Martirio de San Lorenzo," in *Obras completas de Gonzalo de Berceo,* edited by Jorge García López and Carlos Clavería (Madrid: Fundación José Antonio de Castro, 2003), pp. 489–506.

Translation into modern Spanish: *Milagros de Nuestra Señora, Vida de Santo Domingo de Silos, Vida de San Millán de la Cogolla, Vida de Santa Oria, Martirio de San Lorenzo,* edited by Amancio Bolaño e Isla (Mexico: Porrúa, 1965), pp. 465–485.

A prolific poet, Gonzalo de Berceo left behind more than thirteen thousand lines of verse. Some Latin hymns are occasionally wrongly attributed to him, and he has often been given credit for composing the contemporaneous masterpiece *Libro de Alexandre* (Book of Alexander). Most scholars, however, do not now accept Berceo's authorship of this work.

Berceo is the first Old Spanish author whose name is known; it was unusual for medieval authors to identify themselves, as Berceo does in *Vida de Santo Domingo de Silos* (circa 1236, The Life of St. Dominic of Silos), *Los Milagros de Nuestra Señora* (before 1246–after 1252; translated as *Miracles of Our Lady,* 1997), and *Vida de San Millán de la Cogolla* (circa 1230, The Life of St. Millán de la Cogolla). Little else is known about him, and most of what is known is from casual references in his surviving works. A few documents mention him, and his name is affixed to others as a witness. He was made a deacon in 1221, a status one could not attain until one was at least twenty-three; he must, therefore, have been born before 1198. In his works he says that he was born in the town of Berceo in the province of La Rioja and the diocese of Calahorra and went to school in the Monastery of San Millán de la Cogolla. He may also have studied at the short-lived university at Palencia and may have been the notary of the San Millán monastery; he may also have been a monk at that monastery and may have been ordained as a priest. Because he was closely connected with the San Millán monastery and its politics throughout his life, it is assumed that he spent most of his life in La Rioja. He apparently died before 1264.

The road to Santiago de Compostela passed through La Rioja, and the San Millán monastery was a natural stopping place for pilgrims and other travelers using the thoroughfare. In addition to Iberian Christians, the traffic included Saracens, Franks, Basques, and Jews; thus, there was a continual flow of influence from the outside, particularly from France. The monastery was within easy walking distance of the town of Berceo and had an outstanding library and a scriptorium that produced books that are now scattered in many collections. It is still the home of the *Glosas Emilianenses* (Glosses of St. Emilianus); since these marginal glosses in Spanish for a Latin text include the first known instance of a recorded Spanish sentence, the monastery is considered the birthplace of Spain's national vernacular tongue.

Berceo is the foremost practitioner of the dominant poetic verse form of the thirteenth century: the *cuaderna vía* (fourfold way). Modeled loosely on French and Latin forms of the period, it is a stable and technically exacting line of fourteen syllables with a pause between the two half-lines; each half-line contains a stressed sixth syllable. There was some flexibility in achieving the required syllable count by dividing or merging adjacent vowels within words or across word boundaries. Four of these "alexandrine" lines—named for the anonymous *Libro de Alexandre*—formed a *copla* (stanza) or *estrofa* (quatrain), with full consonantal rhyme at the end of each line and, normally, some form of prosodic closure at the end of each verse, although clever run-on phrasing did occur. The fashion was associated with learned clerics who reworked stories inherited from foreign, often Latin, sources and showed off their skills by dubbing it a *mester de clerecía* (clerics' handiwork). This poetic form was launched either by Berceo or by the poet of the *Libro de Alexandre*—the two may well have been acquaintances or even classmates in Palencia—and endured through the fourteenth century.

Most medieval writers do not consider originality a virtue, and Berceo is no exception. He continually refers to his written sources and complains when they do not furnish him enough information. But he excels in churchly turns such as figurative usage, spiritual allegory, and typology. He calls the literal meaning the *corteza* (bark) and the figurative meanings the *meollo* (kernel or pith). Readers of his works thus need to be familiar with medieval symbolism.

Joaquín Artiles has documented Berceo's use of the rhetorical devices recommended in medieval manuals, but his expressiveness shows itself best in his mastery of the *cuaderna vía* and the bipartite constructions imposed, or at least suggested, by it. His persona is that of a country clergyman, and many of his homespun references are rural in nature; yet, he does not hesitate to quote Latin or to make erudite references a lay audience could not have been expected to understand. It is, therefore, difficult to determine what sort of readership he had in mind. He does indicate that his poetry is meant to be read aloud, but in the Middle Ages all reading was vocal.

Berceo's extant works fall into three groups. The first group, lives of saints of local interest, comprises *Vida de San Millán, Vida de Santo Domingo de Silos, Poema de Santa Oria* (date uncertain, Poem of St. Aurea), and *El Martirio de San Lorenzo* (date uncertain, The Martyrdom of St. Lawrence). The second group, works centering on the Virgin Mary, consists of *Los Milagros de Nuestra Señora, Loores de Nuestra Señora* (date uncertain, Praise of Our Lady), and *El Duelo de la Virgen* (date uncertain, The Virgin's Lament). The final group, doctrinal works, is made up of *Del Sacrificio de la misa* (date uncertain, The Sacrifice of the Mass), *Himnos* (date uncertain, Hymns), and *Los Signos del Juicio Final* (date uncertain, The Signs of Judgment Day).

Berceo seems to have begun his writing career with *Vida de San Millán de la Cogolla.* Much of the work is devoted to promoting his home monastery and is based on documents that he must have known were self-serving forgeries. Near the end he gives his name: "Gonzalvo fue so nomne qui fizo est tractado, / en Sant Millán de Suso fue de ninnez crïado; / natural de Verceo ond sant Millán fue nado" (Gonzalvo was his name who wrote this work / in San Millán de Suso he served from his childhood; / born in Berceo, where San Millán was born). Berceo's first work does not show the skill of his later ones in rhetorical adornment, references to the Bible and other religious texts, or the employment of symbolism and allegory. But when it is compared with its principal Latin source, the seventh-century *Vita Beati Emiliani* (The Life of St. Emilianus), by St. Braulio of Saragossa, *Vida de San Millán de la Cogolla* can be seen to demonstrate some rhetorical and poetic devices and to show an ability to translate gracefully instead of lapsing into a slavish, word-by-word rendition. In book 1 (lines 1 to 108) the shepherd boy Millán shows outstanding academic ability: "Fue en poco de tiempo el pastor psalteriado, / de imnos et de cánticos sobra bien decorado, / en toda la doctrina maestro profundado, / faziése el maestro misme maravellado" (In but a short time the shepherd learned his psalms, / learned extremely well hymns and canticles, / in all doctrine a profound master, / he surprised even the master himself). His studies completed, Millán goes into the wilderness and becomes a hermit. In spite of the simplicity of the work, Berceo employs learned topoi such as the *puer senex* (young man who is old in learning) to characterize the learned saintly man who is forced to move farther into the wilderness when crowds of people come out to see him. He also uses the topos of inexpressibility—"De la su santa vida, qui vos podra decir?" (Who could tell you about his

blessed life?)—and refers to Satan by various epithets, such as "el mortal guerrero" (the lethal warrior). Millán lives in the wilderness for forty years, in holiness and much loved by God, then returns to take holy orders; he is sent to the church of St. Eulalia in Berceo, where he performs his priestly duties so splendidly that, to avoid the envy of other clerics, he returns to the wilderness.

The second book (lines 109 to 319) begins with a contest suggested by Satan between himself and Millán to see who will stay in the mountains. Berceo's language becomes more colorful as he warms to his task: "Luego que esto disso la bestia enconada / quiso en el sant omne meter mano irada, / abraçarse con elli, pararli çancajada; / mas non li valió todo una nuez foradada (After the poisonous beast had said this, / he tried to lay an angry hand on the blessed man, / to wrestle with him, to make a sudden trick move; / but all that was no more use to him than a nut with a hole in it). Berceo loved homespun expressions such as "nuez foradada" (nut with a hole in it [that is, a wormy nut]); later, Satan quotes a similar folksy proverb: "mal día l'amasco al qui ha mal vecino" (a bad day dawns for him who has a bad neighbor), and a sick man comes to Millán whom doctors have not helped "quanto val un dinero" (a nickel's worth). Many of the miracles wrought by Millán are for servants of the powerful, as when he cures a blind girl or casts the demon whose favorite trick is throwing excrement on the food of a character named Honorio's food. God protects Millán and keeps his sanctuary secure.

As the end of Millán's life draws near, the devil returns and accuses him of all sorts of crimes but is defeated again. Attacked by a citizen of Cantabria named Abundancio, Millán predicts correctly that Cantabria will be destroyed and that his attacker will be the first to die. When he himself is about to expire, he gathers his friends around him. At his death all of the *ordo justorum* (order of the Just)—patriarchs, prophets, apostles, martyrs, confessors, and virgins—gather to rejoice. As Millán's soul ascends to heaven, a fellow cleric, Aselmus, and his aides carve out a tomb and bury the deceased priest with all honors. Berceo ends the second book with the founding of the monastery: "Después fezo vertudes el confessor ondrado, / porque ganó grant precio, máes que tenié ganado; / fue el so monesterio ricament eredado, / ont es Dios ý servido, e Sant Millán nomnado" (Afterward the honored confessor performed miracles / from which he gained great praise, more than he had already gained; / his monastery was richly endowed, whence God is served there, and it is called San Millán).

Book 3 (lines 319 to 489) describes the posthumous miracles of the saint. The Muslim ruler Abderramán forces the Christians to pay the Moors a yearly tribute of a large number of virgins. God signals his displeasure with northern Spain in such a way that many fear that the Last Judgment has come. Count Fernán González of Castile and King Remiro of Leon decide to stop paying the tribute, and the Moors, after a long deliberation that includes consultation with the stars, attack Leon. Remiro proposes that the Christians promise support for St. James in the amount of three small *meajas* (coins) if the saint will aid them; González and the Castilians agree, and the count suggests the same for San Millán: "Frontero es del regno, cuerpo envergonçado, / padrón de espannoles, el apóstol sacado; / onrémoslo, varones, demos li esti dado. / respondiéronli todos: A, Sennor, de mui buen grado" (He is the protector of the kingdom, an honored person, / patron saint of the Spanish, excepting the apostle [St. James]; / let us honor him, sirs, let us give him this gift. / They all answered: "Gladly, my lord"). Aided by the apparitions of St. James and San Millán, the Christians slay Moors left and right; Abderramán sees that all is lost and flees. Both Christian rulers confirm the *votos* (monetary support) they have promised the two saints, and Berceo carefully details who owes what. He ends his tale with the formula *Tu autem, Domine* (But thou, Oh Lord) used by monks to signal the end of a public reading.

Vida de Santo Domingo de Silos is about another saint from La Rioja: Domingo was born in Cañas, near the town of Berceo. Berceo's longest verse narrative, it was at one time also his most popular. The life of the saint is treated in book 1 (stanzas 1 through 288), which includes some of Berceo's most frequently quoted verses: "Quiero fer una prosa en romanz paladino / en qual suele el pueblo fablar con so vezino, / ca non só tan letrado por fer otro latino. / Bien valdrá, como creo, un vaso de bon vino (I would like to write a poem in plain Spanish, / such as the people are accustomed to speak with their neighbors, / for I am not learned enough to do it in Latin. / It will be worth, as I think, a glass of good wine). Like San Millán, Domingo begins as a shepherd boy. The description of his studies provides insight into Berceo's own schooling: Domingo not only reads the Psalter, hymns, Canticles, Gospels, and Epistles but also tries to understand their deeper spiritual sense. He rises rapidly through the four minor orders of porter, acolyte, lector, and exorcist. One had to be literate to go on to become a subdeacon, or reader of the Epistles, and a deacon, or reader of the Gospels, before rising to the rank of *misacantano* (priest), who is sanctioned to "sing" or celebrate the Mass. Domingo

achieves this rank and then becomes a hermit. After a year and a half of desert life, he enters the San Millán monastery as a monk. His superiors test him by giving him the task of returning to his native village of Cañas to repair and reform the Chapel of St. Mary. Domingo begs, works, and enriches the church with books and vestments. He is invited back to San Millán and ultimately becomes its prior. King García of Nájera demands tribute from the monastery, and Domingo makes his famous answer to the monarch's threats: "Puedes matar al cuerpo, la carne maltraer, / mas non has en la alma, reï, ningún poder; / dizlo el evangelio que es bien de creer" (You can kill the body, mistreat the flesh, / but you have over the soul, king, no power; / the gospel tells us this [Matt. 10:28], and it is good to believe it). Forced to leave the kingdom of Nájera, Domingo goes to the kingdom of León, on the other side of the mountain from San Millán. At this point Berceo tells the story of Liciniano, who prays for aid for the Monastery of San Sebastián in Silos, which has fallen into decay, though there are still monks living there. The abbot decides that Domingo should reform and repair the monastery. Domingo has a vision of three crowns earned in heaven by good works on Earth; Berceo inserts the story of the translation of the relics of Vicente, Sabina, and Cristeta to the monastery of San Pedro de Arlanza, revealing the saint's ability to prophesy.

Book 2 (stanzas 289 through 532) is devoted to the miracles Domingo worked during his lifetime, which, according to Berceo, are too many to tell. Following Grimaldus, his source narrative, Berceo puts Domingo's death at the end of book 2. Domingo gives a long parting speech of advice to his charges, and the patriarchs, apostles, martyrs, confessors, and virgins (the *ordo justorum*) and the founder of his monastic order, St. Benedict, are pleased to see the angels take him to heaven. Book 3 (stanzas 533 through 777) is devoted to the miracles that took place after Domingo's death and, Berceo assures the reader, are still taking place. Stanzas 754 through 777 are an epilogue added to arrive at the mystical number 777.

The thirteenth century has been called the Century of Mary because of her dominant place in the literature and religious thought of the period. Berceo contributed several works on Mary, beginning with the *Loores de Nuestra Señora*. (This title is the traditional one; Berceo does not use the expression *Nuestra Señora* for Mary. The Silos manuscript has the title *Laudes a la Virgen Madre*.) After Satan tricked Adam and Eve, he knew that a woman would crush his head (Gen. 2:15); but he did not know when, so he needed to be ever watchful. Berceo lists the patriarchs, the Old Testament precursors of Mary, and mentions what are to become her allegorical names: the Burning Bush (Exod. 3:2), the Rod of Aaron (Num. 17:1–11), the Rod of Jesse with the Seven Gifts of the Holy Ghost (Isa. 11:1–2), the Bridechamber (Ps. 18:6), the Fleece of Gideon (Judg. 6:36–40), the Well-Closed Gate (Ezek. 44:1–3). He then lists the prophets: Jacob, Daniel, Jeremiah, Moses, Zachariah, Isaiah, and, in a common bridge to the New Testament, John the Baptist. He weaves the story of the birth of Christ into his exposition of the sayings of the prophets:

> Nueve meses folgó en el tu sancto seno,
> bien fasta que el tiempo de la pariçon veno;
> quando's plegó la hora e el cuento fue pleno,
> fijo pariste et padre sobre lecho de feno.
>
> (Nine months He rested in your blessed womb
> until the time of birth-giving came;
> when the hour arrived and the time was fulfilled
> you bore Son and Father on a bed of straw.)

Berceo then notes the miracles, found throughout the Middle Ages in nonbiblical legendary accounts, that occurred at Christ's birth.

In an action that is contrary to the usual medieval story, though not unknown in earlier works, Mary performs the circumcision of Jesus. Berceo couples Balaam's prophecy (Num. 24) with the advent of the Wise Men, as was common at the time, and tells of the flight into Egypt, Herod's death by his own hand, the return from Egypt, and the presentation in the temple. Taking advantage of every opportunity to display his learning, Berceo makes use of the *puer senex* topos and says, in keeping with the usual medieval notion, that Christ was baptized not because he needed to be cleansed of original sin but in order to sanctify water. He details the entry into Jerusalem, the Last Supper, the betrayal, and the mystery of bread and wine. His recounting of the story is fairly straightforward, but he cannot resist adding that, as theologians believed in the Middle Ages, Christ was crucified on the day and at the hour that Adam had been deceived. When the Crucifixion takes place, Christ reminds Mary of the prophecy of Simeon that a sword will pierce her heart (Luke 2:35):

> Madre, la su dolor a ti mal quebrantava,
> el gladio del tu Fijo la tu alma passava,
> lo que disso el vieio por verdat se provava:
> tal Madre por tal fijo, ¿qué mira si's quexava?"
>
> (Mother, his pain hurt you badly,
> the sword of your Son passed through your soul,
> what the old man said revealed itself to be true:
> such a Mother for such a Son, what wonder, if she was aggrieved?)

Berceo moves on to the Resurrection: "Resuscitó don Christo–en buena nos levamos!" (Christ arose–we are coming to the good part!), continually interspersing his discourse with praises of Mary. He condemns those who guarded Christ's sepulchre and relates how Herod and others who harmed Christ died, the ten apparitions of Christ after the Resurrection, his first appearance to Mary Magdalene, and his ascension to heaven. Berceo then returns to Mary with a rendition of the Magnificat, Mary's song of praise (Luke 1:46–55). He realizes that he promised to speak of Pentecost but cannot avoid speaking of the virtues of the number 7, giving examples from Scripture. When he speaks of the seven gifts of the Holy Spirit, he is reminded of Pentecost and the apostles, including the four evangelists with their emblematic tetramorphs: Matthew, a man; Luke, an ox; Mark, a lion; and John, an eagle.

Berceo then passes to the Last Judgment, when the apostles will judge humanity; offers a short résumé of the torments of the damned; and moves on to the joys of the blessed. Stanza 196 again pauses to praise Mary and returns to one of his favorite themes: Mary as Star of the Sea. As he says, the epithets he uses for Mary seem inexhaustible, including "Salió quando tu naciste de la spina rosa" (When you were born a rose arose among thorns) and the comparison of Mary to glass:

> En el vidrio podría asmar esta razón,
> como lo pasa el rayo del sol sin lesïón;
> tú así engendréste sin nulla corruptión,
> como si te passasses por una visïón
>
> (By the example of glass one may contemplate this mystery,
> as the ray of the sun passes through it without harm;
> so did you give birth without any corruption,
> just as if you were going through an apparition.)

He ends with a prayer to Mary to intercede with God for him:

> Aun merced te pido por el tu trobador,
> qui est romance fizo, fue tu entendedor,
> seï contra tu fijo por élli rogador,
> recábdali limosna en casa del Criador
>
> (Still I ask you mercy for your troubadour
> he who made this romance was your worshiper,
> be a beseecher for him to your son,
> procure for him alms in the house of the Creator.)

Loores de Nuestra Señora is Berceo's best doctrinal poem, since it contains so much theological instruction–much of it, as he says, hidden.

Coplas 1 through 7 in the manuscript of the Vida de San Millán de la Cogolla *(Monastery of Santo Domingo de Silos, MS. 56, folio 195r)*

Most medieval literatures include "Laments of the Blessed Virgin Mary"; most of these works depend on the *De lamentatione Beatae Virginis Mariae,* which is often attributed to St. Bernard of Clairvaux. Such is the case with Berceo's *Duelo de la Virgen,* a 210-stanza poem on the "mater dolorosa" (dolorous mother). Berceo's familiar use of the Bible and homespun style emerge when he reports that St. Bernard importunes Mary so fervently and so frequently that she feels compelled to give in: "Disso Santa María: Apensemos de tornar, / non quiere esti Monge darnos ningún vagar" (Blessed Mary said: "Let us think of yielding, / this monk is going to give us no rest"). She comes down to Earth and visits St. Bernard so that they may compose "una prossa" (a poem) together. With his prompting, she tells of the day Christ was taken, his torture, the cross, the crown of thorns, the scourging, and the scorning. Each of the acts of Christ on the cross is repeated. On Friday evening Joseph of Arimathea asks for Christ's body; meanwhile, Mary never leaves the cross, embracing it and trying to touch her son. She weeps, and the elements cry with her. Joseph of Arimathea and Nicodemus remove Christ from the cross in verses that could almost be a description of the celebrated sculpture *The Descent from the Cross* in the cloister of the monastery at Silos. Mary goes to stay with John but can neither eat nor sleep, and the others give voice to sorrow all around her. The Jews demand that Pilate place a guard around the tomb, lest the disciples steal Jesus and say that he has arisen. Pilate grants them the right to guard the sepulchre, suggesting that they make up songs against the Christians. They do so, playing instruments and singing offensive songs. The high point of the *Duelo de la Virgen,* the watchman's song *Eya velar* (Oh, keep watch), is one of Berceo's few departures from the *cuaderna vía* stanza: "Eya velar, eya velar, eya velar! / Velat aljama de judios, eya velar, / que non vos furten el *su* dios, eya velar" (Oh, keep watch, oh, keep watch, oh, keep watch! / Keep watch, ghetto of the Jews, oh, keep watch, / lest they steal from you their God, oh, keep watch).

The *Milagros de Nuestra Señora* is Berceo's masterpiece and his most popular work; dozens of modern editions exist. The title is the invention of an influential twentieth-century scholar, Ramón Menéndez Pidal; Berceo never uses *Nuestra Señora,* preferring *la Gloriosa* in all of his compositions. None of the miracle stories is original: twenty-four have well-known Latin antecedents, and the twenty-fifth recounts a Spanish miracle. The prologue alone seems to be Berceo's own work, but even it is a gathering of commonplaces and expressions. It is an extended allegory of the Virgin Mary as the "unplowed field" of Gen. 2:5. Berceo names himself a pilgrim who exem-

plifies humanity: he rests in this field and enjoys the flowers or spiritual beauties of Mary, the songs of the birds, and so forth: "Yo, Maestro Gonçalvo de Verceo nomnado, / yendo en romería, caecí en un prado / verde è bien sencido, de flores bien poblado, / logar cobdiciaduero pora omne cansado (I, Master Gonzalvo de Berceo by name, / going on a pilgrimage, happened upon a meadow, / green and quite unplowed, well populated with flowers, / a pleasant place for weary man). The pilgrimage is a typical opening gambit in medieval literature: life itself is described as a pilgrimage in 1 Pet. 2:11, Heb. 11:13–16, and 2 Cor. 5:6, and in the medieval commentaries on these passages the field unpierced by delving man is a common metaphor for the Virgin Mary. Berceo equates the shade of the trees with Mary's cloak, which protects human beings. The trees are the miracles of Mary, and the birds that sing in them are Church Fathers, such as Augustine and Gregory, and others who sing her praises day and night in the church. The streams that run from each corner of the meadow are the four evangelists. The flowers that increase rather than decrease in number when they are plucked are the epithets applied to the Virgin Mary. Berceo gathers together many of these attributes of Mary from hymns and treatises of the medieval Church and weaves them into a tapestry of praises. Finally, he decides to "climb into the trees" to recount some of her miracles, which are without number: the "milagro de la casulla de San Ildefonso" (miracle of the Chasuble of St. Ildefonsus of Toledo), "el sacristán fornicario" (the fornicating sacristan), "el clérigo y la flor" (the cleric and the flower), "el galardón de la Virgen" (The Reward of the Virgin), "el pobre caritativo" (the charitable poor man), "El ladrón devoto" (the pious thief), "San Pedro y el monje lozano" (St. Peter and the lusty monk), "el romero engañado por el diablo" (the pilgrim deceived by the devil), "el clérigo simple" (the simpleton priest), "los dos hermanos" (the two brothers), "el labrador avaro" (the greedy rustic), "el prior y Uberto el sacristán" (the prior and Hubert the sacristan), "Jerónimo, el nuevo obispo de Pavia" (Jerome, the new bishop of Pavia), "la imagen milagrosamente respetada por el incendio (the image miraculously respected by the fire), "la boda y la Virgen" (the wedding and the Virgin), "el judiezno" (the little Jewish boy), "la iglesia de Santa María profanada" (The profaning of the Church of Holy Mary), "Cristo y los judíos de Toledo" (Christ and the Jews of Toledo), "la preñada salvada por la Virgen" (the pregnant woman saved by the Virgin), "el monje beodo" (the drunken monk), "la abadesa preñada" (the pregnant abbess), "el náufrago salvado por la Virgen" (the shipwrecked traveler saved by the Virgin), "el mercader de Bizancio" (Jew lends to Christian), "el milagro de Teófilo" (the miracle of Theophilus), and "la iglesia robada" (the plundered church).

Berceo also translated at least three Latin hymns, including *Veni Creator Spiritus* (Come Creator Spirit), one of the most famous hymns of the Middle Ages; *Ave maris stella* (Hail, Star of the Sea), sung on almost all feast days of the Virgin Mary; and *Christe qui lux es et dies* (Oh Christ, Who Art Light and Day), the favorite hymn of many national churches. Though short, the hymns are excellent examples of Berceo's mature art.

Only the first twenty-two stanzas *of Los signos del Juicio Final* are devoted to the Fifteen Signs of Doomsday, a set piece extremely common in the literature and art of the Middle Ages. Berceo's work is a fairly close translation of the Latin *Quindecim signa ante judicium* (Fifteen Signs of Doomsday) once attributed to St. Jerome. He tells of the fifteen things that will happen at the end of the world and of the nearness of the last day. Stanzas 23 through 47 are about the torments of the damned, and stanzas 48 through 76 are about the life of the blessed: "Cambiemos la materia, en otro son cantemos" (Let us change the subject, let us sing a different song). The poem ends with a depiction of Judgment Day.

Another of Berceo's "doctrinal" works is *Del sacrificio de la misa,* 297 stanzas that explain the spiritual significance of each part of the Mass and show how the Old Testament prefigures the New "acordarlos en uno, facerlos saludar" (to bring them together as one, make them greet one another). Referring to the birds that were sacrificed in the temple to Christ, he says that "La palomba significa la su simplicidat, / la tórtora es signo de la su castidat (The dove signifies his simplicity, / the turtledove is a sign of his chastity). The goat that was sacrificed signifies Christ's human nature, the scapegoat his divine nature. Allegorical interpretations of the Mass were common in the Middle Ages; scholars cannot be sure which source Berceo used, although all of his explanations can be found in previous works. Berceo is convinced, however, that the Mass will remain a mystery: "la missa es oficio tan complido, que saber no lo puede ningún omne nacido" (the Mass is such a complete [perfect] office that no man born [of woman] can understand it). His effort to explain it has exhausted him: "días ha que lazdramos, queremos ir folgar" (we have been suffering [working hard] for days, we are ready to go rest).

The *Poema de Santa Oria* is a 205-stanza life of a saint and recluse who was buried at San Millán de Suso. She is little known outside of La Rioja, and her Latin life, written by Muño, is lost. The poem is mostly devoted to three of her visions. According to Berceo's own declaration, it is a work of his old age; it is believed to be his next-to-last poem.

El Martirio de San Lorenzo is Berceo's only life of a non-Riojan saint. While the third-century Roman deacon was one of the favorite saints of the Middle Ages, one suspects that he drew Berceo's attention because a peak named after Lorenzo dominated Berceo's birthplace and was the site of an oratory devoted to him. Lorenzo is born in Huesca and trained by a relative, Valerio, with whom he goes on a mission to Rome. Lorenzo stays in Rome to serve Pope Sixtus as a deacon and caretaker of the poor. When Decius becomes emperor in 249, he begins persecuting Christians. He demands that Sixtus sacrifice to idols and give up the Church treasures; Sixtus refuses, and Decius orders him beheaded. Lorenzo begs Sixtus to be allowed to die with him or even take his place, but Sixtus assures Lorenzo that a greater fame is reserved for him. Lorenzo gives all of the treasure of the Church to the poor and assures Sixtus that the treasure is safe and can be recovered at any time. When he is captured by Decius's lieutenant, Valeriano, and ordered to give up the treasure, Lorenzo asks for and is granted a three-day reprieve. At the end of the three days he brings a large number of Christians with him and announces that they are his Church's treasure. Valeriano sees that he has been tricked and demands that Lorenzo either sacrifice to the gods or be tortured to death. Roasted on a gridiron, the saint jauntily asks to be turned so that his other side will be well done. These words are probably the last that Berceo wrote; the composition of the poem may have been interrupted by his death.

Gonzalo de Berceo was never totally forgotten by those interested in medieval Spanish literature, but interest in his work increased when his entire corpus was first edited by Tomás Antonio Sánchez in 1780. Nineteenth-century studies of Berceo were mostly by dilettantes such as Henry Wadsworth Longfellow, who made some of the earliest translations of his works into English, until the Generation of 1898 rediscovered Berceo. They, however, conceived him as a sort of ingenuous primitive, which hindered appreciation of the literary artistry of his works. Although outstanding scholarship was done in the early part of the twentieth century by Antonio García Solalinde and C. Carroll Marden, it remained for the second half of the century to gain a critical understanding of Berceo. In 1963 Erika Lorenz dispelled the notion of Berceo as a naive primitive, and work on the manuscripts began again. Between 1967 and 1981 Brian Dutton produced a new edition of the corpus that includes a commentary and an investigation of Berceo's sources. A journal, *Berceo,* was founded in 1946 to publish studies of his work. New editions of his writings included the admirable *Obra completa* (1992, Complete Works); it was coordinated by Isabel Uría Maqua, who published a Berceo bibliography with Fernando Baños Vallejo in 1997.

Bibliography:

Isabel Uría Maqua and Fernando Baños Vallejo, "Bibliografía de Gonzalo de Berceo," *Boletín bibliográfico de la Asociación Hispánica de Literatura Medieval,* 10 (1997): 269–338.

References:

Joaquín Artiles, *Los recursos literarios de Berceo,* Biblioteca Románica Hispánica, volume 2, Estudios y Ensayos, no. 81 (Madrid: Gredos, 1964);

Mercedes Brea, "El milagro de Teofilo: Texto dramático y texto narrativo," in *Actas del V Congreso de la Asociación Hispánica de Literatura Medieval, Granada, 27 septiembre–1 octubre 1993,* 4 volumes, edited by Juan Paredes (Granada: Universidad de Granada, 1995), I: 415–428;

Thomas M. Capuano, "La correspondencia artistica entre 'De los signos que apareceran . . .' de Berceo y la escultura del siglo XIII," *Hispania,* 71, no. 4 (1988): 738–742;

M. C. Díaz y Díaz, *Libros y librerías en La Rioja altomedieval* (Logroño: I. E. R., 1978);

Marta Ana Diz, *Historias de certidumbre: Los Milagros de Berceo* (Newark, N.J.: Juan de la Cuesta, 1995);

Brian Dutton, "Berceo's Watch-Song 'Eya Velar,'" *Modern Language Notes,* 89, no. 2 (1974): 250–259;

Dutton, *A New Berceo Manuscript: Madrid, Biblioteca Nacional Ms. 13149* (Exeter, U.K.: University of Exeter, 1982);

David A. Flory, *Marian Representations in the Miracle Tales of Thirteenth-Century Spain and France* (Washington, D.C.: Catholic University of America, 2000), pp. 22–46;

Claudio García Turza, ed., *Actas de las III Jornadas de estudios berceanos,* Centro de Estudios Gonzalo de Berceo, volume 6 (Logroño: Instituto de Estudios Riojanos, 1981);

E. Michael Gerli, "Poet and Pilgrim: Discourse, Language, Imagery, and Audience in Berceo's *Milagros de Nuestra Señora,*" in *Hispanic Medieval Studies in Honor of Samuel G. Armistead,* edited by Gerli and Harvey L. Sharrer (Madison, Wis.: Hispanic Seminary of Medieval Studies, 1992), pp. 139–151;

Gerli, "La tipología bíblica y la introducción a los *Milagros de Nuestra Señora,*" *Bulletin of Hispanic Studies,* 62, no. 1 (1985): 7–14;

Francisco Javier Grande Quejigo, *Hagiografía y difusión en "La Vida de san Millán de la Cogolla" de Gonzalo de Berceo,* Centro de Estudios Gonzalo de Berceo, volume 18 (Logroño: Instituto de Estudios Riojanos, 2000);

George D. Greenia, "Berceo, autor del 'Alixandre'?" in *Actas del IX Congreso de la Asociacion Internacional de Hispanistas,* edited by Sebastian Neumeister, Dieter Heckelmann, and Franco Meregalli, 2 volumes (Frankfurt am Main: Vervuert, 1989), I: 215–222;

Patricia E. Grieve, "The Spectacle of Memory/Mary in Gonzalo de Berceo's *Milagros de Nuestra Señora,*" *Modern Language Notes,* 108, no. 2 (1993): 214–229;

Mary Jane Kelley, "Spinning Virgin Yarns: Narrative, Miracles, and Salvation in Gonzalo de Berceo's *Milagros de Nuestra Señora,*" *Hispania,* 74, no. 4 (1991): 814–823;

Rufino Lanchetas, *Gramática y vocabulario de las obras de Gonzalo de Berceo* (Madrid: Rivadeneyra, 1900);

Erika Lorenz, "Berceo, der 'Naive': Über die Einleitung zu den Milagros de Nuestra Señora," *Romanistisches Jahrbuch,* 14 (1963): 255–268;

James W. Marchand, "Berceo the Learned: The *Ordo Prophetarum* in the *Loores de Nuestra Señora,*" *Kentucky Romance Quarterly,* 31 (1984): 291–304;

Marchand, "Gonzalo de Berceo's *De los signos que aparesceran ante del juicio,*" *Hispanic Review,* 45, no. 3 (1977): 283–295;

Marchand and Spurgeon Baldwin, "Singers of the Virgin in Thirteenth-Century Spain," *Bulletin of Hispanic Studies,* 71, no. 2 (1994): 169–184;

Marchand and Baldwin, "Two Notes on Berceo's *Sacrificio de la misa,*" *Modern Language Notes,* 89, no. 2 (1974): 250–259;

C. Carroll Marden, "Cuatro poemas de Berceo," *Anejos de la Revista de Filología Española,* anejo 9 (1928);

Jesús Montoya Martínez, "El alegorismo, premisa necesaria al vocabulario de los *Milagros de Nuestra Señora,*" *Studi Mediolatini e Volgari,* 30 (1984): 167–190;

Montoya Martínez, "El 'milagro literario' en Berceo a la luz de la retorica medieval," *Incipit,* 20–21 (2000–2001): 13–42;

Montoya Martínez, "El prólogo de Gonzalo de Berceo al libro de los *Milagros de Nuestra Señora,* composición numérica," in *La lengua y la literatura en tiempos de Alfonso X,* edited by Fernando Carmona and Francisco J. Flores (Murcia: Universidad de Murcia, 1985), pp. 347–363;

Dana A. Nelson, "El *Libro de Alixandre* y Gonzalo de Berceo: Un problema filológico," *La corónica,* 28, no. 1 (1999): 93–136;

T. Anthony Perry, *Art and Meaning in Berceo's Vida de Santa Oria* (New Haven: Yale University Press, 1968);

Albert Poncelet, *Index miraculorum Beatae Virginis Mariae quae latine sunt conscripta* (Brussels: Société des Bollandistes, 1902);

Rafael Sala, *La lengua y el estilo de Gonzalo de Berceo: introducción al estudio de la vida de Santo Domingo de Silos* (Logroño: Instituto de Estudios Riojanos, 1983);

Joël Saugnieux, *Berceo y las culturas del siglo XIII* (Logroño: Instituto de Estudios Riojanos, 1982);

Joseph T. Snow, "Gonzalo de Berceo and the Miracle of Saint Ildefonso: Portrait of the Medieval Artist at Work," *Hispania*, 65, no. 1 (1982): 1–11;

San Millán de Cogolla en su XV centenario (1473–1973) (Logroño: Editorial Ochoa, 1974);

Olivia C. Suszynski, *The Hagiographic-Thaumaturgic Art of Gonzalo de Berceo: Vida de Santo Domingo de Silos* (Barcelona: Hispam, 1976);

Isabel Uría Maqua, *Panorama crítico del mester de clerecía* (Madrid: Castalia, 2000);

Uría Maqua, "Sobre la transmisión manuscrita de las obras de Berceo," *Incipit*, 1 (1981): 13–23;

J. K. Walsh, "Sanctity and Gender in Berceo's *Santa Oria*," *Medium-Aevum*, 57, no. 2 (1988): 254–263;

Benedicta Ward, *Miracles and the Medieval Mind: Theory, Record, and Event, 1000–1215* (Philadelphia: University of Pennsylvania Press, 1982);

Julian Weiss, "Writing, Sanctity, and Gender in Berceo's *Poema de Santa Oria*," *Hispanic Review*, 64, no. 4 (1996): 447–465.

La gran conquista de Ultramar

(thirteenth century)

Cristina González
University of California, Davis

Manuscripts: The text is extant in four incomplete manuscripts dating from the late thirteenth to the early fifteenth centuries: Biblioteca Nacional, Madrid, MSS. 1187, 1920, and 2454; and Biblioteca Universitaria de Salamanca, MS. 1698.

First edition: *La gran conquista de Ultramar* (Salamanca: Hans Giesser, 1503).

First modern edition: *La gran conquista de Ultramar,* edited by Pascual de Gayangos (Madrid: Biblioteca de Autores Españoles, 1858).

Standard editions: *La gran conquista de Ultramar,* 4 volumes, edited by Louis Cooper (Bogotá: Publicaciones del Instituto Caro y Cuervo, 1979); *Text and Concordances of the Gran Conquista de Ultramar (BNM R-518, R-519),* edited by Ray Harris-Northall (Madison, Wis.: Hispanic Seminary of Medieval Studies, 1994) [microfiches].

Partial editions: *The Texts and Concordances of Biblioteca Nacional Manuscript 1187,* edited by Louis Cooper and Francis M. Waltman (Madison, Wis.: Hispanic Seminary of Medieval Studies, 1985 [microfiches]); *La Gran Conquista de Ultramar: Biblioteca Nacional MS 1187,* edited by Cooper and Waltman (Madison, Wis.: Hispanic Seminary of Medieval Studies, 1989); *La leyenda del Cavallero del Cisne,* edited by María Teresa Echenique (Barcelona: Aceña, 1989).

La gran conquista de Ultramar (The Great Conquest of Lands beyond the Seas), the only Castilian chronicle about the Crusades, is a long work that survives in four manuscripts and one early-sixteenth-century printing. None of the manuscripts is complete; together they cover a little less than three quarters of the story, which appears in complete form in the edition printed in Salamanca in 1503. In addition to several modern editions of the work that transcribe most, but not all, of the manuscripts, there are two editions of the complete work. The first, published in 1858 by Pascual de Gayangos, follows Biblioteca Nacional, MS. 1187, as well as the Salamanca imprint; the second, published in 1979 by Louis Cooper, is based on the 1503 edition alone.

The most studied issue surrounding *La gran conquista de Ultramar* is its authorship. The Salamanca edition attributes the work to King Alfonso X *el sabio* (the Learned), who was born in 1221 and reigned from 1252 to 1284; this attribution was not questioned until Gayangos argued in the prologue to his edition that the work was composed in the fourteenth century. Other critics thought that some of the passages to which Gayangos pointed in support of his dating were later interpolations. Gayangos succeeded, however, in raising doubts about Alfonso X's authorship. Scholars tried to settle the question by attributing *La gran conquista de Ultramar* to Alfonso's son and successor, Sancho IV, who was born in 1258 and reigned from 1284 to 1295. That attribution has not been universally accepted either. Christina González and Fernando Gómez Redondo favor the theory that the chronicle was started by Alfonso X, continued under Sancho IV, and completed at a later date.

The oldest manuscript, Biblioteca Nacional, MS. 1187, attributes the work to Sancho IV. This copy, however, contains only the end of the chronicle and states that it is about the children and grandchildren of the Swan Knight, which would indicate that the adventures of the Swan Knight himself are not included in it. Therefore, the attribution of this part of the narrative to Sancho does not guarantee that he was also the author of the beginning of the work. Indeed, Biblioteca Nacional, MS. 1920, which also attributes the work to Sancho, says that he ordered the scribe to translate the work "from the conquest of Antioch on." This statement could mean that the segment of the chronicle covered by manuscript 1920 was the part executed by this particular scribe, or it could refer to the portion of *La gran conquista de Ultramar* undertaken under Sancho. Since Biblioteca Nacional, MS. 1698, attributes the work to Alfonso X, this attribution was not the invention of the editor of the 1503 edition. Furthermore, Gayangos did not take into account the fact that various scribes often composed medieval chronicles over long periods of time at the behest of various kings. The attributions to Alfonso and Sancho in the various texts of *La gran conquista de Ultramar,* and the passages that appear to be of a later date, are thus not necessarily contradictory.

In addition to having a passion for commissioning chronicles, Alfonso was obsessed with the Holy Land. His letters and wills, as well as the autobiographical poems in the *Cantigas de Santa Maria* (translated as *Songs of Holy Mary of Alfonso X, the Wise,* 2000) reveal that he dreamed of following in the steps of Louis IX of France by leading a Crusade. His temporary capture of the city of Salé on the North African coast during the first years of his reign shows his early interest in launching Crusading efforts from Spanish shores. This commitment seems to have increased in the last years of his life, when he disowned his second-born son, Sancho, in favor of the descendants of his deceased elder son, Fernando, who were Louis IX's grandchildren on their mother's side. This act expressed his hope that the French and Spanish would unite and defeat the Moors on all fronts.

If Alfonso had reasons to commission a chronicle about the Crusades, Sancho had motives for continuing it. Although the works that Sancho is known to have commissioned were quite different from those supported by his father–they included no chronicles–he did continue to support his father's team of historical writers. During Sancho's reign Pope Nicholas IV called for a new Crusade in light of recent disasters in the Holy Land, and there was a gathering of nobles in Valladolid in 1292 to discuss the matter. As the situation was unfolding, Sancho significantly advanced the Spanish Reconquest by taking Tarifa, which is in the southernmost part of the Iberian Peninsula–the area closest to North Africa. Sancho refers to both enterprises in his best-known work, the *Castigos y documentos* (Chastisements and Documents), in which he specifically mentions the siege of Antioch. It would, therefore, make sense for him to have ordered the continuation of *La gran conquista de Ultramar* from that point onward.

It is not known which historians were assigned the writing of *La gran conquista de Ultramar.* Evelyn S. Procter notes that in the 1260s and 1270s, when Alfonso X was seeking the crown of the Holy Roman Empire, many learned men from northern Italy went to work for him as scribes and notaries. Employed by the imperial chancellery, which was independent from the royal scriptorium and presumably less busy, these scholars wrote extensive literary works, as well as legal documents, in French, Latin, and Castilian. For example, Bonaventura de Siena wrote the *Livre de l'eschiele*

Mahomet (Book of the Ladder of Muhammad) and some documents related to the negotiations between Alfonso and Louis IX regarding the marriage of their children Fernando and Blanche. Egidio Tebaldi de Parma composed a Latin version of the *Quatripartitum* (Four-Part Treatise) and legal instruments pertaining to negotiations between Alfonso and Louis's heir, Philip III, with respect to Fernando and Blanche's children. Other Italian scholars in Alfonso's employ during those years include Rufino de Parma, Pietro de Regio, Johan de Messina, and Johan de Cremona. According to Procter, when Alfonso renounced his candidacy to the Holy Roman throne in 1275, the assignments given the royal scriptorium changed; but some of its Italian scholars continued to work for him, and there is evidence that Egidio Tebaldi de Parma, Pietro de Regio, and Johan de Cremona were still in Castile in the 1280s. In addition to their main duties, they dealt with the political and cultural exchanges between Castile and France. They had personal reasons to be interested in the Crusades, since the cities of northern Italy, which desired control over North African shipping routes, had participated in Louis IX's expeditions and supported Alfonso's candidacy to be Holy Roman Emperor in the hope that Castilian military assistance would help them wrest control of the sea-lanes from Morocco. After the death of Alfonso, Sancho employed several of these Italian scholars. De Cremona, for example, was still in Castile in the 1290s and continued to work on royal projects. José Amador de los Ríos believes that he and Johan de Chipre, who was also employed by Sancho, were involved in the composition of the work.

La gran conquista de Ultramar is a translation of several French works from the twelfth and thirteenth centuries. They include the chronicle *Eracles* (Heraclitus) and the courtly epic poems *Chanson du Chevalier au Cygne* (Song of the Swan Knight), *Chanson de Godefroi de Bouillon* (Song of Godfrey of Bouillon), *Chanson des Chétifs* (Song of the Stunted Ones), *Chanson d'Antioche* (Song of Antioch), *Chanson de Jerusalem* (Song of Jerusalem), *Berte aus grans pies* (Bertha of the Big Feet), and *Mainet* (The Youthful Exploits of Charlemagne). Critics have been at odds about the true genre of the work: some consider it fiction, others history, and most a hybrid of the two. As a result, the various episodes have been studied independently, and the overall structure was not analyzed until González and Gómez Redondo did so in the 1990s. The best-known part of the work is the Swan Knight episode, which has traditionally been considered a chivalric romance novel inserted into a chronicle. When *La gran conquista de Ultramar* is approached as a unified whole, however, the links between the Swan Knight episode and the rest of the chronicle become clearer: the Swan Knight is a chivalric archetype whose

Opening of the manuscript of La gran conquista de Ultramar *(Biblioteca Nacional, Madrid, MS. 1920, folio 1r)*

life is faithfully followed by his grandson, Godfrey of Bouillon. In *La gran conquista de Ultramar* the successes and failures of the Christians in the Holy Land depend on whether they follow or deviate from the model offered by the Swan Knight and Godfrey. The work as a whole is, therefore, a chivalric chronicle. Its narrative logic is reproduced in the *Amadís de Gaula* (Amadís of Gaul) and other chivalric romances of the Golden Age, long accounts of the ups and downs of courtly knights involved in Crusade-like adventures in distant lands.

The prologue of *La gran conquista de Ultramar* affirms that God gave human beings intelligence and the five senses for the purpose of obtaining knowledge; hearing is the sense most closely associated with intelligence and most necessary to acquiring knowledge; and people must cultivate the sense of hearing by listening to tales of the good deeds of their ancestors:

> Por ende, nos, don Alfonso, rey de Castilla, de Toledo, de León e del Andaluzíam mandamos trasladar la ystoriade todo el fecho de Ultramar, de como passó, según oýmos leer en los libros antiguos, desque se levantó Mahoma hasta que el rey Luys de Franci, hijo del rey Luys e de la reina doña Blanca, e nieto del rey don Alfonso de Castilla, pasó a Ultramar e puñó en servir a Dios lo más que él pudo.

> (Therefore, I, don Alfonso, King of Castile, of Toledo, of León and of Andalusia, ordered the translation of the history of all the overseas exploits, of how they happened, as I heard them read from old books, from Muhammad's rise until King Louis [IX] of France, son of King Louis [VIII] and of Queen doña Blanca [Blanche of Castile], and grandson of King don Alfonso [VIII] of Castile, went overseas and tried to serve God as much as he could.)

Unlike the *Estoria de España* (History of Spain) and the *General estoria* (General History), chronicles commissioned by Alfonso X that cover long periods and the actions of good and bad people, *La gran conquista de Ultramar* deals with the limited time span of the Crusades and features the deeds of the valiant and pure among the Christian forces rather than those of their morally unworthy allies. The emphasis on hearing in the prologue suggests that it is a more emotional, and perhaps proselytizing, enterprise than the two chronicles, which emphasize the importance of sight and are more intellectual in nature. Leonardo Funes points out that Alfonso's chronicles are rationalistic works that explain events as produced by causes other than divine providence. Thus, the *Estoria de España* and the *General estoria* prompt readers to reflection, while the goal of *La gran conquista de Ultramar* is action: to incite Spanish Christians to fight the Moors by establishing that all Muslims are evil. The first chapter of the work states

that Muhammad took all the vices, called them virtues, and gave them to his people as laws. By explicitly stating that the adherents of Islam are willfully perverse, the narrative implicitly establishes that their Christian rivals are good.

The prologue and chapters 1 through 29 of book 1 of *La gran conquista de Ultramar* survey the bad Christian kings and good Muslim leaders who rule immediately before the Crusades and tell how relationships between Christians and Moors deteriorate until Peter the Hermit incites the Pope to call for a Crusade. For fighting the Moors, the Christians' sins will be forgiven. The noblemen who are going overseas are enumerated; among them is Godfrey of Bouillon, grandson of the Swan Knight. The chronicle announces that the adventures of both heroes will be narrated later. Chapters 30 through 46 then deal with the experiences of four undisciplined groups of poor knights, peasants, and wanderers who go on the Crusade before the great noblemen. As they traverse Europe, ostensibly on their way to the Holy Land, they start killing their fellow believers. The contradiction between the ideals of the Crusade and its historical failures is explained by saying that not all Crusaders are righteous; God indicates who is good and who is bad through miracles such as delaying the death of a just man and accelerating the death of a wicked one. Noblemen are presented as having more rectitude and self-control than the general populace. The lack of leadership among the first wave of Crusaders, which included few noblemen and none of great stature, is emphasized.

The adventures of the Swan Knight are introduced in chapter 47. If they had been related when they were first mentioned, in chapter 29, they would have seemed oddly out of place; but the disasters narrated in chapters 30 through 46 have made it clear that the Crusading enterprise is extremely complex and difficult and requires extraordinarily strong leadership. The exploits of the Swan Knight now appear as a necessary introduction to the exemplary adventures of Godfrey of Bouillon, the knight who is called to restore virtue to the Christians and bring destruction to Muslims and thereby repair the chaos into which the world has fallen.

The story of the Swan Knight is told in chapters 47 through 138 of book 1 and is divided into three parts, each of which follows the pattern of a specific type of folktale. The first part is an "accused wife" tale. The Oriental king Popleo and his wife, Gisanca, plan to marry their daughter, Isonberta, against her will. She escapes in a boat to the land of Count Eustacio, and they wed against his mother's wishes. While Eustacio is away at war, Isonberta gives birth to seven children. Her mother-in-law alters Isonberta's letter to Eustacio

Title page for the only complete extant medieval version of the poem, printed by Hans Giesser in Salamanca in 1503
(Biblioteca Nacional, Madrid)

to say that Isonberta has seven puppies. Eustacio writes and asks that they be cared for until he returns, but his mother changes his letter to instruct that Isonberta and her children be killed. The man who is given the assignment does not carry it out, and the children turn into swans. Eventually, all but the youngest recover their human shape. When Isonberta is brought to trial years later, her oldest son, who is always accompanied by his swan sibling and is, therefore, called the Swan Knight, fights for her freedom and wins. Since the Swan Knight's mother came from the Orient, he is a bridge between East and West. This fact gives his descendant, Godfrey of Bouillon, the right to rule in Jerusalem.

In the second part of the Swan Knight's story, which takes the form of the traditional "dragon-slayer" tale although no dragon is present, Duke Bartolot of Bouillon dies, and Rayner de Saxoña tries to take his land away. The duke's widow, Cathalina, and his daughter, Beatriz, complain to the emperor but cannot find a knight who will fight for them until the Swan Knight arrives. The struggle is long and bloody; realizing that he is losing, Rayner invokes the devil and promises to become a Muslim. The Swan Knight kills him, cuts off his head, marries Beatriz, and becomes the new duke of Bouillon.

In the third part, based on the "animal spouse" tale, the Swan Knight tells Beatriz that she must not ask his name and place of birth if she does not want to lose him. They have a daughter, Ida. All is well until, at the end of seven years, Beatriz feels compelled to ask the forbidden question. The Swan Knight leaves, never to be seen again. He leaves behind the archetype of the chivalric hero the Christians need to conquer Jerusalem.

The adventures of Godfrey of Bouillon take up chapters 139 through 231 of book 1, all 244 chapters of book 2, and the first 113 chapters of book 3. They are also divided into three parts. The first is about Godfrey's birth and early adventures. In reality, he was probably the second son of Eustacio of Boloña and Ida of Bouillon, but *La gran conquista de Ultramar* presents him as their first son; in folklore the hero is either the oldest son or the youngest son, and Godfrey's model, the Swan Knight, was the eldest. The most meaningful episode in Godfrey of Bouillon's early adventures is a dragon-slayer-type tale. A maiden's cousin invades her land; she complains to the emperor, and Godfrey goes to fight for her. His duel with the maiden's cousin is modeled after the Swan Knight's struggle with Rayner. Unlike his grandfather, however, Godfrey shows extraordinary chastity and does not accept the lady's offer of herself and her land.

The second part of Godfrey's adventures concerns his trip from Bouillon to Jerusalem. Although historically other leaders were more important, the chronicle presents Godfrey as equal to them in rank and as their moral superior. On the death of the bishop of Puy, Godfrey becomes the spiritual leader of the expedition. The narrative pays a great deal of attention to minor characters who exemplify some of the virtues that Godfrey exhibits, including Folquer Uver of Chartres, a humble Crusader who kills Sultan Aliadan of Persia. To explain this deed, the chronicle says that Uver is a descendant of the tutor of Carlos Maynete (Charlemagne). The adventures of Carlos Maynete, which are a combination of three tales, including a dragon-slayer tale, are inserted at this point. Because of their illustrious ancestors, Godfrey and Uver succeed where more-distinguished knights fail.

In the third part of the tale Godfrey's candle miraculously ignites at the meeting where the leaders of the Crusade are to determine the next king of Jerusalem, and he is elected. Instead of accepting a crown and scepter from the noblemen, he puts on a crown of thorns and takes a staff from the leader of the people. This action represents the conquest not only of the Moors by the Christians but also of the Christians' own sinful passions, and it constitutes the climax of *La gran conquista de Ultramar*. After Godfrey's untimely death from an illness, the chronicle remarks that his virtues, including his chastity, were unparalleled, and that whatever follows will be necessarily anticlimactic.

From chapter 94 of book 3 to chapter 110 of book 4 the kingdom is inherited by a series of kings, all members of Godfrey's family, who end up losing Jerusalem. Godfrey was young, healthy, and in control of his passions. His younger brother, Baldovin I, is not chaste, and neither are Baldovin III and Amaric. Baldovin II and Uver are too old; Baldovin V is too young; and Baldovin IV has leprosy, considered a venereal disease

in the Middle Ages, which was believed to have been caused by his ancestors' lust. *La gran conquista de Ultramar* thus builds on the historical facts that Godfrey was single and Baldovin IV was a leper to create a dialectical relationship between chastity and lust that explains the failure of the family to safeguard Jerusalem. In addition, Godfrey's successors lack leadership ability: they cannot keep the Christian forces united and even create new dissensions among the Crusaders. The family's decadence coincides with the rise of Saladin, the Islamic prince who takes Jerusalem away from the Christians. *La gran conquista de Ultramar,* therefore, explains the loss of Jerusalem by the decay of the Swan Knight's lineage.

After the fall of Jerusalem to Saladin, *La gran conquista de Ultramar* loses its linear structure and becomes increasingly diffuse. Chapters 117 through 377 of book 4 of the chronicle, instead of following the lives of the kings, narrate various events interlaced with their lives. Eventually, it abandons even that narrative structure in favor of a focus on the major events of the succeeding years, in the fashion of the annals. The writers were obviously in a hurry to get from the past to the present, as was to be expected in a work whose goal was to incite its readers to continue the Crusades.

Toward the end of *La gran conquista de Ultramar* there is an allusion to Alfonso X's victory over the Moors, which connects the Crusade to the Holy Land to the Spanish Reconquest:

> Esta es la ystoria de todo lo que hasta este tiempo passó entre los cristianos e moros en la tierra de Ultramar e hechos otros. E en aquel año mismo de la encarnación del Señor, de mil e dozientos e sesenta e quatro, desbarató el rey de Castilla al rey de Granada, entre Córdoba e Sevilla, e muriorn quatro mil moros de cavallo, e de pie gran gente en demasía.

> (This is the story of all the things that happened overseas between Christians and Muslims until the present time, and other events. And in that same year of the Incarnation of our Lord of 1264, the King of Castile defeated the King of Granada between Cordova and Seville, and four thousand Moors on horse and an exceedingly high number of people on foot died.)

The narrative ends in 1271, after Louis IX's expeditions to North Africa.

Alfonso X could have had *La gran conquista de Ultramar* begun at any time after 1271 but most likely did so after receiving a letter from Pope Nicholas III in 1280 asking him to reconcile with Philip III of France and start a new Crusade. To impress Alfonso with the seriousness of the situation, the Pope had his letter carried by a Templar knight who had just arrived from the Holy Land. But the Pope was not successful; Louis IX was the last Crusader king. The Pope did, however, spark enough of the Crusading spirit in Alfonso X and in his son, Sancho IV, to inspire them to carry out the massive work of composing this chronicle, which became the swan song of the Crusades and the first stage in the development of chivalric literature in the Iberian Peninsula.

References:

José Amador de los Ríos, *Historia crítica de la literatura española,* volume 4 (Madrid: José Fernández Cancela, 1863), pp. 23–29;

Antonio Ballesteros Beretta, *Alfonso X el Sabio,* edited by José Manuel Pérez-Prendes (Barcelona: Salvat / Madrid: Consejo Superior de Investigaciones Científicas / Murcia: Academia Alfonso X el Sabio, 1963);

Suzanne Duparc-Quioc, "*La Chanson de Jérusalem* et *La gran conquista de Ultramar,*" *Romania,* 56 (1940–1941): 32–48;

Leonardo Funes, *El modelo historiográfico alfonsí: Una caracterización* (London: Papers of the Medieval Hispanic Research Seminar, Queen Mary and Westfield College, 1997);

Fernando Gómez Redondo, *Historia de la prosa medieval castellana,* volume 1: *La creación del discurso prosístico: El entramado cortesano* (Madrid: Cátedra, 1998), pp. 1029–1092;

Cristina González, "Alfonso X el Sabio y *La Gran Conquista de Ultramar,*" *Hispanic Review,* 54 (1986): 67–82;

González, *La tercera crónica de Alfonso X: "La gran conquista de Ultramar"* (London: Tamesis, 1992);

John E. Keller, "Some Observations on Realism in the *Gran conquista de Ultramar:* Episode of *El Caballero del cisne,*" *Ariel,* 2 (1973): 17–20;

Richard P. Kinkade, "Sancho IV: Puente literario entre Alfonso el Sabio y Juan Manuel," *PMLA,* 87, no. 5 (1972): 1039–1051;

George T. Northup, "*La gran conquista de Ultramar* and Its Problems," *Hispanic Review,* 2 (1934): 287–302;

Evelyn S. Procter, *Alfonso X of Castile, Patron of Literature and Learning* (Oxford: Clarendon Press, 1951);

Agapito Rey, "Las leyendas del ciclo carolingio en la *Gran conquista de Ultramar,*" *Romance Philology,* 3 (1949–1950): 172–181;

Francisco Rico, *Alfonso el sabio y la "General estoria"* (Barcelona: Ariel, 1984);

Christine R. Stresau, "*La gran conquista de Ultramar:* Its Sources and Composition," dissertation, University of North Carolina, 1977.

Rodrigo Jiménez de Rada
(after 1170 – 10 June 1247)

Lucy K. Pick
University of Chicago

WORKS: *Breviarium historiae catholicae* (before 1214)

Manuscripts: The work is preserved in two medieval manuscripts: Real Biblioteca del Monasterio de El Escorial, MS. X.I.10, which represents an early redaction of the work by the author, and Biblioteca Universitaria, Madrid, MS. 138, containing his final version. The eighteenth-century Biblioteca Provincial de Toledo, MS. 54–57 also transmits the finished version.

Standard edition: *Breviarium historiae catholicae,* edited by Juan Fernández Valverde, Corpus Christianorum Continuatio mediaevalis Volume 72A–B (Turnhout: Brepols, 1992).

Dialogus libri vitae (1214)

Manuscript: The work is preserved in one manuscript from the beginning of the fifteenth century: Biblioteca Universitaria Salamanca, MS. 2089.

Standard edition: *Dialogus libri vitae,* edited by Juan Fernández Valverde and Juan Antonio Estévez Sola, Corpus Christianorum Continuatio mediaevalis, Volume 72C (Turnhout: Brepols, 1999).

Two letters to Diego García (1218)

Manuscript: The letters respond to the dedication by Diego García of his *Planeta* to the archbishop and are found with the *Planeta* in Biblioteca Nacional, Madrid, MS. 10108 (Vitr. 5–8).

Standard edition: "Apendice," in *Dialogus libri vitae,* edited by Juan Fernández Valverde, Corpus Christianorum Continuatio mediaevalis, Volume 72C (Turnhout: Brepols, 1999), pp. 429–433.

Historia de rebus Hispaniae sive Historia Gothica (31 March 1243)

Manuscripts: The work is preserved in thirty-one manuscripts, including Real Biblioteca del Monasterio de El Escorial, MS. Ç.IV.12, Biblioteca Universitaria de Madrid, MS. 143, and Biblioteca Pública de Córdoba, MS. 131.

Early editions: *Rerum in Hispania Gestarum Chronicon,* edited by Sancho de Nebrija (Granada, 1545);

De rebus Hispaniae in *Hispaniae Illustratae,* volume 2, edited by Andreas Schott (Frankfurt am Main, 1603); *De rebus Hispaniae,* edited by Cardinal F. de Lorenzana, in *Sanctorum Patrum Toletanorum Opera,* volume 3 (Madrid, 1793), republished by María Desamparados Cabanes Pecourt in *Roderici Toletani Antistitis Opera* (Valencia: Anubar, 1968); *Crónica,* edited by Agustín Ubieto Arteta (Valencia: Anúbar, 1971).

Standard edition: *Historia de rebus Hispaniae sive Historia Gothica,* edited by Juan Fernández Valverde, Corpus Christianorum Continuatio mediaevalis, Volume 72 (Turnhout: Brepols, 1987).

Edition in Spanish: *Historia de los hechos de España,* edited by Juan Fernández Valverde (Madrid: Alianza, 1989).

Historia Romanorum; Historia Hunnorum, Vandalorum et Suevorum, Alanorum et Silingorum; Historia Ostrogothorum (31 March 1243)

Manuscripts: These three short histories circulated in many of the codices that contain the *Historia de rebus Hispaniae sive Historia Gothica,* including Real Biblioteca del Monasterio de El Escorial, MS. Ç.IV.12; Biblioteca Universitaria de Madrid, MS. 143; and Biblioteca Pública de Córdoba, MS. 131.

Early editions: *Rerum in Hispania Gestarum Chronicon,* edited by Sancho de Nebrija (Granada, 1545); *De rebus Hispaniae,* in *Hispaniae Illustratae,* volume 2, edited by Andreas Schott (Frankfurt am Main, 1603); *De rebus Hispaniae,* edited by Cardinal F. de Lorenzana, in *Sanctorum Patrum Toletanorum Opera,* volume 3 (Madrid, 1793).

Standard edition: *Historia Romanorum; Historia Hunnorum, Vandalorum et Suevorum, Alanorum at Silingorum; Historia Ostrogothorum,* edited by Juan Fernández Valverde, Corpus Christianorum Continuatio mediaevalis, volume 72C (Turnhout: Brepols, 1999).

Historia Arabum (1245)

Manuscripts: This work circulated with the *Historia de rebus Hispaniae sive Historia Gothica* and in several independent manuscripts, including Catedral de Segorbe, MS. G.1, and Biblioteca Capitular de Toledo, MS. 27–26.

Early editions: *Historia Arabum,* in *Hispaniae Illustratae,* volume 2, edited by Andreas Schott (Frankfurt am Main, 1603); *Historia Arabum,* edited by Cardinal F. de Lorenzana, in *Sanctorum Patrum Toletanorum Opera,* volume 3 (Madrid, 1793); *Historia Arabum,* edited by Thomas Erpenius and Iacobus Golius (Leiden, 1625).

Standard editions: *Historia Arabum,* edited by J. Lozano Sánchez (Seville: Secretariado de Publicaciones de la Universidad de Sevilla, 1974); *Historia Arabum,* edited by Juan Fernández Valverde, Corpus Christianorum Continuatio mediaevalis, volume 72C (Turnhout: Brepols, 1999).

Prayer (1209–1247)

Manuscript: Biblioteca Capitular de Toledo, MS. 37–27.

Standard edition: José Janini and Ramón Gonzálvez, *Manuscritos litúrgicos de la catedral de Toledo* (Toledo: Diputación Provincial, 1977), pp. 294–296.

Archbishop of Toledo from 1209 to 1247, Rodrigo Jiménez de Rada was a leading adviser to King Fernando III of Castile and León and a staunch defender of his own ecclesiastical privileges. He is best known for his role in the crucial Christian victory over the Almohad Muslim dynasty at the battle of Las Navas de Tolosa in 1212 and for writing several works of history that trace the emergence of the kingdoms of Spain from the Roman, Visigothic, and Arabic past to his own day. His most visible monument is the Cathedral of Toledo, whose construction he initiated to replace the mosque the Christians had been using since their capture of the city from the Muslims in 1085. Throughout his career as archbishop he pressed the papacy to recognize the primacy of his see in Spain, and he sought control over bishoprics newly released from Muslim control.

Few facts about Jiménez de Rada's life are certain before his nomination as archbishop. Biographers have favored a date of birth sometime after 1170. He was nominated bishop of Osma no earlier than 1207; he never actually occupied the post, but under canon law he could not have received this appointment before the age of thirty. Jiménez de Rada's father was the Navarrese noble Jimeno Pérez de Rada; his mother was Eva de Hinojosa, a member of a noble Castilian family with lands near the border with Navarre. Her brother Mar-

tín de Hinojosa was abbot of Santa María de Huerta and a likely early influence on Jiménez de Rada.

Jiménez de Rada studied in Paris, where he drafted a will in 1201 in which he asked to be buried at Huerta. When he returned to Spain is not known, although it has been surmised that he joined the court of Alfonso VIII of Castile on his arrival. After his nomination to head the diocese of Osma, he was transferred to the archbishopric of Toledo; he arrived there in early 1209 or possibly in December 1208. He held the position until he drowned in the Rhône on 10 June 1247 on the way back from a visit to Pope Innocent IV in Lyons.

The first of Jiménez de Rada's known works to be completed was the *Breviarium historiae catholicae* (Breviary of Catholic History), which traces sacred history from the Creation to the dispersal of the Apostles to preach to the Gentiles; it is interspersed with fragments of secular history. The *Historia scholastica* (Scholatic History), probably composed before 1214, of Peter Comestor provided the *Breviarium historiae catholicae* with its internal structure and much of its content. Jiménez de Rada supplemented the *Historia scholastica* with substantial gleanings from the *Glossa ordinaria,* the standard medieval biblical commentary. He intended the *Breviarium historiae catholicae* to introduce to the Iberian Peninsula the kind of theological discourse that was in vogue in Paris during his student days, especially in the field of biblical exegesis. Juan Fernández Valverde suggests that the work may have been compiled for the fledgling university at Palencia.

Jiménez de Rada departs from his model in two important respects. The first is the account of the relationship between God and Creation and the unfolding of the work of the first six days at the beginning of the *Breviarium historiae catholicae.* Jiménez de Rada describes the moment of creation in Neoplatonic terms:

> Per uerbum quod erat in principio fecit ut essent omnia quantum ad mundum archetipum . . . id est, per uerbum quod est Sapiencia procedens ex ore Altissimi disposuit et ornauit omnia iuxta illud: Sapiencia disponit omnia suauiter suauitate mirifica Creatoris.

> (Through the Word which was in the beginning He caused all things to be according to the World-archetype . . . that is, through the Word, which is Wisdom proceeding from the mouth of the Almighty, He arranged and furnished the world according to it: Wisdom arranged all things sweetly with the wonderful sweetness of the Creator.)

This use of Neoplatonic vocabulary contradicts Comestor's employment of the Creation story to attack Platonism and reveals a Neoplatonic intellectual influence from Jiménez de Rada's student days in Paris.

The second major modification of his model is that Jiménez de Rada concludes the *Breviarium historiae catholicae* not at the end of the Gospels, as Comestor does, nor at the end of Acts of the Apostles, like Peter of Poitiers's continuation of the *Historia scholastica,* but in the middle of Acts, where Paul and Barnabas announce that they will turn their attention to the Gentiles, since the Jews have repulsed the Christian message. Jiménez de Rada also uses this verse in his prologue to cap his outline of the contents of the book and thus shift the spotlight of history from the Jews to the Gentiles. The focus on Gentile history in his later works thus continues the story where it leaves off at the end of the *Breviarium historiae catholicae.*

The *Dialogus libri vitae* (Dialogue of Life), an anti-Jewish polemic, has only recently been added to Jiménez de Rada's canon. Despite its title, the work is not the debate between a Jew and a Christian that was a common format in polemical texts of the period. Instead, Jiménez de Rada anticipates and presents Jewish objections in his own words, addressing his imagined Jewish interlocutor in the second person as if he is speaking to a specific individual. The structure of the work is thus as close to a typical theological compendium of Christian doctrine as it is to a typical anti-Jewish treatise.

The *Dialogus libri vitae* is made up of a prologue, in which Jiménez de Rada outlines his methodology and approach, followed by eight "books" or chapters. He opens the prologue by blaming human *varietas* (inconstancy or changeableness) for causing people to depart from God's plan and for influencing them to worship idols. God, as he had promised Abraham, gave his Law through Moses to the descendants of Israel. The true fulfillment of God's promise to Abraham was not the letter of the Law but was hidden inside that letter: that is, God concealed the New Testament inside the Old. Jiménez de Rada chides his Jewish adversary for misreading the Bible: Jews not only do not understand the full meaning of Scripture; they have deliberately prevented others from penetrating it by constructing fables to explain difficult prophecies. Their "changeableness" is deliberate and blameworthy. But Jiménez de Rada also condemns Christians who strive after temporal things when they could be seeking the truth by studying the Bible. These are the people, he says, for whom he is writing his work. Absent from the prologue is any statement concerning conversion of the Jews or efforts to proselytize them.

Jiménez de Rada's polemic is constructed around the question of which religion interprets the Bible correctly. In book 1 he discusses the existence of God and the Trinity, using many concepts of twelfth-century French theology. In book 2 he addresses the Incarna-

tion, interpreting a series of Old Testament prophecies to show that they predict the events of Christ's life. His interpretations are commonplaces found in sources such as the *Glossa ordinaria*. In book 3 he considers the invalidation of Jewish law, the mission of the Apostles, and the transfer of the covenant to the Gentiles. In book 4 he describes the triumph of the Church and the discrediting of the Jews. These books reflect the standard topics and ordering of anti-Jewish treatises and of theological summae and rely on traditional Christian biblical exegesis to argue that Jews only understand the Old Testament "carnally"–that is, literally–while Christians, who appreciate its full spiritual meaning, read it allegorically to find the foreshadowing of the New Testament in its stories and themes. Book 5 is the linchpin of the treatise: here Jiménez de Rada accuses the Jews of misrepresenting even the literal sense of the Bible and of disagreeing among themselves about what they read. He points out what he regards as inconsistencies in their interpretation of passages regarding the coming of the Messiah, the Messianic Age, the general resurrection, and the world to come. The final three books deal with topics that are unusual for an anti-Jewish text: book 6 finds evidence for the Sacraments in the Old Testament; book 7 describes the actions of the Antichrist; and book 8 deals with the general resurrection and the Last Judgment.

Jiménez de Rada did not complete the secular histories for which he is best known until several decades after he finished his two works of sacred history, the *Breviarium historiae catholicae* and the *Dialogus libri vitae;* but the same preoccupation with philosophical unity and its fragmentation suffuses these later works. Moreover, he announced his plans to write his last completed work, the *Historia Arabum* (History of the Arabs), in his first, the *Breviarium historiae catholicae*. According to their modern editor, Fernández Valverde, the common thread of the secular histories is that they recount the invasions of Spain from the first, by Hercules, to what Jiménez de Rada hoped would be the last, by the Arabs. The first work in the series to be completed was the *Historia de rebus Hispaniae sive Historia Gothica* (History of the Affairs of Spain or History of the Goths). The Goths of the title are the Visigoths, who began as heretical Arian invaders but ended up as the orthodox Catholic unifiers of Spain. He then completed the *Historia Romanorum* (History of the Romans); the *Historia Hunnorum, Vandalorum et Suevorum, Alanorum et Silingorum* (History of the Huns, Vandals and Sueves, Alans and Silingues), on the failed barbarian invasions of Spain; and the *Historia Ostrogothorum* (History of the Ostrogoths), which ends with the Ostrogoths scattered and partly absorbed into the Visigoths. All of these books were finished by 31 March 1243. The series ends

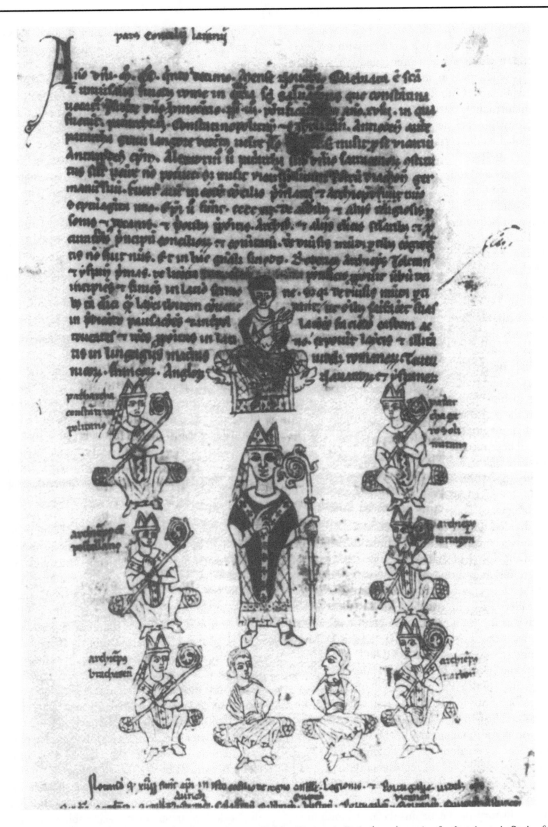

Page from a cartulary of the Toledo Cathedral. The illustration shows Rodrigo Jiménez de Rada (center) arguing for the primacy in Spain of the See of Toledo at the Fourth Lateran Council in 1215, surrounded by Pope Innocent III on his throne; the patriarchs of Constantinople and Jerusalem; the archbishops of Compostela, Tarragona, Braga, and Narbonne; and two clerks (Biblioteca Nacional, Madrid, MS. Vitr. 15-5, folio 22r).

with the long-promised *Historia Arabum,* which was completed in 1245. In addition to a concern with invaders of Spain, these works share a preoccupation with the origins of peoples and an interest in the triumph of Christian truth and Catholic orthodoxy through the creation, maintenance, fracture, and recovery of Christian hegemony. Jiménez de Rada's perspective is encyclopedic, global, and integrative.

Jiménez de Rada's best-known work, both during the Middle Ages and today, is his history of Spain from Noah to his own time: the *Historia de rebus Hispaniae sive Historia Gothica.* The first redaction of this masterwork was completed before the death of King Alfonso IX of León in 1229 and the second and final redaction in 1243, during the reign of Fernando III. The popularity of the work is demonstrated by the many manuscripts of it, as well as medieval translations and abridgments into Castilian, Leonese, and Catalan and several early print editions. In the thirteenth century it was an important source for the compilers of Alfonso X's *Estoria de España* (History of Spain).

Jiménez de Rada's approach both to history and to theology centers around the idea of divine unity. According to him, political and religious division and disunity in the world are an inevitable consequence of the Fall of humanity and reflect the human distance from God. These themes are explored in the *Historia de rebus Hispaniae sive Historia Gothica.* Jiménez de Rada begins with the world united under Noah after the Flood: everyone lived by the same customs and spoke the same language. This unity proved short-lived: the land was divided among Noah's sons, and God splintered the universal language as punishment for the construction of the Tower of Babel. Hatreds arose between linguistic groups, and war arose. Spain is at its most unified, and therefore closest to God, when it is under the spiritual leadership of Toledo. Toledo first appears in the narrative as the triumphant *urbs regia* (royal city) of the Visigoths. According to Jiménez de Rada, the Muslims did not so much conquer it as find it bereft of inhabitants and repopulate it with Arabs and Jews. Recaptured by Alfonso VI, it was reestablished as the preeminent see of Spain. Jiménez de Rada discusses his own role as archbishop of Toledo and primate of Spain, listing the properties that accrued to his see and stressing that the leading religious figures accompanying military expeditions act only as his representatives.

The *Historia de rebus Hispaniae sive Historia Gothica* has been looked to for inspiration for centuries by those who see the history of the peninsula as a continuing quest to restore the political unity lost at the Muslim conquest, because the title seems to make Visigothic identity and experience synonymous with Spain itself, and because Jiménez de Rada traces his tale from

Gothic high point to Muslim conquest to Christian recovery. This argument is not, however, the one Jiménez de Rada actually makes. He is untroubled by political disunity and does not reduce *Hispaniae* (the Spains) to the singular *Hispania.* He deals at greater length with Castile and León than with other regions, but he also recounts the origins, genealogies, and some of the history of the kingdoms of Navarre, Aragon, and Portugal. There is no suggestion anywhere in his writings that he looks to the day when the whole peninsula will be united under a king of Castile. The *Historia de rebus Hispaniae sive Historia Gothica* is thus much more than a pro-Castilian version of Lucas de Tuy's contemporary pro-Leonese *Chronicon mundi* (circa 1236, Chronicle of the World). Spain is already united, in Jiménez de Rada's understanding: Toledo is the spiritual capital not just of Castile but of all of Spain, whether the Spanish kingdoms are united under one king or not.

In the prologue to the *Historia Arabum* Jiménez de Rada explains that he is narrating the depredations perpetrated by the Muslims, who are, he hopes, the last of the oppressors of Spain. He himself has tried to put an end to their devastation, and if God wills, Spain may be preserved from further partitioning by "gladiators," as he collectively describes the previous invaders of the peninsula. Spain has been cut up into five kingdoms since the Muslim invasion—he presumably has in mind Muslim al-Andalus and the Christian kingdoms of Castile and León, Portugal, Navarre, and Aragon—and has had to endure Christian deserters to the Saracen side. Jiménez de Rada credits his hero, Alfonso VIII, with reviving Gothic strength by defeating the Almohad ruler at Las Navas de Tolosa, and he announces his own project of describing Islamic history from the time of Muhammad to help weak Christians avoid being tempted by Muslim blandishments. At the time of Muhammad's birth "Arabia et Affrica inter fidem Catholicam et heresim Arrianum et perfidiam Iudaycam et ydolatriam diuersis studiis traherentur" (Arabia and Africa were being pulled by conflicting desires, between Catholic faith, Arian heresy, Jewish faithlessness, and idolatry). Muhammad's father, under the influence of a Jewish magician friend who cast a horoscope for the boy, vacillated between Christianity and Judaism. After the deaths of Muhammad's parents and grandparents, his uncle, Abu Talib, took him in and had him tutored by the Jewish magician "in naturalibus scienciis et lege Catholica et Iudayce perfidie documentis; unde et ipse postmodum aliqua de fide Catholica, aliqua de lege ueteri in sue secte subsidium usurpauit" (in natural sciences, and the Catholic law, and the written record of Jewish perfidy; whence he afterwards usurped something of the Catholic faith and something of the old Law for the support of his sect). Jiménez de

Rada thus characterizes Islam as a religion that dishonestly cobbles together aspects of Christianity and Judaism, and he blames a Jew for providing Muhammad with the building blocks for the false creed. He demonstrates that Muslim rule leads from unity toward greater division, which is a sign of movement away from God, by showing Muslim leaders fighting against each other as well as against Christians, recounting rebellions against Muslim authority by local communities, and depicting a general state of festering, internecine quarrels.

Rounding out Jiménez de Rada's Latin writings are two letters acknowledging Diego García's dedication to him of *Planeta* (1218, Planet) and a penitential poem transcribed at the end of a Toledan liturgical manuscript. While he has not been known for involvement in vernacular literary production, there is a close link between his *Dialogus libri vitae* and the *Auto de los Reyes Magos* (Drama of the Magi), a short play that predates any other extant Castilian dramatic text by two hundred years. The work survives in a single exemplar copied by a thirteenth-century hand onto the final folios of a manuscript that once belonged to the Cathedral of Toledo but is now Biblioteca Nacional MS. Vitr. 5–9. The penmanship of the copyist of the *Auto de los Reyes Magos* is similar to that of subscriptions on legal charters drafted by canons from Toledo during Jiménez de Rada's tenure as archbishop. Ramón Menéndez Pidal originally dated the script to the early thirteenth century but subsequently redated it to the mid twelfth century on linguistic grounds: language in the *Auto de los Reyes Magos* is similar to that in the *Cantar de mio Cid* (Song of My Cid; translated as *Poem of the Cid*, 1879), which, according to Menéndez Pidal, was finished by the middle of the twelfth century; therefore, the *Auto de los Reyes Magos* must date to the same time. The scholarly consensus now, however, is that the *Cantar de mio Cid* was written in the late twelfth or early thirteenth century; scholars have not yet recalculated the dating of the *Auto de los Reyes Magos*. Rafael Lapesa located parallels for the many lexical peculiarities in the text in other early-thirteenth-century writings from Castile in general and from Toledo in particular; these discoveries were part of his effort to document the Toledan origins of the play against Joan Corominas's suggestion that the author was from Aragon or Navarre.

Early scholars believed that the extant text is a fragment, but David Hook and Alan Deyermond have convincingly argued that it is reasonably complete. In the penultimate scene Herod sends the three Magi on their way, soliloquizes in a rage about the possibility of a new king more powerful than he, and orders his majordomo to summon his two chief counselors. In the final scene the counselors enter and tell the king that

they have brought their writings, "los meiores que nos auemos" (the best that we have). Herod asks if the king foretold by the three Magi is prophesied in their books. One answers that he finds it written nowhere. The other says,

> ¡Hamihala, cumo eres enartado!
> ¿por que eres rabi clamado?
> Non entendes las profecias
> las que nos dixo Ieremias.
> Par mi lei, nos somos erados.
> ¿por que non somos acordados?
> ¿por que non dezimos uertad?

> (By Allah, how you are deceived!
> Why are you called a rabbi?
> You do not understand the prophecies
> that Jeremiah told us.
> By my law, we have wandered.
> Why are we not in agreement?
> Why do we not speak the truth?)

The pair end by confessing that they neither know nor speak the truth. This scene, in which Jews disagree among themselves, is unique in medieval literature about the Magi and makes for an effective and dramatic climax to the play.

There is reason to believe that the *Auto de los Reyes Magos* was intended to be performed publicly to convey to a Romance-speaking audience the defense of Christianity in Jiménez de Rada's scholarly Latin *Dialogus libri vitae* and that it was created around the time of the Christian victory at Las Navas de Tolosa. The notion that even the authorities among the Jews disagree among themselves is the central theme of the *Dialogus libri vitae* but is not a feature of other Christian polemics, even the few that show an awareness of rabbinic exegesis, and this view is mirrored in the concluding passage of the *Auto de los Reyes Magos*. The complexity of Jiménez de Rada's arguments in the *Dialogus libri vitae* suggests that it was the inspiration for the *Auto de los Reyes Magos* and not the other way around.

An explicit link between the *Auto de los Reyes Magos* and the *Dialogus libri vitae* is the reference to the Book of Jeremiah in the final scene of the former, which Julian Weiss takes to refer to Jer. 23:5: "Behold the day will come, says the Lord, and I will raise up a righteous branch from David, and a king will reign and he will be wise and he will issue judgment and justice in the land." The third king paraphrases that verse in his opening speech in the *Auto de los Reyes Magos*. Jer. 23:5 was not one of the liturgical readings for Epiphany, nor does the exegesis of it in the *Glossa ordinaria* connect it to the Magi. It does have an important place in the *Dialogus libri vitae*, however: it is the first biblical verse quoted in book 2, where it is used to support the Incarnation of

Christ against the Jewish notion of a Messiah who will be purely human. The prominent position of the verse indicates its importance to Jiménez de Rada as a prophecy of the Christian Messiah, whose life he outlines in the remainder of book 2. Jiménez de Rada's comparatively long chapter on the Adoration of the Magi in book 2 makes extended allusions to the verse, connecting it to the recognition of Christ by the Gentile kings. Jiménez de Rada speaks of one who comes "de regum germine venerat" (from the line of kings) "de qua David stiterat oriundus" (from the city of David), and he explains that the Messiah "in paterno domicilio sibi solium ordinavit" (reigned on a throne in his father's house). The Gentiles were to be the ones to preserve the justice of this royal branch, and the power of this eternal branch was to be demonstrated by the creation of a new star. The prominence of Jer. 23:5 in both the *Auto de los Reyes Magos* and the *Dialogus libri vitae* cannot be a coincidence.

The *Auto de los Reyes Magos* was also designed to convey the importance of conquering the Muslims still in Spain and the inevitability of their final defeat. This intention is evident when the play is compared to the section of the *Historia de rebus Hispaniae sive Historia Gothica* that describes the battle of Las Navas de Tolosa. This section is usually read as an extended praise of the kingdom of Castile, but this reading obscures the extent to which it describes the expedition of three kings—of Castile, Aragon, and Navarre—to another king, the Almohad caliph. These three kings, like the biblical ones, are Gentiles because of their Visigothic origins; but also like their biblical counterparts they are bearers of Christian truth who confront a non-Christian king bent on violence against innocents. In *Historia de rebus Hispaniae sive Historia Gothica* Jiménez de Rada uses explicitly Trinitarian language to describe their action in concert: "Sicque regum ternarius in sancte Trinitatis nomine processerunt" (And so the threefold kings set out in the name of the holy Trinity). The three act as one throughout the account: they ascend the mountain to occupy the castle of Ferral; they follow the path through the mountains indicated by a mysterious shepherd; and they each take charge of a wing when they engage in battle. The caliph treats them as a unity, swearing "unde et epistolas misit Biaciam et Giennium quod tres reges obsederat intra triduum capiendos" (he sent letters to Baeza and Jaén that he will capture the three kings in three days). Thus, the events of the battle of Las Navas de Tolosa—the attack by three kings on another of a different faith—are given a biblical resonance in the *Historia de rebus Hispaniae sive Historia Gothica,* while in the *Auto de los Reyes Magos* three Gentile kings whose faith allows them to behave as one also encounter an unbelieving king. A

link between the Almohad caliph and the Jewish Herod is plausible, given the tradition that Herod's family were foreign-born usurpers, non-Jewish in origin. Jiménez de Rada cites this tradition in the *Breviarium historiae catholicae,* where he calls Herod's grandfather "king of the Arabs." The rabbi in the *Auto de los Reyes Magos* uses what must be a Christian author's understanding of an Arabic interjection to refer to God: "Hamihala" (By Allah). This interjection tells the audience that the long-ago action in Herod's palace can be seen to be repeating itself in their own lifetime at a Muslim court.

The hypothesis of a connection between the *Auto de los Reyes Magos* and the *Dialogus libri vitae* solves problems that have vexed scholars concerning the play. It explains why the unusual ending is entirely appropriate, and it accounts for the reference to Jeremiah. The language of the play also makes sense as a product of Jiménez de Rada's Toledo. Linguistic historians such as Corominas and Gerold Hilty have detected traces of the Arago-Navarrese dialectic within the Castilian: Jiménez de Rada's cathedral included canons and officeholders from all over the peninsula and beyond, and in a region of high mobility and relatively new written vernaculars, as Spain was at the time, the detection of linguistic footprints only hints at the origins of the author; it does not determine the origin of the text. At the very least, Jiménez de Rada could have commissioned the *Auto de los Reyes Magos* and influenced its form and content. But if he personally wrote the play, his authorship might explain the traces of Arago-Navarrese: Jiménez de Rada's father's family estates were in the part of Spain, near the confluence of the Ebro and Aragon Rivers, where those dialects were spoken, and his mother came from the Castilian side of the Ebro. Jiménez de Rada's involvement with the *Auto de los Reyes Magos* would also explain the existence of this unique early Castilian example of what is generally thought to be a French dramatic form: Jiménez de Rada could have become familiar with dramatic staging while he was a student in Paris.

Scholars are only beginning to sort out the diverse pieces of the puzzle that make up Rodrigo Jiménez de Rada's writings and career. Recent critical editions of his texts will bring his work to a broader public and make his accomplishments vivid, but some themes already stand out. Jiménez de Rada was preoccupied with the relationship between divine unity and the created world throughout his life. As archbishop he sought to make his own social and political landscape resemble this idealized unity more closely by containing the threat of those of different religions and by placing the entire Iberian Peninsula under his spiritual control as primate of Spain. This program of unity is defended, and its underpinnings explained, in his historical and theological writings.

References:

M. Ballesteros Gaibros, *Don Rodrigo Jiménez de Rada* (Madrid: Labor, 1943);

Eduardo Estella Zalaya, *El fundador de la Catedral de Toledo: Estudio histórico del pontificado de D. Rodrigo Ximénes de Rada en la sede toledana, con la documentación original del Archivo Capitular 1208–1247* (Toledo: A. Medina, 1926);

Juan A. Estévez Solá, "Las leyendas de Alejandro magno en el *Breuiarium Historie Catholice* del Toledano," in *Actas del primero congreso nacional de latin medieval: León, 1–4 de diciembre de 1993,* edited by Maurilio Pérez González (León: Universidad de León, Secretariado de Publicaciones, 1995), pp. 257–263;

Juan Fernández Valverde, "Datación y autenticidad del *Dialogus Libri Vite* de Rodrigo Jiménez de Rada," in *Actas del primero congreso de latin medieval,* pp. 105–106;

Javier Gorosterratzu, *Don Rodrigo Jiménez de Rada* (Pamplona: T. Bescansa, 1925);

Hilda Grassotti, "Don Rodrigo Ximénez de Rada, gran señor y hombre de negocios en la Castilla del siglo XIII," *Cuadernos de Historia de España,* 55–56 (1972): 1–302;

Gerold Hilty, "La lengua del *Auto de los Reyes Magos,*" in *Logos semantikos,* edited by Brigitte Schlieben-Lange (Madrid: Gredos, 1981), pp. 289–302;

David Hook and Alan Deyermond, "El Problema de la Terminación del *Auto de los Reyes Mago,*" *Anuario de Estudios Medievales,* 13 (1983): 268–278;

Rafael Lapesa, "Mozárabe y catalán o gascón en el *Auto de los Reyes Magos,*" in *Estudios de historia lingüística española* (Madrid: Paraninfo, 1985), pp. 138–156;

Peter Linehan, *History and the Historians of Medieval Spain* (Oxford: Clarendon Press, 1993);

Derek W. Lomax, "Rodrigo Jiménez de Rada como historiador," in *Actas del Quinto Congreso Internacional de Hispanistas celebrado en Bordeaux del 2 al 8 de septiembre de 1974,* edited by Maxime Chevalier, François Lopez, Joseph Perez, and Noël Salomon (Bordeaux: Instituto de Estudios Ibéricos e Iberoamericanos, Université de Bordeau III, 1977), pp. 587–592;

Florencio Marcos Rodríguez, "El 'Dialogus libri vitae' del arzobispo Jiménez de Rada," *Salmanticensis,* 9 (1962): 617–622;

Georges Martin, "Luc de Tuy, Rodrigue de Tolède, leurs traducteurs, et leurs compilateurs alphonsins. Comparaison segmentaire d'une lexicalisation," *Cahiers de linguistique hispanique médiévale,* 14–15 (1990): 173–206;

Ramón Menéndez Pidal, *Cantar de mio Cid: Texto, gramática, y vocabulario* (Madrid: Bailly-Baillière é Hijos, 1908);

Menéndez Pidal, ed., "Auto de los Reyes Magos," *Revista de archivos, bibliotecas, y museos,* 4 (1900): 453–462;

Lucy K. Pick, *Conflict and Coexistence: Archbishop Rodrigo and the Muslims and Jews of Muslim Spain* (Ann Arbor: University of Michigan Press, 2004);

Pick, "Michael Scot in Toledo: *Natura Naturans* and the Hierarchy of Being," *Traditio,* 53 (1998): 93–116;

Pick, "Rodrigo Jiménez de Rada and the Jews: Pragmatism and Patronage in Thirteenth-Century Toledo," *Viator,* 28 (1997): 203–222;

Timoteo Rojo Orcajo, "La Biblioteca del Arzobispo don Rodrigo Jiménez de Rada y los manuscritos del monasterio de Santa María de Huerta," *Revista Ecclesiastica,* 1 (1929): 196–219;

Julian Weiss, "The *Auto de los Reyes Magos* and the Book of Jeremiah," *La corónica,* 9, no. 2 (1981): 128–130;

Geoffrey West, "The Destiny of Nations: Treatment of Legendary Material in Rodrigo of Toledo's *De Rebus Hispaniae,*" in *The Medieval Mind,* edited by Ian Macpherson and Ralph Penny (London: Tamesis, 1997), pp. 517–533.

Juan Manuel
(5 May 1282 - 1348)

Laurence de Looze
University of Western Ontario

WORKS: *Crónica abreviada* (before 1325)

Manuscript: Biblioteca Nacional, Madrid, MS. 1356.

Standard edition: "Crónica abreviada," in *Obras Completas,* volume 2, edited by José Manuel Blecua (Madrid: Gredos, 1983), pp. 505–877.

Libro de la caça (1325–1326?)

Manuscript: Biblioteca Nacional, Madrid, MS. 6376.

Standard edition: "Libro de la caza," in *Obras Completas,* volume 1, edited by José Manuel Blecua (Madrid: Gredos, 1982), pp. 515–596.

Libro del cauallero e del escudero (between 1326 and 1328)

Manuscript: Biblioteca Nacional, Madrid, MS. 6376.

Standard edition: "Libro del cavallero et del escudero," in *Obras Completas,* volume 1, edited by José Manuel Blecua (Madrid: Gredos, 1982), pp. 35–116.

Libro de los estados (1326–1330)

Manuscript: Biblioteca Nacional, Madrid, MS. 6376.

Standard editions: *Libro de los estados,* edited by Robert Brian Tate and Ian Macpherson (Oxford: Clarendon Press, 1974); "Libro de los estados," in *Obras Completas,* volume 1, edited by José Manuel Blecua (Madrid: Gredos, 1982), pp. 191–502.

El conde Lucanor (1335)

Manuscripts: Biblioteca Nacional, Madrid, MSS. 6376, 4236 (*olim* M-100 and 19,426); Real Academia de la Historia, Madrid, MS. 9-29-4/5893, (*olim* 9-27-3 = E-78); Real Academia Española, Madrid, MS. 15.

First publication: *El conde Lucanor: Compuesto por el excelentissimo principe don Iuan Manuel, hijo del Infante don Manuel, y nieto del sancto rey don Fernando,* edited by Gonçalo de Argote de Molina (Seville: Hernando Díaz, 1575).

Standard editions: "El Conde Lucanor," in *Obras Completas,* volume 2, edited by José Manuel Blecua (Madrid: Gredos, 1983), pp. 7–503; *El conde*

Juan Manuel; detail from the Altarpiece of Santa Lucia in the Cathedral of Murcia (from <http://www.ensayistas.org/filosofos/spain/ Juan-Manuel/>)

Lucanor, edited by Guillermo Serés (Barcelona: Crítica, 1994).

Editions in English: *Count Lucanor; or, The Fifty Pleasant Tales of Patronio,* translated by James York (Westminster: Pickering, 1868; New York & London: White & Allen, 1889); *El Conde Lucanor: A Collection of Mediaeval Spanish Stories,* translated by

John England (Warminster, U.K.: Aris & Phillips, 1987); *El conde Lucanor: The Book of Count Lucanor and Patronio. A Translation of Don Juan Manuel's* El conde Lucanor, translated by John E. Keller, L. Clark Keating, and Barbara E. Gaddy (New York: Peter Lang, 1993).

Tractado de la Asunción de la Virgen María (after 1335)
   Manuscript: Biblioteca Nacional, Madrid, MS. 6376.
   Standard edition: "Tractado de la asunción de la Virgen María," in *Obras Completas,* volume 1, edited by José Manuel Blecua (Madrid: Gredos, 1982), pp. 503–514.

Libro infinido (1336–1337)
   Manuscript: Biblioteca Nacional, Madrid, MS. 6376.
   Standard edition: "Libro enfenido," in *Obras Completas,* volume 1, edited by José Manuel Blecua (Madrid: Gredos, 1982), pp. 141–189.

Libro de las armas (after 1337)
   Manuscript: Biblioteca Nacional, Madrid, MS. 6376.
   Standard edition: "Libro de las armas," in *Obras Completas,* volume 1, edited by José Manuel Blecua (Madrid: Gredos, 1982), pp. 117–140.

In 1575 Gonçalo de Argote de Molina published a short biography of the fourteenth-century writer Juan Manuel as part of the prefatory material to the first printed edition of Juan Manuel's *El conde Lucanor* (1335; translated as *Count Lucanor; or, The Fifty Pleasant Tales of Patronio,* 1868). The six-page biography ends with the text of the inscription on Juan Manuel's tomb at the Dominican monastery he founded at Peñafiel and is followed by ninety-seven pages on the genealogy of Juan Manuel's family. The edition also includes an essay on Spanish poetry, glossaries of archaic words, and a notice from the editor to the "curioso lector" (interested reader). Juan Manuel would undoubtedly have been happy to know that not only the text of his greatest work but also a detailed genealogy and an account of his deeds were included in the first published edition of *El conde Lucanor,* since these matters were of great importance to him. He combined, albeit with difficulty at times, the active life of a powerful noble with the contemplative pursuits of a writer. And although he is now remembered primarily as one of the greatest medieval Spanish writers, to his contemporaries he was, above all, a major political figure and a prime actor in the tumultuous events of the period.

Juan Manuel is one of the two most important vernacular Spanish writers of the fourteenth century; the other is Juan Ruiz, Archpriest of Hita, celebrated for his *Libro de buen amor* (circa 1330–1343; translated as *Book of Good Love,* 1933). Scholars are often wont to contrast the two. First, while virtually nothing is known of the life of Juan Ruiz–whose name may, in fact, be a fourteenth-century version of "John Doe"–the opposite is true of Juan Manuel, who was the nephew of King Alfonso X *el Sabio* (the Learned) of Castile and one of the most powerful nobles of his day. Second, unlike Juan Ruiz, whose reputation is based entirely on a single work, Juan Manuel has left a substantial oeuvre. Finally, while Juan Ruiz's *Libro de buen amor* is in many respects a potpourri whose meanings are hard to pin down, Juan Manuel is generally considered a didactic writer–though treatments of his "didacticism" have occasionally been discussions of the author's putative intentions rather than of what the writings actually imply. In "The Structures of Didacticism: Private Myths and Public Fictions," in *Juan Manuel Studies* (1977), edited by Ian Macpherson, Peter N. Dunn calls Juan Manuel's didacticism an attempt "to represent the variety and greatness of the world, and to present this world as a mind which is capable of reflecting on it." A great deal is known about what Juan Manuel thought regarding a wide range of issues and the knowledge he wished to impart to others. Well known also are the intellectual influences on Juan Manuel, above all the writings of his uncle, Alfonso X, who was one of the towering literary figures of the previous century, and those of the Dominican religious order, of which Juan Manuel was a great supporter.

Juan Manuel was born on 5 May 1282 into a world of almost constant political conflict. His father, also named Juan Manuel, had been an *infante* (royal prince), the youngest child of St. Ferdinand III, king of Castile and brother of Alfonso X. When the elder Juan Manuel died in 1284, the two-year-old inherited the title of *adelantado* (governor) of Murcia, the front line in the Reconquest of Spain from the Muslims by the Christian kings. In later life he also saw himself as the intellectual heir of Alfonso X. In many of his literary works, including the two greatest, the *Libro de los estados* (1326–1330, Book of the Estates) and *El conde Lucanor,* Juan Manuel identifies himself as the son of the *infante* Juan Manuel and the *adelantado* of Murcia. He does not mention, however, that he was denied the title of *adelantado* more than once for significant periods because of his conflicts with the Castilian king Alfonso XI.

Juan Manuel's mother, Countess Beatrice of Savoy, died when he was eight. She had overseen his education; comments he makes in the *Libro de los estados* indicate that his studies suffered after her death, in part because fawning instructors hesitated to give him stern correction. A recurrent motif of Juan Manuel's writings is a self-deprecating attitude that stresses his *poco entendimiento* (limited understanding) of complex philosophical and theological issues, but this modesty is balanced by an extraordinary assurance regarding political and social matters. The self-confidence Juan Manuel displays when he addresses practical problems implies a greater degree of success than he enjoyed in his real-life actions.

In 1294 the Muslims invaded the territory of Murcia from nearby Granada; because of his tender age, Juan Manuel states in his *Libro de las armas* (after 1337, Book of Arms), he was not allowed to take an active part in these battles. By September of that year he was deeply embroiled in the political intrigues of the Iberian Peninsula—involvement that was inevitable for a person in his position during what his biographer, Andrés Giménez-Soler, calls "the most confused period of Castile's history." A problem of dynastic succession had been brought on by the fact that the crown prince of Castile, Fernando de la Cerda, had died in 1275, while his father, Alfonso X, was still alive. Alfonso had named his own younger son, Sancho IV, known as "the Brave," his heir instead of the dead crown prince's eldest son, Alfonso, but had later disinherited him without naming a new heir. Sancho had taken the throne on the death of Alfonso X in 1284 but throughout his reign had to defend his throne against Alfonso de la Cerda and the latter's supporters. Juan Manuel backed Sancho; when Sancho died in 1295, however, the support Juan Manuel had received from the Castilian crown began to wane. Juan Manuel devotes the entire final section of the *Libro de las armas* to Sancho IV's death more than forty years earlier and narrates an extraordinary deathbed confession Sancho allegedly made to him. The passage is a tour de force that calls on all of Juan Manuel's powers as a writer: after ordering everyone except Juan Manuel to leave the room, Sancho movingly explains to the youthful narrator that King Ferdinand III, their common grandfather, gave his benediction to Juan Manuel's father who passed it along to the author. In almost biblical fashion, then, the last-born son, Juan Manuel's father, was allegedly made the chosen one over his older brothers; by extension, the younger Juan Manuel is cast as morally superior to the current ruling Castilian house. Giménez-Soler and Reinaldo Ayerbe-Chaux take the passage at face value; but for all the drama of the scene, one has only Manuel's word for it, and he is hardly a disinterested observer. Questions of historical veracity aside, it is clear that Juan Manuel capitalizes in the *Libro de las armas* on this alleged interview with Sancho IV to provide a justification, many years after the fact, for his long series of bitter conflicts with the House of Castile.

Juan Manuel's lands in Murcia came under attack from Castile and Aragon, and in 1296 he lost some of his most important towns, including Elche. At seven-teen he married Princess Isabel of Majorca; she died two years later, in 1301. In 1303 he negotiated a pact to marry Princess Constanza of Aragon that specified that in return for his recognition of her father, Jaime II, as his lord, Jaime would return the city of Elche to Juan Manuel and defend him against most of his enemies, especially Castile. Because Constanza was only three years old, the marriage was put off for eight years. Constanza was given over to Juan Manuel in 1306; her father was assured that she would reside at the fortress at Villena and that the marriage would not be consummated for another six years. Ferdinand IV of Castile was so troubled by the alliance between Juan Manuel and Jaime II of Aragon that he plotted to assassinate Juan Manuel. That plan came to naught, but another murder, the details of which remain unexplained to this day, did take place: in 1306 Juan Manuel's half sister Violante was killed by her husband, Prince Alfonso of Portugal.

Juan Manuel has been chastised for committing what Giménez-Soler calls "one of the most shameful acts of the history of Castile." He had joined, albeit reluctantly, in a prolonged action with Aragon and Castile against the Moors in Almería. In a crucial battle in 1310 he deserted along with Prince Juan, the younger brother of Sancho IV, rendering the campaign a failure. Juan Manuel claimed that Ferdinand IV had asked him to make sure that Prince Juan was not endangered, but Ferdinand was so furious that the two Juans had to seek refuge for several months in León. The marriage of Juan Manuel and Constanza was finally celebrated on 3 April 1311, two months after the bride's twelfth birthday. The couple had two daughters.

In 1313 Fernando IV died, leaving as heir his one-year-old son Alfonso XI. Alfonso XI's mother also died in 1313, and the child sovereign's grandmother took over as regent until her own death in 1321. The regency then consisted of the most powerful Spanish nobles, including Juan Manuel. Alfonso dismissed them in 1325, in part for the rapaciousness of their projects during the regency. Soon afterward, the young Castilian king sought to marry Juan Manuel's daughter Constanza. Juan Manuel's *El conde Lucanor* includes the tale of a man who purchases a piece of great wisdom: it turns out to be the simple advice not to act before one knows a situation entirely. Juan Manuel did the exact opposite when presented with the offer to marry his daughter to Alfonso XI: he could not pass up the chance to put his daughter on the throne that had once belonged to Alfonso *el Sabio*. This action proved to be the single biggest mistake of his political career, because Alfonso XI had no intention of carrying through with the marriage. By the time Juan Manuel realized that he had been tricked, his daughter was being held by

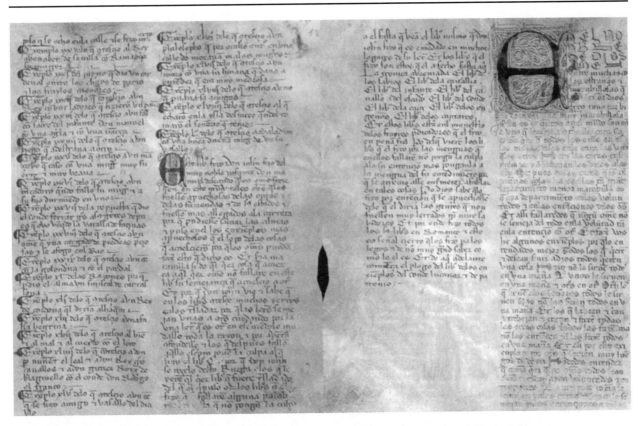

Manuscript for the table of contents, anteprólogo, *and first-person prologue of Juan Manuel's* El conde Lucanor
(Biblioteca Nacional, Madrid, MS. 6376)

Alfonso XI in the fortress of Toro, and the Castilian king was in negotiations to marry the daughter of Alfonso IV of Portugal. The repudiation of his daughter by a young king for whom Juan Manuel had considerable disdain, and Alfonso's presumptuousness in holding her hostage in his realm, were terrible humiliations. Juan Manuel divested himself of his feudal obligations to the king and declared war on Castile.

Juan Manuel's wife died in August 1327, followed in November by her father, Jaime II of Aragon. The marriage to Constanza had secured Juan Manuel's alliance with Aragon, and Jaime had interceded on Juan Manuel's behalf more than once in his disputes with the Castilian Crown. Alfonso XI took immediate steps to cement an alliance between Castile and Aragon through the marriage of his sister to the new king of Aragon, Alfonso IV. This action left Juan Manuel in a position of extreme weakness, and he sought the aid of the Muslim ruler of Granada. Exemplum 28 of *El conde Lucanor* tells of the Christian knight don Llorenço Suárez, who served the Moorish kings in Granada; that service, it is suggested, might cost him God's everlasting mercy. That Juan Manuel would conclude an alliance with non-Christians against a Christian sovereign indicates the extremity of his predicament. Don Llorenço

redeems himself by continuing to serve the Christian church even as he serves a Muslim sovereign; in his negotiations with Granada, Juan Manuel tried to tread the kind of fine line he later attributed to Llorenço Suárez: his letters stipulate that while he was prepared to stand aside during conflicts between the Muslim leader and Christian kings, he would not actually fight with the Muslims against a Christian sovereign. Unfortunately for Juan Manuel, his letters pledging an alliance with the Muslim ruler fell into the hands of agents of the king of Castile and made his situation even more dire.

Desperate to shore up his position, Juan Manuel contracted a marriage with Blanca Núñez de la Cerda—the wing of the Castilian royal family against which he had stood when he had supported Sancho IV for the kingship of Castile many years earlier. The marriage was solemnized in 1329 and produced two children, Fernando and Juana. Also in 1329 a peace treaty between Juan Manuel and Alfonso XI was negotiated by Pope John XXII, and Juan Manuel's daughter Constanza was returned to him.

Juan Manuel had problems not only with his king but also with his subjects, who more than once rejected him as their *adelantado* in Murcia. As a result, in rescinding and then reinstating Juan Manuel's title Alfonso XI was in part responding to the unhappiness of Juan Manuel's subjects. One provision of the 1329 settlement between Juan Manuel and Alfonso XI was the official restitution of Juan Manuel's title in Murcia, which was proclaimed in a royal decree of 29 January 1330. War broke out between the two again in 1334, and another peace accord was reached three years later.

In 1339 Juan Manuel's daughter Constanza married Crown Prince Pedro of Portugal. During their truces Juan Manuel and the Castilian king participated in joint campaigns against the Moors; hostilities between the two would then resume. In an alliance with Alfonso XI, Juan Manuel won the Victory of Salado in 1340 and the Conquest of Algeciras in 1344. In his *Libro de los estados* Juan Manuel refers to "este tiempo que es turbio" (this period that is tumultuous). He died in 1348.

Juan Manuel's daughter Juana married Enrique of Trastámara in 1350. When Alfonso IV of Portugal died in 1357, Crown Prince Pedro became King Pedro I, and Constanza became queen. Juana became queen of Castile when her husband took the throne as Enrique II in 1369. Their son Juan, born in 1358, became King Juan I of Castile in 1379. In the end, then, the twists of history permitted Juan Manuel to place both of his daughters on major thrones of the Iberian Peninsula. And though he failed in his attempt to put Constanza on the Castilian throne, Juana's son—his grandson—achieved the goal that had eluded him in his own life.

If Juan Manuel's place in history depended on the events of his political life, he would be a rather minor figure. His significance, however, stems from his writing, and here his stature is great. Juan Manuel's own comments show that he accorded considerable importance to his literary work, and despite ritual reiterations that his knowledge was slight, he clearly held the same high opinion of himself as an author that he had of himself as a political player. In his *Libro infinido* (1336–1337, Book without End) he considers whether a nobleman should spend so much time writing literary works. He claims to have been criticized for composing books but says that this charge will not make him desist. He notes that his books do good, not ill, and adds that in any event it is better to spend time writing books "than playing darts or participating in other base things." He also directs the reader to a proverbial summation in *El conde Lucanor*. The playful intertextual reference reveals that he recognizes himself as the creator of a literary corpus. This writerly self-consciousness can be situated within the pan-European fourteenth-century rise of the semiprofessional author, proud of his literary production, aware of the relationships among his writings, who authorizes and authenticates his "complete works." In

this respect Juan Manuel has much in common with contemporaries such as Giovanni Boccaccio and Dante in Italy and Guillaume de Machaut in France, as well as such later fourteenth-century figures as Jean Froissart and Geoffrey Chaucer. In several places Juan Manuel mentions that he deposited an authorized copy of a "complete-works" manuscript in the library of the Dominican monastery he founded at Peñafiel; at the beginning of *El conde Lucanor* he charges the reader to compare dubious readings in other manuscripts with the Peñafiel copy, which, he says, he corrected himself.

The Peñafiel manuscript has been lost; the most authoritative surviving manuscript is MS. 6376 in the Biblioteca Nacional in Madrid, which includes seven of Juan Manuel's eight extant works. *El conde Lucanor* appears in four other manuscripts, which include no other work by Juan Manuel; *El conde Lucanor* appears by itself in two of the manuscripts and is collected with works by other authors in the remaining two. Four of the five manuscripts with *El conde Lucanor,* including MS. 6376, are from the fifteenth century, while the fifth is a sixteenth-century humanist production. There are, thus, five versions—six, if one takes the 1575 edition by Argote de Molina into account—of *El conde Lucanor.* The *Crónica abreviada* (before 1325, Abbreviated Chronicle) is the only work that does not appear in MS. 6376.

The general prologue to MS. 6376 contains a list of Juan Manuel's works that claims to include "todos los libros que yo fasta aquí he fechos" (all the books I have composed up until now). A second list is found in the *anteprólogo* (preprologue) to *El conde Lucanor* in all five manuscripts of that work, including MS. 6376; the 1575 Argote de Molina edition of *El conde Lucanor* provides yet a third list. The list in the general prologue to MS. 6376 includes titles that are absent from the list in the *anteprólogo;* on the other hand, the *anteprólogo* lists a work that does not appear among the titles in the general prologue to MS. 6376: *El conde Lucanor* itself. One wonders why the general prologue fails to mention one of the most important works the manuscript contains.

More problematic is the issue of distinguishing between titles that are merely alternates for extant works and titles that refer to writings that are now lost. Titles in the Middle Ages were not fixed in the way modern ones are. For example, Juan Manuel's *Libro infinido* also goes by the title *Libro de castigos et de consejos* (Book of Punishment and Advice), and what the general prologue to MS. 6376 and modern critics call the *Libro de los estados* is known in the *anteprólogo* and the Argote de Molina list as the *Libro del infante* (Book of the Prince). *El conde Lucanor* is also known by several titles, which might represent various stages of revision: in the *anteprólogo,* as found in all five manuscripts, it is called both the *Libro del conde* (Book of the Count) and the

Libro de los enxienplos del conde Lucanor et de Patronio (Book of the Exempla of Count Lucanor and of Patronio), while Argote de Molina lists the work as the *Libro de los exemplos* (Book of Exempla). Two quite different titles, *Libro del conde* and *Libro de los exemplos,* thus refer to one and the same work. The general prologue names some works that have certainly been lost and some, such as the *Reglas de trobar* (Rules of Poetry) and the *Crónica cumplida* (Full Chronicle), that may never have existed. The *anteprólogo* in the manuscripts and the Argote de Molina edition mentions an unknown *Libro de los sabios* (Book of the Learned Men) that Blecua thinks might be another alternate title for the *Libro infinido,* a suggestion with which Guillermo Serés, the editor of a 1994 edition of *El conde Lucanor,* concurs; Giménez-Soler, on the other hand, proposes that it might be an alternate title for the *Libro de los estados,* and Ayerbe-Chaux believes that it is one of what he sees as three or four titles of *El conde Lucanor.* The lists in the medieval manuscripts group the works not chronologically but generically or thematically. Nevertheless, by means of internal evidence and intertextual references, one can sketch out a rough chronology of the eight extant works.

What appears to be Juan Manuel's earliest extant writing, the *Crónica abreviada,* is a chronicle of political events; Juan Manuel states in the prologue that it is a summary of the *Crónica d'Espanna* (Chronicle of Spain) by his uncle Alfonso X, and it is, indeed, a chapter-by-chapter recapitulation of the topics detailed in the more extensive chronicle. The *Libro de la caça* (1325–1326? Book of the Hunt) is exemplary of the interests of a man of Juan Manuel's historical period and status. The principal topic is falconry–a complex skill, part art and part science, that was much studied by fourteenth-century aristocrats; Juan Manuel's French contemporary Machaut also wrote a minor work on falconry, the *Dit de l'alerion* (1340s; translated as "The Tale of the Alerion," 1994). Juan Manuel says that he will not treat the subject of fishing. In this work he introduces a technique he develops in his later writings: that of presenting a more or less fictionalized version of himself. Here the third-person expression "dize don Iojan" (Juan Manuel says) frequently punctuates the text.

The *Libro del cauallero e del escudero* (between 1326 and 1328, Book of the Knight and the Squire) also treats falconry and, like the *Libro de la caça,* eschews discussion of fishing because, as the wise old knight says in chapter 42, "I haven't practiced fishing as much as hunting." This time Juan Manuel inserts himself into the text in the first person as the author of the work. His pronouncements "yo, don Iohan, fijo del infante don Manuel, adelantado . . . de Murcia" (I, don Juan, son of the prince, don Manuel, governor . . . of Murcia) and "yo, don Iohan . . . fiz este libro" (I, don Juan . . .

made this book) are repeated in subsequent works. The work is structured as a dialogue between an experienced character and an inexperienced one, another technique that became standard in much of his writing. The questions and answers take place here between the wise, aged knight and a newly knighted young man–the squire of the title. In the first pages the squire goes to court; according to the caption heading to chapter 3, he falls asleep on his horse–a commonplace of medieval literature. How the squire meets the old knight is unknown, since at this point a lacuna of four folios occurs in MS. 6376; the text resumes in chapter 16 with the discussion between the two well under way. Each chapter then consists of the response the old knight gives to a question supposedly posed by the young man. Some of the issues have to do with the natural world; the knight explains, for example, what trees and rocks and earth are. But the main interest has to do with knighthood: what is chivalry? How does one become a knight? At the end of the work a reversal occurs as the old knight questions the young one in a kind of "final examination." Indebted to Ramon Llull, who wrote the *Libre del orde de cavalleria* (circa 1276, Book of the Order of Chivalry; translated as *Here begynneth the Table of this present booke Intytled the Book of the ordre of chyualry or knyghthode,* 1484), and Alfonso X, the *Libro del cauallero e del escudero* integrates itself harmoniously into Juan Manuel's overriding concerns in his work with questions of honor and *estado* (estate or class).

The *Libro de los estados,* probably composed between 1326 and 1330, ranges with great artistry over the classes of medieval society. The loosely structured work, in which material appears to have been interpolated or revised on several occasions, as Leonardo Funes argued in 1984 and 1986, uses the dialogue format Juan Manuel exploited in the *Libro del cauallero e del escudero;* but here the discussion among the old knight, Julio; a young prince (the infante of the alternate title, *Libro del infante*), and, to a lesser extent, the prince's father, King Morabán, functions as a frame within which Julio recites various exempla or tales. The influence of the Dominicans, a teaching order who regularly used exempla to spice up their sermons, can be seen here. The two-tiered text provides the flexibility to accommodate such disparate elements as a defense of the Christian faith, an Eastern legend, and current events in fourteenth-century Spain.

The *Libro de los estados* is divided into two books: the first addresses the secular life and the second the spiritual life. The exempla are often quickly summarized rather than being narrated in detail; the most extensive single tale is the legend of Barlaam and Josaphat, which occupies the first forty-seven chapters of book 1. Popular in the Middle Ages, the Barlaam

Page from a later manuscript of El conde Lucanor *(Real Academia Española, Madrid, MS. 15, folio 25r)*

and Josaphat story was believed erroneously to have been written by John of Damascus; in fact, it is a Christianized version of the life of Gautama Buddha that originated in the East and traveled westward through a series of translations. There has been much debate regarding which version of the tale Juan Manuel adapted for his work, but there is a high degree of consensus as to the shifts in emphasis he introduced. One major change is the reduction of the three encounters to a single one with a corpse; an even more substantial alteration is the downgrading of the ascetic orientation that would be found in almost any source Juan Manuel might have used. The rejection of the life of this world as transitory and without importance would not be palatable to a writer concerned to show that one could seek salvation without abandoning one's worldly status. Juan Manuel's approach reveals an indebtedness to the thinking of St. Thomas Aquinas, a Dominican and the greatest theologian of the High Middle Ages, who held that this world presents many opportunities for salvation and does not need to be rejected categorically. The second book of the *Libro de los estados* is less concerned with salvation per se than with how to live a moral life within the boundaries of one's estate in this world. In his discussion of the *estados* in society, Juan Manuel follows the usual medieval division into three orders: those who pray, the churchmen; those who bear arms and defend the realm, the knights; and those who till the land, the peasants.

Juan Manuel's greatest work, and the most complex by far in terms both of organization and of textual history, is the *El conde Lucanor*, composed in 1335. In this work the techniques he used in his earlier writings are redeployed in brilliant ways. Like the *Libro de los estados*, *El conde Lucanor* operates on two levels: a frame in which Count Lucanor comes to a wise counselor, Patronio, with a problem, and an exemplum told by Patronio that provides, by analogy, guidance on how to solve the problem. Lucanor interprets the advice encoded in the exemplum and successfully applies it to his situation. At the end of each of the fifty encounters the author, Juan Manuel, steps into the text, announces that the tale has pleased him greatly, and sums up its lesson in a *cobla* (couplet). The work has often been compared unfavorably to other fourteenth-century frame narratives, especially Boccaccio's *Decameron* and Chaucer's *Canterbury Tales;* the criticism most commonly voiced is that Juan Manuel fails to develop the dramatic possibilities of the framing situation as Boccaccio and Chaucer do. But the *Libro de los estados* shows that Juan Manuel could create a lively frame narrative if he chose to do so; the repetitive and formulaic frame in *El conde Lucanor* thus is designed to direct the reader's attention to the exempla. The narrative frame, the question-and-answer format, and the

exempla work together in consummate fashion to provide fifty object lessons in courses of conduct for a nobleman who wishes to succeed in the world. The same techniques as in previous works and the same concerns for prudence and the maintenance of one's honor and estate are present here, but with a new emphasis on the need for interpretation.

The five extant manuscript copies of *El conde Lucanor*—more than of any of Juan Manuel's other works—as well as the printed edition of 1575 suggest that *El conde Lucanor* was his most widely read text. But the variances among the versions have complicated the interpretation of the work. The *anteprólogo* asks that no reading be accepted as definitive until it has been compared with the Peñafiel manuscript, corrected by the author's own hand; this request is quite different from the one made in the *Libro de los estados* and in many other medieval works that the reader take the liberty to alter the text as needed. But it would hardly be feasible for every reader of *El conde Lucanor* to make a trip to Peñafiel; in addition, there are reasons for suspecting that the *anteprólogo* was not written by Juan Manuel.

In the "complete-works" MS. 6376 and the sixteenth-century humanist manuscript, the narrative frame and fifty exempla constitute the first of five books. Books 2 through 5 are much shorter and quite different in content. At the beginning of book 2 the Juan Manuel figure announces that he will leave off the "declarado" (clear) discourse of book 1 and opt for a more "oscuro" (obscure) mode of expression. Books 2 through 4 consist of proverbs of dwindling quantity—one hundred in book 2, fifty in book 3, and thirty in book 4—and increasing obscurity. These aphoristic statements increasingly tax the interpretive powers both of Lucanor and of the reader. In book 3 every fourth proverb is an example of rhetorical complexity; others tread a fine line between meaningfulness and meaninglessness, especially as they approach pure tautology as in "Error is error" or "Life without life is not life." In book 4 Patronio declares that it will henceforth be impossible for readers to understand the most obscure proverbs; the syntax of almost half of them has been scrambled, rendering them virtually impossible to decipher. Book 5 says that the whole world is a "figura"—a vast metaphorical text to be read for one's salvation. Laurence de Looze argues (2000, 2001) that the five-part version of *El conde Lucanor* comprises a series of graded tutorials in hermeneutics, each more difficult than the last, until the reader is returned in book 5 to the sociopolitical world of book 1 with the charge and the skills to read it figuratively. Book 5 is also concerned with how a person such as Juan Manuel who is deeply enmeshed in that world can nevertheless achieve salvation.

Despite the fact that MS. 6376 is generally considered the most authoritative extant text of the work, most nineteenth- and twentieth-century critics treated *El conde Lucanor* as though only book 1 existed; the three English and one German translations, for example, are of book 1 only. More recently, scholars such as de Looze, Marta Ana Diz, and Paolo Cherchi have assumed that books 2 through 5 are legitimate factors in the interpretation of the meaning of *El conde Lucanor*.

The five manuscripts and the printed edition of *El conde Lucanor* tell much about the varying receptions of the work by fifteenth- and sixteenth-century readers, copyists, and editors. The large size and luxuriousness of the fifteenth-century MS. 6376–it seems almost certain that it was meant to be illustrated, as Maria Rosa Lida de Malkiel first proposed, although the miniatures were never painted into the spaces left for them–indicate that it was produced for an elite readership. By contrast, the single-work sixteenth-century codex, Biblioteca Nacional MS. 19,426, is humanist rather than medieval in character and is typical of an academic "glance back" at an earlier age. Devoid of rubrication and color, it has more in common with Argote de Molina's 1575 edition than with the other handwritten copies. Although Argote de Molina includes only book 1 of the text, he adds the biography of the author, the genealogical study, an extrapolation of all of the *coblas* (often regularizing the meter and rhyme), and an essay on Castilian poetry. These additions also attest to a humanist interest in "old" literature that is quite different from the interests that motivated medieval reproductions of the text. The fifteenth-century MS. 9-29-4-5893 in the Real Academia de la Historia in Madrid, despite also being a single-work copy of book 1 of *El conde Lucanor,* takes a "medieval" approach to the text in terms of layout and rubrication. MS. 4236 in the Biblioteca Nacional and MS. 15 in the Real Academia Española in Madrid are also medieval versions of book 1 alone, and in that sense similar to MS. 9-29-4-5893, but both associate *El conde Lucanor* with other works that are not by Juan Manuel. Hence, in these instances the unifying feature is not the author but literary or generic considerations. MS. 15 follows *El conde Lucanor* with the *Libro de Sendebar,* a frame narrative that was first translated from Arabic by Alfonso X's brother Fadrique around 1253 and that probably influenced Juan Manuel's use of framing. MS. 15 carries over the disposition and rubrication of *El conde Lucanor* to the *Libro de Sendebar,* as though they were parts of a larger whole.

The least studied of Juan Manuel's works is the brief *Tractado de la asunción de la Virgen María,* which appears to have been composed after 1335. In style it is quite typical of his literary endeavors, and it shows Dominican influence in its insistence on the Virgin's assumption into heaven in both body and spirit. The theological subject matter, however, is a departure from the norm for Juan Manuel, who is concerned in almost all of his other writings with sociopolitical affairs in fourteenth-century Spain.

The *Libro infinido,* probably written in 1336–1337, is a summary of the kinds of knowledge Juan Manuel considers crucial for a fourteenth-century nobleman. Each chapter begins with a direct address to his son Fernando and goes on to treat a particular subject. Juan Manuel claims to be basing his advice on real-life experiences that turned out well. The work ends with a typology of the *maneras de amar* (kinds of friendship) among noblemen.

Composed after 1337, the *Libro de las armas* is an almost propagandistic work in which Juan Manuel presents his vision of the social and political status that he believed should be his. He again uses the question-and-answer format: the Juan Manuel figure is now cast in the wise counselor's role, "answering" the questions that the cleric Juan Alfonso puts to him. In the course of the work he comments on many issues that touch on his family, including its coat of arms, of which he gives a detailed explication. Particularly compelling is the dramatic account of Sancho IV's alleged deathbed confession.

Scholarly attention has been paid to the question of the audience for which Juan Manuel was writing in the early and middle fourteenth century. Those readers would have been aristocrats like himself, and Juan Manuel addresses, above all, the practical concerns of a man of his class, whether in manuals on technical arts such as the *Libro de la caça* on hunting, the lost *Libro de los engeños* (Book of Devices) on the art of war, and the *Reglas de trobar* on poetry–if, in fact, he ever wrote such a text–or in treatises on how to conduct oneself such as the *Libro de los estados,* the *Libro del cauallero e del escudero,* the *Libro de las armas,* and *El conde Lucanor.* Juan Manuel repeatedly insists that he does not have the training or education to treat deep philosophical and theological subjects, which he would almost certainly have done in Latin; all of his writing is in the Spanish vernacular.

Juan Manuel's works are deeply involved in the world in which he lived, even when they are presented as disinterested encounters between an initiate and a wise counselor in a setting devoid of localization in time and space. The paramount importance of maintaining one's honor and estate, which Juan Manuel consistently attributes to his characters, was a constant concern of the author in his real life. The temptation to read his works as autobiographical is all the more keen because of his practice of creating a literary version of himself in his prologues. This stance, the first of its kind in Spanish letters, is found in the works of the greatest non-Spanish writers of the fourteenth century: Dante and Boccaccio in Italy, Machaut and Froissart in France, and Chaucer in England. While there are many affinities between the "Juan Manuel" in the prologues and the real-life author, particularly in terms of their philosophies and ideologies, they cannot simply be conflated. In "Yo, don Johán, fijo del infante don Manuel. . . ," a preliminary study in Serés's 1994 edition of *El conde Lucanor*, Germán Orduna distinguishes two levels of fictionality in the references to "Juan Manuel" in the works: some are in the first person, and others take the third-person form of "my friend, Juan Manuel"; none of these authorial appearances, Orduna argues, can be deemed autobiographical. Juan Manuel's pronouncements regarding his paucity of knowledge, while reiterated in the prologue of work after work, probably have more to do with the "humility topos" of classical and medieval literature than with the real Juan Manuel's sense of himself; overwhelming evidence points to his extraordinary self-confidence regarding his opinions and convictions. The calm, humble, and measured Juan Manuel depicted in these literary self-portraits is quite different from the proud, scheming political player revealed in the historical documents. Critics have also pointed out that Juan Manuel often did not follow in his real life the counsels he urges on others in his literary works.

Care must also be taken in approaching the seemingly autobiographical aspects of the dedicatory passages in the prologues to most of Juan Manuel's works. The rhetorical strategy of presenting one's literary composition as a response to a request by a friend or powerful lord is as old as Plato and characterizes much medieval literature. Juan Manuel dispenses with this formula only in the *Cronica abreviada* and the *Libro de la caça,* in each of which he presents himself as continuing a work begun by his great literary and political model, Alfonso X, and in *El conde Lucanor.* In each of his other prologues he claims to have composed the work in order to send it to a friend. Only in the prologues to the *Libro de las armas* and the *Libro infinido* does he say that he composed the work at the specific request of someone; in the other instances he simply announces that he sent the book to a particular person. He begins the *Tractado de la Asunción de la Virgen María* with a direct address to the prelate Ramon Masquefa, to whom he then relates the gist of a conversation he supposedly had with his father-in-law, Jaime II of Aragon. He says that he composed the *Libro de los estados* and the *Libro del cauallero e del escudero* for his brother-in-law, Juan, the archbishop of Toledo. The latter dedication employs the "insomnia" topos of medieval literature, which was highly developed in the fourteenth century: Juan Manuel says that he wrote his book during his hours of

Title page for the first printed edition of Juan Manuel's work (from <http://www.cervantesvirtual.com/servlet/SirveObras/bne/08147395399159262110046/portada.jpg>)

insomnia and now sends it to his brother-in-law as reading material for the latter's own sleepless hours. He also suggests that the archbishop might be inclined to translate the work into Latin, just as Juan Manuel asked him to translate a book the archbishop had written on the Paternoster from Latin into Spanish. Juan Manuel proves himself highly conversant with this elegant literary banter, but whether any of it represents reality is doubtful.

Juan Manuel says that his cleric friend Juan Alfonso requested that he compose the *Libro de las armas.* Little is known about Juan Alfonso or why he might have wanted Juan Manuel to write such a work. The claim is especially intriguing since Juan Manuel alleges that Juan Alfonso specifically wished him to write about three matters, the third of which is the deathbed confession in which Sancho IV supposedly gave his blessing to Juan Manuel's bloodline over Alfonso XI's. One wonders why it would matter to Juan Alfonso to have this story published; on the other hand, Juan Manuel's interest in putting the incident before his readership is obvious. One is led to suspect that a delicate game is being played here. Similarly, Juan Manuel attributes the order to compose the *Libro infinido* to his then twelve-year-old son Fernando. More than one critic has pointed out that it seems unlikely that a boy would make such a request of his father; it is much more plausible that a father would find that his son, on the cusp of manhood, would do well to have a book in which the father put all the worldly wisdom he had culled over the years. The claim that Fernando requested the book is probably a graceful way of justifying the composition of the work.

El conde Lucanor does not have an opening dedication. Instead, in both the first-person prologue and the perhaps spurious *anteprólogo* Juan Manuel takes full responsibility as the creator and the originator of the work. This stance indicates the evolving view of authorship in the fourteenth century. At the beginning of book 2, when the text shifts from anecdotal exempla to increasingly obscure proverbs, there is a dedicatory nod to Juan Manuel's friend Jaime de Xérica that has led some critics to believe that Jaime requested Juan Manuel to continue his work beyond book 1 and others to hypothesize a complaint by Jaime regarding Juan Manuel's writing style. All Juan Manuel actually says, however, is that Jaime "told me that he would like for my books to speak more obscurely, and asked of me that if I should make some other book, it not be so clear." The critics have passed over the "if-clause" in this statement, which merely alleges that Jaime de Xérica made a suggestion regarding what Juan Manuel might do should he decide to write more books. Shortly afterward, Juan Manuel adroitly uses Jaime de Xérica's supposed comment to assert that readers should blame his friend and not him for any unpleasant obscurity in the succeeding books, because "he made me compose it like this." Boccaccio and Machaut also claim that they are writing certain works because of the desires and complaints of their friends and readers.

One thing that is known about the relationship of Juan Manuel's literary endeavors to his life is that the most difficult period in personal terms, the years 1327 to 1340, was also the most fruitful for him as a writer. Most of his major works were written during this time, including the *Libro infinido* and his masterpieces, *Libro de los estados* and *El conde Lucanor*. This relationship should again make one cautious about assuming that what happens in Juan Manuel's literary works is a reflection of his real life. The confidence with which the counselor figures in Juan Manuel's writings propose solutions to contemporary sociopolitical problems is quite different from the difficulties Juan Manuel had in navigating his way politically between 1327 and 1340. He describes the world not as he knew it but, rather, as a man of his upbringing hoped it might be. He gives his readers what he considers the best models on which to base their conduct; he knows, however, that the reality in which the reader might try to imitate those models will necessarily deviate from the harmonious balance he has created in his works.

Juan Manuel's writings have stood the test of time, and *El conde Lucanor* in particular has been given canonical status. Many modernized Spanish versions exist, and the work has become part of the secondary-school curriculum in Spain. It has benefited from excellent philological studies by Serés, Alberto Blecua, and José Manuel Blecua. Nevertheless, it has been largely neglected by critics of fourteenth-century literature. In 1972 Daniel Devoto was able to summarize all of the scholarship on *El conde Lucanor* in a single volume. Since then, Diz and Aníbal A. Biglieri have devoted book-length studies to the work. Still, to this day it is almost unknown to scholars of the period who are not specifically working in the field of Spanish letters. Even among Hispanists, some 90 percent of the scholarship on *El conde Lucanor* has been on book 1 only; the number of essays on books 2 through 5 can literally be counted on one's fingers. As for Juan Manuel's other writings, the excellent editions by José Manuel Blecua and by Robert Brian Tate and Ian Macpherson open many new avenues of study for adventurous readers.

Bibliography:

Daniel Devoto, *Introducción al estudio de Don Juan Manuel y en particular de* El conde Lucanor: *Una bibliografía* (Madrid: Castalia, 1972).

Biography:

Andrés Giménez-Soler, *Don Juan Manuel: Biografía y estudio crítico* (Saragossa: Academía Española, 1932).

References:

Reinaldo Ayerbe-Chaux, "*El libro de los proverbios del conde Lucanor y de Patronio,*" in *Studies in Honor of Gustavo Correa,* edited by Charles B. Faulhaber, Richard P. Kinkade, and T. A. Perry (Potomac, Md.: Scripta Humanistica, 1986), pp. 1–10;

Aníbal A. Biglieri, *Hacia una poética del relato didáctico: Ocho estudios sobre* El Conde Lucanor, North Carolina Studies in the Romance Languages and Literatures, no. 233 (Chapel Hill: University of North Carolina Press, 1989);

Alberto Blecua, *La transmisión textual de* "El Conde Lucanor" (Barcelona: Bellaterra, 1980);

James F. Burke, "Frame and Structure in the *Conde Lucanor*," *Revista Canadiense de Estudios Hispánicos*, 8 (1984): 263–274;

Paolo Cherchi, "*Brevedad, oscuredad,* synchysis in *El Conde Lucanor* (Parts II–IV)," *Medioevo Romanzo*, 9 (1984): 361–374;

Laurence de Looze, "*El Conde Lucanor,* Part V, and the Goals of the Manueline Text," *La corónica*, 28, no. 2 (2000): 129–154;

de Looze, "The 'Nonsensical' Proverbs of Juan Manuel's *El Conde Lucanor,* Part IV: A Reassessment," *Revista Canadiense de Estudios Hispánicos*, 25 (2001): 199–221;

A. D. Deyermond, *A Literary History of Spain*, volume 1: *The Middle Ages* (London: Benn / New York: Barnes & Noble, 1971), pp. 109–118;

Marta Ana Diz, *Patronio y Lucanor: La lectura inteligente "en el tiempo que es turbio"* (Potomac, Md.: Scripta Humanistica, 1984);

Peter N. Dunn, "Don Juan Manuel: The World as Text," *Modern Language Notes*, 106 (1991): 223–240;

Dunn, "Framing the Story, Framing the Reader: Two Spanish Masters," *Modern Language Review*, 91 (1996): 94–106;

Umberto Eco, "Two Problems in Textual Interpretation," *Poetics Today*, 2 (1980): 145–161;

Leonardo Funes, "La capitulación del *Libro de los estados:* Consecuencias de un problema textual," *Incipit*, 4 (1984): 71–91;

Funes, "La leyenda de Barlaam y Josafat en el *Libro de los estados* de don Juan Manuel," *Letras*, 15–16 (1985): 84–91;

Funes, "Sobre la partición original del *Libro de los estados,*" *Incipit*, 6 (1986): 3–26;

Funes, "El trabajo intertextual de Don Juan Manuel y la apertura del relato en el *Libro de los estados,*" *Journal of Hispanic Philology*, 12 (1988): 102–112;

Funes and Sun-me Yoon, "Motivación y verosimilitud en el relato-marco del *Libro de los estados,*" *La corónica*, 19 (1991): 100–111;

María Rosa Lida de Malkiel, "Tres Notas sobre Don Juan Manuel," *Romance Philology*, 4 (1950–1951): 155–194;

Ian Macpherson, ed., *Juan Manuel Studies* (London: Tamesis, 1977);

Joseph F. O'Callaghan, *A History of Medieval Spain* (Ithaca, N.Y.: Cornell University Press, 1975), pp. 403, 408, 410–411, 421, 431, 466–467, 510–512;

Alberto Vàrvaro, "La cornice del *Conde Lucanor,*" in *Studi di letteratura spagnola,* edited by Carmelo Samonà (Rome: Tipografia P.U.G., 1964), pp. 187–195.

Libro de Alexandre

(early thirteenth century)

Amaia Arizaleta
Université de Toulouse le Mirail

Manuscripts: The text is extant in two nearly complete manuscripts that apparently belong to two branches of the textual tradition with different readings. The older manuscript, called "O" for its former owner, the duke of Osuna, is Biblioteca Nacional, Madrid, M.S. Vitr. 5-n°10 and dates from the end of the thirteenth century or the beginning of the fourteenth. The language is Castilian with some Leonese dialectical characteristics. It has 2,510 stanzas and was corrected by a different hand in the fifteenth century. Manuscript "P," Bibliothèque Nationale, Paris, MS. Esp. 488, dates from the fifteenth century. Its language is also Castilian but with some Aragonese traits. The Paris manuscript is composed of 2,639 stanzas. There are also a manuscript fragment dating from the fourteenth century and quotations in works of the fifteenth and seventeenth centuries. Modern editors have mainly used manuscript P as the base text of their editions. Stanzas from all sources total 2,675 and are commonly numbered according to the system proposed by Raymond S. Willis in his paleographic edition of the two major manuscripts.

First publications: Francisco de Bivar, *Marci Maximi . . . Continuatio Chronici* (Madrid, 1651); Gutierre Díaz de Games, *Victorial* (Madrid, 1762); *Poema de Alexandre,* in *Colección de poesías castellanas anteriores al siglo XV,* volume 3, edited by Tomás Antonio Sánchez (Madrid: Antonio de Sancha, 1782).

Paleographic edition: *El Libro de Alexandre: Texts of the Paris and the Madrid Manuscripts,* edited by Raymond S. Willis (Princeton: Princeton University Press, 1934).

Standard editions: *Libro de Alexandre,* edited by Jesús Cañas Murillo (Madrid: Editora Nacional, 1978); *Libro de Alejandro,* Versión de Elena Catena (Madrid: Castalia, 1985).

Critical reconstructions: *Gonzalo de Berceo: El libro de Alixandre,* edited by Dana Arthur Nelson (Madrid: Gredos, 1979); *Libro de Alexandre,* edited by Francisco Marcos Marín (Madrid: Alianza, 1987).

Critical edition: *Libro de Alexandre,* edited by Juan Casas Rigall (Madrid: Castalia, 2007).

The anonymous thirteenth-century *Libro de Alexandre* (Book of Alexander) has a fundamental place in the history of medieval Spanish literature because of its metric and thematic influence. Composed of more than ten thousand verses, it is one of the longest works of Castilian romance. It is also the first poem written in *cuaderna vía* (fourfold way), a Castilian strophic form composed of four monorhymed verses of fourteen syllables with a caesura in the middle of each line. Widely embraced by Iberian writers in the thirteenth century, *cuaderna vía* was used for the entire hagiographic corpus of Gonzalo de Berceo and the anonymous epic *Poema de Fernán González* (Poem of Fernán González). In the fourteenth century it is found in Juan Ruiz's *Libro de buen amor* (Book of Good Love), the anonymous *Libro de la miseria d'omne* (Book of the Misery of Mankind), and the *Rimado de palacio* (Rhymed [History] of the Palace), by Pero López de Ayala. In the fifteenth century Íñigo López de Mendoza, Marquis of Santillana, celebrated the *Libro de Alexandre* as a prestigious native model of metrical accomplishment.

The *Libro de Alexandre* is a biography of Alexander the Great that combines nonfictional and fictional elements. The poet adroitly exploits the potential of the epic genre to promote an agenda that includes the diffusion of classical learning, lessons for a just and wise life, and a political ideology concerning good rulers. But he seems to have wanted to construct more than a finely crafted epic with an encyclopedic reach: he has left ample evidence of his interest in the creation of literature.

The initial stanzas amount to a declaration of formal principles of poetic composition and serve as a sort of manifesto for the arrival in Castile of a new manner of composing verses. The author proclaims the power of writing as a guarantor of a warrior's fame, promising that "meten al que bien lidia luego en escriptura" (they will put into writing whoever can fight well). For medieval authors the life of Alexander was second only to the Bible as a source of exemplary behavior, both good and bad, and in Spain writers regarded the *Libro de Alexandre* as an essential model in content and rhetorical style. Its influence can easily be discerned in the *Poema de Fernán González*, the *General estoria* (General History) of Alfonso X *el Sabio* (the Learned), and Ruiz's *Libro de buen amor*. The fifteenth-century author Gutierre Díaz de Games included eighteen stanzas from the poem in his historiographical *Victorial*.

The identity of the author remains unknown. At one point the poet refers to himself as a member of the educated clergy–"somos los simples clérigos" (we are simple clerics)–a disingenuous avowal undermined by the vast Latin learning reflected in the work. There are only the slightest of clues to the poet's region of birth, although most critics concur with Emilio Alarcos Llorach that he was a native Castilian who savored his vernacular idiom and effectively marshaled its strengths and charms. One of the two surviving manuscripts betrays linguistic traits of the eastern (Leonese) border of Castile and the other of the western (Aragonese) border, but these features were more than likely introduced by later copyists and not by the author himself.

José de Pellicer Salas Ossau y Tovar in 1663 and Tomás Antonio Sánchez in his edition of 1782 attributed the poem to Alfonso X, although there is no textual evidence to substantiate the claim. Tomás Antonio Sánchez's 1782 edition of the late-thirteenth- or early-fourteenth-century manuscript that is now in the Biblioteca Nacional in Madrid attributes the work to Juan Lorenzo de Astorga; but the discovery in the nineteenth century of a fourteenth-century manuscript in Paris cast doubt on this attribution, because the explicit (the concluding annotation by the scribe on the production of the book) of that manuscript does not mention Lorenzo and, more significantly, attributes the work to Gonzalo de Berceo. But to complicate matters further, stanza 1528 of the Paris manuscript includes the name "Lorente," and stanza 1386 of the Madrid manuscript contains the name "Gonzalo"; thus, both witnesses refer to the supposed author by the same two different names. Scholars such as Dana Arthur Nelson have endorsed Berceo's authorship, while others, including Ian Michael, have sought a hidden code that might help resolve the enigma. Scholars also continue to debate whether the confused state of the texts reflects a common but mangled source, scribal errors, or even some sort of elaborate inside joke.

Isabel Uría suggests that the poem was the work not of one author but of a team, perhaps working under a master poet who merged the segments he farmed out and gave them polish and unity. Her theory is based on the complexity and vastness of the poem, elements that have led some scholars to compare the *Libro de Alexandre* with some of the grand compilations assembled under the patronage and initiative of Alfonso X.

There is, at least, unanimous agreement concerning the terminus ad quem for the *Libro de Alexandre*: between 1250 and 1252 the poet of the *Poema de Fernán González* relied on the *Libro de Alexandre* as one of his principal sources. As to the terminus a quo, the *Libro de Alexandre* must have been written after 1182, the date of composition of its main textual source, Gautier de Châtillon's Latin epic the *Alexandreis*.

Three periods have been proposed for the composition of the *Libro de Alexandre*. The latest, around 1250, seems unlikely for two reasons. First, the *Libro de Alexandre* seems to have served as a model for a series of works that were written, by all accounts, shortly after 1230. Second, while Raymond S. Willis suggested that an allusion to Seville means that the poem could not have been written before the reconquest of that city in 1248, the "Seville" reading is present only in the Madrid manuscript; the Paris manuscript refers to a different city, Soria. Even if Seville were cited in both manuscripts, mention of its name would not necessarily imply that the poem was written after the return of the city to Christian rule; it was an admired urban environment even under the Moors.

The period between 1215 and 1230 has received wider scholarly acceptance. At the end of the nineteenth century Gottfried Baist declared that an allusion to the king of Sicily indicated that the poem was written not long after 1228, the year Frederick II Hohenstaufen, the king of Sicily, took part in the Fifth Crusade. But the poem says that a king of Sicily sent Alexander a splendid cuirass and that monarchs from Morocco, Germany, France, and Spain also sent gifts to the unvanquished Macedonian prince; the text does not unambiguously allude to Frederick II. And since the king of Germany sends Alexander a tribute distinct from that sent by the Sicilian monarch, Germany must be an independent country with no formal ties to Sicily. Those ties, however, dated back to the marriage of Frederick's parents, Henry VI Hohenstaufen and Constance, heiress to the throne of Sicily. The Spanish poet was probably just following his principal source, the *Alexandreis*.

Alarcos Llorach suggests an earlier date in the period: 1217, the year Damietta, a Muslim stronghold on the Egyptian coast whose name appears in the poem, fell to Crusader armies; but long before its seizure, Damietta was synonymous with great wealth, the topic that brings it into the catalogue of fame of this poem. A flourishing city on the Nile Delta, it was partic-

Page from manuscript "O," the older of two surviving nearly complete manuscripts of the Libro de Alexandre, *copied in the late thirteenth or early fourteenth century (Biblioteca Nacional, Madrid, MS. Vitr. 5-n°10, folio 45v)*

ularly renowned in the Middle Ages for its linen. The anonymous Spanish storyteller compares the city's wealth to that of the chair of Darius, the legendary potentate of Persia, affirming that the rings that adorn the chair are so costly that not even the combined income of the merchants of Damietta could rival their value. His allusion to this city parallels his references to Pisa and Lombardy as paragons of abundance and prosperous merchant enclaves. Given the lateness of both manuscripts and evidence of willful intervention by later scribes, neither the reference to the king of Sicily nor that to Damietta has any decisive value for settling on a date of composition for the *Libro de Alexandre*.

A date between 1215 and 1230 has found a certain degree of acceptance among researchers mostly because the only place in the Iberian Peninsula in the thirteenth century where one could obtain the necessary classical schooling to write the work was the short-lived university at Palencia, which was founded around 1212 and attracted teachers from across Europe. Uría and Enzo Franchini suggest that one or more students could have undertaken the composition of the *Libro de Alexandre* when the university was at its apogee between 1220 and 1240. But European teachers had converged on Palencia since at least 1178 and had fashioned the city's *studium generale* into an important center of learning before the founding of the university.

A third theory is that the poem was composed as early as 1201 to 1207. Stanza 1779 describes the Persian king Darius's tomb and mentions the length of time between the date of his death and the year of Creation; then, in an elaborate display of versified mathematics, it calculates the year of the composition of the *Libro de Alexandre* in reference to the date of Darius's death. Willis was the first to interpret the stanza as a reliable declaration of the date of the poem, concluding that the poet meant his roundabout calculations to come out to 1201 or 1202. Niall Ware worked out a date of 1204, while Francisco Marcos Marín proposed a range of years from 1202 to 1207. It seems certain that the poet wanted to provide a firm date; but either he could not produce the wording to emulate the precision achieved by his Latin model, or his formulation was garbled by subsequent copyists who rewrote the lines to give a better—or their own—year.

The poem is based on the life of Alexander the Great, but the poet has spliced in the story of the Trojan War, as well as assorted digressions of varying length and purpose. Michael points out in *The Treatment of Classical Material in the "Libro de Alexandre"* (1970) that "this multiple form of composition has some connections with the medieval *artes poeticae* and contemporary forms in painting and sculpture, as well with the *artes praedicandi* and medieval musical forms." The narrative of

Alexander's life can be divided into three principal parts. The first, stanzas 7 through 198, follows him from birth to his coronation. Alexander's education under the tutelage of the philosopher Aristotle includes assurances that the young prince will become a knight and king endowed with exemplary wisdom. These stanzas also report Alexander's anguish over tribute Greece has to pay to Persia. Aristotle counsels a bold counterstroke that hastens the prince toward his ceremonial knighting. A fundamental part of the investiture rite is the enumeration of the magic articles, some fashioned by fairies, that are received by the prince along with the fierce white charger Bucephalus. Armed, mounted, and authorized to lead men into battle, Alexander defeats the haughty King Nicholas of Armenia, seizes control of Nicholas's realm, and takes revenge on Pausanias, the assassin of his father, King Philip. He then assumes the crown as the new king of Macedonia.

The second and by far the longest part of the poem, stanzas 199 through 2,265, narrates Alexander's conquests, beginning with Athens. After the conquest of Thebes and the army's landfall on Asia Minor, Alexander delivers a prolonged account of the history of Troy that is based on popular medieval Latin sources. After this loving tribute to the type of fame to which he aspires, Alexander marches toward his confrontation with Darius, his principal rival for sovereignty over the known world. After diverse skirmishes and perils, the two armies face each other at Issus, where Alexander carries the day. He advances without pause, seizing the cities of Tyre and Gaza, entering Jerusalem, and making his way to the sacred temple of Ammon in Egypt. The poet describes the death of Darius's captured wife and her honorable burial at the command of the hero. The second battle with Darius takes place at Arbela (also called Gaugamela) and concludes with Alexander's definitive victory and the Persian king's flight. Alexander enters Babylon too late to forestall Darius's assassination at the hands of the traitors Bessus and Narbazanes. The poet shows the hero's greatness as Alexander weeps at the loss and the valor of his foe.

Alexander consorts with the Amazonian queen Thalastris in acquiescence to her offer to bear him a son, and he weds the barbarian Roxanne, but these trysts are brief digressions from the second great military engagement of this section of the poem: the confrontation with Porus, king of India. The narrative of Alexander's encounter with this monarch echoes the spirit and themes of his Persian campaign: two battles, two victories for Alexander, and a finale in which the conqueror displays his appreciation of his rival's noble qualities.

The third part of the poem (stanzas 2,266 through 2,675) tells of the hero's descent into the depths of the ocean in what amounts to an early ancestor of the diving bell, his flight in a gondola hoisted by tame griffins, and encounters with diverse and exotic peoples. It also departs from Alexander's exploits to serve up a description of hell populated by allegorized sins, including the Macedonian's own principal fault: overweening pride. Divine anger at the youth's efforts to fathom the secrets of nature moves the goddess Pride to seek the help of Satan to destroy Alexander. Treason, one of the devil's personal ministers, enlists the help of Jobas and Antipater to poison Alexander. The crime takes place in Babylon, where Alexander has established a tented palace that has previously been described as a magnificent microcosm of the world itself. Aware of his betrayal and impending death, Alexander takes leave of his men, makes his will, and dies with dignity, commending his soul to God. The account ends with expressions of loss and bereavement by the hero's subjects and family and descriptions of the discord that reigns among those who inherit his empire.

The *Libro de Alexandre* shows how a moral and practical schooling and a curious, almost presumptuously demanding mind are as much a guarantee of success as are military strategy and charismatic governance. The second and third parts of the poem, which recount Alexander's conquests of territory and of forbidden knowledge, are inextricably bound to the first part, in which the future king is presented as the overachieving disciple of the polymath Aristotle. He conquers the world and the hearts of his followers and foes alike but cannot limit his zeal to what is allowed to mortals. The work lays out the necessity of blending practical and theoretical knowledge with the wisdom of the ancients—a shrewd endorsement of the instruction available from scholars such as the *Libro de Alexandre* poet. A good Christian cleric, the storyteller had to respect tradition's judgment on the hero, which ascribed his untimely end to divine retribution for his excess of curiosity and pride. The poet makes it clear that the dangers that most often lie in wait for a powerful monarch are pride, ambition, discord among subjects, and, above all, treason. But God does not directly annihilate Alexander: death befalls the Macedonian through the actions of Treason's accomplices.

Another theme of the *Libro de Alexandre* is the transformative power—and danger—of knowledge. Though the third part of the poem narrates Alexander's mythic exploits, testimony to the Macedonian's desire for all forms of knowledge can be found throughout the work and serves both to delineate his character and to display the author's own erudition. The poem demonstrates the poet's mastery of grammar and rhetoric, which is not surprising in a university-trained cleric capable of composing such a vast work as the *Libro de Alexandre*. But Alexander also has a firm command of dialectics and is interested in medicine, music, and astronomy, all of which are treated with confident adroitness. The first part of the poem delineates Alexander's acquisition of the scholar's tools, and the two remaining parts show how those tools make an able ruler. Only at the end of the hero's life, after the warrior's tasks have been accomplished, is the reader shown how the thirst for knowledge, indulged to excess, leads to the destruction of the hero.

The principal source of the *Libro de Alexandre* is the *Alexandreis,* a classically inspired Latin epic that became a widely used medieval school text. It was supplemented by the French vernacular *Roman d'Alexandre* (Tale of Alexander), which includes fantastic elements, and the late Latin *Historia de Proeliis* (History of Battles), a conflation of Alexander's more-fabulous adventures with his historical deeds. All three works were written after 1150. Other sources provided the finishing touches to a text that became an authoritative resource in itself. From the Silver Age schoolbook *Ilias Latina* (Latin Iliad) came the material for the digression concerning the Trojan War, and tidbits were taken from Isidore of Seville's *Etymologies* (circa 635), an encyclopedic work built around mostly fanciful word histories. Echoes of the second-century *Physiologus* (Physical Science), the third- or fourth-century *Disticha Catonis* (Verses of Cato the Philosopher), several of Ovid's classical Latin compositions, the Old and New Testaments, and the *Mythographii Vaticani* (Vatican Manuscript of Mythical Tales) can also be found in the poem. The poet does not just translate and conflate his source texts: he transforms the material and creates a homogeneous whole, adding touches from his personal stock of rhetorical grace notes and his interpretative stance. The passages dedicated to medicine and astronomy, for example, seem to be drawn from the *Alexandreis* but polished with elements taken from the *Etymologies*.

Most scholars consider the *Libro de Alexandre* the first poem in the *mester de clerecía* (craft or art form of clerics) style. The term, which is applied to all *cuaderna vía* poems composed in writing in the thirteenth century, was coined by nineteenth-century critics from two words in the second stanza of the *Libro de Alexandre:* "mester traigo fermoso, non es de joglaría, / mester es sin pecado, ca es de clerezía" (I present a comely craft, which is not like that of the minstrels, / it is a sinless art, since it is that of the clergy). The opening stanza also includes the poet's self-imposed rules for generating *mester de clerecía* poems: "fablar curso rimado por la quaderna vía, / a sílabas contadas, ca es grant maestría" (to compose a rhymed discourse in the fourfold way, counting the syllables, because that is great art). The lines are of rigorously equal length—fourteen syllables—

divided into equal hemistiches, each of which has an obligatory stress on the sixth syllable, and are combined into four-line stanzas with a single rhyme. This type of versification was unknown in Castilian romance poetry before the *Libro de Alexandre,* and to this day Spanish metrics refers to this sort of line as an "alexandrine."

The *cuaderna vía* meter distinguishes the *Libro de Alexandre* from oral epic tales, although Uría has pointed out that the cadence and stability of the rhythm make the poem well suited for memorization and recitation. The entire poem, or parts of it, could also have been sung; the May poem that precedes the account of Alexander's marriage to Roxanne would have lent itself well to performance along the lines of the *mayas* (May songs) of popular tradition.

The *Libro de Alexandre* perfectly combines what Horace defined as the main functions of literature: to teach and to entertain. The poet says in the exordium that "debe de lo que sabe omne largo seer" (one must be generous with his knowledge) but also that "qui oír lo quisiere . . . / avrá de mi solaz, en cabo grant plazer (whosoever should want to listen to it [my tale] . . . / will have from me pleasure and great comfort in the end). The pleasure depends to a great degree on an able combination of *clerecía* and *juglaría* (minstrelsy). Although the poem belongs to a self-declared clerical genre, the appearance of formulaic language proper to the art of the minstrels would have served as bait with which to lure a public familiar with their poems. Among the most obvious formulas are the frequent gestures toward an audience of listeners, thanking them for attending to the tale and inviting them to be impressed with this or that detail. Also, in imitation of the popular Spanish epic the *Libro de Alexandre* poet deploys a phrase found in the opening lines of the anonymous *Cantar de mio Cid* (circa 1200, Song of My Cid; translated as *Poem of the Cid,* 1879), "De los sus ojos tan fuertemientre llorando" (Crying from those eyes of his), which is rendered here as "llorando de los ojos" (crying from his eyes). Another telling instance is the phrase "el rey Alexandre de la barva onrada" (King Alexander, he of the noble beard), which parallels beard imagery in the *Cantar de mio Cid.* Although, as Michael has argued, "they are not part of an active oral device" but "the dying reflection in a more learned work of what had been a flourishing epic convention," these expressions were still characteristic marks of the minstrel's art and would have been recognized as such by the public. Other evidence of habits of oral composition include the recycling of phrases and words to create modified lines that sustain a tone and style and reinforce a recurring image, as when the narrator says, referring to Aeneas, "tan rabioso com' una sierpe fiera" (he came

on raging like a savage serpent), and a few lines later, "Andaba tan rabioso com' una sierpe brava" (He came on raging like an angry serpent). There are also recurrent echoes of the vernacular idiom in popular turns of phrase and folk sayings, such as homespun asides on someone who "just as well should never have been born," repeated uses of "Christians and Moors" to mean "everyone," and humorous observations about Venus promising Paris that she will make Helen want to place him "under her curtains," Menalaus finding his "inn swept clean" of his young wife, and Achilles rushing at a foe like a greedy man lunging for a glass of wine. Still, the poet keeps his level of discourse elevated by ponderous reflections on high moral themes, direct allusions to classical personages and authors, and a regular sprinkling of Latinisms.

The author of *Libro de Alexandre* thus does not look down on minstrel poetry, as was once supposed, but pays implicit homage to it by using its technical devices and tone. Above all, however, the work displays the learned rhetoric characteristic of the schoolman's voice. The author has studied the arts of the trivium, and the poem is an instrument for teaching an unlearned public. This idea is promoted in the text when the narrator says that Alexander "mandó venir los sabios que sabían las naturas, / que entendían los signos e las cosas escuras; / mandóles que guardasen, segund las escripturas, / qué signos demostraban estas tales figuras" (made the wise men come, the ones who knew the secret arts, / who understood signs and obscure matters; / he made them interpret, according to what is written in books / what signs these figures and portents revealed). The poet demonstrates how what appears hidden can be placed within anyone's reach through exegesis; all that is required is that wise men interpret the recondite and explain it to the unlearned. The poet evidently thought that he was such an interpreter, and his choice of the vernacular facilitates his instruction.

Although it is full of sober moralizing themes, the text is also an immense repository of battles and legends. Its novelesque quality must have made it attractive to a public that might have included noble and clerical households. While the latter would have had a greater taste for the moral perspectives, the work could have served as a sort of catechetical tool for the ruling class. In this respect the *Libro de Alexandre* is a predecessor of the Spanish romances of chivalry: it is the story of a young protagonist who is endowed through instruction with many virtues, launches himself on a quest for the unknown, and vanquishes a thousand enemies; he is chivalrous at court and at home in a magical and marvelous world.

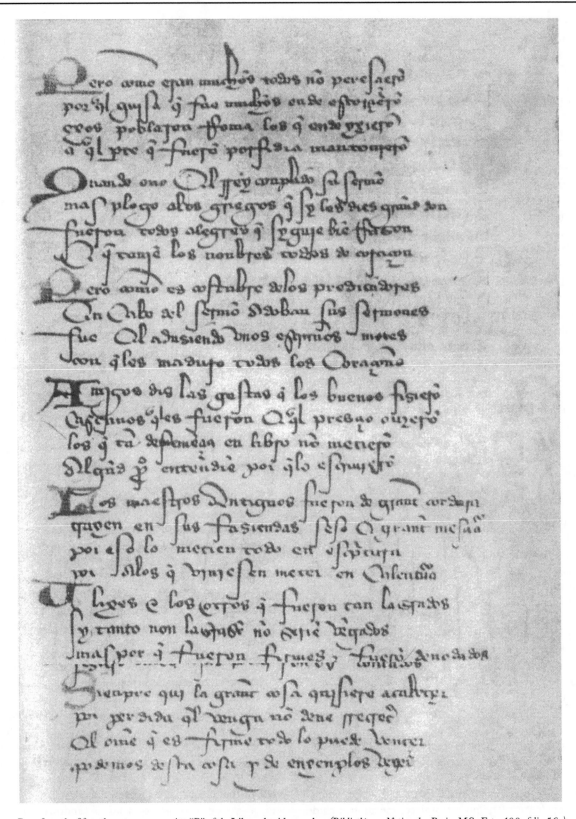

Page from the fifteenth-century manuscript "P" of the Libro de Alexandre *(Bibliothèque Nationale, Paris, MS. Esp. 488, folio 56v)*

In the thirteenth century Alexander was regarded as a model of monarchy and conquest, the greatest sovereign the world had ever known. Several medieval monarchs, such as Philip II of France, claimed to be contemporary avatars of Alexander; Frederick II Hohenstaufen represented himself as a resurrected Alexander and entered Jerusalem with great pomp, just as the Macedonian king had done. (The *Libro de Alexandre* stages this peaceful visit to the Holy City with a Jewish high priest dressed as a Christian bishop coming out to greet the entering hero.) Thus, one of the generic models of the *Libro de Alexandre* may have been the *speculum principum* (mirror of princes), a handbook assembled from heroic and exemplary narratives, conversations between a sage and the prince entrusted to his tutelage, and philosophical considerations on right rule and effective leadership.

Michael points out that the *Libro de Alexandre* Christianizes pagan source material and allows it to be interpreted according to the reader's "own intellectual, moral and emotional criteria." The definitive lesson of the work from a moral point of view is the vanity of worldly things and the pettiness of human actions: "Alexandre que era rëy de grant poder, que nin mares nin tierra non lo podién caber, en una foya ovo en cabo a caer que non pudo de término doze piedes tener" (Alexander, who was a king of great power, whom seas and land could not contain, came to rest into a furrow of no more than twelve feet in length). Gnomic works such as the *Libro de los doze sabios* (Book of the Twelve Wise Men), the *Libro de los buenos proverbios* (Book of Sound Proverbs), and the *Bocados de Oro* (Choice Golden Morsels) include scenes of philosophers convening around Alexander's tomb. In the final stanzas of the poem the hero at the moment of death "mandó que lo echassen del lecho en el suelo" (demanded to be taken from the bed to the floor). This scene, depicting the humility of a man who returns to dust and ashes, is common in descriptions of the deaths of other Western monarchs and saints, including King Louis IX of France and St. Francis of Assisi. In Alfonso X's *Estoria de España* (History of Spain) Alfonso's father, King Fernando III of Castile and León (who, like his cousin Louis IX, was both a king and a saint), in the face of his imminent death "fizo una muy maravillosa cosa de grant omildat: ca a la ora que lo asomar vio, dexose derribar del lecho en tierra" (did a wonderful thing of great humility: when he saw it [the consecrated Host] come, he let himself slip from the bed onto the earth). Everything indicates that the authors of the *Estoria de España* and those of the *General estoria,* both of which were composed in the decade 1270 to 1280, took the *Libro de Alexandre* as a source of content and inspiration.

It is also possible that the poem served as a "mirror of princes" for Fernando III or Alfonso X, even if it was not written with this end in mind. Alexander is, above all, a king at war. Over their long and embattled reigns Fernando and Alfonso acquitted themselves with superb skill on the battlefield. In the historical context of the Iberian Peninsula of the thirteenth century, those coincidences could not have gone unnoticed. The battles waged by the Macedonian general would have found keen and appreciative ears in Iberian courts. The many verses dedicated to military strategy, the camaraderie among soldiers, the establishment of the leader's authority, and the enumeration of successive battles cannot have failed to entertain courtiers whose livelihood and glory were based on the seizure of neighboring lands. The text presents a concrete image of the function of royal power: it is the sovereign's duty to make war on his enemies, whether near or far. In an impossible feat of anachronism, the poem even declares that Alexander wants to conquer the Iberian Peninsula and the kingdom of Castile. The author uses this narrative device to praise the Castilians: "desque oviés a Africa en su poder tornada, entrar en Europa, toda la mar passada, enpeçar en España, una tierra señada, tierra de fuertes gentes e bien encastillada" (once Africa was under his control he would enter Europe, crossing the sea, to begin in Spain, a noteworthy land, a land strong in peoples and strong in castles). In this way he draws his hero close to the immediate experience of his audience.

The young Alexander is knighted before being crowned, and that ceremony is recounted in more verses than the coronation. It is possible to read the prince's placing the sword on himself as an approximation of the self-dubbing of Alfonso VIII of Castile. Alfonso VIII presented himself as the head of a chivalric order destined to fight against the infidel; after the rout at Alarcos in 1195, he began to elaborate a new monarchical ideology, based on virtue and victory, that led to his decisive defeat of the Muslims at the Navas de Tolosa in 1212. The *Libro de Alexandre* may be a witness to this change of political direction.

The *Libro de Alexandre* is a work of extraordinary richness: it places the adventurous life of Alexander the Great within a universe of incredible encounters, voyages to far-off lands, exotic delights, scientific information, luxury, mythology, and salvation and perdition. There is still no consensus among specialists about the author's attitude toward his hero: some, such as Uría and Franchini, believe that he condemns Alexander as an incarnation of pride; others, including Michael and Arizaleta, think that Alexander is redeemed by emulating monarchical and intellectual ideals. The poem is an encyclopedia of received knowledge, a repository of folklore, a didactic treatise, and a work that carries a heavy ideological burden.

References:

Emilio Alarcos Llorach, *Investigaciones sobre el Libro de Alexandre* (Madrid: Consejo Superior de Investigaciones Científicas, 1948);

Amaia Arizaleta, "Alexandre en su *Libro,*" *La corónica,* 28 (2000): 3–20;

Arizaleta, "La jerarquía de las fuentes del *Libro de Alexandre,*" in *Actas del VI Congreso de la Asociación Hispánica de Literatura Medieval: Alcalá de Henares, 12–16 de septiembre de 1995,* 2 volumes, edited by José Manuel Lucía Megías (Alcalá de Henares: Universidad de Alcalá, 1997), I: 183–189;

Arizaleta, *La translation d'Alexandre: Recherches sur les structures et les significations du Libro de Alexandre* (Paris: Klincksieck, 1999);

Gottfried Baist, "Eine neue Handschrift des Spanischen Alexandre," *Romanische Forschungen,* 6 (1891): 292;

Peter A. Bly and Alan Deyermond, "The Use of *figura* in the *Libro de Alexandre,*" *Journal of Medieval and Renaissance Studies,* 2 (1972): 151–181;

Marina Scordilis Brownlee, "Pagan and Christian: The Bivalent Hero of the *Libro de Alexandre,*" *Kentucky Romance Quarterly,* 30 (1983): 263–270;

Juan Manuel Cacho Blecua, "El saber y el dominio de la naturaleza en el *Libro de Alexandre,*" in *Actas del III Congreso de la Asociación Hispánica de Literatura Medieval: Salamanca, 3 al 6 de octubre de 1989,* 2 volumes, edited by María Isabel Toro Pascua (Salamanca: Universidad de Salamanca, 1994), I: 197–207;

Cacho Blecua, "La tienda en el *Libro de Alexandre,*" in *La lengua y la literatura en tiempos de Alfonso X: Actas del Congreso Internacional, Murcia, 5–10 marzo 1984,* edited by Fernando Carmona and Francisco J. Flores (Murcia: Universidad de Murcia, 1985), pp. 109–134;

George Cary, *The Medieval Alexander* (Cambridge: Cambridge University Press, 1956);

Brian Dutton, "A Further Note in the *Alexandre* Enigma," *Bulletin of Hispanic Studies,* 48 (1971): 298–300;

Dutton, "The Profession of Gonzalo de Berceo and the Paris Manuscript of the *Libro de Alexandre,*" *Bulletin of Hispanic Studies,* 37, no. 3 (1960): 137–145;

Charles F. Fraker, "*Aetiologia* in the *Libro de Alexandre,*" *Hispanic Review,* 55 (1987): 277–299;

Fraker, *The Libro de Alexandre: Medieval Epic and Silver Latin* (Chapel Hill: University of North Carolina Department of Romance Languages, 1993);

Fraker, "The Role of Rhetoric in the Construction of the *Libro de Alexandre,*" *Bulletin of Hispanic Studies,* 65 (1988): 353–368;

Enzo Franchini, "El IV Concilio de Letrán, la apócope extrema y la fecha de composición del *Libro de Alexandre,*" *La corónica,* 25 (1997): 31–74;

Olegario García de la Fuente, *El latín bíblico y el español medieval hasta el 1300,* volume 2: *El Libro de Alexandre* (Logroño: Instituto de Estudios Riojanos, 1986);

Eugenio García Gascón, "Los manuscritos P y O del *Libro de Alexandre* y la fecha de composición del original," *Revista de Literatura Medieval,* 1 (1990): 31–39;

Jorge García López, "De la prioridad cronológica del *Libro de Alexandre,*" in *Actas del II Congreso de la Asociación Hispánica de Literatura Medieval: Segovia, del 5 al 19 de Octubre de 1987,* 2 volumes, edited by José Manuel Lucía Megías, Paloma García Alonso, and Carmen Martín Daza (Alcalá de Henares: Universidad de Alcalá, 1991), I: 341–354;

Fernando Gómez Redondo, *Historia de la prosa medieval castellana,* volume 1: *La creación del discurso prosístico: El entramado cortesano* (Madrid: Cátedra, 1998);

Marta Haro Cortés, *La imagen del poder real a través de los compendios de castigos castellanos del siglo XIII* (London: Queen Mary and Westfield College, 1996);

José Hernando Pérez, *Hispano Diego Garcia, escritor y poeta medieval, y el "Libro de Alexandre"* (Burgos: J. Hernando Pérez, 1992);

Gerold Hilty, "Fecha y autor del *Libro de Alexandre,*" in *Actas del VI Congreso Internacional de la Asociación Hispánica de Literatura Medieval,* I: 813–820;

María Rosa Lida, "La leyenda de Alejandro en la literatura medieval," *Romance Philology,* 15 (1961–1962): 413–423;

Francisco Marcos Marín, "Establecimiento de la fecha del *Libro de Alexandre,*" *Zeitschrift für Romanische Philologie,* 112 (1996): 424–437;

Marcos Marín, "Libro de Alexandre," in *Diccionario filológico de Literatura Medieval Española,* edited by Carlos Alvar and José Manuel Lucía Megías (Madrid: Castalia, 2002), pp. 754–762;

Ramón Menéndez Pidal, ed., *Alfonso X: Primera Crónica General* (Madrid: Gredos, 1955);

Ian Michael, "The Alexandre Enigma: A Solution," in *Medieval and Renaissance Studies in Honour of Robert Brian Tate,* edited by Michael and Richard A. Cardwell (Oxford: Dolphin, 1986), pp. 109–121;

Michael, "A Comparison of the Use of Epic Epithets in the *Poema de Mio Cid* and the *Libro de Alexandre,*" *Bulletin of Hispanic Studies,* 38 (1960): 32–41;

Michael, *The Treatment of Classical Material in the "Libro de Alexandre"* (Manchester, U.K.: Manchester University Press, 1970);

Dana Arthur Nelson, *Gonzalo de Berceo y el "Alixandre": Vindicación de un estilo* (Madison: Hispanic Seminar of Medieval Studies, 1991);

José de Pellicer Salas Ossau y Tovar, *Informe del origen, antigüedad, calidad y sucesión de la Excelentísma Casa de Sarmiento de Villamayor* (Madrid, 1663);

Francisco Rico, "La clerecía del mester," *Hispanic Review,* 53 (1985): 1–23, 127–150;

David J. A. Ross, "Alexander Iconography in Spain: The *Libro de Alexandre,*" *Scriptorium,* 21 (1967): 83–86;

Isabel Uría, *Panorama crítico del mester de clerecía* (Madrid: Castalia, 2000), pp. 177–213;

Niall Ware, "The Date of Composition of the *Libro de Alexandre:* A Reexamination of Stanza 1799," *Bulletin of Hispanic Studies,* 42 (1965): 252–254;

Ware, "Gonçalo, Lorenço, Lorente: An Alexandre Enigma," *Bulletin of Hispanic Studies,* 44 (1967): 41–43;

Raymond S. Willis, *The Debt of the Spanish "Libro de Alexandre" to the French "Roman d'Alexandre"* (Princeton: Princeton University Press, 1935);

Willis, "*Mester de clerecía*: A Definition of the *Libro de Alexandre,*" *Romance Philology,* 10 (1956–1957): 212–224;

Willis, *The Relationship of the Spanish "Libro de Alexandre" to the "Alexandreis" of Gautier de Châtillon* (Princeton: Princeton University Press, 1934).

Libro de Apolonio

(late thirteenth century)

Michèle S. de Cruz-Sáenz

Manuscript: The work is preserved in folios 1r–64v of Real Biblioteca del Monasterio de El Escorial, MS. K.III.4, a fourteenth-century codex consisting of eighty-five folios of Ceuta paper measuring 250 by 180 millimeters. The text is written in a single column of twenty to twenty-two lines per folio. The manuscript also contains unique Spanish verse redactions of the *Vida de madona Santa María Egipciaqua* and the *Libre dels tres reys d'Orient.*

First publication: "Libre de Appollonio," in *Colección de poesías castellanas anteriores al siglo XV,* volume 3, edited by Tomás Antonio Sánchez (Madrid: A. de Sancha, 1782).

Paleographic edition: *Libro de Apolonio: Estudios, ediciones, concordancias,* 3 volumes, edited by Manuel Alvar (Madrid: Fundación Juan March / Valencia: Castalia, 1976); *Text and concordances of Escorial MS. K.III.4,* edited by Michèle S. de Cruz-Sáenz (Madison, Wis.: Hispanic Seminary of Medieval Studies, 1992).

Standard editions: *Libro de Apolonio: An Old Spanish Poem,* 2 volumes, edited by C. Carroll Marden, Elliott Monographs in the Romance Languages and Literatures, nos. 11–12 (Baltimore: Johns Hopkins University Press / Paris: Champion, 1917, 1922); *Libro de Apolonio: Estudios, Ediciones, Concordancias,* 3 volumes, edited by Manuel Alvar (Madrid: Fundación Juan March / Valencia: Castalia, 1976); *Libro de Apolonio: Introducción, edición y notas,* edited by Alvar (Barcelona: Planeta, 1984); *Libro de Apolonio,* edited by Carmen Monedero (Madrid: Castalia, 1987); *Libro de Apolonio,* edited by Dolores Corbella Díaz (Madrid: Castalia, 1992), online at <http://www.cervantesvirtual.com/>.

Modernized edition: *Libro de Apolonio,* edited by D. Pablo Cabañas (Madrid: Castalia, Odres Nuevos, 1955).

Edition in English: *The Book of Apollonius,* translated by Raymond L. Grismer and Elizabeth Atkins (Minneapolis: University of Minnesota Press, 1936).

The *Libro de Apolonio* (translated as *The Book of Apollonius,* 1936) is an anonymous thirteenth-century Castilian translation and revision of a tenth-century Latin version of Simphosius's sixth-century *Historia Apollonii Regis Tyri* (History of Apollonius, King of Tyre), which is itself based on a third-century Latin translation of a no-longer-extant Greek original. It consists of 656 four-verse stanzas, plus two additional verses, for a total of 2,626 verses. The poem is written in *cuaderna vía* (fourfold way): stanzas of four monorhymed verses of fourteen syllables, with each verse separated into hemistichs by a medial caesura. The *cuaderna vía* was the preferred meter and stanza of works of the *mester de clerecía* (craft of the clerics), which also include the *Libro de Alexandre* (early thirteenth century, Book of Alexander), the writings of Gonzalo de Berceo, and Juan Ruiz's *Libro de buen amor* (circa 1330–1343; translated as *Book of Good Love,* 1933).

The *Libro de Apolonio* is extant only in Escorial Manuscript K.III.4, a fourteenth-century codex that probably originally belonged to the library of Jerónimo Zurita. His manuscripts were deposited in the monastery of Aula Dei in Saragossa in 1571. It later turned up in the library of the Conde-Duque de Olivares and still later in the Convento del Ángel in Seville. Each verse begins with a majuscule in the left margin; these letters are touched up with color, sometimes gold. C. Carroll Marden notes that "While the handwriting is clear, the frequency of erasures, blotted letters, rewritten words, syllables and letters, shows a coolness somewhat surprising on the part of a scribe who is at such pains to write clearly." Abbreviation strokes are found above words that seem to be spelled out fully; the most common example is a tilde over the word *mucho* (much) that might indicate the pronunciation *muncho* or might mean nothing at all.

The plot of the *Libro de Apolonio* is taken from the *Historia Apollonii Regis Tyri* but is reinterpreted to make it relevant to a thirteenth-century audience, and the work becomes an encyclopedia of medieval mores and customs. The protagonist is a mythical hero with classical overtones, but he is also the incarnation of a chivalrous ideal imbued with the respect for knowledge that characterized King Alfonso X *el Sabio* (the Learned) of Castile and León.

The poet begins his tale with an invocation to God and the Virgin Mary and solicits their assistance in composing in the "nueva maestría" (new mastery) a romance of King Apollonius, who was destined to lose his daughter and his wife only to recover them later. The wife of King Antioch, founder of the city of the same name, dies, leaving him with a daughter of unequaled beauty who is wooed by princes from near and far. The devil causes Antioch to fall in love with his daughter, and against her will she submits to the incestuous relationship. Her shame leads her to try to starve herself to death, but an old woman persuades her that she is not responsible for the situation and advises her to conceal what has happened. The king forestalls her engagement to anyone else by posing a riddle to the suitors in which a confession of his incest is hidden "La verdura de ramo es come la rayz, / De carne de mi madre engruesso mi serviz" (The verdor of the limb is like the root, / Of the flesh of my mother I increase my service); when they fail to solve it, they are beheaded. Many have fallen victim when Apollonius, the monarch of the city of Tyre, presents himself as a suitor and pledges his city for the princess's dowry. Apollonius solves the riddle, understands the sin it implies, and berates Antioch for his conduct. Rather than lose his daughter, Antioch declares the answer false; but instead of beheading Apollonius, he gives the latter thirty days to devise another solution. Apollonius returns to Tyre and studies the riddle but cannot find another answer.

Fearing exposure, Antioch sends his servant Taliarcus to kill Apollonius. In Tyre, Taliarcus finds a depressed citizenry. When he asks why, he is told that Apollonius, ashamed of his failure to solve the riddle, has sailed away to an unknown destination. Taliarcus returns to Antioch and reports Apollonius's self-banishment. Antioch promises to reward anyone who kills or captures Apollonius.

Apollonius drops anchor in Tarsus, where he is warned of Antioch's threat to his life. He is invited to stay in the home of Estrangilius, a city councilman. Estrangilius tells him of the scarcity of grain in the city, and Apollonius offers to sell the city a hundred thousand bushels of grain, which he has aboard his ships, for the price at which it is sold in Tyre. In appreciation, the people erect a statue of Apollonius in the marketplace. On Estrangilius's advice, Apollonius leaves Tarsus to spend the winter in Pentapolin. Two hours into the voyage a storm capsizes the ships, and all perish except Apollonius.

Apollonius washes up, unconscious, on a beach in Pentapolin. Recovering his senses, he laments his circumstances and asks a fisherman for assistance. The fisherman takes Apollonius home and shares his meager food and clothing with the king. Apollonius promises to double the value of the fisherman's services when he recovers his fortune. The fisherman accompanies him to the city gate, where Apollonius joins some youths who are playing a ball game.

King Architrastes arrives with his entourage and, noticing the stranger's superior skill, orders Apollonius to play with him. After the game, he invites Apollonius to dinner. When Apollonius does not appear at the table, Architrastes dispatches a squire to find him; the squire reports that Apollonius refuses to enter the palace because he is improperly attired, and the king sends out appropriate raiment. At the table Architrastes introduces his daughter, Luciana, to Apollonius and tells her of the newcomer's athletic skill. Apollonius recounts his lamentable adventures, and Luciana plays the *vihuela* (an early guitar) to soothe him. Everyone praises her musical gifts except Apollonius; when Architrastes asks why he is silent, Apollonius says that she played well but not expertly. Entreated to perform himself, he requests a bow. The king orders that his best bow be given to Apollonius. Everyone says that he plays better than Apollo or Orpheus, and Luciana offers Apollonius two hundred *quintales* of gold and as many of silver, plus food, wine, and personal servants, to be her music teacher. During her studies Luciana and Apollonius fall in love, and she becomes weak and thin and finally desperately ill from desire.

One day Architrastes and Apollonius are out walking and meet three young princes who had proposed to Luciana and had agreed to accept her father's decision as to which one would marry her. The king informs them that his daughter is ill and that the doctors are not certain that she will live but tells them to put their dowry offers in letters to Luciana, who will choose among them. He places Apollonius in charge of bearing the letters to Luciana. When he delivers them, she asks for his advice. He tells her that she should marry someone better than any of these three. She writes to her father that she chooses the pilgrim who was saved from the sea. The king, not understanding, gives the letter to Apollonius to interpret. Blushing, Apollonius confesses that the letter refers to him. Architrastes and Apollonius return to the palace, and Architrastes asks Luciana whom she wants to marry. She answers that if she cannot marry Apollonius, she does not wish to live. The king accedes to her wishes; she recovers from her lovesickness; and the couple marry.

Seven months later, Apollonius is walking on the beach and sees a beautiful ship at anchor. He learns that

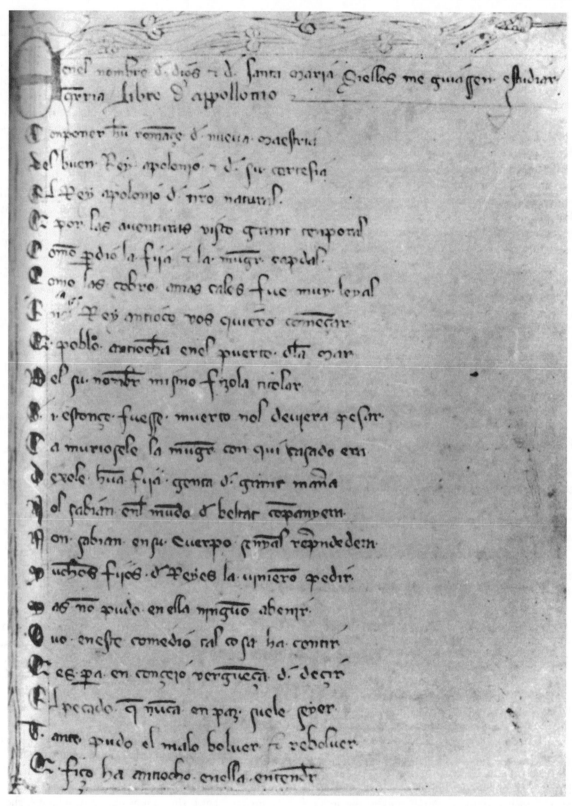

Manuscript page from the introduction to the Libro de Apolonio *(Real Biblioteca del Monasterio de El Escorial, MS. K.III4, folio 1r)*

the vessel is from Tyre, that Antioch and his daughter are dead, and that the people are awaiting Apollonius's return. Apollonius tells the pregnant Luciana of his wish to claim Antioch's kingdom and asks her to accompany him. En route Luciana gives birth to a daughter, Tarsiana, but falls gravely ill "en falsa muerte" (in a false death). A superstitious helmsman tells the king that the body must be thrown overboard, or else all on board will perish. The body is placed in a coffin with money and a letter and cast into the sea.

On the third day the coffin washes up at the port of Ephesus and is discovered by a physician walking along the shore. He has it taken to his house. When his apprentice begins to embalm the "corpse," he notices a faint pulse. Luciana is revived, and the physician and his apprentice care for her during her recuperation. To safeguard her chastity until her husband returns, they build a temple to the goddess Diana and install Luciana as its priestess.

Apollonius docks at Tarsus and entrusts his daughter and her nursemaid, Licorides, to Estrangilius. Vowing not to cut his nails or his hair until he can marry his daughter well, he withdraws to Egypt. Estrangilius and his wife, Dionisa, raise the child, and by the age of twelve she has mastered all the arts but is ignorant of her heritage. The dying Licorides tells Tarsiana that she is the child of Apollonius and Luciana and that her father is in Egypt. With Licorides dead, Dionisa plots to murder her stepdaughter and use the princess's adornments and treasure to marry her own daughter well. Dionisa engages a man named Theophilus to kill Tarsiana while she is praying at Licorides' grave. When he grabs her by the hair, she pleads for time to commend her soul to God. He agrees; but while she is praying, pirates appear, and Theophilus flees. He reports to Dionisa that he has accomplished the task, and she sends him away to die in servitude.

The pirates take Tarsiana to the slave market in Mytilene, where Prince Antinagorus takes a liking to her and tries to purchase her. But a pimp doubles his bid, and Antinagorus lets his rival purchase the girl with the intention of renting her from him afterward. He does so; but after hearing her story, he pays the fee and leaves her untouched. All of her other clients react similarly. Tarsiana then persuades her master that she can earn even more money for him by performing on the *vihuela,* and the enterprise proves quite successful.

Apollonius returns to Tarsus and asks for his daughter. Dionisa tells him that she died of a heart ailment and orders an ornate sepulcher set up. But when Apollonius goes to see it, tears will not come; some inner sense tells him that his daughter is not buried there. Grief stricken, he embarks for Tyre; but the ship encounters a fierce storm and washes up on the shore

of Mytilene. Apollonius orders his men to take on food and sequesters himself in his bedchamber. Antinagorus is strolling by the port; he approaches the ship, and the crew invites him aboard. To console the grieving Apollonius, Antinagorus calls for Tarsiana to sing to him, but the sweetness of her songs accomplishes nothing. Tarsiana sits next to Apollonius and poses several riddles, which he readily solves. The riddles show Apollonius that Tarsiana is his daughter, and his sadness turns to joy. Antinagorus asks Apollonius for his daughter's hand, and Apollonius cuts his long nails and beard. The marriage is promptly celebrated, and the whole city rejoices. Antinagorus calls the city council together, announces that Apollonius will give the city 500,000 gold marks, and demands that Tarsiana's master be punished. The council condemns the pimp to be stoned to death and his body thrown to the dogs. They also order a statue of Apollonius and Tarsiana to be erected in the marketplace.

Apollonius, his daughter, and his new son-in-law leave for Tyre, planning to stop in Tarsus on the way, but an apparition advises Apollonius to go first to Ephesus and visit a temple dedicated to Diana. There he discovers that the priestess is Luciana, the wife he had given up for dead and who never knew her own daughter. No one can take Tarsiana from her mother's arms. After lingering for a time in Ephesus, the ships sail on to Tarsus. The family and their attendants are joyously received by the people; only Estrangilius and Dionisa lament their return. After Apollonius's report to the city council, Theophilus is summoned to appear before them. He relates the details of the murder plot, and the council orders Dionisa burned and Estrangilius hanged.

Apollonius assumes the kingship of Antioch, and then he, Luciana, Tarsiana, and Antinagorus sail for Pentapolin. King Architrastes, who had given Apollonius and Luciana up for dead, rejoices on their arrival. Tarsiana gives birth to a son, who is named Architrastes after his grandfather. The elder Architrastes dies, and the kingdom passes to Apollonius. Not forgetting his promise of old to the fisherman who saved him in Pentapolin, the grateful monarch rewards the man richly. Apollonius and Luciana return to Tyre, where they die many years later.

Marden notes in his 1917 edition of the *Libro de Apolonio* that "With the original story ready at hand, it was possible for the Spanish poet to devote more than usual attention to the development of characters and to other accessories, and to reveal a personal touch far removed from that of a mere translator or versifier." The *Libro de Apolonio* conflates the genres of romance and hagiography: by repeatedly invoking God and moralizing the action of the tale, the poet infuses the work with the didacticism characteristic of the *mester de clerecía*. Marina Scordilis Brownlee cites several instances where the poet seeks to justify his moralizing by invoking an anthropomorphized Christian morality. For example:

> Confonda Dios tal rey de tan mala mesura,
> Bivía en pecado y asmaba locura,
> Que querié matar al omne que dixera derechura,
> Que abrió la demanda que era tan escura.

> Esto façié el pecado, que es de tal natura,
> Ca en otros muchos que en mucho atura
> A pocos días dobla que traye gran abascura;
> Traye mucho enxemplo desto la escriptura.

> (May God damn a king of so poor judgment
> Who lived in sin and devised such madness
> Who wanted to kill any man who might respond truthfully
> Who solved the riddle that was so dark.

> This was prompted by Sin, whose nature is such
> That many others whom he presses upon at length,
> He soon bends to his great darkness;
> Learned writings have many examples of this.)

The reference to learned writings in this passage is one of many places in which the poet celebrates the written word. Apollonius uses his books to try to find an alternative solution to the riddle posed by King Antioch:

> Ençerróse Apolonio en sus cámaras privadas,
> Do tenié sus escritos y sus estorias notadas.
> Rezó sus argumentos, las fazañas pasadas,
> Caldeas y latinas, tres o cuatro vegadas.

> En cabo, otra cosa non pudo entender
> Que al rey Antioco pudiese responder;
> Çerró sus argumentos, dexóse de leer,
> En laçerio sin fruto non quiso contender.

> (Apollonius cloistered himself in his private chambers,
> Where he had his books and well-studied tales.
> He sorted through his treatises, the past deeds of famous men,
> Texts in Caldean and Latin, three or four times over.

> In the end could not find another way
> That he might answer the King of Antioch,
> He closed his manuals on enigmas, and stopped his reading.
> He resigned himself to the uselessness of the struggle.)

Later, after he solves the riddles put to him by Tarsiana:

> –Bien, dixo Tarsiana, has a esto respondido;
> Paresçe bien que eres clérigo entendido.

> (–You have responded very well to this, said Tarsiana;
> It seems clear that you are a learned scholar.)

Further references to literacy occur when Architrastes requests that Luciana's three suitors state their assets in letters to her so that she may choose among them and when Luciana writes her response to her father. Twice people honor Apollonius by erecting statues of him, each time with an engraved tribute. Even the unlettered fisherman counsels Apollonius that life's roughest lessons confirm the wisdom transcribed by the ancients:

> "Nunqua sabrién los omnes qué eran aventuras
> Si no probasen pérdidas o muchas majaduras,
> Quando han pasado por muelles y por duras,
> Después se tornan maestros y creen las escripturas."

> ("Men would never know what their experiences meant
> If they did not suffer its hard knocks,
> When they've experienced good times and bad,
> Then they become teachers and trust their learned sources.")

Brownlee observes that although the Latin word *peregrinus* can mean "foreigner" as well as "pilgrim," the Spanish poet is careful to use *peregrino* synonymously with *palmero* (bearer of palms, that is, pilgrim) and *romero* (pilgrim to Rome and, in general, any pilgrim). By seeking wisdom through his wandering, despite the hardships he endures, Apollonius is converted from the "foreign traveler" he was in the classical text to a Christian pilgrim:

> El rey Apolonio, un noble caballero,
> Señor era de Tiro, un reçio cabdalero;
> Ése fue vuestro padre, agora es palmero,
> Por tierras de Egipto anda como romero.

> (King Apollonius, a noble knight,
> Lord was he of Tyre, a redoubtable lord;
> That man was your father, now he is a pilgrim,
> Through the lands of Egypt he roams as a pilgrim.)

As Egypt was a site of Christian asceticism rather than of pilgrimage, Apollonius's sojourn there transforms him from a king into a Christian Everyman. This transformation is indicated by references to divine providence and God's secret designs, as well as by formulaic invocations of God and expressions of faith.

Alan Deyermond concludes that the *Libro de Apolonio* is superior to its Latin model, the *Historia Apollonii Regis Tyri,* in structure, intellectual quality, and use of dialogue, and that the poet's descriptions reflect a Spanish reality. Doris Clark has shown that the nine riddles in the *Libro de Apolonio* are not mere translations of the Latin, indicating that the poet was familiar with popular versions of the riddles. Brownlee calls the work "suspenseful entertainment literature" that is highly original in form. The tale of Apollonius is recounted in act 1 of

William Shakespeare's *Pericles, Prince of Tyre* (performed circa 1607; published 1609).

References:

Manuel Alvar, "Apolonio, clérigo entendido," in *Symposium in honorem prof. M. de Riquer* (Barcelona: Universitat de Barcelona, Quaderns Crema, 1986), pp. 51–73;

Henry H. Arnold, "A Reconsideration of the Metrical Form of *El libro de Apolonio*," *Hispanic Review*, 6, no. 1 (1938): 46–56;

Joaquín Artiles, *El Libro de Apolonio: Poema español del siglo XIII* (Madrid: Gredos, 1976);

Marina Scordilis Brownlee, "Writing and Scripture in the *Libro de Apolonio:* The Conflation of Hagiography and Romance," *Hispanic Review*, 51 (1983): 159–174;

Wilfredo Casanova, "*El Libro de Apolonio:* Cristianización de un tema clásico," dissertation, Yale University, 1970;

Doris Clark, "Riddles in the *Libro de Apolonio*," in *Medieval Hispanic Studies Presented to Rita Hamilton*, edited by Alan D. Deyermond (London: Tamesis, 1976), pp. 31–43;

Dolores Corbella Díaz, *Estudio del léxico del Libro de Apolonio*, 2 volumes (La Laguna, Tenerife, Canary Islands: Universidad de La Laguna, 1986);

Alan Deyermond, "Emoción y ética en el *Libro de Apolonio*," *Vox Romanica*, 48 (1989): 153–164;

Deyermond, "Motivos folkóricos y técnicas estructurales en el *Libro de Apolonio*," *Filología*, 13 (1968–1969): 121–149;

Christopher Donahue, "Alteraciones escribaniles y la reconstrucción del *Libro de Apolonio*," in *Discursos y representaciones en la edad media: Actas de las VI Jornadas Medievales*, edited by Aurelio González and Lillian von der Walde, Moheno Publicaciones Medievalia, no. 22 (Mexico City: Universidad Nacional Autónoma de México, 1999), pp. 141–151;

María Cristina Gates, "Zonas de pertinencia: Lo público y lo privado en el *Libro de Apolonio*," *Medievalia*, 23 (1996): 22–32;

José Luis Girón Alconchel, *Comentario de textos de clerecía: Alexandre y Apolonio* (Madrid: Arco/Libros, 2002);

Patricia E. Grieve, "Building Christian Narrative: The Rhetoric of Knowledge, Revelation, and Interpretation in *Libro de Apolonio*," in *The Book and the Magic of Reading in the Middle Ages*, edited by Albrecht Classen (New York: Garland, 1998), pp. 149–169;

Anita Benaim Lasry, "The Ideal Heroine in Medieval Romances: A Quest for a Paradigm," *Romance Quarterly*, 32 (1985): 227–243;

John R. Maier, "The *Libro de Apolonio* and the Imposition of Culture," in *La Chispa '87: Selected Proceedings. The Eighth Louisiana Conference on Hispanic Languages and Literatures, Tulane University, New Orleans, 1987* (New Orleans: The Conference, 1987), pp. 169–176;

Sean McDaniel, "The Wandering Merchant King: Timoneda's Rewriting of the History of Apollonius," *Revista Canadiense de Estudios Hispánicos*, 23 (1998): 85–100;

J. C. Musgrave, "Tarsiana and Juglaría in the *Libro de Apolonio*," in *Medieval Hispanic Studies Presented to Rita Hamilton*, edited by Alan Deyermond (London: Tamesis, 1976), pp. 129–138;

C. Calvert Phipps, "El incesto, las adivinanzas, y la música: diseños de geminación en el *Libro de Apolonio*," *El Crotalón*, 1 (1984): 807–818;

Carmen S. Rivera, "Defending their Honor: Women's Voices in *El libro de Apolonio*," *Cincinnati Romance Review*, 13 (1994): 24–30;

Isabel Uría Maqua, "El *Libro de Apolonio*, contrapunto del *Libro de Alexandre*," *Vox Romanica*, 56 (1997): 193–211.

Libro del Caballero Zifar

(circa 1300 – 1325)

George D. Greenia
College of William and Mary

and

Frank A. Domínguez
University of North Carolina at Chapel Hill

Manuscripts: The *Libro del Caballero Zifar* survives in two manuscripts: Biblioteca Nacional, Madrid, MS. 11.309, copied in the early fourteenth century, from which nine folios are missing, and Bibliothèque Nationale, Paris, MS. Esp. 36, copied toward the end of the fifteenth century. MS. Esp. 36 is one of the most intensively illuminated Spanish manuscripts, with 242 miniatures.

First publication: *Libro del cauallero de dios que auia por nombre Cifar* (Seville: Jacobo Cromberger, 1512; reprinted, 1529).

Modern editions: *Historia del Cavallero Cifar,* edited by Heinrich Michelant (Tübingen: Vereins, 1872); *El Libro del Cavallero Zifar,* edited by Charles P. Wagner (Ann Arbor: University of Michigan Press, 1929); *El Cavallero Zifar,* edited by Martín de Riquer (Barcelona: Ariel, 1951); *Libros de caballerías españoles: El caballero Cifar, Amadís de Gaula, Tirant el Blanco,* edited by Felicidad Buendía (Madrid: Aguilar, 1960); *Libro del Caballero Zifar,* edited by Joaquín González Muela (Madrid: Castalia, 1982); *Libro del Caballero Zifar,* edited by Cristina González (Madrid: Cátedra, 1983); *Libro del Cauallero Çifar,* edited by M. A. Olsen (Madison, Wis.: Hispanic Seminary of Medieval Studies, 1984); *Edición crítica del* Libro del caballero Zifar, edited by J. M. Lucía Megías (Alcalá de Henares: Universidad de Alcalá, 1993 [microfiche]); *Texto y concordancias del* Libro del caballero Çifar: *BNP MS. Esp. 36,* edited by Francisco Gago Jover (Madison, Wis.: Hispanic Seminary of Medieval Studies, 1994 [microfiche]).

Edition in English: *The Book of the Knight Zifar: A Translation of* El libro del Cavallero Zifar, translated by Charles L. Nelson (Lexington: University Press of Kentucky, 1983).

The *Libro del Caballero Zifar* (circa 1300; translated as *The Book of the Knight Zifar: A Translation of* El libro del cavallero Zifar, 1983) is among Castile's earliest works of prose fiction and is a major forerunner of the genre of chivalric literature that became one of the strongest currents of Spanish fiction in the fifteenth and sixteenth centuries. Its occasional designation as the *Libro del caballero de Dios* (Book of the Knight of God) comes from a passage in one of the two surviving manuscripts (Biblioteca Nacional, Madrid, MS. 11.309): "e por ende es dicho este libro del cauallero de dios" (and lastly, this book is called the book of the knight of God). The title of the earliest print edition (1512) is *Libro del cauallero de dios que auia por nombre Cifar* (The Book of the Knight of God Who Was Named Cifar). One medieval book catalogue referred to the work as the *Libro del cauallero Sifar,* and that title, or some variant of it, was standard after the Middle Ages; it was adopted by the first modern editor, Heinrich Michelant, in 1872 and remains the most common designation used by critics and bibliographers.

The main pieces of evidence as to the date of composition of the work are the description of the Roman Holy Year of 1300 in the prologue and an allusion to the Jubilee pilgrimage of 1300 in the closing paragraphs. Some of the translations of oriental folktales and Latin sources were probably done prior to 1300, while passages such as the retrospective justification of Queen María de Molina's regencies during the minorities of her son and grandson are likely to have been composed after 1300; but the compilation of the work must have been completed before the memory of the Holy Year events had faded. Fernando Gómez Redondo dates the book to the period 1295 to 1325.

The work is hundreds of pages in length. Of the two medieval copies, the Madrid manuscript, from the early fourteenth century, is humbler in appearance than Bibliothèque Nationale, Paris, MS. Esp. 36, which was copied toward the end of the fifteenth century. The

Illumination from the manuscript of the Libro del Caballero Zifar: *Zifar and Grima watch helplessly as their older son, Garfin, is carried off by a lioness (Bibliothèque Nationale, Paris, MS. Esp. 36, folio 32v)*

Madrid manuscript has been associated with the scholarly circle of the bishop's palace in Toledo, which may have been the site of the composition of the work a century earlier. From the thirteenth through the fifteenth centuries Toledo prospered under a series of illustrious archbishops and cardinals who held the status of ecclesiastical primate of Spain: when addressing the Iberian Peninsula, Rome dealt first with Toledo, and Toledo represented the Spanish church to Rome and to monarchs and nobles at home and abroad. The engagement of its clerical hierarchy in national and international politics was constant, and the bishop's private library and that of the cathedral were progressively enriched by manuscripts and archived documents and the intellectuals who drew on them.

The *Libro del Caballero Zifar* is a repository of narrative traditions as disparate as hagiography, tales of military exploits and battles, the popular vernacular sermon, the Byzantine novel of elaborate travels and narrow escapes, medieval debate literature, the manual for princes, stories of fantastic adventures with magical beings, and translations of the wisdom of the Orient retold through stories of talking animals and of common people in trying circumstances. The clerical circles of Toledo could have provided both the initial interest

in this large repertoire of sources and the scholarly ability to translate and merge them.

The Paris manuscript of the *Libro del Caballero Zifar* is celebrated for its princely dimensions and 242 illustrations, many of which spread across large areas of the pages. It is the only illuminated romance novel known to have been produced in medieval Iberia, despite the great popularity of other works of this genre such as *Amadís de Gaula* (fourteenth century, Amadis of Gaul) and Joanot Martorell and Marti Joan de Galba's *Tirant lo Blanc* (1490, Tirant the White). The "miniatures" of the *Libro del Caballero Zifar* are really salon paintings, beautifully drawn, brightly colored, and frequently adorned with gold leaf. The elaborate clothing worn by the characters reflects the fashions of the early 1470s and indicates an audience of nobles or, at least, of patrons of the visual arts. Who commissioned this lavish manuscript is not known–E. Michael Gerli suggests that it might have been King Enrique IV–but it was clearly enjoyed by a limited group of insiders. The manuscript reveals something of the grandiose pretensions of its makers: not a folio is missing, and nearly every illustration and illuminated capital letter is finished. The elaborate miniatures reflect a middlebrow reading of the pious didactic romance of a king triumphing over distressing circumstances through his own virtue and the nobility of his family.

The two early print editions, published in Seville in 1512 and 1529, survive in unique witnesses in Paris and Madrid, respectively. The pressruns would have been limited to a few hundred copies, but the fact that only one copy of each edition is extant hints that the rest may have been worn out by heavy use. Tales of chivalric adventures were consumed in great quantity in sixteenth-century Spain; but while the *Amadís de Gaula, Tirant lo Blanc,* and many others achieved enduring fame and pervasive influence at home and abroad, the *Libro del Caballero Zifar* was all but forgotten until the modern period.

The book was probably composed in various stages, with some of the folktales and exemplary stories being translated prior to their incorporation into the didactic section that makes up roughly the third quarter of the work. Parts of the frame narrative were likely composed between 1301 and 1321, and a third phase may have occurred from around 1321 to 1325. Although some critics suggest a somewhat later period of composition, they agree that the spirit of the work is suffused with Alfonso XI's policy of reining in the independent and combative Castilian nobility. The first explicit mention of the *Libro del Caballero Zifar* as a literary composition is in Juan García de Castrogeriz's *Glosa castellana al "Regimiento de príncipes" de Egidio Romano* (1350, Castilian Gloss to the "Rule of Princes" of Giles of Rome).

Francisco J. Hernández thinks that Ferrand Martínez, the "arçidiano de Madrid" (archdeacon of Madrid) mentioned in the prologue, may have been the author of the work. He spent years as a secretary and notary in the royal courts of Spain and simultaneously in the chanceries of various bishops, including several in Toledo. His authorship of the *Libro del Caballero Zifar* has not been widely accepted, despite a total lack of evidence for any other possible author. It is possible that the text was reworked over time by a succession of scholars; the prologue says: "pero esta obra es fecha so emienda de aquellos que la quisieren emendar . . . ca quanto mas es la cosa emendada tanto mas es loada" (but this work is offered for correction by those who can emend it . . . for the more a work is emended the more it is praised).

One of the templates for Zifar's story appears to be the life of St. Eustachius, although there is disagreement among critics as to whether the inspiration for the plot comes from a French or an oriental folkloric tradition or from a narrative autochthonous to the Iberian Peninsula that owes much to Catalan or Galician antecedents. All critics divide the work into sections, although the divisions vary; none are labeled as such in the earliest witnesses. The most common divisions are the prologue, which seems essentially historical; "El caballero de Dios" (The Knight of God), the adventures of Zifar until he becomes king of Mentón; the "Rey de Mentón" (King of Mentón) section, which includes the tale of the "Caballero Atrevido" (Rash Knight); "Castigos del rey de Mentón" (Sayings of the King of Mentón), as told to Zifar's passively attentive sons; and "Los Hechos de Roboán" (The Adventures of Roboán), the fantastic exploits of Zifar's younger son. Although these divisions are postmedieval, they make one of the central problems of the *Libro del Caballero Zifar* obvious: either the work posseses a scanty unity, dependent on the mere presence of consistently named characters, or it is constructed according to a concept of unity that is quite different from modern ones.

The prologue tells how Ferrand García, an archdeacon of Toledo, managed to gain the Pope's consent to recover the body of Cardinal Gonzalo García Gudiel, who had died and been entombed in Rome during the Holy Year observances. Such consent had never been given before, and the state procession homeward to Spain acquired the trappings of the welcoming of the relics of a national hero and saint. The prologue shares some compositional principles with medieval works such as Juan Ruiz's *Libro de buen amor* (circa 1330–1343; translated as *Book of Good Love,* 1933) and the prologue to the works of Juan Manuel, which illustrate the power of God to overcome all barriers.

In the work proper the celebrated Indian knight Zifar suffers from a family curse: he cannot keep a horse alive under him for more than ten days, although out of self-interest his king keeps him supplied with mounts during wartime. But the sovereign finally gives up: the cost is too great, and other knights, who are jealous of Zifar's fame and prowess, persuade the king to bar him from combat. Zifar reveals his disappointment to his wife, Grima, and confides to her his grandfather's prophecy that from the grandfather's lineage a man would come who would revolt against a bad king and take over the kingdom. The distraught knight and his family leave the kingdom, with Zifar on foot and his wife and their sons, Garfín and Roboán, riding on two horses. They come to the city of Galapia, which is being besieged by a neighboring count. The count's nephew refuses to allow Zifar to enter the city and challenges him to a duel. Zifar mounts his wife's horse, kills the nephew, and enters the city. There he becomes a military adviser to the widowed lady of Galapia, whose name is also Grima (according to Robert M. Walker, "Zifar" means "traveler" and "Grima" means "noble" in Arabic), and defeats the besieging forces. In the confusion of the battle, however, Grima of Galapia believes that all is lost and falls dead from grief; but she miracu-

Illumination from the manuscript of the Libro del Caballero Zifar: *Grima tosses the corpses of her abductors overboard, while the Christ child guides her ship from the crow's nest (Bibliothèque Nationale, Paris, MS. Esp. 36, folio 37)*

lously recovers through the intercession of the Virgin. She then comes to an understanding with the count, whose son she forces into a strategic marriage to cement the truce. No longer needed in Galapia, Zifar leaves to continue wandering with his family; his departure distresses the townsfolk, who wish him to stay.

A restful interlude on the banks of a stream, during which Grima cradles Zifar's head in her lap and tenderly picks lice out of his hair as he naps–the medieval audience apparently found this scene intimate and touching–is broken when Garfín is carried off by a lioness. In the city of Falac, Roboán becomes lost among the maze of streets. Unbeknownst to Zifar and Grima, Garfín is still alive; he is reunited by chance with Roboán, and they become the foster children of a rich Falac burger and his wife. Finally, Grima is abducted by sailors who were to ferry the bereft couple to the kingdom of Orbín. A miraculous voice prompts the sailors to fight over Grima, and they all kill each other. She emerges from belowdecks to a scene of carnage but plucks up her courage and throws the corpses overboard. At the behest of the Virgin Mary, Jesus Christ pilots Grima's ship and its considerable treasure to

Galán in the kingdom of Orbín. Grima dwells there in dignified semiseclusion for nine years, until God directs her to sail back to her birthplace to die among her people.

Meanwhile, Zifar meets a hermit who consoles him just as his current horse meets the same fate as his previous ones. Near the hermitage is the shed of a fisherman, who has given shelter to a *ribaldo* (comic rogue). The *ribaldo* probes Zifar's character with a series of questions to determine whether he is given to passion or is a sensible man; convinced of Zifar's goodness, the *ribaldo* offers to become his squire. Before they depart, the hermit has a prophetic dream in which he sees the knight crowned and standing atop a tower. The vision is explained by a disembodied voice that reveals that Zifar will lift the siege of the city of Mentón, become its king, and marry the former king's daughter.

The events come to pass as predicted; but the princess is two years too young to become Zifar's consort, which temporarily solves his quandary as to whether to risk polygamy or give Grima up for dead. The two years of grace expire; but rather than confess that he fears committing unintentional adultery, Zifar tells his bride that he must expiate a sin he committed by two further years of chastity. She accedes to his pious request, and the union remains unconsummated.

On her way to Orbín, Grima visits Mentón and meets the king and his still-virgin wife. Zifar is now bearded and fat and speaks in a strange dialect he acquired in his new kingdom, but he and Grima recognize each other; they remain silent about their relationship before the young queen. Zifar bestows on Grima a property on which she can build a charitable hostel for travelers.

Garfín and Roboán's foster parents send them to the increasingly famous king of Mentón with the hope that he will incorporate them into his household and eventually knight them. They stop at Grima's hostel; she recognizes them as her long-lost sons and reveals her identity to them. After feasting to celebrate their reunion, they all retire, exhausted, to the same bed. A porter who sees them together goes to the king and queen and accuses the three of promiscuity. Zifar, not recognizing the young men, is forced by his unflinching sense of justice to condemn Grima to be burned. First, however, he questions the youths, who reveal their relationship to Grima and, therefore, to Zifar. Grima is vindicated, and Garfín and Roboán are knighted and brought into the royal household.

With the help of the *ribaldo,* who has been knighted and is now known as the "Caballero Amigo" (Friendly Knight), the youths capture the rebellious Count Nasón and bring him to Zifar. The rest of the rebels, including Nasón's nephew, were defeated in a conflict so gruesome that Zifar cuts his sons' description of the battle short. He condemns the rebels to be burned at the stake and Nasón's ashes to be thrown into a magical body of water that becomes the site of the adventure of the Caballero Atrevido.

Although only a few pages long and barely anchored in the framing story line, the tale of the headstrong knight is one of the best-known episodes in the book. The Rash Knight (the adjective *atrevido* also means "bold" and "daring") arrives at the lake where Count Nasón's ashes were scattered and is swept into an enchanted kingdom. There he is seduced by a wondrous lady, actually a devil in disguise, who promises him the lordship of her realm in exchange for his unquestioning obedience. The trappings of courtly pleasure abound, from fine clothing to gleaming gemstones that illuminate the homes by night. But even at the feast in honor of the knight's ascension to their lordship, the subjects maintain an unearthly speechlessness. The entertainment includes acrobats who climb sunbeams and slide down them as if on sturdy ropes. Time passes here at a dizzying rate: trees mature and bear fruit in one day, and the livestock give birth in seven.

Pregnant from their first night together, the she-devil produces a son in a week. In another week the boy is a grown man. The knight passes another lady of the city and is overcome by temptation. When he and his son return to the palace, the demon has resumed her true form and sits furiously gnawing on the black hearts of Count Nasón and his equally evil great-grandfather. An earthquake hurls the Caballero Atrevido back to his own world along with his son, who is baptized Alberto Diablo.

The main plot resumes with Zifar giving the county that had belonged to Nasón to his older son, Garfín. The virgin queen conveniently expires eight days before Zifar's two-year vow of chastity is to end; on her deathbed she tells Zifar that he should marry again. This advice is seconded by a disembodied voice, which tells him to ask the principal nobles of the kingdom to pledge their support to whatever their king requests. He explains his personal history and wishes to his vassals, and they agree that they would prefer to have Grima as their queen than not to have him as their king. The final chapters of the "Rey de Mentón" section bring closure to the story to this point: Zifar gives the hermit who had befriended him money to build a monastery; the Caballero Amigo rewards the fisherman who had been his host before his fortunes improved; and Roboán obtains Zifar's permission to go out into the world to seek adventure.

The next section, "Castigos del rey Mentón," is a collection of sayings that "chastise" or correct the behavior of Garfín and Roboán—and, through them, the reader; it does nothing to advance the main plot. The sayings alternate between exempla—short stories used to drive home a moral—and direct instruction by Zifar to his sons on proper comportment and values. Each pronouncement is introduced by a phrase such as "De commo el rey Mentón . . ." (How the king of Menton . . .) or "Del Ejemplo que el Rey de Mentón dió . . ." (The Example that the king of Menton gave . . .). This compendium of learned and popular tales is largely taken from the medieval anthology of wisdom stories *Flores de Filosofía* (circa 1275, Flowers of Philosophy), the code of noble conduct laid out in the second section of Alfonso X's *Siete partidas* (1256–after 1272, Seven-Part Law), the Eastern exempla in the popular *Poridat de Poridades* (circa 1250, Secret of Secrets), and the anthology of tales in the *Castigos del rey don Sancho IV* (1292–1293, Lessons of King Sancho IV), composed on the orders of Alfonso's son and successor. A manual of virtuous and chivalric acts, it is one of innumerable such medieval treatises written to instruct princes in just rule. The illustrators of the Paris manuscript, who apparently divided up the work among themselves, made no effort to represent the action in the tales recounted by

mer et ella commo conellos et no auie
conndo entodo aql dia conel grand plazer

qla vido assy yazer entre aqllos dos
estudieros fue muy espantado por la

Illumination from the manuscript of the Libro del Caballero Zifar: *Grima, reunited with her sons, Garfín and Roboán, is discovered sharing their bed (Bibliothèque Nationale, Paris, MS. Esp. 36, folio 70v)*

Zifar; instead, they produced a succession of static tableaux of Zifar talking to his sons, the trio frozen in their seats in various interior or exterior spaces, clad in different raiment, and with no physical resemblance between the depiction of each character from one image to the next. The commissioning patron seems to have required at least one miniature per two-page spread, and the artists complied by taking the path of least resistance.

The first tale is representative of the exempla: a king seeking a cure for his faithless ways consults a physician who is examining urine specimens. The doctor prescribes a penitential recipe, a compound of "roots of the fear of God and the marrow of his commandments, the bark of good will and the acorns of humility," and so forth. Even with the promise of a lifelong cure for his body and soul, the king complains about how bitter the draft will be. The physician responds that the king should heed the ensuing tale of the hunter and the lark. And so the tales and direct instruction accumulate over scores of pages.

The final section of the *Libro del Caballero Zifar* recounts the adventures of Zifar's younger son, Roboán. With the rest of the family settled and secure, and his brother Garfín the heir apparent, Roboán sets out to seek his own fortunes elsewhere. With the Caballero Amigo as his trusted lieutenant and sometime ambassador and a force of three thousand soldiers, the prince journeys to the realm of Pandulfa. As he liberates the land from the incursions of a neighboring king, he and the beautiful Princess Seringa fall in love. Roboán must move on to new adventures, but he promises Seringa that he will return.

The emperor of Trigrida inducts Roboán into his personal entourage and treats him as a son. But evil counselors prompt Roboán to pose a question the monarch has forbidden to be asked: why he never laughs. The punishment that immediately befalls the youth is banishment and condemnation to learn firsthand the sobriety that produces such mirthlessness. The emperor takes Roboán to a secret wharf, where the youth boards a magic skiff. It bears him to Las Islas Dotadas (The Blessed Isles), an earthly paradise of courtly perfection. The enchanted land is ruled by Lady Nobility, who captivates and marries him. His discretion and self-control are put to repeated tests in lengthy, learned conversations with her and in encounters with demons disguised as damsels who put his relationship with his flawless consort to the test. For his idle pleasure he begs Lady Nobility first for her hawk, then for her greyhound, and finally for her noblest steed, which bolts out of control and carries him, helpless, out of the enchanted realm and back to Trigrida. He now knows the dejection that prevents the emperor from smiling, and he shares the ruler's sad fate.

Roboán returns to Seringa and marries her in a union of wisdom like that of his parents. The family is reunited for the wedding celebrations in Pandulfa, an expansive realm with marvels such as piles of wondrous sapphires whose mere presence can cure the most violent bleeding. Even more wondrous is the good government the highest levels of nobility display, with their unfailing justice, temperate mercy, and attentiveness to learned clergy.

Interpolated throughout the *Libro del Caballero Zifar* are short episodes and exemplary tales on a wide range of themes taken from an equally wide variety of sources. These interruptions are not palatable to modern readers, but they may have lent themselves well to oral delivery. Kenneth Scholberg, Charles P. Wagner, A. F. Bolaños, Juan M. Cacho Blecua, and Edwin J. Webber argue that the work is unified by the characters of Zifar, his sons, and the Caballero Amigo, and, most of all, by the characters' recollections of what has been said in earlier episodes; but the fact remains that the various sections display quite different types of narrative.

The *Libro del Caballero Zifar* offers lessons for every stratum of medieval society. Liars are shown to disrupt the safety of the community; lying is a criminal offense and a classic feature of all evildoers. When a military officer repents of his transgressions, he wins the renewed allegiance of the knights he has led to defeat. But in the moral universe of this novel, betrayal is the greatest of evils. The she-devil of the enchanted lake discloses herself to the Caballero Atrevido as the Mistress of Treason, and he betrays her with another woman. On the other hand, Zifar avoids betraying his first wife during his double marriage.

Universal literacy is assumed in the work: lists of combatants are drawn up before battles are joined; affairs of state are conducted in carefully crafted letters and diplomatic documents that are transcribed in full; and a well-read daughter debates with her father toward the end of the Caballero Atrevido episode. Much more is made, however, of the oral transmission of wisdom and of proving virtue through action. A good leader improves his or her subjects through moral instruction; that teaching role requires that the ruler possess a large measure of piety but without crossing over into the activities proper to the clergy. Zifar's assistance to Lady Grima of Galapia includes schooling her in fitting conduct for a ruler, such as military strategy, the protocols of administration, presiding over a court, and safe-

guarding her dead husband's armor, a possession that may be lent out but not alienated from the estate. Finally, reticence and discretion should always be the opening gambit of the noble in spirit. Zifar is unwilling to enter the privy council of the besieged widow Grima until he is formally summoned; he is reluctant to negotiate directly with an opponent conquered on another's behalf; and Grima refuses to state her business to a knight who boards her ship in a foreign port.

Attention to legal niceties and the practicalities of medieval life and statecraft laces the entire narrative. Rulers must recruit their fighters and supply them with war matériel. Peace delegations travel on *palafrenes* (palfreys), normal riding horses, not on the *corceles* (war chargers) used in battle. (Most horses in the Middle Ages did double duty as needed, but their tack and livery identified their intended purpose.) After one engagement, Zifar places guards over the booty scattered on the battlefield to make sure that it is not looted before it can be gathered and inventoried.

The *Libro del Caballero Zifar* documents various medieval Spanish social practices. All weddings were celebrated on Sundays. Judicial torture to extract confessions was to be applied in such a way that the tortured party provided information that only the guilty person would know. The son of a defeated general had to be released from his shackles before he could express his intent to marry. A woman receiving a proposal of marriage was legally required to remain silent so that a male relative could speak on her behalf. In a dynastic marriage that sealed a truce to end a war in which the groom's side lost, reparations were merged with the groom's contribution; the victorious clan did not need to provide a dowry for the bride.

The book is not without touches of humor. When the *ribaldo,* captured and condemned to death by enemies in an early episode, is placed on a horse with his hands tied and a noose around his neck, he calls out to Zifar to "hurry before they hang me!" and is desperate not to hear his captors holler "giddyap" to the horse. The lower-class squire who is trying to assimilate the manners and wisdom of his betters is a stock comic figure; Sancho Panza in Miguel de Cervantes's *Don Quixote* (1605, 1615) is the best-known example. In the *Libro del Caballero Zifar* the *ribaldo* succeeds completely, becoming a knight, a count, and a royal emissary. But the humor can also be humiliating mockery, as when Zifar taunts Count Nasón before sentencing him to mutilation and death.

Despite its probable clerical origins, the *Libro del Caballero Zifar* is not dogmatic about religious principles or preoccupied with theological issues. The overt moral lessons are clearly aimed at the ruling class, but the majority of learned clerics connected to the bishop's

Illumination from the manuscript of the Libro del Caballero Zifar: *the Caballero Atrevido is seduced by the she-devil of the enchanted lake of traitors (Bibliothèque Nationale, Paris, MS. Esp. 36, folio 86v)*

palace and library in Toledo would have come from this social stratum. What distinguishes the book from a purely secular work by a nobleman of the same period, such as Alfonso X or Juan Manuel, is its message that reliance on clerics is essential for acquiring the wisdom required of rulers. The episode of Zifar and the hermit corresponds to the "desert experience" of holy men who withdraw from society to seek strength and good counsel before reengaging with the world. The story includes supernatural elements such as apparitions, dream visions, odors of inexplicable sweetness, and mysterious but refreshing breezes. These phenomena never drive the plot of the story but serve only to confirm the resolve of the characters and encourage them to continue on courses they have already chosen.

There are some biblical echoes, as well. The sufferings of Zifar are much like those of Job, and his modesty and discretion after his triumphs are reminiscent of Christ's instruction to the apostles not to reveal his true identity until later. Zifar's identify is repeatedly concealed: when he wears the borrowed armor of the

widow Grima's deceased husband, when he is dressed as a madman in the *ribaldo*'s borrowed clothes, when he fights as an anonymous knight in livery lent by a steward of the king of Mentón, and when he is posing as the steward's nephew. His true identity is only gradually revealed to others. Through this deferred recognition and his endurance of trials Zifar grows in virtue and into his life's role. Although only 20 percent of the novel passes before Zifar is renamed the Knight of God, the other protagonists must learn the same lessons in new contexts; but they have the benefit of the superior wisdom of their kingly mentor.

The *Libro del Caballero Zifar* did not receive the attention of later generations of readers, either in Spain or outside the peninsula, that many other Castilian chivalric narratives of this period did. There was apparently enough interest to justify the two early print editions in 1512 and 1529. Faint echoes of it can be found in subsequent literary works; but even among the most avid readers of this genre, Cervantes and Lope de Vega, the traces are slight. Today, however, the *Libro del Caba-*

llero Zifar is celebrated as a time capsule that archives the noble wisdom and aspirations of the late Middle Ages and, in the illuminations of the Paris manuscript, the idealized self-image of courtly life in the late fifteenth century.

Bibliographies:

Marilyn A. Olsen, "Tentative Bibliography of the Libro del cauallero Zifar," *La corónica,* 11, no. 2 (1983): 327–335;

Juan M. Cacho Blecua, "Bibliografía del Libro del cavallero Zifar (1983–1998)," *La corónica,* 27, no. 3 (1999): 227–250;

Carlos Alvar and José Manuel Lucía Megías, *Diccionario filológico de literatura medieval española* (Madrid: Castalia, 2002), pp. 773–776.

References:

J. Acebrón Ruiz, "Psicomaquía: El proceso interior de la aventura en el *Libro del Cavallero Zifar,*" in *Actas do XIX congreso internacional de lingüística e filoloxía románicas,* edited by Ramón Lorenzo (La Coruña: Fundación Pedro Barrié de la Masa, Conde de Fenosa, 1994), pp. 801–810;

Reinaldo Ayerbe-Chaux, "Las Islas Dotadas: Texto y miniaturas del manuscrito de París, clave para su interpretación," in *Hispanic Studies in Honor of Alan D. Deyermond: A North American Tribute,* edited by John Miletich (Madison, Wis.: Hispanic Seminary of Medieval Studies, 1986), pp. 31–50;

Vincent Barletta, "Agency and Intertexts: Natural Philosophy as Christian Ethics in the *Libro del cauallero de Dios,*" *Hispanic Review,* 72, no. 2 (2004): 239–259;

Barletta, "Por ende deuemos creer: Knowledge and Social Practice in the *Libro del cauallero de dios,*" *La corónica,* 27, no. 3 (1999): 13–34;

Barletta and Michael Harney, "Society and Culture in the *Libro del caballero Zifar,*" *La corónica,* 27, no. 3 (1999): 7–12;

Pere Bohigas Balaguer, "Orígenes de los libros de caballería," in *Historia general de las literaturas hispánicas,* edited by Guillermo Díaz-Plaja (Barcelona: Vergara, 1969), pp. 519–541;

A. F. Bolaños, "Cifar y el ribaldo: ortodoxia y novedad de dos personajes literarios," *Thesaurus,* 44 (1989): 159–167;

Erasmo Buceta, "Algunas notas históricas al prólogo del Cauallero Zifar," *Revista de filología española,* 17 (1930): 18–36;

Buceta, "Nuevas notas históricas al prólogo del Cavallero Zifar," *Revista de filología española,* 17 (1930): 419–422;

James F. Burke, *History and Vision: The Figural Structure of the* Libro del Cavallero Zifar (London: Tamesis, 1972);

Burke, "The *Libro del Cavallero Zifar* and the Fashioning of the Self," *La corónica,* 27, no. 3 (1999): 35–44;

Burke, "The *Libro del Cavallero Zifar* and the Medieval Sermon," *Viator,* 1 (1970): 207–221;

Burke, "The Meaning of the Islas Dotadas Episode in the *Libro del Cavallero Zifar,*" *Hispanic Review,* 38 (1970): 56–68;

Juam M. Cacho Blecua, "Los 'castigos' y la educación de Garfín y Roboán en *El Libro del Cavallero Zifar,*" in *Nunca fue pena mayor: Estudios de literatura española en homenaje a Brian Dutton,* edited by Ana Menéndez Collera and Victoriano Roncero López (Cuenca: Universidad de Castilla-La Mancha, 1996), pp. 117–135;

Cacho Blecua, "La configuración literaria del ribaldo en el *Libro del cavallero Zifar:* Modelos cultos y folclóricos," in *Actas de la Asociación Hispánica de Literatura Medieval,* edited by Margarita Freixas, Silvia Iriso, and Laura Fernández (Santander: Consejería de Cultura del Gobierno de Cantabria/Año Jubilar Lebaniego/Asociación Hispánica de Literatura Medieval 1, 2000), pp. 426–440;

Cacho Blecua, "Del exemplum a la estoria ficticia: La primera lección de Zifar," in *Tipología de las formas narrativas breves románicas medievales,* edited by Juan Paredes and Paloma Gracia (Granada: University of Granada Press, 1998), pp. 209–236;

Cacho Blecua, "Del Liber consolationis et consilii al Libro del cavallero Zifar," *La corónica,* 27, no. 3 (1999): 45–66;

Cacho Blecua, "El género del Cifar (Cromberger 1512): La invención de la novela," in *Seminario hispano-francés organizado por la Casa de Velázquez,* edited by Jean Canavaggio (Madrid: Casa de Velázquez, 1997), pp. 93–116;

Ivy Corfis, "The Fantastic in *Cavallero Zifar,*" *La corónica,* 27, no. 3 (1999): 67–86;

M. Ana Diz, "El mundo de las armas en el Libro del Caballero Cifar," *Bulletin of Hispanic Studies,* 61, no. 3 (1979): 189–199;

E. Michael Gerli, "Zifar redivivus: Patronage, politics, and the Paris manuscript of the *Libro del caballero Zifar,*" *La corónica,* 27, no. 3 (1999): 87–103;

Gordon H. Gerould, "Forerunners, Congeners, and Derivatives of the Eustace Legend," *PMLA,* 19 (1904): 335–448;

Fernando Gómez Redondo, "El *Libro del Cavallero Zifar,*" in his *Historia de la Prosa Medieval Castellana,* volume 2: *El desarrollo de los géneros. La ficción caballeresca y el orden religioso* (Madrid: Cátedra, 1999), pp. 1371–1459;

Gómez Redondo, "Los públicos del Zifar," in *Studia in honorem Germán Orduna,* edited by Leonardo Funes and José Luis Moure (Alcalá de Henares: Universidad de Alcalá, 2001), pp. 279–297;

Michael Harney, "Law and Order in the *Libro del caballero Zifar,*" *La corónica,* 27, no. 3 (1999): 125–144;

Harney, "The *Libro del caballero Zifar* as a Refraction of the Life of Saint Eustace," in *Saints and Their Authors: Studies in Medieval Hispanic Hagiography in Honor of John K. Walsh,* edited by Jane Ellen Connolly, A. D. Deyermond, and Brian Dutton (Madison, Wis.: Hispanic Seminary of Medieval Studies, 1990), pp. 71–82;

Francisco J. Hernández, "Ferrán Martínez, 'Escrivano del rey,' canónigo de Toledo y autor del *Libro del Cavallero Zifar,*" *Revista de Archivos, Bibliotecas y Museos,* 81, no. 2 (1978): 289–325;

Hernández, "*El Libro del Cavallero Zifar:* Meaning and Structure," *Revista Canadiense de Estudios Hispánicos,* 2, no. 2 (1978): 89–121;

Ronald G. Keightley, "Models and Meanings for the *Libro del caballero Zifar,*" *Mosaic,* 12, no. 2 (1978): 55–73;

Keightley, "The Story of Zifar and the Structure of the *Libro del caballero Zifar,*" *Modern Language Review,* 63, no. 2 (1978): 308–327;

A. H. Krappe, "La leggenda di S. Eustachio," *Nuovi Studi Medievali,* 3 (1926–1927): 223–258;

María Rosa Lida de Malkiel, "La leyenda de Alajandro en la literatura medieval," in her *La tradición clásica en España* (Barcelona: Ariel, 1975), pp. 165–187;

José Manuel Lucía Megías, "Los castigos del rey de Mentón a la luz de Flores de filosofía: Límites y posibilidades del uso del modelo subyacente," *La corónica,* 27, no. 3 (1999): 145–165;

Lucía Megías, "La descripción del Otro Mundo en el *Libro del Cavallero Zifar,*" *Anthropos,* 154–155 (1994): 125–130;

Lucía Megías, "Fantasía y lógica en los episodios maravillosos del Libro del caballero Cifar," *Parole,* 3 (1990): 99–111;

Edward J. Mullen, "The Role of the Supernatural in *El Libro del Cavallero Zifar,*" *Revista de Estudios Hispánicos,* 5 (1971): 257–268;

Neryamn R. Nieves, "The Centrality of the Oriental in the *Libro del Caballero Zifar,*" *Romance Quarterly,* 49, no. 4 (2002): 270–279;

Germán Orduna, "La élite intelectual de la escuela catedralicia de Toledo y la literatura en la época de Sancho IV," in *La literatura en la época de Sancho IV,* edited by Carlos Alvar and José Manuel Lucía Megías (Alcalá de Henares: Universidad de Alcalá, 1996), pp. 53–62;

Orduna, "Las redacciones del *Libro del Cauallero Zifar,*" in *Studia in honorem prof. M. de Riquer,* volume 4, edited by L. Vela (Barcelona: Crema, 1991), pp. 283–299;

Jules Piccus, "Refranes y frases proverbiales en el *Libro del Cavallero Zifar,*" *Nueva Revista de Filología Hispánica,* 18, nos. 1–2 (1965–1966): 1–24;

Francisco Rico, ed., *Libro del caballero Zifar: Códice de París,* volume 2: *Estudios* (Barcelona: Moleiro, 1996);

Jesús D. Rodríguez Velasco, "*El Libro del cavallero Zifar* en la edad de la virtud," *La corónica,* 27, no. 3 (1999): 167–185;

Justina Ruiz de Conde, *El amor y el matrimonio secreto en los libros de caballerías* (Madrid: Aguilar, 1948);

Kenneth Scholberg, "La comicidad del *Caballero Zifar,*" in *Homenaje a R. Rodríguez Moñino,* volume 2 (Madrid: Gredos, 1962), pp. 157–163;

Scholberg, "A Half-Friend and a Friend and a Half," *Bulletin of Hispanic Studies,* 35, no. 4 (1958): 187–198;

Scholberg, "The Structure of the *Caballero Cifar,*" *Modern Language Notes,* 79, no. 2 (1964): 113–124;

Wendell Smith, "Marital Canon-Law Dilemmas in *El libro del cauallero Zifar,*" *La corónica,* 27, no. 3 (1999): 187–206;

Luciana de Stéfano, "*El Caballero Zifar:* Novela didáctico-moral," *Thesaurus,* 27, no. 2 (1972): 173–260;

Robert M. Walker, *Tradition and Technique in* El libro del Cavallero Zifar (London: Tamesis, 1974);

Edwin J. Webber, "The *Ribaldo* as Literary Symbol," in *Florilegium Hispanicum,* edited by John S. Geary (Madison, Wis.: Hispanic Seminary of Medieval Studies, 1983), pp. 131–138.

Libro de miseria d'omne

(circa 1300 – 1340)

Jane E. Connolly
University of Miami

Manuscript: The only extant copy of the *Libro de miseria d'omne* is Biblioteca Menéndez Pelayo, Santander, MS. 77. According to Miguel Artigas, the first editor of the poem, the copy dates from the last quarter of the fifteenth century, but more-recent scholars have placed it in the first half of the century. The manuscript is damaged, and Artigas estimates that two folios, containing approximately twenty-two strophes, are missing.

First publication and paleographic edition: Miguel Artigas, "Un nuevo poema por la cuaderna vía," *Boletín de la Biblioteca Menéndez y Pelayo,* 1 (1919): 32–37, 87–95, 153–161, 210–216, 328–338; 2 (1920): 41–48, 91–98, 154–163, 233–244.

Standard editions: *Libro de miseria d'omne,* edited by Pompilio Tesauro (Pisa: Giardini, 1983); "Critical Edition of the *Libro de miseria d'omne*," edited by Jane E. Connolly, in her *Translation and Poetization in the "Quaderna Vía": Study and Edition of the "Libro de miseria d'omne"* (Madison, Wis.: Hispanic Seminary of Medieval Studies, 1987), pp. 119–221.

The *Libro de miseria d'omne* (Book on the Misery of Humanity) is a poetic adaptation of the *De Miseria Condicionis Humane,* an encyclopedic prose treatise written in Latin by Lothar of Segni three years before his accession to the Papacy as Innocent III in 1198. The theme of Lothar's work, *contemptu mundi* (contempt for or rejection of the world), had been in vogue for a hundred years prior to the composition of the *De Miseria Condicionis Humane;* the purpose of works on this theme was to humble human beings by forcing them to confront the wretchedness of their condition. The *De Miseria Condicionis Humane* was the most influential work of its kind: many translations appeared in nine languages, and authors such as Eustache Deschamps, Christine de Pisan, Geoffrey Chaucer, and John Wyclif quoted from or adapted it. Lothar states in his prologue that he wrote the text during recent difficulties with the aim of putting down pride, the foremost of all sins. Unlike the Latin treatise, the *Libro de miseria d'omne* is an anony-mous work and offers few clues to the poet's identity. The place and date of composition and the intended audience are also unknown, and the text does not include an overt declaration of purpose.

The Latin treatise is divided into three books, each examining a commonplace of *contemptu mundi:* the misery of the human condition, the evil that humans do, and the Last Judgment. The Spanish poet retains the tripartite structure but does not follow the source material slavishly. He adds fluidity through the use of transitions, and he reorders much of the material. The poem thus gains a narrative coherence that the source lacks.

The first book of the *Libro de miseria d'omne,* which constitutes 250 of the 502 extant stanzas, opens with an often graphic depiction of the vileness of human nature: it moves from conception to birth, bodily functions, and, finally, the decrepitude of old age. The poet then discusses the futility of all human endeavors. People strive and scheme endlessly to increase their knowledge and wealth, but such efforts are in vain; humans can never learn what God knows, and their energies would be better expended pursuing him instead of riches. After condemning the labors of the wealthy, the poet turns to the suffering of the poor. This theme is only briefly suggested in the *De Miseria Condicionis Humane,* but the *Libro de miseria d'omne* deals with the destitute in poignant detail: they wander scantily clothed in the dead of winter with no hope of shelter, rejected by their families, friends, and neighbors. The poet places particular emphasis on the power of money to buy friends and honor, observing that a prosperous pig herder is held in high esteem, while the impoverished son of a great emperor counts for naught. The passage that follows, while inspired by the *De Miseria Condicionis Humane,* is narrated with such emotional force and in such detail that its connection to the source seems remote: telling of the abuses of servants by masters, the poet offers the example of a servant who is terrified when his angry master unexpectedly arrives home after an unsuccessful hunt. Comparing the servant to a mouse cowering in a hole, the poet says that he must unwillingly kiss the master's hand and extend hospitality to him, only to have himself, his family, and his livestock displaced by the master, who occupies the entire house and eats the servant's food. Although social inequity is a favorite subject of the poet, this episode is so scathing in tone that it has become the most frequently cited passage in the *Libro de miseria d'omne*. Some scholars view it as revolutionary for its time, but similar depictions of social abuses are found in the *Proverbios de Salamón* (fourteenth century[?], Solomon's Proverbs) and Juan Ruiz's *Libro de buen amor* (circa 1330–1343; translated as *Book of Good Love,* 1933). Nonetheless, they attest to the distance of the *Libro de miseria d'omne* from its source, which could never be characterized as a text fomenting social change.

The poem continues with a comparison of the woes of the celibate and of the married. While the chaste are afflicted with the temptations of the flesh and are therefore encouraged to marry, marriage is not an easy solution for men, because wives are frequently nagging and have an unquenchable thirst for wealth and attention. Although the description of the *mala mujer* (shrew) closely follows the *De Miseria Condicionis Humane,* many of the misogynistic notes struck here and elsewhere in the *Libro de miseria d'omne* have parallels in other poems written in *cuaderna vía* (alexandrine verse), the verse form first employed in the *Libro de Alexandre* (circa 1220–1230, Book of Alexander), including the *Proverbios de Salamón,* the *Libro de buen amor,* and the *Castigos de Catón* (late thirteenth century, Chastisements of Cato).

The final category of human misery described in the *De Miseria Condicionis Humane* is the tribulations of saints and of evil men. The *Libro de miseria d'omne* ignores the latter and replaces the generalities about saints in the source with brief narratives of six martyrs, including St. Laurence, who was "de los pobres much amado" (greatly loved by the poor) and "nascido fue en España" (was born in Spain); the latter detail would surely interest a Spanish audience.

The poet next turns to the roots of all of this misery in humanity's three enemies: the devil with his arsenal of deadly sins; the world, which deceives mortals with temporal wealth; and the flesh, which fights against the soul's purest desires. Pleasure, wealth, and happiness are transitory, and the only certainty in life is death. People should, therefore, be mindful of death's proximity, love life less, and mend their ways, or they risk God's wrath and the loss of their souls. People can die in many painful manners, from hanging and roasting to being beaten and starving, and their bodies may be left to be consumed by wild beasts. The first book concludes with the message that there is no earthly justice: the innocent are punished while the guilty go free, and the pious are vilified while the arrogant are honored.

The second book is a commentary on sin. The poet defines the sins of greed, gluttony, drunkenness, lust, ambition, and pride; gives the characteristics of each; and provides examples from the Bible and from everyday life. Pride is traditionally the chief of all deadly sins, and the poet states that it is the first and last of all vices; following the *De Miseria Condicionis Humane,* however, he places it at the end of his inventory of sins. The catalogue begins with a long tirade against excessive greed—*codicia* (covetousness) or *avaricia* (avarice)—which is the root of other sins and "cosas malas" (bad things): fornication, pride, sacrilege, theft, quarrel, simony, murder, and war. Greed is clearly of supreme importance to the poet: he dedicates sixty-five stanzas to it—possibly more, as the missing folios occur at this point—and includes references to it in the discussion of each of the other sins. Although he attributes a panoply of vices to greed, he gives particular attention to the selling of justice, noting that widows and orphans have little hope of a fair hearing unless they can offer gifts to the judges. These corrupt judges line their coffers with bribes and "non quiere catar al pobre más qu'al puerco enlodado" (give as little consideration to the poor as to a muddy pig). The poet warns such judges, and all avaricious people, that they will meet God's ire on Judgment Day and that they had best not mortgage their souls for riches that will turn to dust.

Since folios are missing from the manuscript, it is difficult to gauge the degree of attention that the poet allots to the next sin, gluttony. It is, however, clear that he departs from the Latin text. Lothar says that gluttony causes the body to be weighed down, the mind to become disturbed, and the intellect to be overcome, adding that the immoderate consumption of rich foods produces abundantly stinking excrement, horrible winds from above and below, and abominable sounds. The *Libro de miseria d'omne* eliminates the indelicate references to bodily functions and merely states that those who eat excessively have difficulty standing. It also presents the effect of gluttony on mental abilities in practical terms: men with swollen bellies cannot reason well with the ladies, and they play their lutes or games poorly. The handling of the source material here may reflect the poet's concern for the sensibilities of his audience, for throughout the *Libro de miseria d'omne* he rephrases, glosses over, or eliminates potentially unsuitable subjects. Such is the case further on where he excises from his consideration of lust the chapters on sodomy and bestiality and their punishment that are found in the Latin work.

Page from the only surviving manuscript of the Libro de miseria d'omne *(Biblioteca Menéndez Pelayo, Santander, MS. 77)*

Of particular interest to students of *cuaderna vía* poetry is the treatment of drunkenness. While Américo Castro believes that the section on the abuse of wine in Ruiz's *Libro de buen amor* is derived from an Arabic source, John K. Walsh attributes it to the *Libro de miseria d'omne*. Both poets advise against the use of wine because it fouls the breath, causes the body to shake, instigates disagreements and fights, and brings about folly and evil. In addition to similarities in theme, Walsh notes common rhyme patterns and even rhyming words and believes that this section is but one of many instances where Ruiz parodies the *Libro de miseria d'omne*. Billy Bussell Thompson also cites this passage as one of several that point to the influence of the *Libro de miseria d'omne* on the *Alhotba arrimada* (fourteenth century [?], Rhymed Sermon), an *aljamiado* (Moorish text written in Romance) poem partially cast in *cuaderna vía*.

Although the poet declares pride the foremost of all sins, he dedicates only twenty-seven strophes to it. He touches on many of the topics included in the eleven chapters on the subject in the Latin treatise but in a markedly condensed fashion. For example, where Lothar dedicates two chapters to the excessive pride of humans in their clothing and ornaments, the *Libro de miseria d'omne* poet merely says in two lines that they take pleasure in their clothes "como si fuesen pavones" (as though they were peacocks). In keeping with the misogynist tone of the *Libro de miseria d'omne*, however, the poet retains and refocuses a section on the use of makeup. Lothar warns that the unnatural alteration of appearance is an attempt to surpass God's creation and is thus an offense to God. He does not specifically mention women as offenders, but in the *Libro de miseria d'omne* women are singled out for plucking their brows and foreheads, painting their eyelids, and using rouge. The poet cautions that such practices risk the loss of God's favor, as well as causing the face to wrinkle and the breath to stink.

The second book of the Latin treatise closes with an assertion that human life is filled with mortal sin and a catalogue of sinners: heretics, schismatics, hypocrites, robbers, usurers, drunkards, adulterers, the impure, the negligent, the desperate, sorcerers, soothsayers, and so on. The Spanish poet similarly views the world as replete with sin; but instead of giving a sweeping list of sinners, he focuses on the vices of specific professions that would be familiar to the audience from their own lives. His first target is the clergy, who fail to pray the canonical hours; they prefer chess and hunting to service to God, the Virgin Mary, and the saints. God will judge such clerics as thieves for living off stolen benefices, and he will harshly examine all prelates who tolerate their corruption. The poet next charges that rather than protecting the social order, knights either fail to prevent injuries to others because of their own self-interest or disrupt the public weal themselves through theft and the seduction of their neighbors' daughters. Such disorder is self-perpetuating, for if the knight is corrupt, so will his son, the *escudero* (page), be. The poet then turns to lower social ranks, describing in one or two strophes the deceptions perpetrated by each profession: merchants who pass off cheap wares as expensive ones; baker women who sell watered-down bread to unsuspecting travelers; fishermen who promise fresh fish but deliver rotten ones; servants who steal from the shopping money; shepherds who tell the master that a sheep they stole was eaten by a wolf; and so on. The sins of these professions result chiefly from greed, and all such sinners will burn if they do not reform. The poet thus brings the second book full circle, returning to the first sin considered, while at the same time introducing the subject of the third book: the suffering of sinners on Judgment Day.

The last book, by far the shortest at seventy-two strophes, begins with the reminder that riches are temporal; the only things that human beings carry with them after death are their prayers and deeds. Regardless of their earthly status, all humans will meet the same end, their decaying bodies gnawed by worms and stinking. Rendering the eight chapters of Lothar's depiction of hell in just fourteen strophes, the poet describes it as a place of endless torment, darkness, and confusion, where each condemned soul will suffer according to its sins while the righteous look down on the scene from heaven with pleasure. Failure to confess one's sins and to lead a virtuous life will result in eternal damnation. The poet compresses and reorders Lothar's chapters dealing with the Judgment Day to present the material more logically, with the awesome events and tribulations preceding the Final Judgment appearing first. Both rich and poor will shrink in fear, but to no avail: all sins have been written down, and none can be hidden. Acting both as accuser and judge, Christ will call the just to join him in heaven and will send the wicked to everlasting suffering in hell.

The final thirty strophes represent a complete departure from the source. Condemned souls will face nine afflictions in hell. First, their eyes will tear from an unquenchable fire stronger than any earthly flame. Second, they will shiver from a cold that could turn a person to ice in the blink of an eye. For their third torment, worms, snakes, and dragons will surround them like fish in the sea. An inescapable stench, the fourth punishment, will be so intolerable that they will desire death. As the fifth agony, demons will incessantly strike the souls with sledgehammers like smiths in forges. The sixth affliction is the palpable darkness, and the seventh is the sins of each soul inscribed by the devil's own hand. For the eighth torture, fire-breathing demons, serpents, and dragons will produce horrible visions. The final punishment is restraints of fire and chains. Each penalty is designed to suit a specific crime. For example, fire will punish the greedy who so ardently sought wealth, and those whose envy gnawed at them like a worm will be surrounded by vermin and snakes.

The *Libro de miseria d'omne* closes with a brief discourse on the seven deadly sins and their antitheses, the seven corporal works of mercy that all good Christians should perform. In addition to good works, the poet admonishes his audience to do penance and avoid all sin.

Some scholars consider the *Libro de miseria d'omne* as contemporary with Pero López de Ayala's *El Rimado de Palacio* (The Poem about the Palace), which was written at the beginning of the fifteenth century and is also composed in *cuaderna vía*. The *cuaderna vía* had fallen into disuse by then; Ayala calls the *El Rimado de Palacio* "versetes algunos de antiguo rrymar" (some verses in antiquated rhyme). When Miguel Artigas published his paleographic edition of the poem in 1919–1920, he classified it as a translation of the *De Miseria Condicionis Humane* and saw in it the decline of the *cuaderna vía*. Literary histories echoed these judgments until the 1980s. The strongest evidence adduced by proponents of the *Libro de miseria d'omne* as a late *cuaderna vía* work is its use of eight-syllable hemistiches instead of the seven syllables characteristic of the early *mester de clerecía* (craft or art form of clerics or the learned), a term applied to all *cuaderna vía* poems composed in writing in the thirteenth century. But the eight-syllable hemistich does not necessarily signify that the *Libro de miseria d'omne* represents the end of the *cuaderna vía*, for it is also found in the *Libro de buen amor*. The arguments that imperfect rhyme and meter are evidence of degeneration do not take into consideration the scribe's effect on the text. Pompilio Tesauro points to at least one level of scribal influence, arguing that the unique copy of the poem represents a Leonese version of an Aragonese original. Just as the scribe might have unconsciously superimposed his own language on the original, he might also have updated the vocabulary and ignored metrical rules that were not familiar to him. Equally important for an assessment of the poem is the fact that it was copied as prose, causing metrical clues to be lost and inviting scribal errors such as the repetition or deletion of words or entire lines.

Comparison of the *Libro de miseria d'omne* to other *cuaderna vía* works shows that it bears strong affinities to the early *mester de clerecía* while having little in common with Ayala's poem. Except for its use of the eight-syllable hemistich, the *Libro de miseria d'omne* follows the metrical and rhyming patterns of the thirteenth-century *cuaderna vía*. From the outset the poet uses many of the common-

places of the early *mester de clerecía*, including the convocation of the public, a petition to be heard, a comparison of his poetic offering to a good meal, and the declaration that his poem is meant to be read and not sung—an implicit reference to the difference between *mester de clerecía* and *mester de juglaría* (minstrel works). This familiarity with the early works is manifested throughout the poem in metrical clichés that also appear in the *Libro de Alexandre* and the *Libro de buen amor* but are absent from the *Rimado de Palacio*. That the poet wanted his audience to interpret his work within the context of the thirteenth-century poems is clear from his borrowing the claim of metrical perfection from the prologue of the *Libro de Alexandre*. Strophe 2 of the latter reads:

> Mester trago fermoso, non es de joglaría,
> mester es sen pecado, ca es de clerecía:
> fablar curso rimado por la cuaderna vía,
> a sílabas cuntadas, ca es grant maestría.

> (I offer a beautiful art, not from the minstrels,
> It is an art free of flaws because it is by the learned/clergy.
> Speaking in the versified way in the alexandrine,
> with counted syllables, is a great skill.)

In comparison, strophe 4 of the *Libro de miseria d'omne* reads:

> Ond todo omne que quisiere este libro bien pasar,
> mester es que las palabras sepa bien silabicar;
> ca por sílavas contadas, que es arte de rimar
> e por la quaderna vía su curso quiere finar.

> (All men who wish to translate this book well,
> It is essential that they know how to count well the syllables in the words;
> Because with counted syllables, which is the art of versifying,
> And in the Alexandrine, its course will be completed.)

While a poet at the beginning of the fourteenth century might expect his words to recall the earlier poem for his audience, such an expectation would seem to be unreasonably remote nearly one hundred years later. Owing to similarities in topic, tone, and even phrase, Walsh believes that the *Libro de miseria d'omne* is part of a cycle of didactic *cuaderna vía* poetry from the late thirteenth and early fourteenth centuries, including *Proverbios de Salamón* and *Castigos de Catón,* that served as a bridge between the early works of *mester de clerecía* and the *Libro de buen amor.* The final years of the thirteenth century and the first years of the fourteenth were a period of political, economic, and social disorder. Chronicles and legal documents attest to increasing poverty and hunger, the plague, and rising complaints from peasants of abuse from the nobility. Such a climate of misery and discord would be expected to produce a work such as the *Libro de miseria d'omne*.

The poet's treatment of his source material not only reveals his understanding that his audience is distinct from Lothar's but also indicates a different intent. On reading the *De Miseria Condicionis Humane* one is struck by its studied rhetoric; modern scholars have called it cold, pedantic, and artificial, and the Spanish poet seems to have had a similar attitude toward his source. At the beginning of the *Libro de miseria d'omne* he states that Pope Innocent, "maestro en las siete artes" (master of the seven arts), wrote the *De Miseria Condicionis Humane* in a highly polished Latin that can only be understood by *letrados* (those educated in Latin). The *Libro de miseria d'omne* poet does not merely translate his source from Latin; he also transforms its elevated rhetoric by eliminating wordplay and complex sentence structures. Whereas Lothar's style is oratorical, the language of the *Libro de miseria d'omne* approaches ordinary speech; scholars have described it as emotional, picturesque, and roguish, adjectives that could not be applied to the *De Miseria Condicionis Humane*. While Lothar frequently deals in abstractions, the Spanish poet focuses on the concrete, drawing examples from everyday life to illustrate his points.

The poet's approach to adapting the *De Miseria Condicionis Humane* gives some hints as to his audience: Tesauro observes that the *De Miseria Condicionis Humane* is a solitary meditation and clearly the product of a written culture, while the *Libro de miseria d'omne* seems more like a dialogue with implied listeners. Unlike Lothar, the poet addresses the audience in the second person as he calls on them to relate what he narrates to their own lived experience and admonishes them to follow his advice. These changes indicate that the poet intended to reach a broader, less-educated audience than that of the *De Miseria Condicionis Humane*.

The *De Miseria Condicionis Humane* is a tour de force on *contemptu mundi* in which the author demonstrates an impressive knowledge of rhetoric, theology, philosophy, and law. While he surely had a didactic aim—his declared intention is to suppress pride—he seldom preaches, preferring to allow his readers to derive whatever lessons they will from the massive accumulation of quotations and biblical exempla. By contrast, at one point the *Libro de miseria d'omne* poet refers to his work as a sermon, and he frequently mentions preachers. Although the work is not structured as a sermon, it adheres to the principles of the mendicant *artes praedicandi* (manuals on the art of preaching): instead of employing the elevated rhetoric found in the *De Miseria Condicionis Humane* and characteristic of the monastic tradition, the poet emphasizes simplicity, uses everyday speech and a limited vocabulary, establishes connec-

tions between disparate topics, explains his meaning, and draws lessons for his audience. What the source material loses in complexity in its adaptation to Spanish, it gains in vitality owing to the poet's penchant for vivid description and reliance on exempla from daily life, both of which were prescribed by the *artes praedicandi* for effective communication with a wide audience. The exclusion of complicated points of philosophy is also in keeping with mendicant preaching, as are the topics that the poet adds: the deadly sins, social criticism, penance, and good works. Moreover, some of the themes of *De Miseria Condicionis Humane,* such as the opposition of heaven and hell and of the vices and virtues, were favorite subjects of the mendicants. (Innocent was the Pope who granted approval to the mendicant Dominican and Franciscan orders, and in 1215 he called the Fourth Lateran Council, which led to the reforms favored by the mendicants.) The *Libro de miseria d'omne* poet may have been a mendicant; in any case, it is certain that he intended to instruct his audience on how to live a Christian life and gain salvation. Throughout the poem he preaches the importance of good works, especially charity and penance, which are the subjects of the final strophes. At one point he argues, in contradiction of Lothar, that God does not want to condemn sinners but hopes that they will save themselves through conversion, confession, and penance. Thus, the *Libro de miseria d'omne* is in essence a sermon in verse designed to instruct the audience in fundamental Christian principles, revealing to them the horrors of eternal damnation while showing them the path to salvation.

References:

Américo Castro, *España en su historia: Cristianos, moros y judíos* (Buenos Aires: Losada, 1948), pp. 377–379;

Jane E. Connolly, *Translation and Poetization in the "Quaderna Vía": Study and Edition of the "Libro de miseria d'omne"* (Madison, Wis.: Hispanic Seminary of Medieval Studies, 1987);

Pompilio Tesauro, "Aragonesismo y leonesismo en el *Libro de miseria de omne,*" *Studi di Letteratura e di Linguistica,* 2 (1983): 225–234;

Tesauro, "Il *Libro de miseria de omne,* sermone in versi," *Studi Ispanici,* 1984 (1985): 9–19;

Billy Bussell Thompson, "La *Alhotba arrimada* (o *Sermón de Rabaddán*) y el mester de clerecía," in *Hispanic Studies in Honor of Alan D. Deyermond: A North American Tribute,* edited by John S. Miletich (Madison, Wis.: Hispanic Seminary of Medieval Studies, 1986), pp. 279–289;

John K. Walsh, "Juan Ruiz and the *mester de clerezía:* Lost Context and Lost Parody," *Romance Philology,* 33 (1979–1980): 62–86.

Ramon Llull

(1232? – 1316?)

Mark D. Johnston
DePaul University

SELECTED WORKS: *Libre de contemplació en Déu* (circa
    1274);
Ars compendiosa inveniendi veritatem (circa 1274);
Liber de gentili et tribus sapientibus (1274–1276?);
Liber principiorum philosophiae (1274–1278?);
Liber principiorum theologiae (1274–1278?);
Liber principiorum iuris (1274–1278?);
Liber principiorum medicinae (1274–1278?);
Liber de sancto spiritu (1274–1283?);
Liber de angelis (1274–1283?);
Doctrina pueril (circa 1276);
Libre del orde de cavalleria (circa 1276);
Libre de Evast e de Aloma e de Blanquerna (circa 1276);
Art demostrativa (circa 1276); translated as *Ars demostra-
    tiva* (circa 1283);
Liber de prima et secunda intentione (1283?);
Liber de XIV articulis Sacrosanctae Romanae Ecclesiae (1283–
    1285);
Liber Tartari et Christiani (1288);
Cent noms de Déu (1288);
Disputatio fidelis et infidelis (1288–1289);
Compendium seu commentum Artis demostrativae (1288–
    1289);
Libre de meravelles (circa 1288–1289);
Ars inventiva veritatis (1290);
Ars amativa boni (1290);
Liber contra Antichristum (1290–1292);
Liber de laudibus beatae Virginis Mariae (1290–1292);
De adventu Messiae (1290–1292);
Quomodo Terra Sancta recuperari potest (1292);
Tractatus de modo convertendi infideles (1292);
Liber de quinque sapientibus (1294);
Arbor philosophiae desideratae (1294);
Liber de affatu (1294);
Desconhort (1295?);
Arbre de sciència / Arbor scientiae (1295–1296);
Liber de anima rationali (1296);
Proverbis de Ramon (1296);
Contemplatio Raymundi (1297);
Tractatus novus de astronomia (1297);
Declaratio Raymundi (1298);

Ramon Llull (from Catalan Review: International Journal of
Catalan Culture, *4 [July–December 1990]; Thomas Cooper
Library, University of South Carolina)*

Arbor philosophiae amoris (1298);

Consolatio Venetorum et totius gentis desolatae (1298);

Cant de Ramon (1299);

Liber de homine (1300);

Medicina de peccat (1300);

Rhetorica nova (1301);

Liber de natura (1301);

Aplicació de l'Art general (1301);

Mil proverbis (1302);

Logica nova (1303);

Liber de regionibus sanitatis et infirmitatis (1303);

Liber de lumine (1303);

Disputatio fidei et intellectus (1303);

Liber de intellectu (1304);

Liber de voluntate (1304);

Liber de memoria (1304);

Ars iuris naturalis (1304);

Liber de praedicatione (1304);

Liber praedicationis contra iudaeos (1305);

Liber de ascensu et descensu intellectus (1305);

Liber de demonstratione per aequiparantiam (1305);

Ars generalis ultima (1305–1308);

Ars brevis (1308);

Liber de novis fallaciis (1308);

Disputatio Raymundi christiani et Hamar saraceni (1308);

Liber de esse Dei (1309);

Liber de probatione quod in Deo sunt tres personae (1309);

Liber acquisitione Terrae Sanctae (1309);

Liber de convenientia fidei et intellectus in obiecto (1309);

Proverbis d'ensenyament (1309);

Liber de modo naturali intelligendi (1310);

Liber reprobationis aliquorum errorum Averrois (1310);

Liber in quo declaratur quod fides sancta catholica est magis probabilis quam improbabilis (1310);

De fallaciis quas non credunt facere aliqui, qui credunt esse philosophantes, contra purissimum actum Dei verissimum et perfectissimum (1310);

Disputatio Raimundi et Averroistae (1310);

Metaphysica nova et compendiosa (1310);

Liber novus physicorum et compendiosus (1310);

Liber correlativorum innatorum (1310);

De conversione subiecti et praedicati et medii (1310);

Disputatio Petri clerici et Raymundi phantastici (circa 1311);

Sermones contra errores Averrois (1311);

Petitio Raymundi in Concilio Generali ad adquiriendam Terram Sanctam (1311);

Liber natalis pueri Christi Jesu (1311);

Liber lamentationis philosophiae (1311);

Liber contradictionis (1311);

Liber de syllogismis contradictoriis (1311);

Liber de novo modo demonstrandi (1312);

Liber de Trinitate et Incarnatione (1312);

Ars confessionis (1312);

Sermones de Ave Maria (1312);

Sermones de decem praeceptis (1312);

Sermones de Pater noster (1312);

Liber de virtutibus et peccatis (1313);

Liber de compendiosa contemplatione (1313);

Liber de Trinitate trinitissima (1313);

Liber de essentia et esse Dei (1313);

Liber de quinque praedicabilibus et decem praedicamentis (1313);

Liber de multiplicatione quae fit in essentia Dei per divinam Trinitatem (1314);

Liber de maiori fine intellectus, amoris et honoris (1315).

Manuscripts: Biblioteca Nazionale Marciana, Venice, MS. lat. VI.200 (2757), 1298 *(Blanquerna);* Biblioteca Central, Barcelona, MS. 12, s. XV *(Libre del orde de cavalleria);* Bibliotheca Ambrosiana, Milan, MS. D 535 inf., x. XV *(Arbre de sciència);* Bayerische Staatsbibliothek, Munich, MSS. Clm. 10498, s. XIV *(Arbor scientiae),* Clm. 10507, s. XIV *(Liber de ascensu et descensu intellectus),* hisp. 60 (604), s. XIV *(Arbre de filosofia desiderat),* hisp. 66, s. XIV *(Doctrina pueril);* Bibliothèque Nationale, Paris, MS. lat. 16116, III, s. XIV *(Arbor philosophiae desideratae);* Bibliotheca Vaticana, Rome, MS. Ottob. lat. 845, s. XIV *(Cent noms de Déu).*

First publications: *Raymundi Lully Doctoris illuminati de noua logica de correlatiuis necnon & de ascensu et descensu intellectus* (Valencia: Alfonso de Proaza, 1512); *Blanquerna: Qui tracta de sinch estaments de persones* (Valencia: Joan Bonllabi, 1521).

Collections: *Opera omnia,* 9 volumes, edited by Ivo Salzinger (Mainz: Ivo Salzinger, 1721–1740); *Obres de Ramon Lull,* 21 volumes, edited by Mateo Obrador y Benassar, Salvador Galmés, Miguel Ferrá, and Miquel Gayà (volumes 1–11, Palma de Mallorca: Comissió Editora Lulliana, 1906–1917; volumes 12–21, Palma de Mallorca: Diputació Provincial de Balears & Institut d'Estudis Catalans, 1923–1950); *Obres essencials,* 2 volumes, edited by Miguel Batllori and others (Barcelona: Selecta, 1957, 1961); *Raimundi Lulli Opera Latina,* 28 volumes to date, edited by Friedrich Stegmüller, Johannes Stöhr, Hermógenes Harada, Aloisius Madre, Helmut Riedlinger, Louis Sala-Molins, Charles H. Lohr, Manuel Bauzà Ochogavía, Fernando Domínguez Reboiras, Abraham Soria Flores, Antoni Oliver, Michel Senellart, Marta M. M. Romano, Francesco Santi, M. Pereira, Theodore Pindl-Büchel, Walburga Büchel, Thomas Le Myésier, Jordi Gayà Estelrich, Walter Euler, Père Villalba Varneda, Viola Tenge-Wolf, Blanca Garí, Jaume Medina, and María Asunción Sánchez Manzano (volumes 1–5, Palma de Mallorca: Maioricensis Schola Lullistica del CSIC, 1959–1967; volumes 6– ; Turnhout:

Brepols, 1978–); *Nova edició de les obres de Ramon Llull,* 7 volumes to date, edited by Domínguez Reboiras, Gayà Estelrich, Antoni Joan Pons i Pons, Gret Schib Torra, Anthony Bonner, Lola Badia, Eugènia Gisbert, and Joan Santanach i Suñol (Palma de Mallorca: Patronat Ramon Llull, 1990–).

Editions in English: *Here begynneth the Table of this present booke Intytled the Book of the ordre of chyualry or knyghthode,* translated by William Caxton (Westminster: William Caxton, 1484); *The Book of the Lover and the Beloved,* translated by E. Allison Peers (London: Society for Promoting Christian Knowledge / New York: Macmillan, 1923); *Thoughts of Blessed Ramón Lull for Every Day,* translated by Peers (London: Burns, Oates & Washbourne, 1925); *The Art of Contemplation,* translated by Peers (London: Society for Promoting Christian Knowledge / New York: Macmillan, 1925); *Blanquerna: A Thirteenth Century Romance,* translated by Peers (London: Jarrolds, 1926); *The Tree of Love,* translated by Peers (London: Society for Promoting Christian Knowledge / New York & Toronto: Macmillan, 1926); *The Book of the Beasts,* translated by Peers (London: Burns, Oates & Washbourne, 1927); *Selected Works of Ramon Llull (1232–1316),* 2 volumes, edited and translated by Anthony Bonner (Princeton: Princeton University Press, 1985); revised as *Doctor Illuminatus: A Ramón Llull Reader,* 1 volume, edited by Bonner, translated by Bonner and Eve Bonner (Princeton: Princeton University Press, 1993); *The New Rhetoric of Ramon Llull: An Edition and Translation of Llull's Rethorica nova,* translated by Mark D. Johnston (Davis, Cal.: Hermagoras Press, 1993); *The Book of the Lover and the Beloved of Ramon Llull: An English Translation with Latin and Old Catalan Versions Transcribed from Original Manuscripts,* translated by Johnston (Warminster, U.K.: Aris & Phillips, 1995).

The Majorcan theologian and philosopher Ramon Llull (known in English as Raymond Lully) was one of the most active lay writers of the European Middle Ages and perhaps the single most prolific vernacular author of the medieval era. He wrote nearly three hundred works in his native Catalan, in Latin, and in Arabic (all of the Arabic works are now lost) during a career that spanned six decades. Despite this copious oeuvre, the details of Llull's biography are frustratingly obscure. The chief source of knowledge about him is a highly selective, quasi-hagiographic *Vita* (Life) composed in 1311 by admirers at the Carthusian house in Vauvert, outside Paris. Only a handful of other docu-

ments testify to his activities: his will, various letters of commendation, and references in the work of contemporaries. His own writings include surprisingly limited autobiographical material, although the colophons of many of his works indicate their dates and places of composition. New scholarly discoveries continue to illuminate his life. The most detailed chronology, with critical discussions of disputed or uncertain events, appears in Anthony Bonner's *Selected Works of Ramon Llull* (1985).

Llull was born on Majorca, probably in 1232. He was the scion of a prosperous, French-descended Catalan merchant family that helped settle the island after King James I "The Conqueror" of Aragon won it from the Arabs in 1229. Llull evidently received the training in vernacular letters and courtesy typical for well-born young men of this era. His earliest instruction perhaps resembled the programs of elementary education described in his *Doctrina pueril* (circa 1276, Instruction for Children) and *Libre de Evast e de Aloma e de Blanquerna* (circa 1276, Book of Evast and Aloma and Blanquerna; translated as *Blanquerna: A Thirteenth Century Romance,* 1926), although these models are rather idealized. The *Vita* says that Llull served as "seneschal" to the young Prince James of Majorca. He married Blanca Picany in 1257; they had two children.

Around 1263 Llull experienced a profound religious awakening that the *Vita* calls a "conversion to penitence." Visions of Christ crucified, which first came to him one night while he was composing a love poem, spurred him to resolve to abandon the world and serve God by evangelizing the Muslims, writing a book of irrefutable apologetic arguments, and campaigning for the establishment of schools to train missionaries in the Oriental languages. After making some pilgrimages, he decided to seek education in Paris, since, according to the *Vita,* he possessed "no knowledge and only a little grammar" (that is, Latin). Such professions of ignorance were, however, a common polemical posture: like other contemporary laypeople who sought to intervene in affairs of the faith at a time when such intervention could easily attract suspicions of heresy, Llull appealed to the higher authority of direct divine inspiration and sought to avoid academic pretensions. His family and friends, including the Dominican leader Ramon de Penyafort, persuaded him to remain on Majorca. During the next ten years he apparently stayed on his native island where he learned "a little grammar." The nature of the Latin instruction he received is unclear. A few grammar teachers were available on the island by this time, but their schools typically served juvenile pupils. The most likely recourse for a wealthy adult such as Llull was private lessons with a tutor. He also practiced Arabic intensively with the aid of a Muslim slave he acquired.

During this decade Llull studied whatever texts of Islamic theology and philosophy he could obtain and read widely in Christian mystical and apologetic theology. The content of these studies is, perhaps, the single most debated point among scholars. Llull's philosophical and theological erudition was, as many critics have noted, somewhat old-fashioned and even elementary. The doctrines and precepts expounded in his oeuvre rarely extend beyond the commonplaces found in popular vernacular, Latin, or Arabic encyclopedias, which may have been the only resources accessible to him on Majorca. After the island's conquest, the materials available for advanced study of Islam would have been limited and rather antiquated. His earliest writings include a vernacular verse rendering of al-Ghazali's treatise on logic, which may have served him as a textbook for studying Arabic; in the poem he announces his intent to educate laypeople who are ignorant of Latin or Arabic and to help them seek knowledge of God above all else. Local religious houses would be a likely venue for Llull to seek instruction in the Western arts, philosophy, and theology. Laypeople interested in more-advanced learning may have been able to audit classes at the convents of the mendicant orders, as Dante did at Santa Maria Novella in Florence. The Dominicans and the Franciscans had houses on Majorca in Llull's day; the Order of Preachers' overseas missions would obviously have interested him, and the *Vita* claims that his final commitment to evangelism resulted from hearing a Franciscan sermon. The *Vita* particularly mentions Llull's association with a "nearby abbey," long identified as the Cistercian house of La Real. The intellectual resources available at this abbey were not extraordinary but easily sufficient for his purposes. Joceyln N. Hillgarth notes in "La Biblioteca de La Real: Fuentes posibles de Llull" (1963, The Library of La Real: Possible Sources for Llull) that a 1386 inventory describes a library of around two hundred volumes, mostly of theology but including works on grammar, logic, and other arts. None of the works held there since the thirteenth century correspond exactly to the few authorities that Llull cites in his writings, a discrepancy that has encouraged some scholars to deny a major role for La Real in Llull's education. The abbey did, however, possess standard encyclopedic works, such as Isidore's *Etymologiae* (Etymologies), Peter Lombard's *Sententiae* (Sentences), and the *Summa* attributed to Alexander of Hales, that match the range of Llull's knowledge of the arts, theology, and philosophy. Any conclusion based on Llull's citation of sources is hazardous, since he regularly rejects arguments based on authority and recasts all ideas in his own terminology. It is, perhaps, emblematic of his overall intellectual vision that Arab Christian apologetic texts such as the anonymous *Contrarietas alfo-*

lica, a work so little known that even the meaning of the title is unclear, and twelfth-century Latin contemplative writers such as Richard of St. Victor appear among the few authorities named in his oeuvre. References to these sources suggest that the two areas of interest Llull probably explored most enthusiastically during his years of private study were controversialist and mystical theology. This dual emphasis is obvious in his first major writing, the *Libre de contemplació en Déu* (circa 1274, Book of Contemplation of God), and informs the structure of his "Great Universal Art of Finding Truth," or *Ars magna* (Great Art), which offers a combined system of meditation and argumentation. As a pious layman studying privately, Llull designed his own curriculum without direction from academic requirements or ecclesiastical superiors and probably excluded any liberal arts or philosophy that he considered irrelevant to his evangelical project.

During a period of meditative seclusion on Mount Randa, probably in 1274, Llull received the inspiration for his Great Art, which he attributed to divine revelation. He built a hermitage on the mountain and worked at the "nearby abbey" on the *Libre de contemplació en Déu* and the *Ars compendiosa inveniendi veritatem* (circa 1274, Compendious Art of Finding Truth), the first redaction of his Great Art.

An encyclopedia of devotional and contemplative practice, the *Libre de contemplació en Déu* is a compendium of all of the doctrines he subsequently expounded. It comprises 366 thirty-paragraph chapters—one for each day of the year—in three "volumes," five "books," and forty "distinctions." The introduction explains the spiritual symbolism of these numerical divisions. The *Libre de contemplació en Déu* treats God in chapters 1 through 29, the material universe in chapters 30 through 102, human nature in chapters 103 through 226, natural and revealed faith in chapters 227 through 268, and love of and devotion to God in chapters 269 to 366. Each chapter opens with an ecstatic salutation to God and offers a meditative exercise. The third volume, consisting of chapters 227 through 366, is especially noteworthy for the gradual introduction of the symbolic letters, charts, and principles that later provided the structure of Llull's Great Art; most scholars regard these chapters as the genesis of Llull's system. The *Libre de contemplació* is, nevertheless, largely expository, relying especially on exempla to illustrate its lessons. Llull claims in the last chapter that the three volumes lead the reader through progressively higher levels of spiritual understanding. Among his most popular writings, it survives in more than two dozen Catalan and Latin manuscripts, including Biblioteca Nazionale Marciana, Venice, MS. lat. VI.200 (2757), a collection of Llull's works professionally prepared in 1298 for presentation to the Doge of Venice.

Around 1275 Prince James of Majorca summoned Llull to have his first writings examined by a friar at the Franciscan theological school in Montpellier. The *Vita* reports the friar's admiration for the piety displayed in Llull's works. In 1276 Llull persuaded James, who had become King James I of Majorca that year, to endow a center at Miramar for training Franciscans as missionary friars; the project eventually failed. Also in 1276 his wife sought an administrator for their affairs, arguing that he was too absorbed in the "contemplative life" to manage their estate. Around 1276 Llull produced some of his best-known vernacular works, including the *Doctrina pueril*, the *Libre del orde de cavalleria* (Book of the Order of Chivalry; translated as *Here begynneth the Table of this present booke Intytled the Book of the ordre of chyualry or knyghthode*, 1484), the *Libre de Evast e de Aloma e de Blanquerna*, and the *Art demostrativa* (Art of Demonstration), a further redaction of his Great Art. He composed the last two works in Montpellier, a city that became a frequent way station in the nearly constant peregrination that he began at this time.

Although all of Llull's writings are didactic in a broad sense, the *Doctrina pueril* and *Libre del orde de cavalleria* are noteworthy as contributions to the medieval literature of *specula* (mirrors), educational treatises designed to guide the training of particular groups or classes. Both texts largely treat their subjects as applications of moral theology. The *Doctrina pueril*, addressed in the second person to a "son," combines an extended catechism with a short encyclopedia of the arts and sciences. The first nine sections, chapters 1 through 72, expound the articles of the faith, the Decalogue, the sacraments, the gifts of the Holy Spirit, the Beatitudes, the joys of the Virgin, virtues, vices, and laws. The last section, chapters 73 through 100, reviews the seven liberal arts, theology, jurisprudence, natural philosophy, medicine, the mechanical arts, moral philosophy, and the seven ages of the world. The content is deliberately commonplace, but the work is remarkable for being entirely in the vernacular. Llull insists on the efficacy of this medium in chapter 73, arguing that children should learn the trivium first in their native language so that they will later understand it better in Latin. The *Doctrina pueril* survives in more than a dozen manuscripts, including versions in French, Provençal, Castilian, and Latin.

The *Libre del orde de cavalleria* was another "best-seller," circulating in more than two dozen manuscripts, with thirteen in French and a Scottish version used by William Caxton as the basis of his English printed text in 1484. Some historians consider it the most popular and influential manual of chivalry of the later Middle Ages. It is certainly not a comprehensive guide to aristocratic education, ignoring important profane pursuits such as hunting, heraldry, warfare, jousting, estate management, and even courtesy. The seven parts of the text treat the origins of knighthood, the order and rank of the knight, the examination of prospective knights, the ceremony of bestowing knighthood, the heavily moralized meaning of a knight's armaments, the proper customs of a knight, and the honor due to knights. Through this exposition Llull develops a cogent definition of knighthood as a divinely sanctioned vocation dedicated to fortifying the Christian commonwealth and defending the faith. He portrays the aristocracy and the clergy as the dual foundations of society and suggests that knights should receive training in schools just as clerics do.

Llull wrote the "spiritual romance" *Libre de Evast e de Aloma e de Blanquerna* during one of his visits to Montpellier in the 1280s and later composed a Latin translation. Multiple manuscripts of both versions survive, and it was among his first texts set in print in the early sixteenth century. Commonly known as *Blanquerna*, it recounts the quest of a Christian hero for devotion to and love of God. Llull originally spelled the name of his hero "Blaquerna," but copyists soon altered it to "Blanquerna," the form commonly used in later editions. The only son of a wealthy merchant couple abandons secular affairs and devotes himself to serving God, persuading his fiancée, Natana, to do the same. She quickly becomes an abbess, while his ecclesiastical career develops more gradually through the ranks of sacristan, abbot, bishop, and finally, Pope, but he renounces the Holy See to become a hermit. Retired from the world, he writes the *Libre de amic e amat* (translated as *The Book of the Lover and the Beloved*, 1923) and the *Art de contemplació* (translated as *The Art of Contemplation*, 1925), which appear as appendices to *Blanquerna*. The main text is divided into five books treating marriage (secular life), religion (regular clergy), prelacy (secular clergy), the apostolic estate (Pope), and eremetic life, providing a complete model of the ideal Christian society as Llull conceives it. At each stage in his career Blaquerna confronts problems ranging from simony and prostitution to conversion of the infidel and devises appropriately pious schemes for resolving them.

The *Libre de amic e amat* offers 366 short paragraphs for daily devotion, modeled, according to the introduction, on the pious exhortations and exempla composed by Sufis. Each paragraph recounts tribulations, travails, or triumphs of the Lover, representing the fervent Christian or the human soul generally, devoted to his Beloved, symbolizing Christ or God. The work is almost lyrical in intensity and adapts some traditional images from both Christian spirituality and

Manuscript illumination showing Llull advancing against falsehood and ignorance, preceded by the faculties of intellect, will, and memory and pulling a wagon containing personifications of his eighteen principles (Landesbibliothek, Karlsruhe, MS. St. Peter perg. 92)

medieval courtly love literature. The use of male figures for both the Lover and the Beloved is striking: whether Llull knew of, or would have accepted for imitation if he did, the classical Arabic device of love poetry addressed by men to boys is unknown. The exquisite and exalted expression of spiritual passion in this work continues to sustain its popularity and has led to its publication in some forty modern translations or editions.

Llull's activities in the early 1280s are uncertain; but in 1287 he visited Rome, hoping to present his plans for the moral reform of Christendom to Pope Honorius IV. The pontiff's death frustrated that under-

taking, and Llull traveled to Paris to seek the support of King Philip IV "the Fair." He evidently wrote his other spiritual romance, the *Libre de meravelles* (Book of Marvels; translated as "Felix, or, The Book of Wonders," 1985), in Paris, perhaps for presentation at Philip's court. Commonly known as *Felix,* the work follows a less linear trajectory than *Blanquerna.* In a brief prologue a "sad and sorrowing man in a foreign land" writes the *Libre de meravelles* and then sends his son, Felix, out into the world as a Christian *viator* (traveler) to marvel at its loss of piety. The text is divided into ten books, representing the hierarchy of beings: God, angels, heaven, elements, plants, metals, animals, humans, paradise, and hell. The plot consists of Felix's successive encounters with seven sages, who relate often-extended edifying stories to him. He also witnesses or intervenes in many morally illustrative incidents, including an adaptation of the Oriental fable *Kalila and Dimna* as "The Book of the Beasts." The *Libre de meravelles* thus employs the device of the hero's journey to concatenate scores of exempla into a kind of moralized encyclopedia, nearly half of which is devoted to questions of moral theology. Felix ends his life's journey as the lay brother of an abbey. After he dies, one of the monks adopts the title of Second Felix and sets out to wander the world, recounting the *Libre de meravelles* and extending it with the new wonders that he encounters. Medieval translations into Latin, Castilian, Italian, and French—the latter charmingly illustrated—testify and contributed to its popularity. Llull's modern reputation as the giant of medieval Catalan literature rests especially on *Blanquerna* and *Felix*. Despite the overtly devotional character and loose narrative structure of the works, both won esteem from some twentieth-century scholars as medieval antecedents of the modern novel.

Llull's *Cent noms de Déu* (1288, Hundred Names for God) presents one hundred titles for God, each explicated in ten verses, as an alternative to the ninety-nine names of God recognized in Muslim devotion. Although Llull's names include many Latinate terms, as his introduction acknowledges, and his explications are heavily theological and philosophical, this work became popular enough to circulate in ten Catalan manuscripts.

In Paris, Llull read from his works before a university audience. Their apparently unfavorable reaction initiated his lifelong antagonism toward the Parisian scholars, whom he came to regard as "Averroists"—Scholastics who embraced the doctrines of the Muslim thinker Averroës (Ibn Rushd) to the detriment of Christian belief. Llull's zeal for promoting his Great Art, his conviction that God had inspired its design, and its idiosyncratic methods and terminology made his work difficult for his academic contemporaries to accept. From the beginning of his career he explicitly presented the Great Art as an alternative to the theology and philosophy of the schools, and the *Vita* explains that he composed many applications of his system specifically to render it intelligible for "simple" people. Llull's dedication to these objectives probably made his antagonistic relationship with the schools inevitable. His dual commitments to contemplation and evangelism suited the cloister and the public plaza far better than the classroom.

Between 1289 and 1291 Llull passed through Montpellier, Genoa, and Rome, preparing an improved redaction of his system, the *Ars inventiva veritatis* (1290,

Art of Finding Truth), with an Arabic translation. He met the Franciscan minister-general, Ramon Gaufredi, during the order's chapter-general of 1289 at Rieti, and he again sought unsuccessfully to present proposals for missions and Crusades at the papal court. Returning to Genoa around 1293, he suffered what the *Vita* describes as a profound spiritual depression, which only abated when he had a vision commanding him to seek salvation through the Dominican Order. Judging the Franciscans more likely to promote his Great Art, Llull ignored this divine counsel and sought their support instead. Recovering from his malaise, he made his first overseas mission, to the North African kingdom of Tunis, in 1293. His success in evangelizing learned Muslims, the *Vita* recounts, soon led to his arrest and expulsion from the kingdom.

Llull spent most of the years 1294 to 1296 in Naples and Rome, where he sought audiences with Popes Celestine V and Boniface VIII with no more success than before. In the verse work *Desconhort* (Disconsolation), probably composed in Rome in 1295, the figure of Ramon pours out to a hermit his disappointment after thirty years of labor promoting his Great Art and missionary plans. Composed in Rome in 1295–1296, his *Arbre de sciència* or, in Latin, *Arbor scientiae* (Tree of Knowledge) is a tremendous compilation of exempla and perhaps the most complete summa of learning that Llull produced. In Llull's oeuvre exempla are, after the methods of his Great Art, the discursive device that he uses most often. Although every redaction and application of his Great Art is encyclopedic, insofar as his system seeks to comprehend all knowledge and being, the *Arbre de sciència* explicitly organizes all divine and mundane affairs into sixteen sections or "trees," each of which is subdivided into "trunks," "branches," "limbs," "leaves," flowers," and "fruits." The first eleven "trees" treat the hierarchy of creation and human affairs: the elements, plants, senses, imagination, human nature, ethics, government, Christian faith, heaven, angels, and paradise. The next three "trees" treat Catholic doctrine regarding the Virgin Mary, Christ, and God. Finally, two lengthy "trees" of exempla and questions explicate even further the content of the first fourteen "trees." The *Arbre de sciència* exists in two Catalan and ten Latin manuscripts, which provided the basis for printed editions in the late fifteenth and early sixteenth centuries with woodcut illustrations of the arboreal structure of the work.

Llull returned to Genoa and then to the court of James II of Majorca before visiting Paris again in 1297. The *Vita* reports that he enjoyed a successful audience with Philip IV and again presented his work to academic audiences. The visit evidently prompted him to pay increased attention to the Aristotelian logic that was so important to his Scholastic peers.

In the final lines of his *Declaratio Raymundi* (Declaration of Ramon), written in Paris in 1298 as a refutation of Scholastic doctrines, Llull invites anyone who reads the treatise to polish its rough manner and blames the lack of "bono dictamine"(good style) in the work on his "quia sufficiens grammaticus non sum nec rhetoricus" (inadequate grammatical and rhetorical training). Some of the first modern scholars to study Llull's oeuvre wondered whether he ever actually mastered Latin, since the *Vita* states that his proficiency in Latin was negligible when he began his crusade for conversion of the unbelievers, and documents from the end of his life indicate that he sought secretaries and translators to assist him. His reliance on their assistance more likely reflects both his advanced age and the devotion of his disciples. His disclaimer at the end of the *Declaratio Raymundi* and similar statements in other works leave little reason to doubt that Llull produced, as best he could, nearly all of the Latin versions of his writings. Their style and diction are consistent enough to make it easy to recognize the few texts that might be the work of hired secretaries or later translators. His Latin syntax typically mirrors the constructions of his native Catalan, especially in the use of subordinate and relative clauses. Furthermore, the idiosyncratic terminology of his Great Art would have been difficult to maintain if he had not had a ready command of Latin. In general, the quality of Latin displayed in his writings differs little from that found in the work of merchants, administrators, and other nonacademic professionals who used Latin as a common koine in later medieval Europe. Indeed, since Llull traveled so extensively but never mentions speaking any languages other than Catalan and Arabic, Latin must have been his necessary medium of communication in the royal and papal courts, at the schools of Paris and Montpellier, and among his enthusiasts in the northern Italian towns. His own experience probably contributed to his advocacy of Latin as a universal language.

The Catalan *Cant de Ramon* (Song of Ramon), evidently written in Paris in 1299, offers an anguished expression of his despair regarding the results of his labors. That same year Llull received official permission from James II of Aragon to proselytize Jews and Muslims in his realm. In Barcelona he wrote for the king the short verse *Dictat de Ramon* (Declaration of Ramon) and an accompanying commentary, both of which were also redacted in Latin; they succinctly and vigorously announce the tenets of the Christian faith that he considered most important to set before unbelievers. He also wrote the *Medicina de peccat* (1300, Cure for Sin), a conventional and popularized exposition of the vices and virtues that draws little from the Great Art, and the *Aplicació de l'Art general* (1301, Application of the General Art), in which he attempts to provide an easy verse summary of his system; its terms and methods seem even harder to grasp in rhyme.

Following his commitment to use the vernacular as a medium of instruction and to render his Great Art as accessible as possible to the less learned, during the first thirty years of his career Llull produced Catalan versions of most of his theological and philosophical works. But after he left Paris in 1299, his Catalan production appears to have diminished considerably: of the nearly 160 works that he wrote after this date, no more than 20 percent are known to exist in vernacular versions. The reasons for this shift in idiom are unclear, although Llull's special attention to the "Averroist" errors of Parisian scholars and his constant efforts to win princely or papal support perhaps led him to use Latin more often as a means of reaching his intended audiences.

Excited by news of Tartar conquests in the Near East, Llull traveled in 1301 to Cyprus, where he unsuccessfully sought support from the island's Christian ruler, King Henry Lusignan II, and attempted, with similar results, to evangelize Eastern Christians. The *Vita* mentions that he also met with Jacques de Molay, the last grand master of the Knights Templars. The meeting probably concerned Llull's proposal for a union of all of the military orders into a single organization devoted to a general Crusade for recovery of the Holy Land, a scheme that he advocates in his *Quomodo Terra Sancta recuperari potest* (1292, How to Recover the Holy Land), *Liber acquisitione Terrae Sanctae* (1309, Book on Acquiring the Holy Land), and *Petitio Raymundi in Concilio Generali ad adquiriendam Terram Sanctam* (1311, Petition of Ramon to the General Council on Acquiring the Holy Land). In a similar vein, the *Tractatus de modo convertendi infideles* (1292, Treatise on Converting Unbelievers) proposes methods for the compulsory conversion of Muslims and Jews in Christian territories. Although Llull does not consistently advocate Crusades and other uses of force throughout his oeuvre, these works counter the impression of ecumenical tolerance conveyed by his accounts of reasoned debates among Christians and unbelievers.

Llull returned to Genoa in 1302 and then traveled to Lyon, where he hoped for an audience with the newly elected Pope Clement V, and perhaps Paris. During the decade between his journey to Tunis and his visit to Lyon he wrote more than seventy works, including the *Liber de quinque sapientibus* (1294, Book of the Five Sages); the *Proverbis de Ramon* (1296, Proverbs of Ramon); the *Liber de ascensu et descensu intellectus* (1305, Book of the Ascent and Descent of the Mind); and the last major redaction of his Great Art, the *Ars generalis ultima* (1305–1308, Final Great Art). By far the most widely read of his contemplative guides, the *Liber de ascensu et descensu intellectus* is perhaps also the most consistent and complete exposition of his theories of spiritual psychology. Extant in twenty-seven Latin manuscripts, it was among his first works to be published in the early sixteenth century.

Although it is not clear whether the layman Llull ever received official permission to preach publicly, he did write works expounding Christian doctrine in the form of sermons. The longest, the *Liber de praedicatione* (Book of Preaching) of 1304, provides a complete cycle of full-length sermons for each Sunday in the liturgical year and for all major saints' days. The *Liber praedicationis contra iudaeos* (1305, Book of Preaching against Jews) presents an annual cycle of brief sermons giving the "true" senses of scriptural passages commonly "misinterpreted" by the Jews. These exegetical exercises may record arguments employed by Llull in addressing Jewish audiences or may have been designed for other Christian proselytizers to use.

Early in 1307 Llull returned to North Africa, eager to debate Islamic theologians and make converts at Bougie, a popular commercial venue for Majorcan traders. The *Vita* recounts in detail his public demonstrations of Christian truth and Muslim error, which he recorded as the *Disputatio Raymundi christiani et Hamar saraceni* (1308, Disputation of Ramon the Christian and Hamar the Muslim) and which provoked the authorities to imprison him until Genoese and Catalan merchants interceded on his behalf. Expelled from Bougie, he lost all of his possessions in a storm at sea en route to Pisa. He was forced to recompose many of his works in progress, including the *Ars generalis ultima.* He also wrote a popular introduction to the *Ars generalis ultima,* the *Ars brevis* (1308, Brief Art; translated as "Ars brevis," 1984).

If Llull had written only his Great Universal Art of Finding Truth, he would still be famous for this comprehensive system of philosophical and theological argumentation that he held to be capable of demonstrating the truth of Christian doctrine to unbelievers. He attributed its basic premises to the divine inspiration received in 1274 at Mount Randa and devoted his life to perfecting its system. Among its many redactions are the Latin versions *Ars compendiosa inveniendi veritatem, Ars demonstrativa* (circa 1283, Art of Demonstration; translated as "Ars demonstrativa," 1985), the *Compendium seu commentum Artis demonstrativae* (1288–1289, Compendious Commentary on the Art of Demonstration), the *Ars inventiva veritatis,* and, finally, the *Ars generalis ultima.* He also produced many other Latin, Catalan, and Arabic summaries or applied expositions of his system, especially the *Ars brevis,* which achieved wide circulation in

later centuries as his most accessible synopsis of the complete Great Art.

Llull's Great Art is an exercise in "natural theology," a program for explaining how all being and knowledge lead to understanding, love, and honor of God. In scope it rivals the great summae of Scholastic contemporaries such as St. Thomas Aquinas. Unlike the Schoolmen of the thirteenth century, however, Llull eschewed the logic and metaphysics of Greek philosophy, especially those of Aristotle, seeking instead to create a system based on categories so obvious and easy to understand that they would be acceptable to Christians and non-Christians alike, whether learned or not.

The foundation of the Great Art is the definition of nine divine attributes as absolute principles of all existence and knowledge: *Bonitas* (Goodness), *Magnitudo* (Greatness), *Aeternitas* or *Duratio* (Perpetuity), *Potestas* (Power), *Sapientia* (Wisdom), *Voluntas* (Will), *Virtus* (Virtue), *Veritas* (Truth), and *Gloria* (Glory). The traditions of Christian, Muslim, and Jewish belief all recognized some such set of attributes in God, and Llull's names for them are based for the most part on terms used in the Bible and the Koran. Llull also defines nine relative principles through which the absolute principles interrelate within the Godhead and throughout creation: *Differentia* (Difference), *Concordantia* (Concord), *Contrarietas* (Contrariety), *Principium* (Beginning), *Medium* (Middle), *Finis* (End), *Maioritas* (Greater Than), *Aequalitas* (Equality), and *Minoritas* (Less Than). Such basic relationships were common categories in virtually all Christian and non-Christian philosophy and logic. Parallel sets of heuristic *Regulae* (Questions ["Who?" "What?" "Where?" and so forth]), *Subiecta* (Subjects [levels of being from God and the planets to humans and the elements]), *Virtutes* (Virtues), *Vitia* (Vices), and other categories extend the application of Llull's absolute and relative principles to any specialized area of inquiry. As Robert D. F. Pring-Mill explains in *El microcosmos lul·lià* (1961, The Llullian Microcosm), the basic categories of the Great Art offer a nearly perfect statement of the medieval worldview: an understanding of the universe and its constitution that was accepted by almost any educated person in Europe or the Mediterranean world during the Middle Ages.

Although Llull presents the Great Art as a program of argumentation, it does not rely on the rules of Aristotelian logic or dialectic employed by his Scholastic contemporaries. Instead, it creates theological or philosophical propositions through simple combinations of its principles and other categories. Llull facilitates this process by designating each principle or category with the letters *B* through *K* of the alphabet—*A* symbolizes their coherence in the Godhead—and then organizing combinations of these letters in circular and tabular *fig-*

urae (charts). This simple mechanical *ars combinatoria* (combinatory art) served Llull's effort to create a general, easily comprehensible method of inquiry and argumentation and contributed to the popularity of his system in later centuries as a veritable "thinking machine." The *figurae* also serve the practice of meditation and contemplation, which are ultimately the objective of his entire system insofar as all inquiry and argumentation should lead to the understanding, love, and honor of God.

Throughout his career Llull revised the Great Art to incorporate useful doctrines from Islamic and Jewish theology, as he understood them, and to accommodate criticisms from the Christian lay and learned audiences that he addressed. Harvey J. Hames has shown that Llull's absolute principles would be especially congenial to practitioners of the cabala, who were widespread in contemporary Judaism–especially among Aragonese Jews–because they recognized a similar set of fundamental divine attributes or *Sefirot*. Llull's study of Islamic doctrines evidently inspired one of the more unusual elements of his Great Art, the identification of the three metaphysical *correlativa innata* (innate correlative principles) of agent, patient, and action for every entity. He names these principles with a neologistic system of suffixes that he claims to borrow from Arabic usage, positing, for example, that the *Bonitas* in any being gives it the capacity to be *bonificativum* or *bonificans* (an agent of Goodness), *bonificabile* or *bonificatus* (a patient or recipient of Goodness), and *bonificare* (an action of Goodness). This metaphysical triad strengthened his demonstrations that every creature manifests the Trinity, the Christian doctrine that Muslims and Jews found the most difficult to accept.

The simple mechanical combination of principles and categories was insufficient by itself to generate effective arguments. Llull's method requires extensive interpretation of the terms combined, as in the *Art demostrativa*, the Catalan version of the *Ars demonstrativa*:

6. *Questió es:* si Deus pot desamar y.

Solució: | a.y. | e.y. | i.z. | e.z. | i.y. | m.y.z. |

(6. *The Question is:* whether God can hate Truth.

Solution: | a.y. | e.y. | i.z. | e.z. | i.y. | m.y.z. |)

The values of the letters are expounded in the first chapters of the *Art demostrativa:* a. = God; b. = Memory remembering; c. = Intellect understanding; d. = Will loving; e. = b., c., and d. acting together; f. = Memory remembering; g. = Intellect understanding; h. = Will hating; i. = f., g., and h. acting together; m. = Will loving or hating; t. = the figure T (combinations of absolute principles, relative principles, and subjects); y. =

Truth; and z. = Falsehood. The letters function as shorthand for the categories, but replacing each letter with its corresponding term does not by itself elucidate the argument, which relies on various tacit assumptions. Llull's "solution" is:

Per la primera cambra que f. menbrà descórrec g. ab t. en les altres cambres, e per asò entès que en la segona cambra es y. amable, e en la tersa es z. airable, e en la quarta e quinta se e. i. airables e contra a. en el la .vj.ª cambra es y. meyns amada que en la segona, e z. es meyns airada que en la tersa. On, con asò sia enaxí, *ergo* si a. desamava o podia desamar y., concordarsia ab z. per totes les cambres, e i. e. en la tersa e en la quarta cambra ab a. aurien concordansa, e asò es inpossíbol: per la qual inpossibilitat c. entén que a. per totes ses cambres à y., que en ses cambres es pus amable que per b. c. d. en e. amable, ni que en f. g. h. la z. desamable per i.

(From the first cell that Memory remembers, the Intellect discourses through the other cells with the Figure T and from this understands that: Truth is desirable in the second cell; Falsehood undesirable in the third cell; in the fourth and fifth cells Memory remembering, Intellect understanding, and Will loving [Falsehood] and Memory remembering, Intellect understanding, and Will hating [Truth] are undesirable and contrary to God; in the sixth cell Truth is less loved than in the second cell and Falsehood is more loved than in the third. Now, since this is so, *therefore*, if God did not love or could not love Truth, He would agree with Falsehood in all the cells, and Memory remembering, Intellect understanding, and Will loving and Memory remembering, Intellect understanding, and Will hating would agree with God in the third and fourth cells, which is impossible. From this impossibility the Intellect understands that in all the cells God has Truth, which in these cells is more lovable for the Memory, Intellect, and Will to love in remembering, understanding, and loving than Falsehood is hateful for the Memory, Intellect, and Will through Memory remembering, Intellect understanding, and Will hating.)

In short, Truth is the best object for the mind to grasp, because Truth "agrees" most with God. For God to hate Truth would be contrary to this agreement, which is impossible.

In later works Llull often replaces the symbolic letters with the terms that they signify, which creates a more readable discourse but does not necessarily articulate more fully the assumptions underlying the manifold relationships of agreement or contrariety that he constantly invokes. Although nearly all of those relationships were commonplaces of his contemporaries' worldview, his letter symbolism and idiosyncratic terminology repelled many who encountered the Great Art. Even those who sympathized with Llull's objec-

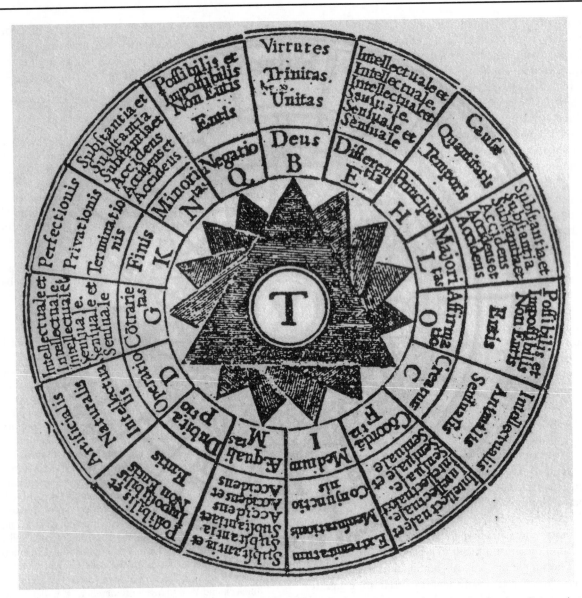

Llull's chart of principles and meanings; from a sixteenth-century edition of the Ars generalis ultima *(from* Catalan Review: International Journal of Catalan Culture, *4 [July–December 1990]; Thomas Cooper Library, University of South Carolina)*

tives could find his arguments unattractively anti-quated, and some later Humanists ridiculed the language of his system as the superlative example of barbarous Scholastic discourse. The Great Art is based on a neoplatonic metaphysics in which the beings of the world all derive their existence from the One Supreme Being, and Llull's method consists almost entirely in tracing relationships of likeness, resemblance, agreement, or concord as evidence of that derivation. His arguments owe little to the Aristotelian metaphysics of causality expounded by his contemporaries in the schools, which would explain in large measure why so few of them embraced his work.

Apart from the various redactions of the Great Art itself, Llull's Latin oeuvre falls into the categories of theology and philosophy–divisions of inquiry that he does not really distinguish, since his Great Art is universal and comprehends all knowledge. His Latin theological writings cover the entire range of Christian belief; nearly all of them deal in some measure with the nature of God and the Trinity. The most complete expressions of Llull's arguments for Catholic doctrine appear in the major polemical works that depict debates between Christian and non-Christian disputants: the *Liber de gentili et tribus sapientibus* (1274–1276? Translated as "The Book of the Gentile and the Three Wise Men," 1985), the *Liber Tartari et Christiani* (1288, Book of the Tartar and Christian), the *Disputatio fidelis et infidelis* (1288–1289, Disputation of the Believer and Unbeliever), the *Liber de quinque sapientibus,* and the *Disputatio Raymundi christiani et Hamar saraceni.* These works, above all, have fostered modern views of Llull as an advocate of reasoned debate, rather than force, for converting Muslims and Jews. The point of departure for the debates recounted in them are invariably the principles and methods of his own Great Art, which provide a "universal" and therefore "natural" basis for discussion between representatives of any religions.

Many of Llull's writings expound the faith for the edification of Christian audiences. He produced various practical guides for meditation and devotion, some of which rigorously apply the principles and methods of his Great Art: the *Ars amativa boni* (1290, Art of Loving the Good), the *Contemplatio Raymundi* (1297, Contemplation of Ramon), the *Arbor philosophiae amoris* (1298, Tree of Philosophy of Love; translated as *The Tree of Love,* 1926), the *Ars confessionis* (1312, Art of Confession), and the *Liber de compendiosa contemplatione* (1313, Book of Compendious Contemplation). Llull's writings on devotion and contemplation were among his most appealing for later readers. The *Arbor philosophiae desideratae* (1294, Tree of Desired Philosophy) offers a popularized application of the Great Art, presented as spiritual advice for a son from a pious father troubled by the lack of true devotion among Christians. Nineteen Latin and two Catalan manuscripts of the work testify to its success as a manual of spiritual instruction.

Throughout his career Llull addressed other topics and occasions as opportunities to present theological instruction or spiritual guidance. His works on particular issues include the *Liber de sancto spiritu* (1274–1283? Book on the Holy Spirit), the *Liber de XIV articulis Sacrosanctae Romanae Ecclesiae* (1283–1285, Book on the Fourteen Articles of the Holy Roman Church), the *Liber de angelis* (1274–1283? Book on Angels), the *Liber contra Antichristum* (1290–1292, Book against the Antichrist), the *Liber de laudibus beatae Virginis Mariae* (1290–1292, Book of Praises of the Blessed Virgin Mary), *De adventu Messiae* (1290–1292, On the Coming of the Messiah), the *Consolatio Venetorum et totius gentis desolatae* (1298, Consolation for the Venetians and All Distressed People), and the *Liber natalis pueri Christi Jesu* (1311, Book on the Birth of Christ Jesus). The doctrines expounded in these and Llull's many other theological or spiritual writings are almost wholly orthodox. As one would expect from a pious layman, he often invites academic or ecclesiastical authorities to correct any errors in his work. The accusations of heresy that later arose against Lullian teachings focused on their claims to "prove" or

"demonstrate" tenets of the faith that orthodox dogma held to be matters of belief alone. The larger spiritual goals of Llull's work–the edification of believers and conversion of unbelievers–were completely uncontroversial.

Llull's Latin writings on philosophy and the arts and sciences offer the most ambitious effort of his era to realize the ideal that his contemporary St. Bonaventure called "retracing the arts to theology." All of Llull's most comprehensive works, from his early *Libre de contemplació en Déu* and the redactions of his Great Art to the *Arbor scientiae,* strive to redirect every branch of philosophy and the arts and sciences to that higher end. Two series of works attempt to apply his system to particular branches of learning. He applied the first version of the Great Art to the major divisions of academic inquiry in the *Liber principiorum philosophiae* (1274–1278? Book of the Principles of Philosophy), the *Liber principiorum theologiae* (1274–1278? Book of the Principles of Theology), the *Liber principiorum iuris* (1274–1278? Book of the Principles of Law), and the *Liber principiorum medicinae* (1274–1278? Book of the Principles of Medicine; translated as "The Principles of Medicine," 1984). His visits to Paris evidently inspired another cycle of writings on the arts and sciences: the *Tractatus novus de astronomia* (1297, New Treatise on Astronomy), the *Rhetorica nova* (1301; translated as *The New Rhetoric of Ramon Llull,* 1993), the *Liber de natura* (1301, Book of Nature), the *Logica nova* (1303, New Logic), the *Liber de regionibus sanitatis et infirmitatis* (1303, Book on the Sources of Health and Illness), the *Liber de lumine* (1303, Book on Optics), the *Ars iuris naturalis* (1304, Art of Natural Law), the *Metaphysica nova et compendiosa* (1310, New Compendious Metaphysics), and the *Liber novus physicorum et compendiosus* (1310, New Compendious Book on Physics). The "new" in several of these titles explicitly announces Llull's desire to reform these disciplines by providing a Christian understanding of the classical and Arabic learning that his peers in the schools wrongly studied for its own sake. In metaphysics, his *Liber correlativorum innatorum* (1310, Book on Innate Correlatives) offers the most detailed explanation of this original doctrine from his Great Art, an innovation that he considered fundamental to demonstrating how the ontological constitution of all beings derived from the Christian Trinity.

Psychology and epistemology–the "study of the soul" in classical and medieval terms–were branches of philosophy that especially concerned Llull. The program of right contemplation and argumentation in his Great Art depends on a model of human nature that he adapted freely from commonplace Western and Islamic doctrines. Early in his career he settled on a scheme of three general levels–

the sensitive, imaginative, and rational—that comprised the complete human being. He always divides the rational level into three faculties of Memory, Will, and Intellect, following a scheme accepted in Christian culture since St. Augustine. This basic model provides the foundation for his major works on psychology and epistemology: the *Liber de anima rationali* (1296, Book on the Rational Soul), the *Liber de homine* (1300, Book on the Human Being), the *Liber de intellectu* (1304, Book on the Intellect), the *Disputatio fidei et intellectus* (1303, Disputation of Faith and Intellect), *Liber de voluntate* (1304, Book on Will), the *Liber de memoria* (1304, Book on Memory), the *Liber de ascensu et descensu intellectus,* the *Liber de convenientia fidei et intellectus in obiecto* (1309, Book on the Common Object of Faith and Intellect), and the *Liber de modo naturali intelligendi* (1310, Book on the Natural Way of Understanding). These works also discuss the more basic "elemental" (chemical and mineral) and "vegetable" (plant) levels of body, as well as the "internal senses" of the mind, distinctions commonly recognized by other medieval authorities. Nonetheless, his model diverges significantly from the adaptations of Aristotelian doctrine taught in the schools, especially in its recognition of the imagination as a separate level of human nature. Treating imagination as a distinct faculty allowed Llull to construct a neatly parallel scheme for explaining how human cognition, when rightly exercised, necessarily leads to spiritual truth, rising from perceptions of the senses through their impressions in the imagination to their apprehension by the mind. His commitment to this theosophic model of human psychology eventually produced one of his most original proposals, the classification of *affatus* (speech) as a sixth perceptual sense. He announced this proposal in his *Liber de affatu* (Book on Speech) of 1294, arguing that speech deserved this status because only words could grasp God. Llull claimed that his discovery of the sixth sense was completely new, though he perhaps adapted the doctrine from contemporary literature on vices and virtues in speaking, which equated the tongue with the organs of sensation as primary instruments of moral conduct.

The fundamentally ethical and spiritual orientation of Llull's psychological model also determines his proposal that all creatures (especially humans) naturally bear a "first intention" of seeking their Creator and a "second intention" of using other creatures for that first intention. Expounded fully in his *Liber de prima et secunda intentione* (1283? Book on the First and Second Intention), this doctrine helps justify Llull's lifelong insistence that his Great Art offers a "natural" and "universal" system of knowledge. Llull's model of human psychology clearly differed from academic teachings yet drew on doctrines familiar enough to his learned Christian or Muslim contemporaries that they could address them—if only to refute them, as one Parisian scholar later did regarding Llull's proposal of speech as a sixth sense.

The methods of argumentation of Llull's Great Art were much less acceptable to his peers in the schools, who regarded Aristotelian logic as the indispensable tool of all inquiry. In striving to create a universally acceptable system of demonstration, Llull relied on ancient principles of neoplatonic philosophy that had contributed little to the Aristotelian dialectical methods cultivated by the Schoolmen. Their inattention to—if not disdain for—his system impelled Llull to argue vigorously for the superiority of his Great Art to Scholastic logic. His *Logica nova* offers a completely "Lullian" interpretation of all the major components of the Schoolmen's methods, from the predicables and categories to syllogistics and sophistics. He subsequently addressed most of these areas in separate treatises: the *Liber de demonstratione per aequiparantiam* (1305, Book on Demonstration through Equipollences), the *Liber de novis fallaciis* (1308, Book of New Fallacies), the *De conversione subiecti et praedicati et medii* (1310, On the Convertibility of Subject, Predicate, and Middle Terms), the *Liber contradictionis* (1311, Book of Contradiction), the *Liber de syllogismis contradictoriis* (1311, Book on Contradictory Syllogisms), the *Liber de novo modo demonstrandi* (1312, Book on the New Method of Demonstration), and the *Liber de quinque praedicabilibus et decem praedicamentis* (1313, Book on the Five Categories and Ten Predicables). In all of these works Llull strives to reinterpret Aristotelian rules of predication and valid inference as relationships of resemblance or congruence like those used in his own Great Art. He freely offers his innovations as corrections to Scholastic dialectic, including a new mode of demonstration through "equipollences" and a new master fallacy of "contradiction." The latter, he argues, embraces all the recognized Aristotelian fallacies, but in fact it depends on interpreting as "equivocal" any predications that contradict Christian belief. Despite their idiosyncracy, Llull's logical innovations contributed significantly to later esteem for his Great Art as an alternative to Scholastic methods. His Renaissance enthusiasts especially appreciated this potential value and labored to revise his system into a nontheosophical, general art of inquiry.

In 1308–1309 Llull traveled to Pisa, Genoa, Marseilles, Montpellier, Poitiers, and Avignon, endeavoring to obtain royal and papal backing for his plans. During this period he wrote the *Liber de esse Dei* (1309,

Book of the Being of God), the *Liber de probatione quod in Deo sunt tres personae* (1309, Book Proving That Three Persons Exist in God), and the *Proverbis d'ensenyament* (1309, Proverbs of Instruction), the last of his three vernacular compilations of proverbs–the earlier ones were the massive *Proverbis de Ramon* (1296, Proverbs of Ramon) and the *Mil proverbis* (1302, Thousand Proverbs). The *Mil proverbis* and the *Proverbis d'ensenyament* are briefer compendia collections, well suited to the popularizing value that Llull clearly appreciated in this genre. The verse form of the *Proverbis d'ensenyament* further suggests a work composed for children; it was perhaps prepared for presentation in one of Llull's appeals to the Aragonese court at this time. Much of the content of these works appears to be original, borrowing little from the many popular medieval vernacular and Latin collections of proverbs. The *Proverbis de Ramon* especially offers many maxims that are simple, concise statements of Lullian doctrine as expounded in his Great Art and other learned writings.

While the results of Llull's new petitions before King Philip and the Papacy are unclear, the *Vita* claims that he received enthusiastic and generous pledges of support from devout private citizens of the Italian towns. Perhaps encouraged by this success, Llull undertook his final visit to Paris late in 1309. While there, he produced at least thirty writings that offer some of his most detailed and direct responses to contemporary Scholastic teachings, including the *Liber reprobationis aliquorum errorum Averrois* (1310, Book Refuting Some Errors of Averroës), the *Liber in quo declaratur quod fides sancta catholica est magis probabilis quam improbabilis* (1310, Book Showing that the Holy Catholic Faith Is More Probable Than Improbable), the *De fallaciis quas non credunt facere aliqui, qui credunt esse philosophantes, contra purissimum actum Dei verissimum et perfectissimum* (1310, On the Fallacies That Some, Who When They Think They Are Philosophizing, Do Not Believe That They Commit against the Most True, Pure, and Perfect Act of God), the *Disputatio Raimundi et Averroistae* (1310, Disputation of Ramon and the Averroist), and the *Sermones contra errores Averrois* (1311, Sermons against the Errors of Averroës). These works provide Llull's most explicit references to particular authorities and their teachings, such as the eternity of the world. For this reason they are especially helpful in understanding his relationship to received tradition and contemporary learning.

The *Vita* reports that the university community responded much more positively to public presentations of his work on this visit than it had previously, describing the "multitude" of students and masters who heard him defend the Great Art. Nonetheless, the *Vita* and his own writings express disappointment with the lack of

widespread enthusiasm for his work among the Parisian Schoolmen. In his allegorical *Liber lamentationis philosophiae* (Book of the Lament of Philosophy), dedicated to King Philip in 1311, the figure of Philosophy decries the way the Schoolmen have perverted her from her true end, the love and knowledge of God. In a letter of recommendation that he provided for Llull, the chancellor of the University of Paris, Francesco Caroccioli, uses scriptural allusions to compare Llull's writings with the poor widow's offering (Mark 12:42 and Luke 21:2) and with the humbler furnishings provided for the Tabernacle by the Israelites (Exod. 25:3–4). Both analogies were commonplaces familiar from St. Jerome's prologue to the Vulgate. The reference to the widow especially suggests a comparison between Llull and traditional images of women as simple messengers of divine wisdom sent to humble the proud. In short, Caroccioli expresses appreciation for Llull's pious zeal but regards his work as quite modest.

Other authorities evidently proffered less flattering assessments. In some works Llull complains bitterly that his contemporaries ignore him and even suggests that they scorn him as a "fool." After leaving Paris in 1311, he depicted his encounter with an adversary there in a treatise facetiously titled *Disputatio Petri clerici et Raymundi phantastici* (Disputation of Peter the Scholar and Ramon the Madman). The label *phantasticus* recalls the term *idiota* habitually used by clerics to condemn heretics or laypeople whose ideas challenged the academic and ecclesiastical monopoly on learning. It also, however, implicitly aligns Llull with St. Francis of Assisi and many previous "fools for God" or "divine jesters" who readily accepted such epithets in recognition of their humble self-sacrifice. Even when reporting his failures, the accounts of Llull's visit to academic centers in the *Vita* strive to suggest his prophetic abilities and capacity for public teaching. To what extent the pious, learned layman Llull could claim authority to preach or teach remains one of the most basic and obscure questions about his entire career. A few documents from his career do refer to him as a *magister* (master), a title applied not only to teachers but also to leaders in many professional and clerical roles. Soon after his death–if not before–this appellation became routine, and his fourteenth-century Aragonese followers eventually elevated him to the level of *doctor* in their literature.

The letter of commendation from Caroccioli was one of forty that Llull solicited from university masters and students, in addition to one from King Philip. He probably obtained these letters as credentials to support his presentation of his proposals at the General Council of Vienne of 1311. The council did implement one of the proposals, the establishment of chairs in Oriental languages at several major universities, although there is no evidence outside of Llull's own writings of his direct participation in the council or in any other princely or papal undertaking.

Early in 1312 Llull returned to Majorca, where he dictated his will and prepared for what proved to be his final round of journeys to promote his proposals. He also wrote at least thirty works on the Trinity, including the *Liber de Trinitate et Incarnatione* (1312, Book of the Trinity and Incarnation), the *Liber de Trinitate trinitissima* (1313, Book of the Most Triune Trinity), the *Liber de essentia et esse Dei* (1313, Book of the Essence and Being of God), and the *Liber de multiplicatione quae fit in essentia Dei per divinam Trinitatem* (1314, Book of the Extension of God's Essence through the Divine Trinity). All of these works apply the system of the Great Art to proving this fundamental tenet of Christian belief as an example of arguments suitable for proselytizing unbelievers and as a defense of his method against its critics. He also wrote a series of catechetical sermons: the *Sermones de Ave Maria* (1312, Sermons on "Ave Maria"), the *Sermones de decem praeceptis* (1312, Sermons on the Decalogue), the *Sermones de Pater noster* (1312, Sermons on the Lord's Prayer), and the *Liber de virtutibus et peccatis* (1313, Book of Virtues and Vices). The *Liber de virtutibus et peccatis* is one of the last major writings for which he provided a vernacular redaction.

In 1313–1314 Llull visited Messina to seek aid from King Frederick III, whose previous support for the Spiritual Franciscans evidently led him to hope that the king might finance his plans for overseas missions. While in Sicily, he composed in Latin more than thirty tractates on theological issues, all expounded through the system of his Great Art. Failing to win support from Frederick, Llull returned to Tunis late in 1314 for one last evangelizing campaign among unbelievers. The sultan of Tunis enjoyed close relations with the Aragonese Crown, and Llull arrived with letters of introduction from King James II. He contacted the king again in 1315 to ask that Friar Simon de Puigcerdà be sent to Tunis to assist him in preparing Latin translations of his works. Llull's last known writing, the *Liber de maiori fine intellectus, amoris et honoris* (Book on the Highest End of Understanding, Love, and Veneration) is dated at Tunis in December 1315. Llull died shortly after completing it, either in the North African city or while returning to Majorca, where he is buried in the Church of St. Francis.

Llull's will arranged for the distribution of his writings among his small communities of devotees in Paris, Majorca, and northern Italy. In the Crown of Aragon his followers grew plentiful enough to attract the investigation of the Inquisition in the fourteenth century. Despite this challenge, Lullism continued to thrive; by 1433 a Lullist school existed in Barcelona, remaining in operation until the end of the century. The rejection of Scholastic methods and doctrines during the Renaissance led to a surge of interest in the Great Art among pedagogical reformers. Llull's sixteenth-century enthusiasts, who included Cornelius Agrippa and Giordano Bruno, freely revised the Great Art and replaced works they found unsatisfactory with new ones that circulated under Llull's name. More than one hundred printed editions of his writings appeared after 1500, ensuring the continued popularity of his Great Art into the early modern era. Bishop John Prideaux's *Heptades logicae* (1639, Seven Logics) listed the Great Art as one of the seven great systems of logic, and the late-seventeenth- and early-eighteenth-century mathematician and rationalist philosopher Gottfried Wilhelm Leibniz acknowledged it as an example for his own efforts to create a *characteristica universalis* (universal symbolic language).

Llull scholars are still trying to determine when, where, or how he might have drawn on new sources of theological and philosophical learning. His extensive travels during his long career would have presented many opportunities to expand his knowledge in all branches of learning; at major academic centers such as Paris and Montpellier he would have found ample libraries and communities of scholars from which to draw fresh ideas or to extend his knowledge. His writings frequently indicate his encounters with new learning, though often only to reject it. Any new concepts or doctrines that might have appealed to him were subsumed into the idiosyncratic structure and terminology of his own system. It is clear that innovations such as the *correlativa innata,* which uses terminology based on Arabic morphology, resulted from new insights or experiences. In some cases Llull developed completely new theories in order to "reform" conventional doctrines for his purposes: in this category belong his claim to have discovered a new "master fallacy" of contradiction and his recognition of speech as a sixth sense. Despite the introduction of these novel theories, throughout his career Llull rehearsed many commonplace arguments and doctrines without revision.

Also difficult to assess is the extent of Llull's engagement with non-Christian communities, especially Muslims and Jews. His command of Arabic and knowledge of Islamic and Jewish learning have encouraged esteem for him as one of the preeminent European Orientalists of his day, on a par with Roger Bacon and Ramon Martí. He possessed a firsthand knowledge of Islamic theology and dubs himself a *christianus arabicus* (Christian familiar with Arabic learning) in some of his works. The basic principles of his Great Art closely parallel in function the divine attributes defined in Jewish cabalist doctrine. Since Llull usually prefers not to cite authorities and to recast all ideas in his own terminology, these and other undisputed indications of his familiarity with Islamic and Jewish learning continue to fuel research on non-Christian sources that could explain more, or even all, of his otherwise inexplicably idiosyncratic work. He must have learned much from personal contact with Muslim and Jewish communities in the western Mediterranean; yet, his references to their cultures are infrequent and anecdotal. His overall knowledge of their theology and philosophy does not match that of a Schoolman such as Martí, and in some areas he evidently relied on existing Christian polemical literature. In his exhaustive study of Llull's knowledge of cabala, Hames concludes that Llull was not a Christian cabalist and probably lacked detailed knowledge of any specific cabalist doctrines. Whatever the extent of Llull's direct debt to Islamic or Jewish learning, he consistently and zealously applied all that he knew to one purpose alone: converting unbelievers to Christianity through demonstration of the necessary truth of the one Faith.

Ramon Llull stands as one of the most remarkable examples of lay learning of his era. His exposition of sophisticated theological and philosophical issues in the vernacular, as well as Latin and Arabic, was unmatched in Western Europe until the end of the Middle Ages. As a vernacular writer, Llull is unquestionably the single greatest contributor to medieval Catalan literature: his prolific production equals the output of all Catalan writers before him. His native language was already well established as a literary idiom in his day, which explains in part his frequent defense of the vernacular as a suitable medium for education. He recommends it especially for teaching those without facility in Latin or of limited intellectual capacity. Thanks to his prolific production and enthusiasm for instruction in the vernacular, modern Catalan scholars seeking to defend their region's heritage against Castilian cultural hegemony within Spain have lionized Llull as a "universal genius" of world literature on a par with Dante or Geoffrey Chaucer. Less-partisan assessments would be more guarded: none of his writings are, in a strict sense, literary; they all serve the exposition of his theological and philosophical concerns. Throughout his work he decries the frivolity and dubious moral value of vernacular prose and poetry composed strictly for entertainment. Several of his own creations attempt to provide edifying alternatives to the chivalric romances and "books of marvels" popular among lay readers of his era. Much of his learned vocabulary consists of Latinisms or Latinate neologisms that did not find general usage in later medieval Catalan. Nonetheless, his use of his native language to expound virtually the entire range of theological and philosophical knowledge contributed to the development of the vernacular as a learned idiom in later medieval Europe. Although his Great Art achieved limited success in bringing Muslims or Jews to embrace the Catholic faith, his writings on devotion and contemplation have continued to satisfy the spiritual needs of Christian readers in every century since his own time.

Bibliographies:

Rudolf Brummer, *Bibliographia Lulliana: Ramon-Llull-Schrifttum 1870–1973* (Hildesheim: H. Gerstenberg, 1976);

Marcel Salleras i Carolà, "Bibliografia [lul•liana] (1974–1984)," *Randa,* 19 (1986): 153–198.

Biographies:

Miguel Batllori and Joceyln N. Hillgarth, eds., *Vida de Ramon Llull: Les fonts escrites i la iconografia coetànies* (Barcelona: Associació de Bibliòfils de Barcelona, 1982);

Anthony Bonner and Lola Badia, *Ramón Llull: Vida, pensament i obra literària* (Barcelona: Empúries, 1988).

References:

Miguel Batllori, *Ramon Llull i el lul•lisme* (Valéncia: E. Climent, 1993);

Miguel Cruz Hernández, *El pensamiento de Ramón Llull* (Madrid: Fundación Juan March, 1977);

Álvaro Galmés de Fuentes, *Ramón Llull y la tradición árabe: Amor divino y amor cortés en el "Llibre d'amic e amat"* (Barcelona: Quaderns Crema, 1999);

Sebastián Garcías Palou, *Ramon Llull y el Islam* (Palma de Mallorca: Institut d'Estudis Balears, 1981);

Harvey J. Hames, *The Art of Conversion: Christianity and Kabbalah in the Thirteenth Century,* The Medieval Mediterranean: Peoples, Economies, and Cultures, 400–1453, volume 26 (Leiden: Brill, 2000);

Joceyln N. Hillgarth, "La Biblioteca de La Real: Fuentes posibles de Llull," *Estudios Lulianos,* 7 (1963): 5–17;

Hillgarth, *Ramon Lull and Lullism in Fourteenth-Century France* (Oxford: Clarendon Press, 1971);

"Homage to Ramon Llull," special issue of *Catalan Review: International Journal of Catlan Culture,* 4 (July–December 1990);

Mark D. Johnston, "*Affatus:* Natural Science as Moral Theology," *Estudios Lulianos,* 30 (1990): 3–30, 139–159;

Johnston, *The Evangelical Rhetoric of Ramon Llull* (New York: Oxford University Press, 1995);

Johnston, *The Spiritual Logic of Ramon Llull* (Oxford: Clarendon Press, 1987);

Felipe Moreno Rodríguez, *La lucha de Ramon Llull contra el averroismo entre 1.309 y 1.311* (Madrid: Universidad Computense de Madrid, 1982);

Antonio Oliver, "El Beato Ramón Llull en sus relaciones con la escuela franciscana de los siglos XII–XIV," *Estudios Lulianos,* 9 (1965): 55–70, 145–165; 10 (1966): 49–56; 11 (1967): 89–119; 13 (1969): 51–65;

Robert D. F. Pring-Mill, "The Analogical Structure of the Lullian Art," in *Islamic Philosophy and the Classical Tradition: Essays Presented by His Friends and Pupils to Richard Walzer on His Seventieth Birthday,* edited by S. M. Stern, Albert Hourani, and Vivian Brown (Columbia: University of South Carolina Press, 1973), pp. 315–326;

Pring-Mill, *El microcosmos lul·lià* (Palma de Mallorca: Editorial Moll, 1961);

Raymond Lulle et le pays d'Oc, Cahiers de Fanjeaux, no. 22 (Toulouse: E. Privat, 1987);

Josep M. Ruiz Simon, *L'Art de Ramon Llull i la teoria escolàstica de la ciència* (Barcelona: Quaderns Crema, 1999);

Joan Tusquets i Terrats, *La filosofia del llenguatge en Ramon Llull: Marc, exposició i crítica* (Barcelona: Balmes, 1993);

Tusquets i Terrats, *Ramon Llull pedagogo de la cristiandad* (Madrid: Consejo Superior de Investigaciones Científicas, 1954);

Dominique Urvoy, *Penser l'islam: Les présupposés islamiques de l'"Art" de Lull* (Paris: Vrin, 1980);

Frances A. Yates, "The Art of Ramon Lull," *Journal of the Warburg and Courtauld Institute,* 17 (1954): 115–173.

Pero López de Ayala

(1332 – 1407)

Eric W. Naylor
University of the South

WORKS: *El Rimado de Palacio* (1367–1407)

Manuscripts: *El Rimado de Palacio* is preserved in full in two codices copied in the middle of the fifteenth century–Biblioteca National, Madrid, MS. 4055 and Real Biblioteca del Monasterio de El Escorial, h.III.19–as well as in fragments. Although neither of the complete versions represents Ayala's archetype, the Madrid manuscript is universally recognized as being nearer to the author's final redaction.

Paleographic edition: *Poesías del Canciller Pero López de Ayala,* 2 volumes, edited by Albert Frederick Kuersteiner (New York: Hispanic Society of America, 1920).

Standard editions: *Obra poética del Canciller Ayala,* edited by José López Yepes (Vitoria: Diputación Provincal, 1974); *Libro de Poemas o Rimado de Palacio,* 2 volumes, edited by Michel García (Madrid: Gredos, 1978); *Libro Rimado del Palacio,* 2 volumes, edited by Jacques Joset (Madrid: Alhambra, 1978); *Rimado de Palacio,* 2 volumes, edited by Germán Orduna (Pisa: Giardina Editori, 1981); *Rimado de Palacio,* edited by Orduna; (Madrid: Clásicos Castalia, 1987); *Libro Rimado de Palacio,* edited by Kenneth Adams (Madrid: Cátedra, 1993); *Rimado de Palacio,* edited by H. Salvador Martínez (New York: Peter Lang, 2000).

Libro de la caça de las aves (1386)

Manuscript: British Library, London, MS. El 16.329.

Editions: *El libro de las aves de caça . . . con las glosas del Duque de Alburquerque,* edited by Pascual de Gayangos and Emilio Lafuente y Alcántara (Madrid: Sociedad de Bibliófilos, 1869); *Libros de cetrería del Príncipe y el Canciller,* edited by José Gutiérrez de la Vega (Madrid: Biblioteca Venatoria, 1879); *Libro de la caza de las aves, texto íntegro,* edited by José Fradejas Lebrero (Madrid: Editorial Castalia, 1959); *Libro de la caça de las aves: El MS 16.329 (British Library, Londres),* edited by John G. Cummins (London: Tamesis, 1986).

Moralia in Job or *Los Morales de San Gregorio* (late fourteenth century)

Manuscripts: *Moralia in Job* is conserved in Biblioteca National, Madrid, MSS. 10136, 10137, and 10138 and Real Biblioteca del Monasterio de El Escorial, MS. b.II.7.

Editions: *Las flores de los "Morales de Job,"* edited by Francesco Branciforti (Messina: Firenze, 1963); *Libro de Poemas o Rimado de Palacio,* volume 2, edited by Michel García (Madrid: Gredos, 1978), pp. 267–376; *Libro Rimado de Palacio,* edited by Kenneth Adams (Madrid: Cátedra, 1993), pp. 497–616.

El Libro del santo omne Job (late fourteenth century)

Manuscript: *El Libro del santo omne Job* is preserved in Biblioteca National, Madrid, MS. 10138, folios 171v–185r.

Edition: *El libro de Job,* edited by Francesco Branciforti (Messina: Firenze, 1962).

Chronicles of the Kings Pedro I, Enrique II, Juan I, Enrique III (begun circa 1380?)

Manuscripts: The chronicles are preserved in many manuscripts, among which are Real Academia de la Historia, Madrid, MSS. 9-26-1-4764 and 9-23-A-14-4765; Biblioteca Nacional, Madrid, MSS. 18 and 10219; Fundación Lázaro Galdiano, Madrid, MS. 463 (Inventario 15276); Real Biblioteca del Monasterio de El Escorial, MSS. K.II.20, X.I.5, Y.I.14, and Z.III.15; and Memorial Library of the University of Wisconsin–Madison, MS. 57. There are two versions: the shorter, called the *Abreviada,* and the longer–the one usually published–known as the *Vulgar.*

Early printing: *Crónica del Rey Don Pedro* (Seville: Printed by Meinardo Ungut & Estanislao Polonio, 1495).

Editions: Jerónimo Zurita, *Enmiendas y advertencias a las coronicas de los reyes de Castilla don Pedro, don Enrique el segundo, don Iuan el primero, don Enrique el tercero que escribió don Pero López de Ayala. . . . compuesto por Gerónimo Zurita* (Saragossa: Herederos de

Diego Dormer, 1683); *Crónicas de los reyes de Castilla,* 2 volumes, edited by Eugenio Llaguno y Amírola (Madrid: A. de Sancha, 1779, 1780); *Crónica del rey don Pedro,* edited by Constance L. Wilkins and Heanon M. Wilkins (Madison, Wis.: Hispanic Seminary of Medieval Studies, 1985); *Crónicas,* edited by José-Luis Martin (Madrid: Planeta, 1991); *Crónica del rey don Pedro y del rey don Enrique, su hermano, hijos del rey don Alfonso onceno,* 2 volumes, edited by Germán Orduna, preliminary study by Orduna and José Luis Moure (Buenos Aires: SECRIT, 1994, 1997).

Livy, *Las décadas de Tito Livio,* translated by Ayala (1401)
   Manuscript: Real Biblioteca del Monasterio de El Escorial, MS. g.I.1.
   Edition: *Las décadas de Tito Livio,* 2 volumes, edited by Curt J. Wittlin (Barcelona: Puvil Libro, 1982).

Giovanni Boccaccio, *Cayda de príncipes,* translated by Ayala (early fifteenth century?)
   Manuscript: Hispanic Society of America, MS. B1196.
   Editions: *Cayda de príncipes,* edited by Isabella Scoma (Messina: La Grafica, 1993); *Caída de príncipes,* edited by Eric W. Naylor (Madison, Wis.: Hispanic Seminary of Medieval Studies, 1994).

Pero López de Ayala is one of the principal intellectual and political figures of the second half of the thirteenth century. Reared and educated in the Castile of the first onslaught of the plague, which coincided with the beginning of the reign of the young King Pedro I, in his later career he became one of the most trusted advisers and representatives of the Trastámara monarchs. He also translated moral works into Castilian and wrote poetry, and at an undetermined point in his career he began to compose *crónicas* (chronicles) of the events that took place during his lifetime in the tradition of the chronicles patronized by Alfonso X *el Sabio* (the Learned) and Alfonso XI. As a poet he was the last author of note who wrote in the already antiquated *cuaderna vía* (four-rhyme quatrain). This type of verse was characteristic of the moral-educational genre *mester de clerecía* (art of the educated), which was in style from the beginning of the thirteenth century through the first half of the fourteenth. But López de Ayala was also a predecessor of a literary type that characterized the fifteenth century, the noble who takes up letters as an avocation; he was the uncle of the prototype of this group, Íñigo López de Mendoza, Marqués de Santillana.

Another nephew, Fernán Pérez de Guzmán, provides a succinct sketch of López de Ayala in his *Loores de los claros varones de España* (before 1452, Praises of the Famous Men of Spain):

Lord Pero López de Ayala, Chancellor of Castile, was a nobleman of distinguished lineage, since on his father's side he was from the house of Haro, from whom the Ayalas descend, and on his mother's side he is from the Cevallos, a great noble house. Some of the Ayala lineage claim descent from a prince of Aragon to whom the king of Castile gave the lordship of Ayala. That is what I found recorded by Lord Fernán Pérez de Ayala, father of the said Lord Pero López de Ayala, although I have never read it in any chronicle nor have I other confirmation of this claim.

The aforementioned Lord Pero López de Ayala was tall, thin, and of distinguished bearing, a man of great perception and authority, who could give good advice, both in peace and in war. He enjoyed high standing with the kings in whose time he lived, for, as a youth, he was very much liked by King Pedro and, afterwards, he was on the Royal Council of King Enrique II and greatly esteemed by him. Juan I and his son Enrique III had great trust and confidence in him. He was involved in many important events, in both war and peace.

He was taken prisoner twice, once at the battle of Nájera and again at Aljubarrota. He was of a sweet disposition, pleasant to be around, had a great moral sense and was God-fearing. He was a devotee of scholarship and dedicated himself to books and chronicles, so much so that although he was a distinguished lord and of great insight in dealing with matters of politics, he was extremely studious by nature. For that reason he spent a great deal of his time reading and studying, not law but rather moral philosophy and history. Thanks to him some works which were previously unknown in Castile are now known, such as the *Titus Livius,* the most noteworthy of the Roman histories, Giovanni Boccaccio's *The Fall of Princes,* the *Morals* of Saint Gregory, the *De summo bono* of Isidore of Seville, *The Consolation of Philosophy* of Boethius, and *The History of Troy.* He wrote a history of Castile beginning with King Pedro and ending with Enrique III. He composed a good book on hunting, for he was a great hunter, and another written in verse about affairs at court.

He had more to do with women than was fitting for such a wise lord as he.

He died at Calahorra, in La Rioja, at the age of seventy-five, in the year 1407.

The Ayala family had its origins in the second-tier nobility of the present-day province of Álava in the Basque country and had moved to Toledo in New Castile. The author's great-great-grandfather, the first to bear the name Pero López de Ayala, was named by the conqueror of Andalusia, Fernando III, "The Saint," to be tutor to his second son, the *Infante* Manuel. Manuel was the father of the powerful feudal magnate Juan Manuel, who was also an author and is known as the founder of Castilian fiction. This alliance involved the Ayala family in the conquest from the Moors of the Murcia region, and several family members held important positions in the newly conquered area. When Alfonso XI came of age in 1312, the Ayalas broke with the Manuel family and joined the party of nobles around the king. They continued to hold high offices in Murcia. Pero López II de Ayala, the author's grandfather, was named *adelantado* (governor) of the area in 1328; in early 1331 the governorship passed back to Juan Manuel. Pero López II married Sancha Fernández Barroso, who came from an influential Toledan family. Her brother, Cardinal Pero Gómez Barroso, seems to have been influential in the education of Pero López de Ayala's father, Fernán Pérez de Ayala. Fernán Pérez inherited the lordship of Salcedo and Ayala after the murder of his older brother in 1332; the brother had gone to Álava to claim the legacy after a distant relative died without legitimate issue, and he was killed by the relative's illegitimate son. Pedro López II had a second family in Murcia with Lady Inés de Azagra; they and their illegitimate sons, Pedro López de Ayala y Azagra and Juan Sánchez de Ayala y Azagra, founded the Murcian branch of the house of Ayala.

Fernán Pérez de Ayala married Lady María de Ceballos in 1332; their son, Pero López III de Ayala, was born that same year at the family seat in Quejana in the part of Álava known as Ayala. Pero López was probably educated in schools for nobles at the court of Alfonso XI and by tutors hired by his father. Alfonso XI died of the plague at the siege of Gibraltar in March 1350 and was succeeded by his son Pedro I, known as "Pedro the Cruel." In 1353 Pero López was serving as a *doncel* (page) for Pedro. In 1359 he captained a ship in a naval expedition against Barcelona during the "War of the Two Pedros" between Castile and Aragon. In 1360 he was rewarded with the post of *alguacil mayor* (chief constable) of Toledo for supporting Pedro in the king's struggle against various Castilian magnates. That same year he personally escorted Lord Vasco, the archbishop of Toledo, out of the city when Pedro ordered Vasco's expulsion from the cathedral and exile to Portugal.

In 1366, according to López de Ayala's account in his *crónica,* he and his father were with Pedro in Burgos. They accompanied the king when he fled south toward Toledo after his illegitimate brother, Count Enrique de Trastámara, and Enrique's French allies entered Castile to depose him. Soon after this flight many nobles deserted Pedro; López de Ayala and his father may have been part of this group or may have changed parties slightly later when Pero López's uncle, Garcí Álvarez, master of the powerful military Order of Santiago, surrendered Toledo to Enrique II, who had recently been crowned in Burgos. The next time López de Ayala

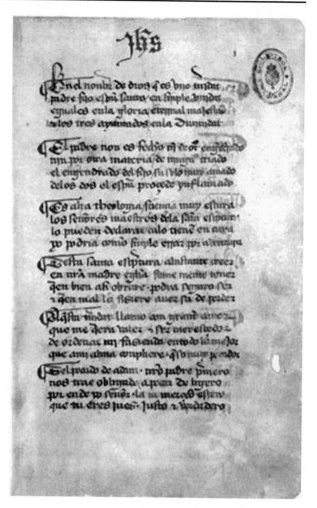

Page from one of two mid-fifteenth-century manuscripts of Pero López de Ayala's El Rimado de Palacio *(Biblioteca Nacional, Madrid, MS. 4055)*

appears in his own *crónica* is at the battle of Nájera in 1367, when he was on the side of Enrique and the bearer of the ensign of the order of knighthood known as La Banda (The Ribbon). At this battle, which was won by Pedro and his English allies, López de Ayala was captured by the English and held for a high ransom; had he been captured by Pedro, he would probably have been killed. Enrique II murdered Pedro in 1369 at Montiel Castle.

Fernán Pérez de Ayala's wife died in 1372. He founded a *mayorazgo* (entailed estate) in 1373. Concurrently he rewrote and published the traditional *fuero* (customary law code) for the district of Ayala, making many alterations to enhance the role of the feudal lord. He also compiled a genealogy of his house. In 1375 he took vows at the Dominican convent in Vitoria. In 1378 he founded a convent of Dominican nuns in the fam-

Endpaper and title page for a 1495 printing of one of López de Ayala's chronicles of the kings of Castile
(Colección Borbón-Lorenzana, Biblioteca de Castilla-La Mancha)

ily's hereditary *casa fuerte* (fortified house) at Quejana to serve as the family pantheon.

After the battle of La Rochelle in 1372, which ensured the control of the English Channel by the Castilian fleet and secured the commercial route to Flanders for the Spanish wool trade, Pero López de Ayala became a specialist in Franco-Castilian relations. He was named chief lord mayor and lord lieutenant of Vitoria, the principal city of Ávila, in 1374 and chief lord mayor of Toledo in 1375. He dealt extensively both with the French court and the Avignon Papacy, which in 1378 became entangled in the Great Schism. The affair was one of López de Ayala's chief occupations. He made seven trips to France between 1378 and 1396, developing close relations with the French monarch, Charles V, and his court.

Enrique II died in 1379 and was succeeded by Juan I. One gathers from López de Ayala's writings that he encouraged the young king to avoid some of the errors made by Alfonso XI and Pedro, such as executing those opposed to royal policies. He was in France in 1382 to announce the arrangement of the marriage, to

be celebrated the following year, of the newly widowed Juan to the heiress to the Portuguese throne, the *Infanta* Beatriz, through a treaty that specified that the king of Castile could never also become the Portuguese monarch. He participated in the battle of Roosebeke on 27 November 1382 as one of the eleven knights entrusted to be the personal bodyguards of the king of France. For this service the king named López de Ayala his chamberlain, a post that guaranteed him a stipendiary appointment at the French court. During this period López de Ayala seems to have been working on the poems that he later recopied as the first 728 strophes of the general anthology of his verses known as *El Rimado de Palacio* (1367–1407, The Poem about the Palace).

The Portuguese king, Ferdinand I, died in October 1383; Juan I claimed the crown in the name of his wife and invaded the country. After a series of engagements, the Castilians and Portuguese met at Aljubarrota on 14 August 1385. Before the battle began, two of the king's principal counselors presented Juan's position to the Portuguese; one of them was López de Ayala. The Castilians were defeated, and López de Ayala was taken

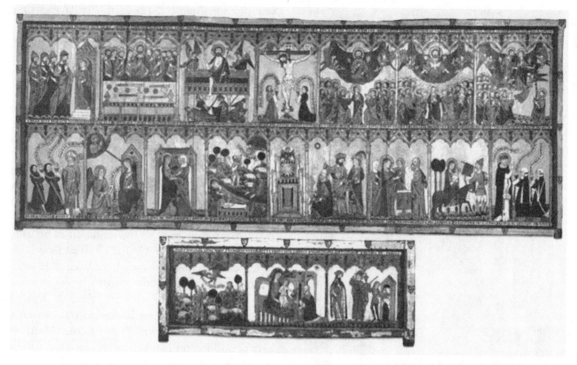

Retable and Frontal of the Virgen del Cabello, *commissioned by López de Ayala for the monastic complex he erected at Quejana in the present-day province of Álava. It is now at the Art Institute of Chicago (from <http://www.cancillerayala.net/img/01_retablo_capilla_funerari.jpg>).*

prisoner. He was held first in Leiria and then in Obidos Castle, awaiting the payment of the huge ransom demanded by his captors. In 1386, during his imprisonment, he finished his *Libro de la caça de las aves* (Manual of Bird Hunting; it is based in part on the Portuguese Pedro Menino's *Libro de Falcoaria* (Book on Falconry, which was apparently written in the early 1380s). He also wrote various short-meter poems, some praising the Virgin, others lamenting his captivity. The ransom was finally raised with the help of a contribution from Charles VI of France, and López de Ayala was released sometime between 1387 and 1389.

Juan died in a fall from his horse in 1390 and was succeeded by his eleven-year-old son, Enrique III. López de Ayala played an important role in the struggle for power among the various factions of the highest nobility and served as a member of Enrique's regency council. He was present at the unsuccessful Embassy of the Three Dukes in the spring and summer of 1395, when the kings of Castile, France, and England tried to force the resignation of the Avignon Pope Benedict XIII (Pedro de Luna). In 1396, according to his chronicle, López de Ayala was in Paris as Enrique's representative at the marriage of the daughter of the French king, Charles VI, to Richard II of England. On his return journey he passed through Avignon to attempt to pressure Benedict to renounce the papal throne. The

culmination of López de Ayala's political career came in 1496 or 1497, when he was named *canciller mayor de Castilla* (lord high chancellor of Castile). During this period he added to the family estate, which he had inherited on his father's death in 1385, more feudal holdings at Salvatierra in Álava. He erected at the convent at Quejana a large tower-chapel in honor of the *Virgen del Cabello* (Virgin of the Hair), a reliquary willed to Sancha Fernández, López de Ayala's grandmother, by her brother, Cardinal Gómez Barroso. It contains not only a bit of hair purportedly from the Virgin but also thirty-three other relics. It is still kept by the nuns at Quejana who, singing in procession the hymn *Ave Maris Stella* (Hail, Thou Star of Ocean), daily transport it back and forth from their choir to an oratory near their cells. López de Ayala also placed two pieces of art in the monastic complex. One is the set of tombs for himself; his wife, Leonor de Guzmán; and his parents. They were probably sculpted in Toledo by the same workshop that executed the tombs of the New Kings and of Cardinal Pedro Tenorio for the cathedral. The other is the internationally known Retable and Frontal of the *Virgen del Cabello*. Now at the Art Institute of Chicago, the Retable has, besides the usual depictions of the life of Mary and of the Crucifixion and Resurrection of Christ, a small area in the center intended to serve as a backdrop for the reliquary with depictions of

Tomb of López de Ayala and his wife at Quejana (from <http://www.cancillerayala.net/img/02_sepulcro.jpg>)

López de Ayala; his son, Fernán; their wives; and two grandchildren.

In 1401 López de Ayala completed his Spanish translation of the Roman historian Livy's *Ad urbe condita* (From the Foundation of the City), or *Decades;* it was derived from Pierre Bersuire's French translation, completed in 1359. Livy shows the decadent state into which Rome has fallen in his own period, and López de Ayala had a similar opinion of his own crisis-filled time. López de Ayala was also no doubt attracted to the work by Livy's concern for literary style.

Certain groups of the nobility, as well as various members of the royal family, had become devotees of a newly founded religious sect, the Geronimites. López de Ayala supported this movement and founded San Miguel del Monte in a high, isolated, circular valley slightly south of Miranda de Ebro, to which he attached quarters for his personal use. There, around 1403, he began to assemble his literary production, particularly his poetic work, into the form in which it is known today.

In a will made shortly before his death on Christmas Day 1406, Enrique III ordered that López de Ayala should continue as lord high chancellor to his

year-old son, Juan II. López de Ayala was unable to perform this last duty, as he died early in 1407.

Of the translations listed as part of López de Ayala's oeuvre by early commentators, three are doubtful. The *Historia destruccionis Trojae* (History of the Destruction of Troy) has not survived and may be spurious, although it is easy to imagine that this subject interested him because it deals with a society in crisis. Neither is it certain that the surviving contemporary translation of Boethius's *De Consolatione Philosophiae* (circa 524, The Consolation of Philosophy) is by López de Ayala, but, again, it is easy to see why someone as passionately interested in the Book of Job as López de Ayala was would also find this work appealing. At least two manuscripts exist of the rendition of St. Isidore of Seville's *De summo bono* (On the Greatest Good) ascribed to López de Ayala, but they have been little studied by philologists or literary historians.

It is also easy to see why López de Ayala would be attracted to Giovanni Boccaccio's *De casibus virorum illustrium* (On the Downfall of Famous Men), written between 1355 and 1360, in which the most unfortunate of men and women, beginning with Adam and ending with contemporary figures, appear to the author in a dream and relate their disastrous lives. The majority of these rich and famous people had behaved badly and had received their just deserts. López de Ayala thought that the same was true of King Pedro the Cruel, whom he regarded as having brought about his own spectacular downfall through sinful behavior.

López de Ayala was fascinated by Job, whose image is one of the figures that decorates the lower part of his tomb. The story of a man deprived of his health and property for no known cause seemed to López de Ayala to parallel events in his own time, such as the plague and the reign of Pedro. The story of Job also stands in counterpoint to the theme of those who brought about their own downfall by their excesses, as in Boccaccio's *De Casibus virorum illustrium*. Four of López de Ayala's works are based on the Book of Job. *El Libro del santo omne Job* (late fourteenth century, The Book of the Holy Man Job) is a translation of the version in the Latin Bible. There is a possibility that it is neither by López de Ayala nor from his scriptorium, but it is bound with a translation of the *Moralia in Job* of Pope Gregory the Great that is definitely Ayala's work. The medieval manuscript of *Moralia in Job* copies the texts, notes, glosses, underlinings, and other markings of López de Ayala's now lost original manuscript. *Las flores de los Morales de Job* (late fourteenth century, The Crème of the *Moralia in Job*) is an alphabetized selection of favorite glosses of the *Moralia*. Finally, a verse translation of the Book of Job and selections from the *Moralia*, probably written around 1400, appears as the final element in his collected poems.

The collection has been named in the modern period the *El Rimado de Palacio* because the best-known portions condemn the volatile system of court favorites and criticize the venality of officials and others connected with public life. The poems are written in *cuaderna vía* and in a short meter related to the Arabic *zéjel*, both of which were popular when López de Ayala was a young man. In no way an experimental poet, he criticized younger poets of the Troubadour revival, such as those whose works were later collected in the *Cancionero de Baena* (1445, Songbook of [Juan Alfonso] de Baena), as frivolous, while they considered him a respectable elder poet.

The anthology consists of various vaguely independent sections. It begins (stanzas 1 through 189) with a confession in which López de Ayala formulaically enumerates his sins in terms of the Ten Commandments, the seven deadly sins, the seven corporal works of mercy, the five senses, and the seven spiritual works of mercy. It is followed (stanzas 190 through 233) by comments on and proposed solutions for the disorders in the contemporary church, especially the Great Schism. Stanzas 234 through 371 address the many ills of civil government and society, including the misdeeds of merchants and lawyers. There follows a treatise on the virtues and vices that ends with a long prayer (stanzas 372 through 422).

Stanzas 423 through 591 comprise the best-known section, "Los fechos del Palacio" (The Affairs of the Palace). Written in the first person, it is a tale of the woes of a man who returns to the court to complete some business after a prolonged absence. He finds everything changed and himself unknown. After spending a great deal of money, he accomplishes little. This part concludes with some moral verse that includes a retelling of the legend of St. Nicholas.

Stanzas 592 through 729, titled "Consejo para governamiento de la república" (Advice for Running Government), are derived from the *De Regimine Principum* (The Principles of Running a Government) of Egidio da Colonna (Egidius Romanus). The next section (stanzas 730 through 921) is a collection of personal poems and lyrics written in long and short verse. Most are of a religious nature, often responding to personal disquietude, and some are directed to the Virgin Mary. One of the best-known invokes the *Virgen del Cabello,* the reliquary in the family chapel at Quejana. This section includes two poems (stanzas 832 through 857) in which he makes suggestions about how to resolve the Great Schism. The last and longest part of the collection (stanzas 922 through 2,170) is the *cuaderna vía* verse adaptation of the Book of Job commingled

with verse passages based on Gregory the Great's *Moralia in Job.*

Pero López de Ayala's best works are his chronicles; their high quality has led him to be regarded as one of the major authors of the Castilian Middle Ages. His career coincided with the disordered reigns of the Castilian monarchs of the second half of the thirteenth century: Pedro I, Enrique II, Juan I, and Enrique III. The considerations that led him to undertake the writing of the history of his time were his strong moral convictions, a desire to analyze the causes of the ills of contemporary society, and the need to justify his family's changing sides during the civil war. His retentive memory, as well as access to official and personal documents, provided the source material for an excellent recounting of the political history of his time. His high position and personal wealth probably also allowed him to employ helpers who could fill in details such as the specific dates that are found in his detailed narratives. These historical-literary works are outstanding because of their conscious historiography, the careful organization of the material, the presentation of events to make a point, the excellent Spanish style, and the impartiality of the presentation. The last aspect may be seen at its best in the treatment of King Pedro, whom the Ayala family deserted after the flight from Burgos when Enrique de Trastámara's advance seemed unstoppable. Despite the author's need to defend his family's actions, nowhere in the chronicles can be found the vituperation often characteristic of those who change sides. Though objective, however, López de Ayala's account makes the necessity for the change clear by showing that Pedro was a cruel man who killed capriciously and thus precipitated his own well-deserved downfall.

Bibliography:

Juan Contreras y López de Ayala, Marqués de Lozoya, *Introducción a la bibliografía del Canciller Ayala* (Bilbao: Junta de Cultura de Vizcaya, 1950).

Biographies:

Luis Suárez Fernández, *El Canciller Pedro López de Ayala y su tiempo, 1332–1407* (Vitoria: Diputación Foral de Álava, 1962);

F. García de Andóin, *El Canciller Ayala: Su obra y su tiempo, 1332–1407* (Vitoria: Obra Cultural de la Caja de Ahorros Municipal de la Ciudad de Vitoria, 1976);

Michel García, *Obra y personalidad del Canciller Ayala* (Madrid: Alhambra, 1982).

References:

Francesco Branciforti, "Regesto delle opere di Pero López de Ayala," in *Saggi e ricerche in memoria di*

Etorre Li Gotti, volume 1 (Palermo: Mori, 1962), p. 289;

José Luis Coy, "La estructura del *Rimado de Palacio,*" in *Hispanic Studies in Honor of Alan D. Deyermond: A North American Tribute,* edited by John S. Miletich (Madison, Wis.: Hispanic Seminary of Medieval Studies, 1986), pp. 71–82;

Coy, *El Rimado de Palacio, Tradición manuscrita y texto original* (Madrid: Paraninfo, 1984);

Rafael Floranes, "Vida literaria del Canciller Mayor de Castilla, D. Pedro López de Ayala," in *Colección de Documentos inéditos para la historia de España,* volumes 19 and 20, edited by Fernández Navarrete (Madrid: Academia de la Historia, 1851, 1852; New York: Millwood, 1960), pp. 5–575, 5–49;

Ignacio González Alvarez, *El Rimado de Palacio: Una visión de la sociedad entre el testimonio y el tópico* (Vitoria: Diputación Foral de Álava, 1990);

Jacques Joset, "Pero López de Ayala dans de *Cancionero de Baena,*" *Le Moyen Age,* 82 (1971): 475–497;

Richard P. Kinkade, "On Dating the *Rimado de Palacio,*" *Kentucky Romance Quarterly,* 18 (1971): 17–36;

Kinkade, "Pero López de Ayala and the Order of St. Jerome," *Symposium,* 26 (1972): 161–180;

Franco Meregalle, *La vida política del Canciller Ayala* (Varese: Istituto Editoriale Cisalpino, 1955);

Eric W. Naylor, "Pero López de Ayala's Translation of Boccaccio's *De Casibus,*" in *Hispanic Studies in Honor of Alan D. Deyermond: A North American Tribute,* edited by Miletich (Madison, Wis.: Hispanic Seminary of Medieval Studies, 1986), pp. 205–216;

Germán Orduna, *El arte narrativo y poético del Canciller Ayala* (Madrid: Consejo Superior de Investigaciones Científicas, 1998);

Fernán Pérez de Guzmán, *Generaciones y Semblanzas,* edited by Robert Brian Tate (London: Tamesis, 1965);

Michaela J. Portilla, *Quejana, solar de los Ayala* (Vitoria: Diputación Foral de Ávila, 1988);

Peter E. Russell, *The English Intervention in Spain and Portugal in the time of Edward III and Richard II* (Oxford: Clarendon Press, 1955);

H. I. Sears, "The *Rimado de Palacio* and *De Regimine Principum* Traditions of the Middle Ages," *Hispanic Review,* 20 (1952): 1–27;

E. B. Strong, "The Rimado de Palacio: López de Ayala's Proposals for Ending the Great Schism," *Bulletin of Hispanic Studies,* 38 (1961): 64–77;

Constance L. Wilkins, *Pero López de Ayala* (Boston: Twayne, 1989).

Leonor López de Córdoba

(December 1362 or January 1363 – 1412?/1430?)

Gregory S. Hutcheson
University of Louisville

WORK: *Memorias* (circa 1400)

Manuscripts: The original manuscript, held for centuries at the Dominican Convent of San Pablo in Cordova, disappeared during Spain's anticlerical movement in the mid nineteenth century. Prior to its disappearance, the text had been transcribed at least twice. A copy dated 1733 turned up more than a century later in the private library of Teodomiro Ramírez de Arellano; it was lost when the library was siphoned off to private collections in the United States. The other copy, comprising nine folio pages, is held by the Biblioteca Colombina in Seville.

Early editions: José María Montoto, "Reflexiones sobre un documento antiguo," *Ateneo de Sevilla,* 16 (1875): 209–214; Feliciano Ramírez de Arellano, Marqués de la Fuensanta del Valle, *Colección de documentos inéditos para la historia de España,* volume 81 (Madrid: Miguel Ginesta, 1883), pp. 33–44; Teodomiro Ramírez de Arellano y Gutiérrez, *Colección de documentos inéditos ó raros y curiosos para la historia de Córdoba,* volume 1 (Cordova, 1885), pp. 150–164.

Standard edition: "Las memorias de doña Leonor López de Córdoba," edited by Reinaldo Ayerbe-Chaux, *Journal of Hispanic Philology,* 2 (1977): 11–33.

Editions in English: "To Restore Honor and Fortune: The Autobiography of Leonor López de Córdoba," translated by Amy Katz Kaminsky and Elaine Dorough Johnson, *New York Literary Forum,* 12–13 (1984): 77–88; "The Memories of Doña Leonor López de Córdoba," translated by Kathleen Lacey, in *Medieval Women's Visionary Literature,* edited by Elizabeth Alvilda Petroff (New York: Oxford University Press, 1986), pp. 329–334; "Autobiografía," translated by Kaminsky and Johnson, in *Water Lilies/Flores del agua: An Anthology of Spanish Women Writers from the Fifteenth through the Nineteenth Century,* edited by Kaminsky (Minneapolis: University of Minnesota Press, 1996), pp. 19–32.

Leonor López de Córdoba's brief *Memorias* (circa 1400, Memoirs; translated as "To Restore Honor and Fortune: The Autobiography of Leonor López de Córdoba," 1984), also known as the *Relación jurada* (Sworn Account), is generally acknowledged as the earliest autobiography in Spanish letters. It remains the earliest work of Spanish literature known to have been composed by a woman.

Born in December 1362 or January 1363 to Martín López de Córdoba and Sancha Carrillo, by birthright Leonor López de Córdoba could claim access to the highest echelons of the Castilian aristocracy. Her mother was the niece of King Alfonso XI and had been raised in the royal household; her father, of somewhat less noble stock, was rewarded by Alfonso's son Pedro I with command of the prestigious military orders of Alcántara and Calatrava. In the *Memorias* López de Córdoba relates that her mother died when she was still a baby and that she was brought up in the company of the infantas. At seven she was married to Ruy Gutiérrez de Hinestrosa, the son of Pedro's head chamberlain. Pedro was at this time embroiled in a dynastic struggle with his half brother Enrique de Trastámara, who had proclaimed himself king of Castile in 1366. After three years of civil war, Enrique's forces, in alliance with the French, dealt a decisive blow to the loyalists at Montiel. Through a ruse devised by the French general Bertrand du Guesclin, Enrique personally killed Pedro in March 1369.

In his *Crónica del rey don Enrique* (Chronicle of King Don Enrique) Pero López de Ayala recounts that Martín López de Córdoba, a loyalist to the last, retreated with Pedro's children and his own household to the fortified city of Carmona in the south of Spain, where he withstood a siege by Enrique's supporters for a year and a half. Weakened by dwindling supplies and the desertion of his forces to Enrique, Martín López de Córdoba negotiated a surrender that guaranteed safe passage out of the realm. In violation of these terms, Enrique had Martín López de Córdoba seized and beheaded in Seville in May 1371. His possessions were confiscated, and his household, including Leonor and her husband, was imprisoned in the arsenal of Seville.

Released in 1379 by order of Enrique's last will and testament, López de Córdoba took up residence with her maternal aunt María García Carrillo in Cordova. Although her husband returned to her seven years later, López de Córdoba makes scant mention of him in the *Memorias*. Of her three or more children she mentions only the oldest, Juan Fernández, who died of the plague around 1400. Other records indicate that her daughter Leonor Gutiérrez de Hinestrosa married don Juan de Guzmán, the son of the count of Niebla, in 1409.

Sometime after her son's death, López de Córdoba emerged as the *privada* (royal favorite) of Catalina, the wife of Enrique III. How she achieved this status is unknown, although she almost certainly capitalized on her father's loyalty to Pedro I, Catalina's grandfather. The dissension caused at court by López de Córdoba's influence over Catalina and active role in matters of state is well documented. Among her most ardent political foes was Enrique III's brother Fernando, the future king of Aragon, who had served as coregent with Catalina during Juan II's minority. Undoubtedly at his instigation López de Córdoba was banished from court sometime after 1408. So taken was the queen with her new *privada,* the young noblewoman Inés de Torres, that she threatened to have López de Córdoba burned at the stake should the latter attempt to return to court. By 1412 López de Córdoba had returned to Cordova, where she remained until her death in either 1412 or 1430. She is buried there in a chapel she founded in the Church of San Pablo.

López de Córdoba's fall from grace did not fail to make an impression on her contemporaries. It was memorialized by the poet Gómez Pérez Patiño in two rather enigmatic pieces included by Juan Alfonso de Baena in his *Cancionero* (circa 1430, Songbook). The *Crónica del rey don Juan II* (Chronicle of King Don Juan II) configures the episode as a cautionary tale for other royal favorites. Even more critical is Fernán Pérez de Guzmán, who in his *Generaciones y semblanzas* (circa 1450–1455, Lineages and Likenesses; translated as *Pen Portraits of Illustrious Castilians,* 2003) condemns López de Córdoba as an upstart and a "frivolous and wretched woman."

López de Córdoba recounts in the *Memorias* the major episodes of her life up to the death of her son around 1400. While there is general agreement that she composed her work in 1412, what remains to be explained is why she neglected to include her tenure at court and subsequent fall from grace. Scholars have speculated that she died before finishing her account or that she was too upset by her recent experiences to commit them to writing. María-Milagros Rivera Garretas and Reinaldo Ayerbe-Chaux reject the 1412 date, proposing that López de Córdoba completed the text sometime before her arrival at court. María Eugenia Lacarra makes a case for reading the text as an excerpt, copied from a longer original in the eighteenth century, for the purpose of advancing the cause of beatification of López de Córdoba's brother Álvaro de Córdoba; promoters of the beatification were presumably less interested in the later period of López de Córdoba's life.

In a formulaic introduction López de Córdoba styles her account as an exemplum intended to bolster the faith of her readers by relating the favors granted to her over the course of her life by the Virgin Mary: "scribolo . . . por que todas las Criaturas que estubieren en tribulacion sean ciertos . . . que si se encomiendan de Corazon á la Virgen Santa Maria que Ella las consolará, y acorrerá, como consoló á mi" (I write it down . . . so that all creatures in tribulation might be assured . . . that if they commend themselves wholeheartedly to the Holy Virgin Mary, she will console them and succor them as she consoled me [all translations of passages from the *Memorias* are by Amy Katz Kaminsky and Elaine Dorough Johnson, 1996]). Such a motive would position her among other authors who composed spiritual testimonies during the late Middle Ages, especially women of a mystical bent such as Julian of Norwich and Margery Kempe. But López de Córdoba's reconstruction of the lineages of her father, her mother, and her husband and her meticulous inventory of her wealth and possessions have led some readers to suggest a more self-serving purpose: the recovery of social prestige lost by her family as a consequence of the change of dynasty.

López de Córdoba begins the narrative portion of the *Memorias* with her father's defense of Carmona and surrender to Enrique de Trastámara. Although her version corresponds in broad strokes to chronicle accounts, she portrays Martín López de Córdoba as a paragon of loyalty not only for his defense of Carmona after Pedro's death but also for his protection of the infantas and negotiation of their safe passage to England. Most telling are the words her father utters to du Guesclin, the "traitor of Montiel," as he is led to the chopping block: "Mas vale morir como Leal, como Yo lo hé echo, que no vivir como vos vivis, haviendo sido Traydor" (It is better to die loyal, as I have done, than to live as you live, having been a traitor). Peter E. Russell points out two liberties taken by López de Córdoba in her narration of these events: the infantas were not present at the siege of Cordova, and du Guesclin was not in Seville at the time of Martín López de Córdoba's execution. Some scholars have attributed these lapses to the author's hazy recollection of events that took place at least thirty years earlier, others to a deliberate revisionism intended to suggest the illegitimacy of the Trastamaran line.

López de Córdoba narrates her father's execution in a curiously detached tone that belies the pathos of the situation. Much more poignant is her account of the nine years she and her father's household spent in the arsenal in Seville. Every detail seems calculated to provoke the reader's sympathy: the weight of the chains, the threat of starvation, the heavy toll taken by a pestilence that breaks out among the prisoners. López de Córdoba's thirteen-year-old brother Lope, "la mas hermosa Criatura que havia enel mundo" (the most beautiful creature there was in the world), is among those stricken; he dies ignobly, "como á moro" (like a Moor), when the jailers refuse to relieve him of his shackles. Equally tragic is the tale of López de Córdoba's brother-in-law, one of five brothers who donned gold necklaces in the Church of Santa María de Guadalupe with the pledge to reunite there one day and offer their necklaces to the Virgin Mary: "por sus pecados el Vno se murió en Sevilla, y el Otro en Lisbona, y el Otro en Ynglaterra, é asi murieron derramados, é se mandaron enterrar con sus Collares de Oro, é los frayles con la codicia despues de enterrado le quitaron el Collar" (for their sins, one perished in Seville and another in Lisbon, and another in England, and so they died scattered, and it was ordered that they be buried with their gold necklaces. But the friars in their greed removed their necklaces after they were buried).

Only López de Córdoba and her husband survive the harsh conditions of imprisonment, gaining their freedom with the death of Enrique in 1379. López de Córdoba's collective account of the trials of her father's household turns now to a dynamic first-person description of her efforts to achieve financial solvency, a theme that predominates in the remainder of the narrative. Striking here is the summary dismissal of her husband's role in these efforts. His quest to recover his birthright ends in utter failure; after seven years, he returns to López de Córdoba's side with little more than a mule and the clothes on his back, leaving her to draw the sober conclusion that "los derechos . . . dependen á los Lugares que hán conque se demandar" (rights . . . depend on the station one has on which to base a claim). For her part, López de Córdoba avails herself of the resources of her mother's family, whose own solvency had been assured by its allegiance to the Trastamaran cause. She seems indebted primarily to the generosity of her aunt María García Carrillo, with whom she takes up residence in Cordova shortly after

her release from prison and remains for some twenty years.

In a much-discussed episode of the *Memorias* López de Córdoba voices her dissatisfaction with the lodgings her aunt provides for her: although adjoining the main house, they require her and her husband to make their way through public streets in order to take meals with the family. Clara Estow and Arturo Roberto Firpo remark that the social anxiety expressed here anticipates the obsession with external appearances characteristic of the poor hidalgo during Spain's golden age. Through negotiations with her aunt and novenas to the Virgin Mary, López de Córdoba secures permission to open a *postigo* (back entrance) affording direct access to the main house. She meets, however, with opposition from the servants: "quando Otro dia quise abrir el postigo, Criadas suyas le havian buelto su Corazon, que no lo hiziese, y fui tan desconsolada, que perdi la paciencia, é la que me hizo mas contradicion con la Señora mi tia se murió en mis manos, comiendose la lengua" (when on the following day I tried to open the passageway, some of her maids had changed her mind, convincing her not to do it; and I was so disconsolate that I lost my patience, and the one who did the most to set my aunt against me died in my hands, swallowing her tongue). The ambiguous wording has left readers to wonder whether the maidservant died of an epileptic seizure, as Ayerbe-Chaux argues, or whether López de Córdoba murdered her, as Ruth Lubenow Ghassemi contends. In either case, the implication is that the woman brought death on herself by attempting to thwart the divine will.

What Encarnación Juárez calls López de Córdoba's "pragmatic religiosity" is manifested again in her efforts to build her estate, an undertaking she first envisions in a dream that borrows much from Spain's rich hagiographical tradition: "Soñaba pasando por Sant Hipolito, tocando el Alva, vi en la pared delos Corrales un arco mui grande, y mui alto, é que entraba yo por alli, y cojia flores dela Sierra, y veia mui gran Cielo, y en esto desperte, é obe esperanza enla Virgen Santa Maria que me daria casa" (I dreamed that when passing by San Hipólito with the morning bells ringing, I saw on the courtyard walls a very big, high arch, and that I entered there and picked flowers from the mountainside, and I saw the vast heavens. At this point I woke up and placed my hope in the Holy Virgin Mary that she would give me a house). To achieve her ends López de Córdoba resorts to piety and prayers, all carefully tabulated and serving, as Amy Suelzer notes, as a bargaining chip with which to secure divine favor: "yo havia ido treinta dias á Maytines ante Santa Maria el Amortecida . . . con aguas o con vientos descalza, é rezabale 63 vezes esta Oracion que se sigue con 66 Aves Marias, en reverencia delos 66 años que Ella vivió con amargura en este mundo, por que Ella me diese Casa" (I had gone barefoot in the wind and rain to morning prayer to the shrine of María el Amortecida, which is in the monastery of the order of San Pablo de Córdoba, and I prayed this prayer to her sixty-three times, followed by sixty-six Hail Marys, in homage to the sixty-six years she lived with bitterness in this world, that she might give me a house). She has the same purpose in mind when she takes in Alonso, a boy most likely orphaned in the anti-Jewish pogroms of 1391, and raises him in the Christian faith.

López de Córdoba is rewarded for her efforts when the monks of San Hipólito offer parcels of their land for sale. Disregarding their objection to having persons of such high station as neighbors, she secures from her aunt the funds with which to buy the property and begin building. She purposefully expresses her ownership of this victory when she concludes: "de labor de mis manos hize en aquel Corral dos Palacios, y una huerta, é Otras dos, ó tres Casas para servicio" (with the labor of my hands I built in that courtyard two palaces and a garden and another two or three houses for the servants).

Discord and prayer remain central themes in the final episode of the *Memorias*. When plague breaks out in Cordova in 1400, López de Córdoba withdraws with her aunt's household to Aguilar. They are joined by Alonso, who has begun to exhibit symptoms of the illness. At López de Córdoba's insistence, a former valet of her father's takes the boy in; the man is stricken and dies, along with a dozen subsequent caretakers: "é por mis pecados treze Personas, que de noche lo velaban, todos murieron" (and for my sins, thirteen people, who kept vigil over him during the night, all died). López de Córdoba again resorts to prayer, offering her twelve-year-old son Juan Fernández to God in exchange for the safekeeping of the rest of her family: "si alguno obiese de llevar, llebase, el mayor por que era mui doliente" (if any of them had to be taken away, it should be the eldest one, for he was in great pain). One night, when no one else remains to keep watch over Alonso, she sends Juan Fernández to his bedside: "é por mis pecados aquella noche le dió la pestilencia e otro dia lo enterré, y el enfermo vivió despues haviendo muerto todos los dichos" (and for my sins, that night he came down with the plague and I buried him the next day. And the sick man survived, but all those I have mentioned died). Here, as well, readers have been perplexed by López de Córdoba's motives, some seeing her as impassive, even cruel, others as duty bound to care for Alonso at the risk of everything she holds dear. Ghassemi speculates that López de Córdoba refused to place her son's life above family honor; in this act, she

argues, López de Córdoba honored the memory of her father, who placed service to Pedro I before the well-being of his own family. Kathleen Amanda Curry reads López de Córdoba's protection of Alonso as a political act that recalls Pedro's favorable policies toward the Jews and defies the anti-Semitism of the Trastamaran camp.

Recourse to prayer is one unifying factor between this episode and previous ones; another is López de Córdoba's volatile relationship with the women of her aunt's household–first the servants who oppose the opening of the *postigo,* and later her aunt's own daughters and daughter-in-law: "mis Primas nunca estaban bien con migo, por el bien que me hacia su madre, y dende alli pase tantas amarguras, que no se podian escribir" (my cousins were never favorably disposed toward me because of the kindness their mother showed me, and from then on I suffered so much bitterness it cannot all be written down). Spurred by the death of Juan Fernández, Carrillo's daughter-in-law Teresa works tirelessly to have López de Córdoba banished from the household, a goal she finally achieves. López de Córdoba records her parting remark to her aunt: "Señora, Dios no me salve si mereci por que" (My lady, may God not grant me salvation if I have done anything to deserve this). In the introduction to his 1977 edition of the *Memorias* Ayerbe-Chaux notes the parallel between López de Córdoba's banishment from her aunt's household at Teresa's urging and her subsequent banishment from Catalina's court. He suggests that this second banishment motivated López de Córdoba to compose her text and that her parting words are directed as much to the queen as they are to her aunt. With these words and a reference to her return to Cordova, López de Córdoba ends her account.

Early editors of the *Memorias*–José María Montoto (1875), Feliciano Ramírez de Arellano, Marqués de la Fuensanta del Valle (1883), and Teodomiro Ramírez de Arellano y Gutiérrez (1885)–considered the text no more than an historical curiosity. Even Adolfo de Castro y Rossi, who deems some passages "equal in greatness to the best of Greek epic," devotes the bulk of his 1902 edition to historical annotation. For much of the twentieth century interest in the *Memorias* was limited to the ways in which it complemented or contradicted the official records of Trastamaran Spain. A. D. Deyermond was the first to demonstrate sustained interest in the literary value of the work. In 1971 he compared the *Memorias* to Pérez de Guzmán's *Generaciones y semblanzas* and Hernando del Pulgar's *Claros varones de Castilla* (1486, Illustrious Noblemen of Castile). In a 1983 essay he admires López de Córdoba's lack of artifice and her "artist's instinct for the telling phrase," even as he calls into question the reliability of her historical narrative. Ayerbe-Chaux is somewhat more indulgent in the introduction to his 1977 edition, where he asserts López de Córdoba's right to narrate history from her own perspective and calls the piece "the first noteworthy example of the autobiographical genre in Spain." Subsequent studies have also focused on the place of the work in the history of autobiography as a genre. Firpo, for example, locates the *Memorias* between medieval modes of autobiography, which are marked by the subject's exemplarity, and modern modes, which are marked by the subject's singularity. Carmen Marimón Llorca anchors López de Córdoba's autobiographical impulse in the vitality and diversity of historiographical discourse in fifteenth-century Castile, while Esther Gómez Sierra argues for the *Memorias* as an "alternative historical narrative," one that achieves a greater degree of reliability than traditional historiography by taking seriously the compulsion to confess.

Feminist considerations of the text were limited initially to efforts to secure for López de Córdoba a place in the medieval Spanish canon. Later efforts have used the *Memorias* as an invaluable source for reconstructing the history of women in late-medieval Spain. Rivera Garretas and Suelzer take on the dichotomies traditionally drawn between public life, associated with the masculine, and private life, associated with the feminine, that have obscured women's agency in the making of history. Rivera Garretas argues for acknowledging private spaces such as those inhabited by López de Córdoba as politically charged and so equally constitutive of history. Suelzer reads the *Memorias* as a deliberate crossing of the boundary between the private and the public that is fueled both by circumstances—the affront to family honor—and by López de Córdoba's independent character. Marimón Llorca analyzes López de Córdoba's participation in the economic and political spheres of late medieval society and concludes that she is representative of a "progressive feminization" of Castilian politics that culminated in the rise of Isabel the Catholic in the latter half of the fifteenth century. Estow investigates López de Córdoba's career as courtier and probes the reasons for the opprobrium she earned from her peers; she speculates that López de Córdoba's relationship with Catalina may have transcended the bounds of propriety. Gregory S. Hutcheson explores López de Córdoba's relationships with women more fully and agrees that they allow for the possibility of same-sex desire.

Louise Mirrer has perhaps done the most to advance feminist readings of the *Memorias*. Taking issue with the commonly held view that a scribe had a heavy hand in the authorship of the work, Mirrer argues for the authenticity of López de Córdoba's voice. Even the highly formulaic language of the opening lines, she maintains, might represent López de Córdoba's struggle for interpretative authority within the public arena of men's writing. By fusing her own life story, steeped in the "female" universe of hagiographical discourse, with the male discourse of letters and learning, López de Córdoba produced a text firmly grounded in a woman-centered and woman-identified epistemology. Hers is a "world of men's absence," just as the *Memorias* is structured around "women's spaces" and validated through the author's identification with a series of powerful foremothers, among them the Virgin Mary. For Mirrer, López de Córdoba's *Memorias* forms part of "program of resistance," a coherent response to the male-constructed female images by which Reconquest Castile attempted to keep its powerful women in check and deprive them of a voice of their own.

The most sustained discussion of the *Memorias* emerges from efforts to decipher authorial intent in composing it. Virtually all modern criticism has moved past the ingenuousness of early readers such as Manuel Serrano y Sanz, who in 1898 praised López de Córdoba for her "profound religious sentiment and inexhaustible charity." That López de Córdoba modeled herself at least in part on exempla and hagiographical accounts is evident in both her opening salvo and her liberal use of tropes such as prayer, displays of charity, and prophetic dreams. But her obsession with lineage and the acquisition of wealth undermines the characterization of the text as a work of devotional literature. Beginning with Ayerbe-Chaux, most critics have admitted to more-opportunistic motives such as reconciliation with María Carrillo or Catalina; recovery of possessions confiscated by Enrique de Trastámara after the execution of Martín López de Córdoba; or redemption of the López family name. Curry discerns broader political motives, perhaps an effort to produce an apologia for the loyalist cause. Ghassemi suggests that even the enigmatic episodes of the death of the maidservant and López de Córdoba's care for the sick Alonso fall in line with an inflexible idealism that places faith, honor, and loyalty above life and limb.

Two readers circumvent the issues of López de Córdoba's political engagement or her material opportunism and return to a more straightforward interpretation of the words with which she opens her account. Rivera Garretas argues that the *Memorias* is in great part just what it claims to be: a record of the favors López de Córdoba believes that she received from the Virgin Mary. Her identification with Mary represents a powerful strategy through which to expand the boundaries of her own identity and find sanction for pursuing projects that traditionally fell outside a woman's domain. In this way Rivera Garretas attempts to move beyond what Ayerbe-Chaux, in his 1977 edition, labeled the "strangeness" of the text, that is, the incongruity between López de Córdoba's seeming piousness and the patent opportunism of her actions. Ayerbe-Chaux himself broke from this interpretation in 1992, rereading the *Memorias* as an intensely personal document: a private examination of conscience that López de Córdoba composed in the wake of her son's death. By recalling the grace she experienced at other tragic moments in her life, López de Córdoba derives the means to confront this most recent tragedy and expiate the overwhelming guilt she feels as a consequence of her role in it.

As a work of literature, Leonor López de Córdoba's *Memorias* had no impact on subsequent authors. Nonetheless, it serves as a touchstone for tracing the rise of autobiography in a society that had just begun steering a course into modernity. It is remarkable both for the complexity of its relationship to reigning discourses, whether historical, hagiographical, or juridical, and the simplicity with which it tells its tale. More important, perhaps, it gives voice and agency to a class that has been understudied in Spanish history, the *ricas hembras* (women of the highest nobility) who participated in the society and politics of late medieval Spain and paved the way for the rise to power of Isabel the Catholic in the final decades of the fifteenth century. It remains an indispensable resource, whether for historians exploring the role of women in historical process or for literary scholars intent on locating in Spanish letters the genesis of an authentically female voice.

References:

Reinaldo Ayerbe-Chaux, "Leonor López de Córdoba y sus ficciones históricas," in *Historias y ficciones: Coloquio sobre la literatura del siglo XV. Actas del coloquio internacional organizado por el Departament de Filologia Espanyola de la Universitat de València, celebrado en Valencia los días 29, 30 y 31 de octubre de 1990,* edited by Rafael Beltrán Llavador, José Luis Canet Vallés, and Josep Lluís Sirera (Valencia: Universitat de València, 1992), pp. 17–23;

Adolfo de Castro y Rossi, "Memorias de una dama del siglo XIV y XV (de 1363 a 1412): Doña Leonor López de Córdoba," *La España Moderna,* 163 (July 1902): 120–146; 164 (August 1902): 116–133;

Kathleen Amanda Curry, "Historia y literatura en las *Memorias de doña Leonor López de Córdoba,*" dissertation, Georgetown University, 1985;

A. D. Deyermond, *A Literary History of Spain: The Middle Ages* (London: Benn / New York: Barnes & Noble, 1971), p. 154;

Deyermond, "Spain's First Women Writers," in *Women in Hispanic Literature: Icons and Fallen Idols,* edited by Beth Miller (Berkeley: University of California Press, 1983), pp. 27–52;

Clara Estow, "Leonor López de Córdoba: Portrait of a Medieval Courtier," *Fifteenth-Century Studies,* 5 (1982): 23–46;

Arturo Roberto Firpo, "Un ejemplo de autobiografía medieval: Las 'Memorias' de Leonor López de Córdoba (1400)," *Zagadnienia Rodzajów Literackich,* 23, no. 1 (1980): 19–31;

Ruth Lubenow Ghassemi, "La 'crueldad de los vencidos:' Un estudio interpretativo de *Las memorias de doña Leonor López de Córdoba,*" *La corónica,* 18, no. 1 (1989–1990): 19–32;

Esther Gómez Sierra, "La experiencia femenina de la amargura como sustento de un discurso histórico alternativo: Leonor López de Córdoba y sus *Memorias,*" *La voz del silencio: Fuentes directas para la historia de las mujeres,* volume 1, edited by Cristina Segura Graiño (Madrid: Asociación Cultural Al-Mudayna, 1992), pp. 111–129;

Gregory S. Hutcheson, "Leonor López de Córdoba and the Configurations of Female-Female Desire," in *Same Sex Love and Desire Among Women in the Middle Ages,* edited by Francesca Canadé Sautman and Pamela Sheingorn (New York: Palgrave, 2001), pp. 251–275;

Encarnación Juárez, "Autobiografía de mujeres en la Edad Media y el Siglo de Oro y el canon literario," *Monographic Review/Revista Monográfica,* 13 (1997): 154–168;

Carmen Marimón Llorca, *Prosistas castellanas medievales* (Alicante: Caja de Ahorros Provincial de Alicante, 1990), pp. 81–102;

Louise Mirrer, *Women, Jews, and Muslims in the Texts of Reconquest Castile* (Ann Arbor: University of Michigan Press, 1996), pp. 139–150;

Fernán Pérez de Guzmán, *Generaciones y semblanzas,* edited by R. B. Tate (London: Tamesis, 1965), p. 34;

María-Milagros Rivera Garretas, "Leonor López de Córdoba: La autorrepresentación," in her *Textos y espacios de mujeres (Europa siglos IV–XV)* (Barcelona: Icaria, 1990), pp. 159–178;

Peter E. Russell, *The English Intervention in Spain and Portugal in the Time of Edward III and Richard II* (Oxford: Clarendon Press, 1955), pp. 163–164;

Manuel Serrano y Sanz, *Apuntes para una biblioteca de escritoras españolas desde el año 1401 al 1833,* volume 2 (Madrid: Establecimiento Tipolitográfico Sucesores de Rivadeneyra, Impresores de la Real Casa, 1898), pp. 16–18;

Amy Suelzer, "The Intersection of Public and Private Life in Leonor López de Córdoba's Autobiography," *Monographic Review/Revista Monográfica,* 9 (1993): 36–46.

Las Mocedades de Rodrigo

(circa 1300)

Matthew Bailey
University of Texas, Austin

Manuscript: The text is extant in a unique manuscript from the early fifteenth century: Bibliothèque Nationale, Paris, MS. Fonds Espagnol 12, folios 188r–201v.

First publication: "Mocedades de Rodrigo," edited by Francisque Michel, *Wiener Jahrbücher für Literatur*, 116 (1846): 1–27.

Editions: *Mocedades de Rodrigo,* edited by Juan Victorio, Clásicos Castellanos, volume 226 (Madrid: Espasa-Calpe, 1982); *Las Mocedades de Rodrigo,* edited by Carlos Alvar and Manuel Alvar, Letras Hispánicas, volume 330 (Madrid: Cátedra, 1997); "Mocedades de Rodrigo," edited by Fátima Alfonso-Pinto, in *"Las Mocedades de Rodrigo": Estudios críticos, manuscrito y edición,* edited by Matthew Bailey, King's College London Medieval Studies, volume 15 (London: King's College London Centre for Late Antique and Medieval Studies, 1999), pp. 185–216; *Mocedades de Rodrigo: Estudio y edición de los tres estados del texto,* edited by Leonardo Funes and Felipe Tenenbaum (London: Tamesis, 2004).

Paleographic editions: A. D. Deyermond, *Epic Poetry and the Clergy: Studies on the "Mocedades de Rodrigo,"* Colección Támesis, Serie A: Monografías, no. 5 (London: Tamesis, 1969), pp. 221–277; Matthew Bailey, ed., *Texto y Concordancias de "Mocedades de Rodrigo"* (Madison, Wis.: Hispanic Seminary of Medieval Studies, 1994 [microfiche]).

Photographic reproductions: Archer M. Huntington, *Crónica Rimada* (New York, 1904); Matthew Bailey, ed., *"Las Mocedades de Rodrigo": Estudios críticos, manuscrito y edición,* King's College London Medieval Studies, volume 15 (London: King's College London Centre for Late Antique and Medieval Studies, 1999), between pp. 182 and 183.

Edition in English: *Las Mocedades de Rodrigo: The Youthful Deeds of Rodrigo, the Cid,* edited and translated by Matthew Bailey (Toronto: Medieval Academy of America, University of Toronto Press, 2007).

Las Mocedades de Rodrigo (circa 1300, The Youthful Deeds of Rodrigo; translated as *Las Mocedades de Rodrigo: The Youthful Deeds of Rodrigo, the Cid,* 2007) is a narrative poem about the young Rodrigo Díaz de Vivar, the eleventh-century hero known in his later years as the Cid. One of only two extant epic poems in Castilian Spanish, it occupies folios 188r through 201v of an early fifteenth-century manuscript whose first 187 folios contain the *Crónica de los reyes de Castilla* (between 1290 and 1300, Chronicle of the Kings of Castile). The hero is a rebellious youth, quite distinct from the mature Díaz portrayed in the other, more celebrated extant Spanish epic, the *Cantar de mio Cid* (circa 1200, Song of My Lord; translated as *Poem of the Cid,* 1879). In the first bibliographical record of the work (1844) Eugenio de Ochoa described it as a patchwork culled from divergent authors and periods, part chronicle and part poorly rhymed verse, with language so uneven and with so little connection between the phrases that it frequently becomes unintelligible. This initial reception was reinforced in 1924 by Ramón Menéndez Pidal's opinion that the poem reflects the decadent taste of late-fourteenth-century Spain. It was considered the handiwork of a deviant bard or *juglar* (minstrel) because it did not respect the heroic figure depicted in the *Cantar de mio Cid,* a work that was considered historically accurate. But the rebellious Rodrigo, not the mature and measured Cid, captured the popular imagination and was repeatedly brought back to life in Spanish chronicles and *romances* (ballads), in the golden-age dramas of Lope de Vega and Guillén de Castro y Bellvís, in France in Pierre Corneille's play *Le Cid* (1637; translated as *The Cid,* 1637), and in Anthony Mann's 1961 movie *El Cid.*

The poem begins with a cattle raid by Rodrigo's father, Diego Laínez, on the lands of Count Gómez de Gormaz. The offended count challenges Diego Laínez to meet him on the field of battle, each to be accompanied by one hundred knights. Against his father's wishes, twelve-year-old Rodrigo joins the fight, kills Gómez de Gormaz, and captures the count's two sons. Gómez de Gormaz's three daughters come to request the release of their brothers; Diego Laínez refers the request to his son, who grants it. The brothers immediately begin plotting reprisals, but the youngest sister, Jimena, asks them to trust her to gain justice from the king in Zamora. Jimena arrives, weeping, at the royal court and beseeches redress for the wrong done to her family. Young King Fernando of León, fearful of the unruly Castilians, is uncertain how to respond. Jimena offers a solution: she will take Rodrigo, "the one who killed my father," as her husband. The king's adviser seizes on the idea, and Rodrigo is summoned to court. Rodrigo and his father are suspicious but acquiesce after taking precautions to protect themselves against the treachery they expect from the king. On their arrival the court falls back in terror at the sight of the enraged Rodrigo. The king quickly summons Jimena, and she and Rodrigo are betrothed. Rodrigo swears that he will not lie with her or kiss the king's hand until he has won five battles. The first four battles involve the Muslim king Burgos, who is raiding Castile with five thousand Moors; the beheading of Martín González, the Navarrese champion representing the king of Aragon in a dispute over the city of Calahorra, in a single combat; five Muslim kings whom Rodrigo defeats after his father and three paternal uncles are killed; and two rebellious Castilian counts who had plotted with the five Muslim kings against King Fernando. The fifth and final battle is a full-fledged military campaign pitting the five kingdoms of Spain, united under King Fernando, against the forces of the king of France, the Holy Roman Emperor, the Pope, and the Patriarch over their demand that Spain pay a yearly tribute. King Fernando designates Rodrigo his standard-bearer; Rodrigo distinguishes himself in victory over the count of Savoy, who hands over his only heir, a daughter, in exchange for his freedom. She is given to Fernando as his concubine. Rodrigo arrives at the gates of Paris with an army of nine hundred knights and demands that the Twelve Peers come out to fight him. The French king refuses, saying that he will only fight King Fernando. An attempt at diplomacy fails when Rodrigo insults the Pope and threatens the king of France. Just as the war is about to recommence, the Savoyard concubine gives birth to a son; he is baptized by the Pope before Fernando can act. In light of this miraculous event a truce of eight years is declared.

There was a long-standing tradition in Spain of using the oral tales of *juglares* in the writing of history, both in the vernacular languages of the Iberian Peninsula and in Latin. Accounts of Rodrigo's youthful exploits began to appear in chronicles with the Latin *Historia Roderici* (circa 1110 or circa 1185, History of Rodrigo), which is generally considered to be largely true to the historical facts. The work offers a genealogy of Rodrigo and recounts some of the deeds that later tradition associates with his youth: his upbringing in the court of Sancho II; his knighting by the king; his valiant efforts in the siege of Zamora; his single combat against the Navarrese champion of the king of Aragón for possession of the city of Calahorra; and his marriage to Jimena, arranged by King Alfonso VI. Other episodes recount his heroics in the battles between Sancho II and Sancho's brother Alfonso VI in Llantada and Golpejera and his victorious single combat against a Saracen of Medinaceli. But the tales grew taller with changing times and distance from the events, reflecting the changing values, attitudes, and social environments of bards and their audiences. One of the variables in the tales is Díaz's attitude toward his king: the mature Díaz of the *Cantar de mio Cid* is loyal to a fault; similarly, in the *Crónica de los reyes de Castilla,* which begins with the reign of Fernando I *el Magno* (the Great), king of León from 1038 to 1065, and narrates some of the episodes that are found in *Las Mocedades de Rodrigo,* he is portrayed as loyal to the king, happy to be of service, and eager to please the monarch. In contrast, the youthful Rodrigo of *Las Mocedades de Rodrigo* is brash, belligerent, and independent; he initially regards the king as an enemy, then as a monarch to be obeyed but not served, and finally as an inept yet necessary leader. The two texts, though they appear in the same manuscript, thus reflect divergent interpretations of the role of the young Rodrigo in the reign of Fernando I. Such differences preclude the possibility of the chronicle having served as a source for the poem. Instead, either the two works are variations on an ever-changing oral narrative tradition depicting the youthful deeds of the Cid, carried on by *juglares* over a period of two hundred years, or the chroniclers transformed the popular rebel figure of the oral narrative tradition into a servant of his king.

The recto of the first folio of the text of *Las Mocedades de Rodrigo* provides a brief historical sketch of the paternal forebears of Rodrigo and Fernando I, who are descended, respectively, from Laín Calvo and Nuño Rasura, the two legendary *jueces* (judges) of Castile. According to tradition, one of these noblemen would defend Castile, while the other led the nobility to the assemblies of the court in León, the ruling kingdom. The sentences almost all begin with the word *Et* (And) and contain no end rhyme or assonance. The use of prose and the desire to provide genealogies for the two protagonists suggest a learned influence. The historical sketch continues on the verso of the same folio as it recounts the legendary deeds of Count Fernán González–Rasura's grandson and so Fernando's ancestor–who freed Castile from its status as a tributary of León. At this point the text turns to verse, and the remainder of the work is composed in assonantal lines of varying length in which the vowel or vowels of the last word of each verse are repeated and receive the stress; the "á-o" assonance predominates. Although at times the assonance is missing, it is the principal compositional mechanism of the poem and clearly associates *Las Mocedades de Rodrigo* with oral verse: Spanish learned poetry of this period employs the alexandrine meter known as *cuaderna vía* (fourfold way), a four-line stanza of fourteen syllables with a single consonantal rhyme.

The life of Fernán González, including some of the deeds recounted in the introduction to *Las Mocedades de Rodrigo*, is the subject of a *cuaderna vía* work, the *Poema de Fernán González* (between 1251 and 1258, Poem of Fernán González), which is most likely a recasting of an oral epic. That poem also precedes the narration of the life of its protagonist with an historical introduction, prompting some scholars to suggest that the *Poema de Fernán González* was a direct model for the historical sketch at the beginning of *Las Mocedades de Rodrigo*, as well as a general inspiration for the writing of the poem. This theory may be correct, but the style and content of the historical sketch in *Las Mocedades de Rodrigo* are essentially oral: the verse is not metrically regular and relies on assonance as a compositional principle; and there are no abstract ideals or concepts, no call to historical destiny or preacherly moralizing as there are in the historical introduction to the *Poema de Fernán González*. Also, while *Las Mocedades de Rodrigo* includes González's crowning achievement of gaining Castilian independence from León, this episode is absent from the learned earlier version.

A. D. Deyermond notes that a connection between the descendants of Rasura and Calvo and the diocese of Palencia is unique to *Las Mocedades de Rodrigo*, setting it apart both from the earlier chronicle versions and from the later ballads, and he uses this feature as a clue for dating the poem and to argue for its learned authorship. The historical introduction details the legendary discovery and recognition of an ancient holy shrine to San Antolín; the transfer of the property from Count don Pedro of Palencia to King Sancho Avarca, the father of Fernando I; its transfer to the bishop of Toledo, who is in flight from the marauding Moors; and its designation as the see of Palencia. In the poem the rights of the see are reaffirmed by Fernando but usurped by the aggression of Pedro's sons. Fernando expresses a wish for the absent Rodrigo to resolve the matter, but the discussion is interrupted by news of a threat from France. It is likely that in a now-lost part of the text Rodrigo returns to Palencia after the truce between Spain and France that constitutes the final episode in the extant poem, fights for the rights of the diocese, and marries Jimena in a ceremony there. Deyermond identifies a diocesan crisis in the mid fourteenth century and argues that the Palencia

material was added around 1360 by a learned writer intent on associating the diocese's claims to the status of papal see with the popular epic hero Díaz. Reviewing Deyermond's thesis in the light of irregularities in line lengths, Thomas Montgomery concludes that the extant poem contains a good deal of evidence of intervention by a learned author in a previously transcribed poetic text.

On the other hand, Georges Martin associates Rodrigo's defiance of royal authority in the poem with the struggles over the throne of León and Castile following its usurpation in 1284 by Sancho IV *el Bravo* (the Brave), the son of Alfonso X *el Sabio* (the Learned). These struggles were especially acute during the regency period of Fernando IV, who ruled from 1295 to 1312 and shed his regents when he came of age. Martin argues that during his minority Fernando IV was ineffective in the face of the power of the old nobility and that this dynamic is reflected in the portrayal in the poem of the relationship between the youthful Fernando I and Rodrigo. Martin also asserts that the *Crónica de los reyes de Castilla* reflects changes in Alfonsine historiography that are attributable to the influence of the genealogy of Rodrigo in the introductory passage of *Las Mocedades de Rodrigo*, most notably the details relating to the *jueces* of Castile. In addition, he points out that the literary influences on the poem are from the thirteenth century and that the linguistic characteristics of the poem do not rule out the possibility of its genesis prior to 1350. Finally, in response to Deyermond's identification of a diocesan crisis in the mid fourteenth century as a motivating factor in the learned reworking of the narrative, Martin points to a crisis in Palencia between 1296 and 1300 that provides a plausible motive for the reassertion of the rights of its diocese in the poem. Martin makes a case for *Las Mocedades de Rodrigo*, or a poem similar to the text that exists today, having influenced the composition of the episodes relating Rodrigo's exploits in the *Crónica de los reyes de Castilla*. He considers the years 1289 to 1312 the likely period of gestation for the poem.

One problem remains to be resolved: in the *Crónica de los reyes de Castilla* Rodrigo does not rebel against a young and incompetent king, as in the poem, but is a faithful and unwavering servant of the mature and accomplished Fernando I. Martin suggests that the writers of the *Crónica de los reyes de Castilla* were familiar with a poem, similar to the extant *Las Mocedades de Rodrigo*, that was composed with Fernando IV as the cowardly royal protagonist and Rodrigo as a temperamental and disrespectful vassal. They then modified this narrative to fit it into the preexisting royal historiography relating to Fernando I. In an article in *"Las Mocedades de Rodrigo": Estudios críticos, manuscrito y edición*

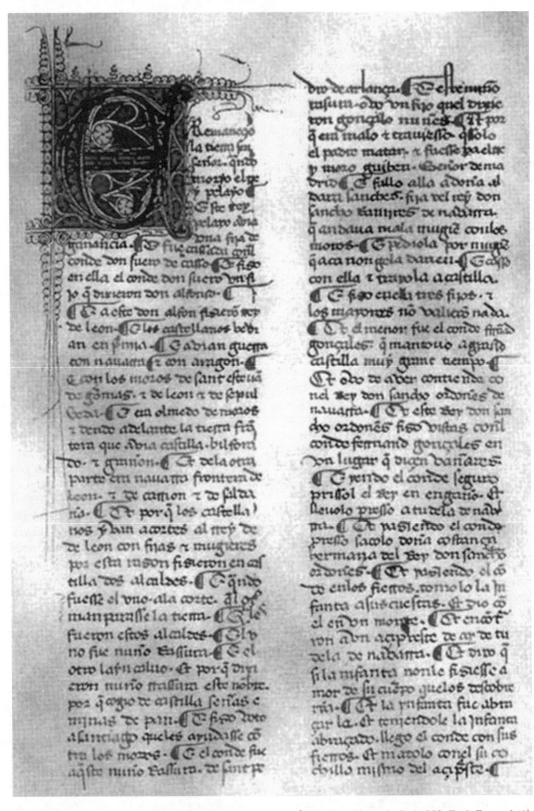

Page from the unique manuscript of Las Mocedades de Rodrigo *(Bibliothèque Nationale, Paris, MS. Fonds Espagnol 12)*

(1999, "Las Mocedades de Rodrigo": Critical Studies, Manuscript and Edition), edited by Matthew Bailey, Mercedes Vaquero proposes a similar manipulation of the source narrative by the compilers of the *Crónica de los reyes de Castilla*. But perhaps more likely is that the *Crónica de los reyes de Castilla* reflects the *Las Mocedades de Rodrigo* at an earlier stage of its development in which Rodrigo remained in the shadow of the adult Fernando I. In time, and owing in part to the troubled minority of Fernando IV, a change in the portrayal of Rodrigo began to occur. It must have taken some time to develop in oral form and may have acquired its structure during the reign of Alfonso XI in the first half of the fourteenth century. The real character of Fernando IV was assimilated then into the oral narrative tradition linking Rodrigo to Fernando I, bringing into being the pitifully inept young Fernando I in *Las Mocedades de Rodrigo*.

Virtually all critics agree that prior to the composition of the *Crónica de los reyes de Castilla* an oral narrative tradition existed in which Rodrigo was portrayed as the young vassal of a mature Fernando I, loyal to his king and eager to be of service. The many chronicle references to his loyal deeds suggest a continuity of tradition up to the completion of the *Crónica de los reyes de Castilla* and the genesis of the rebellious Rodrigo as a subsequent development. Regardless of the specific period during which this transformation occurred, it is clear that Rodrigo's rebellious exploits represent a second oral tradition that came to eclipse in popularity and vitality the earlier narrative tradition of the mature Rodrigo, the Cid. The chronicle references, the *Las Mocedades de Rodrigo,* and the later Cidian *romances* bear witness to this vitality and confirm Menéndez Pidal's assertion that the Spanish oral-narrative tradition "vive en variantes" (lives through mutations).

In addition to the real-world situations identified by Martin, myth also played a role in shaping the narrative tradition of Rodrigo's *mocedades*. Apart from Rodrigo's single combat against the Navarrese champion of the king of Aragon for the city of Calahorra, which is narrated in the *Historia Roderici* and the *Carmen Campidoctoris* (circa 1194, Poem of the Champion), the deeds recounted in *Las Mocedades de Rodrigo* seem to have no basis in history. The bards therefore turned to familiar myths such as the rite of initiation of the male warrior, a myth that is also reflected in the Spanish *Cantar de mio Cid* and *Siete infantes de Lara* (Seven Princes of Lara); the French *Chanson de Roland* (Song of Roland); the various pan-European versions of the Tristan legend; and the Irish saga *Táin Bó Cúailnge* (The Cattle Raid at Cooley), with its young hero Cúchulainn. All are permutations of an Indo-European initiation myth first identified by Georges Dumezil in 1942. Episodes in

Las Mocedades de Rodrigo that Montgomery has linked to the *Táin Bó Cúailnge* include Rodrigo's first battle, in which he kills Jimena's father; his antisocial behavior at the king's court; his forced betrothal to Jimena in retribution for the death of her father; his vow not to consummate his marriage until he has won five battles in the field; the French campaign; and an episode of *furor belli* (war-like fury) associated with the historical single combat for Calahorra.

In his hostile attitude toward his king, the young Rodrigo is reminiscent of other Castilian epic heroes such as Fernán González, Bernardo del Carpio, and Gonzalo, the protagonist of the tragic *Siete infantes de Lara*. The story of the young Charlemagne, known as Mainet in the two Spanish prose versions of his childhood, shares the initiatory aspects of Rodrigo's *mocedades* and appears in chronicles contemporary with *Las Mocedades de Rodrigo*. French twelfth- and thirteenth-century chansons de geste include a subgenre of stories about young heroes who, like Rodrigo, are aggressive and disrespectful of their elders, and *Las Mocedades de Rodrigo* shows familiarity with some of these figures.

The presence in *Las Mocedades de Rodrigo* of figures from French epic indicates that the fictional account of the invasion of France led by Fernando I and the child-warrior Rodrigo might be a Castilian response to the incursions into Spain by the protagonists of the *Chanson de Roland*. The heroes of the Carolingian epic cycle, first recorded in Spain in the *Nota Emilianense* (1075, San Millianese Notes), lost their luster as Castile gained in stature; the conquest of the Moorish kingdom of Valencia by Díaz showed that the heroes of French epic song were no longer needed to fight the Moors in Spain. In *Las Mocedades de Rodrigo* a young warrior emerges to challenge the old guard and set a new standard of conduct that leads to the defeat and humiliation of the enemies of Castile. Once this task is accomplished, a woman subdues his passions by becoming his wife and the bearer of his children.

Key episodes of *Las Mocedades de Rodrigo* were recreated in *romances* composed more than two hundred years later—long after memories of historical events could influence the increasingly embellished story line. These short narrative poems were enormously popular during the fifteenth and sixteenth centuries. The love-hate relationship of Rodrigo and his wife to be, Jimena, fired the imaginations of *juglares* and their audiences, and the *romances* explore its implications with exuberance. This oral tradition formed the basis for much of the golden age drama of Spain. The best known of the plays exploring the dramatic tension generated by "sleeping with the enemy" is Castro's most celebrated work, *Las Mocedades del Cid* (circa 1612). Castro adapts the story by having Jimena and Rodrigo already in love when Rodrigo's father is shamed by Jimena's father, the count of Orgaz. Although this situation requires deadly redress, Rodrigo and Jimena's passion is too strong to die. In the end they marry, but not before Jimena and her repeated cries for justice are ridiculed and Rodrigo's mythic stature is reduced to that of a lovelorn but obedient son. Corneille's best-known work, *Le Cid*, was not based on the medieval poem but was inspired by Castro's drama.

Bibliography:

Eugenio de Ochoa, *Catálogo razonado de los manuscritos españoles existentes en la Biblioteca Real de París, seguido de un suplemento que contiene los de las otras tres bibliotecas públicas (del Arsenal, de Santa Genoveva y Mazarina)* (Paris: Imp. Real, 1844), pp. 105–110.

References:

Manuel Alvar, ed., "Romances referentes a Rodrigo," in his *Cantares de gesta medievales* (Mexico City: Porrúa, 1991), pp. 181–186;

Samuel G. Armistead, "The Earliest Historiographic References to the *Mocedades de Rodrigo*," in *Estudios literarios dedicados a Helmut Hatzfeld*, edited by Josep M. Solà-Solé, Alessandro Crisafulli, and Bruno Damiani (Barcelona: Hispam, 1974), pp. 25–34;

Armistead, "*The Enamored Doña Urraca* in Chronicles and Balladry," *Romance Philology*, 11 (1957–1958), 26–29;

Armistead, "La gesta de las mocedades de Rodrigo": Reflections of a Lost Epic Poem in the "Crónica de los reyes de Castilla" and the "Crónica general de 1344," dissertation, Princeton University, 1955;

Armistead, "A Lost Version of the 'Cantar de gesta de las Mocedades de Rodrigo' Reflected in the Second Redaction of Rodriguez de Almela's 'Compendio historial,'" *University of California Publications in Modern Philology*, 38, no. 4 (1963): 299–336;

Armistead, "The Structure of the *Refundición de las Mocedades de Rodrigo*," *Romance Philology*, 17 (1963–1964): 338–345;

Armistead, *La tradición épica de las "Mocedades de Rodrigo,"* Acta Salmanticensia, Estudios Filológicos, no. 280 (Salamanca: Ediciones Universidad de Salamanca, 2000);

Armistead, "An Unnoticed Epic Reference to Doña Elvira, Sister of Alfonso VI," *Romance Philology*, 12 (1958–1959): 143–147;

Matthew Bailey, "Las asonancias inusitadas de las *Mocedades de Rodrigo*," *Revista de poética medieval*, 3 (1999): 9–30;

Bailey, ed., *"Las Mocedades de Rodrigo": Estudios críticos, manuscrito y edición*, King's College London Medi-

eval Studies, volume 15 (London: King's College London Centre for Late Antique and Medieval Studies, 1999);

Gloria Beatriz Chicote, "Jimena, de la épica al romancero: Definición del personaje y convenciones genéricas," in *Caballeros, monjas y maestros de la Edad Media (Actas de las "V Jornadas Medievales")*, edited by Lillian von der Walde, Concepción Company, and Aurelio González (Mexico City: Universidad Nacional de México, Colegio de México, 1996), pp. 75–86;

Crónica de los reyes de Castilla, edited by Matt Mayers, Spanish Series, no. 119 (Madison, Wis.: Hispanic Seminary of Medieval Stuides, 1997);

Crónica de veinte reyes, edited by José Manuel Ruiz Asencio and Mauricio Herrero Jiménez (Burgos: Ayuntamiento, 1991);

Crónica geral de Espanha de 1344, 4 volumes, edited by Luis Filipe Lindley Cintra (Lisbon: Academia Portuguesa da Historia, 1951–1990);

A. D. Deyermond, *Epic Poetry and the Clergy: Studies on the "Mocedades de Rodrigo,"* Colección Támesis, Serie A: Monografías, no. 5 (London: Tamesis, 1969);

Georges Dumézil, *Horace et les Curiaces* (Paris: Gallimard, 1942; New York: Arno Press, 1978);

Richard Fletcher, *The Quest for El Cid* (Oxford: University Press, 1991);

John Gornall, "The Cid's Youthful Deeds: Decadent *Mocedades* or Pristine *Enfances*," *Journal of Hispanic Research*, 3 (1994–1995): 69–79;

"Historia Roderici," edited by Emma Falque, in *Chronica Hispana Saeculi XII, Pars I*, Corpus Christianorum, Continuatio Mediaeualis, volume 71 (Turnhout: Brepols, 1990), pp. 1–98;

Georges Martin, *Les juges de Castile: Mentalités et discours historique dans l'Espagne médiévale*, Annexes des Cahiers de Linguistique Hispanique Médiévale, no. 6 (Paris: Séminaire d'Études Médiévales Hispaniques, Université de Paris-XIII, 1992);

Gonzalo Martínez-Díez, *El Cid histórico* (Barcelona: Planeta, 1999);

Ramón Menéndez Pidal, *La España del Cid* (Madrid: Plutarco, 1929);

Menéndez Pidal, *Poesia juglaresca y juglares: Aspectos de la historia literaria y cultural de España*, Publicaciones de la *RFA*, no. 7 (Madrid: Centro de Estudios Históricos, 1924), pp. 406–413;

Alberto Montaner Frutos, "La *Gesta de las Mocedades de Rodrigo* y la *Crónica particular del Cid*," *Actas del I Congreso de la Asociación Hispánica de Literatura Medieval: Santiago de Compostela, 2 al 6 de diciembre de 1985* (Barcelona: PPU, 1988), pp. 431–444;

Montaner Frutos, "Las quejas de doña Jimena: Formación y desarrollo de un tema en la épica y el romancero," in *Actas: II Congreso Internacional de la asociación Hispánica de Literatura Medieval (Segovia, 5 al [9] de octubre de 1987),* volume 2, edited by José Manuel Lucía Megías and others (Alcalá de Henares: Universidad de Alcalá, 1992), pp. 475–507;

Thomas Montgomery, "The Lengthened Lines of the *Mocedades de Rodrigo,*" *Romance Philology,* 38, no. 1 (1984–1985): 1–14;

Montgomery, *Medieval Spanish Epic: Mythic Roots and Ritual Language* (University Park: Pennsylvania State University Press, 1989), pp. 29–41;

Montgomery, "Las *Mocedades de Rodrigo* y los romances," in *Josep María Solà-Solé: Homage, homenaje, homenatge (miscelánea de estudios de amigos y discípulos),* volume 2, edited by Antonio Torres-Alcalá and others (Barcelona: Puvill, 1984), pp. 119–133;

David G. Pattison, "The *Crónica ocampiana:* A Reappraisal," in *Letters and Society in Fifteenth-Century Spain: Studies Presented to P. E. Russell on His Eightieth Birthday,* edited by Alan Deyermond and Jeremy Lawrence (Llangrannog, Wales: Dolphin, 1993), pp. 137–147;

Roger Wright, "The First Poem on the Cid: The *Carmen Campi Doctoris,*" *Papers of the Liverpool Latin Seminar, Second Volume 1979,* edited by Francis Cairns, ARCA, Classical and Medieval Texts, Papers and Monographs, no. 3 (Liverpool: Francis Cairns, 1979), pp. 213–248.

Petrus Alfonsi
(Pedro Alfonso, Pierre Alphonse)
(*flourished 1106 – circa 1125*)

John V. Tolan
Université de Nantes

WORKS: *Dialogi contra Iudaeos* (1110)

Manuscripts: The work survives in sixty-three medieval manuscripts, including Bibliothèque de l'Arsenal, Paris, MSS. 553, 769, 941; Bibliothèque Nationale, Paris, MSS. lat. 10624, 10722, 5080, 14069; Biblioteca Universitaria, Salamanca, MS. 2579; Biblioteca Provincial, Tarragona, Códice Misceláneo 55–126; and Biblioteca de la Catedral, Tortosa, MS. 15.

Medieval Catalan translation: "Una versión catalana desconocida de los *Dialogi* de Pedro Alfonso," edited by J. Ainaud de Lasarte, *Sefarad,* 3 (1943): 359–376.

Early edition: *Dialogi contra Iudaeos* (Cologne: Johann Gymnich, 1536).

Modern editions: *Dialogi contra Iudaeos,* Maxima bibliotheca veterum patrum, volume 21 (Lyon: Anissonios, 1677); "Dialogi contra Iudaeos," in *Patrologiae latinae cursus completus,* edited by J. P. Migne, 217 volumes (Paris: Migne, 1844–1864), CLVII: 527–672.

Standard edition: Pedro Alfonso de Huesca, *Diálogo contra los Judíos,* edited by Klaus-Peter Mieth, Spanish translation by Esperanza Ducay (Huesca: Instituto de Estudios Altoaragoneses, 1996).

Tabulae Astronomicae (adaptation of al-Khwârizmi's *Zij al-Sindhind*) (1116)

Manuscripts: Two medieval manuscripts survive: Lambeth Palace Library, London, MS. 67; and Corpus Christi College, University of Oxford, MS. 283.

Standard edition: *The Astronomical Tables of al-Khwârizmi, Translated with the Commentaries of the Latin Version edited by H. Suter,* edited by O. Neugebauer, Historisk-filosofisde Skrifter: Udgivet af det Kongelige Danske Videnskabernes Selskab, volume 4, no. 2 (Copenhagen: Munksgaard, 1962).

Petrus Alfonsi (from Disciplina Clericalis, *translated by Esperanza Ducay, edited by María Jesús Lacarra, 1980; Thomas Cooper Library, University of South Carolina)*

Epistola ad Peripateticos in Francia (1120s?)

Manuscript: One twelfth-century manuscript survives: British Museum, London, MS. Arundel 270.

Standard edition: "Epistola ad Peripateticos in Francia," with English translation ("Letter to the

Peripatetics in France"), in John V. Tolan, *Petrus Alfonsi and His Medieval Readers* (Gainesville: University Press of Florida, 1993), pp. 163–181.

Disciplina clericalis (date uncertain)

Manuscripts: The *Disciplina clericalis* survives in seventy-six medieval manuscripts, including Archivo General de la Corona de Aragón, Barcelona, MS. 123; Biblioteca de San Lorenzo de El Escorial, Codex latin Q.I.14; Biblioteca de la Catedral, Cordova, MS. 150; and Biblioteca Provincial, Tarragona, 55.

Early edition: *Disciplina clericalis* (Paris: J. Labouderie, 1824).

Standard edition: *Disciplina Clericalis,* edited by Alfons Hilka and Werner Söderhjelm, Acta Societatis Scientiarum Fennicae, volume 38, no. 4 (Helsinki, 1911).

Editions in English: "Peter Alphonse's Disciplina clericalis (English Translation), from the Fifteenth Century Worcester Cathedral Manuscript F.172," edited by William H. Hulme, *Western Reserve University Bulletin,* new series 22, no. 3 (1919); *The Scholar's Guide: A Translation of the Twelfth-Century* Disciplina Clericalis *of Pedro Alfonso,* translated by Joseph Ramon Jones and John Esten Keller (Toronto: Pontifical Institute, 1969); *The Disciplina Clericalis of Petrus Alphonsi,* translated by P. R. Quarrie (Berkeley & Los Angeles: University of California Press, 1977).

Petrus Alfonsi is one of the key actors in the transmission and assimilation of Arabic scientific, literary, and religious texts and ideas to Latin Europe in the early twelfth century. His impact is attested in the survival of roughly 160 manuscripts of his works, in the frequent use made of them by key authors from the twelfth century to the sixteenth, and in their wide diffusion through early printed editions. Just as Alfonsi adapted elements of the Arabic and Hebrew traditions to the needs and tastes of twelfth-century Latin Europe, his later readers, scribes, and anthologizers reworked his texts to fit their own interests and preoccupations.

Alfonsi was born a Jew in al-Andalus (Muslim Spain) and was originally named Moses. He was educated in Hebrew and Arabic; his writings show familiarity with the Talmud; with texts of Arabic astronomy, medicine, and philosophy; and with the Arabic wisdom traditions. He converted to Christianity and was baptized on 29 June 1106 in the Huesca cathedral. He explains in his *Dialogi contra Iudaeos* (1110, Dialogues against the Jews) that he took the name Petrus in honor of St. Peter and Alfonsi in honor of his godfather, King Alfonso I of Aragon. He may have played a role in Alfonso's court, perhaps as royal physician and astrologer.

Alfonsi composed the *Dialogi contra Iudaeos* to respond to Jews who accused him of abandoning his former faith out of contempt for God's law, misunderstanding of the Prophets, and lust for worldly gain; he seeks to "destroy their objections with reason and authority." He says that he has named the Jewish debater Moses, because that was his own name when he was a Jew; he gives the Christian debater his new name, Petrus. The twelve dialogues fall into three parts. In the first four dialogues Petrus contends that Judaism is no longer valid—that Jews "obey the law only in part, and that part is not pleasing to God." Much of his argument turns on rationally and scientifically based attacks on the Talmud. In the fifth dialogue he attacks Islam, presenting Muhammad as a fraud and a pseudoprophet and Muslim rituals such as ablutions, fasting, and pilgrimage as sullied by their pagan origins. In the final seven dialogues he attempts to show that the basic doctrines of Christianity contradict neither reason nor the Old Testament. In the end Moses is convinced and meekly converts to Christianity.

Alfonsi's dialogues brought three important new elements to anti-Jewish polemic in Latin. The first was his attack on the Talmud, a text almost unknown to previous Latin authors. Alfonsi's denunciations gave it a greater profile as the authoritative body of teachings that Christian polemicists would have to confront and moved the arena of dispute from abstractions about Old Testament Judaism into a face-off between living communities. The second novel element was his use of scientific and philosophical arguments to show the irrationality of the beliefs he opposed; this strategy was common in the Arab world but was new to Latin Christendom. The third was Alfonsi's charge that because of their espousal of the unreasonable and antibiblical tenets of the Talmud, Jews were no longer faithful to their divine covenant and that, therefore, contemporary Judaism was a heretical deviation from classical Judaism. The previous consensus among Christian anti-Jewish polemicists had been, on the contrary, that Jews erred in their literalist readings of Holy Writ and in clinging obstinately to the Old Law instead of embracing the Christian New Dispensation. Alfonsi's charge contributed to an intensification of anti-Judaism and to accusations against the Jews of moral "contumacy"—the perverse election of evil over an unmistakable good.

The popularity of Alfonsi's work both within and well beyond the Iberian Peninsula furthered an increasing tendency to link anti-Jewish and anti-Muslim polemics: whereas earlier anti-Jewish polemicists had for the most part contented themselves with arguing for

Christian interpretations of the Torah (the first five books of the Bible, called the Pentateuch by Christians) and the Prophets, Alfonsi focused on the Talmud and the Koran as illicit pseudorevelations that formed the bases for two heretical doctrines. According to Alfonsi, the Talmud and the Koran could be attacked, and certain key elements of Christian doctrine, such as the Trinity, could be proven, through scriptural and rational-scientific argumentation. Jews and Muslims, if they allowed themselves to be rational, could thus be brought to the Christian truth, as Moses is in the dialogues. The conflation of anti-Jewish and anti-Muslim argumentation and an increasing Christian insistence on the irrationality of both rival faiths represent a crucial turning point in Christian portrayal of Islam and Judaism in medieval Europe.

The *Dialogi contra Iudaeos* became the most widely read and used medieval anti-Jewish text; it survives in sixty-three manuscripts and in variant or abridged versions in sixteen additional manuscripts. The work was already popular in the first quarter of the twelfth century at the Parisian abbey of St. Victor, whose canons took particular interest in Alfonsi's presentation of Jewish scriptural exegesis. In the twelfth and thirteenth centuries it was found principally in Benedictine and Cistercian monasteries in France and England. It also proved popular among those interested in Islam; some scribes recopied only the anti-Islamic fifth dialogue, and Humbert of Romans, fifth master general of the Dominican order, recommends it in his thirteenth-century *Tractatus de prædicatione crusis contra Saracenos infideles et paganos* (Tract on the Preaching of the Cross against the Saracens, Infidels, and Pagans) along with the Latin translation of the Koran as essential reading for understanding the religion of the adversary. Dozens of medieval writers on Islam, including Petrus de Pennis, Marino Sanudo, and Jacobus de Voragine, based their descriptions of Muhammad's life, of Muslim law, and of the pilgrimage rites at Mecca on Alfonsi's fifth dialogue. The *Dialogi contra Iudaeos* also crops up in unexpected places: Robert Grosseteste relies on the astronomical information from the dialogues in his *De sphaera* (circa 1214–1235, On the Spheres), and Joachim of Fiore co-opts the Trinitarian arguments, which Alfonsi had tried to make more palatable to Jewish readers by inventing a cabalistic explanation for a Triune godhead, as an inspiration for his theory of three successive epochs of world history devoted to the Father, the Son, and the Holy Spirit.

The *Dialogi contra Iudaeos* proved most popular among anti-Jewish polemicists, who redeployed Alfonsi's arguments in works that were often derivative, out of touch with the primary sources in Hebrew and Arabic, and savage. In particular, his attack on the irrationality of the Talmud became a mainstay of

anti-Jewish antipathy: Peter the Venerable, abbot of Cluny, used the dialogues in his vitriolic *Adversus Iudeorum inveteratam duritiem* (1143, Against the Inveterate Stubbornness of the Jews), as did Theobald of Saxony in the thirteenth-century *Pharetra fidei contra Iudaeos* (Quiver of the Faith against the Jews) and Ramon Martí in *Pugio fidei* (circa 1278, Dagger of the Faith). Jerónimo de Santa Fe cited Alfonsi at the disputation between Christians and Jews held at Tortosa between 1412 and 1414. Francisco Machado reused Alfonsi's arguments in his diatribe against Portuguese *conversos* (Jewish converts to Christianity) in his *Espelho de Christãos novos* (1541, Mirror of New Christians).

In the thirteenth century some scribes began taking it upon themselves to change the text of the dialogues, expunging what seemed to them superfluous, such as Alfonsi's scientific arguments, or unorthodox, such as his conception of the Trinity. One anonymous thirteenth-century redactor removed Moses from the text, transforming the *Dialogi contra Iudaeos* into a one-sided and harsh anti-Jewish diatribe. Vincent de Beauvais includes a similarly distilled monologue extracted from Alfonsi's text in his *Speculum historiale* (circa 1250, Mirror of History), a work that survives in more than two hundred medieval manuscripts.

Sometime between 1110 and 1116 Alfonsi taught astronomy in England; according to one manuscript of his *Disciplina clericalis* (Clerical Instruction), he served for a time as royal physician to King Henry I. In 1116 he produced his *Tabulae astronomicae* (Astronomical Tables), a somewhat flawed Latin version of al-Khwârizmi's *Zîj al-Sindhind*. Two of his students in England are known by name: Walcher of Malvern composed a text on how to predict eclipses based on Alfonsi's teachings, and Adelard of Bath revised and improved Alfonsi's Latin version of al-Khwârizmi's text.

Alfonsi seems to have been in France sometime in the 1120s, since during that decade he wrote the *Epistola ad Peripateticos in Francia* (Letter to the Peripatetics in France). In this work he complains about his lack of students, professes his astronomical expertise, and lambastes Latin intellectuals for preferring the study of grammar and logic to the "hard science" of astronomy: these ignoramuses, who prefer to read Macrobius's commentary on Cicero's *Somnio Scipionis* (The Dream of Scipio) rather than study Arabic astronomy with Alfonsi, are like goats in a vineyard who eat the leaves instead of the ripe, sweet grapes. He gives an impassioned argument for the influence of stellar movements on earthly events, claiming that astronomical knowledge is essential for promoting human welfare, especially in the practice of medicine. That the impact of Alfonsi's scientific works was short-lived is attested by the small number of surviving manuscripts and the

Page from a manuscript of the Chastoiement d'un père à son fils, *with an illumination that depicts Alfonsi teaching a student (Bibliothèque Nationale, Paris, MS. Français 726, folio 119r)*

infrequent use of his works in later scientific treatises. He nevertheless played an important role in introducing and promoting Arabic science in Latin Europe in the early twelfth century.

It is unclear when Alfonsi composed his most popular text, the *Disciplina clericalis*. In his prologue he presents it as a work of philosophy meant to inspire the reader "to follow the path that leads to the kingdom of heaven." He calls it the *Disciplina clericalis,* he explains, because it is meant to make the cleric disciplined; it is a sort of "mirror" or lesson book not for princes but for the new clerical elite of Latin Europe, which in Alfonsi's mind probably resembled the community of ʿulama (learned men) of his native al-Andalus. The main protagonists are narrators who are referred to variously as philosophers or as Arabs but who blend together to form an archetypal sage who "castigates" or counsels his charge by recounting pithy moral pronouncements along with fables to make them memorable and convincing. The link between a dictum, such as "All fear those who fear God; but those who do not fear God fear all," "The insatiable will always suffer hunger for something more," or "Kings are like fires. If you draw too close you get burned, but if you withdraw completely you're left out in the cold," and the associated tale is often made explicit by the narrator in the formula "do not do X [something immoral] lest Y [something bad] befall you, as happened to Z [a person or an animal]." The listener, typically a son or student of the narrator, begs to hear the story, and the narrator delivers it. The *Disciplina clericalis* gives advice to kings about justice and humility, warns of the wiles of women, instructs on the cultivation of neighbors and social ties, reflects on the fleeting nature of earthly fame, and ultimately counsels a retreat into spiritual solitude to contemplate the awesome power of God. Despite invocations of Christ in the prologue and epilogue, the *Disciplina clericalis* is essentially a work of *adab* (oriental Wisdom literature) that reflects a philosophical asceticism predating the three monotheistic religions of the medieval Mediterranean. Socrates is cast in one tale as an ascetic "hermit," and two other stories narrate the adventures of pious pilgrims, some to Mecca and others to Jerusalem, equally motivated by a desire for prayer.

In the prologue Alfonsi says, "I have composed a book, partly from the proverbs and castigations of the philosophers, partly from Arabic proverbs, castigations, fables and verses, partly from comparisons with animals and birds." His sources seem to be such moralizing works as Abu al-Wafa al-Mubashshir ibn Fatik's *Mukhtar al-hikam* (Selection of Aphorisms) and fable and story collections in Arabic such as the *Kalila wa Dimna* (Kalila and Dimna) and *Sinbadnameh* (The Book of Sindbad), although Alfonsi's Latin versions are not close translations of any extant Arabic texts, and some of the aphorisms and fables may have come to him orally. He says that God compelled him "to compose this book and translate it into Latin," probably meaning that he culled the sayings and stories from various Arabic sources, as well as from memory, and reshaped them into his own Latin versions. Wise "sentences" were celebrated in Arabic, in the Talmud, in classical Latin texts that percolated through the Middle Ages, and, through Ecclesiastes, in Christian Scripture. Alfonsi was probably under all of these influences.

The *Disciplina clericalis* was enormously popular throughout the Middle Ages and beyond in part because it made few demands on those with a spotty education and was useful to those who preached to such people. It survives in seventy-six medieval manuscripts in widely varying versions that reflect the divergent interests of their copyists and intended readers. Twelfth-century scribes tended to perceive the *Disciplina clericalis* as a work of "pagan" wisdom and placed it in codices alongside Roman moralists such as Seneca or contemporary moralists such as Lotharius (Lothar of Segni), who reigned as Pope Innocent III from 1198 to 1216. Albertanus of Brescia's twelfth-century *Liber consolationis et consilii* (Book of Consolation and Counsel) quotes Alfonsi along with Seneca, Cassiodorus from the sixth century, and Hugh of St. Victor from the eleventh century. In the "Tale of Melibeus" in *The Canterbury Tales* (circa 1375–1400) Geoffrey Chaucer cites Alfonsi five times, along with Cicero, Seneca, Cato the Elder, Cassiodorus, Lotharius, and Old Testament Wisdom literature; Alfonsi and Lotharius are the only medieval writers to whom Melibeus and his wife, Prudence, refer by name, and they quote only the proverbs, not the fables, from the *Disciplina clericalis*.

In the early thirteenth century Jacques de Vitry adapted five of Alfonsi's fables as exempla for his sermons, modifying them and changing their morals to fit his own didactic purposes. Many thirteenth-century Franciscan and Dominican preachers followed suit, and not a few medieval manuscripts of the *Disciplina clericalis* reflect this use: it accompanies collections of exempla and preachers' and confessors' manuals. The fables most useful as exempla were retained and given more pointedly Christian morals; additional exempla were added; and sometimes the aphorisms were omitted. The fables of the *Disciplina clericalis* appear in anthologies of exempla such as those of the thirteenth-century Dominicans Humbert of Romans and Etienne Bourbon. The fifteenth-century Castilian *Libro de los exemplos por abc* (Book of Exemplary Tales [Arranged] by the ABCs) reproduces twenty-nine of the thirty-four exempla of the *Disciplina clericalis*.

Various other texts in Latin and in other European languages deploy the fables of the *Disciplina clericalis* for didactic purposes, including several *specula principum* ("mirrors" or handbooks for princes): among them are Egidius Romanus's *De regimine principum* (On the Rule of Princes), which was translated into Castilian in the fourteenth century as *Glosa castellana al regimiento de príncipes* (The Castilian Gloss on the Rule of Princes); the late-thirteenth-century *Castigos e documentos para bien vivir ordenados por el rey don Sancho IV* (Lessons and Documents for Right Living Commissioned by King don Sancho IV); and the fifteenth-century *Espéculo de los legos* (Manual for Laymen). The *Disciplina clericalis* served as a minor source for a brief passage on table manners in Alfonso X's vast legal code, the *Siete Partidas* (Seven Divisions of the Law), and for the *Libro del caballero Zifar* (Book of the Knight Zifar), a fourteenth-century Castilian chivalric romance that includes many instructive fables; it even provided the epitaph in Canterbury Cathedral of Edward, the "Black Prince" of Wales, who died in 1376. The most distinguished Castilian descendant of the *Disciplina clericalis* is Juan Manuel's early-thirteenth-century *El conde Lucanor* (Count Lucanor), an anthology of fables recited by the learned Patronio to the young count in his tutelage in which lapidary morals are matched to shrewd and subtle tales that are as well crafted as they are ambiguous. For many of these texts, it is impossible to know whether the author had read the *Disciplina clericalis* itself, a vernacular translation, or a text derived from the *Disciplina clericalis*.

While the preachers and moralists used the *Disciplina clericalis* fables as exempla for sermons and handbooks for princes, other readers abandoned their didactic function and transformed them into short stories. Giovanni Boccaccio turns four of the fables into episodes in his *Decameron* (circa 1348–1353). Whereas Alfonsi uses bare plots and stereotyped characters, Boccaccio describes settings, develops rounded characters, adds plot twists, and infuses the stories with humor. For example, story 4 of day 7 completely changes the moral message of Alfonsi's fable 14, "The Well," one of a series warning of the wiles of women. In Alfonsi's brief version a young husband tries to insure the fidelity of his wife by locking her in the house and keeping the keys under his pillow at night; but she repeatedly gets him drunk and sneaks out at night to rendezvous with a lover. His suspicions aroused, he feigns inebriation, discovers her betrayal, and locks her out in the dark. She pretends to throw herself into a well in distress, tossing in a large stone to create the requisite sound effect. When the husband rushes out to the well, she slips back into the house, locks the door, and accuses him of going out every night with prostitutes. His relatives and the neighbors believe her fabrication, and the shame of infidelity falls on the naive husband rather than on the faithless wife. Boccaccio sweeps aside Alfonsi's moral of the lustful and scheming nature of women and gives the characters distinct personalities. He places the tale in Arezzo, with the husband a rich man named Tofano and the wife a beauty named Ghita. While not especially virtuous, Ghita is clearly the victim; and Tofano's two fatal flaws, abnormal jealousy and a propensity to drink, precipitate his well-deserved ruin. Molière, apparently borrowing the core narrative from Boccaccio, made the same story the basis of his comedies *La Jalousie du Barbouillé* (1660, The Jealousy of Barbouillé) and *Georges Dandin, ou Le Mary confondu* (1668, Georges Dandin, or The Defeated Husband).

Miguel de Cervantes adapted fable 12 of the *Disciplina clericalis*, "The King and His Storyteller," into the "cuento de las cabras" (story of the goats) in *Don Quixote* (1605–1615). In Alfonsi's version an insomniac king has his storyteller recount long tales late into the night. One evening the raconteur begins an account of a villager who crosses a stream to go to town, where he buys two thousand sheep; on his return, he finds the stream flooded and begins to ferry the sheep across two by two. At this point the storyteller nods off; the king wakes him, eager to hear the rest of the tale. The storyteller responds: "The river is wide, the boat is small, and the sheep are numerous. Let the peasant ferry his sheep across first and then I will finish the story." A foolish demand is met with a literary excuse for not meeting it. Two fifteenth-century Castilian texts, the *Libro de los exemplos por abc* and the *Esopete ystoriado* (Illustrated Aesop), include the fable, and one of them may have been Cervantes's source. Sancho Panza tells the tale to Don Quixote during the "noche de las batanes" (night of the mills) as a stalling tactic to prevent Quixote from venturing forth into a battle that they think they hear in the distance (it turns out to be the sound of a fuller's mill). In Sancho's version a shepherd, forlorn because of an unrequited love, decides to immigrate to Portugal with his three hundred goats. He arrives at the Guadiana and finds only a small fishing boat in which the goats have to be ferried one by one. "He takes one across, comes back for the next, takes it across, comes back again," says Sancho, asking Quixote to keep track of the number of goats that have made the crossing. Quixote, annoyed, tells Sancho to consider that the goats have crossed and get on with the tale, but Sancho replies that since he has lost track of the number of goats that have crossed he is unable to remember the rest of the story, which, as a result, is "tan acabada como mi madre" (as finished [dead] as my mother). Alfonsi's 180-word fable is a moral reproof for unreasonableness; in Cervantes's version, which is ten times as long, the reproof is elevated to the absurd and–thanks to

Sancho's desperate digressions and Quixote's demands that he get to the point—is comically prolonged.

The *Disciplina clericalis* was translated many times and into many languages during the Middle Ages. In the early thirteenth century an anonymous Norman translator produced a verse rendering, *Le chastoiement d'un père à son fils* (Counsels of the Father to His Son), in which the various philosopher-narrators of the Latin text become a single father "chastising" his son and references to Arabic culture are expunged. Around the same time another French verse translation appeared that also came to be known as *Le Chastoiement d'un père à son fils*. At the end of the century an anonymous Picard produced a prose translation titled *Disciplines de Clergie* that closely follows Alfonsi's original and became the source of a fifteenth-century Gascon translation. The manuscripts of the French translations tend to accompany translations of classical moral texts and works about the wonders of the East.

An English prose translation of the *Disciplina clericalis* dates from the fifteenth century: the translator, who was apparently more interested in telling good stories than in Alfonsi's didactic purposes, reorganizes much of the material and excises many of the tangential proverbs and fictional frames that introduce the fables, leaving a collection of short stories laced with a few random sayings by nameless philosophers. In some places he takes liberties with the original, and in others he has misunderstood the Latin. Individual fables were also translated into French and English, and partial medieval translations of the *Disciplina clericalis* are extant in Italian, Icelandic, and Hebrew.

In the late Middle Ages fables from the *Disciplina clericalis* began to circulate in collections of Aesopian fables. In 1477 Heinrich Steinhöwel published fables of Aesop in Latin and in his own German translation, to which he appended fables from Avianus, Poggio Bracciolini, and fifteen "pleasant fables of Alfonce." He retells the stories in his own words, and William Caxton, in turn, takes great liberties in his 1484 English translation of Steinhöwel's work. The stories from the *Disciplina clericalis* were best known in this form—in collections of Aesopian fables sometimes attributed to Aesop, sometimes to "Alfonce"—from the sixteenth to the nineteenth centuries. The fifteenth-century *Esopete ystoriado* includes Castilian versions of nineteen of the fables from the *Disciplina clericalis*, thus reintroducing them into the peninsula in printed form.

The works of Petrus Alfonsi provide a glimpse into how the Latin West adapted and transformed the intellectual and cultural legacy of the Arab world. Alfonsi imported into England and France the aphorisms and fables of the Eastern Wisdom traditions, astronomical texts, and his own interpretations of the

Koran and Talmud suffused with Hispano-Arab religious polemics. He shaped this knowledge to fit the needs and desires of his pan-European Latin readers. His rationalistic religious disquisitions reflect the faith-seeking-understanding concerns of the theologians of the twelfth-century renaissance. He passionately defended astronomy, and his affirmation that the study of nature could reveal God's designs for creation is in accordance with the thinking of contemporary theologians such as Thierry of Chartres or William of Conches. Finally, the moral aphorisms of the *Disciplina clericalis* are directed to the edification of a proud new educated clerical elite. His readers, copyists, and continuers perpetuated the process of "naturalization" of the Jewish and Arabic elements of Alfonsi's thought, using the *Dialogi contra Iudaeos* to inform a new, harsher anti-Judaism and mining the *Disciplina clericalis* for their sermon tales and instructive fables.

References:

Anna Sapir Abulafia, *Christians and Jews in the Twelfth-Century Renaissance* (New York: Routledge, 1995);

Abulafia, "Jewish-Christian Disputations and the Twelfth-Century Renaissance," *Journal of Medieval History,* 15 (1989): 105–125;

Cecilia Almba, "Tradiciones judías en la *Disciplina clericalis* de Pedro Alfonso," *Sefarad,* 52 (1992): 21–28;

Jacques Berlioz and Marie Anne Polo de Beaulieu, "La capture du récit. La *Disciplina clericalis* de Pierre Alphonse dans les recueils d'*exempla* (XIIIe–XIVe s.)," *Crisol,* new series 4 (2000): 33–58;

Claude Bremond, "Postérité orientale d'un *exemplum* de Pierre Alphonse," in *Tipología de las formas narrativas breves románicas medievales,* edited by Paloma Gracia Juan Paredes (Granada: Editorial Universidad de Granada, 1998), pp. 311–381;

Alfred Büchler, "A Twelfth-Century Physician's Desk Book: The *Secreta Secretorum* of Petrus Alphonsi Quondam Moses Sephardi," *Journal of Jewish Studies,* 37 (1986): 206–212;

Thomas E. Burman, *Religious Polemic and the Intellectual History of the Mozarabs, 1050–1200* (Leiden: Brill, 1994);

Charles Burnett, "Adelard of Bath and the Arabs," *Rencontres de cultures dans la philosophie médiévale: Traductions et traducteurs de l'antiquité tardive au XIVe siècle. Actes du colloque international de Cassino, 15–17 juin 1989,* edited by Marta Fattori and Jacqueline Hamesse (Louvain: Institut des Etudes médiévales de l'Université catholique de Louvain, 1990), pp. 89–107;

Burnett, *The Introduction of Arabic Learning into England* (London: British Library, 1997);

Burnett, "The Works of Petrus Alfonsi: Questions of Authenticity," *Medium Aevum*, 66 (1997): 42–79;

Victoria Burrus and Harriet Goldberg, eds., *Esopete ystoriado (Toulouse, 1488)* (Madison, Wis.: Hispanic Seminary of Medieval Studies, 1990);

Jeremy Cohen, "The Mentality of the Medieval Jewish Apostate: Peter Alfonsi, Hermann of Cologne, and Pablo Christiani," in *Jewish Apostasy in the Modern World,* edited by Todd M. Endelman (New York: Holmes & Meier, 1987), pp. 20–47;

Gilbert Dahan, *Les Intellectuels chrétiens et les Juifs au moyen âge* (Paris: Cerf, 1990);

Dahan, "L'usage de la *ratio* dans la polémique contre les Juifs, XIIe–XVe siècles," in *Diálogo filosófico-religioso entre Cristianismo, judaísmo, e islamismo durante la edad media en la península iberica,* edited by Horacio Santiago Otero (Turnhout: Brepols, 1994), pp. 289–308;

Thomas Klein, "'Arabs' siue 'De dimidio et integro amico': Mittelalterliche Paraphrasendichtung am Beispiel der Petrus-Alfonsi-Rezeption im 13. und 14. Jahrhundert," *Mittellateinisches Jahrbuch,* 33 (1998): 67–84;

M. Kniewasser, "Die antijüdische Polemik des Petrus Alphonsi (getauft 1106) und des Petrus Venerabilis von Cluny (+1156)," *Kairos,* new series 2 (1980): 34–76;

Pieter Sjoerd van Koningsveld, "Petrus Alphonsi, een 12de eeuwse schakel tussen islam en christendom in Spanje," in *Historishce betrekkingen tussen moslims en christenen,* edited by Koningsveld, Midden oosten en islampublicatie, volume 9 (Nijmegen: Midden oosten en islampublicaties, 1982);

María Jesús Lacarra Ducay, *Pedro Alfonso* (Saragossa: Diputación General de Aragón, 1991);

Lacarra Ducay, "La renovación de la artes liberales de Pedro Alfonso," in *De Toledo a Huesca: Sociedades medievales en transición a finales des siglo XI (1080–1100),* edited by Carlos Laliena Corbera and Juan F. Utrilla Utrilla (Saragossa: Institución Fernando el Católico [C.S.I.C.], 1998), pp. 131–138;

Lacarra Ducay, ed., *Estudios sobre Pedro Alfonso* (Huesca: Instituto de Estudios altoaragoneses, 1996);

Dorothee Metlitzki, *The Matter of Araby in Medieval England* (New Haven: Yale University Press, 1977);

José Maria Millás Vallicrosa, "La aportación astronómica de Pedro Alfonso," *Sefarad,* 3 (1943): 65–105;

Millás Vallicrosa, "Un nuevo dato sobre Pedro Alfonso," *Sefarad,* 7 (1947): 136–137;

Guy Monnot, "Les citations coraniques dans le "Dialogus" de Pierre Alphonse," *Islam et Chrétiens du Midi (xiie–xive s.), Cahiers de Fanjeaux,* 18 (1983): 261–277;

C. Nedelou, "Sur la date de la naissance de Pierre Alphonse," *Romania,* 35 (1906): 462–463;

Sveinbjörn Rafnsson, "Sagnastef í íslenskri menningarsögu," *SAGA, tímarit Sögufélags,* 30 (1992): 81–121;

Fiona Robb, "Did Innocent III Personally Condemn Joachim of Fiore?" *Fiorensia: Bollettino del centro internazionale di studi giochimiti,* 7 (1993): 77–91;

Horacio Santiago Otero, "Pedro Alfonso," in *Biblioteca bíblica ibérica medieval,* by Santiago Otero and Klaus Reinhardt (Madrid: Consejo Superior de Investigaciones Científicas, Centro de Estudios Históricos, 1986), pp. 250–258;

Santiago Otero and Klaus Reinhardt, "Los *Dialogi* de Pedro Alfonso: Tradición manuscrita e impresa," *Azafea,* 1 (1985): 33–43;

H. Schwarzbaum, "International Folklore Motifs in Petrus Alfonsi's *Disciplina Clericalis,*" *Sefarad,* 21 (1961): 267–299; 22 (1962): 17–59, 321–344; 23 (1963): 54–73;

Bernard Septimus, "Petrus Alfonsi on the Cult at Mecca," *Speculum,* 56 (1981): 517–533;

A. G. Solalinde, "Una fuente de las *Partidas*: La *Disciplina Clericalis* de Pedro Alfonso," *Hispanic Review,* 2 (1934): 241–242;

J. Stalzer, "Stücke der *Disciplina Clericalis* des Petrus Alfonsi in lateinischen Versen der Berliner Handschrift Diez, B28," *Jahresbericht des k.k. Staats-Realgymnasiums in Graz,* 3 (1911–1912): 1–36;

Heinrich Steinhöwel, *Steinhöwels Äsop,* edited by Hermann Öserley, Bibliothek des litterarischen Vereins in Stuttgart, volume 127 (Tübingen: Litterarischer Verein in Stuttgart, 1873);

Jürgen Stohlmann, "Orient-Motive in der lateinischen Exempla-Literatur des 12. und 13. Jahrhunderts," in *Orientalische Kultur und europäisches Mittelalter,* edited by Albert Zimmerman, Ingrid Craemer-Ruegenberg, and Gudrun Vuillemin-Diem (Berlin & New York: De Gruyter, 1985), pp. 123–150;

Barry Taylor, "Wisdom Forms in the *Disciplina clericalis* of Petrus Alfonsi," *La corónica,* 22, no. 1 (1993): 24–40;

John V. Tolan, "Peter the Venerable on the 'Diabolical Heresy of the Saracens,'" in *The Devil, Heresy, and Witchcraft in the Middle Ages: Essays in Honor of Jeffrey B. Russell,* edited by Alberto Ferreiro (Leiden: Brill, 1998), pp. 345–367;

Tolan, *Petrus Alfonsi and His Medieval Readers* (Gainesville: University Press of Florida, 1993);

Tolan, "Reading God's Will in the Stars: Petrus Alfonsi and Raymond de Marseille Defend the New Arabic Astrology," *Revista Española de Filosofia Medieval,* 7 (2000): 13–30;

Tolan, *Saracens: Islam in the Medieval European Imagination* (New York: Columbia University Press, 2002).

Poema de Alfonso XI
(1348)

Juan Victorio
Universidad Nacional de Educación a Distancia

Manuscript: The poem survives in two copies. Real Biblioteca del Monasterio de El Escorial MS. III.Y.9 lacks the initial and probably the final folios and has many other lacunae, and some of the extant folios are out of sequence. The text begins with the infancy of Alfonso XI and breaks off, just before his death thirty-nine years later, on folio 61v; enough space is left on the folio for another stanza. It is copied in two columns on both sides of the folios in two fifteenth-century hands, the first of which is responsible for the initial 1,170 stanzas and the second for the remaining 1,286. The other manuscript, Real Academia de la Lengua, MS. 213, is a copy made from Escorial III.Y.9 that contains the same faults as that manuscript and was probably made to save it from further degradation through use.

First editions: Thirty-four stanzas in Gonzalo Argote de Molina, *Nobleza de Andalucía* (Seville: Fernando Diaz, 1588); "Poema de Alfonso Onceno, rey de Castilla y de Leon," in *Biblioteca de Autores Españoles,* volume 57, edited by Florencio Janer (Madrid: Atlas, 1952), pp. 477–551.

Edition: *El poema de Alfonso XI,* edited by Yo ten Cate, *Revista de Filología Española,* anejo 65 (Madrid, 1956).

Critical edition: *Poema de Alfonso Onceno,* edited by Juan Victorio (Madrid: Cátedra, 1991).

The *Poema de Alfonso XI* (1348, Poem of Alfonso XI) is unique among medieval Castilian epic poems in that it narrates events contemporary with the writing of the poem. It is also the only epic poem about a king; the protagonists of the *Cantar de mio Cid* (circa 1200, Song of My Lord; translated as *Poem of the Cid,* 1879), the *Poema de Fernán González* (between 1251 and 1258, Poem of Fernán González), the legends of Bernardo del Carpio, and the recovered verses of *Los Siete Infantes de Salas* (The Seven Princes of Salas) are about vassals. The *Poema de Alfonso XI* has been called a rhymed chronicle and appears to have been written side by side with a prose chronicle of the same king. At a time when few

people could read, and fewer still would have had access to a prose chronicle, a poem recited at court in praise of the inner qualities of Alfonso XI encouraged unity of spirit and promoted the Reconquest.

On the death of his father, King Fernando IV of Castile, in 1312, Alfonso XI was one year old. A struggle ensued among powerful nobles to become his tutors and thereby to become de facto regents of the kingdom. Internecine warfare and instability ensued until the fourteen-year-old Alfonso forced the three nobles then acting as his tutors to resign. He married his cousin María, the daughter of Alfonso IV of Portugal, but then fell in love with another noblewoman, Leonor de Guzmán. The affair led to a war with Portugal; Pope Benedict XII intervened to reestablish peace between the kings and redirect their hostilities against the Muslim Benimers (Marinids) of North Africa, who had just crossed the Strait of Gibraltar with a large army. The Christian forces met with great success in the campaign against the Moorish invaders, which came to be known as "la batalla del Estrecho" (the Battle of the Straits). But in 1350, as he was besieging Gibraltar, Alfonso XI succumbed to the Black Plague—the only European monarch to die in this early outbreak of the disease. These events are recorded in contemporary prose chronicles and in the *Poema de Alfonso XI.*

The poem must have been composed between the conquest of Algeciras in 1344, the last event narrated, and the initial preparations for the siege of Gibraltar in 1349, after which concern for promoting the king would have faded. Alfonso had gathered a true crusading army for the siege, with reinforcements from England, Germany, and France complementing his forces. The need of those troops to know the character of the king who had called them into battle would justify the writing of a poem in praise of a living monarch. Another indication that the poem was composed during Alfonso's lifetime is that it narrates his relationship with Guzmán, which resulted in tensions between the king and his official consort, the war with Portugal, and Alfonso's preference for his children by his lover over those by his wife. The rightful heirs became estranged from their father, and the persecution and annihilation of Alfonso's favorites began as soon as he died. His son and successor, Pedro *el Cruel* (the Cruel)–known to his allies as *el Justiciero* (the Justice Worker)–would not have permitted the inclusion of the Guzmán affair. Finally, the narrative is in the present tense–not the historical present but the present of the narrator and his audience. For example, the narrator says: "Don Johán quiero dexar, que ha / su tierra percebida; del muy / noble rey fablar que Dios / mantenga en vida" (I wish to finish speaking of don Juan, who is / now interred; and speak of the very / noble king, whom God / preserve). It would be impossible for the narrator to make this comment if Alfonso, the king about whom he is speaking, were dead. The many instances of the phrase "deste rey que Dios defienda" (may God protect this king) show that Alfonso was still alive when the poem was crafted.

In stanza 1,842 the narrator says, "La profecía conté e / torné en dezir llano; / yo, Ruy Yáñez, la noté / en lenguaje castellano" (I told and related the prophecy in a plain style; I, Ruy Yáñez, set it down in the Castilian language), thus seeming to reveal the author's name. But while the pronoun *yo* (I) appears frequently in the poem, it is formulaic, as are the alternations of verbs such as *fablaré* (I shall speak) and *fablemos* (let us speak). Furthermore, the name Ruy Yáñez appears only once, in the middle of the composition, and not at the beginning or the end, as was the standard practice. The stanza deals with the prophecy by Merlin, mentioned in the preceding stanzas, of a victory for the Christian army over the Saracens; another prophecy of Merlin appears earlier in the poem, in stanzas 243 through 247, without an author's name but, again, with a first-person *yo*. Neither prophecy is directly related to events in the *Poema de Alfonso XI*. Thus, Ruy Yáñez may be a later compiler who introduced himself into the poem. Some scholars have found traces of the Leonese or Portuguese dialects in the poem and have argued that the author was from the northwestern Iberian Peninsula, perhaps from Portugal. The question then arises why a poet from a kingdom that had recently warred against Castile would be attached to the Castilian court to praise the deeds of a Castilian king. It is just as improbable that the poem was first written in Portuguese and then translated into Castilian, because its immediate audience was clearly Castilian.

Imperfections in the rhyme scheme led Diego Catalán to posit a first redaction in a northwestern dialect, because they disappear when the poem is read aloud in one of those tongues. But 90 percent of the rhymes are perfect in Castilian and would fail if the poem were read in any of the other dialects. It makes more sense simply to grant the author some phonological and poetic latitude in making words such as "fidalgo/Santiago" (hidalgo/Santiago) and

"torneo/comedio" (tournament/he thought) and the proper names "Ossorio/Duero" rhyme, even though in normal speech they would not. The best surmise is that the poem was written, as it claims, in "lenguaje castellano" (the Castilian tongue), by a reasonably skilled wordsmith who lacked social distinction and, therefore, remained anonymous.

The metrical form of the *Poema de Alfonso XI* is unique among Spanish epic poems. Other epics are written in either the *mester de juglaría* (minstrelsy of the popular jongleurs) or the *mester de clerecía* (minstrelsy of learned clerics). Each of the 2,456 stanzas of the *Poema de Alfonso XI* consists of four octosyllabic lines with a consonantal *ABAB* rhyme. The metrical form is the same as that used by Shem Tov in his *Proverbios morales* of about the same period.

Though the text of the *Poema de Alfonso XI* is continuous, the events narrated can be divided into blocks of stanzas. The first, comprising stanzas 1 through 152, extends from the infancy of Alfonso until he assumes the rule of Castile. This section thus narrates his tutelage by some of the great nobles of Castile and the wars against the Moors, during which Pope John XXII urged the struggle against the king of Granada. The main thrust of this initial part of the poem is the sad state of Castile during the minority of the king:

> Los tutores a las tierras se
> fueron quanto podían: non
> dexaron fazer guerras bien
> así como solían.
>
> Cada día azes parando,
> estragando a los menores,
> todas las tierras robando
> matando los labradores.
>
> (The tutors returned to their lands as
> often as they could: they did not
> let the war go on as well as before.
>
> Each day they interfered with the troops,
> despoiled the weak,
> robbed everyone,
> killed the peasants.)

The first major appearance of Alfonso XI occurs in stanza 87, when he takes stock of the condition of Castile and, like heroes of other Castilian epic poems, implores God to intercede. The author of the *Poema de Alfonso XI* is fully conscious of the role of Fernán González, an ancestor of the king, and the Cid as models to emulate. Confident of his success, the king assumes power.

In the second narrative block, stanzas 153 through 389, Alfonso deposes his tutors, Juan *el Tuerto* (the One-Eyed) and Juan Manuel, who then sign a treaty of mutual assistance against him. To allay the threat, Alfonso proposes to marry Juan Manuel's daughter, Costanza.

The powerful nobleman believes such a marriage advantageous to his security and interests and agrees to it. Juan *el Tuerto* is called to appear before the king; he believes that his clan, too, is to marry into the king's family. The summons proves to be a trap, and Juan *el Tuerto* is killed. Alfonso then reneges on his promise to marry Costanza and forces her father to flee Castile. The rest of this section concerns the pacification and ordering of the kingdom and the establishment of secure alliances with Portugal and Aragon: Alfonso marries Maria, the daughter of the Portuguese king Alfonso IV, and arranges the marriage of his sister Leonor to King Alfonso IV *el Benigno* (the Benign) of Aragon. This part of the poem also recounts his meeting and falling in love with Guzmán. The poet does not condemn this affair, which proved so injurious to Castilian interests; on the contrary, the relationship is presented as divinely sanctioned.

The third grouping, stanzas 390 through 527, begins with the crowning of the king in Burgos. The official ceremonies and the merriment that follow are described in detail, from the parades of ships on wheels to the enumeration of the musical instruments played during the festivities: "laudes" (lutes), "vihuelas" (Spanish guitars), "rabés" (violins), "salterios" (psalters), "guitarras serraniscas" (mountain guitars), "exabebas moriscas" (Moorish flutes), "gaitas" (bagpipes), and "arpas de don Tristón" (Sir Tristam's harps). Also discussed are the political situation in Moorish Africa that leads to the subsequent invasion by the Benimerins, raids by the neighboring kingdoms of Navarre and Aragon, and the struggle to overcome the remaining resistance to Alfonso within Castile. In a break with chronology, this part of the poem also recounts the births of the king's children by Maria and Guzmán.

The fourth block of stanzas, 528 through 887, describes the war with Portugal encouraged by Alfonso's jilted wife and the fractious nobility–especially Juan Manuel, who had been humiliated by the king and who now intends to marry his daughter Costanza to the son of the king of Portugal. The fierce struggle provokes the intervention of Pope Benedict XII, who urges the two kings to turn their attention to the Benimerin threat to the peninsula. They negotiate a settlement that includes Juan Manuel's making peace with his king. Stanzas 888 through 1,643 provide an account of "la batalla del Estrecho"–the Castilian king's crusade against the Moors, sometimes with and sometimes without the aid of Portugal. The great victory at the Salado River and the siege of Algeciras make up the balance of the poem. The narrative then breaks off.

The form and objectives of the *Poema de Alfonso XI* could not be more different from those of the medieval chronicles dedicated to the king. Besides the obvious contrast between poetry and prose, the poet adopts a more emotional tone than the chroniclers. He describes the characters and their actions in a more impressionistic manner, particularly when discussing Alfonso XI and Guzmán, showing a partiality for the latter that makes him seem to be writing at the king's behest. The same ability to create literary portraits is shown in his descriptions of Moorish characters, where he is more credible and less starkly demonizing than other writers of the period. His descriptions of war are somewhat repetitious, but the accounts of the reverses afflicting Castile tend toward pathetic realism. The poet is particularly good at expressing emotions, as in the "planto" (plaint or outcry) put in the mouth of the Marinid sultan Albohacén (Abu al-Hasan 'Ali) on the death of his son, Albomalique, whom he calls "lumbre destos ojos míos" (light of my eyes). Earlier, Albomalique's own lamentation after losing the battle of Salado and his wives is no less moving: "Mezquino, ¿por qué vivo? / ¡Ay, rey triste, sin ventura!, ¡ay, / rey vil, ay, rey captivo!, ¡ay, rey / lleno de amargura" (Oh, wretch, why do I live? / Oh, sad king, without hope! Oh, / vile king, captive king! Oh, king / filled with bitterness). The author is clearly more comfortable with the lyric tradition than the epic, and some of his stanzas would be worthy of inclusion in an anthology of the best of medieval poetry.

References:

Samuel G. Armistead and James T. Monroe, "Mis moros mortaricaca: Arabic Phrases in the *Poema de Alfonso XI* (Strophe 1709b–d)," *La corónica*, 17, no. 2 (1989): 38–43;

Diego Catalán, "Las estrofas mutiladas en el ms. E del *Poema de Alfonso XI*," *Nueva Revista de Filología Hispánica*, 13 (1959): 325–334;

Catalán, "Hacia una edición crítica del Poema de Alfonso XI," in *Hispanic Studies in Honour of I. González Llubera,* edited by Frank Pierce (Oxford: Dolphin, 1959), pp. 105–118;

Catalán, "La historiografía en verso y en prosa de Alfonso XI a la luz de los nuevos textos," *Boletín de la Real Academia de la Historia*, 154 (1964): 79–126;

Catalán, "La oración de Alfonso XI en el Salado," *Boletín de la Real Academia de la Historia*, 131 (1952): 247–273;

Catalán, *Poema de Alfonso XI: Fuentes, dialecto, estilo* (Madrid: Gredos, 1953);

Catalán, "Un romance histórico de Alfonso XI," in *Estudios dedicados a Menéndez Pidal,* volume 6 (Madrid, 1956), pp. 259–285;

Gifford Davis, "National Sentiment in the *Poema de Fernán González* and in the *Poema de Alfonso Onceno*," *Hispanic Review*, 16 (1948): 61–68;

V. González López, "El *Poema de Alfonso XI* y el condado de Trastamara," *Miscelânea de estudos a Joaquim de Carvalho*, 9 (1963): 963–983;

Juan Victorio, "El desordenado amor de Alfonso XI," *Historia*, 16, no. 41 (1979): 110–112.

Poema de Fernán González

(between 1251 and 1258)

Frank A. Domínguez

University of North Carolina at Chapel Hill

Manuscript: The *Poema de Fernán González* survives in a single damaged manuscript, Real Biblioteca del Monasterio de El Escorial, MS. IV.b.21, copied between 1460 and 1480. The story breaks off before the end, possibly because of the poor condition of the source manuscript from which it was copied. The *Poema de Fernán González* is bound with four other works. Folios 136*r* to 190*v*, on which the poem appears, show evidence of two or three scribal hands.

First publications: "Poema de Fernán González," in *Ensayo de una biblioteca española de libros raros y curiosos,* volume 1, edited by Bartolomé José Gallardo (Madrid: M. Rivadeneyra, M. Tello, 1863), pp. 763–804; "Leyendas del conde don Fernando de Castilla, conocidas con el nombre de poema del conde Fernan Gonzalez," edited by Florencio Janer, in *Poetas castellanos anteriores al siglo XV,* edited by Janer, Tomás Antonio Sánchez, and Pedro José Pidal, Biblioteca de autores españoles, volume 57 (Madrid: M. Rivadeneyra, 1864), pp. 389–804.

Paleographic and facsimile editions: "*Poema de Fernan Gonçalez:* A Palaeographic Edition of the Escorial Manuscript IV.b.21," edited by Jacob Riis Owre, dissertation, University of Minnesota, 1934; *Historia del conde Fernán González: A Facsimile and Paleographic Edition,* edited by John S. Geary (Madison, Wis.: Hispanic Seminary of Medieval Studies, 1987); *Poema de Fernán González: Edición facsímil del manuscrito depositado en el monasterio de el Escorial,* edited by José Manuel Ruiz Asencio (Burgos: Excmo. Ayuntamiento de Burgos, 1989); *Libro de Fernán González,* edited by Itzíar López Guil (Madrid: CSIC, 2001).

Standard editions: *Poema de Fernán González,* edited by C. Carroll Marden (Baltimore: Johns Hopkins Press, 1904); *Poema de Fernán González,* edited by Luciano Serrano (Madrid: Junta del milenario de Castilla, 1943); "Poema de Fernán González," in *Reliquias de la poesía épica española,* edited by Ramón Menéndez Pidal (Madrid: Espasa-Calpe, 1951),

Statue of Fernán González in the Santa María Arch in Burgos (from <http://www.sandovaldelareina.com>)

pp. 39–161; *Poema de Fernán González,* edited by Alonso Zamora Vicente (Madrid: Clásicos Castellanos, 1970); *Poema de Fernán González,* edited by Juan Victorio (Madrid: Cátedra, 1981); *Poema de Fernán González,* edited by John Lihani (East Lansing, Mich.: Colleagues Press, 1991); *Poema de Fernán González,* edited by Miguel Ángel Muro (Logroño: Gobierno de la Rioja, Instituto de Estudios Riojanos, 1994); *Libro de Fernán González,* edited by Itzíar López Guil (Madrid: CSIC, 2001).

Editions in modern Spanish: *Poema de Fernán González,* translated by E. Alarcos Llorach (Madrid: Castalia "Odres Nuevos," 1951); *Poema de Fernán*

González, translated by Miguel Ángel Pérez Priego (Madrid: Alhambra, 1986).

The *Poema de Fernán González* (Poem of Fernán González) is an anonymous thirteenth-century *mester de clerecía* (craft or art form of clerics or the learned) epic poem that celebrates the feats of the most famous warrior of medieval Spain after Rodrigo Díaz de Vivar, who was also known as the Cid. The historical Fernán González, who was born in 929, took advantage of the instability of the Christian states and their constant warfare against the Moors to establish the virtual independence of the region of Castile and become its first hereditary count. His actions presaged Castile's emergence as a kingdom in its own right and its political and military dominance during the Reconquest of Spain. Fernán González is, therefore, a key figure in the founding myth of the nation.

In the tenth century the Muslim caliphate of Cordova comprised most of what is now Spain; it was bordered on the north and northeast by several small Christian principalities. These Christian states included the county of Barcelona and the kingdoms of Navarre, which contained the county of Aragon; León; Asturias; and Galicia. The king of León was also king of Galicia, Asturias, and a border territory that was known as Castile because of its many castles. The four kingdoms ran east to west along the northern coast and were bisected by the pilgrimage road to Santiago de Compostela. Their boundaries were fluid, because primogeniture had not yet been adopted: kings divided their possessions among their children, who often quarreled with each other for a more advantageous share of the inheritance and sometimes ended up losing everything to a stronger sibling.

Exploiting Leonese weakness, Fernán González used a cunning marriage strategy to turn a post that was equivalent to that of military and administrative governor of Castile into a hereditary fief for his family. It retained this quasi-independent hereditary status until 1029, when it was acquired by the kingdom of Navarre through the marriage of González's descendant doña Mayor to Sancho III. On his death in 1035 Sancho willed his properties to his sons as independent kingdoms. García Sánchez became king of Navarre, and the counties of Aragon, Sobrabe-Ribagorza, and Castile became kingdoms under Ramiro I, Gonzalo Sánchez, and Fernando I, respectively. In 1037 Fernando defeated and killed his brother-in-law, Bermudo III, king of León. For the remainder of his reign Fernando was known as king of Castile and León.

Castile's location on the easternmost edge of the kingdom of León made it the scene of sporadic battles with neighboring Navarre to the east. It also exposed Castile to frequent Moorish raids from the south and made it the logical region from which to launch the reconquest of Toledo, a goal that would have been more difficult if the caliphate of Cordova had not disintegrated between 1009 and 1031 into small independent kingdoms centered around the principal Muslim cities of Saragossa to the east, Toledo in the middle, and Badajoz to the west. Toledo fell to Alfonso VI, king of Castile and León, in 1085. More than a century of intermittent warfare ensued as the Christians fought off invasions by the Almoravides and the Almohades. During this period, however, the Toledan lands were being resettled by Christians and progressively integrated into Castile. Once this base was secured, Fernando III *el Santo* (the Saint) was able to launch a series of spectacularly successful campaigns: he conquered the Kingdom of Cordova in 1236, Murcia in 1243–1244, Jaén in 1246, and Cadiz and Seville in 1248. The themes of the *Poema de Fernán González* resonate more with the ideology surrounding these reconquests of the mid thirteenth century, when the poem was composed, than with the struggles of the tenth century. By the thirteenth century the historical Fernán González was remembered primarily as the quasi-legendary founder of the county of Castile and progenitor of its kings; he was buried at the monastery of San Pedro de Arlanza.

A few charters, legal documents, and early chronicles reveal that Fernán González succeeded his father as count of Lara in the late 920s, that he was closely related by blood to the kings of León and Navarre, and that he died in 970. Later historical accounts—the *Liber regum* (1194–1211, Book of Kings) and the *Crónica najerense* (circa 1150–1173, Chronicle of Najera)—make him a descendant of Nuño Rasura, one of the two fabled judges of Castile who ruled during a power vacuum in the county. The other judge, Laín Calvo, was reputed to be the ancestor of the Cid. The first mention of the two judges, however, dates from the end of the twelfth century. The earliest extant literary material celebrating the deeds of the first count of Castile is also scant. It includes, in addition to the *Poema de Fernán González,* three historical romances of even later date and the *Primera Crónica General* (circa 1272, First General Chronicle), also known as the *Estoria de España* (History of Spain), which incorporates a prose version of his story. Although Gonzalo de Berceo's *Vida de San Millán de la Cogolla* (circa 1230, The Life of St. Emilianus de la Cogolla), *Las Mocedades de Rodrigo* (circa 1300, The Youthful Exploits of Rodrigo), and the *Crónica de 1344* (Chronicle of 1344) include episodes involving Fernán González, the *Poema de Fernán González* and the *Primera Crónica General* are the only fairly complete early medieval treatments of his life to survive. The two and three-quarters centuries that separate the death of the count from these texts make them unreliable historical sources.

Nearly all scholars maintain that both the *Poema de Fernán González* and the portion of the *Primera Crónica General* dedicated to the count are based on oral epic poems that have not survived, one of which was recast as the *Poema de Fernán González*. The fact that the *Poema de Fernán González* includes scenes and events that are missing from the version in the *Primera Crónica General*, and vice versa, has been explained by the theories that the authors of the two works relied on different poems or different versions of the same poem or that the authors of the *Primera Crónica General* were mainly concerned with the figure of the king, while the writer of the *Poema de Fernán González* was not interested in anything that detracted from the count's centrality to the narrative. Details in the *Poema de Fernán González* that are absent from the *Primera Crónica General* could also be traced to texts such as the *Liber Regum,* Lucas de Túy's *Chronicon Mundi* (circa 1236, Chronicle of the World), or Rodrigo Jiménez de Rada's *De rebus Hispaniae* (circa 1243, History of Spain). The *Chronicon Mundi* and *De rebus Hispaniae* are among the first works consistently to espouse the notion of the *goticismo* (gothicism) of the Spanish people—the belief that the royal house of Castile descended from the ancient kings of the Visigoths—and to conceive of the Reconquest as a restoration of the Visigothic kingdom. The chronicles gave the idea a new ideological impetus and coherence that provided the justification for the conquests of Fernando III. *Goticismo* pervades the *Poema de Fernán González,* leading one to suspect that these chronicles may be among the *escritos* (writings) to which the poet often refers to give authority to his own work.

Most *mester de clerecía* poems have religious subjects, and the *Poema de Fernán González* is sometimes called a religious epic. The author prefaces the story of the Castilian count with an extensive historical excursus that begins with the Creation, quickly moves to the Visigothic "conquest" of Spain, and ends with its loss and "reconquest." The poem includes prophecies of future events, divine interventions, praying by the characters before and after battles, comparisons of González to individuals who had previously received God's help, and the pledging of a fifth of Castile's war booty to God via the monastery of San Pedro de Arlanza.

The work shows the effects of the religious and educational changes that took place in the eleventh and twelfth centuries. Fernando I and Alfonso VI favored Cluniac liturgical and educational reforms, which slowly displaced the Mozarabic rite in favor of the Roman rite; at the same time, monasteries that followed the rule of St. Benedict were established, French churchmen were appointed to high-ranking positions, and the

Carolingian minuscule replaced Visigothic script. This Europeanization of Spanish institutions accelerated in early-thirteenth-century Castile with the establishment of the first universities in Spain—in particular, the University of Palencia, founded around 1208 to 1212, where Tello de Meneses gathered "sapientes a Gallis et Italia" (learned men from France and Italy) and the study of prosody received preferential treatment. Many of the clergy attached to the northern monasteries in the region must have been educated at Palencia.

The bookish aura of the *Poema de Fernán González* is in keeping with an author who has received some educational training. The style, structure, and content of the poem seem to be influenced by the University of Palencia's educational reforms and the appearance of a new type of *escolar* (scholar), superbly skilled in Latin, who often served in the capacity of notary or found employment in the retinue of important nobles or Church hierarchs. Some of the texts that these learned men and their pupils, including the author of the *Poema de Fernán González,* would have read and that have a bearing on the poem are the Bible and its commentaries, the *Liber Regum,* the *Chronicon Mundi,* the *De rebus Hispaniae,* the *Liber Calixtinus* (circa 1130–1140, Book of Calixtus), the *Crónica Silense* (1115, Chronicle of Silos), hagiographical works, and the *Alexandreis* (circa 1180, Alexandriad) of Walter (or Gautier) de Châtillon. Popular in the schools of the time, the *Alexandreis* influenced *mester de clerecía* compositions such as the *Libro de Alexandre* (circa 1202–1207, Book of Alexander) and the works of Berceo.

The *Poema de Fernán González* is one of several thirteenth-century poems associated with northern monasteries established on or near the pilgrimage route to Santiago de Compostela. The *Cantar de mio Cid* (circa 1200, Song of My Lord; translated as *Poem of the Cid,* 1879) was associated with the monastery of San Pedro de Cardeña; the *Vida de San Millán de la Cogolla,* the *Vida de Santa Oria* (Life of St. Oria), and the *Milagros de Nuestra Señora* (Miracles of Our Lady) with San Millán de la Cogolla; the *Vida de Santo Domingo* (Life of St. Dominic) with Santo Domingo de Silos; and the *Poema de Fernán González* with San Pedro de Arlanza. These poems were probably read aloud to instruct and entertain the ever-increasing number of pilgrims who visited monasteries along the Camino de Santiago (road to Santiago). The works often establish ties between their heroes and the founding of the monasteries; the *Poema de Fernán González* claims that San Pedro de Arlanza was founded on a preexisting hermitage by Fernán González, who selected it as his burial place. In reality, it was founded by the count's father, Gonzalo Fernández, in 912; and although Fernán González was buried there, no evidence exists of a donation to the monastery that is as extensive as that claimed in the poem. One suspects that the hero's pledge to San Pedro de Arlanza of a fifth of his booty is included to counteract a rival claim made by a document known as the *Votos del conde Fernán González* (Oath of Count Fernan Gonzalez) or *Privilegio de los Votos* (Privilege of the Oaths) that was thought to have been given by the count to the monastery of San Millán de la Cogolla. That document, which survives in three separate charters and is cited in Berceo's *Vida de San Millán de la Cogolla,* pledges that Fernán González and Ramiro I of Navarre will pay the monastery of San Millán de la Cogolla an annual tithe exacted from the cities and villages of Castile and Navarre in celebration of a victory over the Moors at Simancas. This donation, like others of the period, is probably a mid-twelfth-century forgery crafted in response to a decline in San Millán de la Cogolla's revenues. San Pedro de Arlanza, however, was going through a serious economic decline in the mid thirteenth century, and its monks must have believed that they had a clearer claim to the tribute of Fernán González than did San Millán de la Cogolla. Critics agree that the poem was probably written by a monk of the monastery of San Pedro de Arlanza or a member of the secular clergy attached to the monastery.

The *Poema de Fernán González* is a *mester de clerecía* poem of 737 *cuaderna vía* (fourfold way) stanzas. Older epics such as the *Cantar de mio Cid* and the *Cantar de Roncesvalles* (beginning of the thirteenth century, Song of Roncesvalles) are written in the *mester de juglaría* (craft of minstrels). *Juglaría* lines are divided by a caesura, are of variable length, are arranged in stanzas of unequal numbers of lines called *series* (series) or *tiradas* (sequences), and are unified by a single assonantal rhyme. The *clerecía* form, on the other hand, seems to be an adaptation of the preferred strophe of the Latin goliardic (medieval university student) poets, who frequently wrote in stanzas of four thirteen-syllable lines each divided by a caesura into half-lines of seven and six syllables. The goliardic form appears in Castilian Latin poetry at the beginning of the twelfth century. *Cuaderna vía* verse, in contrast, is written in Spanish rather than Latin; each stanza consists of four lines with the same consonantal rhyme; each line comprises fourteen syllables divided by a caesura into equal half-lines; and each half-line bears syllabic stress on its penultimate syllable. Because the *Libro de Alexandre* is generally believed to be the first poem written in *cuaderna vía,* the line is often called *alejandrino* (alexandrine), but it should not be confused with the French alexandrine, which has twelve syllables. Francisco Rico is among the scholars who attribute the *cuaderna vía* adaptation of the goliardic stanza and verse form to poets educated at the University of Palencia; they supposedly considered it superior to the untidy traditional verse of the *mester de juglaría*

because of its regularity and its association with learning and writing.

The *Poema de Fernán González* is not divided into chapters or sections, but the plot has recognizable narrative segments of varying lengths. Stanzas 1 through 70 describe the history of Spain from its beginnings until the fall of the Visigothic kingdom; the early Reconquest is recounted in stanzas 71 through 173. The author maintains that when the pagan Visigoths entered Spain, they were unknowingly acting at the behest of Christ. They were "venturados" (fortunate) in receiving God's favor in spite of their lack of belief, but they were "vnos pueblos loçanos" (a hearty and proud people) who immediately recognized the error of their ways and became Christians: "Resçibyeron los godos del ánima vautysmo, / fueron luz e estrella de tod' el cristianismo; / alçaron cristiandat, vaxaron paganismo: / el cond' Ferrán Gonçález fyzo aquest mismo" (The Goths received baptism for their souls, / they were the light and star of Christendom; / they promoted Christianity and abandoned paganism: / Count Fernán González did the very same). From then on, the Visigoths were the "pueblo escogido" (chosen people).

Despite being the chosen people, the Visigoths suffered a progressive degeneration in their kings from the strength of Recceswinth and Wamba to the weakness of Egica and the early death of Wittiza. The reign of the last Visigothic king, Rodrigo, is characterized by the envy and greed of Wittiza's sons; the disloyalty of his vassal Count don Yllán, who is charged with gathering the tribute of the Moors of Africa but instead paves the way for an invasion; and the blindness of Rodrigo, who follows Yllán's treacherous proposal of disarmament, turning his arms into plowshares and leaving the kingdom defenseless. (The *Poema de Fernán González* does not mention, as other sources do, that Yllán was provoked by the king's rape of his daughter.)

The *Poema de Fernán González* reenacts a central pattern of loss and redemption in which Spain is identified with paradise; a doomed king such as Rodrigo is an Adamic figure cast in opposition to Fernán González, the restorer of the Visigothic line, who is a Christ figure. Successes are followed by disasters because of the personal flaws of kings, who are encouraged in their "sins" by the continual tricks and evil counsel of the devil. Fernán González's youth and strength are likened to the virtues of the Visigothic kings Recceswinth and Wamba; Rodrigo's vain fight against the invasion of the Moors and his death are part of the punishment of his people, which is relived later in the trials of the Asturian kings as they struggle to recover lost territory.

The disunity of Rodrigo's people and their failure to protect Spain against an invader strains for a time the special bond that united the Visigoths to God and leads to a prayer and lamentation over the cruelty of the Moorish invasion. The lament proper (stanzas 105 through 113) derives from the *Ordo commendationis animae* (Prayer of commendation for the soul) for the gravely ill and appears in one form or another in several other poems of the period. The *Ordo commendationis animae* reviews examples of people who suffered loss followed by gain and concludes with the commendation of the soul of the departed to God. The *Poema de Fernán González* does the same but divides the prayer into two parts. The Visigoth's prayer catalogues holy men and women who throughout history have received God's protection when threatened with violence by unbelievers: St. Peter, St. Catherine, Queen Esther, St. Marina, King David, the falsely accused Suzanna, the prophet Daniel, Matthew the Evangelist, the three youths saved from the fiery furnace, and John the Evangelist. The prayer professes that "Somos mucho errados e contra Ty pecamos, / pero cristianos somos e la tu Ley guardamos; / el tu nonbre tenemos, por tuyos nos llamamos, / tu merçet atendemos, otra non esperamos" (We have much erred and sinned against you, / but we are Christians and have kept your commandments; / we bear your name and consider ourselves yours, / we hope for your mercy and await no other). The prayer remains unanswered until the beginning of the section devoted to Fernán González.

Stanzas 114 through 144 review the early history of the Spanish Reconquest from Pelayo, "syeruo del Crÿador" (servant of the Creator), through Fafila, a "muy mal uaron" (very evil man); Alfonso I, "una lança dudada" (a stalwart lance); and Fruela, "que fue malo provado" (who was a known evil man), to Alfonso II *el Casto* (the Chaste), "un rey de grand valor" (a king of great worth). Stanzas 145 through 158 digress to relate the history of the fictional Bernardo del Carpio before concluding with a hymn in praise of Spain. The hymn has its ultimate roots in Isidore of Seville's *Historia Gothorum* (History of the Goths), which includes a similar text. It also owes much to medieval chronicles that incorporate and adapt Isidore's text, among them Lucas de Túy's *Chronicon mundi* and the *De rebus Hispaniae* of Rodrigo Jiménez de Rada, who was bishop of Toledo from 1209 to 1247 and preached a crusade against the Moors in 1211. The encomium begins with a description of Spain's temperate climate, abundance of pasturage, and fruit trees. Then it focuses on the northern section, "la montaña" (the mountainous region), identified with Castile, which is particularly plentiful in cows, sheep, pigs, linen, wool, wax, wheat, and wine, as well as hunting, fishing, mining, and cloth dying. Three attributes distinguish the Spanish above all: their country has been singled out by God as the burial place of the apostle Santiago (St. James the Greater); they have

endured martyrdom for their faith; and their "mesura" (measuredness) or "seso" (thoughtfulness) is world renowned. Castilians are special among Spaniards because of their loyalty to their lords and because they were the beginning of a great enterprise. The placement of the praise of Spain at the end of the section dedicated to the loss of the country underscores both the enormity of the loss and the magnitude of the future gain and also serves as a bridge connecting the story of the Visigoths to the early kings of Asturias and León and to the count of Castile.

Stanzas 159 to 173 return to the Reconquest. Alfonso II dies, and the Christians are unsure who should succeed him: "Eran en muy grran[d] coyta espannones caydos, / duraron muy grran[d] tienpo todos desavenidos, / commo omnes syn sennor, tristes [e] doloridos, / dezian: 'Mas nos valdrrya nunca s[e]er nasçidos'" (The Spanish fell into deep dejection, / they could not agree for long time, / like men without a Lord, sad and afflicted, / they said: "Better that we had not been born"). Two men, the Judges of Castile, are appointed to deal with the interregnum following the king's death; one of them, Nuño Rasura, is an ancestor of Fernán González.

Fernán González's youth and early exploits are recounted in stanzas 174 through 224. Like Wamba, Pelayo, and the Judges of Castile, Fernán González does not hold power early in life. Wamba at first hid to avoid accepting the crown; Pelayo was found in a cave, "fanbryento e lazrado" (hungry and suffering); Nuño Rasura and Laín Calvo were elected late in their lives by the people in a moment of desperation; and Fernán González did not know his own noble lineage. As an infant the future count was kidnapped and brought up by a "povreziello que labraba carbon" (poor coal maker). The prose accounts of the life of Fernán González do not mention this character but have the count raised by an old knight. According to Jean Paul Keller, the idea that he was kidnapped by a coal maker comes from a faulty reading in a French translation of a Latin life of St. Eustace that served as a model for this section of the *Poema de Fernán González*. In the Latin version some "pastores" (shepherds) and "aratores" (plowmen) save Eustace's sons from being killed by a wolf and a lion. The French translation renders *pastores* as "car li boviers" (cowherds); but in one manuscript a French scribe mistakenly copied *car li boviers* as *charbonniers* (coal makers). This scribe or another one crossed out the error and wrote in "car li boviers" above the cancelled words. It is surmised that the error was uncorrected in some other manuscripts of the translation and that one of them was a source for the author of the *Poema de Fernán González*. Whatever the origin of the detail, the poem builds on the concept, characteristic of folklore, of the unlikely

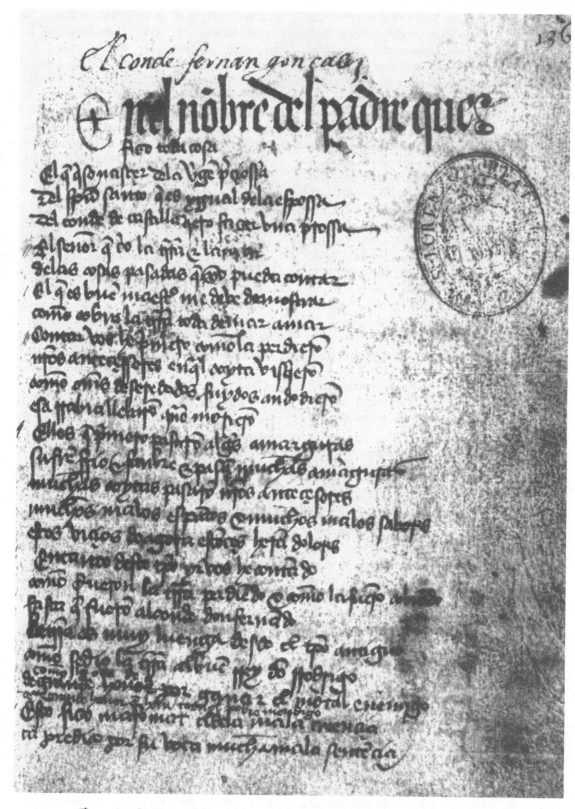

The opening of the Poema de Fernán González *in the only surviving manuscript (Real Biblioteca del Monasterio de El Escorial, MS. IV.b.21, folio 136r)*

beginnings of important leaders and places. For example, the summary of the life of Pelayo emphasizes the parallels between the tentative early development of the Reconquest—"Fyncaron las Asturyas, un pequeño lugar" (The Asturias remained a small territory)—and Castile, which is described as "vn pequeño ryncón" (a small corner) composed of "solo un alcaidía" (only one jurisdiction) that is "pobre e de poca valía" (poor and of little worth). Castile is, however, a breeder of strong men.

From the beginning Fernán González pledges himself to the service of God and his people. His first words in the poem are a continuation of the prayer of the Visigoths: "Señor, Tú me ayuda, que só muy pecador, / que yo saque a Castyella del antigo dolor" (Lord, help me, a great sinner, / that I might to redeem Castile from its ancient grief). The earlier general prayer that reflected on the end of the Visigothic period becomes more specific as Fernán González asks God to help him redeem Castile and pledges his vassalage to God.

Shortly thereafter (stanzas 226 through 245), Fernán González is pursuing a wild boar; the animal takes refuge in a small hermitage at Arlanza where three monks live in poverty. Fernán González refuses to shed blood in a holy place and is rewarded for his piety with a prophecy about his future. This incident may derive from the legend of St. Eustace, in which an important Roman general named Placidus hears a voice during a deer hunt that prophesies that regardless of the tribulations that he may undergo at the hands of the devil, he will be victorious; he immediately converts to Christianity as Eustace. In the *Poema de Fernán González* the prophecy is delivered not by a disembodied voice but by Pelayo, one of the hermits: "Fágote, el buen conde, de tanto sabydor, / que quier' la tu fazienda, guiar el Crÿador, / vençrás tod' el poder del moro Almozor" (I will let you know, good count, / that God wishes to guide your efforts, / you will completely vanquish the Moor Almanzor [al-Mansur 'Ali]). After continuing in this vein for several stanzas, Pelayo implores the count not to forget Arlanza in victory: "Mas ruégote, amigo, e pýdote de grado, / que quando tú ovyeres el canpo arrancado, / véngasete en mientes d'est' convento lazrado, / e non se te olvide el pobre ospedado" (But I plead and ask you plainly, / that when you have vanquished your foes, / you remember this impoverished monastery, / and not forget our humble hospitality). In response, the count promises to give one-fifth of his gains in battle to Arlanza. As a vassal of the king of León, the count is compelled to give the monarch a fifth of his spoils; the pledge to give a fifth of the booty to Arlanza marks a symbolic breaking of his bond of vassalage to the king and foreshadows his later anguish at

having to kiss the king's hand as a pledge of vassalage: Castile should bow only to God.

Fernán González kills the invading King Sancho of Navarre during the battle of Era Degollada (stanzas 279 through 324) and then slays the count of Tolosa, who comes to avenge his lord (stanzas 325 through 377). In short order a new invasion by Almanzor begins (stanzas 378 through 386). That invasion provokes the count's second visit to Arlanza, where he asks for God's aid in a prayer that again recalls the earlier supplication of the Visigoths (stanzas 388 through 398). This time, however, like a nobleman asking his lord for protection against a foe, his petition is for God to intervene in the fight against Almanzor at Hacinas on behalf of the Castilians. The monk Pelayo, who has died and become a saint in heaven, and San Millán answer the prayer in a dream. San Pelayo tells the count that as a vassal of God he will have the aid of Santiago Matamoros (St. James the Moorslayer), of Pelayo himself, of San Millán, and of the host of heaven. Another otherworldly voice, which turns out to be San Millán's, confirms the prophecy and directs the disposition of the count's men down to the last detail. The battle seems to be almost lost when Fernán González appeals to heaven in prayer once more. A voice, presumably that of San Millán, responds: "Ferrando de Castiella, oy te creçe grand' bando" (Ferdinand of Castile, today your side is greatly enlarged). Thereupon Santiago and his host join the fight.

Through this association with Santiago the poet relates the battle of Hacinas to the continuing struggle between God and the devil that informs the poem and that, as his audience knows, will culminate in the founding of Castile. The scene also further connects Arlanza to Fernán González through the interment of the Castilian dead at the monastery and the count's promise to join them there when he, too, is laid to rest. (Although the burial of the laity within the precincts of a church was prohibited in the sixth century, the practice had become common in Castile's churches and monasteries by the thirteenth century.) Around 1275 the body of the Cid was moved to a more prominent space inside the church of the monastery of Cardeña; the remains of Wamba were taken from Pampliega to Burgos in the second half of the thirteenth century; and Fernán González's body was probably moved into the chapter house behind the altar of the church of San Pedro de Arlanza in 1274 (it was moved to the nearby Colegiata de Covarrubias [Collegiate Church of Covarrubias] in the nineteenth century). With these relocations the monasteries were probably seeking to increase donations from those who wished to be buried close to relics of ancient heroes and saints.

Forced to attend the *cortes* (assembly) of León, even though he does not want to swear fealty to King Sancho Ordóñez, Fernán González sells the king a horse that belonged to Almanzor and a hawk for a thousand marks. He tricks the monarch into agreeing that the sum will increase exponentially each day that it is not paid. Fernán González is then himself tricked by the queen of León, Teresa. She is the sister of Sancho of Navarre, whom Fernán González had killed in the battle of Era Degollada. She offers marriage to her niece, Sancha, as a way of settling accounts and avoiding a feud. The count meets with Sancho of Navarre's son, García of Navarre, at Cirueña and realizes that Teresa and García are actually seeking revenge. He seeks refuge in a church, but García forcibly removes him and imprisons him in chains in Castroviejo. A Lombard count on a pilgrimage to Santiago de Compostela visits Fernán González in jail and intercedes with Princess Sancha on his behalf. The Lombard count's praise of Fernán González's worthiness causes Sancha to fall in love with him sight unseen. After obtaining a promise of marriage from Fernán González, she secretly frees him from the prison and carries him on her back because he is chained–a common test of a heroine's strength in folklore. On their way to Castile they meet an evil archpriest; Sancha tricks the archpriest into thinking that she will have sex with him, and she and the count kill the naked cleric with his own knife. This incident is more worthy of French *fabliaux* (short narrative pieces, often of a sexual nature) than of an epic poem.

The marriage of Fernán González and Sancha was an actual event, and the counts of Castile eventually became kings through their descent from Sancha. But the incidents leading up to the marriage are pure fiction, as are some of the characters involved. From a literary point of view, however, the episode allows the poet to introduce the theme of love into his narrative. According to Itzíar López Guil, editor of a 2001 edition of the *Poema de Fernán González,* Fernán González goes through the four stages of the courtly lover: from *fenhedor* (timid lover) to *pregador* (supplicant), *entendedor* (suitor), and, finally, to *drutz* (chosen favorite). The scene is also influenced by the exempla (exemplary tales) and the French *fabliaux* with their deep folkloric roots.

After the marriage, García of Navarre invades Castile. Fernán González captures him but releases him when Sancha intercedes for her uncle. The count fights the Moors at Sahagun, then returns to León and asks the king for payment for the horse and hawk. Three years have passed, and the amount has grown so huge that the only way the king can redeem his debt is by ceding Castile to the count. The episode is one of the best known in the poem, but it has no basis in fact. The historical Sancho Ordóñez was too fat to hunt with a hawk or to ride a horse. W. J. Entwistle discovered an example of the redemption of a people at the cost of a single horse in Jordanes's *Getica,* a sixth-century history of the Goths, and L. P. Harvey and David Hook revealed the folkloric roots of the motif in a tale about one man's desire for another man's hunting animals leading to a ruinous bargain.

The poem limps on through further battles with the Moors and with García of Navarre at Valpirre before breaking off because of the manuscript's mutilation. In his 1970 edition of the *Poema de Fernán González* Alonso Zamora Vicente hypothesizes that the oral song on which the work is based ended with the independence of Castile from León and that the author of the written version added further episodes. One can only speculate as to the true nature of the lost ending. María Eugenia Lacarra believes that the logical conclusion of a text that seeks to relate the beginnings of the kingdom of Castile to the deeds of Fernán González and, through him, to the monastery of San Pedro de Arlanza had to end with Fernán González's death and his interment in the monastery. The connection of the poem with the monastery has led J. B. Avalle Arce to call it a hagiographical text and Giorgio Perissinotto to consider it an ecclesiastical epic that co-opts the deeds of the count for the benefit of the monastery. By the middle of the thirteenth century, when the poem was probably composed, the Reconquest had advanced to Iberia's southern shores under Fernando III, and only Granada remained as an independent Muslim principality. This movement of the frontier, first to Toledo and then to Cordova and Seville, led to a progressive decline in the influence and importance of the northern monasteries as royal munificence shifted south to support the military orders, new religious foundations, and the resettlement of the freshly conquered lands. *Clerecía* works such as the *Poema de Fernán González* may have been a propagandistic attempt by clever monks to recover the importance that the monasteries had enjoyed in the cultural and political life of León, Navarre, and Castile and to stake a claim on their continued patronage by the Castilian Crown. The *Poema de Fernán González* not only espouses the continuity, propounded by historians such as Lucas de Túy and Rodrigo Jiménez de Rada, between the Visigothic kings and the Christians who undertook the Reconquest but also links the Reconquest to the intercession of San Pelayo, a monk of Arlanza, who makes God's protection of Castile rely in part on the monastery's intercession.

The triumphs of Fernán González may also have been meant to foreshadow the total reconquest of Castilian territory from the Moors, a feat that may have been thought to have been achieved when the *Poema de Fernán González* was created. Fernando III, who died in 1252, claimed in his will to have conquered Murcia and Granada and to have received the homage of their Moorish lords, in effect completing the Reconquest. In 1246, before taking Seville, Fernando had the tomb of Fernán González opened and perhaps took a relic of the count with him on his final campaigns.

The *cuaderna vía* stanza of the *mester de clerecía* has been largely ignored since the sixteenth century because of the very feature that made it popular during the Spanish Middle Ages: its rigidity. Although it can be supple in the hands of a skilled poet such as Berceo, it can be monotonously repetitive to modern ears. In addition, the sections of the *Poema de Fernán González* are not artfully joined, either because of the poet's limitations or because of the corruption of the text. The virtual disappearance of the *cuaderna vía* stanza and of the *Poema de Fernán González* in particular did not mean that the exploits of Fernán González were unknown. In the fifteenth, sixteenth, and seventeenth centuries the life of the first count of Castile provided material for many ballads and for works such as the anonymous *Estoria del noble caballero el conde Fernán González con la muerte de los siete infantes de Lara* (1511, History of the Noble Knight Count Fernán González with the Death of the Seven Crown Princes of Lara), Gonzalo de Arredondo's *Vida rimada de Fernán González* (Rhymed Life of Fernán González) in the early sixteenth century, and Lope de Vega's play *El conde Fernán González* (1627, Count Fernán González). The legend has also served as the basis for many modern works.

In the eighteenth and nineteenth centuries interest in folklore and the epic and the search for the origins of the nation-state and the roots of national character brought renewed attention to the *Poema de Fernán González*. Much of the early critical labor was concerned with refining the text of the work and providing historical information about its main character. The poem was published by Bartolomé José Gallardo in the first volume of his *Ensayo de una biblioteca española de libros raros y curiosos* (Essay on a Spanish Library of Rare and Curious Books) in 1863 and by Florencio Janer in volume fifty-seven of the *Biblioteca de autores españoles* in 1864, but it had its first serious presentation with the publication of C. Carroll Marden's edition in 1904. Ramón Menéndez Pidal's *Reliquias de la poesía española* (1951) includes the *Poema de Fernán González* with other texts in which Fernán González's story appears. Paleographic and facsimile editions were published by John S. Geary in 1987, José Manuel Ruiz Asencio in 1989, and López Guil, whose text includes both a paleographic and a critical edition, in 2001. Among critical editions, those of Zamora Vicente and Juan Victorio (1981) disagree the

most sharply: Zamora Vicente thinks that the verse of the *Poema de Fernán González* is irregular because of the influence of an earlier folk epic on which it was based, while Victorio believes that the metrical regularity of the poem was altered by careless copyists and attempts to restore it.

References:

Samuel G. Armistead, "La perspectiva histórica del *Poema de Fernán González*," *Papeles de Son Armadans*, 21 (1961): 9–18;

Gonzalo de Arredondo, *Vida Rimada de Fernan Gonzalez*, edited by Mercedes Vaquero, Exeter Hispanic Texts, no. 44 (Exeter, U.K.: University of Exeter Press, 1906);

J. B. Avalle Arce, "El *Poema de Fernán González:* Clerecía y juglaría," *Philological Quarterly*, 51 (1972): 60–73;

Matthew Bailey, *The* Poema del Cid *and the* Poema de Fernán González*: The Transformation of an Epic Tradition* (Madison, Wis.: Hispanic Seminary of Medieval Studies, 1992);

Bailey, "Las últimas hazañas del conde Fernán González en la *Estoria de España*: La contribución alfonsí," *La corónica*, 24, no. 2 (1996): 31–40;

Isidro G. Bango Torviso, "El espacio para enterramientos privilegiados en la arquitectura medieval española," *Anuario del Departamento de Historia y Teoría del Arte*, 4 (1992): 93–132;

J. G. Casalduero, "Sobre la composición del *Poema de Fernán González*," *Anuario de Estudios Medievales*, 5 (1969): 181–206;

Wilfredo Casanova O., "El conde Ferran Gonçales de los fechos grranados," *Boletín del Instituto de Filología de la Universidad de Chile*, 22 (1971): 27–36;

Vera Castro Lingl, "The Count's Wife in *La condesa traidora*, the *Poema de Fernán González*, and the *Romanz del infant Garcia:* How Many Sanchas?" *Bulletin of Hispanic Studies*, 73 (1996): 371–378;

Louis Chalon, *L'Histoire et l'épopée castillane au moyen age* (Paris: Champion, 1976), pp. 389–475;

René Cotrait, *L'Histoire et poésie: Le comte Fernán González. Recherches sur la tradition gonzalienne dans l'historiographie et la littérature des origines au* Poema (Grenoble: Allier, 1977);

Alan Deyermond, *Epic Poetry and the Clergy* (London: Tamesis, 1968);

W. J. Entwistle, "The Liberation of Castile," *Modern Language Review*, 19 (1924): 471–472;

Luciano Formisano, "Cuaderna via ajuglarada nel *Poema de Fernán González*," *Actas del Congreso Internacional Murcia, 5–10 mar. 1984*, in *La lengua y la literatura en tiempos de Alfonso X*, edited by Fernándo Carmona and Francisco J. Flores (Murcia: Dept.

de Letras Románicas, Facultad de Letras, Universidad de Murcia, 1985), pp. 181–194;

A. M. Garrido Moraga, *Concordancias del* Poema de Fernán González (Málaga: Universitat Autònoma de Barcelona: Universidad de Málaga, 1987);

Garrido Moraga, *La estructura del poema de Fernán González* (Rome: Bulzoni, 1987);

John S. Geary, "The Death of the Count: Novelesque Invention in the *Crónica de Fernán González*," *Bulletin of Hispanic Studies*, 69 (1992): 321–334;

Geary, *Formulaic Diction in the* Poema de Fernán González *and the* Mocedades de Rodrigo: *A Computer-Aided Analysis* (Madrid: José Porrúa Turanzas, 1980);

Geary, "The 'tres monjes' of the *Poema de Fernán González*: Myth and History," *La corónica*, 19, no. 2 (1991): 24–42;

E. Michael Gerli, "The *Ordo Commendationis Animae* and the Cid Poet," *Modern Language Notes*, 95, no. 2 (1980): 436–441;

José Gómez Pérez, "Una crónica de Fernán González, escrita por orden del emperador Carlos V," *Revista de Archivos, Bibliotecas y Museos*, 64 (1958): 551–581;

Fernando Gómez Redondo, "La materia épica en la *Atalaya de las coronicas* del Arcipreste de Talavera: El caso de Fernán González," in *Actas del Coloquio Internacional organizado por el Departamento de Filologia Espanyola de la Universitat de Valencia, celebrado en Valencia los dias 29, 30 y 31 de oct. de 1990, Historias y ficciones: Coloquio sobre la literatura del siglo XV*, edited by Rafael Beltrán Llavador, José Luis Canet Vallés, Josep Lluís Sirera, and Evangelina Rodriguez (Valencia: Department of Filologia Espanyola, Universidad de Valencia, 1992), pp. 57–71;

L. P. Harvey and David Hook, "The Affair of the Horse and Hawk in the *Poema de Fernán González*," *Modern Language Review*, 77 (1982): 840–847;

José Hernando Pérez, "Nuevos datos para el estudio del *Poema de Fernán González*," *Boletín de la Real Academia Española*, 66 (1986): 135–152;

Jean Paul Keller, *The Poet's Myth of Fernán González* (Potomac, Md.: Scripta Humanistica, 1990);

John E. Keller, "El misterioso origen de Fernán González," *Nueva Revista de Filología Hispánica*, 10 (1956): 41–44;

Keller, "The Structure of the *Poema de Fernán González*," *Hispanic Review*, 25 (1957): 235–246;

María Eugenia Lacarra, "La mujer ejemplar en tres textos épicos castellanos," *Cuadernos de Investigación Filológica*, 14 (1988): 5–20;

Lacarra, "*El significado histórico del* Poema de Fernán González," *Studi Ispanici* (1979): 9–41;

John Lihani, "Las manifestaciones de la técnica juglaresca en el *Poema de Fernán González*," in *Actas del I Congreso Internacional sobre la juglaresca*, edited by Manuel Criado de Val (Madrid: EDI-6, 1986), pp. 239–245;

Manuel Márquez-Sterling, *Fernán González, First Count of Castile: The Man and the Legend* (Jackson: University Press of Mississippi, 1980);

Georges Martin, *Les Juges de Castille: Mentalités et discours historique dans l'Espagne médiévale*, Annexes des *Cahiers de linguistique hispanique médiévale*, 6 (Paris: Klincksieck, 1992);

Josefina Nagore de Zand, "La alabanza de España en el *Poema de Fernan González* y en las crónicas latino-medievales," *Incipit*, 7 (1987): 35–67; 9 (1989): 13–31;

Justo Pérez de Urbel, *El conde Fernán González* (Burgos: Institución Fernán González, 1970);

Giorgio Perissinotto, *Reconquista y literatura medieval: Cuatro ensayos* (Potomac, Md.: Scripta Humanistica, 1987), pp. 53–87;

Lawrence Rich, "Fernán González en la *Primera Crónica General* y la función paradigmática del texto," in *Selected Papers of the Fifth Biennial Northeast Regional Meeting of the American Association of Teachers of Spanish and Portuguese: Reflections on the Conquest of America Five Hundred Years After*, edited by F. William Forbes, Faith Teresa Méndez, Mary Anne Vetterling, Barbara H. Wing, and Elena Poniatowska (Durham: University of New Hampshire, 1996), pp. 217–229;

Rich, "Kings and Counts: Pragmatics and the *Poema de Fernán González* in the *Primera crónica general*," *La corónica*, 25, no. 2 (1997): 103–113;

Francisco Rico, "La clerecía del mester," *Hispanic Review*, 53, no. 1 (1985): 1–23; no. 2 (1985): 127–150;

Connie L. Scarborough, "Characterization in the *Poema de Fernán González*: Portraits of the Hero and the Heroine," in *Proceedings of the 1981 SEMA Meeting, Literary and Historical Perspectives of the Middle Ages*, edited by Patricia W. Cummins, Patrick W. Connor, Charles W. Connell, Raymond J. Cormier, and Gatch Milton (Morgantown: West Virginia University Press, 1982), pp. 52–65;

José Luis Senra Gabriel y Galán, "La escultura románica y sus problemas de interpretación: El llamado sepulcro 'de Mudarra' procedente del monasterio de San Pedro de Arlanza," *Archivo español de arte*, 72, no. 285 (1999): 25–38;

Senra Gabriel y Galán, "Peregrinaciones y reliquias en las rutas hacia Compostela: Hérores y santos a la vera del camino," in *Peregrinación y santuarios en los archivos de la Iglesia: Santoral hispano-mozárabe en las diócesis de España. Actas del XV Congreso de la Asociación celebrado en Santiago de Compostela, 13 al 17 sep-*

tiembre 1999, 2 volumes, edited by Agustín Hevia Ballina, Memoria Ecclesiae, nos. 18–19 (Oviedo: Asociación de Archiveros de la Iglesia en España, 2001), I: 277–292;

K. Sneyders de Vogel, "Le *Poema de Fernán González* et la *Crónica general,*" *Neophilologus,* 8 (1922): 161–180;

Fernando de Toro Garland, "El Arcipreste, protagonista literario del medievo espanol: El caso del 'mal Arcipreste' del Fernán González," in *El Arcipreste de Hita: El libro, el autor, la tierra, la epoca. Actas del I Congreso Internacional sobre el Arcipreste de Hita,* edited by Manuel Criado de Val (Barcelona: S.E.R.E.S.A, 1973), pp. 327–336;

Toro Garland, "Las citas de Almanzor, una clave del problema cronológico del *Poema de Fernán González,*" in *Actas del I Congreso Internacional sobre la juglaresca, La juglaresca,* edited by Manuel Criado de Val (Madrid: EDI-6, 1986), pp. 229–238;

Mercedes Vaquero, "Spanish Epic of Revolt," in *Epic and Epoch: Essays on the Interpretation and History of a Genre,* edited by Steven M. Oberhelman, Van Kelly, and Richard J. Golsan (Lubbock: Texas Tech University Press, 1994), pp. 146–163;

Alexandre Veiga, "*El Poema de Fernán González:* Sobre el más problemático texto de clerecía y sus problemas de edición crítica," in *Iberia cantat: Estudios sobre poesía hispánica medieval,* edited by Juan Casas-Rigall and Eva M. Díaz Martínez (Santiago de Compostela: Universidade de Santiago de Compostela, 2002), pp. 187–212;

Juan Victorio, "*Poema de Fernán González* et *Mocedades de Rodrigo,*" *Marche Romane,* 23–24 (1973–1974): 151–155;

Beverly West, *Epic, Folk, and Christian Traditions in the* Poema de Fernán González (Madrid: J. Porrúa Turanzas / Potomac, Md.: Studia Humanitatis, 1983).

Razón de amor con los denuestos del agua y el vino

(1230 – 1250)

Enzo Franchini
University of Zurich

Manuscript: The sole extant manuscript is Bibliothèque Nationale, Paris, MS. lat. 3576, folios 124r–126r.

First publications: Alfred Morel-Fatio, "Textes castillans inédits du XIIIe siècle," *Romania,* 16 (1887): 364–382; Ramón Menéndez Pidal, "*Razón de amor con los denuestos del agua y el vino,*" *Revue Hispanique,* 13 (1905): 602–618; republished, with corrections, as "Siesta de abril," in his *Crestomatía del español medieval,* volume 1, third edition, revised by Rafael Lapesa and María Soledad de Andrés (Madrid: Gredos, 1982), pp. 92–99.

Standard edition: Enzo Franchini, *El manuscrito, la lengua y el ser literario de la Razón de amor* (Madrid: Consejo Superior de Investigaciones Científicas, 1993).

Edition in modern Spanish: Leo Spitzer, *Estilo y estructura en la literatura española* (Barcelona: Crítica, 1980), pp. 81–102.

Edition in English: Charles C. Stebbins, "The *Razón de amor*: An Old Spanish Lyrical Poem of the 13th Century," *Allegorica,* 2, no. 1 (1977): 144–171.

The anonymous 264-verse poem *Razón de amor con los denuestos del agua y el vino* (1230–1250, Treatise on Love with the Debate between Water and Wine), generally known simply as the *Razón de amor,* was discovered in 1887 by the French Hispanist Alfred Morel-Fatio in the middle of the manuscript MS. lat. 3576 in the Bibliothèque Nationale in Paris. This manuscript is the only known witness of the *Razón de amor,* which occupies folios 124r through 126r. Folios 1 through 122 comprise a set of Latin Sunday sermons; folio 123 is a set of Hispano-Latin imprecations against bad weather from the early thirteenth century; folios 126v through 128v consist of a confessor's manual in Navarro-Aragonese, *Los diez mandamientos* (circa 1275, The Ten Commandments); and folios 129 through 168 are a collection of saints' day sermons in Latin. The two Latin sermon collections are in the same southern French copyist's hand and are datable to the end of the

twelfth century or the beginning of the thirteenth century; the three short Spanish texts in the middle were copied at a later date. In contrast to the majority of Spanish debate poems of the twelfth and thirteenth centuries, such as the *Disputa del alma y el cuerpo* (Dispute between the Soul and the Body) and the *Elena y María* (Elena and María), which are incomplete, the *Razón de amor* has been preserved intact.

The poem is composed in rhymed couplets of mostly nine-syllable lines. The language is close to that of Gonzalo de Berceo and of the *Libro de Alexandre* (Book of Alexander) and, therefore, datable to the second quarter of the thirteenth century. Enzo Franchini's thorough analysis of the language in his edition of the work (1993) identifies it as essentially Castilian, with the majority of non-Castilian forms probably a residue of Aragonese. The site of composition was assuredly within the realm of Aragon, whose dialect is present most unmistakably in words in rhyme position; the features of that dialect were multiplied and distributed more uniformly through the text as a subsequent scribe gave free rein to his native oral habits. The maiden's speeches, which are the more-lyrical passages in the poem, are stylized renditions of tropes of Galician-Portuguese, the tongue that became Iberia's lyrical language par excellence, but they are prompted by their literary sources and have nothing to do with the birthplace of the poet or the audience for which he composed his text. The mention of the village of Moros in verse 264 supports the hypothesis that the poet came from a frontier zone between Castile and Aragon, and the Latin verbs *scripsit* (he wrote) and *feçit* (he made) in the *explicit* (formula marking the end of the text) leads one to think of the Lupus (Lope) de Moros credited in the closing lines as the author of the poem, rather than as merely the copyist of this particular manuscript.

The poem begins with a first-person autobiographical prologue in the style of the Provençal *vidas* (troubadour biographies):

Qui triste tiene su coraçón
benga oyr esta razón.
Odrá razón acabada,
feyta d'amor e bien rymada.
Vn escolar la Rimó
que sie[m]pre dueñas amó.
Mas ssie[m]pre ouo tryança
en Alemanja y en Fra[n]çia;
moró mucho en Lombardía
por aprender cortesía.

(Whoever is sad of heart
Come hear these reflections.
He will hear a thoughtful account
Composed of love and fine rhyme.
A scholar composed it
who always loved the ladies.
Yet, he always embraced refinement
in Germany and France
and dwelt in Lombardy
to learn courtesy.)

In April, after a full meal in the midday heat, the speaker, a young cleric, is sitting under an olive tree in a garden of Edenic beauty. In front of him is an apple tree whose branches bear two goblets; the lower one brims with a fine wine that the mistress of the orchard placed there as a love potion for her beloved to drink on his arrival, while the upper vessel holds cool water from a spring that wells up at the foot of the tree.

Because of the heat, the speaker doffs some of his clothes and stretches out in the grass. In a reverie he sees himself draw near an unquenchable wellspring and is amazed at the refreshingly cool ambience that can be felt for a hundred paces around it. Within it is a spreading carpet of flowers that perfumes the air with otherworldly scents. He takes a refreshing draft from the fountain and plucks an especially lovely flower, which inspires him to sing of *fin amor* (refined love), as in the French tradition. But before he can do so, a damsel appears in the orchard, dazzling him with her beauty and noble countenance. A formal set piece follows: a description of a lovely girl composed in strict accord with the dictates of medieval rhetoric but with specifically Hispanic components—hair cut short above her ears, black eyes—that do not appear in poetry from north of the Pyrenees.

The maiden is gathering flowers and singing a classic lover's lament and panegyric to her beloved. She bemoans the absence of the object of her affections, sighs over his scholarly ability and gentle ways, and expresses jealousy and fear that he will be stolen by a noble lady but also an unshakable confidence in her own beauty. At the conclusion of her monologue the speaker reveals that he has been eavesdropping; but he does so with such courteous refinement that the girl has

none of the apprehension about sexual importuning commonly felt by the shepherdesses in Provençal and goliardic *pastourelles* (short narrative poems in which a knight relates his attempt to seduce a shepherdess). He gets up, takes the maiden's hand, and reclines with her at the foot of the olive tree. She discloses that she has fallen in love with an unknown youth whose virtues have been recounted to her by his envoy. The narrator asks whether she has received any love tokens; her answer leads to a scene of *anagnorisis* (recognition) between these apparent strangers. Overjoyed, the maiden kisses the scholar on the mouth and eyes and launches into a Galician-Portuguese *cantiga d'amigo* (woman's song about her beloved) with the hallmark parallelistic structure of such compositions:

¡Dios señor, a ti loa[do]
quant conozco meu amado.
Agora é tod bien [comigo]
quant conozco meo amjgo!

(Lord God, be praised
now that I met my beloved.
Now I enjoy all happiness
now that I met my beloved!)

After an interlude of tender exchanges, the maiden assures the cleric of her love and retires because of the late hour. The narrator's attempt to fall asleep is frustrated by another reverie or dream vision in which a white dove with a tiny bell tied to its leg approaches the fountain. Medieval falconers attached bells to the legs of their birds and sent them to chase doves; the bell became a symbol of the "love chase" in courtly poetry, with the falcon representing the man pursuing the woman, symbolized by the dove. Here the dove takes on the attribute of the predator, symbolizing the Hispanic maiden's seduction of the cleric. Frightened by the presence of the speaker, the dove instead flies up into the apple tree and bathes in the vessel of cool water. Some of the water splashes into the goblet of wine, triggering a playful verbal brawl between the two liquids. The debaters alternate between insults and boasts, the water using skillfully measured arguments and the wine making impulsive retorts. The poem itself then voices a demand in the voice of a *juglar* (minstrel) not unlike that in the closing lines of the *Cantar de mio Cid* (circa 1200, Song of My Lord; translated as *Poem of the Cid,* 1879): "Mi Razón aquí la fino, / e mandat-nos dar uino" (Here I end my account, / so order wine for us). The poem concludes with a Latin *explicit* of a type common in medieval works; but the Spanish poet replaces the usual *vivat* (may he live) with *bibat* (may he drink), thus converting the closing lines into a waggish play on words in the spirit of the goliards:

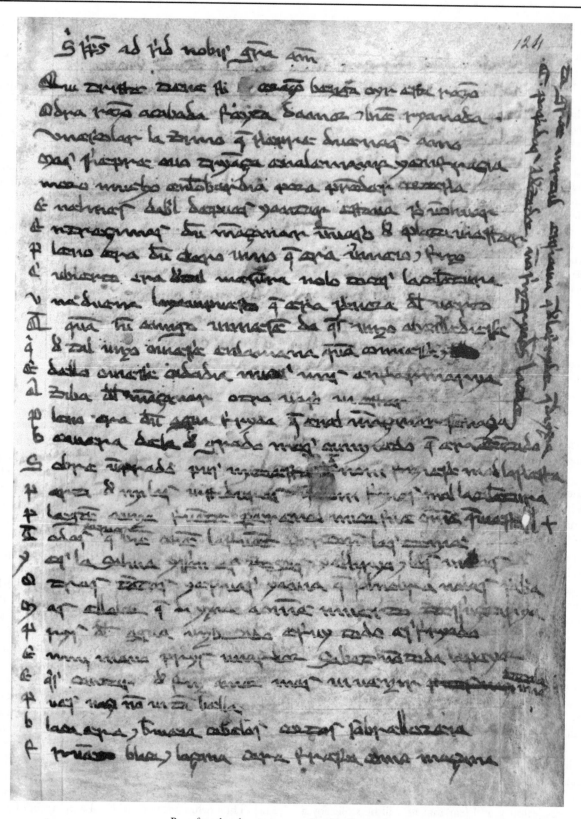

Pages from the sole extant manuscript of the Razón de amor con los denuestos del agua y el vino
(Bibliothèque Nationale, Paris, MS. lat. 3576, folios 124r and 125v)

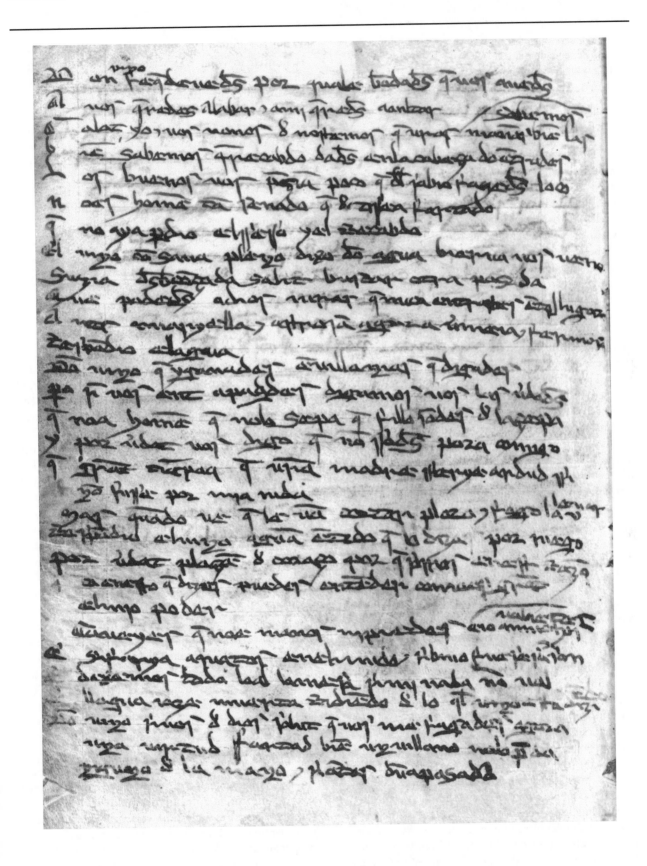

Qui me scripsit scribat,
se[m]per cum domino bibat.
Lupus me feçit, de Moros.

(Let the one who wrote me keep writing,
And let him always drink with the Lord.
Lupus from Moros created me.)

The debate between water and wine is an adaptation of the twelfth-century Latin poem *Denudata veritate* (Naked Truth), which is preserved in two manuscripts in Paris, one in Oxford, and among the compositions in the celebrated *Carmina Burana* (Songs of Beuern) in the Bayerische Staatsbibliothek in Munich. Matching features between the *Razón de amor* and the *Denudata veritate,* a poem saturated with the spirit of the goliards, are so many and so clear that no doubt remains about their relationship. While vernacular versions of the water/wine debate exist in German, Czech, and Basque, among the nine surviving versions in Romance languages–Spanish, French, Italian, and Rhaeto-Romanic–the *Razón de amor* is the oldest known.

The sources of the lovers' tryst in the garden are less certain. The lyrical opening scenes betray a deep familiarity with the poetic repertoire, from which the poet has drawn a generic rhetoric that he has then personalized and polished. He clearly wants to show off his learning and expansive literary tastes; one can detect an undercurrent of pride in the refinement that, he thinks, sets him apart both from knights and from coarse peasant types. That sense of superiority runs through the first part of the poem as a leitmotiv.

Alicia C. de Ferraresi and Dorothy Clotelle Clark believe that Provençal troubadour poetry is the dominant influence on the poem, while Daniel N. Cárdenas finds an intimate association with the Arthurian tradition. Silvestro Fiore proposes that the structure of the *Razón de amor* is taken from the Provençal *tenso* (debate song), a formal arrangement ultimately derived from Arabic and Mesopotamian poetic conventions. Colbert I. Nepaulsingh argues that the *Razón de amor* owes much to the Song of Songs; but this well-loved biblical text left echoes in almost all medieval love lyric, both Latin and vernacular. Margo De Ley has enumerated some of the similarities between the prologue and the Provençal *vida* and *razó* (explanation of the circumstances that gave rise to a poem); the name of the latter is borrowed by the Spanish poet to baptize his work a *"razón,"* and the period of popularity of the *razó* meshes with codicological and linguistic evidence for the dating of the work. Margaret Van Antwerp points out that the *Razón de amor* is laced with symbolic motifs drawn from popular folk lyrics: the cool water; the *alborada* (song of the rendezvous of lovers at dawn); the lovers' immersion in a refreshing, cleansing, transforming bath; and the bird.

What is known of popular medieval Castilian lyric is limited to what was written down beginning in the fifteenth century, but these themes are found in texts from earlier times, such as the *kharjas* and the Galician-Portuguese *cantigas d'amigo,* that are accepted as learned versions of popular poetry. Given the linguistic evidence, one can hardly doubt that the studiously artful Galician-Portuguese lyric left its mark on the *Razón de amor.* The lyrical segments, which are placed in the mouth of the maiden, follow the content and to some extent the form of the *cantiga d'amigo* genre. One could also argue that the poet had some acquaintance with schoolmen's treatises on love such as Andreas Capellanus's *De amore* (circa 1185, On Love) and Boncompagno da Signa's *Rota Veneris* (circa 1205, The Wheel of Venus). Finally, it would be hard to overlook the influence of the Latin poetry of the goliards. It is plausible that the poet, like his speaker, spent some time at French, German, or Lombard universities, where he came to know the milieu and Latin compositions of those itinerant scholars and may even have become one of them. Although the first part of the *Razón de amor* is an artful pastiche, it is not a mere jumble of materials: it was composed by a craftsman who fused his disparate elements into an original creation. The forms may be venerable, but the sense is new–a goal of all medieval poetry.

While the first generation of critics after the discovery of the manuscript uniformly contended that the work is made up of two autonomous poems clumsily cobbled together by an inept scribe, the opposite view has been steadily gaining ground since Leo Spitzer published his analysis of the text in 1950. As early as 1905 Ramón Menéndez Pidal pointed to the absence of any dividing line that cuts "the two halves apart with scissors," because the vessels of water and wine, whose accidental mixing provides the impetus for the debate, are present from the outset. The goblets, therefore, are not incidental to the idealized garden but are an integral part of its design. The dualism of water and wine is one of several pairs, along with the apple and olive trees, standing up and lying down, the hot day and the cold fountain, and the maiden and her suspected courtly rival.

The Edenic garden, the apple tree, the fountain, the water, the wine, and the white dove have prompted starkly different interpretations. Alfred Jacob holds that the *Razón de amor* is a mystical work imbued with Christian symbolism; Enrique de Rivas sees it as heretical propaganda; and André Michalski reads it as a description of an initiatory rite into the mysteries of alchemy, which celebrated the distillation of alcohol as a purified essence of all matter. Critics such as Spitzer, de Ferraresi, and Olga Tudorica Impey, in contrast, accept the work as what it claims to be: a poem that ponders love in courtly terms. Franchini is convinced that the *Razón de amor* deals with two conflicting kinds of love: *amor purus* (chaste love) and *amor mixtus* (physical love); the speaker personifies the *fin amador* (refined suitor) who aspires to the ideal of *amor purus* and rejects *amor mixtus*. This stance contrasts with the goliardic lyrics and the Provençal *pastourelles,* where rape is a frequent outcome of male desire. Capellanus's *De amore* explains these two antithetical conceptions of love using the same metaphor of water and wine as is found in the *Razón de amor.*

The speaker is an exemplar of foreign fashions, but the maiden is of Iberian extraction. Part of the charm of the encounter between these lovers is the confrontation of two literary types who represent distinct geographical and ideological worlds. The song of *fin amor* that the opening verses of the poem herald is never voiced; just as the speaker is about to launch into it, the girl appears and makes him fumble in his intent, just as the sudden apparition of the white dove prevents him from falling asleep at the transition to the second part of the poem:

> e quis cantar de fin amor.
> Mas ui uenir una doncela.
> (And I wished to sing of fine love.
> But I saw a maiden approach.)

> Por uerdat, quisieram adormjr
> mas u<n>na palomela uj.
> (In truth I wanted to fall asleep
> But I saw a dove.)

His song is silenced, while hers is delivered "en alta voz" (in full voice). Furthermore, the speaker picks "una flor, sabet, non toda la peyor" (a flower, and not the humblest one), indicating his refined tastes; the maiden, however, feels no need to make choices: accepting uncritically all that nature has to offer, she picks "flores" (flowers) without qualification and in the plural. The speaker, a picky suitor, is cosmopolitan, international, and a representative of a notion of love whose origins lie beyond the Pyrenees in Germany, France, and Lombardy, while the ideological world of the maiden is that of Spain, named in her song as the lands reconquered by Christian Iberia: "Más amaría contigo estar / que toda España mandar" (More would I love being with you, / Than ruling all of Spain).

Another signal of the distance between the world of courtly love and that of the maiden are the gifts the two lovers exchange. The love tokens given by the speaker are "alfayas" (gems), the kind of gifts recommended to the courtly lover by Capellanus in the *De amore;* the damsel, despite her noble lineage, bestows on

her unknown suitor a simple sash, more symbolic of her self-surrender than of material worth–a present that shows up innumerable times in the *cantigas d'amigo* and in traditional Hispanic folk lyric. It is also telling that the maiden is jealous of a "cortesa" (courtly) rival but believes that her beauty can overpower the pretty gestures of the woman of courtly ways. Thus, the Spanish girl's thoughts are turned toward physical attractiveness and not toward the social and moral attainments of courtliness. The description of the maiden focuses on her flawless body and sumptuous clothing. There is no mention of the speaker's appearance, only of his youth, irreproachable behavior, and personal attainments such as reading, writing, and singing. The girl takes the lead in their amorous encounter, inverting the typical roles of a courtly couple. Her effusive pining in her song does not suggest *fin amor* but simply *amor.* After she appears, the poem veers away from courtly male love and the Provençal *cansós* and their Iberian counterparts, the *cantigas d'amor* (love songs in the male voice), and toward a woman's love lyric in the style of the *cantigas d'amigo.* Just as the courtly current carries the weight of sophisticated, refined, and spiritualized love, subject to specific norms of social conduct and filtered through the male gaze, this woman's song is joined to a far deeper Iberian folk tradition of natural love free of all artifice, as exemplified in *villancicos* (homespun Hispanic folk songs). It is a sensual, spontaneous, and expressive love unfettered by the codes imposed by the courtly system. The maiden's love is lusty, and her appearance in the poem begins a major shift in theme: the love of this girl draws the young cleric further and further from his ideal of *amor purus* and allows the *Razón de amor* to be read as the confession of a seduction.

An already venerable pattern, well known in classical antiquity and celebrated in the Middle Ages in the Latin poetry of the *Carmina Burana* and the Ripoll manuscript of the *Carmina erotica* and in vernacular lyric, was the *quinque lineae amoris* (five steps of love): *visus* (sight), *alloquium* (conversation), *tactus* (touch), *basia* (kisses), and *factum, actus,* or *coitus* (intercourse). Since there can be little doubt that the author of the *Razón de amor,* familiar with university life and goliardic poetry, knew the progression of the *quinque lineae amoris,* one should not be surprised to find these steps structuring his work. The sequence is seen in the first part of the poem through the fourth step, the kiss, followed by the tactical retreat of the young lady, who has taken the lead in making the first moves. While the *quinque lineae amoris* is not unknown in courtly poetry, it progresses much more quickly in goliardic verse. In the *Razón de amor* the process is so accelerated that, after the first sighting *(visus)* and the verbal exchanges *(alloquium),* the maiden rushes through the touching stage to the kiss, which occurs precisely at the midpoint of the poem.

Consideration of the *quinque lineae amoris* leads one to suspect that the debate between water and wine is really a veiled consideration of the fifth and final step, the *factum*. The physical consummation may be represented allegorically, as it is in Guillaume de Lorris Jean de Meun's *Roman de la Rose* (circa 1230–1275, Story of the Rose), in the dream produced by the ignited imagination of the speaker after the maiden has left. He succumbs to her charms, which are presented metaphorically as the white dove, and the *factum* plays itself out in a virtual fashion through the ensuing contest. The second part of the *Razón de amor* depicts the inner turmoil of the cleric, who is torn between his desires for *amor purus* and *amor mixtus*, through an entertaining allegory deliberately and systematically laced with ambiguities. From the moment the dove makes its appearance, the poet relies on ambivalent symbols and images that function antithetically as their erotic and sexual connotations alternate with allusions to self-control and chastity. The dove itself is an ancient Christian symbol of virginity and spirituality but in many medieval texts is also a reference to erotic union and fertility. Similarly, the dove's bathing ritual can be understood either as the cleansing act of baptism or as a rite of intimacy that often precedes sexual intercourse in Hispanic folk lyric.

The *amor mixtus* is formally achieved in the commingling of the water and wine. This mode of symbolizing sexual union is a recurrent theme in the poetry of the wandering scholars of the *Carmina Burana* and similar texts and occurs in popular lyric, as well. The motif may be a degradation of the sense that the mixture of water and wine holds in the Catholic liturgy, where the priest sprinkles a few drops of water into the chalice of wine during the Mass, symbolizing the union of humankind with Christ's blood. To this analysis can be added the goliards' predilection for punning and profane games played with sacred language. The goliards were capable Latinists who indulged themselves in typically sophomoric double entendres. Nouns such as *commixtio* (commingling) and *conjunctio* (conjoining, or coupling), both of which appear in the *Denudata veritate*, were commonly subverted to stand for the act of sex. But in the twelfth century the mixture of water and wine was also a symbol for *temperantia* (temperance), one of Pope Gregory the Great's four cardinal virtues, with many iconographic representations in manuscript illuminations.

The commingling of water and wine is the point of departure for the debate between the two liquids. The poem moves from the interwoven narration and lyricism of the first part to the incessant dialogue of the second half, which, for all its theatrical qualities, lacks real drama. It has the feel of a rowdy, if clever, stunt by a fellow student of the goliards, but only on the surface: just below one can feel the opposing pull, at once carnal and chaste, of the dove, the bath, and the little bell. The challenges exchanged between the water and wine are symbolic of the erotic tensions that built to the point of the kiss–after which, according to tradition, the movement of love was practically irreversible and its consummation all but inevitable.

The normal conclusion of a debate, the assignment of victory to one of the opponents, is missing in the *Razón de amor*. Its absence indicates that the poet did not conceive the second half of his composition as an independent work but as an integral part of the poem. He has not chosen the genre of the debate to cater to the tastes of his anticipated audience; instead, he takes advantage of the ambiguity of the allegorical setting and the debate genre to reflect his own inner turmoil as he moves back and forth between the desires of the flesh, spurred on by his biological urges and the dictates of courtly love, and the precepts of chastity imposed by his clerical state. The poet handles this conflict in a self-conscious and self-mocking way that is difficult to appreciate at first glance. The central notion of the *Razón de amor* is summed up in strophe 70 of the *Carmina Burana*: "In trutina mentis dubia / fluctuant contraria / lascivus amor et pudicitia" (Onto the scales of one's mind / pour opposing currents: / cloying love and scouring modesty).

There may well have been an historical and social motivation for the writing of the *Razón de amor*. In the third and fourth decades of the thirteenth century the church was pursuing a campaign of repression, including threats of excommunication and cancellation of benefices, against the notorious incontinence and concubinage of Spanish clerics. The poet of the *Razón de amor* was faced with this drama on a daily basis and may have been moved to carry it into the literary realm, transforming his theme into an exemplary tale with an autobiographical veneer. Resistance to the effort to impose celibacy was so fierce that in 1251 Pope Innocent IV was forced to withdraw most of the sanctions.

References:

Daniel N. Cárdenas, "Nueva luz sobre *Razón de amor y denuestos del agua y del vino* (sugerida por un análisis fono-morfosintáctico)," *Revista Hispánica Moderna*, 34 (1968): 227–241;

Dorothy Clotelle Clarke, *Early Spanish Lyric Poetry: Essays and Selections* (New York: Las Americas, 1967), pp. 39–58;

Margo De Ley, "Provençal Biographical Tradition and the *Razón de amor*," *Journal of Hispanic Philology*, 1 (1976–1977): 1–17;

Alicia C. de Ferraresi, *"Locus amoenus* y vergel visionario en *Razón de amor,"* *Hispanic Review,* 42 (1974): 173–183;

Ferraresi, *"Razón de Amor,"* in her *De amor y poesía en la España medieval: Prólogo a Juan Ruiz* (Mexico City: Colegio de México, 1976), pp. 43–118;

Ferraresi, "Razón de amor," in her "Religio amoris en la poesía castellana de la Edad Media," dissertation, Stanford University, 1973, pp. 47–158;

Ferraresi, "Sentido y unidad de *Razón de amor,"* *Filología,* 14 (1970): 1–48;

Silvestro Fiore, "La tenson en Espagne et Babylonie: Volution ou polygenèse?" in *Actes du IVe Congrés de l'Association Internationale de Littérature Compareé/Proceedings of the IVth Congress of the International Comparative Literature Association, Fribourg, 1964,* volume 2, edited by François Jost (The Hague: Mouton, 1966), pp. 982–992;

Enzo Franchini, *Los debates literarios en la Edad Media* (Madrid: Ediciones del Laberinto, 2001), pp. 43–79, 219–225;

Olga Tudorica Impey, "La estructura unitaria de *Razón de amor,"* *Journal of Hispanic Philology,* 4, no. 1 (1979): 1–24;

Alfred Jacob, "The *Razón de Amor* as Christian Symbolism," *Hispanic Review,* 20 (1952): 282–301;

Helen McFie, *The Medieval Debate between Wine and Water in the Romance Languages: Tradition and Transformation* (Philadelphia: University of Pennsylvania Press, 1981);

André Michalski, *La* Razón *de Lupus de Moros: Un poema hermético* (Madison, Wis.: Hispanic Seminary of Medieval Studies, 1993);

Colbert I. Nepaulsingh, "The Song of Songs and the Unity of the *Razón de amor,"* in his *Towards a History of Literary Composition in Medieval Spain* (Toronto: University of Toronto Press, 1986), pp. 41–62;

Enrique de Rivas, "La razón secreta de la Razón de amor," in his *Figuras y estrellas de las cosas,* Monografías y Ensayos, no. 14 (Maracaibo: Facultad de Humanidades y Educación, Universidad de Zulia, 1969), pp. 93–110;

Leo Spitzer, *"Razón de Amor,"* *Romania,* 71 (1950): 145–165;

Margaret Van Antwerp, "*Razón de amor* and the Popular Tradition," *Romance Philology,* 32 (August 1978): 1–17.

Juan Ruiz, Arcipreste de Hita

(flourished circa 1330 – 1343)

Steven D. Kirby

Eastern Michigan University

WORK: *Libro de buen amor* (circa 1330–1343)

Manuscripts: The work is preserved in three primary manuscripts, all of which are incomplete to varying degrees but, taken together, furnish a nearly complete text: the early-fifteenth-century MS. 2.663 at the Universidad de Salamanca, the "Gayoso" manuscript (officially MS. 19) in the Real Academia Española in Madrid, and the "Toledo" manuscript, now catalogued as MS. Vitr. 6-1 (formerly Hh-101) in the Biblioteca Nacional in Madrid. Most standard editions are based mainly on MS. 2.663, with gaps supplied in all but a few cases from the Gayoso manuscript; incidental minor corrections derive from the highly fragmentary Toledo manuscript. The work also exists in a fragmentary Old Portuguese translation, and scattered minor fragments survive in miscellaneous manuscripts of the fifteenth and sixteenth centuries.

First publication: *Poesías del Arcipreste de Hita,* volume 4 of *Colección de poesías castellanas anteriores al siglo XV,* edited by Tomás Antonio Sánchez (Madrid: Sancha, 1790).

Standard editions: *Libro de buen amor,* edited by Jean Ducamin (Toulouse: Privat, 1901); *Arcipreste de Hita: Libro de buen amor,* 2 volumes, edited by Julio Cejador y Frauca, Clásicos castellanos, volumes 14 and 17 (Madrid: Espasa-Calpe, 1913); *Libro de buen amor: Selección,* edited by María Rosa Lida de Malkiel (Buenos Aires: Losada, 1941); *Libro de buen amor,* edited by Giorgio Chiarini (Milan: R. Ricciardi, 1964); *Libro de buen amor,* edited by Manuel Criado de Val and Eric W. Naylor (Madrid: Consejo Superior de Investigaciones Científicas, 1965; revised and enlarged, 1972); *Libro de buen amor,* edited by Joan Corominas (Madrid: Gredos, 1967); *Libro de buen amor,* 2 volumes, edited by Jacques Joset, Clásicos castellanos, volumes 14 and 17 (Madrid: Espasa-Calpe, 1974); *Libro de buen amor,* edited by Alberto Blecua (Barcelona: Planeta, 1983); *Libro de buen amor,* edited by G. B. Gybbon-Monypenny (Madrid: Castalia, 1988); *Libro de buen amor,* edited by Joset (Madrid: Taurus, 1990); *Libro de buen amor,* edited by Blecua (Madrid: Cátedra, 1992); *Libro de buen amor,* edited by Marcella Ciceri (Modena: Mucchi, 2002); *Libro de buen amor,* edited by Steven D. Kirby (Newark, Del.: Cervantes/European Masterpieces, 2007).

Editions in English: *Book of Good Love,* translated by Elisha Kent Kane (New York: Rudge, 1933); *Book of Good Love,* translated by Rigo Mignani and Mario A. Di Cesare (Albany: State University of New York Press, 1970); *Libro de buen amor,* edited and translated by Raymond S. Willis (Princeton: Princeton University Press, 1972); *The Book of the Archpriest of Hita (Libro de buen amor),* translated by Mack Singleton (Madison, Wis.: Hispanic Seminary of Medieval Studies, 1975); *Book of True Love,* edited by Anthony N. Zahareas, translated by Saralyn R. Daly (University Park: Pennsylvania State University Press, 1978); *Book of Good Love,* edited by Melveena McKendrick, translated by Elizabeth Drayson MacDonald (London: Dent, 1999).

Juan Ruiz, archpriest of the small northern Castilian town of Hita, is the foremost author of the Spanish Middle Ages. His one work, the *Libro de buen amor* (circa 1330–1343; translated as *Book of Good Love,* 1933), a poem of 7,273 verses in 1,728 stanzas, is an astonishingly original creation for its time, and its enduring appeal has engaged the attention of scholars around the world.

Ruiz begins his book with a prose introduction structured as a sermon, stating his virtuous intentions—or, at least, those of the merry narrator and inept swain bearing his name—followed by another introduction in verse containing the customary invocations to heavenly powers. He notes the human being's need to blend joys with cares and invokes Aristotle's authority to discuss the all-too-human drive to seek physical love. The poet boasts of his formidable literary skill but exhorts the

Antes.....CAX, 17_2o.
Ahora --Cajon - -103-26.

DIALOGO
entre la Quaresma y Carnal
en Uarios Apologos en
Endechas Castellanas
Fecho Era de 1368.

ITEM
Una Vision de Filiberto.

Este Dialogo es del Arcipreste de Hita
Juan Ruiz qe floreció en tiempo del
Arzobispo Dn Gil de Albornoz.

Está incompleto, y la fha el fin ~~~~~~~~~~
~~~~~~ esto
errato: la razon es porqe Juan d Hita le compuso
en la Carcel en que le mandó poner el Arzobispo
Dn Gil Cuio señor fue Arzobispo trece años desde el
1337 hasta el de 1350: luego la cuida fha de la era

Title page for the "Toledo" manuscript of the Libro de buen amor *(Biblioteca Nacional, Madrid, MS. Vitr. 6-1)*

reader to understand the poem's meaning correctly; he illustrates the dangers of confusing pious motives with vulgar ones by means of a burlesque, almost slapstick debate between the Romans and the Greeks. He recounts his first attempt at an amorous engagement in a debate format, using artfully construed Aesopian fables to illustrate his points. This failed attempt at courting a discreet lady and his next fiasco, with a common baker girl, prompt a diatribe against Don Amor (Sir Love), who appears to him in a vision in the form of a gentleman. After relating a series of cleverly retold fables that exemplify how the seven deadly sins are a consequence of physical love, the frustrated would-be lover receives instruction from Don Amor and then from Lady Venus. He learns from them whom to love, what sort of go-between to employ, which character flaws to avoid, and how to be diligent in the pursuit of love. Thanks to the coaching he has received, his next attempt is successful; but the affair is short-lived. After a transitional adventure with a strange old woman who takes advantage of him, the narrator makes an erotic pilgrimage to the mountains and is again trumped in his amorous pursuits by a series of four rough-and-ready shepherd girls with cartoonish looks and bruising sexual appetites. His unsatisfying experiences in the mountain passes lead him to seek refuge and do penance at a nearby shrine, where he meditates on Christ's sacrifices.

The next long section of the poem is given over to a vivid allegorical depiction of a battle between personifications of Flesh (love) and Lent as the Lenten season approaches. Flesh triumphs with the end of Lent. The triumphal reception of Lord Love by all of society, including the clergy, leads the narrator again to think of his own love life and to seek new erotic adventures with an elderly woman, the waggishly nicknamed "Trotaconventos" (Convent Trotter), as his expert go-between. An unsuccessful attempt with an upstanding noble lady leads the go-between to suggest that he seek the love of a nun. This tryst produces another debate conducted by a witty exchange of Aesopian fables. The nun accepts the narrator as her confidant; the relationship is ostensibly platonic. Two months later, the nun dies. An approach to a Moorish girl results in a humiliating rebuff in Arabic. This failure inspires the poet to consider which musical instruments are good for Arabic-language songs and the similarities between his book and such an instrument. Shortly thereafter, his go-between dies, and the poet composes a tirade against death, an extravagant tribute to the deceased madame, and a poetic epitaph for her. He then begins to bring his book to a formal close by advising the reader how to combat worldly temptations. He ironically praises the virtues of women of small stature: like pepper, the tinier they are,

the spicier; and if they become a source of sin, the smaller the woman, the smaller the sin. He then humorously lists the fourteen character flaws of his messenger boy. He ends the book by again exhorting the reader to understand his true meaning and good intentions. Two of the manuscripts contain additional material that some critics do not consider integral parts of the *Libro de buen amor:* poems about the Virgin Mary, an extended satire on clerical misconduct, and two songs to be sung by blind men.

Ruiz's central theme is love in all of its manifestations, both secular and sacred, and he uses people's diverse reactions to love as a vehicle for social satire and religious parody. While the bulk of the poem—6,213 verses in 1,554 quatrains—is narrative in tone, Ruiz incorporates into his work 1,060 verses in 174 stanzas of lyric poetry; in so doing he establishes himself as the first major writer to compose lyrics in Castilian instead of Galician-Portuguese or Catalan. His mastery of complex versification and exuberant rhyme allow him to find distinctive and clever means of expression and to display impressive virtuosity at almost every turn, even when manipulating a conventional form.

The *Libro de buen amor* was widely influential among Spanish poets in the fourteenth and fifteenth centuries and was read and excerpted by scholars in the sixteenth century; it then disappeared for two hundred years, probably because its verse forms were deemed antiquated. Today, however, the rich ambiguity of Ruiz's writing inspires the admiration of academic critics and general readers alike.

On nearly all other aspects of this poem and its author, there is a notable lack of consensus. The disagreement begins with the poet's stated name and ecclesiastical position. The commonness of the surname Ruiz and the lack of external documentation of him as an archpriest of Hita led scholars such as Manuel Criado de Val to suspect that the name might be a pseudonym. In 1984 a legal document dated around 1330 surfaced in Spain with a list of witnesses that included a Juan Ruiz, identifying him as archpriest of Hita and calling him "venerable"; but that evidence is as sketchy as the information in his own book. The lusty and wayward cleric is an established Spanish literary type; whether or not the historical Ruiz was truly ill behaved, he at least exploited brilliantly the stock figure of the rollicking churchman. Ruiz also incorporates into his work what appears to be a physical description of himself as reported by his go-between that is so rich in detail, down to the proud barrel chest and resonant voice, that generations of scholars believed it to be an accurate self-portrait. Elisha Kent Kane, André S. Michalski, and Peter N. Dunn, however, have shown that the features attributed to Ruiz are a combination of

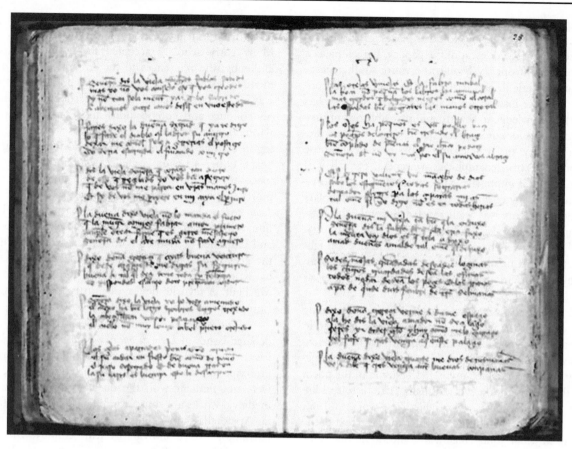

Pages from the "Toledo" manuscript of the Libro de buen amor *(Biblioteca Nacional, Madrid, MS. Vitr. 6-1)*

rhetorical commonplaces and medical characteristics associated with men of sanguine temperament.

Yet, it is possible to draw some conclusions about the poet from the text of his work. His familiarity with ecclesiastical doctrine and culture was extensive, since he speaks confidently and authoritatively about scriptural exegesis, the liturgical calendar, saints, confession and penance, and the nature of temptation, as well as being able to spin off traditional set pieces such as the denouncement of the seven deadly sins; the catalogue of the arms of the Christian against the world, the flesh, and the devil; and the struggle between Flesh and Lent. Even allowing for wide familiarity with such matters among the medieval public, the range and depth of Ruiz's knowledge sets him apart from most of his lay contemporaries. At several points in the poem Ruiz also displays an impressive familiarity with both civil and canon law. In one instance, using a cast of animal litigants and lawyers, he presents an entire fictionalized lawsuit in verse, employing the exact procedural language, formulas, and terminology of early Spanish courts.

Ruiz's awareness of ethnic diversity is evident in the few words of Arabic he uses and in his familiarity with certain Jewish religious observances and foods. These elements could be explained by the inherent multiculturalism of medieval Spain rather than by any real contact with Moors and Jews, though both groups were present in Hita at that time. There is no doubt, however, that Ruiz was familiar with the musical traditions and performance of Semitic groups in medieval Spain. His claim to have composed many musical works for Jewish and Moorish performers is believable because of his familiarity with virtually the full range of available instruments and the sounds they produced: in one passage he discusses which instruments are not appropriate for Arabic performers, and in another he lists many medieval instruments and characterizes the tone or appearance of each.

Ruiz's familiarity with Spanish geography also supplies clues to his background. He displays detailed knowledge of Hita and the topography of the neighboring Guadarrama Mountains. He has firsthand knowledge of nearby Segovia and of more-distant Toledo, the seat of ecclesiastical authority in his region. He also mentions Belorado, Burgos, and Castro Urdiales, stopping points along the pilgrimage roads to Santiago de

Compostela, suggesting that he may have made the journey himself. Allusions to other places are more generalized: Rome as the seat of the papacy, Barcelona as a city of great prosperity, Seville as a warm southern capital, and Bougie in northern Africa as a source of monkeys. In some instances it is apparent that the poet has used his knowledge to construct implausible or impossible itineraries for comic effect, because his audience presumably knew the realities and rigors of travel in those regions. Yet, his geographical awareness, even if it is secondhand, is impressive, and so much of his information has the ring of direct experience that most scholars believe that Ruiz was well traveled beyond what was required to supervise local priests under his authority. Much of the misbehavior he reports in his poem might reflect conduct he observed or heard about in performing his archpriestly duties, such as hearing confessions and disciplining wayward priests and nuns.

One final body of supposed evidence regarding Ruiz concerns the prose rubrics or headings included in the Salamanca manuscript of the poem. Early researchers accepted these headings at face value, but Julio Cejador y Frauca contended in his 1913 edition of the poem that they were not the work of Ruiz. The historical linguist Joan Corominas, who edited the work in 1967, determined the headings to be older than the text of the poem. In 1994 John Dagenais conjectured that they may reflect the reactions of an early reader of the work. In 1997 Jeremy N. H. Lawrance demonstrated that they are extraneous to the poem both textually and literarily. It appears likely that the headings are commentaries on the text by a scribe. They are useful as signposts for readers of the poem.

The proper title of the book has been debated; among the candidates, *Libro de buen amor* has the advantage that the poet himself explicitly calls his book by this name at several points. The problem is that *buen amor* as used by Ruiz appears to mean different things on different pages. He contrasts *buen amor*, which he says means the love of God, with *loco amor*, the mad and uncontrolled carnal lust of this world. But at other times it is evident that *buen amor* also means skillful sexual love. The *Libro de buen amor* is thus ambiguous even in its title.

Some critics contend that the title should be *Libro del Arcipreste de Hita* (Book of the Archpriest of Hita), because the poem was so styled by two early readers and because this title allegedly better reflects the unity conferred by the narrator/author's personality. But it is clearly preferable in artistic terms that title and text both reflect the same coherent aesthetic aim—in this case, a challenging literary ambiguity that is present at all levels, from beginning to end. Hence, *Libro de buen amor* is the best title.

The book is an erotic autobiography that purports to be a negative example to others to avoid sin. Many early scholars accepted the autobiography as authentic; the references to the Archpriest's imprisonment, for example, led some critics to posit that the poet was incarcerated because of the objectionable nature of his conduct and compositions and that he compiled, wrote, or revised the *Libro de buen amor* while languishing in ecclesiastical confinement for as long as thirteen years. Other scholars contend that imprisonment is a metaphor for spiritual suffering while confined to one's mortal flesh. The range of experience recounted in the *Libro de buen amor* supports the idea that the work is fiction rather than memoir. G. B. Gybbon-Monypenny and Laurence de Looze argue that the work belongs to the genre of erotic pseudo-autobiography as practiced by writers such as St. Augustine and Guillaume de Machaut. A favorite device of courtly literature, across Europe, it was likely to be familiar to Ruiz.

The question of unity has been one of the most debated issues in *Libro de buen amor* scholarship and criticism. The problem arose because scholars in the overly prescriptive second half of the eighteenth century, who were not familiar with the distinctive ways in which medieval works are constructed, failed to find the familiar Aristotelian unities in the book. Studies of medieval narratology have shown that Ruiz employs the technique of "interlaced narrative," which was widely used in the period, to unify his work: themes are initiated, go dormant for a while, then reappear through a passing allusion to another event, person, or situation.

Phonetic unity is provided by words and names that repeat a sound, such as *cárçel, çaraças, Garçía,* and *Garoza.* Semantic associations are set up between key words such as *provar* and *servir,* which reappear in various contexts to establish thematic consistency. Rhyme is manipulated to structure and underscore meaning; for instance, Ruiz uses consecutive rhyme (the same rhyme sound in two consecutive stanzas) to emphasize the importance of key passages. Finally, on many occasions he drives home the meaning of a stanza by making a proverb or proverb-like expression the final verse of it. These phenomena are not immediately apparent, but careful analysis confirms their presence.

Medieval sermons constitute one of the primary sources of the *Libro de buen amor,* but it is clear that Ruiz used a wide variety of other material. The prose prologue has been linked to the learned vernacular sermon and to Augustinian teachings, but it probably owes more to medieval *Accessus ad Auctores* (Introduction to Recommended Authors) commentaries on literary works. Ruiz shows an extensive knowledge of classical and medieval rhetorical treatises: he uses the techniques of *amplificatio* (amplification) and *abbreviatio* (abbreviation) in his adaptation of sources, expanding the twelfth-century Latin drama *Pamphilus de amore,* for example, to double its original length by incorporating details and material of his own devising. Other sources Ruiz uses include the Bible, ecclesiastical doctrine and practice, civil and canonical law, Aesopian fables, and various vernacular literary works. The adaptation of such wide-ranging source material is a key merit of the work but also one of the primary obstacles to its effective study.

The first challenge a reader of the *Libro de buen amor* faces is to discern the author's literal meanings. In the prologue Ruiz emphasizes his desire to benefit his readers with a work that is rich in moral and didactic content, but he observes that if some readers wish—against his recommendation—to follow the path of mad and heedless love, they will find examples in his book that will be useful to them, as well. In the fables "los griegos y los romanos" (the Greeks and the Romans) and "el nasçimiento del fijo del rey Alcarás" (the Birth of the son of King Alcaraz) he shows that nonverbal communication can be misconstrued from charitable or hostile perspectives; he indicates the importance of correctly understanding language by placing these tales near the beginning of the *Libro de buen amor.* He uses many other exemplary tales, from Aesop and other sources, in a similar manner to drive home such points as the need to avoid drunkenness, diligence in courtship, not to leave a new bride alone too long, indulging in too much sex, and how to choose an appropriate or ideal woman to love. This more or less utilitarian advice is accompanied by explicit or implicit instruction on the proper construction of a literary work. At one point he shows how each of five different astrological forecasts of the cause of a person's death could contain a germ of truth and how all of them together could be true. To the reader accustomed to plainspoken lessons this pose by Ruiz is at once entertaining and infuriating, delightful and disconcerting.

Parody in the *Libro de buen amor* ranges from the subtle to the obvious. For instance, the discord between Flesh and Lent is presented as a lighthearted allegory. In a battle among dining options, fish and other sea creatures allowed on a Lenten table engage in combat for dominance with tantalizing cuts of meat. The canonical-hours section of the poem employs Latin liturgical phrases to imply sexual activity. The Latin source of the Aesop fable of the wolf and vixen in court before Judge Sir Ape is expanded to twenty times its original length by the incorporation of medieval legal procedures from King Alfonso X's *Siete partidas* (1256–1265, Seven-Part Law), which it parodies. Humor is omnipresent in the *Libro de buen amor* except in its prayer poems. Ruiz unabashedly parodies Church doctrines and makes fun of monks and their concubines.

Ruiz invents or adapts words to meet his needs. Describing his love for a woman named Cruz, for instance, he says that he "cruiziava" (excruciated) for her. The invented word incorporates his surname while also alluding to the woman's name and to the Crucifixion. In "Juan Ruiz's Manipulation of Rhyme," included in *Libro de buen amor Studies* (1970), edited by Gybbon-Monypenny, K. W. J. Adams notes that many first attestations of Spanish words are rhyme words found in the *Libro de buen amor* and that many of these words appear in the third or fourth verses of his stanzas—testimony to his dwindling supply of "normal" words late in his stanzas. At times he resorts to syntactical rhyme, such as *muy mal va* with *malva;* at other times he uses a place-name with a comical sound such as "vil forado" (vile hole) to make a play on words between the dwelling of a she-wolf and the town Belorado. He describes a wayward "monja" (nun) as a "podrida toronja" (rotten orange).

The one thing of which Ruiz never makes fun is his own literary attainments. Even when he issues the common medieval invitation to readers to alter his work if they wish, he adds the caveat—unique to the *Libro de buen amor*—that they are to do so only if they know how to write poetry well.

The poet invokes heavenly powers to inspire him to create a book devoted to the theme of Good Love, which, he asserts, is the love of God, not lust as practiced by most people. If the work is to succeed, the reader must be a full partner and endeavor to understand the author's intended message. The process of creation will be complicated because of the inherent ambiguity of language, but this same ambiguity will enrich the *Libro de buen amor* by producing humorous misunderstandings and requiring the use of debate, astrology, and authority. Debates occur between Ruiz and Don Amor in the first half of the book and between Trotaconventos and Doña Garoza in the second half; even the four mountain-girl adventures can be considered debates or negotiations. As to astrology, Ruiz discloses that he was born under the "sign" of Venus and is, therefore, destined to seek love without really knowing how. Early in the book Ruiz appeals to the authority of Aristotle when he alludes to humankind's natural impulses to eat and reproduce; throughout the rest of the book he uses Spanish proverbs to appeal to his audience with more-recognizable and palatable "philosophical" authority. Proverbs are for Ruiz, as they were centuries later for Miguel de Cervantes, an essential compositional tool. But the poet also treats his literary art as authoritative and calls himself one troubadour in a thousand. Near the end of the poem he claims to have written his book as a manual on how to write poetry.

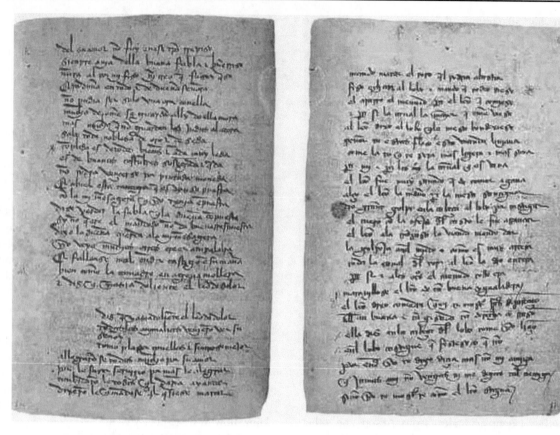

Pages from the "Gayoso" manuscript of the Libro de buen amor *(Real Academia Española, Madrid, MS. 19)*

An important element in the construction of the *Libro de buen amor* is the allegorical vision in which the narrator receives instruction. First, he learns from Don Amor and Lady Venus that love is not merely a feeling but a technique to be learned and practiced. The narrator's relationship with Don Amor is initially strained because of the bumbling would-be lover's lack of success to that point: the narrator reviles Don Amor as a liar and a fraud and orders him away. But Don Amor shows considerable forbearance and stays to give abundant practical advice. When he leaves, Lady Venus appears and gives additional advice. In this way the narrator and the reader receive a male and a female perspective on the amorous process.

Another important allegory in the poem is the Flesh-Lent combat. This allegory represents the struggle between flesh and asceticism in suggestive ways, including veiled allusions to sexual encounters and even to the sexual organs. As a cultural document, this extended passage is of the greatest value because it shows how combat challenges were issued and received, the legalistic technicalities that were invoked, the details of penance imposed on Sir Meatseason, and the alliances between Flesh and Jewish butchers.

Perhaps the most important allegory, however, is the implicit one of the human being's journey through life, exploring it, experiencing it, and ultimately facing his or her inescapable mortality. This allegory is subtly woven throughout the *Libro de buen amor;* it occasionally surfaces clearly, as in the passages devoted to the mountain girls, but it is present in all of the pseudo-autobiographical sketches.

Religious imagery is found everywhere in the *Libro de buen amor,* from the invocation of heaven and the Virgin Mary at the outset, to the narrator's asking God to free him from the prison where he is languishing unjustly, and the piously couched debate between Trotaconventos and Doña Garoza. It appears in the finale to the mountain-girls episode when the traveler meditates at Santa María del Vado and in the Flesh-Lent debate and its aftermath. There is no denying a religious inspiration, and possibly even a religious audience, for the *Libro de buen amor,* though it clearly transcends that context in many passages. But while devotional and meditative imagery is pervasive, the author incorporates hunting and predatory imagery when he offers warnings to women who are the objects of male stalking, implying that they are not safe in the society in which he and they live. This blend of religious and predatory imagery points to the context in which Ruiz was writing: the sermon. Modern scholarship has shown that medieval sermons were eclectic works in which the sacred and the profane were combined as preachers sought to achieve memorable effects and lasting results by shocking their congregations.

As indicated by the title, love is the paramount theme of the *Libro de buen amor*. Ruiz argues at the outset of his poem that he is advocating the practice of Good Love, which, he says, is God's love or clean love. Some critics have suggested that the abundance of failed amorous affairs is depicted for the purpose of driving home the point that only God's love or that of the Virgin Mary are constant, reliable, and truly rewarding and that the aim of the book is to turn men and women from lust for each other to the love of God. Yet, the obvious relish with which the narrator presents his carnal quests shows that he was more than a little interested in this activity, as well. Most modern critics are reluctant to believe that the work is essentially a sophisticated tract against worldly love. His suit to win Doña Garoza leads to courtly conversation and deference rather than erotic adventure, and his "success" in this instance is foreshortened by his lady's premature demise. His fondness for his go-between, Trotaconventos, leads the narrator to compose a heartfelt dirge for her late in the poem. Near the end there is the clearly ironic praise of short women in which the Archpriest reveals misogynistic sentiments or, perhaps, only adopts such a pose as a gesture to the misogyny that was widespread in the later Middle Ages. In any case, the poet prizes women most highly when they are in his "service" in one sense or another. But his experiences take place during a lifelong journey that inevitably ends in death and disappointment. Perhaps for this reason he finds the courtly model unappealing, with one notable exception: the only woman consistently worthy of the narrator's devotion is the Virgin Mary, and his dedication to her never flags from the beginning of the poem to the end.

Trotaconventos is an even more memorable character than the protagonist himself. The skilled old crone knows the ways and the wiles of erotic love and the psychological strengths and weaknesses of its practitioners. She demands respect; when the Archpriest makes the mistake of uttering a tasteless joke at her expense, she punishes him by revealing to the young lady who has his attention at the time that he is in pursuit of her. The lesson leads him to furnish a list of the insulting terms one must never use to refer to a bawd. The bawd herself advises her client to call her Good Love; he does so, leading Adolfo Bonilla y San Martín to posit that the title might be construed as the "Book of Go-Betweenery."

One of the most memorable episodes in the book is the narrator's trip to the Guadarrama Mountains to "try all things." There he is accosted successively by four shepherd girls with stronger sexual desires and greater physical strength than his. His submission to the demands of his hostesses constitutes another amorous failure: the sexual gratification he achieves is diminished by the fact that it is not on his terms. The depiction of the mountain girls draws on the folkloric myth of the wild woman, a sylvan creature feared because of her great strength and uncontrollable appetites, especially sexual ones.

The range of female characters in the book indicates that the Archpriest envisions physical love in two contexts, urban and rural. Doña Endrina is the quintessential urban lover and is in the clutches of the equally urban Trotaconventos. The *serrana* (mountain-girl) episodes show the rural, wild, and uncivilized side of love removed from the pressures polite society exerts on its members to conform. Religious love, on the other hand, knows no urban or rural boundaries, since it is applicable to all situations and places.

Ruiz presents two lists of the seven deadly sins, one of which has eight sins; an explanation of the arms of the Christian to fight off the world, the flesh, and the devil; and the combat between the forces of Flesh and those of Lent. He incorporates these traditional themes into his lessons on love: lovers run the risk of committing most or all of the sins enumerated; the arms against the world, the flesh, and the devil are three "enemies" of the erotic experience; and the Flesh-Lent contest, while comically depicted, is serious in its implications for the Christian interested in complying with the dietary restrictions imposed by his or her faith, although the Archpriest merrily interpolates erotic imagery and symbolism into his account.

Time appears in at least three different forms in the *Libro de buen amor*, sometimes in combination: chronological, liturgical, and allegorical. Chronological time appears in the trial of the wolf and vixen before Sir Ape, Judge of Bougie, in which a specific year–1263–and a twenty-day continuance are mentioned. Chronological time is also involved in the lengths of time required for the traveler to walk from town to town. Liturgical time is more subtle. In the *serranas* episode the attentive reader notes that the journey begins on St. Emeterius's Day, 3 March, and is linked to Carnival and Lent and the year 1329, though the year is never explicitly mentioned and only surfaces when the reader painstakingly verifies the dates and times by using perpetual calendars and treatises on technical chronology. The traveler returns to the approximate starting point of his journey; thus, his trip is cyclical in the same way that liturgical time, in which events recur every year, is cyclical. The fact that the traveler arrives at Santa María del Vado during Lent and does penance connects the *serranas* episode to the Flesh-Lent combat. As the combat draws to a close, Lady Lent is permitted by the calendar to avoid further conflict with Sir Flesh and go on pilgrimage because the Lenten season is over. The *Libro de buen amor* also uses the canonical hours as objects of parody and erotic suggestion: the poet combines the hours of Prime, Tierce, Sext, Nones, and so forth with liturgical phrases to suggest daylong concern with, and possible involvement in, erotic activity by clergy. This passage is one of the subtlest, funniest, and most creative in the book. Allegorical time is exploited when the narrator describes the tent of Don Amor, on which each month is depicted by showing the typical activities associated with it. This passage, inspired by the Old Spanish *Libro de Alexandre* (early thirteenth century, Book of Alexander), is an impressive example of ekphrasis (verbal description of artwork).

Any appraisal of Ruiz's achievement must address his linguistic mastery. That Ruiz displays the most extensive and varied lexicon of any writer of the Spanish Middle Ages is documented in the glossaries, vocabularies, and concordances of José María Aguado (1929), Henry B. Richardson (1930), Rigo Mignani, Mario A. Di Cesare, and George Fenwick Jones (1977). By far the bulk of Ruiz's vocabulary is in the standard Castilian dialect; there are persistent traces of Leonese, as well, but they are perhaps attributable to copyists rather than to the author. Beyond vocabulary, Ruiz displays bold innovations in syntax, sometimes when he is under pressure to complete a challenging rhyme or to furnish a witty final line to a stanza. The *Libro de buen amor* is written almost entirely in verse, primarily in quatrains of fourteen-syllable lines in the *mester de clerecía* (mastery of clerics) style, though with abundant variations in syllable count.

The intended audience of the *Libro de buen amor* has been a persistent problem for critics since the work reemerged in the mid eighteenth century. Episodes such as the trial of the wolf and vixen before Sir Ape could best be relished by legal professionals, though ordinary citizens could enjoy the displays of legalese without understanding the impressive accuracy of the presentation. Clerics would appreciate theologically based sections such as the digression on confession, but all ordinary believers could get something out of even the most doctrinal passages. Beyond such learned elements, however, there is ample material drawn from folklore, such as the episodes with the mountain girls, which would appeal mostly but not exclusively to the common people. The question of whether the work was intended for public performance or private reading is far from resolved.

The beginning of literary criticism of the *Libro de buen amor* dates from the autumn of 1750, when Fray Martín Sarmiento inspected the Gayoso and Toledo manuscripts and wrote that it would be dangerous to publish the work because of scabrous material such as the canonical-hours passage. Sarmiento's remarks are reproduced in the revised and enlarged edition (1972) of Criado de Val and Eric W. Naylor's paleographic edition of the *Libro de buen amor*. A milestone in the early history of Ruiz criticism is the final volume of the four-volume *Colección de poesías castellanas anteriores al siglo XV* (Collection of Pre-Fifteenth-Century Castilian Poetry), a cornerstone of Spanish medieval studies published by subscription between 1779 and 1790 by the librarian Tomás Antonio Sánchez. Sánchez situates Ruiz in the fourteenth century, identifies his poetry as written almost entirely in Spanish alexandrines (fourteen-syllable lines, as opposed to the twelve-syllable French alexandrine), and states that he has not received the praise that he is due. Sánchez discovered the Salamanca manuscript but says that even with three codices, there are still gaps in the work. He adds that some of the variant readings between manuscripts appear to result from Ruiz's revisions of the work. Sánchez links the poet to Guadalajara and Alcalá de Henares and deduces that he was dead by 1351, since Pedro Fernández is named in a document as archpriest of Hita in January of that year.

The fourth volume of José Amador de los Ríos's Spanish literary history appeared in 1863 and includes a fifty-page chapter on Ruiz in which Amador de los Ríos rejects what he considers easy comparisons of the Archpriest to François Rabelais and Geoffrey Chaucer and states that the varying judgments presented of him are evidence of his greatness. Amador de los Ríos observes that Ruiz received inspiration from all possible sources and likens his work to a great lake into which all area rivers flow. His refutation of claims that Ruiz imitated northern French models furnishes a model of scholarly precision that many subsequent critics would have done well to follow. He critiques the notion that Ruiz was imprisoned and examines and reaffirms Juan Antonio Pellicer's discovery that the central episode of the *Libro de buen amor*—the pursuit of Doña Endrina by Don Melón de la Huerta—is founded on the *Pamphilus de amore*. (Pellicer's comments are incorporated into the prologue to Sánchez's 1790 edition of the poem.) Amador de los Ríos concludes by affirming the unity of the book, defending the fundamental virtue of the Archpriest despite the fictitious adventures the poet presents for satirical purposes, and repeating his claim of world-class greatness for Ruiz. Despite his overzealous defense of the Archpriest's morals, Amador de los Ríos's chapter remains one of the most important stud-

Page from the most complete manuscript of the Libro de buen amor, *copied in the fifteenth century (Universidad de Salamanca, MS. 2.663)*

ies of the *Libro de buen amor*. It also paved the way for a study later in the century that influenced critical thinking on Ruiz for generations: that of Marcelino Menéndez y Pelayo in 1892.

Menéndez y Pelayo's essay marks a new direction in Ruiz studies and constitutes the cornerstone of all subsequent work on the writer. Unlike such pioneers as Sarmiento, Amador de los Ríos, Luis Josef Velázquez, and Ferninand Wolf, whose works are fundamentally descriptive in nature and aimed at making Ruiz better known, Menéndez y Pelayo is concerned with the Archpriest's literary merit. For the first time Ruiz is examined in terms of his positive achievements and not in relation to the connections of his poem to various literary traditions. Menéndez y Pelayo regards Ruiz as the first real stylist in Spanish poetry and as the greatest poet of medieval Spain. The Archpriest's free treatment of traditional themes and sources receives due notice. Menéndez y Pelayo also offers a groundbreaking attempt at a structural analysis of the poem instead of a mere plot summary, and he presents a detailed program for the exhaustive study of the *Libro de buen amor* that has still not altogether been accomplished: the editing of the text stands at a high point, but studies of Ruiz's language have not achieved comparable excellence. Juan Gutiérrez Cuadrado's article "La lengua del *Libro de Buen Amor*," in *Estudios de frontera: Alcalá la Real y el Arcipreste de Hita* (1996), edited by Francisco Toro Ceballos and José Rodríguez Molina, is a welcome exception in this regard. Menéndez y Pelayo states that the Archpriest was no paragon of virtue but expresses admiration for his skills as a satirist. Probably the greatest merit of Menéndez y Pelayo's study, apart from its thoroughness and vision, is its enthusiasm and zeal. Menéndez y Pelayo, known for his conservatism in many areas, responds with evident excitement to his subject and does not let moral concerns affect his judgment. This open-minded enjoyment conferred on Ruiz a respectability that had previously been withheld or bestowed only grudgingly. Moreover, with the appraisal of Menéndez y Pelayo, Ruiz ceased to be a figure of historical or antiquarian interest and began to be seen as a writer of wide relevance and appeal.

Less than a decade after Menéndez y Pelayo's landmark critical study came the next crucial tool in the progressive analysis of Ruiz's work and art: Jean Ducamin's paleographic edition of the *Libro de buen amor,* published in Toulouse, France, in 1901. This edition set new standards within Hispanism for the careful and painstaking presentation of early texts. For the first time, medieval manuscripts were transcribed with the utmost care, and while abbreviations were expanded for the ease of readers, the expansions were printed in italics to indicate that they were interpretations by the editor. The demanding and costly process enabled readers, in effect, to audit the editor's work.

The first book-length monograph on the Archpriest was published by Julio Puyol y Alonso in 1906. Cejador y Frauca's widely circulated 1913 two-volume *Clásicos castellanos* edition made the full text of the work available at a more affordable price than Ducamin's vastly superior edition. The accessibility of Cejador y Frauca's edition and Ruiz's well-established prestige as a "canonical" author by the turn of the twentieth century led to a stream of impressive scholarship on the *Libro de buen amor* from the 1920s through the end of the century. Ramón Menéndez Pidal was the first important link in this chain with his epoch-making *Poesía juglaresca y juglares: Aspectos de la historia literaria y cultural de España* (Minstrel Poetry and Minstrels: Aspects of the Literary and Cultural History of Spain), which was published in 1924, has never been out of print since, was substantially revised in 1957, and was republished with full scholarly apparatus (except for the useful photographic illustrations) in 1991. Menéndez Pidal links Ruiz to the minstrelsy movement in medieval Spain and argues that he was sympathetic to popular forms of entertainment that would not ordinarily appeal to clerical authors. Though subsequent scholarship has questioned the degree to which Ruiz was influenced by minstrelsy and now emphasizes his learned qualities, Menéndez Pidal's pages on him remain classics. With the endorsement of the writer by both of Spain's greatest medievalists, Menéndez y Pelayo and Menéndez Pidal, studies on Ruiz abounded for the next seventy-five years.

The single most important work on the *Libro de buen amor* after Ducamin's edition is Félix Lecoy's 1938 book-length study of Ruiz's literary sources. Lecoy argues that while exotic Semitic originals may have exercised some minor influence on certain sections of the book, virtually all of the *Libro de buen amor* is modeled on Christian and European sources. Lecoy's scrupulous presentation of his findings provided a solid foundation for real critical analysis, which was not long in coming.

While many capable scholars gave attention to Ruiz in the next two decades, the name that dominates *Libro de buen amor* scholarship in this period is that of María Rosa Lida de Malkiel. Her publications span the decades from 1940 through 1961 and include an exceptionally solid though only partial 1941 edition of the *Libro de buen amor* with scholarly introduction and notes. Two lengthy articles dealing with the influence, interpretation, unity, didacticism, and autobiographical nature of the *Libro de buen amor,* several reviews, and miscellaneous note-length articles collected in her *Juan Ruiz: Selección del* Libro de buen amor *y estudios críticos*

(1973, *Juan Ruiz: Selection from the Libro de buen amor and Critical Studies*). A 1961 book version of her lectures on the *Libro de buen amor* and Fernando de Rojas's *Celestina* (circa 1496–1499, translated as *The Spanish Bawd,* 1631) represents the last and best of her thinking on the poem.

The 1960s produced a body of *Libro de buen amor* scholarship that is impressive in both quantity and quality. In 1964 Giorgio Chiarini produced the first truly critical edition of the *Libro de buen amor.* Though controversial at the time, his work has stood the test of time and has gained in reputation. In 1965 Criado de Val and Naylor published a full paleographic transcription of all three primary manuscripts and most of the fragments. Their work, revised and enlarged in 1972, remains the reference standard. The historical linguist and lexicographer Corominas produced what he called a critical edition of the text in 1967; time has shown it to be unreliable, though his linguistic notes and commentaries are generally of great value.

But the real breakthrough of the 1960s was Anthony N. Zahareas's *The Art of Juan Ruiz, Archpriest of Hita* (1965). This book was as significant as the works of Ducamin and Lecoy, but their contribution was essentially positivistic—transcribing the texts and tracing the sources; Zahareas was the first to examine the *Libro de buen amor* primarily as a work of literary communication, rather than as an archaeological artifact. Zahareas does not ignore historical considerations, but he uses them only as starting points and rapidly advances beyond them to produce a persuasive explication of the text and its techniques, both didactic and humorous. Paramount among the widely accepted conclusions offered in this book is that Ruiz consciously exploited the intrinsic ambiguity of language for literary effect.

In 1970 Gybbon-Monypenny edited an anthology of studies of Ruiz's poem. Two years later, an international congress was held on Ruiz in Madrid; the proceedings, edited by Criado de Val, were published in 1973. Raymond S. Willis published a scholarly bilingual edition of the text in 1972, and in 1974 Jacques Joset brought out a major new edition of the *Libro de buen amor* to replace the long-antiquated Cejador y Frauca edition in the same series. In 1977 Luis Beltrán published a linear commentary on the poem. In the same year an elaborate computer-generated concordance to the *Libro de buen amor* by Mignani, Di Cesare, and Jones appeared. Two years later, John K. Walsh published a landmark article in which he argues that Ruiz parodies the entire body of clerical poetry and that much of the parody is difficult to grasp today because of the loss of texts.

New editions appeared in the 1980s: a provisional one by Alberto Blecua in 1983 and a long-awaited one

by Gybbon-Monypenny in 1988. The most useful single publication of this period, however, was Joset's *Nuevas investigaciones sobre el "Libro de buen amor"* (1988, New Investigations on the *Libro de buen amor*). This slender volume offers a summary of the status of various fundamental questions regarding the poem, as well as an updated bibliography. Also useful for background on the Archpriest as an ecclesiastical figure is Henry Ansgar Kelly's monograph *Canon Law and the Archpriest of Hita* (1984), though its conclusions as to chronology and legal background must be used with caution.

The most important theoretical and critical work on the *Libro de buen amor* during the 1990s was Dagenais's *The Ethics of Reading in Manuscript Culture: Glossing the* Libro de buen amor (1994), which persuasively argues for new and heightened scrutiny of the manuscripts themselves instead of reliance on "homogenized" critical editions that deliberately or inadvertently conceal the evidence of reception of the work by early copyists and readers. This book generated considerable discussion in the journal *La corónica* between 1997 and 1999. Just as the twentieth century began for *Libro de buen amor* studies with Ducamin's great edition of the text, the century ended with an implicit indictment of all editing in advocating a return to manuscripts or facsimiles themselves.

The *Libro de buen amor* is not easy to translate in a satisfactory manner. Nonetheless, there have been six complete renderings of Ruiz's poem into English. The first was Kane's rollicking and free version of 1933. The 1970s produced four versions: that of Mignani and Di Cesare in prose in 1970, Willis's prose paraphrase in 1972, Mack Singleton's mixture of verse and prose in 1975, and Daly's verse version, concluding a draft begun by Hubert Creekmore, in 1978. Elizabeth Drayson MacDonald's 1999 version translates the work line by line but in prose. The poem has also been translated into Dutch, German, Italian, and French.

The availability of modern personal computers for textual manipulation will permit detailed investigations of such elements as sound patterns in the text; preliminary work in this direction has been published by Steven D. Kirby (1999). A searchable CD-ROM of the manuscripts of the book, with exhaustive concordances and word lists, was published in 2004 by Kirby and Naylor. With the technology available today and that which will become available in the future, it is difficult to conceive of the new directions research will take in the next decades and generations. What is certain, however, is that the richness and complexity of Juan Ruiz's masterpiece will continue to challenge readers and scholars as it has since it was rediscovered in the eighteenth century.

Bibliography:

German Orduna, Georgina Olivetto, and Hugo O. Bizzari, "El *Libro de buen amor:* Bibliografía," *Boletín bibliográfico de la Asociación Hispánica de Literatura Medieval,* 8 (1994): 231–376.

References:

José María Aguado, *Glossario sobre Juan Ruiz, poeta castellano del siglo XIV* (Madrid: Talleres Espasa-Calpe, 1929);

José Amador de los Ríos, *Historia crítica de la literatura española,* volume 4 (Madrid: José Fernández Cancela, 1863), pp. 155–204;

Rica Amran, ed., *Autour du* Libro de buen amor (Paris: Indigo, 2005);

Nicolás Antonio, *Bibliotheca hispana vetus,* 2 volumes, second edition, edited by Francisco Pérez Bayer (Madrid: Ibarra, 1788); translated into Spanish by Gregorio de Andrés Martínez and others as *Biblioteca hispana antigua,* 2 volumes (Madrid: Fundación Universitaria Española, 1998);

Luis Beltrán, *Razones de buen amor: Oposiciones y convergencias en el libro del arcipreste de Hita* (Madrid: Fundación Juan March/Editorial Castalia, 1977);

Alberto Blecua, "Juan Ruiz, Arcipreste de Hita: *Libro de buen amor,*" translated by Carlos Alvar and José Manuel Lucía Megías, in *Diccionario filológico de literatura medieval española: Textos y transmisión* (Madrid: Castalia, 2002), pp. 739–744;

Blecua, "Los textos medievales castellanos y sus ediciones," *Romance Philology,* 45 (1991): 73–88; translated by Steven B. Raulston as "Medieval Castilian Texts and Their Editions," in *Scholarly Editing: A Guide To Research,* edited by D. C. Greetham (New York: Modern Language Association of America, 1995), pp. 459–485;

Adolfo Bonilla y San Martín, "Antecedentes del tipo celestinesco en la literatura latina," *Revue Hispanique,* 15 (1906): 372–386;

Manuel Criado de Val, ed., *El Arcipreste de Hita: El libro, el autor, la tierra, la época. Actas del I Congreso Internacional sobre el Arcipreste de Hita* (Barcelona: S.E.R.E.S.A., 1973);

Criado de Val, ed., *Los orígenes del español y los grandes textos medievales:* Mio Cid, Buen Amor, y Celestina (Madrid: Consejo Superior de Investigaciones Científicas, 2001);

John Dagenais, *The Ethics of Reading in Manscript Culture: Glossing the* Libro de buen amor (Princeton: Princeton University Press, 1994);

Laurence de Looze, *Pseudo-Autobiography in the Fourteenth Century: Juan Ruiz, Guillaume de Machaut, Jean Froissart, and Geoffrey Chaucer* (Gainesville: University Press of Florida, 1997);

Xavier Domingo, *Erótica hispánica* (Paris: Ruedo Ibérico, 1972), pp. 59–68;

Peter N. Dunn, *Verdad y verdades en el* Libro de buen amor (Mexico City: Colegio de México, 1970);

Daniel Eisenberg, "Juan Ruiz's Heterosexual 'Good Love,'" in *Queer Iberia: Sexualities, Cultures, and Crossings from the Middle Ages to the Renaissance,* edited by Josiah Blackmore and Gregory S. Hutcheson (Durham, N.C.: Duke University Press, 1999), pp. 250–274;

Juan Ignacio Ferreras, *Las estructuras narrativas del* Libro de buen amor (Madrid: Endymión, 1999);

G. B. Gybbon-Monypenny, "Autobiography in the *Libro de Buen Amor* in the Light of Some Literary Comparisons," *Bulletin of Hispanic Studies,* 34 (1957): 63–78;

Gybbon-Monypenny, ed., *"Libro de buen amor" Studies* (London: Tamesis, 1970);

Louise M. Hayward and Louise O. Vasvari, eds., *A Companion to the* Libro de buen amor (Woodbridge, U.K. & Rochester, N.Y.: Tamesis, 2004);

Carlos Heusch, ed., *El* Libro de buen amor *de Juan Ruiz, Archiprêtre de Hita* (Paris: Ellipses, 2005);

Jacques Joset, *Nuevas investigaciones sobre el "Libro de buen amor"* (Madrid: Cátedra, 1988);

José Jurado, *Bibliografía sobre Juan Ruiz y su* Libro de buen amor (Madrid: Consejo Superior de Investigaciones Científicas, 1993);

Elisha Kent Kane, "The Personal Appearance of Juan Ruiz," *Modern Language Notes,* 45 (1930): 103–109;

Henry Ansgar Kelly, *Canon Law and the Archpriest of Hita* (Binghamton, N.Y.: Medieval and Renaissance Texts and Studies, 1984);

Steven D. Kirby, "La función estética de la rima consecutiva en el *Libro de buen amor,*" *Revista de Filología Española,* 79 (1999): 101–121;

Kirby and Eric W. Naylor, eds., *Texts and Concordances of the* Libro de buen amor *(Gayoso, Salamanca and Toledo Manuscripts)* (New York: Hispanic Seminary of Medieval Studies/Hispanic Society of America, 2004 [CD-ROM]);

Jeremy N. H. Lawrance, "The Rubrics in MS. S of the *Libro de buen amor,*" in *The Medieval Mind: Hispanic Studies in Honour of Alan Deyermond,* edited by Ian Macpherson and Ralph Penny (London: Tamesis, 1997), pp. 223–252;

Félix Lecoy, *Recherches sur le* Libro de buen amor *de l'Archiprêtre de Hita* (Paris: Droz, 1938); edited by Alan D. Deyermond (Farnborough, U.K.: Gregg International, 1974);

María Rosa Lida de Malkiel, *Juan Ruiz: Selección del Libro de buen amor y estudios críticos,* preface by Yakov Malkiel, prologue by Alberto Vàrvaro (Buenos

Aires: Editorial Universitaria de Buenos Aires, 1973);

Lida de Malkiel, *Two Spanish Masterpieces:* The Book of Good Love *and* The Celestina (Urbana: University of Illinois Press, 1961);

Francisco López Estrada, "Manifestaciones festivas de la literatura medieval castellana," in *Formas carnavalescas en el arte y la literatura,* edited by Javier Huerta Calvo (Barcelona: Ediciones del Serbal, 1989), pp. 63–117;

Ramón Menéndez Pidal, *Poesía juglaresca y juglares: Aspectos de la historia literaria y cultural de España* (Madrid: Centro de Estudios Históricos, 1924), pp. 37, 41, 48, 64, 108, 264–276, 462–467; revised and enlarged as *Poesía juglaresca y juglares: Orígenes de las literaturas románicas* (Madrid: Espasa-Calpe, 1991), pp. 56, 60, 65, 79, 80, 114, 268–283, 487–493;

Marcelino Menéndez y Pelayo, ed., *Antología de poetas líricos castellanos desde la formación del idioma hasta nuestros días,* volume 1 (Madrid: Viuda de Hernando, 1892);

André S. Michalski, "Description in Medieval Spanish Poetry," dissertation, Princeton University, 1964, pp. 94–101;

Rigo Mignani, Mario A. Di Cesare, and George Fenwick Jones, *A Concordance to Juan Ruiz,* Libro de buen amor (Albany: State University of New York Press, 1977);

Margherita Morreale, "*El libro de buen amor* de Juan Ruiz, Arcipreste de Hita," in *Grundriss der romanischen Literaturen des Mittelalters,* volume 9: *La littérature dans la Peninsule Ibérique aux XIVe et XVe siècles,* edited by Walter Mettmann, fascicule 4, tome 2 (Heidelberg: Carl Winter, 1985), pp. 53–73;

Oliver T. Myers, "Symmetry of Form in the *Libro de buen amor,*" *Philological Quarterly,* 51 (1972): 74–84;

Eric W. Naylor, "El intellectum tibi dabo del prólogo del *Libro del [sic] buen amor,*" *Letras,* 41 (1999–2000): 19–26;

Naylor, "'Nunca le digas trotera' (*Libro de buen amor,* 926c)," in *Homenaje al Profesor Antonio Vilanova,* volume 1, edited by Adolfo Sotelo Vázquez and María Cristina Carbonell (Barcelona: Universidad de Barcelona, Departamento de Filología Española, 1989), pp. 461–474;

José Luis Pérez López, "El códice T del *Libro de buen amor* en su biblioteca: averroistas y goliardos," *La corónica,* 31, no. 1 (2002–2003): 69–106;

Pérez López, "La fecha del *Libro de buen amor,*" *Incipit,* 22 (2002): 95–132;

Pérez López, "El *Libro de buen amor* a la luz de algunos textos litúrgicos de la Catedral de Toledo," *Revista de Poética Medieval,* 6 (2001): 53–85;

Julio Puyol y Alonso, *El arcipreste de Hita* (Madrid: Sucesora de M. Minuesa de los Ríos, 1906);

César Real de la Riva, "El *Libro de buen amor,* de Juan Ruiz, Arcipreste de Hita," in *Grundriss der romanischen Literaturen des Mittelalters,* volume 9, pp. 59–90;

Henry B. Richardson, *An Etymological Vocabulary to the* Libro de buen amor *of Juan Ruiz, Arcipreste de Hita* (New Haven: Yale University Press / London: M. Milford, Oxford University Press, 1930);

William W. Ryding, *Structure in Medieval Narrative* (The Hague: Mouton, 1971);

Colin Smith, "Juan Ruiz: *The Book of Good Love,*" in *The New Pelican Guide to English Literature,* volume 1: *Medieval Literature,* part 2: *The European Inheritance,* edited by Boris Ford (Harmondsworth, U.K.: Penguin, 1983), pp. 275–286;

Francisco Toro Ceballos and Bienvenido Morros, eds., *Juan Ruiz, Arcipreste de Hita y el* Libro de buen amor: *Actas del Congreso Internacional del Centro para la Edición de los Clásicos Españoles* (Alcalá la Real: Ayuntamiento de Alcalá la Real/Centro para la Edición de Clásicos Españoles, 2004)–available on-line at <http://cvc.cervantes.es/obref/arcipreste_hita/>;

Toro Ceballos and José Rodríguez Molina, eds., *Estudios de Frontera: Alcalá la Real y el Arcipreste de Hita* (Jaén: Diputación Provincial de Jaén, 1996);

Luis Josef Velázquez, *Orígenes de la poesía castellana* (Málaga: Francisco Martínez de Aguilar, 1754), pp. 36–44;

Mary-Anne Vetterling, "Los siete pecados capitales en el *Libro de buen amor* a la luz de la teoría del entrelazamiento," in *Actas del XIII Congreso de la Asociación Internacional de Hispanistas: Madrid, 6–11 de Julio de 1998,* volume 1: *Medieval; Siglo de Oro,* edited by Florencio Sevilla and Carlos Alvar (Madrid: Castalia, 2000), pp. 244–248;

John K. Walsh, "Juan Ruiz and the *mester de clerezía:* Lost Context and Lost Parody in the *Libro de buen amor,*" *Romance Philology,* 33 (1979): 62–86;

Sarah Jane Williams, "An Author's Role in Fourteenth-Century Book Production: Guillaume de Machaut's 'Livre ou je met toutes mes choses,'" *Romania,* 90 (1969): 433–454;

Ferdinand Wolf, *Studien zur Geschichte der spanischen und portugiesichen nationalliteratur* (Berlin: Asher, 1859), pp. 98–139;

Domingo Ynduráin, *Las querellas del buen amor: Lectura de Juan Ruiz* (Salamanca: Seminario de Estudios Medievales y Renacentistas, 2001);

Anthony N. Zahareas, *The Art of Juan Ruiz, Archpriest of Hita* (Madrid: Estudios de Literatura Española, 1965).

Santa María Egipçiaca

(thirteenth–fourteenth centuries)

Dayle Seidenspinner-Núñez
University of Notre Dame

WORKS: *Vida de madona Santa María Egipçiaqua* (early thirteenth century)

Manuscript: Real Biblioteca del Monasterio de El Escorial, MS. K.III.4.

Editions: *La Vida de Santa María Egipçiaca, traducida por un juglar anónimo hacia 1215,* edited by María S. de Andrés Castellanos, BRAE, anejo 11 (Madrid: Real Academia Española, 1964); *Vida de Santa María Egipçiaca: Estudios, vocabulario, edición de los textos,* 2 volumes, edited by Manuel Alvar, (Madrid: Consejo Superior de Investigaciones Cientíificas, 1970, 1972); *The Life of Saint Mary of Egypt: An Edition and Study of the Medieval French and Spanish Verse Redactions,* edited by Michèle Schiavone de Cruz-Sáenz (Barcelona: Puvill, 1979).

Estoria de Santa María Egipçiaca (fourteenth century)

Manuscript: Real Biblioteca del Monasterio de El Escorial, MS. h.I.13.

Editions: *Vida de Santa María Egipçiaca: Estudios, vocabulario, edición de los textos,* volume 2, edited by Manuel Alvar (Madrid: Consejo Superior de Investigaciones Cientíificas, 1972), pp. 151–167; *Estoria de Santa María Egipçiaca,* edited by Roger M. Walker (Exeter, U.K.: University of Exeter Press, 1972).

Vida de Santa María Egipçiaca (fourteenth century)

Manuscripts: Real Biblioteca del Monasterio de El Escorial, MS. h.III.22; Biblioteca Nacional, Madrid MS. 780.

Edition: *Vida de Santa María Egipçiaca: A Fourteenth-Century Translation of a Work by Paul the Deacon,* edited by Billy Bussell Thompson and John K. Walsh (Exeter, U.K.: University of Exeter Press, 1977).

De Santa María de Egipto (fourteenth century)

Manuscripts: Real Biblioteca del Monasterio de El Escorial M.S.S. h.I.14, Escorial MS. MS.II.6, and K.II.12; Biblioteca Menéndez y Pelayo MS. 8; Biblioteca de la Fundación Lázaro-Galdiano, Madrid MS. 419.

Edition: *Vida de Santa María Egipçiaca: A Fourteenth-Century*

Statue (1465) of Santa María Egipçiaca with her three loaves of bread in the chapel of the Château de Châteaudun (from Manuel Alvar, Vida de Santa María Egipçiaca: Estudios, vocabulario, edición de los textos, *volume 1, 1970; Thomas Cooper Library, University of South Carolina)*

Translation of a Work by Paul the Deacon, edited by Billy Bussell Thompson and John K. Walsh (Exeter, U.K.: University of Exeter Press, 1977).

In medieval Spain few legends compared in importance, popularity, number of manuscripts, and influence to that of Santa María Egipçiaca (St. Mary the

Egyptian). In the legend Mary is a spoiled child who flees her parents' home at age twelve and travels to Alexandria, where she becomes a celebrated prostitute. One day she encounters a group of pilgrims bound for Jerusalem and offers to sell her body to the sailors in exchange for passage on the ship. During the voyage she seduces everyone—the young and foolish, as well as the old and wise. In Jerusalem she attempts to visit a temple with a group of pilgrims on the Feast of the Ascension, but her entrance is mysteriously barred. Suddenly aware of her iniquity, Mary repents, prays to the Virgin, and is admitted to the temple, where a voice directs her to journey to the desert beyond the River Jordan to spend the rest of her life in atonement. Taking three loaves of bread with her, she becomes a hermit in the desert. For the first seventeen years she suffers temptations of the flesh, but she spends the next thirty years in perfect inner peace. In the harsh conditions of the desert her clothes wear away and the great beauty she once flaunted is grotesquely transformed: her naked body blackens and shrivels. She is discovered by Zosimas, a perfection-minded monk who has come to spend the forty days of Lent in the desert. During Lent the following year Mary crosses the Jordan by walking on the water to receive communion from Zosimas. She dies the next year, and Zosimas buries her with the assistance of a docile lion. The monk then returns to the monastery to tell his brothers Mary's story, and her exemplary spiritual perfection and penitence inspire the monks to improve their own conduct.

A figure of extraordinary devotion in both the East and the West during the Middle Ages, Mary first appears in the fifth century in Cyril of Scythopolis's life of St. Cyriacus the Hermit as a minor character who miraculously lives for many years as a hermit in the Palestinian desert with little or no food. Her hair grows so long that it covers her body after her clothes wear away. Discovered by two monks, she tells them that she was a cantoress in a church in Jerusalem but escaped to do penance in the desert so that her beauty would not be a source of temptation to men. She dies shortly afterward, and the monks bury her in a nearby cave; Cyril claims to have visited her tomb. Another version of the story was transmitted orally to John Moschus (circa 550–619), who recorded it in his *Pratum Spirituale* (The Spiritual Meadow).

The earliest known life of St. Mary the Egyptian was written in Greek and falsely attributed to Sophronius, the patriarch of Jerusalem (circa 560–638) to confer greater authenticity on it. The legend recorded—or composed—by Pseudo-Sophronius combines the tale of the penitent from Cyril's life of Cyriacus with St. Anthony's encounter with the hermit Paul of Thebes in the desert. In this version Mary is depicted for the first

time as the former Alexandrian prostitute whose extravagant penitence serves as atonement for her past. But Pseudo-Sophronius did not write his work to glorify Mary; instead, he presents her as a counterexemplum to illustrate for his monastic audience the central lesson in the life of the holy monk Zosimas. Zosimas arrogantly believes that he has achieved spiritual perfection until he learns that the monks of the monastery of St. John, near the River Jordan, lead more-austere lives than his, subsisting on bread and water and spending all of Lent in solitude in the desert. Zosimas joins these ascetic monks during their Lenten exercise and discovers Mary, who tells him the story of her life. He then realizes that there are levels of asceticism and humility to which he can only aspire.

Three independent early-medieval Latin translations of Pseudo-Sophronius's work survive: a late-ninth-century translation by Paul the Deacon, which is a learned version destined for court or monastic circles and had little impact on the vernacular tradition during the Middle Ages (it became widely known after the invention of printing because of its inclusion in the *Vitae Patrum* [Lives of the Desert Fathers], first printed in 1478 and frequently reprinted afterward); a much shorter and less accurate translation in the eleventh-century collection *Vitae Sanctorum Patrum* (Lives of the Holy Fathers) from the Benedictine monastery of Monte Cassino; and a Hispano-Latin version in a collection of devotional works dated 954 (Escorial MS. a-II-9), whose importance in the transmission of the story of Mary of Egypt to the vernacular was established by Jerry R. Craddock in 1966. A fourth translation in the *Acta Sanctorum* (Acts of the Saints), formerly considered the most elegant and accurate version in Latin and the source of the medieval vernacular versions, was revealed by Craddock to be the work of Daniel Papebrochius, the seventeenth-century compiler of the collection.

These early Latin translations of the Greek text generated other versions in Latin and in the vernacular. Among the Latin reworkings of the story are verse redactions by Flodoard of Rheims (894–966); Hildebert of Lavardin, Archbishop of Tours (1056–1135); and a twelfth-century monk of the Abbey of St. Evroult in Normandy. Influential Latin prose versions appear in the *Speculum Historiale* (Mirror of History), by Vincent de Beauvais (circa 1190–1264), and in the widely disseminated collection of saints' lives, the *Legenda Aurea* (Golden Legend), by Jacobus de Voragine (1228/1230–1298), which presents an abridgment of the *Speculum Historiale* account.

By the thirteenth century vernacular versions of the legend were proliferating. Extant texts include an

Painting by the Renaissance artist Franciabigio (Francesco di Cristofano) of Santa María Egipçiaca receiving communion from St. Zosimas (from Manuel Alvar, Vida de Santa María Egipçiaca: Estudios, vocabulario, edición de los textos, *volume 1, 1970; Thomas Cooper Library, University of South Carolina)*

Anglo-Saxon translation from the ninth century; a short Anglo-Norman poem by Adgar from the late twelfth century; the anonymous Old French poem *La Vie de Sainte Marie l'Egyptienne* (The Life of St. Mary the Egyptian) from the late twelfth or early thirteenth century; an anonymous Anglo-Norman poem, the Old Spanish *Vida de madona Santa María Egipçiaqua* (Life of Our Lady St. Mary the Egyptian), and a Middle English verse life in the *Liber Festivalis* (Book of Feasts), all from the early thirteenth century; a Franco-Venetian translation from the thirteenth century; a prose adaptation of *La Vie de Sainte Marie l'Egyptienne* from the late thirteenth century; an Old French *Vie de Sainte Marie l'Egyptienne,* by Rutebeuf (flourished 1245–1285); a poem by Martin de Thorout dated 1290; the Italian poem *De Maria Egyptiaca* (On Mary the Egyptian), by Bonvesin da Riva (circa 1240–1315); an Italian prose translation of Pseudo-Sophronius by Domenico Cavalca, who died in 1342; two Portuguese translations of Pseudo-Sophronius from the fourteenth century; a fourteenth-century Portu-

guese translation of the *Legenda Aurea* account; and the Old Spanish *Estoria de Santa María Egipçiaca* (History of Saint Mary the Egyptian), *Vida de Santa María Egipçiaca* (Life of St. Mary of Egypt), and *De Santa María de Egipto* (Of St. Mary of Egypt), all from the fourteenth century. There are also redactions of the story in Celtic, German, Dutch, Norwegian, Armenian, Ethiopian, Syrian, Ukranian, Greek, and Arabic.

The Latin and vernacular versions that follow the structure of Pseudo-Sophronius maintain the emphasis of the Eastern monastic tradition that engendered the legend: they focus on Zosimas's battle with pride and the lesson in humility he learns from Mary's example. Mary appears late in the narrative and recounts her life in the first person; the reader learns much of Zosimas's vainglory and spiritual quest but few details of Mary's sinful past. In contrast, the more-popular vernacular texts initiate a Western tradition in which Mary is the central figure. A third-person narrator presents the life of Mary from childhood to death, and Zosimas does not appear until halfway through the tale;

while dramatic and vivid accounts are given of Mary's sinfulness and perversity in her youth and of the stark contrast with her austere penitence, the most important feature of Pseudo-Sophronius's story—Zosimas's pride in his own saintliness and his path back to humility—is omitted.

More than a dozen manuscripts of *sanctorales* (collections of saints' lives) in Old Spanish exist, most of which derive from Voragine's *Legenda Aurea*. Medieval compilers selected material from various sources, omitting some saints and focusing on others who were favored by or meaningful to their monastery, order, or region. It is common to find several consecutive lives from the *Legenda Aurea* combined with a longer life of a saint of special importance that replaces the abbreviated life in the *Legenda Aurea* and the occasional insertion of a new local or national saint. Thus, in the compilations represented by Biblioteca Nacional MS. 780 and Escorial MS. h-III-22, translations of Paul the Deacon's more elaborate version of the life of Mary are substituted for Voragine's brief account. Independent Spanish translations of Voragine's narrative appear in five other collections. Billy Bussell Thompson and John K. Walsh observe in an article in *La corónica* (1986–1987) that the most important saints in medieval Spain, as gauged by the number of literary renditions of their legends or by the frequency of their invocation in literature, were Mary Magdalene, Mary the Egyptian, Ildefonsus, Catherine of Alexandria, and James. Their veneration was surpassed only by that of the Virgin, and their legends were recited so frequently that they generated episodes in folklore.

Although the Old Spanish translations of Paul the Deacon and of Voragine maintain the structure and emphasis of the Eastern version that focuses on Zosimas, the other two treatments—the early-thirteenth-century poem *Vida de madona Santa María Egipçiaqua* and the fourteenth-century prose work *Estoria de Santa María Egipçiaca*—are translations of French originals, representing the Western tradition in which Mary is the protagonist. Both texts derive from the anonymous late-twelfth- or early-thirteenth-century Old French *Vie de Sainte Marie l'Egyptienne,* the *Vida de madona Santa María Egipçiaqua* directly, and the *Estoria de Santa María Egipçiaca* through an intermediate French prose version of the poem. The *Vida de madona Santa María Egipçiaqua* survives in a unique manuscript copied in the late fourteenth century by an Aragonese scribe; the Spanish poet worked from a twelfth-century French manuscript that is no longer extant (none of the eight surviving manuscripts of the Old French *Vie* served as the source of the *Vida de madona Santa María Egipçiaqua*). The French prose version of the life of Mary the Egyptian survives in five manuscripts and represents a free adaptation of the verse *Vie de Sainte Marie l'Egyptienne* that

incorporates Paul the Deacon's Latin version for its ending; the Old Spanish *Estoria de Santa María Egipçiaca* is a remarkably faithful translation of its French model.

While the education required for translation, the religious themes, and the moral intention indicate that both the *Vida de madona Santa María Egipçiaqua* and the *Estoria de Santa María Egipçiaca* were written by ecclesiastical authors, and while both works, given their common dependence on the *Vie de Sainte Marie l'Egyptienne,* tell the same story with the same sequence of events, the two texts address different audiences. The *Vida de madona Santa María Egipçiaqua* is designed for a broad spectrum of listeners; many of its stylistic features—rhymed octosyllabic couplets, oral formulas, repetitions and summaries, dramatization, and use of descriptive detail—suggest that it was written to be performed by minstrels as part of the campaign for religious instruction of the masses promoted by the Fourth Lateran Council, summoned by Pope Innocent III in 1215. The poet insistently expounds the religious lessons and doctrine that Mary's life represents, from the opening homily on the nature of sin, the importance of confession, the necessity of penitence, and the extent of divine mercy to the closing exhortation to the audience to mend their ways and pray to St. Mary of Egypt to intercede on their behalf and effect their salvation. The *Estoria de Santa María Egipçiaca,* on the other hand, is intended for private devotional reading or to be read aloud to a small group of educated listeners who are less in need of religious instruction and capable of following its sophisticated style.

Part of the appeal that the St. Mary of Egypt legend exercised on the medieval imagination lies in its dramatic juxtaposition of the themes of flamboyant sexuality and extreme asceticism. The *Vida de madona Santa María Egipçiaqua* poet presents two contrasting portraits of Mary. A detailed seductive picture of the beautiful but corrupt harlot appears in lines 205 through 244:

> Abié redondas las orejas,
> blanquas como leche dovejas;
> ojos negros, e sobreçejas;
> alba fruente, fasta las çernejas.
> La faz tenié colorada,
> como la rosa cuando es granada;
> boqua chica e por mesura
> muy fermosa la catadura.
> Su cuello e su petrina,
> tal como la flor dell espina.
> De sus tetiellas bien es sana
> tales son como maçana.
>
> (She had round ears,
> white as sheep's milk;
> dark eyes and eyebrows;
> her forehead white to her hairline.

Her face was blushed,
like a full-blown rose;
her mouth small and well proportioned,
her visage very lovely.
Her neck and her chest
were like a white rose.
Her little breasts were robust
just like two apples.)

An equally elaborate description of the ugly but saintly anchorite is given in lines 720 through 758:

Las sus orejas, que eran albas,
mucho eran negras e pegadas.
Entenebridos abié los ojos;
abié perdidos los sus mencojos.
La boca era empeleçida,
e derredor muy denegrida.
La faz muy negra e arrugada
de frío viento e de la elada
La barbiella e el su grinyón
semeja cabo de tizón.

Tan negra era la su petrina,
como la pez e la resina.
En sus pechos no abiá tetas,
como yo cuido eran secas.

(Her ears, which used to be white,
were very black and sticky.
Her eyes were cloudy:
she had lost her eyelashes.
Her mouth was covered with hair,
and blackened around.
Her face was darkened and wrinkled
from the cold wind and the frost.
Her chin and her grinyón
were like the end of a burnt stick.

Her chest was as black
as pitch and as resin.
Her breasts had no nipples,
for I think they were dry.)

These two rhetorical portraits, present in the French poem but amplified in detail and lyricism in the *Vida de madona Santa María Egipçiaqua,* graphically present the contrast between the physical beauty that masks the harlot's morally corrupt interior and the external repugnance that cloaks the penitent's inner spiritual perfection. The portraits function both diachronically, by contrasting the past of preconversion sinfulness and the present of postconversion sanctity, and synchronically by opposing Mary's outer physical appearance with her inner spiritual reality—outer beauty versus inner ugliness before conversion, outer ugliness versus inner beauty after conversion—and graphically illustrate the themes of conversion, penitence, sin, and salvation.

The hagiographic category to which St. Mary of Egypt belongs is that of St. Mary Magdalene, the prototype of the harlot saint; the category also includes St. Mary the Harlot, St. Pelagia, and St. Thais. In its most reductive form the harlot-saint paradigm represents a beautiful, sexually active young woman, her moment of conversion, and her ultimate transformation through penance. Mary the Harlot is raised from age seven by her uncle, the ascetic hermit Abraham; ashamed to face her saintly uncle after being tricked and debauched by a young monk, she joins a brothel in Alexandria. Abraham journeys to Alexandria, disguises himself as a prospective client, and convinces his fallen niece that God will forgive her if she does penance. Mary returns with her uncle to the desert, leads an exemplary life of penitence and abnegation, performs miraculous cures, and on her death is recognized as a saint. The great beauty of Pelagia, a hetaera in Antioch, delights even the venerable Bishop Nonnus, who later converts and baptizes her. The former prostitute distributes her wealth to the poor and, disguised in Nonnus's tunic, journeys to Jerusalem, where she dwells as the ascetic and holy monk Pelagius. On her death, her wasted body is discovered to be that of Pelagia, formerly the glory of Antioch. Thais is a famous fourth-century Alexandrian courtesan who is reconverted by Paphnutius, a holy abbot who disguises himself to enter her chamber. Paphnutius seals his penitent in a narrow, doorless cell for three years, until she is sufficiently purified to receive communion; she dies fifteen days after leaving her prison. The stories of the harlot saints Pelagia of Antioch, Thais the courtesan, and Mary the niece of Abraham were often presented as a set of texts, along with the life of Mary of Egypt or Mary Magdalene; all are well represented in Old Spanish collections.

There is considerable contamination between the legends of Mary Magdalene and Mary of Egypt. In the Western apocryphal tradition, Mary Magdalene is conflated with three other women: Mary of Bethany, the sister of Martha and Lazarus; the unnamed woman sinner who annointed Jesus' feet; and the also unnamed woman taken in adultery. While the unnamed women are never specified as prostitutes in the New Testament, the sinfulness of the apocryphal Mary Magdalene is clearly identified with prostitution. After the resurrection, Mary Magdalene, her sister Martha, and their brother Lazarus sailed to Marseilles after the resurrection; from there Mary traveled to the forest of Sainte Baume near Aix, where she lived in prayer and penitence in expiation of her former wickedness and ultimately received communion from the monk Maximin. Both Mary Magdalene and Mary the Egyptian, then, are converted prostitutes turned anchorites in the wilderness; both receive the Eucharist—from St. Maximin

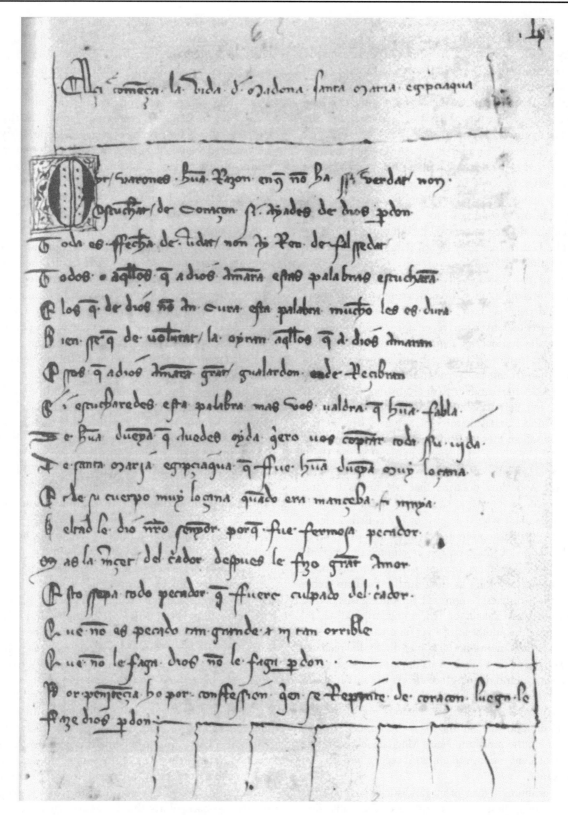

The opening of the verse Vida de madona Santa María Egipçiaqua *(Real Biblioteca del Monasterio de El Escorial, MS. K.III.4, folio 65r)*

and St. Zosimas, respectively–at the hour of their deaths; and both are lifted up, chastely wrapped in their hair, by angels. In works of art both Marys are typically depicted with long flowing hair that covers their bodies; they are virtually indistinguishable, unless they are labeled or accompanied by their iconographic tags–the penitent Magdalene by a flask of perfume and the Egyptian by three loaves of bread.

In medieval Europe these stories of prostitute saints proved to be a dramatically effective vehicle for the exposition of Christian doctrine. The issues of confession, penance, and the Eucharist, intrinsic to the conversion from prostitution to sanctity, were being debated and defined in the twelfth and thirteenth centuries. The Fourth Lateran Council required annual confession and communion of all Christians and formalized the doctrine of transubstantiation; it also launched a campaign for the educational reform of the clergy and religious instruction of the masses. By dramatizing acts of conversion, repentance, confession, and penance, the harlot-saint legends communicated doctrine to the reader or listener more immediately and directly than teaching or sermonizing, as concrete experiences to be shared rather than as abstract concepts or theories. The denouement of each dramatic sequence is another fundamental theme of Catholic Christianity–the gift of salvation–and a primary reason for the popularity and circulation of the harlot stories in the West, for the spectacular example of the prostitute saints illustrates the appealing doctrine that no one is beyond God's grace.

Consonant with the spirit of the Fourth Lateran Council, which also promoted an ambitious program of proselytization of the Jews, the prostitute-saint legends offer a New Testament reading of an Old Testament commonplace, evoking as they do the familiar archetype of the seductress-temptress Eve. During this period the Virgin was exalted for redeeming original sin by representing the antithesis of Eve; on a parallel but perhaps more human and literal plane, the harlot reenacts Eve's sin, dramatizes her conversion, and through rigorous purgation and divine grace effects her salvation. In the Old Testament and in Judaism, the prostitute or fallen woman is a symbol of religious apostasy, condemnation, and sin; in the New Testament and in Christianity, the prostitute Mary Magdalene becomes a symbol of conversion, redemption, reconciliation, and divine grace.

In addition to their propagandistic value and symbolic richness, these legends possess considerable dramatic force: the delicate undercurrent of love between Pelagia and Nonnus; the aged hermit Abraham, who, like the Good Shepherd, rescues his lost and despairing niece; and the humility of Mary the anchorite that inspires the love and admiration of the arrogant Zosimas are powerful themes. Thus, like other hagiographic tales, the harlot-saint legends were eminently adaptable to the romance conventions that dominated medieval literary taste. Formally, both the Old French *Vie de Sainte Marie l'Egyptienne* and the Old Spanish *Vida de madona Santa María Egipçiaqua* are written in rhymed couplets, the typical form of verse romances; stylistically, they include detailed descriptions, romance formulas, and interlacing techniques; and thematically, motifs common to hagiography and romance include women escaping disguised as men, as in the Pelagia tale, and friendly animals, as in the case of the lion who aids Zosimas.

Probably because saints' legends were ideal vehicles for the mass religious instruction promulgated by the Fourth Lateran Council and because the cross-pollination of hagiography and romance produced an efficacious mix of entertainment and edification, the thirteenth century was a period of extraordinary success for hagiographic poems in the vernacular in both France and Spain. In both countries, however, this flourishing was followed by an equally conspicuous decline in the fourteenth century. In "Literary Problems of Hagiography in Old French" (1976) Peter F. Dembowski analyzes the disappearance of Old French hagiographic verse romances, and his arguments apply to the decline of such works in Old Spanish. According to Dembowski, the very triumph of the genre paradoxically determined its demise: secular romances could be added to or continued, but the presumed canonicity of the myths precluded the possibility of such alterations; since nothing new could be added, hagiographic poems ceased to be composed.

The decline of the verse *vitae* was facilitated by contemporary attacks on imaginative literature in general and poetic narratives in particular: verse became associated with lies and prose with the truth. Beginning in the late thirteenth century, hagiographic poems were eclipsed by two new forms of "more authentic" hagiography: prose versions of the poems, such as the fourteenth-century *Estoria de Santa María Egipçiaca,* and prose translations of the more-authoritative Latin sources, such as the fourteenth-century translation into Old Spanish of Paul the Deacon's Latin version. The genre was further weakened, also beginning in the late thirteenth century, by compilations of the lives of the saints. These compendia presented severely abridged forms of the *vitae;* abbreviation was necessary because of the scope of the works–particularly those that arranged the lives by month and feast day–and possible because most of the legends were already known to everyone. Thus, in Voragine's hugely popular *Legenda Aurea* the story of St. Mary of Egypt is drastically reduced; as Dembowski

The opening of the prose Estoria de Santa María Egipçiaca *(Real Biblioteca del Monasterio de El Escorial, MS. h.I.13)*

notes, to "appreciate the beauty of the legend in Jacobus's version, one must know it beforehand. He does not really narrate the story, he does not move his reader, he offers a résumé, he calls on us to contemplate the story we already know."

A parallel process of abridgment may be observed in the plastic arts. The oldest extant visual representation of St. Mary of Egypt is a twelfth-century chapiter from the Monastery of San Esteban that depicts six scenes in narrative sequence: Mary barred from entering the temple, her prayer to the Virgin, Mary receiving alms to buy three loaves of bread and washing her hair in the Jordan, the anchorite meeting with Zosimas, the lion digging the grave; and Mary's burial. Manuel Alvar reproduces the scenes in the first volume of his edition of the work (1970). Later paintings and sculptures focus with far greater economy on a single scene or depict the traditional iconographic representation of Mary. As in the case of the hagiographic shorthand of Voragine, there is no longer a need to narrate; the viewer is invited to contemplate a myth whose details are already well known. A summary inventory of medieval and golden-age art dealing with Mary of Egypt establishes the predominance of three major themes: the young penitent carrying three loaves of bread, Mary receiving communion from Zosimas, and the aged ascetic. Art history thus corroborates the evidence of literary history that St. Mary the Egyptian, like her sister prostitute saints, was iconographically associated with the Eucharist, conversion, and penance. Moreover, medieval martyrologies assigned St. Mary of Egypt a feast day in early April; thus, it would be celebrated in conjunction with Lent or Easter, reaffirming her association with themes of penance, salvation, conversion, and the Eucharist.

Literature, art, and the liturgical calendar combined to impress the image of the harlot saint on the mind of the medieval reader. The myth of the harlot saint evolved in early hagiographic legends of St. Mary Magdalene, St. Mary the Egyptian, St. Thais, St. Pelagia, and St. Mary the Harlot and was poeticized and amplified into full-scale romance in the thirteenth-century hagiographic poems. Verse romances such as the Spanish *Vida de madona Santa María Egipçiaqua* and the Old French *Vie de Sainte Marie l'Egyptienne* so effectively disseminated and popularized the harlot-saint legend that later versions could circulate in the form of prose abridgments, reminders to a contemporary audience of a fuller, well-known, and much-loved legend.

References:

Manuel Alvar, *Vida de Santa María Egipçiaca: Estudios, vocabulario, edición de los textos,* 2 volumes (Madrid: Consejo Superior de Investigaciones Cientíificas, 1970, 1972);

Enrica J. Ardemagni, "Hagiography in Thirteenth-Century Spain: Intertextual Reworkings," *Romance Languages Journal,* 2 (1990): 313–316;

Alfred T. Baker, "La vie de Sainte Marie Egyptienne," *Revue de Langues Romanes,* 59 (1916–1917): 145–401;

Fernando Baños Vallejo, *La hagiografía como género literario en la Edad Media: Tipología de doce vidas individuales castellanas* (Oviedo: Departamento de Filología Española, 1989);

Baños Vallejo, "Hagiografía en verso para la catequesis y la propaganda," in *Saints and Their Authors: Studies in Medieval Hispanic Hagiography in Honor of John K. Walsh,* edited by Jane E. Connolly, Alan Deyermond, and Brian Dutton (Madison, Wis.: Hispanic Seminary of Medieval Studies, 1990), pp. 1–11;

Peter Brown, *The Cult of the Saints: Its Rise and Function in Latin Christianity* (Chicago: University of Chicago Press, 1981);

Anthony J. Cárdenas, "The Desert Experience as Other World in the Poem *Vida de Santa María Egipçiaca,*" *Romance Languages Journal,* 7 (1995): 413–418;

Lynn Rice Cortina, "The Aesthetics of Morality: Two Portraits of Mary of Egypt in the *Vida de Santa María Egipçiaca,*" *Hispanic Journal,* 2 (1980): 41–45;

Jerry R. Craddock, "Apuntes para el estudio de la leyenda de Santa María Egipçiaca en España," in *Homenaje a Rodríguez-Moñino: Estudios de erudición que le ofrecen sus amigos o discípulos hispanistas norteamericanos,* volume 1 (Madrid: Castalia, 1966), pp. 99–110;

Peter F. Dembowski, "Literary Problems of Hagiography in Old French," *Medievalia et Humanistica,* new series 7 (1976): 117–130;

Dembowski, ed., *La Vie de Sainte Marie l'Egyptienne: Versions en ancien et en moyen français* (Paris & Geneva: Publications Romanes et Françaises, 1976);

Guillermo Díaz-Plaja, "*Vida de Santa María Egipçiaca,*" in *Studia Hispanica in Honorem R. Lapesa,* volume 3, edited by E. de Bustos (Madrid: Gredos, 1975), pp. 233–240;

Theodore L. Kassier, "The Rhetorical Devices of the Spanish *Vida de Santa María Egipçiaca,*" *Anuario de Estudios Medievales,* 8 (1972–1973): 467–480;

Derek Lomax, "The Lateran Reforms and Spanish Literature," *Iberoromania,* 1 (1969): 299–313;

John R. Maier, "Sainthood, Heroism, and Sexuality in the *Estoria de Santa María Egipçiaca,*" *Revista Canadiense de Estudios Hispánicos,* 8 (1984): 424–435;

Peter L. Podol, "The Stylized Portrait of Women in Spanish Literature," *Hispanófila,* 71 (1901): 1–21;

Connie L. Scarborough, "The *Vida de Santa María Egipciaca* and Julia Kristeva's Theory of Abjection," *Medievalia*, 20 (1995–1996): 14–19;

Michèle Schiavone de Cruz-Sáenz, *The Life of Saint Mary of Egypt: An Edition and Study of the Medieval French and Spanish Verse Redactions* (Barcelona: Puvill, 1979);

Schiavone de Cruz-Sáenz, "La *Vida de Santa María Egipcíaca*: texto juglaresco u obra de clerecía," in *La juglaresca: Actas del I Congreso Internacional sobre la Juglaresca*, edited by Manuel Criado de Val (Madrid: EDI-6, 1986), pp. 275–281;

Joseph T. Snow, "Notes on the Fourteenth-Century Spanish Translation of Paul the Deacon's *Vita Sanctae Mariae Aegyptiacae, Meretricis*," in *Saints and Their Authors*, pp. 83–96;

Michael Solomon, "Catarsis sexual: La *Vida de Santa María Egipciaca* y el texto higiénico," in *Erotismo en las letras hispánicas: Aspectos, modos y fronteras,* edited by Luce López-Baralt and Francisco Márquez Villanueva (Mexico City: Centro de Estudios Lingüísticos & Literarios, Colegio de México, 1995), pp. 425–437;

Ellen Swanberg, "*Oraisons* and Liaisons: Romanesque Didacticism in *La Vie de Sainte Marie l'Egyptienne*," *Romance Notes*, 23 (1982–1983): 65–71;

Swanberg, "The Singing Bird: A Study of the Lyrical Devices of *La vida de Santa María Egipçiaca*," *Hispanic Review*, 47 (1979): 339–353;

Billy Bussell Thompson and John K. Walsh, "Old Spanish Manuscripts of Prose Lives of the Saints and Their Affiliations. I: Compilation A (The *Gran Flos Sanctorum*)," *La corónica*, 15 (1986–1987): 17–28;

Carlos Alberto Vega, "Erotismo y ascetismo: Imagen y texto en un incunable hagiográfico," in *Erotismo en las letras hispánicas*, pp. 479–497;

Walsh and Thompson, *The Myth of the Magdalen in Early Spanish Literature (With an Edition of the "Vida de Santa María Madalena" in MS h-I-13 of the Escorial Library)* (New York: Lorenzo Clemente, 1986);

Benedicta Ward, *Harlots of the Desert: A Study of Repentance in Early Monastic Sources* (Oxford: A. R. Mowbray, 1987);

Marina Warner, *Alone of All Her Sex: The Myth and Cult of the Virgin Mary* (New York: Knopf, 1976);

Raymond S. Willis, "Mary Magdalene, Mary of Bethany, and the Unnamed Woman Sinner: Another Instance of Their Conflation in Old Spanish Literature," *Romance Philology*, 24 (1970): 89–90.

Shem Tov de Carrión
(Isaac Ibn Ardutiel)
(flourished circa 1350 – 1360)

Norman Roth
University of Wisconsin–Madison

WORKS: *Ma'aseh ha-Rav: Milhemet ha-et ve-ha-misparayim* (1345)

Manuscript: Only a microfilm of the sole known manuscript exists; the original was apparently destroyed by Nazis.

Editions: "Milhemet ha-et ve-ha-misparayim," edited by Eliezer Ashkenazi, in his *Divrey akhamim* (Metz: Samuel, 1849); excerpts from Ashkenazi edition in Hayyim Shirmann, ed., *ha-Shirah ha-'ivrit bi-sefarad u-Provens,* volume 2 (Jerusalem & Tel Aviv, 1956), pp. 531–540; translated by F. Díaz Esteban as "El debate del cálamo y las tijeras," *Revista de la Universidad de Madrid,* 18 (1968): 62–102; *Ma'aseh ha-Rav: Milhemet ha-'et veha-misparayim,* edited by Maya Fruchtman and Yehuda Nini (Tel Aviv: Universitat Tel-Aviv, 1980).

Edition in English: "The Battle of the Pen and the Scissors," translated by Clark Colahan, in *Shem Tov: His World and His Words,* by Sanford Shepard (Miami: Universal, 1978), pp. 79–97.

Proverbios morales (circa 1350)

Manuscripts: Cambridge University Library, MS. Add. MS. 3355; Biblioteca Nacional, Madrid, MS. 9216 (*olim* Bb-82); Biblioteca de la Real Academia Española, Madrid, MS. R-M-73 (*olim* Biblioteca Antonio Rodríguez Moñino, MS. V-6-73); Biblioteca del Monasterio de El Escorial, MS. b.IV.21 (*olim* iv-N-28; iv-B-24); Archivo Diocesano de Cuenca, expediente inquisitorial Legajo 6, no. 125, fifteenth century.

Early editions: Excerpts from Escorial MS. b.IV.21 published as "Consejos y documentos," in *Colección de poesías castellanas anteriores al siglo XV,* 4 volumes, edited by Tomás Antonio Sánchez (Madrid: A. Sancha, 1779–1790), I: 179–184; IV: 12ff. "Proverbios morales" [Biblioteca Nacional, Madrid, MS. 9216], edited by George Ticknor, in his *History of Spanish Literature,* volume 3 (London:

Murray, 1849; New York: Harper, 1849), pp. 436–464; "Proverbios morales," in *Colección de poesías castellanas anteriores al siglo XV,* 1 volume, edited by Sánchez, revised by Florencio Janer (Madrid: M. Rivadeneyra, 1864), pp. 351–372.

Editions: *Proverbios morales* [Cambridge, Biblioteca Nacional, Escorial, and Real Academia Español manuscripts], edited by Ignacio González Llubera (Cambridge: Cambridge University Press, 1947); González Llubera, "A Transcription of Ms. *C* of Sem Tob de Carrión's *Proverbios morales,*" *Romance Philology,* 4 (1950–1951): 217–256; *Proverbios morales,* edited by Eduardo González Lanuza and Antonio Portnoy (Buenos Aires: Sociedad hebraica Argentina, 1958); *Glosas de sabiduría, o, Proverbios morales y otras rimas,* edited by Agustín García Calvo (Madrid: Alianza, 1974); Luisa López Grigera, "Un nuevo códice de los Proverbios morales" [Cuenca manuscript], *Boletín de la Real Academia Española,* 56 (1976): 221–281; *Proverbios morales,* edited by Sanford Shephard (Madrid: Castalia, 1985); *Proverbios morales,* edited by Theodore Anthony Perry (Madison, Wis.: Hispanic Seminary of Medieval Studies, 1986); *Proverbios morales,* edited by Marcella Ciceri (Modena: Mucchi, 1998); *Proverbios morales,* edited by Paloma Díaz-Mas and Carlos Mota (Madrid: Cátedra, 1998).

Edition in English: *The Moral Proverbs of Santob de Carrión: Jewish Wisdom in Christian Spain,* translated by Theodore Anthony Perry (Princeton: Princeton University Press, 1987).

Viduiy ha-gadol

Edition in English: "The Penitential Prayer," translated by Clark Colahan, in *Shem Tov: His World and His Words,* by Sanford Shepard (Miami: Universal, 1978), pp. 98–106.

Pages from a manuscript of Shem Tov de Carrión's Proverbios Morales, *composed circa 1350 (Cambridge University Library, MS. Add. 3355)*

TRANSLATION: Israel ben Joseph Israeli, *Mivot zemaniyot.*

Shem Tov means "good name" in Hebrew and was a common name of Jews in medieval Spain. Shem Tov de Carrión is the pseudonym of Isaac Ibn Ardutiel, who is known in Spanish as "Santo" and "Santob." He was born in the first half of the fourteenth century. According to the colophons of some of the manuscripts of his *Proverbios morales* (circa 1350, Moral Proverbs; translated as *The Moral Proverbs of Santob de Carrión: Jewish Wisdom in Christian Spain,* 1987), he was a rabbi. Around 1345 he translated a legal work on the rules of prayer by Israel ben Joseph Israeli from Judeo-Arabic into Hebrew. He lived at some point in Carrión de los Condes, near Burgos, and one of the manuscripts of his legal translation states that he wrote it in Soria. Scholars have paid little attention to this translation, nor has sufficient notice been taken of the implications of the fact that Shem Tov was fluent in Arabic. It means that he could not have been born either in Soria or in Carrión de los Condes, where, by his own account, Jews did not know Arabic. The only possibilities are Aragon, Toledo, or Andalusia, places where Jews knew Arabic; Aragon is excluded by his expert knowledge of Castilian.

Proverbios morales was at least Shem Tov's second work: he had completed the legal translation, and probably also his own Hebrew composition, *Ma'aseh ha-Rav: Milhemet ha-et ve-ha-misparayim* (translated as "The Battle of the Pen and the Scissors," 1978), in Soria in 1345. In this poem, which is appended to the Escorial manuscript of *Proverbios morales,* the speaker is alone on a bitterly cold and snowy day. In his solitude he turns his attention to his pen: "who has his pen and ink–it is sufficient for him more than friends." He compares the pen to the sword as a "second tongue," referring to the "tongue," or edge, of the sword. But when he tries to write with the pen, he discovers that the ink has frozen. In anger he strikes the pen on the table, and it breaks. After quarreling with the pen over its neglect of its duty, he tries to write with his fingernail; but the frozen ink breaks the nail. The pen exclaims in triumph, "Do not judge your companion until you stand in his place," a quotation from the Mishnah *Avot* (Ethics of the Fathers). Finally, he has the idea to "write" with scissors by cutting out the letters of the poem from another manuscript and pasting them in sequence on a new piece of paper. He considers the experiment a success, but the pen is not ready to give up its position and engages in a debate with the scissors. The pen points

Page from a second manuscript of the Proverbios Morales *(Biblioteca Nacional, Madrid, MS. 9216)*

out that it takes much longer to write with scissors: "before you have written one line, I will have written the whole Bible!" The scissors respond that the commandments were engraved—that is, "cut out"—on the tablets that God gave to Moses. The poet puts an end to the dispute by declaring that the pen has many advantages, but he cannot forget the "goodness" of the scissors, which helped him when he was unable to write with the pen. The editors of the 1980 edition of this lighthearted satire suggest that it may be an "allegory," with the snow and cold representing the oppression of the Jews; if the same composition had been written anonymously in Spanish or in Arabic, no one would think to search for any such allegorical meanings.

Américo Castro calls *Proverbios morales* "the first case of authentic lyric expression in Castilian"; it is the first purely literary work written in Castilian by a Jew. The 745-stanza poem comprises a series of aphorisms from Jewish and Christian sources advocating a life of cautious circumspection rather than pursuing wealth, power, or fleeting happiness. Merging Semitic poetics with vernacular Spanish compositions, it is written in heptasyllabic quatrains rhyming *abab,* a verse form that was first used by Juan Ruiz, Arcipreste de Hita, but was perfected by Shem Tov. Tomás Navarro Tomás calls the *Proverbios morales* the most important example of this form in medieval Spanish poetry.

Although the colophon of *Proverbios morales* says that the author was a Jew, early in the eighteenth century it was assumed that Shem Tov was a *converso* (Jewish convert to Christianity), and both the *Doctrina de la discriçión* (Doctrine of Reason) or *Doctrina cristiana* (Christian Doctrine), actually by Pedro de Veragüe, and the *Danza de la muerte* (Dance of Death) were erroneously attributed to him. Tomás Antonio Sánchez realized the error of the attributions in the late eighteenth century and was the first to state in print that Shem Tov was not a *converso.* Nevertheless, no less an authority than José Amador de los Ríos continued to adhere to this notion until the 1861–1865 revised edition of his *Historia crítica de la literatura española* (Critical History of Spanish Literature), where he wrote that Shem Tov was, indeed, a Jew. The poet Iñigo López de Mendoza, Marqués de Santillana, who lived in Carrión de los Condes in the fifteenth century, wrote in a letter to the constable of Portugal that "Rabbi Santo wrote many good things, among them the *Proverbios morales.*" Nevertheless, the work was known incorrectly as *Consejos y documentos* (Counsels and Documents) until Florencio Janer recognized its correct title in 1864.

Shem Tov apparently began writing the *Proverbios morales* before the death of Alfonso XI *el Sabio* (the Learned) in 1350, at which time he changed the dedication to honor the new king, Pedro I. In the preface to the *Proverbios morales* Shem Tov says that no one could "understand" (that is, believe or imagine) that so great a king as Alfonso XI had died. Agustín García Calvo, the editor of a 1974 edition of the work, notes that a motivation for the writing of the work might be that Alfonso had borrowed a substantial sum from Shem Tov and had not repaid it. Probably, however, the poet is offering general advice on moral behavior not only to the king but also to the nobles of Castile.

In his dedication to Pedro, Shem Tov writes (these lines were cited by the Marqués de Santillana in his letter to the constable of Portugal):

> Por nasçer en el espino
> Non val la rosa çierto
> Menos, nin el buen vyno
> Por nasçer en el sarmiento.
> Non val el açor menos
> Por nasçer de mal nido,
> Nin los enxemplos buenos
> Por los dezir judío

> (Because upon a thorn it grows,
> The rose is not less fair;
> And wine that from the vine-stock flows
> Still flows untainted there.
> The goshawk, too, will proudly soar,
> Although his nest sits low;
> And gentle teachings have their power,
> Though 'tis the Jew says so. [translation by George Ticknor])

The Jewish historian Fritz (Yitzhak) Baer was responsible for misleading Ignacio González Llubera, the editor of a 1947 edition of the *Proverbios morales,* into thinking that Shem Tov had "suffered persecution" at the hands of Alfonso XI. Although there is no evidence for this claim, it is accepted by the editor of a 1986 edition of the *Proverbios morales,* Theodore Anthony Perry. Perry believes that the text includes a "coded message" about the "oppression" of the Jews; the lines in question, however, refer to nothing of the sort and conclude with the clear statement by the poet: "Why should I be worse than other Jews, who have benefits from the king?"

Nevertheless, the period in which the *Proverbios morales* was written was one of uncertainty and insecurity for Christians as well as Jews. The latter were subjected to a series of hostile measures enacted by the *cortes* (infrequent parliament of nobles) and the king, culminating in calls for special taxation of the Jews, proposals to remove them from banking into agriculture, and outbreaks of violence against them. In addition, the plague was raging; although the disease affected Castile much less than Aragon and Catalonia and Jews much less than Christians, it still had

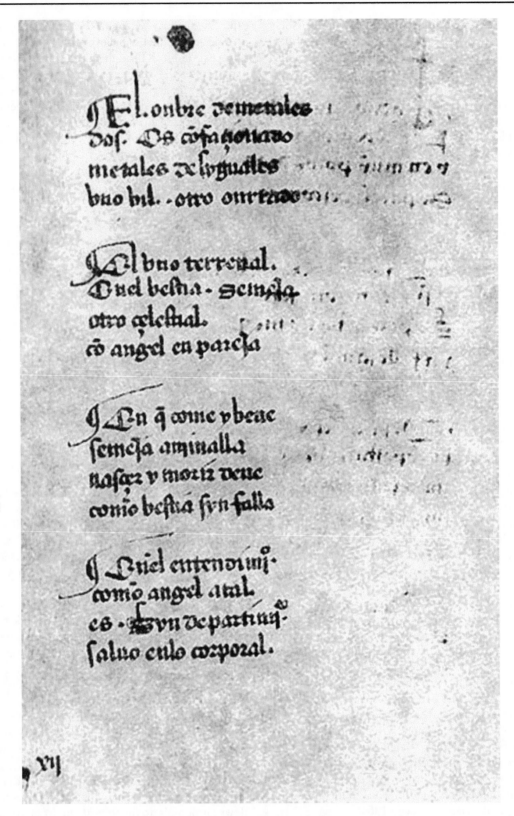

Page from a third manuscript of the Proverbios Morales *(Real Biblioteca del Monasterio de El Escorial, MS. B.IV.21)*

a devastating impact. Alfonso XI himself died as a result of the plague—the only European monarch to suffer this fate. His son, who earned the perhaps not altogether just title *el Cruel* (the Cruel), agreed to various restrictive laws against Jews at the first *cortes* he convened, at Valladolid in 1351. They included some of the measures his father had instituted, as well as new ones such as restrictions on dress and conspicuous consumption and requiring Jews to live in separate areas of towns. On the other hand, Pedro refused to consent to other measures against the Jews that were presented to him by the *cortes.*

In 1355 Pedro's half brother Enrique, who was in rebellion against the king, attacked Toledo, where his soldiers robbed and killed many Jews. Pedro accused the queen, who was involved in the rebellion against her husband, and other rebels in the city of stealing the treasure kept in the home of the royal treasurer and chief tax collector, Samuel Levi (ha-Levy). But eventually the king turned against Levi, who had long been in government service: in constant need of money, Pedro listened to accusations that Levi was not surrendering all of the funds he had collected. In 1360 Pedro ordered the arrests of Levi and of all his relatives throughout the kingdom; Levi was imprisoned, tortured, and killed in Seville. Nevertheless, other Jews continued to serve in government positions, including tax collection. In any case, these events happened well after Shem Tov had completed his work, and there is no justification for attempts to find allusions to persecution of the Jews in the *Proverbios morales.* Maya Fruchtman and Yehuda Nini, the editors of the 1980 edition of *Ma'aseh ha-Rav: Milhemet ha-'et veha-misparayim,* point out that there is even less basis for reading into the work, as Sanford Shepard does in the introduction to his 1985 edition of *Proverbios morales,* a "response" to Abner of Burgos, a Jew who converted to Christianity, took the name Alfonso de Valladolid, and engaged in polemics against the Jews.

The *Proverbios morales* includes many commonsense epigrams that are applicable to everyone. When Shem Tov writes that "No man is poor but the covetous; none rich except he who is content with what he has," he is referring not just to Jews but to a universal human experience. His source is the Spanish anthology of *sententiae Bocados de oro* (circa 1260, Golden Nuggets), and a similar statement appears in the *Avot:* "Who is rich? He who is content with his lot." Turning specifically to the nobles, Shem Tov observes that those who constantly seek honor for themselves and wander from place to place to obtain it are in danger of going astray because of envy or fear that others may surpass them; and they do not take into account death, which equalizes all. Perry notes the influence here of the Jewish phi-

losopher Moses Maimonides' *Dalalat al-ha'irin* (1191, The Guide for the Perplexed). Shem Tov contrasts with such people the truly noble man, who strives to be good, deals with others according to their stations in life, is simple and pleasant with the lower class, and shows "grandeza" (generosity or true greatness) to the "desconoçidos" (less fortunate). If he is poor, the truly noble man is happy and content; if rich, he is simple and modest. The "villano" (vile or base person) who abases himself before his superiors but is haughty and pretentious with those beneath him is the opposite in every way of the noble character. Justly famous are the lines in which Shem Tov praises books: "There is no better companion than a book / and having with it a debate is worth more than peace." This praise of books has antecedents in works by various other Jewish writers of medieval Spain.

Appended to the *Proverbios morales* in the Escorial manuscript is a satirical poem in which Shem Tov tells of sending a certain contemptible person a letter in which the words were cut out with scissors and pasted in. The recipient thought that such a form of writing was a compliment to his intelligence, but Shem Tov says that he used it only because he did not wish to waste ink on this person. This form of writing was known among Muslims in medieval Spain and perhaps also among Jews; it continued as a popular Jewish art form in Europe until the modern era.

The editors of the 1980 edition of *Ma'aseh ha-Rav: Milhemet ha-et ve-ha-misparayim* note that there has been confusion about the poems Shem Tov wrote because of difficulties in the manuscript record. Aside from his major liturgical poem *Viduiy ha-gadol* (The Great Confession; translated as "The Penitential Prayer," 1978) and the lengthy *Yam Qohelet,* which remains unpublished, all of his poems are found within, or at the end, of the text of *Ma'aseh ha-Rav* and should not be considered separate pieces. *Yam Qohelet* (Sea of Ecclesiastes) borrows its opening words, "Ma-rom me-rishon," and its overall structure from a poem by Yedayah ben Abraham Bedersi. Shem Tov exceeded Bedersi's poem in length by two thousand lines, all beginning with the letter *m* as in Bedersi's composition.

Just as Spanish works were attributed to Shem Tov de Carrión that were not his, two Hebrew works have been wrongly ascribed to him: *Ma'aseh Sofar* (circa 1600), which Moritz Steinschneider accepted as authentic but which the editors of *Ma'aseh ha-Rav* have shown to be erroneously attributed to Shem Tov, and the cabalistic book *Sefer ha-pe'e,* about which the editors of *Ma'aseh ha-Rav* have raised doubts. It is likely that the latter was written long after Shem Tov's time, possibly by an unknown Italian author.

Bibliography:

John Zemke, *Critical Approaches to the* Proverbios Morales *of Shem Tov de Carrión: An Annotated Bibliography* (Newark, Del.: Juan de la Cuesta, 1997).

References:

Emilio Alarcos Llorach, "La lengua de los *Proverbios morales* de don Sem Tob," *Revista de filología española,* 35 (1951): 249–309;

Alarcos Llorach, "Notas sobre don Santo de Carrión," in *Actas del I Congreso de historia de Palencia,* volume 4 (Valladolid: Diputacion Provincial de Palencia, 1987), pp. 231–243;

José Amador de los Ríos, *Historia crítica de la literatura española,* 7 volumes (Madrid: J. Rodriguez, 1861–1865), IV: 468;

Yitzhak Baer, *Die Juden in christlichen Spanien,* 2 volumes (Berlin: Akademie-Verlag, 1929, 1936); translated by Louis Schoffman as *A History of the Jews in Christian Spain,* 2 volumes (Philadelphia: Jewish Publication Society of America, 1961, 1966);

Americo Castro, *España en su historia* (Buenos Aires: Losada, 1948), p. 562;

Clark Colahan and Alfred Rodríguez, "Traditional Semitic Forms of Reversibility in Sem Tob's *Proverbios morales,*" *Journal of Medieval and Renaissance Studies,* 13 (1983): 33–50;

Agustín García Calvo, "Razón y escritura en don Sem Tob," in *Jornadas Extremeñas de Estudios Judaicos: Raíces hebreas en Extremadura: Del candelabro a la encina: Hervás, 16, 17, 18 y 19 de marzo de 1995: Actas* (Badajoz: Junta de Extremadura, Consejería de Cultura y Patrimonio; Diputación Provincial de Badajoz, Departamento de Publicaciones, 1996), pp. 419–434;

Jacques Joset, "Opposition et réversibilité des valeurs dans les *Proverbios morales,*" *Marcheromane* (1973): 171–189;

Joset, "Pour une archeologie de l'autobiographie: De quelques modalités du yo dans les Proverbios morales de Santob de Carrion," in *L'Autobiographie dans le monde hispanique: Actes du Colloque international de la Baume-les-Aix, 11–12–13 mai 1979,* (Aix-en-Provence: Publications Université de Provence; Paris: Champion, 1980), pp. 77–94;

Otto Kurz, "Libri cum characteribus ex nulla materia compositis," *Israel Oriental Studies,* 2 (1970): 240–247;

Armando López Castro, "Pensamiento y lenguaje en los *Proverbios morales* de Sem Tob," in *Medioevo y literatura: Actas del V Congreso de la Asociación Hispánica de Literatura Medieval (Granada, 27 septiembre–1 octubre 1993),* 4 volumes, edited by Juan Paredes (Granada: Universidad de Granada, 1995), III: 61–69;

Tomás Navarro Tomás, *Métrica española* (New York: Las Americas, 1966), p. 77;

J. A. de la Pienda and Clark Colahan, "Relativistic Philosophic Traditions in Santob's *Proverbios morales,*" *La corónica,* 23 (1994): 46–62;

Norman Roth, "Satire and Debate in Two Famous Medieval Poems from al-Andalus: Love of Boys vs. Girls, the Pen and Other Themes," *Maghreb Review,* 4 (1979): 105–113;

Sanford Shepard, *Shem Tov: His World and His Words* (Miami: Universal, 1978);

Leopold Stein, "Cartas literarias acerca del rabi don Sem Tob," in *Untersuchungen über die Proverbios morales von Santob de Carrion: Mit besonderem Hinweis auf die Quellen und Parallelen* (Berlin: Mayer & Müller, 1900);

Moritz Steinschneider, *Jüdische Literatur* (Leipzig: Gieditsch, 1850); translated by William Spottiswoode as *Jewish Literature from the Eighth to the Eighteenth Century: With an Introduction on Talmud and Midrash. A Historical Essay* (London: Longman, Brown, Green, Longmans & Roberts, 1857; New York: Herman Press, 1965);

Restituto del Valle Ruiz, *Estudios literarios* (Barcelona: Gili, 1903), pp. 235–257;

John Zemke, "A Neglected Fragment of Shem Tov's *Proverbios morales,*" *La corónica,* 17 (1988): 76–89;

Zemke, "Shem Tov de Carrión's *Proverbios morales:* A Sermon Addressed," *Romance Philology,* 51, no. 2 (1997): 194–210.

Appendix:
Literary Genres in Thirteenth- and Fourteenth-Century Spain

Alfonsine Legal Codes

José Sánchez-Arcilla Bernal

Universidad Complutense de Madrid

WORKS: *Espéculo* (1252–1255)

Manuscripts: Two medieval manuscripts survive: Biblioteca Nacional, Madrid, MSS. 10123 (fourteenth century) and Res. 125 (a fifteenth-century copy of MS. 10123).

First publication: "El Espéculo o espejo de todos los derechos," in *Opúsculos legales del rey don Alfonso el Sabio, publicados y cotejados con varios códices antiguos por la Real Academia de la Historia,* volume 1 (Madrid: Imprenta Real, 1836).

Standard edition: *Leyes de Alfonso X,* volume 1: *Espéculo,* edited by Gonzalo Martínez Díez and José Manuel Ruiz Asencio (Ávila: Fundación Sánchez Albornoz, 1985); *Espéculo: Texto jurídico atribuido al Rey de Castilla Don Alfonso X, el Sabio,* edited by Robert A. MacDonald (Madison, Wis.: Hispanic Seminary of Medieval Studies, 1990).

Setenario (circa 1256?)

Manuscripts: Three medieval manuscripts of this work survive: Real Biblioteca del Monasterio de El Escorial, MS. P.II.20 (fourteenth century); Biblioteca de la Catedral de Toledo, MS. 43-20 (fourteenth century); and Hispanic Society of America, New York, MS. HC 397/573 (a fourteenth-century copy of the *Primera partida* with interpolations from the *Setenario*).

First publication and standard edition: *Setenario,* edited by Kenneth H. Vanderford (Buenos Aires: Instituto de Filología, 1945; republished with an introduction by Rafael Lapesa, Barcelona: Crítica, 1984); *Electronic text and concordances of the Setenario by Alfonso el Sabio Biblioteca Capitular de Toledo, MS 43-20,* edited by Xenia Bonch-Bruevich (Madison, Wis.: Hispanic Seminary of Medieval Studies, 1999 [computer optical disc]).

Fuero real (1256)

Manuscripts: Twenty-seven principal medieval manuscripts survive: Real Biblioteca del Monasterio de El Escorial, MSS. K.II.16 (fifteenth century), K.III.25 (fourteenth century), Z.I.5 (fifteenth century), Z.II.8 (fourteenth century), Z.III.5 (fifteenth century), MS. Z.III.11 (fourteenth century), Z.III.13 (thirteenth century), Z.III.16 (thirteenth–fourteenth centuries), and Z.III.17 (fourteenth century); Palacio de Perelada, Gerona, MS. 95 A-VI (fifteenth century); Arquivo Nacional de Torre do Tombo, Lisbon, MS. No. 4 do maço 6 dos forais antigos (thirteenth century); Academia de la Historia, Madrid, MS. V-6-75 (fourteenth century); Biblioteca Nacional, Madrid, MSS. 710 (fourteenth century), 6501 (fourteenth century), 6655 (fourteenth century), 691 (fourteenth–fifteenth centuries), 8417 (fourteenth–fifteenth centuries), 5764 (fifteenth century), 10166 (fifteenth century), and 17809 (fourteenth century); Hispanic Society of America, New York, MS. B2568, present location unknown (thirteenth century); Free Library, Philadelphia, Lewis European MS. 245 (thirteenth century); Biblioteca Universitaria Salamanca, MSS. 2673 (thirteenth–fourteenth centuries) and 1862 (fourteenth–fifteenth centuries); Biblioteca de la Catedral de Toledo, MSS. 43-21 (fourteenth century) and 43-22 (fourteenth century).

First publication: "Fuero real," edited by Alfonso Díaz de Montalvo (Seville: Alfonso del Puerto, 1483).

Standard edition: *Fuero real,* in *Opúsculos legales del rey don Alfonso el Sabio, publicados y cotejados con varios códices antiguos por la Real Academia de la Historia,* volume 2 (Madrid: Imprenta Real, 1836), pp. 1–169; *El fuero real de Burgos: European MS 245 Philadelphia Free Library,* edited by Ivy A. Corfis (Madison, Wis.: Hispanic Seminary of Medieval Studies, 1987); *Leyes de Alfonso X,* volume 2, edited by Gonzalo Martínez Díez and José Manuel Ruiz Asencio (Ávila: Fundación Sánchez Albornoz, 1988); *Fuero real,* edited by Azucena Palacios Alcaine (Barcelona: Promociones y Publicaciones Universitarias, 1991).

Leyes para los adelantados mayores (1255?)

Manuscripts: One medieval manuscript and later copies exist: Real Biblioteca del Monasterio de El

Escorial, MS. Z.II.8 (fourteenth century); Academia de la Historia, Madrid, MS. 213, Abella XVII (date uncertain); British Library, London, 205, MS. Add. 9916 (copied 1700–1800); Academia Española, Madrid, MS. 214 (eighteenth century); Hispanic Society, New York, MS. 269 HC380/685/1 (eighteenth century).

First publication and standard edition: "Leyes para los adelantados," in *Opúsculos legales del rey don Alfonso el Sabio, publicados y cotejados con varios códices antiguos por la Real Academia de la Historia,* volume 2 (Madrid: Imprenta Real, 1836), pp. 171–177; *Leyes de los adelantados mayores: Regulations, Attributed to Alfonso X of Castile, Concerning the King's Vicar in the Judiciary and in Territorial Administration,* edited by Robert A. MacDonald (New York: Hispanic Seminary of Medieval Studies, 2000).

Siete partidas (1256–after 1272)

Manuscripts: More than eighty medieval manuscripts survive, many with only a portion of the text, including Biblioteca de Cataluña, Barcelona, MSS. 942 (fourteenth century) and 15 (fifteenth century); Arquivo Distrital e Biblioteca Pública, Braga, MS. 175 (fourteenth century); Real Biblioteca del Monasterio de El Escorial, MSS. L.II.22 (fourteenth century), M.I.1 (fourteenth century), M.I.2 (fourteenth century), M.I.4 (fourteenth century), N.I.5 (fourteenth century), N.I.7 (fourteenth century), and Y.II.1 (fourteenth century); Biblioteca Nacional, Madrid, MSS. 12793 (fourteenth century), 12794 (fourteenth century), 12795 (fourteenth century), 12897 (fourteenth century), 22 (fifteenth century), 580 (fifteenth century), 708 (fifteenth century), 6725 (fifteenth century), and Vit. 4-6 (fifteenth century).

First publication: *Siete partidas,* edited by Alfonso Díaz de Montalvo (Seville: Meynardo Ungut & Lançalvo Polono, 1491).

Standard editions: *Siete partidas,* edited by the Real Academia de la Historia (Madrid: Imprenta Real, 1807); *Las "Siete Partidas" del sabio rey don Alfonso el X, con las variantes de más interés, y con la glosa del lic[enciado] Gregorio López,* edited by Ignacio Sonponts y Barba, Ramón Martí de Eilaxa, and José Ferrer y Subirana (Barcelona: A. Bergnes, 1843–1844); *Primera partida Alfonso X el Sabio: Según el manuscrito Add. 20.787 del British Museum,* edited by Juan Antonio Arias Bonet, Guadalupe Ramos, and José Manuel Ruiz Asencio (Valladolid: Universidad de Valladolid, Secretariado de Publicaciones, 1975); Dwayne E. Carpenter, *Alfonso X and the Jews: An Edition of and Commentary on* Siete Partidas *7.24 "De los judíos,"* Modern Philology, no. 115 (Berkeley, Los Angeles & London:

University of California Press, 1986); *Partida segunda de Alfonso X El Sabio: Manuscrito 12794 de la B.N.,* edited by Aurora Juárez Blanquer, Antonio Rubio Flores, Cristóbal Torres Delgado, and Jesús Montoya Martínez (Granada: Impredisur, 1991); *Las Siete Partidas (El Libro del Fuero de las Leyes),* edited by José Sánchez-Arcilla Bernal (Madrid: Reus, 2004).

Edition in English: *Las Siete Partidas,* edited and translated by Samuel Parsons Scott (Chicago: American Bar Association, 1931); republished as *Las Siete Partidas,* 5 volumes, introduction by Robert I. Burns, S.J. (Philadelphia: University of Pennsylvania Press, 2001).

Leyes de estilo (date uncertain)

Manuscripts: Five medieval manuscripts survive: Real Biblioteca del Monasterio de El Escorial, MSS. Z.II.8 (fourteenth century), Z.II.14 (fifteenth century), Z.III.11 (fourteenth century), and Z.III.17 (fourteenth century); Biblioteca Nacional, Madrid, MS. 5764 (fourteenth–fifteenth centuries).

First publication: *Leyes de estilo* (Salamanca: Leonardo Hutz & Lope Sanz, 1497).

Standard editions: "Leyes de estilo" in *Opúsculos legales del rey don Alfonso el Sabio, publicados y cotejados con varios códices antiguos por la Real Academia de la Historia,* volume 2 (Madrid: Imprenta Real, 1836), pp. 233–352; *Text and Concordance of the Leyes del estilo MS. 5764, Biblioteca Nacional, Madrid,* edited by Terrence A. Mannetter (Madison, Wis.: Hispanic Seminary of Medieval Studies, 1989 [2 microfiches and 1 guide]); *Texts and Concordances of the Leyes del estilo Escorial MSS. Z.II.8, Z.II.14 and the 1497 and 1500 Salamanca incunables,* edited by Mannetter (Madison, Wis.: Hispanic Seminary of Medieval Studies, 1993 [8 microfiches and 1 guide]).

Leyes nuevas (circa 1260)

Manuscripts: Eleven medieval manuscripts survive: Real Biblioteca del Monasterio de El Escorial, MSS. P.III.2 (thirteenth century), Z.III.13 (thirteenth century), Z.III.16 (thirteenth–fourteenth centuries), K.III.25 (fourteenth century), Y.II.5 (fourteenth century), Z.II.5 (fifteenth century), and Z.II.6 (fifteenth–sixteenth centuries); Palacio de Perelada, Gerona, MS. 95 A-VI (fifteenth century); Biblioteca Nacional, Madrid, MS. 6655 (fourteenth century); Biblioteca de la Catedral Toledo, MSS. 43-21 (fourteenth century) and 43-22 (fourteenth century).

First publication and standard edition: "Leyes nuevas," in *Opúsculos legales del rey don Alfonso el Sabio, publicados y cotejados con varios códices antiguos* *por la Real Academia de la Historia,* volume 2 (Madrid: Imprenta Real, 1836), pp. 179–209; *La colección conocida con el título "Leyes nuevas" y atribuida a Alfonso X el Sabio,* edited by José Lopez Ortiz, Publicaciones del Instituto Nacional de Estudios Jurídicos, Serie 1, Publicaciones periódicas, edición especial del *Anuario de historia del derecho español,* 16 (Madrid: Ministerio de Justicia y Consejo Superior de Investigaciones Científicas, 1945).

Ordenamiento de las tafurerías (1276)

Manuscripts: Seventeen medieval manuscripts exist: Real Biblioteca del Monasterio de El Escorial, MSS. Z.I.6 (1347), Z.II.14 (fourteenth century), Z.II.5 (late fourteenth century), Z.I.8 (early fifteenth century), Z.I.9 (early fifteenth century), Z.II.4 (early fifteenth century), and Z.II.6 (fifteenth–sixteenth centuries); Biblioteca Nacional, Madrid, MSS. 5784 (mid fourteenth century), 23 (fifteenth century), and 691 (fifteenth century); Biblioteca de Palacio, Madrid, MS. II-1963 (fifteenth century); Museo Lázaro Galdiano, Madrid, MS. 439 (mid fourteenth century); Hispanic Society of America, New York, MS. B2193 (mid fourteenth century); Biblioteca Universitaria Salamanca, MSS. 1962 (fourteenth century), 2056 (fourteenth century), and 1862 (fifteenth century); Biblioteca de Santa Cruz, Valladolid, MS. 139 (early fifteenth century).

First publication: Excerpts in Alfonso García de Madrigal, *Doctrinal de los caualleros* (Burgos: Fadrique Alemán, 1497); "Ordenamiento de las tafurerías," in *Opúsculos legales del rey don Alfonso el Sabio, publicados y cotejados con varios códices antiguos por la Real Academia de la Historia,* volume 2 (Madrid: Imprenta Real, 1836), pp. 211–231.

Standard edition: *Libro de las Tahurerías: A Special Code of Law, Concerning Gambling, Drawn up by Maestro Roldán at the Command of Alfonso X of Castile,* edited by Robert A. MacDonald (Madison, Wis.: Hispanic Seminary of Medieval Studies, 1995).

The legacy of Alfonso X *el Sabio* (the Learned) in the realm of European law is legendary. His fame among cultural historians rests on his astonishing contributions to medieval poetry, history, and astronomy, but his thirteenth-century legal codes are also distinguished as the first successful, if imperfect, merger of the independent streams of jurisprudence that were in competition throughout his realms.

Alfonso inherited laws from highly disparate sources, including the Visigoths, who entered Spain around 500 and whose legal practices were encoded in Alaric's *Breviarium* (506, Breviary) and in the *Forum Iudi-*

Original design by the sculptor Gaetano Cecere for the marble bas-relief of Alfonso X that hangs in the chamber of the United States House of Representatives to honor him as one of the world's greatest lawgivers (photograph courtesy of José Sánchex-Arcilla)

cium (sixth century, Law Code of the Judges), which was translated into the vernacular as the *Fuero juzgo.* There were also the vastly influential body of canon law used by the Church, the widespread regional and municipal *fueros* (law codes) and *cartas puebla* (legal codes for established towns and frontier settlements), and a welter of native customary laws that Alfonso tried to supersede with more reliably consistent bodies of legislation. Finally, there was the recovery and systematization of ancient Roman law that was part of a wave of legal work emanating from thirteenth-century Italian centers of learning and government, some of whose best scholars Alfonso imported to assist with his legislative initiatives.

The Alfonsine legacy determined the essentials of subsequent Spanish and Latin American legal systems; it was also a major influence in the formulation of the Napoleonic Code and, through it, of the laws of Louisiana. The American Bar Association commissioned the first complete translation of Alfonso's *Siete partidas* (1256–after 1272, Seven Divisions of the Law) into English (1931); and the United States Congress acknowledged the Spanish monarch as one of the world's greatest lawgivers by authorizing his bust to be placed in the House of Representatives.

The diverse corpus of literature produced under Alfonso X, including laws, guarantees him a place in the international Hispanic and Western canons. His legislative programs have, however, spawned much controversy among researchers, partly because of the lack of critical editions of the *Siete partidas* and the other law codes that are supposed precursors or derivatives of it, such as the *Espéculo* (1252–1255, Mirror), the *Fuero real* (1256, Royal Code), and the *Setenario* (date uncertain, Sevenfold Law Book). In addition to these large-scale projects, Alfonso was the de facto author of more-modest legal manuals such as the *Leyes para los adelantados mayores* (1255? Laws for Frontier Governors), the *Leyes nuevas* (circa 1260, New Laws), and the *Ordenamiento de las tafurerías* (1276, Manual for Gambling Houses).

Extant copies of the *Setenario* are incomplete and found only in late manuscripts. The title indicates that the work was conceived of as being divided into seven parts, but the surviving texts consist of laws grouped categorically. Alfonso refers to the work by name in his preface, saying that "desque ouimos este libro compuesto e ordenado pusiémosle nombre Setenario" (ever since we had this book written and arranged we called it the *Sevenfold Law Book*); this passage suggests that the king finished the work and that the misfortunes of time and transmission have resulted in its survival in partial form. But its first editor, Kenneth H. Vanderford, raised the possibility that the work was never completed and came into Alfonso's possession in its truncated state at the time of the death of the true author, Alfonso's father, Fernando III, in 1252. If so, in the preface Alfonso is merely eulogizing his father's intent to sustain the sevenfold compositional scheme announced in the title of the work. On the other hand, internal references suggest that Alfonso pushed the work into finished form after Fernando's demise. It is not clear what parts of the *Setenario* were finished by 1252 or even when it was begun. The version that survives gives the impression that even with Alfonso's input, it was essentially the handiwork of theologians and philosophers rather than working jurists, since it deals with faith and the sacraments of baptism, confirmation, confession, and the Eucharist, all of which matches up well with the preoccupations of the first *partida*. These links to the first *partida,* which was apparently at least in draft form by 1256, lead one to think that the *Setenario* was finished by then.

According to the prologue, Fernando intended the *Setenario* to be part of his legacy to his heirs so they could govern wisely and justly. Alfonso apparently took care to preserve the only copy ever made: his 1283 will specifies that his rightful heir should take possession of

"illum librum quem nos fecimus fieri, *Septenarius* appellatus" (that book which we had made, called the *Sevenfold Law Book*). It is not certain what specific textual sources were used in the elaboration of this code, although some were apparently nonjuridical, nor is there certainty of its precise relation to the far larger *Siete partidas*.

The *Espéculo* is contained in a fourteenth-century codex in the Biblioteca Nacional in Madrid under the title *Este es el Libro del Fuero que fizo el rey Don Alfonso, fijo del muy noble rey D. Fernando e la muy noble reina Doña Beatriz, el cual es llamado Espéculo, que quiere tanto como decir espejo de todos los Derechos* (This Is the Book of the Code That Don Alfonso Made, Son of the Very Noble Don Fernando and the Very Noble Queen Beatriz, Which Is Called *Speculum,* Which Means the Mirror of All Laws). The use of the past tense makes one suspect that it was added later—probably in the fourteenth century, when this copy was made—and that the original title could well have been *Libro del fuero* (Book of the Code). The codex does not reveal when or where the work was created. Although still the subject of much discussion, the work has benefited from the publication of two modern critical editions.

In its present state the *Espéculo* consists of five books, but it was planned as a more extensive work. While some passages correspond with the *Siete partidas* line by line, it offers a distinct set of guidelines on the issue of rights of royal succession. Because the *Siete partidas* employs a protocol that would have favored the infantes de la Cerda, the prematurely orphaned sons of Alfonso's first son, while the *Espéculo* settles rights to the throne in favor of Sancho IV, his second son and eventual successor, there has been speculation that the latter work was cobbled together during Sancho's reign. This notion is supported by the parallels between its language and that of other texts from the same post-Alfonsine period.

The prologue presents the work as an effort to correct "libros de fueros minguados" (deficient law codes) and "non conplidos" (inconsistent codes), as well as "fazañas desaguisadas e sin derecho" (misapplied and unfair oral precedents). The monarch's aim was to provide a general text that would standardize the best practices and to place it in every town under his jurisdiction.

Alfonso also states his sources for this "Libro del fuero": "E catamos e escogiemos de todos los fueros lo que más valié e lo mejor, pusiémoslo, y también del Fuero de Castiella como de León como de los otros logares que nos fallamos que eran derechos e con razón" (And we examined and selected from all the [preexisting] codes what was most apt and best, and we set it all down, relying, too, on the Codes of Castile and Léon and from other texts that we found well made and

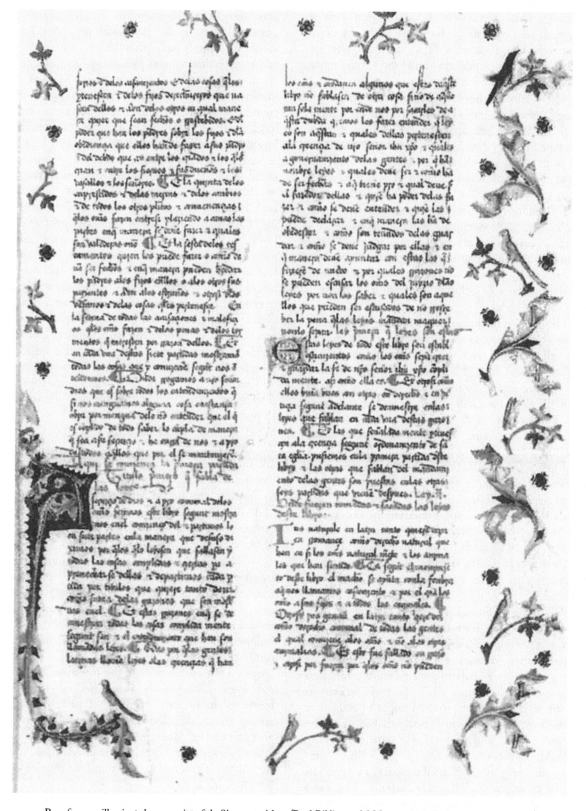

Page from an illuminated manuscript of the Siete partidas *(Real Biblioteca del Monasterio de El Escorial, MS. Z.I.14)*

reasonable). This statement is undoubtedly an attempt to drape his new code in the borrowed authority of its predecessors, as well as to validate its sway over his recently combined kingdoms and the even more recently conquered border territories.

Noteworthy in the *Espéculo* is the declaration of the king's *potestas condendi legis* (monopoly over producing legislation); the principle was taken from Roman law, as stated in the *Forum Iudicium,* and was also a declaration of his exclusive right to name *alcaldes* (judges). Whether the *Espéculo* was conceived of as a theoretical work to guide later codes of practical applied law, as Jerry R. Craddock suggests, or as a mature reflection of principles after early attempts at settling inconsistencies and gaps in case law as practiced across Spanish Christendom, the level of jurisprudence is more refined, better buttressed by Roman law, and more adorned with the formal niceties of Scholastic precision of thought than other law codes.

The *Fuero real,* conceived of as a model municipal law code, is extant in more than thirty manuscripts; all seem to rely on a distant common source text that is now lost. These copies lack a unified name, leading scribes to make up titles such as *Libro del fuero* (Book of the Code), *Fuero de las leyes* (Code of Laws), and even *Libro de flores* (Book of Flowers). A dozen of the surviving witnesses contain a dated *explicit* (final text of a book or manuscript) with a named place of production. Their authenticity is unquestionable, because the *explicit* exactly matches the text used in 1255, and the royal seal they bear was used in a manuscript prepared by the king's chancery for the northern Spanish town of Santo Domingo de la Calzada. The dates transcribed in these twelve copies vary because they indicate when the copies were made, not when the *Fuero real* was composed.

All of the manuscripts of the *Fuero real* with intact opening folios state that Alfonso X gave "este fuero que es escripto en este libro porque se judguen comunalmientre varones e mugeres. E mandamos que este fuero sea guardado para siempre e ninguno sea osado de venir contra ello" (the code written in this book so that men and women might be judged in the same way. We furthermore order that this code be preserved forever and that no one dare contravene it). The king's identity is as clear as his wish to compose a code merging traditional practices or common law with canonical and Roman currents. The *Fuero real* is divided into four books with subdivisions in titles and laws that embrace clear fields of legal concern. Book 1 surveys "public law" that applies to all, such as political allegiance to the monarch and his immediate family, and shows due deference to the

autonomy of religious law and the clerical institutions governed by it. Book 2 deals with procedural matters, including appropriate jurisdiction, witnesses, documentary testimony and proofs, statutes of limitation, swearing of oaths, handing down sentences, and bringing closure to lawsuits and their appeals. Book 3 covers personal law: marriage, dowry, inheritance, legal guardianship for minors, and commercial law—buying and selling, gifts, legal fees, and loaned and rented properties. Finally, book 4 encompasses the penal code; it includes items that modern readers would consider religious prohibitions, such as bans on Christians becoming Jews and on Jews proselytizing Christians. But there are also protections for Jews, such as a cap of 25 percent on the interest a moneylender can charge them and freedom from forced labor on their Sabbath. Other sections of the penal code deal with disputes or matters of legislative oversight, including regulation of physicians and surgeons; compensation for insults, defamation, and battery; sexual comportment with minors, members of religious orders, slaves, and prostitutes; murder; the plundering of graves; desertion from the military; and an odd assortment of provisions on topics from pilgrimage to salvaging flotsam and jetsam after a shipwreck. In "The Legislative Works of Alfonso el Sabio" (1990) Craddock notes several deficiencies in the *Fuero real:* procedural matters such as court costs are tucked among commercial regulations; proscriptive rules about Jews are included, but none about the greater number of Muslim subjects of the realm; and the examples cited are curious—insults, for instance, are illustrated by the surely sporadic slight of burying one's foe's head in the mud.

The *Fuero real* was aimed at providing a legal framework for municipalities that had obsolete customary codes or lacked a comprehensive and integrated common law. Resistance to the proposed model municipal code swelled among the stubbornly independent nobles and overtaxed town councils until Alfonso X had to retreat from his initial insistence on the normativity of the *Fuero real,* but its internal logic, along with the inherited local codes' tendency to impede the flow of people and goods across the realm, led to its eventual, if grudging, acceptance. Its preeminence grew to the point that Alfonso's great-grandson, Alfonso XI, could mandate use of the *Fuero real* as the standing municipal code for all of his realms.

The *Siete partidas* was the largest-scale effort of the Alfonsine team of legal scholars and legislators and the major source for most of the Hispanic world's subsequent national laws. The king's personal investment in and identification with this code could not be clearer, for he embedded his own name in it: the initial letters of the seven books spell out "A-L-F-O-N-S-O." Craddock sums up the content in "The Legislative Works of Alfonso el Sabio" (1990):

> The first partida [book] presents general legal principles and a treatise on canon law. The second combines the two *Espéculo* books dealing with the king's household and military law. The third merges the last two books of the *Espéculo* (which regulate . . . judicial personnel and procedure). The fourth partida takes up matrimonial law and diverse sorts of personal relations, including feudal obligations between lord and vassal; the fifth contains commercial law; the sixth contains the law of inheritance; and the seventh is a penal code.

A critical edition has yet to be undertaken of the more than five score manuscripts of the *Siete partidas,* few of which contain the entire work or a clear indication of how they relate to other copies. The first *partida* has appeared in a serious modern edition, but it relies on only a few of the available sources. The work was unstable by the fourteenth century, as its promulgator, Alfonso XI, recognized when he marshaled all his authority to sanction the *Siete partidas* as Spain's definitive legal code in the year before his death in 1350. After that point its success was swift and decisive. The expanding influence of the *Siete partidas* was proven within a few decades by its translation into Catalan, Galician-Portuguese, Portuguese, and the Limousin dialect of French. The first print edition was prepared by the jurist Díaz de Montalvo in Seville in 1491 and republished with annotations in Venice in 1501, in Burgos and in Lyon in 1528, and in Alcalá de Henares in 1542. This edition was criticized for occasionally differing from manuscripts that were still in regular use at the time. Gregorio López's fresh attempt at editing the work was widely accepted and was reprinted in Salamanca in 1565, twice in 1576, and in 1580; in Valladolid in 1587–1588; in Madrid in 1598 and 1610–1611; in Valencia in 1757 and 1759; in Madrid again in 1789, 1828, 1829–1831, and 1843–1844; and in Barcelona in 1844. It became the edition of consensus of the *Siete partidas* and was confirmed as official by the Spanish legal establishment in 1889. It is not known, however, what source manuscripts or editorial criteria López followed. The reliability of his edition was questioned in the eighteenth century, and at the beginning of the nineteenth century the Real Academia de la Historia (Royal Academy of History) undertook a new critical edition of the *Siete partidas* that was published in three volumes in 1807. The academy based its version of the first *partida* on a pair of manuscripts from the fourteenth and fifteenth

centuries and used a single fourteenth-century manuscript for the rest. While the academy's edition has not won legal or critical acceptance, it has the advantage of reproducing from the surviving manuscript record amplified versions of the first four titles in the *Siete partidas.*

Some of the earlier manuscripts give the years 1256 to 1263 as dates for the composition of the *Siete partidas.* The claim of a seven-year period may have been a literary conceit to complement the sevenfold divisions that structure the work. Most of the surviving copies do not refer to these dates.

The legal sources of the *Siete partidas* are not known with certainty, although one can point with confidence to Gratian's *Decretum* and Gregory IX's *Decretals* for aspects of canon law and to various provisions derived from Roman law. One can also discern a reliance on Aristotle, Plutarch, Seneca, the Bible, St. Augustine, St. Thomas Aquinas, the *Flores de Filosofía* (1240–1260, Flowers of Philosophy), the *Poridat de Poridades* (circa 1250, Secret of Secrets), Petrus Alfonsi's *Disciplina clericalis* (date uncertain, The Discipline of Clerics; translated as "Peter Alphonse's Disciplina clericalis [English Translation], from the Fifteenth Century Worcester Cathedral Manuscript F.172," 1919), and *Calila e Dimna* (first half of the thirteenth century, Calila and Dimna). Specifically legal works consulted include the *vulgata* version of the *Libri Feudorum* (Book of Law Codes) and, for maritime law, the French *Rooles de Oleron,* published in 1671 as the *Les us & coutumes de la mer* (translated as *The Ancient Sea-Laws of Oleron, Wisby and the Hanse-towns,* 1686).

The origins and evolution of the Alfonsine legislative corpus were debated by scholars in the twentieth century. Alfonso García-Gallo posited that the *Espéculo* was the seminal work of the king and his team of jurists and became the core of the frontier and municipal codes that were granted by Alfonso within Castile and that reached into the zones of war and resettlement. It was the starting point for later drafts of codes that grew into the *Siete partidas.* According to García-Gallo, the *Fuero real* was a posthumous offshoot of the same wellspring of jurisprudence and was meant to replace and normalize the local codes that had spread throughout the realms of twelfth- and thirteenth-century Spain. Aquilino Iglesia Ferreirós, however, later established that the *Fuero real* was granted to the town of Campoamor in 1269, proving that the text was finished and being bestowed on localities by royal fiat fifteen years before Alfonso's death. Iglesia Ferreirós defended the more traditional critical view that the *Espéculo,* the *Fuero real,* and the *Siete partidas* were all begun and completed between 1255 and 1265.

Primera partida

Titulo.j.

Comieça la primera partida que fabla de todas las cosas que pertenescen ala se catholica: q̃ faze al õbre conoscer a dios por creencia.

Titulo primero. que fabla delas leyes. y por quantas razones es este libro ptido por titulos. y en que manera.

Seruicio d dios z a pro comunal delas gẽtes: faze mos este libro se gũro que mostra mos enel comiẽ ço del. E ptimos lo en siete partes: enla manera q̃ di rimos de suso. E por q̃ los que lo leyesen fallassen ay todas las co sas cõplidas z ciertas por aprouecharse dellas: departimos cada vna partida por titulos: que quiere tãto dezir como suma delas razões que son mostradas enel. z estas razones en q̃ se mue stran todas las cosas conplidamẽte segũ son z el entẽdimiẽto q̃ ban son llamadas leyes. Mas q̃las gentes latinas llamã leyes alas creencias q̃ ban los onbres: z cuydaria algunos q̃ estas de ste libro no fablasen de otra cosa sino de aq̃llo tã sola mẽte. pot ende nos por sacar los desta dub da. queremos les fazer enteder q̃ leyes son estas z de q̃ lugares fuerõ tomadas z sacadas z q̃les dellas pertenescẽ ala se dela creencia õ nṙo señor ibesu xpo: z quales pertenescẽ al gouernamien to delas gẽtes: z poriq̃ ban nonbre leyes. z q̃les deuẽ ser estas leyes: z como deuẽ ser fechas. z a

que tienẽ pro. z qual deue ser el fazedor dellas: z quiẽ ha poder delas fazer. z como se deue en tender. z quiẽ las puede declarar. z en q̃ manera las deuẽ obedescer. z como son temidos delas guardar. z como se deuẽ iudgar por ellas: z en que manera deuẽ ayuntar las que fiziere de nue uo cõ estas. z por quales razones no se puedẽ escusar los onbres del iuyzio dlas leyes por de zir q̃no las saben. z quales son aquellos q̃ pue dẽ ser escusados de no rescebir la pena q̃ las ley es mãdan maguer no las sepan. z sobre todo di remos delas virtudes delas leyes.

Ley.primera.que leyes son estas.

Estas leyes de todo este libro son establecimi entos como los õbres sepan guardar la se d nṙe stro señor ibesu cristo conplidamẽte assi como el la es. Otrosi como biuã los onbres vnos cõ o tros en derecho z en iusticia segũd adelante se muestra enlas leyes q̃ fablan en cada vna destes razones: z las q̃ señalada mente pertenescen ala creencia segũd ordenamiento de santa yglesia pusimos enla primera partida deste libro: z las otras que fablan del mantenimiento delas gen tes son puestas enlas seys partidas que se sigue despues.

Ley.ij.onde fueron sacadas las leyes deste libro.

Ius naturale en latin: tãto quiere dezir en ro mãce como derecho natural q̃ bã enst los õbres naturalmente. z avn las otras animalias q̃ han sentido. Ca segũd el mouimiẽto deste derecho el masculo se ayũta conla fenbra: aq̃ nos llama mos casamiẽto: z por el criã los onbres a sus fi jos z todas las animalias. Otrosi ius gentium en latin. tãto quiere dezir como derecho comũal de todas las gẽtes: el qual cõuiene alos onbres z no alas otras animalias. z este fue fallado cõ razon. z otrosi por fuerça poriq̃ los õbres no po drian bien beuir entresi en cõcordia z en paz. sy todos no vsasen dl. ca por tal derecho como este cada vn onbre conosce lo suyo apartada mente z son deptidos los campos z los termios dlas villas. E otrosi son temidos los õbres de loar a dios z obedescer a sus padres z a sus madres z a su tierra: q̃ dizẽ en latin patria. Otrosi cõsie te este derecho q̃ cada vno se pueda anparar cõ tra aquellos q̃ desõtra o fuerça le quisierẽ fazer z avn mas q̃ toda cosa q̃ fagan por anparamien to de fuerça q̃ le quierã fazer cõtra su psona q̃ se en tiende q̃ lo faze con derecho: y delas mãda miẽtos destas dos cosas. E destas dos maneras

ā 4

Page of the first printed edition of the Siete partidas, *edited by Alfonso Díaz de Montalvo and published in Seville in 1491 (Biblioteca de la Institución Colombina, Seville)*

These opposing interpretations can be combined into an historical narrative that salvages parts of both: when Alfonso took the throne in 1252, his father, Fernando III, had already begun adapting the old *Forum Iudicium* to the needs of the thirteenth century and had rechristened it the *Fuero juzgo;* Alfonso continued this process by introducing the code into the southern flank of his realm, which had recently been reconquered from the Moors. The lords and townships of Castile and Extremadura were accustomed to creating their own local codes, which permitted self-governance and erected barriers against outside taxation and tribute. Alfonso had good reason to believe that his replacement of those local codes with the *Fuero juzgo* would meet resistance, as would his claim to an exclusive royal right to validate existing and new laws and to force the normalization of conflicting local procedures. The *Fuero juzgo* would have been an apt tool for this legislative program, but Alfonso may have sensed that its authority was tenuous: the Crowns of Castile and León had only recently been united, and they held separate *cortes* (parliaments) until well into the following century. This scenario lends support to Iglesia Ferreirós's thesis that one of the king's principal objectives was promoted in each of the works produced during his lifetime: the unification of local laws in the *Espéculo,* the exclusive royal right to enact laws in the *Fuero real,* and the comprehensive reformulation of national law in the *Siete partidas.* In reality, the distinctions are not so clear-cut: the objectives overlap in each work, any one of which could have been sufficient to defend all three principles.

Modern scholarship on Alfonso's ambitions as a legislator and lawgiver may rely too heavily on premises that conform to later—in some cases, much later—legal protocols. The modern sequence of sanctioning, promulgating, and publishing a body of law may lead one to imagine conflicts and tensions that were not present in the Middle Ages: the *Fuero real* needed no legitimizing act of promulgation for the realm as a whole to take effect, nor would any legislative body have had to give its approval. The *cortes* of Castile and León were consultative assemblies of prelates and nobles where consensus had to be built if royal initiatives were to make headway against local interests. But all trained jurists, both civil and ecclesiastical, agreed that the ultimate *potestas condendi legis* resided with the king. Alfonso's codes are uniformly mute on the authority of the ceremonial *cortes,* and this silence is a telling witness to the narrow scope of their participation in his legislative operations.

Whether one takes the position of García-Gallo, Craddock, and Robert A. MacDonald that the *Espéculo* was a finished code issued by the king with the full force of law or agrees with Iglesia Ferreirós and Gonzalo Martínez Díez that it was absorbed into other works, there is no doubt that Alfonso's jurists completed two major legal projects in an amazingly short time. The *Espéculo* and the *Fuero real* came into being between 1252 and 1256 despite the wanderings of a highly mobile court that rarely spent more than a few months at a time in any one place. This achievement surely implies separate teams of jurists working on distinct assignments. The *Espéculo* seems to have been an initiative inherited from Fernando III's regime that served as a model first for the *Fuero real* and then for the *Siete partidas,* but not in the way theorized by scholars such as Iglesia Ferreirós. Their long-respected view was that the limited *Espéculo* was abandoned and the more ambitious *Siete partidas* was launched to further Alfonso's imperial pretensions: the king spent years, beginning in 1256, building a case for his candidacy for Holy Roman Emperor, only to have his hopes dashed by the Pope in a private audience in Beaucaire in southern France in 1275. But the *Espéculo,* the *Fuero real,* and the *Siete partidas* all claim that they are equal in legislative authority to kings. The conclusion is that Alfonso was not seeking to confirm his monopoly over the passage of laws by advancing to imperial rank; that power was already his by right.

The issue still remains of the extent to which the *Siete partidas* had the force of law during Alfonso X's reign. Many scholars hold that since it was not formally promulgated—decreed normative by royal mandate in a solemn assembly—until Alfonso's great-grandson, Alfonso XI, did so in the *Ordenamiento de Alcalá* in 1348, it never got out of the workshop and into public use before Alfonso X's death in 1284. Yet, it could not simply have been shelved after Alfonso died and only dusted off for its 1348 debut as a national law code. There must have been a swelling current of interest and institutional investment in the *Siete partidas* for Alfonso X's fourteenth-century successor to feel certain of its universal acceptance more than eighty years after its first formulation. The language of the promulgation suggests that some editorial work and updating had become necessary by 1348, perhaps to correct disparities in the manuscripts:

> Fasta aquí non se falla que fuesen publicadas por mandado del Rey, nin fueron habidas nin resçibidas por leyes . . . pero nos mandamos las requerir e conçertar e emendar en algunas cosas que cumplía. . . . Et por que sean çiertas e non haya rrazón de tirar e emendar e mudar en ellas cada uno lo que quisiere, mandamos fazer de ellas dos libros, uno sellado con nuestro sello

de oro, et otro sellado con nuestro sello de plomo para tener en la nuestra cámara, por que en lo que duda ouiere, que las concierten con ellas.

(Until now [the *Siete partidas*] were not accepted as proclaimed by order of the king nor held nor received as law . . . but we ordered them collated and harmonized and corrected in those things that were proper. . . . And so that they may be reliable and there be no reason for anyone to delete or emend or change anything one might want, we order two books [official copies] to be made of them, one sealed with our golden seal and the other with our leaden seal, to be retained in our chambers so that anyone in doubt can consult them.)

The new redaction of the *Siete partidas* by Alfonso XI in 1348 and the establishment of official proof copies may imply that older conflicting copies were destroyed to avoid further divergences; few manuscripts copied prior to that date survive, and none from the royal Alfonsine scriptorium that was at work in the 1250s and 1260s.

Alfonso X continued the development of the *Fuero juzgo*, a unified legal code begun by his father, Fernando III, that upheld the king's exclusive prerogatives as lawgiver. Alfonso set himself the project of extending his legislative oversight over central Castile and the Extremaduras on its western flank, but the refurbished *Fuero juzgo* had a Leonese character that did not reflect the legal practices or the needs of the newly conquered territories. He therefore undertook a comprehensive reworking of the laws that would tie the preexisting local *fueros* into a unified whole. The result was the *Espéculo*. But the output of his jurists exceeded even the king's expectations, so he had them set the *Espéculo* aside around 1254 in favor of a more succinct document that would be better suited to immediate local needs. The result was the *Fuero real*, which he began granting in 1256 to communities that wished to bring themselves under the king's legislative purview. Meanwhile, he launched the project of compiling a corpus of laws to deal with all civic and private needs and to serve him and his successors in perpetuity. The result was the *Siete partidas*. In the years that followed, short versions of the *Espéculo* were pulled out to create the *Leyes de los adelantados mayores* and *Ordenanzas* that were sent to the magistrates of Valladolid in 1258. The *Siete partidas* reached its definitive form by 1263, and the eclipse of the *Espéculo* was complete.

The progressive imposition of Roman law as a normative pattern in Castilian jurisprudence encouraged native legal scholars from the start of the fourteenth century to rely increasingly on the *Siete partidas*. The Latin codes that were the ultimate authority in other parts of medieval Europe could be sidestepped in Castile in favor of a homegrown vernacular code that benefited from association with the expanding historical prestige of the Learned King. Until its final promulgation by his great-grandson, Alfonso XI, it underwent incremental additions and adjustments; but once a standard version was authorized, competing renditions of the code were swept aside. Throughout the fourteenth and fifteenth centuries copies of the *Siete partidas* multiplied and spread across Iberia. Alfonso X's legislative contribution had reached its final crystallization and begun its long career as the progenitor and core of all Spanish law.

References:

Juan Antonio Arias Bonet, "Sobre presuntas fuentes de las Partidas," *Revista de la Facultad de Derecho de la Universidad Complutense,* 9 (July 1985): 11–23;

Ivy A. Corfis, *Texts and Concordances of the "Siete partidas," October 25, 1491* (Madison, Wis.: Hispanic Seminary of Medieval Studies, 1997);

Jerry R. Craddock, "La cronología de las obras legislativas de Alfonso X el Sabio," *Anuario de Historia de Historia del Derecho Español,* 51 (1981): 365–418;

Craddock, "The Legislative Works of Alfonso el Sabio," in *Emperor of Culture: Alfonso X the Learned of Castile and His Thirteenth-Century Renaissance,* edited by Robert I. Burns, S.J. (Philadelphia: University of Pennsylvania Press, 1990), pp. 182–197;

Craddock, *The Legislative Works of Alfonso X, el Sabio* (London: Grant & Cutler, 1986);

Craddock, "El Setenario: Última e inconclusa refundición alfonsina de la primera Partida," *Anuario de la Historia del Derecho Español,* 56 (1986): 441–466;

Alfonso García-Gallo, "El *Libro de las Leyes* de Alfonso el Sabio: Del *Espéculo* a las *Partidas,*" *Anuario de la Historia del Derecho Español,* 21–22 (1951–1952): 345–528;

García-Gallo, "Nuevas observaciones sobre la obra legislativa de Alfonso X," *Anuario de la Historia de Derecho Español,* 46 (1976): 509–570;

García-Gallo, "La obra legislativa de Alfonso X. Hechos e hipótesis," *Anuario de la Historia del Derecho Español,* 54 (1984): 97–161;

Aquilino Iglesia Ferreirós, "Alfonso X el Sabio y su obra legislativa: Algunas reflexiones," *Anuario de la Historia del Derecho Español,* 50 (1980): 445–465;

Iglesia Ferreirós, "Alfonso X, su labor legislativa y los historiadores," *Historia Instituciones Documentos,* 9 (1982): 9–112;

Iglesia Ferreirós, "Cuestiones alfonsinas," *Anuario de la Historia del Derecho Español,* 55 (1985): 95–149;

Iglesia Ferreirós, "Fuero Real y Espéculo," *Anuario de la Historia del Derecho Español,* 52 (1982): 111–191;

Iglesia Ferreirós, "La labor legislativa de Alfonso X el Sabio," in *España y Europa: Un pasado jurídico común. Actas del I Simposio Internacional del Instituto de Derecho Común, Murcia, 26–28 de marzo de 1985,* edited by Antonio Pérez Martín (Murcia: Instituto de Derecho Común, 1986), pp. 275–599;

Robert A. MacDonald, "El Espéculo atribuido a Alfonso X, su edición y problemas que plantea," in *España y Europa,* pp. 611–654;

MacDonald, "Problemas políticos y derecho alfonsino considerado desde los tres puntos de vista," *Anuario de la Historia del Derecho Español,* 54 (1984): 25–53;

Gonzalo Martínez Díez, "Los comienzos de la Recepción del Derecho Romano en España y el Fuero Real," in *Diritto Comune e Diritti locali nella Storia dell'Europa* (Milan: A. Giuffrè, 1980), pp. 253–262;

Joseph F. O'Callaghan, *Alfonso X, the Cortes, and Government in Medieval Spain,* Variorum Collected Studies Series, No. CS608 (Aldershot, U.K. & Brookfield, Mass.: Ashgate, 1998);

J. M. Pérez-Prendes, "Las Leyes de Alfonso X el Sabio," *Revista de Occidente,* 43 (1984): 67–84;

José Sánchez-Arcilla Bernal, *La obra legislativa de Alonso X el Sabio. Historia de una polémica,* in *El Scriptorium alfonsí: De los Libros de Astrología a las "Cantigas de Santa María"* (Madrid: Fundación Universidad Complutense, 1999), pp. 17–81.

Early Medieval Spanish Theater

Karoline Manny
Seminole Community College

WORKS: Tropes

Quem quaeritis in sepulchro (Silos, eleventh century)

Quem quaeritis in sepulchro (Silos, eleventh century)

Quem quaeritis in sepulchro (Huesa, eleventh or twelfth century; copied: Saragossa, fifteenth century)

Quem quaeritis in presepe pastores, dicite (Huesa, eleventh or twelfth century; copied: Saragossa, fifteenth century)

Quem quaeritis in sepulchro (Compostela, twelfth century; copied: Compostela, fifteenth century)

Quem quaeritis pastores, dicite (León, thirteenth century; copied: Toledo and Palencia, fourteenth century)

Cantus Sibyllae (León, thirteenth century; copied: Palencia, fourteenth century)

Pastores dicite (Toledo, early sixteenth century; copied: Saragossa, Guadix, Palencia, and Segovia), sixteenth century)

Edition: Richard B. Donovan, ed., *The Liturgical Drama in Medieval Spain* (Toronto: University of Toronto Press, 1958).

Auto de los Reyes Magos (twelfth century)

Manuscript: One manuscript is housed in the Biblioteca Nacional, Madrid, MS. 1193.

Edition: *Teatro Medieval,* edited by Fernando Lázaro Carreter (Madrid: Editorial Castalia, 1958), pp. 97–115.

The greatest obstacle to the study of early medieval Spanish theater is the lack of extant examples. Latin religious tropes (brief texts interpolated into the church service) are relatively abundant in eastern Spain, but western Spain preserves only ten examples. Vernacular drama fares considerably more poorly. The earliest known extant Spanish drama, the *Auto de los Reyes Magos* (Drama of the Magi), was written in the second half of the twelfth century; the next known extant examples, the sketches of Gómez Manrique, were written in the fifteenth century. No copy of a drama written between those dates is known to exist.

This hiatus of more than two centuries has led to considerable controversy among medieval scholars as to the nature of Castilian drama prior to Juan del Encina. Because there are so few examples, some scholars have attempted to reconstruct early Spanish theater from church and court documents, travel accounts, and records of activities that are not commonly thought of as classically dramatic in nature, such as dialogues, debates, mock battles, minstrels' songs, and mime performances. Thus, the definition of drama itself becomes blurred, and other scholars question whether such documents are truly evidence of the existence of a vigorous theater in medieval Spain.

The debate over medieval Spanish theater begins with the question of its origins. One point on which critics agree is that Greek classical drama was unknown during the Spanish Middle Ages. Latin theater, on the other hand, fared better. Many medieval Spanish authors and chroniclers refer to the ancient Roman dramatists Plautus, Terence, and Seneca. For example, Antonio Vilaragut translated Seneca's *Hercules and Medea* near the end of the fourteenth century, and Enrique de Villena cites Terence in his *Consolatoria* (1423, Consolatory). Latin drama of the eleventh to the fourteenth centuries undeniably influenced literature in the peninsula. The *comedias elegíacas* (elegiac comedies) of the eleventh and twelfth centuries oscillated between narration and dialogue. An example of this type of play is *Pamphilus,* which had a great influence on Juan Ruiz's *Libro de buen amor* (circa 1330–1343; translated as *Book of Good Love,* 1933). The fourteenth-century Italian *comedias humanísticas* (humanistic comedies) were another important influence on peninsular literature; Petrarch (Francesco Petrarca, 1304–1374) is the most important writer of this genre. The influence of the *comedias humanísticas* on such works as Fernando de Rojas's *Tragicomedia de Calisto y Melibea* (circa 1495, Tragicomedy of Calisto and Melibea; translated as *The Spanish Bawd, Represented in Celestina; or, The Tragicke-Comedy of Calisto and Melibea,* 1631) is well established.

Another certainty is that medieval Spain was familiar with the liturgical trope. The word *trope,* from the Latin *tropus* (turn), was originally a musical term designating one to five lines that were inserted into the Mass to illustrate a passage of the liturgy. Normally associated with the Roman-French rite of the Catholic liturgy, tropes for the Mass were recorded in tropers (books of tropes) and graduals, while tropes for the Divine Office were recorded in breviaries and ordinaries, also called *consuetudo, liber consuetudinis, directorium, agenda,* and *consueta.* The troper or breviary contained the words, while the gradual or ordinary contained descriptions or "stage directions." If one of these sources is lost or separated from its partner, modern researchers are left with half a work; such has been the case with several discoveries in Spain.

In Europe the most primitive tropes are the *sequentia* (sequences): brief interludes based on the singing of the Alleluia on Easter Sunday. The Benedictine monk Notker Balbulus (840–910) is best known for the production of these pieces in Saint Gall, Switzerland. Later tropes can be divided into five groups. The *Visitatio Sepulchri* (Visit to the Sepulchre) tropes are performed during the Easter cycle of the liturgical year and dramatize the antiphon *Quem quaeritis in sepulchro?* (Whom do you seek in the grave?), when the Angel of God announces the Resurrection of Christ to the three Marys after the Crucifixion. The *Officium Pastorum* (Adoration of the Shepherds) tropes are included in the Nativity cycle and dramatize the antiphon *Quem viditis pastores, dicite?* (Whom do you see, shepherds?), when the shepherds are seeking the newborn Christ. The *Ordo Prophetarum* (Prophets) tropes arise from a sermon, *Contra judaeos, paganos et arianos* (Against Jews, Pagans, and Arrians), which was occasionally delivered on Christmas during the fifth and sixth centuries instead of the *Officium Pastorum.* In the *Ordo Prophetarum* Old Testament personages such as Moses, Isaiah, Jeremiah, Daniel, and David testify to the divinity of Jesus. One of these characters, Sibila Eritea, gave rise to the *Cantus Sibyllae* (Song of Sibyl), which was popular in Spain. The *Ordo* or *Officium Stellae* (The Three Kings and the Star), another Nativity variant, has the theme of the adoration of the Magi. The final group of tropes comprises those dramatizing the lives of the saints. The number of these religious plays extant today and their diffusion throughout Europe are indicative of their popularity.

Three major theories of the development of vernacular drama have been advanced. The first maintains that medieval drama evolved directly from the primitive tropes of the Mass. This theory seems to be supported by the prevalence of religious plays in the fifteenth century. The second theory is that medieval drama grew out of the influence of classical Latin theater. This theory accounts for the appearance of works

such as the *Tragicomedia de Calisto y Melibea.* The final theory offers a compromise: they argue that medieval theater arose as a result of the influence of both classical and religious sources. No consensus has been reached on this issue among Spanish scholars.

The first clearly dramatic form in the Iberian Peninsula was the liturgical trope; but because of the Arab presence in medieval Spain, and because the Mozarabic rite of the Catholic liturgy, which has never been proven to produce liturgical tropes, dominated the peninsula, the number of tropes is not as large there as it is in the rest of Europe. Nevertheless, eastern Spain, Cataluña in particular, was greatly influenced in the Middle Ages by France, an important producer of religious tropes. Because of this influence the eastern dioceses converted to the Roman-French liturgy in 800, much earlier than the rest of Spain. Not surprisingly, then, most of the extant tropes in Spain originate in the dioceses of Barcelona, Girona, Vic, and Urgell.

The earliest Latin Easter play found in Spain is the *Verses Pascales de III Mariis* (The Paschal Verses of the Three Marys) from the eleventh century; it is contained in the Ripoll troper. Another codex from Ripoll dating to the beginning of the twelfth century conserves a more extensive Resurrection play. A valuable find was the thirteenth-century version of the Resurrection plays copied by Andrés de Almunia in Vic; not only the text but also the stage directions are extant for this collection. Finally, the Girona chapter library houses a fourteenth-century *consueta* with descriptions of eight plays; the breviary that contained the scripts for these plays is lost.

The eastern peninsular area was not only the greatest source of liturgical tropes in Iberia but was also a source of innovation. The antiphon *Ubi est Christus* (Where is Christ?) appears to have been invented in St. Martial de Limoges. Critics cite this innovation as evidence that the tropes in the eastern provinces are not merely copies of French texts.

Some critics argue that when western Spain converted to the Roman-French rite in 1085, many of the clergy, especially the Cluny monks, were not anxious to include innovation, especially theater, in the liturgy. Thus, the first *Visitatio Sepulchri* in western Spain appeared in the eleventh century, the first Nativity cycle drama in the twelfth century, and the first *Cantus Sibyllae* in the thirteenth century. Ten tropes found in ten cities in western Spain are extant. The earliest is the eleventh-century *Visitatio Sepulchri* trope, found in a breviary in the Monastery of Silos. Another, slightly more sophisticated, trope of the same century was found in another breviary in the Silos Monastery. Also from the late eleventh and early twelfth centuries are two tropes from the Huesca Cathedral: a *Visitatio Sepulchri* and an *Offi-*

cium Pastorum. Duplicates of these tropes were found in fifteenth-century breviaries in Saragossa. A twelfth-century *Visitatio Sepulchri* in the French-Catalan rite is housed in the Compostela Cathedral. The *Ordo Prophetarum* finally made an appearance in western Spain in the thirteenth century with the *Cantus Sibyllae* in the León Cathedral. This piece is copied in a fourteenth-century breviary in Palencia. The León Cathedral also houses a thirteenth-century nativity trope from the *Officium Pastorum,* which was copied in fourteenth-century manuscripts in Toledo and Palencia. By the fifteenth century the *pastores dicite* (shepherds say) trope appears in Toledo and Palencia, a trope of the *Sibila* tradition is found in Palencia, and a *Processio Sibyllarum* (Procession of the Sybils) and a *Planctus Passionis* (Lament of the Passion) occur in Salamanca. One of the most important findings is a *Visitatio Sepulchri* trope, with accompanying stage directions, from the mid fifteenth century in Compostela. The stage directions and references preserved with the other tropes reveal that altar boys, choirboys, and priests impersonated angels, the three Marys, the shepherds, and the Magi and occasionally used special robes as costumes. These playlets generally took place in front of the choir, lectern, and altar.

The tropes are in Latin; but Spain was the origin of one of only three twelfth-century religious plays in a vernacular language: the *Auto de los Reyes Magos* (the others are the *Jeu d'Adam* [Play of Adam] and the *Seinte Resureccion* [Holy Resurrection], both in French). The term *auto* is typically reserved for one-act religious plays performed outside on carts or inside the church during the Corpus Christi celebration, while *representación* is a more generic term that is applied to any short dramatic piece in the Middle Ages; thus, some critics refer to the twelfth-century play as the *Representación de los Reyes Magos* (Performance of the Magi). The 147-verse fragment was found in the Toledo Cathedral in the eighteenth century by Felipe Fernández Vallejo. Based on Matthew's Gospel, it relates the story of the Three Wise Men's search for the Christ child and Herod's reaction to his birth. Modern editors have divided the play into five scenes. The first scene contains the monologues of the Wise Men as they gaze separately upon the Star of Bethlehem. In the second scene the Wise Men meet and decide to go together to adore Jesus. In the third scene the Wise Men tell Herod of the birth of Christ. In the fourth scene Herod wonders if there could actually be a king above him. The fifth scene depicts Herod's conversation with his rabbis.

The *Auto de los Reyes Magos* is written in polymetric verse, which varies depending on who is speaking and the serious or comical nature of the dialogue. This variation is a fundamental feature of later Spanish drama. The quality of the verse is also outstanding. Many crit-

ics have praised the lyricism of the poetry, especially in the monologues of the Wise Men.

The characterization of the biblical personages in the play is also significant. They are faithful to the biblical models but at the same time are portrayed through their dialogue as fully developed characters. Herod is the best example: the spectator sees Herod's doubt when he hears of the birth of Christ, his fear as he wonders if there could be a king over him, and his foolishness as he speaks with his rabbis. Critics also call attention to the author's skill in creating conflict, which is fundamental to the development of theater. The structure of the work is noteworthy, as well: this early play has distinct scenes that take place in a variety of settings: the homes of the three Magi and Herod's palace. Furthermore, it begins in medias res, as renaissance theater did later. Scholars generally agree that *Auto de los Reyes Magos* is a highly sophisticated, complex play for its time.

The Latin tropes and the vernacular *Auto de los Reyes Magos* are the only known extant examples of early medieval Spanish theater. Scholars note many reasons for the relatively low number of survivals. In the case of religious drama, the primary cause is the destruction of church records through damage to the cathedrals. Fires in the cathedrals of Astorga and Zamora undoubtedly destroyed some theatrical pieces, and Napoleonic looting of the León Cathedral may have resulted in the loss of valuable records. Much destruction would also have accompanied the *desamortización* (secularization) of church property. Many works may have been lost because the various parts were usually written on separate pages, to be handed out to the individual actors; thus, often no single manuscript ever existed. Nonreligious drama stood little chance of being preserved before the arrival of the printing press in Spain, because the Church had a virtual monopoly on scribing. Any work that was not religious had no value to the church and thus would not have been copied or stored in church libraries.

Regardless of the cause, before the mid fifteenth century Spain can claim only one vernacular work. Many scholars conclude that prior to this time Spain was a barren field with regard to dramatic production, but other critics point out that the number of known works has nearly doubled since this debate began in the 1950s. For example, all but two of the ten extant tropes were unknown before Donovan's study in 1958. Significantly, Donovan makes it clear that his research was not exhaustive but was confined to consulting breviaries and only five customaries from specific cathedrals in Castile; of the five customaries, four contained tropes. Donovan admits that there is room for much more research. Charlotte Stern and John Lihani agree

The entire text of the Auto de los Reyes Magos *(Biblioteca Nacional, Madrid, MS. Virt.5-9, folios 67v-68r)*

that more research is needed and cite the many references to nonextant dramas in chronicles, church decrees, travelers' accounts, and other nonliterary documents. In many cases the quality of the descriptions of liturgical and court drama is so high that some scholars assert that one can learn as much from them as one would from reading the plays themselves.

Scholars concede that not all documents that mention plays or spectacle can be considered proof that drama existed in medieval Spain. For example, Law 34, Title 6, of Part 1 of the *Siete partidas* (1256–1276, Seven-Part Law) of King Alfonso X *el Sabio* (the Learned) of Castile and León prohibits the clergy from participating in plays during the Mass that distract from the service but permits such plays if they inspire devotion. Humberto López Morales argues convincingly that this reference does not indicate the existence of liturgical drama, since the *Siete partidas* was copied from the *Espéculo* (1254, Mirror of Laws) and embellished by Spanish jurists who were heavily influenced by their studies in Italy. On the other hand, Stern argues,

equally convincingly, that Law 34 is not the only reference in the *Siete partidas,* nor in the chronicles in general, to drama. Whether or not the *Siete partidas* is evidence that liturgical drama was performed in Spain in the thirteenth century, it is proof that literate people in Spain were aware of such drama—if not before, then certainly after, reading Law 34. Permission to perform plays that inspire devotion constitutes an invitation and encouragement to do so.

Stern has compiled a wealth of other documents that seem to indicate that drama existed in early medieval Spain. Some refer specifically to dramatic performances. The earliest known reference is in the *Campesinos vasallos del Obispo Suero de Zamora* (1254–1286, Peasant Vassals of Bishop Suero de Zamora), which mentions a performance of the *Representación de Nuestro Señor* (Performance of Our Lord). The *Hechos del Condestable Don Miguel Lucas de Iranzo* (second half of the fifteenth century, Deeds of Constable Don Miguel Lucas de Iranzo) records various court celebrations, including performances of the *Representación de los Reyes Magos* and the *Estoria de Nascimiento de Nuestro Señor* (History of the Birth of Our Lord), as well as mock battles with dragons, jousting, dancing and singing, and allegorical performances.

The documents of greatest value to the study of nonextant theater in early medieval Spain are those that describe the Corpus Christi celebrations. These celebrations, founded by Pope Urban IV in 1264, usually involve parades through city streets that end in the cathedral, and the parades employ carts on which plays are enacted. The first Corpus Christi parade in Spain took place in Barcelona in 1322. In the rest of eastern Spain, Corpus Christi celebrations developed quickly thereafter: in Vich in 1330, in Lérida in 1340, in Valencia in 1355, and in Palma de Mallorca in 1377. The first reference to an *entremés* (short farce or interlude) performed during a Corpus Christi celebration comes from Barcelona in 1391 and describes the Garden of Eden with the characters of Adam and Eve.

As was the case with the tropes, Corpus Christi celebrations developed later in western than in eastern Spain. The most valuable document for the study of the Corpus Christi celebrations in western Spain is the *Libro de Cuentos y de Cabildo* (second half of the fifteenth century, Book of Accounts and of the Chapter). It records the titles of thirty-one plays used during the Corpus Christi celebration in Toledo and describes the materials purchased to perform them, the route the pageant followed, where it stopped to enact the plays, and the decorations of the carts. It also contains two play fragments. Carmen Torroja Menéndez and María Rivas Palá have done the most thorough study of the *Libro de Cuentos y del Cabildo*. They describe the expenditures listed for the various years, which include wax for the candles; wood for the pageant wagons; cloth, paper, and paint to decorate the wagons' figures; and payments to the artisans who created the materials for the festival. Additionally, there are references to payments for minstrels, and in 1445 the first payments to actors for the "juegos" (performances). In 1456 they note the first references to "representaciones." By the time Alonso de Campo took charge of the celebrations in 1481, their theatrical nature is certain. The Corpus Christi parade then consisted of as many as 92 to 130 pageant carts; some had monsters, giants, or other figures, while others were used for performances of *autos* at stops along the parade route and at the end of it.

Court documents describe festivals surrounding the coronation of kings or their arrival in towns. Many of these festivals included dramatic spectacles. The *Crónica de Alvar García de Santa María* (Chronicle of Alvar García de Santa María) describes the 1414 celebrations for the coronation of Fernando I de Antequera as king of Aragon, which included pageant wagons with alle-

gorical floats—a wheel of fortune that toppled pretenders to the throne and a wooden city under siege—and jousts. The Aljafería palace in Saragossa was decorated with a fire-breathing griffin and a Canopy of Heaven. People impersonating angels and the prophets played musical instruments during banquets; between courses they staged political allegories, the allegory of the vices and virtues, and a *Dance of Death*.

A similar account in the *Crónica de don Álvaro de Luna* (1423, Chronicle of don Álvaro de Luna) describes don Álvaro's tastes in entertainment:

> ordenó alli en Tordesillas muchas fiestas e muy ricas justas e otros entremeses en los cuales el rey e toda su corte ovieron mucho placer e alegría. . . . todos los caballeros, escuderos e pajes procuraron de salir muy nueva e apuestamente en todos los otros entremeses. . . . don Álvaro fue muy inventivo e mucho dado a fallar invenciones e sacar entremeses en fiestas o en justas o en guerra en las cuales invenciones muy agudamente significaba lo que quería.

> (he ordered in Tordesillas many parties and rich jousts and interludes in which the king and all his court took much pleasure and happiness. . . . all the knights, squires, and pages appeared in all the interludes. . . . don Álvaro was very creative and given to innovation and putting on interludes in parties or jousts or mock-battles in which his inventions sharply represented what he meant.)

In 1428 the people welcomed Leonor, the daughter of King Fernando, into Valladolid with a staging of the *Passo de la Fuerte Ventura* (Pass of Arms of Misfortune), and an *entremés* with eight women on horseback followed by a pageant wagon carrying a "goddess" and twelve singers. Plays were also used to describe negative political events: in 1431 a mock deposition of the Maestro of Santiago was staged, and in 1465 an effigy of Enrique IV of Castile was deposed in the *Farsa de Ávila* (Farce of Ávila).

Finally, in addition to records that mention or describe performances, there are many documents that describe laws surrounding dramatic performances. Most of these references are similar to the *Siete Partidas*. The *Concilio de Valladolid* (1228–1229, Council of Valladolid) condemns "joglares et rashechadores" (minstrels and performers) in the church. Chapter 137 of the *Libro de confesiones* (1312–1317, Book of Confessions) attacks actors who disguise themselves as devils and animals, take off their clothes and blacken themselves, and make irreverent jumps and gestures. Chapter 140 accepts actors who sing, play instruments, relate the deeds of kings and princes, and perform in reputable places but condemns those who sing obscene songs; jump, dance, and cavort; and distort their bodies. The *Concilio de*

Valladolid condemns the invitation of Jews and Moors into the churches to perform on Saints' Days. The *Sínodo de Cuéller* (1325, Synod of Cuéller) says that "Otrosí, en las iglesias non se deuen fazer juegos si non sean juegos de las fiestas así como de las Marías e del monumentos pero an de catar los clérigos que por tales juegos non distrayan el divinal oficio" (In churches they ought not do plays if they are not plays about the festival days such as that of the Marys and the monuments but the clergy ought to sing those plays that do not distract from the Divine Office). The *Concilio de Aranda* (1473, Council of Aranda) forbids lewd spectacles in the church but encourages honest religious works. These references lend credence to the idea that dramatic performances were so common in some areas that laws had to be made to govern them. When the one reference in *Siete Partidas* was discovered, it seemed likely that it was merely an imitation of an earlier law. Now that research has unearthed so many more references, especially ones that are so specific in nature, many scholars are beginning to concede that Spain had a rich tradition of medieval drama. Especially in the eastern peninsula dramatic spectacle accompanied most important events in the lives of the citizenry—religious seasons and the coronations or depositions, marriages, and arrivals into town of political figures.

There is a movement among scholars to expand the definition of drama beyond the classic definition, which requires impersonation, scripted dialogue, action, and conflict, to include other activities described in court and church records. These scholars argue that the medieval mind had not established or even contemplated literary definitions of theater and certainly would not have comprehended the formal theories proposed by Renaissance and modern scholars. Therefore, they contend, medieval people might have considered any spectacle to be dramatic in nature, and they study descriptions in chronicles and church documents that depict a variety of spectacles to determine how these events might have contributed to the development of drama. Some references are to minstrels, who most likely performed epic poetry. In 1116 social strife between Cluniac monks and minstrels led to the expulsion of the latter from Sahagún. The *Chronica Adefonsi Imperatoris* (1126–1157, Chronicle of Alfonso the Emperor) describes the wedding of Alfonso VII's daughter, with minstrels and *juglaresas* (female minstrels) singing and playing instruments. In 1238 Jaime I was honored in Saragossa with "baylls e jochs e solaces diuerses" (dances and games and diverse activities). In 1269 Alfonso *el Sabio* was welcomed in Valencia with tournaments, wild men, mock battles with oranges, and galley ships on wheels in the streets. In 1286 the coronation of Alfonso III of Aragon was celebrated with

mock battles between two ships on wheels. In 1327 the coronation of Alfonso IV was celebrated in the Aljafería with hundreds of minstrels, knights, wild men, and other entertainers. In 1399 the coronation of Martín I of Aragon was celebrated with a procession that included floats with a castle and singers pretending to be sirens and angels. The courtyard was decorated with a representation of the Canopy of Heaven, and knights staged mock battles with a model of a dragon. These instances all involve entertainers that dress up and impersonate characters. Although there was usually no dialogue involved, these scenes were highly dramatic in nature.

Again, many references to such events are criticisms of them by the pious or describe laws that governed them. In 1202 the *Fuero de Madrid* (Law of Madrid) set fees for entertainers who entered the city on horseback to prevent overpaying them and thereby attracting more entertainers. In 1258 the *cortes* (parliament) of Valladolid mandated that *joglares* and *soldaderas* (female entertainers) should be rewarded by the king once a year and that "non anden en su casa sino aquéllos que él tovier por bien" (only those whom he invited should go to his house). In his *Libro de los estados* (1326–1330, Book of the Estates) Juan Manuel states: "allí [durante vigilias] se dicen cantares et se tañen estrumentos et se fablan palabras et se ponen posturas que son todas al contrario de aquello para que las vigilias fueran ordenadas" (there [during vigils] they sing and play instruments, and say words, and put themselves in postures that are contrary to that for which the vigils were ordained). The *Concilio Provincial de Toledo* (1324, Toledan Provincial Council) criticizes *soldaderas* who dance to entertain bishops.

Some scholars argue that although these accounts may be of interest to historians or cultural studies, drama requires conflict acted out by people impersonating characters; since minstrels and debaters did not impersonate others, their work cannot be considered drama. But the scholars who defend these references as evidence of medieval theater define two extremes of activity in early medieval Spain: nonliterary spectacles such as jousting, singing, dancing, contorting, and gesticulating; and presenting texts such as epic poems, Bible stories, and morality sermons to an audience with little dramatic quality in their delivery. These extremes seem to coalesce in later court celebrations, where jousting and tilting evolved into mock battles that took place on primitive stages such as galley ships or carts with façades of castles. Songs, dances, and gesticulating developed into mimed, sometimes allegorical, performances on carts, in which performers sang or gestured to represent or imitate other people. Although these activities have little literary value, their developing theatricality, seen in the use of a stage and props and in clear imitation, is undeniable. In fact, there is evidence that medieval people did regard them as drama. In book 3 of the *Doctrinal de caballeros* (written circa 1444, published 1487, Catechism of Knighthood), Alfonso de Cartagena refers to "torneos e justas e actos que agora nuevamente aprendemos que llaman entremeses" (tournaments and jousts and other actions that we now are learning are called interludes).

Given the lack of extant works, the early history of the development of drama in medieval Spain is fraught with controversy. Scholars have drifted away from the previously generally accepted theory that Spain had no medieval dramatic tradition and now admit the existence of some sparse liturgical theater and palace entertainment, especially in the fourteenth century and later. As new research detects additional evidence of theatrical production, the debate over what constituted drama in early medieval Spain continues.

References:

Luigi Allegri, "La idea de teatro en la Edad Media," *Insula,* 527 (November 1990): 1–2, 31–32;

Ana María Alvarez Pellitero, "Del Officium Pastorum al auto pastoril renacentista," *Insula,* 527 (November 1990): 17–18;

Dino Bigongiari, "Were There Theatres in the Twelfth and Thirteenth Centuries?" *Romanic Review,* 37 (1946): 201–224;

Suzanne Byrd, "The Juglar: Progenitor of the Spanish Theater," *American Hispanist,* 4 (March–April 1979): 20–24;

Alan Deyermond, "The Lost Genre of Medieval Spanish Literature," *Hispanic Review,* 43 (1975): 231–259;

Richard B. Donovan, *The Liturgical Drama in Medieval Spain* (Toronto: University of Toronto Press, 1958);

Leandro Fernández de Moratín, *Discurso histórico sobre los orígenes del teatro español* (Buenos Aires: Schapire, 1946);

Clifford Flanigan, "The Roman Rite and Origins of the Liturgical Drama," *University of Toronto Quarterly,* 43 (1974): 263–284;

Joaquín Forradellas Figueras, "Para los orígenes del teatro español," *Bulletin Hispanique,* 72 (1972): 328–330;

O. B. Hardison, *Christian Rite and Christian Drama in the Middle Ages: Essays in the Origin and Early History of Modern Drama* (Baltimore: Johns Hopkins University Press, 1965);

Humberto López Morales, "El 'Auto de los Reyes Magos': Un texto para tres siglos," *Insula,* 527 (1990): 20–21;

López Morales, "El concilio de Valladolid de 1228 y el teatro medieval castellano," *Boletín de la Academia Puertorriqueña de la Lengua Española,* 14 (1986): 61–68;

López Morales, "Nueva hipótesis sobre el teatro medieval castellana," *Revista de Estudios Hispánicos-Puerto Rico,* 1–4 (1972): 7–19;

López Morales, "Nuevo examen del teatro medieval," *Segismundo,* 4 (1972): 113–124;

López Morales, *Tradición y creación en los orígenes del teatro castellano* (Madrid: Alcalá, 1968);

José López Yepes, "Una Representación de las Sibilas y un *Planctus Passionis* en el Ms. 80 de la Catedral de Córdoba," *Revista de Archivos, Bibliotecas y Museos,* 80 (1997): 545–567;

Francisco Mendoza Díaz-Maroto, "El Concilio de Aranda (1473) y el teatro medieval castellano," *Criticón,* 26 (1984): 5–15;

Alexander A. Parker, "Notes on the Religious Drama in Medieval Spain and the Origins of the 'Auto Sacramental,'" *Modern Language Review,* 30 (1935): 170–182;

Francisco Ruiz Ramón, *Historia del teatro español desde sus orígenes hasta mil novecientos* (Madrid: Alianza, 1967);

N. D. Shergold, *A History of the Spanish Stage from Medieval Times until the End of the Seventeenth Century* (Oxford: Clarendon Press, 1967);

Charlotte Stern, *The Medieval Theater in Castile* (Binghamton, N.Y.: Medieval and Renaisance Texts and Studies, 1996);

Carmen Torroja Menéndez and Mariá Rivas Palá, *Teatro en Toledo en el siglo XV: "Auto de la Pasión" de Alonso del Campo* (Madrid: Anejos de la Real Academia Española, 1977);

Ángel Valbuena Prat, *Historia del teatro español* (Barcelona: Noguer, 1956);

J. E. Varey, "A Note on the Councils of the Church and Early Dramatic Spectacles in Spain," in *Medieval Hispanic Studies Presented to Rita Hamilton,* edited by Alan Deyermond (London: Tamesis, 1976), pp. 241–244;

Francis George Very, *The Spanish Corpus Christi Procession: A Literary and Folkloric Study* (Valencia: Tipografía Moderna, 1962);

Karl Young, *The Drama of the Medieval Church,* 2 volumes (Oxford: Clarendon Press, 1933).

Jewish Literature of Medieval Spain

John Zemke

University of Missouri, Columbia

Saadya ben Joseph (882–942)

WORKS: *Kitab fatsih lughat al-ʿibraniyyin*

Manuscripts: Russian State Public Library, St. Petersburg, MS. Hebr. Ar. 3073; Bodleian Library, University of Oxford, MS. Heb. e27; University of Cambridge Library MSS. T-S. K7-19, T-S. Ar. 32-39, and T-S. Ar. 31-247; Jewish Theological Seminary, New York, MS. ENA 3220-6.

Editions: "Kitab fatsih lughat al-ʿibraniyyin," in *Or rishon behokhmat halashon: Sefer Tsahut leshon haʿIvrim,* volume 2, edited by Aron Dotan (Jerusalem: Rabbi David Moses and Amalia Rosen Foundation, 1997).

Haegron

Manuscripts: Russian State Public Library, St. Petersburg, MSS. Hebr. Ar. I 3067 and Hebr. Ar. I 3072; University of Cambridge Library, MSS. T-S. K 7/38, T-S. D 1/19, T-S. 8 K/12, T-S. N.S. 309/80, and T-S. 302/75.

Edition: *Haegron,* edited by Nehemya Allony (Jerusalem: Academy of the Hebrew Language, 1969).

Kitab al-sabʿin

Modern edition: "Kitab al-sabʿin," edited by Nehemya Allony, in *Ignace Goldziher Memorial Volume,* 2 volumes, edited by Samuel Löwinger and Joseph Somogyi (Budapest: Globus, 1958), II: 1–48.

Menahem Ibn Saruq (910–976)

WORKS: *Mahberet Menahem*

Manuscripts: British Library, London, MSS. Add. 27214 and Ar. Or. 51; Bodleian Library, University of Oxford, MS. Opp. 627; Biblioteca Medicea-Laurenziana, Florence, MS. Plut. 88.9; Staats- und Universitätsbibliothek, Hamburg, Cod. Heb. 48; Burgerbibliothek, Bern, MS. Cod. 200; Preussischer Kulturbesitz, Berlin, MS. Or. Fol. 120; Bibliotheek van der Rijksuniversiteit, Leiden, Cod. Or. 4722; Bibliothèque nationale, Paris, MS. Héb. 1214; Biblioteca Palatina, Parma, MSS. 3508 and 2781; Vatican Library, Rome, MS. 460.

First publication: *Mahberet Menahem,* 2 volumes, edited by Hirschel Filipowski (London: Hevrat yeshanim, 1854).

Modern editions: "Mahberet Menahem," in *Hashirah haʿivrit besefarad ubeprovens,* 2 volumes, edited by Jefim Schirmann (Tel Aviv: Devir, 1954, 1956), I: 3–31; *Menahem ben Saruq, Mahberet,* edited by Ángel Sáenz-Badillos (Granada: Universidad de Granada, 1986).

Dunash ben Labrat (circa 920 – circa 990)

WORKS: *Teshuvot de Dunash*

Manuscripts: British Library, London, MS. Ar. Or. 51; Bodleian Library, University of Oxford, Opp. 627; Staatsbibliothek, Berlin, MS. Or. Oct. 243; Biblioteca Medicea Laurenziana, Florence, MS. Plut. 88.9; University of Cambridge Library, MSS. T-S. Miscel. 36/6, T-S. 9/2, and T-S. N.S. 301/73; Bibliotheek van der Rijksuniversiteit, Leiden, Cod. Or. 4722; Biblioteca Palatina, Parma, MS. 3508.

Editions: *The Objections of Dunash to the Mahberet of Menahem,* edited by Herschell Filipowski (London: Hevrat yeshanim, 1855); *Teshuvot de Dunash ben Labrat,* edited and translated by Angel Sáenz-Badillos (Granada: Universidad de Granada, 1980).

Critical edition: "Teshuvot de Dunash," edited by Nehemya Allony, introduction by Herschell Filipowski, *Beit Mikra* (1965): 45–63.

Diwan

Manuscripts: Jewish Theological Seminary, New York, MS. ENA 2678; Bodleian Library, University of Oxford, MS. 1100; British Museum, London, MSS. 655 and 1056; Russian State Public Library, St. Petersburg; University of Cambridge Library, MSS. T-S. 8K 15/8 and T-S. N.S. 143/46; private collection of the widow of Jacques Nissim Mosseri, Paris, MSS. VIII 202 and VIII 387; Bodleian Library, University of Oxford, MS. Hebr. D. 75.

Editions: *Dunash ben Labrat: Shirim,* edited by Nehemya Allony (Jerusalem: Mosad Rav Kuk, 1947); selections in *Hashirah haʿivrit besefarad* *ubeprovens,* 2 volumes, edited by Jefim Schirmann (Tel Aviv: Devir, 1954, 1956), I: 31–41; *El divan poético de Dunash ben Labrat,* edited by Carlos del Valle Rodríguez (Madrid: CSIC, 1988).

Riddles

Manuscripts: Jewish Theological Seminary, New York, MS. ENA 3702; Russian State Public Library, St. Petersburg.

Edition:, Nehemya Allony, "Ten of Dunash ben Labrat's Riddles," *Jewish Quarterly Review,* 36 (1945–1946): 141–146.

Judah ben David Hayyuj (circa 945–circa 1000)
WORKS: *Kitab al-tanqit*

Manuscript: Bodleian Library, University of Oxford, MS. 1453.

Edition: *Kitab al-tanqit,* edited by John W. Nutt (London: Asher, 1870).

Kitab al-afal dhawat huruf al-lin

Manuscript: British Library, London, MS. 982.5.

Editions: "Gramatische Werke des r. Jehuda Chajjug: Sifre Dikduk merosh hamedakdekim R. Yehuda Hayyug," edited by Leopold Dukes, in *Beiträge zur Geschichte der aeltesten Auslegung und Spracherklärung des Alten Testamentes,* edited by Dukes and Heinrich Ewald (Stuttgart: A. Krabbe, 1844); *Kitab al-afal dhawat huruf al-lin,* edited by Morris Jastrow (Leiden: Brill, 1897); *Sheloshah sifre dikduk,* edited by David Tene (Jerusalem: Hebrew University, 1969).

Edition in English: *Two Treatises on Verbs Containing Feeble and Double Letters by R. Jehuda Hayyug of Fez, Translated into Hebrew from the Original Arabic by R. Moses Gikatilia of Cordova; to Which Is Added the Treatise on Punctuation by the Same Author Translated by Aben Ezra: Edited from Bodleian MSS. With an English Translation,* edited and translated by John W. Nutt (London & Berlin: Asher, 1870).

Sefer teshuvot talmide Menahem ben Yaakov Ibn Saruq al teshuvot Dunash ben Labrat: teshuvot talmid Dunash Ibn Labrati

Manuscript: Biblioteca Palatina, Parma, MS. 3508, folios 181v–193v.

Editions: *Sefer teshuvot talmide Menahem ben Yaakov Ibn Saruq al teshuvot Dunash ben Labrat: teshuvot talmid Dunash Ibn Labrati,* edited by Solomon Gottlieb Stern (Vienna: Solomon Gottlieb Stern, 1870); *Teshuvot de los discípulos de Menahem contra Dunash ben Labrat,* edited and translated by Santiago Benavente Robles (Granada: Universidad de Granada, 1986).

Joseph Ibn Abitor (circa 950–after 1024)
WORK: *Piyyutim*

Manuscripts: Bodleian Library, University of Oxford, MS. 2712; Jewish Theological Seminary,

New York, MS. ENA 629; University of Cambridge Library, MS. T-S. H6/58; British Library, London, MS. Or. 557B.

Editions: "Piyyutim," in *Die religiöse Poesie der Juden In Spanien,* edited by Michael Sachs (Berlin: Beit, 1845), pp. 9–11; selections in *Hashirah haivrit besefarad ubeprovens,* 2 volumes, edited by Jefim Schirmann (Tel Aviv: Devir, 1954, 1956), I: 53–65; "Piyyutim," in *Shirim hadashim min hagenizah,* edited by Schirmann (Jerusalem: Israel Academy of Sciences and Humanities, 1965), pp. 149–156; "Piyyutim," in *Yetsirato shel Yosef Ibn Avitur: sugim vetavniyot bepiyutav,* 2 volumes, edited by Ezra Fleischer (Jerusalem: Hebrew University, 1970); "Piyyutim," in *Shirat haqodesh haivrit biyeme habenayim,* edited by Fleischer (Jerusalem: Keter, 1975), pp. 382, 396–399, 411.

Isaac Ibn Khalfun (circa 965–after 1020)
WORK: *Diwan*

Manuscripts: Hungarian Academy of Sciences, Budapest, MS. Kaufmann 72; University of Cambridge Library, MSS. T-S. Misc. 35.58, T-S Box K8, T-S. Misc. Box 23, K 16c, T-S Misc. 23.9c; T-S Misc. 35.58, T-S Misc. 35.61, T-S K 8.39, and T-S 8K 14/2; Bodleian Library, University of Oxford, MSS. Heb. D. 36 and 2776/3.

Editions: Selections in *Hashirah haivrit besefarad ubeprovens,* 2 volumes, edited by Jefim Schirmann (Tel Aviv: Devir, 1954, 1956), I: 66–73; *Shire rabbi Yitzhak Ibn Khalfun,* edited by Aharon Mirsky (Jerusalem: Mosad Bialik, 1961); María José Cano, *Yishaq ibn Jalfun poeta cortesano cordobés* (Granada: Universidad de Granada, 1988); *Isaac ben Jalfón de Córdoba: Poemas,* edited and translated by Carlos del Valle Rodríguez (Madrid: Aben Ezra Ediciones, 1992); Ann Brener, "Isaac Ibn Khalfun: A Professional Poet of the Eleventh Century," dissertation, Cornell University, 1999.

Jonah Ibn Janah (Abu-l-Walid Merwan Ibn Janah) (circa 985–circa 1040)
WORKS: *Kitab al-mustalhaq*

Manuscripts: Bodleian Library, University of Oxford, MSS. 1453, 1454, 1455, and 1456; British Library, London, MSS. 952, 953, and 982.3–4.

Edition: "Kitab al-mustalhaq," in *Opuscules et traités d'Abou'l-Walid Merwan Ibn Djanah de Cordoue: Texte arabe, publié avec une traduction français,* edited and translated by Joseph and Hartwig Derenbourg (Paris: Imprimerie Nationale, 1880), pp. 1–246.

Kitab al-tanqih (Kitab al-lumac and Kitab al-utsul)

Editions: *Sefer hariqmah,* translated by Judah Ibn

Tibbon, edited by Baer Goldberg and Raphael Kirchheim (Frankfurt am Main, 1856); *The Book of Hebrew Roots by Abu'l Walid Marqan Ibn Ganah,* 2 volumes, edited by Adolf Neubauer (Oxford: Clarendon Press, 1873, 1875); *Kitab al-utsul,* edited by Neubauer (Oxford: Clarendon Press, 1875); *Le livre des parterres fleuris: Grammaire hébraique,* edited by Joseph Derenbourg (Paris: Vieweg, 1886); *Le livre des parterres fleuris d' Abou'l-Walid Merwan Ibn Djanah,* translated by Moses Metzger (Paris: E. Bouillon, 1889); *Sefer hashorshaim: Würzelworterbuch der hebräischen Sprache,* translated by Ibn Tibbon, edited by Wilhelm Bacher (Berlin: Selbstverlag des Vereins M'Kize Nirdamim [Dr. A. Berliner], printed by H. Itzkowski, 1896); *Sefer hariqmah,* translated by Ibn Tibbon, edited by Michael Wilensky (Berlin: Akademie-Verlag, 1930); *Sefer hariqmah,* translated by Ibn Tibbon, edited by David Tene (Jerusalem: Academy of the Hebrew Language, 1964).

Moses Ibn Gikatilla (circa 1000–circa 1080)
WORKS: *Kitab 'al tadhkir w'al-ta'anith*
  Manuscripts: Bodleian Library, University of Oxford, MSS. 1457 and 1467.
  Editions: *Two Treatises on Verbs Containing Feeble and Double Letters by R. Jehuda Hayyug of Fez, Translated . . . by R. Moses Gikatilia of Córdoba,* edited and translated by John W. Nutt (London & Berlin: Asher, 1870); Samuel A. Poznanski, *Moses Ibn Chiquitilla und die Fragmente seiner Schriften* (Leipzig: J. C. Hinrichs, 1895); "Kitab 'al tadhkir w'al-ta'anith," in *Novye materialy dlia kharakteristiki IEkhudy Khaïi-udzha, Samuila Nagida i niekotorykh drugikh predstaveitelei evreiskoi filologicheskoi nauki v X, XI i XII viekie,* edited by Pavel Kokovcov (Petrograd: Tip. imperatorskoi akademii nauk, 1916), pp. 59–66.

Diwan
  Editions: Israel Davidson, "Moses Ibn Chiqatilla as Poet," *Hebrew Union College Annual,* 1 (1924): 599–601; "Diwan," in *Hashirah ha'ivrit besefarad ubeprovens,* 2 volumes, edited by Jefim Schirmann (Tel Aviv: Devir, 1954, 1956), I: 294–297.

Judah Ibn Balcam (eleventh century)
WORKS: *Kitab al-tajnis*
  Editions: "Kitab al-tajnis," edited by Pavel Kokovcov, in *Novye materialy dlia kharakteristiki IEkhudy Khaïiudzha, Samuila Nagida i niekotorykh drugikh predstaveitelei evreiskoi filologicheskoi nauki v X, XI i XII viekie* (Petrograd: Tip. imperatorskoi akademii nauk, 1916), pp. 69–108; "Kitab al-tajnis," edited by Nehemya Allony, *Beit Mikra* (1964): 87–122; Shraga Abramson, ed., *Sheloshah sefarim shel*

Rav Yehuda Ibn Balcam (Jerusalem: Kiryat Sefer, 1975).
  Critical edition: "Kitab al-tajnis," edited by Shraga Abramson, in *Sefer Yalon,* edited by Saul Lieberman (Jerusalem: Kiryat Sefer, 1963), pp. 51–149.
Shaar taame sheloshah sefarim Emet
  Edition: *Shaar taame sheloshah sefarim Emet: Abhand-lung über die Poetischen Accente der 3 Bücher,* edited by Gabriel I. Polak (Amsterdam: Levisson, 1858).
Commentary on the Twelve Minor Prophets
  Edition: Samuel Poznanski, "The Arabic commentary of Abu Zakariya Yahya (Judah Ben Samuel) Ibn Balcam on the Twelve Minor Prophets," *Jewish Quarterly Review,* new series 15 (1924–1925): 1–53.
Poetry
Edition: Jefim Schirmann, *Hashirah ha'ivrit besefarad ubeprovens,* 2 volumes (Tel Aviv: Devir, 1954, 1956), I: 298–300.

Samuel the Nagid (Ismail ibn Nagrelca) (993–1055/1056)
WORKS: *Rasacil al-rifaq*
  Edition: "Rasacil al-rifaq," in *Opuscules et traités d'Abou'l-Walid Merwan Ibn Djanah de Cordoue: Texte arabe, publié avec une traduction français,* edited by Joseph and Hartwig Derenbourg (Paris: Imprimerie Nationale, 1880), pp. lix–lxvi.
Kitab al-istighnac
  Edition: "Kitab al-istighnac," edited by Pavel Kokovcov, in *Novye materialy dlia kharakteristiki IEkhudy Khaïiudzha, Samuila Nagida i niekotorykh drugikh predstaveitelei evreiskoi filologicheskoi nauki v X, XI i XII viekie* (Petrograd: Tip. imperatorskoi akademii nauk, 1916), pp. 205–224.
Hilkhata gavrata
  Edition: *Hilkhata gibarvata: Hilkhot Hanagid,* edited by Mordecai Margulies (Jerusalem: Judah Leb & Mini Epstein/Academy for Jewish Research, 1962).
Diwan
  Manuscripts: Sassoon family estate, Letchworth, U.K., MS. 589; Jewish Theological Seminary, New York, MSS. ENA 1834, 2163, and 2648; fragments in Bodleian Library, University of Oxford, MSS. 242.18 and 2861, and in University of Cambridge Library, MSS. T-S. N.S.108/41 and T-S. N.S.108/76.
  Editions: *Zikkaron rabbi Shemuel Ibn Yosef Halevi,* edited by Abraham E. Harkavy (St. Petersburg: Avraham Eliyahu Harkavi, 1879); *Kol shire rabbi Shemuel Hanagid,* edited by Heinrich Brody (Warsaw: Tushiyah, 1910); *Diwan of Shemuel Hanagid:*

According to a Unique Manuscript with an Index of Poems, 3 volumes, edited by David S. Sassoon (Oxford & London: Oxford University Press, Humphrey Milford, 1934); *Rabbi Shemuel Hanagid: Ben Mishle,* edited by Shraga Abramson (Tel Aviv: Mahbarot lesifrut, 1948); *Rabbi Shemuel Hanagid: Ben Qohelet,* edited by Abramson (Tel Aviv: Mahbarot lesifrut, 1953); *Rabbi Shemuel Hanagid: Shire milhamah,* edited by A. M. Habermann (Tel Aviv: Mahbarot lesifrut, 1963); *Divan Shemuel Hanagid, II. Ben Mishle,* edited by Dov Yarden (Jerusalem: Dov Yarden, 1982); *Divan Shemuel Hanagid, III. Ben Qohelet,* edited by Dov Yarden (Jerusalem: Dov Yarden, 1992).

Piyyutim

Editions: *Rabbi Shemuel Hanagid: Diwan vekolel bo sefer Ben Tehillim,* edited by Abraham M. Habermann (Tel Aviv: Mahbarot lesifrut, 1947); selections in *Hashirah ha'ivrit besefarad ubeprovens,* 2 volumes, edited by Jefim Schirmann (Tel Aviv: Devir, 1954, 1956), I: 74–168; selections in *Shirim hadashim min hagenizah,* edited by Schirmann (Jerusalem: Israel Academy of Sciences and Humanities, 1965), pp. 159–165; *Diwan Shemuel Hanagid, I. Ben Tehillim,* edited by Dov Yarden (Jerusalem: Hebrew Union College Press, 1966).

Editions in English: *The Jewish Poets of Spain, 900–1250,* edited and translated by David Goldstein (Harmondsworth, U.K.: Penguin, 1971), pp. 47–76; *Jewish Prince in Moslem Spain: Selected Poems of Samuel Ibn Nagrela,* edited and translated by Leon J. Weinberger (Tuscaloosa: University of Alabama Press, 1973); *The Penguin Book of Hebrew Verse,* edited and translated by T. Carmi (Harmondsworth, U.K.: Penguin, 1981), pp. 285–301; *Poemas desde el campo de batalla,* translated by Ángel Sáenz-Badillos and Judit Targarona (Cordova: El Almendro, 1988); *Selected Poems of Shemuel Hanagid,* translated by Peter Cole (Princeton: Princeton University Press, 1996); *Grand Things to Write a Poem on: A Verse Autobiography of Shemuel Hanagid,* translated by Hillel Halkin (Jerusalem: Gefen, 2000).

Joseph Ibn Hisdai (flourished early eleventh century)
WORK: *Shira yetomah*
Editions: "Shira yetomah," in *Hashirah ha'ivrit besefarad ubeprovens,* 2 volumes, edited by Jefim Schirmann (Tel Aviv: Devir, 1954, 1956), I: 169–170; *The Penguin Book of Hebrew Verse,* edited and translated by T. Carmi (Harmondsworth, U.K.: Penguin, 1981), p. 302.

Solomon ben Judah Ibn Gabirol (Abu Ayyub Sulayman ibn Yahya Gabirul) (circa 1020–circa 1057)

WORKS: *Mekor hayyim*
Manuscript: Bibliothèque Nationale, Paris, MS. Héb. 239.
Editions: "Kitab al-hadiqa; Likkutim mesefer mekor hayyim (La source de vie)," translated by Shem Tov ben Joseph Ibn Falaquera in *Mélanges de philosophie juive et arabe,* edited by Salomon Munk (Paris: Franck, 1859), pp. 3–148; *Avencebrolis (Ibn Gebirol): Fons vitae ex arabico in latinvm translatvs ab Iohanne Hispano et Dominico Gvndissalino,* edited by Clemens Baeumker (Münster: Aschendorff, 1895); *Ibn-Gebirol (Avicembron): La Fuente de la vida,* 2 volumes, translated by Federico de Castro y Fernández (Madrid: B. Rodríguez Serra, 1901); *Mekor hayyim,* edited by Jacob Blaustein (Jerusalem: Mahbarot Lesifrut, 1926); Shlomo Pines, "*Sefer arugat habosem,* haqetaim, mitokh *Sefer mekor hayyim," Tarbiz,* 27 (1958): 218–233; *Mekor hayyim,* edited by Noah Bar-On (Tel Aviv: Mahbarot lesifrut, 1964); *Salomon Ibn Gabirol: Livre de la source de vie (Fons vitae),* translated by Jacques Schlanger (Paris: Aubier Montaigne, 1970).
Editions in English: *The Fountain of Life,* translated by Harry E. Wedeck (New York: Philosophical Library, 1962); *The Fountain of Life,* translated by Alfred B. Jacob (Stanwood, Wash.: Sabian Publication Society, 1987).

Itslah al-'akhlaq
Manuscripts: Real Biblioteca del Monasterio de El Escorial, MS. G.IV.4, folios 144–166r; Jewish Theological Seminary, New York, MS. ENA 82.
Early translation: Judah Ibn Tibbon, *Tikkun middot hanefesh* (c. 1161–c. 1167).
Early imprint: Isaac Hayim Hazan (Constantinople: Moses ben Eleazar, 1550).
Editions: *Sefer Goren Nakhon* (Lunéville: Bet Avraham Prizek, 1807; Brooklyn, N.Y.: Ahim Goldenberg, 1993); *R. Shelomoh ben Gabirol: Sefer Tikkun Midoth hanefesh,* translated by Judah Ibn Tibbon, edited by Noah Bar-On (Tel Aviv: Mahbarot lesifrut, 1951); *La corrección de los caracteres,* translated by Joaquín Lomba Fuentes (Saragossa: Universidad de Zaragoza, 1990).
Edition in English: *The Improvement of Moral Qualities,* edited and translated by Stephen Wise (New York: Columbia University Press, 1902).

Keter malkhut
Manuscripts: Bodleian Library, University of Oxford, MSS. 108.2, 1239, 1967; British Library, London, MSS. 626.1, 633.1, 678.6, 692.5, 693.1, Add. 14763/IV; University of Cambridge Library, MS. Add. 658; Jewish Theological Seminary, New York, MS. ENA 900.
Early imprints: *Libro de las oraciones,* edited and

translated by Yom Tob Atias (Ferrara?, 1552); *Poma aurea Hebraicae lenguae . . . in tria opuscula distributa,* translated by Donati Francesco (Rome: Stephanus Paulinus, 1618); *Keter malchut de R. Selomoh hijo de Gabirol,* translated by Ishac Nieto (Leghorn, 1769).

Editions: José M. Millás-Vallicrosa, *La poesía sagrada hebraicoespañola,* second edition (Madrid: CSIC, 1948), pp. 205–224; *Keter malkhut,* edited by I. A. Zeidman (Jerusalem: Mahbarot lesifrut, 1950); *Solomon Ibn Gabirol: Keter malkhut,* edited by Paula Bernadette and David N. Barocas (New York: Foundation for the Advancement of Sephardic Studies and Culture, 1972); *La couronne royale,* translated by Paul Vuillaud (Paris: Dervy, 1984).

Editions in English: *The Kingly Crown,* translated by B. Lewis (London: Vallentine, Mitchell, 1961); *A Crown for the King,* translated by David Slavitt (New York: Oxford University Press, 1998); *Selected Poems of Solomon Ibn Gabirol,* translated by Peter Cole (Princeton: Princeton University Press, 2001).

Diwan

Manuscripts: Schocken Institute for Jewish Research of the Jewish Theological Seminary of America, Jerusalem, MSS. 37 and 22; Bodleian Library, University of Oxford, MS. 1970; University of Cambridge Library, MS. T-S. N.S.108/28; Jewish Theological Seminary, New York, MS. ENA 627.

Edition: *Shire Shelomoh ben Solomon Ibn Gabirol,* edited by Haim N. Bialik and Yehoshua Hana Rawnitzki, 6 volumes (Berlin & Tel Aviv: Devir, 1924–1930).

Piyyutim

Manuscripts: Bodleian Library, University of Oxford, MSS. 1026 and 1176; University of Cambridge Library, MS. Add. 33788; Jewish Theological Seminary, New York, MS. ENA 2161.

Editions: *Azharot: Cantiques de Salamon Ibn Gabirol (Avecibron),* edited by Senior Sachs (Paris: L. Guerin, 1868); *Piyyutim* (Leghorn: Shelomo Bilforte, 1885); *Shire haqodesh lerab Shelomo Ibn Gabirol,* 2 volumes, edited by Dov Yarden (Jerusalem: Dov Yarden, 1971, 1973); *Poesía religiosa,* translated by María José Cano (Granada: Universidad de Granada, 1992); Jefim Schirmann, ed., *Shirim hadashim min hagenizah,* (Jerusalem: Israel Academy of Sciences and Humanities, 1965), pp. 166–184.

Editions in English: *Selected Religious Poems of Solomon Ibn Gabirol,* edited by Israel Davidson, translated by Israel Zangwill (Philadelphia: Jewish Publication Society of America, 1924); *Selected Poems of Solomon*

Ibn Gabirol, translated by Peter Cole (Princeton: Princeton University Press, 2001).

Diwan

Editions: *Shire Shelomoh; shirim yakarim,* edited by Leopold Dukes (Hanover: Telgener, 1858); "Diwan," in *Hashirah ha'ivrit besefarad ubeprovens,* 2 volumes, edited by Jefim Schirmann (Tel Aviv: Devir, 1954, 1956), I: 176–285; *Qobets shire hol,* edited by Nehemya Allony and Dov Yarden (Jerusalem, 1968); *Shelomoh Ibn Gabirol shire hol,* edited by Schirmann and Heinrich Brody (Jerusalem: Schocken Institute for Jewish Research of the Jewish Theological Seminary of America, 1974); *Shire hahol lerabbi Shelomoh Ibn Gabirol,* 2 volumes, edited by Yarden (Jerusalem: Dov Yarden, 1975, 1976); *Poesía secular,* translated by Elena Romero (Madrid: Alfaguara, 1978); *Poemas seculares,* translated by María José Cano (Granada: Universidad de Granada, 1987); *Selected Poems of Solomon Ibn Gabirol,* translated by Peter Cole (Princeton: Princeton University Press, 2001).

Ha'anaq

Manuscript: Bodleian Library, University of Oxford, MS. 2489.D 1.

Editions: "Ha'anaq," edited by Jacob Egers, in *Jubelschrift zum neunzigsten Geburtstag des Dr. L. Zunz* (Berlin: L. Gerschel, 1884), pp. 192–196; *Shire Shelomoh ben Solomon Ibn Gabirol,* 6 volumes, edited by Hayyim Nahman Bialik and Yehoshua Hana Rawnitzki (Berlin & Tel Aviv: Devir, 1924–1930); *Ibn Gabirols 'Anak,* edited by Ernst Neumark (Leipzig: Teicher, 1936); "Ha'anaq," in *Hashirah ha'ivrit besefarad ubeprovens,* 2 volumes, edited by Jefim Schirmann (Tel Aviv: Devir, 1954, 1956), I: 176–285; Angel Sáenz-Badillos, "El 'anaq, poema lingüístico de Selomoh Ibn Gabirol," *Miscelánea de Estudios Árabes y Hebreos,* 29 (1980): 5–29.

Mibhar hapeninim

Manuscripts: University of Cambridge Library, MSS. Add. 1224.3 and Dd.4.2.5.

Early imprints: *Mibhar hapeninim,* edited by Solomon ben Perez (Soncino: Joshua Soncino, 1484); *Mibhar hapeninim* (Venice, 1546).

Editions: *Mibhar hapeninim,* edited by A. M. Habermann (Jerusalem: Sifriyat Hapoalim, 1947); *Selección de Perlas,* translated by David Gonzalo Maeso (Barcelona: Ameller, 1977).

Edition in English: *Solomon Ibn Gabirol's Choice of Pearls,* edited and translated by Abraham Cohen (New York: Bloch, 1925).

Isaac Ibn Ghiyyat (1038–1089)
WORK: *Diwan*

Manuscripts: University of Cambridge Library, MSS. T-S. K 16/86, T-S. H11/25, and T-S. H 11/10.

Editions: "Diwan," in *Die religiöse Poesie der Juden in Spanien,* edited by Michael Sachs (Berlin: Beit, 1845), pp. 11–17; selections in *Hashirah ha'ivrit besefarad ubeprovens,* 2 volumes, edited by Jefim Schirmann (Tel Aviv: Devir, 1954, 1956), I: 301–326; "Diwan," in *Shirim hadashim min hagenizah,* edited by Schirmann (Jerusalem: Israel Academy of Sciences and Humanities, 1965), pp. 185–195; *The Poems of R. Isaac Ibn Ghiyyat, 1038–89,* edited by Yonah David (Jerusalem: Akhshav, 1987); Sarah Kats, *R. Isaac Ibn Ghiyyat: Monograph* (Jerusalem: Rueben Mas, 1994).

Bahya ben Joseph Ibn Paquda (1040?–1110?)
WORKS: *Al-hidaja 'ila faraid al-qulub*

Manuscripts: Bodleian Library, University of Oxford, MS. 1225; Bibliothèque Nationale, Paris, MS. 756.1.

Early imprints: *Sefer hovot halevavot,* translated by Judah Ibn Tibbon (Naples: Joseph Ashkenazi, 1489); *Sefer hovot halevavot,* edited by Isaac Hayim Hazan (Constantinople: Moses ben Eleazar, 1550); *Hovot halevavot: Obrigaçam dos coraçoens,* translated by Samuel ben Isaac Abbas (Amsterdam: David de Castro Tartas, 1670); *Hovot halevavot. Livro yamado en Ladino obligasion de los korasones* (Venice: Moses Solomon Ashkenazi, 1712); *Sefer hovot halevavot* (Amsterdam: Props, 1715).

Editions: *Sefer hovot halevavot,* edited by David Slucki (Leipzig: C. W. Vollrath, 1864); *Torat hovot halevavot,* edited by Isaac Goldman (Warsaw: A. Klein, 1875); *Al-hidaja 'ila faraid al-qulub des Bachja Ibn Josef Ibn Paquda,* edited by A. S. Yahuda (Leiden: Brill, 1912); *Sefer hovot halevavot,* edited by A. Zirfoni (Tel Aviv: Mahbarot lesifrut, 1949); *Les devoirs du cour,* translated by André Chouraqui (Paris: Desclee de Brouwer, 1972); *Sefer hovot halevavot,* edited by Joseph Kafah (New York: Feldheim, 1984).

Critical edition: *Torat hovot halevavot,* edited by Isaac Benjacob (Leipzig: P. A. Brakhoiz, 1846).

Editions in English: *Duties of the Hearts,* translated by Moses Hyamson (New York: Bloch, 1925); *Book of the Direction to the Duties of the Heart,* translated by Menahem Mansoor (London: Routledge & Kegan Paul, 1973).

Piyyutim

Manuscript: University of Cambridge Library, MS. Or. 2245.

Editions: "Piyyutim," in *Shaar hashir: The New-Hebrew School of Poets of the Spanish-Arabian Epoch,* edited by Heinrich Brody and Karl Albrecht (Leipzig: Hinrichs, 1905; London: Williams & Norgate, 1906; New York: Lemcke & Beuchner, 1906), pp. 61–62; "Piyyutim," in *Shirim hadashim min hagenizah,* edited by Jefim Schirmann (Jerusalem: Israel Academy of Sciences and Humanities, 1965), pp. 203–208.

Kitab ma'ani al-nafs

Editions: *Résumé des réflexions sur l'âme de Bahya ben Joseph Ibn Pakouda, traduites de l'arabe en hébreu,* edited by Isaac Broydé (Paris: Levinzohn-Kilemnik, 1896); *Kitab macani al-nafs,* edited by Ignác Goldziher (Berlin: Weidman, 1907).

Levi ben Jacob Ibn Altabban (flourished late eleventh century)
WORK: *Piyyutim*

Manuscripts: Jewish Theological Seminary, New York, MSS. ENA 2225, 2923, and 3109; Bodleian Library, University of Oxford, MSS. 1081, 1133, 1137, 1139, 1145, 1162, 1164, 1190, 1970, 1971, 1972, Heb. e 93, and Heb.e 184; Staatsbibliothek, Berlin, MSS. 91, 180, Acc. 1928/386; Vatican Library, Rome, MS. Barberini Or. 18; University of Cambridge Library, MSS. T-S. H 5/22, H 15, 8H 17/17, and Or. 2242; Hebrew National Library, Jerusalem, MSS. 8⁰ 421 and 8⁰ 3312; Ben-Tsvi Institute, Jerusalem, MS. 1119; British Library, London, MS. 699; Bibliotheek van der Rijksuniversiteit, Leiden, Cod. Or. 94; Jews' College Halberstamm-Montefiore, London, MS. 203; Schocken Institute for Jewish Research of the Jewish Theological Seminary of America, Jerusalem, MSS. 22, 36, and 37; Sassoon family estate, Letchworth, U.K., MS. 902.

Editions: "Piyyutim," in *Die religiöse Poesie der Juden in Spanien,* edited by Michael Sachs (Berlin: Beit, 1845), p. 39; "Piyyutim," in *Shaar hashir: The New-Hebrew School of Poets of the Spanish-Arabian Epoch,* edited by Heinrich Brody and Karl Albrecht (Leipzig: Hinrichs, 1905; London: Williams & Norgate, 1906; New York: Lemcke & Beuchner, 1906), pp. 120–123; selections in *Hashirah ha'ivrit besefarad ubeprovens,* 2 volumes, edited by Jefim Schirmann (Tel Aviv: Devir, 1954, 1956), I: 329–339; *Shire Levi Ibn Altaban,* edited by Dan Pagis (Jerusalem: Israel Academy of Sciences and Humanities, 1967).

Joseph Ibn Sahl (?–circa 1123)
WORKS: *Piyyutim*

Manuscripts: Bodleian Library, University of Oxford, MS. 1971; Schocken Institute for Jewish Research of the Jewish Theological Seminary of America, Jerusalem, MS. 37; University of Cambridge Library, MSS. T-S. N.S. 275 and T-S. N.S. 108; British Library, London, MS. Or. 5557/F.

Editions: "Piyyutim," in *Shaar hashir: The New-*

Hebrew School of Poets of the Spanish-Arabian Epoch, edited by Heinrich Brody and Karl Albrecht (Leipzig: Hinrichs, 1905; London: Williams & Norgate, 1906; New York: Lemcke & Beuchner, 1906), pp. 86–87; "Piyyutim," in *Hashirah ha⁽ivrit besefarad ubeprovens,* 2 volumes, edited by Jefim Schirmann (Tel Aviv: Devir, 1954, 1956), I: 358–361; "Piyyutim," in *Shirim hadashim min hagenizah,* edited by Schirmann (Jerusalem: Israel Academy of Sciences and Humanities, 1965), pp. 209–214.

Moses Ibn Ezra (Abu Harun) (circa 1055–circa 1139)
WORKS: *Kitab zahr al-riyad Sefer ha⁽anaq*
    Manuscript: Bodleian Library, University of Oxford, MS. 1972.
    Editions: *Kitab zahr al-riyad,* edited by Baron David Günzberg (Berlin: Mekitse Nirdamim, 1886); *Prolegomena zu Moses Ibn Ezra's Buch der tajnis,* "Piyyutim," edited by Tobias Lewenstein (Halle: C. A. Kraemerer, 1893); *Mishebetset hatarshish,* edited by Saul Joseph Abdallah (Vienna & London: S. Krauss, 1926).

Maqalat al-hadiqa fi ma⁽ni al-majaz wa al-haqiqa
    Manuscripts: Hebrew University Library, Jerusalem, MS. 5701 (*olim* MS. Sassoon 412); Russian State Public Library, St. Petersburg, MS. 2331; Jewish Theological Seminary, New York, MS. ENA 4022.
    Editions: *Shirat Israel,* translated by Benzion Halper (Leipzig: Abraham Joseph Steibl, 1924); David S. Sassoon, *Ohel Dawid: Descriptive Catalogue of the Hebrew and Samaritan Manuscripts in the Sassoon Library, London,* 2 volumes (London: Oxford University Press, Humphrey Milford, 1932); *Kitab al-muhadara walmudhakara, Liber discussionis et commemorationis (poetica hebraica),* edited and translated by A. S. Halkin (Jerusalem: Mekitse Nirdamim, 1975); *Maqalat al-hadi qa fi ma⁽ni al-majaz wa al-haqiqa,* 2 volumes, edited and translated by Montserrat Abumalhan Mas (Madrid: CSIC, 1985, 1986).

Piyyutim
    Manuscripts: Bodleian Library, Oxford, MSS. 1051, 1058, 1064, 1073, 1074, 1076, 1081, 1082, 1083, 1084, 1087, 1091, 1093, 1094, 1119, 1150, 1162, 1163, 1164, 1168, 1180, 1188, 1189, 1190, 1191, 1192, 1193, 1194, 1198, 1575, 2703, 2709, 2837, 2838, 2839, 2842, and Heb. e. 184; Staatsbibliothek, Berlin, MSS. 89, 103, 186, and 386; Lenin State Library, Moscow, MSS. 197 and 198; Vatican Library, Rome, MSS. 18, 57, 314, 319, 320, and 553; Royal Library, Vienna, MSS. 97, 99, and 103; Madrid University Collection, MS. 15; British Library, London, MSS. 605, 606, 607, 616, 619, 621, 622, 626, 627, 629, 630, 633, 636,

637, 685, 695, 699, 700, 701, 702, 703, 704, 705, 706, 707, 709, 711, 712, 713, 714, 715, 716, 717, 720, 721, 726, and 728; Jews' College Halberstamm-Montefiore, London, MSS. 17, 129, 190, 194, 195, 196, 203, 213, 215, and 244; Bibliothèque Nationale, Paris, MSS. 593, 594, 598, 600, 601, 604, 605, 606, 609, 614, 616, 617, 618, 620, 621, 625, 631, 633, 634, 648, 649, 656, 657, 658, 666, 1330, 1331, and 1332; Biblioteca Palatina, Parma, MSS. 521, 772, 835, 997, 1192, 1377, and 1390; Royal Library, Copenhagen, MS. 30; Schocken Institute for Jewish Research of the Jewish Theological Seminary of America, Jerusalem, MS. 5, 22, 23, 36, 71; Sassoon family estate, Letchworth, U.K., MSS. 416 and 634.
    Editions: "Piyyutim," in *Die religiöse Poesie der Juden in Spanien,* edited by Michael Sachs (Berlin: Beit, 1845), pp. 20–39; "Piyyutim," in *Shirim hadashim min hagenizah,* edited by Jefim Schirmann (Jerusalem: Israel Academy of Sciences and Humanities, 1965), pp. 219–230; *Shire haqodesh,* edited by Simeon Bernstein (Tel Aviv: Masadah, 1965).

Diwan
    Manuscripts: Schocken Institute for Jewish Research of the Jewish Theological Seminary of America, Jerusalem, MSS. 22 and 37; Bodleian Library, University of Oxford, MSS. 1970 and 1972; Lenin State Library, Moscow, MS. 1332; Westminster College, University of Cambridge, MS. Fragmenta Cairensia II.95; University of Cambridge Library, MS. T-S. H14; British Library, London, MS. Or. 5557 F.
    Modern editions: *Otsar shirat yisrael bisefarad,* volumes 7 and 8, edited by Haim N. Bialik and Yehoshua Hana Rawnitzki (Jerusalem: Devir, 1928); *Diwan. Moshe Ibn Ezra. Shire hahol,* 3 volumes, edited by Heinrich Brody (Berlin & Jerusalem: Schocken, 1935–1977); selections in *Hashirah ha⁽ivrit besefarad ubeprovens,* 2 volumes, edited by Jefim Schirmann (Tel Aviv: Devir, 1954, 1956), I: 362–418; Dan Pagis, ed., "Shire hahol shel Mosheh Ibn Ezra," dissertation, Hebrew University, 1967.
    Editions in English: *Selected Poems of Moses Ibn Ezra,* edited by Heinrich Brody, translated by S. de Solis Cohen (Philadelphia: Jewish Publication Society of America, 1934); *The Jewish Poets of Spain, 900–1250,* edited and translated by David Goldstein (Harmondsworth, U.K.: Penguin, 1971), pp. 105–115; *The Dream of the Poem: Hebrew Poetry from Muslim and Christian Spain, 950–1492,* translated and edited by Peter Cole (Princeton: Princeton University Press, 2007), pp. 122–136.

On the Prophet Moses

Edition: Wilhelm Bacher, "Ein unbekanntes Werk Moses Ibn Esras," *Monatschrift für Geschichte und Wissenschaft des Judentums,* 51 (1907): 343–349.

Judah ben Samuel Halevi (Abu–l-Hasan) (circa 1075–July 1141)

WORKS: *Diwan*

Manuscripts: Schocken Institute for Jewish Research of the Jewish Theological Seminary of America, Jerusalem, MS. 37; Bodleian Library, University of Oxford, MSS. 1970 and 1971.

Editions: *Diwan des Abu-l-Hasan Jehuda ha-Lev,* edited by Heinrich Brody, 4 volumes (Berlin: Mekitse Nirdamim, 1894–1930; Farnborough, U.K.: Gregg International, 1971); *Kol shire Rabbi Yehuda Halevi,* edited by Israel Zemorah, 3 volumes (Tel Aviv: Mahbarot lesifrut, 1945); selections in *Hashirah ha'ivrit besefarad ubeprovens,* 2 volumes, edited by Jefim Schirmann (Tel Aviv: Devir, 1954, 1956), I: 425–536; "Diwan," in *Shirim hadashim min hagenizah,* edited by Schirmann (Jerusalem: Israel Academy of Sciences and Humanities, 1965), pp. 234–256; "Diwan," in *Antología poética,* translated by Rosa Castillo (Madrid: Altalena, 1983); *Yehuda Ha-Levi, poemas,* translated by Ángel Sáenz-Badillos and Judit Targarona (Madrid: Santillana, 1994).

Piyyutim

Manuscripts: University of Cambridge Library, MSS. Add. 33788, T-S. N.S.108/77, T-S. H 15/93, 58, 5, T-S. H11/58, T-S. H14/45, T-S. N.S.275/31, T-S. H15/108, 101, T-S. N.S.96/11, MS. T-S. H14/92, 55, T-S. N.S.194/30; Stadt- und Universitätsbibliothek, Frankfurt am Main, MSS. Geniza 4 and 155.

Editions: *Piyyutim. Shire haqodesh,* 4 volumes, edited by Dov Yarden (Jerusalem: Dov Yarden, 1978–1985).

Edition in English: *Selected Poems of Jehudah Halevi,* edited by Heinrich Brody, translated by Nina Salaman (Philadelphia: Jewish Publication Society, 1924).

Kitab al-radd wa-'d-dali l fi 'd-din adh-dhalil

Manuscripts: Bodleian Library, University of Oxford, MS. 5424 (Damascus, 1463), a nearly complete manuscript; Bodleian Library, University of Oxford, MSS. 1228 and Heb. d. 611; University of Cambridge Library, MS. T-S. Arabic N.S. 308, T-S. Arabic 46, T-S. Arabic N.S. 223, T-S. Arabic 12, and T-S. Arabic N.S. 301; British Library, London, MS. Or. 5564A; Jewish Theological Seminary, New York, MS. ENA 3624; Alliance Israélite Universelle, Paris, MS. Geniza V.A. 82.

Early imprints: *Sefer hakuzari,* translated by Judah Ibn Tibbon (Fano: Soncino, 1506); *Sefer hakuzari,* translated by Ibn Tibbon (Venice, 1507); *Liber cosri,* translated by Johann Buxtorf (Basel: Georg Deckeri, 1660); *Sefer hakuzari,* translated by Ibn Tibbon (Berlin: Gedruckt in der orienthalischen Freyschule, 1795).

Editions: *Sefer hakuzari,* translated by Judah Ibn Tibbon, edited by David Cassel (Leipzig: F. Voigt, 1869); *Kitab al-radd wa-'d-dali l fi 'd-din adh-dhalil: Das buch al-Chazari aus dem arabischen des Abu-l-Hasan Jehuda Hallewi,* edited by Hartwig Hirschfeld (Breslau: W. Koebner, 1885); *Sefer hakuzari,* translated by Ibn Tibbon, edited by A. Tsifroni (Tel Aviv: Mahbarot lesifrut, 1964); *Liber cosri,* translated by Johann Buxtorf (Farnborough, U.K.: Gregg International, 1971); *Liber cosri,* translated by Buxtorf, edited by Tsifroni (Jerusalem, 1967); *Kitab al-radd wa-'d-dali l fi 'd-din adh-dhalil,* edited by David H. Baneth and Haggai Ben-Shammai (Jerusalem: Judah Magnes Press, 1977).

Modern translations: *Kitab al khazari,* translated by Hartwig Hirschfeld (London: Routledge / New York: Dutton, 1905); *The kuzari: An Argument for the Faith of Israel* (New York: Schocken, 1964); *Cuzary,* translated by Jesús Imirizaldu (Madrid: Editora Nacional, 1979).

Meamar ʿ al hamiskalim

Manuscript: Schocken Institute for Jewish Research of the Jewish Theological Seminary of America, Jerusalem, MS. 37.

Edition: Jefim Schirmann, "Judah Halevi's Treatise on Meters," *Studies of the Research Institute for Hebrew Poetry,* 6 (1945): 319–322.

Letters

Edition: S. D. Goitein, "Documents in the Handwriting of Judah Halevi," *Tarbiz,* 25 (1956): 393–412.

Abraham Ibn Ezra (1089–1164)

WORKS: *Diwan*

Manuscript: Staatsbibliothek, Berlin, MS. 186.

Editions: *Reime und Gedichte des Abraham Ibn Ezra,* 2 volumes, edited and translated by David Rosin (Breslau: W. Köbner, 1885, 1894); *Diwan des Abraham Ibn Esra mit seiner Allegorie Hai ben Mekiz,* edited by Jacob Egers (Berlin: Itzkowski, 1886); *Qobets hokhmat harabbi Abraham Ibn Ezra,* 2 volumes, edited by David Kahana (Warsaw: Ahiasaf, 1894); selections in *Shaar hashir: The New-Hebrew School of Poets of the Spanish-Arabian Epoch,* edited by Heinrich Brody and Karl Albrecht (Leipzig: Hinrichs, 1905; London: Williams & Norgate, 1906; New York: Lemcke & Beuchner, 1906), pp. 137–

148; "Diwan," in *Shirim hadashim min hagenizah,* edited by Jefim Schirmann (Jerusalem: Israel Academy of Sciences and Humanities, 1965), pp. 267–276.

Edition in English: *Twilight of a Golden Age: Selected Poems of Abraham Ibn Ezra,* translated by Leon J. Weinberger (Tuscaloosa: University of Alabama Press, 1997).

Piyyutim

Manuscripts*:* Bodleian Library, University of Oxford, MS. 1968; University of Cambridge Library, MSS. T-S. Misc. 10, T-S. Misc. 22, and T-S. N.S. 96; private collection of the widow of Jacques Nissim Mosseri, Paris, MS. P16.

Edition: "Piyyutim," in *Die religiöse Poesie der Juden in Spanien,* edited by Michael Sachs (Berlin: Beit, 1845), pp. 40–44; *Shire hakodesh shel Avraham Ibn Ezra,* 2 volumes, edited by Israel Levin (Jerusalem*:* Israel Academy of Sciences and Humanities, 1975, 1980).

Sefer moznayim

Manuscripts: Bodleian Library, University of Oxford, MSS. 1467.1b and 14863b.

Early imprint: *Mozne leshon hakodesh,* edited by B. Ben Meeli Hacohen (Altona, 1770); *Mozne leshon hakodesh,* edited by Wolf Heidenheim (Offenbach: Tsevi Hirsch Shpits, 1791).

Editions: *Sefer otiyyot hanuah, Sefer poolei hakefel, Sefer hanikkud,* edited by Leopold Dukes (Frankfort am Main, 1844); "Sefer moznayim," edited by L. Jiménez Patón, dissertation, Universidad Complutense, 1985.

Sefat yeter, Yesod diqduq, hu, Sefat yeter

Manuscripts: Vatican Library, Rome, MS. 460; Bodleian Library, University of Oxford, MS. 2566.

Edition: *Sefat yeter, Yesod diqduq, hu, Sefat yeter,* edited by Nehemya Allony (Jerusalem: Mosad Rav Kook, 1984).

Sefer hahaganah

Editions: *Sefat yeter,* edited by Mordecai Leib Bisliches (Pressburg: Anton Schmid, 1838); *Sefat yeter,* edited by Gabriel H. Lippmann (Frankfurt am Main: G. H. Lippmann, 1843); *Sefer hahaganah,* edited by Lippmann (Frankfurt am Main: G. H. Lippmann, 1843); "Sefer hahaganah," edited by Yigal Oshri, M. A. thesis, Bar-Ilan University, 1988.

Sefert tsahot

Manuscripts: Bodleian Library, University of Oxford, MSS. 392, 1467, 2566, 221.10, 1468, and Angelica A.1.2; Bibliothèque Nationale, Paris, MSS. Héb. 1221, 1222, 1223, 1224, and 1251; Vatican Library, Rome, MS. hebr. 403; Biblioteca Nacional, Madrid, MS. 5460; Stadt- und Univer-

sitätsbibliothek, Frankfurt am Main, MS. hebr. Oct. 5; University of Cambridge Library, MS. Add. 3111; Jewish Theological Seminary, New York, MS. 2885; private collection of Manfred R. Lehmann, Cedarhurst, N.Y., MS. 91/1; Biblioteca Palatina, Parma, MS. 30.1.

Early imprint: *Diqduqim,* edited by Elías Levita (Venice, 1546).

Editions: *Sefer tsahot,* edited by Gabriel H. Lippmann (Fürth: D. J. Zürndorfer, 1827); *Sefer tsahot,* edited and translated by Carlos del Valle Rodríguez (Salamanca: Universidad Pontificia, 1977).

Sefer haʿibbur

Manuscripts: Bodleian Library, University of Oxford, MSS. 916.8, 2020, and 2021.1.

Edition: *Sefer haʿibbur,* edited by Solomon J. Halberstam (Lyck, Poland: Mekitse Nirdamim, 1874).

Sefer mispar

Manuscripts: British Library, London, MS. 1085.7; Bodleian Library, University of Oxford, MSS. 2018.2, 2019.1–2, and 2065.2; Jewish Theological Seminary, New York, MS. ENA 305.

Editions: *Sefer mispar,* edited by Gabriel H. Lippmann (Fürth: D. J. Zürndorfer, 1839); *Sefer mispar,* edited and translated by Moses Silberberg (Frankfurt am Main: Koiffmann, 1895); "Sefer mispar," edited by E. Ruiz González, dissertation, Universidad Complutense, 1994.

Critical edition: "Sefer mispar," edited by Michael Wilensky, *Devir,* 2 (1924): 274–302.

Safah berurah

Early imprint: *Safah berurah* (Constantinople: Astruc Detolon, 1530).

Edition: *Safah berurah,* edited by Gabriel H. Lippmann (Fürth: D. J. Zürndorfer, 1839).

Sefer hashem

Manuscripts: Bodleian Library, University of Oxford, MSS. 1234.7, 1235.2, 1278.3, 1318.19, 1465.10, 1816.3, and 2218.3c.

Edition: *Sefer hashem,* edited by Gabriel H. Lippmann (Fürth: D. J. Zürndorfer, 1834).

Sefer haehad

Manuscripts: Bodleian Library, University of Oxford, MSS. 1234.6, 1235.3, and 2006.2; British Library, London, MSS. 1073.6 and 1085.8.

Edition: *Sefer haehad,* edited by Simhah Pinsker and Michael A. Goldhart (Odessa: L. Nishe & A. Sederboim, 1867).

Yesod hamispar

Manuscripts: London, British Library 1073.4; Bodleian Library, University of Oxford, MS. 1234.4, 2218 3b.

Editions: *Yesod hamispar,* edited by Simhah Pinsker, in *Mavo el hanikkud hashuri* (Vienna, 1863); *Yesod hamispar,* edited and translated by Moses Silberberg (Frankfurt am Main: Y. Koffmann, 1895).

Mispete hamazzalot

Manuscript: Bodleian Library, University of Oxford, MS. 2025b.

Sefer hamoladot

Manuscripts: Bibliothèque Nationale, Paris; Bodleian Library, University of Oxford, MSS. 2023.1, 2025c, and 2518.2c; Jewish Theological Seminary, New York, MS. ENA 3702.

Translation: *De nativitatibus* (Venice: Erhard Ratdolt, 1485).

Reshit hokhmah

Manuscripts: Bibliothèque Nationale, Paris, MSS. 259, 1044, 1045, 1047, 1055, 1056, and 24276; Jewish Theological Seminary, New York, MS. ENA 746; Bodleian Library, University of Oxford, MSS. 458.2, 1269.8, 1822.6, 2010.2, 2024.1, 2025.1a, and 2518.2g; Real Biblioteca del Monasterio de El Escorial, MS. Estante j.N.19.

Editions: *Reshit hokhmah,* edited and translated by Raphael Levy and Francisco Cantera (Baltimore, Md.: Johns Hopkins University Press, 1935); *Le Livre des fondements astrologiques; Le Commencement de la sapience des signes,* translated by Jacques Halbronn (Paris: Retz, 1977).

Edition in English: *The Astrological Works of Abraham Ibn Ezra,* edited and translated by Raphael Levy (Baltimore: Johns Hopkins University Press / Paris: Presses Universitaires, 1927).

Sefer hate͑amim

Manuscripts: Bodleian Library, University of Oxford, MS. 1662; Bibliothèque Nationale, Paris, MS. 1055.

Editions: *Sefer hate͑amim,* edited by Judah L. Fleischer (Jerusalem: Mahbarot lesifrut, 1951); *Le Livre des fondements astrologiques; Le Commencement de la sapience des signes,* translated by Jacques Halbronn (Paris: Retz, 1977).

Sefer hamibharim

Manuscripts: Bodleian Library, University of Oxford, MSS. 2023.1, 2025f, 2026.1b, and 2518.2c.

Edition: *Sefer hamibharim,* edited by Meir ben Isaac Bakal (Jerusalem: Bakal, 1996).

Sefer ha͑olam

Manuscripts: Bibliothèque Nationale, Paris, MS. 1055; Bodleian Library, University of Oxford, MSS. 2023.1c, 2026.1c, 2027.1, and 218.2f.

Edition: "Sefer ha͑olam," edited by Judah L. Fleischer, *Otsar ha-Hayyim,* 13 (1937): 38–56.

Sefer hameorot

Manuscripts: Bibliothèque Nationale, Paris, MS. 1055; Bodleian Library, University of Oxford, MSS. 2023.1 and 2518.2b.

Edition: "*Sefer hameorot,*" edited by Judah L. Fleischer, *Sinai,* 5 (1932): 40–51.

Sefer keli nehoshet

Manuscripts: British Library, London, MSS. 1002.4–5, 10015.4; Bodleian Library, University of Oxford, MSS. 1736.2, 2024.1, 2025d, 2246.8, and 2518.2b; Jewish Theological Seminary, New York, MS. ENA 2276.

Edition: *Keli nehoshet,* edited by Hirsch Edelmann (Königsberg: Hartung, 1845).

Sefer ha͑asamim

Edition: *Sefer ha͑asamim,* edited by Menasseh Grossberg (London: E. Z. Rabbinowitz, 1901).

Yesod mora

Manuscripts: Bodleian Library, University of Oxford, MSS. 1234, 1235, 1254, 1278, and 2079; Vatican Library, Rome, MSS. 49, 105, 405, and 419; Jewish National and University Library, Jerusalem, MSS. 2132 and 3308; British Museum, London, MSS. Add. 27.038 and Add. 27.131; Bibliothèque Nationale, Paris, MSS. 680 and 1221; Palatine Library, Parma, MS. 314.

Early imprints: *Yesod mora* (Constantinople, 1529); *Yesod mora* (Venice, 1666); *Yesod mora* (Hamburg, 1770).

Edition: *Yesod mora,* edited by Meyer Waxman (Jerusalem: Hokhmat Israel, 1930).

Edition in English: *The Secret of the Torah,* translated by H. Norman Strickman (Northvale, N.J.: Jason Aronson, 1995).

Iggeret shabbat

Manuscripts: British Library, London, MS. 1073.2; Bodleian Library, University of Oxford, MSS. 1234.2, 2218.3a, and 2289.2a.

Edition: *Iggeret shabbat,* edited by Leopold Dukes (Leghorn: E. M. Ottolenghi, 1840).

Hai ben mekits

Manuscripts: University of Cambridge Library, MS. Add. 1502/2; Bodleian Library, University of Oxford, MS. 1968; Vatican Library, Rome, MS. 286.2; Jewish Theological Seminary of America, New York, MSS. Mic 2316.2 and Rab 1462.4; Palatine Library, Parma, MS. 88.2; Staatsbibliothek, Berlin, MS. 186.

Early imprints: *Hai ben mekits* (Amsterdam, 1733); *Hai ben mekits* (Constantinople: Jonah ben R. Jacob, 1736); *Hai ben mekits* (Berlin: Isaac Shpayer, 1766).

Edition: *Hai ben mektis,* edited by Israel Levin (Tel Aviv: Tel Aviv University, 1983).

Edition in English: "Hay ben meqitz: An Initiatory Tale," edited by Aaron W. Hughes, in his *The Texture of the Divine: Imagination in Medieval Islamic and Jewish Thought* (Bloomington: Indiana University Press, 2004), appendix.

Perushe hatorah lerabbi Ibn Ezra

Manuscripts: Bodleian Library, University of Oxford, MSS. 214–221.5, 222, 223, 225.2, and 246.1; British Library, London, MSS. 191, 192.1, 193, and 194.

Editions: Selections in *Hashirah ha'ivrit besefarad ubeprovens,* 2 volumes, edited by Jefim Schirmann (Tel Aviv: Devir, 1954, 1956), I: 569–623; *Kitvei Rabi Abraham Ibn Ezra,* 4 volumes (Jerusalem: Makor, 1970)–comprises volume 1, *Sefer haehad, Sefer hashem,* and *Sefer ha'olam;* volume 2, *Keli nehoshet, Sefer ha'asamim, Yesod mora,* and *Sefer ha'ibbur;* volume 3, *Sefer sahot* and *Sefer sefat yeter;* and volume 4, *Sefer hamispar; Perushe hatorah lerabbi Ibn Ezra,* 3 volumes, edited by Asher Weiser (Jerusalem: Mahbarot lesifrut, 1977); *Yalkut Abraham Ibn Ezra,* edited by Israel Lewin, Israel Matz Hebrew Classics, volume 1 (New York & Tel Aviv: Edward Kiev Library Foundation, 1985).

Solomon Ibn Parhon (twelfth century)

Work: *Mahberet he'arukh*

Manuscripts: Bodleian Library, University of Oxford, MSS. 1463, 1464, and 1465.

Edition: *Mahberet he'arukh,* edited by Solomon Gottlieb Stern (Pressburg: Anton A. Schmid, 1844).

Joseph ben Isaac Qimhi (circa 1105–circa 1170)

WORKS: *Sefer zikkaron*

Manuscripts: Bodleian Library, University of Oxford, MSS. 695.4, 1465.9, 1472.2, and 1784.4; British Library, London, MS. 969; University of Cambridge Library, MS. Add. 1740.

Edition: *Sefer zikkaron,* edited by Wilhelm Bacher (Berlin: Izkowski, 1888).

Sefer hagalui

Edition: *Sefer hagalui,* edited by Henry J. Mathews (Berlin: Itzkowski, 1887).

Shekel hakodesh

Manuscripts: Bodleian Library, University of Oxford, MSS. 1975, 1976.1, and 1180.17.

Edition and edition in English: *Shekel hakodesh,* edited and translated by Hermann Gollancz (London: Oxford University Press, 1919).

Sefer haberit

Editions: *Sefer haberit,* in *Milhemet hovah* (Constantinople, 1710); *Sefer haberit,* edited by Frank Talmage (Jerusalem: Mosad Byalik, 1974).

Edition in English: *The Book of the Covenant of Joseph Kimhi,* translated by Frank Talmage (Toronto: Pontifical Institute of Mediaeval Studies, 1972).

Abraham Ibn Daud (circa 1110–1180)

WORKS: *Sefer haqabbalah*

Manuscripts: Jewish Theological Seminary, New York, MSS. ENA 1737 and 2237; Bodleian Library, University of Oxford, MSS. Heb. 9 and 162.

Early imprints: *Sefer haqabbalah* (Naples, 1489); *Sefer haqabbalah* (Mantua, 1514).

Editions: "Sefer haqabbalah," in *Mediaeval Jewish Chronicles,* 2 volumes, edited by Adolph Neubauer (Oxford: Clarendon Press, 1887, 1895), I: 47–84; Jaime Bages, "Libro de la tradición," *Revista del Centro de Estudios de Granada y su reino,* 11 (1921): 105–178; *Libro de la tradición,* translated by Lola Ferré (Barcelona: Ríopiedras, 1990).

Edition in English: *The Book of Tradition (Sefer Ha-Qabbalah),* edited and translated by Gerson D. Cohen (London: Routledge & Kegan Paul, 1967).

Al 'aqida al-raf'a (1160–1161)

Manuscript: *Emunah nisaah* (1391), translated by Samuel Ibn Motot, Biblioteca Comunale, Mantua, MS. 81.

Early translation: *Emunah haramah,* translated by Solomon Ibn Labi, edited and translated by Simon Weil (Frankfurt am Main: Anstalt, 1852).

Edition in English: *The Exalted Faith,* edited by Gerson Weiss, translated by Norbert M. Samuelson (Rutherford, N.J.: Fairleigh Dickinson University Press / London: Associated University Presses, 1986).

Judah Ibn Tibbon (circa 1120–circa 1190)

WORKS: Bahya Ibn Paquda, *Sefer hovot halevavot,* translated by Ibn Tibbon (1161)

Manuscripts: University of Cambridge Library, MS. Add. 658; Bodleian Library, University of Oxford, MSS. 1226, 1617, and 1548.8; British Library, London, MS. 897; Jewish Theological Seminary, New York, MS. ENA 1086.

Early imprint: Bahya Ibn Paquda, *Sefer hovot halevavot,* edited by Solomon ben Perez (Naples: Joseph Ashkenazi, 1489).

Editions: *Sefer hovot halevavot,* edited by David Slucki (Leipzig: C. W. Vollrath, 1864); *Sefer hovot halevavot,* 2 volumes, edited by Pinhas Yehudah Lieberman (Jerusalem, 1969, 1971); *Sefer hovot halevavot,* edited by Joaquín Lomba Fuentes (Madrid: Fundación Universitaria Española, 1994).

Solomon Ibn Gabirol, *Mibhar hapeninim,* translated by Ibn Tibbon

Early imprint: *Mibhar hapeninim,* edited by Solomon ben Perez (Soncino: Joshua Soncino, 1484).

Ibn Gabirol, *Tikkun middot hanefesh,* translated by Ibn Tibbon (circa 1161–circa 1167)

Manuscripts: British Library, London, MSS. 867 and 1063.

Early imprint: Solomon Ibn Gabirol, *Tikkun middot hanefesh,* edited by Isaac Hayim Hazan (Constantinople: Moses ben Eleazar, 1550).

Judah Halevi, *Kuzari,* translated by Ibn Tibbon (1167)

Manuscript: University of Cambridge Library, MS. Add. 545; Jewish Theological Seminary, New York, MS. ENA 297.

Early imprint: Judah Halevi, *Kuzari* (Fano: Soncino, 1506).

Jonah Ibn Janah, *Sefer hariqmah,* translated by Ibn Tibbon (circa 1171)

Manuscript: Bodleian Library, University of Oxford, MS. 2509.

Edition: Jonah Ibn Janah, *Sefer hariqmah,* edited by Baer Goldberg and Raphael Kirchheim (Frankfurt am Main, 1856).

Ibn Janah, *Sefer hashorashim,* translated by Ibn Tibbon (1171)

Manuscript: Bodleian Library, University of Oxford, MS. 2509.

Edition: *Sefer hashorashim: Würzelworterbuch der hebräischen Sprache,* edited by Wilhelm Bacher (Berlin, 1896).

Saadya Gaon, *Sefer ha'emunot vehade'ot,* translated by Ibn Tibbon (1186)

Early imprint: *Sefer ha'emunot vehade'ot* (Constantinople: Solomon Yaabez, 1562).

Goren nakhon (= *Sefer tappuah*)

Early imprint: *Goren nakhon* (= *Sefer tappuah*) (Riva di Trento, 1562).

Edition: *Goren nakhon* (= *Sefer tappuah*) (Lunéville: Avraham Prizek, 1807).

Tsawwa'ah

Edition: "Sawwa'ah," in *Hebrew Ethical Wills,* 2 volumes, edited by Israel Abrahamson (Philadelphia: Jewish Publication Society of America, 1934), I: 51–93.

Maimonides (Moses ben Maimon) (30 March 1135 – 13 December 1204)

WORKS: *Makalah fi tsina'at al-mantik*

Manuscripts: Bibliothèque Nationale, Paris, MS. Héb. 1202; Bodleian Library, University of Oxford, MS. 2424.11; translated by Moses Ibn Tibbon as *Milot hahigayon,* Jewish Theological

Seminary, New York, MSS. Halberstam 491 and ENA 389, 399, and 2771; Bibliothèque Nationale, Paris, MSS. 673, 969, 970, and 983; Bodleian Library, University of Oxford, MSS. 227.4, 1268.2, 1271.6, 1318.1, 1319.1, and 1322.2.

Early imprints: *Makalah fi tsina'at al-mantik; Milot hahigayon,* translated by Sebastian Münster (Basel, 1527); *Makalah fi- sina'at al-mantik; Milot hahigayon* (Venice, 1552).

Editions: *Makalah fi tsina'at al-mantik; Milot hahigayon,* edited by Leon Roth and David H. Baneth (Jerusalem: Judah L. Magnes, Hebrew University, 1934); *Maimonides' Treatise on Logic,* edited by Israel Efros (New York: American Academy for Jewish Research, 1938); *Maimonides' Arabic Treatise on Logic,* edited by Israel Efros (New York: American Academy for Jewish Research, 1966).

Iggeret hashemad

Manuscripts: British Library, London, MS. 454; Bodleian Library, University of Oxford, MSS. 2218.2b and 2214.2; translated by Samuel Ibn Tibbon, Bodleian Library, University of Oxford, MSS. 158.4, 1254.4, and 1270.1; translated by Judah ben Salomon al-Harizi, Bodleian Library, University of Oxford, MS. 2496.3.; Jewish Theological Seminary, New York, MS. ENA 2405.

Editions: *Iggeret hashemad* (Breslau, 1850); *Iggeret hashemad* (Vienna, 1857); *Iggerot,* edited by Joseph Kafah (Jerusalem: Mossad Rav Kuk, 1972).

Al-Risaah al-yamaniyyah; Iggeret teman

Manuscript: British Library, London, MS. 1081.

Editions: *Petah tikvah,* translated by Nahum Hama\u1d9caravi (Basel, 1629); *Iggeret teman,* translated by Samuel ben Judah Ibn Tibbon (Vienna, 1857); *Iggerot,* edited by Joseph Kafah (Jerusalem: Mossad Rav Kuk, 1972).

Edition in English: *Letters of Maimonides,* edited and translated by L. D. Stitskin (New York: Yeshiva University Press, 1977).

Kitab al-siraj

Manuscripts: Bodleian Library, University of Oxford, MSS. 393–407.1.

Early imprint: *Kitab al-siraj, Mishnah Avot* (Naples, 1492).

Edition: *Perush le-masekhet Avot,* edited by M. D. Rabinovits (Jerusalem: Mosad ha-Rav Kuk, 1961).

Editions in English: *The Commentary to Mishnah Aboth,* translated by Arthur David (New York: Bloch, 1968); *Living Judaism: The Misnah of Avot,* edited and translated by Paul Forchheime (Jerusalem: Feldheim, 1974); *Ethical Writings of Maimonides,* translated by Raymond L. Weiss and

Charles Butterworth (New York: New York University Press, 1975).

Mishneh Torah

Manuscripts: British Library, London, MSS. 485–497; Bodleian Library, University of Oxford, MSS. 568–613, 641.10, 844.2, and 859.3.

Early imprints: *Mishneh Torah* (Rome?: Solomon ben Judah & Obadiah ben Moses, circa 1473–1475); *Mishneh Torah,* edited by Eliezer ben Samuel (Soncino: Gerson Soncino, 1490); *Mishneh Torah* (N.p.: Moses Ibn Shealtiel, 1491); *Mishneh Torah* (Constantinople, 1509);

Edition: *Mishneh Torah* (Vilna, 1900).

Editions in English: *The Mishneh Torah by Maimonides,* edited and translated by Moses Hyamson (New York: Bloch, 1937); *The Book of Knowledge and The Book of Adoration,* edited and translated by Hyamson (London, 1940); *The Book of Knowledge from the Mishnah Torah of Maimonides,* translated by H. M. Russell and J. Weinberg (Edinburgh: Royal College of Physicians of Edinburgh, 1981; New York: Ktav, 1983).

Mishnah Demai

Manuscript: Bodleian Library, University of Oxford, MS. 1919.

Edition: *Mishna demai: Der Commentar des Maimonides zum Tractat Demai. Arabischer Text mit hebräischer Uebersetzung und Anmerkungen,* edited by Joseph Ziv (Berlin: H. Itzkowski, 1891).

Kitab al-faraʿid

Manuscript: British Library, London, MSS. 503 and 505.

Early imprints: *Kitab al-faraʿid. Sefer hamitsvot,* translated by Moses Ibn Tibbon (Lisbon, 1492); *Kitab al-faraʿid* (Amsterdam: Y. Atias, 1660).

Dalalat al-haʾirin

Manuscripts: Bibliotheek van der Rijksuniversiteit, Leiden, MSS. 18 and 221; Bibliothèque Nationale, Paris, MSS. Héb. 760, 761, and 758; Bodleian Library, University of Oxford, MSS. Hebr. 1236–1249, 407, 2508, and 2422; British Library, London, MSS. Or. 1423 and Or. 2423; Royal Library, Berlin, MS. Or. Qu. 579; Jewish Theological Seminary, New York, MS. ENA 343.

Early imprint: *Doctor perplexorum,* translated by Johann Buxtorf (Basel, 1629).

Editions: *Dalalat al-haʾirin. Le guide des egarés, traité de théologie et de philosophie par Moïse Maïmonide,* 3 volumes, edited and translated by Salomon Munk (Paris: A. Franck, 1856–1866); *Dalalat al-haʾirin,* edited by Issachar Joel (Jerusalem: J. Junovitch, 1930); *Dalalat al-haʾirin,* 3 volumes, edited by Yosef Kafah (Jerusalem: Mossad Rav Kuk, 1972).

Edition in English: *The Guide of the Perplexed,* 2 volumes, translated by Shlomo Pines (Chicago: University of Chicago Press, 1963).

Moreh nevukhim

Manuscripts: Translated by Samuel ben Judah Ibn Tibbon: (1204) British Library, London, MSS. Harleian 7586A, Harleian 7586B, Harleian 5507, Harleian 5525, Add. 27068, and Add. 14763; Jewish Theological Seminary, New York, MSS. ENA 265, 308A, and 1772; Bibliothèque Nationale, Paris, MSS. Héb. 685 and 691; Real Biblioteca del Monasterio de El Escorial, MS. G.II. 17; translated by Judah al-Harizi (1205–1213): Bibliothèque Nationale, Paris, MS. Héb. 682.

Early imprints: *Moreh nevukhim,* translated by Judah al-Harizi (Rome?, 1473–1475?); *Moreh nevukhim,* translated by Samuel ben Judah Ibn Tibbon (Italy, 1480); *Moreh nevukhim,* translated by Ibn Tibbon (Venice, 1551); *Moreh nevukhimn* (Sabionetta, 1553); *Moreh nevukhim,* translated by Ibn Tibbon (Jessnitz: Israel bar Abraham, 1742); *Moreh nevukhim,* translated by Ibn Tibbon (Berlin, 1791).

Editions: *Moreh nevukhim,* translated by Samuel ben Judah Ibn Tibbon, edited by Simon Scheyer (Frankfurt am Main: Ferdinand Hauch, 1838); *Moreh nevukhim,* 3 volumes, translated by Judah al-Harizi, edited by Leon Schlossberg and Simon Scheyer (London: Bagster, 1851–1879); *Moreh nevukhim,* translated by al-Harizi (Berlin: H. Itzkowski, 1891); *Moreh nevukhim,* translated by Ibn Tibbon, edited by Judah Kaufman (Tel Aviv: Shevil, 1935); *Moreh nevukhim,* translated by al-Harizi, edited by Scheyer and Salomon Munk (Tel Aviv: Mahbarot lesifrut, 1952); *Guía de perplejos,* translated by David Gonzalo Maeso (Madrid: Editorial Nacional, 1984).

Edition in English: *The Guide for the Perplexed,* translated by M. Friedländer, revised edition (London: Routledge & Kegan Paul, 1904).

Iggeret tehiyyat (1191)

Manuscripts: British Library, London, MS. Add. 27542; *Iggeret tehiyyat hametim,* translated by Samuel ben Judah Ibn Tibbon, Oxford, Bodleian Library, MSS. 158.5, 1254.5, and 1270.1.

Early imprints: *Iggeret tehiyyat hametim,* (Constantinople: Solomon ben Isaac Yaabets, 1569); *Iggeret tehiyyat hametim,* translated by Samuel ben Judah Ibn Tibbon (N.p., 1629); *Sefer hamisvot* (Amsterdam: Y. Atias, 1660).

Editions: *Mainonides' Treatise on Resurrection (Makala fi tehiyyat hamestim),* edited by Joshua Finkel (New York: American Academy for Jewish Research,

1939); *Iggeret tehiyyat hametim,* edited by A. S. Halkin, *Qobets al yad* (*Minora Manuscripta Hebraica*), 9 (1989): 129–150.

Makalah fi al-Tauhid. Meamar hayihud

Manuscript: Bodleian Library, University of Oxford, MS. 1317.2.

Edition: *Makalah fi al-Tauhid. Meamar hayihud* (Berlin, 1846).

Makalah fi al-Sa'adah

Manuscript: Bibliothèque Nationale, Paris, MS. Héb. 7193.

Early imprint: *Perakhim hahatslahah* (Salonica, 1567); *Makalah fi al-Sa'adah* (Constantinople, 1569).

Solomon Ibn Saqbel (before 1140)
WORKS: *Neum Asher ben Judah*

Editions: "Neum Asher ben Judah," edited by J. H. Schorr, *Hehalutz,* 3 (1856): 154–158; "Neum Asher ben Judah," edited by Jefim Schirmann, *Studies of the Research Institute for Hebrew Poetry,* 2 (1936): 152–162, 193; "Neum Asher ben Judah," in *Hashirah ha'ivrit besefarad ubeprovens,* 2 volumes, edited by Schirmann (Tel Aviv: Devir, 1954, 1956), I: 554–565, II: 685; Ángeles Navarro Peiro, "Ibn Saqbel's *Ne'um Asher ben Judah,*" *Sefarad,* 36 (1976): 339–351; David S. Segal, "*Mahberet Neum Asher ben Yehudah* of Solomon Ibn Saqbel: A Study of Scriptural Citations," *Journal of the American Oriental Society,* 102 (1982): 17–26.

Edition in English: "Asher in the Harem" translated by Raymond P. Scheindlin, in *Rabbinic Fantasies,* edited by David Stern and Mark J. Mirsky (Philadelphia: Jewish Publication Society, 1990), pp. 269–294.

Benjamin ben Jonah of Tudela (circa 1130–circa 1175)
WORKS: *Sefer masa'ot*

Manuscript: British Library, London, MS. 27.089.

Early imprints: *Sefer masa'ot* (Constantinople: Soncino, 1543); *Sefer masa'ot* (Ferrara: Abraham Ibn Usque, 1556); *Itinerarium Beniamini Tudelensis . . . Arias Montano interprete,* translated by Benito Arias Montano (Antwerp: Christophorous Pantinus, 1575); *Sefer masa'ot* (Fribourg: Sifroni, 1583); *Sefer masa'ot,* edited and translated into Latin by Constantine L'Empereur (Leiden: Elzevir, 1633); *Sefer masa'ot* (Amsterdam: Gaspar Stern, 1696); *Sefer masa'ot* (Altdorf, 1762); *Sefer masa'ot* (Sultzbach: Aaron ben Meshulam Zalman, 1782); *Voyages de Rabbi Benjamin fils de Jona de Tudele,* translated by Jean Philippe (Amsterdam: Baratier, 1734).

Editions: *Sefer masa'ot* (Zolkiev, 1805); *Sefer masa'ot*

(Lemberg, 1859); *Sefer masa'ot* (Warsaw, 1884); *Die reisebeschreibungen des R. Benjamin von Tudela,* edited by Eleazar Grünhut (Jerusalem: J. Kaufmann, 1903); *Viajes de Benjamín de Tudela,* translated by Ignasi A. González Llubera (Madrid: Sanz Calleja, 1918); *Libro de Viajes de Benjamín de Tudela,* translated by José Ramón Magdalena Nom de Déu (Barcelona: Ríopiedras, 1982).

Critical edition and edition in English: *The Itinerary of Benjamin of Tudela,* edited and translated by Marcus N. Adler (London: Henry Frowde, 1907).

Editions in English: *Benjamin of Tudela's Itinerary,* 2 volumes, edited and translated by Adolf Asher (London & Berlin: A. Asher, 1840, 1841); *The Itinerary of Benjamin of Tudela: Travels in the Middle Ages,* edited by Michael A. Signer (Malibu, Cal.: Joseph Simon/Pangloss Press, 1983).

Joseph ben Meir Ibn Zabara (circa 1140–?)
WORKS: *Sefer sha'ashuim*

Manuscript: Lenin State Library, Moscow, MS. Baron David Günzberg.

Early imprint: *Sefer sha'ashuim,* edited by Isaac Akrish (Constantinople, 1577).

Editions: Yehiel Bril, ed., "The Book of Delight," *Lebanon,* 2 (1865); *Sefer sha'ashuim,* edited by Yehiel Bril, introduction by Senior Sachs (Paris: Bril, 1866); *Sefer sha'ashuim,* edited by Israel Davidson (New York: Jewish Theological Seminary of America, 1914); *Sefer sha'ashuim,* edited by Davidson (Berlin: Eshkol, 1925); *Llibre d'ensenyaments delectables,* translated by Ignasi González-Llubera, Biblioteca Hebraico-Catalana, volume 2 (Barcelona: Editorial Alpha, 1931); *Libro de los entretenimientos,* translated by Marta Forteza-Rey (Madrid: Editora Nacional, 1983); *Sefer sha'ashuim,* edited by Judith Dishon (Jerusalem: A. Mas, 1985).

Edition in English: *The Book of Delight,* translated by Moses Hadas (New York: Columbia University Press, 1932).

Battei hanefesh

Edition: "Battei hanefesh," in *Sefer sha'ashuim,* edited by Israel Davidson (Berlin: Eshkol, 1925), pp. 169–173.

Marot hasheten

Edition: "Marot hasheten," in *Sefer sha'ashuim,* edited by Israel Davidson (Berlin: Eshkol, 1925), pp. 151–168.

Ofan

Edition: "Ofan," in *Shaar hashir: The New-Hebrew School of Poets of the Spanish-Arabian Epoch,* edited by Heinrich Brody and Karl Albrecht (Leipzig: Hinrichs, 1905; London: Williams & Norgate, 1906;

New York: Lemcke & Beuchner, 1906), pp. 168–170.

Shelosh halatsot

Edition: *Shelosh halatsot,* edited by Israel Davidson (New York: A. H. Rozenberg, 1904).

Judah ben Isaac Ibn Shabbetai (1168–after 1225)
WORKS: *Minhat Yehudah sone' hanashim*

Manuscripts: British Library, London, MSS. Add. 26.945 (1281), Add. 27.113 (1282), and Add. 26.945 (1818); Bodleian Library, University of Oxford, MSS. Mich. 260 and Can. Or. 29.

Early imprint: *Minhat Yehudah sone' hanashim* (Constantinople: Eleazar ben Gerson Soncino, 1543).

Editions: "Minhat Yehudah sone' hanashim," edited by Eliezer Ashkenazi, in *Ta'am Zekenim,* volume 5, edited by R. Kirchheim (Frankfurt am Main: Verlag der hebraische-antiquarischen Buchhandlung, 1854), pp. 1a–12b; "Minhat Yehudah sone' hanashim," in *Shalosh mekamot 'al hanashim,* edited by Abraham M. Habermann (Jerusalem: Ben-Uri, 1970).

Critical edition: "Minhat Yehudah sone' hanashim," edited by Mati Hus, dissertation, Hebrew University, 1991.

Edition in English: "Misogynist," translated by Raymond P. Scheindlin, in *Rabbinic Fantasies: Imaginative Narratives from Classical Hebrew Literature,* edited by David Stern and Mark J. Mirsky (Philadelphia: Jewish Publication Society, 1990), pp. 269–294.

Milhemet hahokhmah veha'osher

Early imprint: *Milhemet hahokhmah veha'osher* (Constantinople: Eleazar ben Gerson Soncino, 1543).

Editions: "Milhemet hahokhmah veha'osher," in *Sefer ben hamalekh vehanazir* (Warsaw: Sh. Halevi Levin, 1884); *Milhemet hahokhmah veha'osher,* edited by Abraham M. Habermann (Jerusalem: Merkaz, 1952).

Divre haalah vehaniddui

Manuscript: Bodleian Library, University of Oxford, MS. Can. Or. 29.

Editions: "Divre haalah vehaniddui," edited by Israel Davidson, *Haeshkol,* 6 (1909): 165–175; selections in *Hashirah ha'ivrit besefarad ubeprovens,* 2 volumes, edited by Jefim Schirmann (Tel Aviv: Devir, 1954, 1956), II: 67–86; Judith Dishon, "A Critical Examination of the Literary Work of Judah Ibn Shabbetai," dissertation, University of Michigan, 1967.

Ezrat nashim

Editions: *Ezrat nashim,* edited by Solomon J. Halberstam, *Jeschurun,* 7 (1871): 40–61; selections in

Hashirah ha'ivrit besefarad ubeprovens, 2 volumes, edited by Jefim Schirmann (Tel Aviv: Devir, 1954, 1956), II: 87–96.

Judah ben Solomon al-Harizi (circa 1170–after 1235)
WORKS: Maimonides, *Dalalat al-ha'irin. Moreh nevukhim,* translated by al-Harizi (1205–1213)

Manuscript: Bibliothèque Nationale, Paris, MS. Héb. 682.

Early imprint: Moses ben Maimon, *Dalalat al-ha'irin. Moreh nevukhim,* translated by Judah al-Harizi (Rome?, 1473–1475?).

Edition: *Moreh nevukhim,* 3 volumes, edited by Leon Schlossberg and Simon Scheyer (London: Bagster, 1851–1879); *Moreh nevukhim,* edited by Mordecai Z. Jolles (Lemberg: Circa Winiarz, 1855–1856); *Moreh nevukhim* (Berlin: H. Itzkowski, 1891); *Moreh nevukhim,* edited by Scheyer and Salomon Munk (Tel Aviv: Mahbarot lesifrut, 1952).

Maimonides, *Kitab al-siraj, Mishnah Avot,* translated by al-Harizi

Manuscripts: Bodleian Library, University of Oxford, MSS. 393–407.

Early imprint: *Kitab al-siraj, Mishnah Avot* (Naples, 1492).

Edition: *Hakdamot leperush hamishna (Introduction to the Mishnah),* edited by M. D. Rabinovits (Jerusalem: Mosad Rav Kuk, 1960).

Maimonodes, *Iggeret tehiyyat hametim,* translated by al-Harizi

Manuscript: Bodleian Library, University of Oxford, MS. 2496.3.

Early imprints: *Iggeret tehiyyat hametim* (N.p., 1629); *Sefer hamisvot* (Amsterdam: Y. Atias, 1660).

Maimonides, *Mishna demai,* translated by al-Harizi

Edition: *Mishna demai: Der Commentar des Maimonides zum Tractat Demai. Arabischer Text mit hebräischer Uebersetzung und Anmerkungen,* edited by Joseph Ziv (Berlin: H. Itzkowski, 1891).

'Ali Ibn Rudwan, *Igeret 'ali haeshmeeli,* translated by al-Harizi

Edition: *Igeret 'ali haeshmeeli,* edited by Menasseh Grossberg (London, 1900).

Hunain Ibn Ishaq, *Adab al-falasifa. Sefer musre haphilosophim,* translated by al-Harizi

Manuscripts: Bodleian Library, University of Oxford, MSS. 851.1, 1140.11, 1436.2, 1437.1, 2183.2, and 2236.5.

Edition: Hunain Ibn Ishaq, *Adab al-falasifa. Sefer musre haphilosophim (Sinnsprüch der Philosophen): Aus dem Arabischen des Honein ibn Ishak ins Hebräische/ übersetzt von Jehuda ben Salomo Alcharisi,* edited by A.

Loewenthal (Frankfurt am Main: J. Kauffmann, 1896).

Galen, *Sefer hanefesh,* translated by al-Harizi
  Manuscript: Bodleian Library, University of Oxford, MS. 2283.11.

Moses Ibn Ezra, *Maqalat al-hadiqa fi maʿna al-majaz wa al-haqiqa. ʿArugat habosem,* translated by al-Harizi
  Edition: "Maqalat al-hadiqa fi maʿna al-majaz wa al-haqiqa. ʿArugat habosem," edited by Leopold Dukes, *Zion,* 2 (1842): 117–123, 134–137, 157–160, 175.

Abu Muhammad al-Qasim al-Hariri of Basra (1054–1122), *Maqamat,* translated by al-Harizi as *Mahberot ʾItiel* (circa 1205–circa 1215)
  Manuscript: Bodleian Library, University of Oxford, MS. 1976.2.
  Editions: *Mahberot ʾItiel,* edited by Thomas Chenery (London: Williams & Norgate, 1852); *Mahberot ʾItiel,* edited by Isaac Perez (Tel Aviv: Mahbarot lesifrut, 1950).

Maqama
  Editions: Hartwig Hirschfeld, "Fragment of an Unknown Work by Judah al-Harizi," *Jewish Quarterly Review,* 16 (1903): 683–688, 693–697; Samuel M. Stern, "A New Description by Judah Al-Harizi of His Tour to Iraq," *Sefunot,* 8 (1964): 145–156; Stern, "An Unpublished *Maqama* by al-Harizi," in *Papers of the Institute of Jewish Studies, London,* volume 1, edited by J. G. Weiss (Jerusalem: Magnes Press, Hebrew University, 1964), pp. 186–201; Yehuda Ratzaby, "An Arabic *maqama* by al-Harizi," *Criticism and Interpretation,* 15 (1980): 5–51; Yehuda Ratzaby, "An Arabic *maqama* by al-Harizi," *Criticism and Interpretation,* 23 (1988): 51–55.

Tahkemoni
  Manuscripts: Bodleian Library, University of Oxford, MSS. 1977, 1978, and 2516; University of Cambridge Library, MSS. Add. 1519, Add. 377.5, and Add. 1525; British Library, London, MSS. 904.4, 926.1, 927, 1048.7, Add. 27.112, Add. 27.113, Add. 14.763, and Harleian 5686; Real Biblioteca del Monasterio de El Escorial, MS. G.IV.8., Jewish Theological Seminary, New York, MSS. ENA 1791 and 1793.
  Early imprints: *Tahkemoni* (Constantinople: Obadiah Sabbakh, 1578); *Tahkemoni* (Amsterdam: Solomon Props, 1729).
  Editions: *Die ersten Makamen aus dem Tahkemoni oder Divan des Charisi,* edited by Saul Isaac Kaempf (Berlin: A. Duncker, 1845); *Tahkemoni,* edited by Armand Kaminka (Warsaw: Ahiasaph, 1899); *Tahkemoni,* edited by Israel Toporovski (Jerusalem: Mahbarot lesifrut, 1952); selections

in *Hashirah haʿivrit besefarad ubeprovens,* 2 volumes, edited by Jefim Schirmann (Tel Aviv: Devir, 1954, 1956), II: 97–206; *The Tahkemoni of Judah al-Harizi,* 2 volumes, translated by Victor E. Reichert (Jerusalem: R. H. Cohen, 1965, 1973); *Las asambleas de los sabios,* translated by Carlos del Valle Rodríguez (Murcia: Universidad de Murcia, 1988).
  Edition in English: *The Book of Tahkemoni: Jewish Tales from Medieval Spain,* edited and translated by David S. Segal (Portland, Ore.: Littman Library of Jewish Civilization, 2001).

Haʿanaq
  Manuscript: Bodleian Library, University of Oxford, MS. 1979.
  Editions: "Haʿanaq. Judah ben Solomon al-Harizi Haʿanaq," edited by Heinrich Brody, in *Festschrift zu Ehren des Dr. A. Harkavy aus Anlass seines am 20. November 1905 vollendeten siebzigsten Lebensjahres: Gewidmet von Freunden und Verehrern,* 2 volumes, edited by David Günzburg and Isaac Markon (St. Petersburg: Printed by H. Itzkowski, Berlin, 1908), I: 309–356; *Haʿanaq,* edited by A. Avronin (Tel Aviv, 1945).

Diwan
  Manuscripts: University of Cambridge Library, MSS. T-S. misc. 25 and Add. 1745; Bodleian Library, University of Oxford, MS. 2712.
  Edition: Samuel M. Stern, "Some Unpublished Poems by al-Harizi," *Jewish Quarterly Review,* 50 (1960): 269–276, 346–364; "Diwan," in *Shirim hadashim min hagenizah,* edited by Jefim Schirmann (Jerusalem: Israel Academy of Sciences and Humanities, 1965), pp. 282–291.

Sefer mazzalot shel adam. Sefer refu'at hageviya
  Early imprints: *Sefer mazzalot shel adam. Sefer refu'at hageviya lerabenu Yehuda al-Harizi* (Salonika, 1593); *Sefer mazzalot shel adam. Sefer refu'at hageviya lerabenu Yehuda al-Harizi* (Amsterdam, 1714).

Anonymous
WORK: *Mishle Sendebar* (before 1316)
  Manuscripts: Bodleian Library, University of Oxford, MSS. Hebr. d. 11 and Or. 135; Bibliothèque Nationale, Paris, MS. Héb. 1282; British Library, London, MS. Harleian 5449; Jews' College Halberstamm-Montefiore, London, MSS. 113 and 185; Jewish Theological Seminary, New York, MS. Steinschneider 11 and Steinschneider 33; Bibliotheca Lipsiensis, Leipzig, MSS. 21 and 32; Biblioteca Palatina, Parma, MSS. 2294, 1049, and 1087; Jewish Theological Seminary, Budapest, MS. 59; Vatican Library, Rome, MS. hebr. 100.3; Hebrew Union College, Cincinnati, MS. Grossman 598.

Early imprint: "Mishle Sendebar," in *Kibbuts Sippurim Shonim* (Constantinople: R. Samuel Ibn Nahmias, 1516); *Mishle Sendebar* (Venice: Juan de Gara, 1605).

Editions: *Les paraboles de Sendebar sur les ruses des femmes*, translated by Eliakim Carmoly (Paris: P. Jannet, 1849); *Mishle Sindbad: Secundus–Syntipas, edirt, emendirt und erklärt. Einleitung und deutung des buches der Sieben weisen meister*, edited and translated by D. Paulus Cassel (Berlin: R. Schaeffer, 1888); *Historia Septem Sapientum: Eine bisher unbekannte lateinische Übersetzung einer orientalischen Fassung der Sieben Weisen Meister (Mischle Sendabar)*, edited by Alfons Hilka, Sammlung Mittellateinischer Texte, volume 4 (Heidelberg: Winter, 1912); *Mishle Sendebar: Sipur mezimat eshet melekh Hodu ve-hokhmat Sendabad ve-shiv'at yo'atse ha-melekh*, edited by Abraham Meir Habermann (Tel Aviv: Mahbarot le-sifrut, 1946).

Critical edition and edition in English: *Tales of Sendebar*, edited and translated by Morris Epstein (Philadelphia: Jewish Publication Society of America, 1967).

Meshulam ben Solomon da Piera (?–after 1260)

WORK: *Diwan*

    Manuscript: Bodleian Library, University of Oxford, MS. 1970.

    Editions: "Diwan," edited by Heinrich Brody, *Studies of the Research Institute for Hebrew Poetry*, 4 (1938): 1–117; selections in *Hashirah ha'ivrit besefarad ubeprovens*, 2 volumes, edited by Jefim Schirmann (Tel Aviv: Devir, 1954, 1956), II: 295–318.

Shem Tov ben Joseph Ibn Falaquera (circa 1225–circa 1295)

WORKS: *Iggeret battei hanhagat haguf vehanefesh*

    Manuscripts: Biblioteca Mediceo Laurenziana, Florence, MS. Plut. II; Bodleian Library, University of Oxford, MSS. 1980, 2901.4, and 2398.2; Biblioteca Universitaria, Basel, MS. R III 2; Bayerische Staatsbibliothek, Munich, MS. 49.7.

    Editions: *Iggeret battei hanhagat haguf vehanefesh or Battei hanhagat haguf habari*, edited by Suessmann Muntner (Tel Aviv: Mahbarot lesifrut, 1950); *Versos para la sana conducción del cuerpo; Versos para la conducción del alma*, translated by María Encarnación Varela (Granada: Universidad de Granada / Salamanca: Universidad Pontificia de Salamanca, 1986).

Iggeret hamusar

    Edition: "Iggeret hamusar," edited by A. M. Haberman, *Qobets 'alyad*, 1 (1936): 43–90; 2 (1937): 231–262.

Tseri hayagon

    Early imprints: *Tseri hayagon*, edited by Rabbi Saul ben Simon (Cremona, 1557); *Tseri hayagon* (Heno: Y. Y. Bosang, 1715).

    Editions: *Tseri hayagon*, edited and translated by David Ottenssosser (Fürth, 1854); *Tseri hayagon* (Jerusalem: Mekor Hayim, 1966); Roberta Klugman Barkan, "Shem Tov Ibn Falaquera's 'Tsori hayagon or 'Balm for Assuaging Grief,' Its Literary Sources and Traditions," dissertation, Columbia University, 1971.

Megilat hazikkaron, Iggeret vikkuah, or Vikkuah hehakham im hehasid

    Manuscripts: British Library, London, MS. Add. 29.925; Ets Haim, Amsterdam, MS. 176; Bibliotheek van der Rijksuniversiteit, Leiden, MS. 15; Königlichen Bibliothek, Munich, MS. 402; Bodleian Library, University of Oxford, MSS. 1600.15, 1822.5, 2091.4, and 2398.2.

    Early imprints: *Iggeret vikkuah*, edited by Isaac Akrish (Constantinople, 1557); *Iggeret vikkuah* (Prague, 1610).

    Editions: *Dialog zwischen einem Orthodoxen und einem Philosophen*, edited by Adolph Jellinek (Vienna: Winter, 1875); Gilbert Dahan, "Epistola Dialogi: Une Traduction Latine de *L'Igeret havikuah* de Shem Tov Ibn Falaqerua: Etude et Édition," *Sefarad*, 39 (1979): 45–85, 237–264.

    Critical edition and edition in English: *Falaquera's Epistle of the Debate: An Introduction to Jewish Philosophy*, edited and translated by Steven Harvey (Cambridge, Mass.: Harvard University Press, 1987).

Reshit hokhmah

    Manuscripts: Jüdisch-theologischen Seminars Saraval, Breslau, MS. 19; Königlichen Bibliothek, Munich, MS. 402; British Library, London, MS. 914 and Add. 29.925.

    Edition: *Schemtob ben Josef Ibn Flaquera's Propaedeutik der Wissenschaften*, edited by Moritz David (Berlin: M. Poppelauer, 1902).

Sefer hama'alot

    Manuscripts: Jüdisch-theologischen Seminars Saraval, Breslau, MS. 19; British Library, London, MSS. 914 and Add. 29.925; Bodleian Library, University of Oxford, MS. 1407.

    Edition: *Das Buch der Grade*, edited by Ludwig Venetianer (Berlin: Calvary, 1894).

Sefer hamevakkesh

    Manuscript: British Library, London, MS. 870.1.

    Early imprints: *Sefer hamevakkesh* (Cracow, 1646); *Sefer hamevakkesh*, edited by Mordecai Tamah (The Hague: Leb Zusmansh, 1772).

    Edition: Selections in *Hashirah ha'ivrit besefarad*

ubeprovens, 2 volumes, edited by Jefim Schirmann (Tel Aviv: Devir, 1954, 1956), II: 329–342.

Edition in English: *Falaquera's Book of the Seeker,* translated by M. Herschel Levine (New York: Yeshiva University Press, 1976).

Deʿot hapilosofim

Manuscripts: Biblioteca Palatina, Parma, MS. 1283 (1416); Bibliotheek van der Rijksuniversiteit, Leiden, MS. 20; Jews' College Halberstamm-Montefiore, London, MS. 273.

Edition: *Un dizionario filosofico ebraio del XIII secolo: L'introduzione al "Sefer Deʿot hapilosofim" di Shem Tob Ibn Falaquera,* edited by Mauro Zonta (Turin: S. Zamorani, 1992).

Sefer hanefesh

Manuscripts: National Library, Vienna, MS. 143 sig.12; Bodleian Library, University of Oxford, MS. 227.3; Jews' College Halberstamm-Montefiore, London, MS. 273; Bibliothèque Nationale, Paris, MS. Heb. 706; University of Cambridge Library, MS. 1214; Talmud Torah, Leghorn, MS. 40; Biblioteca Palatina, Parma, MS. 1283.

Editions: *Sefer hanefesh,* edited by Naftali Hertz Grosman (Lemberg, 1835); *Sefer hanefesh,* edited by Israel H. Klein (Warsaw: Alexander Ginaz, 1864); *Sefer hanefesh* (Warsaw, 1924); *Libro del alma,* translated by Ana María Riaño López (Granada: Universidad de Granada, 1990).

Critical edition and edition in English: "Sefer hanefesh," edited and translated by Raphael Jospe, in his *Torah and Sophia: The Life and Thought of Shem Tov Ibn Falaquera* (Cincinnati: Hebrew Union College Press, 1988), pp. 265–350.

Shelemut hamaʿasim

Manuscripts: Vatican Library, Rome, MS. 391; Bibliothèque Nationale, Paris, MS. Héb. 700.

Edition in English: "Shelemut hamaʿasim," edited and translated by Raphael Jospe, in his *Torah and Sophia: The Life and Thought of Shemhi Tov Ibn Falaquera* (Cincinnati: Hebrew Union College Press, 1988), pp. 411–438.

Iggeret hahalom

Manuscript: British Library, London, MS. 1083.6.

Edition: "Iggeret hahalom," edited by H. Malter, *Jewish Quarterly Review,* 1 (1910–1911): 151–183, 451–491.

Moreh hamoreh (1280)

Manuscripts: Jews' College Halberstamm-Montefiore, London, MS. 273; Bibliothèque Nationale, Paris, MSS. Heb. 706 and Heb. 700; University of Cambridge Library, MS. Add. 1214.

Edition: *Moreh hamoreh,* edited by Mordecai Leib Bislidhes (Pressburg: Anton Schmid, 1837).

Likkutim misefer mekor hayyim

Manuscript: Bibliothèque Nationale, Paris, MS. Heb. 700.

Edition: "Likkutim misefer mekor hayyim," in *Mélanges de philosophie juive et arabe,* edited by Salomon Munk (Paris: Franck, 1859), pp. 1–148.

Likkutim misefer haʿatsamim hahamishah

Edition: "Likkutim misefer haʿatsamim hahamishah," edited by David Kaufmann, in his *Studien über Salomon Ibn Gabirol* (Budapest: Jahresbericht der Landes-Rabbinerschule in Budapest, 1899), pp. 17–51.

Mikhtav ʿal devar hamoreh

Edition: *Mikhtav ʿal devar hamoreh,* edited by Mordecai Leib Bislidhes (Pressburg: Anton Schmid, 1837).

Diwan

Edition: "Diwan," in *Hashirah haʿivrit besefarad ubeprovens,* 2 volumes, edited by Jefim Schirmann (Tel Aviv: Devir, 1954, 1956), II: 329–342.

Issac ben Solomon Ibn Sahula (1244–?)

WORKS: *Meshal Hakadmoni* (1281)

Manuscripts: Bodleian Library, University of Oxford, MS. hebr. E 49; University of Cambridge Library, MS. T-S. K 22/6.

Early imprints: *Meshal Hakadmoni* (Brescia: Gerson Soncino, circa 1491); *Meshal Hakadmoni* (Venice: Meir Parenzo, circa 1548); *Meshal Hakadmoni* (Frankfurt am Main, 1693); *Meshal Hakadmoni* (Frankfurt am Main, 1799); *Meshal Hakadmoni* (Venice: Meir Parenzo, n.d.).

Editions: *Meshal Hakadmoni,* edited by Israel Zemorah (Tel Aviv, 1953); selections in *Hashirah haʿivrit besefarad ubeprovens,* 2 volumes, edited by Jefim Schirmann (Tel Aviv: Devir, 1954, 1956), II: 349–412.

Editions in English: "The Sorcerer," translated by Raymond P. Scheindlin, in *Rabbinic Fantasies,* edited by David Stern and Mark J. Mirsky (Philadelphia: Jewish Publication Society, 1990), pp. 295–311; *Meshal Haqadmoni: Fables from the Distant Past. A Parallel Hebrew-English Text,* edited and translated by Raphael Loewe (Oxford & Portland, Ore.: Littman Library of Jewish Civilization, 2004);

Diwan

Manuscript: Bibliotheek van der Rijksuniversiteit, Leiden, MS. K 22/6.

Todros ben Judah Halevi Abulafia (1247–after 1298)

WORK: *Gan hameshalim vehahidot*

Manuscripts: Private collection of Saul Abdalla

Joseph, Hong Kong; Schocken Institute for Jewish Research of the Jewish Theological Seminary of America, Jerusalem, MS. 37; Jewish Theological Society, New York, MS. ENA 1856.

Editions: *Gan hameshalim vehahidot,* edited by Moses Gaster and Saul Abdalla Joseph (London: A. Goldston, 1926); *Gan hameshalim vehahidot, Diwan of Don Todros son of Yehuda Abu-l-'Afiah,* 3 volumes, edited by David Yellin (Jerusalem: Weiss, 1932–1934); Bernard Chapira, "Contribution à l'étude du divan de Todros Ben Iehouda Halévi Aboulafia," *Revue des Etudes Juives,* new series, 5 (1941–1945): 1–33; selections in *Hashirah ha'ivrit besefarad ubeprovens,* 2 volumes, edited by Jefim Schirmann (Tel Aviv: Devir, 1954, 1956), II: 413–448.

Abraham ben Samuel Halevi Ibn Hasdai (late twelfth century–thirteenth century)

WORKS: *Sefer hatappuah*

Manuscripts: British Library, London, MSS. 867.7, 869.2, 870.2, 904.13, 918.4, and 1083.3; Bodleian Library, University of Oxford, MSS. 1176, 851, 1409.3, 1436, 1600.7, 2243.10, and 2287.11.

Early imprints: "Sefer hatappuah," in *Likkutei hapardes* (Venice: Daniel Bomberg, 1519); *Sefer hatappuah* (Frankfurt am Main, 1693); *Sefer hatappuah* (Amsterdam, 1715).

Editions: *Sefer hatappuah,* translated by J. Musen (Lemberg: S. L. Kugel, 1873); *Reah ha-tapuah,* edited by Abraham Menahem Mandel (Warsaw: Schriftgisser, 1881).

Moznei tsedek

Manuscript: Bodleian Library, University of Oxford, MS. 1334.4.

Edition: *Moznei tsedek,* edited by Jacob Goldenthal (Leipzig & Paris: Geghardt & Reisland, 1839).

Sefer hayesodot

Manuscripts: Bodleian Library, University of Oxford, MSS. 1316.1 and 1368.2.

Edition: *Sefer hayesodot,* edited by S. Fried (Drogobych: A. H. Zupnik, 1900).

Bilwahar wa-Yudasaf, *Ben hamelekh vehanazir,* translated and adapted by Ibn Hasdai

Manuscripts: British Library, London, MS. 866; Bodleian Library, University of Oxford, MS. 502.2; Jewish Theological Seminary, New York, MS. 1879.

Early imprints: *Ben hamelekh vehanazir* (Constantinople, 1518); *Ben hamelekh vehanazir* (Mantua: Venturino Ruffinelli, 1557); *Ben hamelekh vehanazir* (Wandsbeck: Israel ben Abraham, 1726).

Editions: *Ben hamelekh vehanazir* (Leghorn: M. Y.

Tobiana, 1835); *Prinz und derwich; oder Die Makamen Ibn-Chisdais,* translated by W. A. Meisel (Stettin: H. Effenbarts, 1847); *Sefer ben hamelekh vehanazir* (Warsaw: S. Halevi Levin, 1884); *Prinz und Derwisch: Ein Indischer Roman enthaltend Die Jugendgeschichte Buddha's in hebräischer Darstellung aus dem Mittelalter; nebst einer Vergleichung der arabischen und griechischen Paralleltexte,* edited by Nathan Weisslowits (Munich: T. Ackermann, 1890); "Ben hamelekh vehanazir," edited by Israel Davidson, in *Sefer Zikkaron A. S. Rabinovitz* (Tel Aviv: Histadrut hasofrim ha'ivrim be Erets Yisrael, 1924), pp. 83–101; *Sefer ben hamelekh vehanazir,* edited by A. M. Habermann (Tel Aviv: Mahbarot lesifrut, 1950); *El príncep i el monjo: D'Abraham ben Semuel Halevi Ibn Hasday,* translated by Tessa Calders i Artís (Sabadell: AUSA, 1987).

Jacob ben El'azar (late twelfth century–thirteenth century.)

WORKS: *Kitab al-kamil*

Manuscripts: Jewish Theological Seminary, New York, MSS. ENA 4186 and ENA 2713; University of Cambridge Library, MS. T-S. Ar. 52/217.

Edition: *Kitab al-kamil, Sefer hashalem,* edited by Nehemya Allony (Jerusalem: American Academy for Jewish Research, 1977).

Kalila vedimna

Manuscript: British Library, London, MS. Harleian 340; Bodleian Library, University of Oxford, MS. Opp. Add. 4⁰ 101.

Early imprints: *Kalila vedimna* (Constantinople, 1513); *Kalila vedimna* (Mantua, 1557).

Editions: *Deux verions hébraïques du livre de Kalilah et Dimnah,* edited by Joseph Derenbourg (Paris: F. Vieweg, 1881); *Sipure Kalilah vedimnah,* translated by Abraham Elmaleh (Tel Aviv: Devir, 1926).

Sefer pardes rimmone

Manuscripts: British Library, London, MS. Or. 2538; Real Biblioteca del Monasterio de El Escorial, MS. G.IV.4, folios 104r–146r; Jews' College Halberstamm-Montefiore, London.

Edition: "Sefer pardes rimmone hahokmah haarugat bosem hamezimmah," edited by Israel Davidson, *Hasofeh lehokhmat Yisra'el,* 10 (1926): 94–105; 11 (1927): 96.

Sefer hameshalim

Manuscript: Königliche Hof- und Staatsbibliothek, Munich, MS. 207.

Editions: "Sefer hameshalim," edited by Jefim Schirmann, *Studies of the Research Institute for Hebrew Poetry,* 5 (1939): 209–266; "Sefer hameshalim," edited by Schirmann, *Sefarad,* 20 (1960): 207–237;

"Sefer hameshalim," edited by A. Navarro, *El Olivo*, 15 (1982): 49–82; *Sipure ahava shel Ya'akov ben El'azar* (Tel Aviv: Tel Aviv University, 1992).

Piyyutim

Edition: Selections in *Hashirah ha'ivrit besefarad ubeprovens,* 2 volumes, edited by Jefim Schirmann (Tel Aviv: Devir, 1954, 1956), II: 207–237, 689.

The Jewish literature of medieval Spain joins biblical and liturgical forms with Arabic and Romance genres. Andalusian society comprised Arabs, Berbers, native Iberian converts to Islam, Christians, Arabized Christians, European slave soldiers, and Jews; the last group paid a poll tax and a land tax in exchange for protection and religious freedom. Radical innovations initiated in the Umayyad caliphate of Cordova between 929 and 1008 matured during the era of the *muluk at-tawa'if* (party kingdoms) from 1031 to 1086, the so-called golden age of Hebrew poetry. The Almohad riots of 1146 provoked a Jewish exodus from al-Andalus that heralded the postclassical period. The Andalusian style survived the expulsions from Spain and Portugal, persisting in Italy and Holland into the nineteenth century.

Andalusian Jewish literature comprises secular and liturgical poetry and rhymed prose (Arabic *saj'*) that parallel Arabic genres. Secular poetry, unknown since the biblical era, has a clear authorial voice that emerges from liturgical communal poetry and breathes the complexity of human experience into conventional and stylized Arabic forms. Poetry and rhymed prose were used to expound various disciplines and to reflect the culture's theocentricism: all sciences adumbrated human knowledge of the Creator and his works. The triliteral root of Hebrew grammar—all verb roots consist of three consonants—and the revival of biblical Hebrew *(tsahot halashon)* in lieu of rabbinic and liturgical registers allowed for a poetic diction sufficiently ductile to transform Arabic themes, imagery, and quantitative-verse rhythms, which rely on long and short syllable patterns, into Hebrew poetry.

Having brought its genius to bear on an assimilated classical legacy of Greek rationalism, Arabic culture extended from Babylonia and Palestine across North Africa to the nascent learning centers of al-Andalus. An Arabized Jewish elite achieved significant advances in philology and made outstanding contributions to exegesis, philosophy, ethics, mysticism, history, travel writing, homiletics, polemics, science, and belles lettres. Samuel the Nagid (Ismail Ibn Nagrel'a), Solomon Ibn Gabirol, Moses Ibn Ezra, Judah Halevi, Abraham Ibn Daud, and Maimonides (Moses ben Maimon) spoke vernacular Arabic or Romance and were also steeped in Hebrew; their mastery of Arabic grammar, literature, and philosophy allowed them to graft

Arabic methods, themes, genres, and poetics onto the Hebrew stock. Arabic was used for science, philology, exegesis, philosophy, and poetics, Hebrew for aesthetic and religious purposes.

Sephardic al-Andalus, a cultural colony of Babylonia until the tenth century, initiated its cultural independence with the ascendancy of the courtier-rabbis and scholars in Berber Muslim courts and the establishment of local Talmudic academies. At the same time, Dunash Ibn Labrat's Hebrew adaptation of Arabic quantitative meter and choice of biblical Hebrew as a literary benchmark configured a secular poetry patterned on Arabic conventions unknown in traditional *piyyutim* (liturgical poetry).

The Muslim ruling class esteemed poetry, making its cultivation necessary for attaining *adib,* the refined cosmopolitanism of the Muslim courts, and that status of high esteem was an incentive for the courtier-rabbis. Ross Brann and Raymond P. Scheindlin believe that the courtier-rabbis' self-conscious acculturation motivated their synthesis of Arabic and Hebrew literature. Recitation of the new secular poetry was a daily affair among the elite, but it is unclear whether most Jews ever heard it.

Immersed in a Hispano-Arabic Andalusian culture that encompassed the opposing principles of *dunya* (the world and its vanity) and *akhira* (the ultimate reality of God), the courtier-rabbis expressed their own cultural ambivalence in the parallel genres of *piyyut* and secular poetry based on Arabic quantitative meters. A reflection of these competing secular and religious spheres is expressed by the recurrent theme of the mature poet who is repentant of his youthful poems.

Craftsmanship, shown in close attention to form, artifice, and technique, is constant among Jewish poets of the Middle Ages. Formal complexity and allusiveness invite comparison with Elizabethan or Metaphysical poetry. Biblical mastery is required to understand the recondite allusions in the works.

Professional poets among the laity competed for patronage with courtier-rabbis by reciting and improvising poems. Such poems were meant to manipulate public opinion by bestowing praise on generous patrons and reviling their enemies; panegyric and satire, wedding songs, eulogies, and dirges regulated social relationships. Poems circulated in manuscript and among *tradents* (specialists in the memorization and recitation of poetry). When a poet died, copyists gathered the manuscripts of his works and assembled his *diwan* (compilation).

The new secular poetry, whose introduction is credited to Solomon Ibn Gabirol, derived its principles, images, rhythms, genres, forms, idiom, and poetics from Arabic poetry, especially *al-badi'* (highly ornamented poetry), the Abbasid modernist style associated with Abu Tammam. It reproduces twelve of the sixteen basic classical Arabic meters, with sixty variants; the accommodation of Arabic quantitative meter violated Hebrew grammar and phonology and sparked criticism in certain quarters. The Andalusian-Hebrew poets rejected the notion that biblical poetry was excluded by Qudama ibn Ja'far's classic definition of Arabic quantitative verse as "metered, rhymed speech expressing a certain meaning."

Secular Arabic and Hebrew Andalusian poetry takes two main forms: the *qasida* (ode) and the *muwashshah* (girdle poem; Hebrew *shir ezor;* plural *muwashshahat*). The *qasida,* consisting of continuous verses in a single meter with invariable end rhyme, is as apt for brief epigrams as for extended odes. It includes a *nasib* (amatory prelude) describing nature, a wine party, or a meditation, and a *takhalluts* (formulaic transition) leading to the main theme. The verse comprises two balanced cola. In the initial verse the cola rhyme, setting the end rhyme for the second colon in all succeeding verses. Rhythmically balanced cola rise and fall in pairs, while syntactically balanced hemistichs organize *shibbuts* or *musiv* (embedded scriptural citations or allusions; Arabic *iqtibas,* to light again from a flame). Structural support comes from *tanjis* (paronomasia) and *mutabaqa* (antithesis). Juxtaposition of startling opposites that resolve in metaphor is a hallmark of this poetry. Many Hebrew courtly poems are *qasida,* including *shire yedidut utehilah* (panegyric; Arabic *madih*), *shire hasheninah* (invective or satire; Arabic *hija'*), and *qinot* (elegies; Arabic *maratih*). *Shire ahavah* (love poetry; Arabic *tashbib*) derives from Arabic *ghazal:* four to six monorhymed verses in classical prosodic patterns. Other genres are *shire hayayin* (wine poetry; Arabic *khamriya*); *shire tiferet* (self-praise; Arabic *fakhr*); *shire hateba'* (nature poetry); *rawdiyat* (descriptions of gardens); *zahriyat* (flower poems); *shire sha'ashu'im* (poems of pleasure), from the Arabic *zurafa* tradition; *teuri* (descriptive poetry; Arabic *wasaf*), which may portray domestic utensils; *hidot* (riddles); *tefillot* (prayers); and *shire perishut umusar* (ascetic verse; Arabic *zuhdiya*). Elements from various genres may be combined in a single poem. Both secular and liturgical poetry adhere to conventions of content, style, and form, but these conventions did not preclude individual expression: though many poems are anonymous, the distinctive voices of the best poets are unmistakable.

Poetry, music, and dance graced the Abbasid wine party. The *raki* (wine bearer) is depicted in many poems as a seductive but unattainable lover. Wine and cup are described metaphorically as gold and silver, fire and ice, precious stones and metal, and soul and body. Epigrams on small objects and improvisation contests entertained the revelers. Judah Halevi achieved fame by improvising a contrafactum (substitution of text without

changing the metrical pattern) on a *muwashshah* by Moses Ibn Ezra, whose prosodic patterns usually confounded his rivals. The thirty-second *maqama* of Judah ben Solomon al-Harizi's *Tahkemoni* (translated as *The Book of Tahkemoni: Jewish Tales from Medieval Spain*, 2001) portrays a contest between a youth and an old man who improvise on themes such as a pen, a letter, a sword, and so forth. A *maqama* (literally, "gate," "marketplace," or "session"; plural, *maqamat*) consists of narrative and rhetorical tours de force in rhymed prose with intercalated metrical poems.

Wine poetry—brief poems in classical quantitative meter—can be descriptive, meditative, or both, and one or more wine poems could be incorporated into the prelude of a *qasida*. Moses Ibn Ezra, whose *Ha'anaq* (The Necklace) catalogues descriptive themes and images, and Samuel the Nagid were the foremost exponents of wine poetry.

Love poetry offers variations on conventional themes derived from a common Hebrew and Arabic stock of images, forms, and styles. The anonymous beloved, comparable to the Provençal *senhal,* is addressed with epithets such as *tsevi* (fawn or gazelle). The beloved may be a young *raki* who embodies a beauty that is neither feminine nor masculine. Love poems are descriptive, comprising portraits of the beloved's body, or petitionary, serving as instruments to advance the love affair. Petitionary poems portray love as a disease and confront the speaker with opponents: the guardians of an indifferent and unattainable beloved who is the source of the lover's endless suffering, and his own friends, to whom he is incomprehensible. The beloved's unique beauty, conveyed by stock clichés, commands the lover's complete devotion and leaves him in solitary frustration.

Many love poems are *muwashshahat,* the sole parallelistic strophic form cultivated by classical Arabic poets. The invention of the *muwashshah* is attributed to Muhammad Ibn Mahmud al-Qabri, the Blind, around 900. Sung to instrumental accompaniment—performance indications survive in some manuscripts—the Hebrew *muwashshah* usually consists of five strophes. Each strophe comprises a *bayt* (house; Arabic *ghusn,* Spanish *mudanza*), whose rhyme varies with each new strophe, and a *qufl* (return; Arabic *simt;* Spanish *vuelta*) of invariable rhyme. A *bayt* matching the rhyme and number of verses of the *qufl* commonly opens the poem. The last *qufl* is the *kharja* (exit; Spanish *jarcha;* plural *kharajat*), verses in vernacular Arabic or Romance intoned by the girl to whom the preceding verses were addressed. The shift in language and tone of the *kharja* emphasizes the main theme of the *muwashshah* by contrasting with it. Mother or friends advise the plaintive girl, or a *raqib* (spy) frustrates the lovers' tryst; well-tended gardens and birds are common images. Scholars consider Romance *kharajat* to be quotations of otherwise unknown songs and, therefore, early witnesses of lyric poetry. Secular Hebrew *muwashshahat* with Romance *kharajat* by Joseph al-Katib, Isaac ben Judah Ibn Ghiyyat, Moses Ibn Ezra, Judah Halevi, Joseph Ibn Saddiq, Abraham Ibn Ezra, and Todros ben Judah Abulafia are extant.

Literary tradition regarded the *piyyut* as wholly different from its secular counterpart. Religious poems to accompany public prayers had appeared in Palestine by the fourth century; poetic cycles keyed to weekly scriptural readings also developed. *Piyyutim* use an esoteric idiom, are generally strophic, and commonly employ acrostics. Tenth-century Andalusian preference for pure Hebrew diction departs from the traditional *piyyut* register, and syllabic meter is replaced by the quantitative meters of secular poetry, notably *marnin* (humming mode).

Paytanim (liturgical poets) composed in traditional style but added new forms: the *muwashshah* and *reshuyot* (preludes), brief monorhyme meditations in Arabic meters or strophes that precede preliminary prayers. Though themes from Arabic *zuhd* (ascetic) poetry, philosophy, and science were adapted, the theme of Israel in exile–traditionally depicted as an abandoned woman awaiting her lover's return–remained constant. Liturgical poets incorporated erotic themes from *qasida* into their poems, couching messianic longing in the language of the Song of Solomon.

Penitential liturgical poems, or *selihot* (supplications), replace the congregational first-person plural with the first-person singular of philosophy. Medieval philosophy was preoccupied with the soul, the nature of humanity, and the relation of the human being to God and the universe, leading to the appearance of such themes in *reshuyot*. *Sefer hamevaqqesh* (1623; translated as *Falaquera's Book of the Seeker*, 1976), by Ibn Falaquera, identifies three degrees of liturgical poetry: prophetic, exemplified by Ex. 15 and Deut. 32; inspired, such as Psalms, Proverbs, and the Song of Solomon; and a third degree corresponding to Andalusian *piyyutim,* that Ibn Falaquera describes as "poems of praise to the Lord, dealing with His wondrous deeds, have been composed by gifted poets; these are of the lowest order."

Angel Sáenz-Badillos notes in "Hebrew Philology in Sefarad: The State of the Question" (2001) that "the connection of grammar with the exegesis of sacred texts, and the connection of the new Hebrew philology with the main schools of Arabic grammar, provides a framework for correctly understanding the Andalusian obsession with grammar and vocabulary." Arabic was considered a refined instrument, capable of philosophical rigor and intimate sentiment, and the Jewish elite

studied classical Arabic literature for the purpose of attaining *adib*. Jewish grammarian-poets answered *ʿarabiyya* (Arabism), the notion of the preeminence of Arabic culture and ethnicity, with *al-ʿibraniyya* (Hebraism): the idea that Hebrew was flawless and divinely ordained and, therefore, superior to all other languages and that Arabic was derivative from it. Under the banner of biblical Hebrew, Andalusian Jews developed a literary aesthetic that achieved unalloyed success through the generation of Meshullam ben Solomon da Piera, who died around 1260.

Saadya Gaon (Saadya ben Joseph) played a decisive role in medieval Hebrew grammar and poetry. Egyptian by birth, he immigrated in 915 to Baghdad, a center of Arabic philological studies. In 928 he was appointed *gaon* (head) of the Babylonian Academy. His prolific writings on philology, liturgy, *halakhah* (religious law), calendars and chronology, philosophy, and polemics and his Arabic translations of the Scriptures led Abraham Ibn Ezra to call him "the chief spokesman in all matters of learning." His *Kitab fatsih lughat al-ʿibra-niyyin* (circa 915–921; Book of Elegance of the Language of the Hebrews), the first normative biblical and rabbinical Hebrew grammar, presents biblical Hebrew as intrinsically eloquent and elegant. Reflecting medieval Abbassid rationalism, his *Haegron* (Collection), a rhyming dictionary written in 902, is the first systematization of poetic rules. Finally, his *Kitab al-sabʿin* (Explanation of the Seventy Isolated Words) anticipates later Andalusian advances in grammar.

The patronage of Eastern scholars by the caliph ʿAbd ar-Rahman III, who ruled from 912 to 961, and his son ʿAl-Hakam II, who succeeded him and reigned until 976, transformed the Umayyad court of Cordova into the center of Arabic philology. Hasdai Ibn Shaprut, a learned and powerful physician, translator, and poet in the court of ʿAbd al-Rahman III, figured decisively in the creation of Andalusian-Hebrew culture. Moses Ibn Ezra describes Ibn Shaprut as a generous and honorable man who brought the sciences to al-Andalus, and Ibn Daud mentions him in connection with the establishment of an independent academy in Cordova. With his support, scholars compiled dictionaries, wrote pioneering studies of grammar, and adapted Arabic rhythmic patterns to Hebrew verse. Waves of migration to Spain from the Near East and North Africa brought Jews into indirect contact, through the pan-Arabic culture, with the great academies in Mesopotamia, Babylonia, and Palestine. Philology, poetry, exegesis, philosophy, and the sciences were the curricula for Andalusian-Jewish elaboration of what Brann, in "The Arabized Jews" (2000), calls "a strictly rationalist method of studying their own heritage."

Menahem Ibn Saruq, Ibn Shaprut's secretary, maintained his patron's wide correspondence. Moses Ibn Ezra praises Ibn Saruq's poetry, but al-Harizi judges it eminently forgettable. Ibn Saruq wrote the first complete dictionary in Hebrew, *Mahberet* (960, Dictionary), to demonstrate the elegance of the language; it inaugurated the influence of Arabic doctrines over Hebrew philology. In the introduction Ibn Saruq states that God endowed humans with speech so that they could express themselves correctly. The Hebrew *tsahot* (correctness) parallels the Arabic categories *fasaha* (eloquent language) and *balagha* (rhetorical eloquence) employed by Saadya Gaon, concepts pivotal to Jews' understanding of their religious culture. Though Ibn Saruq eschewed Arabic cognates in elucidating biblical Hebrew, later philologists used Arabic exclusively in their discipline. Another Hebrew grammar written in Hebrew did not appear until Abraham Ibn Ezra's in 1145.

Ibn Saruq's dictionary elicited withering attacks from Dunash ben Labrat, and a polemic ensued between the students of the two masters. When Ibn Saruq was accused of heresy, Ibn Shaprut dismissed him. Influential among non-Arabists, *Mahberet* was superseded by the work of Ibn Saruq's students, who introduced the theory of the triliteral verbal root.

The aristocratic grammarian-poet Dunash ben Labrat studied in Baghdad with Saadya Gaon and became a leading figure in Ibn Shaprut's entourage. His comparative Hebrew-Arabic morphology elucidated Hebrew forms, and his accommodation of Arabic quantitative-meter prosody, which violated rules of Hebrew prosody based on tone and stress, contributed decisively to Andalusian-Hebrew poetry. His *Teshuvot de Dunash* (Objections of Dunash) points out 160 errors in Ibn Saruq's grammar. The condemnation was contested by Menahem's students Isaac Ibn Kapron, Isaac Ibn Gikatilla, and Judah ben David Hayyuj in *Teshuvot al Dunash ben Labrat* (Objections to Dunash ben Labrat). Replying to 55 of his strictures, they decry Dunash's use of Arabic and Aramaic and the imposition of Arabic meters on Hebrew poetry. Dunash's pupil Yehudi ben Sheshet responded, and the controversy continued throughout the period. Nevertheless, Dunash had blazed the trail that later grammarians followed.

Hayyuj connected the Arabic triliteral root with the Hebrew verb: he recognized no verbs that contained fewer than three letters and maintained that all derivations could be explained by *qiyas* (analogy). Applying Arabic theory, he laid the methodological foundations for Hebrew grammar, phonology, and lexicography. He also derived rules from the analysis of biblical texts. His *Kitab al-tanqit* (The Book of Vocalization) examines vowels, while *Kitab al-afal dhawat huruf al-lin* (The Weak and Geminative Verbs) and *Kitab al-dhawat al-mathalayn* (Book of Reduplicated Verbs) study verbs. He championed philological exegesis and helped make biblical Hebrew the aesthetic standard. Moses Ibn Ezra calls him the first to grasp the weak verb. Ibn Daud notes that Hayyuj "reestablished the principles of the Hebrew language–these having been forgotten throughout the Diaspora."

The first great Andalusian *paytan,* the Talmudist Joseph Ibn Abitor, studied with Rabbi Moses ben Hanokh in Cordova. Ibn Daud recounts that after Hanokh's death, rivals blocked Ibn Abitor's elevation to chief of the academy, and he was forced to flee to the East. Later, he was invited to lead the academy but declined. Ibn Abitor translated the Talmud into Arabic for Caliph al-Hakam II. Three hundred of his *piyyutim* are extant; though they are written in Eastern style, their innovative forms and themes became the standard. In 1021 he composed an Arabic quantitative-verse threnody for victims of pogroms in Palestine. Moses Ibn Ezra considered him superior to Ibn Saruq and ben Labrat. Al-Harizi esteems his poetry as "lovely and excellent" and notes that Ibn Abitor was the first Andalusian to compose liturgical poems for the Day of Atonement.

The son of a North African émigré, the *paytan* and professional poet Isaac Ibn Khalfun lived in Cordova before fleeing to Toledo in 1013. Seventy-five of his secular and liturgical poems are extant. His *diwan* includes poems he sent to Samuel the Nagid and others dedicated to the Saragossan courtier Yequti'el Ibn Hasan. He wrote the first extant Andalusian-Hebrew love poem around 1000; it comprises four verses that trace a downward spiral from confidence to despondence. Moses Ibn Ezra applies to Ibn Khalfun the epithet "the poet" and mentions his travels in service of patrons. Al-Harizi says that the poems are "forceful, but some of them are dried up and blasted."

Jonah Ibn Janah wrote a systematic biblical-Hebrew grammar, *Kitab 'al-mustalhaq* (1012, The Book of Criticism), that corrects and supplements Hayyuj's work. A polemic with Samuel the Nagid ensured dissemination of Hayyuj's discoveries. *Kitab al-tanqih* (circa 1040, Book of Detailed Investigation), Ibn Janah's magnum opus, includes "Kitab 'al-luma^c" (Book of Colored Flowerbeds) and "Kitab 'al-utsul" (Book of [Hebrew] Roots); Judah Ibn Tibbon translated it into Hebrew in 1171. Ibn Janah perceived the need for accurate texts to facilitate grammar study. Meant to cultivate elegance, his study of biblical syntax anticipates modern scholarship. His biblical lexicography remained unsurpassed until the nineteenth century.

The Cordovan poet and exegete Moses Ibn Gikatilla, a friend of Samuel the Nagid's, lived in Saragossa and southern France. His commentaries incorporate philological insights. His translations of Hayyuj's main treatises, which incorporate his own observations, made Hayyuj's revolution available to non-Arabists. Fragments of his *Kitab 'al tadhkir w'al-ta'anith* (Treatise on Masculine and Feminine Genders) survive. Moses Ibn Ezra emphasizes Ibn Gikatilla's oratorical and poetic skills in Arabic and Hebrew, while Ibn Daud notes his "verses of consolation to fortify the hearts of Israel."

Basing it on the work of Hayyuj and Ibn Janah, the Talmudist Judah Ibn Balᶜam prepared *Kitab al-tajnis* (The Book of Homonyms), a grammar textbook with philological commentary on most of the Bible. Composed for poets and biblical expositors, it circulated widely. A guide to cantillation (an inflectional system for public recitation) of Psalms, Proverbs, and Job, *Shaar taame shelosha sefarim emet* (Cantillation for the Three Books), is attributed to him. Lengthy quotations from earlier Bible commentators make his work a valuable historical repository. Moses Ibn Ezra notes his phenomenal memory but also his contentiousness and megalomania. Ibn Balᶜam attacked Moses Ibn Gikatilla's reliance on halakhic hermeneutics (interpretation of Scripture according to rabbinic oral tradition and Holy Law) in lieu of grammatical method.

Samuel the Nagid was a member of a prominent Mérida family descended from Jerusalemite aristocracy. He studied with the Talmudist Rabbi Hanokh ben Moses and mastered Hebrew, Arabic, and Greek sciences. Poet, philologist, halakhist, warrior, statesman, learned in Islamic law, and supremely self-confident, he claimed to be the King David of his day. His life and wisdom embody the courtier-rabbi archetype: in *The Compunctious Poet: Cultural Ambiguity and Hebrew Poetry in Muslim Spain* (1991) Brann says that Joseph ibn Hisdai's '*Shirah yetomah*' (The Singular Song) envisions Samuel the Nagid "as the prophet Samuel incarnate!" Judah Ibn Tibbon does the same in *Tsawwa'ah* (circa 1190, Ethical Will).

The Berber overthrow of the Umayyad caliphate in 1013 precipitated Samuel's flight to Málaga. Legend recounts that he composed letters in his spice shop for a maidservant of the *hajib* (vizier) and that their eloquence and beautiful calligraphy gained him entry to the court of the caliph Habbas. After several reverses, he became secretary to *Hajib* Abu al-ᶜAbbas in 1020; seven years later was named the first *nagid*, the Jewish community's chief leader. The death of Habbas in 1038 precipitated a struggle between his elder son, Badis, and the court favorite, Bullugin, for the succession. Samuel backed Badis, who, once installed, elevated him to vizier. As chief minister and commander of the army, Samuel directed Granada's diplomatic and military affairs. According to the historian Abu l-ᶜAbbas Ahmad b.

Muhammad Ibn Idhari, "the king raised him above every other rank and dignity." Chronic warfare with Seville and its allies revealed a consummate strategist and tactician possessing what Jefim Schirmann calls "the temperament of a gambler and an adventurer." He brought Granada wealth and power among the *taifas*, the small, independent kingdoms into which the Caliphate of Cordova had fragmented between 1009 and 1031. "Shira," (Song), celebrating the death of his archenemy, the Almerian vizier Ibn Abi Musa at the battle of Alfuente in 1038, records his capacity for violent hatred; he also persecuted members of the Karaite sect of Jews in villages along the Christian frontier.

Ibn Daud places Samuel, who appointed judges, among "the first of the generation of the rabbinate" who heralded the eclipse of Babylonian preeminence in jurisprudence. Ibn Gabirol says that with his *Hilkhata gavrata* (1049, Laws of the Mighty), a compilation of *halakah* that influenced Ibn Ghiyyat, Isaac Alfasi, and Judah al-Bargeloni, Samuel usurped absolute authority in matters of religious law from Hai Gaon of Pumbedita in Babylonia.

Samuel maintained a wide correspondence, supported academies of learning, sent funds to synagogues in Jerusalem, purchased copies of the Mishna and Talmud, and assembled an extraordinary library. His poetry is an important biographical record. He sent war poems home from the battlefield to his eldest son, Yehosef. Brushes with death and near defeats turned into victories strengthened his conviction that he was under divine protection. He composed ninety elegies recounting his elder brother Isaac's illness and death in 1041.

As a grammarian and lexicographer, Samuel helped write *Rasaᶜil al-rifaq* (Epistles of the Companions) against Ibn Janah and also wrote a now-lost grammar, *Kitab al-hujja* (The Book of Evidence), in reply to Ibn Janah. Abraham Ibn Ezra claims that Samuel wrote twenty-two philological treatises; all are now lost except for fragments of *Kitab al-istighna* (The Book of Amplitude). This work, a comprehensive dictionary in Arabic, is thought to have been the crown jewel of Hebrew lexicography; its unique arrangement listed under each entry all definitions and forms of the biblical-Hebrew root, with exegetical and lexicographical notes from multiple sources.

Instrumental in introducing Arabic quantitative verse into Hebrew—his social and cultural stature helped guarantee its acceptance—Samuel's secular love poetry synthesizes Arabic motifs, biblical diction, and love motifs that are often taken from the Song of Solomon; he also introduced the *muwashshah* into Hebrew literature. Al-Harizi says that Samuel "bared his mighty arm in the craftsmanship of poetry, and his rhetoric was powerful. He brought forth hidden things to light." Ibn Daud wrote: "In the days of Hasdai the Nasi they began to chirp, and in the days of Samuel the Nagid they sang aloud." Technical virtuosity–he devised sixty-one variations on fourteen basic meters–and a rich storehouse of motifs, themes, forms, and figures of speech manifest his vast literary erudition. His poems include love and wine songs, panegyrics, polemics, epigrams, dirges, and meditations; unique in Hebrew and lacking Arabic models, his autobiographical poems recount events and his attitude toward them.

Three collections of Samuel's work are extant: *Ben Tehillim* (After Psalms), *Ben Mishle* (After Proverbs), and *Ben Kohelet* (After Ecclesiastes). Superscriptions evince biblical antecedents and imply, according to Brann's *The Compunctious Poet*, that "the Nagid was proposing a typological correspondence between his work and that of David and Solomon." According to Moses Ibn Ezra, the 222 poems of *Ben Tehillim* introduced Arabic quantitative meters and themes into Hebrew poetry "in a way no one before or after did." Yehosef began copying the poems at age eight; he later wrote a preface that anticipates modern polemic in discounting interpretation of the homoerotic poems in other than allegorical terms. Perhaps at his father's direction, Yehosef added superscriptions that allude to dates of composition.

The 1,197 dense and complex wisdom poems of *Ben Mishle* may have formed the basis for al-Harizi's judgment that "most of [Samuel's] poems are profound and difficult and require commentary." Samuel's youngest son, Eliassaf, copied the poems and arranged them alphabetically by first letter and further subdivided them by meter–a variation on standard *diwan* organization, which is alphabetical by rhyme scheme. An introductory twenty-two-word motto is acrostically reiterated in as many sections, one for each letter of the alphabet. Eliassaf's preface discusses their contradictory and antithetical rhetoric.

The 411 poems of the anonymously edited *Ben Kohelet* are similarly arranged, again with an acrostic iteration of the initial motto, but lack a preface or superscriptions. They were copied repeatedly and circulated widely, and several appear, intact or as fragments, in *Ben Kohelet, Ben Tehilim,* and *Ben Mishle.* They elicited high praise from Moses Ibn Ezra: "And it *[Ben Kohelet]* is the most sublime and admirable of HaNagid's compositions, and it is more beautiful and more profound than *Ben Tehillim* and *Ben Mishle,* because it was written after its author reached middle age."

Convalescing after a military campaign, Samuel fell ill, perhaps from exhaustion, and died in 1056. He was buried outside the Elbira Gate, and Ibn Khalfon, Ibn Hisdai, Ibn Gabirol, and Ibn Ghiyyat eulogized him. Moses Ibn Ezra quotes an elegy by the Arabic poet

ᶜAbdah Ibn al-Tabib: "His death was not the loss of one person, but with him the building of an entire people was demolished." The historian Abu Marwan Hayyan b. Khalaf b. Husayn Ibn Hayyan assesses Samuel:

> this accursed Jew was in himself one of the most perfect men, although God had denied him His guidance. He excelled in learning, endurance, intelligence and wit, charm of character, perseverance, astuteness, cunning, self-control and natural courtesy. He knew how to act according to the requirements of the moment, how to flatter his enemies and remove suspicion from their heart by his fine manners. What an uncommon man!

Yehosef, who succeeded his father as vizier, was killed in the massacre of Granadan Jewry on 20 December 1066. Two decades later, the Almoravid invasion brought the *taifa* period to a close.

Samuel the Nagid's secular poetry came to light in the nineteenth century. Abraham E. Harkavy published an edition in 1879. David S. Sassoon's three-volume 1934 edition of *Ben Tehillim* reflects a unique 1584 manuscript in which the poems are grouped according to length, while Dov Yarden's 1982 edition arranges them thematically: war, friendship and praise, wit, elegy and condolence, nature, light verse, wine, love, prayers, and miscellaneous. The texts are vocalized and commentaries are supplied in 1947 and 1963 editions by A. M. Habermann, 1948 and 1953 editions by Shraga Abramson, and a 1966 edition by Yarden.

Joseph Ibn Hisdai's sole extant poem, *Shira yetomah* (circa 1045, The Unique Song), is the prelude to a panegyric for his childhood friend Samuel the Nagid and is renowned for its virtually perfect fusion of form and content. Moses Ibn Ezra lauds its description of imaginary events, parallelism, and metaphor, and Al-Harizi emphasizes its "sweetness and smoothness."

Solomon ben Judah Ibn Gabirol *hakatan* (the little one) is credited with introducing *al-badiᶜ* (the modernist style of the Abbasid poets) into Hebrew literature. His works are regarded, along with those of Judah Halevi, as the epitome of Andalusian-Hebrew literature. Born in Málaga around 1020 and educated in Saragossa, Ibn Gabirol lost his father when he was quite young. Autobiographical poems portray him as a small, ugly, disagreeable, and impoverished misanthrope suffering from a chronic skin disease. Moses Ibn Ezra notes that his friend's superior intelligence often succumbed to a contentious temper. Arrogant and individualistic, a mystic conscious of his genius, Ibn Gabirol wrote, "I am the master and the song is my slave / . . . /and though I am only sixteen years of age / my heart has the wisdom of an eighty-year-old!" The youthful *paytan* completed *Azharot* (Exhortations), poems for the first two days of Shavuot, around 1036. These uniquely structured expressions of triumph over self-defeat eschew conventional complexity. Reminiscent of mystical biblical interpretation, they fuse Arabic idioms and images in unconventional, paradoxical, and revelatory images permeated by science, especially astronomy. The first Andalusian-Jewish philosopher, Ibn Gabirol wrote *Keter malkhut* (The Royal Crown), which contrasts the glory of the Omnipotent with human powerlessness. The work is a synthesis of poetry, philosophy, and prayer that draws on mystical Midrashim, Neoplatonic cosmology, and astronomy. After praising God and meditating on his attributes, the speaker surveys the universe and ascends from the sublunar world through the encompassing celestial spheres until he reaches the outermost sphere, where the formation and function of the soul are explained. After a final confession of sins, he petitions for divine compassion. Today the Sephardic rite for the Day of Atonement includes a reading of the poem.

A champion of Hebrew, Ibn Gabirol vents his displeasure over neglect of the holy tongue in *Ha'anaq* (circa 1039, The Necklace). A poetic summary of grammar, it extols Hebrew and expounds the analogy that words are to the alphabet as form is to matter. Abraham Ibn Ezra regarded the work as crucial for understanding Hebrew; he reports that it consisted of four hundred verses; only ninety-eight are extant.

The assassination in 1039 of his patron, Yequtiel Ibn Isaac Hasan, threw Ibn Gabirol into material want, and he fled from Saragossa to Granada and thence to Valencia. Moses Ibn Ezra relates that "the knight of the word" finally abandoned worldly affairs and dedicated himself to physics and astronomy; Abraham Ibn Ezra claims that Ibn Gabirol attempted to predict the Day of Judgment.

According to Moses Ibn Ezra, the subtlety of Ibn Gabirol's poetry is equal to that of the Arab poets, and his elegies, dirges, *shire tiferet,* love poems, meditations, and mordant satires radiate incomparable beauty. Al-Harizi alludes to their metaphors: "He alone ascended to the highest rank in poetry, and metaphor gave birth to him on the knees of intelligence." His elegy for Ibn Isaac Hasan, *Biyeme Yequti'el asher nigmaru* (In the Days of Yequtiel), is considered one of the great triumphs of medieval secular poetry. Ibn Gabirol's philosophical writings were attacked by Ibn Daud but influenced Neoplatonists such as Moses Ibn Ezra and Joseph Ibn Zaddik; they were ultimately eclipsed by the rise of Aristotelianism. Ibn Gabirol's ideas and terminology appear in the cabala, especially in the writings of Isaac Ibn Latif. Ibn Gabirol was admired by Ibn Falaquera, who cites him in *Moreh hamoreh* (1280, Guide to the Guide), and Abraham Ibn Ezra and David Qimhi quote his allegorical interpretations in their Bible commentar-

ies. *Itslah al-'akhlaq* (circa 1045, The Improvement of Moral Qualities) treats practical morality and psychology. A Hebrew translation, *Tikkun middot hanefesh,* was done by Judah Ibn Tibbon in 1167.

A now-lost Arabic treatise, *Yanbu al-hayya* (Fountain of Life), expounded Ibn Gabirol's philosophy; it is preserved in *Fons vitae* (circa 1150, The Source of Life), a Latin translation by Johannes Hispalensis and Dominicus Gundissalinus, and in a unique manuscript, *Mekor hayyim,* which is a partial translation by Ibn Falaquera. In dialogue a master and pupil discuss concepts such as the existence of a spiritual substance that sustains corporeal form. The treatise was once attributed to a Muslim or Christian theologian named Avicebron, a corruption of "Ibn Gabirol"; Ibn Gabirol's authorship was established in the nineteenth century by Salomon Munk, who identified fragments of *Mekor hayyim* with *Fons Vitae. Sefer al hanefesh* (The Book on the Soul) and *Mibhar hapeninim* (circa 1045, Selection of Pearls) are also attributed to Ibn Gabirol; a document found in the Cairo Geniza (the storehouse of the Ben Ezra Synagogue) supports his authorship of *Mibhar hapeninim.*

Ibn Gabirol's secular poetry is largely panegyric. Poetry is portrayed erotically as a desirable girl; the speaker takes refuge in wisdom and God, contrasts himself with an uncomprehending society, complains against Time (Fate), laments worldly misery, and mourns his failure to delight in the world and in love. Some of Ibn Gabirol's nature poems probably served as panegyric preludes: the patron's largesse is likened to nature's plenitude. The winter poems *Avei shehakim* (Tempest at Dawn) and *Yeshallem hasetav nidro* (Autumn's Vow) are especially prized by critics. Ibn Gabirol's wisdom poetry depicts a devotee of knowledge preparing his soul to rejoin the Godhead on release from the illusory sublunar world of matter and the senses. Highly introspective poems address perennial themes of the transience and vanity of earthly life and the immortality of the soul. The many riddles attached to Ibn Gabirol's letters and in dialogues to relieve the monotony of identical rhyme suggest a didactic purpose.

The first *paytan* who fully incorporated Hispano-Arabic conventions into *piyyut,* Ibn Gabirol also composed in the Eastern style with its complex strophic forms. He initiated the *reshut* (prelude) genre: short, metrical monorhyme poems recited before preliminary prayers during Sabbath and festival morning services; his *reshuyot* served as models for later generations. Inclusion of his *piyyutim* in the prayer book confirms his status as religious poet of the Sephardim.

Following custom, Ibn Gabirol composed acrostic *piyyut,* most of which begin with the letter *shin.* Brief poems set the name "Solomon" once; in longer poems it is reiterated or combined with that of his father, Judah. Devotional poems blend philosophical motifs with traditional liturgical themes. Private contemplative poems are also extant. Earlier *piyyutim* petition God on behalf of the community; the Andalusian poets, particularly Ibn Gabirol, address the soul, speak of its relationship with God, or present a petitioner who humbly beseeches him for succor and compassion. Full of yearning for deliverance from exile, Ibn Gabirol's national poetry entreats God as a woman does her lover, pouring out her complaints while receiving his comfort and promises of deliverance.

Isaac Ibn Ghiyyat, jurist and head of the Lucena academy, among whose students were Moses Ibn Ezra, Joseph Ibn Sahl, and Joseph Ibn Saddiq, composed an elegy for Samuel the Nagid, "the lamp of the west," and supported the widow and son of the murdered Yehosef Ibn Nagrelᶜa. His legal decisions contain allusions to Sephardic customs in which he often follows Samuel the Nagid's *Hilkhata gavrata*. Of his Arabic Talmud commentaries, only *Kitab al-siraj* (Book of the Candle) is extant; of his Bible commentaries only a volume on Ecclesiastes is preserved. Four hundred mainly Andalusian-style *piyyutim* of Ibn Ghiyyat are also extant. Full of philosophical, cosmological, and astronomical allusions, they are considered among the best of the period; his *muwashshahat* are especially beautiful. Moses Ibn Ezra describes Ibn Ghiyyat as a brilliant teacher, jurist, and grammarian whose liturgical poetry surpasses all predecessors. Ibn Daud praises him as a Talmudist, teacher, and poet "learned in Greek wisdom." Al-Harizi finds Ibn Ghiyyat's poetry difficult.

The biography of liturgical poet and Neoplatonic philosopher Bahya ben Joseph Ibn Paquda is slight—he was a *dayyan* (judge) who was perhaps connected with the Banu Hud dynasty in Saragossa. He composed *piyyutim*, but his renown rests on *Al-hidaja 'ila faraid al-qulub* (Duties of the Hearts), a theological treatise on ethics and social criticism and one of the most original works of medieval Jewish literature in Spain. Ibn Paquda's thought is anchored by the tenet that genuine observance of the Law nurtures a love of God that overwhelms the soul. Revered by the pious, it was translated by Judah Ibn Tibbon as *Hovot halevavot* in 1161, by Joseph Qimhi around the same year, and thereafter into many languages. Its ten chapters are organized according to the soul's degree of nearness to God, a common scheme of Arabic *zuhd* literature. *Kitab maʿani al-nafs* (Attributes of the Soul), previously attributed to Ibn Paquda, has been shown not to be his work.

Levi ben Jacob Ibn Altabban's grammar book *Sefer hamafteah* (The Key), considered essential by Abraham Ibn Ezra, is no longer extant. Moses Ibn Ezra praises him as learned teacher, poet, and exegete, while al-Harizi numbers him among those who "shake out poetic phrases as one shakes out straw." Seventy *piyyutim* by Ibn Altabban, more than half of them strophic, survive. Their delicate lyricism reflects the influence of Ibn Gabirol. The poems were forgotten for centuries; many were otherwise attributed, especially to Judah Halevi. Ibn Altabban's penitential hymns lament the disasters that befell the Saragossa Jewish community after Alfonso I conquered the kingdom in 1118.

Joseph Ibn Sahl, disciple of Ibn Ghiyyat, poet, scholar, and jurist resident in Cordova from 1113 until his death around 1123, exchanged poems with Moses Ibn Ezra and Judah Halevi and wrote an elegy for Ibn Ghiyyat. Few of his poems survive. Ibn Daud emphasizes his piety. Moses Ibn Ezra considers him the jewel of his generation, noble and intelligent, a wise jurist and eloquent poet whose compositions shows abundance and sweetness, strength and fluidity, and are eminently memorable and declamatory. Al-Harizi places him at the "rear-guard of the camp of poetry. Rhetoric was born on the knees of Joseph."

The poet laureate of the Andalusian-Hebrew school, Moses Ibn Ezra fled with his family from Granada to Lucena after the murder of Yehosef Ibn Nagrelᶜa. He studied with Ibn Ghiyyat and was instructed in Arabic and Hebrew subjects, acquiring mastery of poetry and the ideas of philosophers such as Plato, Aristotle, and Plotinus. The family soon returned to Granada; there Ibn Ezra moved in the sophisticated courtier-rabbi milieu, acquiring the Arabic honorific *sahib al-shurta* (his excellency). Halevi was his lifelong friend. A consummate Arabist, he praises Arabic poetic genius in his Hebrew rhetoric.

Almoravid riots in 1090 shattered Granada's affluent Jewish community. The Ibn Ezra family fortune was confiscated, and Moses' brothers scattered to Cordova and Toledo. Moses remained in Granada with his wife and children until a threat on his life, which somehow involved his elder brother Isaac's daughter, compelled him to abandon his family in 1095; his brother Joseph supported them in his absence.

Ibn Ezra's relations with his brothers and children deteriorated, and their entreaties for his return to al-Andalus were rebuffed. Wandering among cities in Castile, Navarre, and Aragon, dependent on patrons, until his death in 1138, he was never reconciled with his family or to his fate as an exile. Poems pleading for money or bearing complaints and recriminations were sent to his brothers. In the sole poem addressed to his brother Judah he laments his separation from his children and the deaths of friends and family and decries the boorish stammerers of the North, among whom he suffers dangers and imprisonment. Bitter and alienated in a world without refinement or culture, he yearns for

Granada. His last dated poem (1138) is an elegy on the death of the mother of his friends Joseph and Isaac.

Ibn Daud describes Ibn Ezra: "R. Moses b. R. Jacob b. Ezra of the family of officials, a great scholar learned in the Torah and in Greek wisdom, and a composer of poems and hymns—he renounced [the pleasures of] this world and looked forward to the world to come—[of such quality] as to melt the heart of his hearers and fill them with awe of their Creator." His scrupulous observance of Arabic quantitative prosody motivates al-Harizi's judgment that "the poetry of Moses Ibn Ezra is more pleasing to poets than to the others because of his rhetoric and the delightful quality of his craftsmanship"; al-Harizi considers many of the poems to be perfect. A classicist, a master of *al-badi* and of traditional imagery, and a virtuoso of poetic structures common to Arabic and Hebrew verse, he revived the traditional neoclassical Arabic *qasida* structure in Hebrew. Ibn Ezra is considered the most sensual poet of the Andalusian-Hebrew school, and the hallmark of his work is intricate construction. His personal poems express an optimism that counters his bitter complaints of worldly misery. While his poetic theory and philosophy evidence his mastery of Abbasid culture, he vouchsafes the superiority of Jewish poets by virtue of their legendary origin among the Jerusalemite aristocracy.

The themes of Ibn Ezra's *Kitab zahr al-riyad* (Book of the Flowers of the Flowerbeds) and its Hebrew title *Sefer ha'anaq* (The Necklace) suggest that his model was Ibn 'Abd Rabbih's anthology *'Iqd* (Necklace). An Arabic rhymed prose introduction and a poem honoring Abraham Ibn Muhajir precede 573 two-to-four-line Arabic-style Hebrew *tajnis*, in which rhyme words are homonyms or other types of paronomasia—an *al-badi* mainstay—that survey the golden-age thematic repertoire. The first theme is the panegyric, followed by love, wine, nature, rural life, the disloyalty of friends, old age, vicissitudes, death, trust in God, and the beauty of poetry. According to Scheindlin, the work is an ideal poetic biography: "from youthful pleasure through the experience of loss to resignation and late piety."

A philosophical *adab* (summary of the knowledge that makes a man courteous and urbane) compilation, *Maqalat al-hadi qa fi ma'ni al-majaz wa al-haqiqa* (The Book of Learning; or, The Enclosed Garden in the Meaning of Metaphor and of Reality) discusses theological implications of figurative language. A section modeled on Saadya Gaon defines and examines *majaz* (figurative language) and contrasts it with *muhkam* (literal speech) and treats the unity and attributes of God, the divine names, motion, the creation of the cosmos, God's laws, nature, and the soul. An exegetical section reviews Hebrew and Arabic terminology for the human body

and explores the metaphorical nature of biblical anthropomorphism.

Late in life Ibn Ezra composed an *adab*-style Arabic treatise on Andalusian-Hebrew poetry, *Kitab al-muhadara wal-mudhakara* (after 1135, The Book of Conversation and Deliberation). Comprehensive in scope, it is the most important medieval work on the subject and an invaluable source for the literary history of the period. The introduction reviews the ideas of the Arabic literary theorists Abu'l-'Abbas 'Abd Allah Ibn al-Mu'tazz, Abu 'l-Faradi Qudama Ibn Ja'far al-Katib al-Baghdadi, the North African Abu 'Ali Hasan Ibn Rashik al-Qayrawani, and Abu 'Ali Muhammad al-Hatimi. In the body of the work Ibn Ezra, answering eight questions posed by a friend, examines the legitimacy of Andalusian-Hebrew poetry and addresses the grounds on which Hebrew poets justify composing in Arabic quantitative-meter style. Chapters 1 and 2 qualify poetry and rhetoric as branches of logic, finding poetry deficient when judged against the standard of truth. Chapter 3 attributes Bedouin poetic eloquence to geography and climate and reviews poetic divination among the nations. Geographical proximity accounts for similarities among Arabic, Hebrew, and Aramaic. Discussion of Hebrew grammar and problems of translation follows. Chapter 4 takes up biblical poetry: by Arabic standards Psalms, Job, and Proverbs qualify as mere *rajaz* (an inferior type of verse); massive loss of manuscripts accounts for the small amount of biblical poetry. Chapter 5 asserts that the superiority of Andalusian-Hebrew poetry derives from the excellence of the poets' Jerusalemite ancestry among the tribes of Judah and Benjamin. A critical review by generation is followed by biographical details about the poets. Chapter 6 copiously illustrates the ethics of poetry with examples from the author's work. A pseudo-Aristotelian aphorism, "the best poem is the most false," introduces a classification of poetry and rhetoric recalling the equations of Aristotle's *Organon:* true = demonstration; more true than false = dialectic; equally true and false = rhetoric; more false than true = speech of the sophists; false = the style of the poets, not the content of their speech. The poet's imagination is the source of poetic falsehood. Chapter 7 investigates inspiration and oneiric poems. Prophetic dreams originate in the intellect and the rational soul and come only to good people; false dreams, which originate in sense-perception and take form in the imagination and common sense, rather than in the intellect and rational soul, are experienced by everyone. The prophetic books illustrate dreams and poetry: the story of Saul exemplifies inspiration, and its interpretation underscores the association of poetry and prophecy. Just as an artisan may dream about his art, so may a poet compose in dreams. Chapter 8, "Advice on

How to Compose Hebrew Poetry According to the Canons of Arabic," takes up more than half of the treatise. The study of grammar, the sine qua non of poetic composition, is prescribed. The theory of "ornamentation" and twenty Arabic figures of speech are treated and illustrated with Arabic, Hebrew, and biblical examples that demonstrate that Scripture has no literary defect and that Arabic-style Andalusian-Hebrew poetry is legitimate. Finally, Ibn Ezra maintains that the poet's craft requires practice for its perfection.

Benzion Halper's Hebrew translation (1924) made *Kitab al-muhadara* accessible to literary historians, who came to view it as prescriptive. David Yellin treats the conspectus of rhetorical ornaments as normative. Dan Pagis compares its explicit poetics with the implicit poetics of Ibn Ezra's poems. Nehemya Allony discusses Ibn Ezra's advocacy of *al-ʿarabiyya* (Arabism). Scheindlin reads the alternating disparagement and praise of poetry as an ambivalent defense of golden-age style, underscoring the legitimacy question. Joseph Dana documents Ibn Ezra's reliance on Arabic criticism and analyzes his prescriptive poetics, erudition, and autobiography. Brann elucidates efforts by "the regenerate poet" to reconcile his loyalties to Arabic secular poetry and culture, on the one hand, and to Hebrew Scriptures and Jewish tradition, on the other hand, by a defense of Andalusian-Hebrew poets, who, as legitimate heirs to ancient Hebrew tradition, owe allegiance to Hebrew poetry.

Ibn Ezra's liturgical poems depict a contrite soul yearning for the Creator, synthesizing confessional and secular elements to create a musical aesthetic of intricate variations on rhyme and rhythm. His 200 *piyyutim* are largely strophic. Brilliant and poignant *selihot* that earned him the epithet *hasalhan* (author of penitential poems) move with great artistic variation across themes of introspection about the absurdity of life, worldly aspiration and achievement, disenchantment, divine judgment, the ruined-encampment motif, and nationalism. Though many are preserved in his *diwan,* the majority are found in prayer books.

Ibn Ezra's *diwan* contains 250 secular poems. In addition to short pieces on the themes from *Haʿanaq,* longer *qasida* poems address friends, family, and social equals. Adherence to poetic tradition dampens the personal inflection of the poet's voice, but self-expression emerges in the distinctive and plaintive exile *qasidas.* Exquisite verses on banquets and romance reveal that bitterness fails to extinguish his poetic joy. Reflective meditations on life and death, feelings on seeing a cemetery, and epigrams on worldly vanity convey profound emotional honesty and stylistic vigor, while blending aestheticism with analytical ethics. Three of Ibn Ezra's writings are known to be lost: a treatise on the excel-

lence of the men of culture and nobility, cited in *Kitab al-muhadara;* a treatise of sincere advice to innocent beginners, mentioned in the *Maqalat al-hadiqa fi maʿni al-majaz wa al-hadiqa;* and a work on the prophet Moses. Poet, theorist, literary historian, philosopher, and moralist, Ibn Ezra was a model Andalusian-Jewish intellectual.

The physician, philosopher, and poet Judah ben Samuel Halevi infused conventional Andalusian-Hebrew poetry with new meaning; inaugurated "Zionides," songs of yearning for Zion; and composed descriptions of his voyage to Egypt. A culminating figure of this period, Halevi achieved mythic stature. Moses Ibn Ezra describes him as a connoisseur of beauty, while Ibn Daud classes him among "great and saintly scholars, who have added strength to Israel with their poems and verses of consolation." Al-Harizi shares Ibn Daud's opinion: "In the poems of prayers, he draws and subdues every heart. In his love-poems his expression is as a layer of dew."

Halevi was born in Tudela under the Banu Hud dynasty around 1075. Little is known of his youth—a letter suggests that it was spent in Christian Spain—but his Arabic and Hebrew training are evident. Visiting Cordova, the precocious poet attended a literary meeting where, pressed to extemporize on a *muwashshah* pattern, he improvised a correct contrafactum. At the invitation of Moses Ibn Ezra he traveled to Granada, beginning a lifelong friendship between the two men. After the Almoravid conquest of Granada in 1090, Halevi established himself in Christian Toledo; his poetry soon brought him renown. A consummate courtier-rabbi, apparently in the service of Alfonso V, he celebrated his patron, Solomon Ibn Ferrizuel. Ibn Ferrizuel's assassination on 3 May 1108 in the Kingdom of Aragon forced Halevi to abandon a panegyric honoring Ibn Ferrizuel for an elegy cursing the "Daughter of Edom." Anti-Jewish violence in Castile prompted Halevi's return to al-Andalus in 1109. While residing in Cordova, he visited notables in Seville, Lucena, Granada, and Almería, and, accompanied by Abraham Ibn Ezra, traveled to North Africa. He composed an epitaph in 1103 for Isaac Alfasi, chief of the Talmudic academy in Lucena, and wrote letters for Alfasi's successor, Joseph Ibn Migash.

Halevi's anticipation of the Muslim empire's collapse and Israel's messianic redemption in 1130 was unfulfilled. A decade later, to the dismay of his family and friends, he embarked by ship for Palestine, arriving in Alexandria on 8 September 1140. Detained in Fustat by his host, Samuel ben Hannaniah, Halevi reentered the courtier-rabbi milieu he had rejected. A period of intense poetic activity ensued in which he composed fifty-one secular poems and four rhymed prose letters.

More than a thousand poems, considered among the most beautiful in Andalusian style, attest Halevi's profound lyricism and mastery of language and musical pattern. Revisiting traditional Arabic themes, he composed panegyrics for Moses Ibn Ezra, Abraham Ibn Ezra, Ibn Zaddik, and Ibn Ghiyyat; poems of friendship and love; wedding songs; *muwashshahat;* elegies; *shire hagalut* (poems of the Diaspora); liturgical poems; mystical love poems; and thirty-five *shire hatsion* (Poems of Zion), passionate works in praise of the Holy Land of a kind unheard since the Psalms. Messianic expectation, implied by allusions and conceits from the Song of Solomon, yearning for Zion, the painful loneliness of exile, and the sea-voyage poems are unique themes in Jewish literature of the period. *Zeman* (Time or Fate), commonly negative, becomes for him providential and redemptive.

Halevi's *Meamar ʿal hamiskalim* (Treatise on Hebrew Meters) illustrates eleven Arabic rhythmic patterns apt for Hebrew poetry but discourages direct imitation of Arabic prosody: "I recalled what was on the mind of the noble Abu's-Sa'id concerning the meters employed by the neo-Hebrew poets who do not consider the corruption of the Hebrew language. In truth, Arabized Hebrew prosody is objectionable for it corrupts the articulation of Hebrew speech." The treatise presents a contradiction that has been noted by critics: Arabic metric prosody is denounced in the course of explaining its musical appeal.

Shortly before abandoning al-Andalus, Halevi completed an apologetic treatise in Arabic: *Kitab al-radd wa-'d-dalil fi 'd-din adh-dhalil* (circa 1130–1140, The Book of Refutation and Proof on the Despised Faith). Judah Ibn Tibbon's 1167 translation bears a title Halevi mentions elsewhere: *Sefer hakuzari* (The Book of the Kuzari). A polemic against Karaism, it defends prophetic faith against Aristotelian proofs of the existence of God and expresses discontent with courtier-rabbi values. An influential formulation of national identity, it has been studied, quoted, and criticized since its first appearance. Book 1 begins as a discussion among Christian and Muslim philosophers, a Jewish sage, and a fictitious eighth-century Khazar king. The respective confessions of the participants are summarized, after which the Christian and Muslim are dismissed. In the remaining four books the Jewish sage and the Khazar king discuss God's revelation and criticize Andalusian-Hebrew poetry for debasing the sublime ancient music of Israel's language. Literary historians have variously construed Halevi's theory and poetic practice as rejection of *hokhmat yevanit* (Greek wisdom) for revealed faith, as rejection of *al-ʿarabiyya* (Arabism) and *adab* for *al-ʿibraniyya,* and as a pietist's quest for redemption.

Solomon Ibn Parhon reports that Halevi "repented before his death, [to] never compose verse again."

The date and circumstances of Halevi's death are unknown. A letter attests his embarkation for Palestine in May 1141; legend has it that on his arrival in Jerusalem, singing a Zionide, a Muslim horseman murdered him. This romantic account is given by Heinrich Heine in *Romanzero* (1851) and by Micah Joseph Lebensohn in *Rabbi Yehudah Halevi* (1869).

The distinguished physician, polymath, and superb poet Abraham Ibn Ezra was raised in al-Andalus, later resided in Toledo and Cordova, and finally lived in exile in various European cities. His friends included Ibn Tsaddik, Ibn Daud, Moses Ibn Ezra, and Halevi, with whom he visited North Africa; legend holds that he married Halevi's daughter. He alludes in his writings to five sons; only one, Isaac, is explicitly mentioned, in two poems that mourn the young man's conversion to Islam. Moses Ibn Ezra emphasizes Ibn Ezra's theological eloquence; al-Harizi characterizes his poems as "a help in trouble and like bountiful rains in a time of drought"; and Ibn Daud accords him the stature of Halevi.

Though he was an accomplished Arabist, Ibn Ezra wrote exclusively in Hebrew. A master of grammar, lexicography, and exegesis, he subscribed to Ibn Hayyuj's principles but rejected triliteralism for a system of his own devising. His translations and writings brought Andalusian-Hebrew culture into Europe. His Bible commentaries reflect vast erudition, rationalist philological method, and Neoplatonic philosophy.

Impoverished by the Almohad invasion of 1140, Ibn Ezra earned his livelihood producing treatises for the communities he visited. *Sefer moznayim* (The Book of Scales), written in Rome in 1140, is a grammar treating nomenclature and verb conjugation and surveying Andalusian philology. He translated three of Hayyuj's works: the *Kitab al-afal dhawat huruf al-lin* as *Sefer otiyyot hanuah vehameshekh,* the *Kitabal-dhawat al-mathalayn* as *Sefer poolei hakefel,* and the *Kitab al-tanqit* as *Sefer hanikkud.* In Lucca he composed now-lost biblical commentaries; a grammar, *Sefer hayesod* (Foundation); a beginning grammar, *Sefat yeter* (1145, The Preferred Language); and *Sefer hahaganah* (The Defense). An apology for Saadya Gaon written in Mantua in 1145, *Sefer Tsahot* (Book of Clarity) is a grammar book whose notes on Andalusian prosody publicized the new style in Europe. In Lucca again between 1146 and 1148, he wrote a series of books on judicial astrology—*Mispete hamazzalot* (Judgments of the Constellations), *Sefer hamoladot* (Book of Nativities), *Reshit hokhmah* (The Beginning of Wisdom), *Sefer hateʿamim* (The Book of Reasons), *Sefer hamibharim* (The Book of Selections), *Sefer haʿolam* (The Book of the World and the Conjunctions), *Sefer hameorot*

(The Book of Lights), and *Keli nehoshet* (The Treatise of the Astrolabe)–and *Sefer haʿatsamim* (Substances), a work on physics and metaphysics. In Verona he composed books on mathematics and on the calendar; *Sefer haʿib-bur* (On Conception); *Sefer mispar* (Number Book); and *Safah berurah* (Pure Language), a defense of the antiquity of Hebrew. In Béziers he composed before 1155 *Sefer hashem* (Book of the Name), a biblical commentary with philosophical reflections on the names of God; and the mathematical treatises *Sefer haehad* (The Book of One) and *Yesod hamispar* (Fundamental Number). In London he wrote a philosophical exegesis of the commandments, *Yesod mora* (1158, Fundamental Teaching), and *Iggeret shabbat* (1158, Treatise on the Sabbath), on the calendar. He moved to Narbonne in 1161. Sources variously place his death there and in Rome, Palestine, London, and Calahorra.

Social criticism, realism, sardonic humor, satire, animal allegory, and parody are hallmarks of Ibn Ezra's poetry. Poems on an old cloak and tormenting flies satirize his poverty. Others portray everyday life, beggars, gamblers, games of chance and of chess. Debate protagonists are less common: the eye, the ear, and the tongue in a *qasida,* the Sabbath and other holidays, summer and winter, people and animals, and, in four *muwashsha-hat,* a boatman and the sea. More than five hundred liturgical poems are *kerovot* (hymns) and *avodot* (services), and their most common form is the *muwashshah.* *Hai ben mekits* (The Journey of the Soul) is a rhymed prose allegory framed as a journey through mystical worlds and heavenly spheres. In search of enlightenment into the mystery of the Creation, the soul leaves home and meets a mysterious old man, the active intellect, who counsels avoidance of three companions: imagination, lust, and anger.

Solomon Ibn Parhon's dictionary, *Mahberet heʿarukh* (Lexicon), based on Ibn Janah's *Kitab al-tanqih,* was completed in Salerno in 1160. A student of Halevi and Abraham Ibn Ezra, Ibn Parhon disseminated the advances in comparative grammar made by Hayyuj and Ibn Janah among Jews in Christian Europe and the Islamic Orient.

Hebrew translations by Joseph Qimhi, his sons Moses and David, Abraham Ibn Ezra, and the Ibn Tibbons spread Andalusian science and culture among European Jews. Exiled from al-Andalus, Joseph Qimhi worked as a teacher in Narbonne. His *Sefer zikkaron* (Book of Remembrance) summarizes Hayyuj and Ibn Janah's classification of Hebrew vowels as five long and five short. *Sefer hagalui* (Open Book) addresses lexicography and exegesis through the polemic between Ibn Saruq and ben Labrat. Qimhi also translated Ibn Paquda's *Al-hidaja ʿila faraid al-qulub* as *Hovot halevavot.* *Shekel hakodesh* (The Holy Shekel) is a metric reprise of

apothegms and proverbs from *Mibhar hapeninim* (Selection of Pearls), a work attributed to Ibn Gabirol. *Sefer haberit* (Book of the Covenant), a dialogue between a Jew and an apostate, is a compilation of anti-Christian polemics that provides glimpses of life in medieval Provence.

The physician, astronomer, philosopher, and historian Ibn Daud wrote *Sefer haqabbalah* (Book of Tradition) in 1160–1161. An anti-Karaite polemic, it chronicles rabbinic tradition. *Al ʿaqida al-rafʿa* (1160–1161, The Exalted Faith) addresses free will and determinism and presents a philosophical defense of Judaism and the accord between revelation and human reason. Though he anticipated Maimonides' Aristotelianism, the latter's preeminence eclipsed Ibn Daud until the late fourteenth century.

The physician Judah Ibn Tibbon was exiled from Granada and settled in Lunel. Encouraged by Rabbi Meshullam da Piera, he translated Andalusian Jewish philosophy into Hebrew, introducing Arabic loanwords and coining Hebraicisms for philosophical terms. Successive Ibn Tibbon generations continued this translation enterprise. Judah's son Samuel translated Maimonides' *Dalalat al-ha'irin* into Hebrew as *Moreh nevukhim* in 1204 in consultation with the author. His grandson Moses made Hebrew translations of Maimonides' *Kitab al-faraʿid* as *Sefer hamitsvot* (Book of Commandments) in 1240 and of *Makalah fi-sina'at al-mantik* as *Milot hahigayon* (Treatise on Logic) in 1256. Of Judah Ibn Tibbon's original writings only a title, *Sod tsahot halashon* (Foundation of Pure Language), and *Tsawwa'ah* are extant. The latter work depicts Samuel the Nagid as the ideal courtier.

The physician, logician, jurist, and theologian Maimonides was a widely influential figure; the extraordinary scope of his work and its inestimable value for subsequent generations mark a watershed in medieval Jewish philosophy. His theological summa and original philosophical vision are characterized by Isadore Twersky as "a fastidious interpretation and thoughtful reformulation of Jewish belief and practice." Maimonides understood from an early age that his exploration of jurisprudence and philosophy would be unprecedented. Profoundly impressed by two chiefs of the Lucena rabbinic academy, Isaac Alfasi and Joseph Ibn Megas, and by his own father, Maimon, who had been a student of Ibn Megas, he proclaimed Ibn Megas his master without ever meeting the rabbi in person. Maimonides' family fled Cordova around 1148 and traveled to Almería; Provence; Fez, Morocco, around 1160; Palestine around 1165; and, finally, Fustat, Egypt, around 1166. Shortly after their arrival in Fustat, Maimonides' father died. Appointed chief of the Jews of Fustat in 1171, Maimonides was later dismissed and then restored to the post. The death at sea of his brother David around 1173 ended the family's commercial transactions with India, and Maimonides succumbed to depression.

A well-known letter written to Samuel ben Judah Ibn Tibbon portrays a contemplative philosopher harried by his duties as physician to Saladin's vizier Al-Fadil. Constant medical consultations and community responsibilities kept Maimonides in a perpetual state of exhaustion. During this period, a son, Abraham, was born. Though he had a delicate constitution, Maimonides' capacity for work was immense. His *Makalah fi-sina'at al-mantik* (Treatise on Logic, 1158) explains logic following Alfarabi; it was translated from Arabic into Hebrew by Moses Ibn Tibbon as *Milot hahigayon* (circa 1256). Other Arabic treatises address historical catastrophe, forced conversion, and faith; they were translated as *Iggeret hashemad* (circa 1161–1162, Epistle on Conversion). *Kitab al-Siraj* (1168, Commentary on the Mishnah) treats *halakha. Sheloshah 'eser 'ikkarim* (The Thirteen Principles), and *Shemone perakim* (Eight Chapters) are well-known excerpts from the *Kitab al-Siraj.* Maimonides divides speech into five classes: prescribed, cautioned against or prohibited, rejected, desired, and permitted; subject matter determines the classification. The nobility of the Hebrew language makes the recitation of a cautioned-against or rejected theme in Hebrew at a wine party or a wedding more reprehensible than that of an Arabic poem. Love lyrics in cadences, terms, phrases, and prophetic words expressing Israel's love of God and his love of Israel are similarly censured.

Iggeret Teman (1172, Epistle to Yemen) was written for Rabbi Jacob ben Nathaniel al-Fayyumi and was translated by Samuel ben Judah Ibn Tibbon around 1210. *Mishneh Torah* (1178, The Code of Maimonides), a comprehensive, authoritative codification and restatement of halakhic rules scattered among multiple sources is fundamentally significant. An introduction, *Kitab al-fara'id* (Book of the Commandments), was translated by Moses Ibn Tibbon as *Sefer hamitsvot* in 1240; Solomon ben Joseph Ibn Ayyub Garneti translated it the same year.

Maimonides' preeminent reconciliation of Aristotelian philosophy with religious faith, *Dalalat al-ha'irin* (translated as *The Guide of the Perplexed,* 1963), was written in 1190. Samuel ben Judah Ibn Tibbon translated it in 1204, as did Judah al-Harizi between 1205 and 1213; it appeared in several translations during the Renaissance. It explains biblical terms and similes and elucidates the true science of the Law, which possesses a literal public face and a hidden metaphorical aspect. Written for his student Rabbi Joseph Ibn Aknin, whose knowledge of metaphysics would allow him to detect recondite meanings, it is also intended for the uniniti-

ated, who will grasp only its literal sense. A master of grammar, lexicography, and exegesis, Maimonides devotes the first forty-five chapters to an explanation of biblical homonyms whose anthropomorphism vexed commentators. He discusses biblical terms applied to God and the angels; demonstrations of God's existence, unity, and incorporeality; prophecy; the divine chariot; providence; actions commanded by God and those done by him; and human perfection and divine providence. According to Shlomo Pines, Maimonides held that Aristotelian philosophy constituted a system for acquiring knowledge that embodied "the supreme achievements of the human intellect when geared to its highest form of activity."

Iggeret tehiyyat hametim (1191, Treatise on Resurrection) was translated by Samuel Ibn Tibbon. *Makalah fi al-Tauhid* (On the Unity of God) was translated by Isaac ben Nathan. *Makalah fi al-Sa'adah* (On Eternal Felicity) was translated anonymously as *Perakhim hahatslahah* (Fortunate Flowers). Maimonides' death in December 1204 was observed with public mourning in Jewish communities.

Al-Harizi calls Solomon Ibn Saqbel, the presumed author of *Neum Asher ben Judah* (Thus Says Asher ben Judah), the first extant Hebrew *maqama,* an expert in the art of poetry. Exceptionally among *maqamat,* Asher ben Judah narrates his own adventure, which is woven from typical motifs. Youthful years of wandering end with his return home, where friends fete the hero with three days of revelry. In the aftermath an apple inscribed with love poems leads to misadventures, and more love poems draw the hero to the beloved's chambers. Tested by her attendants, he gains entry; drawing aside her veil, he discovers the bearded visage of her father, who remonstrates the hero for his indiscretion but agrees to the couple's betrothal. It is then revealed that the whole affair was a hoax played by his friends, making the story a cautionary tale about fiction. Manuscript attributions to Abu Job ben Sahal and Solomon ibn Sahl have called Ibn Saqbel's authorship into question.

Benjamin ben Jonah of Tudela wrote *Sefer masa'ot* (circa 1173, Book of Travels), a commercial traveler's firsthand account of people and places from Spain to the Middle East that reflects thorough knowledge of trades and businesses, with secondhand reports on more-remote places. An anonymous prologue, probably by the editor, describes Benjamin as a learned rabbi versed in the Bible and the Talmud, classical history, and philosophy. Detailed descriptions of Jewish communities; relations between Christian West and Islamic East; cities and their inhabitants, defenses, climate, agriculture, and customs; and of mercantile centers, the commercial routes connecting them, and the number of days required to travel between them make *Sefer masa'ot* an irreplaceable primary source on the twelfth-century Mediterranean world.

Departing from Tudela for Saragossa, Benjamin descends the Ebro through Tortosa, Tarragona, Barcelona, and Gerona to Marseille. There he embarks for Genoa, Lucca, Pisa, and Rome, traveling along the coast to Salerno and then crossing to the Adriatic. From Otranto he makes for Corfu and journeys by land to Patros, Tebas, Salonica, and Constantinople. After touring the Aegean Islands, including Rhodes, and visiting Cyprus, he arrives in Curicus. He then follows the Turkish-Syrian coast to Jerusalem, Damascus, and Aleppo, heads east to Mosul, and travels down the Tigris River valley to Baghdad. Ceylon and China are mentioned, but it is unlikely that he reached them. From Basra he returns to Spain, presumably by ship, traveling around the Arabian peninsula and through Helwan, Fayyum, Cairo, Alexandria, Mesina, and Rome. Jewish communities in Germany, Prague, and Russia are mentioned, and the account ends with allusions to communities in France. Though his date of departure is unknown, the prologue mentions the Hebrew year 4933 (1172/1173) as the time of his return. The journey could have taken as few as five and as many as fourteen years to complete.

Joseph ben Meir Ibn Zabarra practiced medicine in Barcelona. *Sefer sha°ashuim* (circa 1200, The Book of Amusements), a pseudo-autobiography of his adventures in al-Andalus and Provence, is dedicated to Sheshet Ben Isaac Benveniste, physician and adviser to King Alfonso II of Aragon. Framed as a dream vision, thirteen *maqamat* relate the main tale. The physician-protagonist Joseph encounters the giant demon Enan Natash, who persuades him to abandon home for a place where his unappreciated learning will be acclaimed. In continuous debate, the pair journey to Enan's home. Their adventures occasion discussion of proper moral and ethical conduct. Tales, parables, and witticisms drawn from Arabic, Greek, Hebrew, and Indian sources relate contemporary medicine, natural science, and psychology. In a surprise climax, the demon metamorphoses into a domestic angel. A eulogy for Sheshet Ben Isaac Benveniste closes the work.

Ibn Zabara also composed a didactic poem, *Battei hanefesh* (The Seats of the Soul), describing human anatomy and the functions of the organs, and *Marot hasheten* (Epistle Dedicatory). *Ofan* (The Wheel), a poem on angelology, is attributed to him. Al-Harizi classifies him among the third tier of poets. In 1904 Israel Davidson edited three prose satires attributed to Ibn Zabara, but of dubious authorship, as *Shelosh halatsot* (Three Satires).

Judah ben Isaac Ibn Shabbetai, a physician and poet who lived in Toledo, Burgos, and Saragossa, wrote *Minhat Yehudah sone hanashim* (The Gift of Judah the

Misogynist), a satirical romance dedicated to Abraham Ibn Alfakhar, courtier-poet in the court of the Castilian king Alfonso VIII. An unreliable narrator relates in rhymed prose and intercalated poems a parody of misogyny. Though the influence of the medieval romances is patent, biblical style and *shibbuts* (quotation of a Bible pericope) mark ironic twists in the narrative structure. Appreciation of the subtleties of narrative requires thorough knowledge of Scripture. A poetic rejoinder, *Ezrat nashim* (1210, The Help of Women), dedicated to Todros ben Jospeh Halevi Abulafia of Burgos and written by a youth known only as Isaac, started a polemic that lasted into the sixteenth century.

Milhemet hahokhmah veha°osher (1214, Dialogue between Wisdom and Wealth), a second satire by Ibn Shabbetai, recounts a debate between the twins Peleg and Joktan on the relative merits of wisdom and wealth. They bring the case before Todros ben Joseph, who declares that wisdom and wealth must cooperate, for both are pillars of society. Finally, *Divre haalah vehaniddui* (The Curse and the Ban) is a caustic denunciation of five prominent Saragossans who persecuted Ibn Shabbetai.

Born in Toledo, the poet and translator Judah ben Solomon al-Harizi served patrons in northern Spain and Provence. He lived in Baghdad, Toledo, and Provence and journeyed to Palestine. He saw himself as a champion of Hebrew and his compositions as models of eloquence for other poets. Between 1205 and 1213 he translated Maimonides' *Dalalat al-ha'irin* as *Moreh nevukhim;* it is more accomplished as literature but less accurate than the Judah Ibn Tibbon version. He also translated Maimonides' *Hakdamot leperush hamishna* (Introduction to the Mishnah), *Iggeret tehiyyat hametim* (Epistle on the Resurrection), and commentary on the *Mishna demai* (Doubtful), which addresses cases in which it is not certain whether the offering of fruit has been given to the priests. Other works he translated include °Ali Ibn Rudwan's *Igeret °ali haeshmeeli* (Epistle on Morals); Hunain Ibn Ishaq's *Adab al-falasifa* (The Book of the Philosopher's Morals); Galen's *Dialogue on the Soul;* and Moses Ibn Ezra's *Maqalat al-hadiqa fi ma°na al-majaz wa al-haqiqa,* which was influential among early cabalists and a fragment of which, known as °*Arugat habosem* (Perfumed Garden), is extant.

Fifty *maqamat* of Abu Muhammad al-Qasim al-Hariri of Basra were translated by the author as *Mahberot 'Itiel* (circa 1205–circa 1215, The Compositions of Itiel); a unique Oxford manuscript preserves twenty-six of the translated *maqamat.* After 1216 al-Hariri traveled to Egypt, Palestine, and Syria, where he was supported by wealthy patrons and composed an Arabic *maqama* about his journey.

Fifty original Hebrew *maqamat,* titled *Tahkemoni,* written after 1216, constitute a major development in post-classical literature. Considered the finest "pure-genre" Hebrew *maqamat,* they are often cited as salient examples of Arabic influence on golden-age literature; Rina Drory, however, argues to the contrary that *Tahkemoni* constitutes a renewal of Hebrew literature by promoting a new literary paradigm. The dedications to Shemuel ben al-Barquli, a noble of Damascus; Yoshiyau ben Yisahai, the exilarch (prince of the exiles, a position of honor recognized by the state) of Baghdad; and Sadid al-Dawla Abd al-Qadir of Aleppo and his son Abu Nasr underscore Hariri's objective of showcasing the expressive beauty of Hebrew. The author claims originality: "I composed this book with new poems, hallowed by the Holy Tongue, with new themes which will revive souls and refresh the dry bones." He cautions the reader is against the deceits of fiction: "All that I have mentioned in their name never was and never happened, it is only fiction." The fifty independent episodes afford a fictional panorama of al-Harizi's world. The two recurrent characters are the narrator, Heman the Ezrahite, and his friend Heber the Kenite, a wandering scholar, poet, and amiable boastful rogue who beguiles one and all. Incidental characters include girls, women, peasants, hunters, soldiers, merchants, swindlers, and physicians. The stories concern amorous intrigues, journeys, battles, an ant and a flea, the months of the year, an unhappy marriage, praise for a fine letter, miserliness and generosity, a poetic contest, the seven virtues, seven virgins, a hunt, a storm-tossed ship, the pen and the sword, a man and a woman, and praise for city life. In the second *maqama* a youth who asserts the superiority of Arabic receives the author's response that Hebrew is foremost but, forsaken, has no audience. Challenged to demonstrate the incomparability of Hebrew, the youth reveals himself to be Heber the Kenite. *Maqama* 3 is an *ars poetica,* and *maqama* 18 presents a panorama of Andalusian-Hebrew poetry and an appraisal of its poets. Al-Harizi expounds his poetic principles: simple words, euphony, and strict meter and grammar, and polished verse are to be preferred; writers should be slow to publish and ruthless with weak constructions: of fifty verses they should discard twenty, and of seventy they should leave forty.

Like Moses Ibn Ezra, Harizi wrote a book titled *Ha'anaq;* Harizi's version comprises 257 strophes of *tajnis.* He also composed a panegyric for Samuel ben Nissim of Aleppo, a *muwashshah* in honor of the exilarch David of Mosul, ten *qasidas* on philosophical questions, and poems in Arabic. A treatise on astrology, *Sefer mazzalot shel adam* (Book of Humanity's Stars), and an Arabic version of the Book of Esther are attributed to him.

Mishle Sendebar (Tales of Sendebar), an anonymous collection of popular stories, illustrates the metamorphosis of Eastern tales into medieval romances. Though the narrative form derives from Indian animal-tale collections, biblical stories and scriptural allusions give the fables a Jewish character. The frame narrative on feminine guile and wickedness is also found in the Eastern version, *The Book of Sindibad,* and the Western version, *The Seven Sages of Rome.* The Hebrew version, considered crucial in the collection's westward drift, is related to the Old Spanish *Libro de los engaños e los asayamientos de las mugeres* (circa 1253, Book of the Deceptions and Wiles of Women). A late-fourteenth- or early-fifteenth-century Latin translation exists.

In the frame story Bibor, a childless king with many wives, is finally blessed with a son; but the boy is stubborn and refuses to study. The king charges the sage Sendebar (Sindibad) with educating the prince in six months; if he fails, he will forfeit his life, and his heirs' property will be confiscated. When the deadline looms, Sendebar divines that the prince is in mortal danger and must keep silent for seven days. The king orders one of his wives to make the boy speak. Rebuffed, she makes false accusations against the prince, and his father sentences him to be executed one week hence. Each day one of the king's advisers tells one or more tales of feminine wile, concluding each with an appeal for clemency for the prince and a warning about women's deceitful natures; the queen counters with stories of evil sons and insists that the sentence be carried out. After seven days, the narratives reveal her treachery, and the prince's sentence is annulled. In all other versions the queen is punished; but in *Mishle Sendebar* the Talmudic Golden Rule is invoked, and she is freed.

Meshulam ben Solomon Da Piera, also known as En Vidas de Gerona, was a notable in the community of Gerona, a center of cabala and antirationalism. During his lifetime Andalusian convention shed some elements and acquired others associated with the troubadours, while retaining its quantitative metric prosody. Da Piera's poetry articulates a pietism that is opposed to Andalusian rationalism. His novel lexicon incorporates Talmudic, midrashic, and medieval vocabulary and excludes the pure biblical idiom. Metaphor is replaced by new ideas, images, characters, and phraseology, and sequential organization gives way to abrupt conceptual transitions and unusual syntactic connections; anadiplosis, reminiscent of Provençal *leixapren,* is typical. Humor, satire, irony, realism, description, mention of place, mannerism, and the bucolic are found in many of his poems. Innovation notwithstanding, da Piera's poetry continues in service to polemics: a member of the pietist circle around the poet and exegete

Moses ben Nahman, da Piera fired poetic salvos against Maimonides. An enemy of courtier rationalism, he endowed Andalusian genres, motifs, and poetics with a new religious sensibility. Da Piera's "satiric persona," the confessed liar-poet through whom he speaks, gives rise to a complex poetic ethic and nuance that contrasts with more-conventional voices from the Andalusian school.

Poet, translator, philosopher, and physician Shem Tov ben Joseph Ibn Falaquera resided in Tudela and possibly also in Provence. A prolific writer whose philosophical treatises manifest an open-minded pursuit of truth, he mainly adheres to Maimonidean tenets but accepts astrology and Neoplatonism. He was renowned for a philosophical commentary on Maimonides' *Dalalat al-ha'irin* and an epitome of Ibn Gabirol's *Mekor hayyim* that reflect a struggle for the intellectual perfection and enlightenment required for salvation. His rhymed prose works disseminate science and philosophy in which he marshals scientific terminology that differs from that of the Ibn Tibbons. He claims authorship of more than twenty thousand verses, of which only seventy-seven are extant; he renounced love poetry in middle age.

Ibn Falaquera's medical writings underscore the psychological aspects of bodily disorders. The mnemonic verses of *Battei hanhagat haguf habari* (Verses on the Regimen of the Healthy Body) and *Battei hanhagat hanefesh* (Verses on the Regimen of the Soul) address diet and ethics, respectively. *Iggeret hamusar* (Treatise on Ethics) recounts, in rhymed prose, the story of a peripatetic youth in search of wisdom. A compilation of Arabic and Jewish aphorisms systematizing norms of conduct, it is a model for his later *Sefer hamevaqqesh*. *Tseri hayagon* (Book of the Seeker. Balm for Sorrow), a *maqama*, shows how true faith, self-discipline, and philosophy bring consolation. *Megilat hazikkaron* (Scroll of remembrance), a discussion of historical and contemporary events, is lost. A popular rhymed-prose dialogue between a Talmudist and a philosopher, *Iggeret havikkuah* (Treatise of the Disputation), reconciles science and faith, underlining the value of philosophy and science for true piety. *Reshit hokhmah* (The Beginning of Wisdom), an encyclopedic review of language, logic, mathematics, physics, metaphysics, and jurisprudence argues that philosophical reflection perfects the intellect and is necessary to achieve true happiness. This idea is continued in *Sefer hama'alot* (Book of Degrees), which identifies three degrees of intellectual perfection: divine, possessed by true prophets (superior); spiritual, characteristic of true philosophers who reason to knowledge (medial); and corporeal, a servant to the body's desires (inferior). Its purpose is twofold: a systematic account of ethics based on psychology, and the harmonization

of reason and faith. It is thought that the fifteenth-century Italian humanist Giovanni Pico della Mirandola studied this text.

Ibn Falaquera returns to questions examined by *Reshit hokhmah* in *Sefer hamevaqqesh*. The autobiographical introduction represents him as a repentant poet who serves his muse a writ of divorce: "I resolved to give up the love poetry of the knights, to reject the songs of the troubadours and minstrels who wander about in the wilderness of desire, for all this is mere vanity and derision." In this rhymed-prose book of conduct with intercalated poems a young peripatetic seeker after truth interviews men of various classes and professions about the liberal arts. The trivium (grammar, rhetoric, and logic) is reviewed in conversations with a wealthy man, a soldier, an artisan, a physician, a pietist, a Hebrew grammarian, and a poet. Each interviewee advocates propositions formulated in verse, aphorism, or tale and defends his art against the seeker's probing until a question is posed that cannot be answered. The second section, in prose, examines the quadrivium (arithmetic, geometry, music, and astronomy) by relating the seeker's studies with a pious Jew, a Torah scholar, a mathematician, an optician, an astrologer, a musician, a logician, a natural scientist, and a philosopher. The reader is warned to separate the form of the work from its content: "For it is like fruit which partly consists of inedible matter; the wise man eats the tasty sections and casts away the worthless peel." Brann sees the work as the confrontation of Ibn Falaquera the philosopher with Ibn Falaquera the poet: it is a rhetorical dialogue meant to free the imagination from mendacious poetry so that it may occupy itself with the truth of philosophy.

De'ot hapilosofim (Opinions of the Philosophers), Ibn Falaquera's most important study of philosophy, was composed to distinguish demonstrated from presumptive opinion in metaphysics and to replace defective Hebrew translations of Arabic writings with his accurate ones. The first seven chapters examine general principles of physics, generation and corruption of elements, minerals, plants, the bodies of animals, the faculties of animals, and the celestial spheres. The final three chapters discuss the opinions of ancient philosophers regarding the active intellect, secondary principles, and God.

Sefer hanefesh (Book of the Soul), a textbook on "the science of the soul" drawn from the *Treatise on Psychology* of Ibn Sina (Avicenna) and the *Middle Commentary* on Aristotle's *De Anima* (On the Soul) by Ibn Rushd (Averroës), examines the existence, definition, and faculties of the soul; the five senses and the common sense; the imagination; the rational and theoretical faculties; memory; appetite; the ancients' opinions; and the active intellect. A sequel, *Shelemut hama'asim* (The

Perfection of Actions), includes ethical sayings, proverbs, and parables from Hunain ibn Ishaq's *Adab al-falasifah* on asceticism, humility, and wisdom, as well as a quotation from Pythagoras. *Iggeret hahalom* (Treatise of the Dream) addresses ethics, physical and spiritual well-being, truth in speech and deed, and speculative truth. *Sefer haderash* (Book of Interpretation), seemingly a commentary on *aggada* (Talmudic legends), is not known to be extant. Other writings offer rationalist allegorical interpretations of biblical verses.

Ibn Falaquera's *Moreh hamoreh,* a commentary on Maimonides' *Dalalat al-ha'irin,* is an obligatory reference for subsequent commentators. *Likkutim misefer mekor hayyim* (Selections from the Book *Fons Vitae*) is a translation of Ibn Gabirol's *Fons Vitae. Likkutim misefer haʿatsamim hahamishah* (Selections from the Book of the Five Substances) translates unidentified Arabic Neoplatonic writings. *Mikhtav al devar hamoreh* (1290, Letter Concerning the Guide), Ibn Falaquera's last extant title, denounces a call for the condemnation of Maimonides' *Dalalat al-ha'irin,* underscoring the antirationalists' ignorance of Arabic philosophy and the inadequate translations of the *Dalalat al-ha'irin.*

Isaac ben Solomon Ibn Sahula, physician, poet, scholar, a disciple of the cabalist Moses of Burgos, and colleague of Moses de Leon, resided in Guadalajara and traveled widely in the practice of medicine. His *Meshal hakadmoni* (1281, Proverb of the Ancient One) is a rhymed-prose handbook of virtues and a compendium of popular science and folktales that exemplifies medieval wisdom literature, instruction, and entertainment: "Secular parables hung outside you will find, but wisdom within and hidden signs." Though *Meshal hakadmoni* is patterned on such works as *Calila and Dimna* and *Voyages of Sindbad the Sailor,* Ibn Sahula censures their seductive qualities and asserts his originality: "I will now create something new. I will take these fables, parables and tales . . . and will wrap them . . . with the words of our Torah, with the divine parables of our prophets, and with the wise riddles and allusions of our Talmudic sages." Some manuscripts and all early editions of the work bear miniatures accompanied by rhymed-couplet legends: "*Proverb of the Ancient One* should please the children also and be loved by them," the author says. A poet consumed by repentance encounters Goliath and four assistants, who endeavor to pervert his piety. In each of the five chapters one of these devil's advocates narrates a complex tale condemning a virtue—wisdom, repentance, good counsel, humility, and fear of God—and praising its corresponding vice; the poet responds with a fable in which a bird or other animal who is an expert in ethics and rabbinic jurisprudence cites the Bible and the Talmud and tells tales of men and women that deride the vice treated in

the devil's advocate's tale. *Meshal hakadmoni* circulated widely in the Middle Ages; it was first printed by Gerson Soncino in Brescia around 1491 and was reprinted many times. A splendid Venetian edition (circa 1547–1549) includes seventy-nine woodcut illustrations.

Todros ben Judah Halevi Abulafia was a dissolute libertine whose knowledge of Arabic culture brought him fame and wealth, then imprisonment and rehabilitation in the court of King Alfonso X *el Sabio* (the Learned) of Castile and León, on whom Halevi Abulafia bestowed a drinking cup engraved with a Hebrew poem. A notorious womanizer, he was excommunicated by religious authorities for maintaining relations with gentile women. Imprisoned in 1281, he wrote confessional poems denouncing profligacy. After being freed, he visited Rabbi Solomon ibn Adret and Rabbi Aaron Halevi in Barcelona and composed devotional poems. His repentance was short-lived, and he returned to the court of Sancho IV before 1289.

Halevi Abulafia's *diwan, Gan hameshalim vehahidot* (The Garden of Parables and Riddles), preserves some 1,100 intensely personal and conventional poems: "I use traditional images. . . . My only aim is to tell my own life and fate." The *diwan* abounds with panegyrics to rich and powerful Jewish viziers and poems honoring Alfonso X, Sancho IV, and Prince Enrique. Virtuoso acrostics dedicated to Isaac ben Solomon ibn Tsadoq reprise the Andalusian theme of the patron beloved for his beauty. More varied in theme and form than its Andalusian Hebrew counterpart, thirteenth-century Jewish secular poetry in Christian Spain acquired elements from the troubadour aesthetic: dates and places, portraits of everyday things, a prison cell, a chess game, and details of love affairs to enhance verisimilitude. Halevi Abulafia's scabrous justification of his preference for Arab over Christian girls as lovers exemplifies the trend. His proclamation of spiritual love for a woman is also an innovation. Halevi Abulafia's obscene and insulting debate with his fellow poet Phineas ben Joseph Halevi suggests the influence of the Provençal *tensó,* in which two rivals attack each other with crass obscenity in alternating strophes; Arabic literature features complaints against Destiny and mocking of personal, political or military enemies and of the ignorant, the arrogant, and the envious but rarely countenances personal insult, mention of physical defects, or cruel and obscene language. Halevi Abulafia deftly deploys the ironic, irreverent, and evasive *tawriya* (double entendre) in his poems.

Abraham ben Samuel Halevi Ibn Hasdai, poet, translator, and Maimonidean rationalist, wrote a defense of David Qimhi, who was attacked for supporting rationalism; entreaties to Judah Ibn Alfakhar and Meir Halevi Abulafia to retract their opposition to Maimonides' *Dalalat al-ha'irin,* and, with his brother Judah, a letter to the Jews of Aragon, Navarre, Castile, and

León denouncing Maimonides' detractors. His translations from Arabic include *Sefer hatappuah* (The Book of the Apple) from *De pomo,* attributed to Aristotle; *Moznei tsedek* (circa 1235–1240, Scales of Justice), from *Mizan al-ʿamal* (Ethics), by al-Ghazzali; *Sefer hayesodot* (The Book of the Elements), from Isaac Israeli's *Elements;* and Maimonides' *Kitab al-faraʿid* as *Sefer hamitsvot.*

Ben hamelekh vehanazir (The Prince and the Dervish) is Ibn Hasdai's translation and adaptation of *Bilwahar wa-Yudasaf,* a version of the *Barlaam and Josaphat* story of the Buddha's youth. A young prince is sheltered from worldly sorrow and death by his father, who raises him on an island. A hermit visits and reveals that this world of desires is an ephemeral dream and that life is a narrow, contemptible prison whose sole purpose is purification of the soul and service to God. Death alone is praiseworthy, for it leads to eternal life. The hermit's homilies are woven from parables, stories, legends, and proverbs, especially *aggada* and Indian-Arabic sources. Except for a prose discussion of the soul, the exempla are in *maqama* style. The central theme is love's purifying potential, and love poems are intercalated throughout the narrative. The eighteenth *maqama* portrays a youth in love and celebrates feminine beauty. Love personified delivers a soliloquy whose elegiac sorrow is characteristic of Ibn Hasdai's lyric sensibility. The hermit urges the prince to forego worldly desire and meditate on God; the boy dismisses the hermit but, deeply moved, resolves to reflect on God and become a prophet of his word. The work achieved great popularity and was widely translated.

The Toledan poet, grammarian, and philosopher Jacob ben Elazar wrote *Kitab al-kamil* (The Complete Book). Known from citations by other grammarians, such as David Qimhi in his *Mikhlol* (Comprehensive [Tract]), it apparently consisted of an exhaustive grammar and lexicon; extant folios of the original were edited by Allony (1977). A master of *shibbuts,* ben Elazar adapted into rhymed prose an Arabic version of the ancient Indian story *Calila and Dimna* at the behest of Benveniste ben Hiyya Aldian. Prefatory poems and the introduction describe it as the law book of the ancient Indians and as containing fables and parables that conceal profound wisdom. *Sefer pardes rimmone hahokmah va-arugat bosem hamezimmah* (Book of the Paradise of the Pomegranates of Science and Bench of Delicious Aromas) comprises twenty-three chapters of philosophy in verse and prose.

Ben Elazar's most important work, *Sefer hameshalim* (circa 1233, The Book of Rhetorical Narratives), comprises ten *maqamat* on themes of love, debate, and adventure. The introduction offers an apology for Hebrew and a polemic against advocates of using Arabic instead of Hebrew; the author endeavors to rehabilitate the holy tongue and reveal its beauty. The *maqamat* are narrated by Lemuel ben Itiel, from the village of Qabtseel. The first *maqama* is an allegory in which the protagonists are the narrator, the soul, and the heart: Lemuel proclaims his desire to know wisdom, and to satisfy him the soul recites a poem on wisdom's origins. A debate on the virtues of poetry and prose is featured in the second *maqama;* the assembly finally pronounces itself in favor of poetry, and the defender of prose leaves in protest. *Maqama* 3 is a poetic competition in which one contestant recites a poem containing five comparisons in one verse; the other fits six comparisons into one verse, improvises a second poem in the same genre, and concludes with a verse containing seven comparisons. *Maqama* 4 is an allegory in which an eloquent prophet conjures two contestants: one has a sword, the other has a reed pen, and each argues for his instrument's virtues. The controversy is resolved when the sword bearer admits that both instruments are subordinate to God. The pen recites a philosophical poem about God and a dissertation on philosophical terminology. *Maqama* 5 is the tale of handsome Sappir, his beloved Shappir, and the villainous seductress Birsha; whether they are humans or animals is unclear. Unable to tell Shappir of his passion for her, Sappir is lured away by Birsha. Awaking to find Sappir gone, Shappir enlists a friend to search for him. They find him at a spring; Sappir's love is rekindled, and Birsha is reproved and taken prisoner. The unscrupulous Aryok adjudicates; Birsha deceives him by claiming that Sappir is her only son, and Sappir must summon all his wits to undo the fraud. Aryok condemns Birsha to death.

In *maqama* 6 Prince Maskil, an extraordinarily handsome youth, encounters the beautiful Penina and takes her to a natural paradise. Their idyll is undone by the arrival of Kushan Rishatayim, a giant black knight, who demands Penina or battle. Volleys of *shire tiferet* poems of self-exaltation and denigration of the opponent leave Maskil exhausted, but Penina inspires him to continue. Combat is joined, and weapons are destroyed and replaced until Kushan Rishatayim succumbs. The way is now clear for Maskil and Penina to marry.

In *maqama* 7 worldly injustice persuades Yashefe that a dissolute life is best. With a band of vagabonds he travels to Egypt, where he finds Yefefiyya and is transformed. Suddenly and mysteriously wealthy, he purchases Yefefiyya, a palace, and all manner of luxuries. Beautiful Yemima, who was encountered en route to Cairo, steals into Yashefe's palace under cover of night and discovers him with Yefefiyya. Yemima kidnaps Yashefe and escapes on horseback. At her encampment Yemima is challenged by a warrior, who is actually Yefefiyya in disguise. A passive spectator of the struggle, Yashefe is astonished when Yefefiyya is disarmed and her disguise falls away. Taking up the vanquished Yefefiyya's arms, Yashefe rages against Yemima, but a lyric reconciliation follows. Masos, the palace administrator, arrives. Recognizing Yemima's virtues, Yashefe determines to keep both her and Yefefiyya. Masos weds Yashefe's sister.

In the eighth *maqama* Lemuel comes to a village of cheats and villains. Presiding at an outdoor assembly, Akhbor, a venerable cheat, exhorts his audience to piety with tales of generosity, while his two servants collect donations. Intrigued, the narrator follows the old man and discovers that the pious fraud lives in a sumptuous palace where he is serenaded by four beautiful maidservants with erotic wine songs. Having feasted, the hypocrite retires to his room followed by a slave girl. Lemuel emerges from his hiding place and enlists four servants to rebuke the old man by pitilessly tugging at his beard.

In *maqama* 9 the handsome Sahar, offended by his father, leaves home. He embarks at Jaffa, but the ship sinks in a storm. Miraculously saved, he swims, lashed to a board, to land at the village of Alep. Sahar passes near the harem where Kima, the king's daughter, resides, and all the women rush to glimpse his extraordinary beauty. Kima throws him an apple inscribed with a love poem. Sahar attempts to visit her, but a eunuch drives Kima to her room. Kima sends him proof of her love, Sahar gains entrance to the palace, and the lovers marry. Kima announces that henceforth their love is to be platonic. Sahar accepts her decision and amuses himself in the palace, whose floors and walls are transparent glass. The return of Kima's father, who opposes Sahar, interrupts the couple's pleasure. He eventually consents to their marriage, and on his death, they ascend the throne.

In the final *maqama* Lemuel snatches a wolf cub from its den and carries it away. In the village of Qedesh in the Galilee, Lemuel adopts an orphan who is ignorant even of his own name. After a time, the narrator delegates management of the house to the youth and of the garden to the wolf; both disappoint him. Four sages exhort the narrator to avoid scoundrels; but seeing nothing virtuous in the sages, he ignores their advice. Disenchanted, he recites poems on the world's wickedness.

Among those who first rediscovered Andalusian-Hebrew literature was Shabbetai Bass, who completed *Sifte yeshenim* (1680, The Lips of the Sleeping) after five years of research in Amsterdam. A model of brevity and accuracy, this first Jewish bibliography of Hebraica enumerates 2,200 titles and attempts a classification of Jewish literature that emphasizes method and system. Johann Christoph Wolf's *Bibliotheca Hebrea* (1715–1733) is based chiefly on *Sifte yeshenim*. Wolf Heidenheim produced a nine-volume edition of the German *Mahzor*

(1800, High Holy Days Prayer Book) with a critical text, German translation, and a Hebrew commentary that is essential for students of *piyyut*. He also edited Abraham Ibn Ezra's *Moznayim* with a commentary in 1791. Solomon Judah Rapoport's dual biography of Saadya Gaon and the great *paytan* Rabbi Eleazar Kalir (1829–1830) is a cornerstone in the literary study of synagogue poetry. Rapoport characterizes Sephardic liturgical poetry as communication between the soul and its Maker and that of the Ashkenazim as communication between Israel and its God; the distinction elicited attacks and defenses.

The advent of *Haskalah* (The Jewish Enlightenment), Reform Judaism, and the *Wissenschaft des Judentums* (Science of Judaism) in nineteenth-century Europe marked the restoration of Andalusian Jewry's literary and cultural legacy. Proponents of *Haskalah* valued rationalism, individualism, and cosmopolitanism and saw in medieval Jewish philosophy and poetry a secular and egalitarian cultural model whose intellectuals pursued knowledge and beauty and spoke to the universalist and nationalist themes underlying their aspirations for emancipation. Not all nineteenth-century scholars who recovered medieval Andalusian-Hebrew poetry, philology, and philosophy supported the *Haskalah* agenda, however. The *Literaturblatt des Orients* (Literary Papers of the Orient), a supplement to the weekly *Der Orient* (The Orient) founded by Julius Fürst in Leipzig in 1840, published many texts by, and studies of, medieval Sephardic authors. German translations and paraphrases of works by Bahya Ibn Paquda (1836), Maimonides (1838, 1839), Joseph Albo (1844), Saadya Gaon (1845), and Judah Halevi (1853) brought Sephardic ethics and philosophy to a wider public.

Leopold Zunz undertook a study of *piyyut* "to justify reforms in the Synagogue." His exhaustive review aspired to incorporate a purportedly continuous tradition into the modern liturgy and account for differences in the same few fundamental prayers that bind all the communities. The fruits of his labor are *Die synagogale Poesie des Mittelalters* (1855–1859, Synagogue Poetry of the Middle Ages) and *Literaturgeschichte des synagogalen Poesie* (1865, Literary History of Synagogue Poetry).

Samuel David Luzzatto, a poet, philologist, commentator, professor at Padua, and one of the greatest scholars of the day, was an opponent of philosophical Judaism who faulted Maimonides' adherence to Aristotelianism. Luzzatto undertook the task of deciphering and scientifically editing relevant manuscripts. His wide correspondence, generosity, and incomparable knowledge increased his influence with peers far beyond his publications. His mastery of Sephardic liturgical poetry underpinned his rebuke of Rapoport's generalizations. He sent examples of "national songs" to Michael Sachs, who omitted them from his *Die religiöse Poesie der Juden in Spanien* (1845, The Religious Poetry of the Jews in Sapin); edited Judah Halevi's *Diwan* (1864); compiled an onomasticon that lists 642 liturgical poets and 4,077 compositions; and oversaw publication of the Roman *Mahzor* (1856).

To Salomon Munk, devotee of medieval Judeo-Arabic literature who went blind cataloguing the Sanskrit and Hebrew manuscripts in the Bibliothèque Nationale, belong two signal achievements: identification of Ibn Gabirol as the author of *Mekor Hayim* in 1846 and publication of the Arabic original of Maimonides' *Dalalat al-ha'irin* with a French translation (1856–1866).

Sachs, a philologist, translator, and Rabbi of Prague, edited *Die religiöse Poesie der Juden in Spanien*. A superb German version of Ibn Gabirol's *Keter malkhut* precedes translations of a dozen Andalusian-Hebrew poets' songs, which are followed by detailed studies and the original poems. In this work Heinrich Heine became acquainted with Judah Halevi, whom he then introduced to the world at large.

In his *Zur Kenntnis der neuhebräischen religiösen Poesie* (1842, Toward an Understanding of neo-Hebraic Religious Poetry) Leopold Dukes justifies the substitution of Sephardic *piyyut* for the entire Ashkenazi liturgy. Dukes wandered the great European public libraries rescuing literary and cultural treasures from oblivion.

Abraham Geiger was a key proponent of Reform Judaism and promoter of the Science of Judaism. He published a history of medieval Jewish literature (1847); a monograph on Maimonides (1850); articles on the Qimhis; *Tsitsim uferahim* (1856, Buds and Flowers), a biography of Judah Halevi with a metrical German translation of some of his poems; and *Salomo Gabirol und reine Dichtungen* (1867, Solomon Ibn Gabirol and Pure Poetry).

Franz Delitzsch, a Lutheran academic and the nineteenth century's foremost Christian Hebraist, traced an unbroken poetic tradition from the close of the scriptural canon to the *Haskalah* in *Zur Geschichte der jüdischen Poesie* (1836, On the History of Jewish Poetry). His periodization of Andalusian-Hebrew literature into "the golden age" of 940 to 1040, "the silver age" of 1040 to 1140, and "the age of roses among the thorns," 1140 to 1240, though now recognized as misleading, stood for years.

Saul Isaac Kaempf, who succeeded Sachs as rabbi of Prague in 1846, published a German translation of al-Harizi's *Tahkemoni* as *Die Ersten Makamen aus dem Tachkemoni, oder Divan des Charisi* (1845, The First *Maqama* of the *Tahkemoni;* or The *Diwan* of al-Harizi) and *Nichtandalusische Poesie andalusischer Dichter aus dem elften, zwölften und dreizehnten Jahrhundert* (1858, Non-Andalusian-Language Poetry Written by Andalusian Poets from the Eleventh, Twelfth, and Thirteenth Century).

The mathematician, linguist, and editor Herschell Filipowski published two important Andalusian-Hebrew grammars: *Mahberet Menahem* (1854, Menahem's Notebook) and *Teshuvot Dunash ben Labrat* (1855, Responses of Dunash ben Labrat). Senior Sachs, who later became Baron David Günzberg's private librarian, was keenly interested in philosophy, mysticism, and poetry and published twenty-nine poems with commentary in *Shirei hashirim asher lishelomo ibn gabirol* (1868, The Poems of Solomon Ibn Gabirol).

Moritz Steinschneider, who attended Franz Bopp's lectures on comparative philology and the history of oriental literatures in Berlin, was a cultural historian of the *Wissenschaft* movement. His encyclopedia essay "Jüdische Literatur" (1850, Jewish Literature) offered the first systematic survey of Jewish literature. He also published the first catalogues of Hebrew books and manuscripts in European public libraries and edited twenty-one volumes of the periodical *Hebräische Bibliographie* (Hebrew Bibliography), a cornucopia of Jewish history and literature, from 1859 to 1882. His *Catalogus Librorum Hebraeorum in Bibliotheca Bodleiana* (1852–1860, Catalogue of the Hebrew Books in the Bodleian Library) sealed his reputation as the greatest Jewish bibliographer of the day, and his *Die Hebräischen Übersetszungen des Mittelalters und Die Juden als Dolmetscher* (1893, The Hebrew Translations of the Middle Ages and the Jews as Translators) is a crucially important book. Under the sway of the dominant periodization scheme of the *Wissenschaft* circle conceived by Solomon Löwisohn in *Vorlesungen über die neuere Geschichte der Juden* (1820, Lectures on the New History of the Jews), Steinschneider held that Arab-Greek culture fostered individualism and fomented the emergence of writers, authors, and distinct disciplines.

The historian Heinrich Graetz published *Leqet shoshanim* (1862, Collection of Roses), an anthology of medieval Hebrew poems. Leser Landshuth undertook original research on *piyyutim* that he published in *ʿAmudei haʿavodah* (1857, The Onamasticon); it treats in detail some four hundred authors and three thousand compositions. David Rosin carefully edited Abraham Ibn Ezra's introductions to his commentaries and short poems, with vocalized texts and rhymed German translations, in *Reime und Gedichte des Abraham ibn Esra* (1885–1894, Verse and Poetry of Abraham Ibn Ezra). Jacob Egers edited the complete *Diwan* of Abraham Ibn Ezra, together with his secular poetry, in 1886.

Albert Harkavy, an outstanding philologist who devoted himself to critical study of the manuscripts collected by the nineteenth-century Karaite scholar Abraham Firkovitch in Palestine, Syria, and Egypt and acquired by the St. Petersburg Imperial Public Library in two sales in 1862–1863 and 1876, published *Zikaron lerishonim* (Chronicle of Early and Later Poets) in 1891; it was the first comprehensive collection of Samuel the Nagid's poems but includes a fraction of what David S. Sassoon published in *The Newly-Discovered Diwan of the Vizier Samu Hannaghid* in 1924. Günzberg published the *ʿAnaq* of Moses Ibn Ezra in 1886. Heinrich Brody, rabbi of Prague, completed Luzzatto's work on Judah Halevi and set himself the task of publishing all of the important medieval poets, beginning with Ibn Gabirol in 1897. His comprehensive knowledge of the literature provided insights into passages that were otherwise meaningless. David Kaufmann published the work of Ibn Gabirol in 1899.

Emphasis on individuals of great cultural achievement is the ideological foundation of the Sephardic paradigm developed by advocates of the *Haskalah*. It offered a Judaism imbued with Hellenic philosophy and science–a classical heritage on a par with German culture, whose ideal was the Greeks; as Ismar Schorsch notes, "Paradoxically, the contact with Islam had made Judaism part of the Western world." Thus, German Reform contributed to the restoration to contemporary Jewish culture of the medieval Andalusian-Hebrew literary legacy.

References:

Nehemya Allony, "Hatsevi vehagamal beshirat sefarad," *Osar yehude sefarad,* 4 (1961): 16–43;

Allony, "The Reaction of Moses Ibn Ezra to ʿArabiyya," *Bulletin of the Institute of Jewish Studies,* 3 (1975): 19–40;

S. W. Baron, *A Social and Religious History of the Jews,* volume 7: *Hebrew Language and Letters* (New York: Columbia University Press / Philadelphia: Jewish Publication Society of America, 1958);

Shabbetai Bass, *Sifte yeshenim* (Amsterdam, 1680);

Isaac Benabu and Joseph Yahalom, "The Importance of the Genizah Manuscripts for the Establishment of the Text of the Hispano-Romance *Kharjas* in Hebrew Characters," *Romance Philology,* 40 (1986): 139–158;

Sandra Benjamin, *The World of Benjamin of Tudela: A Medieval Mediterranean Travelogue* (Madison, Wis. & London: Fairleigh Dickinson University, Associated University Presses, 1995);

Esther Bienenfeld, "*Meshal hakadmoni* by Isaac b. Solomon ibn Sahula (Brescia: Gerson Soncino, circa 1491): The Book and Its Illustrations," dissertation, Hebrew University, 1991;

Ross Brann, *The Compunctious Poet: Cultural Ambiguity and Hebrew Poetry in Muslim Spain* (Baltimore: Johns Hopkins University Press, 1991);

Heinrich Brody, *Divan: ve hu sefer kolel kol shire abir ha meshorerim, Yehuda Halevi,* 4 volumes (Berlin: Mekitse Nirdamim, 1901–1930; Farnborough, U.K.: Gregg International, 1971);

Brody, *Shir hashirim: sefer kolel kol hashire hol shel Shelomoh Ibn Gabirol,* 2 volumes (Berlin: M. Poppelauer, 1897, 1900);

Brody and Karl Albrecht, eds., *Shaar hashir: The New-Hebrew School of Poets of the Spanish-Arabian Epoch* (Leipzig: Hinrichs, 1905; London: Williams & Norgate, 1906; New York: Lemcke & Beuchner, 1906);

T. Carmi, ed. & trans., *The Penguin Book of Hebrew Verse* (Harmondsworth, U.K.: Penguin, 1981);

Joseph Dan, "Hashir kelebush mekushat," *Hasifrut,* 2 (1968): 110–175;

Dan, *Poetics of Medieval Hebrew Literature according to Moses Ibn Ezra* (Jerusalem: Devir, 1982);

Israel Davidson, "The Study of Medieval Hebrew Poetry in the Nineteenth Century," *Proceedings of the American Academy for Jewish Research,* 21 (1929): 33–48;

Franz Delitzsch, *Zur Geschichte der jüdischen Poesie* (Leipzig: Tauchnitz, 1836);

Aviva Doron, *Poet in the King's Courtyard: Todros Halevi Abulafia. Hebrew Poetry in Christian Spain* (Tel Aviv: Devir, 1989);

Rina Drory, "Literary Contacts and Where to Find Them: on Arabic Literary Models in Medieval Jewish literature," *Poetics Today,* 14 (1993): 277–302;

Leopold Dukes, *Moses ben Esra aus Granada: Darstellung seines Lebens und literarischen Wirkens nebst hebräischen Byelagen und deutschen Überstezungen* (Altona: Bonn, 1839);

Dukes, *Zur Kenntnis der neuhebräischen religiösen Poesie* (Frankfurt am Main: Bach, 1842);

Ismar Elbogen, *Jewish Liturgy: A Comprehensive History,* translated by Raymond P. Scheindlin (Philadelphia: Jewish Publication Society / New York: Jewish Theological Seminary of America, 1993);

Herschell Filipowski, *Mahberet Menahem* (London: Hevrat Meorere Yeshenim, 1854).

Ezra Fleischer, "The 'Gerona School' of Hebrew Poetry," in *Rabbi Moses Nahmanides (Ramban): Explorations in His Religiosity and Literary Virtuosity,* edited by Isadore Twersky (Cambridge, Mass.: Harvard University Press, 1983), pp. 35–49;

Fleischer, "Piyyut," in *Encylopaedia Judaica,* volume 13 (Jerusalem: Encyclopaedia Judaica / New York: Macmillan, 1971), pp. 574–603;

Margit Frenk, "La lírica pretrovadoresca," in *Les genres lyriques,* edited by Erich Köhler, Grundriss der romanischen Literaturen des Mittelalters, volume 1, fascicle 2 (Heidelberg: Winter, 1979), pp. 25–79;

Michael Friedlander, *Essays on the Writings of Abraham Ibn Ezra* (London: Society of Hebrew Literature, 1877);

Abraham Geiger, *Divan des Castiliers, Abu'-l-Hassan Judah Halevi* (Breslau: J. U. Kern, 1851);

Geiger, *Jüdische Dichtungen der spanischen und italienschen Schule* (Leipzig: O. Leiner, 1856);

Geiger, *Moses ben Maimon: Studien. 1. Heft* (Breslau: L. J. Weigert & A. Gosohorsky, 1850);

Geiger, *Salomo Gabirol und seine Dichtungen* (Leipzig: O. Leiner, 1867);

Geiger, *Tsitsim uferahim* (Leipzig: L. Shenvais, 1856);

Moshe Gil and Ezra Fleischer, *Yehuda Halevi and His Circle: 55 Geniza Documents* (Jerusalem: World Union of Jewish Studies, 2001);

S. D. Goiten, "The Biography of Rabbi Judah Halevi in the Light of the Genizah Documents," *Proceedings of the American Academy for Jewish Research*, 28 (1959): 41–56;

Isaac Goldberg, *Solomon Ibn Gabirol: A Bibliography of His Poems in Translation* (Washington, D.C.: Word Works International Editions, 1998);

Ignác Goldziher, *Muhammedanische Studien*, 2 volumes (Halle: Niemeyer, 1889, 1890); edited and translated by S. M. Stern and C. R. Barber as *Muslim Studies*, 2 volumes (Albany: State University of New York Press, 1973, 1977);

Heinrich Graetz, *Leqet shoshanim* (Breslau: Schletter, 1862);

Baron David Günzberg, *Sefer ha'anaq; hu hatarshish* (Berlin: Mekitse Nirdamim, 1886);

Abraham S. Halkin, "Judeo-Arabic literature," in *The Jews: Their Religion and Culture*, 3 volumes, edited by Louis Finkelstein, fourth edition (New York: Schocken, 1971), II: 121–154;

Halkin, "The Medieval Jewish Attitude toward Hebrew," In *Biblical and Other Studies*, edited by Alexander Altmann (Cambridge, Mass.: Harvard University Press, 1963), pp. 233–248;

Albert Harkavy, *Zikaron lerishonim vegam haaharonim*, 5 volumes (St. Petersburg: Bermana & Rabinovicha, 1891);

Klaus Heger, *Die bisher veröffentlichten har_as und ihre deutungen* (Tübingen: Niemeyer, 1960);

Wolf Heidenheim, *Mahzor* (Franfkurt am Main: Wolf Heidenhaim & Baruch Bashevits, 1800);

Richard Hitchock, *The Kharjas: A Critical Bibliography* (London: Grant & Cutler, 1977);

Benjamin Hrushovski, "Prosody, Hebrew," in *Encylopaedia Judaica*, volume 13, pp. 1195–1203;

Raphael Jospe, *Torah and Sophia: The Life and Thought of Shem Tov Ibn Falaquera* (Cincinnati: Hebrew Union College Press, 1988);

Saul Isaac Kaempf, *Nichtandalusischer Poesie Andalusischer Dichter aus dem Elften, Zwölften und Dreizehnten Jahrhundert* (Prague: C. Bellmann, 1858);

David Kaufmann, *Studien über Salomon Ibn Gabirol* (Pressburg: A. Alkalay, 1899);

Neal Kozodoy, "Reading Medieval Hebrew Love Poetry," *AJS Review*, 2 (1977): 111–129;

Leser Landshuth, *'Amudei ha'avodah* (Berlin, 1857);

Israel Levin, *Abraham Ibn Ezra: His Life and His Poetry* (Tel Aviv: Hakibuts hameuhad, 1969);

Solomon Löwisohn, *Vorlesungen über die neuere Geschichte der Juden* (Vienna: Karl Ferdinand Beck, 1820);

Samuel David Luzzatto, *Diwan: Yehudah Halevi* (Lyck: Mekitze Nirdamim, 1864);

Luzzatto, *Mavo lemahzor kaminhag bene Roma* (Leghorn: Sh. Belforte, 1856);

Henry Malter, *Life and Works of Saadia Gaon* (Philadelphia: Jewish Publication Society of America, 1921);

Ivan Marcus, "Beyond the Sephardic mystique," *Orim*, 1 (1985): 35–53;

George Margoliuth, *Catalogue of the Hebrew and Samaritan Manuscripts in the British Museum*, 4 volumes (London: British Museum, 1899–1935);

María Rosa Menocal, Raymond P. Scheindlin, and Michael Sells, eds., *The Literature of al-Andalus* (Cambridge: Cambridge University Press, 2000);

Aharon Mirsky, "The Principles of Hebrew Poetry in Spain," in *The Sephardi Heritage: Essays on the Historical and Cultural Contribution of the Jews of Spain and Portugal*, volume 1, edited by R. D. Barnett (London: Vallentine, Mitchell, 1971; New York: Ktav, 1971), pp. 186–247;

Angeles Navarro Peiro, *Literatura Hispanohebrea (Siglos X–XIII)* (Cordova: E. Almendro, 1988);

Navarro Peiro, *Narrativa Hispanohebrea (Siglos XII–XV)* (Cordova: E. Almendro, 1988);

Adolf Neubauer and Arthur E. Cowley, *Catalogue of the Hebrew Manuscripts in the Bodleian Library and in the College Libraries of Oxford: Including MSS. in Other Languages, Which Are Written with Hebrew Characters, or Relating to the Hebrew Language or Literature, and a Few Samaritan MSS.*, 2 volumes (Oxford: Clarendon Press, 1886, 1906; revised edition, 1 volume, Oxford & New York: Oxford University Press, 1994);

Dan Pagis, *Hebrew Poetry of the Middle Ages and the Renaissance* (Berkeley: University of California Press, 1991);

Pagis, *Hiddush umasoret beshirat hahol: sefarad veitalia* (Jerusalem: Keter, 1976);

Pagis, *Shirat hahol vetorat hashir lemoseh ibn ezra uvney doro* (Jerusalem: Bialik, 1970);

Pagis, "Trends in the Study of Medieval Hebrew Literature," *AJS Review*, 4 (1979): 125–141;

Pagis, "Variety in Medieval Rhymed Narratives," *Scripta Hierosolymitana*, 27 (1978): 79–98;

Solomon Judah Rapoport, "Biographies," *Bikure ha'itim,* 11 (1829–1830): 95–123;

Tova Rosen-Mokod, *Laezor shir. Al shirat-haezor ha'ivrit biyeme-habenayim* (Haifa: Haifa University Press, 1985);

Michael Sachs, ed., *Die religiöse Poesie der Juden in Spanien* (Berlin: Beit, 1845);

Senior Sachs, ed. and trans., *Shirei hashirim asher lishelomo ibn gabirol* (Paris: Guerin, 1868);

Ángel Sáenz-Badillos, *Diccionario de autores judíos (Sefarad, Siglos X–XV)* (Cordova: El Almendro, 1988);

Sáenz-Badillos, "Hebrew Invective Poetry: The Debate between Todros Abulafia and Phineas Halevi," *Prooftexts,* 16 (1996): 49–73;

Sáenz-Badillos, "Hebrew Philology in Sefarad: The State of the Question," in *Hebrew Scholarship and the Medieval World,* edited by Nicholas de Lange (Cambridge: Cambridge University Press, 2001), pp. 38–59;

Nahum M. Sarna, "Hebrew and Bible Studies in Medieval Spain," in *The Sephardi Heritage,* I: 323–366;

Raymond P. Scheindlin, *The Gazelle: Medieval Hebrew Poems on God, Israel, and the Soul* (Philadelphia & New York: Jewish Publication Society, 1991);

Scheindlin, "Rabbi Moses Ibn Ezra on the Legitimacy of Poetry," *Medievalia et Humanistica,* new series 7 (1976): 101–115;

Scheindlin, *Wine, Women, and Death: Medieval Hebrew Poems on the Good Life* (Philadelphia & New York: Jewish Publication Society, 1986);

Arie Schippers, *Spanish Hebrew Poetry and the Arabic Literary Tradition* (Leiden: Brill, 1994);

Jefim Schirmann, "The Ephebe in Medieval Hebrew Poetry," *Sefarad,* 15 (1955): 55–68;

Schirmann, "Samuel Hannagid: The Man, the Soldier, the Politician," *Jewish Social Studies,* 13 (1951): 99–126

Schirmann, ed., *Hashirah ha'ivrit besefarad ubeprovens,* 2 volumes (Tel Aviv: Devir, 1954, 1956);

Schirmann, ed., *Shirim hadashim min hagenizah* (Jerusalem: Israel Academy of Sciences and Humanities, 1965);

Ismar Schorsch, "The Myth of Sephardic Superiority," *Leo Baeck Institute Year Book,* 34 (1989): 47–66;

Bernard Septimus, *Hispano-Jewish Culture in Transition* (Cambridge, Mass.: Harvard University Press, 1982);

Colette Sirat, *A History of Jewish Philosophy in the Middle Ages* (Cambridge: Cambridge University Press / Paris: La Maison des Sciences de l'Homme, 1985);

Moritz Steinschneider, *Catalogus Librorum Hebraeorum in Bibliotheca Bodleiana,* 5 volumes (Berlin: Friedlaender, 1852–1860);

Steinschneider, *Die hebräische Übersetzungen des mittelalters und die Juden als Dolmetscher* (Berlin: Kommissionsverlag des Bibliographischen bureaus, 1893);

Steinschneider, "Jüdische Literatur," in *Allgemeine Encyklopädie der Wissenschaften und Künste,* second section, volume 27, edited by Hermann Brockhaus, Johann Samuel Ersch, Johann Gottfried Gruber, and others (Leipzig: Gleditsch, 1850), pp. 357–471;

Norman A. Stillman, "Aspects of Jewish Life in Islamic Spain," in *Aspects of Jewish Culture in the Middle Ages,* edited by Paul E. Szarmach (Albany: State University of New York Press, 1979), pp. 51–84;

Stillman, *The Jews of Arab Lands: A History and Source Book* (Philadelphia: Jewish Publication Society of America, 1979);

Adena Tannebaum, "On Translating Medieval Hebrew Poetry," in *Hebrew Scholarship and the Medieval World,* edited by Nicholas de Lange (Cambridge: Cambridge University Press, 2001), pp. 171–185;

Isadore Twersky, *Introduction to the Code of Maimonides (Mishneh Torah)* (New Haven & London: Yale University Press, 1980);

Johann Christoph Wolf, *Bibliotheca Hebrea,* 4 volumes (Hamburg: Christiani Liebezeit, 1713–1733);

David Yellin, *Torat hashira hasefardit,* second edition (Jerusalem: Judah Magnes, Hebrew University Press, 1972);

Yellin and Israel Abrahams, *Maimonides* (Philadelphia: Jewish Publication Society of America, 1904);

J. Zedner, *Catalogue of the Hebrew Books in the Library of the British Museum* (London: Trustees of the British Museum, 1867);

Israel Zinberg, *A History of Jewish Literature,* volume 1: *The Arabic-Spanish Period,* edited and translated by Bernard Martin (Cleveland: Case Western Reserve University Press, 1972);

Leopold Zunz, *Literaturgeschichete des synagogalen Poesie* (Berlin: L. Gerschel, 1865);

Zunz, *Die synagogale Poesie des Mittelalters,* 2 volumes (Berlin: Springer, 1855, 1859).

The *Kharjas*

Vincent Barletta
Stanford University

Arabic manuscripts: Zaytuna Library, Tunis, MS. 4583; National Library, Tunis, ʿAbd al-Wahhab MS. 18623; private library of Mohammed al-Nifar; private library of the heirs of Georges S. Colin, MS. G. S. Colin).

Hebrew manuscripts: New York Public Library, MS. Adlera; British Library, London, MSS. 5557D and Or. 5557p; University of Cambridge Library, MSS. Loan 63, H.15, SK 14, 108, 96, 114, and 111; University of Oxford Library, MSS. 1971, 1970, 2853, hbre 100, and 1972-253; Berlin Library, MSS. 103 and 186; Frankfurt Library, MS. 159; Jerusalem Library, MS. Schocken 37.

Editions: *Diwan des Abraham Ibn Esra mit seiner Allegorie Hai Ben Mekiz: Zum ersten male aus der ein-zigen handschrift,* edited by Jacob Egers (Berlin: Itzkowski / Frankfurt am Main: Kaufmann, 1886); *Selected Poems of Jehudah Halevi,* edited by Heinrich Brody (Philadelphia: Jewish Publication Society, 1928); Samuel M. Stern, "Les vers finaux en espagnol dans les muwashshahs hispanohebraiques: Une contribution à l'histoire du *muwassahas* et à l'étude du vieux dialecte espagnol 'mozarabe,'" *Al-Andalus,* 13 (1948): 299–346; Emilio García Gómez, "Veinticuatro jaryas romances en muwassahas árabes (ms. G. S. Colin)," *Al-Andalus,* 17 (1952): 57–127; García Gómez, "Dos nuevas jarchas romances (XXV y XXVI) en muwassahas árabes," *Al-Andalus,* 19 (1954): 369–391; Jefim Schirmann, "Un nouveau poème hébreu avec vers finaux en espagnol et en arabe," in *Homenaje a Millás Vallicrosa,* volume 2 (Barcelona: Consejo Superior de Investigaciones Cientificas, 1956), pp. 347–353; Klaus Heger, *Die bisher veröffentlichten Hargas und ihre Deutungen* (Tübingen: Niemeyer, 1960); García Gómez, *Las jarchas romances de la serie árabe en su marco* (Madrid: Sociedad de Estudios y Publicaciones, 1965); James T. Monroe, *Hispano-Arabic Poetry: A Student Anthology* (Berkeley & Los Angeles: University of California Press, 1974); Stern, *Hispano-Arabic Strophic Poetry,* edited by L. P. Harvey (Oxford: Clarendon Press, 1974); Alan Jones, *Romance Kharjas in Andalusian Arabic Muwassah Poetry: A Paleographical Analysis* (Oxford: Ithaca Press, 1988); Josep María Solà-Solé, *Las jarchas romances y sus moaxajas* (Madrid: Taurus, 1990); Federico Corriente Córdoba, *Poesía dialectal árabe y romance en Alandalús* (Madrid: Gredos, 1997).

The Arabic term *kharja* (also *xarja;* Spanish *jarcha*), along with its variant, *markaz,* refers to the final segment (Arabic *qufl*) of the Andalusi poetic form known as the *muwashshah* (Spanish *moaxajá*). The *muwashshah,* which is closely related to the more colloquial *zajal* (plural *azjal;* Spanish *zéjel*), developed as a performative poetic genre in al-Andalus during the tenth century. Outside the context of poetry, *kharja* can mean "exit," "departure," or "salient part"; all of these meanings are relevant to the poetic *kharja,* given its placement as a kind of "exit segment" at the end of the *muwashshah* and given the important role it plays in the poem. For scholars of Spanish literature the *kharja* is significant because of its early development, combined with the fact that sixty-eight of them, found in Arabic and Hebrew *muwashshahat,* were composed at least partially in a dialect of Ibero-Romance particular to al-Andalus.

The earliest written source for the history and development of the *muwashshah* is provided in the early twelfth century by Ibn Bassam of Santarem, who deals with the origins of the form in his *al-Dhakhira fi mahasin ahl al-jazira* (Treasury of the Charms of the [Andalusian] Peninsula). According to Ibn Bassam, the genre was originated either by Mohammed ibn Mahmud al-Qabri at the court of the emir ʿAbdullah ibn Mohammed al-Marwani, who died in 912, or by Ibn ʿAbd Rabbihi, the author of the *Kitab al-ʿiqd al-farid* (Book of the Peerless Garland), who died in 940. Ibn Bassam defines the *muwashshah* as

measures that the people of Andalus used copiously in the [erotic genres of] *ghazal* and *nasib,* such that carefully guarded bosoms and even hearts, are broken upon hearing them. The first to compose the measures of these *muwashshahat* in our country, and to invent their method of composition, as far as I have determined, was Mohammed ibn Mahmud al-Qabri, the Blind. He

315

used to compose them after the manner of the hemistichs of classical Arabic poetry (except that most of them were [composed] after the manner of the nonexistent, hypothetical meters that are not used [in classical Arabic poetry]), adopting colloquial Arabic and Romance diction, which he called the *markaz,* and basing the *muwashshah* upon it, without any *tadmin* [i.e., internal rhyme] in [the *markaz*] or in [the] *aghsan.* It has been claimed [as an alternate tradition] that Ibn ᶜAbd Rabbihi, the author of the *Kitab al-ᶜiqd* [The book of the garland], was the first to [compose] *muwashshahat* of this type among us. Then appeared Yusuf ibn Harun al-Ramadi who was the first to extend the use of *tadmin* into the *marakiz,* employing it at every caesura he came to, but in the *markaz,* exclusively. The poets of our age continued after this fashion, such as Mukarram ibn Saᶜid and Abu l-Hasan's two sons. Then there appeared our ᶜUbada [ibn Ma' al-Sama'], who invented [the technique of] *tadfir;* that is to say, he reinforced the caesurae in the *aghan* by adding *tadmin* to them, just as al-Ramadi had reinforced the caesurae in the *markaz.* The measures of these *muwashshahat* lie beyond the scope of this anthology, since the majority of them are not [composed] after the manner of the meters [found] in the classical poems of the Arabs [translated by Samuel G. Armistead and James T. Monroe].

In his *Muqaddimah* (Prolegomenon), written at the end of the fourteenth century, Ibn Khaldun supports Ibn Bassam's findings regarding al-Qabri and the origins of the genre but rejects the claims of the "alternate tradition" with respect to Ibn ᶜAbd Rabbihi. He says that the *muwashshahat*

> were invented in al-Andalus by Muqaddam ibn Muᶜafa al-Qabri, a poet under the emir ᶜAbdullah ibn Mohammed al-Marwani. Ahmad ibn ᶜAbd Rabbihi, the author of the *ᶜIqd,* learned this [type of poetry] from him. [Muqaddam and Ibn ᶜAbd Rabbihi] were not mentioned together with the recent (authors of *muwashshahat*), and thus their *muwashshahat* fell into desuetude. The first poet after them who excelled in this subject was ᶜUbada al-Qazzaz, the poet of al-Mutasim ibn Sumadih, the lord of Almería [translated by James T. Monroe].

Tova Rosen notes that a striking feature of both Ibn Bassam's and Ibn Khaldun's remarks is the notion that whoever the "first author" of *muwashshahat* was, he was almost certainly "not a popular bard but a learned poet who also had an ear for colloquial Arabic and Romance expressions, which he used as endings *(markazes)* to his poems." This point is exceedingly important for *muwashshah* studies, as it underscores the central role of citation and intertextuality in the development, composition, and performance of the genre, while highlighting its essentially elite status within Andalusi poetic discourse.

The question of origins is the most polemical aspect of *kharja* research. The pressing question for Hispanists is whether or not the Romance *kharjas* stem from a preexisting and fully formed Romance lyric tradition, while for Arabists the issue of primary interest is how Andalusi strophic poetry as a whole derived from Arabic poetic genres inherited from the East. Much of the often acrimonious debate surrounding the *kharjas,* which reached its highest levels during the 1980s, has been the result of the perceived incommensurability of these two scholarly projects. Rosen, Federico Corriente Córdoba, and Dwight Reynolds have brought together arguments from both disciplines to form what they claim is a more contextualized, performance-oriented understanding of Andalusi language and culture.

The formal and structural aspects of the *muwashshah,* rather than broader thematic issues in either the *muwashshahat* or the *kharjas,* have largely provided fuel for scholarly discussions centered on the question of the origins of the *kharjas.* As Corriente Córdoba puts it, "el verdadero caballo de batalla entre teóricos de estos géneros ha sido siempre la estructura métrica" (the true point of contention among theorists of these genres has always been metrical structure).

While Ibn Bassam's principal interest in the *muwashshah* seems to revolve around the absence of classical Arabic meters and the development of systems of internal rhyme within its verses, there is nonetheless a fair amount of material, ambiguously presented though it is, in his treatment of meter. One wonders, for example, what he means when he states that al-Qabri "used to compose [the measures of the *muwashshah*] after the manner of the hemistichs of classical Arabic poetry." He might mean that the lines of the *muwashshah* contain caesurae, as classical, Khalilian *abyat* (verses; singular *bayt*) do; or he could mean that the verses of the *muwashshah* were considered to be the same length as a hemistich of classical verse. James T. Monroe argues that Ibn Bassam is intentionally ambiguous on this point "in order to allow for either possibility." In any case, he does much to stir up debate and little to resolve it, as even the Arabic term *ashtar,* which Monroe translates literally as "hemistich," has produced confusion: in his study of Ibn Bassam, Samuel M. Stern, citing what he believes to have been a peculiarity of Andalusi usage, translates the term as "meter," from which follows the paradoxical notion that the composers of *muwashshahat* followed the classical meters as a rule–except that they ignored this rule most of the time. What stands out, however, is Ibn Bassam's comment regarding al-Qabri's early use of "colloquial Arabic and Romance diction" as the basis for the *muwashshah.*

J. A. Abu-Haidar notes that in the introduction to the *al-Dhakhira fi mahasin ahl al-jazira* Ibn Bassam states that he has little respect for or interest in poetry of any sort. Abu-Haidar translates a key passage:

> I have saved myself the humiliation of [writing] poetry, and would rather not lay the soles of my feet where poetry lay. . . . What have I got to do with it, when the greater part of it is the deceit of crooks, and the attire of the haughty and arrogant. The serious part of it is affectation and fantastic deception, and the lighter side is senselessness and delusion.

Abu-Haidar points out that Ibn Bassam's account of the *muwashshah* was almost certainly taken from a book by ʿUbada bin Ma al-Sama; thus, Ibn Bassam probably had little taste for the *muwashshah* and little personal knowledge of it but somewhat selectively copied information he found in an earlier work. In light of Abu-Haidar's arguments, it is possible that the ambiguity in the *al-Dhakhira fi mahasin ahl al-jazira* regarding the metrical system of the *muwashshah* has more to do with Ibn Bassam's lack of knowledge than with any conscious attempt at subtlety.

The next known author to deal with the question of meter in the *muwashshahat* is Ibn Sana' al-Mulk (1155–1211), who discusses the *muwashshah* and *kharja* extensively in his treatise *Dar al-tiraz fi ʿamal al-muwashshahat* (House of Style: The Production of *Muwashshahat*). His rich, if largely doctrinaire, account of Andalusi strophic poetry remains the most important external resource for understanding the form and meaning of the *muwashshah* and the *kharjas*. Dealing with the question of meter, and probably using some unknown Andalusi author as his source, he writes that the *muwashshahat*

> have no prosody [ʿarud] other than singing [talhin], no *darb* [the last foot of the second hemistich of a classical line] other than the musical beat [darb], no *watads* ["pegs," as in "tent pegs"] other than the pegs of instruments, no *sababs* ["rope," as in "tent rope"] other than their strings; by this prosody alone can the regular be distinguished from the irregular and the sound from the unsound. The majority of them are based on the compositions for musical [urghun] instruments . . . , and singing them to other than musical instruments is derivative and an extension [translated by James T. Monroe].

Stressing the performative roots of *muwashshah* composition and prosody, Ibn Sana' al-Mulk thus situates the metrical system of the genre within the rhythms of Andalusi music and language use. This notion is not far from Corriente Córdoba's contention regarding the performative and eminently regional nature of the genre in its formative period:

> las especiales características prosódicas del habla andalusí con respecto al árabe estándar y oriental requirieron una adaptación del ʿarud, que era enmascarada por los poetas andalusíes en la composición de casidas mediante una adpoción íntegra de las exigencias tradicionales, aun las que no decían nada al oído andalusí, pero no así siempre en el caso de la poesía estrófica, por su relación con el habla local, lo que no podía naturalmente entenderse en Oriente y daría lugar a la ya comentada y famosa afirmación de Ibn Sana'almulk . . . , en el sentido de que la mayor parte de los buenos poemas de este tipo se apartaban más o menos radicalmente del ʿarud.

> (the special prosodic characteristics of Andalusi speech with respect to Standard and Eastern Arabic required an adaptation of the classical system of meters. This adaptation was masked by Andalusi poets in their composition of qasidas, monorhymed poems of sixty to one hundred verses, each divided into hemistichs through the wholesale adoption of traditional conventions–even those that sounded odd to the Andalusi ear–but not always in the case of strophic poetry (due to the latter's relation to local speech), which would logically not be understood in the East and would make possible the much-discussed and famous comment made by Ibn Sana' al-Mulk . . . , in the sense that the majority of the good poems of this type departed more or less radically from the ʿarud.)

In this brief argument Corriente Córdoba combines two notions that have become central to *muwashshah* and *kharja* studies: that the *muwashshah*, like the *zejel*, was an essentially performative genre that was seldom divorced from musical accompaniment and that the *muwashshah*, though mostly written in classical Arabic and classical Hebrew and to some extent reflecting Eastern aesthetic and cultural values, was a fundamentally Andalusi poetic genre shaped by verbal interaction within the multilingualistic Andalusi speech community. While Corriente Córdoba disagrees with Monroe and Samuel G. Armistead regarding the place of Romance meters and popular song forms in the "prehistory" of the *muwashshah*, he nonetheless argues for an approach to the genre that takes into account its organic link to the communities that composed, performed, and enjoyed it within al-Andalus.

While Ibn Khaldun focuses on the stanzaic structure of the genre, he does deal briefly with the question of meter:

> The *muwashshahat* consist of "branches" [ghusn] and "strings" [simt] in great number and different meters. A certain number [of "branches" and "strings"] is called a single verse [stanza]. There must be the same number of rhymes in the "branches" [of each stanza] and the same meter [for the "branches" of the whole poem] throughout the whole poem [translated by James T. Monroe].

The reference to the "different meters" employed in the *muwashshahat* and the uniformity of meter within each poem may be an attempt by Ibn Khaldun to evade a difficult issue: like Ibn Bassam, he seems to have had little direct knowledge of the *muwashshah,* taking much of his text directly from the thirteenth-century *Kitab al-muqtataf min azahir al-turaf* (Selection from the Flowers of Novelty), by the Andalusi writer Ibn Saʿid al-Maghrebi.

Modern scholars have made use of the comments of Ibn Bassam, Ibn Sana' al-Mulk, and Ibn Khaldun, as well as the multilingual character of the *kharjas* themselves, in a variety of ways. Inspired by early editions and studies of the *kharjas* such as those by Adolf Friedrich Graf von Schack (1865) and Martin Hartmann (1896), Spanish scholars such as Marcelino Menéndez y Pelayo, Julián Ribera, Dámaso Alonso, Ramón Menéndez Pidal, and Rafael Lapesa established an interpretive frame for the Romance *kharjas* that is centered on Castile and the Castilian language. This project, which rested on a liberal reading of the Romance elements found in the few known *kharjas* and a belief that the meters employed in the *muwashshahat* originated in Romance lyric forms rather than in the Khalilian meters of classical Arabic, accelerated dramatically in 1948 after Stern published interpretations of Romance *kharjas* in the Hebrew *muwashshahat* in the *genizah* (hiding place) of the Ezra Synaguge in Cairo. While based on solid work by Semitic scholars such as Stern, the strong "Hispanic" reading that many scholars gave the *kharjas* depended on a fair amount of philological license. For the most part, the Romance *kharjas* that were presented to readers, often in textbook anthologies, had been stripped from their textual setting within the *muwashshahat.* For many researchers in Europe—especially in Spain—and North America, as well as for readers of the anthologies, the *kharjas* presented irrefutable evidence of a traditional Romance lyric that had developed on "Spanish" soil at least two centuries before the earliest Provençal poetry and three centuries before the *scuola siciliana* (Sicilian School) described by Dante in his *De vulgari eloquentia* (circa 1304–1307, On Vernacular Speech). Alonso's rhetorical question is characteristic of this view: "Habrá atracción mayor que el mundo recién descubierto de las jarchas, que cambia nuestras ideas sobre el origen de la lírica del Occidente europeo?" (Can there be a greater attraction than the recently discovered world of the *kharjas,* which changes our ideas about the origin of the Western European lyric?).

Alonso's claim is informed by powerful nationalistic ideologies that intersected with the broader cultural politics of Spain after the end of its civil war and the establishment of the Franco regime in 1939. Similar ideologies and institutional practices inform the broader philological search for ways to reconstruct the spoken language of the Mozarabs, the minority Christian communities living in al-Andalus; and the Romance *kharjas*—most of which contain a good deal of colloquial Arabic—came to represent invaluable textual witnesses of a Romance vernacular spoken and, more importantly, sung in al-Andalus alongside regional dialects of Arabic and, to a lesser extent, Tamazight and Tarifit.

More-recent Romance scholars, including some who do not specialize in Andalusi language and literature, have questioned the philological and interpretive practices of this earlier generation with respect to the *kharjas*. Mary Jane Kelley, for example, casts doubt on the "popular" or "traditional" status of the *kharjas,* arguing that the feminine voice that they supposedly present should be viewed through the filter of their use and recontextualization by learned male poets. Similarly, Consuelo López-Morillas points out that while the *kharjas* "may well be rooted in popular forms of speech . . . once grafted onto the *muwashshah* they were subject to such learned reworking to fit the aesthetics of the genre that their language became artificial and conventional." Anthony P. Espósito goes even further, arguing that any philological attempt to access the "popular forms of speech" potentially encoded within the Romance *kharjas* mimics a surgical procedure, a transplant in which the poetic organ is excised and subsequently grafted onto another entity. Such an operation is needed given that these early lyric manifestations, supposedly popular and voiced by women in a natural setting, are found framed in a radically different poetic context, assembled in codicils of courtly (not popular) origin, and claimed to be in great part written by men. The debate regarding the status of the *kharjas* as faithful transcriptions of a fundamentally traditional Romance lyric expression performed in al-Andalus or as learned, elite revisions of such works is likely to continue for some time.

Scholars specializing in Andalusi language and literature have naturally had the most to say about the relation of the metrical system of the *muwashshah* and its relation to the question of the genre's origins. In 1965 and more extensively in 1974, for example, Emilio García Gómez addressed this issue and concluded that the most appropriate way to analyze the metrical system of the *muwashshahat* and *azjal* that did not clearly follow classical Arabic meters is through a focus on stress-based rhythms such as those found in "la antiquísima poesía romance" (the oldest of Romance poems). Understanding García Gómez's argument and those of scholars such as Abu-Haidar, Armistead and Monroe, Corriente Córdoba, Richard Hitchcock, Alan Jones, and Otto Zwartjes requires some familiarity with classical Arabic and Romance metrical systems.

The meters from which the *muwashshah* and the *zajal* deviate are the sixteen recognized ones normally employed in classical Arabic poetry. These meters originated in the pre-Islamic period but were codified in the eighth century by the Arab scholar al-Khalil bin Ahmad—whence the term *Khalilian* to designate them. Like classical Latin poetry, classical Arabic meters are based on the length of syllables rather than on syllabic stress or number of syllables, and each *bayt* (verse) is typically divided by a caesura into two equal *shatrayn* (hemistichs). A *bayt* from a *ghazal* in Abu Mohammed ᶜAli ibn Ahmad ibn Saᶜid ibn Qazm's *Tawq al-hamama* (The Dove's Neck-Ring) demonstrates how the system works:

> Awadduk wuddan laysa fihi ghadada wa baᶜdu mawaddat al-rrijali sarabu.
> (I love you with a love that has no waning, while some men's loves are midday mirages [translated by James T. Monroe].)

In the Khalilian system the meter of this *bayt* is known as *tawil* (long). Each foot of a *tawil* verse is made up of a short syllable followed by two long ones:

$$\text{\textasciicircum} -- | \text{\textasciicircum} -- | \text{\textasciicircum} -- | \text{\textasciicircum} \ -- | \quad \text{\textasciicircum} -- | \text{\textasciicircum} -- | \text{\textasciicircum} -- | \text{\textasciicircum} --$$

The pattern is repeated throughout the *bayt*. There is a tremendous amount of regularity to classical verses; but the alternation of long and short syllables avoids the almost mechanical repetitiveness of similar attempts to standardize Castilian verses, such as the *cuaderna vía* (fourfold way) poetry of the thirteenth century.

Andalusi Arabic, however, employs a quite different system of prosody from classical Arabic. Corriente Córdoba argues that the characteristics of colloquial Andalusi Arabic speech required speakers, singers, and poets to carry out various adaptations of the classical system; these adaptations, while not manifested in the highly prestigious and eminently Eastern *qasida* tradition as it manifested itself in al-Andalus, were employed in the autochthonous *muwashshah* and *zajal*. In other words, Corriente Córdoba is suggesting that the origins of the unique (in medieval Arabic, at least) metrical features of Andalusi lyric may be found in the language practices of Andalusi Arabic speakers. Whether such practices included the wholesale use of metrical systems with origins in early Romance popular lyrics continues to be debated.

A verse from a *muwashshah* shows how the metrical system suggested by Armistead and Monroe might work in practice. The poem is by Mohammed ibn ᶜUbada al-Qazzaz, a poet mentioned by both Ibn Bassam and Ibn Khaldun: "Jifani yaᶜishu liwaqfi ᶜalayhi | law bilnnafsi rishu latirtu ilayhi" (My eyelids live only to know him | if my soul had feathers I would fly to him

[translated by James T. Monroe]). On the classical Arabic system of vowel length, the meter of this verse can be represented as:

$$\text{\textasciicircum} -- | \text{\textasciicircum} - \text{\textasciicircum} | \text{\textasciicircum} \ \text{\textasciicircum} - | \text{\textasciicircum} \ \text{\textasciicircum} \ \text{\textasciicircum} | \quad \text{\textasciicircum} -- | \text{\textasciicircum} - \text{\textasciicircum} | \text{\textasciicircum} \ \text{\textasciicircum} - | \text{\textasciicircum} \ \text{\textasciicircum} \ \text{\textasciicircum}$$

To bring even this much syllabic regularity to the verse requires a good deal of effort; and, needless to say, it does not follow any of the classical Khalilian meters. In keeping with their theory that the *muwashshahat* have more than a tangential relationship to Romance systems of meter, Armistead and Monroe claim that the rhythm of this *muwashshah* can be described as dactylic; accordingly, the verse might be read "Jifáni yaᶜíshu liwáqfi ᶜaláyhi | law bílnnafsi ríshu latírtu iláyhi." Armistead and Monroe do not maintain that the metrical system of the *muwashshahat* is in any exclusive sense a Romance one; rather, they, along with a growing number of scholars in Arabic and Romance literatures, argue that it is fundamentally Andalusi.

Al-Andalus was characterized throughout its history by a significant degree of cultural and linguistic contact and exchange among Christian, Jewish, and Muslim communities from various regions of the Iberian Peninsula and the Maghreb. Rosen refers to this phenomenon when she writes of the "fluid and diverse linguistic situation of the peninsula's population" and the effect that this fluidity and diversity had on performative genres such as the *muwashshah* throughout the area between the Pyrenees and the Atlantic Ocean. Writing in support of Armistead and Monroe's theory, María Rosa Menocal describes the sociocultural ramifications of this rethinking of the metrical origins of the *muwashshah* while opening the possibility of multidirectional, cross-cultural contact and influence:

> Such an approach has been especially important in terms of the origins question, since it has successfully established that the *kharjas* (or at least the proto-*kharjas*, the poems that provide the inspiration for the final strophes of the *muwashshah*, and in some cases exact verses or whole refrains) are an important part of the common Romance corpus of popular lyric of medieval Europe. As such, in fact, the successes of this scholarship provide significant evidence for the sort of revisionist medieval image we are proposing here. They clearly indicate, through the relationships that have been established between the reflexes of popular poetry adopted by courtly Arabic poetry and the examples of other Romance popular forms, that what we are dealing with is a community of popular poetry that was as much a part of the Arabic cultural orbit as of the Romance/Latin world.

It is possible to exaggerate the mutual influence of Romance and Arabic poetic production and performance in medieval Iberia; for example, Arabic poets never ceased to look to the cultural centers of the East for inspiration, artistic training, and validation. But the cultural and linguistic boundaries between the communities were largely porous.

In regard to stanzaic structure, the *muwashshah* typically begins with a two-verse rhyming segment known as the *matla'*. Ibn Sana' al-Mulk points out in the *Dar al-tiraz* that a *muwashshah* that begins with a *matla'* was typically called *tamm* (complete), while one without the *matla'* was referred to as *aqra* (bald). In his 1965 edition of forty-three Arabic *muwashshahat* that employ Romance *kharjas*, García Gómez maintains Ibn Sana' al-Mulk's terminology in part: he describes *muwashshahat* without a *matla'* as *aqra* but refers to those with a *matla'* as "having a *preludio* [prelude]." Stern investigates the two terms employed by Ibn Sana' al-Mulk and concludes that "while there is no further evidence for the term *tamm*, the name *aqra* is regularly employed in the *diwan* [poetic anthology] of Ibn ʿArabi to designate poems which have no *matla'*." Stern's comments and García Gómez's editorial practice highlight the fact that Ibn Sana' al-Mulk's terminology was by no means in widespread use throughout al-Andalus during the late twelfth century; there is, nonetheless, an important distinction to be made between those *muwashshahat* that begin with a *matla'* and those that do not. Like the *estribilho* (refrain) of the Galician-Portuguese *cantigas* (songs), it is likely that the presence or absence of the *matla'* had a significant impact on the performance of a given poem.

After the *matla'*—or at the beginning of a *muwashshah* that does not begin with one—comes the opening *ghusn*. The *ghusn* (plural *aghsan*), which in Arabic means "twig" or "branch," is a segment (*qufl*) with an independent rhyme scheme; the rhyme scheme normally changes from stanza to stanza, which is why these segments are metaphorically referred to as "branches." The opening *ghusn* is followed by a two-verse segment known as the *simt* (plural *asmat*), a term that literally refers to the "string" or "thread" of a pearl necklace. Using Ibn Sana' al-Mulk's terminology, one can say that the *simt* has the same rhyme scheme as the *matla'* and all other *asmat* in the case of a *muwashshah tamm* and the same rhyme scheme as all other *asmat* in the case of the *muwashshah aqra*.

The *muwashshah* generally consists of five to seven stanzas in addition to the two-verse *matla'*, when the latter is present, as opposed to the potentially limitless number of stanzas in the more colloquial *zajal*. There are thus usually five *aghsan* and six *asmat* in a *muwashshah*, the first *simt* being the *matla'*, when the latter is present, and the last being the *kharja*. The simplest rhyme scheme of a *muwashshah* is AA | BBBAA | CCCAA | DDDAA | EEEAA | FFFAA, although a cer-

tain amount of variation is possible; for example, the *matla'*, *simt*, and *kharja* may have an AB rather than an AA rhyme. The meter can follow a relatively wide range of schemes, as long as the same meter is employed throughout the poem.

A more concrete sense of the structural scheme of a *muwashshah* is provided by one written by Abu Bakr Mohammed ibn al-Hassan al-Kumayt al-Gharbi for Ahmad al-Musta'in of Saragossa, who died in 1110. It has an Andalusi Romance *kharja* and a two-verse *matla'*:

Li 'admuʿun tastahillu mudh shahita l-khillu.

Li-llahi 'ashku l-ghadata ma sanaʿ l-baynu!
Lam tabqa li bi-l-buka'i baʿda-humu ʿaynu.
Ya naqidan li-l-ʿuhudi! Hal yajmulu l-maynu?
Ila mata tastahillu ma laisa yuhillu?

Taʿsan li-sarfi z-zamani min hakamin yajfu,
lam yabqu li sahibun ma- waddatu-hu tasfu!
Wa-'asbahtu fi maʿsharin qulubu-hum gulfu,
waslu-humu mudmahallu, wa-wuddu-hum ghillu.

Ha 'ana bayna l-hayati wa-l-mawti mawqufu.
Qad ʿalima l-ʿalimuna anniya mashghufu.
Man liya bi-katmi l-hawa, wa-sirri maʿrufu?
In kana khatbi yajillu, fa-s-sabru 'ajallu.

A-ya qamaran talican ʿala gusnin zahi!
Law-la-ka, lam adri ʿan hi- yadi r-rada ma hi.
Adnayta jismiya hawa, fa-qul li, bi-llahi;
Dhaka l-ʿidharu l-mutillu, sawlajun am sillu?

Lamma jafa-ni l-habibu, hasbiya bi-t-tihi,
wa-lam utiq katma-hu hi- dhara r-rada fi-hi,
shadawtu-hu muʿlinan ka- khawdin tuganni-hi:
Non kerh, bonh khallellh illa s-samarellh.

(I weep without solace since the one whom I love departed.

I complain to God of the dawn that brought this separation. I have no eyes left from so much crying after his departure. Oh, breaker of promises! Is a lie perhaps a proper thing? For how long will you allow what is not right?

A curse on the passing of time, handed out by a tyrannical judge! I am now without any friend whose affection is pure. I wake up each morning among people whose hearts are hard. Their friendship is a thing that comes apart and their love is hatred.

I am here uncertain, between life and death. The wise men have already determined that I am crazy with love. How will I hide my love, when my secret is already known? But if my suffering is great, then my patience is even greater.

Oh moon on high, above a flowering branch! If not for you, I would not know the term of death, what it is. My body is consumed by love, so tell me, by God: this wisp of beard, is it a curved scepter or an adder?

When my beloved caused me pain, I responded with pride. And, not being able to contain myself, for fear of dying, I recited to him, speaking like a young girl who sings to her beloved:

"I want no lover but the dark-skinned one.")

The *muwashshah* begins with a *matla'* made up of an AA rhyme scheme *(-illu)*. This rhyme scheme is repeated in all of the *asmat* that follow, including the *kharja (khillello/ samarello)*. The *aghsan* share an independent rhyme within the last hemistich of each verse; there is no internal rhyme.

In theme this *muwashshah* closely follows the classical *ghazal* genre, although the form is quite different–a *ghazal* consists of five to fifteen monorhymed couplets with no enjambment: the compact expression of endless longing, as well as some of the figurative images, are elements that many Arabic and Hebrew *muwashshahat* share with the *ghazal*. Particularly powerful is the speaker's figurative contemplation of the beloved's wisp of presumably dark and curly beard hair as either a curved scepter, a symbol of legitimate masculine authority, or a venomous black adder, a symbol of deceit, danger, and perdition. Other *muwashshahat,* especially Hebrew ones, compare the black curl of hair that crosses the beloved's cheek with the tail of a scorpion protecting a rose in bloom.

Thematically the Arabic *muwashshah* can be divided into three general types: panegyrics, lyrics, and wine songs. In this respect, as Stern argues, "there is nothing that would distinguish it from the main stream of Arabic poetry." Stern goes on to cite Ibn Sana' al-Mulk and Ibn Khaldun:

> That the subjects of the *muwashshah* are identical with those of the *shi'r* was already clearly stated by Ibn Sana' al-Mulk (fol. 15ᵛ): "The *muwashshah* treats of the same subject as the various kinds of *shi'r*, i.e., love, praise, mourning *(marthiya)*, invective *(hija')*, frivolity *(mujun)*, and asceticism *(zuhd)*." Similarly Ibn Khaldun (iii. 390): "In this genre one makes erotic or panegyrical verses as in the *qasida*."

Later in their development, the *muwashshahat* also began to be used increasingly for religious purposes, although the formal and linguistic liberties that the genre takes with classical Arabic genres, especially the *qasida,* never ceased to provoke a certain amount of tension for religious poets and their audiences. Within the Jewish communities of al-Andalus, however, there was little concern with maintaining any sort of rigorous adherence to classical Arabic meters and poetic forms. The *muwashshah* was quickly taken up by Jewish poets, who composed their *kharjas* in classical Hebrew, Hispano-Romance, and Andalusi Arabic for religious purposes.

While the *muwashshah* by al-Kumayt al-Gharbi maintains its lyric theme throughout the poem, such is often not the case. *Muwashshahat* tended to be polythematic, moving fluidly between praise of a patron or of wine and the direct and often plaintive address of a beloved. According to Rosen,

> A typical polythematic poem is tripartite. It usually begins with one or two introductory strophes addressing a beloved man or woman or singing the praises of wine. Then, employing some transitional device, the speaker shifts for the next one or two strophes to the eulogy of his patron. There follows a second transition, so that the poem concludes with one or two strophes elaborating the themes of love or wine. These last strophes furnish the context for the erotic or impudent kharja that ends the poem. Whereas the first shift, from love to praise, corresponds to the *takhallus* of the qasida, the second shift, from praise back to love, is peculiar to the muwashshah. This typical tripartite structure results from the combination of the conventional two-part qasida with the requirement that the muwashshah end with an erotic theme culminating in the kharja.

For modern readers the shift back and forth of the *muwashshah* between panegyric, lyric, and other themes can be somewhat jolting. Rosen's comments make clear, however, that there is order to this thematic play, and that this order ultimately revolves around the *kharjas*.

Scholars thus should not treat the *kharjas* as mere extractable ending lines for otherwise complete compositions but as the nucleus of the *muwashshah* itself. As Ibn Sana' al-Mulk argues in the *Dar al-tiraz,* "the *kharja* is the spice of the *muwashshah,* its salt and sugar, its musk and amber. It is the close of the *muwashshah;* it must, therefore, be beautiful; it is its seal; nay, it is the beginning, although it is at the end." Ibn Sana' al-Mulk goes so far as to place the *kharja* at the forefront of the process of composition of the *muwashshahat:*

> What I mean by saying it is the beginning is that the composition of the poem must begin with it. The composer must start with it before committing himself to a particular meter or rhyme, while he is still perfectly free; and whenever there occurs to him an expression or a meter which is light to the heart, agreeable to the ear, natural to the soul, sweet to the taste, he can take it and use it, consider it and compose on it; and build the *muwashshah* on it, having found the basis, holding the tail fast and putting the head on it [translated by Samuel M. Stern].

Ibn Sana' al-Mulk is describing a process by which the last segment, or tail, "wags" an entire strophic composition. One wonders how literally, or, indeed, how seriously to take what he says, given his geographic distance from al-Andalus and his temporal distance from the period during which the *muwashshah* took shape.

One potentially productive way to engage the *kharjas* and the *muwashshah,* as well as Ibn Sana' al-Mulk's comments, is to focus on what is evident (however elusive) from a consideration of both the internal discursive features of the genre and the external sources: the profoundly intertextual and explicitly citational character of the *kharja*. Ibn Sana' al-Mulk says:

> It is the rule—indeed, it is the law—in the *kharja* that the transition to it should be effected by a jump and by suddenly passing from one subject to another; in addition, it should be a phrase put in the mouth of some other person, animate or inanimate. The most common thing is to put it into the mouth of boys or women or drunkards of either sex. The strophe immediately preceding the *kharja* must contain an expression like: "he said," "I said," "she said," "I sang," "he sang," or "she sang" [translated by Samuel M. Stern].

Inherently recontextualized and multilingual components of Andalusi strophic poems, the *kharjas*—whether written in Romance, Andalusi Arabic, or some combination of the two, and leaving aside the small subgroup of panegyrical and religious *kharjas* written in classical Arabic and Hebrew—provide a potentially rich and complex textual locus for the study of Andalusi language use, musical composition, and communicative practice.

The known Romance *kharjas,* collected by Corriente Córdoba and divided into the Arabic (A) and Hebrew (H) series, can be translated as:

A1: Ibrahim, oh sweet name, come to me at night or, if you do not want to, I shall come to you; tell me where I shall find you.

A2: Tell how long an absence shall I endure; how much wailing by this woman in love, if you are not here.

A3: Go away, go away! What nerve he has: he (even) wishes to wake my relatives.

A4: Blond one, enough burning me (with passion), my tormenter; in spite of the guardian, tonight you are my prince.

A5: Mercy, mercy, oh beautiful one; tell me: why do you want, by God, to kill?

A6: My beloved's indifference hurts me to the point of breaking me: what shall I do, Mama? I cannot bear it any longer.

A7: Be off, you witch; this blond one with beautiful passion, scarcely have I seen fear (in him).

A8: My beloved, lovesick for me, seems to want a cure; he did not even wish to see me: put yourself in my place.

A9: I shall not go with you unless you raise my anklets up to my earrings.

A10: This shameless one, Mama, this troublemaker, he kisses me by force and (now) my buttocks are sore.

A11: If you love me the way one might love a beautiful person, kiss me and lead me by the necklace, you with the little cherry mouth.

A12: Without him the festival becomes like a fast, (since) I have restricted the joys of my heart to him.

A13: I want no handsome lover but the dark-skinned one.

A14: Mama, oh what a beloved! Below his lovely blond hair, that pale neck and little red mouth.

A15: He didn't want even to say a word to me; my worry (about him) drives sleep away from me, Mama.

A16: Who cuts apart my soul? Who tears my soul from me?

A17: I will not sleep, Mama; in the morning I will make up my beautiful face for Abu-l-Qasim.

A18: As if he (were) a boy from the outside, no more would I hold him to my bosom.

A19: Oh, compassionate Mother, in the morning I will make up my beautiful face for Abu-l-Óajjaj.

A20: If you knew, my lord, whose kisses you would have! I would offer you my little mouth, red like cistus flowers.

A21: Mama, my beloved has gone away and will not return; tell (me), Mama, what shall I do? He has not left (me) even a little kiss.

A22: Today is a bright day, the day of the feast of the summer solstice; I shall wear my brocaded suit and shatter my lance (in sport).

A23: Do not bite me, my beloved, I flinch at that; I wear such a fine garment that I recoil at that.

A24: I said: how exciting you are for me, little mouth, sweet like I do not know what.

A25: Mercy, my love, you will cause me grief with your absence; kiss my little mouth, beautiful one; to Huesca you will not go.

A26: From embraces with beauty spots you are bitten as if by teeth as sharp as spears: what a horrid way to kill people.

A27: My friend, believe me, I'd be glad to die. How can he know everything? . . . By God, what shall I do?

A28: Because I have loved a boy from the outside as he has loved me, his guardian wants to keep him away from me.

A29: Oh heart of mine, you wish to love beauty; come on, take refuge in the *(sura)* Yasin . . . and distance yourself from the (rough) sea.

A30: Mama, what good is the *(sura)* Yasin for lovesickness? If I'm going to die, bring Ibn Alhajib to me as a remedy and I shall be cured.

A31: Mama, I suffer so much from promises and excuses; (but) let him forsake me, for if I were to cut things off it would not become me.

A32: You frown at me whenever I appear; how many troubles are of my doing? Without cause you have allowed the killing of someone beautiful. Tell me, Mama, what shall I do?

A33: Come with me—don't be troublesome, bearing grudges is unbecoming; join me in love.

A34: A curse on the beautiful one who hurts a lover; I believed that I had found teeth to defend me, not someone to bite me, Mama.

A35: Tell me, Mama, for fuck's sake: do my relatives suspect that I'll abandon my hopes of getting paid in full for what he bought on credit?

A36: Little mouth like a necklace, sweet like honey; come, kiss me, my darling, come to me, join me in love, because I am dying.

A37: You already know my complaint, that I think I am suffering harm. Go away, get away from me, not without a good reason to run away.

A38: Mama, this boy has to be all mine, lawfully or unlawfully.

A39: I have been asked who my lord is; (Listen) everyone, the name given to him is, perhaps, Badrillo.

A40: What will I do or what will become of me, my love? Don't leave me.

A41: My love hurt me, he didn't want my heart; his eyes are fickle in granting favor and he is not upset by my possible death.

A42: You satisfy me in nothing, you don't want to change; loafing is your custom now as before.

H1: Come, my lord, come, the future heir to so many of Fortune's gifts; come, son of Ibn Addayyan.

H2: Tell me if you are a fortune-teller and can truthfully tell the future; tell me when my beloved Ishaq will come to me.

H3: Since my Cidillo came, such good tidings; it is as if a ray of sun shone over Guadalajara.

H4: I shall tell you, little sisters: who will contain my illness? Without my beloved I cannot live: where shall I go asking for him?.

H5: Without him the festival becomes like a fast; how my heart burns for him [a slight variation of A12].

H6: My God, how will I live with this thieving dove? He threatens to part even before saying hello.

H7: Boy from the outside, may you soon sleep on my bosom [a slight variation of A18].

H8: Do not take hold of me, my beloved, I flinch at that; I wear such a fine garment that I recoil at that [a slight variation of A23].

H9: My heart is leaving me; oh God, will it ever return to me? My beloved hurts me so badly; (my heart) is ill, when will it get better?

H10: Just when you have truly gotten better, you shatter again from longing and get worse.

H11: Keep my necklace as security for my condition, Mama; my lord wants to see my white neck, he doesn't want my jewelry.

H12: She is an unfortunate woman, you all see it, tormented by her own aunt; sell your love to others, harlot who is not paid up front.

H13: Go to Seville in the clothing of a merchant, so that you may get for me a letter from Ibn Muhajir.

H14: What shall I do, Mama? My beloved is at the door.

H15: Tell me: What will I do? How will I live? I will die for my beloved, you must know this.

H16: What will I do or what will become of me, my love? Don't leave me [identical to A40].

H17: Good morning–tell me where you're coming from; I already know that you love someone else; you do not love me.

H18: So much love, so much love, my dear, (that) my healthy eyes became ill; now they hurt so badly.

H19: Go away, you shameless one, get away from here, for you don't have good intentions for me.

H20: Oh dark-skinned one, oh joy of my eyes, who will be able to bear (your) absence, my beloved?.

H21: Because I have loved a boy from the outside as he has loved me, his guardian wants to keep him away from me [identical to A28].

H22: Mama, what does it say in the Scriptures? "Women are irrational." (That's why) I am fickle, for whom will my love last?

H23: What will I do, Mama? My beloved is going away with such intense brightness; I wish that I did not love him.

H24: If you cared for me, you with the illustrious name, if you cared for me, you would take me with you.

H25: . . . to you I will fly; . . . I will be able to give it to you.

H26: Love is little comfort; hold a throbbing heart and then suffer.

Bibliographies:

Richard Hitchcock, *The Kharjas: A Critical Bibliography* (London: Grant & Cutler, 1977);

Hitchcock and Consuelo López-Morillas, *The Kharjas: A Critical Bibliography. Supplement 1* (London: Grant & Cutler, 1996);

Henk Heijkoop and Otto Zwartjes, "A Supplementary Bibliography of Andalusi Strophic Poetry," *Bibliotheca Orientalis*, 55 (1998): cols. 642–726.

References:

J. A. Abu-Haidar, *Hispano-Arabic Literature and the Early Provençal Lyrics* (Richmond, U.K.: Curzon, 2001);

Abu-Haidar, "The Muwashshahat and the Kharjas Tell Their Own Story," *Al-Qantara*, 26, no. 1 (2005): 43–98;

Dámaso Alonso, "Cancioncillas 'de amigo' mozárabes (Primavera temprana de la lírica europea)," *Revista de Filología Española*, 33 (1949): 297–349;

Alonso, "Perspectivas del hispanismo actual," in *Actas del Segundo Congreso Internacional de Hispanistas, Nijmegen, 20–25 de agosto de 1965*, edited by Jaime Sánchez Romeralo and Norbert Paulussen (Nijmegen: Instituto Español de la Universidad de Nimega, 1967), pp. 17–23;

Samuel G. Armistead, "A Brief History of *Kharja* Studies," *Hispania*, 70 (1987): 8–16;

Armistead, "Pet Theories and Paper Tigers," *La corónica*, 14, no. 1 (1985): 55–70;

Armistead, "Speed or Bacon? Further Meditations on Professor Alan Jones," *La corónica*, 10, no. 2 (1982): 148–155;

Armistead and James T. Monroe, "Beached Whales and Roaring Mice: Additional Remarks in Hispano-Arabic Strophic Poetry," *La corónica*, 13, no. 2 (1985): 206–242;

Richard Bauman and Charles L. Briggs, "Poetics and Performances as Critical Perspectives on Language and Social Life," *Annual Review of Anthropology,* 19 (1990): 59–88;

Briggs and Bauman, "Genre, Intertextuality, and Social Power," *Journal of Linguistic Anthropology,* 2 (1992): 131–172;

Federico Corriente Córdoba, "Modified ʿArud: An Integrated Theory for the Origin and Nature of Both Andalusi Arabic Strophic Poetry and Sephardic Hebrew Verse," in his *Poesía estrófica* (Madrid: Universidad Complutense–Instituto de Cooperación con el Mundo Árabe, 1991), pp. 71–78;

Corriente Córdoba, *Poesía dialectal árabe y romance de Alandalús* (Madrid: Gredos, 1997);

Corriente Córdoba and Angel Sáenz-Badillos, "Nueva propuesta de lectura de las *xarajat* con texto romance de la serie hebrea," *Revista de Filología Española,* 74 (1994): 283–289;

Alan Deyermond, "Las jarchas y la lírica tradicional," in *Historia y crítica de la literatura española,* volume 1: *Edad Media,* edited by Francisco Rico (Barcelona: Grijalbo, 1979), pp. 47–82;

Anthony P. Espósito, "The Monkey in the Jarcha: Tradition and Canonicity in the Early Iberian Lyric," *Journal of Medieval and Early Modern Studies,* 30, no. 3 (2000): 463–477;

Emilio García Gómez, "Métrica de la moaxaja y métrica española: Aplicación de un nuevo método de medición completa al 'Gais' de Ben al-Jatib," *Al-Andalus,* 39 (1974): 1–256;

Martin Hartmann, *Das arabische Strophengedicht, I: Das Muwassah* (Weimar: Felber, 1897);

Richard Hitchcock, "The Interpretation of Romance Words in Arabic Texts: Theory and Practice" *La corónica,* 13, no. 2 (1985): 243–254;

Hitchcock, "Las jarchas treinta años después," *Awraq,* 3 (1980): 19–25;

Hitchcock, "Sobre la 'mama' en las jarchas," *Journal of Hispanic Philology,* 2 (1977): 1–9;

Hitchcock, "Some Doubts about the Reconstruction of the *Kharjas,*" *Bulletin of Hispanic Studies,* 50 (1973): 109–119;

Alan Jones, "*Eppur si muove,*" *La corónica,* 12, no. 1 (1983): 45–70;

Jones, "Romance Scansion and the *Muwassahat:* An Emperor's New Clothes?" *Journal of Arabic Literature,* 11 (1980): 36–55;

Jones, "Sunbeams from Cucumbers? An Arabist's Assessment of the State of *Kharja* Studies," *La corónica,* 10, no. 1 (1981): 38–53;

Mary Jane Kelley, "Virgins Misconceived: Poetic Voice in the Mozarabic Kharjas," *La corónica,* 19, no. 2 (1991): 1–23;

Rafael Lapesa, "Sobre el texto y lenguaje de algunas jarchas mozárabes," *Boletín de la Real Academia Española,* 40 (1960): 53–65;

Consuelo López-Morillas, "Language," in *The Literature of Al-Andalus,* edited by María Rosa Menocal, Raymond Scheindlin, and Michael Sells (Cambridge: Cambridge University Press, 2000), pp. 33–59;

Ramón Menéndez Pidal, "Cantos románicos y andalusíes, continuadores de una lírica latina vulgar," *Boletín de la Real Academia Española,* 31 (1951): 187–270;

Menéndez Pidal, *Discurso acerca de la primitiva poesía lírica española, leído en la inauguración del curso de 1919 a 1920* (Madrid: Jiménez & Molina, 1919);

Marcelino Menéndez y Pelayo, "De las influencias semíticas en la literatura española," in his *Estudios y Discursos de crítica histórica y literaria* (Santander: Consejo Superior de Investigaciones Científicas, 1941), pp. 192–217;

María Rosa Menocal, *The Arabic Role in Medieval Literary History* (Philadelphia: University of Pennsylvania Press, 1987);

James T. Monroe, "¿Pedir peras al olmo? On Medieval Arabs and Modern Arabists," *La corónica,* 10, no. 2 (1982): 121–147;

Monroe, "Poetic Quotation in the *Muwassah* and Its Implications: Andalusian Strophic Poetry as Song," *La corónica,* 14, no. 2 (1986): 230–250;

Monroe, "Zajal and Muwashshaha," in *The Legacy of Muslim Spain,* edited by Salma Khadra Jayyusi (Leiden & New York: Brill, 1992), pp. 398–417;

Dwight Reynolds, "Music," in *The Literature of Al-Andalus,* pp. 60–82;

Reynolds, "Musical 'Membrances of Medieval Muslim Spain,'" in *Charting Memory: Recalling Medieval Spain,* edited by Stacy Beckwith (New York: Garland, 2000), pp. 155–168;

Julián Ribera, "El Cancionero de Abencuzmán," in his *Disertaciones y opúsculos,* volume 1 (Madrid: Estanislao Maestre, 1928), pp. 3–92;

Tova Rosen, "The Muwashshah," in *The Literature of Al-Andalus,* pp. 165–189;

Adolf Friedrich Graf von Schack, *Poesie und Kunst der Arabe in Spanien und Sicilien* (Berlin: Hertz, 1865);

Samuel M. Stern, *Hispano-Arabic Strophic Poetry,* edited by L. P. Harvey (Oxford: Clarendon Press, 1974);

Otto Zwartjes, *The Andalusian Xarja-s: Poetry at the Crossroads of Two Systems?* (Nijmegen: Catholic University of Nijmegen, 1995);

Zwartjes, *Love Songs from al-Andalus: History, Structure and Meaning of the Kharja* (Leiden: Brill, 1997).

Latin Histories and Chronicles of Medieval Spain

Manuel Alejandro Rodríguez de la Peña
Universidad Autónoma de Madrid

WORKS: Anonymous, *Gesta Comitum Barcinonensium et Regum Aragonie* (1208–1276)

Edition: *Gesta Comitum Barcinonensium, textos llatí i catalá editats i anotats,* edited by L. Barrau-Dihigo and Jaime Massó Torrents (Barcelona: Imprenta de la casa de caritat, 1925).

Rodrigo Jiménez de Rada, *Breviarium Historiae Catholicae* (before 1214)

Manuscripts: Real Biblioteca del Monasterio de El Escorial, MS. X.I.10; Biblioteca Universitaria de Madrid, MS. 138; Biblioteca Provincial de Toledo, MSS. 54–57, eighteenth century.

Modern edition: *Roderici Ximenii de Rada Opera Omnia,* edited by Juan Fernández Valverde, Corpus Christianorum Continuatio Medievalis, volume 72, part 2 (Turnhout: Brepols, 1992).

Lucas de Tuy, *Liber de Miraculis Sancti Isidori* (circa 1223)

Manuscript: Archivo de San Isidoro, León, códice no. LXIII.

Modern edition: "Liber de Miraculis Sancti Isidori," in *Sancti Martini Legionensis Presbyteri et Canonici Regularis, Ordinis Sancti Augustini, in Regio Cœnobio Legionensi D. Isidoro Hispalensi Sacro: Opera Omnia,* edited by Jacques-Paul Migne, Patrologia Latina, volume 208 (Paris: Migne, 1855), cols. 9–24.

Edition: *Libro de los miraglos* [sic] *de San Isidro arçobispo de Seuilla, primado y doctor excelle[n]tissimo de las Españas successor del apostol Santiago en ellas: co[n] la hystoria de su vida y fin y de su trasladacio y del glioso doctor S[an]to Martino su canonis y co[m]panero, en q[ue] se co[n]tiene[n] muchas cosas deuotas et puechosas pa la co[n]ciencia: para saber las antiguidades de España,* translated by Juan de Robles (Salamanca: Alonso Porras, Lorenço de Lion Dedey, 1525).

Edition in modern Spanish: *Milagros de San Isidoro,* translated by Juan de Robles, edited by Julio Pérez Llamazares, introduction by Antonio Viñayo González (León: Universidad de León, Secretariado de Publicaciones/Cátedra de San Isidoro de la Real Colegiata de León, 1992).

Lucas de Tuy, *Vita Sancti Martini Legionensis* (circa 1230)

Editions: *Libro de los miraglos* [sic] *de San Isidro arço-*
bispo de Seuilla, primado y doctor excelle[n]tissimo de las Españas successor del apostol Santiago en ellas: co[n] la hystoria de su vida y fin y de su trasladacio y del glioso doctor S[an]to Martino su canonis y co[m]panero, en q[ue] se co[n]tiene[n] muchas cosas deuotas et puechosas pa la co[n]ciencia: para saber las antiguidades de España, translated by Juan de Robles (Salamanca: Alonso Porras, Lorenço de Lion Dedey, 1525); *Santo Martino de León: Vida y obras narradas por el Tudense,* edited by Antonio Viñayo González (León: Editorial Isidoriana, 1984); *Santo Martino de León (1130–1203): Vida, prólogos y epílogos parenéticos de sus tratados,* edited by Antonio Viñayo González (León: Editorial Isidoriana, 2002).

Lucas de Tuy, *Chronicon mundi* (circa 1236)

Manuscripts: Biblioteca Nacional, Madrid, MSS. 10441 (*olim* Toledo 27-28) and 898; Biblioteca de Palacio, Madrid, MS. 2-C-3; Biblioteca Nacional, Lisbon, MS. 353; Real Academia de la Historia, Madrid, MS. G-2; Biblioteca Universitaria Salamanca, MSS. 203 and 2248; Biblioteca San Isidoro, León, MSS. 20 and 41; Vatican Library, Rome, MS. lat. 7004; Kungliga Biblioteket, Stockholm, MS. D 1272a.

Early edition: *Hispaniae Illustratae Scriptores,* edited by Andreas Schott, 4 volumes (Frankfurt am Main, 1608), IV: 1–116.

Edition in Spanish: *Crónica de España por Lucas, obispo de Tuy,* edited by Julio Puyol (Madrid: Revista de Archivos, Bibliotecas y Museos, 1926).

Modern editions: *Obra sacada de las cronicas de Sant Isidoro, arcebispo de Sevilla,* edited by Regina af Geijerstam and Cynthia M. Wasick (Madison, Wis.: Hispanic Seminary of Medieval Studies, 1988); Olga Valdés García, *El "Chronicon Mundi" de Lucas Tuy* (Salamanca: Universidad de Salamanca, 1999 [microform]); *Lucae Tudensis Chronicon mundi,* edited by Emma Falque Rey, in *Lucae Tudensis Opera omnia,* volume 1 (Turnhout: Brepols, 2003).

Juan de Soria(?), *Chronica Latina Regum Castellae* (circa 1236)

Manuscript: Biblioteca de la Real Academia de la

Historia, Madrid, MS. 9/450 (*olim* G-1), folios 89–122.

Editions: Georges Cirot, "Une Chronique latine inédite des rois de Castille (1236)," *Bulletin Hispanique,* 22 (1920): 1–153; *Crónica Latina de los Reyes de Castilla,* edited and translated into Spanish by Luis Charlo Brea (Cádiz: Servicio de Publicaciones de la Universidad, 1984; revised edition, Madrid: Akal, 1999); *Chronica Latina,* in *Textos Medievales,* volume 11, edited by María Desamparados Cabanes (Saragossa: Anúbar, 1985); *Chronica hispana saeculi XIII,* edited by Luis Charlo Brea, Juan A. Estévez Sola, and Rocío Carande Herrero, Corpus Christianorum Continuatio Medievalis, volume 73 (Turnhout: Brepols, 1997), pp. 9–118.

Edition in English: *The Latin Chronicle of the Kings of Spain,* edited by Joseph F. O'Callaghan (Tempe: Arizona Center for Medieval and Renaissance Studies, 2002).

Jiménez de Rada, *Historia de rebus Hispaniae sive historia Gothica* (circa 1243)

Manuscripts: Real Biblioteca del Monasterio de El Escorial, MS. Ç.IV.12; Biblioteca Universitaria de Madrid, MS. 143; Biblioteca Pública de Córdoba, MS. 131.

First publication: *De rebus Hispaniae* (Granada: Sancho de Nebrija, 1545).

Edition: *Patrum Toletanorum quotquot extant opera,* volume 3, edited by Cardinal F. de Lorenzana (Madrid, 1793), pp. 1–208; republished in *Roderici Toletani Antistitis Opera,* edited by María Desamparados Cabanes (Valencia: Anúbar, 1968).

Standard edition: *Roderici Ximenii de Rada Opera Omnia,* edited by Juan Fernández Valverde, Corpus Christianorum Continuatio Medievalis, volume 72, part 1 (Turnhout: Brepols, 1987).

Editions in Spanish: *Historia de los hechos de España,* edited by Juan Fernández Valverde (Madrid: Alianza, 1989); *Crónica: "Additiones" a "De rebus hispanie" de Rodrigo Jiménez de Rada,* edited and translated into Spanish by Benito Morer de Torla, Juan Fernández Valverde, and Juan Antonio Estévez Sola (Huesca: Instituto de Estudios Altoaragoneses / Saragossa: Prensas Universitarias de Zaragoza, 2002).

Jiménez de Rada, *Historia Romanorum; Historia Hunnorum, Vandalorum et Suevorum, Alanorum at Silingorum; Historia Ostrogothorum* (31 March 1243)

Manuscripts: Real Biblioteca de El Escorial, MS. Ç.IV.12; Biblioteca Universitaria de Madrid, MS. 143; Biblioteca Pública de Córdoba, MS. 131.

Early editions: *Rerum in Hispania Gestarum Chronicon,* edited by Sancho de Nebrija (Granada, 1545);

De rebus Hispaniae, in *Hispaniae Illustratae,* volume 2, edited by Andreas Schott (Frankfurt am Main, 1603); *De rebus Hispaniae,* edited by Cardinal F. de Lorenzana, in *Sanctorum Patrum Toletanorum Opera,* volume 3 (Madrid, 1793).

Standard edition: *Historia Romanorum; Historia Hunnorum, Vandalorum et Suevorum, Alanorum at Silingorum; Historia Ostrogothorum,* edited by Juan Fernández Valverde, Corpus Christianorum Continuatio mediaevalis, Volume 72C (Turnhout: Brepols, 1999).

Jiménez de Rada, *Historia Arabum* (circa 1245)

Manuscripts: Catedral de Segorbe, MS. G.1; Biblioteca Capitular de Toledo, MS. 27–26.

First publication: *Historia Arabum,* edited by Andreas Schott, in *Hispaniae Illustratae,* volume 2 (Frankfurt am Main, 1603).

Editions: *Tarikh al-Muslimin: Min sahib shari'at al-Islam Abi al-Qasim Muhammad ilá al-dawlah al-Atabakiyah,* edited by Thomas Erpenius and Iacobus Golius (Leiden: Typographia Erpeniana Linguarum Orientalium, 1625); *Historia Arabum,* in Roderici Ximenii de Rada, *Toletanae ecclesiae praesulis, opera praecipua complectens,* edited by Francisco Antonio Lorenzana (Madrid: Iochimi Ibarra, 1793); republished as *Roderici Toletani Antistitis Opera,* edited by María Desamparados Cabanes (Valencia: Anúbar, 1968).

Modern editions: *Historia Arabum,* edited by J. Lozano Sánchez (Seville: Secretariado de Publicaciones de la Universidad de Sevilla, 1974); *Historia Arabum,* edited by Juan Fernández Valverde, in *Roderici Ximenii de Rada opera omnia,* Corpus Christianorum Continuatio Medievalis, volume 72, part 2 (Turnhout: Brepols, 1992).

Juan Gil de Zamora, *De Preconiis Hispaniae* (circa 1278–1282)

Manuscripts: Bibliothèque Nationale, Paris, MSS. nouvelle acq. latin 175 and latin 12925; Real Biblioteca del Monasterio de El Escorial, MS. Q.II.7; Biblioteca Nacional, Madrid, MSS. 6353 and 1348; Biblioteca de Palacio, Madrid, MS. 1091.

Edition: "Joannes Aegidius Zamorensis, *De Preconiis Hispaniae,*" edited by Manuel de Castro y Castro, thesis, Universidad de Madrid, 1955.

Edition in Spanish: "Alabanza de España," in *Maremagnum de escrituras; Dictaminis epithalamium; Libro de las personas ilustres; Formación del príncipe,* edited and translated by José-Luis Martín (Zamora: Ayuntamiento de Zamora, 1995).

Gil de Zamora, *Liber Illustrium Personarum* (circa 1285)

Manuscripts: Burgo de Osma Biblioteca Capitular 18 (fragment); Biblioteca de Palacio, Madrid,

MS. II. 1903-II. 1347.

Edition: F. Fita, "Biografías de San Fernando y de Alfonso el Sabio por Gil de Zamora," *Boletín de la Real Academia de la Historia,* 5 (1884): 321–323.

Edition in Spanish: "Libro de las personas ilustres," in *Maremagnum de escrituras; Dictaminis epithalamium; Libro de las personas ilustres; Formación del príncipe,* edited and translated by José-Luis Martín (Zamora: Ayuntamiento de Zamora, 1995).

Jofré de Loaysa, *Chronica* (circa 1305)

Manuscript: Bibliothèque de l'Arsenal, Paris, MS. 982, folios 92v–97r.

Editions: Antonio Morel-Fatio, "*Chronique des Rois de Castille,*" *Bibliothèque de l'Ecole des Chartes,* 59 (1898): 325–378; *Crónica,* edited by Agustín Ubieto Arteta (Valencia: Anúbar, 1971).

Edition in Spanish: *Crónica de los reyes de Castilla: Fernando III, Alfonso X, Sancho IV y Fernando IV (1248–1305),* translated by Antonio García Martínez, second edition (Murcia: Academia Alfonso X el Sabio, 1982).

Anonymous, *Chronica de San Juan de la Peña* (circa 1369–1372)

Manuscripts: Biblioteca Capitular de la Catedral de Valencia, MS. 198, fourteenth century; Biblioteca Nacional, Madrid, MS. 18080, folios 158–228, fourteenth century, and 1684, end of fourteenth or beginning of fifteenth century.

Edition: *Crónica de San Juan de la Peña,* edited by A. Ubieto Arteta (Valencia: Graf Bautista, 1961).

Edition in English: *The Chronicle of San Juan de la Peña: A Fourteenth-Century Official History of the Crown of Aragon,* translated by Lynn H. Nelson (Philadelphia: University of Pennsylvania Press, 1991).

Throughout the eleventh and twelfth centuries the kingdoms of León and Castile, Aragon, and Navarre were the poor relations of their northern neighbors in chronicle production. The monastic scriptoria of France and England hummed with activity, but peninsular historiography languished; for example, no Latin chronicle was produced in the kingdom of León and Castile after the *Chronica Naierense* (1169–1174, Chronicle of Nájera) until the 1230s. Then, in a span of less than ten years, the situation was transformed by the appearance of three Latin chronicles: Lucas de Tuy's *Chronicon Mundi* (circa 1236, Chronicle of the World); the anonymous *Chronica Latina Regum Castellae* (circa 1236, Latin Chronicle of the Kings of Castile), attributed to Juan de Soria; and Rodrigo Jiménez de Rada's *Historia de rebus Hispaniae sive Historia Gothica* (1243, History of the Affairs of Spain or History of the Goths). The transformation coincided with the acceleration of the reconquest of Andalusia and with cultural stirrings

evidenced by the development of the *mester de clerecía* (art of clerics) style in poetry and the foundation of the universities of Palencia and Salamanca.

It would be difficult to exaggerate the importance of these three authors and their Latin chronicles: they mark a qualitative and quantitative break with the dry, annalistic treatment of earlier peninsular experiments in the genre. The works of Lucas and Jiménez de Rada, in particular, forged a path for the vernacular historiography promoted by King Alfonso X *el Sabio* (the Learned). Without these episcopal forerunners, the Alfonsine *Estoria de España* (circa 1270–circa 1284, History of Spain) and *General estoria* (circa 1272–circa 1280, General History or History of the World) would have been inconceivable. All three authors were closely associated with their reigning kings, and their chronicles serve those kings' causes. The language in which they were written limited their circulation to a learned public and did not secure any significant diffusion for them beyond the Pyrenees.

Lucas's *Chronicon mundi* was the first to be completed. His reputation has undergone a wholesale rehabilitation: far from the rustic simpleton and purveyor of miracle stories characterized by Benito Sánchez Alonso in 1941 and Francisco J. Fernández Conde in 1987, he has been shown to have been a subtle writer possessed of a calculating mind and a man of cosmopolitan culture uncommon among the peninsular prelates of his day. Although the reevaluation of his work is still in progress and will be much advanced by Emma Falque Rey's 2003 edition of his chronicle, there is already a general appreciation of his skill in falsifying the historical record—his almost Machiavellian capacity for manipulating, as well as inventing, sources to serve the present interests of the kingdom of León and to preserve its identity in the immediate aftermath of its reunification with Castile in 1230. His propagandistic purpose has been characterized by Peter Linehan as a form of historiographical terrorism against the hegemonic ambitions of the kingdom of Castile and the church of Toledo.

Little is known about Lucas's life; it is not even clear that he was Spanish. Linehan suggests that he may have been one of the French or Italian scholars recruited by King Alfonso VIII of Castile to staff the university of Palencia, and he questions Henrique Flórez's claim (1767) that before being elected bishop of Tuy, Lucas was *magister scolarum* (master of scholars) in Palencia. Lucas himself only mentions in his *De altera vita* (1236, On the Second Life) that he journeyed to Paris and to Rome sometime before 1234.

Whatever his origins might have been, Lucas's devotion to the kingdom and the city of León is plain. As deacon of the church of San Isidoro he compiled a collection of miracles performed by the patron saint of the church (circa 1223). Sometime after 1230 the widow of Alfonso IX of León, Queen Berenguela, commissioned him to write his chronicle. He completed this task in or after 1236, the year Berenguela's son Fernando III conquered Cordova. For Lucas that event signaled the defeat of Spanish Islam and the expunging of the shame of Spain. For him Fernando III was, therefore, a "blessed king."

Lucas declares in the prologue to the *Chronicon mundi* that St. Isidore the historian is the model for the first three books of the work, covering the period from the Creation to the Visigoths, although in book 3 he also makes use of other sources. With the purpose of falsifying the past for contemporary purposes, Lucas introduces into the text of Isidore's "Praise of Spain" an equally expansive praise of León, the "patria et civitas" (homeland and capital) and cradle of martyrs. In book 4, dealing with developments since 711, Lucas comes into his own by supplementing with his fertile imagination the reduced number of sources available and creates a history directed against a nobility that he sees as perennially intent on destroying the king's peace; against Castile, which is forever "bellatrix" (war-like) because, imbued by the subversive spirit of the same nobility, it confronts "fidelis" (faithful) León; and against Toledo.

Jiménez de Rada has long been regarded as the most important and influential Latin chronicler of medieval Spain and the chief ideologist of the Castilian court. Although of Navarrese origin and, according to tradition, an alumnus of the universities of Paris and Bologna, he made his mark in Castile as royal prelate in the service of Alfonso VIII and Fernando III and as archbishop of Toledo from 1208 until his death in 1247. More warrior than reformer, he was lukewarm in his enthusiasm for the implementation of the moral reforms of the Fourth Lateran Council of 1215 and was disgraced at Rome for speculating in Crusade revenues.

An early work of Jiménez de Rada's is the monumental *Breviarium historiae catholicae* (before 1214, Breviary of Catholic History), a biblical history in nine books covering the period between the Creation and, 5,198 years later, Christ's Passion on 25 March of the year 33 (Jesus was thought to have died on 25 March, just as he had been conceived on 25 March; this notion explains why Christmas comes exactly nine months after the 25 March Feast of the Annunciation). Jiménez de Rada closely follows Peter Comestor's *Historia scholastica* (circa 1170, Scholastic History). Jiménez de Rada's editor Juan Fernández Valverde suggests that the *Breviarium historiae catholicae* was designed to provide early-thirteenth-century Spain with the benefits of Parisian theological scholarship. To judge by its extremely limited manuscript diffusion, it was not a best-seller.

Linehan and Georges Martin describe Jiménez de Rada's historiographical activities as being in the service of Castile and against the Leonese objectives. Linehan suggests that Jiménez de Rada became aware of Lucas's chronicle and its explosive content in 1239, when one of his agents visited San Isidoro de León in search of evidence for a legal case against the archbishop of Tarragona. Jiménez de Rada decided to refute Lucas's *Chronicon mundi* by using it as the main source for his *Historia de rebus Hispaniae sive Historia Gothica*. Fernández Valverde states that the *Chronicon mundi* "served him as the armature of his narrative onto which he grafted all the rest, and in that way he kept in play multiple versions of his tale from which he could select what he found most convincing." Jiménez de Rada's objective was to harmonize the neo-Gothic ideal of *praeclara Gothorum posteritas* (the preeminent Visigothic heritage) with the ambitions of Castile to be the "cabeça del reinado" (head of the kingdom) and of the church of Toledo to be the peninsula's most important see. Although no less preoccupied than Lucas with the Visigoths, he eschews his predecessor's ostensibly universal schema in favor of one that provides room for genealogies of the rulers of Navarre, Aragon, and Portugal to emphasize the hegemony of the kingdom of Castile and, by extension, of its ecclesiastical counterpart, the church of Toledo.

The *Historia de rebus Hispaniae sive Historia Gothica,* a work composed, in its author's own words, in response to Fernando III's request for an account of Spanish *antiquitas* (ancient history), took on the character of a story of *strenuitas* (vitality, fortitude) lost and found, of the *patria* (homeland, nation) perishing and then reviving through feats of patriotism, and of the protocol of the Gothic revival. Castile's rulers are Jiménez de Rada's ideal monarchs. They are characterized, above all, by their *sapientia* (wisdom) and their *strenuitas,* with Alfonso VIII, the author's favorite king, presented as a paradigm in the chapter dedicated to his virtues.

As ex officio chancellor of the kingdom, and as an almost obsessive accumulator of papal privileges in his church's interest, Jiménez de Rada enjoyed unrivaled access to raw materials from which to create a history of the previous century and a half; in striking contrast to his English contemporary Matthew Paris, however, he made virtually no use of those materials. He follows Lucas's account for the years prior to 1209, editing it to suit his requirements; for example, he deletes all references to the so-called Division of Wamba and completely recasts the legend of the Judges of Castile. He uses Jordanes's *Getica* (551, History of the Goths) to supply gaps in Isidore's *Historia de regibus Gothorum, Van-*

The opening of a manuscript of Rodrigo Jiménez de Rada's Historia de rebus Hispaniae sive historia Gothica
(Biblioteca Pública de Córdoba, MS. 13)

dalorum et Suevorum (History of the Kings of the Goths, Vandals and Suebi)—rebuking that author, in passing, for various omissions—and in Lucas's *Chronicon mundi* itself. He also makes use of the *Chronicle of the Moor al-Rasi* and French epic material.

For the final books of *Historia de rebus Hispaniae sive Historia Gothica,* covering the years 1209 to 1243, Jiménez de Rada is his own source. The narrative uses the first-person singular or plural as he depends largely on personal recollections of events he had witnessed or, more often than not, dominated. He reports, for example, that he played a decisive role at the battle of Las Navas de Tolosa in 1212, strengthening Alfonso VIII's resolve and urging on the counterattack of the victorious Christian host. For the years 1212 to 1217 Jiménez de Rada's history remains an essential source to this day.

Thereafter the pace of the chronicle slackens; the change coincides with Jiménez de Rada's momentary fall from grace after the brief reign of the child-king Enrique I, during which the royal chancery had been entirely in his hands. At the end of 1217 supervision of the office was transferred to the chancellor, Juan de Soria, and the archbishop was no longer in a position to further his own church's interests. After that year, Jiménez de Rada's main area of activity was outside royal government. The ninth and final book of the chronicle is slightly briefer than its predecessors, and its treatment of Fernando III is markedly cooler than that of Alfonso VIII in the earlier books.

Jiménez de Rada also wrote historical sketches of the successive inhabitants of Spanish soil: the *Historia Romanorum* (1243, History of the Romans), which is interesting only for its toponymical content; the fifteen-chapter *Historia Hunnorum, Vandalorum, Suevorum, Alanorum et Silingorum* (1243, History of the Huns, Vandals and Sueves, Alans and Silingues), derived from Jordanes and St. Isidore; the *Historia Ostrogothorum* (1243, History of the Ostrogoths); and the *Historia Arabum* (circa 1245, History of the Arabs). His final work, the *Historia Arabum* is remarkable for displaying the author's knowledge of Arabic-language sources and for being the earliest account of al-Andalus (Moorish Spain) from the pen of a peninsular ecclesiastic. A question that has not been settled is whether Jiménez de Rada was in any real sense the author of this work or of any of the others attributed to him. Linehan notes that he may have exercised a general supervision over his writings as Alfonso X *el Sabio* did in the following generation.

The unique manuscript of the third Latin history, the *Chronica Latina Regum Castellae,* lacks both a prologue and an indication of authorship. Various authors have been proposed since Georges Cirot discovered the manuscript in 1912. Derek W. Lomax's review of the

question in 1963 established that the critical consensus favored Juan de Soria, Fernando III's chancellor and successively bishop of Osma and of Burgos, although in 1995 Luis Charlo Brea suggested stylistic reasons for attributing the final chapters to a second author.

After a rapid review of the first two centuries of Castilian history, beginning with the death of Fernán González and—surprisingly—failing to include his deeds, the *Chronica Latina Regum Castellae* dedicates sixty-seven of its seventy-five chapters to the eighty-year period between the accession of the "nobilis et gloriosus" (noble and glorious) Alfonso VIII and the conquest of Cordova. The narrative concludes in 1236, the same year as Lucas's. Described by Lucas as "sapientissimus" (highly learned), Juan possessed a fluent Latin style and brought to his task knowledge not only of the Bible but also of Horace, Virgil, Lucan, and, perhaps, Seneca. His preoccupation with uncanonical royal marriages (that is, those that were classified by the Church as incestuous) reveals a degree of sensitivity to papal reform not evident in the work of Jiménez de Rada, with whom he attended the Fourth Lateran Council.

What particularly distinguishes this chronicle is the firsthand knowledge it displays of Fernando III's activities. When Juan embarked on it in 1223, he was in charge of the king's chancery and was therefore able to refer to the texts of treaties, wills, and other government records. For example, he reports verbatim Fernando's speech of 1224 announcing the resumption of military action in al-Andalus. While he does not disguise his hostility toward Alfonso IX of León, his vision rises above narrow peninsular prejudice to encompass the wider world: Fernando's victories are characterized as blows struck for the "exaltation of the name of Jesus Christ" rather than for the aggrandizement of the kingdom of Castile. It is not known whether Juan, who introduced the use of the vernacular to the Castilian chancery, chose to write his chronicle in Latin to reach a wider audience. In any case, the *Chronica Latina Regum Castellae* is not one of the sources of the Alfonsine *estorias.*

Strictly speaking, the *De preconiis Hispaniae* (1278–1282, The Glories of Spain) of Juan Gil de Zamora is not a work of history but a didactic treatise for the instruction of the Infante Sancho, to whom it is dedicated. But it includes a huge number of historical exemplars for the prince to emulate, including Aristotle, who is claimed to have been a Spaniard. His *Liber illustrium personarum* (circa 1285, Book of Illustrious Persons) is a series of biographies and hagiographies of notable figures of the Spanish past, including Fernando III and Alfonso X.

The *Chronica* (circa 1305) of Jofré de Loaysa was conceived as a continuation of Jiménez de Rada's *Histo-*

ria de rebus Hispaniae sive Historia Gothica and covers the years 1243 to 1305. Originally written "in romancio" (in romance), it was translated into Latin at Jofré's request by Armandus de Cremona, canon of Toledo. The son of a Catalan knight of the same name, who had come to Castile as a member of the household of Alfonso X's wife, Violante of Aragon, Jofré served in the royal chancery and on diplomatic missions abroad and after lengthy litigation secured the valuable archdeaconry of Toledo. In 1282 he abandoned Alfonso X in favor of the rebellious Infante Sancho. Writing during the anarchical minority of Sancho's son, Fernando IV, he laments in equal measure the irresponsibility of Sancho's imperial aspirations and the early death in 1295 of Fernando. A civil servant par excellence, he is careful otherwise not to reveal where his sympathies lie. His other principal loyalty was to the church of Toledo, whose pretensions to the primateship receive his unqualified support. As a close collaborator of the archbishop of Toledo, Gonzalo Pérez Gudiel, Sancho IV's principal minister for much of his reign, Jofré was probably involved in that prelate's campaign to recast the Alfonsine *Estoria de España* to magnify Toledo's importance in Spanish history. No copy of the original vernacular version of the *Chronica* has survived, and only a single late manuscript of Armandus's Latin translation exists.

In the Crown of Aragon the *Crónica de San Juan de la Peña* (translated as *The Chronicle of San Juan de la Peña: A Fourteenth-Century Official History of the Crown of Aragon,* 1991) was composed at the behest of Pere IV *el Ceremoniós* (the Ceremonious) between 1369 and 1372, possibly to serve as a preamble to the vernacular chronicle of his reign. The original Latin text, together with the Catalan and Aragonese versions into which it was immediately translated, provided the principal source for Aragonese and Navarrese historiography throughout the fifteenth century. Ambitious in conception, it begins with the mythical coming of Tubal and a general treatment of the history of Spain borrowed from Jiménez de Rada's *Historia de rebus Hispaniae sive Historia Gothica;* it then concentrates on the deeds of the kings of Aragon and the counts of Barcelona down to the death of Alfonso IV in 1336. It constitutes the earliest attempt to present the affairs of the separate territories of the Crown of Aragon as constituent parts of a single whole.

References:

Luis Charlo Brea, "¿Un segundo autor para la última parte de la *Crónica Latina de los Reyes de Castilla?*" in *Actas I Congres Nacional de Latín Medieval: León, 1–4 de diciembre de 1993,* edited by Maurilio Pérez González (León: Universidad de León, Secretariado de Publicaciones, 1995), pp. 251–256;

Francisco J. Fernández Conde, "El biógrafo contemporáneo de Santo Martino: Lucas de Tuy," in *Santo Martino de Leon: Ponencias del I Congreso Internacional sobre Santo Martino en el VIII centenario de su obra literaria (1185–1985),* edited by Antonio Viñayo González (León: Isidoriana Editorial, 1987), pp. 303–335;

Henrique Flórez, *De la Iglesia de Tuy* (Madrid, 1767);

Julio González, "La crónica latina de los reyes de Castilla," in *Homenaje a don Agustín Millares Carlo,* volume 2 (Las Palmas de Gran Canaria: Caja Insular de Ahorros de Gran Canaria, 1975), pp. 55–79;

Hilda Grassotti, "Don Rodrigo Ximénez de Rada, gran señor y hombre de negocios en la Castilla del s. XIII," *Cuadernos de Historia de España,* 55–56 (1972): 1–302;

Francisco J. Hernández, "La corte de Fernando III y la casa real de Francia: Documentos, crónicas, monumnetos," in *Fernando III y su tiempo (1201–1252)* (Ávila: Fundación Sánchez-Albornoz, 2003), pp. 103–155;

Hernández, "La hora de don Rodrigo," *Cahiers de linguistique et de civilisation hispaniques mediévales,* 26 (2003): 15–71;

Hernández, "Noticias sobre Jofré de Loaisa y Ferrán Martínez," *Revista Canadiense de Estudios Hispánicos,* 4 (1980): 281–309;

Hernández and Peter Linehan, *The Mozarabic Cardinal: The Life and Times of Gonzalo Pérez Gudiel* (Florence: SISMEL/Edizioni del Galluzzo, 2004);

Peter Linehan, "Dates and Doubts about D. Lucas," *Cahiers de linguistique et de civilisation hispaniques Médiévales,* 24 (2001): 201–217;

Linehan, *History and the Historians of Medieval Spain* (Oxford: Clarendon Press, 1993);

Linehan, "On Further Thought: Lucas of Tuy, Rodrigo of Toledo and the Alfonsine Histories," *Anuario de Estudios Medievales,* 27 (1997): 415–435;

Linehan, *Past and Present in Medieval Spain* (Aldershot, U.K.: Variorum / Brookfield, Vt.: Ashgate, 1992);

Linehan, "Reflexiones sobre historiografía e historia en el siglo alfonsino," *Cahiers de Linguistique Hispanique Médiévale,* 23 (2000): 101–111;

Derek W. Lomax, "The Authorship of the *Chronique Latine des rois de Castille,*" *Bulletin of Hispanic Studies,* 40 (1963): 205–211;

Lomax, "Rodrigo Jiménez de Rada como historiador," in *Actas del Quinto Congreso Internacional de Hispanistas,* edited by Maxime Chevalier (Bordeaux: Instituto de Estudios Ibericos e Iberoamericanos, Universidad de Bordeaux III, 1977), pp. 587–592;

Georges Martin, *Les juges de Castille: Mentalités et discours historique dans l'Espagne médiévale* (Paris: Klincksieck, 1992);

Martin, "Luc de Tuy, Rodrigue de Tolède, leurs traducteurs et leurs compilateurs alphonsins: Comparaison segmentaire d'une lexicalisation," *Cahiers de Linguistique Hispanique Médiévale,* 14–15 (1989–1990): 173–206;

Bernard F. Reilly, "Rodrigo Jiménez de Rada's Portrait of Alfonso VI of León-Castile in the *De Rebus Hispaniae:* Historical Methodology in the Thirteenth Century," *Estudios en homenaje a D. Claudio Sánchez Albornoz en sus 90 años,* volume 3 (Buenos Aires: Instituto de Historia de España, 1985), pp. 87–97;

Reilly, "Sources of the Fourth Book of Lucas of Tuy's *Chronicon Mundi,*" *Classical Folia,* 30 (1976): 127–137;

Manuel Alejandro Rodríguez de la Peña, "El paradigma de los reyes sabios en el de *Rebus Hispaniae* de Rodrigo Jiménez de Rada," in *Sevilla 1248: Congreso internacional commemorativo del 750 aniversario de la conquista de la ciudad de Sevilla por Fernando III, rey de Castilla y León, Sevilla, Real Alcázar, 23–27 de noviembre de 1998,* edited by Manuel González Jiménez (Madrid: Centro de Estudios Ramón Areces, 2000), pp. 757–765;

Benito Sánchez Alonso, *Historia de la historiografía española,* 2 volumes (Madrid: Consejo Superior de Investigaciones Científicas, 1941, 1944);

Roger Wright, "Latin and Romance in the Castilian Chancery (1180–1230)," *Bulletin of Hispanic Studies,* 73 (1996): 115–128.

Medieval Spanish Debate Literature

Andrew M. Beresford
University of Durham

WORKS: Anonymous, *Disputa del alma y el cuerpo* (circa 1145–1172)

Manuscript: Archivo Histórico Nacional, Madrid, clero pergaminos: carpeta 272, no. 22.

First modern edition: José M. Octavio de Toledo, ed., "Visión de Filiberto," *Zeitschrift für Romanische Philologie,* 2 (1878): 40–69.

Editions: Manuel Alvar, ed., *Antigua poesía española lírica y narrativa,* fourth edition, Colección Sepan Cuantos, 151 (Mexico City: Porrúa, 1985), pp. 127–142; Fernando Gómez Redondo, ed., *Poesía española,* volume 1: *Edad Media: Juglaría, clerecía y romancero,* Páginas de Biblioteca Clásica, no. 1 (Barcelona: Crítica, 1996), pp. 211–220.

Standard editions: *"Disputa del alma y el cuerpo y Auto de los Reyes Magos,"* edited by Ramón Menéndez Pidal, *Revista de Archivos, Bibliotecas y Museos,* 4 (1900): 429–462, republished in his *Textos medievales españoles: Ediciones críticas y estudios,* Obras Completas, volume 12 (Madrid: Espasa-Calpe, 1976), pp. 161–169; Enzo Franchini, ed., *Los debates literarios en la Edad Media,* Arcadia de las Letras, no. 9 (Madrid: Laberinto, 2001), pp. 215–217.

Anonymous, *Disputa entre un cristiano y un judío* (circa 1230–1250)

Manuscript: Biblioteca de San Lorenzo de El Escorial, Madrid, MS g-IV-30, folio 22v.

Standard editions: Américo Castro, ed., *"Disputa entre un cristiano y un judío," Revista de Filología Española,* 1 (1914): 173–180; Enzo Franchini, ed., *Los debates literarios en la Edad Media,* Arcadia de las Letras, no. 9 (Madrid: Laberinto, 2001), pp. 227–228.

Anonymous, *Elena y María* (circa 1280)

Manuscript: Biblioteca Duquesa de Alba, Madrid, MS. LXXXVI, folios 1r–25v.

Editions: Manuel Alvar, ed., *Antigua poesía española lírica y narrativa,* fourth edition, Colección Sepan Cuantos, volume 151 (Mexico City: Porrúa, 1985), pp. 159–177; Fernando Gómez Redondo, ed., *Poesía española,* volume 1: *Edad Media: Juglaría, clerecía y romancero,* Páginas de Bib-

lioteca Clásica, no. 1 (Barcelona: Crítica, 1996), pp. 237–246.

Standard editions: *"Elena y María (disputa del clérigo y del caballero): Poesía leonesa inédita del siglo XIII,"* edited by Ramón Menéndez Pidal, *Revista de Filología Española,* 1 (1914): 52–96, republished in his *Textos medievales españoles: Ediciones críticas y estudios,* Obras Completas, volume 12 (Madrid: Espasa-Calpe, 1976), pp. 119–159; Enzo Franchini, ed., *Los debates literarios en la Edad Media,* Arcadia de las Letras, no. 9 (Madrid: Laberinto, 2001), pp. 229–234.

Anonymous, *Visión de Filiberto* (circa 1360)

Manuscript: Biblioteca Nacional, Madrid, MS. Vitrina 6-1, folios 37v–48v.

Standard editions: José M. Octavio de Toledo, ed., "Visión de Filiberto," *Zeitschrift für Romanische Philologie,* 2 (1878): 41–69; Enzo Franchini, ed., *Los debates literarios en la Edad Media,* Arcadia de las Letras, no. 9 (Madrid: Laberinto, 2001), pp. 235–247.

Anonymous, *Disputa del cuerpo e del ánima* (circa 1382)

Manuscripts: Bibliothèque Nationale, Paris, MS. esp. 230, folios 225r–228r; Bibliothèque Nationale, Paris, MS. esp. 313, folios 179v–181v.

First modern edition: José M. Octavio de Toledo, ed., "Visión de Filiberto," *Zeitschrift für Romanische Philologie,* 2 (1878): 40–69.

Editions: Manuel Alvar, ed., *Antigua poesía española lírica y narrativa,* fourth edition, Colección Sepan Cuantos, no. 151 (Mexico City: Porrúa, 1985), pp. 127–142; Fernando Gómez Redondo, ed., *Poesía española,* volume 1: *Edad Media: Juglaría, clerecía y romancero,* Páginas de Biblioteca Clásica, no. 1 (Barcelona: Crítica, 1996), pp. 211–220.

Standard editions: Erik von Kræmer, ed., *Dos versiones castellanas de la disputa del alma y el cuerpo del siglo XIV,* Mémoires de la Société Néophilologique, volume 18.3 (Helsinki: Suomalaisen Kirjallisuuden Kirjapaino, 1956), pp. 40–53; Enzo Franchini, ed., *Los debates literarios en la Edad Media,*

Arcadia de las Letras, no. 9 (Madrid: Laberinto, 2001), pp. 249–252.

Anonymous, *Revelación de un hermitaño* (circa 1382?)

Manuscript: Biblioteca de San Lorenzo de El Escorial, Madrid, MS. b.IV.21, folios 129v–35v.

First modern edition: Tomás Antonio Sánchez and Florencio Janer, eds., *Poetas castellanos anteriores al siglo XV,* Biblioteca de Autores Españoles, volume 57 (Madrid: M. Rivadeneyra, 1864), pp. 387–388.

Editions: José M. Octavio de Toledo, ed., "Visión de Filiberto," *Zeitschrift für Romanische Philologie,* 2 (1878): 40–69; Fernando Gómez Redondo, ed., *Poesía española,* volume 1: *Edad Media: Juglaría, clerecía y romancero,* Páginas de Biblioteca Clásica, no. 1 (Barcelona: Crítica, 1996), pp. 211–220.

Standard editions: Erik von Kræmer, ed., *Dos versiones castellanas de la disputa del alma y el cuerpo del siglo XIV,* Mémoires de la Société Néophilologique, volume 18.3 (Helsinki: Suomalaisen Kirjallisuuden Kirjapaino, 1956), pp. 40–53; Enzo Franchini, ed., *Los debates literarios en la Edad Media,* Arcadia de las Letras, no. 9 (Madrid: Laberinto, 2001), pp. 253–258.

Rodrigo Cota, *Diálogo entre el Amor y un viejo* (circa 1465–1485)

First edition: Hernando del Castillo, ed., *Cancionero general de muchos y diversos autores* (Valencia: Cristóbal Kofman, 1511), folios 72v–75r.

Editions: R. Foulché-Delbosc, ed., *Cancionero castellano de siglo XV,* volume 1, Nueva Biblioteca de Autores Españoles, volume 19 (Madrid: Casa Editorial Bailly Balliere, 1915), pp. 580–587; Alvaro Alonso, ed., *Poesía de Cancionero,* Letras Hispánicas, no. 247 (Madrid: Cátedra, 1995), pp. 307–327.

Standard editions: *Diálogo entre el Amor y un viejo,* edited by Elisa Aragone (Florence: Le Monnier, 1961), pp. 67–106; Enzo Franchini, ed., *Los debates literarios en la Edad Media,* Arcadia de las Letras, no. 9 (Madrid: Laberinto, 2001), pp. 269–277.

Anonymous, *Diálogo entre el Amor, el viejo y la hermosa* (circa 1490?)

Manuscript: Biblioteca Nazionale di Napoli, Naples, MS. XIII.G.42, folios 132r–141r.

First modern edition: Alfonso Miola, ed., "Un testo drammatico spagnuolo del XV secolo," in *Miscelanea di filologia e linguistica in memoria di N. Caix e Ugo Angelo Cannello* (Florence: Successori Le Monnier, 1886), pp. 175–189.

Editions: Ana M. Álvarez Pellitero, ed., *Teatro Medieval,* Colección Austral, no. A157 (Madrid: Espasa-Calpe, 1990), pp. 209–213; Ronald E. Surtz, ed., *Teatro Castellano de la Edad Media,* Clási-cos Taurus, volume 13 (Madrid: Taurus, 1992), pp. 51–54; Miguel Ángel Pérez Priego, ed., *Teatro Medieval,* volume 2: *Castilla* (Barcelona: Crítica, 1997), pp. 117–143.

Standard editions: *Diálogo entre el Amor y un viejo,* edited by Elisa Aragone (Florence: Le Monnier, 1961); Enzo Franchini, ed., *Los debates literarios en la Edad Media,* Arcadia de las Letras, no. 9 (Madrid: Laberinto, 2001), pp. 279-287.

Antonio López de Meta, *Tractado del cuerpo e de la ánima* (circa 1489?)

First edition: *Tractado del cuerpo e de la ánima* (Saragossa: Pablo Hurus, 1489?); *La contienda del cuerpo e alma* (Toledo: Juan de Villaquirán, 1515–1520).

Modern edition: Cyril A. Jones, ed., "Algunas versiones más del debate entre el cuerpo y el alma," in *Miscelanea di Studi Ispanici 1963,* Instituto di Letteratura Spagnola e Ispano-Americana, no. 6 (Pisa: Università, 1963), pp. 110–134.

Although the mostly anonymous medieval Spanish debate literature is not a major field of current academic research, it includes works that are of considerable value to the study of the development of intellectual and rhetorical discussion in Spain, as well as of the history of ideas in general. With the exception of the work of Enzo Franchini and a few brief comments on the sources and influences of the debate in large-scale histories of Spanish literature, the majority of such works have seldom been treated as a group; instead, they are usually absorbed into other contexts, where their individual characteristics are blurred or lost. Early minstrel-like compositions such as the *Disputa del alma y el cuerpo* (circa 1145–1172, Dispute between the Soul and the Body) and *Elena y María* (circa 1280, Helen and Mary), for instance, are frequently read alongside texts such as the thirteenth-century *Vida de Santa María Egipçiaca* (thirteenth–fourteenth centuries, Life of St. Mary of Egypt) and *Libre dels tres reys d'Orient* (Book of the Three Kings of the East) as examples of early Spanish popular narrative poetry. The later body-and-soul debates, on the other hand, are treated as manifestations of the late-medieval obsession with death and the afterlife and read in conjunction with works such as the late-fourteenth-century *Dança general de la Muerte* (General Dance of Death) and Jorge Manrique's *Coplas por la muerte de su padre* (1479, Verses on the Death of His Father).

While this neglect is partly the result of the absence of a single comprehensive study of the debate, it can also be attributed to the chronology of debate production, where unexplained intervals of fifty or even seventy years are common. This apparently sporadic production has provided critics with problems in attempting to trace the development of the various

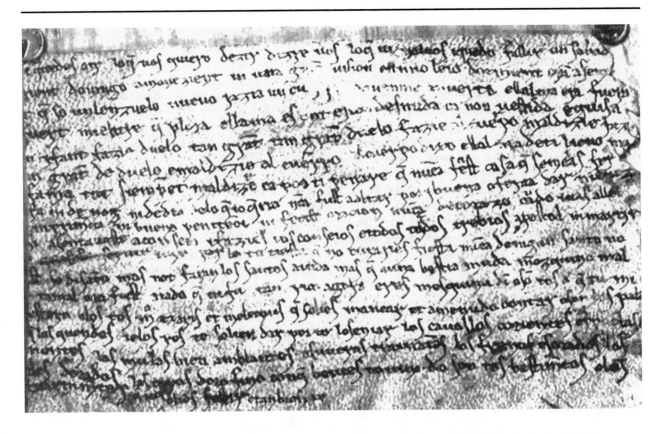

Page from a manuscript of the Disputa del alma y el cuerpo, *composed circa 1145–1172 (Archivo Histórico Nacional, Madrid, clero pergaminos: carpeta 272, no. 22)*

debate forms, as well as in determining the provenance of individual works and traditions.

Several factors are commonly mentioned as fueling interest in the genre. The founding of the universities, in which oral debate was a central intellectual exercise, and the circulation of Latin, Hebrew, Arabic, and French literary debates in the Iberian Peninsula have been cited as major influences. Equally important are the impact of the Provençal *tensó* (debate) and the wrangling language and disputatious rhetoric of the courtroom, as, for instance, in the concluding stages of the *Cantar de mío Cid* (circa 1200; translated as *Poem of the Cid*, 1879), in which a trial serves as a prelude to judicial combat. Yet, none of these factors accounts for the eclectic variety of early Spanish debate literature or the interest in works in which debates are intercalated within more-substantial narratives. Of particular note are the piquant debates that form part of Juan Ruiz's *Libro de buen amor* (circa 1330–1343; translated as *Book of Good Love*, 1933) or those in Alfonso Martínez de Toledo's misogynist diatribe *Arcipreste de Talavera* (1428, Archpriest of Talavera; translated as *Little Sermons on Sin*, 1959), also known as *Corbacho* (The Whip). The evolution of the debate can also be seen in the elaboration of

the stylized *preguntas y respuestas* (questions and answers) fashion in the late-fourteenth- and fifteenth-century *cancioneros* (courtly songbooks), in which groups of writers entered into poetic exchanges on such issues as predestination, the Immaculate Conception, and the actual and theoretical status of women in society.

The earliest extant debate in Spanish is the *Disputa del alma y el cuerpo,* a seventy-four-line fragment copied onto the back of a single sheet of loose parchment in the Monastery of San Salvador de Oña in Burgos. Although the parchment dates from 1201, it is believed that the dispute was composed earlier—according to Juan-Ramón Mayol-Ferrer, as early as 1145 to 1172—and that the surviving version is a defective and incomplete copy of a lost original. Evidence to support this assumption includes the idiosyncratic manner in which the poem is arranged: despite the use of rhyme and a preponderance of heptasyllables (seven-syllable lines), the text was copied as a sequence of carelessly formed prose lines extending over about a third of the space available on the parchment. This scribal interference has produced textual corruption, particularly of rhyme: the modernization, for instance, of the rhyme word *fora* (outside) as *fuera* leads in the following line to the substitution of the hybrid form *plera* (weeping) for the Old Spanish *plora* that would have been found in the original. The most enigmatic aspect of the *Disputa del alma y el cuerpo* is its relationship to its source, the Old French *Un samedi par nuit* (One Saturday Night), also known as *Le Debát de l'âme et du Corps* (The Debate between the Soul and the Body), which comprises more than a thousand lines. The *Disputa del alma y el cuerpo* attempts to rework the French original into Spanish; but if the Spanish version had been of equivalent length, it could never have been copied into the space provided by the parchment. According to Antonio G. Solalinde's calculations, however, another 150 lines could have been included; it is perplexing, therefore, that the scribe stopped in midsentence when he had enough space to continue.

The *Disputa del alma y el cuerpo* is the earliest known in a series of Spanish body-and-soul debates, works that drew on a pan-European tradition of mortality literature inspired by the *contemptu mundi* (contempt for the world) theme and a broad amalgam of hagiographic commonplaces that have been dated to the age of the Desert Fathers. The body-and-soul debates serve to inculcate spiritual dogma by offering a sequence of arguments that stress the dangers of an imperfect balance between the earthly demands of the body and the spiritual aspirations of the soul. The body, the reader is routinely told, faltered in its religious obligations, normally by doting on earthly ephemera, while the soul failed to wield its greater intellectual might to suppress the predilections of the flesh. The *Disputa del alma y el cuerpo* makes use of this tradition but develops several ideas that became familiar features of later debates. Among them are the manipulation of the dream-vision format and the development of the folkloric belief that the souls of the dead wander the earth each seventh night until cockcrow. Other aspects of the poem have an unmistakable early-thirteenth-century flavor. The introduction, for instance, is highly reminiscent of the engaging, minstrel-like tone of the *Vida de Santa María Egipçiaca* and the *Libre dels tres reys d'Orient*. The most noticeable similarity is a dominant first-person narrator who addresses the audience collectively as "vos" (you [plural]) and whets its appetite by promising an interesting and true tale:

Si quereedes oír
lo que vos quiero dezir,
dizré vos lo que vi,
nol' vos ý quedo fallir.

(If you would like to hear
what I should like to tell you,
I shall tell you what I saw
without a single omission.)

Solalinde has demonstrated that the minstrel-like introduction to the *Disputa del alma y el cuerpo* is one of many departures from *Un samedi par nuit* that show that the Spanish poet was eager to draw on native traditions and to rework his original to afford his poem a greater degree of verbal intensity and stylistic cohesion. This pattern continues throughout the debate. The soul's opening speech is reduced to two areas: criticism of the body's spiritual failings followed by a diatribe in the form of a reworking of the *ubi sunt* (where are they?) topos. While the French original revolves around the body's threefold failure to give charitable offerings, to respect the Church, and to value the intercession of the saints, the Spanish version produces a gradual funneling effect as the soul moves from criticism of money to an invective against status symbols. The tone of the second section is particularly caustic as the soul upbraids the body for the ultimate futility of its lust for money:

Dime, ¿ó son tos dineros
que tú mitist en estero? ¿ó los tus moravedís
azarís et melequís
que soliés manear
et a menudo contar?

(Tell me, where are the coins
you tucked into your purse? Where are the maravedís,
azarís and *melequíes* [coins from Christian and Moorish mints]
you would so often
play with and count?)

It then criticizes the body's penchant for conspicuous consumption, lambasting its attachment to a series of familiar status symbols:

¿Ó son los palafrés
que los cuendes e los res
te solién dar
por te lonseniar?
¿los cavallos corrientes
las espuelas punientes? . . . las copas de oro fino
con que bebiés tu vino?

(Where are the riding mounts
that counts and kings
would give you
for your pleasure?
The chargers
and sharp spurs? . . . the cups of fine gold
from which you would drink?)

The poem breaks off at this point. One assumes that the remainder would have followed the pattern of *Un samedi par nuit*: the soul would have concluded its arguments; the body would have defended itself; and the devil would have appeared and dragged the terrified soul to hell.

Like the *Disputa del alma y el cuerpo*, the *Disputa entre un cristiano y un judío* (circa 1230–1250, Dispute between a Christian and a Jew) is a fragment of what might once have been a much longer debate; only the Christian's attacks on Judaism have been preserved in the work, which occupies the final folio of a codex of Latin doctrinal texts. This debate is not one between equals that is destined to end in a stalemate but would almost certainly have concluded with the Jew capitulating and asking to receive the sacrament of baptism. It is, then, a "vertical" or pedagogical debate, in which the more persuasive side eventually wins the argument by drawing the assent of the opponent, as opposed to a "horizontal" debate, in which equals field arguments for listeners to consider but a resolution is not reached. The *Disputa entre un cristiano y un judío* reflects the atmosphere of religious intransigence that is also present in works as diverse as the *Cantar de mio Cid*, the *Auto de los Reyes Magos* (circa 1215, Drama of the Magi), and Gonzalo de Berceo's *Los Milagros de Nuestra Señora* (before 1246–after 1252; translated as *Miracles of Our Lady*, 1997). The speaker's detailed knowledge of Jewish concepts, uncompromising ferocity, mordant sarcasm, and visceral disgust at traditional caricatures of Jewish ritual such as the *mezizá*, the supposed suction of blood during circumcision (in fact, the rabbi spits on the wound, an application of folk medicine that makes use of the antiseptic qualities of saliva), has led critics such as Américo Castro and Nicasio Salvador Miguel to conclude that the piece could only have been composed by a Jew who had converted to Christianity. (The criticism of the *mezizá* includes one of the most outrageous comparisons in early Spanish literature as the Christian informs the Jew that during circumcision the rabbi's mouth becomes akin to the vagina of a menstruating woman: "Onde, quando bien vós mensuraredes, fonta vos ý yace et muy grand, que la boca de vuestro rabí que compieça vuestra oración feches coño de mujer" [So, when you really think about it, the practice is a terrible affront, that you should make the mouth of your rabbi who intones your prayer like the cunt of woman].) Critics have suggested that the hostility to Judaism places the most probable date of composition of the debate between 1230 and 1250, when Fernando III's military expansion was at its peak. Fernando Gómez Redondo thinks that the writer chose prose over verse because of the theological complexity of the piece and maintains that the Christian speaker selects the specific subjects he does—the law and the commandments, the status of the Sabbath, and the identity and nature of God—to entice the Jew into a series of theological minefields. Gómez Redondo also notes the crude but effective way in which the debate is structured by the use of simple parallelistic formulae such as "Agora fablemos de sabaat" (Now let's speak of the Sabbath) and "Agora fablemos de creer verdadero Deus" (Now let's speak of belief in the true God). This sort of analysis has made it possible to challenge the assumption that the text is an historical curiosity detached from the mainstream development of early Spanish prose.

Apart from the mysterious and majestic *Razón de amor con los denuestos del agua y el vino* (1230–1250, Treatise on Love with the Debate between Water and Wine; excerpt translated as "The *Razón de amor:* An Old Spanish Lyrical Poem of the 13th Century," 1977), the only thirteenth-century debate to focus specifically on romantic and sexual issues is *Elena y María,* a fragmentary poetic text written largely in octosyllabic (eight-syllable) couplets and most likely composed in or around 1280. The survival of the poem has been a matter of luck rather than prudent conservation, for the fourteenth-century manuscript in which it is contained is a pocket-sized copy that was probably designed to be used by a *juglar* (minstrel) in performance. The text has been badly damaged, and the introduction, several exchanges in the central and later portions of the poem, and the conclusion have been lost. *Elena y María* can be classified as a knight-clerk debate, even though the discussion is actually carried on by the mistresses of the knight and the clerk, and can be located within a tradition of goliardic and courtly literature that focused on two of the three medieval estates: the *oradores* (prayer-makers [clergy]) and the *defensores* (defenders [knights]); the *labradores* (laborers [peasants and workers]) were excluded. Charles Oulmont traces the development of the knight-clerk debate in French works such as *Phillis et Flora* (Phyllis and Flora) and *Le Jugement d'amour* (The Judgment of Love), in which an impressive degree of literary artifice embraces descriptions of idyllic landscapes, flowering gardens, and competitions between birds. Although the Spanish poem borrows elements from the earlier tradition, it is not modeled on any known source. The result is that in place of a gentle lyrical exchange, readers are presented with a harsh, uncompromising look at society through the eyes of a pair of women who appear at times to be more interested in belittling each others' arguments than in advancing their own claims to superiority. In consequence, readers gain an impression not of two distinct suitors but of four. In María's view her clerical lover is a respected pillar of the community, authoritative, financially stable, and attentive to her every need, while the knight is a lazy and cowardly parasite who spends much of his time gambling and pawning his possessions to survive. Elena, in contrast, sees the knight as a passionate and exhilarating courtly lover who has taken a

Pages from the manuscript of Elena y María, *composed circa 1280 (Biblioteca Duquesa de Alba, Madrid, MS. LXXXVI)*

solemn vow to defend society and the priest as a worthless and sexually depraved scoundrel whose living is made at the expense of others. The division between the views of the two female rivals is as great as the typology of their names suggests: while Elena's recalls Helen of Troy, María's relates her to the Virgin Mary.

Criticism of the poem has generally focused on the lost conclusion and the question of which party would have been adjudged to have won the argument. Ramón Menéndez Pidal, who published the first edition of the text in 1914, raised the possibility that it might have defied tradition by granting victory to Elena; this outcome seemed likely to him in view of the negative portrait of clerical concubinage in the poem. Guiseppe Tavani proposes that the debate would have ended without a clear resolution, as both parties condemn themselves so robustly with their own words that victory becomes impossible. Kevin C. Reilly argues that the perceived materialism of the poet would have led him to side with the more prosperous of the two protagonists and grant the victory to María. John D. Perivolaris, in turn, has drawn attention to some flaws in Reilly's reasoning. The debate over the outcome of the lost conclusion seems set to continue.

Three versions of the body-and-soul debate were produced in little more than twenty-five years of the latter half of the fourteenth century. The appearance of these works can be attributed to a large extent to a prolonged series of catastrophes that struck the Iberian Peninsula during the period, including the outbreak of the Black Death between 1348 and 1350, with cyclical outbreaks thereafter; the political instability that followed the demise in 1349 of Alfonso XI, the only European monarch to die of the plague; and the beginning in 1378 of the Great Schism, with rival popes in Rome and Avignon bestowing favors on those who pledged their loyalties to one faction or the other. With the Church no longer exercising a spiritual monopoly, heretical cults spread throughout Spain and other parts of Europe, and a breakdown of social order was becoming increasingly inevitable. These problems produced a profound pessimism that eventually filtered into the literature of the period in a newly acquired sense of savagery and macabre realism that contrasts with the lighter and more contemplative tone of the earlier debates.

The earliest of the three fourteenth-century body-and-soul debates, the *Visión de Filiberto* (circa 1360,

Vision of Filiberto), is a short prose text reworked not from the *Disputa del alma y el cuerpo* but from the Latin *Dialogus inter corpus et animam* (Dialogue between the Body and the Soul), an influential poem commonly attributed to the goliardic poet Walter Mapes (circa 1140–circa 1209). The *Visión de Filiberto* exists in a single manuscript that also includes a copy of the *Libro de buen amor;* it has not been edited since 1878, when it appeared along with several other manifestations of the theme in a pioneering edition by José M. Octavio de Toledo. (Franchini's 2001 edition reprints Octavio de Toledo's text, introducing some of his own emendations.) The *Visión de Filiberto* then fell into neglect for many years and was dismissed by critics such as Pierre Groult as a derivative and unimaginative reinterpretation of the subject. But the discovery of a direct line of textual influence between the *Visión de Filiberto* and the two later poetic debates has led to greater appreciation of the importance of the piece. In his study of the development of medieval Spanish prose Gómez Redondo comments on the effectiveness of the structure of the *Visión de Filiberto* and its sophisticated handling of levels of narration, while Franchini offers a far-reaching summary of the critical background of the debate along with an appreciation of its internal rhetorical development.

Filiberto is a French prince who renounced his birthright to live as a monk. Late one night when he is at prayer his commitment to a life of asceticism is rewarded with a vision in which he witnesses a debate between a soul and the lifeless body it once occupied. Although the soul is not given a specific physical form—in the *Disputa del alma y el cuerpo* it assumes the likeness of an infant–the *Visión de Filiberto* dramatizes the identities of the two protagonists by exploring a wide range of reactions and emotions. The soul initially assumes a high moral stance, accusing the body of greed, avarice, and corruption. Its haughty arrogance is soon deflated as the body, not in anger but in a staid and bookish manner, painstakingly inverts the soul's major arguments. For example, the soul claimed that its former partner was too powerful to be controlled; the body responds, "aún non me puedo nin tengo fuerça para me defender de cosa tan pequeña como son estos busanos que me rroen los costados" (I am neither able nor have the strength to defend myself against such tiny things as these worms that are gnawing their way inside my ribs). The accusations and recriminations are silenced by the entrance of a pair of devils. In a clear echo of some of the most lurid aspects of medieval iconography–typified by the *transi* (cadaver tomb), on which the traditional serene effigy was replaced by a representation of the decomposing corpse–the devils are characterized as

repulsive monsters whose snouts emit a flurry of serpents, snakes, and scorpion-like creatures. The devils apprehend the soul and inflict on it punishments that include whipping, poisoning, and pouring molten lead into its orifices. Filiberto awakes from his vision and offers the readers a series of recommendations as to how they might avoid a similar fate. Through the interpretations proffered by its emotionally detached narrator, the *Visión de Filiberto* draws attention to the danger of failing to maintain a satisfactory equilibrium between the demands of the body and the responsibilities of the soul.

The *Visión de Filiberto* is the major source of the *Disputa del cuerpo e del ánima* (Dispute of the Body and the Soul), a poetic debate that has survived in two slightly differing manuscripts, one of them incomplete, in the Bibliothèque Nationale in Paris. The *Disputa del cuerpo e del ánima* represents the high point of interest in the body-and-soul theme in late-medieval Spain, for in addition to the polished sophistication of the verbal altercation itself, the poem makes use of an imaginative symbolic framework that turns the vision into a terrifying learning experience for the narrator. The dating of the vision is unusually precise: one o'clock in the morning on 1 January 1382. Although this date has been interpreted by some critics as evidence of the time of composition, it is more likely a literary fiction pointing either to a period of personal difficulty in the author's life or to one of the social, religious, and political problems that were affecting Spain at the time. The narrator is not a reworked version of Filiberto but an everyman figure whose anxiety about and preoccupation with death are manifested in insomnia. He finds himself in a deep, dark valley where he stumbles across a body in an advanced state of putrefaction. The description suggests that its physical state is the result not of a natural process but of the many disfiguring sins that it committed during its lifetime–a direct antithesis to the many hagiographic legends in which the lifelong virtues of a saint are manifested posthumously by freedom from physical corruption. The body is accompanied by a soul in the form of a white bird. Although the debate embraces several arguments that are familiar from the earlier tradition, the achievement of the *Disputa del cuerpo e del ánima* resides in the adept and sophisticated manner in which they are deployed. A striking example is the soul's first speech: after reprimanding the body for its dedication to the seven deadly sins, it changes tack to give voice to a sonorous and elegiac rendition of the *ubi sunt* topos:

"¿Adó tus moradas? ¿Dó es tu arreo,
tu oro e tu plata e tu gran aver,
tus joyas muy ricas e tu gran poder?"

(Where are your dwellings? Where are your trappings,
your gold and your silver and your great wealth,
your priceless jewels and your vast power?)

In contrast to previous debates, where the topos creates a tone of vituperative antagonism, here it underlines the desperate futility of worldly pursuits. In the accompanying moral the soul considers the effortless way in which its former partner was undermined: "Mira agora que fue todo nada: / todo fizo fin en una braçada" (Look now, how it all came to naught: / it all came to an end with the sweep of an arm). Like its counterpart in the *Visión de Filiberto,* the body initially responds with an attitude of bookish obtuseness. Before long, however, it adopts a more temperate and lyrical tone that borrows much from the rhetoric of courtly love:

> Tú mi señora e yo tu servidor:
> mis pies e mis manos por ti se movieron;
> adó tú mandaste, allá anduvieron.
> Yo era la morada e tú el morador
>
> (You were my mistress and I your servant:
> my feet and hands bestirred themselves for you;
> wherever you ordained, there they went.
> I was the dwelling and you the dweller.)

As the debate continues, the speeches become shorter and shorter. Finally, a devil emerges from behind a thicket to claim the soul. Witnessing the tortures meted out to the soul causes the narrator to awake from the vision, but shortly afterward he loses consciousness again in a state of shock. The debate ends without an explicit moral being drawn; but the fact that the body lies lifeless on the ground while its soul is banished to the flames of hell emphasizes the dangers of failing to maintain a satisfactory equilibrium between body and soul.

The *Disputa del cuerpo e del ánima* provided the basis for another poem on the subject, the *Revelación de un hermitaño* (circa 1382? Revelation to a Hermit), which exists in a single manuscript with the *Dança general de la Muerte* and Santob de Carrión's *Proverbios morales* (circa 1350, Moral Proverbs; translated as *The Moral Proverbs of Santob de Carrión: Jewish Wisdom in Christian Spain,* 1987). This poem, which also draws material from the *Visión de Filiberto,* is distinctive in that in place of the macabre resolutions of previous debates, it describes the fate of a soul that repented at the eleventh hour and was rewarded with salvation. Although critics such as Groult and Erik von Kræmer initially received the poem favorably, later studies have demonstrated that its attempt to steer the *Disputa del cuerpo e del ánima* toward an optimistic conclusion produces a series of structural and stylistic anomalies. The most startling occurs in the opening rubric: although readers are initially informed that the narrator is a hermit who experienced a vision while at prayer, as in the *Visión de Filiberto,* the first stanza contradicts this information by saying that he was lying in bed. Much of the rest of the debate is identical to that of the *Disputa del cuerpo e del ánima;* but in the end the soul is saved, while the body is allowed to rot silently into the ground. This disparity destroys the delicate metaphorical symmetry achieved in the *Disputa del cuerpo e del ánima,* and despite the attractiveness of the final section, which includes a lengthy sermon-like intervention by an angel, the structural and stylistic anomalies detract from the overall literary and aesthetic value of the piece. The *Revelación de un hermitaño* provides an insight into the obsession with mortality that took a florid form in many works composed during the period, but it is the least accomplished of the various treatments of the theme.

The majority of debates composed in the fifteenth century circulated not as independent compositions but in the various *cancioneros* (courtly songbooks) that were compiled at that time and comprise a total of around eight thousand poems by hundreds of writers. The relationships among the various *cancioneros* have been better understood since the publication in 1990–1991 of Brian Dutton's and Jineen Krogstad's seven-volume *El cancionero castellano del siglo XV, c. 1360–1520* (The Castilian Songbook of the Fifteenth Century, circa 1360–1520), which attempts to gather all of these works in a single collection. As far as the debate genre is concerned, however, scholars have yet to establish a definitive listing of the relevant poems or to consider the ways in which they differ from other works in dialogue form. Some of the more significant debates that have yet to receive critical attention include Juan Rodríguez del Padron's *El debate de alegría y del triste amante* (Debate between Happiness and the Sad Lover), a far-reaching work on the subject of love that has been considered only in a brief study by Martin S. Gilderman, where it is read as a dialogue rather than as a debate; three poems by Pedro de Cartagena that comprise debates between the Tongue and the Heart, the Heart and the Eyes, and the Lover and the God of Love; Estamariu's *Debat duna senyora et de su voluntad* (Debate between a Lady and Her Free Will); Furtado's *Debate con su capa* (Debate with His Cape); and Cristóbal de Castillejo's *Diálogo con su pluma* (Debate with His Quill). Serious critical investigation has been afforded only to three examples of the genre: Rodrigo Cota's influential *Diálogo entre el Amor y un viejo* (probably between 1465 and 1485, Dialogue between Love and an Old Man); an anonymous reworking of that debate, the *Diálogo del viejo, el Amor y la hermosa* (late fifteenth century, Dialogue between the Old Man, Love, and the Fair Maiden); and the *Tractado del cuerpo e de la ánima* (circa 1490? Treatise on the Body and the Soul), by Antonio López de Meta.

Cota's *Diálogo entre el Amor y un viejo* was first printed in the *Cancionero general de muchos y diversos autores* (General Songbook of Many and Diverse Authors), edited by Hernando del Castillo and published in Valencia in 1511. It consists of 630 octosyllabic lines prefaced by a short prose introduction that summarizes the main narrative thread. The protagonist is an old man who has for many years shut himself away in a tumbledown cabin in a walled garden where he can be free of Love and its machinations. But one day the garden is invaded by Love, which sets about tempting the old man to fall into its clutches once again. The old man resists Love's advances, characterizing it as a trespassing thief:

> Cerrada estava mi puerta:
> ¿a qué vienes? ¿por dó entraste?
> Di, ladrón, ¿por qué saltaste
> las paredes de mi huerta?
>
> (My door was closed:
> what have you come for? Where did you get in?
> Tell me, thief, why did you scale
> the walls of my garden?)

The old man's initial hostility to Love arose from a series of bitter youthful experiences when he fell in love and suffered grievously at its hands. Now, with his physical powers in decline, he sees Love as a dangerous tyrant capable of stirring up a gamut of destructive emotions. The symbolic garden in which he lives is an inversion of the traditional *locus amoenus* (lovers' meeting place), a location characterized by flowers, running water, and greenery: the old man's garden is overgrown and choked with weeds. Natural beauty and fecundity have declined into an atmosphere of sterility and death in keeping with the old man's physical state.

Love responds to the old man's lengthy series of accusations with a considerable degree of subtlety, encouraging him almost imperceptibly to focus on the joys of youth and the pleasures he once experienced. The old man begins to wonder whether it might be possible to recover the virility of his youth and fall in love once more. Eventually, he succumbs, as he had feared, to temptation. Just as he does so, however, Love cruelly changes tack, promising him not the joys he had anticipated but the scorn of a hard-hearted maiden destined never to reciprocate his feelings. Broken by the capricious power of Love's final condemnation, the old man concludes the poem by characterizing his adversary as a venomous serpent—one of many images in the work drawn from the Bestiary—and asking a bitter rhetorical question: "¿A dó estavas, mi sentido?, / dime, ¿cómo te dormiste?" (Where were you, my senses? / Tell me, how could you have been asleep?).

Cota's debate was reworked in a more expansive format in the 725-line *Diálogo del viejo, el Amor y la hermosa*. The poem exists in a single manuscript in the National Library of Naples and was first edited in 1886 by Alfonso Miola. The poem duplicates the sequence of Cota's work but devotes a slightly greater degree of attention to characterization, making the old man's transformation from hostility to love to welcoming it a more hesitant process. The outcome, however, is identical: having tempted the old man into feeling nostalgia for his lost youth, Love condemns him to frustration. Thus, the debates in this poem and in Cota's are "vertical" ones, for in each instance the dialogue takes place not between equals but between the allegorical and all-powerful force of Love and a frail old man who is seduced by its words and made once more to suffer the pangs of romantic infatuation that had for many years lain dormant.

Because of their vivid imagery both poems, and particularly the later one, have been read by some critics as plays rather than as debates. There is little evidence, however, that either was designed for performance; and with some individual speeches embracing more than 150 lines of verse, it is difficult to understand how they might have been staged or how audiences could have maintained an interest in works so lacking in dramatic action. Perhaps the most perplexing result of the drama-versus-debate controversy is that while Cota's poem has generally been classified as a debate and has not been edited from the original manuscript since the edition of Elisa Aragone in 1961, the later work is available in most anthologies of medieval drama. The disparity has led some critics to wonder whether the debate, a significant if minor genre of medieval Spanish literature, has been classified, perhaps unconsciously, by other scholars as inferior to the drama, of which few examples have survived.

López de Meta's 344-line *Tractado del cuerpo e de la ánima* is by far the longest medieval body-and-soul debate. It is also the only such Spanish work that does not appear to have been modeled on a foreign original. Although it includes a good deal of fresh material, it makes use of the existing format by locating the debate within a dream vision that takes place in the dead of night. The narrator falls asleep while wearing a blindfold, a detail that suggests metaphorical blindness, and dreams of a verbal altercation between the body and soul of what was once a handsome young man. The soul upbraids the body for doting on its physical appearance and, exploiting an aesthetically pleasing aspect of numerical symbolism, balances discussions of the Seven Deadly Sins and the Seven Corporal Works of Mercy. The body responds with customary obtuseness; but in contrast to the tone of courtly love present in earlier works, it characterizes its bond with the soul as a student-teacher relationship and accuses the soul of sloppiness and indiscipline. After the soul offers a series of further recriminations, an angel appears and reads from a written sentence that condemns the body to rot into the ground and the soul to roast in hell, and a devil promptly arrives to administer the punishments. At this point the narrator awakes and begins to pray, drawing a series of general morals that he eventually turns on himself:

Roguemos a Dios por su piedad
. . . que quiera guardar la gente christiana
del falso amigo y de su saeta,
e a vos, y a mí, Anton López de Meta
nos lieve a la gloria que es muy sobirana.

(Let us pray to God for his mercy
. . . so that he might protect Christian peoples
from the treacherous enemy and his darts,
as well as you and me, Antonio López de Meta,
may he deliver us unto that most sovereign glory.)

The switch to the first person is arresting, and in many ways it forms an apt colophon not simply to the *Tractado del cuerpo e de la ánima* itself but also to the development of literary disputation in the Middle Ages as a whole. Although debates continued to be written in the golden age and beyond, particularly on the relationship between body and soul, they never achieved the refreshing and candid directness of their earlier counterparts. The *Tractado del cuerpo e de la ánima* is thus the swan song of the medieval Spanish debate tradition; it is by no means the most aesthetically pleasing composition, but it is the last to deal with a series of complex moral and theological issues that were soon eclipsed by more immediate and socially relevant concerns.

References:

Juan F. Alcina, "Un fragmento de la *Visio Philiberti* y la tradición hispana del diálogo del alma y el cuerpo," *Nueva Revista de Filología Hispánica,* 40 (1992): 513–522;

Carlos Alvar, "La *vaquilla* y el *solimán* y otras cuestiones del *Diálogo entre el Amor y un viejo,*" *Revista de Filología Española,* 58 (1976): 67–79;

Manuel Alvar, "Rasgos dialectales en la *Disputa del alma y el cuerpo* (siglo XIV)," in *"Strenae": Estudios de filología e historia dedicados al profesor Manuel García Blanco,* Acta Salmanticensia: Filosofía y Letras, volume 116 (Salamanca: Universidad de Salamanca, 1962), pp. 37–41;

T. Batiouchkof, "Le Débat de l'âme et du corps," *Romania,* 20 (1891): 1–55, 513–578;

Andrew M. Beresford, "Antonio López de Meta's *Tractado del cuerpo e de la ánima* and the Hispanic Body-and-Soul Tradition," *Bulletin of Hispanic Studies* (Liverpool), 74 (1997): 139–150;

Beresford, "The *Disputa del cuerpo e del ánima* and the *Visión de Filiberto:* A Reappraisal of Sources," *La corónica,* 23 (1995): 3–15;

Beresford, Review of Enzo Franchini's *Los debates literarios en la Edad Media, La corónica,* 32 (2004): 227–231;

Beresford, "Theme, Style, and Structure in the *Disputa del cuerpo e del ánima,*" *Revista de Literatura Medieval,* 8 (1996): 73–90;

Michel-André Bossy, "Medieval Debates of Body and Soul," *Comparative Literature,* 28 (1976): 144–163;

Tatiana Bubnova, "El debate del clérigo y del caballero: evolución del tema," in *Voces de la Edad Media: Actas de las Terceras Jornadas Medievales,* edited by Concepción Company, Aurelio Gómez, Lilian van der Walde, and Concepción Abellán, Publicaciones Medievalia, no. 6 (Mexico City: Universidad Nacional Autónoma de México, 1993), pp. 93–104;

Francisco Cantera Burgos, *El poeta Ruy Sánchez Cota (Rodrigo Cota) y su familia de judíos conversos* (Madrid: Universidad de Madrid, 1970);

Augusto Cortina, "Rodrigo de Cota," *Revista del Ayuntamiento de Madrid,* 6 (1929): 151–165;

Emilio Cotarelo, "Algunas noticias nuevas acerca de Rodrigo de Cota," *Boletín de la Real Academia Española,* 13 (1926): 11–17, 140–143;

A. D. Deyermond, *A Literary History of Spain,* volume 1: *The Middle Ages* (London: Benn / New York: Barnes & Noble, 1971);

Deyermond, "The Use of Animal Imagery in Cota's *Diálogo* and in Two Imitations," in *Etudes de philologie romane et d'histoire littéréaire offerts à Jules Horrent a l'occasion de son soixantième anniversaire,* edited by Jean Marie d'Heur and Nicoletta Cherubini (Liège, 1980), pp. 133–140;

Guillermo Díaz Plaja, "Poesía y diálogo: *Elena y María,*" *Estudios Escénicos,* 6 (1960): 65–82;

Brian Dutton and Jineen Krogstad, eds., *El cancionero castellano del siglo XV, c. 1360–1520,* 7 volumes, Biblioteca Española del siglo XV: Serie Maior, volumes 1–7 (Salamanca: Universidad de Salamanca, 1990–1991);

Miguel M. García Bermejo-Giner, "De nuevo sobre Rodrigo de Cota," in *Actas del III Congreso de la Asociación Hispánica de Literatura Medieval: Salamanca, 3 al 6 de octubre de 1989,* edited by María Isabel Toro Pascua, 2 volumes (Salamanca: Biblioteca Española del Siglo XV & Departamento de

Literatura Española e Hispanoamericana, 1994), I: 379–387;

Martin S. Gilderman, *Juan Rodríguez de la Cámara* (Boston: Twayne, 1977);

Gaudioso Giménez Resano, "Anotaciones lingüísticas al *Disputa entre un cristiano y un judío*," in *Actas de las III Jornadas de Estudios Berceanos,* edited by Claudio García Turza, Colección Centro de Estudios Gonzalo de Berceo, no. 6 (Logroño: Instituto de Estudios Riojanos, 1981), pp. 91–100;

Richard F. Glenn, "Rodrigo Cota's *Diálogo entre el Amor y un Viejo*: Debate or Drama?" *Hispania,* 48 (1965): 51–56;

Fernando Gómez Redondo, *Historia de la prosa medieval castellana,* 3 volumes (Madrid: Cátedra, 1998–1999);

Gómez Redondo, ed., *Poesía española,* volume 1: *Edad Media: Juglaría, clerecía y romancero,* Páginas de Biblioteca Clásica, volume 1 (Barcelona: Crítica, 1996);

Pierre Groult, "La *Disputa del alma y el cuerpo:* Fuentes e originalidad," in his *Literatura espiritual española: Edad Media y Renacimiento,* translated by Rodrigo A. Molina, Biblioteca del Hispanismo, volume 4 (Madrid: Imprenta Universitaria, 1980), pp. 99–109;

Cyril A. Jones, ed., "Algunas versiones más del debate entre el cuerpo y el alma," in *Miscelanea di Studi Ispanici 1963,* Instituto di Letteratura Spagnola e Ispano-Americana, no. 6 (Pisa: Università, 1963), pp. 110–134;

Gregory B. Kaplan, "Rodrigo Cota's *Diálogo entre el Amor y un viejo*: A *Converso* Lament," *Indiana Journal of Hispanic Literatures,* 8 (1996): 7–30;

Charles H. Leighton, "Sobre el texto del *Diálogo entre el Amor y un Viejo*," *Nueva Revista de Filología Hispánica,* 12 (1958): 385–390;

Margarita Lliteras, "Sobre el proceso de traducción de la *Disputa del alma y el cuerpo* (fragmento de Oña)," *Cuadernos de Filología: Studia Linguistia Hispanica,* 2, no. 3 (1986): 105–129;

José Miguel Martínez Torrejón, "Debate y disputa en los siglos XIII y XIV castellanos," in *Medioevo y literatura: Actas del V Congreso de la Asociación Hispánica de Literatura Medieval (Granada, 27 septiembre–1 octubre 1993),* 4 volumes, edited by Juan Paredes (Granada: Universidad de Granada, 1995), III: 275–286;

Juan-Ramón Mayol-Ferrer, "Sobre la fecha de la *Disputa del alma y el cuerpo*," *Bulletin Hispanique,* 97 (1995): 253–260;

Colbert I. Nepaulsingh, *Towards a History of Literary Composition in Medieval Spain,* University of Toronto Romance Series, volume 54 (Toronto: University of Toronto Press, 1986);

Charles Oulmont, *Les débats du clerc et du chévalier* (Paris: Champion, 1911);

John D. Perivolaris, "Further Observations on the Conclusion of *Elena y María:* An Answer to Kevin C. Reilly," *La corónica,* 22 (1994): 118–122;

Kevin C. Reilly, "The Conclusion of *Elena y María:* A Reconsideration," *Kentucky Romance Quarterly,* 30 (1983): 251–262;

Francisco Rico, "Review of Rodrigo Cota, *Diálogo entre el Amor y un viejo,* edited by Elisa Aragone," *Revista de Filología Española,* 46 (1963): 485–490;

H. Salvador Martínez, "*El Viejo, el Amor y la Hermosa* y la aparición del tema del desengaño en el teatro castellano primitivo," *Revista Canadiense de Estudios Hispánicos,* 4 (1980): 311–328;

Nicasio Salvador Miguel, *Debate entre un cristiano y un judío: Un texto del siglo XIII* (Ávila: Caja de Ahorros, 2001);

Antonio Salvador Plans, "*Disputa entre un cristiano y un judío*: Estudio lingüístico," *Glosa,* 1 (1990): 59–97;

Lourdes Simó, ed., *Juglares y espectáculo: Poesía medieval de debate* (Barcelona: DVD, 1999);

Antonio G. Solalinde, "*Disputa del alma y el cuerpo*" and "La *Disputa del alma y el cuerpo:* Comparación con su original francés," in *Poemas breves medievales,* edited by Ivy A. Corfis, Spanish Series, no. 39 (Madison, Wis.: Hispanic Seminary of Medieval Studies, 1987), pp. 29–34, 81–95;

Guiseppe Tavani, "Il dibattito sul chierico e il cavaliere nella tradizione medoiolatina e volgare," *Romanistiches Jarbuch,* 15 (1964): 51–84;

Barry Taylor, "Cota, Poet of the Desert: Hermits and Scorpions in the *Diálogo entre el Amor y un Viejo,*" in *The Medieval Mind: Hispanic Studies in Honour of Alan Deyermond,* edited by Ian Macpherson and Ralph Penny (London: Tamesis, 1997), pp. 457–468;

Roger M. Walker, "Two Notes on Spanish Debate Poems," in *Medieval Studies in Honor of Robert White Linker by His Colleagues and Friends,* edited by Brian Dutton, James Woodrow Hassell, and John Esten Keller (Madrid: Castalia, 1973), pp. 177–184;

Thomas Wright, ed., *The Latin Poems Commonly Attributed to Walter Mapes* (London: John Bowyer Nichols, 1841).

Medieval Spanish Epics

Alberto Montaner
Universidad de Zaragoza

WORKS: Cycle of the Counts of Castile

Fernán González: Chronica Naierensis (circa 1185–1190); *Poema de Fernán González* (between 1251 and 1258); Alfonso X, *Estoria de España* (1270–1274).

La Condesa traidora: Chronica Naierensis (circa 1185–1190); Alfonso X, *Estoria de España* (1270–1274).

Los siete infantes de Lara: Alfonso X, *Estoria de España* (1270–1274); *Crónica geral* (1344).

Romanz del Infante García: Chronica Naierensis (circa 1185–1190); Lucas de Tuy, *Chronicon Mundi* (1236); Rodrigo Jiménez de Rada, *Historia de rebus Hispaniae sive Historia Gothica* (1243); Alfonso X, *Estoria de España* (1270–1274).

El abad don Juan de Montemayor: Rodríguez de Almela, *Compendio historial* (1491).

Manuscripts: *Poema de Fernán González:* Real Biblioteca del Monasterio de El Escorial, MS. IV.b.21, copied between 1460 and 1480. Rodrigo Jiménez de Rada, *Historia de rebus Hispaniae sive Historia Gothica:* Real Biblioteca del Monasterio de El Escorial, Ç.IV.12; Biblioteca Universitaria de Madrid, MS. 143; and Biblioteca Pública de Córdoba, MS. 131. Alfonso X, *Estoria de España:* Real Biblioteca del Monasterio de Escorial, MSS. Y.I.2 and X.I.4.

Cycle of the Kings of Navarre-Aragon

Sancho Abarca: Liber Regum (circa 1200); Rodrigo Jiménez de Rada, *Historia de rebus Hispaniae sive Historia Gothica* (1243); Alfonso X, *Estoria de España* (1270–1274); *Crónica de San Juan de la Peña* (circa 1370).

La reina calumniada: Chronica Naierensis (circa 1185–1190); Rodrigo Jiménez de Rada, *Historia de rebus Hispaniae sive Historia Gothica* (1243); Alfonso X, *Estoria de España* (1270–1274); *Crónica de San Juan de la Peña* (circa 1370).

La Campana de Huesca: Alfonso X, *Estoria de España* (1270–1274); *Crónica de San Juan de la Peña* (circa 1370).

Manuscripts: *Liber Regum:* Biblioteca General de la Universidad de Zaragoza, MS. 255, early thirteenth century. Rodrigo Jiménez de Rada, *Historia*

de rebus Hispaniae sive Historia Gothica: Real Biblioteca del Monasterio de El Escorial, MS. Ç.IV.12; Biblioteca Universitaria de Madrid, MS. 143; and Biblioteca Pública de Córdoba, MS. 131. Alfonso X, *Estoria de España:* Real Biblioteca del Monasterio de Escorial, MSS. Y.I.2 and X.I.4. *Crónica de San Juan de la Peña:* Real Biblioteca del Monasterio de El Escorial, MSS. L.II.13, sixteenth century, and N.I.13, sixteenth century; Biblioteca Nacional, Madrid, MS. 2078, sixteenth century.

Editions: Ramón Menéndez Pidal, *Reliquias de la poesía épica española* (Madrid: Espasa-Calpe, 1951), republished with prologue by Diego Catalán (Madrid: Gredos, 1980); *Crónica de San Juan de la Peña,* Latin text edited by Antonio Ubieto (Valencia: Anubar, 1961); *Crónica de San Juan de la Peña,* Aragonese text edited by Carmen Orcástegui Gros (Saragossa: Institución "Fernando el Católico," 1985); Fernando Gómez Redondo, ed., *Poesía Española, 1: Edad Media; Juglaría, Clerecía y Romancero,* Páginas de Biblioteca Clásica (Barcelona: Crítica, 1996); Carlos Alvar and Manuel Alvar, eds., *Épica medieval española,* Letras Hispánicas, no. 330, second edition (Madrid: Cátedra, 1997).

Edition in modern Spanish: Rosa Castillo, ed., *Leyendas épicas españolas,* prologue by Enrique Moreno Báez (Madrid: Castalia, Odres nuevos, 1971).

Carolingian Cycle

Mainete: Lucas de Tuy, *Chronicon mundi* (1236); Rodrigo Jiménez de Rada, *Historia de rebus Hispaniae sive Historia Gothica* (1243); Alfonso X, *Estoria de España;* Juan Gil de Zamora, *Liber illustrium personarum* (circa 1280); *Gran Conquista de Ultramar* (end of thirteenth century).

Roncesvalles (circa 1270).

Bernardo del Carpio: Lucas de Tuy, *Chronicon mundi* (1236); Rodrigo Jiménez de Rada, *Historia de rebus Hispaniae sive Historia Gothica* (1243); Alfonso X, *Estoria de España* (1270–1274).

Peregrinación de Luis VII: Lucas de Tuy, *Chronicon*

344

mundi (1236); Rodrigo Jiménez de Rada, *Historia de rebus Hispaniae sive Historia Gothica* (1243); Alfonso X, *Estoria de España* (1270–1274).

Manuscripts: Lucas de Tuy, *Chronicon mundi:* Biblioteca Nacional, Madrid, MSS. 10441 (*olim* Toledo 27-28) and 898; Biblioteca de Palacio, Madrid, 2-C-3; Biblioteca Nacional, Lisbon, MS. 353; Real Academia de la Historia, Madrid, MS. G-2; Biblioteca Universitaria, Salamanca, MSS. 2248 and 203; Biblioteca San Isidoro, León, MSS. 20 and 41; Vatican Library, Rome, MS. lat. 7004; Kungliga Biblioteket, Stockholm, MS. D 1272a. Rodrigo Jiménez de Rada, *Historia de rebus Hispaniae sive Historia Gothica:* Real Biblioteca del Monasterio de El Escorial, MS. Ç.IV.12; Biblioteca Universitaria de Madrid, MS. 143; and Biblioteca Pública de Córdoba, MS. 131. Alfonso X, *Estoria de España:* Real Biblioteca del Monasterio de El Escorial, MSS. Y.I.2 and X.I.4. *Roncesvalles:* Archivo General de Navarra, Pamplona, MS. 212, circa 1310. Juan Gil de Zamora, *Liber illustrium personarum* (circa 1280): Biblioteca Nacional, Madrid, MS. 18,657, seventeenth century. *Gran Conquista de Ultramar:* Biblioteca Nacional, Madrid, MSS. 1187, 1920, and 2454; Biblioteca Universitaria de Salamanca, MS. 1698.

Editions: Ramón Menéndez Pidal, "*Roncesvalles:* Un nuevo cantar de gesta español del siglo XIII," *Revista de Filología Española,* 4 (1917): 105–204, republished in his *Textos medievales espanoles: Ediciones críticas y estudios* (Madrid: Espasa-Calpe, 1976), pp. 7–99; Menéndez Pidal, *Reliquias de la poesía épica española* (Madrid: Espasa-Calpe, 1951), republished with prologue by Diego Catalán (Madrid: Gredos, 1980); Martín de Riquer, *Chanson de Roland–Cantar de Roldán y el Roncesvalles navarro* (Barcelona: El Festín de Esopo, 1983); Fernando Gómez Redondo, ed., *Poesía Española, 1: Edad Media; Juglaría, Clerecía y Romancero,* Páginas de Biblioteca Clásica (Barcelona: Crítica, 1996); Carlos Alvar and Manuel Alvar, eds., *Épica medieval española,* Letras Hispánicas, no. 330, second edition (Madrid: Cátedra, 1997).

Edition in modern Spanish: Rosa Castillo, ed., *Leyendas épicas españolas,* prologue by Enrique Moreno Báez (Madrid: Castalia, Odres nuevos, 1971).

Cycle of the Cid (Rodrigo Díaz de Vivar)
Carmen Campidoctoris (circa 1181–1190).
Mocedades de Rodrigo: Crónica de Castilla (circa 1295–1312).
Mocedades de Rodrigo (circa 1350–1360).
Cantar de Sancho II: Chronica Naierensis (circa 1185–1190); Rodrigo Jiménez de Rada, *Historia de rebus*

Hispaniae sive Historia Gothica (1243); Alfonso X, *Estoria de España* (1270–1274).
Cantar de mio Cid (circa 1200); Alfonso X, *Estoria de España* (1270–1274).
Epitafio épico del Cid (circa 1400?).

Manuscripts: *Carmen Campidoctoris:* Bibliothèque Nationale, Paris, MS. lat. 5132, end of twelfth century–beginning of thirteenth century. *Mocedades de Rodrigo:* Paris, Bibliothèque National, MS. Espagnol 12, late fourteenth century. *Cantar de mio Cid* (circa 1200): Biblioteca Nacional, Madrid, MS. Vitr. 7–17, fourteenth century. Rodrigo Jiménez de Rada, *Historia de rebus Hispaniae sive Historia Gothica:* Real Biblioteca del Monasterio de El Escorial, MS. Ç.IV.12; Biblioteca Universitaria de Madrid, MS. 143; and Biblioteca Pública de Córdoba, MS. 131. Alfonso X, *Estoria de España:* Real Biblioteca del Monasterio de El Escorial, MSS. Y.I.2 and X.I.4.

Editions: Juan de Velorado, *Crónica particular del Cid* (Burgos: Fadrique Alemán de Basilea, 1512); Alan Deyermond, *Epic Poetry and the Clergy: Studies on the "Mocedades de Rodrigo"* (London: Tamesis, 1969); *Mocedades de Rodrigo,* edited by Juan Victorio (Madrid: Espasa-Calpe, 1982); Matthew Bailey, ed., *Las "Mocedades de Rodrigo": Estudios críticos, manuscrito y edición,* King's College London Medieval Studies, no. 15 (Exeter, U.K.: Short Run Press, 1999); *Carmen Campidoctoris, o Poema latino del Campeador,* edited by Alberto Montaner and Ángel Escobar (Madrid: España Nuevo Milenio, 2001); *Mocedades de Rodrigo: Estudio y edición de los tres estados del texto,* edited by Leonardo Funes and Felipe Tenenbaum (London: Tamesis, 2004).

Edition in modern Spanish: Rosa Castillo, ed., *Leyendas épicas españolas,* prologue by Enrique Moreno Báez (Madrid: Castalia, Odres nuevos, 1971).

"New Epic"
Poema de Alfonso XI (1348).
Fray Gonzalo de Arredondo, *Vida rimada de Fernán González* (circa 1495).

Manuscripts: *Poema de Alfonso Onceno:* Real Biblioteca del Monasterio de El Escorial, MS. Y.III.9, fourteenth century; Real Academia Española, MS. 213, 1490–1510. Fray Gonzalo de Arredondo, *Vida rimada de Fernán González:* Biblioteca Nacional, Madrid, MSS. 2788, sixteenth century, and 894, seventeenth century; Real Biblioteca del Monasterio de El Escorial, MS. Y.III.2, sixteenth century; Academia de la Historia, Madrid, MS. 9/2057, seventeenth century.

Edition: Gonzalo de Arredondo, *Vida rimada de*

Fernán González, edited by Mercedes Vaquero (Exeter, U.K.: Exeter Hispanic Texts, 1987).

The epic was the first principal form of narrative poetry to emerge during the Spanish Middle Ages. Like every literary genre, it is characterized by certain features. The preferred meter is an ametric line of variable length, an internal pause or caesura, accentual rhythms, and assonant rhyme. The common strophic form is a series of verses that share a single rhyme scheme. Stylistic attributes include the use of formulas or set phrases, epic epithets, fluctuating verb tenses, pathetic fallacy, scant description, a preset expository structure that flows back and forth between the tensions caused by an affront and its resolution, a theme of vengeance or heroism in battle, and a protagonist who is an avenging or warrior hero. These traits distinguish epic from other forms of narrative poetry of the same period–in particular, from shorter hagiographic works, such as the *Vida de Santa María Egipciaca* (early thirteenth century, Life of St. Mary the Egyptian), which coincide with epic in their casual use of verb tenses and varying stretches of monorhymed ametric verses but tend to lack caesuras; feature a different strophic form, the couplet; are structured biographically, with the episodes connected only by the presence of the protagonist; and emphasize the theme of the holiness, manifested above all through miracles, of their saintly subjects.

Epic is also distinguished from the learned narrative poetry that emerged in the thirteenth century by the use in the latter of *cuaderna vía* (fourfold way), which is marked by regular verses of invariable length, an alexandrine line with consonant rhyme, and a strict strophic form of monorhymed quatrains. *Cuaderna vía* also has distinctive stylistic traits such as hyperbaton, a taste for Latinate vocabulary, greater scope for description, and a texture full of literary tropes. There is far less unity of plot in *cuaderna vía* poems, which tend toward biography rather than, as in the epic, to resolution of conflict. Themes may be hagiographic, as in Gonzalo de Berceo's *Vida de San Millán de la Cogolla* (circa 1230, The Life of St. Millán de la Cogolla); heroic, as in the *Libro de Alexandre* (early thirteenth century, Book of Alexander); or novelesque, as in the *Libro de Apolonio* (late thirteenth century; translated as *The Book of Apollonius,* 1936). The protagonist may lose some of his dominance, and, although he remains central to the story, his character may be more nuanced.

A similar array of differences separates the epic from narrative poetry in *arte mayor* (poems of more than eight syllables), which replaced *cuaderna vía* in the fifteenth century. This form is marked by a twelve-syllable line split by a caesura, two persistent accents per half-line, and a strophe of eight lines. Its elegant and refined style is characterized by Latin words and syntax.

Finally, the "new epic" is narrative poetry with eight-syllable lines in quartets or quintets that retains some traces of the old epic in its heroic themes and central characters and some use of formulaic diction but veers toward true biography and strives for greater historical accuracy. These works are better termed "rhymed chronicles" or historiography in verse than epics. Two works commonly grouped under this rubric are the *Poema de Alfonso XI* (1348, Poem of Alfonso XI) and the *Vida rimada de Fernán González* (circa 1495, Rhymed Life of Fernán Gonzalez), by Fray Gonzalo de Arredondo; the latter work, however, is best linked to other sorts of narrative poems in five-line strophes from the fifteenth and beginning of the sixteenth centuries.

True epic is more closely related to yet another genre: narrative prose epic legends, which show similar traits of plot, theme, and protagonist. It is not always easy to differentiate between epic poetry and narrative prose epic legends, because the lion's share of medieval Spanish epic survives not in its original verse but in reworked prose versions inserted into historical narratives. This practice often makes it nearly impossible to determine whether an undeniably epic passage in a chronicle came from a poem or from a prose legend and whether the legend was passed along through a vernacular oral tradition or in a Latin work. As a result, the best approach is to separate those works that are unambiguous epics, or clearly inspired by lost epics, from those whose genealogy has been lost.

Among works of clear parentage are four poems: the *Cantar de mio Cid* (circa 1200, Song of My Lord; translated as *Poem of the Cid,* 1879), known from a single manuscript from around 1300 to 1350 that was copied from a lost exemplar dated 1207; the fragmentary *Roncesvalles* (circa 1270), the sole copy of which was produced around 1310; *Las Mocedades de Rodrigo* (1350–1360, The Youthful Deeds of Rodrigo), dealing with the exploits of a young and quite different Rodrigo (Ruy) Díaz de Vivar than the sober hero of the *Cantar de mio Cid;* and the *Epitafio épico del Cid* (circa 1400? Epitaph of the Cid), included among the appendices Juan de Velorado added to the first edition of the *Crónica particular del Cid* (1512). Because of its brevity, only the last of these works is complete. Just a few pages are missing from the *Cantar de mio Cid,* comprising no more than two hundred to four hundred lines, or 5 to 10 percent of the total. But *Las Mocedades de Rodrigo* lacks its conclusion and probably some internal passages, while the *Roncesvalles* is a fragment of barely a hundred lines, a mere 5 percent of what some scholars believe to have been the original total. In a separate category is the *Poema de*

Fernán González (between 1251 and 1258, Poem of Fernán Gonzalez), the sole surviving copy of which is incomplete and dates from the end of the fifteenth century: its content is patently epic, but in form it is a narrative in *cuaderna vía*.

Other medieval Spanish epics are of uncertain origin and transmission. Sometimes the historians who appropriated these works for their chronicles reveled in their poetic lineage, alluding to *cantares* (sung stories) or *fablas de gestas* (tales of great deeds). The situation is more doubtful when they merely note that "algunos dizen" (some say), which usually means that they are inserting undocumented reports from the oral tradition as opposed to their preferred source, Latin chronicles. All one knows with certainty in these cases is that they are not passing along a learned source; it is unclear whether they are relying on a prose legend or an epic poem. Sometimes an abundance of short phrases with assonantal rhyme allows one to hear the echoes of an early verse text that has been tucked, scarcely changed from its original state, into an historical account. But the presence of periodic assonance in an epic passage does not guarantee poetic roots: it could result from mere chance or from the stylized patterns of the chroniclers, who favored a singsong cadence and composition in rhymed prose.

Related to these issues is the problem of successive reworkings or recastings of a given narrative. Medieval literature in general is characterized by a presumption of shared ownership of texts; as common property, these works were susceptible to being freely appropriated and reworked by later writers and even by copyists. This situation obtained with epic poems and also with their prose versions; thus, it is often impossible to tell whether an epic tale in a chronicle was converted to prose by the compilers of that chronicle or by an earlier historian whose work is being used in a subsequent piece of historiography. Unless there is strong evidence to the contrary, the most cautious approach is to presume the second scenario: the reworking of an earlier chronicle that was already a prose version of an epic source.

In the earliest Latin histories of the Spanish High Middle Ages, the *Chronica Albeldensia* (Chronicle of Albelda), composed in 881 with additions from 882 to 976, and the *Chronica Adefonsi III* (Chronicle of Alfonso III), composed around 885 to 910, one finds legendary matter on the theme of the "Fall of Spain"—the Islamic invasion and the defeat of King Rodrigo, the last of the Visigoths—as well as the rise of Pelayo to king of Asturias and his victory at Covadonga, which is traditionally honored as the launching point of the Reconquest of the Iberian Peninsula. Nonetheless, these sources, despite their epic cast, show unmistakable signs

Tomb in the Collegiate Church Covarrubias of Sancho II, who was murdered while beseiging his sister, doña Urraca, in the city of Zamora. The siege and murder are depicted in the Cantar de Sancho II *(photograph courtesy of Alberto Montaner).*

of clerical and historiographical composition, which makes their derivation from epic legends or epic poems fairly improbable. Only in the *Chronica Naierensis* (circa 1185–1190, Chronicle of Nájera) can one find the first vestiges of decisively epic themes. It focuses on the earliest events in Castilian history: the imprisonment of Conde (Count) Fernán González and the stories of the Infante García, the *Condesa traidora* (Traitorous Countess), and the *Reina calumniada* (Maligned Queen). But there are also tales that have overtones of epic legend and deal with more-recent happenings, such as the fratricidal warfare between 1068 and 1072 among Sancho II of Castile, Alfonso VI of León, and Princess Urraca—episodes in which the Cid is a prominent personage. Even if in several of the earlier cases one could justifiably speak of epic legends as source material, it is highly doubtful that these passages were based on full epic poems, and with the later tales it would be safer to suppose oral reports showing the first signs of conversion into legend.

Not until the thirteenth century does one find fresh epic material in Latin texts. Most of this material is encountered in the two great Latin histories of the period, the *Chronicon mundi* (1236, Chronicle of the World), by Bishop Lucas de Tuy, and the *Historia de rebus Hispaniae sive Historia Gothica* (1243, History of the Affairs of Spain or History of the Goths), sometimes shortened to *De rebus Hispaniae,* by Rodrigo Jiménez de Rada, archbishop of Toledo. Along with some epic material previously included in the *Chronica Naierensis,* both works present the first accounts of the purely legendary Bernardo del Carpio; a précis of the *Mainete,* a poem about the youth of Charlemagne; and a legendary version of the 1154 pilgrimage made by Louis VII of France to Santiago de Compostela. But the works that incorporate the largest amounts of epic material, derived both from poetic and from legendary sources, are the early vernacular histories. The *Liber Regum* (Book of Kings), an historical compilation composed in the Navarro-Aragonese dialect around the end of the twelfth century, includes passages of a legendary character concerning the royal dynasty of Pamplona and the Cid. The high point among these vernacular prose works occurs almost a century later with the *Estoria de España* (History of Spain), commissioned by Alfonso X *el Sabio* (the Learned), the earliest version of which was drafted between 1270 and 1274. There, together with recastings of the stories included in the earlier works, are the epic poems *Los siete infantes de Lara* (The Seven Young Noblemen of Lara), the *Cantar de Sancho II* (Song of Sancho II), the *Cantar de mio Cid,* and the *Poema de Fernán González,* the last two of which are derived from the verse compositions known today. For its time, the *Estoria de España* was the most complete assembly of epic accounts of the Spanish Middle Ages.

The *Estoria de España* received several reworkings and continuations. Alfonso personally presided over a thorough revision, the *Versión crítica* (Critical Version), which is reflected in the *Crónica de veinte reyes* (circa 1282–1284, Chronicle of Twenty Kings). This series of manuscripts offers a fairly faithful prose rendition of the *Cantar de mio Cid* but eliminates traces of royal weakness as it freely reworks the *Mainete,* the story of Bernardo del Carpio, and the *Poema de Fernán González* with an eye to strengthening the figure of the monarch and validating his power. The *Versión amplificada* (1289, Extended Version), which was developed under the supervision of King Sancho IV and is basically a stylistically retooled version of the *Estoria de España,* also makes ideological adjustments. In particular, the section on Fernán González is revised to exalt the Castilian *conde*

over his Leonese king and, by extension, to emphasize the role of the upper Castilian nobility in the defense of the kingdom.

Works of historiography crafted in the fourteenth century and part of the fifteenth still used the *Estoria de España* as a point of departure, earning the label *crónicas alfonsíes* (Alfonsine chronicles). One feature they inherited from their model, and accentuated, is the incorporation of epic material. The *Crónica de Castilla* (circa 1295–1312, Chronicle of Castile), for example, is the first to include the mélange of history and legend surrounding the Cid, folding in the beginnings of his career from *Las Mocedades de Rodrigo* with the *Cantar de Sancho II,* the episode of "La Jura de Santa Gadea" (The Oath at St. Agatha), and the *Cantar de mio Cid.* A substantive change introduced at this point was the insertion of legendary material of a hagiographic nature derived from the *Leyenda del Cid* (Legend of the Cid), generated by the monks of the monastery of San Pedro de Cardeña, where the Cid was buried in 1102. The *Crónica geral de Espanha* (General Chronicle of Spain) of 1344, developed under the supervision of the Conde de Barcelos and revised around 1400, is a Portuguese translation of the *Versión amplificada* and the *Crónica de Castilla* augmented with fresh material, including a reworking of *Los siete infantes de Lara.* The *Crónica geral de Espanha* is the most complete repertoire of epic tales in the Spanish Middle Ages.

A final source of information on the existence of lost epic poems, and one no less problematic than the chronicles, is the *romances* (traditional Spanish ballads). These narrative songs are composed in eight-syllable lines with assonantal rhyme in every other line. Although documented from the beginning of the fifteenth century, they are likely to have emerged in the late fourteenth century. Some of these ballads include episodes derived from, or at least inspired by, epic *cantares.*

It is not certain that the ballad genre was produced by the fragmentation of earlier full-scale epic poems, a thesis proposed by Ramón Menéndez Pidal, or if they arose as an independent form of lyrical narrative that later absorbed epic content. In any case, the *romances viejos* (old ballads), set down from the living oral tradition in the first half of the sixteenth century, contain epic material and often overlap in content with epic poems documented directly or indirectly in earlier sources. The difficult part is pinning down the nature of that overlap, since they sometimes display great similarity to a source in epic poetry, while at other times, given the distinctive recasting in ballad style, there seems to be little connection.

The uncertainties arising from the transmission of medieval Spanish epic stories also include their origins and chronology. One possibility is that these epic songs were created at the time of the events themselves as *cantos noticieros* (news songs). They would have been faithful to the facts at first, but over time they would have been expanded and adorned with increasingly fanciful descriptions and incidents. Another possibility is that they were composed much later, around the time their existence is first recorded. The absence of evidence of the hypothetical *cantos noticieros* leads one to favor the second thesis, allowing for the possibility of oral and, perhaps, even written tales supplying the more or less historical core of the stories. The existence of at least some earlier epic compositions in prose or in verse that are now lost can hardly be doubted, but the bulk of medieval Hispanic epic was worked out in the thirteenth and fourteenth centuries.

These epic tales can be grouped by theme into four major clusters or cycles. In chronological order of their subject matter they are the Carolingian Cycle, which retells the Spanish exploits of Charlemagne and his champions in the eighth century; the Counts of Castile Cycle, set when Castile was an independent county under the aegis of León at the end of the tenth century; the Navarro-Aragonese Cycle, about the kings of Pamplona in the tenth through the twelfth centuries; and the Cycle of the Cid, dedicated to the life and adventures of Rodrigo Díaz de Vivar at the end of the eleventh century. The Cycle of the Counts of Castile seems to be the most archaic in terms of story line, the social institutions reflected in it, the expressive modes used to tell its stories, and the early allusions to it—it is first documented in the *Chronica Naierensis* in the late twelfth century. These factors have led some scholars to consider this cycle the foundation of Hispanic epic, in spite of the tenuous dating of its origin. In fact, however, the earliest extant allusions to the existence of epic accounts go back to the end of the eleventh century and refer to the Carolingian Cycle, which allows for the possibility that Spanish epic is a native reworking of French originals. At least the dates of the Cycle of the Cid are clear: it begins with the *Cantar de mio Cid,* composed around 1200, although some data about the hero's deeds can be found a bit earlier.

The Cycle of the Counts of Castile embraces, in chronological order by subject matter, the *Poema de Fernán González, La Condesa traidora, Los siete infantes de Lara,* the *Romanz del Infante García* (Romance of the Prince García), and *El abad don Juan de Montemayor* (The Abbot Sir John of Montemayor). All are set between 942 and 1037, when Castile was an independent county, and tend to stress the conflicts within kingdoms and families over clashes with the Muslim foe: feats of war are overshadowed by personal affronts and the vengeance they provoke. Another persistent feature is the looming presence of the fearsome Andalusian warlord Almanzor, whose menacing figure serves as a constant foil to the central Christian figures even when his historical period—981 to 1002—fails to coincide with theirs. These stories have been celebrated for their historicity, which would imply a date of composition fairly close to the actual events, but their supposed accuracy in most cases derives from the persistence of legendary fictions that dissolve in the face of the facts.

The earliest reference to the legends of Fernán González occurs in the twelfth-century *Chronica Naierensis;* it amounts to little more than a passing reference to the imprisonment of the Castilian count by Sancho I of Navarre in 960. According to the chronicle, the king's sister freed González in exchange for his pledge to marry her, a promise he fulfilled. The incident is pure fiction and is so briefly noted by the *Chronica Naierensis* historiographer that one cannot believe that a whole epic song, now lost, stands behind it. Much later in the thirteenth century an anonymous monk of San Pedro de Arlanza, a monastery that is said to have been founded by the count and that is also his burial site, composed the *Poema de Fernán González.* This poem offers a complete survey of the legendary accretions that surround the count's life, including his resistance to the attacks of Almanzor's Muslim troops, his war with the Navarrese monarch, and his trick to obtain the independence of Castile from León. The episode of the princess Doña Sancha engineering the count's release from prison is included, which only proves that the poet knew the legend and not that he reworked an epic poem that was available to him but is now lost.

The *Crónica geral de Espanha* of 1344, a more faithful adaptation of the *Poema de Fernan González* than that in the *Estoria de España,* includes an episode from the count's life that is absent from the truncated extant copy of the poem and is thoroughly epic in character; the tale also survives in the traditional ballad *Castellanos y leoneses* (Castilians and Leonese). Nothing can be claimed definitively about its source; hypothesizing a lost epic poem is unwarranted, since the tale could have come from an earlier epic-styled ballad or a narrative prose source. The latter possibility is suggested by the allusion in the *Crónica geral de Espanha* to its exemplar being an *estoria,* a word never used to signal legendary material in either prose or verse.

The oldest references to *La Condesa traidora* also appear in the *Chronica Naierensis,* but, unlike the anecdote about Fernán González, the story of *La Condesa traidora* has an actual plot. The countess of Castile—the wife of Fernán González's son, Count García Fernández—is receptive to the amorous advances of Almanzor, who promises to make her his wife and, therefore, queen. To get rid of her husband, the countess has his horse fed with chaff and persuades him to dismiss his knights so that they can celebrate Christmas at home. She then informs Almanzor that the count is without forces to resist him, and Almanzor attacks. In the subsequent battle García Fernández's, horse falters; the injured count is taken prisoner by the Muslims and dies five days later. Still hoping to marry Almanzor, the countess prepares a poisoned drink for her son, Sancho García, the new count. Warned by a captive Muslim woman, Sancho García offers the drink to his mother. She refuses the cup; but the count forces her to drink from it, and she dies.

This story of ambition, crime, and punishment, with its ancient motif of the evil schemer falling into his or her own trap, is not mentioned by Jiménez de Rada in the *Historia de rebus Hispaniae sive Historia Gothica,* which includes a completely different version of the death of García Fernández; but it does appear in the *Estoria de España* of Alfonso X, where it is modified by the addition of new legendary components and by adapting the version in the *Chronica Naierensis* to the more factual version of Jiménez de Rada, which is the fundamental source of the story. In the *Estoria de España* García Fernández marries a French noblewoman, Argentina, who flees with a French count when her husband's illness provides her with the opportunity. García Fernández, disguised as a pilgrim, pursues her. The French count's daughter, Sancha, promises to help García Fernández take his revenge in return for his promise to marry her. Sancha leads him to the bedroom of the French count and Argentina, and he decapitates them. García Fernández takes Sancha back to Castile and marries her. With the passage of time, Sancha begins to plot against her husband. The tale continues with the horse that is fed chaff; the attempt to poison her son, Sancho; and the countess's death at Sancho's hand. It ends with the young count establishing the monastery of Oña to expiate the guilt of killing his own mother. There is no proof that an epic poem was the source for this legend.

The third legend of the Cycle of the Counts of Castile is that of the murder in León in 1029 of the infante García, the son of Count Sancho. The narrative of this incident in the *Chronica Naierensis* can hardly be characterized as legendary: it briefly relates that when García went to León to marry Sancha, the sister of Vermudo III of León, members of a hostile family, the Vela, sneaked into the palace where he was lodging and murdered him while his followers were engaged in a display of arms with the Leonese. The only detail that may allude to the existence of a legend is the mention of the war games, a frequent motif of epic legends; but that detail is absent from Jiménez de Rada's version.

In the *Romanz del Infante García* the marriage of García and Sancha is arranged, and García goes to León accompanied by his brother-in-law Sancho *el Mayor* (the Elder), the king of Navarre. On the way they are involved in a fight at the castle of Monzón, whose lord, Fernán Gutiérrez, becomes a vassal of García. In León the bulk of García's men remain outside the walls of the city with Sancho's men. The children of Count Vela, who was banished from Castile in the time of García's father, Count Sancho, come from their lands in La Somoza to take revenge on García. They traitorously pledge vassalage to him and then, during a display of arms with the Castilian knights, provoke a quarrel that results in the killing of the count's guard. They then kill García in spite of his pleas and those of Sancha, who is ill treated during the murder. As Sancho *el Mayor* tries to enter León, the traitors throw García's body over the walls at him. While the Castilians and Navarrese bury the count in the monastery of Oña, his murderers lay siege to Monzón. Fernán Gutiérrez secretly sends word to Sancho *el Mayor* of their presence at Monzón. Sancho arrives, lifts the siege, and executes all of the traitors except Fernán Laínez, who escapes to the mountainous region of La Somoza. Sancho pursues him at the behest of Princess Sancha, who makes his death a condition of her marriage to the infante Fernando, the second son of Sancho *el Mayor* who, in time, will become the celebrated King Fernando I. Sancho captures Fernán Laínez and hands him to over to Sancha. She mutilates but does not kill him and orders him taken through Castile and León on a mule as a lesson to others of the consequences of treason.

Los siete infantes de Lara takes place in the time of Count García Fernández, who appears briefly in the song. During the festivities that accompany the wedding of Ruy Blázquez and Lambra, a dispute arises between the seven young noblemen of Salas, who are the groom's nephews, and the bride's cousin, Álvar Sánchez, over who won the chivalric games that were held as part of the celebration. Álvar Sánchez is killed, and Ruy Blázquez and Gonzalo González, the youngest of the infantes, are seriously wounded. García Fernández and Gonzalo Gustioz, the father of the infantes, intervene to keep the conflict from escalating. After the count departs with Gonzalo Gustioz and the infantes' uncle, Lambra, desiring revenge for the death of her cousin, sends a squire to challenge Gonzalo González; but the infantes kill the squire, who has sought refuge with Lambra's nurse. The murder is a new affront to Lambra, and when her husband returns, she demands vengeance. Ruy Blázquez pretends to make peace with Gonzalo Gustioz and his seven sons and sends the father to deliver a letter to Almanzor in Cordova; unbeknownst to Gonzalo Gustioz, the letter asks Almanzor to cut off his head. Appalled at such treachery, Almanzor takes pity on Gonzalo Gustioz and imprisons him instead. During his captivity Gonzalo Gustioz is cared for by a beautiful Moorish woman, with whom he has a son, Mudarra. Meanwhile, Ruy Blázquez has his nephews and Muño Salido, their *ayo* (caretaker), ambushed by the Moors and decapitated. The heads are taken to Cordova, where their father sees them and makes a sorrowful lament. Almanzor allows him to leave Castile with the heads of his sons and the *ayo*. Mudarra grows up, is knighted by Almanzor, and goes to Castile to seek satisfaction for the deaths of his brothers and the insult to his father. After he reveals his identity to Gonzalo Gustioz, they go to the count's court. Mudarra challenges Ruy Blázquez, who refuses to fight. Mudarra ambushes and kills him and later has Lambra burned.

The earliest known version of *Los siete infantes de Lara* appears in Alfonso X's *Estoria de España;* but some of its features have led scholars to believe that a song with this theme existed as early as the year 1000. The plot relies on well-known folkloric motifs that have parallels in French and Germanic epics. The only points in which the poem coincides with history involve the appearance of a few royal personages and the submission of the Christian principalities to Almanzor; but Almanzor's invasion left such a lasting impression that his appearance in the poem does not suffice to date the work to his time. Evidence that the poem was composed later includes details in the version in the *Estoria de España* that link it to the thirteenth century.

The story of *Los siete infantes de Lara* is repeated in the *Crónica geral de Espanha* of 1344; but while the tale begins in the same way as in the *Estoria de España,* the denouement is amplified and substantially modified. In the *Crónica geral de Espanha* Mudarra is recognized by Gonzalo Gustioz; is accepted as a son by his wife, Sancha; converts to Christianity; and is knighted by Count García Fernández, against whom Ruy Blázquez had rebelled. Mudarra attacks Ruy Blázquez's lands, occupies his castles and villages, pursues him tirelessly, and finally imprisons him after single combat. Mudarra takes Ruy Blázquez to Sancha, who has him raised on a dais and stoned and lanced to death. Lambra receives a similar death later.

The final legend of the Cycle of the Counts of Castile, *El abad don Juan de Montemayor,* tells of the defense of Montemayor when it is attacked by Almanzor. The tale, which is devoid of any historical foundation, is attested at a rather late date: the first allusion occurs in the mid thirteenth century, and the first extant version is from the fifteenth. It is unlikely to have used an epic poem as its source.

The Cycle of the Kings of Navarre-Aragon consists of two epic legends and a possible epic poem of

Portrait of Alfonso VI, king of Castile and León from 1072 to 1109, from the Cartulario of the Cathedral of Santiago de Compostela (photograph courtesy of Alberto Montaner)

later date. The legends are *Sancho Abarca* and *La reina calumniada* (The Maligned Queen); the poem, whose existence critics have hypothesized, is *La Campana de Huesca* (The Campaign of Huesca), which relates events of 1135–1136. This Aragonese vernacular composition is known only through a summary in the *Crónica de San Juan de la Peña* (circa 1370, Chronicle of San Juan de la Peña), first set down in Latin and translated into Aragonese and Catalan by command of Pedro IV of Aragon. The three legends re-create critical moments in the succession to the throne of the House of Navarre: that of Sancho Garcés II Abarca in 970; the division of the kingdoms of Castile, Aragon, and Navarre among the heirs of Sancho III *el Mayor,* who died in 1035; and the problem caused by the succession of Ramiro II *el Monje* (the Monk) as king of Aragon on the death of his brother, Alfonso I *el Batallador* (the Fighter), in 1134.

The Carolingian Cycle includes epic materials concerned with the incursion of Charlemagne and his twelve knights into Spain in 778 and the Spanish reaction to that incursion. According to the chronology of the events related, the cycle is composed of the *Mainete* (The Youthful Exploits of Charlemagne), the *Roncesvalles,* and *Bernardo del Carpio.* The *Peregrinación de Luis VII* (Pilgrimage of Louis VII) is linked to this cycle by its protagonist, though it refers to events that took place in the mid twelfth century. Although they receive Spanish elaboration, most of these legends are imported products that show the influence of the pilgrimage route to Santiago de Compostela and the French settlement of newly reconquered territories. The only exception is *Bernardo del Carpio,* an anti-Carolingian story that gainsays the French intervention in Spanish history.

The spread in the Iberian Peninsula of the story of the French defeat at Roncesvalles is well attested since the end of the eleventh century, when an anonymous monk summarized the story in the *Nota Emilianense,* a marginal note in a manuscript at the monastery of San Millán de la Cogolla. The structure of the *Nota Emilianense* suggests the existence of an annal as its source, while its adoption of Hispanized forms of proper names, such as *Rodlane* instead of *Roland* or the Latinized form *Rotolandus,* could be a clue to the existence of an autochthonous romance source or even an epic poem. If such a work existed, its content did not coincide with that of the *Chanson de Roland* (circa 1190, Song of Roland): the *Nota Emilianense* includes some characters who are foreign to that work, though they are present in other French epic songs. There is evidence of the circulation of an epic poem on this theme in the twelfth century, but the actual remains of a poem date from the thirteenth century: the one-hundred-verse *Roncesvalles* fragment, which came to light in the early twentieth century when Fernando de Mendoza found two loose folios that had been saved as a bookmark. Dated by some scholars at the beginning of the twelfth century and by others at its end, the fragment brings together materials from the *Chanson de Roland* and other legends and includes some original material, as well. One of the most notable of the new elements is the lament of Charlemagne and his peers when they discover the bodies of the French warriors, which is similar to that of Gonzalo Gustioz before the heads of his sons in *Los siete infantes de Lara.* The many romances about characters mentioned in the poem have led some critics to suppose that the *Roncesvalles* is a fragment of a long epic poem of perhaps five thousand lines. Other critics, however, think that the original poem was a self-contained elegy for the fallen French and that the extant work lacks just a few lines at the beginning and end.

The *Roncesvalles* provides indirect evidence of the existence of a longer French poem, the *Mainet* (circa 1150), that is now lost. That poem is summarized in Jiménez de Rada's *Historia de rebus Hispaniae sive Historia Gothica,* and the *Estoria de España* includes a Castilian version of it. There has been considerable discussion as to whether the two Hispanic versions were based on a Spanish epic or translated independently from a French one. Comparison of the convergent accounts in the Spanish works to the versions circulated in France during the thirteenth century points to an early Spanish borrowing that took the primitive French poem as its point of departure. The Alfonsine prosification, in contrast, combines a direct translation of a French version of the *Mainete* contained in the *Crónica fragmentaria* or *carolingia* (end of the fourteenth century, Fragmentary or Carolingian Chronicle) and in the *Gran Conquista de Ultramar* (circa 1293, The Great Conquest of the Lands beyond the Sea); the Carolingian legends were also grafted onto it toward the end of the fourteenth century.

In the *Estoria de España* Mainete breaks with his father, Pippin, and seeks refuge in the Moorish kingdom of Toledo. There he is welcomed by King Galafre and the king's daughter, Galiana. Soon after his arrival, the city is besieged by another Moorish king, Bramante, who intends to marry Galiana by force. Galiana asks Mainete to fight for her and provides him with weapons in exchange for his promise to marry her. Mainete performs great deeds in the battle and kills Bramante, acquiring the sword Durandarte as a spoil of war. Shortly afterward, he learns of Pippin's death and returns to France with his men; Galafre's opposition to his departure is overcome by Galiana's cunning. Galiana escapes later and meets Mainete in Paris. She becomes a Christian, and she and Mainete are married. Mainete is crowned king of the French and eventually acquires the name by which he is known to history: Charlemagne.

The tale in the French *Mainet* might be an echo of an earlier French legend in which Alfonso VI of León and the Moor Zaida fall in love, sight unseen, from reports of their beauty and nobility; she is baptized; and he releases fortresses around Toledo as a dowry gift. Some scholars have postulated the existence of a Castilian epic song about these events, but the evidence at hand only points to an oral anecdote that was collected by Jiménez de Rada in his *Historia de rebus Hispaniae sive Historia Gothica* and borrowed from that work by Alfonso X's team of historians, who expanded it in the *Versión amplificada.*

The same sources transmit the *Peregrinación de Luis VII,* which is also found in the earlier *Chronicon mundi* of Lucas de Tuy and was expanded in the *Versión amplificada.* This legend of the historical pilgrimage of Louis to Santiago de Compostela in 1153–1154 was seemingly influenced by the French epic poem *Le pèlerinage de Charlemagne* (first half of the twelfth century, The Pilgrimage of Charlemagne), although the Spanish version never seems to have taken the poetic form of its French source. According to the story, the true objective of Louis's pilgrimage is to assure himself of the legitimacy of his wife, Isabel, the daughter of Alfonso VII *el Emperador* (the Emperor). Louis is duly convinced, as well as dazzled by the wealth and power of the Castilian king.

In its anti-French tone the legend is related to *Bernardo del Carpio*. The entirely fictional hero of this work—who was still believed in Miguel de Cervantes's generation to have been an historical personage—opposes Charlemagne and his peers in the Spanish epic. The oldest version of *Bernardo del Carpio* appears in Lucas de Tuy's *Chronicon mundi* and in Jiménez de Rada's *Historia de rebus Hispaniae sive Historia Gothica;* it is the most extensive epic narrative included in the latter work. According to the *Historia de rebus Hispaniae sive Historia Gothica,* Jimena, the sister of Alfonso II *el Casto* (the Chaste), the king of Asturias, marries Count Sancho in secret and bears a son, Bernardo. When the king learns of the marriage, he has the count imprisoned in perpetuity in the castle of Luna, puts his sister in a convent, and raises Bernardo as his son because he lacks an heir. In old age Alfonso is weary of governing and proposes to abdicate in favor of Charlemagne. The French monarch accepts, but the Asturian magnates, especially Bernardo, are opposed and persuade Alfonso to change his mind. Charlemagne is enraged by the breach of promise and crosses the Pyrenees at the head of an army. The advance is checked by a coalition of Hispanic peoples under the command of Alfonso and Bernardo, who inflict a great defeat on the French king and force him to turn back to his own lands. Years later, under the reign of Alfonso III *el Magno* (the Great), Bernardo, seething over the imprisonment of his father, rebels against the king, fortifies himself in the castle of Carpio, and helps the Moors to raid the Asturian frontier. The king frees Count Sancho and reconciles with Bernardo, who goes on to achieve great victories against the Moors, especially in the defense of the city of Zamora. Two legends seem to come together in *Bernardo del Carpio:* that the French defeat at Roncesvalles was owed to Spanish forces and not to the Moors, a legend that perhaps initially referred to a warrior of the Pyrenees named Bernardo de Ribagorza; and a legend about family conflicts that derives from the Navarro-Aragonese or Castilian Count Cycles.

The detailed version of *Bernardo del Carpio* in the *Estoria de España* adds to the material in the *Chronicon mundi* and the *Historia de rebus Hispaniae sive Historia Gothica* what "algunos dizen en sus romances et en sus cantares" (some say in their romances and in their songs).

The *Estoria de España* makes Bernardo the son of Timbor, Charlemagne's sister, and Sancho Díaz de Saldaña, who seduced her while she was on a pilgrimage to Santiago de Compostela. It also offers a different version of the battle of Roncesvalles in which the troops of Marfil, the Moorish king of Saragossa, participate along with those of Alfonso *el Casto* and Bernardo. Finally, it adds an episode in which noble Asturian relatives of Bernardo reveal to him through some ladies his father's identity and the fact that he is languishing in prison; the scene is similar to the revelation to Mudarra in the *Crónica geral de Espanha* of 1344. Bernardo asks the king to free his father, but Alfonso refuses.

The original epic song probably continued with Bernardo's reaction to the king's refusal; but the *Estoria de España,* following the chronology of Jiménez de Rada, leaves this confrontation unresolved and goes on to treat the reign of Alfonso III *el Magno.* But it includes another tradition about Bernardo in which Bernardo distinguishes himself in battle against the Moors under Alfonso *el Magno;* after his military triumphs, he asks for the liberty of his father. The king repeatedly grants the request but never follows through. Tired of the impasse, Bernardo challenges the king and is banished. He then wages war against Alfonso from Saldaña and from the castle of Carpio, which he erects. After many losses, the magnates counsel freeing the count to make peace with the nettlesome Bernardo. But by this time the count has died, and Bernardo receives only his body. Bernardo, infuriated, goes to Paris, where he comes before Charlemagne and declares himself to be a nephew of the French monarch. Charlemagne's court is scandalized and rejects him. Bernardo goes back over the Pyrenees, repopulates the Canal de Jaca (Valley of Jaca), and takes several strongholds from the Moors. He gives the outposts to his son, Galín Galíndez, and they eventually devolve to the dynasty of the counts of Aragon.

The Cycle of the Cid consists of the poems *Las Mocedades de Rodrigo,* about the Cid's youth; *Cantar de Sancho II,* about his early manhood; *Cantar de mio Cid,* about his maturity, and *Epitafio épico del Cid,* about his posthumous fame. The charisma of its hero has made the legend of the Cid one of the most important epic cycles of the Middle Ages and one of the great myths of universal literature. The cycle originated at the end of the twelfth or beginning of the thirteenth century, when the *Cantar de mio Cid* was written down. The *Cantar de mio Cid* is an important nexus of legends and texts through which one can track the development of the Spanish epic. The poem is less about vengeance than about the prowess of the Cid, and it fuses the essential Spanish epic with stylistic novelties imported from French epic.

A Latin poem of the mid twelfth century, the *Praefatio de Almería* (Preface [or Poem] of Almería), refers to "Ipse Rodericus, Meo Cidi sepe uocatus, / de quo cantatur quod ab hostibus haud superatur" (That Rodrigo, often called the Cid, / of whom is it sung that he was never conquered by the enemy). Although the allusion might be to the Cid's public fame, it has often been claimed that the reference is to the *Cantar de mio Cid*, which Menéndez Pidal dated as early as 1140. The institutions, material culture, and literary models reflected in the *Cantar de mio Cid*, however, are those of about 1200. The song was later incorporated into the *Estoria de España*, from which it passed to the *Crónica de Castilla*. These works change the ending of the story under the influence of the prose *Estoria del Cid*, written in the monastery of Cardeña, where the Cid was buried.

The *Cantar de mio Cid* is formally divided into three *cantares* (sections), but its plot is bipartite. In the first part, which covers the first two *cantares*, the Cid, calumniated by envious courtiers, is banished by King Alfonso VI and leaves his family in Cardeña. The exiled Cid lives on the booty he wins from the Moors, of which he sends ever greater portions to Alfonso in an effort to regain the king's favor. After many military victories, which include taking Castejón and Alcocer from the Muslims and defeating the Count of Barcelona, a haughty Christian lord, the Cid acquires his greatest prize, the Moorish capital of Valencia and its region, and establishes his own lordship there. The king is impressed by the Cid's achievements and pleased by the tribute the Cid has turned over to him without being required to do so, and he pardons the hero in a solemn public ceremony. At this time the infantes de Carrión, two young aristocrats of the highest nobility, ask for the Cid's daughters' hands in marriage. Despite the Cid's misgivings, the weddings take place.

The second part of the plot structure, which comprises the third *cantar*, begins with several events that reveal the infantes' cowardice and provoke the laughter of the Cid's retainers. To take revenge on those knights and the chivalrous world they represent, the infantes leave Valencia with their dutiful wives, whom they abandon at the Robledo de Corpes after giving them a brutal beating. At a court called by King Alfonso, the Cid asks for judicial redress for the affront and challenges the infantes to a duel. They are stripped of their wealth after a trial before the king; they and their older brother are stripped of their honor in a series of single combats with the Cid's champions, and they are defamed in perpetuity before the whole court. In contrast, the Cid's daughters marry the princely heirs of Navarre and Aragon.

The *Cantar de Sancho II* incorporates historical matter to which references can be found in the *Chronica Naierensis*. Critics assume two sources for those references in the latter work: the *Cantar de Sancho II* itself and a Latin composition, the *Carmen de Morte Sanctii Regis* (Poem about the Death of King Sancho). It is, however, difficult to find a literary argument in the Latin chronicle, which treats Sancho historically and adds just a few touches from legend for the benefit of rhetorical expansion. It is more likely that the Latin historian composed the gist of the story himself, adding in biblical and classical reminiscences and some oral history. Jiménez de Rada's much more sober account of Sancho II's meteoric career repeats the legendary episodes found in the *Chronica Naierensis*.

The *Estoria de España* alludes explicitly to an epic poem and provides a prose version of it, though one cannot tell exactly where that version begins and ends because of the intercalation of passages from Jiménez de Rada's *Historia de rebus Hispaniae sive Historia Gothica* and probably also from the *Chronica Naierensis*. The *Cantar de Sancho II* may have begun with the breakup of the united kingdoms among the sons of Fernando I, with Sancho taking Castile, Alfonso receiving León, and García inheriting Galicia; the cities of Toro and Zamora were reserved for endowing Fernando's daughters, Urraca and Elvira. Sancho refuses to agree to the division of the joint thrones, and the tensions soon lead to war. García takes Zamora; Sancho intervenes, while Alfonso remains neutral. Sancho defeats García in the battle of Santarén and imprisons him in the castle of Luna. After Galicia is reincorporated into his kingdom, Sancho defeats Alfonso and then dispossesses his sister Elvira. This part of the account seems to derive not from a lost *cantar* but from the Latin prose of the *Historia de rebus Hispaniae sive Historia Gothica;* it is possible that the *cantar* went directly from the defeat of García to the siege of Zamora, which belonged to Urraca.

Sancho sends the Cid as his ambassador to propose that Urraca exchange Zamora for a less militarily sensitive lordship. Urraca refuses on the advice of her military commander Arias Gonzalo and is supported by the town council. Sancho tries to take the city by force, but the great loss of life leads the Cid's rival, Count García Ordóñez, to ask that the city be reduced by hunger rather than by assault. The siege lasts for seven years, and life in the city becomes unbearable. Arias Gonzalo proposes the surrender of the city, but Vellido Adolfo, a knight who is enthralled with Urraca, offers to lift the siege if Urraca grants him her favors. Urraca accedes, though in a somewhat ambiguous fashion, and Vellido Adolfo pretends to flee Zamora after provoking the wrath of Arias Gonzalo in order to make his change in allegiance credible. Vellido Adolfo gains Sancho's

Portrait of doña Urraca, the sister of Sancho II and his successor, Alfonso VI, from the Cartulario of the Cathedral of Santiago de Compostela
(photograph courtesy of Alberto Montaner)

confidence and, under the pretext of showing him some weaknesses in the city wall, separates him from his followers and kills him with a spear. He then flees back to Zamora, pursued by the Cid. Inside the city he is taken prisoner by Arias Gonzalo.

Meanwhile, the Castilians accuse the Zamorans of treason as accomplices of Vellido Adolfo. The Zamorans are granted the right to send five successive combatants to fight the Castilian champion, Diego Ordóñez, the large number a concession to the fact that they are not warriors but members of the city council. Arias Gonzalo and four of his sons agree to go. Diego Ordóñez vanquishes the sons, but on killing the fourth he steps outside the officially marked battle zone and forfeits the contest. The judicial confrontation is, therefore, inconclusive. The Castilians offer the crown to Alfonso, who is exiled in Toledo; but before allowing him to take the throne, the Cid makes him swear at the church of St. Agatha in Burgos that he had nothing to do with the death of his brother Sancho. Following the tense scene of the swearing, Alfonso is declared monarch of the joint kingdoms of Castile and León, and Galicia is made a permanent tributary province.

The presumed beginning of the *Cantar de Sancho II* with the dramatic division of the kingdoms is narrated in a quite different manner by the *Versión crítica* of the *Estoria de España*, which identifies its source as a *Cantar del rey Fernando* (Song of King Fernando). As the title does not refer to a song about the siege of Zamora, the core incident of the *Cantar de Sancho II*, it is probable that the *Versión crítica* is based on a shorter poem that only referred to the division of the patrimony of Fernando I. Similarly, the end of the *Cantar de Sancho II,* the oath in the church of St. Agatha, is covered more extensively in the *Crónica de Castilla* and with telltale traces of the assonance pattern of its verses. Scholars are of varying opinions about this version. Some think that the *Versión crítica* is a prose adaptation of a more detailed version of the *Cantar de Sancho II;* others believe that the poem follows a separate *cantar* devoted exclusively to the oath; and still others hypothesize a later *refundición* (reworking or recasting) of the *Cantar de Sancho II* that treated the beginning and end of the story more extensively. Such a *refundición* would have created a continuous cycle about the entire life of the Cid, the sort of comprehensive arrangement that is found in French epics.

As is frequently the case in European epics, the last of the poems to be composed is devoted to the youthful exploits of its hero. *Las Mocedades de Rodrigo* was unknown to, or at least ignored by, the compilers of the *Estoria de España* around 1270, although it seems that the redactors of the *Versión crítica* knew of its existence around 1284. The *Crónica de Castilla,* composed around 1295 to 1312, provides a complete prose version of *Las*

Mocedades de Rodrigo. In that version Rodrigo kills Jimena's father for no specified reason and then defeats a Moorish invasion. Jimena proposes to Fernando I of Castile that he marry her to the Cid in what was known in the Middle Ages as a "compensatory marriage": as her husband, the Cid will provide the protection that she lost when he killed her father. The king presents the idea to the Cid, who accepts but swears that the union will not be consummated until he has expiated the death of Jimena's father by vanquishing five foes in battle. The second part of the poem is devoted to those battles; but they are not clearly distinguished, either because the poem did not cover that number of battles or because the compilers of the *Versión crítica* altered that section. After the Cid's promise is fulfilled, he and Fernando I join forces in a fictitious battle against the hegemonic pretensions to Spain of France and the Pope. The foreign intruders are forced to desist and recognize Fernando as *par de emperador* (peer of an emperor).

An epic verse version of *Las Mocedades de Rodrigo* survives in a unique manuscript copy commonly dated between the end of the thirteenth century and around 1330. Two historical details, however, argue against a date before 1330: Fernando I's investiture as a knight and the change in the heraldic arms of the lordship of Aguilar de Campóo. The investiture ceremony follows the style of the investiture of Alfonso XI in 1332, and the change in the coat of arms did not take place until around 1345. It is more likely that the poem dates from 1350 to 1360. This version of *Las Mocedades de Rodrigo* retains the plot of the one in the *Crónica de Castilla* with a few changes. It begins with a long historical introduction about the origins of Castile that culminates in the deeds of Rodrigo and the reign of Fernando, who is presented at court as a child by his *ayo* and needs the support of Rodrigo's clan. This incident is, perhaps, a reminiscence of the politically contentious minorities of Fernando IV and Alfonso XI at the end of the thirteenth and the beginning of the fourteenth centuries. The young Cid portrayed in this poem has a degree of insolence and even occasional rebellion that, however, do not make him swerve in his loyalty to the Crown of Castile. A final crucial characteristic of the verse *Mocedades de Rodrigo* is its dogged and self-interested inclusion of the history and circumstances of the diocese of Palencia at the time of its writing. Scholars agree that this *Mocedades de Rodrigo,* despite taking the form of a true epic poem with all the antiquity and authority that this status implies, is a learned composition and a piece of propaganda meant to sustain Palencia's claims to lucrative property.

Finally, the *Epitafio épico del Cid,* which dates from before 1447, was engraved next to the Cid's tomb at Cardeña. It summarizes the Cid's heroic career, including his most famous legendary exploit: his posthumous victory over the Moorish troops of King Bucar of Morocco, in which his armor-clad body was tied upright to the saddle of his horse. It is so brief that it can be reproduced in its entirety as a sample of the style of medieval Castilian epic poems:

> Cid Ruy Díez só que yago aquí encerrado
> e vencí al rey Bucar con treinta e seis reyes de paganos;
> estos treinta e seis reyes, los veinte e dos murieron en el campo.
> Vencílos sobre Valencia desque yo muerto encima de mi cavallo.
> Con ésta son setenta e dos batallas que yo vencí en el campo.
> Gané a Colada e a Tizona, por ende Dios sea loado.
> Amén.

> (I am the Cid Ruy Diaz, who lies buried here.
> I defeated king Búcar along with thirty-six other pagan kings;
> Of these thirty-six kings, twenty-two died on the field of battle.
> I vanquished them in Valencia, where [I rode] on my horse [into battle] as a corpse.
> With this encounter, I won sixty-two battles.
> I won Colada and Tizón, let God be praised.
> Amen.)

References:

Carlos Alvar y Ángel Gómez Moreno, *La poesía épica y de clerecía medievales,* Historia Crítica de la Literatura Hispánica, no. 2 (Madrid: Taurus, 1988);

Samuel G. Armistead, "The *Mocedades de Rodrigo* and Neo-Individualist Theory," *Hispanic Review,* 46 (1978): 313–327;

Armistead, *La Tradición Épica de las "Mocedades de Rodrigo"* (Salamanca: Universidad de Salamanca, 2000);

Matthew Bailey, ed., *Las "Mocedades de Rodrigo": Estudios Críticos, Manuscrito y Edición,* King's College London Medieval Studies, no. 15 (London: Center for Late Antique and Medieval Studies, King's College, 1999);

Francisco Bautista, "Pseudo-historia y leyenda en la historiografía medieval: La Condesa Traidora," in his *El relato historiográfico: Textos y tradiciones en la España medieval* (London: Department of Hispanic Studies, Queen Mary, University of London, 2006), pp. 59–101;

Bautista, "Sobre la materia carolingia en la *Gran conquista de Ultramar* y en la *Crónica fragmentaria,*" *Hispanic Research Journal,* 3 (2002): 209–226;

Bautista, "La tradición épica de las *Enfances* de Carlomagno y el *Cantar de Mainete* perdido," *Romance Philology,* 56 (2003): 217–244;

Diego Catalán, *La Épica Española: Nueva Documentación y Nueva Evaluación* (Madrid: Fundación Ramón Menéndez Pidal/Universidad Complutense, 2001);

Louis Chalon, *L'Histoire et l'Epopée Castillane du Moyen Age: Le cycle du Cid, le cycle des comtes de Castille* (Paris: Champion, 1976);

Alan Deyermond, *El "Cantar de Mio Cid" y la Épica Medieval Española* (Barcelona: Sirmio, 1987);

Deyermond, *Epic Poetry and the Clergy: Studies on the "Mocedades de Rodrigo"* (London: Tamesis, 1969);

Deyermond, *La Literatura Perdida de la Edad Media Castellana: Catálogo y Estudio,* volume 1: *Épica y Romances* (Salamanca: Universidad de Salamanca, 1995);

Deyermond, "Medieval Spanish Epic Cycles: Observations on Their Formulation and Development," *Kentucky Romance Quarterly,* 23 (1976): 281–303;

William J. Entwistle, "On the *Carmen de morte Sanctii regis,*" *Bulletin Hispanique,* 30 (1928): 204–219;

Julio Escalona Monge, "Épica, crónicas y genealogías en torno a la historicidad de la *Leyenda de los Infantes de Lara,*" *Cahiers de Linguistique Hispanique Médiévale,* 23 (2000): 113–176;

Inés Fernández-Ordóñez, ed., *Alfonso X el Sabio y las Crónicas de España* (Valladolid: Universidad de Valladolid/Centro para la Edición de los Clásicos Españoles, 2000);

José Fradejas Lebrero, *Estudios Épicos: "El Cerco de Zamora,"* Aula Magna, no. 5 (Ceuta: Instituto Nacional de Enseñanza Media, 1963);

Fradejas Lebrero, "La Poesía Épica," in *Enciclopedia Temática de Aragón,* volume 7: *Literatura,* edited by Manuel Alvar (Saragossa: Moncayo, 1988), pp. 62–91;

Charles F. Fraker, "Sancho II: Epic and Chronicle," *Romania,* 95 (1974): 467–507;

Enzo Franchini, "El fragmento épico de *Roncesvalles*: Estado de la cuestión y nuevas observaciones," *La corónica,* 24, no. 1 (1995): 90–110;

Paloma Gracia, "La Leyenda de la Condesa Traidora: Observaciones sobre su Estructura y Significación," in *Actas del VI Congreso Internacional de la Asociación Hispánica de Literatura Medieval (Alcalá de Henares, 12–16 de septiembre de 1995),* volume 1 (Alcalá de Henares: Universidad de Alcalá, 1997), pp. 721–728;

Carlos Laliena Corbera, *La Campana de Huesca,* Aragón Cien Temas, no. 69 (Saragossa: CAI, 2000);

Francisco López Estrada, *Panorama crítico sobre el "Poema del Cid,"* Literatura y Sociedad, no. 30 (Madrid: Castalia, 1982);

López Estrada and others, eds., *La cultura del románico: siglos XI al XIII* (Madrid: Espasa-Calpe, 1995);

Albert B. Lord, *The Singer of Tales,* Harvard Studies in Comparative Literature, no. 24 (Cambridge, Mass.: Harvard University Press, 1960);

Georges Martin, "L'Escarboucle de Saint-Denis, le roi de France et l'empereur d'Espagne," in *Saint-Denis et la Royauté: Études Offertes á Bernard Guenée* (Paris: Publications de la Sorbonne, 1999), pp. 439–462;

Martin, *Histoires de l'Espagne Médiévale: Historiographie, Geste, Romancero,* Annexes des Cahiers de Linguistique Hispanique Médiévale, no. 11 (Paris: Klinksieck, 1997);

H. Salvador Martínez, *El "Poema de Almería" y la épica románica* (Madrid: Gredos, 1975);

Maria Luisa Meneghetti, "Almanzor, Çorraquín Sancho e i Primi Passi dell'Epica Castigliana," *Medioevo Romanzo,* 23 (1998): 313–325;

Ramón Menéndez Pidal, *La épica medieval española desde sus orígenes hasta su disolución en el romancero,* edited by Diego Catalán and María del Mar de Bustos (Madrid: Espasa-Calpe, 1992);

Menéndez Pidal, *La epopeya castellana a través de la literatura española* (Madrid: Espasa-Calpe, 1959);

Menéndez Pidal, *La Leyenda de los Infantes de Lara,* third edition (Madrid: Espasa-Calpe, 1969);

Ian Michael, "Orígenes sobre la Epopeya en España: Reflexiones sobre las Últimas Teorías," in *Actas II Congreso Internacional de la Asociación Hispánica de Literatura Medieval (Segovia, del 5 al 19 de Octubre de 1987),* volume 1 (Alcalá de Henares: Universidad de Alcalá, 1992), pp. 71–88;

Alberto Montaner Frutos, "La *Gesta de las Mocedades de Rodrigo* y la *Crónica Particular del Cid,*" in *Actas del I Congreso de la Asociación Hispánica de Literatura Medieval (Santiago de Compostela, 1985)* (Barcelona: PPU, 1988), pp. 431–444;

Montaner Frutos, "La huida de Vellido, ¿por las puertas o el postigo? (o De la *Chronica Naierensis* y las fuentes alfonsíes)," in *Actas del X Congrés de l'Associació Hispànica de Literatura Medieval (Alacant, 16–20 de setembre de 2003),* 3 volumes (Alacant: Institut Interuniversitari de Filologia Valenciana, 2005), III: 1179–1197;

Montaner Frutos, "La mora Zaida, entre historia y leyenda (con una reflexión sobre la técnica historiográfica alfonsí)," in *Historicist Essays on Hispano-Medieval Narrative: In Memory of Roger M. Walker,* edited by Barry Taylor and Geoffrey West (London: Modern Humanities Research Association, 2005), pp. 272–352;

Thomas Montgomery, *Medieval Spanish Epic: Mythic Roots and Ritual Language* (University Park: Pennsylvania State University Press, 1998);

David G. Pattison, *From Legend to Chronicle: The Treatment of Epic Material in Alphonsine Historiography,* Medium Aevum Monographs, new series, no. 13 (Oxford: Society for the Study of Mediaeval Languages and Literature, 1983);

Pattison, ed., *Textos Épicos Castellanos: Problemas de Edición y Crítica* (London: Queen Mary and Westfield College, 2000);

José Ramírez del Río, *La Leyenda de Cardeña y la épica de Al-Andalus: La victoria póstuma del Cid* (Seville: Signatura, 2001);

Carola Reig, *El Cantar de Sancho II y Cerco de Zamora,* Anejos de la Revista de Filología Española, no. 37 (Madrid: CSIC, 1947);

Erik von Richthofen, *La metamorfosis de la épica medieval* (Madrid: Fundación Universitaria Española, 1989);

Alberto del Río Nogueras, "Leyendas Épicas en el Aragón Medieval: Sancho Abarca en los Orígenes del Reino," in *I Curso sobre Lengua y Literatura en Aragón (Edad Media),* edited by José María Enguita (Saragossa: Institución "Fernando el Católico," 1991), pp. 133–157;

Colin Smith, "Toward a Reconciliation of Ideas about Medieval Spanish Epic," *Modern Language Review,* 89 (1994): 622–634;

Antonio Ubieto Arteta, *Historia de Aragón: Literatura Medieval* (Saragossa: Anubar, 1981);

Mercedes Vaquero, "Señas de Oralidad en Algunos Motivos Épicos Compartidos: *Siete Infantes de Lara, Romanz del Infant García* y *Cantar de Sancho II,*" in *Actas del XII Congreso de la Asociación Internacional de Hispanistas (21–26 de agosto de 1995, Birmingham),* volume 1: *Medieval y Lingüística* (Birmingham, U.K.: University of Birmingham, 1998), pp. 320–327;

John K. Walsh, "Religious Motifs in the Early Spanish Epic," *Revista Hispánica Moderna,* 36 (1970–1971): 165–172.

Medieval Spanish Exempla Literature

Eloísa Palafox
Washington University in St. Louis

WORKS: *Calila e Dimna* (first half of the thirteenth century)

Manuscripts: A: Real Biblioteca del Monsterio de El Escorial, MS. h.III.9 (*olim* III.e.18; v.M.11), end of the fourteenth or beginning of the fifteenth century; B: Real Biblioteca del Monasterio de El Escorial, MS. X.III.4 (*olim* III.e.20; v.M.21), end of the fifteenth century; P: Biblioteca Universitaria Salamanca, MS. 1763; and O: Archivo de la Cathedral Oviedo, MS. 18.

First publications: *Exemplario contra los engaños y peligros del mundo* (Saragossa: Pablo Hurus, 1493; Burgos: Friedrich Biel, 1498).

Edition in Castilian: *Calila e Dimna,* edited by Pascual Gayangos, Biblioteca de Autores Españoles, volume 51 (Madrid: Biblioteca de Autores Españoles, 1860).

Critical edition: *Calila e Dimna,* edited by José Manuel Cacho Blecua and María Jesús Lacarra (Madrid: Castalia, 1984).

Sendebar or *Libro de los engaños e los asayamientos de las mugeres* (mid thirteenth century)

Manuscripts: *Sendebar* is the only known Castilian version of the so-called oriental branch of this work. It is contained in manuscript P: Biblioteca de la Academia Española, Madrid, MS. 15, known as the codex of Puñonrostro (fifteenth century). There is also an "occidental branch" of the work, identified by the critics as *Siete sabios,* with one known manuscript in Castilian: *Novella que Diego de Cañizares de latín en romançe declaró y trasladó de un libro llamado Scala Çeli,* Biblioteca Nacional, Madrid, MS. 6.052, folios 1r–16v (end of the fifteenth century).

First publications: *Libro de los siete sabios de Roma* (Seville: Jacobo Cromberger, 1510; Burgos: Juan de la Junta, 1530); *Historia lastimera del Príncipe Erasto,* translated by Hurtado de la Vera (Antwerp: Juan Stelsio, 1573).

First modern edition: Domenico Comparetti, *Ricerche intorno al Libro di Sindibad* (Milan: G. Bernardoni, 1869).

Editions: *Versiones castellanas del Sendebar,* edited by Ángel González Palencia (Madrid & Granada: Consejo Superior de Investigaciones Científicas, 1946); *El libro de los engaños,* edited by John E. Keller, Studies in Romance Languages and Literatures, volume 20 (Chapel Hill: University of North Carolina Press, 1959; revised edition, University, Miss.: Romance Monographs, 1983).

Critical edition: *Sendebar,* edited by María Jesús Lacarra (Madrid: Cátedra, 1989).

Facsimile edition: *Códice de Puñonrostro: El Conde Lucanor y otros textos medievales,* preface by José Manuel Blecua (Madrid: Real Academia Española, 1992).

Editions in English: Domenico Comparetti, *Researches Respecting the Book of Sindibad,* translated by Henry Coote (London: Published for the Folklore Society by E. Stock, 1882); *Sendebar,* edited by John E. Keller (Chapel Hill: University of North Carolina Press, 1956).

Barlaam e Josafat (mid thirteenth century)

Manuscripts: P: *Libro de Berlan e del rrey Josapha de India,* part of codex *Leyes de Palencia,* Biblioteca Universitaria Salamanca, MS. 1877, fifteenth century; G: *El libro del bien aventurado Barlaan e del infante Josafa, fijo del rrey Avenir,* Biblioteca Nacional, Madrid, MS. 18017, second half of fifteenth century; S: *La estoria del rrey Anemur e del Josaphat e de Barlaam,* University Library, Strasbourg, MS. 1829 (*olim* Cod. Hispan. 10), fifteenth century. These three manuscripts seem to be copies of earlier ones that are now lost.

Editions: Friedrich Lauchert, "La estoria dey Anemur e de Iosaphat e de Barlaam," *Romanische Forschungen,* 7 (1893): 331–402; *Barlaam e Josafat,* edited by Gerhard Moldenhauer (Halle: Niemeyer, 1929); *Barlaam e Josafat,* edited by John E. Keller and Robert W. Linker, introduction by Olga T. Impey and John E. Keller (Madrid: Consejo Superior de Investigaciones Científicas, 1979).

Paleographic and critical edition: Severino

fuertes su fuerça es cobardes ⁊ mala andança contra sy
por q̃ sabedes q̃nta mejoria ha la fuerça q̃ auedes sobre las
otras bestias fuestes atreujdos contra mj ⁊ beujstes ala
fuente q̃ le dizen el mj nonbre ⁊ tomastes mj agua ⁊ be
ujstes la vos ⁊ vr̃as compañas yo vos defiendo q̃ no ven
gades y mas ⁊ sy no yo vos cegare ⁊ vos matare ⁊ sy
auedes dubda desto q̃ vos enbio dezir yo ala fuente el
ay me fallaredes q̃ yo sere conbusco luego ⁊ marauillose
el rey delos elifantes delo q̃ le dezia la liebre

fuese con ella pa la fuente ⁊ vido la lus dela luna en el
agua dixo la liebre tomad del agua con vr̃a manga
orlañad vr̃o rostro ⁊ adorad la luna ⁊ pedid le merçed q̃ vos
pdone et quando tomo del agua con su manga mojose el
agua ⁊ semejole q̃ trem̄a la luna ⁊ dixo el elifante ala
liebre q̃ ha la luna sy se ensaño contra mj por q̃ metj la man
ga en el agua dixo la liebre asy es como vos dezides ⁊ fe
juntose el elefante delo q̃ fiziera ⁊ enclinose a ella ⁊ fecho
se en preses ⁊ fizole plito ⁊ omenaje q̃ nunca tornaria mas
en aql lugar el nj los otros elefantes

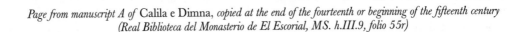

Page from manuscript A of Calila e Dimna, *copied at the end of the fourteenth or beginning of the fifteenth century*
(Real Biblioteca del Monasterio de El Escorial, MS. h.III.9, folio 55r)

Carnero Burgos, "Barlaam e Josafat," dissertation, Universidad Complutense, 1990.

Castigos del rey don Sancho IV (1292–1293)

Manuscripts: A: Biblioteca Nacional, Madrid,
MS. 6559; B: Biblioteca Nacional, Madrid, MS.
6.603 (*olim* S-23); C: Biblioteca Nacional, Madrid,
MS. 3.995 (*olim* P-23); E: Real Biblioteca del
Monasterio de El Escorial, MS. Z.III.4 (*olim*
III.N.24; ij-e-13). All of these manuscripts are fifteenth-
century copies of earlier versions of the text.

First modern edition: "Castigos e documentos
del rey don Sancho," in *Escritores en prosa anteriores
al siglo XV,* edited by Pascual Gayangos, Biblioteca
de Autores Españoles, volume 51 (Madrid: BAE,
1860), pp. 79–228.

Critical editions: *Castigos e documentos para bien
vivir ordenados por el rey don Sancho IV,* edited by
Agapito Rey (Bloomington: Indiana University
Press, 1952); *Castigos e documentos del rey don Sancho
IV,* edited by Hugo O. Bizzarri (Madrid:
Iberoamericana, 2001).

Libro de los gatos (second half of the fourteenth century)

Manuscripts: M: Biblioteca Nacional, Madrid,
MS. 1182 (*olim* F-119; 129-9-A), first half of the fifteenth century; V: Archivo Real de la Chancillería, Pleitos Civiles Moreno 940-1, Fenecidos
c-940/2, beginning of sixteenth century, a fragment.

Editions: *El libro de los gatos,* edited by John E.
Keller (Madrid: Consejo Superior de Investiga-
ciones Científicas, 1958); *Libro de los gatos,* edited
by Bernard Darbord, introduction by Daniel
Devoto (Paris: Séminaire d'études médiévales his-
paniques de l'Université de Paris-XIII, 1984);
María Jesús Díez Carretas, "El *Libro de los gatos*:
Fragmento de un nuevo manuscrito," in *Actas del
VI Congreso Internacional de la Asociación Hispánica de
Literatura Medieval, Universidad de Alcalá, 12–16 de
septiembre de 1995* (Alcalá de Henares: Servicio de
Publicaciones, 1997), pp. 571–580.

Espéculo de los legos (end of the fourteenth or beginning of
the fifteenth century)

Manuscripts: Five fifteenth-century Castilian manu-
scripts of the work are known: A: Biblioteca
Nacional, Madrid, MS. 94 (*olim* B-109); B: Biblio-
teca Nacional, Madrid, MS. 117 (*olim* B-108); C:
Biblioteca Nacional, Madrid, MS. 18.465, 15; D:
Real Biblioteca del Monasterio de El Escorial,
MS. X.III.I (*olim* II.M.22; III-c-23); E: Biblioteca
Universitaria Salamanca, MS. 1859.

Edition: *El* Espéculo de los Legos: *Texto inédito del
s. XV,* edited by José María Mohedano Hernández
(Madrid: Instituto Miguel de Cervantes, Consejo
Superior de Investigaciones Científicas, 1951).

Clemente Sánchez de Vercial, *Libro de los exemplos por
a.b.c.* (end of the fourteenth or beginning of the
fifteenth century)

Manuscripts: M: Biblioteca Nacional, Madrid,
MS. 1.182 (*olim* F-119; C-127-9-A), first half of the
fifteenth century; P: Bibliothèque Nationale, Paris
Esp. 432, last quarter of the fifteenth century.

Edition: *Libro de los exemplos por a.b.c.,* edited by
John E. Keller (Madrid: Consejo Superior de
Investigaciones Científicas, 1961; revised edition,
corrected by Keller and Connie Scarborough,
Madrid: Ars Libris, 2000).

Calila e Dimna (first half of the thirteenth century,
Calila and Dimna), *Sendebar* (mid thirteenth century),
Barlaam e Josafat (mid thirteenth century, Barlaam and
Josafat), the *Castigos del rey don Sancho IV* (1292–1293,
Lessons of King Sancho IV), the *Libro de los gatos* (sec-
ond half of the fourteenth century, Book of Cats), the
Espéculo de los legos (end of the fourteenth or beginning of
the fifteenth century, Mirror of Lay People), and the
Libro de los exemplos por a.b.c. (end of the fourteenth or
beginning of the fifteenth century, Book of Exempla
Aphabetically Arranged) are some of the most important prose works written in Castilian during the Middle
Ages that contain exemplary tales. They are certainly
not the only ones: the exemplum was a prevalent didactic tool in the Middle Ages. Many exempla were
inserted into historical chronicles, books of chivalry,
and books of lineages. Among the texts written in verse
that include narrations and images used in an exemplary way are poems written in the tradition of *cuaderna
vía* (fourfold way), such as the *Libro de Alexandre* (early
thirteenth century, Book of Alexander), Juan Ruiz's
Libro de buen amor (circa 1330–1343; translated as *Book of
Good Love,* 1933), and the *Libro Rimado de Palaçio* (fourteenth century, Rhymed Book of the Palace). Intimately
connected with the secular exemplum tale are the religious varieties of short narrative, which include the
great thirteenth-century collections of Marian miracles:
Gonzalo de Berceo's *Los Milagros de nuestra Señora* (before
1246–after 1252, translated as *Miracles of Our Lady,*
1997) and the preeminent *Cantigas de Santa Maria* (circa
1257–1282; translated as *Songs of Holy Mary of Alfonso X,
the Wise,* 2000), by King Alfonso X *el Sabio* (the
Learned).

Certain texts written in Latin greatly influenced
those written in Castilian. The most important are the
Disciplina clericalis (date uncertain, Discipline of Clerics;
translated as "Peter Alphonse's Disciplina clericalis
[English Translation], from the Fifteenth Century
Worcester Cathedral Manuscript F.172," 1919), by
Petrus Alfonsi, the oldest collection of exempla written
in the Iberian Peninsula in the beginning of the twelfth

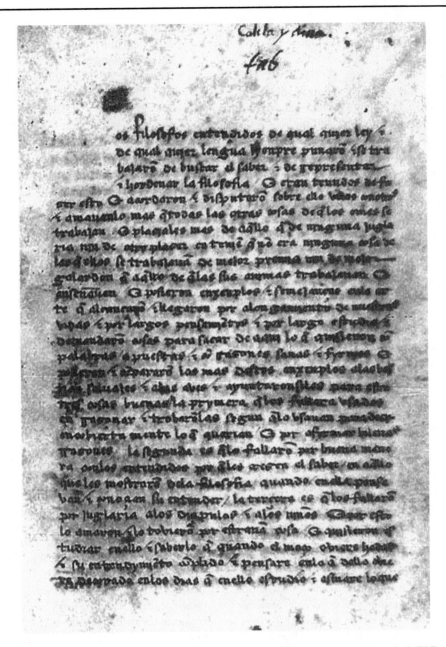

Page from manuscript B of Calila e Dimna, *copied at the end of the fifteenth century (Real Biblioteca del Monsterio de El Escorial, MS. X.III.4)*

century and one with no known medieval translations into Castilian; the *Fabulae* (Fables) attributed to Aesop, which was not translated into Castilian until the end of the fifteenth century (and then from a Latin/German bilingual edition); and the *Facta e dicta memorabilia* (Memorable Sayings and Deeds), by Valerio Maximo, which was translated into Catalan by the end of the fourteenth century and, relying on this Catalan version and a French version, into Castilian by the end of the fifteenth century.

Many Castilian manuscripts containing exempla have not been studied or edited in modern times. María

Jesús Lacarra mentions *Exemplos muy notables* (Very Notable Examples), Biblioteca Nacional, Madrid, MS. 5626, with forty-two exempla, and the *Ejemplos del yermo* (Examples of the Desert), Biblioteca Menéndez Pelayo, Santander, MS. 10. The latter seems to be a translation of one of the many medieval versions of the *Vitae Patrum* (Lives of the Church Fathers). There are also collections of exempla that are part of treatises of religious instruction about the sacraments, especially confession, such as the *Libro de confesiones* (Book of Confessions), Biblioteca Nacional, Madrid, MS. 9535, and the miscellaneous codex *Enxienplos muy provechosos* (Very Profitable

Examples), Biblioteca Nacional, Madrid, MS. 8744 and Biblioteca Menéndez Pelayo, Santander, MS. 77. Finally, there are exempla in the various Castilian versions of the *Viridarium Consolationis* (Garden of Consolation); in the *Tratado de vicios y virtudes* (Treatise on the Vices and Virtues), Biblioteca Nacional, Madrid, MS. 10.252; and in the Castilian versions of the *Fiore di virtù* (Flowers of Virtue), Biblioteca Nacional, Madrid, MS. 2882 and works printed after 1491.

The first problem that modern scholars face when studying the exemplum is defining the genre. In his classical 1927 book on the subject, Jean Thiébaut Welter explains that the word *exemplum* was used in the Middle Ages to refer to a narration, story, fable, parable, or description that was employed to support a doctrinal, religious, or moral discourse. The exemplum could be historical or legendary, sacred or profane, and Eastern or Western in origin. It could be inspired by a contemporary event or taken from classical antiquity or from the experience of preachers and scribes; it could also be found in bestiaries, natural-history treatises, or the popular folk tradition. Every narration or description inherited from the past or recently created in the present could be read, used, and understood as an exemplum. Salvatore Battaglia notes that it is not necessary that the exemplum be an edifying story: one could also resort to "negative" exempla to illustrate the inappropriateness of certain behaviors. What is essential, however, is that the exemplum be used as evidence in the defense of a certain teaching. In most exemplary texts the morals are explicit, but in a few they are reduced to a brief saying or a humorous comment. In some texts the act of teaching itself is integrated in fictional form into the exemplum.

Battaglia argues that the medieval mind conceived of human history as a series of events that are repeated over and over again. For this reason collections of exempla could be presented as exhaustive reservoirs of codes of behavior, with "proved" experiences and "testimonies" to explain and regulate every situation. The authority of the exemplum springs from its being presented as belonging to the whole series of human experiences, transmitted from generation to generation. It was often introduced in sermons and writings as either received from an authoritative oral source or a respected written text.

The flourishing of the didactic mode in general and of the exemplum in particular is related to the recommendation of the Fourth Lateran Council of 1215 concerning the need to give religious instruction to uneducated clergy and laymen. This recommendation led to papal approval of the mendicant orders, the Dominicans and Franciscans, whose main objective was to fulfill that goal by preaching. For this purpose the rhetorical techniques of the sermon were adapted for vernacular tongues in ways that would be attractive and persuasive to the masses. One of the main resources of this popular type of sermon was the exemplum. It is surely not a coincidence that both *Calila e Dimna* and *Sendebar* were translated into Castilian during the decades following the Fourth Lateran Council. The popularity of moralizing narratives coincided with that of other types of didactic discourse such as "mirrors of princes," dialogues, and compilations of proverbs, sentences, and popular sayings ranging from biblical dicta to classical sententiae and the irrepressible Spanish *refrán* (pithy folk wisdom). All of these types of discourse often appear together in the same texts. María Jesús Lacarra Ducay points out some of the most important themes found in exemplary texts: knowledge, wisdom, power, mistrust, misogyny, the fight against evil, and the search for goodness and justice.

Calila e Dimna consists of three introductions and fifteen chapters. The first introduction, written by the Arab translator Ibn al-Muqaffa', deals with the importance of searching for, acquiring, and preserving knowledge. The second introduction is the story of Berzebuey, a Persian royal physician who travels to India in search of medicinal plants and discovers that the only real medicine is the knowledge found in Indian books. He translates these books into the Persian version of *Calila e Dimna*. The narrator of the third introduction is Berzebuey himself, who explains how he came to the conclusion that the most important type of knowledge is that which helps preserve the health of the soul for this life and the next. Each of the fifteen chapters consists of a dialogue between an Indian king, Diçelem, and his philosopher, Burduben. At the beginning of the chapter the king asks a question, and the philosopher answers with multiple exemplary narratives that are often embedded inside one another in a "Chinese box" structure. Calila and Dimna are wolves or jackals who appear in some of the exempla and act as the bad and good advisers, respectively, of an all-too-impressionable lion king. Because the exempla are presented as advice to a royal figure, the book can be placed in the group of didactic texts known as "mirrors of princes."

The Old Castilian translation of the text was produced around 1251 and was probably commissioned by Alfonso X before he ascended to the throne. It was based on an eighth-century Arabic work attributed to Ibn al-Muqaffa'; the Arabic version, in turn, was a translation of a Persian version of around 570. The ultimate roots of *Calila e Dimna,* however, are Indian and are related to the *Panchatantra,* eighty-seven animal fables and magic tales compiled between the third and fifth centuries A.D.

The Old Castilian translation has been preserved in two more or less complete manuscripts. Despite

Page from the codex of Puñonrostro of Sendebar, *or,* Libro de los engaños e los asayamientos de las mugeres *(Biblioteca de la Academia Española, Madrid, MS. 15)*

many differences, they seem to derive from the same archetype, which eventually evolved in two different branches. Manuscript A (Real Biblioteca del Monsterio de El Escorial, MS. h.III.9), from the end of the fourteenth or beginning of the fifteenth century; manuscript B (Real Biblioteca del Monsterio de El Escorial, MS. X.III.4), from the end of the fifteenth century, contains some sections that are not in A: Ibn al-Muqaffa's introduction, chapters 12 and 13, the end of the "Estoria de Berzebuey" (History of Berzebuey), and the end of chapter 11; it also has some folia and chapter titles that are missing from A. There are also two surviving fragments of the translation: P (Biblioteca Universitaria Salamanca, MS. 1763), which includes only the preliminary texts and is related to the Hebrew version of Jacob ben Eleazer; and O (Archivo de la Cathedral Oviedo, MS. 18), consisting of Ibn al-Muqaffa's introduction. At the end of the thirteenth century Juan de Capua, a *converso* (Jewish convert to Christianity), translated *Calila e*

Dimna into Latin from a Hebrew translation of the Arabic version. This Latin version, known as the *Directorium humanae vitae alias parabolae antiquorum sapientum* (Advice for the Lives of People and Other Parables of Ancient Wisdom), was translated into Castilian and published with the title *Exemplario contra los engaños y peligros del mundo* (Collection of Exempla against the Deceptions and Dangers of This World) in 1493 and again in 1498. Capua's version of *Calila e Dimna,* rather than the Old Castilian translation ordered by Alfonso X, was translated into other European languages. The first edition of the Old Castilian translation of *Calila e Dimna* was prepared in 1860 by Pascual Gayangos, who based his edition on A and filled in the gaps with B.

The narrative frame of the mid-thirteenth-century collection of exempla known as *Sendebar* is the story of a prince who has been placed in the hands of a philosopher, Çendubete, by his father, the king. Çendubete commits himself to transfer all his knowledge to the

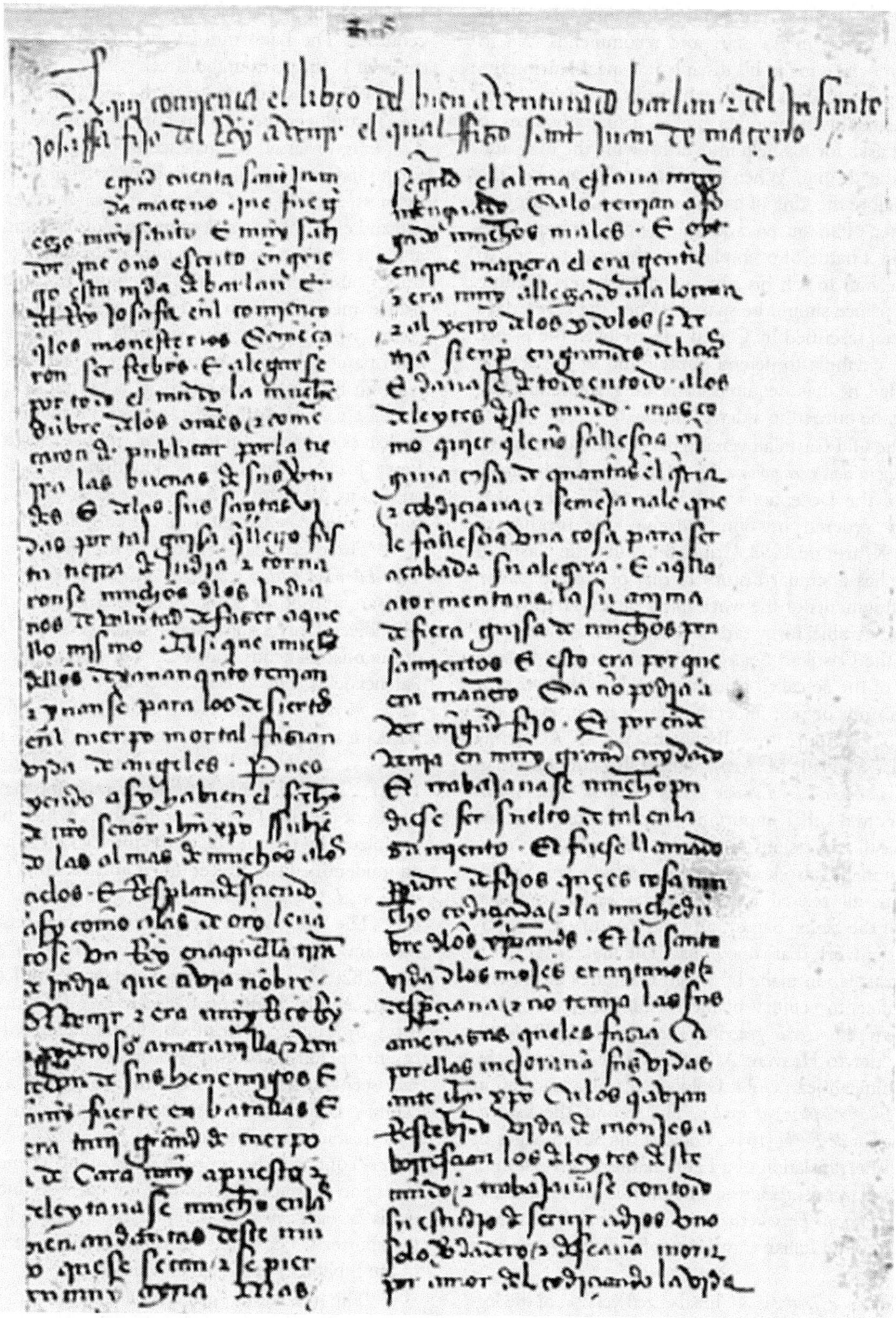

Page from a manuscript of El libro del bien aventurado Barlaan e del infante Josafa, fijo del rrey Avenir, *copied in the second half of the fifteenth century (Biblioteca Nacional, Madrid, MS. 18017)*

prince in six months. At the end of that time Çendubete reads the future in the stars and recommends that to avoid a mortal danger, his disciple not speak during the following seven days. When the prince returns to the royal palace, his stepmother makes sexual advances to him and asks for his help in overthrowing the king and seizing the throne. When he refuses, she accuses the prince before the king of having made the same proposals to her. The queen and the king's advisers then engage in a battle of exempla, with the queen trying to persuade him to kill his son and the advisers arguing that the prince should be spared. When the seven days of silence prescribed by Çendubete are over, the prince tells five exempla to defend himself and to display the knowledge he has acquired. The king condemns the queen to be burned in a dry cauldron.

The Old Castilian version of *Sendebar,* also known as the *Libro de los engaños e los asayamientos de las mugeres* (Book of the Deceptions and Wiles of Women), was probably ordered by don Fadrique, the brother of Alfonso X, around 1253. Critics think that the Castilian *Sendebar* has a similar history to that of *Calila e Dimna,* but no fragments of the work in its earlier Hindu, Persian, and Arabic forms are known to have been preserved; the Castilian *Sendebar* is thus the oldest known version of the so-called oriental branch of the work. It survives only in one fifteenth-century manuscript, the codex of Puñonrostro (Biblioteca de la Academia Española, Madrid, MS. 15), which also contains Juan Manuel's *El conde Lucanor* (1335, Book of Count Lucanor) and other important vernacular texts. Three other Castilian versions of *Sendebar,* belong to the "occidental branch," also known as *Siete sabios* (Seven Sages). They are all related to the *Historia septem sapientibus* (Story of the Seven Sages), a twelfth-century Latin version of the work that is now lost. The first, *Novella,* is a partial translation made by Diego Cañizares at the end of the fifteenth century of the Dominican Jean Gobi's *Scala Coeli de diversis generibus exemplorum* (1323–1330, The Ladder to Heaven: A Collection of Exempla), by the Dominican Jean Gobi; Gobi's text was a translation of the *Historia septem sapientibus.* The second, the *Libro de los siete sabios de Roma* (1510, Book of the Seven Sages of Rome), is a translation of a Latin manuscript version of the *Historia septem sapientibus.* The third is the *Historia lastimera del Príncipe Erasto* (1573), a translation by Hurtado de la Vera of an Italian translation of the twelfth-century Latin version.

Barlaam e Josafat is a Christianized version of the legend, whose Indian origins date from the sixth century B.C., of the conversion of Siddhartha Gautama from Hinduism to become the Buddha. A Manichaean version was written in Turkish in the third century A.D. and was later translated into Arabic. Georgian and Greek translations were made of the Arabic version in the eighth and ninth centuries. The Latin translations, the first of which was made in 1048, are from the Greek.

When Josafat is born to the Indian king Avenir, a royal astrologer predicts his conversion to Christianity. The king orders the construction of a secluded palace for Josafat, hoping to keep him away from Christianity, ugliness, and old age. But one day Josafat leaves the palace and encounters a sick man, an old man, and a leper, and the experience makes him realize that terrestrial things are precarious and fleeting. Eventually, the prince meets Barlaam, a hermit disguised as a merchant, who uses various exempla to convert him to Christianity. After his conversion, Josafat has a dispute with an astrologer, disguised as a hermit, sent by his father. He converts the astrologer and his father; the latter leaves the kingdom to Josafat and becomes a hermit. Later, Josafat turns over the kingdom to another man and joins Barlaam in his cave. After Barlaam dies, Josafat remains a hermit until the end of his own life.

Three Castilian versions of the work are known. The *Libro de Berlan e del rrey Josapha de India* (Book of Barlaam and of the King Josafat of India), known as P (Biblioteca Universitaria Salamanca, MS. 1877), is part of the miscellaneous codex *Leyes de Palencia* (Legends of Palencia). *El libro del bien aventurado Barlaam e del infante Josafa, fijo del rrey Avenir* (The Book of the Well-Adventured Barlaam and of the Prince Josafat, Son of the King Avenir) is known as G (Biblioteca Nacional, Madrid, MS. 18017). These fifteenth-century manuscripts seem to be copies of the first Castilian translation, which had been completed by the middle of the thirteenth century from an unidentified twelfth-century Latin version. The third version, *La estoria del rrey Anemur e del Josaphat e de Barlaam* (The Story of the King Anemur and of Josafat and Barlaam) known as S (University Library, Strasbourg, MS. 1829), is a shorter work adapted from the thirteenth-century Latin *Speculum historiale* (Mirror of History), by Vincent of Beauvais. The unidentified twelfth-century peninsular Latin version and the *Speculum historiale* seem to have had a common origin in a twelfth-century Latin work, now lost, known as the *Vulgata.* The Castilian translations of the *Flos Sanctorum* (Lives of Saints) contain a shortened version of the legend of Barlaam and Josafat by Jacob of Voragine, who included it in his *Legenda aurea* (1275, The Golden Legend). One of the shorter versions has been preserved in MS. 12.689 of the Biblioteca Nacional in Madrid.

The first edition of *Barlaam e Josafat,* published by Friedrich Lauchert in 1893, is based on the shorter version of manuscript S. In 1929 Gerhard Moldenhauer edited manuscript P along with a version of the legend that appears in one of the manuscripts of the *Flos sanctorum* (Biblioteca Nacional, Madrid, MS. 12.689). The most complete modern edition was prepared by John E. Keller and Robert W. Linker in 1979; it includes parallel editions of manuscripts P and G and a separate edition of manuscript S. A 1990 doctoral dissertation by Severino Carnero Burgos includes a paleographic edition of P and G and a critical edition based on P, with annotations and emendations taken from G and S.

The *Castigos del rey don Sancho IV* was the work of a monarch whose learning and patronage of literature are eclipsed only by those of his father, Alfonso X the Learned. During his short and troubled reign of 1284 to 1295 Sancho sponsored projects such as *Los lucidarios* (The Elucidations), *El libro de los tesoros* (The Book of Treasures), and the continuation of the royal histories begun by the teams of scholars assembled by his father. The Castilian text of the *Castigos del rey don Sancho IV*, composed around 1292, is a mirror of princes addressed by Sancho to his son Fernando IV, who was only about six when the anthology was put together and nine when he came to the throne. In the introduction Sancho notes that he composed the work in the same year that he reconquered Tarifa from the Moors. The book is divided into chapters, each devoted to a particular piece of advice given to the prince, such as chapter 9, "De cómmo deue omne amar justiçia" (Of How One Should Love Justice), and chapter 40, "De cómmo se non deue omne pagar del omne traydor" (Of How One Should Not Surround Oneself with Traitors). Various more or less developed exempla are used to illustrate the recommendations. Many of the teachings were appropriate not only for princes but also for the general Christian readership of the time. The *Castigos del rey don Sancho IV* draws on a wide variety of sources, including the Bible; Cicero; Seneca; medieval versions of the Trojan War; Peter Lombard; Petrus Alfonsi's *Disciplina clericalis* (date uncertain, The Discipline of Clerics; translated as "Peter Alphonse's Disciplina clericalis [English Translation], from the Fifteenth Century Worcester Cathedral Manuscript F.172," 1919); Giles of Rome (Aegidius Romanus), and Alfonso X's *Siete partidas* (before 1265, Seven-Part Law) and *Cantigas de Santa Maria* (circa 1257–1282; translated as *Songs of Holy Mary of Alfonso X, the Wise*, 2000).

There are two known versions of the work. The short version, which is the oldest, is found in three manuscripts–B, C, and E (Real Biblioteca del Monasterio de El Escorial, MS. Z.III.4)–and some fragments. Manuscript E is the closest to a lost 1293 subarchetype that was copied from the first manuscript–the archetype–which was finished in 1292. Manuscripts B and C and the fragments seem to have come from another subarchetype of the first half of the fourteenth century. The long version is found in manuscript A (Biblioteca Nacional, Madrid, MS. 6559). This version, written

after 1345, also comes from the 1293 subarchetype but is interpolated with a Castilian translation of Giles of Rome's *De regimine principum* (1279, On the Conduct of Rulers). The title commonly used today was imposed on manuscript A in the fifteenth century. The only modern edition of the long version was prepared by Pascual Gayangos in 1860, using B as a base with additions and corrections from A. The modern editions of the short version by Agapito Rey (1952) and Hugo O. Bizzarri (2001) are based on manuscript E, but they follow different editorial criteria.

The *Libro de los gatos,* a collection of exempla from the second half of the fourteenth century, is a partial translation of the English cleric Odo de Chériton's Latin *Fabulae* (circa 1224–1225). It includes exempla from a variety of sources and is permeated by the ideals of the Fourth Lateran Council, which tried to correct the excesses of the clergy. Only one complete manuscript of the *Libro de los gatos* is known to exist: manuscript M (Biblioteca Nacional, Madrid, MS. 1182), from the first half of the fifteenth century. In this Castilian translation the criticism of immoral customs and social excesses is even more accentuated than in the Latin original. There is neither an introduction nor a framing narrative; most of the fifty-eight chapters include only one exemplum, but a few chapters have more than one, for a total of sixty-four. The title *Libro de los gatos* lacks any clear connection to the contents of the work. Manuscript M was edited by John E. Keller in 1958 and by Bernard Darbord in 1984. A fragment known as manuscript V (Archivo Real de la Chancillería, Pleitos Civiles Moreno 940-1, Fenecidos c-940/2) from the beginning of the sixteenth century was edited by María Jesús Díez Carretas in 1995 and published in 1997.

The *Espéculo de los legos* is a Castilian translation from the end of the fourteenth or beginning of the fifteenth century of the Latin *Speculum Laicorum* (Mirror of Lay People), compiled in England by the end of the thirteenth century. To facilitate its use in the preparation of sermons the book is divided into chapters, each devoted to a particular subject, such as chapter 45, "De la humildad" (On Humility), and chapter 65, "De la paciencia" (On Patience). Each chapter has an introduction and a variable number of exempla. Three of the five known fifteenth-century Castilian manuscripts of this translation are at the Biblioteca Nacional: A (MS. 94), B (MS. 117), and C (MS. 18.465, 15). Manuscript D is at the Real Biblioteca del Monasterio de El Escorial (MS. X.III.I), and manuscript E is at the Biblioteca Universitaria Salamanca (MS. 1859). The only modern edition was prepared by José María Mohedano Hernández in 1951; it is based on manuscript A, the most elaborate and carefully produced of the five known medieval manuscripts.

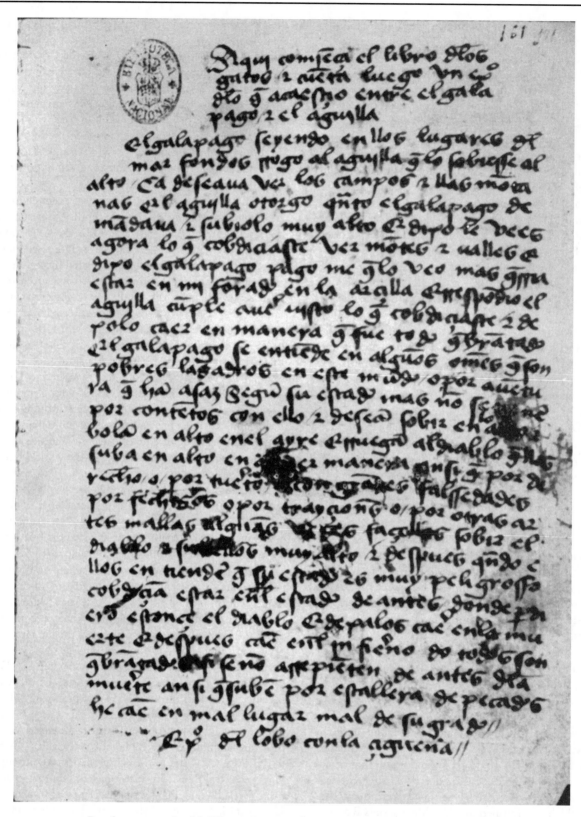

Page from a manuscript of the Libro de los gatos *(Biblioteca Nacional, Madrid, MS. 1182, folio 161r)*

The largest collection of exempla in medieval Spanish is the *Libro de los exemplos por a.b.c.* It was prepared between 1429 and 1438 by Clemente Sánchez de Vercial, who studied law at Salamanca and became a canon in León and an archdeacon in Valderas. The work takes its name from the alphabetical order of its tales. Of the two known manuscripts, M (Biblioteca Nacional, Madrid, MS. 1.182), from the first half of the fifteenth century, comprises 395 entries; and P (Bibliothèque Nationale, Paris, MS. Esp. 432), from the last quarter of the fifteenth century, comprises 438. Manuscript M lacks the dedication, the first seventy-one entries, and entry 216 that appear in P; M, however, has eighteen numbered entries with exempla and three entries without exempla that do not appear in P. The introduction is only a dedication by the author to a friend with a brief explanation of his objective: "por que non solamente a ti mas aun a los que non saben latín fuese solaz" (to entertain not only you but also those who are not acquainted with Latin). There is no frame narrative. Each entry includes one or more exempla and has a thematic heading in Latin that announces the moral of the story and is followed by the same moral in a rhyming couplet in Spanish. The exempla chosen for this text seem to have come from various clerical and Latinate sources; there are few tales from the native Spanish tradition. The modern edition of this work was prepared by Keller in 1961; a corrected edition appeared in 2000, with an updated introduction, a bibliography, an index of exempla, and a comparative chart of the exempla in the two known manuscripts by Connie Scarborough.

At least four other major medieval Castilian works contain important secular collections of short tales and exempla. The *Libro del cavallero Zifar* (Book of the Knight Zifar), a lengthy narrative from around 1300, is the earliest chivalric romance in Castilian; it mixes in other genres, including a light dose of hagiography and a heavier one of the Byzantine novel, full of heartbreaking separations, unexpected reversals of fortune, and happy reunions. Every part of the *Libro del cavallero Zifar* contains embedded exempla, but they are most dense in the third quarter of the book as part of the teachings delivered by King Zifar to his sons under the heading "Castigos del rey de Mentón" (The Lessons of the King of Mentón). The first part of the *Libro del conde Lucanor,* which is by far the longest, is entirely composed of exemplary stories set in a frame tale in which the young Prince Lucanor poses various dilemmas to his counselor, Patronio. Juan Manuel's deft manipulation of his source stories transforms them into novel literary creations that explore the epistemology of narrative itself. The *Libro de buen amor* is a rollicking anthology of amorous misadventures and worldly wisdom composed by an author of uncertain identity who calls himself the Archpriest Juan Ruiz and who also appears as the protagonist. He and many other speaking characters in his book tell fables and tales coyly cast to support the feints and gestures of amorous teasing. Finally, the *Arcipreste de Talavera* (1438, Archpriest of Talavera; translated as *Little Sermons on Sin,* 1959), also known as *El corbacho* (The Scourge), is a misogynist screed composed by Alfonso Martínez de Toledo. His uproariously funny, though savage, tales of feminine deception, frivolity, and lust are generally works of his own invention with few if any ties to preceding versions. Martínez de Toledo's work is mostly a dense framing sermon on the temptations of this world, a prolonged haranguing lecture punctuated with telling examples of fallen states and bad conduct. The passages about wayward women, in particular, are endowed with mocking transcriptions of the speech of misbehaving people.

A large number of additional medieval Castilian works also contain some exemplary material, much of it woven into a continuous narrative stream, as in *El victorial; crónica de don Pero Niño, conde de Buelna, por su alférez Gutierre Díez de Games* (The Victorial, The Chronicle of Don Pedro the Child by his Field Marshall, by Gutierre Díaz de Games, circa 1379–circa 1450), and many chivalric novels such the *Amadís de Gaula* (Amadis of Gaul) in Castilian and the *Tirant lo Blanch* (Tirant the White) in Catalan, and countless ballads in the Spanish *romancero* (ballad tradition).

Non-Castilian Iberian literary traditions produced a respectable corpus of works in the exemplum tradition. Among them are the Portuguese *Livros de linhagens* (Book of Lineages) and the *Recull de eximplis e miracles, gestes e faules ordenades per a.b.c.* (early fifteenth century, Anthology of Examples, Miracles, Heroic Deeds and Fables, organized Alphabetically) a Catalan abbreviated translation of the *Alphabetum Narrationum* (Alphabet of Stories) of Arnold of Liège, which is, perhaps, the largest collection of exempla in any medieval vernacular. Despite its title, this book has little in common with the Castilian *Libro de los exemplos por a.b.c.*

The exemplum genre had a long life in Iberia, extending past the Middle Ages. Francisco Delicado's *La lozana andaluza* (1528, The Lusty Andalusian Girl), Pedro Mejía's *Silva de varia lección* (1540, Forest of Diverse Readings), the anonymous *Lazarillo de Tormes* (1554), Juan de Timoneda's *Patrañuelo* (1565, Engaging Tales), and Miguel de Cervantes's masterpiece *Don Quixote* (1605, 1615) are notable for their embedded short exemplary narratives.

References:

Carlos Alvar and José Manuel Lucía Megías, *Diccionario Filológico de Literatura Medieval Española, Textos y transmisión* (Madrid: Castalia, 2002);

Salvatore Battaglia, "Dall'esempio alla novela," *Filologia Romanza,* 7 (1960): 21–84;

Battaglia, "L'esempio medievale, 1: L'esempio nella retorica antica," *Filologia Romanza,* 6 (1959): 45–82;

Ralph Steele Boggs, *Index of Spanish Folktales* (Helsinki: Academia Scientiarum Fennica, 1930);

Claude Brémond, Jacques Le Goff, and Jean-Claude Schmitt, *Typologie des sources du Moyen Age occidental . . . L'Exemplum,* edited by Léopold Génicot (Turnhout: Brepols, 1972);

Pedro Cátedra, "Los *exempla* de los sermones castellanos de San Vicente Ferrer," in *Ex-Libris: Homenaje al profesor José Fradejas Lebrero,* volume 1, edited by José Romera Castillo, Ana María Freire López, and Antonio Lorente Medina (Madrid: Universidad Nacional de Educación a Distancia, 1993), pp. 59–94;

Alan Deyermond, "The Sermon and Its Uses in Medieval Castilian Literature," *La corónica,* 8, no. 2 (1980): 127–145;

Yves-René Fonquerne and Aurora Egido, *Formas breves del relato: Coloquio de la Casa de Velázquez-Departamento de Literatura de la Universidad de Zaragoza, Madrid, Febrero de 1985* (Madrid & Saragossa: Secretariado de Publicaciones, Universidad de Zaragoza and Casa de Velázquez, 1986);

Harriet Goldberg, *Motif-Index of Folk Narratives in the Pan-Hispanic Romancero* (Tempe: Arizona Center for Medieval and Renaissance Studies, 2000);

Goldberg, *Motif-Index of Medieval Spanish Folk Narratives* (Tempe, Ariz.: Medieval and Renaissance Texts and Studies, 1998);

Fernando Gómez Redondo, *Historia de la prosa medieval castellana,* 2 volumes (Madrid: Cátedra, 1998, 1999);

Marta Haro Cortés, *Los compendios de castigos del siglo XIII: técnicas narrativas y contenido ético,* Anejo 14 de la Revista *Cuadernos de Filología* (Valencia: Universidad de València, 1995);

Haro Cortés, *La imagen del poder real a través de los compendios de castigos castellanos del siglo XIII* (London: Department of Hispanic Studies, Queen Mary and Westfield College, 1996);

Haro Cortés and José Agagüez Aldaz, "El *exemplum* medieval castellano, Una aproximación bibliográfica," *Memorabilia,* 4 (2000): 1-33;

John E. Keller, *Motif-Index of Mediaeval Spanish Exempla* (Knoxville: University of Tennessee Press, 1949);

Richard P. Kinkade, "El reinado de Sancho IV: puente literario entre Alfonso el Sabio y Juan Manuel," *Publications of the Modern Language Association,* 87 (1972): 1039-1051;

María Jesús Lacarra Ducay, *Cuentística medieval en España: los orígenes* (Saragossa: Universidad de Zaragoza, 1979);

Lacarra Ducay, *Cuento y novela corta en España,* volume 1: *Edad Media* (Barcelona: Crítica, 1999);

Lacarra Ducay, *Cuentos de la Edad Media* (Madrid: Castalia, 1986);

Derek W. Lomax, "The Lateran Reforms and Spanish Literature," *Iberorromania,* 1 (1969): 299-313;

Francisco López Estrada, *La prosa medieval (Orígenes–siglo XIV),* Literatura Española en Imágenes, no. 6 (Madrid: La Muralla, 1974);

López Estrada, "Prosa narrativa de ficción," *Grundriss der Romanischen Literaturen des Mittelalters,* 9, no. 1 (1985): 15-53;

José Antonio Maravall, "La concepción del saber en una sociedad tradicional," in his *Estudios de historia del pensamiento español,* volume 1 (Madrid: Ediciones Cultura Hispánica, 1973), pp. 215-272;

Rameline E. Marsan, *Itinéraire Espagnol du conte médiéval, VIIIe–XVe siècles* (Paris: Klincksieck, 1974);

Jesús Montoya Martínez, Aurora Juárez Blanquer, and Juan Paredes Núñez, eds., *Narrativa breve medieval románica* (Granada: Ediciones TAT, 1988);

Eloísa Palafox, *Las éticas del* exemplum, *Los* Castigos del rey don Sancho IV, *El* conde Lucanor *y el* Libro de buen amor, Publicaciones de Medievalia, no. 18 (México: Universidad Nacional Autónoma de México, 1998);

Juan Paredes Núñez, *Formas narrativa breves en la literatura románica medieval: problemas de terminología* (Granada: Universidad de Granada, 1986);

Paredes Núñez, *Las narraciones de los "Livros de linghagens"* (Granada: Universidad de Granada, 1995);

Petrus Alfonsi, *Disciplina clericalis,* edited and translated by María Jesús Lacarra Ducay and Esperanza Ducay, Nueva Biblioteca de Autores Aragoneses, volume 3 (Saragossa: Guara, 1980);

José Antonio Pinel Martínez, *Cuentos de la Edad Media* (Madrid: Castalia, 1999);

J. C. Schmitt, "Recueils franciscaines d'*exempla* et perfectionnement des techniques intellectueles du XIII au XIV siècle," *Bibliothèque de l'Ecole des Chartes,* 135 (1977): 5-21;

Stith Thompson, *Index Exemplorum: A Handbook of Medieval Religious Tales* (Helsinki: Akademia Scientiarum Fennica, 1969);

Thompson, *Motif-Index of Folk Literature* (Bloomington & London: Indiana University Press, 1966);

Jean Thiébaut Welter, *L'Exemplum dans la littérature religieuse et didactique du Moyen Age* (Paris & Toulouse: Occitania, 1927; New York: AMS Press, 1973);

Paul Zumthor, *Essai de poétique médiévale* (Paris: Seuil, 1972).

Medieval Spanish Spiritual Literature, 1369–1500

Mark D. Johnston
DePaul University

WORKS: *Tratado de devoção* [fourteenth century]: excerpt edited by J. Cornu as "Anciens textes portugais," *Romania*, 11 (1882): 357–390;

Vida de Sancto Amaro [fourteenth century]: edited by Otto Klob as "*A vida de Sancto Amaro*, texte portugais du XIVe siècle," *Romania*, 30 (1901): 504–518;

Passion poems [fourteenth century]: edited by E. Moliné i Brasés as "Passió, mort, resurrecció y aparicions de N. S. Jesucrist," *Estudis Universitaris Catalans*, 3 (1909): 65–74, 155–159, 260–264, 344–351, 459–463, 542–546; 4 (1910): 99–109, 499–508; edited by Pere Bohigas as "El repertori de manuscrits catalans de la Institució Patxot," *Estudis Universitaris Catalans*, 16 (1931): 213–310;

Recull d'eximplis e miracles, gestes, faules e altres ligendes ordenades per A-B-C [fourteenth century], 2 volumes, edited by Mariano Aguiló (Barcelona: Alvar Verdaguer, 1981);

Lothar of Segni (later Pope Innocent III), *Libro de miseria d'omne* [circa 1300]: edited by Pompilio Tesauro as *Libro de miseria de omne* (Pisa: Giardini, 1983); edited by Jane Ellen Connolly as *Libro de miseria d'omne*, in her *Translation and Poetization in the Cuaderna Vía: Study and Edition of the* Libro de miseria d'omne (Madison, Wis.: Hispanic Seminary of Medieval Studies, 1987), pp. 119–221; edited by Vincenzo Minervini as *Il "Llibre del plant de l'hom": Versione catalana del "Liber de miseria humane conditionis de Lotario Diacono"* (Fasano di Brindisi: Schena, 1996);

Pedro Fernández Pecha, *Soliloquios entre el alma y Dios y el alma consigo misma* [1373–1402]: edited by A. Custodio Vega as "Los 'Soliloquios' de Fr. Pedro Fernández Pecha, fundador de los Jerónimos de España," *La Ciudad de Dios*, 175 (1962): 710–763;

Francesc Eiximenis, *Lo chrestià* [1379–1391]: edited by Jorge E. J. Gracia as *Com usar bé de beure e menjar: Normes morals contingudes en el Terç del Crestià* (Barcelona: Curial, 1977); edited by Curt J. Wittlin and others as *Dotzè llibre del crestià* (Girona: Col·legi Universitari de Girona, Diputació de Girona, 1986);

Pedro de Veragüe, *Doctrina de la discrición* [late fourteenth century]: edited by Raúl A. Del Piero, in *Dos escritores de la Baja Edad Media castellana (Pedro de Veragüe y el Arcipreste de Talavera, cronista real)*, Anejos del *Boletín de la Real Academia Española*, no. 23 (Madrid: Real Academia Española, 1970), pp. 5–79;

Escorial Bible I.ii.19 [late fourteenth century], edited by Mark G. Littlefield (Madison, Wis.: Hispanic Seminary of Medieval Studies, 1992);

Gutierre de Toledo, *Quaderno* [1377–1389]: edited by Antonio C. Floriano as "Un catecismo castellano del siglo XIV," *Revista española de pedagogía*, 3 (1945): 87–99;

Aymó de Cescars, *Lausor de la divinitat* [1380–1399]: edited by Paul Meyer as "Nouvelles catalanes inédites," *Romania*, 29 (1891): 193–215;

Pero López de Ayala, *Rimado de palacio* [1380–1403], edited by Germán Orduña (Madrid: Castalia, 1987);

Corpus Christi poems [1390]: edited by Amadeu Pagès as "Poésies catalanes inédites du Ms. 377 de Carpentras," *Romania*, 42 (1913): 174–203;

Eiximenis, *Libre dels àngels* [1392]: excerpts edited by Andrés Ivars as "El 'Llibre dels Angels' de Fr. Francisco Eiximenis y algunas versiones castellanas del mismo," *Archivo Ibero-Americano*, 19 (1923): 108–124;

Antoni Canals, *Scala de contemplació* [1398–1400]: edited by Juan Roig Gironella as "*Scala de contemplació* en traducción catalana de Fray Antonio Canals," *Analecta Sacra, Tarraconensia*, 46 (1973): 129–263;

Eiximenis, *Primer volumen de Vita christi de fray Francisco Xymenes* [circa 1400] (Valencia: Ungut & Pegnitzer, 1496);

St. Bernard of Clairvaux, *O Tratado das Meditações de Sam Bernardo* [circa 1400], edited by José Nogueira de Carvalho (Coimbra, 1942);

Pedro de Luna (Pope Benedict XIII), *Libro de las consolaciones de la vida humana* [circa 1400], in *Escritores en prosa anteriores al siglo XV*, edited by Pascual de Gayangos, Biblioteca de Autores Españoles, no.

51 (Madrid: M. Rivadeneyra, 1860), pp. 561–602;

Clemente Sánchez de Vercial, *Libro de los enxiemplos por a.b.c.* [circa 1400], in *Escritores en prosa anteriores al siglo XV,* edited by Pascual de Gayangos, Biblioteca de Autores Españoles, no. 51 (Madrid: M. Rivadeneyra, 1860), pp. 443–542; *Libro de los exenplos por a.b.c.,* edited by John E. Keller and Connie L. Scarborough (Madrid: Edilán, 2000);

Tratado de viçios e virtudes [circa 1400], edited by Cleveland Johnson Jr. (Potomac, Md.: Scripta Humanistica, 1994);

Boosco deleitoso [early fifteenth century]: edited by Augusto Magne as *Boosco deleitoso: Ed. do texto de 1515, com introdução, anotações, e glossário* (Rio de Janeiro: Instituto Nacional do Livro, 1950);

Bíblia medieval Portuguêsa [early fifteenth century], edited by Serafim Silva Neto (Rio de Janeiro: Instituto Nacional do Livro, 1958);

St. Vincent Ferrer, "Le sermon en langue vulgaire prononcé a Toulouse par S. Vincent Ferrier le Vendredi saint 1416," edited by Clovis Brunel, *Bibliothèque de l'École des Chartes,* 111 (1953): 5–53;

Canals, *Scipió e Aníbal, De providència (de Sèneca), De arra d'ànima (d'Hug de Sant Víctor)* [1416–1419?], edited by Martí de Riquer (Barcelona: Els nostres clàssics, 1935);

Felip de Malla, *Memorial del pecador remut: Manuscrit de Barcelona* [1419–1423], 3 volumes, edited by Manuel Balasch, Els nostres clàssics, Col•leció A, volumes 118, 119, and 123 (Barcelona: Barcino, 1981–1986);

Pedro Marín, *Los sermones atribuidos a Pedro Marín* [1430], edited by Pedro M. Cátedra (Salamanca: Universidad de Salamanca, 1990);

Ludolph of Saxony, *Vita Christi,* excerpts edited by Augusto Magne, in *O livro de Vita Christi in lingagem portugués* [1430–1446] (Rio de Janeiro: Instituto Nacional do Livro, 1956);

André Dias, *Laudes e cantigas espirituais* [1435], edited by Mario Martins (Roriz: Mosteiro de Singeverga, 1951);

Lope Fernández de Minaya, *Espejo del alma, Tratado breve de penitencia, Libro de las tribulaciones* [circa 1438], edited by Fernando Rubio, Biblioteca de Autores Españoles, volume 171 (Madrid: Atlas, 1964), pp. 220–301;

Alfonso Martínez de Toledo, *Vidas de San Ildefonso y San Isidoro* [1444], edited by José Madoz (Madrid: Espasa-Calpe, 1962);

Juan Alfonso de Baena, *Cancionero* [1445–1454], edited by Brian Dutton and Joaquín González Cuenca (Madrid: Visor, 1993);

Martín de Córdoba, *Tratado de la predestinación* [after 1454], edited by Rubio, Biblioteca de Autores Españoles, volume 171 (Madrid: Atlas, 1964), pp. 121–155;

João Alvares, *Imitação de Cristo* [1467–1468], edited by Artur de Magalhães Basto, *Anais das Bibliotecas e Arquivos,* 17 (1943–1945): 39–48, 75–84, 191–197;

Castelo perigoso [fifteenth century], edited by Augusto Magne, *Revista Filológica,* 4, no. 15 (1942): 183–202; 5, no. 18 (1942): 81–87; *Verbum* (Rio de Janeiro), 2 (1945): 116–123, 233–238, 458–469; 3 (1946): 79–89, 191–201, 298–307;

Iñigo de Mendoza, *Coplas de Vita Christi* [late fifteenth century]: edited by Julio Rodríguez Puértolas as *Fray Iñigo de Mendoza y sus coplas de Vita Christi* (Madrid: Gredos, 1968);

Diego de San Pedro, *Las siete angustias de Nuestra Señora* [1491] and *La pasión trovada* [circa 1475], in his *Obras completas,* 3 volumes, edited by Dorothy S. Severin and Keith Whinnom (Madrid: Castalia, 1973–1979), I: 150–165; III: 101–238;

Ambrosio de Montesino, *Coplas sobre diversas devociones y misterios de nuestra santa fe católica* [1485], introduction by Henry Thomas (London: British Museum, 1936);

Isabel de Villena, *Llibre anomenat Vita Christi* [1490], 3 volumes, edited by Ramon Miquel i Planas (Barcelona: Alvar Verdaguer, 1916);

Andrés de Li, *Summa de paciencia* (Saragossa: Hurus, 1493);

Juan de Padilla, *Los doze triunfos de los doze apóstoles* [circa 1500], edited by R. Foulché-Delbosc, in *Cancionero castellano del siglo XV,* volume 1, Nueva Biblioteca de Autores Españoles, volume 19 (Madrid: Bailly-Bailliére, 1912), pp. 288–423;

Ludolph of Saxony, *Uita cristi romançado por fray Ambrosio,* 4 volumes (Alcalá de Henares: Stanislaus Polonus, 1502–1503).

Late-fourteenth- and fifteenth-century Iberia produced more vernacular religious literature than all previous medieval centuries combined. The profusion of such material resulted largely from the convergence of two historical developments: the rise in vernacular literacy among laypeople and the growth in practices of piety that emphasized individual devotion.

The maturation of Castilian, Catalan, and Portuguese as literary idioms from the twelfth to the fifteenth centuries is well documented and follows the same pattern of development seen in the other major national languages of western Europe. Although the degree of literacy in the general population is difficult to quantify, anecdotal evidence testifies to rising expectations of education among the middle and

Page from a Castilian Bible (Real Biblioteca del Monasterio de El Escorial, MS. i.j.3)

upper classes. As elsewhere in later medieval Europe, new and more-personal modes of Christian spirituality spread in Iberia. The range of pious practices known as the *Devotio Moderna* (Modern Devotion) in northern Europe especially emphasized the individual's struggle for direct experience of divine grace and revelation. Similar developments appeared in Iberia, where they included sometimes-extravagant public displays of penance or rapture but more often involved intensive private exercises of meditation, contemplation, and prayer guided by images or written materials. These works typically presented striking descriptions to encourage their audience's imagination and emotional reaction and prompt a fuller personal response to the events depicted. This increased emphasis on individual devotion fostered a market for spiritual texts that spanned all literate classes of society. The surge in the production of vernacular spiritual literature continued trends that had existed from the first emergence of Castilian, Catalan,

and Portuguese as literary idioms: religious works figured prominently among the major early monuments of each language. By the middle of the fourteenth century, religious writings constituted most of the vernacular works circulating in Iberia and elsewhere in Europe, outnumbering by far the historical or imaginative texts usually celebrated as landmarks in the formation of the national literatures during the later Middle Ages.

This impressive corpus of vernacular religious writing has not attracted extensive modern attention. For Castilian, only the 1980 anthology by Pedro Sainz Rodríguez attempts a comprehensive survey; for Catalan and Portuguese the best treatments remain sections from the general literary histories by Martí de Riquer (1964) and José Antonio Saraiva (1966). One reason for neglect of this literature among modern readers may be that so much of it seems derivative and repetitive; yet, these apparently negative qualities in fact point to important cultural functions of the texts. Until the end of the Middle Ages most vernacular spiritual literature consisted of translations or adaptations of Latin works by clerical authors. In Portugal the Cistercian house of Alcobaça led the spiritual life of the nation, thanks in part to its steady production of translations of devotional works from Latin and other vernacular languages. Dissemination of learned material in local idioms was a powerful channel for the transmission of advanced learning to the laity. Before the fourteenth century, these translations or adaptations were often singular—even idiosyncratic—creations produced to satisfy the needs of a particular vernacular reader or circle of readers. As more and more religious writings circulated in the vernacular, they helped to establish expectations of vocabulary, imagery, style, and tone that became literary norms for both readers and writers. As authors employed these norms to create new works of spiritual literature independently of Latin models, they fostered the transmission of often novel ideas and images throughout lay culture at large. In Iberia the many spiritual writers of the later Middle Ages, who are little known and less read today, laid the foundation on which great mystical authors of the sixteenth century such as St. Theresa and St. John of the Cross erected their celebrated literary monuments.

The cultural hegemony of the Church in the western Middle Ages makes it almost impossible to find any medieval vernacular text that does not reflect Christian beliefs, but religious writings composed for the direct edification or guidance of the Christian reader belong to four genres: exempla and sermon collections; manuals of instruction or guidance; hagiography, Marian literature, and lives of Christ; and works of devotion, contemplation, or meditation. While these categories are not mutually exclusive—collections of exempla often served as texts for the practice of devotion—they represent levels of increasing spiritual sophistication. Vernacular collections of exempla and sermons usually offered Christian piety in its simplest form. Works of instruction or guidance typically provided more-formal theological or spiritual education. Lives of saints and of Christ demanded active readers seeking to imitate these holy exemplars. Guides to devotion and meditation best served readers prepared to renounce secular affairs, partially or completely, in favor of a life of contemplation.

The use of exempla—brief fictional, historical, or scientific anecdotes—to illustrate an argument in a speech was a staple of the classical rhetorical practice inherited by Western medieval culture. The Dominican and Franciscan preachers of the thirteenth century made the exemplum a fundamental component of their public sermons, which were almost always delivered in the vernacular. Theorists of preaching argued that the

concrete details of vivid exempla would hold popular audiences' limited attention and impress the truths of Christian doctrine on their unsophisticated minds. By the middle of the thirteenth century several well-indexed compendia of exempla in Latin had become standard reference works for Dominican and Franciscan preachers. Theologians debated the limits of credulity or decency that friars should observe in the choice of anecdotes to enliven their sermons. In the later Middle Ages the mendicant friars' constant recourse to exempla had an impact on the development of vernacular literature that would be difficult to underestimate. Spreading quickly and aggressively throughout Western Europe, the friars put into circulation a vast body of common folklore, facts of natural science, historical knowledge, and pious legend. Disseminated orally from the pulpit, this mass of anecdotal information became a stock resource of vernacular literature that was adapted by lay authors in works of instruction, entertainment, and social criticism.

For literate lay audiences accustomed to hearing preachers illustrate their sermons with engaging anecdotes, vernacular collections of exempla were attractive texts for meditation or devotion. A fourteenth-century compiler at Alcobaça created a Portuguese *Tratado de devoção* (Treatise on Devotion), consisting of exempla on the virtues and vices, with particular attention to the horrible punishment awaiting sinners in hell. The chapter on chastity includes a brief anecdote:

> Onde côta huu padre santo que passava cõ seus discipollos pera huu loguar, e vio estar hua molher muito afeitada e tornou muy triste e começou de chorar. E os discipollos perguntarõlhe porque chorava assy. E el rrespondeo e disse: "Filhos, choro polla minha negligencia, que non trabalho por aparecer a Deus tanto como aquella molher trabalha por aparecer ao mudo."

> (Where it tells how a holy father was passing with his disciples through a place, and he saw there a woman wearing much makeup and he became very sad and began to cry. And his disciples asked why he cried so. And he responded, saying "My children, I cry over my own neglect, for I labor not to appear before God as that woman labors to appear before the world.")

Although such collections occasionally—and often inaccurately—attribute their anecdotes to some ancient, biblical, or medieval authority, they usually introduce their stories with the simple claims "They say . . ." or "It is told. . . ." Such anonymous citation reflects the wide, unattributed circulation of this material as a common resource for preachers but also gives the anecdote a kind of generalized authority as an experience universally applicable to any audience. The short exemplum from the *Tratado de devoção* offers little more than a holy man's pithy comment, a feature that illustrates the highly elastic character of the material gathered in such collections, as well as the discursive kinship between exempla and aphorisms. Exempla easily collapsed into sententiae, and the latter easily swelled into stories.

By far the largest of these compilations, with more than seven hundred entries, is the fourteenth-century Catalan *Recull d'eximplis e miracles, gestes, faules e altres ligendes ordenades per a-b-c* (Selection of *Exempla*, Miracles, Deeds, Fables, and Other Legends Alphabetically Arranged). The title reflects the heterogeneous character of the material typically gathered in these collections. Many perpetuate ancient conventions of wisdom literature by offering each anecdote as a separate passage for study. Clemente Sánchez de Vercial follows this format in his *Libro de los exemplos por a.b.c.* (circa 1400, Alphabetical Book of Exempla), the largest exempla collection in Castilian. A typical passage reads:

> *Mulieris caro ignis dicitur esse.*
> De la mujer te guarda, yo te ruego,
> Ca la su carne quema commo fuego.
> Dicen que un monje queriendo pasar á su madre vieja un rio, envolvió sus manos en la ropa; é díjole la madre: "Fijo, ¿por qué envolviste las manos?" E él le dijo: "Porque el cuerpo de la mujer es fuego, é llegando á tí, acordárseme-ha de las otras mujeres."

> (*A woman's flesh is called fire.*
> Of woman beware, I implore you, For her flesh burns like fire.
> They say that a monk, trying to cross a river with his old mother, wrapped his hands in his clothes. His mother asked him: "Son, why did you wrap your hands?" And he told her: "Because a woman's flesh is fire, and being near you will remind me of other women.")

Sánchez de Vercial employs a common convention of medieval wisdom literature, the inclusion of a Latin epigram, rendered freely into vernacular couplets, which the accompanying exemplum explicates. Preachers often used exempla in this way to explain biblical citations or other authoritative maxims as a device for amplifying their material. The alphabetical organization of epigrams that structures the *Libro de enxemplos por a.b.c.* imitates reference works for preachers; such works also arranged their material topically for easier consultation, and compilations for lay readers often followed this convention, as well.

Sermons were also popular as pious literature, appearing often in compendia of devotional texts. An outstanding example of such compilations is Madrid, Biblioteca Nacional MS. 9433, prepared shortly before 1430 by Master Pedro Marín for Pedro Fernández de Velasco, the future count of Haro. The volume includes a treatise on moral theology; some original sermons evidently by Master Pedro; and other sermons copied, without attribution, from St. Vincent Ferrer. This tacit plagiarism demonstrates the appeal of the great mendicant preachers of the later Middle Ages, who developed the popular sermon into a public performance through their reliance on techniques for dramatically retelling sacred events. Early Franciscan and Dominican preachers had enhanced their sermons with dramatic gestures and mimicry, and their successors extended such techniques to include the use of props and audience response. Among contemporary Iberian preachers, none achieved greater renown than St. Vincent Ferrer. Hundreds of admirers followed him during his preaching tours of Iberia and southern France; on some occasions his audiences reportedly surpassed ten thousand. His listeners routinely included at least a few learned devotees who transcribed his words verbatim; thus, more than two hundred of his sermons are extant, often with Latin versions designed for consultation by other preachers. The description of the Virgin at the foot of the cross, from St. Vincent Ferrer's six-hour retelling of the Passion narrative, recorded in Occitan at Toulouse on Easter Sunday 1416, illustrates the use of dramatic monologues that invited his audiences' emotional participation in the events recounted:

> E quant la beneyta Verges Maria levet los huelhs en sus e vit lo seu beneyte filh pendut en la crotz e an ayschi orriblamen turmentant e crucificat e coronat de terriblas espinas sobre lo chap, podetz esmagenar qual dolor ni qual tristor inextimabla era aquela de la beneyta Verges Maria, car tantost que ela vit en aquel estat, ela tombet en terra coma morta, que a grans penas om la poc resperir. E quant ela se fo resperida, ela volc anar al seu beneyte filh, e quant ela y cujava anar, ela no se podia sostener de la gran dolor e engoyscha que passava.

> (And when the Blessed Virgin Mary raised her eyes upward and saw her Blessed Son hanging on the cross and so horribly tortured and crucified and crowned with terrible thorns on his head, you can imagine how much pain and what inestimable sadness was the Blessed Virgin Mary's, for as soon as she saw him in that condition, she fell down to the ground as though dead and could hardly breathe. And when she had recovered, she wanted to go to her Blessed Son, but when she tried to walk there, she could not stand up from the great pain and anguish that she suffered.)

The invitation to imagine the Virgin's suffering before the cross reveals the quintessential mechanism of most later medieval devotional practices: stimulating the senses and imagination to achieve a kind of virtual spiritual experience. The unique manuscript of this ser-

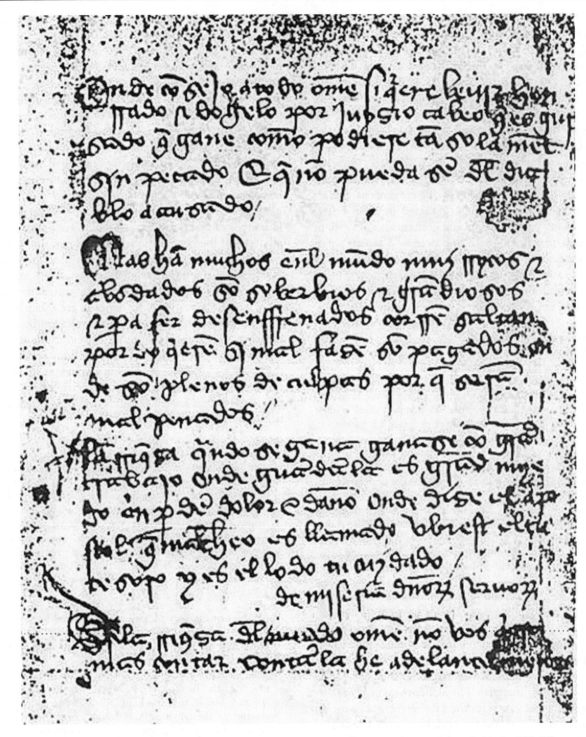

Page from the only extant manuscript of the Libro de miseria de omne *(Biblioteca Menendez Pelayo, Santander, MS. 77)*

mon, Bodleian Douce 162, also contains a vernacular text recounting the dramatic events of Christ's appearance to Mary after the Resurrection, Pentecost, and the Ascension, as well as a section on the capital sins drawn from a French source. Such a compendium would be ideal for inspiring a lay reader to contrition and peni-

tence during Lent. Thanks to the generations of clergy who preached every week or every day throughout the later Middle Ages, the sermon became perhaps the best-known discursive genre, secular or sacred, in medieval literature. The collections studied by Pedro M. Cátedra, Fernando González Ollé, and Josep Moran i

Ocerinjauregui constitute only a tiny fraction of the material that remains unedited in manuscripts. As Francisco Rico has argued, the sermon lent itself to adaptations for nearly every literary purpose from the scurrilous to the mystical.

The rise of literacy among the laity and the Church's campaign to establish a uniform orthodoxy among the faithful stimulated the production of vernacular texts for religious instruction and spiritual guidance. In Iberia this production included the Bible itself, even though fear that misunderstanding holy writ would foster heresy had led Church and secular authorities to ban laypeople from using vernacular translations of Scripture; James I of Aragon did so in 1233. Nonetheless, complete and partial renditions of the Bible into the Iberian Romance languages appeared throughout the later Middle Ages, including several in Castilian and a complete Portuguese version commissioned in the early fifteenth century by King John I. The continued production of Bible translations perhaps served the needs of Iberian clergy, who were reputed to lack adequate Latin training and thus to be in greater need of vernacular versions of Scripture. For lay audiences late-medieval religious authors also synthesized Scripture in compendia of Catholic dogma and moral theology. These works often added considerable material from apocryphal sources, liturgical glosses, and popular legends.

By far the most ambitious instructional project of this era in Iberia was *Lo chrestià* (The Christian), by Francesc Eiximenis. The Franciscan theologian originally planned the work as a thirteen-volume encyclopedia of Catholic belief and learning, but between 1379 and 1391 he completed only the first three and the twelfth volumes, dealing with natural and revealed law, grace, sin, and government, because of his many administrative and diplomatic duties. Eiximenis also composed many shorter works of religious instruction and spiritual guidance. Other Iberian authors also sought to offer succinct, yet comprehensive, treatments of Catholic devotional practice, doctrine, and spiritual advice. The Castilian *Doctrina de la discriçión* (Instruction on Discretion) or *Tratado de la doctrina* (Treatise of Instruction), by Pedro de Veragüe, dates from the later fourteenth century and offers 157 four-line stanzas of simple religious and moral instruction evidently intended for children, such as: "Esto pensé ordenar / para el njnno admenjstrar / que es muy malo despulgar / el çammarón" (I wished to prepare this / for guiding a child, / for it is very hard to delouse an old hide). The homely diction used throughout the treatise makes it a kind of country cousin to the manuals for educating children that were popular among urban and courtly readers. The first half of the *Tratado de la doctrina* pre-

sents rudiments of catechism and moral theology; the second half offers general advice on conduct and customs, such as:

> Es obra maraujillosa
> buena muger e fermosa
> [e] rica, e generosa
> de parientes.

> (A marvelous thing
> is a woman good, beautiful,
> [and] rich, with many
> relatives.)

The consistently sententious character of Veragüe's verses places his treatise in the long tradition of advice literature composed of aphorisms and proverbs.

Many works supported the clergy's task of instructing the faithful on the catechism. Some were clearly destined for priests whose education or knowledge of Latin was deficient. Gutierre de Toledo, a learned theologian who was bishop of Oviedo from 1377 to 1389, composed a summary *Quaderno* (Notebook) of Catholic doctrines in Castilian for the priests of his diocese to learn by heart so that they would be better able to instruct their parishioners. Lay readers evidently expected a more attractive presentation of such material; vernacular authors strove to provide it, creating almost a minor genre of catechetical guides composed with literary artifice in verse or prose. In Catalan, Aymó de Cescars wrote the *Lausor de la divinitat* (Praise of Divinity) between 1380 and 1399 to instruct laypeople, while apologizing for his own limited education. In 347 lines, almost entirely consisting of rhymed couplets, he explains in simple terms the life of Christ, the Last Judgment, the sacraments, the Ten Commandments, works of mercy, and penance.

The practice of confession was a major concern of later medieval devotion. Along with penance, it inspired a considerable "literature of conscience." Guides to the assessment and satisfaction of penitential debts were one of the first original genres of Christian moral literature in the early Middle Ages. After the Fourth Lateran Council made annual confession by all Christians obligatory in 1215, a copious body of material arose on the theory and practice of revealing and requiting one's sins. At least ten Catalan guides to confession appeared in the latter half of the fourteenth century. Castilian court writers offered many verse and prose treatments of confession, as well; the outstanding example is the opening stanzas of the *Rimado de palacio* (The Poem about the Palace), a lengthy work of social and moral criticism written between 1367 and 1407 by the one-time royal chancellor Pero López de Ayala.

Among the best-composed works of vernacular penitential literature are the two books of the *Espejo del alma* (1438, Mirror of the Soul), by the Augustinian friar Lope Fernández de Minaya. Book 1 reviews the pleasures and temptations of this world, the death that awaits everyone, and the pleasures of paradise that one must strive to recall. Book 2 tells how the conscience must become a mirror for the soul in which one examines the blemishes of sin in order to cleanse them away. In the most polished parts of his work Fernández de Minaya effortlessly manipulates standard rhetorical techniques to combine traditional imagery, theological erudition, and commonplace examples. The entire chapter on signs of wrath states:

Cómo la saña es tan manifiesta que, sin señales, la conoce hombre en sí, e cómo tiene señales de fuera esta dicha pasión

Las señales de la saña de parte de dentro son manifiestas a cada uno en sí mismo, que non las conviene escribir, que cada uno siente en sí de dentro quando se turba o se ensaña. Pero las señales de fuera, segund las pone Sant Gregorio, son estas: "El coraçón salta, el cuerpo tiembla, la lengua se traba, el rostro se enciende, los ojos se turban e non conosce hombre a sus amigos, fabla e non entiende lo que dize."

(How Wrath Is So Obvious That, Even without Signs, One Recognizes It within Oneself, and How This Passion Shows Itself Externally

The signs of wrath from within are so obvious to anyone within himself that it is unnecessary to describe them, since everyone feels inside when he is angry or upset. But the outward signs, as Saint Gregory puts them, are thus: "The heart leaps, the body trembles, the tongue stammers, the face reddens, the eyes are agitated and a man does not know his friends, he speaks without understanding what he says.")

The appeal to self-knowledge underscores the examination of conscience that the *Espejo del alma* teaches, while the authoritative citation from Pope Gregory the Great's *Moralia in Job* (579–596) reinforces individual experience with common physiological information from a Doctor of the Church. This collation of appeal to the reader's experience with citation of authority effectively equates their probative value. The *Tratado breve de penitencia o de las señales por do se conoce quando es verdadera* (Brief Treatise on Penance or on the Signs from Which One Knows It Is True) follows the *Espejo del alma* as a practical guide to contrition, confession, and penance.

In addition to these more-comprehensive guides to Christian devotion, various specialized works offered instruction on spiritual or theological questions of particular urgency. In Catalan, Eiximenis composed the *Libre dels àngels* (Book of Angels) in Valencia in 1392. Eiximenis avers that "ací no entenem a curar de parlar curiós, ne subtil, ne artificial, ne a grans clergues, mas a persones simples e devotes" (so we do not seek to speak provocatively, or subtly, or artfully, nor for high clerics, but for simple and devout people). His effort was evidently successful, as the cult of angels flourished in fifteenth-century Catalonia, and the work was printed in Barcelona in 1494. Also useful as indicators of increased demand for religious learning among the laity are the many verse compositions on theological questions by court poets collected in the *cancioneros* (songbook) of the era. The *Cancionero de Baena,* compiled around 1430 for the court of King Juan II of Castile by the royal scribe Juan Alfonso de Baena, includes dozens of poems in which lay and clerical courtiers treat doctrinal issues—from the Virgin to moral theology to predestination. Predestination inspired an extended series of questions and replies by Ayala, Ferrán Sánchez Talavera, Friar Diego de Valencia, Ferrán Manuel de Lando, and Friar Alfonso de Medina. The significance of these poems as contributions to contemporary theological debate remains unclear, but their value as displays of courtly wit and literary skill are obvious. The danger of this playful intrusion into questions of dogma perhaps moved the theologian Martín de Córdoba to compose his *Tratado de la predestinación* (after 1454, Treatise on Predestination), a sober doctrinal treatise that uses exempla to be intelligible to as wide an audience as possible.

The copious literature of instruction and guidance also included treatises offering spiritual counsel in the face of the world's troubles. Translations of widely circulated Latin works dominated this subgenre. The popular *De misera humanae conditionis* (1195, On the Misery of the Human Condition), by Lothar of Segni, who became Pope Innocent III in 1198, appeared in Castilian as the *Libro de miseria d'omne* (circa 1300–1340, Book on the Misery of Humanity) and was also translated into Catalan and Portuguese, while a Latin treatise by Pope Benedict XIII quickly appeared in Castilian as *Libro de las consolaciones de la vida humana* (circa 1400, Book on the Consolation of Human Life). The demand for such works is evident from their appearance among the first printed works of the later fifteenth century. The Saragossan *converso* (convert from Judaism) Andrés de Li dedicated his *Summa de paciencia* (1493, Summa on Patience) to Princess Isabel of Portugal, eldest daughter of the Catholic Monarchs, Fernando and Isabel (better known to English speakers as Ferdinand and Isabella); it found a place in the personal library of Queen Isabel. The *Summa de paciencia* draws from the long tradition of works on this theme to teach the virtue of patience with stories from biblical and classical sources and from popular devotional literature.

By far the most sophisticated vernacular work of spiritual instruction and guidance in late-medieval Iberia was the *Memorial del pecador remut* (Memorial for the Redeemed Sinner), composed around 1419 to 1423 by the Catalan theologian Felip de Malla. Trained at the University of Paris, de Malla earned fame for his sacred oratory and represented the Crown of Aragon at the Council of Constance in 1418. According to the prologue, this long text bears the title *Memorial* because its purpose is to recall doctrine regarding redemption; in fact, de Malla extends his account of redemption to cover the entire spectrum of Catholic theology in dense Scholastic prose using elaborate periodic phrases and occasional passages in Latin. He structures his text with diverse narrative devices–dialogues, colloquies, soliloquies, amazing and terrifying visions, journeys, disputations, debates, and formal speeches–set in the mouths of angels; sibyls; Old Testament prophets; personifications of the Virtues, Theology, and the Cross; Fathers of the Church; the Virgin; and pagan philosophers.

The audience for de Malla's work was apparently educated Aragonese courtiers and clerics who appreciated the display of theological doctrine and classical erudition in the "allegorical" or Italianate style, which was also promoted by Castilian writers such as Juan de Mena and Juan de Padilla. De Malla's insistent recourse to hyperbaton and subordination perhaps served to create an effect of difficulty in the vernacular, offering lay readers an experience of the obscurity that medieval theological exegesis traditionally regarded as necessary for conveying great truths. Although this difficult style had its detractors, the *Memorial del pecador remut* was popular enough to appear in editions printed in Gerona in 1483 and in Barcelona in 1495.

Lives of saints had been a basic genre of vernacular religious literature since at least the late twelfth century, as the 1990 volume of studies edited by Jane E. Connolly, A. D. Deyermond, and Brian Dutton amply documents. As Fernando Baños Vallejo shows, hagiographic narratives provided models of unshakable faith and self-sacrifice, usually employing familiar narrative conventions. In Castilian these works often used the verse form known as the *mester de clerecía* (clerics' art) or *cuaderna vía* (fourfold way): stanzas consisting of four lines of fourteen syllables, with each stanza using a single full rhyme. Both the genre and the verse declined in popularity after 1300 and were replaced by new styles of literature and piety. Most of the hagiographic texts put in circulation after this time appear to be translations of the major Latin collections prepared for use by

mendicant preachers. Billy Bussell Thompson and John K. Walsh found four major Castilian manuscripts from around 1400 that include selective redactions of the enormously popular *Legenda aurea* (1275, The Golden Legend), by the Italian Jacob of Voragine. At least half a dozen other Castilian hagiographical collections survive from that era, with texts from various sources. The compilation now catalogued as Biblioteca Nacional, Madrid, MS. 10252 perhaps served as a preacher's sourcebook. It includes a *Tratado de viçios e virtudes* (Treatise of Vices and Virtues), a partial life of Jesus, and a selection of saints' lives. Acquisition of this manuscript by the celebrated fifteenth-century aristocratic poet Iñigo López de Mendoza, Marquis de Santillana, demonstrates the appeal of such works for educated lay readers. Especially interesting in this regard is Real Biblioteca del Monasterio de El Escorial, MS. h.I.13, a late-fourteenth-century anthology of pious legends. Most of these legends were literal translations or adaptations of French sources, which illustrates the growing strength of the vernacular languages as literary media independent of Latin, as well as the great attraction for lay readers of pious adventure stories. Thomas D. Spaccarelli suggests that the volume may have served as reading matter for pilgrims en route to Santiago de Compostela. From Portugal during this same period, Alcobaça MS. 266 includes lives of Sts. Alexis, Euphrasia, Mary the Egyptian, Pelagia, and Tarsis, as well as the fantastical life of St. Amarus, whose quest for a glimpse of paradise supposedly required two centuries of marvelous travels. Crossing the Red Sea like the ancient Israelites, Amarus and his companions

virõ jazer hua jnssoa muy grande eem muy rryqua terra e muy auondada detodallas cousas quedeus no mudo quis dar, eauya nome fonte clara e aportarõn aly. Eas jentes daly eram dasmais fermosas criaturas queauy[a] no mudo ne mais louçãas, ne mais corteses, essynados detodo bem, efezerõlhe mujta honrra, edauãlhe todallas cousas que lhe faziam mester. Eera terra tam saborosa e tam sãa que nuqua hy morya neguu denehua dóór que ouuesse se nõ deuilhice, e uiuya hy ohome treztos años cõmunalmete.

(saw ahead a huge island in a very rich land, well furnished with all the things that God saw fit to give, and it was called Clear Spring and they went there. And the people there were among the most beautiful creatures on earth and the most handsome and most courteous, endowed with every blessing, and they received him with great honor and gave him all the things that he needed. And it was such a delightful and healthy land that no one died there from any affliction that might arise except old age, and yet, there a man commonly lived three hundred years.)

These saintly adventures, like the pious legends collected in Escorial MS. H.I.13, must have entertained lay readers as much as the tales of Marco Polo or Sir John Mandeville.

Eventually, vernacular writers returned to cultivating individual saints' lives with new purposes and styles. Alfonso Martínez de Toledo, chaplain to King Juan II of Castile and notorious as author of the misogynistic denunciation of profane love *Arcipreste de Talavera* (1438, The Archpriest of Talavera; translated as *Little Sermons on Sin*, 1959), also known as *El Corbacho* (The Scourge), is believed to have written the *Vida de San Isidoro* (1444, Life of St. Isidore) and *Vida de San Ildefonso* (1444, Life of St. Ildephonsus) to celebrate two great figures of the Spanish Church. Padilla, a monk of the Carthusian house of Santa María de las Cuevas in Seville, used an elaborate allegorical style inspired by Dante in his *Los doze triunfos de los doze apóstoles* (circa 1500, The Twelve Triumphs of the Twelve Apostles). The learned Franciscan Ambrosio de Montesino included short lyrics on Sts. John, Mary Magdalene, and Francis in his *Coplas sobre diversas devociones y misterios de nuestra santa fe católica* (Verses on Various Devotions and Mysteries of Our Holy Catholic Faith). Printed in Toledo around 1485, this short volume consists largely of pieces on the lives of Christ and the Virgin. The "Romance de la Magdalena" (Ballad of Mary Magdalene) exemplifies the adaptation of the traditional ballad as a genre of spiritual literature:

> Por las cortes de la gloria
> y por todo lo poblado
> nuevas de la madalena
> excelentes han bolado
> que su coraçon rreal
> quien lo hizo lo ha mudado
> en casa del fariseo
> donde estava convidado.

> (Through the court of Glory
> and through all the town,
> news of the Magdalene,
> wonderful, has gone round,
> that her noble heart,
> by its Maker has been altered,
> at the Pharisee's house,
> where He came for shelter.)

Montesino employs the ballad's characteristic diction, occasional use of hyperbaton; narrative devices, such as an opening announcement of news; and standard-meter, eight-syllable lines with assonance in alternating lines, to tell the story of Mary Magdalene's encounter with Christ. Such "sacred ballads" became a popular genre of devotional literature in the sixteenth century.

Late-medieval piety focused on the Holy Family, especially the Virgin Mary, and collections of miracles attributed to the Virgin became a major devotional genre. More-specialized compositions recounted the *loores* (praises) and *gozos* (joys) of the Virgin. Court writers of the era wrote many poems on these inspiring moments from Mary's life, which were usually seven in number. Catalan authors especially applied to Marian themes the genres and style of the Provençal troubadour lyric, which still dominated poetic invention in the kingdom of Aragon. The *Castelo perigoso* (Dangerous Castle), a fifteenth-century Portuguese translation from the work of a French Carthusian, offered its readers an elaborate courtly allegory of Mary as a castle defended by the Virtues, Graces, and other allegorized ideals in the fashion of a courtly romance. The continuing vitality of Marian devotion generated another topical genre, the *dolores* or *angustias* (pains) of the Virgin, often symbolized by seven swords or daggers and formally recognized by the Church in 1423 as an official subject of celebration. Diego de San Pedro included a version of his *Las siete angustias de Nuestra Señora* (The Seven Pains of Our Lady) in his courtly novel of amorous intrigue *Arnalte y Lucenda* (Arnalte and Lucenda), published in 1491. The collocation of these purely devotional verses within a profane composition confirms the popularity of Marian genres among aristocratic audiences.

The exemplary story of Christian suffering was, of course, that of Jesus himself, and lengthy narratives of his life became a staple of later medieval devotional literature. The thirteenth-century *Meditationes Vitae Christi* (Meditations on the Life of Christ) attributed to St. Bonaventure probably inaugurated this genre, but the *Vita Christi* (Life of Christ) composed by the fourteenth-century Dominican-turned-Carthusian Ludolph of Saxony achieved the greatest circulation through vernacular translations and adaptations. This new literature focused on the humanity of Jesus—his virtues, self-denial, and final suffering—and invited readers to take Christ's life as an exemplary guide for their own behavior. The impact of Ludolph's work was tremendous in fifteenth-century Iberia, where he and his text became known simply as "The Carthusian." One of two Portuguese translations done by 1446 served as the basis for a printed edition prepared under Franciscan supervision and published at Alcobaça by Bernardo de Alcobaça in 1495 as the first printed book in the Portuguese language. Several Castilian and Catalan versions also appeared in the fifteenth century before Fernando and Isabel commissioned Montesino to produce a carefully researched translation into Castilian that Cardinal Francisco Jiménez de Cisneros published in Alcalá de Henares in 1502–1503. Ana María Alvarez Pellitero has

Opening page from the manuscript of the Cancionero de Baena *(Bibliothèque Nationale, Paris, MS. Esp. 37)*

shown that Montesino's labors made important literary and lexicographical contributions to the development of Castilian as a national idiom.

Various Iberian writers made original contributions to the genre. Eiximenis was among the first; his version was translated into Castilian by Friar Hernando de Talavera and printed in 1496. The Franciscan Iñigo de Mendoza's four-thousand-line *Coplas de Vita Christi* (late fifteenth century, Verses on Christ's Life) treats only events from the Incarnation to the Massacre of the Innocents; it recounts each incident almost as a separate story, often with patently satirical amplifications on secular topics. The noble-born Valencian abbess Isabel de Villena left a Catalan *Vita Christi* incomplete at her death in 1490. Her version offers only selected episodes from Christ's life, though it amplifies them with many details designed to engage the reader's imagination and, thus, to inspire more-intense devotion. It also gives special attention to the role of Mary, occasionally using her to exhort the reader as effectively as St. Vincent Ferrer or any preacher addressing audiences of the faithful. Devotional literature evidently offered a major avenue of literary self-expression for women in late-medieval Iberia.

Christ's Passion became a central focus of later medieval devotion and was recounted in many vernacular compositions, especially in verse; enthusiasm for this subject survives today in the annual performance of Passion Plays, which were first staged during this era. Portions of two Catalan poems, one extant in 668 lines and the other in 2,458 lines, survive from the fourteenth century. This subject attracted various Castilian court poets of the 1470s, including San Pedro and Montesino, and their works appeared in printed editions during the 1480s. The success of these compositions from the late fifteenth century resulted at least in part from their heavy reliance on vivid, often profane, details drawn with equal liberty from the Bible, apocryphal sources, and purely secular traditions. Jane Y. Tillier suggests that the proliferation of such works in the *cancioneros* influenced the development of the term *passion* in the love lyric. Of all the contributions to vernacular Passion literature, San Pedro's *La Pasión trovada* (circa 1475, The Rhymed Passion) proved the most popular, even though it was scarcely the most innovative or interesting. *La Pasión trovada* alternates explicitly marked apostrophes to the reader from *el auctor* (the author) with sections narrating *el testo* (the text [or "story"]), as when Christ prays at the Garden of Gethsemane:

[El auctor] Siente agora, peccador,
lo que su alma sentía
de aquel Dios tu Salvador

cuando tan fuerte sudor
todo su cuerpo cubría.
¿Quién dubda que no estuviesse
en grave tribulación?
¡O quién contrición toviesse,
que pensándolo pudiesse
quebrantar el coraçón!
[Buelve al testo]
Pues estando el Rey del cielo
su oración continuando,
cubierto con aquel velo
de amargura y desconsuelo,
llegó el ángel relumbrando.

([The author] Feel now, sinner,
what the soul felt
of that God your Savior
when such great sweat
covered His whole body.
Who would doubt that He was
in grave tribulation?
Oh whoever feels contrition,
in considering it should
be broken-hearted!
[Returning to the text]
So as the King of Heaven
continued his prayer,
covered with that veil
of bitterness and grief,
a shining angel arrived.)

El auctor overtly guides the reader's response to the anguish of Jesus, whose troubled emotional state is obvious from the physical details described. The *testo* continues with a long exhortatory speech by the visiting angel of comfort, a dramatic invention based on the brief reference to this divine messenger in Luke 22:43. The simple style, direct engagement of the reader, and prolific elaboration of detail in *La Pasión trovada* partly explain why it went through frequent, often anonymous, reprintings well into the nineteenth century, outlasting nearly thirty subsequent contributions by other poets.

For modern readers some of the most interesting, because most literary, spiritual writings from late-medieval Iberia are works of devotion and mysticism that express the individual soul's quest for experience of the divine presence. These works are probably far less numerous than those created for the many processions, festivals, and rituals that offered to laypeople—particularly organized groups such as guilds and confraternities—an opportunity for the collective exercise of devotion. The new feasts dedicated to theological doctrines such as Corpus Christi especially stimulated the composition of works celebrating their veneration. Seven poems in honor of Corpus Christi, composed in Valencia around 1390 by poets from the literary circle of Cardinal James of Aragón, use the forms and music of courtly lyric to praise the Eucharist:

> Cant pus hi vau pensan, lo seny mi fayl,
> Tant veig lo cors de natura mudat,
> Que'l vi e'l pa veig transsubstanciat
> En carn e sanch d'aquell veray mirayll,
> On se mostrech, sots l'umenal figura,
> La Deitat, cuberta de carn pura,
> E fuech ensemps ver Deus ez hom mortals,
> Al Payre seu en deitat equals.

> (Whenever I consider this, my mind reels,
> seeing the body so changed in nature,
> seeing the wine and bread transubstantiated,
> into the flesh and blood of that true miracle,
> which manifests, in human form,
> the Deity, clothed in pure flesh,
> at once true God and mortal man,
> equal to his Father in deity.)

The difficulty of rhyming words such as *transsubstanciat* did not impede these poets from offering a lively exposition of orthodox doctrine combining traditional spiritual imagery with troubadour verse conventions. Devotional lyrics of this sort also appear throughout the many Castilian *cancioneros* of the era. While such compositions hold little appeal for modern tastes, their copious production demonstrates the capacity of the vernacular languages to express popular enthusiasm for the basic doctrines of Catholic belief.

The creation of vernacular texts for use in public celebrations of piety is best illustrated in the work of Master André Dias, who composed the collection *Laudes e cantigas espirituais* (1435, Praises and Spiritual Songs) for Lisbon's confraternity Bom Jesus (Sweet Name of Jesus). The group included many tradesmen and craftsmen, and Dias's introduction invites them to dance and sing accompanied by instruments including the drum and guitar. Dias's verses are close in spirit to the *Laudi* (1276–1306, Praises), Franciscan hymns by the Italian Jacopone da Todi, on which they are based:

> Dilecto Jesus Christo quem de ti se recorda, e te chama
> Sempre em seu coração te ama
> e em ti se alegra e baila e canta,
> e eu cantar e alegrar-me quero
> por teu amor,
> ó doce senhor.

> (Beloved Jesus Christ, whoever remembers and invokes you,
> always loves you in his heart,
> rejoicing in you, dancing and singing,
> and I love to rejoice and sing
> for love of you,
> oh sweet lord.)

The *Laudes* demonstrates again how the genres of devotional expression promoted by the mendicant preachers easily crossed national boundaries throughout late-medieval Europe. The friars also encouraged veneration for the Name of Jesus in the fifteenth century, and it became especially popular in Portugal, as the Bom Jesus confraternity indicates.

For the devout who sought a more intimate experience of divine grace, there was no lack of works that offered to guide the soul in its quest for God. This literature included translations of popular Latin meditative and contemplative works. During a visit to Flanders in 1467–1468 Friar João Alvares made a direct Portuguese translation of the *Imitatio Christi* (between 1390 and 1440, Imitation of Christ), attributed to Thomas à Kempis. The impact of northern mysticism in Iberia appears limited before 1500, but many other currents of earlier medieval mystical literature were available to Castilian, Catalan, and Portuguese authors. The monks of Alcobaça disseminated a Portuguese version of *O Tratado das Meditações de Sam Bernardo* (circa 1400, The Treatise of Meditations of St. Bernard). Antoni Canals translated Hugh of St. Victor's *Sololiquium de arrha animae* (circa 1115–1133, Soliloquy on the Soul's Ransom) into Catalan as *De arra de ànima* (1416–1419?), and his knowledge of twelfth-century contemplative theology is obvious in his compendious *Scala de contemplació* (1398–1400, Ladder of Contemplation). Dedicated to King Martin of Aragon, the *Scala de contemplació* comprises three books, each divided into chapters that could serve as daily or occasional texts for meditation: book 1 treats the form and function of contemplation and includes chapters on each level of earthly creation; book 2 offers contemplations on the levels of the heavenly hierarchy; and book 3 covers the levels of paradise and their respective occupants.

Works such as the *Scala de contemplació* best served readers seeking retreat from this world to lead a life of solitary contemplation. Severe ideals of monastic asceticism and penitential self-examination appear in the few writings left by Pedro Fernández Pecha. Born into a noble family that served the Castilian court, he abandoned secular affairs to become a hermit and cofounder in 1373 of the Hieronymite Order in Spain. His two *Soliloquios entre el alma y Dios y el alma consigo misma* (1373–1402, Soliloquies between the Soul and God and of the Soul with Itself) express an intensely ascetic piety:

> ¡O Señor mio! Non me acates segund el que yo so; mas acátame segund el que tu eres, en cuya memoria non son siempre las injurias, e cuyo deseo non es vengança, e cuyo plazer non es tormentar, e cuya voluntad non es dura. Vey, Señor, la mi fealdad, e apiádate de my: vey la mi enfermedad, e sáname: vey la mi tribulación, e duélete: vey la mi mezquindat, e guarésceme: vey los

mis tormentos, e amercendéate: vey la mi mengua, e abúndame.

(Oh my Lord! Consider me not according to what I am, but consider me instead as you are: remembering no offense, desiring no revenge, taking no pleasure in torment, and never hard of heart. See, Lord, my ugliness and pity me; see my sickness and heal me; see my tribulation, and feel pain for me; see my smallness, and protect me; see my torments, and relieve me; see my lack, and provide for me.)

The relatively simple diction and lack of theological erudition in the soliloquies reinforce their focus on the fundamental relationship of the individual soul to God. The hard scrutiny of conscience required by late-medieval practices of confession and penance undoubtedly helped to prepare laypeople to pursue the intensely inward devotion represented in Fernández Pecha's treatise.

The mystical ideals of late-medieval Iberia find their most elaborate expression in the lengthy *Boosco deleitoso* (Garden of Delight), an anonymous Portuguese work of the early fifteenth century. Written in the "Dantesque" style cultivated by court authors of the era, it combines an extended allegory with frequent quotations from Italian and classical authors, including seventy chapters translated from Petrarch's *De vita solitaria* (1346, On the Solitary Life). In the *Boosco deleitoso* the Soul, troubled by Sin, seeks assistance from the Virtues. All reject it except Mercy, which leads the Soul to a great palace where it meets Scripture, undergoes judgment from Justice, and hears advice from a host of patristic and medieval theologians, as well as from virtuous pagan philosophers such as Cicero, Seneca, and Quintilian. The Soul decides to pursue a life of ascetic retreat, retires into a wilderness where it can purge its sins, and, once prepared, is led to a mountaintop to contemplate the divine glory. There the Soul apprehensively awaits God's visit, afraid that it is not truly ready. The scenario of the Lover preparing the bridal chamber for the Beloved, adapted from centuries of medieval commentary on the Song of Songs, combines with the equally traditional imagery of the soul's inner chambers. Afterward, the Soul exults over the rapture of its encounter with God:

¡O amigos! Se vós soubésseis por prova e por experiência e por gosto estas cousas que tenho ditas, cuido que custosamente sofreríeis as trevas da nossa vida, assim como eu fazia. Porque eu dizia muitas vezes em meu coração: O quando será isto? Ó se será isto? Ó se verei isto? ¿Quando? ¿Quando? ¿Quando?"

(Oh friends! If you could know from trying or experiencing or tasting these things I tell, I believe that you would readily suffer the travails of this life, as I have

done. For I often said in my heart "Oh when will this be? When will it happen? When will it appear? When? When? When?")

Although the Soul's jubilant discourse extends over several chapters, these ecstatic exclamations bring the *Boosco deleitoso* to the verge of apophatic mysticism, the experience of the divine that exceeds the bounds of language. In this respect the *Boosco deleitoso* is, despite its unimaginative allegorical format and lengthy quotations from Italian authors, perhaps the most ambitious vernacular mystical work of fifteenth-century Iberia. Its use of lively dialogue and detailed description of settings especially recall the vivid sermons and explicit accounts of the Passion that contemporary audiences also enjoyed. The *Boosco deleitoso,* as much as any work of spiritual literature from this period, demonstrates the perfection of the vernacular languages as vehicles of religious belief and practice in late medieval Iberia.

References:

Ana María Alvarez Pellitero, *La obra lingüística y literaria de Fray Ambrosio Montesino* (Valladolid: Universidad, Departamento de Lengua y Españolas, 1976);

Fernando Baños Vallejo, *La hagiografía como género literario en la Edad Media: Tipología de doce vidas individuales castellanas* (Oviedo: Departamento de Filología Española, 1989);

Pedro M. Cátedra, *Dos estudios sobre el sermón en la España medieval* (Bellaterra: Universidad Autónoma de Barcelona, 1981);

Cátedra, *Sermón, sociedad y literatura en la Edad Media: San Vicente Ferrer en Castilla (1411–1412). Estudio bibliográfico, literario y edición de los textos inéditos* (Valladolid: Junta de Castilla y León, Consejería de Cultura y Turismo, 1994);

Jane E. Connolly, A. D. Deyermond, and Brian Dutton, eds., *Saints and Their Authors: Studies in Medieval Hispanic Hagiography in Honor of John K. Walsh* (Madison, Wis.: Hispanic Seminary of Medieval Studies, 1990);

Fernando González Ollé, ed., *Sermones navarros medievales: Una colección manuscrita (siglo XV) de la Catedral de Pamplona* (Kassel: Edition Reichenberger, 1995);

Albert Hauf, *D'Eiximenis a Sor Isabel de Villena: Aportació a l'estudi de la nostra cultura medieval* (Barcelona: Institut de Filologia Valenciana, 1990);

María Amor Martín Fernández, *El mundo mitológico y simbólico de Juan de Padilla, "El Cartujano": Estudio de "Los doce triunfos de los doce Apóstoles"* (Cordova: Publicaciones del Monte de Piedad y Caja de Ahorros de Córdoba, 1988);

Mário Martins, *A Bíblia na literatura medieval portuguêsa* (Lisbon: Instituto de Cultura Portuguêsa, 1979);

Jesús Montoya Martínez, *Las colecciones de milagros de la Virgen en la edad media (el milagro literario)* (Granada: Universidad de Granada, 1981);

Josep Moran i Ocerinjauregui, ed., *Les homílies de Tortosa* (Barcelona: Publicacions de l'Abadia de Montserrat, 1990);

Francisco Rico, *Predicación y literatura en la España medieval* (Cádiz: Instituto de Estudios Gaditanos, 1977);

Martí de Riquer, *Història de la literatura catalana,* volume 2 (Barcelona: Ariel, 1964);

Pedro Sainz Rodríguez, ed., *Antología de la literatura espiritual española,* volume 1: *Edad Media* (Madrid: Universidad Pontificia de Salamanca & Fundación Universitaria Española, 1980);

José Antonio Saraiva, *História da cultura em Portugal,* volume 1 (Lisbon: Jornal do Fôro, 1950);

Saraiva, *História de la literatura portuguesa,* fifth edition (Porto: Porto Editora, 1966);

Dayle Seidenspinner-Núñez, ed., *The Writings of Teresa de Cartagena* (Cambridge & Rochester, N.Y.: D. S. Brewer, 1998);

Thomas D. Spaccarelli, *A Medieval Pilgrim's Companion: Reassessing "El libro de los huéspedes" (Escorial MS. H.I.13)* (Chapel Hill: University of North Carolina Studies in the Romance Languages and Literatures, 1998);

Ronald E. Surtz, *Writing Women in Late Medieval and Early Modern Spain: The Mothers of Saint Teresa of Avila* (Philadelphia: University of Pennsylvania Press, 1995);

Billy Bussell Thompson and John K. Walsh, "Old Spanish Manuscripts of Prose Lives of the Saints and Their Affiliations. 1: Compilation A (The *Gran flos sanctorum*)," *La Corónica,* 15 (1986–1987): 17–28;

Jane Y. Tillier, "Passion Poetry in the *Cancioneros,*" *Bulletin of Hispanic Studies,* 62 (1985): 65–78;

David J. Viera, *Bibliografía anotada de la vida i la obra de Francesc Eiximenis (1340?–1409?)* (Barcelona: Rafael Dalmau, 1979).

Books for Further Reading

Alborg, Juan Luis. *Historia de la literatura española.* Madrid: Gredos, 1966.

Allen, Don Cameron. *Mysteriously Meant: The Rediscovery of Pagan Symbolism and Allegorical Interpretation in the Renaissance.* Baltimore: Johns Hopkins Press, 1970.

Alvar, Carlos, Angel Gómez Moreno, and Fernando Gómez Redondo. *La prosa y el teatro en la Edad Media.* Madrid: Taurus, 1991.

Alvar and José Manuel Lucía Megías, eds. *Diccionario filológico de literatura medieval española: Textos y transmisión.* Madrid: Castalia, 2002.

Auerbach, Erich. *Literary Language and Its Public in Late Latin Antiquity and the Middle Ages,* translated by Ralph Manheim, foreword by J. M. Ziolokowski. Bollingen Series, volume 74. Princeton: Princeton University Press, 1993.

Auerbach. *Mimesis: The Representation of Reality in Western Literature,* translated by Willard Trask. Princeton: Princeton University Press, 1953.

Baños Vallejo, Fernando. *Las vidas de santos en la literatura medieval española.* Madrid: Laberinto, 2003.

Bishko, Charles Julian. *Studies in Medieval Spanish Frontier History.* London: Variorum Reprints, 1980.

Blanco Aguinaga, Carlos, Julio Rodríguez Puértolas, and Iris M. Zavala. *Historia social de la literatura española (en lengua castellana),* 3 volumes. Madrid: Castalia, 1978–1979.

Bloch, R. Howard. *Medieval Misogyny and the Invention of Western Romantic Love.* Chicago: University of Chicago Press, 1991.

Brann, Ross. *Power in the Portrayal: Representations of Jews and Muslims in Eleventh- and Twelfth-Century Islamic Spain.* Princeton: Princeton University Press, 2002.

Breisach, Ernst. *Historiography: Ancient, Medieval, and Modern.* Chicago: University of Chicago Press, 1983.

Brownlee, Marina S., Kevin Brownlee, and Stephen J. Nichols, eds. *The New Medievalism.* Baltimore & London: Johns Hopkins University Press, 1991.

Bruyne, Edgar de. *The Esthetics of the Middle Ages,* translated by Eileen Hennesey. New York: Ungar, 1969.

Burns, Robert I., S.J. *The Crusader Kingdom of Valencia.* Cambridge, Mass.: Harvard University Press, 1967.

Cañas Murillo, Jesús. *La poesía medieval: De las jarchas al Renacimiento.* Madrid: Anaya, 1990.

Casas Rigall, Juan, and Eva María Díaz Martínez, eds. *Iberia cantat: Estudios sobre poesía hispánica medieval.* Santiago de Compostela: Universidade de Santiago de Compostela, Servicio de Publicacións e Intercambio Científico, 2002.

Castro, Américo. *La realidad histórica de España*. Madrid: Porrúa, 1954.

Catalán, Diego. *La Épica Española: Nueva Documentación y Nueva Evaluación*. Madrid: Fundación Ramón Menéndez Pidal / Universidad Complutense, 2001.

Cátedra, Pedro M. *Amor y pedagogía en la Edad Media: Estudios de doctrina amorosa y práctica literaria*, Acta Salmanticensia, Estudios Filológicos, no. 212. Salamanca: Universidad de Salamanca, 1989.

Chaytor, Henry John. *From Script to Print: An Introduction to Medieval Vernacular Literature*. Cambridge: Cambridge University Press, 1945.

Chejne, Anwar G. *Islam and the West: The Moriscos, a Cultural and Social History*. Albany: State University of New York Press, 1983.

Collins, Roger. *Early Medieval Spain: Unity in Diversity, 400–1000*. New York: St. Martin's Press, 1983.

Curtius, Ernst. *European Literature and the Latin Middle Ages*, translated by Willard R. Trask. New York: Pantheon, 1953.

Dangler, Jean. *Mediating Fictions: Literature, Women Healers, and the Go-Between in Medieval and Early Modern Iberia*. Lewisburg, Pa.: Bucknell University Press, 2001.

De Lange, N. R. M. *Hebrew Scholarship and the Medieval World*. New York: Cambridge University Press, 2001.

Deyermond, A. D. *Historical Literature in Medieval Iberia*. London: Department of Hispanic Studies, Queen Mary and Westfield College, 1996.

Deyermond. *A Literary History of Spain: The Middle Ages*. London: Benn / New York: Barnes & Noble, 1971. Translated by Deyermond as *Historia de la literatura española: La Edad Media*, twelfth edition. Letras e Ideas: Instrumenta, no. 1. Barcelona: Ariel, 1987.

Deyermond. *La literatura perdida de la Edad Media castellana: Catálogo y estudio*, volume 1: *Epica y romances*. Salamanca: Universidad de Salamanca, 1995.

Díaz-Plaja, Guillermo. *A History of Spanish Literature*. New York: New York University Press, 1971.

Dillard, Heath. *Daughters of the Reconquest*. Cambridge & New York: Cambridge University Press, 1984.

Dronke, Peter. *Medieval Latin and the Rise of the European Love Lyric*, second edition. Oxford: Clarendon Press, 1968.

Fletcher, Angus. *Allegory: The Theory of a Symbolic Mode*. Ithaca, N.Y.: Cornell University Press, 1964.

Franchini, Enzo. *Los debates literarios en la Edad Media*. Madrid: Laberinto, 2001.

García Velasco, Antonio. *La mujer en la literatura medieval española*. Málaga: Aljaima, 2000.

Gerbet, Marie-Claude. *Les noblesses espagnoles au Moyen Age, XIe–XVe siècle*. Paris: Colin, 1994. Translated by María José García Vera as *Las noblezas españolas en la Edad Media: Siglos XI–XV*. Madrid: Alianza, 1997.

Gerli, E. Michael, and Samuel G. Armistead, eds. *Medieval Iberia: An Encyclopedia*. New York: Routledge, 2003.

Gimeno Casalduero, Joaquín. *La creación literaria de la Edad Media y del Renacimiento: Su forma y su significado*. Madrid: Porrúa Turanzas, 1975.

Gimeno Casalduero. *Estructura y diseño en la literatura castellana medieval*. Madrid: Porrúa Turanzas, 1975.

Glick, Thomas. *Islamic and Christian Spain.* Princeton: Princeton University Press, 1979.

Goldberg, Harriet. *Motif-Index of Medieval Hispanic Epic Legends.* Tempe: Arizona Center for Medieval and Renaissance Studies, 2003.

Gómez Redondo, Fernando. *Historia de la prosa medieval castellana,* volume 1: *La creación del discurso prosístico: El entramado cortesano.* Madrid: Cátedra, 1998.

González López, Emilio. *Historia de la literatura española: Edad Media y Siglo de Oro.* New York: Las Americas, 1962.

Green, Otis H. *Spain and the Western Tradition,* 3 volumes. Madison: University of Wisconsin Press, 1963.

Hardison, O. B. *Christian Rite and Christian Drama in the Middle Ages: Essays in the Origins and Early History of Modern Drama.* Baltimore: Johns Hopkins Press, 1965.

Hassán, Iacob M., and Ricardo Izquierdo Benito, eds. *Judíos en la literatura española.* Cuenca: Ediciones de la Universidad de Castilla-La Mancha, 2001.

Karras, Ruth Mazo. *Sexuality in Medieval Europe: Doing unto Others.* New York & London: Routledge, 2005.

Keen, Maurice. *Chivalry.* New Haven: Yale University Press, 1984.

Keller, John E., and Annette Grant Cash. *Daily Life Depicted in the* Cantigas de Santa María. Lexington: University Press of Kentucky, 1998.

Khadra Jayyusi, Salma, ed. *The Legacy of Muslim Spain,* 2 volumes. Leiden: Brill, 1993.

Kristeller, Paul. *Renaissance Thought and Its Sources.* New York: Columbia University Press, 1979.

Lanz, Eukene Lacarra, ed. *Marriage and Sexuality in Medieval and Early Modern Iberia.* New York: Routledge, 2002.

Lapesa, Rafael. *De la Edad Media a nuestros días: Estudios de historia literaria.* Madrid: Gredos, 1967.

Le Gentil, Pierre. *La poésie lyrique espagnole et portugaise á la fin du Moyen Age,* 2 volumes. Rennes: Philon, 1949, 1953.

Lewis, C. S. *The Allegory of Love.* Oxford & New York: Oxford University Press, 1977.

Lewis. *The Discarded Image.* Cambridge: Cambridge University Press, 1965.

Linehan, Peter. *History and the Historians of Medieval Spain.* Oxford: Clarendon Press, 1993.

López Morales, Humberto. *Historia de la literatura medieval española.* Madrid & Madison, Wis.: Hispanova, 1974.

Mackay, Angus. *Spain in the Middle Ages: From Frontier to Empire 1000–1500.* London: Macmillan, 1977.

Mann, Vivian B., Thomas Glick, and Jerrilyn Denise Dodds, eds. *Convivencia: Jews, Muslims, and Christians in Medieval Spain.* New York: Braziller in association with The Jewish Museum, 1992.

McInnis, Judy B., and Juan Espadas, eds. *Models in Medieval Iberian Literature and Their Modern Reflections:* Convivencia as Structural, Cultural and Sexual Ideal. Newark, Del.: Juan de la Cuesta, 2002.

Menocal, María Rosa. *The Ornament of the World: How Muslims, Jews, and Christians Created a Culture of Tolerance in Medieval Spain.* Boston: Little, Brown, 2002.

Menocal, Raymond F. Scheindlin, and Michael Sells, eds. *The Literature of Al-Andalus*. Cambridge: Cambridge University Press, 2000.

Mettmann, Walter. *La Littérature dans la Péninsule Ibérique aux XIVe et XVe siècles*. Heidelberg: Winter, 1985.

Meyerson, Mark D. *Christians, Muslims, and Jews in Medieval and Early Modern Spain: Interaction and Cultural Change*. Notre Dame, Ind.: University of Notre Dame Press, 1999.

Montgomery, Thomas. *Medieval Spanish Epic: Mythic Roots and Ritual Language*. University Park: Pennsylvania State University Press, 1998.

Murphy, James J. *Rhetoric in the Middle Ages: A History of Rhetorical Theory from St. Augustine to the Renaissance*. Berkeley: University of California Press, 1974.

Nelson, Janet L., and Peter Linehan. *The Medieval World*. London & New York: Routledge, 2001.

O'Callaghan, Joseph F. *Alfonso X, the Cortes, and Government in Medieval Spain*. Aldershot, U.K. & Brookfield, Mass.: Ashgate, 1998.

O'Callaghan. *A History of Medieval Spain*. Ithaca, N.Y.: Cornell University Press, 1975.

O'Callaghan. *The Learned King: The Reign of Alfonso X of Castile*. Philadelphia: University of Pennsylvania Press, 1993.

O'Callaghan. *Reconquest and Crusade in Medieval Spain*. Philadelphia: University of Pennsylvania Press, 2003.

Orcástegui Gros, Carmen. *La historia en la Edad Media: Historiografía e historiadores en Europa Occidental, siglos V–XIII*. Madrid: Cátedra, 1991.

Pagis, Dan. *Hebrew Poetry of the Middle Ages and the Renaissance*. Berkeley: University of California Press, 1991.

Panofsky, Irwin. *Renaissance and Renaissances in Western Art*. New York: Harper & Row, 1972.

Pattison, David G. *From Legend to Chronicle: The Treatment of Epic Material in Alphonsine Historiography*. Oxford: Society for the Study of Mediaeval Languages and Literature, 1983.

Pieper, Josep. *Scholasticism: Personalities and Problems of Medieval Philosophy*. New York: Pantheon, 1960.

Post, Chandler Rathfon. *Medieval Spanish Allegory*. Cambridge, Mass.: Harvard University Press / London: Humphrey Milford, Oxford University Press, 1915.

Powers, James F. *A Society Organized for War*. Berkeley: University of California Press, 1988.

Reilly, Bernard F. *The Medieval Spains*. Cambridge & New York: Cambridge University Press, 1993.

Rico, Francisco. *Historia y crítica de la literatura española*, volume 1: *Edad Media*. Barcelona: Crítica, 1980.

Rico. *El pequeño mundo del hombre*. Madrid: Castalia, 1970.

Río, Ángel del. *Historia de la literatura española*. New York: Holt, Rinehart & Winston, 1963.

Rubio Tovar, Joaquín. *La prosa medieval*. Madrid: Playor, 1982.

Rucquoi, Adeline. *Histoire médiévale de la Péninsule Ibérique*. Paris: Seuil, 1993.

Russell, Peter E. *Traducciones y traductores en la Península Ibérica (1400–1550)*. Bellaterra: Universidad Autónoma de Barcelona, 1985.

Sánchez Albornoz, Claudio. *España: Un enigma histórico*. Madrid: Fundación Universitaria, 1975.

Scholberg, Kenneth R. *Sátira e invectiva en la España medieval*. Madrid: Gredos, 1971.

Seniff, Dennis P. *Literature and the Law in the Middle Ages: A Bibliography of Scholarship*. New York: Garland, 1984.

Stillman, Norman A. *The Jews of Arab Lands: A History and Source Book*. Philadelphia: Jewish Publication Society of America, 1979.

Ward, Philip. *The Oxford Companion to Spanish Literature*. Oxford: Clarendon Press, 1978. Translated and adapted by Gabriela Zayas as *Diccionario Oxford de literatura española e hispanoamericana*. Barcelona: Crítica, 1984.

Whinnom, Keith. *Spanish Literary Historiography: Three Forms of Distortion*. Exeter, U.K.: University of Exeter, 1967.

Wright, John Kirtland. *The Geographical Lore of the Time of the Crusades*, 2 volumes. New York: American Geographical Society, 1925.

Zumthor, Paul. *Éssai de poétique médiévale*. Paris: Seuil, 1972. Translated by Philip Bennett as *Toward a Medieval Poetics*. Minneapolis: University of Minnesota Press, 1992.

Zumthor. *Introduction a la poésie orale*. Paris: Seuil, 1983. Translated by Kathryn Murphy-Judy as *Oral Poetry: An Introduction,* foreword by Walter J. Ong. Minneapolis: University of Minnesota Press, 1990.

Contributors

Conrado Guardiola Alcover . . . . *Rutgers, The State University of New Jersey*

Amaia Arizaleta . . . . *Université de Toulouse le Mirail*

Matthew Bailey . . . . *University of Texas, Austin*

Vincent Barletta . . . . *Stanford University*

Andrew M. Beresford . . . . *University of Durham*

Jane E. Connolly . . . . *University of Miami*

Michèle S. de Cruz-Sáenz . . . .

Frank A. Domínguez . . . . *University of North Carolina at Chapel Hill*

Enzo Franchini . . . . *University of Zurich*

Cristina González . . . . *University of California, Davis*

George D. Greenia . . . . *College of William and Mary*

Patricia E. Grieve. . . . . *Columbia University*

Gregory S. Hutcheson . . . . *University of Louisville*

Mark D. Johnston . . . . *DePaul University*

Richard P. Kinkade . . . . *University of Arizona*

Steven D. Kirby . . . . *Eastern Michigan University*

Laurence de Looze . . . . *University of Western Ontario*

Karoline Manny . . . . *Seminole Community College*

James W. Marchand . . . . *University of Illinois at Urbana-Champaign*

Alberto Montaner . . . . *Universidad de Zaragoza*

Eric W. Naylor . . . . *University of the South*

Eloísa Palafox . . . . *Washington University in St. Louis*

Pablo Pastrana-Pérez . . . . *Western Michigan University*

Lucy K. Pick . . . . *University of Chicago*

Manuel Alejandro Rodríguez de la Peña . . . . *Universidad Autónoma de Madrid*

Norman Roth . . . . *University of Wisconsin–Madison*

José Sánchez-Arcilla Bernal . . . . *Universidad Complutense de Madrid*

Dayle Seidenspinner-Núñez . . . . *University of Notre Dame*

Joseph T. Snow . . . . *Michigan State University*

John V. Tolan . . . . *Université de Nantes*

Juan Victorio . . . . *Universidad Nacional de Educación a Distancia*

Janice Wright. . . . . *College of Charleston*

John Zemke . . . . *University of Missouri, Columbia*

Cumulative Index

Dictionary of Literary Biography, Volumes 1-337
Dictionary of Literary Biography Yearbook, 1980-2002
Dictionary of Literary Biography Documentary Series, Volumes 1-19
Concise Dictionary of American Literary Biography, Volumes 1-7
Concise Dictionary of British Literary Biography, Volumes 1-8
Concise Dictionary of World Literary Biography, Volumes 1-4

Cumulative Index

DLB before number: *Dictionary of Literary Biography*, Volumes 1-337
Y before number: *Dictionary of Literary Biography Yearbook*, 1980-2002
DS before number: *Dictionary of Literary Biography Documentary Series*, Volumes 1-19
CDALB before number: *Concise Dictionary of American Literary Biography*, Volumes 1-7
CDBLB before number: *Concise Dictionary of British Literary Biography*, Volumes 1-8
CDWLB before number: *Concise Dictionary of World Literary Biography*, Volumes 1-4

Cumulative Index

H

J

L

ISBN-13: 978-0-7876-8155-5
ISBN-10: 0-7876-8155-5

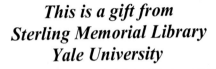

BARCELÓ

Photographs by

JEAN MARIE del MORAL

Introduction by Patrick Mauriès

Thames & Hudson

First published in the United Kingdom in 2003 by
Thames & Hudson Ltd, 181A High Holborn, London WC1V 7QX

www.thamesandhudson.com

British Library Cataloguing-in-Publication Data
A catalogue record for this book is available from the British Library

ISBN 0-500-23810-3

Printed and bound in Germany by Steidl, Göttingen

Contents

Reading Barceló

by Patrick Mauriès

When Jean-Marie del Moral knocked at Miquel Barceló's door one grey Paris day in November 1985, he had no way of knowing what a long journey through space and time he was about to embark upon. At first, there was no reply. Had he been forgotten? Had there been a misunderstanding? Somewhat perplexed, the photographer decided to wait outside the door, and after a while, at the end of the street there appeared a dark, stocky figure, blond hair flying in the wind. Enter Barceló, as friendly yet reserved, as open yet driven by his own obsessions as he is today.

At the time, the young painter was little known and was preparing his first exhibition at Leo Castelli's New York gallery. He was at the start of the steep trajectory that within a few years would lead him to fame and to the very highest reaches of the art world. He had been 'recommended' to del Moral by another artist, Miguel Angel Campano, a friend of Antonio Saura. There could have been no better way of bringing a painter to the photographer's attention than the recognition of other artists.

Barceló and del Moral, painter and photographer, have something else in common: roots in the same distinctive region of Spain, from which they have been obliged for different reasons to tear themselves away. In del Moral's case it was familial and political exile, when his staunch republican parents left Catalonia after the fascists took power. In Barceló's case, it was wilful wandering, one local tradition perhaps not being enough for him. This shared origin does not imply any regionalism or nationalism, however: Catalonia could be described as a multi-faceted place, open to dissemination and cross-fertilization. 'I am Catalan, but I am universal,' said Miró, and Tàpies, Dalí or Fenosa could have said the same. A certain logic might even be detected in the fact that it was the supreme cultural crossroads of Paris that was the eventual meeting place for Barceló and del Moral.

Propped against the walls stood the paintings for the New York exhibition, and the photographer saw the same signs and felt the same shock to the system that he had felt several years earlier, on being admitted into the studio of Miró, a visit that had resulted in his own transformation from a current-affairs photographer into a visual chronicler of contemporary art. (Faithful to his family's concern for social issues, del Moral had previously spent several years as a photojournalist, covering strikes and social issues for publications including *L'Humanité*.) In a tacit, friendly agreement, Barceló immediately allowed him the same freedom that Miró once had: freedom to wander through the studio at will and to follow him at his own creative speed. That agreement fixed one of the key aspects of this book, turning it, in an echo of Barceló's own travels, into a book of motion, or a book of reportage if reportage means following the pulse of life itself, as it intertwines with the life of art. What distinguishes this project from its legendary analogues, such as those by Brassaï or David Duncan on Picasso, is that here the painter holds back nothing about himself; every moment of his life and his work is open, freely offered. The arrangements of objects, details of the studio, still-life images only serve to boost and amplify this dynamic.

This aspect is made even more striking by the fact that Barceló is essentially a nomadic artist, for whom variation and movement, as well as density, design, texture, surface, the sensual substance of the most varied of places, can permeate like a shadow through to the very heart of a work, infiltrating and saturating the substance of the canvases and sketches themselves. These shifting qualities are apparent in several of the parallel and juxtaposed photographs on the pages which follow. From weeding out to setting down, from dripping to glazing, the imaginative world of raw materials is clearly one of the basic motors of Barceló's creativity. In this way, he seems to be clinging on backwards – or upside down – to the (mainstream?) currents of contemporary art whose only raison d'être is mind games and pure, intellectual construction (incidentally, this is also a revolution in the sense of a full circle, and definitely not a step backwards from his own starting point).

We realize how challenging his view of the nature of things is when we see the images of Barceló contemplating, with palpable tension and intensity, the star-like shape of a cut tomato or half a lemon, the flaking scales of a dead fish or the clotted blood of an animal's head. Contemplation itself holds nothing Apollonian for him; when he chose to reintroduce into his paintings the dimension that Viennese art historians call the Haptic, in which the gaze is made to move across and sensually experience, in an almost dream-like fashion, the texture and the surface of the canvas itself, he does so with a striking violence and deliberation, with what seems to be all the strength he can muster.

These pictures also illuminate another aspect of Barceló's work: his need to physically confront the reality of objects, including the materials in front of him; the antagonistic aspect of the process, in which the artist stands constantly and deliberately on the shifting border between self-control and utter dispossession. See, for example, how in several of these shots he is *lost in the picture*, in all senses of the term; in the sea, inside a soft clay pot, in a huge curving dome, in front of an arid mountain landscape, in the water of a river, or beneath the surface of a huge, suspended canvas. Or see how he often stands on the unstable edge of such a construction. He seems to need this resistance, this dizziness, to move forwards; he truly seems to need to tear something out of raw material, and inversely, to leave behind him the muscular imprint of a human body.

At the same time, he presents no heroic facade; he is the very opposite of the mythical man of action, who would be opposed to the reflexive or speculative. Del Moral attacks the now widespread and politically motivated cliché of the artist as a non-intellectual, or anti-intellectual, a creator who is even more admirable for being able to escape the contingencies of 'culture'. In fact, the photographer takes every opportunity to show the complete reverse: Barceló is a painter who both reads and writes, and does so with the same appetite, the same voracious, insatiable curiosity that characterizes his art, and with the same desire to find an unexpected angle, a chanced-upon, unusual perspective, that allows his work to move forwards (I will not say progress).

Del Moral himself admits that he has let himself be carried along by this movement, and that he has learned a lot from watching the painter tackling, taking over and transforming the dryness, aridity and meagre resources of the lands of Africa, the polar opposite of Barceló's own homeland, the seascapes and flourishing plantlife of the island of Majorca. One gaze follows another and finds itself irrevocably altered; a tale or chronicle that is suddenly interrupted (or concentrated, or revealed) by chance incidents, revelatory details. Barceló himself is a book that has now been opened to countless other gazes, other readers.

Born on the island of Majorca, Miquel Barceló spent time in Barcelona, Naples, New York and Vilanova do Milfontes in Portugal before settling in Paris at the age of twenty-eight, to work in a huge run-down apartment on the avenue de Breteuil. Here he produced the paintings that were shown the following year (April–May 1986) at Leo Castelli's gallery in New York. His work was first internationally recognized in 1982, the year that Rudi Fuchs selected him to take part in Dokumenta 7, Kassel.

11 December 1985.

4 December 1985. Preliminary drawing for *Fish Cut Into Seven Pieces*.

1985. *The Sink*, page from notebook.

3 - J'aligne quelques
objects par ordre d'antiquité:

un fossile de poissons
une pointe de flèche en silex
une figure votive ibérique
une bouteille de vieux calvados
une rose.
J'apprécie le résultat mais
j'évite soigneusement
d'en tirer une conclusion
quelconque (

For translation, see page 254.

13 December 1985. On the ground, *Ink*. Against the wall, *Chinese Restaurant With Frogs*.

Chinese Restaurant With Frogs, 1986

4 December 1985.

27 January 1986. Miquel Barceló.

He returns to the stifling heat of Barcelona, where he spends the whole summer painting a cupola, twelve metres across, for the Mercat de les Flors theatre on the site of Barcelona's old flower market. In the same year, the Spanish Ministry of Culture award him the Premio Nacional de Artes Plásticas. Miquel Barceló is still only twenty-nine years old.

23 July 1986. The artist and his brushes.

23 July 1986. Day One.

23 July 1986. Day One – first break.

15 August 1986. Day 24.

On the eastern side of the island of Majorca, in Farrutx, Barceló makes his home at the foot of a majestic mountain. He has a huge studio built with large windows that open on to the surrounding hills, covered in almond trees. He stays there every summer, working every day, like a baker making his daily bread. He shows his work regularly at the gallery of Bruno Bishofberger in Zurich (his dealer since 1984) and in galleries around the world: Barcelona, Nîmes, Rotterdam, the Whitechapel Gallery in London, the Centre Pompidou and the Jeu de Paume in Paris.

24 October 1998. The artist in his tower.

27 October 1987. *Fifteen Holes*, work in progress.

6 September 1988. On location.

6 September 1987. The large studio.

41

3 August 1991. Back from Africa.

24 October 1988. *Zeros* and *Desert Crossing* against the wall.

3 August 1991. Poster for the Nîmes festival on the studio wall.

3 August 1991. Barceló's studio, with his Ségou paintings in the background.

20 September 1997. Painting an orange… and eating it.

20 September 1997. Cauliflower for a still life.

9.11.96 nov/96

Nuit d'insomnie.
Moitié rêve d'un
tableau : l'artiste
a la baignoire. fait
avec savon pour
machine a laver !
la mousse ...
soupe d'artiste ...
de l'eau tiède ...
A la fin je m'endors
le matin a 7h. la
vision persiste.

21 September 1997.

21 September 1997. Preserved fish head.

21 September 1997. Preserved turkey.

Je ne regrette pas mes vieux tableaux.
Je me réjouis ~~que je les aurais~~ de les avoir déjà
peints et de ne pas devoir le faire maintenant.
– même ceux ~~que je~~ que j'aime moins –
Aux moments – comme aujourd'hui, comme si
souvent, dernièrement, de plus en plus, —
où j'efface le travail de la journée – ou de la semaine
c'est pareil — ~~où~~ rien n'est sec, les images que
j'ai tant cherché, disparaissent ~~ø~~ avec la
facilité stupéfiante que disparaissent p. ex.,
mes dessins, où la mémoire d'un visage qu'on croyait
qu'il était là pour toujours ,, tout balayée avec
ce grand pinceau balayé de clown, lourd, dégoulinant
cette peinture un peu moini qui sent mal,
De l'eau sale ,,, comme ces grosses machines
que démolissent immeubles encore chaux de vie,
et qui laissent entrevoir au coin d'un mur rose
pigeon malade, espace ~~comptablement~~ prétencieux
et ridicule, comme cettes pages, — une carte postal d'un
paradis 2ème classe ou le portrait d'un ~~ø~~ acteur que la
fille du machiniste ~~ne connais plus~~ mais ~~ø~~
qui servit de pochoir de dessin à la fille qui logeait la

PÉMOLITION

21 September 1997. Severed birds' heads.

21 September 1997. Donkey's skull.

21 September 1997. Sea urchins and rubber fish.

21 September 1997.

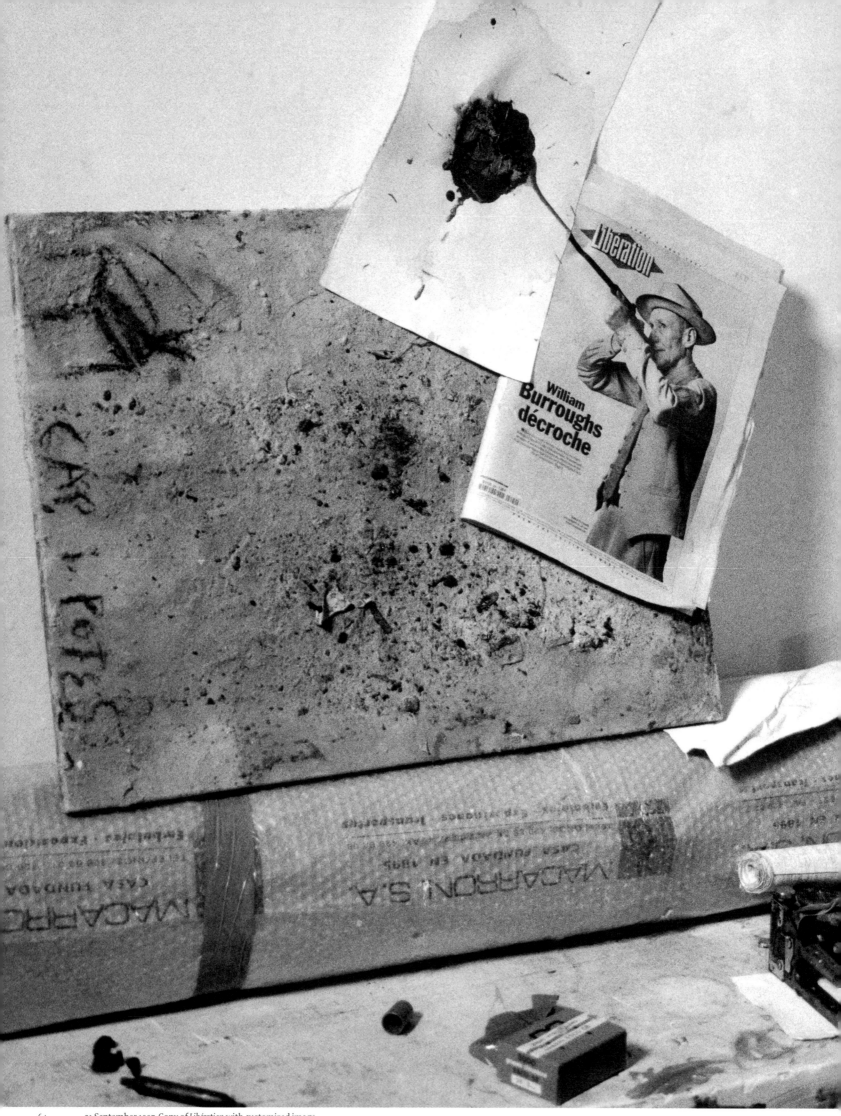

21 September 1997. Copy of *Libération* with customized image.

20 September 1997. Portrait of the flamenco singer Camarón de la Isla, pinned to the studio wall.

Landscape for the Blind on a Red Background, 1989

21 September 1997. *Monkey* and *Painter's Pet*, two sculptures on the studio roof.

21 September 1997. In the big studio.

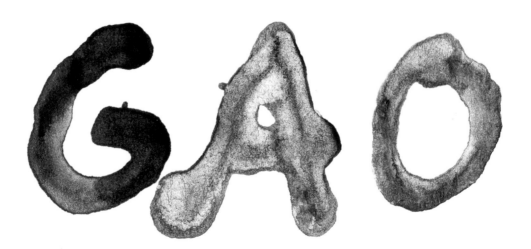

The first trip to Africa. Barceló stays in Gao, Mali, for several months. He rents two houses, one to live in and one to work in. The heat and desert dust prevent him from painting; to console himself, he draws endlessly in large sketchbooks by the river at sunset. The rest of the time, between two bouts of fever, he spends his days exploring the deserts around Gao.

MAYO
lunes
Ntra. Sra. de la. Luz

NOTAS:

ENTRADAS

SALIDAS

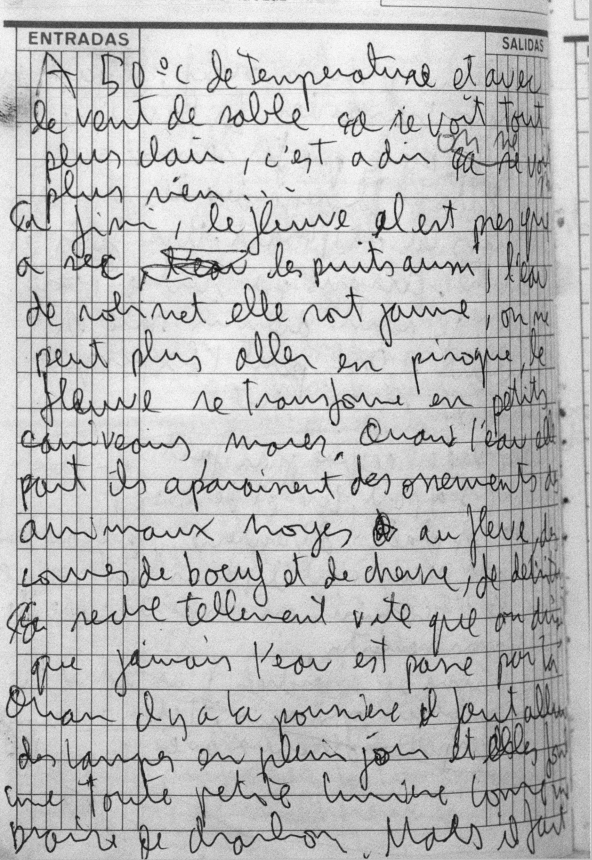

A 50°c de Temperatura et avec
le vent de sable ça se voit tout
plus clair, c'est à dire ça ne
plus rien
la firi, le fleuve el est presque
a sec, des puits aussi, l'eau
de robinet elle soit jaune, on ne
peut plus aller en pirogue le
fleuve se transforme en petits
caniveaux morez, Quand l'eau elle
part ils aparaînent des ornements des
animaux noyez au fleve des
cornes de boeuf et de chevre, je delib
seche tellement vite que on dit
que jamais l'eau est passé par là
Quand il y a la poussiere il faut allu
des lampes en plein jour et elle y
une toute petite lumiere comme un
braise de charbon, Mais il fait

For translation, see page 254.

25 May 1988. View of the river from the studio.

25 May 1988. The artist looking out onto the river and sketching.

The River Niger, 1988.

26 May 1988. Opposite Barceló's house.

27 May 1988. Barceló outside his house.

26 May 1988. View from the terrace of the house.

Barceló returns to Mali and settles in Ségou, in a huge colonial house on the riverside that he rents for several months. From the terrace or balcony, there's an unbeatable view of the market, the boats and the life of the river. Two rooms become studio space and small-scale canvases begin to pile up. Barceló buys a boat, and sketches as he travels along the river.

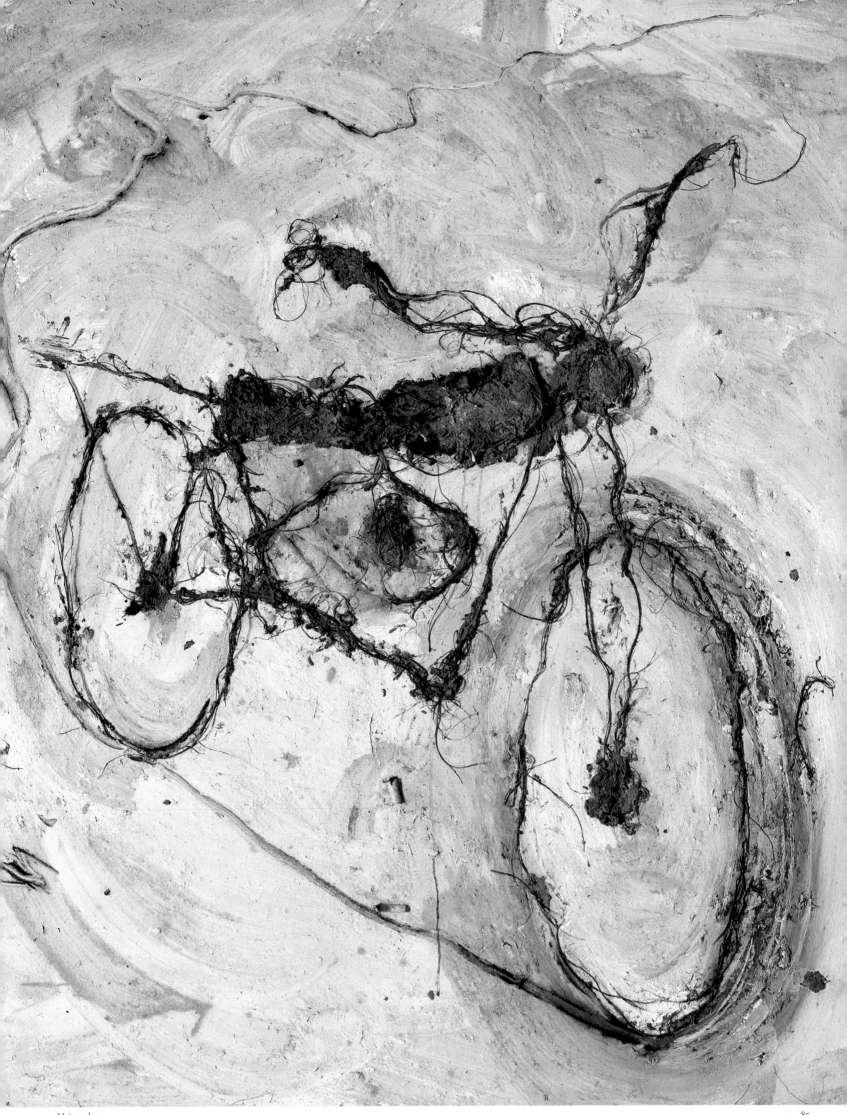

Motorcycle, 1991

8 April 1991. The studio.

J'étais à poil pour faire une douche,
la salle de bains n'est qu'un trou
entre carreaux et deux robinets.
Soudain j'ai vu une grosse araignée,
mais grosse, la plus grosse que j'ai jamais
vu, 25 cm au moins. Noire, bien décidée,
j'avais rien pour la tuer, même pas
une éponge, Tous mes vêtements étaient
dans une autre chambre...
J'ai pissé dessus, longtemps
de pipi jaune a coté des comprimées
de vitamines de l'araignée
s'est recroqueville et n'a plus bougé.
Alors je l'ai jeté dans le trou et
j'ai pris ma douche

 For translation, see page 254.

8 April 1991. Barceló paints on his balcony.

8 April 1991. View of the riverside from Barceló's terrace.

Riverside, 1991

9 April 1991. Barceló's bedroom.

12 April 1991. Out on the river.

11 April 1991. Swimming

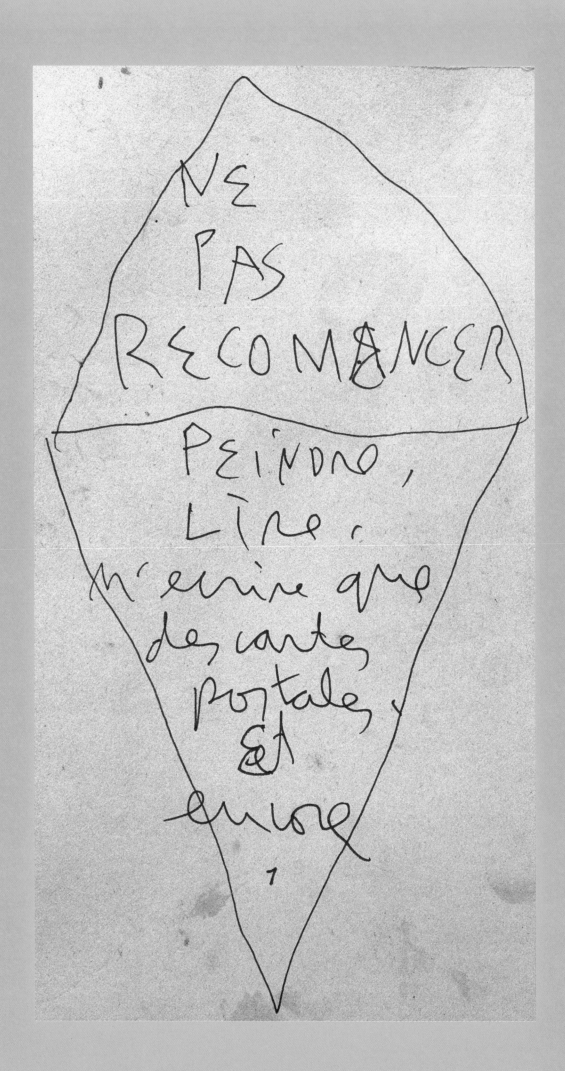

11 April 1991. Scattered paper on the balcony.

9 April 1991. Pirogues in the boatmaker's yard.

Back in Mali. The Dogon people offer to build Barceló a house and studio on a cliff top overlooking the desert. He returns every year to work for a few months. His Dogon friends regularly come to the studio to pose for him. He alternates between painting, drawing, ceramics, reading and writing. News from the rest of the world reaches him via a crackling transistor radio.

6 February 2000. Portrait of Bamo.

6 February 2000. Bamo posing.

6 February 2000. Another portrait of Bamo.

12·XII·92

On était allé loin dans la brousse voir le forgeron qui fait les portes et fenêtres de chez moi.
Au retour on pensait s'arrêter au marché de Banan mais il y avait pas de bière avant quelques heures alors on a continué jusqu'a Ireli. J'ai laissé la voiture a l'ombre chez un enseignant sonrai de Gao a quelques 7 km d'Ibi. Là on a trouvé deux touristes hollandais moitié morts. Depuis presque une semaine ils étaient partis de ~~~~ Bankas avec de faux guides faux dogons pour faire toute la falaise a pied. Ils avaient la dysenterie et ~~~~ deshydratation. plus de 40° de fièvre. On les a amené au dispensaire.

J'ai attendu au campement qu'ils finisse avec le docteur et j'ai comande pour eux une chambre et une bouteille d'eau avec deux verres. A mon retour, deja plus tranquiles ils m'ont demandait combien d'argent je mais encore chancelants voulait ~~—~~. Je m'hi atendait — le docteur m'avait dit qu'ils était a deux doigts de mourir.

Je me suis intalé pour lire et ecrire dans une grote un peut loin de chez moi, ou la falaise de temps en temps Somine vient avec moi ou bien avec une garaffe de 4 litres de bier dolo

7 February 2000. Onion-pickers.

7 February 2000. *The Onion-Pickers.*

7 February 2000. Barceló working on *The Onion-Pickers*.

7 February 2000. The studio.

5 February 2000. In the kitchen.

7 February 2000. Abo, Debamo, Dolo and Barceló.

6 February 2000. The painter's house, 6 a.m.

4 February 2000. Bedroom doorway.

4 February 2000. In the bedroom.

7 February 2000. A vain attempt to find Radio España Internacional, to hear a football match between Real Madrid and FC Barcelona.

4 February 2000. Books in the corner of the bedroom.

5 February 2000. Lunch.

White Ogobara, 1996.

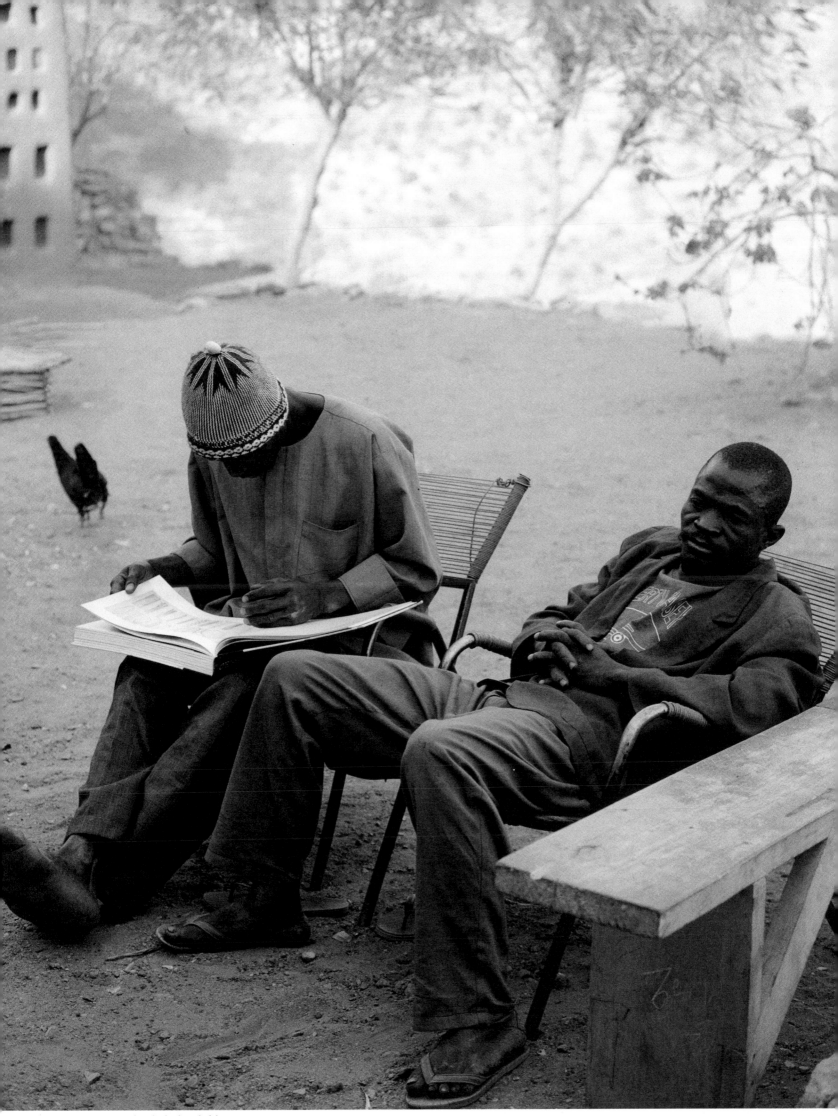

6 February 2000. Ogabara looks thoughtful.

7 February 2000. View of the house and studio.

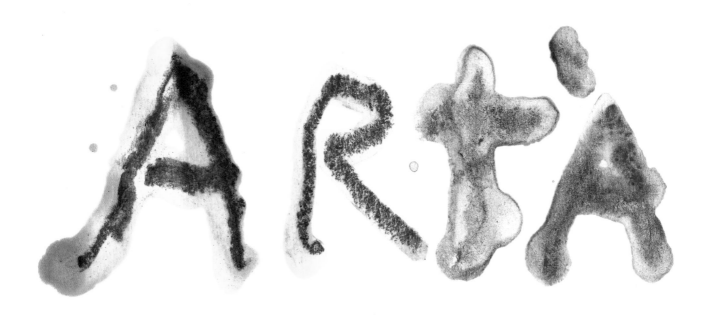

Barceló goes to Artà in Majorca, to the studio of the ceramicist Jeroni Girard, where he experiments with traditional terracotta techniques. Defying convention, Barceló becomes a sculptor, piling, deforming and hollowing clay to create animal skulls, some of which are later cast in bronze.

20 September 1997. Huge clay skulls.

21 September 1997. Large skull.

20 September 1997. Pile of skulls.

Studio I, 1997

20 September 1997. A necklace of skulls.

20 September 1997. Small skull on large skull.

Big white paintings, desert landscapes. Working in Paris close to the Parc des Buttes-Chaumont, his workshop is also white, with tiled walls. He produces his first plaster sculptures. Barceló is thirty-two years old, his reputation still in the ascendant.

15 June 1990. Tower of skulls.

1 March 1989. Sculpture maquette on a cigarette packet.

19 April 1989. Cigarette break.

MIQUEL BARCELÓ
IN MALI

15 June 1990. The white studio.

156   1 March 1989. On the phone to José María Sicilia.

18 June 1990. Barceló in front of *River of Milk I*.

Invited to Palermo for the Sul Novecento festival, for which he designs the posters, Barceló sets up studio in the disused church of Santa Eulalia dei Catalani, in the Vucceria district. He draws in charcoal on the walls and produces a series of large works on whitewashed newsprint. The whole collection, together with some ceramics made in Majorca, becomes the installation *Cristo della Vucceria*.

4 October 1998. Hotel room in the Albergo delle Palme.

26.X.98 Palermo, De retour.

Cette fois je suis a l'hotel delle Palme.
J'ai demandé au porteur laquelle était
la suite de Wagner et il m'a dit: celle-ci
puis en notant j'ai lu a la porte: suite
Raymond Roussel: Et voila le lieu
ou le bonhomme mourut il y a ...
Les problemes recommencent comme
si rien n'était, tout le monde se
fache entre eux, il parent et puis
chaqu'un voudrait nous voir tete a tete.
Je connais la musique desormais,
J'ai acheté un nouveau poste et
quelques nouveaux CD. Demain
matin je commence enfin travailler.

Une chose de faite: l'affiche
pour le festival. Recto verso puisque
recto seul ça posait des problemes
a la mairie, ce que je comprends
c'est d'ailleurs mieux comme ça.

C'est drôle, mais je préfère écrire avec
cette plume Mont Blanc que j'ai
depuis 10 ans et que j'avais prise en
rogne et que j'ai retrouvée dans un
tiroir. C'est peut être là que je fais
la différence entre écrire et
dessiner : question de plume.

Al ... delle Palme.

4 October 1998. Festival poster.

4 October 1998. View from hotel room.

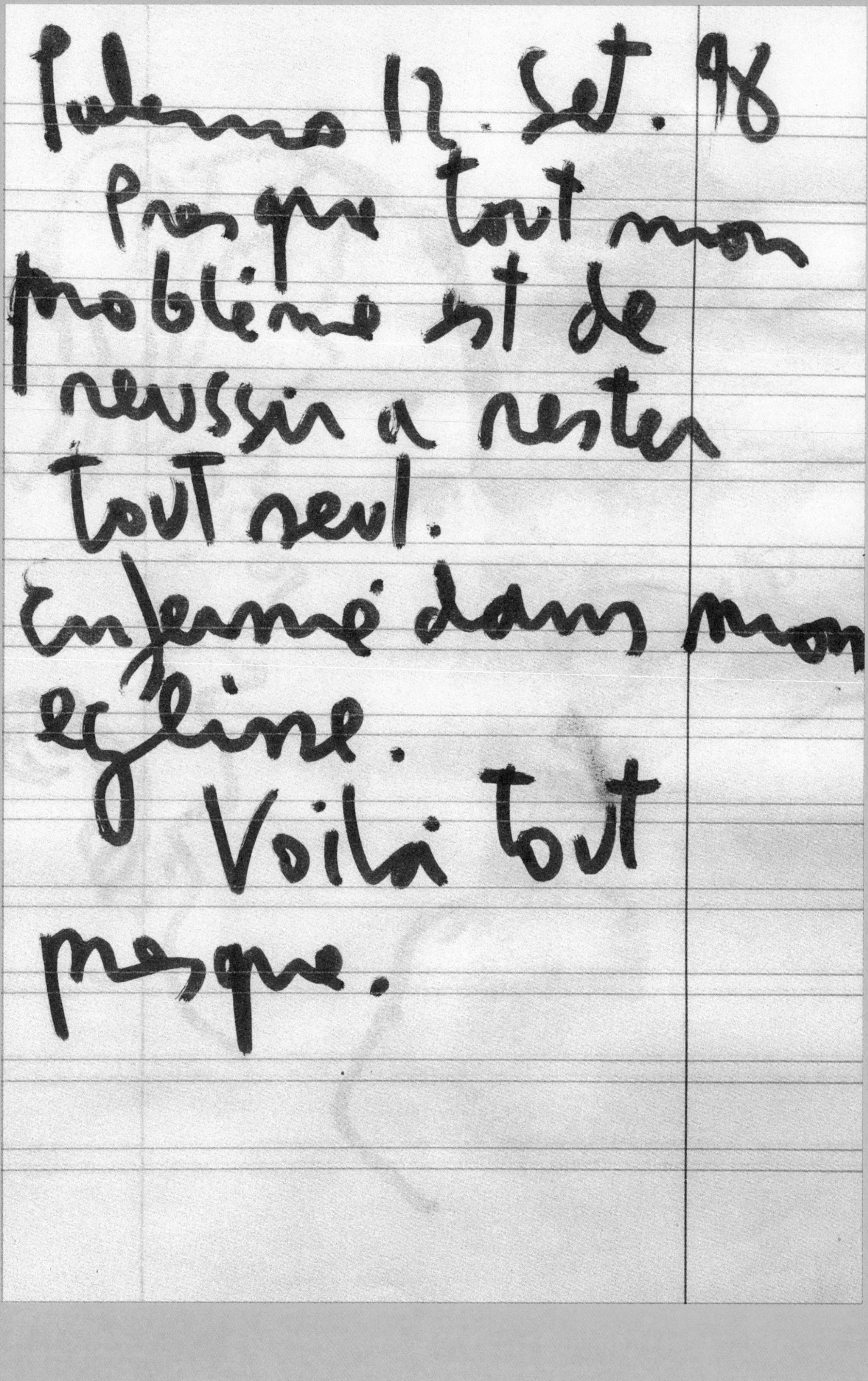

Palermo 12. Set. 98

Presque tout mon
problème est de
réussir a rester
tout seul.
Enfermé dans mon
eglise.
Voila tout
presque.

For translation, see page 255.

Dans la petite malle par laquelle
j'entre par derrière à
l'église où j'écris ceci, dans
une maison. Ils ont un
cheval de course. Pas dans
une écurie ni cour mais
dans la salle à manger.
Son nom est grand écrit
sur le mur en haut de la TV:
TORRE D'ALMA. C'est clair
que c'est le roi de la maison.
puisque les enfants, les chiens
et la voiture sont toujours dans
la rue.

5 October 1998. *The Fall of Icarus* on back wall.

5 October 1998. The racehorse Torre d'Alma.

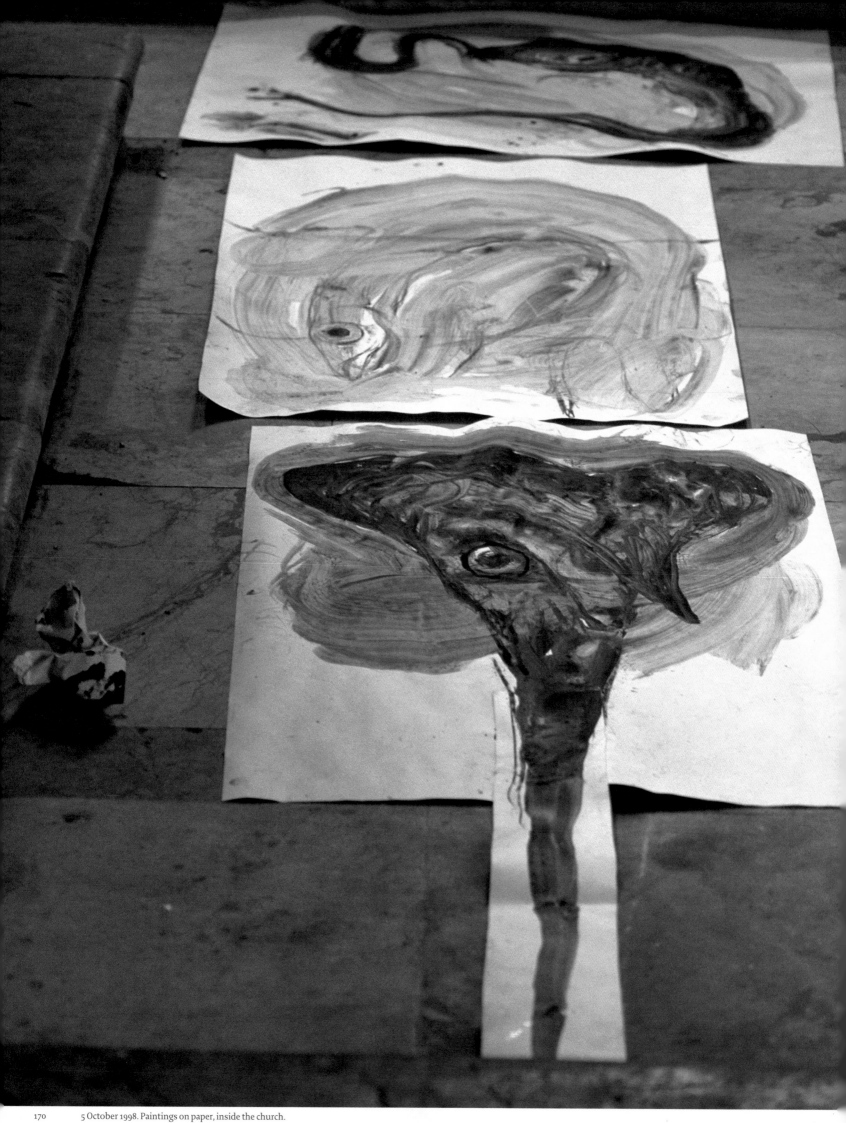

5 October 1998. Paintings on paper, inside the church.

5 October 1998. Charcoal drawing on the church wall.

4 October 1998.

6 October 1998. *Root Christ* on the ground.

6 October 1998. Charcoal sketches on the church wall.

4 October 1998. Unused festival poster design.

4 October 1998. Charcoal drawings on the church wall.

4 October 1998. Drawing table.

When the Musée des Arts Décoratifs in Paris suggests an exhibition of his ceramic works, Barceló wants to create some new ones for the show. He stays near the French town of Angers at the studio of Armelle and Hugo Jakubec. He works on a very large scale, punching the interior of giant jars. Some do not survive this assault.

2 November 1999.

2 November 1999. Getting right inside the work.

19. X. 99 Angers

Je ne suis pas a Angers, en fait,
sinon dans un petit village que
je sais pas le nom encore.
Je fais de la céramique.
Je suis censé d'en faire de grandes,
Je voudrais faire des bas reliefs d'un
seul tenant, sans carreaux, comme
des tableaux, par terre, que je puisse
m'y promener dessus. Grands
comme des façades, comme des parois
des falaises. Bon, pour l'instant
tout s'effondre, s'effritte.
Je connais pas cette argile encore
Je me suis levé de bonne heure
demain aussi. Voilà

3 November 1999. Total collapse.

3 November 1999. Charcoal portraits on the wall of the ceramics studio.

Barceló's works on paper are the subject of an exhibition that tours the world. Organized by the Museo Nacional Centro de Arte Reina Sofía in Madrid, it then travels to Granada in Spain, São Paulo in Brazil, Montevideo in Uruguay and Tel Aviv in Israel.

18 January 2002. Barceló makes etchings.

18 January 2002. The press.

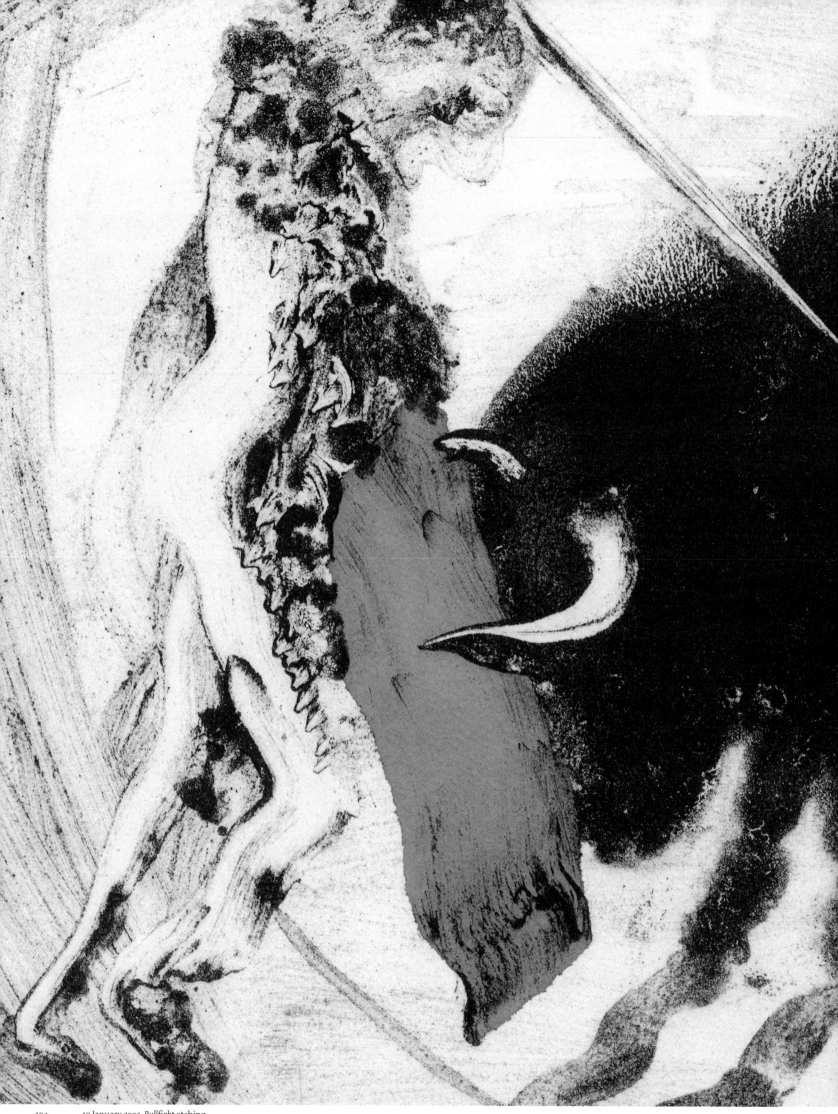

19 January 2002. *Bullfight* etching.

19 January 2002. Lanzarote countryside.

19 January 2002. Lanzarote countryside.

Barceló's current studio in Paris has gone through several changes and transformations over the years. As well as two large rooms intended for single, monumental paintings, the artist has space for drawing, sculpting, and occasionally cooking. He is forty-six years old.

9 June 1996. The studio kitchen.

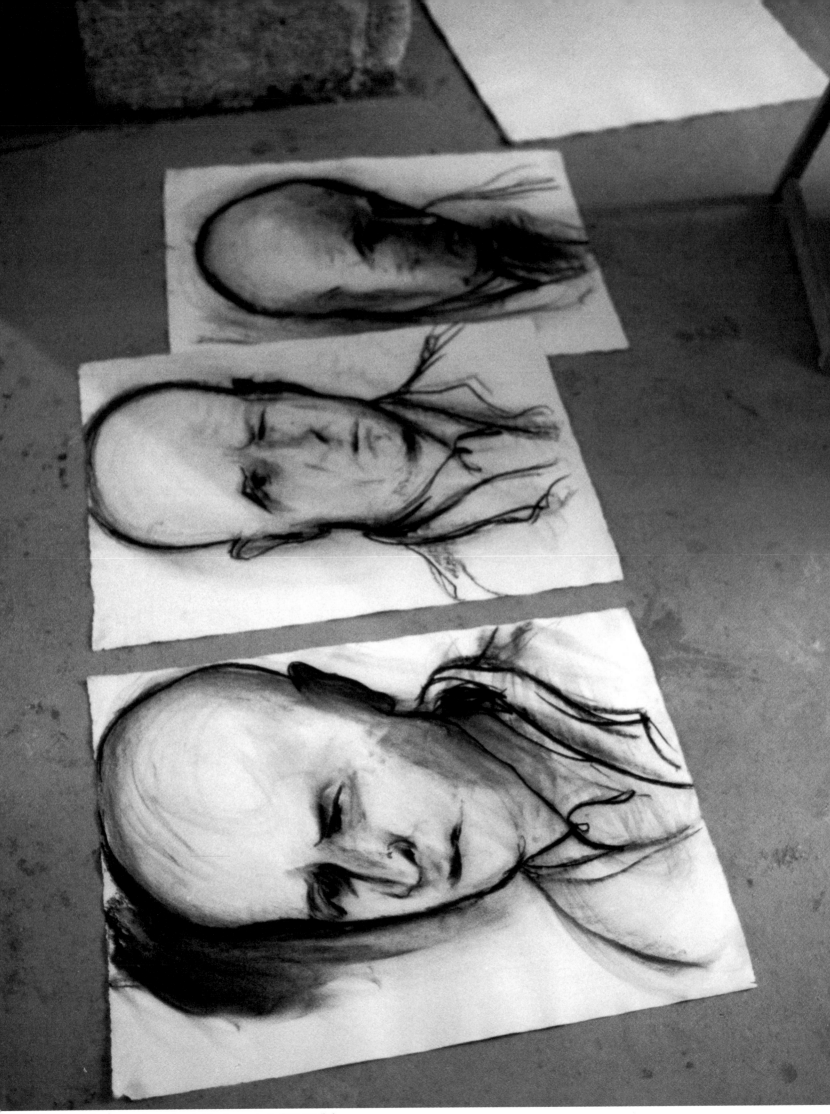

27 January 1993. Preparatory sketches for a portrait of Castor Seibel.

27 January 1993. Castor Seibel poses for a portrait.

27 January 1993. Miquel Barceló and Castor Seibel.

13 Mai

Au contraire d'Ingres et des portraitistes de succès — Warhol — Mes modèles semblent avoir pris 10 ou 15 ans, dans le meilleur des cas. — Survivants d'une hécatombe, convalescents pensionnaires d'un hôpital de vie — Cécile prétend aussi que tous mes portraits ont l'air méchant, pourtant les modèles ont l'air de s'y reconnaître, peut être me félicitent pour s'échapper s'enfuir échapper à cette con seulement pour en finir, enfin,

De toute façon, p. ex, tout le monde se reconnaîtrait devant une crane de mo comme personne ne doute que la radiographie qu'exhibe le docteur ne soit pas vraiment la sienne

En Afrique, la gent ne reconnaît pas eux eux mêmes vus de profil

10 May 1994. Corner of the studio.

29 June 1993. Sculpture studio.

20 June 1997. Artist and onion.

9 June 1997. *Self-portrait* and other works.

6 June 1997. Studio floor.

5 July 1994. The *In Extremis* series.

7 July 1994. The *In Extremis* series.

In Extremis IV, 1994

5 July 1999. Barceló working on a still life.

5 July 1999. The studio floor.

7 July 1994. A tomato about to be squashed.

7 July 1994. A painted tomato.

Three Tomatoes, 1994

26 March 1992. Studio wall.

4 July 1999. Still life detail.

10 May 1999. Painter with pipe.

29 June 1997. The sculpture studio.

The Sculpture Studio, 1993

9 June 1997. Bunch of flowers.

10 June 1994. Rejected poster design for Roland Garros.

5 April 1995. *Ball de la carn* (Meat Dance).

29 June 1993. Sculpture studio.

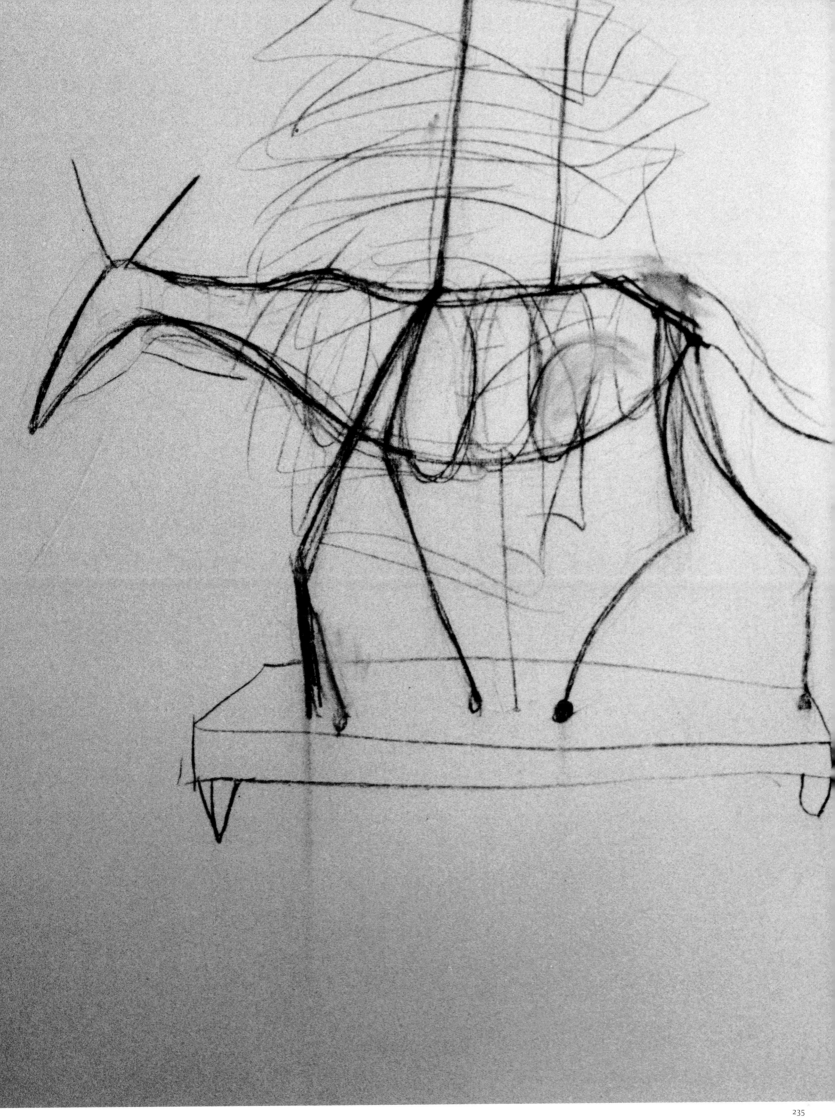

5 July 1999. 31°C.

5 July 1999. *Albino Gorilla.*

plûtot. Je regarde, rarement, des gros livres de Velázquez, Hals, Rembrant Goya, J'y vois plus clair, desfois, surtout avant me coucher, et puis le jour après c'est pareil. No, pas pareil : c'est pire il m'arrive de regretter même certains portraits d'il y a 405 mois que je trouvait ~~...~~ alors pire que nuls,

J'ai voyageais un peu, dernierement, puisque certains de mes vieux ~~mes~~ tableaux, etaient exposés dans differentes villes, Je reçois des eloges comme des gifles, pire puisque je peux pas les rendre, je dois remercier et sourire comme les ~~mas~~ chretiens conseillent. Mes vieux tableaux pires que tout puisque ils sont meme pas, ne sont plus de moi, Si au moins je pouvait etre fier de mon oeuvre passée, Autrefois je l'etait il parais, desfois Mais c'est fini tout cela. Je ne suis

5 July 1999. Barceló and cat.

7 November 2001. Studio with upside-down canvases.

2 December 2001. Dried flowers in the drawing studio.

2 May 2002. Costume for Lanzarote carnival in the drawing studio.

2 May 2002. In the drawing studio.

2 June 1998. In the sculpture studio.

AJUNTAMENT DE FELANITX

Oficina de Portocolom:	971 826 084
Policia local:	971 582 200
Centre de Salut:	971 580 254
Creu Roja:	971 582 885
Casa de Cultura:	971 582 274
Guàrdia Civil:	971 580 090
Pavelló Guillem Timoner:	971 582 101

Plaça de la Constitució, 1 - Telèfon 971 580 051 Fax 971 583 271 e. mail: felanitx.general@ bitel.es

MATEU OBRADOR I BENNÀSSAR
(Felanitx 1852 - Palma 1909). Home de personalitat polifacètica. Fou periodista, fundador i director de revistes, pedagog, poeta líric, autor teatral i crític literari. Però per damunt de tot, la glòria de Mateu Obrador redica en l'edició acurada, amb introduccions i notes, de les obres de Ramon Llull: *Llibre d'Amic e Amat, Doctrina Pueril, Llibre de l'Ordre de Cavalleria, Llibre de Contemplació en Déu, Llibre de les bèsties.*
Altres obres publicades: *L'alt En Jaume d'Aragó, Lecciones de Geografía e Historia Comerciales, La nostra Arqueologia.*
L'Ajuntament el declarà fill il·lustre l'any 1906 i hi fou proclamat l'any 1967.

FEBRER 2001

	LLUNA NOVA	QUART CREIXENT	LLUNA PLENA	QUART MINVANT
	Dia 23	Dia 1	Dia 8	Dia 15

DILLUNS	DIMARTS	DIMECRES	DIJOUS	DIVENDRES	DISSABTE	DIUMENGE
			1 St. Cecili	**2** Presentació del Senyor	**3** FESTA A SON PROENÇ St. Blai	**4** St. Joan de Brito
5 Sta. Àgueda	**6** Sts. Màrtirs del Japó	**7** St. Ricard	**8** St. Jeroni Emilià	**9** Sta. Apol·lònia	**10** Sta. Escolàstica	**11** La Mare de Déu de Lorda
12 Sta. Eulàlia	**13** St. Benigne	**14** Sts. Ciril i Metodi	**15** St. Joan B. de la Concepció	**16** Sta. Juliana	**17** Sts. Fundadors dels Servites	**18** Sta. Bernadeta
19 St. Àlvar	**20** St. Eleuteri	**21** St. Pere Damià	**22** La Càtedra de St. Pere	**23** St. Policarp	**24** St. Modest	**25** St. Cèsar
26 St. Nèstor	**27** Bta. Francesca Coïsi	**28** Directora de Centre St. Teòfil				

7 November 2001. Studio kitchen.

6 November 2001. Watercolour studio.

6 November 2001. Watercolours for *The Divine Comedy*.

4 December 2002. *Mobili* on fire.

Barceló's notebooks
Text in English

p.15 A few objects I've arranged in order of age:

A fossilized fish

A flint arrowhead

An Iberian votive figure

A bottle of aged calvados

A rose

I like the result but I'm carefully avoiding drawing any conclusions from it.

p.53 *9 November 1996*

Sleepless night. Half asleep, I glimpse a picture: the artist in a bathtub, made with dishwasher detergent! The foam... artist soup... warm water.... Eventually I fall asleep at 7 o'clock in the morning. The vision lingers on.

p.58 I don't miss my old paintings. I'm happy that I've already painted them and that I don't have to do them now, even the ones I don't really like. When – like today, like so often, more and more lately – I scrub away the day's work – or the week's work, it's all the same – nothing has dried, and the images I've sought for so long disappear with the same astonishing ease as, for example, our friends or the memory of a face that we believed would be there forever. All swept away with that big clown's brush, heavy and oozing with slightly damp, foul-smelling paint. Dirty water... like those great machines that demolish apartment blocks still warm with life and that let us glimpse on the corner of a pink wall a sick pigeon, trapped, pretentious and ridiculous – like this page – a postcard from a second-class paradise, or the portrait of an actor that the driver's daughter no longer recognizes, which was used as a stencil by the girl who used to live there. DEMOLITION

p.71 *Monday, 9 May*

At a temperature of 50°C and in a sandstorm, you can't see anything clearly, in fact nothing can be seen at all.

It's over, the river is almost dry, so is the well, the water from the tap comes out yellow, you can't travel by boat any more, the river is turning into little channels and ponds. When the water is gone, you can see the bones of animals drowned in the river, horns of bulls and goats, which I draw. It dries up so quickly that you would think that the water had never come this way. When the dust is up, we have to turn on the lamps in the middle of the day, and they give off very little light, like coal embers. But we must...

p.88 I had stripped off to have a shower, the bathroom is just a hole in the ground with two taps. Suddenly I saw a huge spider, really huge, the biggest I've ever seen, at least 25 cm across. Black and very determined; I had nothing to kill it with, not even a sponge, and all my clothes were in the other room....

I pissed on it, my pee was yellow with vitamin tablets. The spider shrivelled up and stopped moving. Then I threw it down the hole and took my shower.

p.102 DO NOT START AGAIN

Paint, read, write nothing but postcards, if that.

p.116 *12 December 1992*

We had gone a long way into the brush to see the blacksmith who is making the doors and windows for my house. On the way back we planned to stop at Banam Market but there was no beer for a few hours so we went on to Ireli. I left the car in the shade at the house of a Donrai teacher from Gao, about 2 km from the village. There we found two half-dead Dutch tourists. Almost a week earlier they had left Bankas with fake Dogon guides to travel the whole cliff on foot. They were suffering from dysentery and dehydration and both had a 40° fever. We took them to the local clinic. I waited at the camp until they had finished with the doctor and I asked for a room for them and a bottle of water with two glasses. When I came back, they were calmer but still shaky, and they asked me how much money I wanted. I wasn't surprised. The doctor said that they had been a hair's breadth away from death.

I settled down to read and write in a cave on the cliff, a short distance from my house. From time to time, Sominé came bringing tea or sometimes a carafe with 4 litres of beer...

p.162 *26 October 1998. Palermo. Back.*

This time I'm at the Albergo delle Palme. I asked the porter which was the Wagner Suite, and he said this one. Then on the way out I read the door: Raymond Roussel Suite. So this is where the guy died, whenever that was.

The problems are starting up again like nothing has happened, it seems like everyone is getting angry with everyone else, then they all want a private word with me. I know the routine now. I've bought a new CD player and some new CDs. Tomorrow morning I'm finally going to start work. I've finished one thing: the poster for the festival. Double-sided, because the city council didn't like the single-sided one, which I can understand. This way is better anyway.

It's funny, but I prefer to write with this Mont Blanc fountain pen that I've had for ten years and that I mislaid and then found again in a drawer. Perhaps that's what I think is the difference between writing and drawing: it's a matter of pens.

p.166 *Palermo, 12 September 1998*

Pretty much my whole problem is managing to stay all alone. Shut up in my church. That's pretty much it.

p.167

In the little alley that I use to get in through the back of the church where I'm writing this, there's a house with a racehorse in it. Not in a stable or in the yard, but in the dining room. Its name is written in big letters above the TV: Torre d'Alma. It obviously rules the house, because the children, the dogs and the car are always out in the street.

p.185 *19 October 1999. Angers*

Actually I'm not in Angers, but in a little village whose name I don't know yet. I'm making ceramics. I'm supposed to be making huge things. I would like to make some one-piece bas reliefs, with no joins, like paintings, on the ground, so that I can walk on top of them. As big as house fronts, as big as cliff faces. Good. At the moment everything is collapsing and crumbling. I haven't got to know this clay yet. I got up early today, tomorrow too. That's all.

p.205

Unlike Ingres and successful portrait painters – like Warhol – my models all seem to come out looking ten or fifteen years older. Survivors of a massacre, life patients in a hospital. Cecile also claims that my portraits have an evil look about them, but the models seem to recognize themselves in them. Perhaps they only say nice things to me so that they can get it over with, get away, run away even, from this cave. At any rate, everyone recognizes themselves when they look at a skull, for example, just as nobody questions whether the X-ray that the doctor is showing them is really themselves.

In Africa, people can't recognize themselves from a profile view.

p.238

...I've been quietly looking through some big books on Velázquez, Hals, Rembrandt, Goya. Sometimes I see them more clearly, especially before I go to bed, and then the next day it's the same. Not even the same – it's worse. I'm even starting to miss some portraits from four or five months ago, which at the time I thought were just awful. I've been doing some travelling lately because some of my old paintings have been on show in different towns. I accept praise like I'd accept a slap: in fact it's worse, because I can't return it. I have to say thank you and smile like those masochist Christians tell you to. It's even worse with my old pictures because they aren't even anything to do with me any more. I wish that I could at least be proud of my old work. I used to be, it seemed, sometimes. But that's all over now. I'm not...

Acknowledgments

I must first express my gratitude to Miquel Barceló who granted me the rare, even unique privilege of accepting my presence in his studio for all these years, even while he was working, and allowing me the utmost freedom to photograph his world. As well as creating the original cover art and section titles for this book, he also gave me access to his private notebooks and kindly granted permission for some previously unseen extracts to be published here. For all of this, he deserves my deepest and most heartfelt thanks.

I also wish to thank all of those who have supported my work, either through exhibitions, in essays and articles, or simply by word of mouth: Antonio Saura, Miguel Angel Campano, Guy Boyer, Maurice Coriat, Christian Gendron, Richard Texier, Josep Miquel García, Pep Subirós, Ferran Cano, Claude Hudelot, Jean-Paul Capitani, Daniel Dobbels, Emmanuel de Roux, Carlo Ducci, Fina Furiol, Bruno Bishofberger, Carles Taché, Jean-Louis Froment, Claude Picasso, Jean-Louis Prat, Thierry Spitzer, Laurent Boudier, Véronique Dabin, Hugo and Armelle Jakubec, Amelia Aranguren, Jeroni Ginard, Philippe Tretiack, Bernard Heitz, Alberto Anaut, Jordi Socias, Menene Gras Balaguer, Alexandra d'Arnoux, Enric Juncosa, Henri-François Debailleux, Ramón Chao, Manolo Valdès, Gisèle Breteau Skira, Kosme de Barañano, Castor Seibel, Christian Caujolle, Jean-Philippe Fournier, Natacha Wolinski, Anne Morin, Oihana Aizarnazabal, Anna Mattirolo, Hervé Hudry.

Thanks also to the following magazines and institutions: *Vogue España*, Rencontres Internationales de la Photographie en Arles, *Vogue Italia*, Fondation Maeght, Universidad Complutense de Madrid, *El País Semanal*, the Biennale du Film d'Art at the Centre Georges Pompidou, the Gulbenkian Foundation, Instituto Valenciano de Arte Moderno (IVAM), *Elle*, *Matador*, Colegio Oficial de Arquitectos de Granada, Fondation ARCO, *Actuel*, *L'Autre Journal*, *El Europeo*, *Beaux Arts*, *City*, *Madame Figaro*, *Lapiz*, *L'Oeil*, Instituto Cervantes, Galleria Nazionale d'Arte Moderna in Rome.

Finally, special thanks to Patrick Mauriès, who initiated and coordinated this project, to Thomas Neurath and all the staff at Thames & Hudson in London, to France Le Queffelec, and to Daniel Bry, whose technical help with the design of this book was invaluable.